Organizational Behaviour

First European Edition

Organizational Behaviour

First European Edition

Robert Kreitner

Angelo Kinicki

Marc Buelens

McGraw-Hill Publishing Company

London • New York • St Loius • San Francisco • Auckland • Bogotá • Caracas
Lisbon • Madrid • Mexico • Milan • Montreal • New Delhi • Panama • Paris
San Juan • São Paulo • Singapore • Sydney • Tokyo • Toronto

Cont. No.   K1430004

Published by

McGraw-Hill Publishing Company

Shoppenhangers Road, Maidenhead, Berkshire, SL6 2QL, England
Telephone 01628 502500
Facsimile 01628 770224

British Library Cataloguing in Publication Data
A catalogue record for this book is available from the British Library.

ISBN 0256-214-20-4

Further information on this title is to be found at http://www.mcgraw-hill.co.uk/buelens

Publisher: Alfred Waller
Desk Editor: Alastair Lindsay

Created for McGraw-Hill by the independent production company
Steven Gardiner Ltd TEL +44(0) 1223 364868; FAX +44(0) 1223 364875

Typeset by Graphic Ideas Studios, London, and printed and bound in Malta by
Interprint Ltd.

Contents *In Brief*

Part One

The World of Organizational Behaviour

Chapter One
Managing Organizational Behaviour for Quality and Results 2

Chapter Two
Managing Diversity: Releasing Every Employee's Potential 28

Chapter Three
Organizational Culture, Values, and Ethics 54

Chapter Four
International OB: Managing Across Cultures 86

Part Two

Individual Behaviour in Organizations

Chapter Five
Individual Differences: Personality, Attitudes, Abilities, and Emotions 116

Chapter Six
Perception and Attributions 148

Chapter Seven
Motivation through Needs, Job Design, and Satisfaction 178

Chapter Eight
Motivation through Equity, Expectancy, and Goal Setting 208

Chapter Nine
Improving Job Performance with Feedback and Rewards 238

Part Three

Group and Social Processes

Chapter Ten
Group Dynamics 268

Chapter Eleven
Power, Politics, Conflict, and Negotiation 298

Chapter Twelve
Individual and Group Decision Making 336

Chapter Thirteen
Teams and Teamwork for the 21st Century 372

Part Four

Organizational Processes

Chapter Fourteen
Organizational Communication in the Computerized Workplace 406

Chapter Fifteen
Behaviour Modification and Self-Management 440

Chapter Sixteen
Leadership 468

Chapter Seventeen
Managing Occupational Stress 500

Part Five

The Evolving Organization

Chapter Eighteen
Organizations: Structure and Effectiveness 532

Chapter Nineteen
Organizational Life Cycles and Design 556

Chapter Twenty
Managing Change in Learning Organizations 582

Glossary 612

Index 616

Contents

Part One
The World of Organizational Behaviour

Chapter One
Managing Organizational Behaviour for Quality
and Results   2

The Manager's Job: Getting Things Done through
Others   6

OB Exercise *Test Your Factual Knowledge
about People at Work*   6

What Do Managers Do? A Skills Profile   7
The New Employment Contract:
A Cautionary Tale   8
21st-century Managers   10

The Field of Organizational Behaviour: Past and
Present   10

The Human Relations Movement   12
The Total Quality Management Movement   13

International OB *Three Coca-Cola Executives
Address the Issue of a Globally Appropriate
Management Style*   15

The Contingency Approach   16

Learning about OB from Theory, Research, and
Practice   16

Learning from Theory   17
Learning from Research   18
Learning from Practice   19

A Topical Model for Understanding and
Managing OB   20

Personal Awareness and Growth Exercise

How Strong Is Your Motivation to Manage?   22

Group Exercise *Timeless Advice*   24

Answers to OB Exercise   27

Chapter Two
Managing Diversity: Releasing Every
Employee's Potential   28

Defining Diversity   31

Dimensions of Diversity   32

OB Exercise *Dimensions of Diversity Affect
Perceptions and Expectations*   33

Affirmative Action and Valuing Diversity   34

Building the Business Case for Managing
Diversity   36

Increasing Diversity in the Workforce   36

Managing Diversity — A Competitive
Advantage   39

International OB *Cultural Insensitivity Affects
Sales*   40

Organizational Practices Used to Effectively
Manage Diversity   43

R Roosevelt Thomas, Jr.'s Generic Action
Options   43

Ann Morrison Identifies Specific Diversity
Initiatives   44

Barriers and Challenges to Managing Diversity   47

Personal Awareness and Growth Exercise

What Is Your Attitude Towards Diversity?   49

Group Exercise *Managing Diversity-Related
Interactions*   50

Chapter Three
Organizational Culture, Values, and Ethics   54

Foundation of Organizational Culture   57

Manifestations of Organizational Culture   57

A Model for Interpreting Organizational
Culture   57

Four Functions of Organizational Culture   58

Types of Organizational Culture   59

OB Exercise *Manifestations of
Organizational Culture at the Ritz-Carlton
and McDonald's*   60

Research on Organizational Cultures   61

Developing High-Performance Cultures   63

What Type of Cultures Enhance an
Organization's Financial Performance?   63

How Cultures Are Embedded in
Organizations   65

The Organizational Socialization Process   66

A Three-Phase Model of Organizational
Socialization   66

Practical Application of Socialization
Research   68

Socialization through Mentoring   69

Functions of Mentoring   69

International OB *Milton Kim Changes
Organizational Culture at Ssangyong
Securities & Investment Co. in Seoul, Korea*   69

Phases of Mentoring   70

Research Evidence on Mentoring   71

Getting the Most Out of Mentoring   72

Organizational Values and Ethics   72

Values Are the Foundation of
Organizational Culture   72

Ethics and Organizational Behaviour   74

Personal Awareness and Growth Exercise

*How Does Your Current Employer Socialize
Employees?*   80

Group Exercise *Investigating the Difference in
Moral Reasoning between Men and Women*   81

Answers to OB Exercise   85

Chapter Four

International OB: Managing Across Cultures   86

Culture and Organizational Behaviour   89

Culture Is Complex and Multilayered   89

Culture Is a Subtle but Pervasive Force   89

A Model of Societal and Organizational
Cultures   90

Ethnocentrism: A Cultural Roadblock in
the Global Economy   91

High-Context and Low-Context Societal
Cultures   91

Towards Greater Cross-Cultural Awareness and
Competence   93

Cultural Perceptions of Time   94

OB Exercise *The Polychronic Attitude Index*   94

Interpersonal Space   95

Language and Cross-Cultural
Communication   96

International OB *Foreign Language Skills Give
Utah an Edge in the Global Economy*   97

Practical Insights from Cross-Cultural Management
Research   100

The Hofstede–Bond Stream of Research   100

Trompenaar's Forms of Relating to
Other People   102

A Contingency Model for Cross-Cultural
Leadership   104

Interpersonal Conflict-Handling Styles   105

Preparing Employees for Successful Foreign
Assignments   105

Why do US Managers, Compared to
Those from Europe and Japan, Have a
Comparatively High Failure Rate in
Foreign Assignments?   105

The Global Manager   106

Avoiding OB Trouble Spots in Foreign
Assignments   106

Personal Awareness and Growth Exercise *How
Do Your Work Goals Compare
Internationally?*   110

Group Exercise *Looking into a Cultural
Mirror*   111

Part Two
Individual Behaviour in Organizations

Chapter Five
Individual Differences: Personality, Attitudes,
Abilities, and Emotions   116

Self-Concept: The I and Me in OB   120

International OB *Culture Dictates the Degree
of Self-Disclosure in Japan and the United
States*   120

Self-Esteem: A Controversial Topic   121

OB Exercise *How Strong Is Your
Organization-Based Self-Esteem (OBSE)?*   122

Self-Efficacy   123

Self-Monitoring   126

OB Exercise *What Are Your Self-Monitoring
Tendencies?*   127

Personality: Dimensions,
Insights, and Issues   128

The Big Five Personality Dimensions   128

Locus of Control: Self or Environment?   129

Attitudes and Behaviour   131

Attitudes versus Values   131

Attitudes and Behavioural Intentions   131

OB Exercise *Where Is Your Locus
of Control?*   131

Attitudinal Research and Application   132

Abilities and Performance   133

Intelligence and Cognitive Abilities   134

Jung's Cognitive Styles Typology   135

Emotions: An Emerging OB Topic   137

Positive and Negative Emotions   137

More Attention Needed   137

Managing Anger   138

Personal Awareness and Growth Exercise

What Is Your Cognitive Style?   141

Group Exercise *Anger Control Role Play*   142

Chapter Six

Perception and Attributions   148

A Social Information Processing Model of Perception   151

Four-Stage Sequence and a Working Example   151

Stage 1: Selective Attention/ Comprehension   152

Stage 2: Encoding and Simplification   153

Stage 3: Storage and Retention   154

Stage 4: Retrieval and Response   155

Managerial Implications   155

OB Exercise *Does a Schema Improve the Comprehension of Written Material?*   155

International OB *Visual Perceptions Vary by Culture*   156

Self-Perception   157

The Halo Effect   157

Stereotypes: Perceptions About Groups of People   156

Research Evidence   158

Stereotype Formation and Maintenance   159

Sex-Role Stereotypes   159

OB Exercise *What Are your Attitudes towards Women Executives?*   160

Age Stereotypes   162

Race Stereotypes   162

Managerial Challenges and Recommendations   163

International OB *Bank of Montreal Proactively Reduces Stereotypes about Women*   163

Self-Fulfilling Prophecy: The Pygmalion Effect   164

Research and an Explanatory Model   164

Putting the Self-Fulfilling Prophecy to Work   166

Causal Attributions   166

Kelley's Model of Attribution   167

Weiner's Model of Attribution   168

Attributional Tendencies   169

Managerial Application and Implications   169

Personal Awareness and Growth Exercise *What Is Your Attributional Style?*   172

Group Exercise *Using Attribution Theory to Resolve Performance Problems*   174

Chapter Seven

Motivation through Needs, Job Design, and Satisfaction   178

What Does Motivation Involve?   181

A Systems Model of Motivation and Performance   181

Historical Roots of Modern Motivation Theories   182

International OB *How a Western Motivation Helped a Japanese Businessman*   183

Motivation Is Only One Factor in the Performance Equation   184

Need Theories of Motivation   185

Maslow's Need Hierarchy Theory   185

McClelland's Need Theory   187

OB Exercise *Assess Your Need Strength with a Thematic Apperception Test (TAT)*   188

Historical Approaches to Job Design   189

Scientific Management   190

Job Enlargement   190

Job Rotation   191

Job Enrichment   191

International OB *Work Culture That Brings No Satisfaction*   192

Job Characteristics Approach to Job Design   193

Overview of the Job Characteristics Model   193

Applying the Job Characteristics Model   196

Practical Implications of the Job Characteristics Model   196

The Causes and Consequences of Job Satisfaction   197

The Causes of Job Satisfaction   197

OB Exercise *How Satisfied Are You with Your Present Job?* 197

    The Consequences of Job Satisfaction 198

Personal Awareness and Growth Exercise

What Is Your Work Ethic? 202

Group Exercise *Applying the Job Characteristics Model* 203

Chapter Eight
Motivation through Equity, Expectancy, and Goal Setting 208

  Adams's Equity Theory of Motivation 210

    The Individual–Organization Exchange Relationship 211

    Negative and Positive Inequity 211

    Dynamics of Perceived Inequity 213

    Expanding the Concept of Equity 213

    Equity Research Findings 214

    Practical Lessons from Equity Theory 214

  Expectancy Theory of Motivation 215

    Vroom's Expectancy Theory 216

OB Exercise *Measuring Perceived Organizational Equity/Fairness* 216

    Porter and Lawler's Extension 218

    Research on Expectancy Theory and Managerial Implications 219

  Motivation through Goal Setting 221

    Goals: Definition and Background 221

    How Does Goal Setting Work? 222

International OB *Japanese Organizations Begin to Reward Performance Instead of Seniority* 222

    Insights from Goal-Setting Research 224

International OB *Veba AG Directs Its Attention to Shareholder Value* 224

    Practical Application of Goal Setting 227

  Putting Motivational Theories to Work 228

Personal Awareness and Growth Exercise *What Outcomes Motivate Employees?* 231

Group Exercise *The Case of the Missing Form* 232

Chapter Nine
Improving Job Performance with Feedback and Rewards 238

Understanding the Feedback Process 241

  Two Functions of Feedback 242

  A Cognitive-Processing Model of Performance Feedback 242

  Sources of Feedback 243

  The Recipient of Feedback 244

OB Exercise *How Strong Is Your Desire for Performance Feedback?* 244

  Behavioural Outcomes of Feedback 245

  Practical Lessons from Feedback Research 246

Nontraditional Feedback: Upward and 360-Degree 246

  Upward Feedback 247

  360-Degree Feedback 248

  Some Concluding Tips for Giving Good Feedback 249

Organizational Reward Systems 249

  Types of Rewards 250

  Organizational Reward Norms 251

  Reward Distribution Criteria 252

  Desired Outcomes of the Reward System 252

  Why Do Rewards Fail to Motivate? 252

Pay for Performance 252

  Putting Pay for Performance into Perspective 253

  Incentive Bonuses and Motivation: A Double-Impact Model 254

  Profit Sharing versus Gainsharing 255

International OB *Gainsharing Helps This Swedish–American Joint Venture Thrive* 257

  Team-Based Pay 258

  Making Pay for Performance Work 259

Personal Awareness and Growth Exercise *What Kind of Feedback Are You Getting?* 261

Group Exercise *Rewards, Rewards, Rewards* 262

Part Three
Group and Social Processes

Chapter Ten
Group Dynamics 268

Groups: Definitions, Types, and Functions   271
   Formal and Informal Groups   272
   Functions of Formal Groups   273
The Group Development Process   273
   Five Stages   273
   Group Development: Research and
   Practical Implications   275
Roles and Norms: Social Building Blocks for
Group and Organizational Behaviour   276
   Roles   276
   Norms   278
OB Exercise *Measuring Role Conflict and
Role Ambiguity*   278
   Relevant Research Insights and Managerial
   Implications   279
Group Structure and Composition   280
   Functional Roles Performed by Group
   Members   280
   Group Size   281
   Effects of Men and Women Working
   Together in Groups   282
   Individual Ability and Group
   Effectiveness   284
OB Exercise *What Is the Degree of
Sexualization in Your Work Environment?*   284
Threats to Group Effectiveness   286
   The Asch Effect   287
   Groupthink   288
   Social Loafing   289
Personal Awareness and Growth Exercise
Is This a Mature Work Group or Team?   292
Group Exercise *A Committee Decision*   293

Chapter Eleven
Power, Politics, Conflict, and Negotiation   298
Organizational Influence Tactics: Getting One's
Way at Work   301
   Eight Generic Influence Tactics   301
   Three Possible Influence Outcomes   302
   Practical Research Insights   302
   How to Extend Your Influence by Forming
   Strategic Alliances   303
Social Power and Empowerment   303
   Dimensions of Power   304
   Research Insights about Social Power   306

OB Exercise *What Is Your Self-Perceived
Power?*   306
   Responsible Management of Power through
   Empowerment   307
International OB *Mercedes-Benz to Employees:
Do Your Own Reorganization*   309
Organizational Politics and Impression
Management   311
   Definition and Domain of Organizational
   Politics   311
   Political Tactics   312
   Impression Management   314
   Research Evidence on Organizational
   Politics and Impression Management   316
OB Exercise *How Much Do You Rely on
Upward Impression Management Tactics?*   316
   Managing Organizational Politics   317
   Women and Organizational Politics   317
Managing Interpersonal and Intergroup Conflict   318
   A Conflict Continuum   318
   Functional versus Dysfunctional Conflict   318
   Antecedents of Conflict   319
International OB *Conflict-Handling in an
International Context*   320
   Stimulating Functional Conflict   321
   Alternative Styles for Handling
   Dysfunctional Conflict   322
   Handling Intergroup Conflict with
   Negotiation and Third-Party Intervention   324
OB Exercise *What Is Your Primary
Conflict-Handling Style?*   324
   Conflict and Negotiation Research
   Evidence   326
   Conflict Management: A Contingency
   Approach   327
Personal Awareness and Growth Exercise *How
Political Are You?*   329
Group Exercise *Bangkok Blowup (A
Role-Playing Exercise)*   330

Chapter Twelve
Individual and Group Decision Making   336
Models of Decision Making   339
   The Rational Model   339
   Simon's Normative Model   341
   The Garbage Can Model   342

International OB *A Garbage Can Process Leads Triton Energy Corp. to Strike Oil in Yopal, Colombia* 344

Dynamics of Decision Making 346

Selecting Solutions: A Contingency Perspective 346

Escalation of Commitment 348

OB Exercise *Making a Decision in an Escalation Situation* 348

Group Decision Making 350

Advantages and Disadvantages of Group-Aided Decision Making 350

Participative Management 352

When Groups should Participate in Decision Making: The Vroom/Yetton/Jago Model 353

Group Problem-Solving Techniques 355

Research on Group Problem-Solving Techniques 358

Creativity 358

Definitions and Stages 359

A Model of Organizational Creativity and Innovation 360

International OB *Matsushita Electric Creates Breadmaker by Combining Tacit and Explicit Knowledge* 360

Personal Awareness and Growth Exercise

What Is Your Decision-Making Style? 365

Group Exercise *Applying the Vroom/Yetton/Jago Decision-Making Model* 366

Chapter Thirteen
Teams and Teamwork for the 21st Century 372

Work Teams: Types, Effectiveness, and Stumbling Blocks 375

A General Typology of Work Teams 375

Work Team Effectiveness: An Ecological Model 378

Why Do Work Teams Fail? 379

Effective Teamwork through Cooperation, Trust, and Cohesiveness 380

Cooperation 381

Trust 383

Cohesiveness 384

Teams in Action: From Quality Circles to Self-Managed Teams 386

Quality Circles 387

Self-Managed Teams 389

OB Exercise *Measuring Work Group Autonomy* 391

Team Building 393

The Purpose of Team Building/High-Performance Teams 394

Developing Team Members' Self-Management Skills 395

International OB *The Wild World of Cross-Cultural Team Building* 396

Personal Awareness and Growth Exercise
How Trusting Are You? 398

Group Exercise *Student Team Development Project* 399

Part Four
Organizational Processes

Chapter Fourteen
Organizational Communication in the Computerized Workplace 406

Basic Dimensions of the Communication Process 409

A Perceptual Process Model of Communication 409

Choosing Media: A Contingency Perspective 411

Interpersonal Communication 413

Assertiveness, Aggressiveness, and Nonassertiveness 414

International OB *Cross-Cultural Awareness Affects Interpersonal Communication* 415

Sources of Nonverbal Communication 416

International OB *Norms for Touching Vary across Countries* 417

Active Listening 418

Women and Men Communicate Differently 421

Organizational Communication Patterns 423

Hierarchical Communication 423

The Grapevine 424

Communication Distortion between Managers and Employees 426

Dynamics of Modern Communications 427

Communication in the Computerized Information Age 427

OB Exercise *A Self-Assessment of Antecedents and Outcomes of Distortion in Upward Communication*   428

Barriers to Effective Communication   430

Personal Awareness and Growth Exercise
Assessing Your Listening Skills   434

Group Exercise *Practising Different Styles of Communication*   435

Chapter Fifteen

Behaviour Modification and
Self-Management   440

What Is Behaviour Modification?   443

Thorndike's Law of Effect   443

Skinner's Operant Conditioning Model   444

Principles of Behaviour Modification   444

A→B→C Contingencies   444

Contingent Consequences   446

International OB *North Americans Modify Behaviour with Classical Music!*   446

Schedules of Reinforcement   448

OB Exercise *A Test of How
Well You Know the
Schedules of Reinforcement*   448

Behaviour Shaping   450

A Model for Modifying Job Behaviour   450

Step 1: Identify Target Behaviour   450

Step 2: Functionally Analyse the
Situation   452

Step 3: Arrange Antecedents and Provide
Consequences   452

International OB *Organizational Behaviour Modification (OB Mod) Successfully Exported to Russia*   454

Step 4: Evaluate Results   455

Some Practical Implications   455

Why OB Mod is so Unpopular in Europe   456

The Anthroposophic Movement   456

Behavioural Self-Management   457

Bandura's Social Learning Theory   457

A Managerial Context for Behavioural
Self-Management   457

Social Learning Model of
Self-Management   458

Research and Managerial Implications   461

Personal Awareness and Growth Exercise *How Are Your B Mod Skills?*   463

Group Exercise *Human Resource
Problem-Solving Team*   463

Chapter Sixteen

Leadership   468

What Does Leadership Involve?   472

What Is Leadership?   472

Leading versus Managing   473

Trait and Behavioural Theories of Leadership   475

Trait Theory   475

Behavioural Styles Theory   477

International OB *Russian Leadership Traits in Three Eras*   478

Situational Theories   480

Fiedler's Contingency Model   480

OB Exercise *Assessing Teacher Leadership Style, Class Satisfaction, and Student Role Clarity*   481

Path–Goal Theory   483

Hersey and Blanchard's Situational
Leadership Theory   484
A Competing Value Approach to
Leadership   485

From Transactional to Charismatic
Leadership   486

What Is the Difference between
Transactional and Charismatic
Leadership?   487

How Does Charismatic Leadership
Transform Followers?   487

Research and Managerial Implications   489

Additional Perspectives on Leadership   490

Graen's Leader–Member Exchange (LMX)
Model of Leadership   490

Substitutes for Leadership   491

Superleadership   493

Coaching   493

Personal Awareness and Growth Exercise *How Ready Are You to Assume the Leadership Role?*   495

Group Exercise *Exhibiting Leadership within the Context of Running a Meeting*   496

Chapter Seventeen

Managing Occupational Stress   500

Defining Stress   503

The Medical Approach to Stress   504
The Clinical Approach to Stress   505
The OB Approach to Stress   505

Important Stressors and Stress Outcomes   508

Stressful Life Events   509

OB Exercise *The Holmes and Rahe Social
Readjustment Rating Scale*   510

Burnout   511

Organizational and Economic Costs
of Stress   513

Moderators of Occupational Stress   513

Social Support   513

International OB *Zeneca Pharmaceuticals
Helps Employees Manage Their Workloads*   514

Coping   515

Hardiness   517

Type A Behaviour Pattern   518

OB Exercise *Where Are You on the Type A–B
Behaviour Continuum?*   519

Stress-Reduction Techniques   520

Muscle Relaxation   521

Biofeedback   522

Meditation   522

Cognitive Restructuring   522

Employment Assistance
Programmes (EAPs)   523

Legal Liabilities of Stress   523

Personal Awareness and Growth Exercise

Are You Burned Out?   525

Group Exercise *Reducing the Stressors in Your
Environment*   527

Part Five
The Evolving Organization

Chapter Eighteen

Organizations: Structure and Effectiveness   532

Defining and Charting Organizations   535

What Is an Organization?   535

Organization Charts   535

The Evolution of Organizational Metaphors   537

Closed versus Open Systems   538

Organizations as Military/Mechanical
Bureaucracies   539

Organizations as Biological Systems   539

International OB *The* Mugama: *Egypt's
Bureaucratic Legacy*   540

Organizations as Cognitive Systems   541

Organizations as Ecosystem
Participants   542

Organizational Metaphors in Perspective
(towards Postmodern Organizations)   543

**The Role of Hierarchy in Today's Downsized,
Reengineered Organizations**   543

How Necessary Is Hierarchy?   544

Substitutes for Hierarchy: A Contingency
Approach   544

Organizational Effectiveness   546

International OB *French Bureaucracy:
Le Systéme "D"*   546

Generic Organizational-Effectiveness
Criteria   547

Multiple Effectiveness Criteria: Some
Practical Guidelines   549

Personal Awareness and Growth Exercise   551

Group Exercise *Stakeholder Audit Team*   552

Chapter Nineteen

Organizational Life Cycles and Design   556

Organizational Life Cycles   559

Organizational Life-Cycle Stages   559

Life-Cycle Timing and Type of Change   559

Organizational Life-Cycle Research and
Practical Implications   562

**The Contingency Approach to Organization
Design**   562

Assessing Environmental Uncertainty   562

Differentiation and Integration: The
Lawrence and Lorsch Study   562

Mechanistic versus Organic
Organizations   565

International OB *W L Gore's Organic Structure
Thrives in Scotland*   566

**Three Important Contingency
Variables: Technology,
Size, and Strategic Choice**   568

The Impact of Technology on Structure
(Woodward and Beyond)   568

Organizational Size and Performance   568

Strategic Choice and Organizational
Structure   570

The Shape of Tomorrow's Organizations   570

New-Style versus Old-Style Organizations   571

Four New Organizational Patterns   571

Personal Awareness and Growth Exercise
Organization Design Field Study   575

Group Exercise *Getting Business Colleges to Swallow Their Own Medicine*   577

Chapter Twenty

Managing Change in Learning Organizations   582

Forces of Change   585

External Forces   585

Internal Forces   587

International OB *Banks Try to Penetrate Untapped Markets in South Africa*   587

Models and Dynamics of Planned Change   588

Types of Change   588

Lewin's Change Model   589

A Systems Model of Change   590

Kotter's Eight Steps for Leading Organizational Change   592

Organization Development   592

Understanding and Managing Resistance to Change   594

Why People Resist Change in the Workplace?   594

Research on Resistance to Change   596

Alternative Strategies for Overcoming Resistance to Change   596

OB Exercise *Assessing an Organization's Readiness for Change*   597

Creating a Learning Organization   598

Defining a Learning Organization   599

Building an Organization's Learning Capability   600

Organizations Naturally Resist Learning   602

Effective Leadership Is the Solution   603

Unlearning the Organization   604

Personal Awareness and Growth Exercise
Applying the Systems Model of Change   607

Group Exercise *Creating Personal Change through Force-Field Analysis*   608

Glossary   612

Index   616

Preface

I don't know whether I have to be grateful or feel sorry for the moment when I agreed to the idea of a European adaptation of Bob Kreitner and Angelo Kinicki's reference book on Organizational Behaviour.

Grateful because it has created the opportunity to meet Bob and Angelo, to have the privilege to work on a world-class text, and to apply all the notions of effective teamwork in my collaborative efforts with Fannie Debussche, without whom this European edition would have ended in my desktop's dustbin.

Sorry, because adapting a brilliantly homogeneous American text has put our nerves to unprecedented tests.

In the end it is the gratefulness that prevails.

Our kick-off meeting in November 1994 in Arizona was one of the most rewarding professional encounters in my career. Bob and Angelo combine a clear concept, long relevant experience, and a relentless drive towards quality. Thank you, Bob and Angelo, for all the feedback, the encouragement, the wisdom, and the perspectives.

At the beginning we had three major objectives in mind:

1. Having a European student-friendly end product. Only a few European students are familiar with quarterbacks, gallons, K-Mart. But they know IKEA, The Body Shop, Virgin…We are very happy to have found highly relevant quotes from European managers, and to have almost exclusive European opening cases.

2. To add some typical European flavours to the dish. Charles Handy once remarked: "An American friend, visiting Britain and Europe for the first time wondered 'Why is it that over here whenever I ask a reason for anything, any institution or ceremony or set of rules, they always give me a historical answer—because…, whereas in my country we always want a functional answer—in order to…'" (Charles Handy, *The Age of Unreason*, London: Random House, 1990, p 3).

3. To add some more historical perspectives and some references to the European cultural heritage.

At the beginning of our work we wanted to highlight the European theoretical perspective. But we were warned by two experts: "When one thinks about management in Europe the image of diversity usually dominates, and the idea of a distinctive European style of management seems like wishful thinking" (Roland Calori and Philippe De Woot in *A European Management Model*, (London: Prentice-Hall, 1994, p 3). At the same time some European work (Hofstede's intercultural dimensions being the most radical example) is readily accepted in the whole world. One cannot deny that 80 per cent of the relevant OB theories are American. Many of them are tested in different cultures. Many are universalistic. Others do not pass the test. Most American authors, including Bob and Angelo, have worked very hard to become more internationally oriented, to overcome Amercian ethnocentrism (for the exact definition of "ethnocentrism" refer to Chapter 3). It also struck us that people all over the world watch the same American series, play the same Japanese video games, admire the same French and Italian designers. More and more people all over the world are hungry for the same business books, ranging from *Reengineering the Corporation* to *Emotional Intelligence*. Applying the same ideas under different circumstances is a contingency approach (for a defintion of "a contingency approach" see Chapter 1). Hence, our objective became "an excellent OB book for European students" and not a book on European OB.

The first European edition is dedicated to Baroness

Cécile Vlerick-Sap, who generously supported this book. She is a truly European woman. The late Professor Vlerick was one of the co-founders of the European Foundation of Management Development. She always helped her husband in fostering the European dimension of management.

Fannie Debussche has sometimes done the impossible to raise the quality level of this book. "Fannie, isn't there a better European example?" "Fannie, I've seen an article written by John Kay. It has to do with ties." "Fannie, what went wrong with those tables?" "Fannie, let's go to London. We have to speak to the editors." "Any news from Angelo?"

A combination of endless patience, careful scrutiny, professional approach, Fannie's name is on every page. It is in a very fine print, only readable by those who have a true OB heart.

My special thanks go to the manuscript reviewers, who for this first European edition were:

Professor Finn Borum, Copenhagen Business School, Denmark.

Dr Martin Gammell, University of Luton, UK.

Professor Roger Gill, Strathclyde Graduate Business School, University of Strathclyde, Scotland.

Dr Stephen Gourlay, Kingston Business School, University of Kingston, UK.

Marc Buelens

One

The World of Organizational Behaviour

One Managing Organizational Behaviour for Quality and Results

Two Managing Diversity: Releasing Every Employee's Potential

Three Organizational Culture, Values, and Ethics

Four International OB: Managing Across Cultures

One

Managing Organizational Behaviour for Quality and Results

When you finish studying the material in this chapter, you should be able to:

1. Identify the Ps in the 4-P cycle of continuous improvement and define the term *management*.

2. Identify at least 5 of the 11 managerial skills in Wilson's profile of effective managers.

3. Describe the new employment contract.

4. Characterize 21st-century managers.

5. Define the term *organizational behaviour,* and explain why OB is a horizontal discipline.

6. Contrast McGregor's Theory X and Theory Y assumptions about employees.

7. Explain the managerial significance of Deming's 85—15 rule.

8. Identify the four principles of total quality management (TQM).

9. Describe the sources of organizational behaviour research evidence.

Why did the Vasa sink?

Stockholm, summer 1628. For three years, carpenters, pit-sawyers, smiths, ropemakers, glaziers, sailmakers, painters, boxmakers, woodcarvers and other specialists had worked on building the Navy's new warship - the Vasa. She was a "royal ship", the seventeenth-century designation for the largest type of naval vessel, designed to be the foremost of Sweden's warships. The new ship aroused the admiration and pride of Stockholmers, but intimidated the countries' enemies. We know that her construction was followed with interest abroad.

By Sunday 10 August, everything was ready for the maiden voyage. The weather was fine and the wind light. On board were around hundred crew members, but also women and children. This was to be a great ceremonial occasion, with pomp and circumstance, so the crew had been given permission to take their families on the first voyage out through the archipelago.

Countless curious spectators gathered in the harbour. They had plenty of time to follow the ship's departure. The wind was from the south-west and, for the first few hundred metres, the Vasa had to be pulled along using anchors. At Tranbodarna, the present-day Slussen, Captain Söfring Hansson issued the order: "Set the foresail, foretop, maintop and mizzen!"

The sailors climbed the rig and set four of the Vasa's 10 sails. The guns fired a salute and slowly, serenely, the Vasa set off on her first voyage.

In a letter to the King, the Council of the Realm described the subsequent course of events: "When the ship left the shelter of Tegelviken, a stronger wind entered the sails and she immediately began to heel over hard to the lee side; she righted herself slightly again until she approached Beckholmen, where she heeled right over and water gushed in through the gun ports until she slowly went to the bottom under sail, pennants and all."

Struck by a powerful gust of wind, the Vasa capsized and sank after a voyage of only 1,300 metres.

Admiral Erik Jönsson witnessed to the terrifying seconds on board when water poured in through the gun ports and the ship began to sink. Jönsson was inside the ship, checking the guns: "By the time I came up from the lower deck, the water had risen so high that the staircase had come loose and it was only with great difficulty that I climbed out."

The Admiral became "so waterlogged and badly knocked about by the hatches" that he was near death for several days. Some fifty people are said to have followed the Vasa into the deep.

News of the disaster did not reach the Swedish King, who was then in Prussia, until two weeks later. He wrote to the Council of Realm in Stockholm that "imprudence and negligence" must have been the cause, and that the guilty parties must be punished.

Were you intoxicated? Had you failed to secure the guns properly? Questions and accusations echoed in the hall of the Royal Castle. Just twelve hours after the loss of the Vasa her Danish-born Captain, Söfring Hansson, stood before the Council of the Realm. He had been taken prisoner immediately afterwards, and the report on his interrogation has survived to this day. "You can cut me in a thousand pieces if all the guns were not secured", he answered. "And before God Almighty I swear that no one on the board was intoxicated." Söfring Hansson thus swore that he was innocent. "It was just a small gust of wind, a mere breeze, that overturned the ship", Söfring Hansson went on to relate. "The ship was too unsteady, although all the ballast was on board." Thus, Söfring Hansson placed the blame on the ship's design—and, by the same token, the shipbuilder.

When the crew were later questioned, they said the same thing. No mistake was made on board. It was impossible to load more ballast. The guns were properly lashed down. It was a Sunday, many people had been to Communion and no member of the crew was drunk. Instead, the fault lay in the unstable construction of the ship: the keel was too small in relation to the hull, the rig and the artillery. "The ship is top-heavy with her masts and yards, sails and guns", they declared.

Shipmaster Jöran Matsson also revealed that the Vasa's stability had been tested before the sailing. Thirty men had run back and forth across the Vasa's deck when she was moored at the quay. After three runs, they had to stop—otherwise, the Vasa would have capsized. Present during the test was Admiral Klas Fleming, one of the most influential men in the Navy. The Admiral's only comment, according to Jöran Matsson, was: "If only His Majesty were at home!"

Those responsible for Skeppsgarden, where the Vasa was built, where then questioned. These were shipbuilder Hein Jakobsson and Arent de Groot, the lessee of Skeppsgarden. One complication was that the actual builder of the Vasa, the Dutchman Henrik Hybertsson, had died the year before. However, Jakobsson and de Groot also swore their innocence. The Vasa conformed to the dimensions approved by the King himself, they said. On board were a number of guns, as specified in the contract.

When the Vasa was salvaged in 1961, it became clear that the guns had not become loose, so they could not have caused the disaster. Present-day technical calculations have also shown that the Vasa is extremely top-heavy, and requires only a moderate wind force to overturn her. Who, then, was at fault?

Admiral Fleming can be blamed partly. He failed to prevent the ship's departure after an unsatisfying stability test, although it was within his power to do so. King Gustavus II Adolphus, too, can be blamed partly, as he wanted a ship with as many guns as possible on board. The shipbuilder, Henrik Hybertsson, was very experienced, the Vasa was very well constructed. Moreover, all ships carrying many guns were very tall and highly unstable. It was therefore impossible to see that the Vasa was top-heavy.[1]

Discussion Question
Why did the Vasa sink?

Sometimes the best place to begin is at the end. This approach is appropriate for the topic of managing people because management is a goal-oriented, or ends-oriented, endeavour. As we will see in the content of this book, a worthy goal for present and future managers is to develop a progressive philosophy for managing our most important resource: people. As Peter Drucker says: "The manager's first task is to make effective the strength of people."[2] Managers such as Virgin boss Richard Branson, The Body Shop's Anita Roddick or IKEA's founder Ingvar Kamprad are so successful because of their conviction that in business, staff should come first:

"Direct contact with people is more valuable than any market survey, " says Ingvar Kamprad.[3] "What I do best is finding people and letting them work. Virgin staff are not mere hired hands. They are not managerial pawns in some gigantic chess game. They are entrepreneurs in their own right," states Richard Branson.[4] "When people say 'I can't do it' or 'I'm only one person', a very effective answer is 'If you think you are too small to be effective, go to bed with a mosquito'," concludes Anita Roddick.[5]

As well as being an inspiring challenge for all managers, these quotes pinpoint three key thrusts of this book. They are described in the following paragraphs.

1. *A human resource development thrust.* Are employees a commodity to be hired and discarded depending on the short-run whims of the organization? Or are they a valuable resource to be nurtured and developed? Sadly, as the massive layoffs from corporate downsizings, reorganizations, and mergers in recent years indicate, the first assumption tends to be the rule.

Too often, large, mismanaged companies that had engaged in undisciplined hiring during more prosperous times simply became smaller, mismanaged companies. While a layoff can be a necessary part of a comprehensive corporate transformation habitual layoffs are a dead end.[6]

ETHICS

More progressive and far-sighted companies treat their employees as a valuable resource, making layoffs the last rather than the first option. They develop "human recycling" programmes through retraining and redeployment.[7]

This book firmly embraces the idea that people are valuable human resources requiring systematic nurturing and development.

2. *A fact-based knowledge thrust.* The field of organizational behaviour is driven by research findings and factual knowledge. This enables current and future managers to identify and eliminate unhealthy preconceptions about people at work. Such preconceptions are commonly based on prejudice, stereotypes, myths, misunderstanding, and ignorance. As a case in point, please take a few moments to respond to the workplace knowledge quiz in the OB Exercise.

How did you do? Are you surprised by some of the answers? For example, stories in the popular press in recent years have left casual observers with the impression that Americans dislike their jobs, the Japanese love their jobs, computers are the answer to everything, and middle managers are practically extinct. In each case, objective facts point in a very different direction.

Our quiz is *not* an intelligence test or an indicator of how well or poorly you will do in your studies. Rather, it serves as a reminder that a key (and fun) part of learning is *surprise*. Factual and research-based surprises challenge us to reject counterproductive ways of thinking. Those who want to be effective managers of people need to have the courage to question themselves and their ways of doing things when faced with a surprising new fact, concept, or application.

3. *A results-oriented managerial thrust.* Few would argue with the claim that we all should know more about why people behave as they do. After all, by better understanding others, we gain greater understanding of ourselves. But from a managerial standpoint, simply acquiring knowledge about organizational behaviour is not enough. That knowledge needs to be put to work to get something accomplished. Managers in all types and sizes of organizations are responsible for getting results. The 4-P model of strategic results in Figure 1–1, focusing on *people, products, processes,* and *productivity,* represents management's agenda for *continuous improvement* in the late 1990s and beyond. This book strives to help today's and tomorrow's managers achieve these challenging and sometimes conflicting results.[8]

The purpose of this chapter is to explore the manager's job, define and examine organizational behaviour and its evolution, and consider how we can learn more about organizational behaviour. A topical model for the balance of the book also is introduced.

The Manager's Job: Getting Things Done through Others

Management

Process of working with and through others to achieve organizational objectives efficiently and ethically.

ETHICS

For better or for worse, managers touch our lives in many ways. Schools, hospitals, government agencies, and large and small businesses all require systematic management. Formally defined, **management** is the process of working with and through others to achieve organizational objectives in an efficient and ethical manner. From the standpoint of organizational behaviour, the central feature of this definition is "working with and through others". Managers play a constantly evolving role. Today's successful managers are no longer the I've-got-everything-under-control order givers of yesteryear. Rather, they need to creatively envision and actively sell bold new directions in an ethical and sensitive manner. Effective managers are team players empowered by the willing and active support of others who are driven by conflicting self-interests. Each of us has a huge stake in how well managers carry out their evolving role. Henry Mintzberg, a respected management scholar, observed: "No job is more vital to our society than that of the manager. It is the manager who determines whether our social institutions serve us well or whether they squander our talents and resources."[9]

OB EXERCISE   *Test Your Factual Knowledge about People at Work*

1. 1 Which country has the highest level of employee satisfaction in Europe?
    a. Switzerland   b.Sweden   c. Spain
2. The lowest percentage of employees in _____ are satisfied with their company.
    a. Mexico   b. Switzland   c. US
    d. Japan   e. Germany
3. An investment in capital equipment (such as machinery and computers) will increase an organization's productivity more than an equal investment in employee education.
    a. True   b. False
4. According to an opinion survey in the UK, a high basic salary is the most important motivation factor.
    a. True   b. False
5. Which group believes more strongly that older workers (50 and older) should step aside for younger workers?
    a. Younger workers   b. Older workers
6. Minorities and women hired under affirmative action guidelines leave the oganization sooner than other recruits.
    a. True   b. False

7. Only 29 per cent of the US workforce in the year 2000 will be white males.
    a. True   b. False
8. In which country are 43 per cent of the managerial jobs held by women?
    a. US   b.Sweden   c. Japan
9. Skill level of the work force will be HR's major concern in the years to come, immediately followed by managing change and information technology.
    a. True   b. False
10. Managers report that they communicate more efficiently thanks to technical innovations such as faxing, e-mail, voice-mail and the Internet.
    a. True   b. False

Answers, interpretations, and sources can be found following the Notes at the end of this chapter.

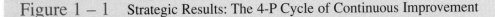

Figure 1 – 1   Strategic Results: The 4-P Cycle of Continuous Improvement

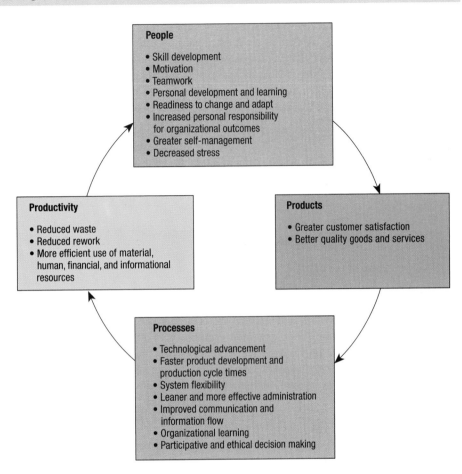

Extending our managerial thrust, let us take a closer look at the skills managers need to perform, the evolving relationship between employer and employee, and the future direction of management.

What Do Managers Do? A Skills Profile

Observational studies by, among others, Rosemary Stewart in Europe and Henry Mintzberg in the USA have found the typical manager's day to be a fragmented collection of brief episodes.[10] It is the brevity of most activities that is the dominant characteristic of a manager's day at all levels in the hierarchy.[11] Interruptions are commonplace, while large blocks of time for planning and reflective thinking are not. In one particular study, four top-level managers spent 63 per cent of their time on activities lasting less than nine minutes each. Only 5 per cent of the managers' time was devoted to activities lasting more than a hour.[12] But what specific tasks do managers' perform during their hectic and fragmented workdays? More recent research evidence gives us some instructive and interesting answers.

Many attempts have been made over the years to paint a realistic picture of what managers do.[13] Diverse and confusing lists of managerial functions and roles have been suggested. Fortunately, a stream of research over the past 20 years by Clark Wilson and others has given us a practical and statistically validated profile of managerial *skills*[14] (see Table 1–1). Wilson's managerial skills profile focuses on 11 observable categories of managerial behaviour. This emphasis on skills is very much in tune with today's results-oriented organizations. Indeed, Wilson's unique skills-assessment technique goes beyond the usual self-report approach with its natural bias. In addition to surveying a given manager about his or her 11 skills, the Wilson approach also asks those who report directly to the manager to answer questions about their boss's skills.

According to Wilson and his colleagues, the result is an assessment of skill mastery, not simply skill awareness.[15] The logic behind Wilson's approach is both simple and compelling. Who better to assess a manager's skills than the people who experience those behaviours on a day-to-day basis—those who report directly to the manager?

The Wilson managerial skills research yields three useful lessons:

1. Dealing effectively with *people* is what management is all about. The 11 skills in Table 1–1 constitute a goal creation/commitment/feedback/reward/accomplishment cycle with human interaction at every turn.

2. Managers with high skills mastery tend to have better subunit performance and employee morale than managers with low skills mastery.[16]

3. *Effective* female and male managers *do not* have significantly different skill profiles,[17] contrary to claims in the popular business press in recent years.[18]

The New Employment Contract: A Cautionary Tale

Employment contract
Mutual written and implied expectations between employer and employee.

Just imagine you work for a large international company and just woke up from a 20-year nap: you would be shocked and worried. Your **employment contract**, defined as the written and implied expectations between employer and employee, would have been completely rewritten (without your input or consent).[19] When you went to sleep, your employer expected you to be loyal, hard working, and obedient. In return, you expected to get a steady stream of salary increases and promotions and the proverbial gold watch upon your retirement from the company. In short, the company was like a nurturing parent who knew what was best for you and your career. You loved and trusted the company.

Now your head spins as you hear things about the so-called new employment

---

Table 1 – 1   **Skills Exhibited by an Effective Manager***

1. **Clarifies goals and objectives** for everyone involved.
   (See Chs. 6, 8, 14, 16, and 18)
2. **Encourages participation**, upward communication, and suggestions.
   (See Chs. 5, 10, 11, 13, 14, and 16)
3. **Plans and organizes** for an orderly work flow.
   (See Chs. 18, 19, and 20)
4. **Has technical and administrative expertise** to answer organization-related questions.
   (See Chs. 1, 2, 9, 14, and 20)
5. **Facilitates work** through team building, training, coaching, and support.
   (See Chs. 3, 4, 7, 9, 13, 14, 15, 16, and 17)
6. **Provides feedback** honestly and constructively.
   (See Chs. 9, 11, 13, 14, 15, and 16)
7. **Keeps things moving** by relying on schedules, deadlines, and helpful reminders.
   (See Chs. 7, 8, 9, 11, 13, 14, 15, 16, and 20)
8. **Controls details** without being overbearing.
   (See Chs. 2, 4, 5, 6, 9, 12, 14, 16, and 17)
9. Applies reasonable **pressure for goal accomplishment.**
   (See Chs. 1, 4, 5, 6, 7, 8, 9, 10, 11, 12, 15, 16, 17, and 18)
10. **Empowers and delegates** key duties to others while maintaining goal clarity and commitment.
    (See Chs. 3, 11, 12, 13, 16, and 19)
11. **Recognizes good performance** with rewards and positive reinforcement.
    (See Chs. 7, 8, 9, 14, 15, and 16)

*Annotated with relevant chapters in this textbook.

Source: Adapted from material in C Wilson, "Identify Needs with Costs in Mind", *Training and Development Journal,* July 1980, pp 58–62; and F Shipper, "A Study of the Psychometric Properties of the Managerial Skill Scales of the Survey of Management Practices", *Educational and Psychological Measurement,* June 1995, pp 468–79.

contract. "Everyone is self-employed." "You own your own employability." "Build a portable career." "No skills, no thrills." "You're paid to add value." "Be willing to stay, but ready to leave." According to this new employment contract, your employer expects you to be a creative self-starter and team-player capable of doing a variety of jobs with a diverse array of people. Your pay will be tied to results, not to years on the job. Moreover, your company expects you to take charge of your own career and act more like a partner than an employee. Complaints and comments by co-workers tell you they don't love and trust the company as before. You turn to one of them and whisper, "What's a stock option? And what on earth is e-mail?" You certainly would have a lot to learn.

The new employment contract, although couched in terms of today's economy in this tale, has immense implications for both individuals and organizations in advanced economies worldwide.

Implications for the Individual   For employees committed to life-long learning, working smarter rather than harder, and making their own opportunities, the new employment contract is a positive situation. Organizational life will give them more opportunities to grow and be rewarded for creating value for internal and external customers. Promotions will be fewer and slower than under the old employment contract because of flatter organizations with fewer layers. But lateral moves from one project or function to another will provide lots of challenge for those who get results. The skills profile for an effective manager in Table 1–1 is a good measuring stick for personal growth and success under the new contract. Meanwhile, the new employment contract is *not* good news for employees with an entitlement mentality. They are the ones who believe the company owes them pay rises and promotions just for showing up at work. They also tend to be inflexible and resistant to change.

Implications for Organizations   According to one management writer, there has been a shift from a "relational contract" to a "transactional contract".[20] Unfortunately, corporations so far have done a better job of defining the employees' end of the bargain than they have their own. It is one thing to say everyone is self-employed, but what are the company's obligations in the new transactional environment? How eager are companies to train employees who might turn around and go to work for a competitor? Employees who feel they are skydiving without a parachute are unlikely to express the loyalty and trust of yesteryear. Yet many executives seem to want it both ways: 21st-century staffing flexibility and 1950s-style employee loyalty. After attending a meeting of human resource professionals in 1996, one observer noted that the biggest complaint "was that high-tech workers have zero company loyalty".[21] Figure 1–2 shows the results of an

Figure 1 – 2   Employee Loyalty in 13 Countries

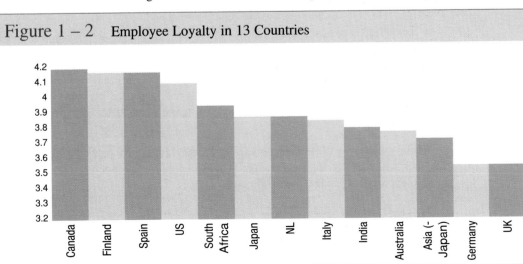

Source: M Hequet, J Gordan, C Lee, M Picard and D Stamps, "Does the new employment contract breed worker loyalty?" *Training*, November 1996, pp 10-12.

international study carried out in 13 countries. On a scale of 1 to 5, with 5 indicating the greatest employee commitment, Canada scores highest, the UK lowest. The researchers asked about employees' perceptions of their companies' focus on customers, quality, and employees, and whether the employees believed better job opportunities existed elsewhere.

Loyalty and trust can be *earned,* but not demanded, in the era of the new employment contract. Companies such as British Airways are doing just that by involving their people as much as possible in achieving change. When Paul Birch, head of business planning, was given the task of seriously cutting BA's cost, he had no other choice than to fire 5,000 employees and outsourcing non-essential services—while maintaining employee trust at the same time. His reaction:

ETHICS

It was not impossible, but difficult. Involuntary redundancies seemed the only way out of this problem. However, we are genuinely committed to involving our people as much as possible in achieving change. As a result we have managed to develop plans which have no enforced redundancies and a very positive voluntary redundancy and retirement scheme with suitable retraining in areas where new skills are required.[22]

In short, employees tend to give what they get. The need for organizational behaviour skills covered in this book—such as managing diversity, motivation, teamwork, communication, leadership, and managing change—is greater than ever.

21st-century Managers

Today's workplace is indeed undergoing immense and permanent changes.[23] Organizations are being "reengineered" for greater speed, efficiency, and flexibility.[24] Teams are pushing aside the individual as the primary building block of organizations.[25] Command-and-control management is giving way to participative management and empowerment.[26] Ego-centred leaders are being replaced by customer-centred leaders. Employees increasingly are being viewed as internal customers. All this creates a mandate for a new kind of manager in the 21st century. Roland Berra, responsible for Corporate Executive Resources at the headquarters of Hoffmann-La Roche in Basel, Switzerland, explains how his company tries to meet the demands of the new developments in business:

In the 80s, Roche management realized that a new world was emerging and that to face the forthcoming challenges, the issue of people development had to be addressed in a different way.

In this context the decisions associated with the 1986 reorganisation which had the furthest reaching implications were:

- commiting the company to promotions from within

- making every line manager directly responsible for people and management

- starting to develop a culture and structures which allow for increased delegation of responsibilities, greater flexibility and innovation and which foster entreprenership at all levels.[27]

Table 1–2 contrasts the characteristics of past and future managers. As the balance of this book will demonstrate, the managerial shift in Table 1–2 is not just a good idea, it is an absolute necessity in the new workplace.

The Field of Organizational Behaviour: Past and Present

Organizational behaviour, commonly referred to as OB, is an interdisciplinary field dedicated to better understanding and managing people at work. By definition,

Table 1 – 2   Evolution of the 21st-Century Manager

	PAST MANAGERS	FUTURE MANAGERS
PRIMARY ROLE	Order giver, privileged elite, manipulator, controller	Facilitator, team member, teacher, advocate, sponsor, coach
LEARNING AND KNOWLEDGE	Periodic learning, narrow specialist	Continuous life-long learning, generalist with multiple specialties
COMPENSATION CRITERIA	Time, effort, rank	Skills, results
CULTURAL ORIENTATION	Monocultural, monolingual	Multicultural, multilingual
PRIMARY SOURCE OF INFLUENCE	Formal authority	Knowledge (technical and interpersonal)
VIEW OF PEOPLE	Potential problem	Primary resource
PRIMARY COMMUNICATION PATTERN	Vertical	Multidirectional
DECISION-MAKING STYLE	Limited input for individual decisions	Broad-based input for joint decisions
ETHICAL CONSIDERATIONS	Afterthought	Forethought
NATURE OF INTERPERSONAL RELATIONSHIPS	Competitive (win-lose)	Cooperative (win-win)
HANDLING OF POWER AND KEY INFORMATION	Hoard	Share
APPROACH TO CHANGE	Resist	Facilitate

Organizational behaviour

Interdisciplinary field dedicated to better understanding and managing people at work.

ETHICS

organizational behaviour is both research- and application-oriented. Three basic levels of analysis in OB are individual, group, and organizational. OB draws upon a diverse array of disciplines, including psychology, management, sociology, organization theory, social psychology, statistics, anthropology, general systems theory, economics, information technology, political science, vocational counselling, human stress management, psychometrics, ergonomics, decision theory, and ethics. This rich heritage has spawned many competing perspectives and theories about human work behaviour. By the mid-1980s, one researcher had identified 110 distinct theories about behaviour within the field of OB.[28]

Organizational behaviour is an academic designation. With the exception of teaching/research positions, OB is not an everyday job category such as accounting, marketing, or finance. Students of OB typically do not get jobs in organizational behaviour, per se. This reality in no way demeans OB or lessens its importance in effective organizational management. OB is a *horizontal* discipline that cuts across virtually every job category, business function, and professional specialty. Anyone who plans to make a living in a large or small, public or private, organization needs to study organizational behaviour.

A historical perspective of the study of people at work helps in studying organizational behaviour. According to a management history expert, this is important because

Historical perspective is the study of a subject in light of its earliest phases and subsequent evolution. Historical perspective differs from history in that the object of historical perspective is to sharpen one's vision of the present, not the past.[29]

In other words, we can better understand where the field of OB is today and where it appears to be headed by appreciating where it has been. Let us examine three significant landmarks in the evolution of understanding and managing people:

1. The human relations movement.

2. The total quality management movement.

3. The contingency approach to management.

The Human Relations Movement

A unique combination of factors during the 1930s fostered the human relations movement. First, following legalization of union—management collective bargaining in the United States in 1935, management began looking for new ways of handling employees. Second, behavioural scientists conducting on-the-job research started calling for more attention to the "human" factor. Managers who had lost the battle to keep unions out of their factories heeded the call for better human relations and improved working conditions. One such study, conducted at Western Electric's Chicago-area Hawthorne plant, was a prime stimulus for the human relations movement. Ironically, many of the Hawthorne findings have turned out to be more myth than fact.

The Hawthorne Legacy   Interviews conducted decades later with three subjects of the Hawthorne studies and reanalysis of the original data with modern statistical techniques do not support initial conclusions about the positive effect of supportive supervision. Specifically, money, fear of unemployment during the Great Depression, managerial discipline, and high-quality raw materials—not supportive supervision—turned out to be responsible for high output in the relay assembly test room experiments.[30] Nonetheless, the human relations movement gathered momentum through the 1950s, as academics and managers alike made stirring claims about the powerful impact that individual needs, supportive supervision, and group dynamics apparently had on job performance.

The Writings of Mayo and Follett   Essential to the human relations movement were the writings of Elton Mayo and Mary Parker Follett. Australian-born Mayo, who headed the Harvard researchers at Hawthorne, advised managers to attend to employees' emotional needs in his 1933 classic, *The Human Problems of an Industrial Civilization*. Follett was a true pioneer, not only as a woman management consultant in the male-dominated industrial world of the 1920s, but also as a writer who saw employees as complex combinations of attitudes, beliefs, and needs. Mary Parker Follett was way ahead of her time in telling managers to motivate job performance instead of merely demanding it, a "pull" rather than "push" strategy. She also built a logical bridge between political democracy and a cooperative spirit in the workplace.[31]

Theory Y
McGregor's modern and positive assumptions about employees being responsible and creative.

McGregor's Theory Y   In 1960, Douglas McGregor wrote a book entitled *The Human Side of Enterprise*, which has become an important philosophical base for the modern view of people at work.[32] Drawing upon his experience as a management consultant, McGregor formulated two sharply contrasting sets of assumptions about human nature (see Table 1–3). His Theory X assumptions were pessimistic and negative and, according to McGregor's interpretation, typical of how managers traditionally perceived employees.

Table 1 – 3   McGregor's Theory X and Theory Y

OUTDATED (THEORY X) ASSUMPTIONS ABOUT PEOPLE AT WORK	MODERN (THEORY Y) ASSUMPTIONS ABOUT PEOPLE AT WORK
1. Most people dislike work; they avoid it when they can.	1. Work is a natural activity, like play or rest.
2. Most people must be coerced and threatened with punishment before they will work. People require close direction when they are working.	2. People are capable of self-direction and self-control if they are committed to objectives.
3. Most people actually prefer to be directed. They tend to avoid responsibility and exhibit little ambition. They are interested only in security.	3. People generally become committed to organizational objectives if they are rewarded for doing so.
	4. The typical employee can learn to accept and seek responsibility.
	5. The typical member of the general population has imagination, ingenuity, and creativity.

Source: Adapted from D McGregor, *The Human Side of Enterprise* (New York: McGraw-Hill, 1960), Ch 4.

To help managers break with this negative tradition, McGregor formulated his Theory Y, a modern and positive set of assumptions about people. McGregor believed managers could accomplish more through others by viewing them as self-energized, committed, responsible, and creative beings. Forty years ago, motivation at work tended to be tackled as single-issue psychology. Typical advice was "people will work harder if you give them more attention." Today, research in Britain reveals that, if, for example, a company gives its people a chance to express themselves, it might feel that the organization is a safe environment in which they can get personally involved. This in turn might make them more committed to their work, so that they produce a larger quantity of better-quality work.[33] According to a study among employees of a Dutch hospital experiencing a tight labour market, job characteristics other than wages, such as labour relations and work content, were found to play a major role in individuals' choices to resign or stay.[34]

New Assumptions about Human Nature   Unfortunately, unsophisticated behavioural research methods caused the human relationists to embrace some naive and misleading conclusions. For example, human relationists believed in the axiom, "A satisfied employee is a hardworking employee". Subsequent research, as discussed later in this book, shows the satisfaction–performance linkage to be more complex than originally thought. A study into the values Europeans feel about, carried out in 1981 and 1990, revealed that, whereas a good salary remains the strongest value, quality of work has increased. Job certainty, on the other hand, has decreased in importance.[35] Table 1–4 represents the evolution in the job-related values in Europe.

Despite its shortcomings, the human relations movement opened the door to more progressive thinking about human nature. Rather than continuing to view employees as passive economic beings, managers began to see them as active social beings and took steps to create more humane work environments. In the above-mentioned study, quality of work included the job's social aspects and job content.[36]

The Total Quality Management Movement

A great deal has been written and said about quality in recent years. So much, in fact, that *total quality management* (TQM) has been dismissed by some as just another fad.[37] Yet TQM programmes are alive and well in the workplace. The European Foundation for Quality Management (EFQM) aims at promoting quality as the fundamental process in total quality. The EFQM-model in Figure 1–3 wants to accompany companies on their

Table 1 – 4	Job-Related Values in Europe	
Characteristic	**1990**	**1981**
good wages	71%	66%
nice colleagues	65%	62%
interesting job	58%	52%
job security	55%	57%
job that corresponds to capacities	54%	47%
job with which you can achieve something	49%	42%
job which enables initiatives	45%	40%
job in which you interact with other people	44%	40%
good timetable	42%	41%
responsible job	40%	36%
valued job	37%	31%
reasonable promotion chances	35%	33%
much leisure time	28%	28%
not much stress	28%	28%

Source: J Kerkhofs, *The Europeans and their Values* (Leuven, Davidfonds, 1997), pp 51-52. This book was published in Dutch as *De Europeanen en hun waarden.*

Figure 1 – 3   The EFQM Model

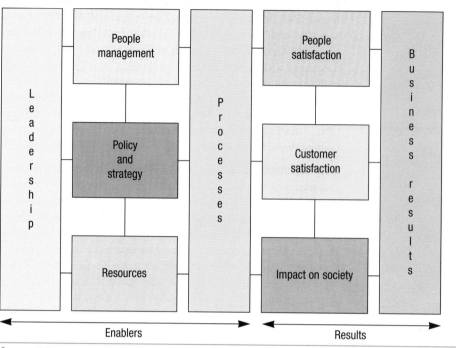

Source: EFQM-homepage: http://www.efqm.org.

way to excellence. The model tells us that "customer satisfaction", "employee satisfaction" and "impact on society" are achieved through "leadership" which drives the "policy and strategy", "people management", "resources", and "processes" leading to excellence in "business results". Each of the nine elements, therefore, is a criterion that can be used to assess the organization's progress along the path to excellence. The "results" indicate what the company has achieved and is achieving; the "enablers" indicate how those results are being achieved.[38] *Training* magazine's 1995 survey of US companies with 100 or more employees found 58 per cent of them pursuing TQM initiatives (more than any other type of programme).[39] Disregarding the underlying principles of TQM because of apparent faddishness would be as unwise as ignoring sound nutrition and exercise guidelines because of endless discussions about dieting. TQM principles have profound practical implications for managing people today.[40]

Total quality management

An organizational culture dedicated to training, continuous improvement, and customer satisfaction.

What Is TQM?   Experts on the subject recently offered this definition of **total quality management:**

TQM means that the organization's culture is defined by and supports the constant attainment of customer satisfaction through an integrated system of tools, techniques, and training. This involves the continuous improvement of organizational processes, resulting in high quality products and services.[41]

Quality consultant Richard J. Schonberger sums up TQM as "continuous, customer-centered, employee-driven improvement".[42] TQM is necessarily employee driven because product/service quality cannot be continuously improved without the active learning and participation of *every* employee. Thus, in successful quality improvement programmes, TQM principles are embedded in the organization's culture.[43]

The Deming Legacy   TQM is firmly established today thanks in large part to the pioneering work of W Edwards Deming.[44] Ironically, the mathematician credited with

Japan's post-World War II quality revolution rarely talked in terms of quality. He instead preferred to discuss "good management" during the hard-hitting seminars he delivered right up until his death at age 93 in 1993.[45] Although Deming's passion was the statistical measurement and reduction of variations in industrial processes, he had much to say about how employees should be treated. Regarding the human side of quality improvement, Deming called for the following:

- Formal training in statistical process control techniques and teamwork.

- Helpful leadership, rather than order giving and punishment.

- Elimination of fear so employees will feel free to ask questions.

- Emphasis on continuous process improvements rather than on numerical quotas.

- Teamwork.

- Elimination of barriers to good workmanship.[46]

One of Deming's most enduring lessons for managers is his 85–15 rule.[47] Specifically, when things go wrong, there is roughly an 85 per cent chance the system (including management, machinery, and rules) is at fault. Only about 15 per cent of the time is the individual employee at fault. Unfortunately, as Deming observed, the typical

---

International Organizational Behaviour
Three Coca-Cola Executives Address the Issue of a Globally Appropriate Management Style

Lynn Oliver, from the [United Kingdom], is responsible for Western Europe training and development. Kees van Langen, from the Netherlands, works with corporate and Asian managers. David Veale, based in the US, is manager of training and development for Coca-Cola Foods. Mr Veale posed the questions mostly by electronic mail, occasionally commenting himself in the responses.

Do you see a homogenization of management practices down the road? Is there one best set of practices that everyone will eventually use?

Oliver: No, I don't because so much is dictated by cultural, political, and religious beliefs. Who owns the business also has an impact. The common trends I see are toward a more people-focused management style. Technology requires skilled, thoughtful people with higher education levels. Higher living standards and the increased mobility of these people give them more of a choice of where to work.

Okay, then. Who has the better or most appropriate management style: Japan, Europe, Great Britain or the US?

Oliver: I don't think any one style is best; there is value for the different approaches depending on the market. If you subscribe to the school of thought that the most successful

businesses of the future will be those with the ability to learn and respond to new and uncharted environments, there may be some evidence that points to the Japanese systems of developing learning ability in people.

van Langen: The burning question is how to foster industry and commerce in a way that promotes collaboration from the strength of expressive individualism. None of the countries has found the answer as yet, so a discussion of who is best begs the question.

Veale: I have to agree with both of you. I can't see a "best" style. I don't really see much difference. Being fast, focused, and flexible in working with customers and producing and distributing great products efficiently are challenges for everyone. Lynn, you are correct in identifying learning as the key. Kees is right as well in that managing a balance between society, the individual and commerce is something that businesses face no matter what their country of origin. If anything, perhaps we in the US could learn to be more collaborative as opposed to adversarial in our approach to addressing social and individual needs. It might make the learning happen more quickly.

SOURCE   Excerpted from D Veale, L Oliver, and K van Langen, "Three Coca-Cola Perspectives on International Management Styles", *Academy of Management Executive*, August 1995, pp 74–77.

manager spends most of his or her time wrongly blaming and punishing individuals for system failures. Statistical analysis is required to uncover system failures.

Principles of TQM   Despite variations in the language and scope of TQM programmes, it is possible to identify four common TQM principles:

1. Do it right the first time to eliminate costly rework.

2. Listen to and learn from customers and employees.

3. Make continuous improvement an everyday matter.

4. Build teamwork, trust, and mutual respect.[48]

Deming's influence is clearly evident in this list.[49] Once again, as with the human relations movement, we see people as the key factor in organizational success.

In summary, TQM advocates have made a valuable contribution to the field of OB by providing a *practical* context for managing people. When people are managed according to TQM principles, everyone is more likely to get the employment opportunities and high-quality goods and services they demand.[50] As you will see many times in later chapters, this book is anchored to Deming's philosophy and TQM principles.

The Contingency Approach

Contingency approach
Using management tools and techniques in a situationally appropriate manner; avoiding the one-best-way mentality.

Scholars have wrestled for many years with the problem of how best to apply the diverse and growing collection of management tools and techniques. Their answer is the contingency approach. The **contingency approach** calls for using management techniques in a situationally appropriate manner, instead of trying to rely on "one best way". According to a pair of contingency theorists:

[Contingency theories] developed and their acceptance grew largely because they responded to criticisms that the classical theories advocated "one best way" of organizing and managing. Contingency theories, on the other hand, proposed that the appropriate organizational structure and management style were dependent upon a set of "contingency" factors, usually the uncertainty and instability of the environment.[51]

The contingency approach encourages managers to view organizational behaviour within a situational context. According to this modern perspective, evolving situations, not hard-and-fast rules, determine when and where various management techniques are appropriate. For example, as discussed in Chapter 16, contingency researchers have determined that there is no single best style of leadership. Organizational behaviour specialists embrace the contingency approach because it helps them realistically interrelate individuals, groups, and organizations. Moreover, the contingency approach sends a clear message to managers in today's global economy: Carefully read the situation and then be flexible enough to adapt (see International OB).

Now that we have reviewed OB's historical evolution, we need to address how we learn about OB through a combination of theory, research, and practice.

Learning about OB from Theory, Research, and Practice

As a human being, with years of interpersonal experience to draw upon, you already know a good deal about people at work. But more systematic and comprehensive understanding is possible and desirable. A working knowledge of current OB theory, research, and practice can help you develop a tightly integrated understanding of why organizational contributors think and act as they do. In order for this to happen, however, prepare yourself for some intellectual surprises from theoretical models, research results, or techniques that may run counter to your current thinking. For instance, one important reason why stress and satisfaction remain popular concepts is the belief that happy,

Figure 1 – 4   Learning about OB through a Combination of Theory, Research, and Practice

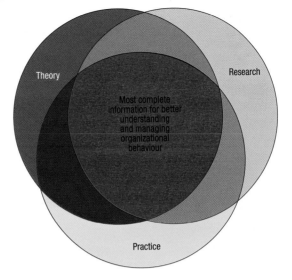

satisfied workers are necessarily more productive workers. Hence, improving the "feel-good-factor" is believed to produce improvements in work performance. This argument has great superficial appeal. But on closer inspection it makes a great deal less sense. For example, feeling particularly happy may make it difficult to concentrate on a complex task, while a person's performance in a repititive, machine-paced job may not depend on how they feel. In addition, there is little research evidence that supports such links.[52]

Therefore, research surprises can not only make learning fun, as mentioned earlier, they also can improve the quality of our lives both on and off the job. Let us examine the dynamic relationship between OB theory, research, and practice and the value of each.

Figure 1–4 illustrates how theory, research, and practice are related. Throughout the balance of this book, we focus primarily on the central portion, where all three areas overlap. Knowledge of why people behave as they do and what managers can do to improve performance is greatest within this area of maximum overlap. For each major topic, we build a foundation for understanding with generally accepted theory. This theoretical foundation is then tested and expanded by reviewing the latest relevant research findings. After interpreting the research, we discuss the nature and effectiveness of related practical applications.

Sometimes, depending on the subject matter, it is necessary to venture into the large areas outside the central portion of Figure 1–4. For example, an insightful theory supported by convincing research evidence might suggest an untried or different way of managing. In other instances, an innovative management technique might call for an explanatory theoretical model and exploratory research. Each area—theory, research, and practice—supports and, in turn, is supported by the other two. Each area makes a valuable contribution to our understanding of, and ability to, manage organizational behaviour.

Learning from Theory

Theory

A story defining key terms, providing a conceptual framework, and explaining why something occurs.

A respected behavioural scientist, Kurt Lewin, once said there is nothing as practical as a good theory. According to one management researcher, a **theory** is a story that explains "why".[53] Another calls well-constructed theories "disciplined imagination".[54] A good OB theory, then, is a story that effectively explains why individuals and groups behave as they do. Moreover, a good theoretical model

1. *Defines* key terms.

2. Constructs a *conceptual framework* that explains how important factors are interrelated. (Graphic models are often used to achieve this end.)

3. Provides a *departure point* for research and practical application.

Indeed, good theories are a fundamental contributor to improved understanding and management of organizational behaviour.[55]

Learning from Research

Because of unfamiliar jargon and complicated statistical procedures, many current and future managers are put off by behavioural research. This is unfortunate because practical lessons can be learned as OB researchers steadily push back the frontier of knowledge. Let us examine the various sources and uses of OB research evidence.

Five Sources of OB Research Insights   To enhance the instructional value of our coverage of major topics, we systematically cite "hard" evidence from five different categories. Worthwhile evidence was obtained by drawing upon the following priority of research methodologies:

Meta-analysis
Pools the results of many studies through statistical procedure.

- *Meta-analyses.* A **meta-analysis** is a statistical pooling technique that permits behavioural scientists to draw general conclusions about certain variables from many different studies.[56] It typically encompasses a vast number of subjects, often reaching the thousands. Meta-analyses are instructive because they focus on general patterns of research evidence, not fragmented bits and pieces or isolated studies.

Field study
Examination of variables in real-life settings.

- *Field studies.* In OB, a **field study** probes individual or group processes in an organizational setting. Because field studies involve real-life situations, their results often have immediate and practical relevance for managers.

Laboratory study
Manipulation and measurement of variables in contrived situations.

- *Laboratory studies.* In a **laboratory study,** variables are manipulated and measured in contrived situations. University students are commonly used as subjects. The highly controlled nature of laboratory studies enhances research precision. But generalizing the results to organizational management requires caution.[57]

Sample survey
Questionnaire responses from a sample of people.

- *Sample surveys.* In a **sample survey,** samples of people from specified populations respond to questionnaires. The researchers then draw conclusions about the relevant population. Generalizability of the results depends on the quality of the sampling and questioning techniques.

Case study
In-depth study of a single person, group, or organization.

- *Case studies.* A **case study** is an in-depth analysis of a single individual, group, or organization. Because of their limited scope, case studies yield realistic but not very generalizable results.[58]

Three Uses of OB Research Findings   Organizational scholars point out that managers can put relevant research findings to use in three different ways:[59]

1. **Instrumental use.** This involves directly applying research findings to practical problems. For example, a manager experiencing high stress tries a relaxation technique after reading a research report about its effectiveness.

2. **Conceptual use.** Research is put to conceptual use when managers derive general enlightenment from its findings. The impact here is less specific and more indirect than with instrumental use. For example, after reading a meta-analysis showing a negative correlation between absenteeism and age,[60] a manager might develop a more positive attitude towards hiring older people.

3. **Symbolic use.** Symbolic use occurs when research results are relied on to verify or legitimize already held positions. Negative forms of symbolic use involve self-serving bias, prejudice, selective perception, and distortion. For example, tobacco industry spokespersons routinely deny any link between smoking and lung cancer because researchers are largely, but not 100 per cent, in agreement about the negative effects of smoking. A positive example would be managers maintaining their confidence in setting

Figure 1 – 5   A Topical Model for What Lies Ahead

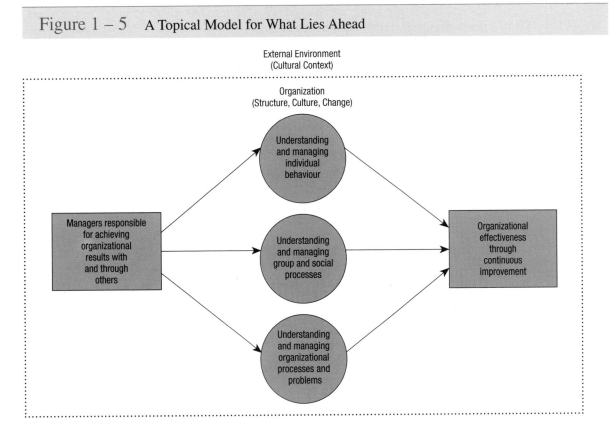

performance goals after reading a research report about the favourable impact of goal setting on job performance.

By systematically reviewing and interpreting research relevant to key topics, this book provides instructive insights about OB.

Learning from Practice

Relative to learning more about how to effectively manage people at work, one might be tempted to ask, "Why bother with theory and research; let's get right down to *how to do it*". Our answer lies in the contingency approach discussed earlier. The effectiveness of specific theoretical models or management techniques is contingent on the situations in which they are applied. For example, one cross-cultural study of a large multinational corporation's employees working in 50 countries led the Dutch researcher Geert Hofstede to conclude that most made-in-America management theories and techniques are inappropriate in other cultures.[61] Many otherwise well-intentioned performance-improvement programmes based on American cultural values have failed in other cultures because of naive assumptions about transferability. In France, the most common medical complaint is *crise de foie* (liver crisis) while in Germany it is *herzinsufficienz* (heart insufficiency). Prescriptions to soothe the digestive system are higher in France, while in Germany digitalis is prescribed six times more frequently to stimulate the heart. These differences have been attributed to the French cultural obsession with food, and the German cultural quest for romanticism. In other words, different countries have very different approaches to medicine. If the practice of medicine is shaped by its cultural origins, why should the practice of management be any different?[62] (International cultures are discussed in Chapter 4.) Fortunately, systematic research is available that tests our "commonsense" assumptions about what works where. Management "cookbooks" that provide only how-to-do-it advice with no underlying theoretical models or supporting research practically guarantee misapplication. As mentioned earlier, theory, research, and practice mutually reinforce one another.

The theory→research→practice sequence discussed in this section will help you better understand each major topic addressed later in this book. Attention now turns to a topical model that sets the stage for what lies ahead.

A Topical Model for Understanding and Managing OB

Figure 1–5 is a topical road map for our journey through this book. Our destination is organizational effectiveness through continuous improvement. Four different criteria for determining whether or not an organization is effective are discussed in Chapter 18. The study of OB can be a wandering and pointless trip if we overlook the need to translate OB lessons into effective and efficient organized endeavour.

At the far left side of our topical road map are managers, those who are responsible for accomplishing organizational results with and through others. The three circles at the centre of our road map correspond to Parts Two, Three, and Four of this text. Logically, the flow of topical coverage in this book (following introductory Part One) goes from individuals, to group processes, to organizational processes and problems, to organizations. Around the core of our topical road map in Figure 1–5 is the organization. Accordingly, we end our journey with organization-related material in Part Five. Organizational structure and design are covered there in Chapters 18 and 19 to establish and develop the organizational context of organizational behaviour. Rounding out our *organizational* context is a discussion of organizational change in Chapter 20. Chapters 3 and 4 provide a *cultural* context for OB.

The broken line represents a permeable boundary between the organization and its environment. Energy and influence flow both ways across this permeable boundary. Truly, no organization is an island in today's highly interactive and interdependent world. Relative to the *external* environment, international cultures are explored in Chapter 4. Organization—environment contingencies are examined in Chapter 19. Chapter 2 examines the OB implications of significant demographic and social trends, and Chapter 3 explores important ethical considerations. These discussions provide a realistic context for studying and managing people at work.

Bon voyage! Enjoy your trip through the challenging, interesting, and often surprising, world of OB.

Summary of Key Concepts

1. *Identify the Ps in the 4-P cycle of continuous improvement and define the term* management. The 4 Ps are people, products, processes, and productivity. Management is the process of working with and through others to achieve organizational objectives in an efficient and ethical manner.

2. *Identify at least 5 of the 11 managerial skills in Wilson's profile of effective managers.* According to the Wilson skills profile, an effective manager (a) clarifies goals and objectives, (b) encourages participation, (c) plans and organizes, (d) has technical and administrative expertise, (e) facilitates work through team building and coaching, (f) provides feedback, (g) keeps things moving, (h) controls details, (i) applies reasonable pressure for goals accomplishment, (j) empowers and delegates, and (k) recognizes and rewards good performance.

3. *Describe the new employment contract.* It is a transactional contract in which employees are expected to be flexible self-starters who are team players with multiple skills. The new contract pays employees for results, not for time spent on the job, and makes employees responsible for their own careers. The company's side of the bargain, in well-managed and ethical organizations, involves giving each employee the opportunity to grow and acquire marketable skills.

4. *Characterize 21st-century managers.* They will be team players who will get things done cooperatively by relying on joint decision making, their knowledge instead of formal authority, and their multicultural skills. They will engage in life-long learning and be compensated on the basis of their skills and results. They will facilitate rather than resist change, share rather than hoard power and key information, and be multidirectional communicators. Ethics will be a forethought instead of an afterthought. They will be generalists with multiple specialties.

5. *Define the term* organizational behaviour *and explain why OB is a horizontal discipline.* Organizational behaviour (OB) is an interdisciplinary field dedicated to better understanding and managing people at work. It is both research- and application-oriented. Except for teaching/research positions, one does not normally get a job in OB. Rather, because OB is a horizontal discipline, OB concepts and lessons are applicable to virtually every job category, business function, and professional specialty.

6. *Contrast McGregor's Theory X and Theory Y assumptions about employees.* Theory X employees, according to traditional thinking, dislike work, require close supervision, and are primarily interested in security. According to the modern Theory Y view, employees are capable of self-direction, of seeking responsibility, and of being creative.

7. *Explain the managerial significance of Deming's 85–15 rule.* Deming claimed that about 85 per cent of organizational failures are due to system breakdowns involving factors such as management, machinery, or work rules. He believed the workers themselves are responsible for failures only about 15 per cent of the time. Consequently, Deming criticized the standard practice of blaming and punishing individuals for what are typically system failures beyond their immediate control.

8. *Identify the four principles of total quality management (TQM).* (a) Do it right the first time to eliminate costly rework. (b) Listen to and learn from customers and employees. (c) Make continuous improvement an everyday matter. (d) Build teamwork, trust, and mutual respect.

9. *Describe the sources of organizational behaviour research evidence.* Five sources of OB research evidence are meta-analyses (statistically pooled evidence from several studies), field studies (evidence from real-life situations), laboratory studies (evidence from contrived situations), sample surveys (questionnaire data), and case studies (observation of a single person, group, or organization).

Discussion Questions

1. Why view the typical employee as a human resource?

2. In your opinion, what are the three or four most important strategic results in Figure 1–1? Why?

3. How would you respond to a fellow student who says, "I have a hard time getting along with other people, but I think I could be a good manager"?

4. Based on either personal experience as a manager or on your observation of managers at work, are the 11 skills in Table 1–1 a realistic portrayal of what managers do?

5. How willing and able are you to work under the new employment contract?

6. What is your personal experience with Theory X and Theory Y managers (see Table 1–3)? Which did you prefer? Why?

7. How would you respond to a new manager who made this statement "TQM is about statistical process control, not about people."?

8. Do you use the contingency approach in your daily affairs? Explain the circumstances.

9. What "practical" theories have you formulated to achieve the things you want in life (e.g., graduating, keeping fit, getting a good job, meeting that special someone)?

10. From a manager's standpoint, which use of research is better: instrumental or conceptual? Explain your rationale.

Personal Awareness and Growth Exercise

How Strong Is Your Motivation to Manage?

Objectives

1. To introduce a psychological determinant of managerial success.

2. To assess your readiness to manage.

3. To discuss the implications of motivation to manage, from the standpoint of global competitiveness.

Introduction

By identifying personal traits positively correlated with both rapid movement up the career ladder and managerial effectiveness, John B Miner developed a psychometric test for measuring what he calls motivation to manage. The questionnaire assesses the strength of seven factors relating to the temperament (or psychological makeup) needed to manage others. One word of caution. The following instrument is a shortened and modified version of Miner's original. Our version is for instructional and discussion purposes only. Although we believe it can indicate the *general* strength of your motivation to manage, it is *not* a precise measuring tool.

Instructions

Assess the strength of each of the seven dimensions of *your own* motivation to manage by circling the appropriate numbers on the 1 to 7 scales. Then add the seven circled numbers to get your total motivation to manage score.

Scoring and Interpretation

Arbitrary norms for comparison purposes are as follows: Total score of 7–21 = Relatively low motivation to manage; 22–34 = Moderate; 35–49 = Relatively high. How do you measure up? Remember, though, high motivation to manage is only part of the formula for managerial success. The right combination of ability and opportunity is also necessary.

Years of motivation-to-manage research by Miner and others has serious implications for global competitiveness. Generally, in recent years, college students in the United States have not scored highly on motivation to manage.[63] Indeed, compared with samples of US college students, samples of students from Japan, China, Mexico, Korea, and Taiwan consistently scored higher on motivation to manage.[64] Miner believes the United States may consequently lag in developing sufficient managerial talent for a tough global marketplace.[65]

In a study by other researchers, MBA students with higher motivation-to-manage scores tended to earn more money after graduation. But students with a higher motivation to manage did not earn better grades or complete their degree programme any sooner than those with a lower motivation to manage.[66]

FACTOR	DESCRIPTION	SCALE
1. Authority figures	A desire to meet managerial role requirements in terms of positive relationships with superiors.	Weak 1-2-3-4-5-6-7 Strong
2. Competitive games	A desire to engage in competition with peers involving games or sports and thus meet managerial role requirements in this regard.	Weak 1-2-3-4-5-6-7 Strong
3. Competitive situations	A desire to engage in competition with peers involving occupational or work-related activities and thus meet managerial role requirements in this regard.	Weak 1-2-3-4-5-6-7 Strong
4. Assertive role	A desire to behave in an active and assertive manner involving activities that in this society are often viewed as predominantly masculine and thus to meet managerial role requirements.	Weak 1-2-3-4-5-6-7 Strong
5. Imposing wishes	A desire to tell others what to do and to utilize sanctions in influencing others, thus indicating a capacity to fulfil managerial role requirements in relationships with subordinates.	Weak 1-2-3-4-5-6-7 Strong
6. Standing out from group	A desire to assume a distinctive position of a unique and highly visible nature in a manner that is role-congruent for managerial jobs.	Weak 1-2-3-4-5-6-7 Strong
7. Routine administrative functions	A desire to meet managerial role requirements regarding activities often associated with managerial work that are of a day-to-day administrative nature.	Weak 1-2-3-4-5-6-7 Strong

Total =

QUESTIONS FOR DISCUSSION

1. Do you believe our adaptation of Miner's motivation to manage instrument accurately assessed your potential as a manager? Explain.

2. Which of the seven dimensions do you think is probably the best predictor of managerial success? Which the least predictive? Why?

3. Miner puts heavy emphasis on competitiveness by anchoring two of the seven dimensions of motivation to manage to the desire to compete. Some observers believe the traditional (win-lose) competitive attitude is being pushed aside in favor of a less competitive (win-win) attitude today, thus making Miner's instrument out of date. What is your position on this competitiveness debate? Explain.

4. Do you believe that low motivation to manage hurts a country's global competitiveness? Explain.

Group Exercise

Timeless Advice

Objectives

1. To get to know some of your fellow students.

2. To put the management of people into a lively and interesting historical context.

3. To begin to develop your teamwork skills.

Introduction

Your creative energy, willingness to see familiar things in unfamiliar ways, and ability to have fun while learning are keys to the success of this warm-up exercise. A 20-minute, small-group session will be followed by brief oral presentations and a general class discussion. Total time required is approximately 40 to 45 minutes.

Instructions

Your instructor will divide your class randomly into groups of four to six people each. Acting as a team, with everyone offering ideas and one person serving as official recorder, each group will be responsible for writing a one-page memo to your current class. Subject matter of your group's memo will be "My advice for managing people today is . . ." The fun part of this exercise (and its creative element) involves writing the memo from the viewpoint of the person assigned to your group by your instructor.

Among the memo viewpoints your instructor may assign are the following:

- Anita Roddick (The Body Shop).

- An ancient Egyptian slave master (building the great pyramids).

- Mary Parker Follett.

- Douglas McGregor.

- A Theory X supervisor of a construction crew (see McGregor's Theories X and Y in Table 1–3).

- W Edwards Deming.

- A TQM coordinator at IKEA

- A contingency management theorist.

- A Japanese auto company executive.

- The chief executive officer of ABB (Asea Brown Bovery, one of the world's leading enterprises in the fields of electrical engineering) in the year 2030.

- Commander of the Starship Enterprise II in the year 3001.

- Others as commanded by your instructor

Use your imagination, make sure everyone participates, and try to be true to any historical facts you've encountered. Attempt to be as specific and realistic as possible. Remember, the idea is to provide advice about managing people from another point in time (or from a particular point of view at the present time).

Make sure you manage your 20-minute time limit carefully. A recommended approach is to spend 2 to 3 minutes putting the exercise into proper perspective. Next, take about 10 to 12 minutes brainstorming ideas for your memo, with your recorder jotting down key ideas and phrases. Your recorder should use the remaining time to write your group's one-page memo, with constructive comments and help from the others. Pick a spokesperson to read your group's memo to the class.

QUESTIONS FOR DISCUSSION

1. What valuable lessons about managing people have you heard?

2. What have you learned about how NOT to manage people?

3. From the distant past to today, what significant shifts in the management of people seem to have taken place?

4. Where does the management of people appear to be headed?

5. All things considered, what mistakes are today's managers typically making when managing people?

6. How well did your group function as a "team"?

Notes

[1]*Vasa* (Sweden: The Vasa Museum)

[2]*Leadership* (Management Centre Europe, 1988)

[3]B Enstrom, "The well tempered king," *Scanorama,* June 1989, p 69.

[4]*Leadership by Richard Branson* (Brussels: AMROP International, 1995)

[5]A Roddick, "Corporate Responsibility: The Body Shop Choice," *efmd Forum,* 95/2, pp 28–33.

[6]See W F Cascio, "Downsizing: What Do We Know? What Have We Learned?" *Academy of Management Executive,* February 1993, pp 95–104; and B Baumohl, "When Downsizing Becomes 'Dumbsizing," *Time,* March 15, 1993, p 55.

[7]For more, see J Stuller, "Why Not 'Inplacement'?" *Training,* June 1993, pp 37–41; and R Henkoff, "Getting Beyond Downsizing," *Fortune,* January 10, 1994, pp 58–64.

[8]Thought-provoking ideas are presented in R Farson, *Management of the Absurd* (New York: Simon & Schuster, 1996).

[9]H Mintzberg, "The Manager's Job: Folklore and Fact," *Harvard Business Review,* July–August 1975, p 61.

[10]See, for example, H Mintzberg, "Managerial Work: Analysis from Observation", *Management Science,* October 1971, pp B97–B110; and F Luthans, "Successful vs. Effective Real Managers," *Academy of Management Executive,* May 1988, pp 127–32. For an instructive critique of the structured observation method, see M J Martinko and W L Gardner, "Beyond Structured Observation: Methodological Issues and New Directions," *Academy of Management Review,* October 1985, pp 676–95. Also see N Fondas, "A Behavioral Job Description for Managers," *Organizational Dynamics,* Summer 1992, pp 47–58.

[11]R Stewart, *Managers and Their Jobs* (Basingstoke: Macmillan Press, 1988)

[12]Se L B Kurke and H E Aldrich, "Mintzberg Was Right!: A Replication and Extension of The Nature of Managerial Work," *Management Science,* August 1983, pp 975–84.

[13]For example, see A I Kraut, P R Pedigo, D D McKenna, and M D Dunnette, "The Role of the Manager: What's Really Important in Different Management Jobs," *Academy of Management Executive,* November 1989, pp 286–93.

[14]Validation studies can be found in E Van Velsor and J B Leslie, *Feedback to Managers, Volume II: A Review and Comparison of Sixteen Multi-Rater Feedback Instruments* (Greensboro, NC: Center for Creative Leadership, 1991); and F Shipper, "A Study of the Psychometric Properties of the Managerial Skill Scales of the Survey of Management Practices," *Educational and Psychological Measurement,* June 1995, pp 468–79.

[15]See F Shipper, "Mastery and Frequency of Managerial Behaviours Relative to Sub-Unit Effectiveness," *Human Relations,* April 1991, pp 371–88.

[16]Ibid.

[17]Data from F Shipper, "A Study of Managerial Skills of Women and Men and Their Impact on Employees' Attitudes and Career Success in a Nontraditional Organization," paper presented at the Academy of Management Meeting, August 1994, Dallas, Texas. The same outcome for on-the-job studies is reported in A H Eagly and B T Johnson, "Gender and Leadership Style: A Meta-Analysis," *Psychological Bulletin,* September 1990, pp 233–56.

[18]For instance, see J B Rosener, "Ways Women Lead," *Harvard Business Review,* November–December 1990, pp 119–25; and C Lee, "The Feminization of Management," *Training,* November 1994, pp 25–31.

[19]For a good overview, see B Ettorre, "Empty Promises," *Training,* July 1996, pp 16–23.

[20]Drawn from W J Byron, "Coming to Terms with the New Corporate Contract," *Business Horizons,* January–February 1995, pp 8–15.

[21].D Jones, "Low Unemployment Makes Employers Less Picky," *USA Today,* July 15, 1996, p 1B.

[22]M Syrett, "Goodbye to Macho Management," *Director,* March 1997, pp 49–53.

[23]Interesting discussions can be found in W Kiechel III, "How We Will Work in the Year 2000," *Fortune,* May 17, 1993, pp 38–52; and A B Shostak, "The Nature of Work in the Twenty-First Century: Certain Uncertainties," *Business Horizons,* November–December 1993, pp 30–34.

[24]Essential sources on reengineering are M Hammer and J Champy, *Reengineering the Corporation: A Manifesto for Business Revolution* (New York: HarperCollins, 1993); and J Champy, *Reengineering Management: The Mandate for New Leadership* (New York: HarperCollins, 1995).

[25]For thoughtful discussion, see G G Dess, A M A Rasheed, K J McLaughlin, and R L Priem, "The New Corporate Architecture," *Academy of Management Executive,* August 1995, pp 7–20.

[26]For an interesting discussion, see M M Broadwell, "Why Command & Control Won't Go Away," *Training,* September 1995, pp 63–68.

[27]R Berra, "People Development at Roche," *Trends. The EAP Review,* October, 1995, pp 15–17.

[28]See J B Miner, "The Validity and Usefulness of Theories in an Emerging Organizational Science," *Academy of Management Review,* April 1984, pp 296–306.

[29]B S Lawrence, "Historical Perspective: Using the Past to Study the Present," *Academy of Management Review,* April 1984, p 307.

[30]Evidence indicating that the original conclusions of the famous Hawthorne studies were unjustified may be found in R G Greenwood, A A Bolton, and R A Greenwood, "Hawthorne a Half Century Later: Relay Assembly Participants Remember," *Journal of Management,* Fall–Winter 1983, pp 217–31; and R H Franke and J D Kaul, "The Hawthorne Experiments: First Statistical Interpretation," *American Sociological Review,* October 1978, pp 623–43. For a positive interpretation of the Hawthorne studies, see J A Sonnenfeld, "Shedding Light on the Hawthorne Studies," *Journal of Occupational Behaviour,* April 1985, pp 111–30.

[31]See M Parker Follett, *Freedom and Coordination* (London: Management Publications Trust, 1949).

[32]See D McGregor, *The Human Side of Enterprise* (New York: McGraw-Hill, 1960).

[33]R McHenry, "Spuring Stuff," *People Management,* July 24, 1997, pp 28–31.

[34]F van de Looy, and J Benders, "Not Just Money: Quality of Working Life as Employment Strategy," *Health Manpower Management,* 1995, vol. 21, nr. 3, pp 27–33.

[35]Translated from J Kerkhofs, *De Europeanen en hun waarden* (Leuven: Davidsfonds, 1997)

[36]Ibid.

[37]J Hall, "Americans Know How to Be Productive if Managers Will Let Them," *Organizational Dynamics,* Winter 1994, p 38.

[37]See, for example, R Zemke, "TQM: Fatally Flawed or Simply Unfocused?" *Training,* October 1992, p 8.

[38]*EFQM,* Brussels Representative Office, Avenue des Pléiadies 15, B–1200 Brussels, 32 2 775 35 11

[39]Data from "Workplace Trends," *Training,* October 1995, p 70.

[40]Instructive background articles on TQM are R Zemke, "A

Bluffer's Guide to TQM," *Training*, April 1993, pp 48–55; R R Gehani, "Quality Value-Chain: A Meta-Synthesis of Frontiers of Quality Movement," *Academy of Management Executive*, May 1993, pp 29–42; P Mears, "How to Stop Talking About, and Begin Progress Toward, Total Quality Management," *Business Horizons*, May–June 1993, pp 11–14; and the Total Quality Special Issue of Academy of Management Review, July 1994.

[41]M Sashkin and K J Kiser, *Putting Total Quality Management to Work* (San Francisco: Berrett-Koehler, 1993), p 39.

[42]R J Schonberger, "Total Quality Management Cuts a Broad Swath–Through Manufacturing and Beyond," *Organizational Dynamics*, Spring 1992, p 18. Also see D K Denton, "Creating a System for Continuous Improvement," *Business Horizons*, January–February 1995, pp 16–21.

[43]See R K Reger, L T Gustafson, S M Demarie, and J V Mullane, "Reframing the Organization: Why Implementing Total Quality Is Easier Said than Done," *Academy of Management Review*, July 1994, pp 565–84.

[44]Deming's landmark work is W E Deming, *Out of the Crisis* (Cambridge, MA: MIT, 1986).

[45]See M Trumbull, "What Is Total Quality Management?" *The Christian Science Monitor*, May 3, 1993, p 12; and J Hillkirk, "World-Famous Quality Expert Dead at 93," *USA Today*, December 21, 1993, pp 1B–2B.

[46]Based on discussion in M Walton, *Deming Management at Work* (New York: Putnam/Perigee, 1990).

[47]Ibid., p 20.

[48]Adapted from D E Bowen and E E Lawler III "Total Quality–Oriented Human Resources Management," *Organizational Dynamics*, Spring 1992, pp 29–41.

[49]See T F Rienzo, "Planning Deming Management for Service Organizations," *Business Horizons*, May–June 1993, pp 19–29.

[50]For example, see J Shea and D Gobeli, "TQM: The Experiences of Ten Small Businesses," *Business Horizons*, January–February 1995, pp 71–77; T L Zeller and D M Gillis, "Achieving Market Excellence through Quality: The Case of Ford Motor Company," *Business Horizons*, May–June 1995, pp 23–31; and P McLagan and C Nel, "A New Leadership Style for Genuine Total Quality," Journal for Quality and Participation, June 1996, pp 14–16.

[51]H L Tosi, Jr., and J W Slocum, Jr., "Contingency Theory: Some Suggested Directions," *Journal of Management*, Spring 1984, p 9.

[52]B Briner, "Feeling for the Facts", *People Management*, January 9, 1997, pp 34–37.

[53]See R L Daft, "Learning the Craft of Organizational Research," *Academy of Management Review*, October 1983, pp 539–46.

[54]See K E Weick, "Theory Construction as Disciplined Imagination," *Academy of Management Review*, October 1989, pp 516–31. Also see D A Whetten's article in the same issue, pp 490–95.

[55]Theory-focused versus problem-focused research is discussed in K E Weick, "Agenda Setting in Organizational Behaviour: A Theory–Focused Approach," *Journal of Management Inquiry*, September 1992, pp 171–82.

[56]Complete discussion of this technique can be found in J E Hunter, F L Schmidt, and G B Jackson, *Meta-Analysis. Cumulating Research Findings across Studies* (Beverly Hills, CA: Sage Publications, 1982); and J E Hunter and F L Schmidt, *Methods of Meta-Analysis: Correcting Error and Bias in Research Findings* (Newbury Park, CA: Sage Publications, 1990). Also see R Hutter Epstein, "The Number-Crunchers Drugmakers Fear and Love," *Business Week*, August 22, 1994, pp 70–71.

[57]For an interesting debate about the use of students as subjects, see J Greenberg, "The College Sophomore as Guinea Pig: Setting the Record Straight," *Academy of Management Review*, January 1987, pp 157–59; and M E Gordon, L A Slade, and N Schmitt, "Student

Guinea Pigs: Porcine Predictors and Particularistic Phenomena," *Academy of Management Review,* January 1987, pp 160–63.

[58]Good discussions of case studies can be found in A S Lee, "Case Studies as Natural Experiments," *Human Relations*, February 1989, pp 117–37; and K M Eisenhardt, "Building Theories from Case Study Research," *Academy of Management Review*, October 1989, pp 532–50. The case survey technique is discussed in R Larsson, "Case Survey Methodology: Analysis of Patterns Across Case Studies," *Academy of Management Journal*, December 1993, pp 1515–46.

[59]Based on discussion found in J M Beyer and H M Trice, "The Utilization Process: A Conceptual Framework and Synthesis of Empirical Findings," *Administrative Science Quarterly*, December 1982, pp 591–622.

[60]See J J Martocchio, "Age-Related Differences in Employee Absenteeism: A Meta-Analysis," *Psychology & Aging*, December 1989, pp 409–14.

[61]For complete details, see G Hofstede, "The Cultural Relativity of Organizational Practices and Theories," *Journal of International Business Studies*, Fall 1983, pp 75–89. For related discussion, see G Hofstede, "Cultural Constraints in Management Theories," *Academy of Management Executive*, February 1993, pp 81–94.

[62]S C Schneider, and J L Barsoux, *Managing across Cultures* (London: Prentice-Hall, 1997)

[63]These research results are discussed in detail in J B Miner and N R Smith, "Decline and Stabilization of Managerial Motivation Over a 20-Year Period," *Journal of Applied Psychology*, June 1982, pp 297–305.

[64]See J B Miner, J M Wachtel, and B Ebrahimi, "The Managerial Motivation of Potential Managers in the United States and Other Countries of the World: Implications for National Competitiveness and the Productivity Problem," in *Advances in International Comparative Management*, vol. 4, eds B Prasad (Greenwich, CT: JAI Press, 1989), pp 147–70; and J B Miner, C C Chen, and K C Yu, "Theory Testing Under Adverse Conditions: Motivation to Manage in the People's Republic of China," *Journal of Applied Psychology*, June 1991, pp 343–49.

[65]See J B Miner, B Ebrahimi, and J M Wachtel, "How Deficiencies in Motivation to Manage Contribute to the United States' Competitiveness Problem (and What Can Be Done about It)," *Human Resource Management*, Fall 1995, pp 363–87.

[66]Based on K M Bartol and D C Martin, "Managerial Motivation among MBA Students: A Longitudinal Assessment," *Journal of Occupational Psychology*, March 1987, pp 1–12.

Answers to OB Exercise

1. a. Switzerland. Employees in Switzerland are by far the most satisfied in Europe. They have the most favourable attitudes in 9 out of the 15 categories judged. In absolute terms, more than 70 per cent of them believe they are efficient, well supervised, produce high-quality work, cooperate well together, receive good company benefits and are satisfied with their jobs. Relatively speaking, in comparison with employees in all other European countries, they also feel that they are better organized, better informed about company matters and better managed. Source: *"Employee Satisfaction: Tracking European Trends,"* London: ISR International Survey Research Ltd, 1995.

2. d. Japan. Results in this survey of 1500 of the world's largest companies were as follows: Switzerland, 82 per cent; Mexico, 72 per cent; Germany, 66 per cent; United States, 65 per cent; France, 58 per cent; Singapore, 53 per cent; Hong Kong, 43 per cent; and Japan, 31 per cent. Source: M J Mandel, "Satisfaction at Work," *Business Week*, June 24, 1996, p 28.

3. b. False. "Analyzing Census Bureau data from more than 3000 US companies, EQW [National Center for Educational Quality of the Workforce] found that, on average, a 10 per cent increase in employees' education level resulted in an 8.6 per cent gain in productivity. By contrast, a 10 per cent increase in the book value of capital equipment increased productivity only 3.4 per cent on average." Source: "Contrary Finding #1: Education Does Matter," *Training*, December 1995, p 19.

4. b. False. A recent opinion survey of 563 general managers has identified that the challenge and interest of the job provided their greatest motivation. Next in order of importance came the authority and freedom to get on with the task. Only 3 per cent of the respondents considered performance-related pay important. Source: Oliver, J. "Cash on Delivery," *Management Today*, August 1996, pp 52–55.

5. b. Older workers. Source: Based on a study of 179 employees working for three organizations in the southeastern United States by B L Hassell and P L Perrewe, "An Examination of Beliefs about Older Workers: Do Stereotypes Still Exist?" *Journal of Organizational Behavior*, September 1995, pp 457–68.

6. a. True. Employees recruited under specific programmes feel treated unfairly and report having fewer promotion opportunities than their colleagues. This feeling results in more employee turnover. Source: P A Galagan, "Trading Places at Monsanto," *Training & Development*, April 1993, pp 45–49.

7. b. False. "White men will make up . . . 45 per cent of the work force by the year 2000, according to a new study." Source: R Sharpe, "Work Week," *The Wall Street Journal*, July 2, 1996, p A1.

8. a. US. In Sweden, only 17 per cent of the managers are women; the figure for Japan is an even lower 9.4 per cent. Source: "Women and Work," *Manpower Argus*, November 1995, p 5.

9. Answer: true. According to a survey by the Human Resources Institute at Eckerd College in St Petersburg, Florida, HR's major concern is the skill level of the workforce, followed by managing change, IT, ageing of the work force; management issues; quality of education; work ethic values and attitudes; managing diversity; improving productivity; employee communications. Source: Laabs, J. J. "Eyeing Future HR Concerns," *Personnel Journal*, January 1996, pp 28–37.

10. b.: False. An international survey among 1300 managers in Great Britain, the US, Singapore and Hong Kong revealed that managers have the feeling they cannot operate efficiently because of the information flow they are faced with. Source: D Lewis, *Dying for Information*, London: Reuters, 1996.

Two

Managing Diversity: Releasing Every Employee's Potential

LEARNING OBJECTIVES

When you finish studying the material in this chapter, you should be able to:

1. Define diversity.

2. Discuss the primary and secondary dimensions of diversity.

3. Explain the differences among affirmative action, valuing diversity, and managing diversity.

4. Demonstrate your familiarity with the demographic trends that are creating an increasingly diverse workforce.

5. Discuss the Mosaic approach to managing diversity.

6. Review the five reasons managing diversity is a competitive advantage.

7. Discuss the organizational practices used to effectively manage diversity as identified by R Roosevelt Thomas, Jr. and Ann Morrison.

8. Identify the barriers and challenges to managing diversity.

Positive action for race: madness, positive discrimination or a sound business approach?

In 1990, the BBC set itself the overall equality objective of reflecting the nation it serves in programmes and in employment. Not so outrageous for a public broadcasting organization, funded by a licence fee whose television programmes are watched by 94% of the population in an average week.

The BBC has a comprehensive equality strategy to meet this goal. It covers gender, race, disability, age, and sexuality. Positive action is one aspect of the strategy to ensure that black and ethnic minority candidates are encouraged to apply for employment or have a chance to acquire the skills to compete for employment in broadcasting.

Targets have been set for the representation of women and black and ethnic minority people in employment to be reached by the turn of the century. Progress is monitored regularly at the corporate centre and each year the director general reviews progress on equal opportunity as part of his performance review with the top management team in each BBC directorate.

So why do the BBC and other broadcasting businesses persist with positive action for black and ethnic minority people? Because:

- It's fundamental to our business. We intend to remain the best public broadcaster in the world and to do that we need diversity to reflect and respond to our audience and the best available talent in programme-making.

- We have a responsibility to provide a service which takes account of the needs and aspirations of all sectors of licence payers. It is a particular source of pride that the BBC has won all five categories of the highly esteemed Commission for Racial Equality Race in the Media Awards.
- There is a chicken and egg link between what we put out on air and whom we employ. The one influences the quality of the other and both affect the image of the BBC as a fair employer and public broadcaster.
- The Government agrees with us. The White Paper on the future of the BBC underlines a responsibility for the BBC to reflect the rich cultural diversity of regions and nations in the United Kingdom.

The criteria under which positive action must be justified are set out in the Race Relations Act 1976. There must be evidence of underrepresentation for black and ethnic minority people doing the particular kind of work, the employer must provide an opportunity for training only and any subsequent employment opportunities must be open to suitable candidates from all racial groups in open competition.

The relatively low representation of black and ethnic minority people in broadcasting and in BBC employment and recruitment monitoring exercises suggest there are barriers which ethnic minorities face to entry into and upward mobility within the broadcasting industry.

Fewer than 2% of BBC journalists and senior producer jobs are held by people classifying themselves as being from ethnic minority groups. According to industry research studies, the figure appears to hold for other television and radio companies. The BBC is based in London and the South East with a presence in other major regional conurbations such as Glasgow, Leeds, Manchester, Bristol and Cardiff where the ethnic minority availability of labour can be higher than the national average of 5.5% and might be as high as 20%. Ethnic minority representation of 2% at this level does not make us comfortably feel that we have the diversity to meet the major challenges facing the industry.

The BBC has been running positive action training schemes for entry into broadcasting since 1988 and several hundred young black people have received valuable training opportunities, as indeed have a far greater number of young white people. Each of the BBC output directorates has run prestigious training schemes, including bi-media journalism, television and radio production training, training for news and current affairs and training in engineering.

The objective of our positive action programmes is to ensure that highly talented members of ethnic minorities have equal access to mainstream BBC opportunities. We do not reduce the selection criteria for positive action training. We apply the same high standards to all applicants irrespective of race and gender and we select on merit.

Since 1990, the broadcasting industry has undergone a sea change. The nature of employment has become increasingly contract-based to staff-specific projects. People can and do work regularly in very different parts of business. The BBC is committed to nurturing and maintaining the skills necessary for a television and radio production base in Britain. Consequently, our approach to positive action is changing to meet the changing nature of the business.

We reviewed the use of positive action in 1990 to establish whether it was still necessary and effective. We moved away from separate training schemes for black and ethnic minority people towards targeting or reserving places on mixed training schemes because we believed that mixed schemes reflect our overriding objective to recognize, value and manage diversity.

Positive action is legal, it's regulated, it's monitored for fair play by the CRE [Commission for Racial Equality] it works. Our recruitment statistics indicate a marked improvement in response rates when we actively encourage applications from suitably qualified or experienced members of ethnic minority groups. There is a noticeable increase in the numbers of black and ethnic minority applicants for mainstream BBC jobs.

Diversity is the life blood of the broadcasting business. The case for encouraging talent from the broadcast base to contribute to the BBC is easily made. The arguments for not doing it? Not wanting to rock the boat; having to explain that the BBC is acting reasonably, and with sound business motives; worse still, not wishing to upset people!

We make omelettes by breaking eggs and mixing. It's a sound, sensible recipe, and we'd like to see a few more cooks using it![1]

Discussion Question
Would you like to work in the type of environment being created at BBC? Explain.

Managers are increasingly being asked to boost productivity, quality, and customer satisfaction while also reducing costs. These goals can only be met, however, through the cooperation and effort of all employees. By creating positive work environments where people feel valued and appreciated, organizations are more likely to foster the employee commitment and performance needed for organizational success. Unfortunately, some organizations are missing the mark.[2]

Without question, it is a difficult challenge to effectively integrate diverse people into the lifeblood of an organization.

Trevor McAuley, an Irishman working at East-Midland's Auto Alloys Foundry (UK), was constantly harassed by Irish comments. When senior management failed to support him, he ended up having time off for stress. According to a recent tribunal's judgement, harassment was the main cause for his final dismissal.[3] A report revealed appalling behaviour in one of British Rail's largest depots: racist graffiti, constant discrimination of four drivers of Asian origin, bias against ethnic minorities in examination procedures, statements about women being physically and mentally unsuitable to become train drivers, blue films during the night shift, . . .[4] When Sarah Locker, a woman police officer received pornographic magazines on her desk and literature making derogatory reference to her Turkish background, she decided to take her complaints to court. She won her case, but she met even more hostility on her return to work, which finally ended in a serious suicide attempt.[5] Sandra Valentine, a woman pilot claimed that she was told by a male colleague: "Women should not be let loose with anything more technical than a knife and fork." Once a senior pilot had announced to passengers: "The first officer is Ms Valentine and, yes, ladies and gentleman, she is a woman. We have them in the front as well as the back these days, so don't blame me."[6]

These examples reinforce the fact that some people do not leave their values, stereotypes, prejudice, and hate at the building entrance. As repugnant as these examples may be, managers nonetheless have to deal with them. What would you have done if you were a manager in one of these situations?

Managing diversity is a sensitive, potentially volatile, and sometimes uncomfortable issue. It is a hot spot in the USA and is now extending to Europe as well. Britain's Rhiannon Chapman declares, "welcoming diversity in the workplace is one of the key management challenges of the '90s."[7] Nevertheless, managing diversity is certainly not top of the bill in Europe. A Dutch study, among 110 public companies on their diversity policies, showed, despite oral agreement to cooperation, the extremely low participation rate of only 26.4 per cent. A non-response analysis showed among other reasons: diversity is unknown; there is no diversity policy; diversity is an unimportant or controversial issue. One company even wrote an elaborate letter to explain their policy of not managing diversity.[8] Yet managers are required to deal with it in the name of organizational survival. Accordingly, the purpose of this chapter is to help you get a better understanding of this important context for organizational behaviour. We begin by defining diversity. Next, we build the business case for diversity and then describe the organizational practices used to manage diversity. The chapter concludes by examining the barriers and challenges associated with managing diversity.

Defining Diversity

Diversity

The host of individual differences that make people different from and similar to each other.

Diversity represents the multitude of individual differences and similarities that exist among people. This definition underscores three important issues about managing diversity:[9] (1) There are many different dimensions or components of diversity. This implies that diversity pertains to everybody. It is not an issue of age, race, or gender. It is not an issue of being heterosexual, gay, or lesbian or of being Catholic, Jewish, Protestant, or Muslim. Diversity also does not pit white males against all other groups of people. Diversity pertains to the host of individual differences that make all of us unique and different from others. (2) Diversity is not synonymous with differences. Rather, it encompasses both differences and similarities. This means that managing diversity entails dealing with both simultaneously. (3) Diversity includes the collective mixture of differences and similarities, not just the pieces of it. Dealing with diversity requires managers to integrate the collective mixture of differences and similarities that exist within an organization.

This section begins our journey into managing diversity by first reviewing the key dimensions of diversity. Because many people associate diversity with affirmative action, this section compares affirmative action, valuing diversity, and managing diversity. They are not the same.[10]

Dimensions of Diversity

Like seashells on a beach, people come in a variety of shapes, sizes, and colours. This variety represents the essence of diversity. A team of diversity experts identified a set of primary and secondary dimensions of diversity to help distinguish the important ways in which people differ (see Figure 2–1). Taken together, the primary and secondary dimensions of diversity constitute one's personal identity.

Primary dimensions of diversity

Personal characteristics that exert an important and sustained impact throughout our lives.

Primary Dimensions of Diversity   **Primary dimensions of diversity** are those human differences that "exert an important impact on our early socialization and a powerful, sustained impact throughout every stage of life."[11] Figure 2–1 shows that the primary dimensions include gender, ethnic heritage, race, mental/physical abilities and characteristics, sexual orientation, and age. There are three additional things to keep in mind about the primary dimensions of diversity. First, some people may have a seventh or eighth core dimension of diversity. For example, religion is a core difference that has a powerful, sustained impact on some individuals' lives but not on others'. Second, primary dimensions are salient to other people; that is, we tend to notice them about each other. Third, primary dimensions of diversity are likely to evoke responses that are associated with biases, prejudices, or stereotypes because they are visible and salient.[12] Take the encounter experienced by a black woman in middle management while vacationing at a resort:

While she was sitting by the pool, "a large, 50-ish white male approached me and demanded that I get him extra towels. I said, 'Excuse me?' He then said, 'Oh, you don't work here,' with no shred of embarrassment or apology in his voice."[13]

Stereotypes most likely influenced this man's behaviour towards the woman.

Secondary dimensions of diversity

Personal characteristics that people acquire, discard, and/or modify throughout their lives.

Secondary Dimensions of Diversity   **Secondary dimensions of diversity** are personal characteristics that contain an element of control or choice. They are individual differences that we acquire, discard, and/or modify throughout our lives. Secondary dimensions are less visible to others, and their power to influence your life is less constant and more individualized than the primary dimensions of diversity. Figure 2–1 lists 11 key secondary dimensions of diversity.

Dimensions of Diversity Dynamically Interact   The primary and secondary dimensions dynamically interact to create numerous diversity combinations. This interaction influences your self-image, values, needs, goals, and expectations. Together, the primary and secondary dimensions of diversity define your diversity identity and affect how you are perceived and treated by others. As an example, read the two scenarios in the OB Exercise, and answer the diagnostic questions before reading on.

One can speculate that Jean-Claude and Aïcha have different needs and priorities based on this limited information. Although precise answers to the diagnostic questions depend on additional unknown information, you can see that the primary and secondary

Figure 2 – 1   Primary and Secondary Dimensions of Diversity

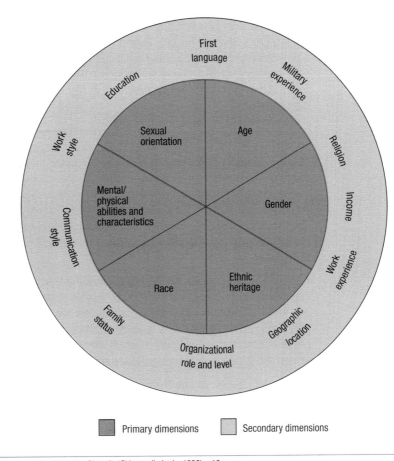

Primary dimensions   Secondary dimensions

Source: M Loden. *Implementing Diversity* (Chicago, IL: Irwin, 1996) p 16.

OB EXERCISE   *Dimension of diversity affect perceptions and expectations*

Jean-Claude is 55 years old. He studied at one of the French 'grandes écoles' and is vice president. He lives in Paris and owns a flat in 'Les grandes Mottes' on the French Mediterranean and is a practising Roman Catholic. His two children are married, and they have children of their own. His wife does volunteer work and is very active in the community. He is in excellent physical health and likes to play tennis and to sail on his catamaran.

Aïcha is a 30-year-old Algerian clerical worker. She is active in an anti- 'Front National' movement and is a single parent. She has two children under the age of 10. She completed secondary school after moving to France and has just begun to attend evening classes at a local school. Aïcha is a practising Muslim. Although her health is excellent, one of her children is developmentally disabled.

Based on this information, answer the following questions:

1. To what extent are Jean-Claude and Aïcha's goals, needs, and priorities similar and dissimilar?.

2. Which employee would prefer the following benefits?
   a. On-site day care
   b. A fitness centre
   c. Tuition reimbursement
   d. An executive bonus plan
   e. A rigorous affirmative action plan
   f. Enhanced retirement benefits
   g. Supervisory training
   h. Financial aid for special education
   I. Corporate membership in a tennis club.

SOURCE   This exercise was adapted from A J Kinicki, *Valuing Diversity* (Chandler, A Z: Angelo Kinicki, 1994), pp 1—5.

dimensions of diversity affect our perceptions and responses towards others. Not only do they influence our self-identity, but they affect how we are treated at work. Consider the case :

Liza Neeson was 17 when she went to work in Belfast for one of United Kingdom's largest security firms. She was the only Roman Catholic in the firm's headquarters, which was based in a Protestant area of the city. After a difficult period with the firm she was sacked and took her case to an employment tribunal. In December 1993, the tribunal, after hearing detailed evidence, awarded her £25,000 for what it described as high-handed, malicious, insulting, and oppressive discrimination.[14]

Affirmative Action and Valuing Diversity

Valuing diversity and managing diversity require organizations to adopt a new way of thinking about differences among people. Rather than pitting one group against another, valuing diversity and managing diversity strive to recognize the unique contribution every employee can make. This philosophy is much different from that of affirmative action. This section highlights the differences among affirmative action, valuing diversity, and managing diversity. Table 2–1 compares these three approaches to managing employee differences.

Kandola & Fullerton define diversity as follows: The basic concept of managing diversity accepts that the workforce consists of a diverse population of people. The diversity consists of visible and non-visible differences which will include factors such as sex, age, background, race, disability, personality, and workstyle. It is founded on the premiss that harnessing these differences will create a productive environment in which everybody feels valued, where talents are being fully utilised and in which organizational goals are met.[15]

Managing diversity means how to deal with personal and cultural differences between employees in order to contribute to their personal development and to increase the productivity.[16]

Affirmative action

Focuses on achieving equality of opportunity in an organization.

ETHICS

Affirmative Action As shown in Table 2 – 1, affirmative action focuses on achieving equality of opportunity in an organization and is often mandated by national or supranational laws. On the promotion of positive action, for example, the Council of the European Communities recommends the member states to adopt a positive action policy designed to eliminate existing inequalities affecting women in working life and to promote a better balance between the sexes in employment, comprising appropriate general and specific measures, within the framework of national policies and practices.[17] The International Labour Office (ILO) labour standards consist of Conventions and Recommendations, that provide a framework of principles for national policies. Conventions are legal instruments, which, when ratified by member states, are binding. They lay down general or technical guidelines to be applied at the national level.[18] Too often companies adopt an affirmative action policy, because laws oblige them to. From this point of view, it is a question of quotas, rather than a conviction. **Affirmative action** or equal opportunities is an artificial intervention aimed at giving management a chance to correct an imbalance, an injustice, a mistake, and/or outright discrimination.[19, 20] South Africa's Standard Bank has set very clear affirmative action standards: Around 40 per cent of Standard Bank's workforce is Asian, black or coloured (ABC). ABCs currently constitute 22 per cent of supervisors and the bank is aiming for a target of 35 per cent in two years' time.[21] Although affirmative action created tremendous opportunities for women and minorities, it does not foster the type of thinking that is needed to effectively manage diversity.[22] Affirmative action is a very artificial way to promote equal opportunities. It is, however, strongly promoted by the European Commission: it recommends acting for women in a way different to that for men, with the obvious aim of redressing the balance.[23] For example, affirmative action is commonly viewed as

Table 2–1   Comparison of Affirmative Action, Valuing Diversity, and Managing Diversity

AFFIRMATIVE ACTION	VALUING DIVERSITY	MANAGING DIVERSITY
Quantitative. Emphasizes achieving equality of opportunity in the work environment through the changing of organizational demographics. Monitored by statistical reports and analysis	*Qualitative.* Emphasizes the appreciation of differences and creating an environment in which everyone feels valued and accepted. Monitored by organizational surveys focused on attitudes and perceptions.	*Behavioural.* Emphasizes the building of specific skills and creating policies which get the best from every employee. Monitored by progress toward achieving goals and objectives.
Legally driven. Written plans and statistical goals for specific groups are utilized. Reports are mandated by laws and decrees.	*Ethically driven.* Moral and ethical imperatives drive this culture change.	*Strategically driven.* Behaviours and policies are seen as contributing to organizational goals and objectives such as profit and productivity and are tied to reward and results.
Remedial. Specific target groups benefit as past wrongs are remedied. Previously excluded groups have an advantage.	*Idealistic.* Everyone benefits. Everyone feels valued and accepted in an inclusive environment.	*Pragmatic.* The organization benefits; morale, profit, and productivity increase.
Opens doors in the organization. Affects hiring and promotion decisions.	*Diversity model.* Assumes that groups will retain their own characteristics and shape the organization as well as be shaped by it, creating a common set of values.	*Synergy model.* Assumes that diverse groups will create new ways of working together effectively in a pluralistic environment.
Resistance due to perceived limits to autonomy in decision making and perceived fears of reverse discrimination.	*Opens attitudes, minds, and the culture.* Affects attitudes of employees.	*Opens the system.* Affects managerial practices and policies.
	Resistance due to fear of change, discomfort with differences, and desire for return to "good old days".	*Resistance due to* denial of demographic realities, the need for alternative approaches, and/or benefits associated with change; and the difficulty in learning new skills, altering existing systems, and/or finding time to work toward synergistic solutions.

Source: L Gardenswartz and A Rowe, *Managing Diversity: A Complete Desk Reference and Planning Guide* (Homewood, IL: Business One Irwin, 1993), p 405.

involving preferential hiring and treatment based on group membership. This view creates tremendous resistance due to perceived injustice, particularly from white males. Affirmative action programmes were also found to negatively affect the women and minorities who supposedly benefited from them. In The Netherlands, Europe Combined Terminals, a container terminal, won a prize for its "women-friendly policy." As Gerda Dekker states: "Our strength is that we just do it. We have not developed endless guidelines, nor do we apply preferential hiring. I too want to be hired because I am the best, and not because some guideline dictates that a place has to be taken by a woman."[24] Research demonstrated that women and minorities, supposedly hired on the basis of affirmative action, felt negatively stigmatized as unqualified or incompetent. They also experienced lower job satisfaction and more stress than employees supposedly selected on the basis of merit.[25] A survey questioning men and women in accountancy, law, banking, construction, and information technology in the UK revealed that women who have succeeded in entering the professions appear to have become disillusioned and frustrated, lowering their ambitions and losing self-confidence.[26] Just the same, without affirmative action's focus on hiring and promoting diverse employees, the true valuing and managing of diversity rarely occurs. An increasing number of people and institutions now question the positive action programmes, and their doubts were affirmed in October 1995 by the European Court of Justice. The all-male court ruled that the use of quotas is sex discrimination against men and is therefore unlawful under the equal treatment directive. This landmark ruling throws into doubt all the systems of positive action giving priority to job applications from women that are favoured by many European states, especially Germany. The ruling was the result of a claim brought by Eckhard Kalanke, a gardener in the Bremen (Germany) parks department. He claimed that a female colleague had been promoted above him because of a law operating in Germany's public sector

Valuing diversity
Emphasizes the awareness, recognition, understanding, and appreciation of human differences.

Managing diversity
Creating organizational changes that enable all people to perform up to their maximum potential.

which requires women with qualifications equal to those of male applicants to be preferred if they are under-represented in certain jobs[27].

Valuing Diversity   Table 2–1 indicates that **valuing diversity** emphasizes the awareness, recognition, understanding, and appreciation of human differences. It revolves around creating an environment in which everyone feels valued and accepted. In essence, valuing diversity entails a cultural change geared towards viewing employee differences as a valuable resource that can contribute to organizational success.[28] This generally takes place through a series of management education and training programs that attempt to improve interpersonal relationships among diverse employees and to minimize blatant expressions of sexism and racism.[29]

Managing Diversity   **Managing diversity** entails enabling people to perform up to their maximum potential. It focuses on changing an organization's culture and infrastructure such that people provide the highest productivity possible. Ann Morrison, a diversity expert, conducted a study of 16 organizations that successfully managed diversity. Her results uncovered three key strategies for success: education, enforcement, and exposure. She describes them as follows:

The education component of the strategy has two thrusts: one is to prepare nontraditional managers for increasingly responsible posts, and the other is to help traditional managers overcome their prejudice in thinking about and interacting with people who are of a different sex or ethnicity. The second component of the strategy, enforcement, puts teeth in diversity goals and encourages behaviour change. The third component, exposure to people with different backgrounds and characteristics, adds a more personal approach to diversity by helping managers get to know and respect others who are different.[30]

More is said about managing diversity later in this chapter.

Building the Business Case for Managing Diversity

The rationale for managing diversity goes well beyond legal, social, and moral reasons. Quite simply, the primary reason for managing diversity is the ability to grow and maintain a business in an increasingly competitive marketplace. Organizations cannot accomplish this objective if employees fail to contribute their full talents, abilities, motivation, and commitment. Thus, it is essential for an organization to create an environment or culture that allows all employees to reach their full potential. Managing diversity is a critical component in creating such an organization.

This section explores the business need to manage diversity by first reviewing the demographic trends that are creating an increasingly diverse workforce. We then review the key reasons effective why management of diversity creates a competitive advantage.

Increasing Diversity in the Workforce

Workforce demographics
Statistical profiles of adult workers.

Workforce demographics, which are statistical profiles of the characteristics and composition of the adult working population, are an invaluable human-resource planning aid. They enable managers to anticipate and adjust for surpluses or shortages of appropriately skilled individuals. The European Union (EU) share of the world population will have fallen from 6.2 per cent in 1992 to 4.4 per cent by 2010, and by 2025 over 20 per cent of the EU population will be over 65 years of age. By 1993, there were only 1,000 net entrants to the European labour market compared with 500,000 in 1970; by the year 2000 more people will be leaving than joining the labour market. It is estimated that by the end of the decade 80 per cent of the net new entrants to the European labour market will be female.[31] These demographics reveal that organizations need to devise strategies to manage the mismatch in labour supply and demand. Moreover, general population demographics give managers a preview of the values and motives of future employees. Demographic changes during the last two or three decades have immense implications for organizational behaviour. This section explores three demographic trends that are creating an increasingly diverse workforce: (1) women continue to enter the workforce in increasing numbers, (2) ethnic minorities and their (grand) children represent a growing share of the labour force, and (3) the workforce is ageing.

Women Entering the Workforce   In the past couple of decades, every country in the Organisation for Economic Cooperation and Development (OECD) has seen a rise in the proportion of women entering the workforce . Since 1980 the number of women with paid jobs has increased by an average of 2 per cent a year. By 2000, women will make up to 80 per cent of Europe's new workers, according to the European Commission. In all rich countries, most women are crowded into a handful of occupations (see Figure 2–2). They are secretaries, shop assistants, cashiers, nurses, kitchen hands, and nannies. The list varies surprisingly little between countries. Even where the proportion of women in the job market is unusually high, such segregation persists. A recent study by the OECD points out that in the Nordic countries fewer than one-tenth of workers are in occupations where the sex balance is roughly equal; and half of all workers are in occupations where their own sex accounts for at least nine employees in ten. Women have not, on the whole, taken men's jobs. But "women's" jobs have expanded in the past couple of decades, while traditional "male" jobs have been disappearing.[32]

Figure 2–3 shows that Sweden (59 per cent) has the highest female participation in the European labour market, directly followed by Denmark (58 per cent) and by Finland

Figure 2–2	Women's Share of Jobs

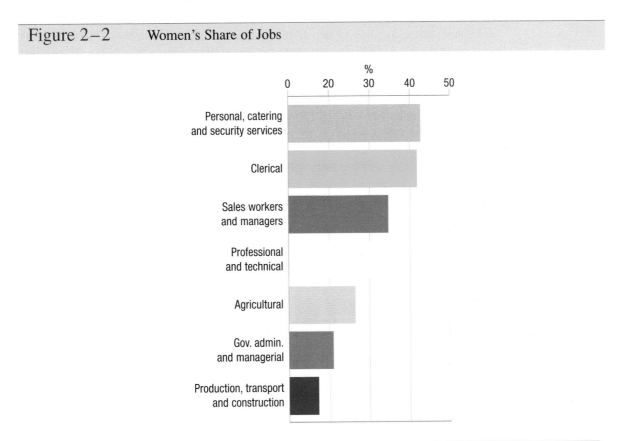

Source: *Bulletin on Women and Employment in the EU.* No 3, p 2. October 1994 (Manchester School of Management, UMIST, UK).

(56 per cent). Of all countries of the European Union, female participation is the lowest in the south-european countries: Italy (34 per cent), Spain (35 per cent) and Greece (36 per cent). Consequently, the gap between male and female participation is the largest in the southern countries: it amounts up to 30 per cent, whereas in Scandinavian countries the difference is limited to 10 per cent.[33]

Hugh Carnegy of *the Financial Times* gives us some historical explanation:

Sweden, perhaps more than any other country, prides itself on the high degree of equality its women have reached in society. The long list of legislative measures goes back to the establishment of equal inheritance rights for women and men in 1845. More recently, it encompasses the steady extension of paid maternity leave, an important encouragement for women joining the workforce. The first legislation giving the right to three months paid leave for women was enacted in 1955. This year a ruling has come into force so that fathers must take at least one month of a couple's current combined 12-month paid leave entitlement on the birth of a child.

Combined with the simultaneous extension of near-universal child care provision, these measures have resulted in 80 per cent of Swedish women joining the workforce, one of the highest levels in the world.

Women have also made startling inroads in politics and government compared with most other countries. The general election last year brought the number of women in the Riksdag up to 40 per cent of the total, compared with a European average for national parliaments of 11 per cent.[34]

In this respect, the European Commission has appointed an equality group to deal with gender discrimination in the senior echelons of the commission.[35]

Ethnic minorities in the European Labour Force   Applications for political asylum in EU member states continue to fall. In the first six months of 1996 they totalled 107,144 compared with 121,651 for the same period of 1995. This was a fall of 12 per cent continuing the trend started in 1993. Germany received over half of all applications, followed by the UK. In 1995, former Yugoslavia ranked first, with Turkey second and Romania third.

The Commission for Racial Equality's (CRE) survey of large companies gives an idea

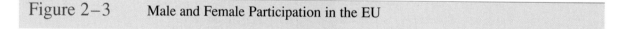

Figure 2–3   Male and Female Participation in the EU

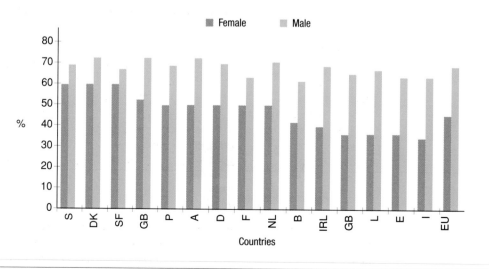

Source: Eurostat, 1995

of race equality measures implemented by major UK companies:[36]

Large Companies and Racial Equality comprised a survey of 168 British firms each with 7,000 or more employees, which began in the summer of 1993 and was completed in autumn 1994.

Of these large companies, 147 (88 per cent) said they had a policy specifically covering racial equality. The larger the company, the more likely it was to have a policy.

Seventy-five companies (45 per cent) said they had implemented, were implementing, or were about to implement an action plan or programme to realize their racial equality policies. Again, it was the large firms that were most likely to have adopted programmes.

Of the 63 companies that had no racial equality policy, 41 (24 per cent) said they did not have any plans to introduce a full equality policy within the next two years.

The main elements of the companies' racial equality programmes were as follows:

- *Ethnic monitoring.* This was mentioned by 85 companies. It would be difficult to imagine a sales or marketing policy that was not subject to close scrutiny, and a racial equality policy is no different.
- *Racial equality training.* Staff responsible for recruitment and selection need to be trained on the legal stipulations, the company's racial equality policy and how to avoid unlawful discrimination. The survey showed that 82 companies provided such training.
- *Racial harassment procedures.* Effective procedures for dealing with racial harassment are a sign that the company will not tolerate such conduct. Seventy-seven companies had formal procedures.
- *Equal opportunity executives.* 42 companies said they employed an executive whose main or sole responsibility was for equal opportunities, including racial equality.
- *Access training, positive action training and "special encouragement".* Using provisions of the Race Relations Act 1976, 40 companies offered general access training, compared with only 21 providing positive action training; and 49 said they encouraged applications from ethnic groups.
- *Targets.* Only 16 companies used numerical targets set on the basis of relevant demographic and business factors. But, says the CRE, many companies that do not feel comfortable with the idea of targets do make effective use of benchmark data. The most popular form of benchmark data, used by 41 companies, was changes in workforce data over time; followed by the 1991 census, used by 39 firms.
- *Contracting arrangements.* 14 companies raised racial equality issues in negotiations with their suppliers and subcontractors.
- *Racial equality objectives as a measure of managers' performance.* 13 companies said they included racial equality objectives among those on which line managers are assessed.

The Ageing Workforce   According to a report issued in 1995 by the International Labour Office older men are rapidly disappearing from their workforces (women seem to be less affected). As Table 2-2 reveals, the number of working men between 60 and 65 has reduced by about 25 per cent in 25 years' time. The major reason is the introduction of early retirement schemes, promoted in many European countries. Moreover, many companies recruit newcomers from recent graduates. At Shell and Unilever, a 28-year-old graduate is considered too old to be recruited if she or he does not have a postgraduate degree.[37] Eastern Europe, and former Soviet republics, too, are expected to encounter significant economic and political problems due to an ageing population.[38]

Managing Diversity—A Competitive Advantage

Some consultants, academics, and business leaders believe that effectively managing diversity is a competitive advantage. This advantage stems from the process in which the management of diversity affects organizational behaviour and effectiveness. Effectively managing diversity can influence an organization's costs and employee attitudes,

Table 2–2   Percentage of Men Between 60 and 64 Who Work

Shedding older men

	1960	1994
Australia	79.6%	48.7%
Austria	66.0%	12.7%
Britain	87.4%	52.2%
Canada	75.8%	47.6%
France*	71.1%	18.2%
Germany	72.5%	34.9%
Japan*	81.9%	75.6%
Netherlands	80.8%	18.0%
Sweden	82.5%	57.8%
United States	77.1%	54.9%

*Legal retirement age of 60

Source: ILO.

recruitment of human resources, sales and market share (See International OB) creativity and innovation, and group problem solving and productivity. This section explores the relationship between managing diversity and each of these outcomes

Lower Costs and Improved Employee Attitudes   Turnover and absenteeism were found to be higher for women and ethnic minorities than for whites. For example, Monsanto learned that ethnic minorities quit more frequently than whites because of poor relationships with their managers, lack of timely promotions, feeling they were not appreciated and being given work that did not improve their skills.[39] Corning Glass also reported that turnover among professional women was double that of men between 1980 and 1987 and that the rate for blacks was 2.5 times that for whites.[40] A Dutch company has built a mosque on the company's premises, not to improve cultural acceptance, but to strengthen its results by reducing absenteeism.[41]

Research revealed that people who were different from their work units in racial or ethnic background were less psychologically committed to their organizations, less satisfied with their careers, and perceived lower managerial discretion on their jobs. A study in the US of 814 blacks and 814 whites revealed that blacks, compared with whites, felt less accepted by their peers, perceived lower managerial discretion on their jobs,

INTERNATIONAL ORGANIZATIONAL BEHAVIOUR

Cultural Insensitivity Affects Sales

Olympia reportedly tried to introduce a photocopier in Chile under the name ROTO. The copiers, however, did not sell well. Why? Two possible explanations: (1) Roto is the Spanish word for "broken," and (2) roto is the word used to delineate the lowest class in Chile.

General Motors was faced with a somewhat similar problem. It was troubled by the lack of enthusiasm among the Puerto Rican dealers for its recently introduced Chevrolet Nova. The word nova means "star" when translated literally. However, when spoken, it sounds like "no va," which, in Spanish, means

"it does not go." This obviously did little to increase consumer confidence in the new vehicle. . . .

In the early 1980s, a German beer company launched a new brand in West Africa and named it EKU. Sales were uneven, and it took the firm two years to figure out the cause. Foreigners and some local tribe members purchased the beer, but one important tribe totally avoided it. Apparently eku was the local slang word in that tribe for "excrement." As word spread, members of other tribes and even the foreigners started drinking it less.

SOURCE: Excerpted from D Ricks, *Blunders in International Business* (Cambridge, MA: Blackwell Business, 1995), pp 35–36.

Career plateau

The end result when the probablity of being promoted is very small.

reached **career plateaus** more frequently, noted lower levels of career satisfaction, and received lower performance ratings.[42] Organizational surveys further revealed that the majority of respondents witnessed some type of hostility and discrimination towards gay and lesbian employees. Gay and lesbian employees also reported higher levels of stress than heterosexual employees. How important is the issue of sexual preference? Up to 10 per cent of the population is estimated to be homosexual.[43] Can any organization afford to squelch the motivation and productivity of possibly 10 per cent of its workforce?

Employees' physical abilities/qualities is another dimension of diversity that needs to be effectively managed. In this context, too, the European Commission takes its responsibility by creating action programmes, such as the Helios programme. The Helios programme was created to promote vocational training and rehabilitation, economic integration, social integration, and an independent way of life for disabled people.[44] Consider the following recruitment policy: a disabled young man with a brilliant degree is told by his employer that, because he is disabled, he will be paid less than other new employees for exactly the same work.[45] The following UK-based companies pay special attention to disabled applicants: P&O's directors claim "full and fair consideration is given to disabled applicants for employment and training, and career development is encouraged on the basis of aptitude and abilities."[46] Cable & Wireless says it gives particular attention to the employment of disabled people.[47] Tarmac's group policy treats all workers equally and gives full consideration to applications for employment from disabled persons.[48]

Improved Recruiting Efforts   Attracting and retaining competent employees is a competitive advantage. This is particularly true given the workforce demographics discussed in the preceding section. Organizations that effectively manage diversity are more likely to meet this challenge because women and ethnic minorities are attracted to such companies. According to Jan Cornet, Personnel Manager at McDonald's in Amsterdam, The Netherlands: "Ethnic minorities will rather apply for a job at McDonald's, as we are known to hire many people of ethnic minorities. It breaks down barriers."[49] What do you think of the following statement, by John Courtis, a UK selection consultant and author of several books on recruitment:

It is probably unwise to recruit women for some Arab countries, and people of the Jewish faith for the same territories, for different reasons. Some gay people will find specific territories and their statutes deeply unsympathetic. Recruiters will be very likely to discriminate when choosing people for these areas, and may be thought incompetent and/or insensitive if they do not. There may sometimes be good reasons for targeting young people. For instance, statistics from a Japanese car maker suggest that repetitive work on a car body production line is best performed by younger employees; middle-aged people cannot keep up.[50]

Increased Sales and Market Share   Workforce diversity is the mirror image of consumer diversity. A survey on 14 well-known UK organizations revealed that two of them had made diversity a strategic issue because they had a need to relate effectively to a more cosmopolitan customer base. For example, one of them now had to sell to some major customers whose purchasing was done by women from an Asian background. Several of the middle-aged, white salesmen, often from engineering backgrounds, had lacked the necessary cultural sensitivity and skills to handle these sales situations successfully. First, the company trained the salesmen and then it recruited an American Filipino woman as a manager within the group. Eventually, some salesmen who could not adjust to the change were moved to other jobs.[51] At Amsterdam's Albert Heyn store located in the popular De Pijp area, boys and girls of 17 different nationalities are filling the shelves, weighing cheese, or sitting behind the desk. The number of colours represented by the workforce almost outnumbers the variety of nationalities the customers represent. Accidental or not? "Our aim is a workforce that reflects the environment," says Erik Muller, spokesman for Albert Heyn. "You will find more coloured people at De Pijp and the Bijlmer than at Wassenaar. The customer is our focus, and he must recognize himself in our staff. We have no special intake policy. We recruit our staff in the immediate neighbourhood of our stores. It happens in a rather natural way, without any calculations. Coloured staff members are however receiving extra assistance, as they usually have more problems in standing up for themselves than their Dutch colleagues.[52] Of school-leavers in Brussels, 39 per cent are not Belgian. A Belgian bank manager puts it crudely: "I'd rather see my clients served by an immigrant, than the immigrant robbing my bank."[53]

It is thus important for companies to market their products so that they appeal to a diverse marketplace. In 1988, the Italian clothing firm Benetton stopped showing its products in its advertisements to put more emphasis on the slogan "United Colors of Benetton". This slogan accompanies provocative pictures, such as a black woman breast-feeding a white baby, a priest in black kissing a nun in white, three children of different colours, sticking out their tongues. It appears that Benetton reports a constant increase in sales.[54] Moreover, just as minorities prefer to work for companies that value diversity, they also may select to buy from such organizations.

The Swedish furniture group, IKEA, routinely employs gay sales staff and uses gay images in some of its advertising. Result: huge numbers of gay shoppers.[55]

In contrast, ski resorts and equipment manufacturers are losing sales because they failed to accommodate female skiers.

In her book Women Ski, Claudia Caibone wonders why even more women don't give up the sport: "The equipment has not met a woman's needs in skiing," she says. "Women's boots may have thicker linings to accommodate the narrower woman's foot," she says. But the newer hard plastic shells are, in nearly all cases, designed for men—meaning the toe boxes are too narrow, the heels too wide and the top of the instep too low for an average woman's foot, she says.

And women's skis are often male-version [skis], painted with different colors. Instead of pretty graphics, what a woman really needs is a softer ski that bends around turns more easily with women's lighter frames, Ms Carbone says.[56]

Increased Creativity and Innovation   Because diverse groups possess a broader base of experience and perspectives from which to analyse a problem, they can potentially improve problem solving and performance A diverse workforce brings to problems multiple solutions based on employees' different knowledge and experiences. "In the service industry especially, making the most of employee potential is how you get ahead of the competition," says Johanne M. Totta, vice president of employee programmes and workplace equality at Canada's Bank of Montreal.[57] Research findings based on short-term groups that varied in terms of values, attitudes, educational backgrounds, and experience supported this conclusion. Heterogeneous groups produced better quality decisions and demonstrated higher productivity than homogeneous groups. Nevertheless, these results must be interpreted cautiously because the experimental samples, tasks, time frames, and environmental situations bear very little resemblance to actual ongoing organizational settings. Recent research has attempted to control for these problems.

Recent studies do not clearly support the proposed benefits of diversity. A study of culturally homogeneous and diverse groups over a period of 17 weeks showed higher performance among homogeneous groups for the first 9 weeks due to the fact that heterogeneous groups experienced less effective group processes than homogeneous groups. Over weeks 10 through 17, however, homogeneous and heterogeneous groups demonstrated similar performance. Additional studies found that work group diversity was significantly associated with increased absenteeism, turnover, and less psychological commitment and intention to stay in the organization.

Based on an extensive literature study and a survey of diversity policy and practices in nearly 300 UK organizations, researchers conclude that only access to talent and enhanced flexibility of the organization are proven benefits. Managing diversity gives better access to valuable potential and reduces turnover costs. The other benefits seem debatable: increased quality, improved customer service and better performing teams.

In summary, research does not clearly support the premise that diversity leads to enhanced problem solving and productivity. It seems that performance is best when there is neither too much nor too little diversity. There are two additional conditions that must be satisfied before diversity can positively contribute to problem solving and performance.

1. Group members must share common values and norms that promote pursuit of the organization's goals.

2. Group members need to be aware of cultural and attitudinal differences of other group members.

Many companies use training programmes to promote this awareness.

Organizational Practices Used to Effectively Manage Diversity

Organizations throughout the world are unsure of what it takes to effectively manage diversity. This is partly due to the fact that top management only recently became aware of the combined need and importance of this issue. Given this awareness, however, some companies are now beginning to implement practices and programmes aimed at both valuing and managing diversity.

So what are organizations doing to effectively manage diversity? Answering this question requires that we provide a framework for categorizing organizational initiatives. Researchers and practitioners have developed relevant frameworks. One was developed by R Roosevelt Thomas, Jr, a diversity expert. He identified eight generic action options that can be used to address any type of diversity issue. A second was proposed by another diversity expert, Ann Morrison. She empirically identified the specific diversity initiatives used by 16 organizations that successfully managed diversity. This section reviews these frameworks in order to provide you with both a broad and specific understanding about how organizations are effectively managing diversity.

R Roosevelt Thomas, Jr's Generic Action Options

Thomas identified eight basic responses for handling any diversity issue. They are presented in Table 2–3. After describing each action option, we discuss relationships among them.[58]

Option 1: Include/Exclude This choice is an outgrowth of affirmative action programmes. Its primary goal is to either increase or decrease the number of diverse people at all levels of the organization.

Option 2: Deny People using this option deny that differences exist. Denial may manifest itself in proclamations that all decisions are colour, gender, and age blind, and that success is solely determined by merit and performance.

Option 3: Assimilate The basic premise behind this alternative is that all diverse people will learn to fit in or become like the dominant group. It only takes time and reinforcement for people to see the light.

Option 4: Suppress Differences are squelched or discouraged when using this approach. This can be done by telling or reinforcing others to quit whining and complaining about issues. The old "you've got to pay your dues" line is another frequently used way to promote the status quo.

Table 2–3	Generic Action Options for Managing Diversity

OPTION	DESCRIPTION
1. Include/exclude	Include by expanding the number and variability of mixture components. Or exclude by minimising the number and variability of mixture components.
2. Deny	Minimize mixture diversity by explaining it away.
3. Assimilate	Minimize mixture diversity by insisting that "minority" components conform to the norms of the dominant factor.
4. Suppress	Minimize mixture diversity by removing it from your consciousness—by assigning it to the subconscious.
5. Isolate	Address diversity by including and setting "different" mixture components off to the side.
6. Tolerate	Address diversity by fostering a room-for-all attitude, albeit with limited superficial interactions among the mixture components.
7. Build relationships	Address diversity by fostering quality relationships—characterized by acceptance and understanding—among the mixture components.
8. Foster mutual adaptation	Address diversity by fostering mutual adaptation in which all components change somewhat, for the sake of achieving common objectives.

Source: Excerpted by permission of the publisher from *Redefining Diversity* © 1996 Roosevelt R Thomas, Jr. Published by AMACOM, a division of American Management Association. All rights reserved.

Option 5: Isolate   This option maintains the current way of doing things by setting the diverse person off to the side. In this way, the individual is unable to influence organizational change. Managers can isolate people by putting them on special projects. Entire work groups or departments are isolated by creating functionally independent entities, frequently referred to as "silos."

Option 6: Tolerate   Toleration entails acknowledging differences but not valuing or accepting them. This option is more successful when people do not frequently interact.

Option 7: Build Relationships   This approach is based on the premise that good relationships can overcome differences. Although this method may create acceptance and understanding of differences, it is frequently used to minimize them. The goal is to focus on similarities rather than the challenges related to differences.

Option 8: Foster Mutual Adaptation   In this option, people recognize and accept differences, and most importantly, agree that everyone and everything is open for change. Mutual adaptation allows the greatest accommodation of diversity.

Conclusions about Action Options   Thomas reminds us to keep five conclusions in mind when trying to pick a course of action: (1) None of the action options is inherently good or bad. All can be legitimately used in either a positive or negative fashion. (2) "Fostering mutual adaptation" is the only approach that unquestionably endorses the philosophy behind managing diversity. (3) Action options can be used alone or in combination. (4) Choosing how to best manage diversity is a dynamic process that is determined by the context at hand. For example, some organizations are not ready for mutual adaptation. The best one might hope for in this case is the inclusion of diverse people. (5) These options apply to any type of collective mixture of differences and similarities. They can be used to guide the process of integrating two merged companies as well as in the context of race and gender.

Ann Morrison Identifies Specific Diversity Initiatives

As previously mentioned, Ann Morrison conducted a landmark study of the diversity practices used by 16 organizations that successfully managed diversity. Her results uncovered 52 different practices, 20 of which were used by the majority of the companies sampled. She classified the 52 practices into three main types: accountability, development, and recruitment.[59] The top 10 practices associated with each type are shown in Table 2–4. They are discussed next in order of relative importance.

Accountability Practices
Focus on treating diverse employees fairly.

Accountability Practices   **Accountability practices** relate to managers' responsibility to treat diverse employees fairly. Table 2–4 reveals that companies predominantly accomplish this objective by creating administrative procedures aimed at integrating diverse employees into the management ranks (practices number 3, 4, 5, 6, 8, 9, and 10). In contrast, work and family policies, practice 7, focus on creating an environment that fosters employee commitment and productivity. Consider the work and family practices at the following companies:

The Boots Company (UK) family-friendly employment policy includes job sharing, term-time and school hours working, holiday play schemes, child minding schemes, career breaks ... [60] The North British Housing Association has a long track record of being a family-friendly employer: it proposes enhanced maternity benefits, flexible working policies, paternity leave and other leave arrangements ... Remarkable at UK's Texaco's is its family leave days (paid time off for emergencies) ... S4C, the Welsh language TV channel, reserved places at a crèche near its Cardiff headquarters, available to staff at a discounted rate.[61]

How would you, as a personnel manager, deal with the following situation:

A London-based uniformed policeman argues that, under the equal opportunities legislation, he should be allowed to wear his hair in a ponytail, or in any other so-called female hair style.

Table 2–4	Common Diversity Practices

ACCOUNTABILITY PRACTICES
1. Top management's personal intervention
2. Internal advocacy groups
3. Emphasis on statistics, profiles
4. Inclusion of diversity in performance evaluation goals, ratings
5. Inclusion of diversity in promotion decisions, criteria
6. Inclusion of diversity in management succession planning
7. Work and family policies
8. Policies against racism, sexism
9. Internal audit or attitude survey
10. Active equal opportunities committee, office

DEVELOPMENT PRACTICES
1. Diversity training programs
2. Networks and support groups
3. Development programs for all high-potential managers
4. Informal networking activities
5. Job rotation
6. Formal mentoring program
7. Informal mentoring program
8. Entry development programs for all high-potential new hires
9. Internal training (such as personal safety or language)
10. Recognition events, awards

RECRUITMENT PRACTICES
1. Targeted recruitment of nonmanagers
2. Key outside hires
3. Extensive public exposure on diversity
4. Corporate image as liberal, progressive, or benevolent
5. Partnerships with educational institutions
6. Recruitment incentives such as cash supplements
7. Internships
8. Publications or PR products that highlight diversity
9. Targeted recruitment of managers
10. Partnership with nontraditional groups

Source: Abstracted from Tables A.10, A.11, and A.12 in A M Morrison, *The New Leaders: Guidelines on Leadership Diversity in America* (San Francisco: Jossey-Bass, 1992).

Women are permitted to wear their hair long provided it is kept away from their face and looks neat. [62]

In addition to improving productivity and satisfaction, a recent study of 398 health professionals demonstrated that work-family programs were associated with lower levels of work-family conflict, depression, health complaints, and blood cholesterol.[63]

Development practices

Focus on preparing diverse employees for greater responsibility and advancement.

Development Practices   The use of development practices to manage diversity is relatively new compared with the historical use of accountability and recruitment practices. **Development practices** focus on preparing diverse employees for greater responsibility and advancement. These activities are needed because most non-traditional employees have not been exposed to the type of activities and job assignments that develop effective leadership and social networks.[64] Table 2–4 indicates that diversity training programmes, networks and support groups, and mentoring programmes are among the most frequently used developmental practices.

Recruitment Practices   **Recruitment practices** focus on attracting job applicants at all levels who are willing to accept challenging work assignments. This focus is critical because people learn the leadership skills needed for advancement by successfully accomplishing increasingly challenging and responsible work assignments. As shown in Table 2–4, targeted recruitment of nonmanagers (practice 1) and managers (practice 9) are commonly used to identify and recruit women and ethnic minorities.[65] Consider the recruitment efforts pursued by Bass and Ford:

Bass (UK) puts serious money into training and development and conducts ethnic monitoring of its graduate recruitment programme in which women often make up a third of the yearly intake.[66] Ford of Britain's record in attracting graduates from ethnic minorities is closely monitored and it has set up two joint union management working parties to analyse the factors influencing the progress of women within the company, and to stamp out sexual and racial harassment.[67]

The Diversity-oriented Organization   Kandola and Fullerton have summed up the six characteristics of the diversity-oriented organization in one word: MOSAIC:[68]

- **M**ission and values.
- **O**bjective and fair processes.
- **S**killed workforce: aware and fair.
- **A**ctive flexibility.
- **I**ndividual focus.
- **C**ulture that empowers.

Mission and Values   The diversity-oriented organization will have a strong, positive mission and core values which make managing diversity a necessary long-term business objective for the organization and a responsibility of all employees. The values must reflect the personal and work needs of all employees.

Objective and Fair Processes   The organization must guarantee objective and fair recruitment, selection, induction and appraisal processes, by always using the most recent techniques.

Skilled Workforce: Aware and Fair   This characteristic first involves having a workforce aware of and guided by the principles of managing diversity. Second, it requires having managers who manage. The emphasis should be on the managing, not on the diversity.

Active Flexibility   There will be increased flexibility in the diversity-oriented organization not only in terms of working patterns but also in all policies, practices, and procedures.

Individual Focus   This characteristic encompasses the previous ones and implies their individual approach and should not be group-focused.

Culture that Empowers   Each action the organization takes must be underpinned by its underlying culture. Features of the empowering culture are:

- Complete delegation of decision-making.
- Total participation and consultation.
- Experimentation is encouraged; failures are accepted.
- Open and trusting culture without any form of discrimination.

Barriers and Challenges to Managing Diversity

We introduced this chapter by noting that diversity is a sensitive, potentially volatile, and sometimes uncomfortable issue. It is therefore not surprising that organizations encounter significant barriers when trying to move forward with managing diversity. The following is a list of the most common barriers to implementing successful diversity programmes.[69]

1. *Inaccurate stereotypes and prejudice.* This barrier manifests itself in the belief that differences are viewed as weaknesses. In turn, this promotes the view that diversity hiring will mean sacrificing competence and quality.

2. *Ethnocentrism.* The ethnocentrism barrier represents the feeling that one's cultural rules and norms are superior or more appropriate than the rules and norms of another culture. This barrier is thoroughly discussed in Chapter 4.

3. *Poor career planning.* This barrier is associated with the lack of opportunities for diverse employees to get the type of work assignments that qualify them for senior management positions.[70]

4. *An unsupportive and hostile working environment for diverse employees.* Diverse employees are frequently excluded from social events and the friendly camaraderie that takes place in most offices.

5. *Lack of political savvy on the part of diverse employees.* Diverse employees may not get promoted because they do not know how to "play the game" of getting along and getting ahead in an organization. Research reveals that women and ethnic minorities are excluded from organizational networks.[71]

6. *Difficulty in balancing career and family issues.* Women still assume the majority of the responsibilities associated with raising children. This makes it harder for women to work evenings and weekends or frequently to travel once they have children. Even without children in the picture, household chores take more of a woman's time than a man's time.

7. *Fears of reverse discrimination.* Some employees believe that managing diversity is a smoke screen for reverse discrimination. This belief leads to very strong resistance because people feel that one person's gain is another's loss.

8. *Diversity is not seen as an organizational priority.* This leads to subtle resistance that shows up in the form of complaints and negative attitudes. Employees may complain about the time, energy, and resources devoted to diversity that could have been spent doing "real work".

9. *The need to revamp the organization's performance appraisal and reward system.* Performance appraisals and reward systems must reinforce the need to effectively manage diversity. This means that success will be based on a new set of criteria. Employees are likely to resist changes that adversely affect their promotions and financial rewards.

10. *Resistance to change.* Effectively managing diversity entails significant organizational and personal change. As discussed in Chapter 20, people resist change for many different reasons.

In summary, managing diversity is a critical component of organizational success. Case studies and limited research inform us that this effort is doomed to failure unless top management is truly committed to managing diversity.

Summary of Key Concepts

1. *Define diversity.* Diversity represents the host of individual differences that make people different from and similar to each other. Diversity pertains to everybody. It is not simply an issue of age, race, gender, or sexual orientation.

2. *Discuss the primary and secondary dimensions of diversity.* Primary dimensions of diversity represent personal characteristics that exert an important and sustained impact throughout our lives. They significantly affect an individual's early socialization and include gender, ethnic heritage, race, mental/physical abilities and characteristics, sexual orientation, and age. Secondary dimensions are personal characteristics that contain an element of control or choice. They are acquired, discarded, and/or modified throughout our lives.

3. *Explain the differences among affirmative action, valuing diversity, and managing diversity.* Affirmative action focuses on achieving equality of opportunity in an organization. It represents an artificial intervention aimed at giving management a chance to correct an imbalance, an injustice, a mistake, and/or outright discrimination. Valuing diversity emphasizes the awareness, recognition, understanding, and appreciation of human differences. Training programmes are the dominant method used to accomplish this objective. Managing diversity entails creating a host of organizational changes that enable all people to perform up to their maximum potential.

4. *Demonstrate your familiarity with the demographic trends that are creating an increasingly diverse workforce.* There are three key demographic trends: (1) women continue to enter the workforce in increasing numbers, (2) ethnic minorities and their (grand) children represent a growing share of the labour force, and (3) the workforce is ageing.

5. *Discuss the MOSAIC-approach to managing diversity.* MOSAIC stands for mission and values, objective and fair processes, skilled workforce: aware and fair, active flexibility, individual focus and culture that empowers.

6. *Review the five reasons managing diversity is a competitive advantage.* (a) Managing diversity can lower costs and improve employee attitudes. (b) Managing diversity can improve an organization's recruiting efforts. (c) Managing diversity can increase sales and market share. (d) Managing diversity can increase creativity and innovation. (e) Managing diversity can increase group problem solving and productivity.

7. *Discuss the organizational practices used to effectively manage diversity as identified by R Roosevelt Thomas, Jr, and Ann Morrison.* There are many different practices organizations can use to manage diversity. R Roosevelt Thomas, Jr, identified eight basic responses for handling any diversity issue: include/exclude, deny, assimilate, suppress, isolate, tolerate, build relationships, and foster mutual adaptation. Thomas recommends five conclusions to consider when trying to pick one of these alternatives. Ann Morrison's study of diversity practices identified three main types or categories of activities. Accountability practices relate to a manager's responsibility to treat diverse employees fairly. Development practices focus on preparing diverse employees for greater responsibility and advancement. Recruitment practices emphasize attracting job applicants at all levels who are willing to accept challenging work assignments. Table 2–4 presents a list of activities that are used to accomplish each main type.

8. *Identify the barriers and challenges to managing diversity.* There are 10 barriers to successfully implementing diversity initiatives: (a) inaccurate stereotypes and prejudice, (b) ethnocentrism, (c) poor career planning, (d) an unsupportive and hostile working environment for diverse employees, (e) lack of political savvy on the part of diverse employees, (f) difficulty in balancing career and family issues, (g) fears of reverse discrimination, (h) diversity is not seen as an organizational priority, (i) the need to revamp the organization's performance appraisal and reward system, and (j) resistance to change.

Discussion Questions

1. Whom do you think would be most resistant to accepting the value or need to manage diversity? Explain.

2. What role does communication play in effectively managing diversity?

3. Does diversity suggest that managers should follow the rule "Do unto others as you would have them do unto you"?

4. Which of the primary and secondary dimensions of diversity is most sensitive or volatile? Discuss your reasoning.

5. Do you think white males are an endangered species? Explain.

6. What is the most critical organizational challenge associated with the increase of ethnic minorities in the workforce? What can be done to facilitate the career success of minorities?

7. Why is underemployment a serious human resource management problem? If you have ever been underemployed, what were your feelings about it?

8. How can interpersonal conflict be caused by diversity? Explain your rationale.

9. Have you seen any examples that support the proposition that diversity is a competitive advantage?

10. Which of the barriers to managing diversity would be most difficult to reduce? Explain.

Personal Awareness and Growth Exercise

What Is Your Attitude Towards Diversity?

Objectives

1. To assess your attitudes towards diversity.

2. To consider the managerial implications of employees' diversity attitudes.

Introduction

Although researchers argue about the direction of the relationship between attitudes and behaviour, most agree they are related. A team of researchers developed a measure of attitudes towards diversity in order to further our knowledge about employees' attitudes and acceptance of diversity programmes.[72] The following survey assesses your attitudes towards diversity on three subscales. The first concerns your attitude towards having co-workers who are minorities. The second subscale measures your attitude towards having minorities in managerial/supervisory positions. Finally, the third subscale assesses your attitude towards the hiring and promotion of minorities. There are no right or wrong answers to the survey. The best answers reflect your real feelings about the issues at hand.

Instructions

Thinking of your current or most recent job, indicate the extent to which you agree with each of the statements shown. Select one number from the following scale for each statement. After completing the survey, use the scoring key to compute a total score for each of the three subscales.

1 = Strongly disagree

2 = Disagree

3 = Neither disagree nor agree

4 = Agree

5 = Strongly agree

_____ 1. If one of my co-workers were racist, I would confront that person and let him or her know of my disapproval.

_____ 2. The most qualified workers in my job seem to be females or minorities.

_____ 3. The minorities in this organization do not have a greater degree of difficulty getting along with others.

_____ 4. If a member of my work group were prejudiced, he or she would be less likely to fit in.

_____ 5. Most of the minority and/or female supervisors in this organization possess the same leadership qualities as do those supervisors who are white or female.

_____ 6. The women I work with do not need to be more assertive to be effective supervisors.

_____ 7. I am equally comfortable with a either a female or male supervisor.

_____ 8. Most of the women and minorities in management do an outstanding job.

_____ 9. It does not bother me that some preferential hiring goes on because we need more of a mix in this organization.

_____ 10. I know many more qualified women or minorities who should have been hired instead of some of the white males that have been hired lately.

_____ 11. We would have a more creative work environment if more women and minorities were hired.

_____ 12. I feel that increasing the hiring of women and minorities can only help this organization.

Scoring Key and Interpretation

Compute a total score for the four survey statements that measure each subscale.

Attitude toward co-workers (1–4)   _____

Attitude towards supervisor (5–8)   _____

Attitude towards hiring and promotion (9–12)   _____

Arbitrary norms for comparisons are as follows: Total subscale score of 4 to 8 = Relatively negative attitude towards the diversity component; 9 to 15 = Moderate attitude towards the diversity component; 16 to 20 = Relatively positive attitude towards the diversity component.

QUESTIONS FOR DISCUSSION

1. What were your attitudes towards diversity along the three subscales? Do you believe these ratings accurately portray your attitude towards diversity? Explain.

2. What are the implications of having either positive or negative attitudes towards diversity? Explain.

3. What would it take to turn a negative attitude towards diversity around to a positive attitude? Discuss.

4. Do you believe an individual's attitude towards diversity affects his or her behaviour? Describe your thinking.

Group Exercise

Managing Diversity-Related Interactions

Objectives

1. To improve your ability to manage diversity-related interactions more effectively.

2. To explore different approaches for handling diversity interactions.

Introduction

The interpersonal component of managing diversity can be awkward and uncomfortable. This is partly due to the fact that resolving diversity interactions requires us to deal with situations we may never have encountered before. The purpose of this exercise is to help you manage diversity-related interactions more effectively. To do so, you will be asked to read three scenarios and then decide how you will handle each situation.

Scenario 1

Philip, who is one of your direct reports, comes to you and says that he and Peter are having a special commitment ceremony to celebrate the beginning of their lives together. He has invited you to the ceremony. Normally the department has a party and cake for special occasions. Christine, who is one of Philip's peers, has just walked into your office and asks you whether you intend to have a party for Philip.

A. How would you respond?

_____

_____

_____

B. What is the potential impact of your response?

_____

_____

_____

C. If you choose not to respond, what is the potential impact of your behaviour?

_____

_____

_____

Scenario 2

You have an open position for a supervisor, and your top two candidates are an ethnic female and a white female. Both candidates are equally qualified. The position is responsible for five white team leaders. You hire the white female because the work group likes her. The team leaders said that they felt more comfortable with the white female. The vice president of human resources has just called you on the phone and asks you to explain why you hired the white female.

A. How would you respond?

_____

_____

_____

B. What is the potential impact of not hiring the ethnic candidate?

_____

_____

_____

C. What is the potential impact of hiring the ethnic candidate?

_____

_____

_____

Instructions

Presented here are three scenarios depicting diversity-related interactions.[73] Please read the first scenario, and then answer the three questions that follow it. Follow the same procedure for the next two scenarios. Next, divide into groups of three. One at a time, each person should present his or her responses to the three questions for the first scenario. The groups should then discuss the various approaches that were proposed to resolve the diversity interaction and try to arrive at a consensus recommendation. Follow the same procedure for the next two scenarios.

Scenario 3

While attending an off-site business meeting, you are waiting in line with a group of team leaders to get your lunch at a buffet. Without any forewarning, one of your peers in the line loudly says, "Thank goodness Steve is at the end of the line. With his size and appetite there wouldn't be any food left for the rest of us." You believe Steve may have heard this comment, and you feel the comment was more of a "weight-related" slur than a joke.

A. How would you respond?

_____

_____

_____

B. What is the potential impact of your response?

_____

_____

_____

C. If you choose not to respond, what is the potential impact of your behaviour?

_____

_____

_____

1. What was the recommended response for each scenario?

2. Which scenario generated the most emotion and disagreement? Explain why this occurred.

3. What is the potential impact of a manager's lack of response to Scenarios 1 and 3? Explain.

Notes

[1]L Holland, "Positive Action for Race: Madness, Positive Discrimination or a Sound Business Approach," *EOR*, November–December 1994, p 48.

[2]P Smulders, M Kompier, P Paoli, "The Work Environment in the Twelve EU-Countries: Differences and Similarities," *Human Relations,* October 1996, pp 1291–1313.

[3]Based on "Race Case Highlights Cost of Harassment," *Personnel Management*, July 1994, p 6.

[4]Based on B Clement, "BR Depot Was Plagued by Race and Sex Harassment," *The Independent on Sunday,* February 6, 1994, p 7.

[5]Based on D Campbell, "Shunned Met Officer Takes Pill Overdose," *The Guardian*, January 7, 1995, p 5.

[6]Based on M Darch, "Go Back and Make Coffee, Woman Pilot Told; Sandra Valentine," *The Times*, January 13, 1995, p 7.

[7]R Chapman, "Discomforting Route to Diversity," *Management Today* , March 1995, p 5.

[8]Adapted from W Nijhof, H Abma, "Diversity in Nederlandse bedrijven," *Opleiding en Ontwikkeling*, June 1994, pp 17–22.

[9]This discussion is based on material in R R Thomas, Jr., *Redefining Diversity* (New York: AMACOM, 1996), pp 4–9.

[10]The difference between affirmative action and diversity is discussed in "Frequently Asked Question about Affirmative Action," *Personnel Journal,* August 1995, p 61.

[11]M Loden, *Implementing Diversity* (Chicago, IL: Irwin, 1996), pp 14–15.

[12]See the related discussion in F J Milliken and L L Martins, "Searching for Common Threads: Understanding the Multiple Effects of Diversity in Organizational Groups," *Academy of Management Review,* April 1996, pp 402–33; and Loden, *Implementing Diversity.*

[13]H Collingwood, "Who Handles a Diverse Work Force Best?" *Working Woman*, February 1996, p 25.

[14]D McKittrick, "Catholic Worker Driven out of Firm by Sectarian Hate: David McKittrick Reports on the Treatment Given to a Teenager by her Loyalist Colleagues," *Independent*, August 22, 1994, p 6.

[15]R Kandola, and J Fullerton, *Managing the Mosaic : Diversity in Action* (London: The Institute of Personnel and Development, 1995), p 8.

[16]Based on W Nijhof, and H Abma, op.cit.

[17]"Council Recommendation of 13 December 1984 on the Promotion of Positive Action for Women," *Official Journal of the European Communities*, No L 331, December 19, 1984, p 34.

[18]"All Women Are Working Women," (Geneva: International Labour Office, 1995), p 3.

[19]For a thorough discussion of affirmative action and its role in managing diversity, see J H Coil III, C M Rice, "Managing Work-Force Diversity in the Nineties: The Impact of the Civil Rights Act of 1991," *Employee Relations Law Journal*, Spring 1993, pp 547–65.

[20]See also R Kandola, and J Fullerton, op.cit.

[21]"Standard Bank Aims to Hit Targets within Next Two Years," *Personnel Management*, December 1994, p 41.

[22]R Thomas Jr, "From Affirmative Action to Affirming Diversity," *Harvard Business Review*, March-April 1990, pp 107–17; and Galagan, P. A. "Navigating the Differences," *Training & Development*, April 1993, pp 29–33.

[23]E Sullerot, *A Practical Manual on How to Create and Run Positive Action Training Programmes for Women Only and How to Create and Run Positive Action Programmes to Promote Women Inside Companies* (Brussels: Commission of the European Communities, Equal Opportunities Unit, 1991), p 1.

[24]Translated from P Gorissen, "Het vrouwvriendelijke beleid van ECT," *Management Team*, February 9, 1996, pp 69–73.

[25]For a thorough review of relevant research, see M E Heilman, "Affirmative Action: Some Unintended Consequences for Working Women," *Research in Organizational Behavior*, vol 16, eds B Staw, and L L Cummings, (Greenwich, CT: JAI Press, 1994), pp 125–69.

[26]Based on L Roberts, "Women: The Office Battlefield," *The Guardian*, November 14, 1994, p 11.

[27]S Overell, "ECJ takes negative view of positive disrimination," *People Management*, November 2, 1995, pp 13–14.

[28]Valuing diversity is discussed by R R Thomas, Jr., *Beyond Race and Gender* (New York: American Management Association, 1991).

[29]Different types of diversity training programs are discussed by P L Nemetz and S L Christensen, "The Challenge of Cultural Diversity: Harnessing a Diversity of Views to Understand Multiculturalism," *Academy of Management Review,* April 1996, pp 434–62; and G Henderson, "Traveling the Path to Diversity," *Security Management*, July 1995, pp 25–26.

[30]A M Morrison, *The New Leaders: Guidelines on Leadership Diversity in America* (San Francisco: Jossey-Bass, 1992), p 78.

[31]R Kandola, J Fullerton, *Managing the Mosaic : Diversity in Action* (London: The Institute of Personnel and Development, 1995), p 30.

[32]"Schools Brief: The War Between the Sexes," *The Economist*, March 5, 1994, pp 79–80.

[33]Eurostat, 1995

[34]Based on H Carnegy, "A Question of Attitude," *The Financial Times*, June 16, 1995, p 16.

[35]Based on J Palmer, "EU Promises to Tackle Sex Bias," *The Guardian*, November 4, 1994, p 13.

[36]Adapted from "The CRE's Survey of Large Companies," *People Management*, February 23, 1994, p 29.

[37]Translated from O Kikkert, "De oorzaken van leeftijdsdiscriminatie," *Personeelsbeleid*, 1994, No 2, pp 17–18.

[38]See A L Otten, "People Patterns: Aging Populations Strain Ex-Communist Nations," *The Wall Street Journal,* February 14, 1994, p B1.

[39]See P A Galagan, "Trading Places at Monsanto," *Training & Development*, April 1993, pp 45–49.

[40]Corning's diversity efforts are discussed in K Kazi-Ferrouillet, "Cracking Corning's Glass Ceiling," *The Black Collegian,* March/April 1992 pp 56–61; and C Hymowitz, "One Firm's Bid to Keep Blacks, Women," *The Wall Street Journal*, February 16, 1989, p B1.

[41]Based on W Nijhof, and H Abma, op.cit.

[42]Details of this study may be found in J H Greenhaus, S Parasuraman, and W M Wormley, "Effects of Race on Organizational Experiences, Job Performance Evaluations, and Career Outcomes," *Academy of Management Journal*, March 1990, pp 64–86.

[43]Based on A van Poppel, "Doelgroep: homo's," *Trends*, April 17, 1995, pp 92–93.

[44]"Council Decision of 18 April 1988 establishing a Second Community Action Programme for Disabled people (Helios)," *Official Journal of the European Communities*, No L 104, pp 38–44.

[45]Morris, A. "Britain's Shameful Wall Must Come Down," *Sunday Times*, January 23, 1994, pp 4–6.

[46]Based on "Company Vitae No 7: P & O," *The Guardian*, October 29, 1994, p 93.

[47]Based on "Company Vitae No 12: Cable & Wireless," *The Guardian*, December 10, 1994, p 35.

[48]Based on "Company Vitae No 8: Tarmac," *The Guardian*, November 5, 1994, p 93.

[49]Adapted and translated from C Broeijer, "Andere koers. McDonald's: geen allochtoon-gericht personeelsbeleid," *Samenwijs*, February 1994, p 273.

[50]J Courtis, "When it's competent not to discriminate," *People Management*, May 31, 1995, p 23.

[51]I Dodds, "Differences can also be strengths," *People Management*, April 20, 1995, pp 42–43.

[52]Translated from Besmo, M. "Mohammed wordt slecht begrepen. Allochtonenbeleid heeft wind mee," *Management Team*, September 29, 1993, pp 135–142.

[53]Based on and translated from G Muelenaer, 'VKW-Projekt: De Uitdaging', *Trends*, February 17, 1994, pp 41–43

[54]Based on R Vézina, and P Olivia, "Toward Understanding of the Role and Effects of Provocation in Advertising," *Marketing: Its Dynamics and its Challenges, Proceedins of the 23rd EMAC Conference*, eds. J. Bloemer, J. Lemmeck and H. Kaspar, Maastricht, NL: University of Lilburg and European Marketing Academy, pp.1117-1134.

[55]See L Buckingham, "Enlightened Attitudes," *The Guardian*, September 10, 1994, p 38.

[56]M Charlier, "Many Women Give Up Skiing; Resorts Shiver," *Wall Street Journal*, February 2, 1995, p B1.

[57]See M Neely Martinez, "Equality Effort Sharpens Bank Edge's," *HRMagazine*, January 1995, pp 38–43.

[58]This discussion is based on Thomas, *Redefining Diversity.*

[59]For complete details and results from this study, see Morrison, *The New Leaders: Guidelines on Leadership Diversity in America.*

[60]Based on A Phillips, "Worst-off among Equals?", *The Guardian*, January 25, 1994, p 15; and K Harper, "Boots to create thousands of jobs with 200 new stores", *The Guardian*, August 30, 1994, p 12; and "Company Vitae No 13: The Boots Company", *The Guardian*, December 17, 1994, p 73.

[61]Based on S Crabb, "Four Reasons to Be Family Friendly", *People Management*, April 6, 1995, pp 40–43.

[62]Based on D Campbell, "Policeman Pleads for Ponytail Equality with Women Officers," *The Guardian*, December 1, 1994, p 2.

[63]Details of this study can be found in L T Thomas and D C Ganster, "Impact of Family-Supportive Work Variables on Work-Family Conflict and Strain: A Control Perspective," *Journal of Applied Psychology,* February 1995, pp 6–15.

[64]Empirical support is provided by H Ibarra, "Race, Opportunity, and Diversity of Social Circles in Managerial Networks," *Academy of Management Journal,* June 1995, pp 673–703; and P J Ohlott, M N Ruderman, and C D McCauley, "Gender Differences in Managers' Developmental Job Experiences," *Academy of Management Journal,* February 1994, pp 46–67.

[65]The pros and cons of targeted recruiting is discussed by J S Lublin, "Firms Designate Some Openings for Women Only," *The Wall Street Journal,* February 7, 1994, pp B1, B4.

[66]Based on "Company Vitae No 16: Bass," *The Guardian*, January 14, 1995, p 63.

[67]Adapted from "Company Vitae No 9: Ford of Britain," *The Guardian*, November 12, 1994, p 84.

[68]Based on R Kandola, and J Fullerton, op. cit.

[69]These barriers were taken from discussions in Loden, *Implementing Diversity;* E E Spragins, "Benchmark: The Diverse Work Force," *Inc.,* January 1993, p 33; and Morrison, *The New Leaders: Guidelines on Leadership Diversity in America.*

[70]The role of promotion opportunities and diversity is discussed by M N Ruderman, P J Ohlott, and K E Kram, "Promotion Decisions as a Diversity Practice," *Journal of Management Development,* 1995, pp 6–23.

[71]See the related discussion in G R Ferris, D D Frink, D P S Bhawuk, and D C Gilmore, "Reactions of Diverse Groups to Politics in the Workplace," *Journal of Management,* 1996, pp 23–44.

[72]M S Montei, G A Adams, L M Eggers, "Validity of Scores on the Attitudes Toward Diversity Scale (ATDS)," *Educational and Psychological Measurement,* April, pp 293–303. Copyright ©W 1996 by Sage Publications. Reprinted by permission of Sage Publications, Inc.

[73]These scenarios were developed by A J Kinicki, *Valuing Diversity* (Chandler, AZ: Angelo Kinicki), pp 4–3, 4–7, 4–10.

Three

Organizational Culture Values, and Ethics

Bureaucrazy

The parable of BT's dress code deserves to be more widely told. After privatization, the company decided it was time to shake off the sloppy dress habits of the public sector. A directive went round telling senior employees that they should adopt suitable business dress.

The directive caused some resentment. Those who opposed it demanded greater clarity and certainty. When they went to the wardrobe in the morning, how could they know what would represent suitable business dress.

After advice from its legal and regulatory affairs department, the company agreed to promulgate a dress code. Senior male employees were expected to wear smart suits, shirts with collars, and ties. It was not long before someone came to the office in a red suit. When criticized, he pointed to the terms of the dress code. The suit was undeniably smart: but it was the smartness of a nightclub rather than a boardroom.

So the dress code had to specify colour. Red was out, grey was in. But what of blue? Some blues were clearly acceptable. The chairman's favourite suit, in fact, was a fetching shade of navy. But bright blues could not be admitted. So how bright was bright? BT research came up with the answer. Brightness is determined by how much light a fabric reflects. A machine could measure this, and one was soon constructed and installed in the reception areas.

But ties posed a more intractable problem. It was simply impossible to define which colours and motifs were acceptable. A clearance procedure seemed the best answer. Anyone who bought a new tie could submit it to the dress code department, which had 42 days to rule on whether or not it was suitable business dress.

This was difficult, since the appropriateness of a tie might depend on the context—the suit and the shirt that went with it. So decisions were rather conservative. This raised the issue of an appeal mechanism.

Delegating discretion over approval of ties to the dress code department made it judge and jury in implementing regulations it had devised. But this violated natural justice. The company agreed that a small group of senior directors, with an independent fashion adviser, would hear complaints from employees who felt their ties had been unreasonably rejected.

But there was the more general problem of changing fashion. After all, it was not so long since every gentleman had gone to work in a wing collar and frock coat. Not only were other forms of dress now acceptable, but wing collars had probably ceased to be acceptable. Not the image of a modern information company. A well-known fashion designer agreed to chair a standing working party to advise the company on fashion trends.

By this time, the dress code extended to 50 pages, largely impenetrable. No sensible employee read it, and when they were given a copy they were told that if they only behaved sensibly they would probably be all right. Knowledge of its contents was confined to the dress department, which by this time consisted of 20 people, mostly lawyers, the union representative who negotiated over it, and a few cranks who enjoyed pointing out inconsistencies and anomalies in the code.

Eventually a new management came in, determined to sweep the dress code department away. They quickly realized there were two alternatives. One was to supply a uniform to all employees. This was obviously an intolerable interference in personal affairs.

The other was to sweep away the dress code and renew the instruction to everyone to wear suitable business dress. If anyone was in genuine doubt as to what constituted suitable business dress—and not many people were—they were advised to have a word with the dress regulator. He had been given this role precisely because of his sound judgement and range of business experience. What the regulator said bound no one, but to ignore his advice was injudicious and might prejudice advancement in the company.[1]

Discussion Question

Do you know an example of an organization where similar processes are usual?

M uch has been written and said about organizational culture, values, and ethics in recent years. The results of this activity can be arranged on a continuum of academic rigour. At the low end of the continuum are simplistic typologies and exaggerated claims about the benefits of imitating Japanese-style *corporate cultures* and values. Here the term corporate culture is little more than a pop psychology buzzword. At the other end of the continuum is a growing body of theory and research with valuable insights but plagued by definitional and measurement inconsistencies.[2] By systematically sifting this diverse collection of material, we find that an understanding of organizational culture is central to learning how to manage people at work in both domestic and international operations.

This chapter will help you better understand how managers can use organizational culture as a competitive advantage. We discuss (1) the foundation of organizational culture, (2) the development of a high-performance culture, (3) the organization socialization process, (4) the role of mentoring in socialization, and (5) the importance of organizational values and ethics.

Foundation of Organizational Culture

Organizational culture
Shared values and beliefs that underlie a company's identity.

Organizational culture is "the set of shared, taken-for-granted implicit assumptions that a group holds and that determines how it perceives, thinks about, and reacts to its various environments".[3] This definition highlights two important characteristics of organizational culture. First, organizational culture influences our behaviour at work. The second key characteristic of organizational culture is that it operates on two levels, which vary in terms of outward visibility and resistance to change.

At the less visible level, culture reflects the values shared among organizational members. At Healthco, a UK-based international pharmaceuticals company, the difference between the two levels became very clear when corporate culture change was implemented. The first part of the change process, focused on behaviour (teamwork, innovation, . . .), is extremely well embedded within the organization. The second stage, the issue of a "values statement" became far less integrated in the company's culture.[4]

At the more visible level, culture represents the normative behaviour patterns accepted by organizational members. These patterns are passed on to others through the socialization process. Culture is more susceptible to change at this level.

Each level of culture influences the other. For example, if a company truly values providing high-quality service, employees are more likely to adopt the behaviour of responding faster to customer complaints. When British Airways began moving towards privatization, a top priority was changing a culture of indifference to a culture of service. Without a culture of service it would not be able to compete in a global marketplace.[5] Similarly, causality can flow in the other direction. Employees can come to value high-quality service based on their experiences as they interact with customers. To improve their customer-oriented philosophy, Center Parcs, the Dutch leisure group specializing in holiday villages has introduced a job rotation system. Four times a year people change jobs for one day. This way, people get acquainted with their colleagues' jobs and meanwhile they learn the clients' needs and wishes at every spot in the parc.[6]

In Europe, business interest in corporate culture dates from the late 1980s, early 1990s. Deregulation and increased competition obliged European companies to reconsider their way of doing business. Companies such as British Airways, SAS, ICI, and Daimler-Benz went through significant culture changes over this period.[7]

To gain a better understanding of how organizational culture is formed and used by employees, this section reviews the manifestations of organizational culture, a model for interpreting organizational culture, the four functions of organizational culture, and the research on organizational cultures.

Manifestations of Organizational Culture

When is an organization's culture most apparent? According to one observer, cultural assumptions assert themselves through socialization of new employees, subculture clashes, and top management behaviour. Consider these three situations, for example: A newcomer who shows up late for an important meeting is told a story about someone who was fired for repeated tardiness. Conflict between product design engineers who emphasize a product's function and marketing specialists who demand a more stylish product reveals an underlying clash of subculture values. Top managers, through the behaviour they model and the administrative and reward systems they create, prompt a significant improvement in the quality of a company's products.

A Model for Interpreting Organizational Culture

A useful model for observing and interpreting organizational culture was developed by a Harvard researcher (see Figure 3–1). Four general manifestations or evidence of organizational culture in his model are shared things (objects), shared sayings (talk), shared doings (behaviour), and shared feelings (emotion). One can begin collecting

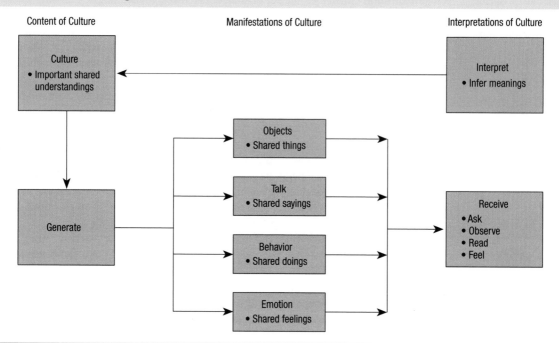

Figure 3 – 1   A Model for Observing and Interpreting General Manifestations of Organizational Culture

cultural information within the organization by asking, observing, reading, and feeling.

The OB exercise provides you with the opportunity to practise identifying the manifestations of organizational culture at the Ritz-Carlton and McDonald's. These examples highlight different manifestations of organizational culture.

Four Functions of Organizational Culture

As illustrated in Figure 3–2, an organization's culture fulfils four functions.[8] To help bring these four functions to life, let us consider how each of them has taken shape at 3M. 3M is a particularly instructive example because it has a long history of being an innovative company—the company was founded in 1902—and it was ranked as the 11th most admired company in the US by *Fortune* in 1996, partly due to its strong and distinctive culture.[9]

1.   *Give members an organizational identity.* 3M is known as being an innovative company that relentlessly pursues new-product development. Chief executive L D "Desi" DeSimone, for example, decreed that 30 per cent of sales must come from products introduced within the past four years. The old standard was 25 per cent in five years. This identity is reinforced by creating rewards that reinforce innovation. For example, "The 3M Corporation has its version of a Nobel Prize for innovative employees. The prize is the Golden Step award, whose trophy is a winged foot. Several Golden Steps are given out each year to employees whose new products have reached significant revenue and profit levels."[10]

2.   *Facilitate collective commitment.* One of 3M's corporate values is to be "a company that employees are proud to be a part of". People who like 3M's culture tend to stay employed there for long periods of time. This collective commitment results in a turnover rate of less than 3 per cent among salaried personnel. Consider the commitment and pride

Figure 3 – 2   Four Functions of Organizational Culture

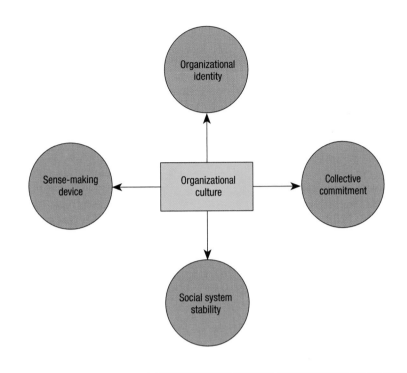

Source: Adapted from discussion in L Smircich, "Concepts of Culture and Organizational Analysis," *Administrative Science Quarterly*, September 1983, pp 339—58.

expressed by Kathleen Stanislawski, a staffing manager. "I'm a 27-year 3Mer because, quite frankly, there's no reason to leave. I've had great opportunities to do different jobs and to grow a career. It's just a great company."[11]

3. *Promote social system stability*. Social system stability reflects the extent to which the work environment is perceived as positive and reinforcing, and conflict and change are managed effectively. This stability is reinforced within 3M through a promote-from-within culture, a strategic hiring policy that ensures that capable college graduates are hired in a timely manner, and a layoff policy that provides displaced workers six months to find another job at 3M before being terminated. Executives also attempt to reduce resistance to change by continually communicating the company's quest for new-product development and continuous improvement of internal processes.

4. *Shape behaviour by helping members make sense of their surroundings*. This function of culture helps employees understand why the organization does what it does and how it intends to accomplish its long-term goals. 3M sets expectations for innovation in a variety of ways. For example, the company employs an internship and coop programme. In 1994, for instance, 30 per cent of 3M's college hires came through an internship or coop programme. 3M also shapes expectations and behaviour by providing detailed career feedback to its employees. New staff are measured and evaluated against a career growth standard during their first six months to three years of employment.

Types of Organizational Culture

Researchers have attempted to identify and measure various types of organizational culture in order to study the relationship between types of culture and organizational effectiveness. This pursuit was motivated by the possibility that certain cultures were more effective than others. Unfortunately, research has not uncovered a universal typology of cultural styles that everyone accepts.[12] Just the same, there is value in providing an example of various types of organizational culture.

Table 3–1 is thus presented as an illustration rather than a definitive conclusion about the types of organizational culture that exist. Awareness of these types provides you with greater understanding about the manifestations of culture.

Table 3–1 shows that there are 12 distinct cultural types or styles. Each type is grounded in a set of **normative beliefs.** Normative beliefs represent an individual's thoughts and beliefs about how members of a particular group or organization are expected to approach their work and interact with others. For example, Table 3–1 reveals that an approval culture is anchored in the belief that conflicts should be avoided and people should agree with, gain the approval of, and be liked by others. In contrast, an oppositional culture encourages and rewards the resolution of conflict.[13] Although an organization may predominately represent one cultural type, it can still manifest characteristics from the others. Research demonstrates that organizations can have functional subcultures, hierarchical subcultures based on one's level in the organization, and social subcultures derived from social activities like a tennis or reading club.[14] Use

Normative beliefs

Thoughts and beliefs about expected behaviour and modes of conduct

OB EXERCISE   *Manifestations of Organizational Culture at the Ritz-Carlton and McDonald's*

Instructions
Read the following descriptions and answer the discussion questions. Answers can be found following the Notes at the end of this chapter.

Ritz-Carlton
The Ritz-Carlton has created a climate and culture that allows them to succeed as an ever-expanding, upscale hotel chain in a very competitive market. At Ritz-Carlton, each hotel employee is part of a team whose members are empowered to do whatever it takes to satisfy a customer. These employees are guided by a credo, called the "Gold Standards", that specifies desired behaviours. More importantly, there are policies, practices, procedures, and routines designed to support and reward employees engaging in these desired behaviours. Ritz-Carlton makes every employee feel like a valued person. The employee motto is "We are ladies and gentlemen serving ladies and gentlemen". Guests and employees alike are treated the right way; there are no mixed messages in Ritz-Carlton's climate and culture.

McDonald's
McDonald's vision is to provide customers with quality, service, convenience, and value (QSCV). Ray Kroc, the founder, wanted a restaurant system known for its consistently high quality and

uniform methods of preparation. He created Hamburger University, which offers a degree in Hamburgerology, to help create this culture. Franchisees, managers, and assistant managers are indoctrinated into McDonald's culture and associated policies and procedures at the University. McDonald's policies and procedures meticulously spell out desired employee behaviours and job responsibilities. For example, they specify how often the bathroom should be cleaned and what colour of nail polish to wear. McDonald's culture is reinforced by using contests and ceremonies to reward those franchisees who best meet their goals. McDonald's recently implemented a set of business practices known as Franchising 2000. Two key components are as follows: franchisees must submit annual financial goals for approval, and a single pricing strategy is established for all products. Franchisees who fail to adhere to the policies and procedures risk losing their franchises when they expire. McDonald's likes to hire executives who have strong traditional values such as loyalty, dedication, and service.

Discussion Questions
1. Identify the shared things, sayings, doings, and feelings at both the Ritz-Carlton and McDonald's.
2. Which organization is based more on control and/or competition?

SOURCE The Ritz-Carlton description was excerpted from B Schneider, A P Brief, and R A Guzzo, "Creating a Climate and Culture for Sustainable Organizational Change", *Organizational Dynamics*, Spring 1996, p 16. Material about McDonald's was obtained from R Gibson, "A Bit of Heartburn: Some Franchisees Say Moves by McDonald's Hurt Their Operations," *The Wall Street Journal*, April 17, 1996, pp A1, A8; and M A Salva-Ramirez, "McDonald's: A Prime Example of Corporate Culture," *Public Relations Quarterly*, Winter 1995/96, pp 30–31.

Table 3 – 1   Types of Organizational Culture

CULTURE	DEFINITION
Achievement	Organizations that do things well and value members who set and accomplish their own goals. Members are expected to set challenging but realistic goals, establish plans to reach these goals, and pursue them with enthusiasm. (Pursuing a standard of excellence)
Self-actualizing	Organizations that value creativity, quality over quantity, and both task accomplishment and individual growth. Members are encouraged to gain enjoyment from their work, develop themselves, and take on new and interesting activities. (Thinking in unique and independent ways)
Humanistic-encouraging	Organizations that are managed in a participative and person-centred way. Members are expected to be supportive, constructive, and open to influence in their dealings with one another. (Helping others to grow and develop)
Affiliative	Organizations that place a high priority on constructive interpersonal relationships. Members are expected to be friendly, open, and sensitive to the satisfaction of their work group. (Dealing with others in a friendly way)
Approval	Organizations in which conflicts are avoided and interpersonal relationships are pleasant—at least superficially. Members feel that they should agree with, gain the approval of, and be liked by others. ("Going along" with others)
Conventional	Organizations that are conservative, traditional, and bureaucratically controlled. Members are expected to conform, follow the rules, and make a good impression. (Always following policies and practices)
Dependent	Organizations that are hierarchically controlled and nonparticipative. Centralized decision making in such organizations leads members to do only what they are told and to clear all decisions with superiors. (Pleasing those in positions of authority)
Avoidance	Organizations that fail to reward success but nevertheless punish mistakes. This negative reward system leads members to shift responsibilities to others and avoid any possibility of being blamed for a mistake. (Waiting for others to act first)
Oppositional	Organizations in which confrontation and negativism are rewarded. Members gain status and influence by being critical and thus are reinforced to oppose the ideas of others. (Pointing out flaws)
Power	Nonparticipative organizations structured on the basis of the authority inherent in members' positions. Members believe they will be rewarded for taking charge, controlling subordinates and, at the same time, being responsive to the demands of superiors. (Building up one's power base)
Competitive	Winning is valued, and members are rewarded for outperforming one another. Members operate in a "win–lose" framework and believe they must work against (rather than with) their peers to be noticed. (Turning the job into a contest)
Perfectionistic	Organizations in which perfectionism, persistence, and hard work are valued. Members feel they must avoid any mistake, keep track of everything, and work long hours to attain narrowly defined objectives. (Doing things perfectly)

Source: Reproduced with permission of authors and publisher from: R A Cooke and J L Szumal, "Measuring Normative Beliefs and Shared Behavioral Expectations in Organizations: The Reliability and Validity of the Organizational Culture Inventory," *Psychological Reports*, 1993, 72, 1299–1330. © *Psychological Reports*, 1993.

Table 3–1 now to characterize both the overall organizational culture of your most recent employer and the style of the specific department in which you work. Do not be surprised if they are different.

Research on Organizational Cultures

Because the concept of organizational culture is a relatively recent addition to OB, the research base is incomplete. Studies to date are characterized by inconsistent definitions and varied methodologies. Quantitative treatments are sparse because there is little agreement on how to measure cultural variables. As a matter of convenience, we review two streams of organizational culture research in this section. One stream has been reported in bestselling books and the other in research journal articles.[15]

Anecdotal Evidence from Bestselling Books about Organizational Culture Initial widespread interest in organizational cultures was stirred by William Ouchi's 1981 bestseller, *Theory Z: How American Business Can Meet the Japanese Challenge*. From a research standpoint, Ouchi's two main contributions were (1) focusing attention on internal culture as a key determinant of organizational effectiveness and (2) developing an instructive typology of organizations based in part on cultural variables.[16]

Close on the heels of Ouchi's book came two 1982 bestsellers: Deal and Kennedy's *Corporate Cultures: The Rites and Rituals of Corporate Life*[17] and Peters and Waterman's *In Search of Excellence*.[18] Both books drew upon interviews and the authors' consulting experience. Each team of authors relied on abundant anecdotal evidence to make the point that successful companies tend to have strong cultures. For example, Peters and Waterman observed:

Without exception, the dominance and coherence of culture proved to be an essential quality of the excellent companies. Moreover, the stronger the culture and the more it was directed toward the marketplace, the less need was there for policy manuals, organization charts, or detailed procedures and rules. In these companies, people way down the line know what they are supposed to do in most situations because the handful of guiding values is crystal clear.[19]

These bestsellers generated excitement about cultural factors such as heroes and stories. They also generated the impression that organizations have one distinct culture. As previously discussed, few people accept this generic conclusion. Finally, these bestsellers failed to break any new ground in the measurement and evaluation of organizational cultures.

Evidence from Research Articles and Management Implications As previously mentioned, little empirical research exists. This is partly due to problems associated with measuring organizational culture. It is a very complex phenomenon to evaluate. Although there is not a uniformly agreed-upon method to assess culture, there are several cultural surveys and interviewing protocols that have been recommended.[20] So, what have we learned to date?

First, John Kotter and James Heskett tried to determine if organizational culture was related to a firm's long-term financial performance. They studied 207 companies from 22 industries for the period 1977 to 1988. After correlating results from a cultural survey and three different measures of economic performance, results uncovered a significant relationship between culture and financial performance.[21] A similar finding was obtained on a longitudinal sample of 11 US insurance companies from the period of 1981 to 1987. More recently, a team of researchers sent a survey measuring culture and subjective and objective indexes of profitability, quality, sales growth, satisfaction, and overall performance to 764 companies. Culture was significantly related to all of these organizational outcomes.[22] Second, studies of mergers indicated that they frequently failed due to incompatible cultures.[23] Third, several studies demonstrated that organizational culture was significantly correlated with employee behaviour and attitudes. For example, culture was associated with (1) the performance and voluntary turnover for a sample of 904 accountants; (2) the organization commitment of 80 Australian manufacturing employees; and (3) the innovativeness, work avoidance, and voluntary turnover of a sample of 4,890 employees working in a variety of organizations.[24] Finally, results from several studies revealed that the congruence between an individual's values and the organization's values was significantly correlated with organizational commitment, job satisfaction, intention to quit, and turnover.[25]

These research results underscore the significance of organizational culture. They also reinforce the need to learn more about the process of cultivating and changing an organization's culture. An organization's culture is not determined by fate. It is formed and shaped by the combination and integration of everyone who works in the organization. As a case in point, a recent longitudinal study of 322 employees working in a governmental organization revealed that managerial intervention successfully shifted the organizational culture towards greater participation and employee involvement. This change in organizational culture was associated with improved job satisfaction and communication across all hierarchical levels.[26] This study further highlights the interplay between organizational culture and organizational change. Successful organizational change is highly dependent on an organization's culture.[27] A change-resistant culture, for instance, can undermine the effectiveness of any type of organizational change. Although it is not an easy task to change an organization's culture, the next section provides a preliminary overview of how this might be done.

Developing High-Performance Cultures

An organization's culture may be strong or weak, depending on variables such as cohesiveness, value consensus, and individual commitment to collective goals. Contrary to what one might suspect, a strong culture is not necessarily a good thing. The nature of the culture's central values is more important than its strength. For example, a strong but change-resistant culture may be worse, from the standpoint of profitability and competitiveness, than a weak but innovative culture. IBM is a prime example: its strong culture, coupled with a dogged determination to continually pursue a strategic plan that was out of step with the market, led to its failure to maintain its leadership in the personal computer market. This strategy ultimately cost the company about 97 billion dollars.[28] This section discusses the type of organizational cultures that enhance an organization's financial performance and the process by which cultures are embedded in an organization and learned by employees.

What Type of Cultures Enhance an Organization's Financial Performance?

Three perspectives have been proposed to explain the type of cultures that enhance an organization's economic performance. They are referred to as the strength, fit, and adaptive perspectives, respectively:

Strength perspective
Assumes that the strength of corporate culture is related to the firm's financial performance.

1. The **strength perspective** predicts a significant relationship between strength of corporate culture and long-term financial performance. The idea is that strong cultures create goal alignment, employee motivation, and needed structure and controls to improve organizational performance.[29]

Fit perspective
Assumes that culture must align with it's business or strategic context.

2. The **fit perspective** is based on the premise that an organization's culture must align with its business or strategic context. Accordingly, there is no one best culture. A culture is predicted to facilitate economic performance only if it "fits" its context.[30]

Adaptive perspective
Assumes that adaptive cultures enhance a firm's financial performance.

3. The **adaptive perspective** assumes that good cultures help organizations anticipate and adapt to environmental changes. This proactive adaptability is expected to enhance long-term financial performance.[31]

A Test of the Three Perspectives   The study by John Kotter and James Heskett partially supported the strength and fit perspectives, findings were completely consistent with the adaptive culture perspective. Long-term financial performance was highest for organizations with an adaptive culture.[32]

Vision
Long-term goal describing "what" an organization wants to become.

Developing an Adaptive Culture   Figure 3–3 illustrates the process of developing and preserving an adaptive culture. The process begins with leadership, that is, leaders must create and implement a business vision and associated strategies that fit the organizational context. A **vision** represents a long-term goal that describes "what" an organization wants to become. Kevin Jenkins, CEO of Canadian Airlines International Ltd, correctly notes, however, that the existence of a corporate vision does not guarantee organizational success:

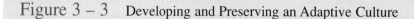

Figure 3 – 3   Developing and Preserving an Adaptive Culture

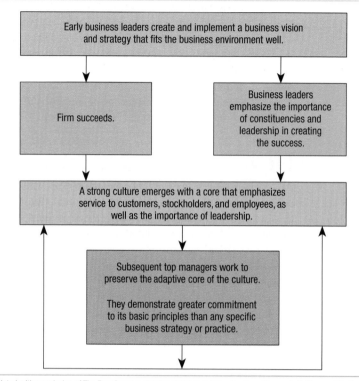

Source: Reprinted with permission of The Free Press, a division of Simon & Schuster, from *Corporate Culture and Performance* by J C Kotter and J L Heskett. Copyright © 1992 by Kotter Associates, Inc and James L Heskett.

"A vision held only by its leadership is not enough to create any real change", indicated Jenkins. "To ensure success, management must continuously—and creatively—articulate the company's vision and goals. This is achieved through open communication systems that encourage employee feedback and facilitate a two-way flow of information. Because the company's ultimate goal must be to satisfy the customer, it is imperative that employees understand what is expected of them as well as their responsibility for achieving results."[33]

As noted by Kevin Jenkins, adaptiveness is promoted over time by a combination of organizational success and a specific leadership focus. Leaders must get employees to buy into a timeless philosophy or set of values that emphasizes service to the organization's key constituents—customers, stockholders, and employees—and also emphasizes the improvement of leadership. An infrastructure must then be created to preserve the organization's adaptiveness. Management does this by consistently reinforcing and supporting the organization's core philosophy or values of satisfying constituency needs and improving leadership. This is precisely what Herb Kelleher, CEO of Southwest Airlines, has done at Southwest Airlines.

Southwest Airlines has grown from a startup company 25 years ago to one of the most consistently profitable airlines by creating a "strong" or widely shared belief in a constituency-oriented culture:

Long before "empowerment" became a management buzzword, Ms Barrett [the No. 2 executive at Southwest] was giving employees freedom from centralized policies. She constantly reinforces the company's message that employees should be treated like customers and continually celebrates workers who go above and beyond the call of duty. And when she sensed the carrier was outgrowing its personality-kid-among-the-impersonal-giants image, she created a "culture committee" of employees charged with preserving Southwest's spirit. . . .

Southwest employees are well-paid compared with counterparts at other airlines. Celebrations are an important part of work, from spontaneous "fun sessions" to Christmas parties beginning in September to a lavish annual awards banquet, where the individual's contribution to the whole is glorified.

At the same time, employees work like crazy between festivities. With that formula, the airline has avoided bureaucracy and mediocrity that infect other companies when they outgrow their entrepreneurial roots.[34]

How Cultures Are Embedded in Organizations

An organization's initial culture is an outgrowth of the founder's philosophy. For example, an achievement culture is likely to develop if the founder is an achievement-oriented individual driven by success. Over time, the original culture is either embedded as is or modified to fit the current environmental situation. Johnson & Johnson, for example, has formally documented its cherished corporate values and ideals, as conceived over four decades ago by the founder's son. The resulting Credo has helped J&J become a role model for corporate ethics.[35] Edgar Schein, a well-known OB scholar, notes that embedding a culture involves a teaching process. That is, organizational members teach each other about the organization's preferred values, beliefs, expectations, and behaviours. This is accomplished by using one or more of the following mechanisms:[36]

1. *Formal statements of organizational philosophy, mission, vision, values, and materials used for recruiting, selection, and socialization.* Philips, for example, published a list of five corporate values, listed together with some practical ideas on how to put them into everyday practice. The five values are: Delight consumers; Value people as our greatest resource; Deliver quality and excellence in all actions; Achieve premium return on Equity and encourage entrepreneurial behaviour at all levels.[37]

2. *The design of physical space, work environments, and buildings.*

3. *Slogans, language, acronyms, and sayings.* For example, the American bank, Bank One, promotes its desire to provide excellent client service through the slogan "whatever it takes." Employees are encouraged to do whatever it takes to exceed customer expectations.

4. *Deliberate role modelling, training programmes, teaching, and coaching by managers and supervisors.*

5. *Explicit rewards, status symbols (e.g., titles), and promotion criteria.* Consider the following reward system: over a period of 31 years, Heiko Hüberle, a bodywork painter at Opel in Wanne-Eickel, was granted DM 50,000 as a result of 150 recommendations for innovations he introduced.[38]

6. *Stories, legends, and myths about key people and events.*

7. *The organizational activities, processes, or outcomes that leaders pay attention to, measure, and control.*

8. *Leader reactions to critical incidents and organizational crises.*

9. *The workflow and organizational structure.* Hierarchical structures are more likely to embed an orientation towards control and authority than a flatter organization.

10. *Organizational systems and procedures.* An organization can promote achievement and competition through the use of sales contests.

11. *Organizational goals and the associated criteria used for recruitment, selection, development, promotion, layoffs, and retirement of people.*

The Organizational Socialization Process

Organizational socialization

Process by which employees learn an organization's values, norms, and required behaviours.

Organizational socialization is defined as "the process by which a person learns the values, norms, and required behaviours which permit him to participate as a member of the organization."[39] As previously discussed, organization socialization is a key mechanism used by organizations to embed their organizational cultures. In short, organizational socialization turns outsiders into fully functioning insiders by promoting and reinforcing the organization's core values and beliefs. At IKEA, for example, seminars are organized to explain the company's roots and values and where the name IKEA comes from. To enhance involvement, trips are organized to the founder's birthplace in Sweden, where everything was started.[40]

This section introduces a three-phase model of organizational socialization and examines the practical application of socialization research.

A Three-Phase Model of Organizational Socialization

One's first year in a complex organization can be confusing. There is a constant swirl of new faces, strange jargon, conflicting expectations, and apparently unrelated events. Some organizations treat new members in a rather haphazard, sink-or-swim manner. More typically, though, the socialization process is characterized by a sequence of identifiable steps.[41]

Organizational behaviour researcher Daniel Feldman has proposed a three-phase model of organizational socialization that promotes deeper understanding of this important process. As illustrated in Figure 3–4, the three phases are (1) anticipatory socialization, (2) encounter, and (3) change and acquisition. Each phase has its associated perceptual and social processes. Feldman's model also specifies behavioural and affective outcomes that can be used to judge how well an individual has been socialized. The entire three-phase sequence may take from a few weeks to a year to complete, depending on individual differences and the complexity of the situation.

Phase 1: Anticipatory Socialization   Organizational socialization begins before the individual actually joins the organization. Anticipatory socialization information comes from many sources. Widely circulated stories about IBM being the "white shirt" company probably deter those who would prefer working in jeans from applying.

All of this information—whether formal or informal, accurate or inaccurate—helps the individual anticipate organizational realities. Unrealistic expectations about the nature of the work, pay, and promotions are often formulated during phase I. Because employees with unrealistic expectations are more likely to quit their jobs in the future, management should use realistic job previews.[42] A **realistic job preview** (RJP) involves giving recruits a realistic idea of what lies ahead by presenting both positive and negative aspects of the job. RJPs may be verbal, in booklet form, audiovisual, or hands-on.

Realistic job preview

Presents both positive and negative aspects of a job.

Phase 2: Encounter   This second phase begins when the employment contract has been signed. It is a time for surprise and making sense as the newcomer enters unfamiliar territory. Behavioural scientists warn that **reality shock** can occur during the encounter phase:

Reality shock

A newcomer's feeling of surprise after experiencing unexpected situations or events.

Becoming a member of an organization will upset the everyday order of even the most well-informed newcomer. Matters concerning such aspects as friendships, time, purpose, demeanor, competence, and the expectations the person holds of the immediate and distant future are suddenly made problematic. The newcomer's most pressing task is to build a set of guidelines and interpretations to explain and make meaningful the myriad of activities observed as going on in the organization.[43]

Figure 3 – 4   A Model of Organizational Socialization

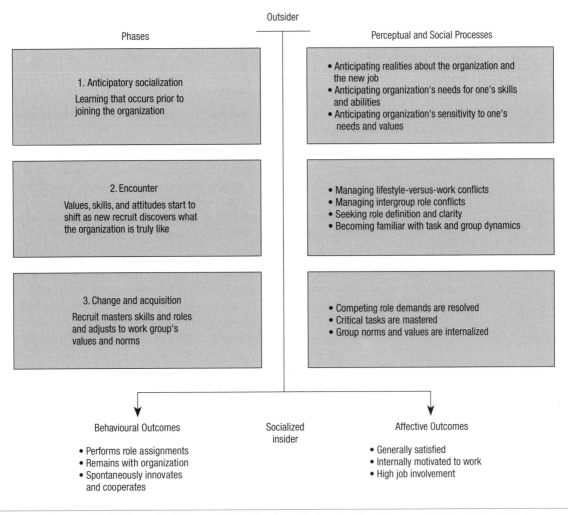

Consider the reality shock Mr Akiro Kusumoto experiences in his new job:

Around a conference table in a large US office tower, three American executives sat with their new boss, Mr. Akiro Kusumoto, the newly appointed head of a Japanese firm's American subsidiary, and two of his Japanese lieutenants. The meeting was called to discuss ideas for reducing operating costs. Mr. Kusumoto began by outlining his company's aspiration for its long-term US presence. He then turned to the current budgetary matter. One Japanese manager politely offered one suggestion, and an American then proposed another. After gingerly discussing the alternatives for quite some time, the then exasperated American blurted out: "Look, that idea is just not going to have much impact. Look at the numbers! We should cut this program, and I think we should do it as soon as possible!" In the face of such bluntness, uncommon and unacceptable in Japan, Mr. Kusumoto fell silent. He leaned back, drew air between his teeth, and felt a deep longing to "return East." He realized his life in this country would be filled with many such jarring encounters and lamented his posting to a land of such rudeness.[44]

Phase 3: Change and Acquisition   Mastery of important tasks and resolution of role conflict signals the beginning of this final phase of the socialization process. Those who do not make the transition to phase 3 leave voluntarily or involuntarily or become network isolates. Senior executives frequently play a direct role in the change and acquisition phase. The International OB discusses how Milton Kim, vice president at Ssangyong Securities & Investment Co. in Seoul, Korea, is trying to change the organizational culture within his organization.

Practical Application of Socialization Research

Past research suggests the following five practical guidelines for the management of organizational socialization.

1. Managers should avoid a haphazard, sink-or-swim approach to organizational socialization because formalized socialization tactics positively influence new staff. Formalized socialization reduced role ambiguity, role conflict, stress symptoms, and intentions to quit while simultaneously increasing job satisfaction and organizational commitment for a sample of 295 recent college graduates. Organizational socialization also positively affected the performance of 150 beginning school administrators.[45]

2. The encounter phase of socialization is particularly important. Studies of newly hired accountants demonstrated that the frequency and type of information obtained during their first six months of employment significantly affected their job performance, their role clarity, their understanding of the organizational culture, and the extent to which they were socially integrated.[46] Managers play a key role during the encounter phase. A recent study of 252 new college graduates further revealed that the quality of the relationship between the new person and his or her manager reduced the negative effects of reality shock and unmet expectations.[47] In summary, managers need to help new people to integrate within the organizational culture.

3. Support for stage models is mixed. Although there are different stages of socialization, they are not identical in order, length, or content for all people or jobs.[48] Managers are advised to use a contingency approach towards organizational socialization. In other words, different techniques are appropriate for different people at different times. Moreover, according to E W Morrison, stage models such as the one discussed above provide no insight in the role of the newcomer in the organization. They do give a clear view on the changes that occur during the socialization. Newcomers are proactive in adjusting to their new environment, they actively take part in the process. A study carried out by E W Morrison involving 240 newly recruited staff accountants in five large American accounting firms has demonstrated the important role of information during socialization. Information-seeking is the first way in which a newcomer will reduce uncertainty about the new environment.[49]

4. The organization can benefit by training new employees to use proactive socialization behaviours. A recent study of 154 entry-level professionals showed that using proactive socialization behaviours effectively influenced the newcomers' general anxiety and stress during the first month of employment and their motivation and anxiety six months later.[50]

5. Managers should pay attention to the socialization of diverse employees. Research demonstrated that diverse employees, particularly those with disabilities, experienced different socialization activities than other newcomers. In turn, these different experiences affected their long-term success and job satisfaction.[51] Polly Platt, author of the book *French or Foe*, has interviewed several expatriates working in France. They feel unwelcomed in their new working environments:

"I arrive the first day and find Monique", says a newly arrived public relations strategist. "She's my new boss. So Monique shows me my desk. Period. No one tells me when lunch is. No one tells me where the bathroom is."

"The first week I'm meeting about 1,000 new people", says an electronics engineer. "I don't speak French and there's no organization chart. How am I supposed to know who all these people are?"[52]

Socialization through Mentoring

Mentoring
Process of forming and maintaining developmental relationships between a mentor and a junior person.

According to Jean-Claude Guez, partner of Andersen Consulting, the French simply assume that people will sense the context and work it out . . . that they're adults, able to manage alone their own destiny.

Mentoring is defined as the process of forming and maintaining an intensive and lasting developmental relationship between a senior person (the mentor) and a junior person (the protégé, if male; or protégée, if female). The modern word *mentor* derives from Mentor, the name of a wise and trusted counsellor in Greek mythology. Terms typically used in connection with mentoring are *teacher, coach, godfather*, and *sponsor*.

Mentoring is an important part of developing a high-performance culture for three reasons. First, mentoring contributes to creating a sense of oneness by promoting the acceptance of the organization's core values throughout the organization. Second, the socialization aspect of mentoring also promotes a sense of membership. Finally, mentoring increases interpersonal exchanges among organizational members.

Functions of Mentoring

Kathy Kram, a Boston University researcher, conducted in-depth interviews with both members of 18 pairs of senior and junior managers. As a by-product of this study, Kram identified two general functions—career and psychosocial—of the mentoring process (see Figure 3–5). Five *career functions* that enhanced career development were sponsorship, exposure-and-visibility, coaching, protection, and challenging assignments. Four *psychosocial functions* were role modelling, acceptance-and-confirmation, counselling, and friendship. The psychosocial functions clarified the participants' identities and enhanced their feelings of competence.[53]

International Organizational Behaviour

Milton Kim Changes Organizational Culture at Ssangyong Securities & Investment Co. in Seoul, Korea

Mr. Chang is one of 260 stockbrokers at Ssangyong Securities & Investment Co. in Seoul who were recently given a $40 pair of suspenders—that sartorial icon of corporate America—and encouraged to wear them to work. . . .

The fashion revolution is the brainchild of Milton Kim, the 34-year-old vice president of Ssangyong who has already shaken up South Korea's brokerage community by introducing such Western management concepts as merit pay and commission-based salaries.

"There's a de facto dress code in South Korea, and it's pretty drab," says Mr. Kim. "I thought [my brokers] needed some color."

Indeed, the 28-year-old Mr. Chang says he used to associate financial service jobs with white shirts and somber navy-blue suits. But inspired by Mr. Kim, Mr. Chang recently bought his own pair of suspenders and now sports them on occasion with colored shirts. . . .

The ultimate test of the new dress code, of course, will be the reaction of customers. At first, customers were "a little shocked" by his floral suspenders, says Mr. Chang. But he says that most have now adjusted to his new look. "One customer even told me I looked very handsome," he says.

But Mr. Chang draws the line at hair mousse. "I don't use mousse because it sticks to my fingers," he says.

SOURCE | Excerpted from N Cho, "First Merit Pay, Now Suspenders Rock Korean Securities Industry," *The Wall Street Journal*, May 9, 1995, p B1. Reprinted by permission of the *The Wall Street Journal* © 1995 Dow Jones & Company, Inc. All Rights Reserved Worldwide

Darryl Hartley-Leonard's experience at Hyatt Hotels exemplifies how important the career and psychosocial functions of mentoring can be to your career. Darryl started as a desk clerk at Hyatt in 1964 and rose to the position of CEO. In an interview with The *Wall Street Journal*, Hartley-Leonard indicated that his relationship with Pat Foley, the general manager who originally hired him, changed his life:

The shy Englishman [Darryl] copied his gregarious boss's style and mannerisms. He learned how to treat employees from Mr. Foley, who washed dishes with the kitchen help and co-signed an $800 note for Mr. Hartley-Leonard's first car. "People would walk through walls for him," he says.

As Mr. Foley's career prospered, so did Mr. Hartley-Leonard's. When Mr. Foley became the resident manager at Hyatt's first big hotel in Atlanta, he hired Mr. Hartley-Leonard as a front-office supervisor. Mr. Foley eventually became president and installed his protégé as executive vice president.

Not surprisingly, Mr. Hartley-Leonard considers mentoring a critical element in his ascent. "If you get five people of equal ability, the one who gets mentoring will have the edge," he says.[54]

This example also highlights the fact that both members of the mentoring relationship can benefit from these career and psychosocial functions. Mentoring is not strictly a top-down proposition, as many mistakenly believe.

Phases of Mentoring

In addition to identifying the functions of mentoring, Kram's research revealed four phases of the mentoring process: (1) initiation, (2) cultivation, (3) separation, and (4) redefinition. As indicated in Table 3–2, the phases involve *variable* rather than fixed time periods. Telltale turning points signal the evolution from one phase to the next. For example, when a junior manager begins to resist guidance and strives to work more autonomously, the separation phase begins. The mentoring relationships in Kram's sample lasted an average of five years. Consider the way in which Scotland's W. L. Gore enhances the socialization process. Each associate, as employees are called, chooses or is allotted a "sponsor", who advises and supports him or her within the company making sure that his or her contribution is recognized and rewarded.

Figure 3 – 5   The Career and Psychosocial Functions of Mentoring

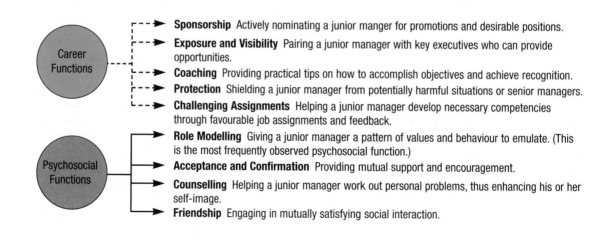

Source: Adapted from discussion in K E Kram, *Mentoring of Work: Developmental Relationships in Organizational Life* (Glenview, IL: Scott, Foresman, 1985), pp 22–39.

"The sponsor is looking for input on what an associate is good at, and what he's not good at, and therefore where training is required. Salary doesn't figure in that relationship, so that makes life better," says Andrew Philip, a leader on product planning and logistics. He is sponsor to four associates—six being the maximum.

Among newcomers, the company finds, doubts and depression commonly begin to set in about a year after they first join. The advice and support of sponsors can then be invaluable. If they survive that period they usually stay a long time.[55]

Research Evidence on Mentoring

Research findings uncovered both individual and organizational benefits of mentoring programmes. Individuals with mentors received more promotions, were more mobile, had greater career satisfaction, and made more income than those without mentors.[56] The impact of mentoring on income was even more pronounced when employees were mentored by white men. For example, a recent study of 1,018 MBA graduates revealed that graduates who were mentored by white men obtained an average annual compensation advantage of $16,840 over those with mentors possessing other demographic characteristics.[57] Mentoring inconsistently affected performance. Research revealed that ability and past experience impacted performance more than career and psychosocial mentoring.[58]

Table 3 – 2   Phases of the Mentor Relationship

PHASE	DEFINITION	TURNING POINTS*
Initiation	A period of six months to a year during which time the relationship gets started and begins to have importance for both managers.	Fantasies become concrete expectations.
		Expectations are met; senior manager provides coaching, challenging work, visibility; junior manager provides technical assistance, respect, and desire to be coached.
		There are opportunities for interaction around work tasks.
Cultivation	A period of two to five years during which time the range of career and psychosocial functions provided expand to a maximum.	Both individuals continue to benefit from the relationship.
		Opportunities for meaningful and more frequent interaction increase.
		Emotional bond deepens and intimacy increases.
Separation	A period of six months to two years after a significant change in the structural role relationship and/or in the emotional experience of the relationship.	Junior manager no longer wants guidance but rather the opportunity to work more autonomously.
		Senior manager faces midlife crisis and is less available to provide mentoring functions.
		Job rotation or promotion limits opportunities for continued interaction; career and psychosocial functions can no longer be provided.
		Blocked opportunity creates resentment and hostility that disrupts positive interaction.
Redefinition	An indefinite period after the separation phase, during which time the relationship is ended or takes on significantly different characteristics, making it a more peerlike friendship.	Stresses of separation diminish, and new relationships are formed.
		The mentor relationship is no longer needed in its previous form.
		Resentment and anger diminish; gratitude and appreciation increase.
		Peer status is achieved.

*Examples of the most frequently observed psychological and organizational factors that cause movement into the current relationship phase.
Source: K E Kram, "Phases of the Mentor Relationship," *Academy of Management Journal,* December 1983, p 622. Used with permission.

Research also supports the organizational benefits of mentoring. In addition to the obvious benefit of employee development, mentoring enhances the effectiveness of organizational communication. Specifically, mentoring increases the amount of vertical communication both up and down an organization, and it provides a mechanism for modifying or reinforcing organizational culture.[59]

Research also investigated the dynamics associated with the establishment of mentoring relationships. Two key findings were uncovered. First, mentoring relationships were more likely to form when the mentor and protégé/protégée possessed similar attitudes, philosophies, personalities, interests, backgrounds, and education.[60] Second, the most common cross-gender mentor relationship involved a male mentor and female protégée. This trend occurred for three reasons: (1) There is an underrepresentation of women in executive-level positions, (2) women perceived more negative drawbacks to becoming mentors than did men, and (3) there are a number of individual, group, and organizational barriers that inhibit mentoring relationships for diverse employees.[61]

Getting the Most Out of Mentoring

A team of mentoring experts offered the following guidelines for implementing effective organizational mentoring programmes:[62]

1. Train mentors and protégés/protégées on how to best use career and psychosocial mentoring.

2. Use both formal and informal mentoring, but do not dictate mentoring relationships.

3. Diverse employees should be informed about the benefits and drawbacks associated with establishing mentoring relationships with individuals of similar and different gender and race.

4. Women should be encouraged to mentor others. Perceived barriers need to be addressed and eliminated for this to occur.

5. Increase the number of diverse mentors in high-ranking positions.

Organizational Values and Ethics

Organizational values and beliefs constitute the foundation of an organization's culture. They also play a key role in influencing ethical behaviour. This final section examines organizational values and ethical behaviour, a pair of intertwined OB topics.

Values Are the Foundation of Organizational Culture

Values
Enduring belief in a mode of conduct or end state.

Value system
Pattern of values within an organization.

Values possess five key components. "**Values** (1) are concepts or beliefs, (2) pertain to desirable end states or behaviours, (3) transcend specific situations, (4) guide selection or evaluation of behaviour and events, and (5) are ordered by relative importance."[63] An organization's **value system** reflects the patterns of conflict and compatibility among values, not the relative importance among values.[64] This definition highlights the point that organizations endorse a constellation of values that contain both conflicting and compatible values. For example, management scholars believe that organizations have two fundamental value systems that naturally conflict with each other. One system relates to the manner in which tasks are accomplished and the other includes values related to maintaining internal cohesion and solidarity.[65] The central issue underlying this value conflict revolves around identifying the main goal being pursued by an organization. Is the organization predominantly interested in financial performance, relationships, or some combination of the two? Moreover, our personal values are influenced by our backgrounds. Generally speaking, Europeans have different values depending on their geographical and religious backgrounds. There are differences between Latin, Germanic,

Slav, catholic, protestant, and orthodox Europeans.[66] To help you understand how organizational values influence organizational culture, we present a typology of organizational values and review relevant research.

A Typology of Organizational Values   Figure 3–6 presents a typology of organizational values that is based on crossing organizational reward norms and organization power structures.[67] Organizational reward norms reflect a company's fundamental belief about how rewards should be allocated. According to the equitable reward norm, rewards should be proportionate to contributions. In contrast, an egalitarian-oriented value system calls for rewarding all employees equally, regardless of their comparative contributions. Organization power structures reflect a company's basic belief about how power and authority should be shared and distributed. These beliefs range from an extreme of being completely unequal or centralized to equal or completely decentralized.

Figure 3–6 identifies four types of value systems: elite, meritocratic, leadership, and collegial. Each value system contains a set of values that is reinforced or endorsed by that type of value system and a set of values that is inconsistent or discouraged by that value system. For example, an elite value system endorses values related to acceptance of authority, high performance, and equitable rewards. This value system, however, does not encourage values related to teamwork, participation, commitment, or affiliation. In contrast, a collegial value system supports values associated with teamwork, participation, commitment, and affiliation, while discouraging values of authority, high performance, and equitable rewards.

Practical Application of Research   Organizations subscribe to a constellation of values rather than to only one and can be profiled according to their values.[68] This, in turn,

---

Figure 3 – 6   A Typology of Organizational Values

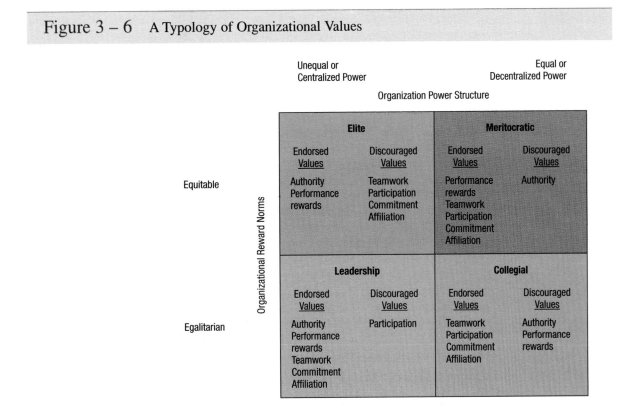

Source: Adapted from B Kabanoff and J Holt, "Changes in the Espoused Values of Australian Organizations 1986–1990," *Journal of Organizational Behavior,* May 1996, pp 201–19.

enables managers to determine whether an organization's values are consistent and supportive of its corporate goals and initiatives. Organizational change is unlikely to succeed if it is based on a set of values that is highly inconsistent with employees' individual values.[69] Finally, a recent study of 85 Australian organizations from 1986–1990 revealed four interesting trends about the typology of organizational values presented in Figure 3–6:[70]

1. Organizational values were quite stable over four years. This result supports the contention that values are relatively stable and resistant to change.

2. There was no universal movement to one type of value system. The 85 organizations represented all four value systems. This finding reinforces the earlier conclusion that there is no one best organizational culture or value system.

3. Organizations with elite value systems experienced the greatest amount of change over the four-year period. elite organizations tended to become more collegial. This finding is consistent with recent results from a national sample of 2,408 US workers. Two-thirds of the survey respondents indicated that they desired more influence or decision making in their jobs.[71]

4. There was an overall increase in the number of organizations that endorsed the individual value of employee commitment. This trend is consistent with the notion that organizational success is partly dependent on the extent to which employees are committed to their organizations.[72]

Ethics and Organizational Behaviour

ETHICS

The issue of ethics and ethical behaviour is receiving greater attention today. This interest is partly due to reported cases of questionable or potentially unethical behaviour. Consider, for example, former French famous politician and businessman, Bernard Tapie's conduct. Although Tapie was continuously declared to be the victim of conspiracies, he was accused, and found guilty of bribery. When Olympique Marseille, his soccer club, won five consecutive league titles and defeated AC Milan to win the Champions Cup in 1993, a player for the Valenciennes football club, was revealed to have been bribed by Tapie.[73]

The line between gifts and bribes is, however, culturally bound, as is confirmed by Yale Richmond in his book on Eastern Europe:[74]

There is, of course, a fine line between a gift and a bribe. Gift giving is an Eastern tradition between friends, acquaintances, and those doing business. The tribute that local Romanian princes paid to the Turks was actually called a *cadou* (gift), and gifts given today by businesspeople will be considered a *cadou,* a sign of respect, rather than a bribe.

OB is an excellent vantage point for better understanding and improving workplace ethics. If OB can provide insights about managing human work behaviour, then it can teach us something about avoiding misbehaviour.

Ethics

Study of moral issues and choices.

Ethics involves the study of moral issues and choices. It is concerned with right versus wrong, good versus bad, and the many shades of grey in supposedly black-and-white issues. Relative to the workplace, the terms business ethics and management ethics are often heard. Moral implications spring from virtually every decision, both on and off the job. Managers are challenged to have moral imagination and the courage to do the right thing. To meet that challenge, present and future managers need a conceptual framework for making ethical decisions.

A Model of Ethical Behaviour   Ethical and unethical conduct is the product of a complex combination of influences (see Figure 3–7). Let us examine key aspects of this model.

At the centre of the model in Figure 3–7 is the individual decision maker. He or she has a unique combination of personality characteristics, values, and moral principles, leaning towards or away from ethical behaviour. The link between values and ethics is

Figure 3 – 7   A Model of Ethical Behaviour in the Workplace

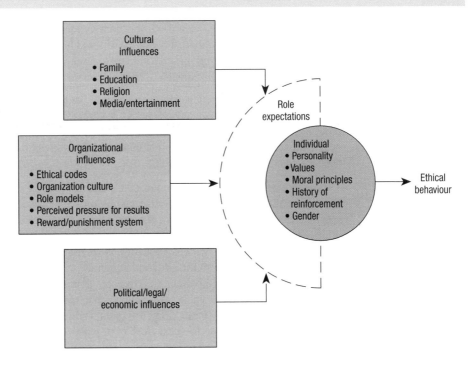

self-explaining. It will come as no surprise that a Canadian study found that students who valued "honesty" higher than average, perceived ethically questionable behaviour as more immoral than subjects who valued "honesty" lower than average. The instrumental value "ambition" was negatively related to the intention to rectify a potentially immoral situation.[75] Personal experience with being rewarded or reinforced for certain behaviours and punished for others also shapes the individual's tendency to act ethically or unethically. Finally, gender plays an important role in explaining ethical behaviour. Men and women have significantly different moral orientations towards organizational behaviour.[76] This issue is discussed later in this section.

Next, Figure 3–7 illustrates three major sources of influence on one's role expectations. People play many roles in life, including those of employee or manager. One's expectations for how those roles should be played are shaped by cultural, organizational, and general environmental factors. Focusing on one troublesome source of organizational influence, many studies have found a tendency among middle- and lower-level managers to act unethically in the face of perceived pressure for results.[77] By fostering a pressure-cooker atmosphere for results, managers can unwittingly set the stage for unethical shortcuts by employees who seek to please and be loyal to the company. Downsizing, business process reengineering and empowerment may all be necessary steps towards creating the lean, mean organization of the late 1990s. But according to accountants at KPMG these management-inspired change programmes also heighten the risk of financial fraud.[78]

Thus, an organization's reward/punishment system can compound the problem of pressure for results. Worse yet, according to a recent study of 385 managers, supervisors who were considered by their subordinates as being consistently ethical tended to have lower salaries than their less ethical peers.[79]

Because ethical or unethical behaviour is the result of person–situation interaction, we need to discuss both the decision maker's moral principles and the organization's ethical climate.

Do Moral Principles Vary by Gender?   Yes, men and women view moral problems and situations differently. This is why research demonstrates that men and women reliably choose alternative solutions to the same moral problems or dilemmas.[80] Carol Gilligan, a well-known psychologist, identified one underlying cause of these gender differences. Her research revealed that men and women differed in terms of how they conceived moral problems. Males perceived moral problems in terms of a **justice perspective** while women relied on a **care perspective**. The two perspectives are described as follows:

> A justice perspective draws attention to problems of inequality and oppression and holds up an ideal of reciprocal rights and equal respect for individuals. A care perspective draws attention to problems of detachment or abandonment and holds up an ideal of attention and response to need. Two moral injunctions, not to treat others unfairly and not to turn away from someone in need, capture these different concerns.[81]

This description underscores the point that men tend to view moral problems in terms of rights, whereas women conceptualize moral problems as an issue of care involving empathy and compassion. In turn, the justice perspective leads males to focus on the "rules of the game." The female perspective, in contrast, is more situational and contextual and results in women focusing on the dynamics and expectations associated with the people involved in the situation at hand.[82]

Although some people believe that the care perspective is more appropriate than the justice approach or vice versa, we believe that men and women have equally valid approaches to ethical behaviour.[83] The key point is for all of us to be aware of these gender differences and to draw on the best from both perspectives when trying to resolve moral or ethical problems.

General Moral Principles   Management consultant and writer Kent Hodgson has helpfully taken managers a step closer to ethical decisions by identifying seven general moral principles (see Table 3–3). Hodgson calls them "the magnificent seven" to emphasize their timeless and worldwide relevance. Both the justice and care perspectives are clearly evident in the magnificent seven, which are more detailed and, hence, more practical. Importantly, according to Hodgson, there are no absolute ethical answers for decision makers. The goal for managers should be to rely on moral principles so their decisions are *principled, appropriate,* and *defensible*.[84] Managers require a supportive organizational climate that translates general moral principles into specific do's and don't's and fosters ethical decisions.

How to Improve the Organization's Ethical Climate   A team of management researchers recommended the following actions for improving on-the-job ethics.[85]

- *Behave ethically yourself.* Managers are potent role models whose habits and actual behaviour send clear signals about the importance of ethical conduct. Ethical behaviour is a top-to-bottom proposition.

- *Screen potential employees.* Surprisingly, employers are generally lax when it comes to checking references, credentials, transcripts, and other information on applicant résumés. More diligent action in this area can screen out those given to fraud and misrepresentation. Integrity testing is fairly valid, but is no panacea.[86]

- *Develop a meaningful code of ethics.* Codes of ethics can have a positive impact if they satisfy these four criteria:

1. They are *distributed* to every employee.

2. They are firmly *supported* by top management.

3. They refer to *specific* practices and ethical dilemmas likely to be encountered by target employees (e.g., salespersons paying kickbacks, purchasing agents receiving payoffs, laboratory scientists doctoring data, or accountants "cooking the books").

Justice perspective
Based on the ideal of reciprocal rights and driven by rules and regulations.

Care perspective
Involves compassion and an ideal of attention and response to need.

Table 3 – 3   The Magnificent Seven: General Moral Principles for Managers

1.   *Dignity of human life: The lives of people are to be respected.* Human beings, by the fact of their existence, have value and dignity. We may not act in ways that directly intend to harm or kill an innocent person. Human beings have a right to live; we have an obligation to respect that right to life. Human life is to be preserved and treated as sacred.

2.   *Autonomy: All persons are intrinsically valuable and have the right to self-determination.* We should act in ways that demonstrate each person's worth, dignity, and right to free choice. We have a right to act in ways that assert our own worth and legitimate needs. We should not use others as mere "things" or only as means to an end. Each person has an equal right to basic human liberty, compatible with a similar liberty for others.

3.   *Honesty: The truth should be told to those who have a right to know it.* Honesty is also known as integrity, truth telling, and honor. One should speak and act so as to reflect the reality of the situation. Speaking and acting should mirror the way things really are. There are times when others have the right to hear the truth from us; there are times when they do not.

4.   *Loyalty: Promises, contracts, and commitments should be honored.* Loyalty includes fidelity, promise keeping, keeping the public trust, good citizenship, excellence in quality of work, reliability, commitment, and honoring just laws, rules, and policies.

5.   *Fairness: People should be treated justly.* One has the right to be treated fairly, impartially, and equitably. One has the obligation to treat others fairly and justly. All have the right to the necessities of life—especially those in deep need and the helpless. Justice includes equal, impartial, unbiased treatment. Fairness tolerates diversity and accepts differences in people and their ideas.

6.   *Humaneness.* There are two parts: (1) *Our actions ought to accomplish good,* and (2) *we should avoid doing evil.* We should do good to others and to ourselves. We should have concern for the well-being of others; usually, we show this concern in the form of compassion, giving, kindness, serving, and caring.

7.   *The common good: Actions should accomplish the "greatest good for the greatest number" of people.* One should act and speak in ways that benefit the welfare of the largest number of people, while trying to protect the rights of individuals.

Source: *A Rock and a Hard Place: How to Make Ethical Business Decisions When the Choices are Tough,* © 1992 Kent Hodgson, pp 69–73. Published by AMACOM, a division of the American Management Association. Used with permission.

4. They are evenly *enforced* with rewards for compliance and strict penalties for non-compliance.

- *Provide ethics training.* Employees can be trained to identify and deal with ethical issues during orientation and through seminar and video training sessions.

- *Reinforce ethical behaviour.* Behaviour that is reinforced tends to be repeated, whereas behaviour that is not reinforced tends to disappear. Ethical conduct too often is punished while unethical behaviour is rewarded.

- *Create positions, units, and other structural mechanisms to deal with ethics.* Ethics needs to be an everyday affair, not a one-time announcement of a new ethical code that gets filed away and forgotten. The Body Shop is using a social or ethical audit to assess how well the company is living up to its ethical standards. Organizational changes are then made on the basis of the audit results.[87]

Consider the case of Fiat, Italy's biggest private company:

To distance itself from the growing political corruption scandal, Fiat decided to issue a new "code of business ethics". It supplements an existing "internal" code regarding issues such as conflicts of interest and insider trading. The document specifically forbids any form of bribery or kickbacks involving the public sector. The ban also applies to any financial inducements to public servants or politicians in covert form, such as sponsorship, advertising or cosmetic "consultancy" agreements. Though not made explicit, the penalty for non-observance would be termination of a worker's contract.[88]

The questionnaire in Table 3–4 consists of 10 questions managers should ask themselves to check their companies' ethical health. It was developed by Values into Action, a Helsinki-based consultancy and is based on responses from 70 senior executives located all over the world.

Table 3 – 4   Values into Action Questionaire[89]

True or false:

1   People in the company conduct their business activities and practices according to the same code of values

2   Because of the current (economic) situation, there is less time to show employees the consideration they deserve as individuals.

3   Survival depends on getting back to basics, cutting costs, and reducing overheads.

4   Faced with a choice, business necessity overrides ethical values.

5   Sometimes there is a gap between ethical values and the way in which the company/or people in it behave.

6   Management trusts employees and employees trust management.

7   Sometimes there is a discrepancy between what executives preach and what they expect their colleagues and employees to practise.

8   People willingly and genuinely want to put the values of the company into practice.

9   We accept and honour our responsibilities towards other 'stakeholders' (those who are taken into account when business decisions are being made, or who are affected by the outcome of business decisions) as well as customers, shareholders, and employees.

10   Frank, fearless, and critical dialogue both upwards and downwards in the company is actively encouraged and practised.

Summary of Key Concepts

1.   *Describe the manifestations of an organization's culture and the four functions of organizational culture.* General manifestations of an organization's culture are shared objects, talk, behaviour, and emotion. Four functions of organization culture are organizational identity, collective commitment, social system stability, and sense-making device.

2.   *Discuss the 12 types of organizational culture.* Organizational culture is grounded in normative beliefs. There are 12 types of organizational culture that are based on separate sets of normative beliefs. The categories of organizational culture include achievement, self-actualizing, humanistic-encouraging, affiliative, approval, conventional, dependent, avoidance, oppositional, power, competitive, and perfectionist.

3.   *Summarize research on organizational culture.* Best-selling books generated interest in organizational culture. Unfortunately, they created the false impression that organizations have one distinct culture, and they failed to break any new ground in the measurement and evaluation of organizational culture. Empirical research has uncovered four key findings: (a) There is a significant relationship between organization culture and a firm's long-term financial performance. (b) Mergers frequently fail due

to incompatible cultures. (c) Organizational culture is significantly related to employee performance, voluntary turnover, organizational commitment, and innovation. (d) The congruence between an individual's values and the organization's values was significantly correlated with organizational commitment, job satisfaction, intention to quit, and turnover.

4.   *Discuss the process of developing an adaptive culture.* The process begins with charismatic leadership that creates a business vision and strategy. Over time, adaptiveness is created by a combination of organizational success and the leaders' ability to get employees to buy into a philosophy or set of values of satisfying constituency needs and improving leadership. Finally, an infrastructure is created to preserve the organization's adaptiveness.

5.   *Summarize the methods used by organizations to embed their cultures.* Embedding a culture amounts to teaching employees about the organization's preferred values, beliefs, expectations, and behaviours. This is accomplished by using one or more of the following 11 mechanisms: (a) formal statements of organizational philosophy, mission, vision, values, and materials used for recruiting,

selection, and socialization; (b) the design of physical space, work environments, and buildings; (c) slogans, language, acronyms, and sayings; (d) deliberate role modelling, training programmes, teaching, and coaching by managers and supervisors; (e) explicit rewards, status symbols, and promotion criteria; (f) stories, legends, and myths about key people and events; (g) the organizational activities, processes, or outcomes that leaders pay attention to, measure, and control; (h) leader reactions to critical incidents and organizational crises; (i) the workflow and organizational structure; (j) organizational systems and procedures; and (k) organizational goals and associated criteria used for recruitment, selection, development, promotion, layoffs, and retirement of people.

6. *Describe the three phases in Feldman's model of organizational socialization.* The three phases of Feldman's model are anticipatory socialization, encounter, and change and acquisition. Anticipatory socialization begins before an individual actually joins the organization. The encounter phase begins when the employment contract has been signed. Phase 3 involves the period in which employees master important tasks and resolve any role conflicts.

7. *Discuss the two basic functions of mentoring and summarize the phases of mentoring.* Mentors help protégés/protégées in two basic functions: career and psychosocial functions. For career functions, mentors provide advice and support in regard to sponsorship, exposure and visibility, coaching, protection, and challenging assignments. Psychosocial functions entail role modelling, acceptance and confirmation, counselling, and friendship. There are four phases of

the mentoring process: (a) initiation, (b) cultivation, (c) separation, and (d) redefinition. Each phase involves variable rather than fixed periods of time, and there are key activities that occur during each phase.

8. *Explain the typology of organizational values.* The typology of organizational values identifies four types of organizational value systems. It is based on crossing organizational reward norms and organization power structures. The types of value systems include elite, meritocratic, leadership, and collegial. Each type of value system contains a set of values that are both consistent and inconsistent with the underlying value system.

9. *Describe how women and men respond to moral problems.* Males and females respond to moral problems in terms of a justice and care perspective, respectively. A justice perspective is based on the ideal of reciprocal rights and is driven by rules and regulations. In contrast, the care perspective involves compassion and an ideal of attention and response to need. Men tend to focus on the "rules of the game" when responding to moral problems, whereas women pay attention to interpersonal dynamics and expectations among people.

10. *Specify at least four actions managers can take to improve an organization's ethical climate.* They can do so by (a) behaving ethically themselves, (b) screening potential employees, (c) developing a code of ethics, (d) providing ethics training, (e) reinforcing and rewarding ethical behaviour, and (f) creating positions and structural mechanisms dealing with ethics.

Discussion Questions

1. How would you respond to someone who made the following statement? "Organizational cultures are not important as far as managers are concerned."

2. What type of organizational culture exists within your current or most recent employer? Explain.

3. Can you think of any organizational heroes who have influenced your work behaviour? Describe them, and explain how they affected your behaviour.

4. Do you know of any successful companies that do not have a positive adaptive culture? Why do you think they are successful?

5. Why is socialization essential to organizational success?

6. Have you ever had a mentor? Explain how things turned out.

7. What type of value system exists within your current classroom? Provide examples to support your evaluation.

8. Which particular source of influence in the left-hand side of Figure 3–7 do you think has had the greatest impact on your ethical behaviour? Explain.

9. Which of the magnificent seven in Table 3–3 is the most important moral principle in your life? Explain. Will this help or hinder you as a manager?

10. What would you say to an individual who says that women are more ethical than men?

Personal Awareness and Growth Exercise

How Does Your Current Employer Socialize Employees?

Objectives

1. To promote deeper understanding of organizational socialization processes.
2. To provide you with a useful tool for analysing and comparing organizations.

Introduction

Employees are socialized in many different ways in today's organizations. Some organizations, such as IBM, have made an exact science out of organizational socialization. Others leave things to chance in hopes that collective goals will somehow be achieved. The questionnaire[90] in this exercise is designed to help you gauge how widespread and systematic the socialization process is in a particular organization.

Instructions

If you are presently employed and have a good working knowledge of your organization, you can complete this questionnaire yourself. If not, identify a manager or professional (e.g., corporate lawyer, engineer, nurse), and ask that individual to complete the questionnaire for his or her organization.

Respond to the items below as they apply to the handling of professional employees (including managers). Upon completion, compute the total score by adding up your responses. For comparison, scores for a number of strong, intermediate, and weak culture firms are provided.

	NOT TRUE OF THIS COMPANY				VERY TRUE OF THIS COMPANY
1. Recruiters receive at least one week of intensive training.	1	2	3	4	5
2. Recruitment forms identify several key traits deemed crucial to the firm's success; traits are defined in concrete terms, and interviewer records specific evidence of each trait.	1	2	3	4	5
3. Recruits are subjected to at least four in-depth interviews.	1	2	3	4	5
4. Company actively facilitates deselection during the recruiting process by revealing minuses as well as pluses.	1	2	3	4	5
5. New staff work long hours, are exposed to intensive training of considerable difficulty, and/or perform relatively menial tasks in the first months.	1	2	3	4	5
6. The intensity of entry-level experience builds cohesiveness among peers in each entering class.	1	2	3	4	5
7. All professional employees in a particular discipline begin in entry-level positions regardless of experience or advanced degrees.	1	2	3	4	5
8. Reward systems and promotion criteria require mastery of a core discipline as a precondition of advancement.	1	2	3	4	5
9. The career path for professional employees is relatively consistent over the first 6 to 10 years with the company.	1	2	3	4	5
10. Reward systems, performance incentives, promotion criteria and other primary measures of success reflect a high degree of congruence.	1	2	3	4	5
11. Virtually all professional employees can identify and articulate the firm's shared values (i.e., the purpose or mission that ties the firm to society, the customer, or its employees).	1	2	3	4	5
12. There are very few instances when actions of management appear to violate the firm's espoused values.	1	2	3	4	5
13. Employees frequently make personal sacrifices for the firm out of commitment to the firm's shared values.	1	2	3	4	5
14. When confronted with trade-offs between systems measuring short-term results and doing what's best for the company in the long term, the firm usually decides in favour of the long term.	1	2	3	4	5
15. This organization fosters mentor–protégé(e) relationships.	1	2	3	4	5
16. There is considerable similarity among high potential candidates in each particular discipline.	1	2	3	4	5

Total score = _____

For Comparative Purposes, some American examples:

SCORES

Strongly socialized firms	65—80	IBM, P&G, Morgan Guaranty
	55—64	AT&T, Morgan Stanley, Delta Airlines
	45—54	United Airlines, Coca-Cola
	35—44	General Foods, PepsiCo
	25—34	United Technologies, ITT
Weakly socialized firms	Below 25	Atari

QUESTIONS FOR DISCUSSION

1. How strongly socialized is the organization in question? What implications does this degree of socialization have for satisfaction, commitment, and turnover?

2. In examining the 16 items in the preceding questionnaire, what evidence of realistic job previews and behaviour modelling can you find? Explain.

3. What does this questionnaire say about how organizational norms are established and enforced? Frame your answer in terms of specific items in the questionnaire.

4. Using this questionnaire as a gauge, would you rather work for a strongly, moderately, or weakly socialized organization?

Group Exercise

Investigating the Difference in Moral Reasoning between Men and Women

Objectives
1. To determine if men and women resolve moral/ethical problems differently.
2. To determine if males and females use a justice and care perspective, respectively, to solve moral/ethical problems.
3. To improve your understanding about the moral reasoning used by men and women.

Introduction
Men and women view moral problems and situations dissimilarly. This is one reason men and women solve identical moral or ethical problems differently. Researchers believe that men rely on a justice perspective to solve moral problems whereas women are expected to use a care perspective. This exercise presents two scenarios that possess a moral/ethical issue. You will be asked to solve each problem and to discuss the logic behind your decision. The exercise provides you with the opportunity to hear the thought processes used by men and women to solve moral/ethical problems.

Instructions
Your instructor will divide the class into groups of four to six. (An interesting option is to use gender-based groups.) Each group member should first read the scenario alone and then make a decision about what to do. Once this is done, use the space provided to outline the rationale for your decision to this scenario. Next, read the second scenario and follow the same procedure: make a decision and explain your rationale. Once all group members have completed their analyses for both scenarios, meet as a group to discuss the results. One at a time, each group member should present his or her final decision and the associated reasoning for the first scenario. Someone should keep a running tally of the decisions so that a summary can be turned in to the professor at the end of your discussion. Follow the same procedure for the second scenario.[91]

Scenario 1
You are the manager of a local toy store. The hottest Christmas toy of the year is the new "Peter Panda" stuffed animal. The toy is in great demand and almost impossible to find. You have received your one and only shipment of 12, and they are all promised to people who previously stopped in to place a deposit and reserve one. A woman comes by the store and pleads with you, saying that her six-year-old daughter is in the hospital very ill, and that "Peter Panda" is the one toy she has her heart set on. Would you sell her one, knowing that you will have to break your promise and refund the deposit to one of the other customers? (There is no way you will be able to get an extra toy in time).

Your Decision:

	WOULD SELL	WOULD NOT SELL	UNSURE
Men			
Women			

Rationale for Your Decision:

Scenario 2

You sell corporate financial products, such as pension plans and group health insurance. You are currently negotiating with Paul Scott, treasurer of a multinational firm, for a sale that could be in the millions of euros. You feel you are in a strong position to make the sale, but two competitors are also negotiating with Scott, and it could go either way. You have become friendly with Scott, and over lunch one day he confided in you that he has recently been under treatment for manic depression. It so happens that in your office there is a staff psychologist who does employee counselling. The thought has occurred to you that such a trained professional might be able to coach you on how to act with and relate to a personality such as Scott's, so as to persuade and influence him most effectively. Would you consult the psychologist?

Your Decision:

	WOULD CONSULT	WOULD NOT CONSULT	UNSURE
Men			
Women			

Rationale for Your Decision:

QUESTIONS FOR DISCUSSION

1. Did males and females make different decisions in response to both scenarios? (Comparative norms can be found in Note 92.)
2. What was the moral reasoning used by women and men to solve the two scenarios?[93]
3. To what extent did males and females use a justice and care perspective, respectively?
4. What useful lessons did you learn from this exercise?

Notes

[1]J Kay, "A question of clarity and certainty," *Financial Times,* February 2, 1996 p. 16.

[2]For a comprehensive review of recent research, see D R Denison, "What IS the Difference Between Organizational Culture and Organizational Climate? A Native's Point of View on a Decade of Paradigm Wars," *Academy of Management Review*, July 1996, pp 619–54.

[3]E H Schein, "Culture: The Missing Concept in Organization Studies," *Administrative Science Quarterly*, June 1996, p 236.

[4]V Hope and J Hendry, "Corporate cultural change — Is it relevant for the organizations of the 1990s," *Human Resource Management Journal,* 1995, p 61–73.

[5]G Egan, "Cultivate your Culture," *Management Today,* April 1994, pp. 39–42.

[6]Based on and translated from G Joseph-Dezaize, "Center Parcs améliore le service aux clients en organisant la rotation des salaires," *L' Essentiel du Management,* March 1996, pp. 50–54.

[7]S C Schneider, and J L Barsoux, *Managing across Cultures* (London: Prentice-Hall, 1997)

[8]Adapted from L Smircich, "Concepts of Culture and Organizational Analysis," *Administrative Science Quarterly*, September 1983, pp 339–58.

[9]The 3M example was based on material contained in R Jacob, "Corporate Reputations: The Winners Chart a Course of Constant Renewal and Work to Sustain Cultures That Produce the Very Best Products and People," *Fortune*, March 6, 1995, pp 54–64; and D Anfuso, "3M's Staffing Strategy Promotes Productivity and Pride," *Personnel Journal*, February 1995, pp 28–34.

[10]J M. Higgins, "Innovate or Evaporate: Seven Secrets of Innovative Corporations," *The Futurist*, September–October 1995, p 45.

[11]Anfuso, "3M's Staffing Strategy Promotes Productivity and Pride," p 28.

[12]See A Xenikou and A Furnham, "A Correlated and Factor Analytic Study of Four Questionnaire Measures of Organizational Culture," *Human Relations*, March 1996, pp 349–71; and Denison, "What IS the Difference Between Organizational Culture and Organizational Climate? A Native's Point of View on a Decade of Paradigm Wars."

[13]The validity of these cultural types was investigated and supported by R A Cooke and J L Szumal, "Measuring Normative Beliefs and Shared Behavioural Expectations in Organizations: The Reliability and Validity of the Organizational Culture Inventory," *Psychological Reports*, 1993, pp 1299–1330.

[14]Subcultural differences are discussed by Schein, "Culture: The Missing Concept in Organization Studies;" R L Klein, G A Bigley, and K H Roberts, "Organizational Culture in High Reliability Organizations: An Extension," *Human Relations*, July 1995, pp 771–93; and S Caudron, "Subculture Strife Hinders Productivity," *Personnel Journal*, December 1992, pp 60–64.

[15]An historical overview of research on organizational culture is provided by H M Trice and J M Beyer, T*he Cultures of Work Organizations* (Englewood Cliffs, NJ: Prentice-Hall, 1993).

[16]See W G Ouchi, *Theory Z: How American Business Can Meet the Japanese Challenge* (Reading, MA: Addison-Wesley Publishing, 1981).

[17]See T E Deal and A A Kennedy, *Corporate Cultures: The Rites and Rituals of Corporate Life* (Reading, MA: Addison-Wesley Publishing, 1982).

[18]See T J Peters and R H Waterman, Jr., *In Search of Excellence* (New York: Harper & Row, 1982).

[19]Ibid., pp 75–76.

[20]The measurement of organizational culture is discussed by Xenikou and Furnham, "A Correlated and Factor Analytic Study of Four Questionnaire Measures of Organizational Culture"; Denison, "What IS the Difference Between Organizational Culture and Organizational Climate? A Native's Point of View on a Decade of Paradigm Wars"; and Cooke and Szumal, "Measuring Normative Beliefs and Shared Behavioural Expectations in Organizations: The Reliability and Validity of the Organizational Culture Inventory."

[21]Results can be found in J P Kotter and J L Heskett, *Corporate Culture and Performance* (New York: The Free Press, 1992).

[22]Results can be found in G G Gordon and N DiTomaso, "Predicting Corporate Performance from Organizational Culture," *Journal of Management Studies*, November 1992, pp 783–98; and D R Denison and A K Mishra, "Toward a Theory of Organizational Effectiveness," *Organization Science*, March–April 1995, pp 204–23.

[23]See S Tully, "Northwest and KLM: The Alliance From Hell," *Fortune*, June 24, 1996, pp 64–72; and J Marren, *Mergers &*

Acquisitions: A Valuation Handbook (Homewood, IL: Business One Irwin, 1993).

[24]See J E Sheridan, "Organizational Culture and Employee Retention," *Academy of Management Journal*, December 1992, pp 1036–56; C Orpen, "The Effect of Organizational Cultural Norms on the Relationship between Personnel Practices and Employee Commitment," *The Journal of Psychology*, September 1993, pp 577–89; and Cooke and Szumal, "Measuring Normative Beliefs and Shared Behavioral Expectations in Organizations: The Reliability and Validity of the Organizational Culture Inventory."

[25]Supportive findings are discussed by S G Harris and K W Mossholder, "The Affective Implications of Perceived Congruence with Culture Dimensions During Organizational Transformation," *Journal of Management*, 1996, pp 527–48; and B Schneider, H W Goldstein, and D B Smith, "The ASA Framework: An Update," *Personnel Psychology*, Winter 1995, pp 747–73.

[26]Results can be found in S Zamanou and S R Glaser, "Moving Toward Participation and Involvement," *Group & Organization Management*, December 1994, pp 475–502.

[27]The relationship between organizational change and culture is discussed by T E Vollman, *The Transformation Imperative: Achieving Market Dominance through Radical Change* (Boston, MA: Harvard Business School Press, 1996); and T Galpin, "Connecting Culture to Organizational Change," *HRMagazine,* March 1996, pp 84–90.

[28]The IBM example was taken from J A Byrne, "Strategic Planning," *Business Week*, August 26, 1996, pp 46–52.

[29]This perspective was promoted by Deal and Kennedy, *Corporate Cultures: The Rites and Rituals of Corporate Life.*

[30]See the discussion in C R Hinings, L Thibault, T Slack, and L M Kikulis, "Values and Organizational Structure," *Human Relations*, July 1996, pp 885–916; and K A Bates, S D Amundson, R G Schroeder, and W T Morris, "The Crucial Interrelationship between Manufacturing Strategy and Organizational Culture," *Management Science*, October 1995, pp 1565–80.

[31]See the discussion in Kotter and Heskett, *Corporate Culture and Performance.*

[32]Ibid.

[33]K Bemowski, "Leaders on Leadership," *Quality Progress,* January 1996, p 43.

[34]S McCartney, "Airline Industry's Top-Ranked Woman Keeps Southwest's Small-Fry Spirit Alive," *The Wall Street Journal*, November 30, 1996, pp B1, B11.

[35]B Dumaine, "Corporate Citizenship," *Fortune*, January 29, 1990, pp 50, 54.

[36]The mechanisms were based on material contained in E H Schein, "The Role of the Founder in Creating Organizational Culture," *Organizational Dynamics*, Summer 1983, pp 13–28.

[37]*The Philips Way. Our Values.*

[38]Adapted and translated from "Goede ideeën brengen op," *Talent,* September 20, 1996, p 1–3.

[39]J Van Maanen, "Breaking In: Socialization to Work," in *Handbook of Work, Organization, and Society*, ed R Dubin (Chicago: Rand-McNally, 1976), p 67.

[40]L Adent Hoecklin, *Managing Cultural Differences for Competitive Advantage* (London: The Economist Intelligence Unit, 1993).

[41]For an instructive capsule summary of the five different organizational socialization models, see J P Wanous, A E Reichers, and S D Malik, "Organizational Socialization and Group Development: Toward an Integrative Perspective," *Academy of Management Review*, October 1984, pp 670–83, table 1. Also see D C Feldman, *Managing Careers in Organizations* (Glenview, IL: Scott, Foresman, 1988), Ch. 5.

[42]Supportive results can be found in M Waung, "The Effects of Self-Regulatory Coping Orientation on Newcomer Adjustment and Job Survival," *Personnel Psychology*, Autumn 1995, pp 633–50.

The impact of RJPs on the acceptance of job offers was investigated by A M Saks, W H Wiesner, and R J Summers, "Effects of Job Previews and Compensation Policy on Applicant Attraction and Job Choice," *Journal of Vocational Behavior*, August 1996, pp 68–85.

[43]J Van Maanen, "People Processing: Strategies of Organizational Socialization," *Organizational Dynamics*, Summer 1978, p 21.

[44]R G Linowes, "The Japanese Manager's Traumatic Entry into the United States: Understanding the American-Japanese Cultural Divide," *The Academy of Management Executive,* November 1993, p p 21. Used with permission.

[45]Results can be found in B E Ashforth and A M Saks, "Socialization Tactics: Longitudinal Effects on Newcomer Adjustment," *Academy of Management Journal*, February 1996, pp 149—78; and R H Heck, "Organizational and Professional Socialization: Its Impact on the Performance of New Administrators," *The Urban Review*, March 1995, pp 31–49.

[46]Results from two separate studies can be found in E W Morrison, "Longitudinal Study of the Effects of Information Seeking," *Journal of Applied Psychology*, April 1993, pp 173–83; and E W Morrison, "Newcomer Information Seeking: Exploring Types, Modes, Sources, and Outcomes," *Academy of Management Journal*, June 1993, pp 557–89.

[47]This study was conducted by D A Major, S W J Kozlowski, G T Chao, and P D Gardner, "A Longitudinal Investigation of Newcomer Expectations, Early Socialization Outcomes, and the Moderating Effects of Role Development Factors," *Journal of Applied Psychology*, June 1995, pp 418–31.

[48]A summary of socialization research is provided by J P Wanous and A Colella, "Organizational Entry Research: Current Status and Future Directions," in *Research in Personnel and Human Resources Management*, eds G R Ferris and K M Rowland (Greenwich, CT: JAI Press, 1989), pp 59–120.

[49]E W Morrison, "Longitudinal study of the effects of information seeking on newcomer socialization," *Journal of Applied Psychology*, vol 78, pp 173–183.

[50]See A M Saks and B E Ashforth, "Proactive Socialization and Behavioural Self-Management," *Journal of Vocational Behavior*, June 1996, pp 301–23.

[51]For a thorough review of research on the socialization of diverse employees with disabilities see A Colella, "Organizational Socialization of Newcomers with Disabilities: A Framework for Future Research," in *Research in Personnel and Human Resources Management*, ed G R Ferris (Greenwich, CT: JAI Press, 1996), pp 351–417.

[52]P Platt, *French or Foe. Getting the Most out of Living and Working in France* (London: Culture Crossings, 1994).

[53]See K E Kram, "Phases of the Mentor Relationship," *Academy of Management Journal*, December 1983, pp 608–25.

[54]H Lancaster, "Managing Your Career: It's Harder, but You Still Can Rise Up from the Mail Room," *The Wall Street Journal*, June 18, 1996, p B1.

[55]T Lester, "The Gores' Happy Family," *Management Today*, February 1993, pp 66–68.

[56]Mentoring research is summarized by B R Ragins, "Diversity, Power, and Mentorship in Organizations," in *Diversity in Organizations: New Perspectives for a Changing Workplace*, eds M M Chemers, S Oskamp, and M A Costanzo (Thousand Oaks, CA: Sage, 1995), pp 91–132.

[57]Results can be found in G F Dreher and T H Cox, Jr., "Race, Gender, and Opportunity: A Study of Compensation Attainment and the Establishment of Mentoring Relationships," *Journal of Applied Psychology*, June 1996, pp 297–308.

[58]See S G Green and T N Bauer, "Supervisory Mentoring by Advisers: Relationships with Doctoral Student Potential, Productivity, and Commitment," *Personnel Psychology*, Autumn 1995, pp 537–61; and G T Chao, P M Walz, and P D Gardner,

"Formal and Informal Mentorships: A Comparison on Mentoring Functions and Contrast with Nonmentored Counterparts," *Personnel Psychology*, Autumn 1992, pp 619–36.

[59]The organizational benefits of mentoring are thoroughly discussed by J A Wilson and N S Elman, "Organizational Benefits of Mentoring," *Academy of Management Executive*, November 1990, pp 88–94.

[60]See Ragins, "Diversity, Power, and Mentorship in Organizations;" and Dreher and Cox, Jr., "Race, Gender, and Opportunity: A Study of Compensation Attainment and the Establishment of Mentoring Relationships."

[61]See B J Tepper, "Upward Maintenance Tactics in Supervisory Mentoring and Nonmentoring Relationships," *Academy of Management Journal*, August 1995, pp 1191–1205; A Vincent, J Seymour, "Profile of Women Mentors: A National Survey," *SAM Advanced Management Journal*, Spring 1995, pp 4–10; and V A Parker and K E Kram, "Women Mentoring Women: Creating Conditions for Connection," *Business Horizons*, March–April 1993, pp 42–51.

[62]These recommendations were based on those presented in Vincent and Seymour, "Profile of Women Mentors: A National Survey."

[63]S H Schwartz, "Universals in the Content and Structure of Values: Theoretical Advances and Empirical Tests in 20 Countries," in *Advances in Experimental Social Psychology*, ed M P Zanna (New York: Academic Press, 1992), p 4.

[64]See Ibid.

[65]See B Kabanoff, "Equity, Equality, Power, and Conflict," *Academy of Management Review*, April 1991, pp 416–41.

[66]Translated from J Kerkhofs, *Europeanen en hun waarden* (Leuven: Davidsfonds, 1997)

[67]This typology and related discussion was derived from B Kabanoff and J Holt, "Changes in the Espoused Values of Australian Organizations 1986–1990," *Journal of Organizational Behavior*, May 1996, pp 201–19.

[68]For an example of profiling organizational values see Xenikou and Furnham, "A Correlational and Factor Analytic Study of Four Questionnaire Measures of Organizational Culture;" and F J Thumin, J H Johnson, Jr., C Kuehl, and W Y Jiang, "Corporate Values as Related to Occupation, Gender, Age, and Company Size," *The Journal of Psychology*, July 1995, pp 389–400.

[69]See T J Galpin, *The Human Side of Change* (San Francisco: Jossey-Bass, 1996); and J Kotter, *Leading Change* (Boston: Harvard Business School Press, 1996).

[70]Results can be found in Kabanoff and Holt, "Changes in the Espoused Values of Australian Organizations 1986–1990."

[71]Details of this study and the general trend toward cooperation and participation is discussed by J T DeLaney, "Workplace Cooperation: Current Problems, New Approaches," *Journal of Labor Research,* Winter 1996, pp 45–61.

[72]See J A Davy, A J Kinicki, and C L Scheck, "A Test of Job Security's Direct and Mediated Effects on Withdrawal Cognitions," *Journal of Organizational Behavior*, in press, 1997; and J Mathieu and D Zajac, "A Review and Meta-Analysis of the Antecedents, Correlates, and Consequences of Organizational Commitment," *Psychological Bulletin*, September 1990, pp 171–94.

[73]Based on R Usher, "Fleurs-de-Lies," *Time*, April 3, 1995, p 29.

[74]Y Richmond, *From Da to Yes* (Yarmouth: Intercultural Press, 1995).

[75]J Finegan, "The Impact of Personal Values on Judgments of Ethical Behaviour in the Workplace," *Journal of Business Ethics,* 1994, 13, 747–755.

[76]See C Gilligan, "In a Different Voice: Women's Conceptions of Self and Morality," *Harvard Educational Review*, November 1977, pp 481–517; and C Gilligan, In a *Different Voice: Psychological Theory and Women's Development* (Cambridge, MA: Harvard University Press, 1982).

[77]For a review of this research, see P V Lewis, "Defining 'Business Ethics': Like Nailing Jello to the Wall," *Journal of Business Ethics*, October 1985, pp 377–83.

[78]T Dickson, "Management: Crime Busters on the Board—Spotting Financial Fraud is Part of the Non-Executive's Role. Tim Dickson on a Few Pointers," *The Financial Times,* May 17, 1995, p 15.

[79]Based on R B Morgan, "Self- and Co-Worker Perceptions of Ethics and Their Relationships to Leadership and Salary," *Academy of Management Journal,* February 1993, pp 200–214.

[80]See L M Dawson, "Women and Men, Morality, and Ethics," *Business Horizons*, July–August 1995, pp 61–68; D K Johnston, "Adolescents' Solutions to Dilemmas in Fables: Two Moral Orientations—Two Problem Solving Strategies," in *Moral Development: Caring Voices and Women's Moral Frames* ed B Puka (New York: Garland Publishing, 1994) pp 99–121; and C Gilligan and J Attanucci, "Two Moral Orientations: Gender Differences and Similarities," *Merril-Palmer Quarterly*, July 1988, pp 223–37.

[81]Gilligan and Attanucci, "Two Moral Orientations: Gender Differences and Similarities," pp 224–25.

[82]"Doing the Right Thing," *The Economist*, May 20, 1995, p 64.

[82]These conclusions were derived from J Dobson and J White, "Toward the Feminine Firm: An Extension to Thomas White," *Business Ethics Quarterly*, July 1995, pp 463–78.

[83]Ibid.

[84]See Ch. 6 in K Hodgson, *A Rock and a Hard Place: How to Make Ethical Business Decisions When the Choices Are Tough* (New York: AMACOM, 1992), pp 66–77. Also see D Vogel, "The Globalization of Business Ethics: Why America Remains Distinctive," *California Management Review*, Fall 1992, pp 30–49.

[85]Adapted from W E Stead, D L Worrell, and J Garner Stead, "An Integrative Model for Understanding and Managing Ethical Behavior in Business Organizations," *Journal of Business Ethics*, March 1990, pp 233–42.

[86]For an excellent discussion of integrity testing and personality tests, see D P O'Meara, "Personality Tests Raise Questions of Legality and Effectiveness," *HRMagazine*, January 1994, pp 97–100.

[87]See "Open Business Is Good for Business," *People Management*, January 1996, pp 24–27.

[88]H Simonian, "Fiat Issues Code of Business Ethics for Workforce," *The Financial Times,* May 12, 1993, p 20.

[89]T Dickson, "Management: Bridging the Ethical Gap–Values May Differ Widely from Behaviour," *The Financial Times,* July 14, 1993, p 14.

[90]This exercise was adapted from Richard Pascale, "The Paradox of 'Corporate Culture': Reconciling Ourselves to Socialization," pp 26–41. © 1985 by the Regents of the University of California. Reprinted/condensed from the *California Management Review*, 27, no. 2, by permission of The Regents.

[91]These scenarios were excerpted from Dawson, "Women and Men, Morality and Ethics," pp 62, 65.

[92]Comparative norms were obtained from Dawson, "Women and Men, Morality and Ethics." Scenario 1: Would sell (28% males, 57% females); would not sell (66% males, 28% females); unsure (6% males, 15% females). Scenario 2: Would consult (84% males, 32% females); would not consult (12% males, 62% females); unsure (4% males, 6% females).

[93]The following trends were taken from Dawson, "Women and Men, Morality and Ethics." Women were likely to primarily respect feelings, ask "who will be hurt?", avoid being judgemental, search for compromise, seek solutions that minimize hurt, rely on communication, believe in contextual relativism, be guided by emotion, and challenge authority. Men were likely to primarily respect rights, ask "who is right?", value decisiveness, make unambiguous decisions, seek solutions that are objectively fair, rely on rules, believe in blind impartiality, be guided by logic, and accept authority.

Answers to OB Exercise

1. Although there are no clear examples of shared objects such as plaques or logos in the Ritz-Carlton example, the policies, practices, procedures, and routines designed to reward employees for providing excellent customer service partially represent shared objects or things. There are two potential shared sayings for the Ritz. One might be "do whatever it takes", and the second could be "we are ladies and gentlemen serving ladies and gentlemen". The "Gold Standards" constitute shared behaviour or doings in that they specify desired employee behaviour within the Ritz.

   Hamburger University represents a shared object or thing within McDonald's. McDonald's vision and its associated acronym of QSCV might well constitute a shared saying. The detailed policies and procedures manual and "Franchising 2000" reflect shared behaviour or doings because they clearly specify desired forms of employee behaviour. Franchisees at McDonald's are likely to share positive emotions about providing customers with quality, service, convenience, and value because their income is directly tied to these customer outcomes.

2. McDonald's culture appears to be more control-oriented than that at the Ritz-Carlton. The Ritz is known for empowering its employees to make decisions, whereas McDonald's directly influences employee behaviour through its meticulous policies and procedures. Both organizations are likely to have a competitive component within their cultures because they operate in very competitive markets

Four

International OB: Managing Across Cultures

LEARNING OBJECTIVES

When you finish studying the material in this chapter, you should be able to:

1. Explain how societal culture and organizational culture combine to influence on-the-job behaviour.

2. Define *ethnocentrism,* and distinguish between high-context and low-context cultures.

3. Explain the difference between monochronic and polychronic cultures.

4. Discuss the cultural implications of interpersonal space and language.

5. Describe the practical lessons from the Hofstede–Bond cross-cultural studies.

6. Explain Trompenaars' five dimensions of cultural differences.

7. Specify why US managers, compared to European and Japanese, have a comparatively high failure rate in foreign assignments, and identify skills needed by today's global managers.

8. Discuss the importance of cross-cultural training relative to the foreign assignment cycle.

When Comecon, the Communist trading bloc, disintegrated in 1990, Hungary's textile industry went into a tailspin. In the three years that followed, the number of textile and apparel jobs fell by one-third. The production of fabric and yarn dropped 60%.

Like other Western businessmen, Michael Smolens recognized an opportunity. But Smolens did them all one better. He didn't just tentatively invest in the country; his new company, Danube Knitwear Ltd, fully embraced Hungary's economy, providing 950 full-time jobs to local workers and investing heavily in new technology for its mill operations.

"We wanted to put something together in a part of the world where there was no competition," says Smolens. "Somewhere with unlimited upside potential."

That potential is beginning to blossom: Danube Knitwear recently opened a sewing facility in Romania. But it hasn't been an easy road. "Here, you're not limited by market size or financing; it's resolving the cultural differences that's a challenge," explains Smolens. . . .

But the cultural differences have taken longer to adjust to than the company had expected. Finding nationals with both experience and willingness to be accountable for challenging responsibilities has been an arduous task, Smolens says. The company has been bringing in younger, inexperienced nationals to train, but unfortunately, that process takes two to five years.

As for the mill labourers, Danube Knitwear continues to learn more about the past work environment and to tailor its management style accordingly. The first step was getting workers used to high Western production standards and motivating them to accept the company's priorities. Hungary's low wage base was seen as a big plus when the company was being formed, but absenteeism has been an ongoing problem. In the plant's first year, employee turnover soared to 120%. Smolens realized he'd have to strengthen his wage structure to keep his workers from abandoning the company for the family farms or the black market. He also moved from awarding attendance bonuses to providing other job incentives—in particular, cultivating a more comfortable, open work environment.

"We're actively soliciting comments from the workers day to day," says [partner Phil] Lighty. "They know what the problems are, but because of the way things used to be in this country, they're not always comfortable sharing them."

"It's a good approach," Smolens adds, "and we do see progress. They're starting to realize that what they say is being taken seriously."[1]

Discussion Question

Are you surprised it took more than money to motivate the employees in a relatively low-wage country such as Hungary? Explain.

Globalization of the economy challenges virtually all employees to become more internationally aware and cross-culturally adept. The path to the top typically winds through one or more foreign assignments today. A prime example is Samir F Gibara, chief executive officer of Goodyear Tire & Rubber, who spent 27 of his 30 years with the company on foreign assignments in Canada, France, Morocco, and Belgium.[2] Even managers and employees who stay in their native country will find it hard to escape today's global economy. Many will be thrust into international relationships by working for foreign-owned companies or by dealing with foreign suppliers, customers, and co-workers. In a recent article entitled, "How You Can Learn to Feel at Home in Foreign-Based Firm," *The Wall Street Journal* offered this perspective:

In foreign-based companies, career success often hinges on a keen understanding of the differences in culture and management style. In any guide to handling these differences, generalizations must be made, even though foreign companies and cultures also vary greatly from each other. Having said that, let's get to the generalizations.

There are advantages to working for foreign employers, including job security. While times are changing, the Japanese still try to build loyalty with job security. The Germans, says [one international recruiter], "go through agony when they have to let someone go."[3]

The global economy is a rich mix of cultures, and the time to prepare to work in it is now.[4] Accordingly, the purpose of this chapter is to help you take a step in that direction by exploring the impacts of culture in today's increasingly internationalized organization. This chapter draws upon the area of cultural anthropology. We begin with a model that shows how societal culture and organizational culture (covered in Chapter 3) combine to influence work behaviour, followed by a fundamental cultural distinction. Next, we examine key dimensions of international OB with the goal of enhancing cross-cultural awareness. Practical lessons from cross-cultural management research are then reviewed. The chapter concludes by exploring the challenge of accepting a foreign assignment.

Culture and Organizational Behaviour

How would you, as a manager, interpret the following situations?

An Asian executive for a multinational company, transferred from Taiwan to the US, appears aloof and autocratic to his peers.[5] In Saudi Arabia an invitation kindly asked that dogs and women be kept at home.[6] In Germany an employee only wants to stay overtime if it is paid for and if a deadline is to be met.[7]

If you attribute the behaviour in these situations to personalities, three descriptions come to mind: arrogant, discriminatory, and unloyal to the company. These are reasonable conclusions. Unfortunately, they are probably wrong, being based more on prejudice and stereotypes than on actual fact. However, if you attribute the behavioural outcomes to *cultural* differences, you stand a better chance of making the following more valid interpretations:

As it turns out, Asian culture encourages a more distant managing style,[8] in Muslim countries women going out are seen as prostitutes,[9] and in Germany overtime is very exceptional: the company has no right to interfere in your private time.[10] You are paid to work between certain hours, and that's it. One cannot afford to overlook relevant cultural contexts when trying to understand and manage organizational behaviour.

Culture Is Complex and Multilayered

Culture
Socially derived, taken-for-granted assumptions about how to think and act.

While noting that cultures exist in social units of all sizes (from civilizations to countries to ethnic groups to organizations to work groups), Edgar Schein defined **culture** as follows:

A pattern of basic assumptions—invented, discovered, or developed by a given group as it learns to cope with its problems of external adaptation and internal integration—that has worked well enough to be considered valid and, therefore, to be taught to new members as the correct way to perceive, think, and feel in relation to those problems.[11]

The word *taught* needs to be interpreted carefully because it implies formal education or training. While cultural lessons may indeed be taught in schools, religious settings, and on the job, formal inculcation is secondary. Most cultural lessons are learned by observing and imitating role models as they go about their daily affairs or as observed in the media.[12]

Culture is difficult to grasp because it is multilayered. Fons Trompenaars, a respected international management scholar and consultant from The Netherlands, offers this instructive analogy:

Culture comes in layers, like an onion. To understand it you have to unpeel it layer by layer. On the outer layer are the products of culture, like the soaring skyscrapers of Manhattan, pillars of private power, with congested public streets between them. These are expressions of deeper values and norms in a society that are not directly visible (values such as upward mobility, "the more-the-better" status, material success). The layers of values and norms are deeper within the onion and are more difficult to identify.[13]

Culture Is a Subtle but Pervasive Force

Culture generally remains below the threshold of conscious awareness because it involves *taken-for-granted assumptions* about how one should perceive, think, act, and feel. Cultural anthropologist Edward T Hall put it this way:

Since much of culture operates outside our awareness, frequently we don't even know what we know. We pick . . . [expectations and assumptions] up in the cradle. We unconsciously learn what to notice and what not to notice, how to divide time and space, how to walk and talk and use our bodies, how to behave as men or women, how to relate to other people, how to handle responsibility, whether experience is seen as whole or fragmented. This applies to all people. The Chinese or the Japanese or the Arabs are as unaware of their assumptions as we are of our own. We each assume that they're part of human nature. What we think of as "mind" is really internalized culture.[14]

In sum, it has been said: "you are your culture, and your culture is you."

A Model of Societal and Organizational Cultures

As illustrated in Figure 4–1, culture influences organizational behaviour in two ways. Employees bring their societal culture to work with them in the form of customs and language. Organizational culture, a by-product of societal culture, in turn affects the individual's values/ethics, attitudes, assumptions, and expectations.[15] The term societal culture is used here instead of national culture because the boundaries of many modern nation-states were not drawn along cultural lines. The former Soviet Union, for example, included 15 republics and more than 100 ethnic nationalities, many with their own distinct language.[16] Societal culture is shaped by the various environmental factors listed in the left-hand side of Figure 4–1. Once inside the organization's sphere of influence, the individual is further affected by the organization's culture. Mixing of societal and organizational cultures can produce interesting dynamics in multinational companies. For example, with French and American employees working side by side at General Electric's medical imaging production facility in the US, unit head Claude Benchimol has witnessed some culture shock:

The French are surprised the American parking lots empty out as early as 5 pm; the Americans are surprised the French don't start work at 8 am. Benchimol feels the French are more talkative and candid. Americans have more of a sense of hierarchy and are less likely to criticize. But they may be growing closer to the French. Says Benchimol: "It's taken a year to get across the idea that we are all entitled to say what we don't like to become more productive and work better."[17]

Same company, same company culture, yet GE's French and American co-workers have different attitudes about time, hierarchy, and communication. They are the products of different societal cultures.[18]

When managing people at work, the individual's societal culture, the organizational culture, and any interaction between the two need to be taken into consideration. For example, American workers' cultural orientation toward quality improvement differs significantly from the Japanese cultural pattern.

Unlike Japanese workers, Americans aren't interested in making small step-by-step improvements to increase quality. They want to achieve the breakthrough, the impossible dream. The way to motivate them: Ask for the big leap, rather than for tiny steps.[19]

Figure 4 – 1   Cultural Influences on Organizational Behaviour

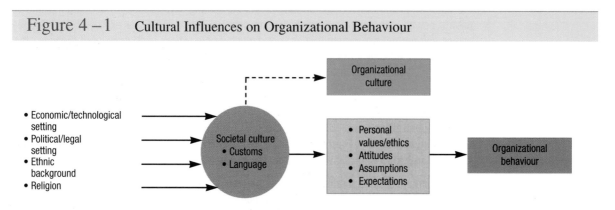

Source: Adapted in part from B J Punnett and S Withane, "Hofstede's Value Survey Module: To Embrace or Abandon?" in *Advances in International Comparative Management,* vol 5, ed S B Prasad (Greenwich, CT: JAI Press, 1990), pp 69–89.

Ethnocentrism: A Cultural Roadblock in the Global Economy

Ethnocentrism

Belief that one's native country, culture, language, and behaviour are superior.

Ethnocentrism, the belief that one's native country, culture, language, and modes of behaviour are superior to all others, has its roots in the dawn of civilization. First identified as a behavioural science concept in 1906, involving the tendency of groups to reject outsiders,[20] the term *ethnocentrism* generally has a more encompassing (national or societal) meaning today. Worldwide evidence of ethnocentrism is plentiful. For example, ethnocentrism led to deadly "ethnic cleansing" in Bosnia and genocide in the African nations of Rwanda and Burundi.

Less dramatic, but still troublesome, is ethnocentrism within managerial and organizational contexts. Experts on the subject framed the problem this way:

[Ethnocentric managers have] a preference for putting home-country people in key positions everywhere in the world and rewarding them more handsomely for work, along with a tendency to feel that this group is more intelligent, more capable, or more reliable. . . . Ethnocentrism is often not attributable to prejudice as much as to inexperience or lack of knowledge about foreign persons and situations. This is not too surprising, since most executives know far more about employees in their home environments. As one executive put it, "At least I understand why our own managers make mistakes. With our foreigners, I never know. The foreign managers may be better. But if I can't trust a person, should I hire him or her just to prove we're multinational?"[21]

Recent research suggests ethnocentrism is bad for business. A survey of 918 companies with home offices in the United States (272 companies), Japan (309), and Europe (337) found ethnocentric staffing and human resource policies to be associated with increased personnel problems. Those problems included recruiting difficulties, high turnover rates, and lawsuits over personnel policies. Among the three regional samples, Japanese companies had the most ethnocentric human resource practices and the most international human resource problems.[22]

Current and future managers can effectively deal with ethnocentrism through education, greater cross-cultural awareness, international experience, and conscious effort.

High-Context and Low-Context Societal Cultures

Cultural anthropologists believe interesting and valuable lessons can be learned by comparing one culture with another. Many models have been proposed for distinguishing among the world's rich variety of cultures. One general distinction contrasts high-context and low-context cultures[23] (see Figure 4–2). On the business front, American corporate downsizing makes Europeans shudder. One French executive, recently returned from a year in New York, was shocked by the "hire-and-fire brutality" of corporate practices in the United States. "In some cases, longtime employees are given just one hour to empty their desks and leave the building, while an armed guard watches. That will never happen here," said the French businessman. Europeans are willing to pay a premium for job security rather than the risk US-style rugged individualism. Recently, 38,000 applicants turned up to take a test and compete for 93 Italian government posts that pay only 12,700 ecus yearly. Italian bureaucrats can't be fired.[24] Managers in multicultural settings need to know the difference if they are to communicate and interact effectively.

High-context cultures

Primary meaning derived from nonverbal situational cues.

Reading between the Lines in High-Context Cultures   People who come from **high-context cultures** rely heavily on situational cues for meaning when perceiving and communicating with another person. Nonverbal cues such as one's official position or status convey messages more powerfully than do spoken words. Thus, we come to better understand the ritual of exchanging *and reading* business cards in Japan. Japanese culture is relatively high-context. One's business card, listing employer and official position, conveys vital silent messages to members of Japan's homogeneous society. An intercultural communications authority explains:

Nearly all communication in Japan takes place within an elaborate and vertically organized social structure. Everyone has a distinct place within this framework. Rarely do people converse without knowing, or determining, who is above and who is below them. Associates are always older or

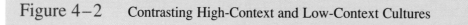

Figure 4–2   Contrasting High-Context and Low-Context Cultures

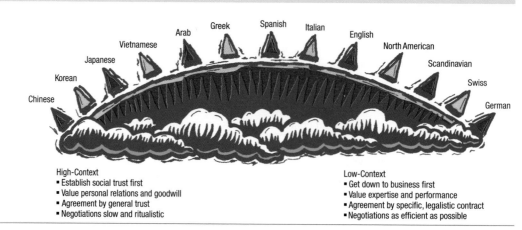

High-Context
- Establish social trust first
- Value personal relations and goodwill
- Agreement by general trust
- Negotiations slow and ritualistic

Low-Context
- Get down to business first
- Value expertise and performance
- Agreement by specific, legalistic contract
- Negotiations as efficient as possible

Source: M Munter, "Cross-Cultural Communication for Managers." Reprinted from *Business Horizons,* May–June 1993, Figure 3, p 72. © 1993 by the Foundation for the School of Business at Indiana University. Used with permission.

younger, male or female, subordinate or superior. And these distinctions all carry implications for the form of address, choice of words, physical distance, and demeanor. As a result, conversation tends to reflect this formal hierarchy.[25]

Verbal and written communication in high-context cultures such as China, Korea, and Japan are secondary to taken-for-granted cultural assumptions about other people.

In Eastern Europe, business practices are more formal, and decision making more hierarchical and lengthy. Titles and honorifics are important. Letters are answered late, if at all.[26]

Low-context cultures

Primary meaning derived from written and spoken words.

Reading the Fine Print in Low-Context Cultures   In **low-context cultures,** written and spoken words carry the burden of shared meaning. True, people in low-context cultures read nonverbal messages from body language, dress, status, and belongings. However, they tend to double-check their perceptions and assumptions verbally. To do so in China or Japan would be to gravely insult the other person, thus causing them to *lose face*.[27] Their positions on the continuum in Figure 4 – 2 indicate the German preoccupation with written rules for even the finest details of behaviour and the American preoccupation with precise legal documents.[28] In high-context cultures, agreements tend to be made on the basis of someone's word or a handshake, after a rather prolonged trust-building period. European-Americans, who have been taught from birth not to take anything for granted, see the handshake as a prelude to demanding a signature on a detailed, lawyer-approved, iron-clad contract.

In his book, *We Europeans,*[29] Richard Hill presents his ethnic map of Europe (Figure 4 – 3), which divides the continental western Europeans into two main groups, the Germanics and the Latins. Latins are identified as high context, whereas Germanics are rather low context. This implies that the Latins need no in-depth background information because they keep themselves informed about everything through friends, family, colleagues, and clients. Hence, their professional and private lives are interrelated. Germanics on the other hand have no informal networks and need more founded information before they go on. Their approach to life is generally segmented and compartmentalized. In eastern Europe family and friends come first as well: rather than going through official channels to get something done, they will first network their families, friends and personal contacts who owe them a favour.[30]

Generally speaking one can say that in southern Europe a working day starts early in the morning and ends at lunch time, whereas a working day in northern Europe starts between 8 and 9 am and ends between 5 and 6 pm. A good indicator for high- or low-context cultures is the way meetings are held in the major European countries.[31]

Figure 4–3	Hill's Ethnic Map of Europe

Source: R Hill, *We Europeans* (Brussels: Europublications, 1995), p 320.

- *France:* detailed agenda, briefing and coordination, interaction between the members through the boss, 15 minutes delay is acceptable.

- *Germany:* very formal, agenda and minutes, coordination and briefing, communication through a senior person, it is very important to be punctual.

- *Italy:* unstructured and informal, people may come and people may go, difficult to impose an agenda, free for all opinions, delay is accepted.

- *Netherlands:* informality of manner, but nevertheless they stick to the basic protocols of keeping an agenda, speaking through the chairman.

- *Spain:* no meetings culture, only to communicate instructions, delay is endemic.

- *United Kingdom:* most important and time-consuming tool, very serious, unpunctuality is the rule!

Towards Greater Cross-Cultural Awareness and Competence

Aside from being high- or low-context, cultures stand apart in other ways as well.[32] Let us briefly review the following basic factors that vary from culture to culture: time, interpersonal space, language, and communication.[33] This list is intended to be indicative rather than exhaustive. Separately or together these factors can foster huge cross-cultural gaps. Effective multicultural management often depends on whether or not these gaps can be bridged.

A qualification needs to be offered at this juncture. It is important to view all of the cultural differences in this chapter and elsewhere as *tendencies* and *patterns,* rather than as absolutes. As soon as one falls into the trap of assuming *all* Germans are this, *all* British are that, and so on, potentially instructive generalizations become mindless stereotypes.[34] Well-founded cultural generalizations are fundamental to successfully doing business in other cultures. But one needs to be constantly alert to *individuals* who are exceptions to the local cultural rule. For instance, it is possible to encounter talkative and aggressive Japanese and quiet and deferential Americans who simply do not fit their respective cultural moulds. Also, tipping the scale against clear cultural differences are space age transportation; global telecommunications, television, and computer networks; tourism; global marketing; and entertainment. These areas are homogenizing the peoples of the world. The result, according to experts on the subject, is an emerging "world culture" in which, someday, people may be more alike than different.[35]

Cultural Perceptions of Time

In North American and northern European cultures, time seems to be a simple matter. It is linear, relentlessly marching forwards, never backwards, in standardized chunks. To the German who received a watch for his or her third birthday, time is like money. It is spent, saved, or wasted.[36] Americans are taught to show up 10 minutes early for appointments. When working across cultures, however, time becomes a very complex matter.[37] Imagine a Swiss's chagrin when left in a waiting room for 45 minutes, only to find a Latin American government official dealing with three other people at once. The North American resents the lack of prompt and undivided attention. The Latin American official resents the North American's impatience and apparent self-centredness.[38] This vicious cycle of resentment can be explained by the distinction between **monochronic time** and **polychronic time**:

Monochronic time

Preference for doing one thing at a time because time is limited, precisely segmented, and schedule driven.

The former is revealed in the ordered, precise, schedule-driven use of public time that typifies and even caricatures efficient northern Europeans and North Americans. The latter is seen in the multiple and cyclical activities and concurrent involvement with different people in Mediterranean, Latin American, and especially Arab cultures.[39]

Polychronic time

Preference for doing more than one thing at a time because time is flexible and multidimensional.

A Matter of Degree   Monochronic and polychronic are relative rather than absolute concepts. Generally, the more things a person tends to do at once, the more polychronic they are.[40] Thanks to computers and advanced telecommunications systems, highly polychronic managers can engage in "multitasking."[41] For instance, it is possible to talk on the telephone, read and respond to computer e-mail messages, print a report, check a pager message, *and* eat a stale sandwich all at the same time. Unfortunately, this extreme polychronic behaviour too often is not nearly as efficient as hoped and, as discussed in

OB EXERCISE   *The Polychronic Attitude Index*

Please consider how you feel about the following statements. Circle your choice on the scale provided: strongly agree, agree, neutral, disagree, or strongly disagree.

	STRONGLY DISAGREE	DISAGREE	NEUTRAL	AGREE	STRONGLY AGREE
I do not like to juggle several activities at the same time.	5	4	3	2	1
People should not try to do many things at once.	5	4	3	2	1
When I sit down at my desk, I work on one project at a time.	5	4	3	2	1
I am comfortable doing several things at the same time.	1	2	3	4	5

Add up your points, and divide the total by 4. Then plot your score on the scale below.

1.0	1.5	2.0	2.5	3.0	3.5	4.0	4.5	5.0
Monochronic								Polychronic

The lower your score (below 3.0), the more monochronic your orientation; and the higher your score (above 3.0), the more polychronic.

Source: A C Bluedorn, C F Kaufman, and P M Lane, "How Many Things Do You Like to Do at Once? An Introduction to Monochronic and Polychronic Time," *Academy of Management Executive*, November 1992, Exhibit 2, p 20.

Chapter 17, can be very stressful.

In a European context, we can say that Latins are polychronic, whereas Germanics are monochronic. In other words the first are schedule-independent and the latter schedule-dependent.[42] In Italy, for example, if something intervenes to make you late, a meeting running overtime, or a surprise visit from someone important, or an unexpected telephone call, then it is understandable. While it is impolite to arrive late for a meeting it is even more impolite to break off the previous one because it is overrunning.[43]

Monochronic people prefer to do one thing at a time. What is your attitude towards time? (You can find out by completing the Polychronic Attitude Index in the OB Exercise.)

Practical Implications Low-context cultures, such as North America and northern Europe, tend to run on monochronic time while high-context cultures, such as that of Latin America and southern Europe, tend to run on polychronic time. People in polychronic cultures view time as flexible, fluid, and multidimensional. The Germans and Swiss have made an exact science of monochronic time. In fact, a new radio-controlled watch made by a German company, Junghans, is "guaranteed to lose no more than one second in 1 million years."[44] Many a visitor has been a minute late for a Swiss train, only to see its taillights leaving the station. Time is more elastic in polychronic cultures. During the Islamic holy month of Ramadan in Middle Eastern countries, for example, the faithful fast during daylight hours, and the general pace of things markedly slows. Managers need to reset their mental clocks when doing business across cultures.

Interpersonal Space

Proxemics

Hall's term for the study of cultural expectations about interpersonal space.

Anthropologist Edward T Hall noticed a connection between culture and preferred interpersonal distance. People from high-context cultures were observed standing close when talking to someone. Low-context cultures appeared to dictate a greater amount of interpersonal space. Hall applied the term **proxemics** to the study of cultural expectations about interpersonal space.[45] He specified four interpersonal distance zones. Some call them space bubbles. They are *intimate* distance, *personal* distance, *social* distance, and *public* distance. Ranges for the four interpersonal distance zones are illustrated in Figure 4–4, along with selected cultural differences.

North American business conversations normally are conducted at about a metre (three- to four-foot) range, within the personal zone in Figure 4–4. A range of approximately a third of a metre (one foot) is common in Latin American and Asian cultures, uncomfortably close for northern Europeans and North Americans. Arabs like to get even closer. Mismatches in culturally dictated interpersonal space zones can prove very distracting for the unprepared. Hall explains:

Figure 4–4 **Interpersonal Distance Zones for Business Conversations Vary from Culture to Culture**

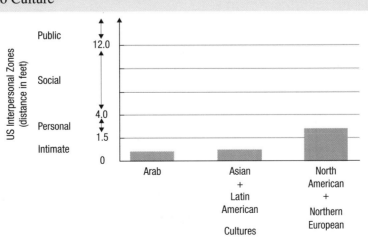

Arabs tend to get very close and breathe on you. It's part of the high sensory involvement of a high-context culture. . . .

The Brit on the receiving end can't identify all the sources of his discomfort but feels that the Arab is pushy. The Arab comes close, the Brits backs up. The Arab follows, because he can only interact at certain distances. Once the Brit learns that Arabs handle space differently and that breathing on people is a form of communication, the situation can sometimes be redefined so the Brit relaxes.[46]

Asian and Middle-Eastern hosts grow weary of having to seemingly chase their low-context guests around at social gatherings to maintain what they feel is a proper conversational range. Backing up all evening to keep conversational partners at a proper distance is an awkward experience as well. Awareness of cultural differences, along with skilful accommodation, are essential to productive intercultural business dealings.

Norwegians, by comparison, can be very jealous of their bubbles of space—to an extent that they even astonished an American visitor. "One of the first things I noticed when I moved to Norway was that Norwegians need a lot of personal space," he remarked to an interviewer. "Once I went into someone's office for an informal chat and sat down on the edge of his desk, some two metres from him. As I did that, I thought he would try to crawl out the window behind him! I had the distinct impression that I was on his territory. Also, I have found that if one reaches out to touch another during a conversation, there will almost immediately be a recoil from the listener."[47]

Language and Cross-Cultural Communication

More than 3,000 different languages are spoken worldwide. What is the connection between these languages and information processing and behaviour? There is an ongoing debate among anthropologists concerning the extent to which language influences perception and behaviour. On one side of the argument, the *relativists* claim each language fosters unique perceptions. On the other side, *universalists* state that all languages share common elements and thus foster common thought processes and perceptions. A study involving subjects from eight countries attempted to resolve this debate. Subjects from the United States, Britain, Italy, Greece, former Yugoslavia, Pakistan, Hong Kong, and Vietnam were shown 15 flash cards, each printed with three pairs of words. Language experts certified the various translations as accurate. The idea was to see if adults from different cultures, speaking different languages, would perceive the same semantic elements in the paired words. Illustrative semantic elements, or basic language building blocks, are as follows: opposite = alive/dead; similar = furniture/bed. The researchers found "considerable cross-cultural agreement on the meaning and use of semantic relations."[48] Greatest agreement was found for semantic opposites (e.g., alive/dead). These findings tip the scale in favour of the universalists. We await additional research evidence for a definitive answer.

If we take a closer look at the language knowledge in Europe, Table 4–1 reveals that

Table 4–1   Percentage of People in 12 Former EC Countries Who Can Take Part in a Conversation in Another Language

	Bel	Dk	Ger	Gr	Sp	Fr	Ire	It	Lux	NL	Por	UK	EU12
Danish	0	100	2	0	0	0	0	0	2	0	0	0	2
Greek	0	0	0	100	0	0	0	0	2	1	0	1	3
Portuguese	1	0	0	0	2	2	0	0	4	1	100	0	3
Dutch	68	1	1	0	0	0	0	0	4	100	0	1	7
Spanish	3	2	2	0	98	10	1	2	4	3	7	3	14
Italian	3	1	1	2	1	4	1	100	15	1	1	2	18
French	70	8	9	4	9	100	14	17	90	90	16	21	29
German	16	47	99	5	1	8	4	3	90	60	1	8	31
English	34	68	35	25	13	30	100	19	46	72	20	100	42
Other	3	5	6	3	25	6	20	1	94	9	1	6	7

Source: *Eurobarometer*, 1994.

English is still the best-known language throughout Europe (42 per cent). Surprisingly, however, more people know German (31 per cent) than French (29 per cent), although French is still the main second language in many schools in Europe. These data imply, however, not that those speaking one or more of the above-mentioned languages should not make any effort to learn other languages, as 58 per cent of the European population still does not understand English, 69 per cent not German, and 71 per cent not French. According to Nigel Brockmann, human resource manager of the publishing arm of the Thomson Corporation, language skills account for part of the success of managers of smaller countries such as Belgium or Switzerland.[49]

Three Cross-Cultural Communication Options   Those attempting to communicate across cultures have three options: (1) stick to their own language, (2) rely on translators, or (3) learn the local language. The first option, preferred by those who insist English has become the language of global business, are at a serious competitive disadvantage. Ignorance of the local language means missing subtle yet crucial meanings, risking

International Organizational Behaviour

Foreign Language Skills Give Utah an Edge in the Global Economy

Bountiful, Utah—In the background are snow-capped mountain peaks, and in the foreground is Kent Derricott, walking around a golf course and carrying a $135 putter. He is talking about the putter, in superlatives—in fluent Japanese.

The scene is part of a 10-minute "infomercial" running on Japanese cable television, in which Mr. Derricott is the pitchman. The idea is to sell American products to the golf-addicted Japanese, at Japanese prices. Sales since June 1995: several thousand putters. "The sales are ahead of forecast. The returns aren't too ugly," Mr. Derricott says.

It is just the latest of Mr. Derricott's adventures in Japan. Over the past 20 years, he has been a Mormon missionary there, a variety-show regular, a TV commentator, and a documentary producer. And it is a tiny slice of what might be called the globalization of the Utah economy.

Utah, population 1.9 million, is one of the last places you might expect to see explosive growth in international trade, lots of foreign-language speakers, and an emerging breed of global executives. After all, the state is landlocked, hundreds of miles from the nearest seaport.

Yet this rugged land, known principally for its mountains and its Mormons, is booming. It ranked No. 2 in job growth among the 50 states last year, relative to workforce size, trailing only Nevada. And while much of its growth is shared by other Rocky Mountain states, a good deal of Utah's international business can be traced, in one way or another, to the pervasive influence of the Mormon faith, formally known as the Church of Jesus Christ of Latter Day Saints.

For more than a century, the Mormons have been sending their young overseas, mostly 19-year-old men dispatched for two-year stints in missions. At the moment, 41,000 Mormons are serving in 302 missions in 111 foreign countries. Some stay on as long-term expatriates, many hail from Utah and return there eventually, and a lot, like Mr. Derricott, go into business, capitalizing on language skills and contacts developed over the years.

"In Utah, 30% of our people speak a foreign language," says Dan Mabey, head of international business development for the state. And thinking internationally seems be a legacy of the Mormon mission experience. "For a lot of these guys, being global is sort of a dominant gene; it's there guiding how they grow right from the beginning," Mr. Mabey says. . . .

"The Mormons have a global rather than a local outlook," says David Birch, president of Cognetics Inc., a Cambridge, Mass., research firm. "You talk about having a branch network—Mormons have a friend in every city in the world."

Utah, he says, "is the No. 1 state, and Salt Lake City-Provo is the No. 1 city in the whole country, in terms of where companies are starting and growing." Though he sees plenty of non-Mormon engines of Utah's growth, he points to the Mormon emphasis on entrepreneurship as a driving force, and to Mormon-supported Brigham Young University.

It is at BYU that the church runs its language institute, a kind of boot camp for missionaries. It can handle 4,000 trainees at a time. BYU also capitalizes on the Mormon overseas experience in its business school curriculum. In some years, 75% of its M.B.A. candidates have been bilingual. Many are missionaries, already setting up importing or exporting business on the side.

"Our competitive advantage is language. We have to take advantage of this," says Lee Radebaugh, a BYU accounting professor who has set up an international management center.

unintended insult, and jeopardizing the business transaction. For example, according to one well-travelled business writer, "In Asia, a 'yes' answer to a question simply means the question is understood. It's the beginning of negotiations. In the Middle East, the response will probably be some version of 'God willing.'"[50] Live translations, translations of written documents and advertisements, and computer e-mail translations are helpful but plagued by accuracy problems.[51] Successful international managers tell us there is no adequate substitute for knowing the local language (see International OB).

General Guidelines for Effective Cross-Cultural Communication   Regardless of which cross-cultural communication option is used, four guidelines from international management scholars Philip R Harris and Robert T Moran are useful:

- *No matter how hard one tries, one cannot avoid communicating.* All behaviour in human interaction has a message and communicates something. Body language communicates as well as our activity or inactivity, the colour of our skin, the colour of our clothes, or the gift we give. All behaviour is communication because all behaviour contains a message, whether intended or not.

- *Communication does not necessarily mean understanding.* Even when two individuals agree that they are communicating or talking to each other, it does not mean that they have understood each other. Understanding occurs when the two individuals have the same interpretation of the symbols being used in the communication process whether the symbols be words or gestures.

- *Communication is irreversible.* One cannot take back one's communication (although sometimes one wishes that he or she could). However, one can explain, clarify, or restate one's message. Once one has communicated, it is part of his or her experience, and it influences present and future meanings. Disagreeing with a Saudi Arabian in the presence of others is an "impoliteness" in the Arab world and may be difficult to remedy.

- *Communication occurs in a context.* One cannot ignore the context of communication that occurs at a certain time, in some place, using certain media. Such factors have message value and give meaning to the communicators. For example, a business conversation with a French manager in France during an evening meal may be inappropriate.[52]

For the most of the past decade, business experts have been promoting the notion of the "international manager" as an inevitable consequence of the increasingly global nature of markets and products.

The reality has not always matched the rhetoric. In spite of the popularity of international comparisons in setting executive pay, the number of senior managers who can move their skills between markets is relatively small.

High-profile examples of executives heading foreign companies, such as Lindsay Owen Jones, the Welsh-born chairman of France's L'Oréal, Bob Bauman, US-born chairman of British Aerospace, and Gerald Hampel, the Austrian managing director of Same, the Italian tractor manufacturer, are rare.

Moreover, many companies that claim to have an international culture do not practise what they preach. A study of 12 leading multinationals by the Massachusetts-based International Consortium for Executive Development Research, a think-tank, suggested that most multinationals are far less globally-minded than they think they are. The companies put relatively less emphasis on issues such as managing a culturally diverse workforce, managing alliances with other companies, and living outside one's home country.

Nonetheless, the creation of "cross-cultural" employees is seen as an increasingly important goal for many companies operating in overseas markets. As a result, they hope to promote the exchange of ideas, expertise, and skills, improve the management of cross-border alliances and create the same quality standards around the world.

Practical difficulties of overcoming cultural barriers are being taken increasingly seriously, according to Kevin Barham of IOC Ashridge, a consultancy and research group based in France. This interest stems largely from companies' experiences with international partnerships in the late 1980s, which often foundered over cultural, rather than strategic, issues.

Research has underlined the difficulties of working with people from different national cultures. Studies by Fons Trompenaars show the difficulty of transferring management techniques between countries.

For instance, performance-related pay often fails in countries such as France, Germany, Italy, and large parts of Asia, where people tend not to accept the notion that "individual members of the group should excel in a way that reveals the shortcomings of other members." Feedback sessions may motivate US managers, but German managers find them "enforced admissions of failure." Trompenaars' research findings are further explored on page 102.

Some management ideas do not translate into other languages. The term "coaching," "brainstorming" and even "teamwork" are either meaningless or have different connotations in different countries.

Even the most international of companies admit the difficulties in getting different nationalities to work well together. "Multinational teams do not happen naturally—on the contrary, the human inclination is to stick to its own kind," according to Percy Barnevik. He headed ABB, Europe's largest electrical engineering group, which is a textbook example of a multinational business with more than four nationalities on its supervisory board and more than 20 at group headquarters.

The question of how to deal with these issues was aired recently by a group of companies, including BP, the oil major; The Thompson Corporation, the Canadian travel and publishing group; and Marks and Spencer, the retailer, in a seminar organized by the Management Training Partnership, a UK-based training company.

The creation of an international manager has, they agreed, become far more complicated than it used to be in the days when expatriates were sent out "to colonize the world." The task now involves greater sensitivity and cultural awareness than it did in the days when managers sent out by head office felt they could simply tell the local people what to do.

International experience does not by itself guarantee an international perspective or the ability to work effectively in different cultures. Nor do training courses represent a panacea, although they play an important part in teaching managers about cultural diversity and the merits of cross-cultural awareness.

"A lot of it is about the personal drive to succeed which is very difficult to train," says David McGill, head of individual learning and development at BP. "Making someone aware of cultural diversity is something that has to start at day one when they join the company."

Language skills account for part of the success of managers from smaller countries. But linguistic abilities, although important, are not the only skill needed by a cross-cultural manager. "We have had some people from the UK who go to a continental subsidiary with hardly any knowledge of the language, but who manage to communicate," says Nicole Huyghens, a Belgian-born manager who works in Marks & Spencer's Paris office. "It is an attitude of mind. Humility is an important quality," she says. "You have to accept you are not going to be as confident or competent as you are in your own environment."

This need to adapt to the culture and values of a foreign country, while representing the culture and values of the parent company can be challenging, says Brockmann. "You cannot go completely native, but cannot be totally rigid," he says.

Finding these footloose, sensitive, and resilient individuals is not easy. There is, for instance, increasing resistance to being moved from employees whose spouses have their own careers.[53]

Practical Insights from Cross-Cultural Management Research

Cross-cultural management
Understanding and teaching behavioural patterns in different cultures.

Nancy Adler, an international OB specialist at Canada's McGill University, has offered the following introductory definition. "**Cross-cultural management** studies the behaviour of people in organizations around the world and trains people to work in organizations with employee and client populations from several cultures."[54] Inherent in this definition are three steps: (1) understand cultural differences, (2) identify culturally appropriate management practices, and (3) teach cross-cultural management lessons. The cross-cultural studies discussed in this section contribute to all three.

The Hofstede–Bond Stream of Research

Instructive insights surfaced in the mid-1980s when the results of two very different cross-cultural management studies were merged. The first study was conducted under the guidance of Dutch researcher Geert Hofstede. Canadian Michael Harris Bond, at the Chinese University of Hong Kong, was a key researcher in the second study. What follows is a brief overview of each study, a discussion of the combined results, and a summary of important practical implications.

The Two Studies   Hofstede's study is a classic in the annals of cross-cultural management research.[55] He drew his data for that study from a collection of 116,000 attitude surveys administered to IBM employees worldwide between 1967 and 1973. Respondents to the attitude survey, which also asked questions on cultural values and beliefs, included IBM employees from 72 countries. Fifty-three cultures eventually were analysed and contrasted according to four cultural dimensions. Hofstede's database was unique, not only because of its large size, but also because it allowed him to isolate cultural effects. If his subjects had not performed similar jobs in different countries for the same company, no such control would have been possible. Cross-cultural comparisons were made along the first four dimensions listed in Table 4–2, power distance, individualism–collectivism,[56] masculinity–femininity, and uncertainty avoidance.

Bond's study was much smaller, involving a survey of 100 (50 per cent women) students from 22 countries and 5 continents. The survey instrument was the Chinese Value Survey (CVS), based on the Rokeach Value Survey.[57] The CVS also tapped four cultural dimensions. Three corresponded to Hofstede's first three in Table 4–2. Hofstede's fourth cultural dimension, uncertainty avoidance, was not measured by the CVS. Instead, Bond's study isolated the fifth cultural dimension in Table 4–2. It was eventually renamed long-term versus short-term orientation to reflect how strongly a person believes in the long-

---

Table 4–2   Key Cultural Dimensions in the Hofstede–Bond Studies

Power distance: How much do people expect inequality in social institutions (e.g., family, work organizations, government)?

Individualism–collectivism: How loose or tight is the bond between individuals and societal groups?

Masculinity–femininity: To what extent do people embrace competitive masculine traits (e.g., success, assertiveness and performance) or nurturing feminine traits (e.g., solidarity, personal relationships, service, quality of life)?

Uncertainty avoidance: To what extent do people prefer structured versus unstructured situations?

Long-term versus short-term orientation (Confucian values): To what extent are people oriented towards the future by saving and being persistent versus being oriented towards the present and past by respecting tradition and meeting social obligations?

Source: Adapted from discussion in G Hofstede, "Cultural Constraints in Management Theories," *Academy of Management Executive*, February 1993, pp 81–94.

term thinking promoted by the teachings of the Chinese philosopher Confucius (551–479 BC). According to an update by Hofstede: "On the long-term side one finds values oriented towards the future, like thrift (saving) and persistence. On the short-term side one finds values rather oriented towards the past and present, like respect for tradition and fulfilling social obligations."[58] Importantly, one may embrace Confucian long-term values without knowing a thing about Confucius.

East Meets West   By merging the two studies, a serious flaw in each was corrected. Namely, Hofstede's study had an inherent Anglo-European bias, and Bond's study had a built-in Asian bias. How would cultures compare if viewed through the overlapping lenses of the two studies? Hofstede and Bond were able to answer that question because 18 countries in Bond's study overlapped the 53 countries in Hofstede's sample.[59] Table 4–3 lists the countries scoring highest on each of the five cultural dimensions. (Countries earning between 67 and 100 points on a 0 to 100 relative ranking scale qualified as "high" for Table 4–3.)

Practical Lessons   Individually, and together, the Hofstede and Bond studies yielded the following useful lessons for international managers:

1. Due to varying cultural values, management theories and practices need to be adapted to the local culture. This is particularly true for made-in-America management theories (e.g., Maslow's need hierarchy theory) and Japanese management practices.[60]

2. High long-term orientation was the only one of the five cultural dimensions to correlate positively with national economic growth.

3. Industrious cultural values are a necessary but insufficient condition for economic growth. Markets and a supportive political climate also are required to create the right mix.

4. Cultural arrogance is a luxury individuals and nations can no longer afford in a global economy.

Table 4–3   Countries Scoring the Highest in the Hofstede–Bond Studies

HIGH POWER DISTANCE	HIGH INDIVIDUALISM	HIGH MASCULINITY	HIGH UNCERTAINTY AVOIDANCE	HIGH LONG-TERM ORIENTATION*
Philippines	United States	Japan	Japan	Hong Kong
India	Australia		Korea	Taiwan
Singapore	Great Britain		Brazil	Japan
Brazil	Netherlands		Pakistan	Korea
Hong Kong	Canada		Taiwan	
	New Zealand			
	Sweden			
	Germany**			

*Originally called Confucian Dynamism.
**Former West Germany

Source: Adapted from Exhibit 2 in G Hofstede and M H Bond, "The Confucius Connection: From Cultural Roots to Economic Growth," *Organizational Dynamics*, Spring 1988, pp 12–13.

Trompenaars's Forms of Relating to Other People

In his study on cultural differences between 28 countries, Fons Trompenaars has developed five relevant dimensions:[61]

1 Universalism–Particularism   Universalism implies that what is good and right can be applied everywhere (abstract societal codes). Typical rule-based cultures are Anglo-Saxon and Scandinavian countries, e.g., The Netherlands, Germany, and Switzerland. Particularist cultures, on the other hand, are more friendship-based. What counts are relationships and unique circumstances. "I must protect the people around me, no matter what the rules say." Typical particularist countries are Russia, Spain, and France.

In practice, we use both judgements. Sometimes universalist rules have no answers to particularist problems. Hence, cooperation between people from both cultures will sometimes cause serious problems: universalists will, for example, accuse particularists of corruption when they "help" a friend, or a family member, whereas universalists will be said to be selfish if they refuse to help an acquaintance. A very detailed contract, drawn by a universalist specifying every legal detail, is seen by the particularist as "if he is not trusted as a business partner." The particularist will first build a relationship with his business partner. Once mutual trust is established, a particularist considers it is not necessary to draw up a detailed contract: the relationship built is the guarantee. (See Table 4–4.)

2 Individualism–Collectivism   Individualist countries, such as the Netherlands and Sweden, are oriented on one self. Collectivist countries are rather group-oriented. Think about the typical family-minded Frenchman.

Regarding oneself as an individual or as part of a group has serious influences on negotiations, on decision-making and on motivation. Pay-for-performance, for example, is welcomed in the USA, the Netherlands, and the UK. More collectivist cultures, such as France, most parts of Asia and Germany, are very reluctant to accept the Anglo-Saxon pay-for-performance systems. They take offence at the idea that one person's performance is related to another's deficiencies. In negotiations and decision making, collectivists will take no decision without prior and elaborate discussions with the home front. Individualists, however, will usually take a decision on their own without prior consent of their colleagues or bosses. In motivation, too, individualism and collectivism play an important role. Individualists work for money rewards, collectivists rather for positive reward and support from their colleagues. (See Table 4–5.)

3 Neutral–Emotional   Showing or not showing our emotion is culturally imbedded. People from countries such as northern America, Europe, and Japan will hardly express their feelings in a first business contact, whereas people from southern countries, like Italy and France are very affective and open. Business contacts between both cultures may cause numerous misunderstandings. Neutral people are considered to have no feelings, emotional people are considered as being out of control. (See Table 4–6.)

Table 4 – 4   Business Areas Affected by Universalism/Particularism

UNIVERSALISM	PARTICULARISM
Focus is more on rules than on relationships	Focus is more on relationships than on rules
Legal contracts are readily drawn up	Legal contracts are readily modified
A trustworthy person is one who honours his or her "word" or contract	A trustworthy person is the one who honours changing circumstances
There is only one truth or reality, that which has been agreed to	There are several perspectives on reality relative to each participant
A deal is a deal	Relationships evolve

Table 4–5   Business Areas Affected by Individualism/Collectivism

INDIVIDUALISM	COLLECTIVISM
More frequent use of "I" and "me"	More frequent use of "we"
In negotiations, decisions typically made on the spot by a representative	Decisions typically referred back by delegate to the organization
People ideally achieve alone and assume personal responsibility	People ideally achieve in groups which assume joint responsibility
Holidays taken in pairs, or even alone	Holiday taken in organized groups or extended family

4 Specific–Diffuse   In specific cultures home and business are strictly separated, contacts are on a contractual basis. In more diffuse cultures both worlds are interrelated, the entire person is involved. In specific-oriented cultures, the relationship you have with a person depends on the common point you have with that person at the very moment. If you are specialized in a certain area you will have the advantage over that subject. If, on the other hand, the other person has more knowledge in another area, the roles will be reversed. In diffuse countries, such as France, one's authority permeates each area of life. In such cultures, everything is connected to everything. In negotiations, for example, your business partner may ask for your background. (See Table 4–7.)

Table 4–6   Business Areas Affected by Neutral/Affective Relationships

EMOTIONAL	NEUTRAL
Show immediate reactions either verbally or nonverbally	Opaque emotional state
Express face and body signals	Do not readily express what they think or feel
At ease with physical contact	Embarrassed or awkward at public displays of emotions
Raise voice readily	Discomfort with physical contact outside "private" circle
	Subtle in verbal and nonverbal expressions

Table 4–7   Business Areas Affected by Specific/Diffuse Relationships

SPECIFIC	DIFFUSE
More "open" public space, more closed "private" space	More "closed" public space, but, once in, more "open" private space
Appears direct, open and extravert	Appears indirect, closed and introvert
"To the point" and often appears abrasive Highly mobile	Often evades issues and "beats about the bush"
Separates work and private life	Low mobility
Varies approach to fit circumstances especially with use of titles (e.g., Herr Doktor Müller at work is Hans in social enviroments or in certain business meetings)	Work and private life are closely linked Consistent in approach, especially with use of titles (e.g., Herr Doktor Müller remains Herr Doktor Müller in any setting)

5 Achievement–Ascription   In achievement-oriented cultures, such as France, emphasis is put on what you have accomplished in ascription-oriented cultures, your person counts. Different countries confer status on individuals in different ways. Anglo-Saxons, for example, will ascribe status to reasons of achievement.

The following situation illustrates that cultural dfferences can lead to serious misunderstandings in business: a Danish paint manufacturing company wanted a large English firm to represent it in Britain. Having received encouraging signals on a first visit, the Danish managers came over a second time and were surprised by the complete lack of interest. Yet they were still not turned down. The British "no" was finally received in a telex of three lines after a total of three visits and much wasted advance planning from the Danish end. Why didn't the English say "no" at the start?[62]

A Contingency Model for Cross-Cultural Leadership

If a manager has a favourite leadership style in his or her own culture, will that style be equally appropriate in another culture? According to a recently proposed model that built upon Hofstede's work, the answer is "not necessarily."[63] Four leadership styles—directive, supportive, participative, and achievement—were matched with variations of three of Hofstede's cultural dimensions. The dimensions used were power distance, individualism–collectivism, and uncertainty avoidance.

By combining this model with Hofstede's and Bond's findings, we derived the useful contingency model for cross-cultural leadership in Table 4–8. Participative leadership turned out to be culturally appropriate for all 18 countries. Importantly, this does not mean that the participative style is necessarily the best style of leadership in cross-cultural management. It simply has broad applicability. One exception surfaced in a more recent study in Russia's largest textile mill. The researchers found that both rewarding good performance with American-made goods and motivating performance with feedback and positive reinforcement improved output. But an employee participation programme actually made performance worse. This may have been due to the Russian's lack of faith

Table 4–8   A Contingency Model for Cross-Cultural Leadership

| COUNTRY | Most Culturally Appropriate Leadership Behaviours | | | |
	DIRECTIVE	SUPPORTIVE	PARTICIPATIVE	ACHIEVEMENT
Australia		X	X	X
Brazil	X		X	
Canada		X	X	X
France	X		X	
Germany*		X	X	X
Great Britain		X	X	X
Hong Kong	X	X	X	X
India	X		X	X
Italy	X	X	X	
Japan	X	X	X	
Korea	X	X	X	
Netherlands		X	X	X
New Zealand			X	X
Pakistan	X	X	X	
Philippines	X	X	X	X
Sweden			X	X
Taiwan	X	X	X	
United States		X	X	X

*Former West Germany.

Source: Adapted in part from C A Rodrigues, "The Situation and National Culture as Contingencies for Leadership Behaviour: Two Conceptual Models," in *Advances in International Comparative Management* vol. 5, ed S B Prasad (Greenwich, CT: JAI Press, 1990), pp 51–68; and G Hofstede and M H Bond, "The Confucius Connection: From Cultural Roots to Economic Growth," *Organizational Dynamics,* Spring 1988, pp 4–21.

in participative schemes, which had been found to be untrustworthy in the past.[64]

Also of note, with the exception of France, the directive style appears to be culturally inappropriate in North America, northern Europe, Australia, and New Zealand. Some locations, such as Hong Kong and the Philippines, require great leadership versatility. Leadership needs to be matched to the prevailing cultural climate. (We will discuss leadership further in Chapter 16.)

Interpersonal Conflict-Handling Styles

In a cross-cultural study of Jordanian, Turkish, and US managers, the collaborative (problem-solving) style of handling interpersonal conflict emerged as the preferred option in all three cultures. Beyond that there was general disagreement about which backup styles were most appropriate.[65] One practical lesson from this study is that even when we find commonalities across cultures, care needs to be taken not to gloss over underlying differences. (Conflict management is covered in detail in Chapter 11.)

Preparing Employees for Successful Foreign Assignments

As mentioned at the opening of this chapter, foreign experience has become a necessary stepping stone on the path to top management. As the reach of global companies continues to grow, many opportunities for living and working in foreign countries will arise.

Why Do US Managers, Compared to Those from Europe and Japan, Have a Comparatively High Failure Rate in Foreign Assignments?

Expatriate

Anyone living or working in a foreign country.

As we use the term here, **expatriate** refers to anyone living and/or working outside their home country. Hence, they are said to be expatriated when transferred to another country and repatriated when transferred back home. Cross-cultural expert Rosalie L Tung, drawing upon her own and others' research, concluded that 30 per cent of the foreign transfers by US multinational companies turn out to be mistakes. The figures for European and Japanese companies are generally below 5 per cent.[66] A "mistake," in this context, means the employee does not perform adequately for the full term of his or her foreign assignment.

Research has uncovered specific reasons for the failure of US expatriate managers. Listed in decreasing order of frequency, the seven most common reasons are as follows:

1. The manager's spouse cannot adjust to new physical or cultural surroundings.

2. The manager cannot adapt to new physical or cultural surroundings.

3. Family problems.

4. The manager is emotionally immature.

5. The manager cannot cope with foreign duties.

6. The manager is not technically competent.

7. The manager lacks the proper motivation for a foreign assignment.[67]

Collectively, *family and personal adjustment problems,* not technical competence, are the main stumbling block for American managers working in foreign countries.

This conclusion is reinforced by the results of a recent survey that asked 72 human resource managers at multinational corporations to identify the most important success factor in a foreign assignment. "Nearly 35 per cent said cultural adaptability: patience, flexibility, and tolerance for others' beliefs. Only 22 per cent of them listed technical and management skills."[68] Consider what happened to Gabriëlle Rosenbaum:

In the beginning, she was thrilled with the idea of her husband's foreign assignment for Philips. As for many Dutch men and women, a foreign assignment was equal to exotic resorts, sunshine, swimming pools, parties, and recreation. Good life was in store for her and her family. Until she, her husband, and their three sons left for Pakistan, where they were confronted with the everyday life of another, Islamic culture. Other habits, norms, and values which lead to serious misunderstandings. How could she reprimand her children in a public place like a restaurant? Her three sons were a gift from God, weren't they? In their next assignment, the empoverished metropolis of Bombay, too, misunderstanding after misunderstanding occurred. At home, in The Netherlands, she had treated people equally, regardless of their position. Why hadn't she realized how confusing such an attitude could be in India, where society is based on castes and contrasts? "In Bombay in particular I realized how badly I had been prepared for this assignment. For my husband it was an enormous challenge to go abroad. He had his job to do, whereas I was left on my own, nobody had cared how I would manage with the three children."[69]

A recent study on differences between Japanese, American, and European multinationals in the area of international human resource management concluded that Japanese companies have international human resource practices that are relatively more ethnocentric than are those of American and European companies, and they do tend to experience more international human resource management problems. The study also concluded that the less ethnocentric a firm's international policies and practices, the less likely it is to experience international human resource management problems.[70]

The Global Manager

On any given day in today's global economy, a manager can interact with colleagues from several different countries or cultures. For instance, at PolyGram, the British music company, the top 33 managers are from 15 different countries.[71] If they are to be effective, managers in such multicultural situations need to develop *global* skills (see Table 4–9). Developing skilled managers who move comfortably from culture to culture takes time. Consider, for example, this comment by the head of Gillette, who wants twice as many global managers on the payroll. Foreign business accounts for 70 per cent of Gillette's annual sales of 6.5 billion ecus. "We could try to hire the best and the brightest, but it's the experience with Gillette that we need. About half of our [expatriates] are now on their fourth country—that kind of experience. It takes 10 years to make the kind of Gillette manager I'm talking about."[72]

Importantly, these global skills will help managers in culturally diverse countries do a more effective job on a day-to-day basis.

Avoiding OB Trouble Spots in Foreign Assignments

Finding the right person (often along with a supportive and adventurous family) for a foreign position is a complex, time-consuming, and costly process.[73] For our purposes, it is sufficient to narrow the focus to common OB trouble spots in the foreign assignment cycle. As illustrated in Figure 4–5, the first and last stages of the cycle occur at home.

Table 4–9	Global Skills for Global Managers	
SKILL	**DESCRIPTION**
Global perspective	Broaden focus from one or two countries to a global business perspective.
Cultural responsiveness	Become familiar with many cultures.
Appreciate cultural synergies	Learn the dynamics of multicultural situations.
Cultural adaptability	Be able to live and work effectively in many different cultures.
Cross-cultural communication	Engage in cross-cultural interaction every day, whether at home or in a foreign country.
Cross-cultural collaboration	Work effectively in multicultural teams where everyone is equal.
Acquire broad foreign experience	Move up the career ladder by going from one foreign country to another, instead of taking frequent home-country assignments.

Source: Adapted from N J Adler and S Bartholomew, "Managing Globally Competent People," *Academy of Management Executive,* August 1992, Table 1, pp 52–65.

Figure 4 – 5   The Foreign Assignment Cycle (With OB Trouble Spots)

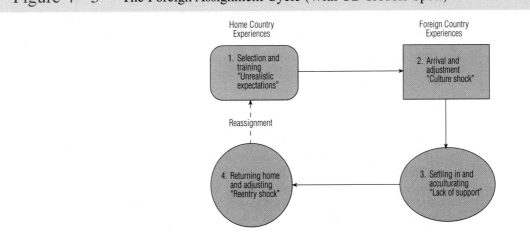

The middle two stages occur in the foreign or host country. Each stage hides an OB-related trouble spot that needs to be anticipated and neutralized. Otherwise, the bill for another failed foreign assignment will grow.

Avoiding Unrealistic Expectations with Cross-Cultural Training   Realistic job previews (RJPs) have proven effective at bringing people's unrealistic expectations about a pending job assignment down to earth by providing a realistic balance of good and bad news. People with realistic expectations tend to quit less often and be more satisfied than those with unrealistic expectations. RJPs are a must for future expatriates. In addition, cross-cultural training is required.

Cross-cultural training is any type of structured experience designed to help employees adjust to a foreign culture. Although costly, companies believe cross-cultural training is less expensive than failed foreign assignments. Programmes vary widely in type and also in rigour.[74] Of course, the greater the difficulty, the greater the time and expense:

- *Easiest.* Predeparture training is limited to informational materials, including books, lectures, films, and videos.

- *Moderately difficult.* Experiential training is conducted through case studies, role playing, assimilators (simulated intercultural incidents), and introductory language instruction.

- *Most difficult.* Departing employees are given some combination of the preceding methods plus comprehensive language instruction and field experience in the target culture. As an example of the latter, PepsiCo Inc. transfers "about 25 young foreign managers a year to the US for one-year assignments in bottling plants."[75]

Which approach is the best? Research to date does not offer a final answer. One study involving US employees in South Korea led the researcher to recommend a *combination* of informational and experiential predeparture training.[76] As a general rule of thumb, the more rigorous the cross-cultural training, the better. Our personal experience with teaching OB to foreign students both in the US and abroad reminds us that there really is no substitute for an intimate knowledge of the local language and culture.[77] This statement is confirmed by John Mole:[78]

Almost everyone interviewed including those interviews given by people working in Denmark and The Netherlands, recommended that anyone embarking on a cross-border relationship should learn the relevant language. Even if the initial contacts speak a second language you soon have to deal with those who do not.

Avoiding Culture Shock   Have you ever been in a totally unfamiliar situation and felt disoriented and perhaps a bit frightened? If so, you already know something about

Culture shock

Anxiety and doubt caused by an overload of new expectations and cues.

culture shock. According to anthropologists, culture shock involves anxiety and doubt caused by an overload of unfamiliar expectations and social cues.[79] First-year students often experience a variation of culture shock. An expatriate manager, or family member, may be thrown off balance by an avalanche of strange sights, sounds, and behaviours. Among them may be unreadable road signs, strange-tasting food, inability to use your left hand for social activities (in Islamic countries, the left hand is the toilet hand), or failure to get a laugh with your sure-fire joke. For the expatriate manager trying to concentrate on the fine details of a business negotiation, culture shock is more than an embarrassing inconvenience. It is a disaster! Like the confused first-year student who quits and goes home, culture-shocked employees often panic and go home early.

Even North Americans coming to work in the UK need some kind of cultural awareness programme. Despite the common language and history, US employees nevertheless experience a culture shock. Problems range from smaller fridges or having to buy drinks on your birthday to lack of discipline in the office.[80]

The best defence against culture shock is comprehensive cross-cultural training, including intensive language study. Once again, the only way to pick up subtle—yet important—social cues is via the local language.

Support During the Foreign Assignment   Especially during the first six months, when everything is so new to the expatriate, a support system needs to be in place. *Host-country sponsors,* assigned to individual managers or families, are recommended because they serve as "cultural seeing-eye dogs." In a foreign country, where even the smallest errand can turn into an utterly exhausting production, sponsors can get things done quickly because they know the cultural and geographical territory.

Dutch Royal Shell founded two organizations which are charged with providing practical information on the living conditions abroad: a network of Shell-families for Shell-families. *Outpost* tries to introduce new expats to existing expats in the same area. A *Spouse Employment Consultant* provides information on the working conditions, the recognition of degrees, work permits, etc.[81]

Avoiding Reentry Shock   Before reading on, consider the case of Trevor Doust:

Trevor Doust is not angry or resentful, just a bit bewildered. Last year he was the high-flying executive vice-president of a joint venture company set up in Japan by John Crane International, the world's leading manufacturer of engineered sealing products. Today, at 50, he is back in the UK and unemployed. He didn't do anything wrong. His only mistake was being out of touch on the other side of the world when his company decided to rationalise and make changes at the top. "If you are reasonably high up the tree," says Doust, "then even in a very large corporation there's a very small group back at the ranch who can be of any use to you. If they change while you're away the new guys don't know you, and if at the same time they retrench a bit you have got a real problem."[82]

Strange as it may seem, many otherwise successful expatriate managers encounter their first major difficulty only after their foreign assignment is over. Why? Returning to one's native culture is taken for granted because it seems so routine and ordinary. But having adjusted to another country's way of doing things for an extended period of time can put one's own culture and surroundings in a strange new light. Three areas for potential reentry shock are work, social activities, and general environment (e.g., politics, climate, transportation, food).

Work-related adjustments were found to be a major problem for samples of repatriated Finnish, Japanese, and American employees.[83] Upon being repatriated, a 12-year veteran of one US company said: "Our organizational culture was turned upside down. We now have a different strategic focus, different 'tools' to get the job done, and different buzzwords to make it happen. I had to learn a whole new corporate 'language.'"[84] Reentry shock can be reduced through employee career counselling and home-country sponsors. Simply being aware of the problem of reentry shock is a big step towards effectively dealing with it.[85] A survey of more than 120 "returnees" by Dr Nick Forster of Cardiff Business School showed that many of them faced difficulties in terms of their career prospects, psychological well-being, and general adaptation to life back home.[86]

Overall, the key to a successful foreign assignment is making it a well-integrated link in a career chain rather than treating it as an isolated adventure.

Summary of Key Concepts

1. *Explain how societal culture and organizational culture combine to influence on-the-job behaviour.* Culture involves the taken-for-granted assumptions collections of people have about how they should think, act, and feel. Key aspects of societal culture, such as customs and language, are brought to work by the individual. Working together, societal and organizational culture influence the person's values, ethics, attitudes, and expectations.

2. *Define ethnocentrism, and distinguish between high-context and low-context cultures.* Ethnocentrism is the belief that one's native culture, language, and ways of doing things are superior to all others. People from low-context cultures infer relatively less from situational cues and extract more meaning from spoken and written words. In high-context cultures, such as China and Japan, managers prefer slow negotiations and trust-building meetings, which tend to frustrate low-context northern Europeans and North Americans who prefer to get right down to business.

3. *Explain the difference between monochronic and polychronic cultures.* People in monochronic cultures are schedule driven and prefer to do one thing at a time. To them, time is like money; it is spent wisely or wasted. In polychronic cultures, there is a tendency to do many things at once and to perceive time as flexible and multidimensional. Polychronic people view monochronic people as being too preoccupied with time.

4. *Discuss the cultural implications of interpersonal space and language.* Anthropologist Edward Hall coined the term proxemics to refer to the study of cultural expectations about interpersonal space. Asians and Latin Americans like to stand close [15–30cm (6–12in)] during business conversations, while North Americans and northern Europeans prefer a larger interpersonal distance [about 1m (3–4ft)]. Conflicting expectations about proper interpersonal distance can create awkward cross-cultural situations. Research uncovered a high degree of agreement about semantic elements across eight cultures.

5. *Describe the practical lessons from the Hofstede–Bond cross-cultural studies.* According to the Hofstede–Bond cross-cultural management studies, caution needs to be exercised when transplanting management theories and practices from one culture to another. Also, long-term orientation was the only one of five cultural dimensions in the Hofstede–Bond studies to correlate positively with national economic growth.

6. *Explain Trompenaars' five dimensions of cultural differences.* Fons Trompenaars distinguishes the following five dimensions, *Universalism–particularism:* what is good and what is bad. *Individualism–collectivism:* being self-oriented or not. *Neutral–emotional:* showing or not showing one's emotion. *Specific–diffuse:* whether private and work relations are strictly separated or not. *Achievement–ascription:* emphasis on what you have achieved or on your person.

7. *Specify why US managers, compared to European and Japanese, have a comparatively high failure rate in foreign assignments, and identify skills needed by today's global managers.* American expatriates are troubled by family and personal adjustment problems. Experts say global managers need the following skills: global perspective, cultural responsiveness, appreciation of cultural synergies, cultural adaptability, cross-cultural communication, cross-cultural collaboration, and broad foreign experience.

8. *Discuss the importance of cross-cultural training relative to the foreign assignment cycle.* The foreign assignment cycle has four stages: selection and training, arrival and adjustment, settling in and acculturating, and returning home and adjusting. Cross-cultural training, preferably combining informational and experiential predeparture sessions, can help expatriates avoid two OB trouble spots: unrealistic expectations and culture shock. There are no adequate substitutes for knowing the local language and culture.

Discussion Questions

1. What are your expectations about being affected by the global economy?

2. Regarding your cultural awareness, how would you describe the prevailing culture in your country to a stranger from another land?

3. What are your personal experiences with ethnocentrism and cross-cultural dealings? What lessons have you learned?

4. Why are people from high-context cultures such as China and Japan likely to be misunderstood by low-context Westerners?

5. Based on your score on the Polychronic Attitude Index, are you relatively monochronic or polychronic? What difficulties do you encounter because of this cultural tendency?

6. In your view, what is the most important lesson for

global managers from the Hofstede–Bond studies? Explain.

7. Based on your personal experience with one or more of the countries listed in Table 4–8, do you agree or disagree with the leadership profiles? Explain.

8. What needs to be done to improve the success rate of managers in foreign assignments?

9. Which of the global manager skills in Table 4–9 do you need to develop? Explain.

10. What is your personal experience with culture shock? Which of the OB trouble spots in Figure 4–5 do you believe is the greatest threat to expatriate employee success? Explain.

Personal Awareness and Growth Exercise

How Do Your Work Goals Compare Internationally?

Objectives

1. To increase your cross-cultural awareness.
2. To see how your own work goals compare internationally.

Introduction

In today's multicultural global economy, it is a mistake to assume everyone wants the same things from the job as you do. This exercise provides a "window" on the world of work goals.

Instructions

Below is a list of 11 goals potentially attainable in the workplace. In terms of your own personal preferences, rank the goals from 1 to 11 (1 = Most important; 11 = Least important). After you have ranked all 11 work goals, compare your list with the national samples under the heading Survey Results. These national samples represent cross-sections of employees from all levels and all major occupational groups. (Please complete your ranking now, before looking at the national samples.)

How important are the following in your work life?

RANK	WORK GOALS
_____	A lot of opportunity to *learn* new things
_____	Good *interpersonal relations* (supervisors, co-workers)
_____	Good opportunity for upgrading or *promotion*
_____	*Convenient* work *hours*
_____	A lot of *variety*
_____	*Interesting work* (work that you really like)
_____	Good *job security*

_____	A *good match* between your job requirements and your abilities and experience
_____	Good *pay*
_____	Good *physical working conditions* (such as light, temperature, cleanliness, low noise level)
_____	A lot of *autonomy* (you decide how to do your work)[87]

QUESTIONS FOR DISCUSSION

1. Which national profile of work goals most closely matches your own? Is this what you expected, or not?

2. Are you surprised by any of the rankings in the four national samples? Explain.

3. What sorts of motivational/leadership adjustments would a manager have to make when moving among the four countries?

Survey Results[88]

Ranking of Work Goals by Country

(1 = Most important; 11 = Least important)

WORK GOALS	UNITED STATES	BRITAIN	GERMANY*	JAPAN
Interesting work	1	1	3	2
Pay	2	2	1	5
Job security	3	3	2	4
Match between person and job	4	6	5	1
Opportunity to learn	5	8	9	7
Variety	6	7	6†	9
Interpersonal relations	7	4	4	6
Autonomy	8	10	8	3
Convenient work hours	9	5	6†	8
Opportunity for promotion	10	11	10	11
Working conditions	11	9	11	10

*Former West Germany.
†Tie.

Group Exercise

Looking into a Cultural Mirror

Objectives

1. To generate group discussion about the impact of societal culture on managerial style.
2. To increase your cultural awareness.
3. To discuss the idea of a distinct (name of your country) style of management.

Introduction

A time-tested creativity technique involves "taking something familiar and making it strange." This technique can yield useful insights by forcing us to take a close look at things we tend to take for granted. In the case of this group exercise, the focus of your attention will be mainstream cultural tendencies in your country (or any other country you or your instructor may select) and management. A 15-minute, small-group session will be followed by brief oral presentations and a general class discussion. Total time required is about 35 to 45 minutes.

Instructions

Your instructor will divide your class randomly into small groups of five to eight. Half of the teams will be designated "red" teams, and half will be "green" teams. Each team will assign someone the role of recorder/presenter, examine the cultural traits listed below, and develop a cultural profile of "that particular country's management style." Members of each red team will explain the *positive* implications of each trait in their cultural profile. Green team members will explain the *negative* implications of the traits in their profiles.

During the brief oral presentations by the various teams, the instructor may jot down on the board or flip chart a composite cultural profile of the managers of that country. A general class discussion of positive and negative implications will follow. Note: Special effort should be made to solicit comments and observations from foreign students and students who have travelled and/or worked in other countries. Discussion needs to focus on the appropriateness or inappropriateness of the country's cultural style of management in other countries and cultures.

As "seed" for group discussion, here is a list of cultural traits identified by researchers[89] (feel free to supplement this short list, e.g., by the traits discussed in this chapter:)

- Individualistic.
- Independent.
- Aggressive/assertive/blunt.
- Competitive.
- Informal.
- Pragmatic/practical.
- Impatient.
- Materialistic.
- Unemotional/rational/objective.
- Hard working.

QUESTIONS FOR DISCUSSION

1. **Are you surprised by anything you have just heard? Explain.**

2. **Is there a distinct management style? Explain.**

3. **Can the management style be exported easily? If it needs to be modified, how?**

4. **What do managers need to do to be more effective at home and in foreign countries?**

Notes

1 Excerpted from "Thread by Thread," *Success,* April 1996, p 8. First appeared in Success magazine April 1996. Written by Kristin Dunlap Godsey. Reprinted with the permission of *Success* magazine. Copyright © 1997 by Success Holdings Company, L.L.C.

2 Based on J S Lublin, "An Overseas Stint Can Be a Ticket to the Top," *The Wall Street Journal,* January 29, 1996, pp B1, B5.

3 Excerpted from H Lancaster, "How You Can Learn to Feel at Home in Foreign-Based Firm," *The Wall Street Journal,* June 4, 1996, p B1. Reprinted by permission of *The Wall Street Journal* © 1996 Dow Jones & Company, Inc. All Rights Reserved Worldwide.

4 For helpful practical advice, see Table 1 in N J Adler and S Bartholomew, "Managing Globally Competent People," *Academy of Management Executive,* August 1992, pp 52–65. Also see T Morden, "International Culture and Management," *Management Decision,* no. 2, 1995, pp 16–21.

5 Based on M Mabry, "Pin a label on a Manager and Watch What Happens," *Newsweek,* May 14, 1990, p 43.

6 F Vuga, "In een moskee trek je je schoenen uit," *Knack,* December 16, 1987, pp 41–44.

7 Adapted from J Mole, *Mind Your Manners* (London: Nicholas Brealey Publishing, 1995).

8 M Mabry, op cit.

9 F Vuga, op cit.

10 J Mole, op cit.

11 E H Schein, *Organizational Culture and Leadership* (San Francisco: Jossey-Bass, 1985), p 9. Also see H H Baligh, "Components of Culture: Nature, Interconnections, and Relevance to the Decisions on the Organization Structure," *Management Science,* January 1994, pp 14–27.

12 For instructive discussion, see J S Black, H B Gregersen, and M E Mendenhall,

Global Assignments: Successfully Expatriating and Repatriating International Managers (San Francisco: Jossey-Bass, 1992), Ch. 2.

[13]F Trompenaars, *Riding the Waves of Culture: Understanding Diversity in Global Business* (Chicago: Irwin, 1994), p 8.

[14]"How Cultures Collide," *Psychology Today,* July 1976, p 69.

[15]See M Mendenhall, "A Painless Approach to Integrating 'International' into OB, HRM, and Management Courses," *Organizational Behavior Teaching Review,* no. 3 (1988–89), pp 23–27.

[16]See C L Sharma, "Ethnicity, National Integration, and Education in the Union of Soviet Socialist Republics," *The Journal of East and West Studies,* October 1989, pp 75–93; and R Brady and P Galuszka, "Shattered Dreams," *Business Week,* February 11, 1991, pp 38–42.

[17]J Main, "How to Go Global—and Why," *Fortune,* August 28, 1989, p 73.

[18]An excellent contrast between French and American values can be found in C Gouttefarde, "American Values in the French Workplace," *Business Horizons,* March–April 1996, pp 60–69.

[19]W D Marbach, "Quality: What Motivates American Workers?" *Business Week,* April 12, 1993, p 93.

[20]See G A Sumner, *Folkways* (New York: Ginn, 1906). Also see J G Weber, "The Nature of Ethnocentric Attribution Bias: Ingroup Protection or Enhancement?" *Journal of Experimental Social Psychology,* September 1994, pp 482–504.

[21]D A Heenan and H V Perlmutter, *Multinational Organization Development* (Reading, MA: Addison-Wesley, 1979), p 17.

[22]Data from R Kopp, "International Human Resource Policies and Practices in Japanese, European, and United States Multinationals," *Human Resource Management,* Winter 1994, pp 581–99.

[23]See "How Cultures Collide," pp 66–74, 97; and M Munter, "Cross-Cultural Communication for Managers," *Business Horizons,* May–June 1993, pp 69–78.

[24]T Stanger, "The Devil Across the Sea," *Newsweek,* November 14, 1994, p 24.

[25]D C Barnlund, "Public and Private Self in Communicating with Japan,"*Business Horizons,* March–April 1989, p 38.

[26]Y Richmond, *From Da to Yes. Understanding the Europeans* (Yarmouth: Intercultural Press, 1995)

[27]The concept of "face" and good tips on saving face in Far East Asia are presented in J A Reeder, "When West Meets East: Cultural Aspects of Doing Business in Asia," *Business Horizons,* January–February 1987, pp 69–74.

[28]The German management style is discussed in R Stewart, "German Management: A Challenge to Anglo-American Managerial Assumptions," *Business Horizons,* May–June 1996, pp 52–54.

[29]R Hill, *We Europeans* (Brussels: Europublications, 1995).

[30]Richmond, op. cit.

[31]Based on J Mole, op cit.

[32]See G Bonvillian and W A Nowlin, "Cultural Awareness: An Essential Element of Doing Business Abroad," *Business Horizons,* November–December 1994, pp 44–50; and K J Fedor and W B Werther, Jr., "Making Sense of Cultural Factors in International Alliances," *Organizational Dynamics,* Spring 1995, pp 33–48.

[33]This list is based on E T Hall, "The Silent Language in Overseas Business," *Harvard Business Review,* May–June 1960, pp 87–96; and R Knotts, "Cross-Cultural Management: Transformations and Adaptations," *Business Horizons,* January–February 1989, pp 29–33.

[34]A discussion of Japanese stereotypes in America can be found in L Smith, "Fear and Loathing of Japan," *Fortune,* February 26, 1990, pp 50–57. Diversity in so-called Eastern Bloc countries in Central and Eastern Europe is discussed in F Luthans, R R Patrick, and B C Luthans, "Doing Business in Central and Eastern Europe: Political, Economic, and Cultural Diversity," *Business Horizons,* September–October 1995, pp 9–16.

[35]Based on discussion in P R Harris and R T Moran, *Managing Cultural Differences,* 3rd ed (Houston: Gulf Publishing, 1991) p 12.

[36]See, for example, N R Mack, "Taking Apart the Ticking of Time," *The Christian Science Monitor,* August 29, 1991, p 17.

[37]For a comprehensive treatment of time, see J E McGrath and J R Kelly, *Time and Human Interaction: Toward a Social Psychology of Time* (New York: The Guilford Press, 1986). Also see L A Manrai and A K Manrai, "Effects of Cultural-Context, Gender, and Acculturation on Perceptions of Work versus Social/Leisure Time Usage," *Journal of Business Research,* February 1995, pp 115–28.

[38]A good discussion of doing business in Mexico is G K Stephens and C R Greer, "Doing Business in Mexico: Understanding Cultural Differences," *Organizational Dynamics,* Summer 1995, pp 39–55.

[39]R W Moore, "Time, Culture, and Comparative Management: A Review and Future Direction," in *Advances in International Comparative Management,* vol. 5, ed S B Prasad (Greenwich, CT: JAI Press, 1990), pp 7–8.

[40]See A C Bluedorn, C F Kaufman, and P M Lane, "How Many Things Do You Like to Do at Once? An Introduction to Monochronic and Polychronic Time," *Academy of Management Executive,* November 1992, pp 17–26.

[41]"Multitasking" term drawn from S McCartney, "The Breaking Point: Multitasking Technology Can Raise Stress and Cripple Productivity," *The Arizona Republic,* May 21, 1995, p D10.

[42]R Hill, op cit.

[43]J Mole, op cit., p 59.

[44]O Port, "You May Have To Reset This Watch—In a Million Years," *Business Week,* August 30, 1993, p 65.

[45]See E T Hall, *The Hidden Dimension* (Garden City, NY: Doubleday, 1966).

[46]"*How Cultures Collide,*" p 72.

[47]R Hill, op cit., p 351.

[48]D Raybeck and D Herrmann, "A Cross-Cultural Examination of Semantic Relations," *Journal of Cross-Cultural Psychology,* December 1990, p 470.

[49]Based on V Houlder, "Management: Cultural Exchanges," *Financial Times,* April 5, 1995, p 19.

[50]G A Michaelson, "Global Gold," *Success,* March 1996, p 16.

[51]Translation services are discussed in D Pianko, "Smooth Translations," *Management Review,* July 1996, p 10. CompuServe's on-line translation service for English, French, Spanish, and German is briefly discussed in L Alderman, "Step into Cyberspace with an E-mailbox," *Money,* April 1995, p 174.

[52]From P R Harris and R T Moran, *Managing Cultural Differences,* 4th ed, p 23.. Copyright 1996 © by Gulf Publishing Company. Used with permission. All rights reserved.

[53]V Houlder, "Culture Shock for Executives," *The Financial Times,* April 5, 1995, p 19.

[54]N J Adler, *International Dimensions of Organizational Behavior,* 2nd ed (Boston: PWS–Kent, 1991). Also see P C Earley and H Singh, "International and Intercultural Management Research: What's Next?" *Academy of Management Journal,* April 1995, pp 327–40; and M B Teagarden et al., "Toward a Theory of Comparative Management Research: An Idiographic Case Study of the Best International Human Resources Management Project," *Academy of Management Journal,* October 1995, pp 1261–87.

[55]For complete details, see G Hofstede, *Culture's Consequences: International Differences in Work-Related Values, abridged ed* (Newbury Park, CA: Sage Publications, 1984); G Hofstede, "The Interaction between National and Organizational Value Systems," *Journal of Management Studies,* July 1985, pp 347–57; and G Hofstede, "Management Scientists Are Human," *Management Science,* January 1994, pp 4–13. Also see V J Shackleton and A H Ali, "Work-Related Values of Managers: A Test of the Hofstede Model," *Journal of Cross-Cultural Psychology,* March 1990, pp 109–18; R Hodgetts, "A Conversation with Geert Hofstede," *Organizational Dynamics,* Spring 1993, 53–61; and P B Smith, S Dugan, and F Trompenaars, "National Culture and the Values of Organizational Employees: A Dimensional Analysis Across 43 Nations," *Journal of Cross-Cultural Psychology,* March 1996, pp 23–164.

[56]For recent research evidence on this key cultural variable, see P C Earley, "East Meets West Meets Mideast: Further Explorations of Collectivistic and Individualistic Work Groups," *Academy of Management Journal,* April 1993, pp 319–48; C H Hui, C Yee, and K L Eastman, "International Replication Note: The Relationship between Individualism–Collectivism and Job Satisfaction," *Applied Psychology: An International Review,* July 1995, pp 276–82; and Y A Fijneman, M E Willemsen, and Y H Poortinga, "Individualism–Collectivism: An Empirical Study of a Conceptual Issue," *Journal of Cross-Cultural Psychology,* July 1996, pp 381–402.

[57]See G Hofstede and M H Bond, "Hofstede's Culture Dimensions: An Independent Validation Using Rokeach's Value Survey," *Journal of Cross-Cultural Psychology,* December 1984, pp 417–33. A recent study using the Chinese Value Survey (CVS) is reported in D A Ralston, D J Gustafson, P M Elsass, F Cheung, and R H Terpstra, "Eastern Values: A Comparison of Managers in the United States, Hong Kong, and the People's Republic of China," *Journal of Applied Psychology,* October 1992, pp 664–71.

[58]G Hofstede, "Cultural Constraints in Management Theories," *Academy of Management Executive,* February 1993, p 90.

[59]For complete details, see G Hofstede and M H Bond, "The Confucius Connection: From Cultural Roots to Economic Growth," *Organizational Dynamics,* Spring 1988, pp 4–21.

[60]See P M Rosenzweig, "When Can Management Science Research Be Generalized Internationally?" *Management Science,* January 1994, pp 28–39.

[61]Based on F Trompenaars, *Riding the Waves of Culture* (London: Economist Books, 1994)

[62]S Brittan "Economic Viewpoint: The folies of the macho manager," *The Financial Times,* December 22, 1994, p 14.

[63]See C A Rodrigues, "The Situation and National Culture as Contingencies for Leadership Behaviour: Two Conceptual Models," in *Advances in International Comparative Management,* vol. 5, ed S B Prasad (Greenwich, CT: JAI Press, 1990), pp 51–68. For a study that found consistent perception of six leadership styles across

four countries (Norway, United States, Sweden, and Australia), see C B Gibson and G A Marcoulides, "The Invariance of Leadership Styles across Four Countries," *Journal of Managerial Issues,* Summer 1995, pp 176–93.

[64]For details, see D H B Welsh, F Luthans, and S M Sommer, "Managing Russian Factory Workers: The Impact of US-Based Behavioural and Participative Techniques," *Academy of Management Journal,* February 1993, pp 58–79.

[65]See M K Kozan, "Cultural Influences on Styles of Handling Interpersonal Conflicts: Comparisons among Jordanian, Turkish, and US Managers," *Human Relations,* September 1989, pp 787–99.

[66]Data from R L Tung, "Expatriate Assignments: Enhancing Success and Minimizing Failure," *Academy of Management Executive,* May 1987, pp 117–26.

[67]Adapted from Tung, "Expatriate Assignments: Enhancing Success and Minimizing Failure," p 117. For a study reporting a strong positive correlation between spousal adjustment and expatriate manager adjustment, see J S Black, "Antecedents to Cross-Cultural Adjustments for Expatriates in Pacific Rim Assignments," *Human Relations,* May 1991, p 497–515.

[68]S Dallas, "Rule No. 1: Don't Diss the Locals," *Business Week,* May 15, 1995, p 8.

[69]Translated from S Jacobus, "Femme globale," *Management Team,* September 22, 1995, pp 111–114.

[70]R Kopp, "International Human Resource Policies and Practices in Japanese, European, and United States Multinationals," *Human Resource Management,* Winter 1994, vol. 33(4), pp 581–599.

[71]Data from B Hagerty, "Trainers Help Expatriate Employees Build Bridges to Different Cultures," *The Wall Street Journal,* June 14, 1993, pp B1, B3. Also see C A Bartlett and S Ghoshal, "What Is a Global Manager?" *Harvard Business Review,* September–October 1992, pp 124–32; B Dumaine, "Don't Be an Ugly-American Manager," *Fortune,* October 16, 1995, p 225; and B Newman, "The New Yank Abroad Is the 'Can-Do' Player in the Global Village," *The Wall Street Journal,* December 12, 1995, pp A1, A12.

[72]C M Farkas and P De Backer, "There Are Only Five Ways to Lead," *Fortune,* January 15, 1996, p 111.

[73]An excellent reference book in this area is Black, Gregersen, and Mendenhall, *Global Assignments: Successfully Expatriating and Repatriating International Managers.*

[74]Ibid., p 97.

[75]J S Lublin, "Younger Managers Learn Global Skills," *The Wall Street Journal,* March 31, 1992, p B1.

[76]See P C Earley, "Intercultural Training for Managers: A Comparison of Documentary and Interpersonal Methods," *Academy of Management Journal,* December 1987, pp 685–98; and J S Black and M Mendenhall, "Cross-Cultural Training Effectiveness: A Review and a Theoretical Framework for Future Research," *Academy of Management Review,* January 1990, pp 113–36. Also see M R Hammer and J N Martin, "The

Effects of Cross-Cultural Training on American Managers in a Japanese-American Joint Venture," *Journal of Applied Communication Research,* May 1992, pp 161–81; and J K Harrison, "Individual and Combined Effects of Behavior Modeling and the Cultural Assimilator in Cross-Cultural Management Training," *Journal of Applied Psychology,* December 1992, pp 952–62.

[77]See G P Ferraro, "The Need for Linguistic Proficiency in Global Business," *Business Horizons,* May–June 1996, pp 39–46. For a recent study demonstrating that employees tend to prefer foreign assignments in culturally similar locations, see S Aryee, Y W Chay, and J Chew, "An Investigation of the Willingness of Managerial Employees to Accept an Expatriate Assignment," *Journal of Organizational Behavior,* May 1996, pp 267–83.

[78]J Mole, Op cit., p 5.

[79]See Harris and Moran, Managing Cultural Differences, pp 223–28; and M Shilling, "Avoid Expatriate Culture Shock," *HR Magazine,* July 1993, pp 58–63.

[80]See R Donkin, "Overwrought, overworked and over here," *The Financial Times,* March 17, 1995, p 1.

[81]Adapted and transalted from M Haenen, "Duimendraaien onder een palmboom," *NRC Handelsblad,* September 7, 1996, p 3.

[82]"The Fading Charms of Foreign Fields," *Management Today,* August 1994, pp 49–51.

[83]See Black, Gregersen, and Mendenhall, *Global Assignments: Successfully Expatriating and Repatriating International Managers,* p 227. Also see H B Gregersen, "Commitments to a Parent Company and a Local Work Unit During Repatriation," *Personnel Psychology,* Spring 1992, pp 29–54; and H B Gregersen and J S Black, "Multiple Commitments upon Repatriation: The Japanese Experience," *Journal of Management,* no. 2, 1996, pp 209–29.

[84]Ibid., pp 226–27.

[85]See J R Engen, "Coming Home," *Training,* March 1995, p 37–40.

[86]N Forster, "The Forgotten Employees? The Experiences of Expatriate Staff Returning to the UK," *International Journal of Human Resource Management,* May 1994, pp 405–425.

[87]This list of work goals is quoted from I Harpaz, "The Importance of Work Goals: An International Perspective," *Journal of International Business Studies,* First Quarter 1990, p 79.

[88]Adapted from a seven-country summary in Ibid., Table 2, p 81.

[89]See A Nimgade, "American Management as Viewed by International Professionals," *Business Horizons,* November–December 1989, pp 98–105; R Calori and B Dufour, "Management European Style," *Academy of Management Executive,* August 1995, pp 61–71; and W A Hubiak and S J O'Donnell, "Do Americans Have Their Minds Set Against TQM?" *National Productivity Review,* Summer 1996, pp 19–32.

Two

Individual Behaviour in Organizations

Five Individual Differences: Personality, Attitudes, Abilities, and Emotions

Six Perception and Attributions

Seven Motivation through Needs, Job Design, and Satisfaction

Eight Motivation through Equity, Expectancy, and Goal Setting

Nine Improving Job Perfomance with Feedback and Rewards

Five

Individual Differences: Personality, Attitudes, Abilities, and Emotions

LEARNING OBJECTIVES

When you finish studying the material in this chapter, you should be able to:

1. Explain the nature and determinants of organization-based self-esteem.

2. Define self-efficacy, and explain its sources.

3. Contrast high and low self-monitoring individuals, and describe resulting problems each may have.

4. Identify and describe the Big Five personality dimensions, and specify which one is correlated most strongly with job performance.

5. Explain the difference between an internal and an external locus of control.

6. Explain how attitudes influence behaviour in terms of the Fishbein and Ajzen model of behavioural intentions.

7. Describe Carl Jung's cognitive styles typology.

8. Distinguish between positive and negative emotions, and explain how they can be judged.

Two World Leaders: Boris Yeltsin and Bill Clinton

Boris Yeltsin

Boris Yeltsin is immense. All alone, he fills the room he is in. Yeltsin is Peter the Great, a rebel, Pugatchev, the legendary rebel from the provinces. Yeltsin talks like a real Russian: he snarls and blusters like a peasant. He doesn't reject being filmed when he is drunk, and stares silently in front of him, as only Russians can do. Sighing, shaking his head, thinking how it will go on with that old Russia.

Yeltsin has never read a book, and he even takes pride in it. He is not drunk with power, like Stalin was.

He promotes no outpaced fantasies, like Khrushchev. No *laissez-faire* like Brezhnev. No coldness like Andropov. No senility like Chernencho. No compromises like Gorbachev.

Yeltsin thinks in a simple and straightforward way. He uses his mind, rather than his brains. And it works even more smoothly after some vodka. He is pure, and simple, somewhat beastly: he does not look, but glares. He does not shake your hand, he claws. It is clear: Yeltsin is a Russian bear.

As a child, he once found a hand grenade in a desolate bunker. It exploded and he lost some fingers. Just because of that handicap, he decided to learn volley ball, and he became an excellent at it!

Yeltsin was born on February 1, 1931 in a hamlet named Butka, near Sverdlovsk. His parents were poor peasants, he has worked enormously at his personal myth. More and more he presented himself as the ethnic Russian who would rebuild the Russian disaster called the USSR.

When, in 1985, Yeltsin came from the provinces to Moscow, to become, after a few months, the capital's party secretary, his working day actually started at 7 am to end around midnight. This endless energy, involving many unwilling apparatchiks, made him very unpopular. There is, however, no doubt that Yeltsin's only intention was to conclude his swift career within the party with a remarkable function: that of the first man of a global power.

Yeltsin presented himself as a real working-class boy who dared to challenge the party Moloch. At the same time, stories went around that Yeltsin, as Moscow's party tsar, had always travelled by public transport, that he had always refused medical treatment from special hospitals intended for the party elite, but that he was, just like any ordinary Russian, satisfied with some simple aspirins from a local hospital. He was even said to queue with his wife in front of stores where the shelves were empty.

From time to time, Yeltsin disappears from the public stage for a couple of weeks, without prior announcement, which is an excellent breeding ground for the rumours about his drinking problem.

The following anecdote shows perfectly the way Yeltsin deals with problems. One day, during an inspection visit in Moscow, he was astonished by the high prices asked in the shops. Surrounded by a mass of infuriated shoppers, he lashed out at the shop manager. The man in vain explained that he had only applied the official recommended prices, and that his price policy was completely legal, that this was the way the free market worked, which Yeltsin certainly knew. But Yeltsin shook his head and ordered the man to reduce his prices to one-tenth. It did not matter to him that in the next street a similar shop, not visited by Yeltsin, applied the official rates. The mighty words of a populist leader had sounded![1]

Bill Clinton

Recent polls have shown that Americans appreciate Clinton's formidable energy and his doughty resilience. And Clinton knows these traits are his biggest advantages. As he told a senior Republican lawmaker last fall, "I'm a lot like Baby Huey. I'm fat. I'm ugly. But if you push me down, I keep coming back. I just keep coming back."

Clinton is a complex, highly intense man who does almost everything at full throttle. He watches several movies each week and reads five or six books at once. He relaxes not by watching a basketball game on TV, or reading, or picking up the telephone, or doing crossword puzzles, but doing all four simultaneously, while worrying an unlit cigar. Clinton fights his schedulers for free time every weekend, but then gets jumpy by midday Sunday and is often working in some fashion by Sunday night. If Clinton's work habits are unorthodox, they are also increasingly successful.

Clinton had such a difficult start, but he wanted it this way: he liked having 20 people report to him, feeding him volumes of

information that he would sit and consider in solitude. He wanted to be his own chief of staff, his own legislative director and his own National Security Adviser. He wanted to be as involved in choosing the dozen presidential scholars coming for lunch as in wrestling with the wording of minor speeches. He was reluctant to let even minor White House proclamations go out without review. He recently barked at an aide who tried to release a statement on ethanol, saying he had to run it by two Midwestern senators, personally. "It's almost a throwback to the old days when Presidents did everything themselves," said an official.

Aides say Clinton is aware of the problem but has trouble taking the steps to correct it. Where once he participated in grueling, two- and three-hour briefings on everything from the budget to the rehiring of fired air-traffic controllers, he has begun to realize that he was having, as he put it, "arguments I didn't need to win." He once insisted on sitting through a briefing on maritime reform only to say afterward, "I shouldn't have spent an hour on that." Observed an official: "He does want to be endlessly involved in the minutiae. He sits down, he smiles, he gets engaged and educates himself. And then he walks out of the room and pitches a fit: 'Why did I have to sit through that?'"

Advisers must also contend with the most creative and chaotic part of Clinton's personality: his desire to constantly roam the mental landscape of the presidency. His 9:15 am meeting with top aides, ostensibly to discuss his schedule, often devolves into a general discussion about whatever is in the news. Clinton holds forth in these sessions, skipping among four or five subjects with as many as 10 officials. Clinton likes to ask whomever he is with for an opinion about whatever is on his mind, whether that person knows much about it or not. In private Clinton will admit to his weakness, likening it to the habit of a schoolboy who enters a public library to browse the history stacks but then loses himself in mysteries. "He can have a 10-minute meeting in two hours," says an aide. . . .

Clinton, his advisers say, needs to "internalize" important decisions, putting together policy proposals, ideas, opinion polls, advice from aides, views of outside experts and comments from everyday people in a kind of cerebral Mixmaster. "Early on, no one understood this," says a veteran of Clinton's campaign. "But a whole lot of things have to happen before it becomes his policy. He needs to think that he has been through a thorough analysis. He has to hear the good options, the bad options, the difficult options, the crazy ideas and the traditional ideas, so that by the time he makes his case to the American people, he knows it fully, he's internalized it." . . .

For Clinton, this enables him to make his case to the public more effectively, and he has developed a high confidence in his ability to sell his ideas once he has internalized them.[2]

Discussion Question

Are Yeltsin's and Clinton's personalities a plus or minus in their role as Presidents?

What makes you *you*? What characteristics do you share with others? Which ones set you apart? Perhaps you have a dynamic personality and dress accordingly, while a low-key friend dresses conservatively and avoids crowds. People's attitudes, abilities, and emotions also vary. Some computer buffs would rather surf the Internet than eat; other people suffer from computer phobia. Sometimes students who skim their reading assignments at the last moment get higher grades than those who study for days. People standing patiently in a long line watch an angry customer shout at a salesperson. One employee consistently does more than asked while another equally skilled employee barely does the job. Thanks to a vast array of individual differences such as these, modern organizations have a rich and interesting human texture. On the other hand, individual differences make the manager's job endlessly challenging. In fact, according to research, "variability among workers is substantial at all levels but increases dramatically with job complexity. In life insurance sales, for example, variability in performance is around six times as great as in routine clerical jobs."[3]

Growing workforce diversity compels managers to view individual differences in a fresh, new way. The case for this new perspective was presented in Britain's *Journal of Managerial Psychology:*

For many years businesses sought homogeneity—a work force that believed in, supported, and presented a particular image. The notion of the company man dressed for success in the banker's blue or corporation's grey flannel suit was *de rigueur.* Those able to move into leadership positions succeeded to the extent they behaved and dressed according to a rather narrowly defined standard.

To compete today, and in preparation for the work force of tomorrow, successful businesses and organizations are adapting to both internal and external changes. New operational styles, language, customs, values, and even dress, are a real part of this adaptation. We now hear leaders talking about "valuing differences," and learning to "manage diversity."[4]

So rather than limiting diversity, as in the past, today's managers need to better understand and accommodate employee diversity and individual differences.[5]

This chapter explores the following important dimensions of individual differences: (1) self-concept, (2) personality traits, (3) attitudes, (4) abilities, and (5) emotions. Figure 5–1 is a conceptual model showing the relationship between self-concept (how you view yourself), personality (how you appear to others), and key forms of self-expression. Considered as an integrated package, these factors provide a foundation for better understanding each organizational contributor as a unique and special individual.

Figure 5 – 1   A Conceptual Model for the Study of Individual Differences in OB

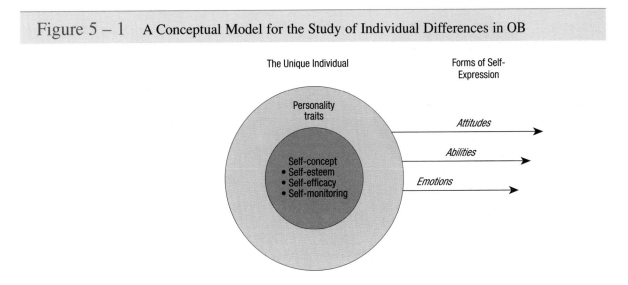

Self-Concept: The I and Me in OB

Self-concept

Person's self-perception as a physical, social, spiritual being.

Cognitions

A person's knowledge, opinions, or beliefs.

Self is the core of one's conscious existence. Awareness of self is referred to as one's self-concept. Sociologist Viktor Gecas defines **self-concept** as "the concept the individual has of himself as a physical, social, and spiritual or moral being."[6] In other words, because you have a self-concept, you recognize yourself as a distinct human being. A self-concept would be impossible without the capacity to think. This brings us to the role of cognitions. **Cognitions** represent "any knowledge, opinion, or belief about the environment, about oneself, or about one's behavior."[7] Among many different types of cognitions, those involving anticipation, planning, goal setting, evaluating, and setting personal standards are particularly relevant to OB.[8] Several cognition-based topics are discussed in later chapters. Differing cognitive styles are introduced in this chapter. Cognitions play a central role in social perception, as will be discussed in Chapter 6. Also, as we will see in

International Organizational Behaviour

Culture Dictates the Degree of Self-Disclosure in Japan and the United States

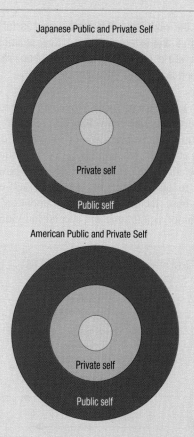

Japanese Public and Private Self

Private self

Public self

American Public and Private Self

Private self

Public self

Private self (the self not revealed to others)
Public self (the self made accessible to others)

Survey research in Japan and the United States uncovered the following distinct contrasts in Japanese versus American self-disclosure:

- Americans disclosed nearly as much to strangers as the Japanese did to their own fathers.

- Americans reported two to three times greater physical contact with parents and twice greater contact with friends than the Japanese.

- The Japanese may be frightened at the prospect of being communicatively invaded (because of the unexpected spontaneity and bluntness of the American); the American is annoyed at the prospect of endless formalities and tangential replies.

- American emphasis on self-assertion and talkativeness cultivates a communicator who is highly self-oriented and expressive; the Japanese emphasis on "reserve" and "sensitivity" cultivates a communicator who is other-oriented and receptive.

SOURCE   Adapted from D C Barnlund, "Public and Private Self in Communicating with Japan," *Business Horizons*, March–April 1989, pp 32–40.
Excerpted from D Veale, L Oliver, and K van Langen, "Three Coca-Cola Perspectives on International Management Styles," *Academy of Management Executive*, August 1995, pp 74–77.

Chapters 7 and 8, modern motivation theories and techniques are powered by cognitions. Successful self-management, covered in Chapter 15, requires cognitive support.

Importantly, ideas of self and self-concept vary from one historical era to another, from one socioeconomic class to another, and from culture to culture.[9] How well one detects and adjusts to different cultural notions of self can spell the difference between success and failure in international dealings. For example, as detailed in the International OB, Japanese—US communication and understanding is often hindered by significantly different degrees of self-disclosure. With a comparatively large public self, Americans pride themselves in being open, honest, candid, and to the point. Meanwhile, Japanese, who culturally discourage self-disclosure, typically view Americans as blunt, prying, and insensitive to formalities. For their part, Americans tend to see Japanese as distant, cold, and evasive.[10] One culture is not right and the other wrong. They are just different, and a key difference involves culturally rooted conceptions of self and self-disclosure.

Keeping this cultural qualification in mind, let us explore three topics invariably mentioned when behavioural scientists discuss self-concept. They are self-esteem, self-efficacy, and self-monitoring. Each deserves a closer look by those who want to better understand and effectively manage people at work.

Self-Esteem: A Controversial Topic

Self-esteem

One's overall self-evaluation.

Self-esteem is a belief about one's own self-worth based on an overall self-evaluation.[11] Self-esteem is measured by having survey respondents indicate their agreement or disagreement with both positive and negative statements. A positive statement on one general self-esteem survey is: "I feel I am a person of worth, the equal of other people."[12] Among the negative items is: "I feel I do not have much to be proud of."[13] Those who agree with the positive statements and disagree with the negative statements have high self-esteem. They see themselves as worthwhile, capable, and acceptable. People with low self-esteem view themselves in negative terms. They do not feel good about themselves and are hampered by self-doubts.[14]

The Battle Over Self-Esteem   The subject of self-esteem has generated a good deal of controversy in recent years, particularly among educators and those seeking to help the disadvantaged. While both sides generally agree that positive self-esteem is a good thing for students and youngsters, disagreement rages over how to improve self-esteem.

Feelings of self-esteem are, in fact, shaped by our circumstances and how others treat us. Researchers who tracked 654 young adults (192 male, 462 female) for eight years found higher self-esteem among those in school or working full-time than among those with part-time jobs or unemployed.[15]

Surprising Research Insights   Is high self-esteem always a good thing? Research evidence provides some surprising answers. In one study, high self-esteem subjects tended to become egotistical and boastful when faced with pressure situations.[16] Other researchers recently found high levels of self-esteem associated with aggressive and even violent behaviour. Indeed, contrary to the common belief that low self-esteem and criminality go hand in hand, youth gang members and criminals often score highly on self-esteem and become violent when their inflated egos are threatened.[17] Our conclusion is that high self-esteem *can* be good, but only *if*—like other characteristics such as creativity, intelligence, and persistence—it is nurtured and channelled in constructive and ethical ways. Otherwise, it can become antisocial and destructive.[18]

From the organization's point of view, high self-esteem can also be a mixed blessing. In nondownsizing organizations, employees with lower self-esteem tend to leave, but in downsizing organizations self-confidence and self-esteem have a positive direct effect on intent to leave.[19] Individuals with the capabilities and the confidence to perform well in other firms tend to leave first. In this way, of course, the downsizing companies are losing not the low performers, but those employees they hoped to retain.

ETHICS

Self-Esteem Across Cultures   What are the cross-cultural implications for self-esteem, a concept that has been called uniquely Western? In a recent survey of 13,118 students from 31 countries worldwide, a moderate positive correlation was found between self-esteem and life satisfaction. But the relationship was stronger in individualistic cultures (e.g., United States, Canada, New Zealand, Netherlands) than in collectivist cultures (e.g., Korea, Kenya, Japan). The researchers concluded that individualistic cultures socialize people to focus more on themselves, while people in collectivist cultures "are socialized to fit into the community and to do their duty. Thus, how a collectivist feels about him- or herself is less relevant to . . . life satisfaction."[20] Global managers need to remember to deemphasize self-esteem when doing business in collectivist ("we") cultures, as opposed to emphasizing it in individualistic ("me") cultures.

Can General Self-Esteem Be Improved?   The short answer is yes. More detailed answers come from recent research. A recent study led to this conclusion: "Low self-esteem can be raised more by having the person think of *desirable* characteristics *possessed* rather than of undesirable characteristics from which he or she is free."[21] (See our related discussions of the self-fulfilling prophecy in Chapter 6 and self-talk in Chapter 15.)

Organization-Based Self-Esteem   The self-esteem just discussed is a global belief about oneself. But what about self-esteem in organizations, a more restricted context of greater importance to managers? A model of organization-based self-esteem was recently developed and validated with seven studies involving 2,444 teachers, students, managers, and employees. The researchers defined **organization-based self-esteem (OBSE)** as the "self-perceived value that individuals have of themselves as organization members acting within an organizational context."[22] Those scoring high on OBSE tend to view themselves as important, worthwhile, effectual, and meaningful within the context of their employing organization. Take a moment to complete the brief OBSE questionnaire in the OB Exercise. This exercise will help you better understand the concept of organization-based self-esteem, as well as assessing the supportiveness of your work setting.

A basic model of OBSE is displayed in Figure 5–2. On the left side of the model are three primary determinants of organization-based self-esteem. OBSE tends to increase when employees believe their supervisors have a genuine concern for employees' welfare. Flexible, organic organization structures generate higher OBSE than do mechanistic (rigid bureaucratic) structures (the organic—mechanistic distinction is discussed in Chapter 19). Complex and challenging jobs foster higher OBSE than do simple,

Organization-based self-esteem

An organization member's self-perceived value.

OB EXERCISE   *How Strong Is Your Organization-Based Self-Esteem (OBSE)?*

Instructions

Relative to your present (or last) job, how strongly do you agree or disagree with each of the following statements?

Arbitrary norms for comparison purposes are: Low OBSE = 10–20; Moderate OBSE = 21–39; High OBSE = 40–50.

	STRONGLY DISAGREE / STRONGLY AGREE			STRONGLY DISAGREE / STRONGLY AGREE
1. I count around here.	1—2—3—4—5	6. I can make a difference around here.		1—2—3—4—5
2. I am taken seriously around here.	1—2—3—4—5	7. I am valuable around here.		1—2—3—4—5
3. I am important around here.	1—2—3—4—5	8. I am helpful around here.		1—2—3—4—5
4. I am trusted around here.	1—2—3—4—5	9. I am efficient around here.		1—2—3—4—5
5. There is faith in me around here.	1—2—3—4—5	10. I am cooperative around here.		1—2—3—4—5
	Total score = _____			Total score = _____

SOURCE   Adapted from discussion in J L Pierce, D G Gardner, L L Cummings, and R B Dunham, "Organization-Based Self-Esteem: Construct Definition, Measurement, and Validation," *Academy of Management Journal,* September 1989, pp 622–48

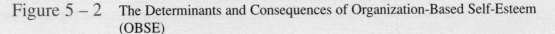

Figure 5 – 2   The Determinants and Consequences of Organization-Based Self-Esteem (OBSE)

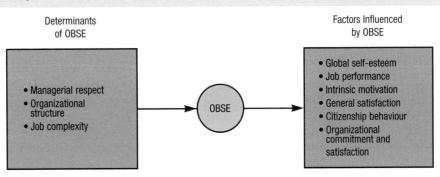

repetitious, and boring jobs. Significantly, these same factors also are associated with greater task motivation.

Factors positively influenced by high OBSE and negatively impacted by low OBSE are listed in the right side of Figure 5–2. Intrinsic motivation refers to personal feelings of accomplishment. Citizenship behaviour involves doing things beneficial for the organization itself. The other consequences of OBSE are self-explanatory. In sum, active enhancement of organization-based self-esteem promises to build a very important cognitive bridge to greater productivity and satisfaction.[23]

Practical Tips for Building On-the-Job Self-Esteem   According to a study by the Society for Human Resource Management, managers can build employee self-esteem in four ways:

1. Be supportive by showing concern for personal problems, interests, status, and contributions.

2. Offer work involving variety, autonomy, and challenges that suit the individual's values, skills, and abilities.

3. Strive for management—employee cohesiveness and build trust. (Trust, an important teamwork element, is discussed in Chapter 13.)

4. Have faith in each employee's self-management ability (see Chapter 15). Reward successes.[24]

Self-Efficacy

Self-efficacy
Belief in one's ability to do a task.

Have you noticed how those who are confident about their ability tend to succeed, while those who are preoccupied with failing tend to fail? **Self-efficacy** is a person's belief about his or her chances of successfully accomplishing a specific task. According to one OB writer, "Self-efficacy arises from the gradual acquisition of complex cognitive, social, linguistic, and/or physical skills through experience."[25] This statement is confirmed by seven British business leaders interviewed by Ruth Tait,[26] when they say that the positive aspirations of parents or school were instrumental in motivating them to succeed and in engendering an early belief in themselves and self-reliance. Childhood experiences have a powerful effect on a person's self-efficacy. Whoopi Goldberg, for example, attributes much of her success as a performing artist to her mother's guidance. Says Goldberg, who grew up in New York City as Caryn Johnson,

My mom encouraged me to explore the city, get on the bus and go watch Leonard Bernstein conduct the young people's concerts, go to the museums and planetarium, Central Park, and Coney Island. There were always things for me to investigate, and she encouraged me to ask a lot of questions.

As kids, my mom instilled in both my brother [Clyde] and me an ideal of what life could and should be, and how we could participate in it. It was never intimated to me that I couldn't be exactly what I wanted to be.[27]

The relationship between self-efficacy and performance is a cyclical one. Efficacy→performance cycles can spiral upwards, towards success or downwards, towards failure.[28] Researchers have documented a strong linkage between high self-efficacy expectations and success in widely varied physical and mental tasks, anxiety reduction, addiction control, pain tolerance, illness recovery, and avoidance of seasickness in naval cadets.[29] Oppositely, those with low self-efficacy expectations tend to have low success rates. Chronically low self-efficacy is associated with a condition called **learned helplessness**, the severely debilitating belief that one has no control over one's environment.[30] Although self-efficacy sounds like some sort of mental magic, it operates in a very straightforward manner, as a model will show.

Learned helplessness

Debilitating lack of faith in one's ability to control the situation.

What Are the Mechanisms of Self-Efficacy? A basic model of self-efficacy is displayed in Figure 5–3. It draws upon the work of Stanford psychologist Albert Bandura. Let us

Figure 5 – 3 A Model of How Self-Efficacy Beliefs Can Pave the Way for Success or Failure

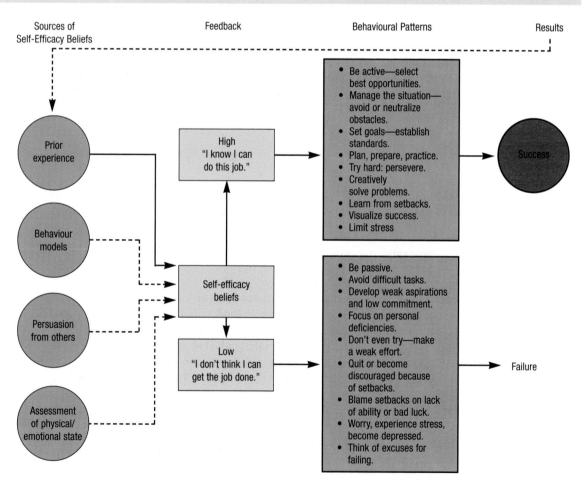

Sources: Adapted from discussion in A Bandura, "Regulation of Cognitive Processes through Perceived Self-Efficacy," *Developmental Psychology,* September 1989, pp 729–35; and R Wood and A Bandura, "Social Cognitive Theory of Organizational Management," *Academy of Management Review,* July 1989, pp 361–84.

explore this model with a simple illustrative task. Imagine you have been told to prepare and deliver a 10-minute talk to an OB class of 50 students on the workings of the self-efficacy model in Figure 5 – 3. Your self-efficacy calculation would involve cognitive appraisal of the interaction between your perceived capability and situational opportunities and obstacles.

As you begin to prepare for your presentation, the four sources of self-efficacy beliefs would come into play. Because prior experience is the most potent source, according to Bandura, it is listed first and connected to self-efficacy beliefs with a solid line.[31] Past success in public speaking would boost your self-efficacy. But bad experiences with delivering speeches would foster low self-efficacy. Regarding behaviour models as a source of self-efficacy beliefs, you would be influenced by the success or failure of your classmates in delivering similar talks. Their successes would tend to bolster you (or perhaps their failure would if you were very competitive and had high self-esteem). Likewise, any supportive persuasion from your classmates that you will do a good job would enhance your self-efficacy. Physical and emotional factors also might affect your self-confidence. A sudden case of laryngitis or a bout of stage fright could cause your self-efficacy expectations to plunge. Your cognitive evaluation of the situation then would yield a self-efficacy belief—ranging from high to low expectations for success. Importantly, self-efficacy beliefs are not merely boastful statements based on bravado; they are deep convictions supported by experience.

Moving to the behavioural patterns portion of Figure 5 – 3, we see how self-efficacy beliefs are acted out. In short, if you have high self-efficacy about giving your 10-minute speech you will work harder, more creatively, and longer when preparing for your talk than will your low-self-efficacy classmates. The results would then take shape accordingly. People programme themselves for success or failure by enacting their self-efficacy expectations. Positive or negative results subsequently become feedback for one's base of personal experience.

Self-Efficacy Implications for Managers   On-the-job research evidence encourages managers to nurture self-efficacy, both in themselves and in others. In one study, for example, the sales performance of life insurance agents was much better among those with high self-efficacy.[32] Self-efficacy requires constructive action in each of the following managerial areas:

1. *Recruiting/selection/job assignments.* Interview questions can be designed to probe job applicants' general self-efficacy as a basis for determining orientation and training needs. Pencil-and-paper tests for self-efficacy are not in an advanced stage of development and validation. Care needs to be taken not to hire solely on the basis of self-efficacy because studies have detected below-average self-esteem and self-efficacy among women and protected minorities.[33]

2. *Job design.* Complex, challenging, and autonomous jobs tend to enhance perceived self-efficacy. Boring, tedious jobs generally do the opposite.

3. *Training and development.* Employees' self-efficacy expectations for key tasks can be improved through guided experiences, mentoring, and role modelling.[34]

4. *Self-management.* Systematic self-management training, as discussed in Chapter 15, involves enhancement of self-efficacy expectations.

5. *Goal setting and quality improvement.* Goal difficulty needs to match the individual's perceived self-efficacy.[35] As self-efficacy and performance improve, goals and quality standards can be made more challenging.

6. *Coaching.* Those with low self-efficacy and employees victimized by learned helplessness need lots of constructive pointers and positive feedback.[36]

7. *Leadership.* Needed leadership talent surfaces when top management gives high self-efficacy managers a chance to prove themselves under pressure.

8. *Rewards.* Small successes need to be rewarded as stepping-stones to a stronger self-image and greater achievements.

A word of caution Self-esteem is clearly related to goal setting, self-management, achievement motivation, notions known to be very culturally sensitive. As the authors of the meta-analysis linking self-esteem and performance, note:

The studies contained within this review have been conducted exclusively in the United States and the United Kingdom. Both cultures may, in general, be described as individualistic in nature. This raises the issue of transferability of the self-efficacy concept to cultures which are more collectivistic in nature.[37]

Self-Monitoring

Consider these contrasting scenarios:

1. You are rushing to an important meeting when a co-worker pulls you aside and starts to discuss a personal problem. You want to break off the conversation, so you glance at your watch. He keeps talking. You say, "I'm late for a big meeting." He continues. You turn and start to walk away. The person keeps talking as if they never received any of your verbal and nonverbal signals that the conversation was over.

2. Same situation. Only this time, when you glance at your watch, the person immediately says, "I know, you've got to go. Sorry. We'll talk later."

In the first all-too-familiar scenario, you are talking to a "low self-monitor." The second scenario involves a "high self-monitor." But more is involved here than an irritating situation. A significant and measurable individual difference in self-expression behaviour, called self-monitoring, is highlighted. **Self-monitoring** is the extent to which a person observes their own self-expressive behaviour and adapts it to the demands of the situation. Experts on the subject offer this explanation:

Self-monitoring

Observing one's own behaviour and adapting it to the situation.

Individuals high in self-monitoring are thought to regulate their expressive self-presentation for the sake of desired public appearances, and thus be highly responsive to social and interpersonal cues of situationally appropriate performances. Individuals low in self-monitoring are thought to lack either the ability or the motivation to so regulate their expressive self-presentations. Their expressive behaviours, instead, are thought to functionally reflect their own enduring and momentary inner states, including their attitudes, traits, and feelings.[38]

In organizational life, both high and low monitors are subject to criticism. High self-monitors are sometimes called chameleons, who readily adapt their self-presentation to their surroundings. Low self-monitors, on the other hand, often are criticized for being on their own planet and insensitive to others.

Importantly, within an OB context, self-monitoring is like any other individual difference—not a matter of right or wrong or good versus bad, but rather a source of diversity that needs to be adequately understood by present and future managers.

A Matter of Degree Self-monitoring is not an either-or proposition. It is a matter of degree; a matter of being relatively high or low in terms of related patterns of self-expression. The OB Exercise is a self-assessment of your self-monitoring tendencies. It can help you better understand yourself. Take a short break from your reading to complete the 10-item survey. Does your score surprise you in any way? Are you unhappy with the way you present yourself to others? What are the ethical implications of your score (particularly with regard to items 9 and 10)?

Research Findings and Practical Recommendations According to recent field research, there is a positive relationship between high self-monitoring and career success. Among 139 MBA graduates who were tracked for five years, high self-monitors enjoyed more internal and external promotions than did their low self-monitoring classmates.[39] Another study of 147 managers and professionals found that high self-monitors had a better record of acquiring a mentor (someone to act as a personal career coach and professional sponsor).[40] These results mesh well with an earlier study that found managerial success (in terms of speed of promotions) tied to political savvy (knowing how to socialize, network, and engage in organizational politics).[41] According to Sumantra Ghoshal, professor of strategic leadership at the London Business School, companies that are able to retain their vitality even after the most savage rationalization have succeed in doing so, among others, because they have lightened the burden of control systems by developing personal values that encourage self-monitoring.[42]

The foregoing evidence and practical experience lead us to make these practical recommendations:

For high, moderate, and low self-monitors: Become more consciously aware of your self-image and how it affects others (the OB Exercise is a good start).[43]

For high self-monitors: Don't overdo it by turning from a successful chameleon into someone who is widely perceived as insincere, dishonest, phoney, and untrustworthy. You cannot be everything to everyone.

For low self-monitors: You can bend without breaking, so try to be a bit more accommodating while being true to your basic beliefs. Don't wear out your welcome when communicating. Practice reading and adjusting to nonverbal cues in various public situations. If your conversation partner is bored or distracted, stop—because they are not really listening.

We now turn our attention to how the self is expressed through personality traits.

OB EXERCISE   *What Are Your Self-Monitoring Tendencies?*

Instructions
In an honest self-appraisal, mark each of the following statements as true (T) or false (F), and then consult the scoring key.

_____ 1. I guess I put on a show to impress or entertain others.

_____ 2. In a group of people I am rarely the centre of attention.

_____ 3. In different situations and with different people, I often act like very different persons.

_____ 4. I would not change my opinions (or the way I do things) in order to please someone or win their favour.

_____ 5. I have considered being an entertainer.

_____ 6. I have trouble changing my behaviour to suit different people and different situations.

_____ 7. At a party I let others keep the jokes and stories going.

_____ 8. I feel a bit awkward in public and do not show up quite as well as I should.

_____ 9. I can look anyone in the eye and tell a lie with a straight face (if for a right end).

_____ 10. I may deceive people by being friendly when I really dislike them.

Scoring Key
Score one point for each of the following answers:

1. T; 2. F; 3. T; 4. F; 5. T; 6. F; 7. F; 8. F; 9. T; 10. T

Score: _____

1–3 = Low self-monitoring

4–5 = Moderately low self-monitoring

6–7 = Moderately high self-monitoring

8–10 = High self-monitoring

SOURCE   Excerpted and adapted from M Snyder and S Gangestad, "On the Nature of Self-Monitoring: Matters of Assessment, Matters of Validity," *Journal of Personality and Social Psychology,* July 1986, p 137.

Personality: Dimensions, Insights, and Issues

Personality

Stable physical and mental characteristics responsible for a person's identity.

Individuals have their own way of thinking and acting, their own unique style or personality. **Personality** is defined as the combination of stable physical and mental characteristics that give the individual his or her identity.[44] These characteristics or traits—including how one looks, thinks, acts, and feels—are the product of interacting genetic and environmental influences. In this section, we introduce the Big Five personality dimensions, issue some cautions about workplace personality testing, and examine an important personality factor called locus of control.

The Big Five Personality Dimensions

Long and confusing lists of personality dimensions have been distilled in recent years to the Big Five.[45] They are extraversion, agreeableness, conscientiousness, emotional stability, and openness to experience (see Table 5–1 for descriptions). Standardized personality tests determine how positively or negatively a person scores on each of the Big Five. For example, someone scoring negatively on extraversion would be an introverted person prone to shy and withdrawn behaviour.[46] Someone scoring negatively on emotional security would be nervous, tense, angry, and worried. A person's scores on the Big Five reveal a personality profile as unique as his or her fingerprints. Yet one important question lingers: Are personality models ethnocentric or unique to the culture in which they were developed? At least as far as the Big Five model goes, recent cross-cultural research evidence points in the direction of "no." Specifically, the Big Five personality structure held up very well in a study of women and men from Russia, Canada, Hong Kong, Poland, Germany, and Finland.[47]

Personality and Job Performance   Those interested in OB want to know the connection between the Big Five and job performance. Ideally, Big Five personality dimensions that correlate positively and strongly with job performance would be helpful in the selection, training, and appraisal of employees. A meta-analysis of 117 studies involving 23,994 subjects from many professions offers guidance.[48] Among the Big Five, *conscientiousness* had the strongest positive correlation with job performance and training performance. According to the researchers, "those individuals who exhibit traits associated with a strong sense of purpose, obligation, and persistence generally perform better than those who do not."[49] Another expected finding: Extraversion (an outgoing personality) was associated with success for managers and salespeople. Also, extraversion was a stronger predictor of job performance than agreeableness, across all professions. The researchers concluded, "It appears that being courteous, trusting, straightforward, and soft-hearted has a smaller impact on job performance than being talkative, active, and assertive."[50]

Issue: Is There an "Ideal" Employee Personality Profile?   Given the complexity of today's work environments, the diversity of today's workforce, and recent research evidence,[51] the quest for an ideal employee personality profile is sheer folly. Just as one

Table 5 – 1   The Big Five Personality Dimensions

PERSONALITY DIMENSION	CHARACTERISTICS OF A PERSON SCORING POSITIVELY ON THE DIMENSION
1. Extraversion	Outgoing, talkative, sociable, assertive
2. Agreeableness	Trusting, good natured, cooperative, soft hearted
3. Conscientiousness	Dependable, responsible, achievement-oriented, persistent
4. Emotional stability	Relaxed, secure, unworried
5. Openness to experience	Intellectual, imaginative, curious, broad minded

Source: Adapted from M R Barrick and M K Mount, "Autonomy as a Moderator of the Relationships between the Big Five Personality Dimensions and Job Performance," *Journal of Applied Psychology*, February 1993, pp 111–18.

shoe does not fit all people, one personality profile does not fit all job situations.

Issue: Why Not Just Forget about Personality?   Personality testing problems and unethical applications do not automatically cancel out the underlying concepts. Present and future managers need to know about *personality* traits and characteristics, despite the controversy over personality testing. Rightly or wrongly, the term personality is routinely encountered both on and off the job. Knowledge of the Big Five encourages more precise understanding of the rich diversity among today's employees. Good management involves taking the time to get to know *each* employee's *unique combination* of personality, abilities, and potential, and then creating a productive and satisfying person–job fit.

Let us take a look at locus of control, another important job-related personality factor.

Locus of Control: Self or Environment?

Individuals vary in terms of how much personal responsibility they take for their behaviour and its consequences. Julian Rotter, a personality researcher, identified a dimension of personality he labelled locus of control to explain these differences. He proposed that people tend to attribute the causes of their behaviour primarily to either themselves or environmental factors.[52] This personality trait produces distinctly different behaviour patterns.

Internal locus of control

Attributing outcomes to one's own actions.

People who believe they control the events and consequences that affect their lives are said to possess an **internal locus of control**. For example, such a person tends to attribute positive outcomes, such as getting a pass grade on an exam, to her or his own abilities. Similarly, an "internal" tends to blame negative events, such as failing an exam, on personal shortcoming—not studying hard enough, perhaps. Many entrepreneurs eventually succeed because their internal locus of control helps them overcome setbacks

---

Table 5 – 2   Words of Caution about Personality Testing in the Workplace

- Rely on reputable, licensed psychologists for selecting and overseeing the administration, scoring, and interpretation of personality and psychological tests.

- Do not make employment-related decisions strictly on the basis of personality test results. Supplement any personality test data with information from reference checks, personal interviews, ability tests, and job performance records.*

- Avoid hiring people on the basis of specified personality profiles. As a case in point, there is no distinct "managerial personality." One study found the combination of mental ability and personality to be responsible for only 21 per cent of the variation in managerial success.**

- Regularly assess any possible adverse impact on women and minorities.

- Be wary of slickly packaged gimmicks claiming to accurately assess personalities. A prime example is *graphology*, whereby handwriting "experts" infer personality traits and aptitudes from samples of one's penmanship. Judging from research evidence, graphology is an inappropriate hiring tool. In a meta-analysis of 17 studies, 63 graphologists did a slightly *worse* job of predicting future performance than did a control group of 51 nongraphologists. Indeed, psychologists with no graphology experience consistently outperformed the graphologists.†

- The rapidly growing use of *integrity* tests to screen out dishonest job applicants seems to be justified by recent research evidence. Dishonest people reportedly have a general lack of conscientiousness that is difficult for them to fake, even on a paper-and-pencil test.‡

Sources: *See M P Cronin, "This Is a Test," *Inc.*, August 1993, pp 64–68; **For details, see J S Schippmann and E P Prien, "An Assessment of the contributions of General Mental Ability and Personality Characteristics to Managerial Success," *Journal of Business and Psychology*, Summer 1989, pp 423–37; †Data from E Neter and G Ben-Shakhar, "The Predictive Validity of Graphological Inferences: A Meta-Analytic Approach," *Personality and Individual Differences*, no. 7, 1989, pp 737–45; and ‡See D S Ones, C Viswesvaran, and F L Schmidt, "Comprehensive Meta-Analysis of Integrity Test Validities: Findings and Implications for Personnel Selection and Theories of Job Performance," *Journal of Applied Psychology*, August 1993, pp 679–703.

and disappointments. They see themselves as masters of their own fate and not simply lucky. But, as *Fortune's* Jaclyn Fierman humorously noted, luck is a matter of interpretation and not always a bad thing:

> For those of us who believe we are the masters of our fate, the captains of our soul, the notion that a career might hinge on random events is unthinkable. Self-made men and women are especially touchy on this subject. If they get all the breaks, it's because they're smarter and harder working than everyone else. If they know the right people, it's because they network the nights away. Luck? Many successful people think it diminishes them.
>
> Hard workers do get ahead, no doubt about it. . . . But then there are folks like Ringo Starr. One day he was an obscure drummer of limited talent from Liverpool; the next day he was a Beatle.
>
> Nobody demonstrates better than Ringo that true luck is accidental, not inevitable.[53]

External locus of control
Attributing outcomes to circumstances beyond one's control.

On the other side of this personality dimension are those who believe their performance is the product of circumstances beyond their immediate control. These individuals are said to possess an **external locus of control** and tend to attribute outcomes to environmental causes, such as luck or fate. Unlike someone with an internal locus of control, an "external" would attribute a passing grade on an exam to something external (an easy test or a good day) and attribute a failing grade to an unfair test or problems at home. A shortened version of an instrument Rotter developed to measure one's locus of control is presented in the OB Exercise. Where is your locus of control: internal, external, or a combination?

Research Findings on Locus of Control   Researchers have found important behavioural differences between internals and externals:

- Internals display greater work motivation.
- Internals have stronger expectations that effort leads to performance.
- Internals exhibit higher performance on tasks involving learning or problem solving, when performance leads to valued rewards.
- There is a stronger relationship between job satisfaction and performance for internals than externals.
- Internals obtain higher salaries and greater salary increases than externals.
- Externals tend to be more anxious than internals.[54]

Implications of Locus of Control Differences for Managers   The preceding summary of research findings on locus of control has important implications for managing people at work. Let us examine two of them.

First, since internals have a tendency to believe they control the work environment through their behaviour, they will attempt to exert control over the work setting. This can be done by trying to influence work procedures, working conditions, task assignments, or relationships with peers and supervisors. As these possibilities imply, internals may resist a manager's attempts to closely supervise their work. Therefore, management may want to place internals in jobs requiring high initiative and low compliance. Externals, on the other hand, might be more amenable to highly structured jobs requiring greater compliance. Direct participation also can bolster the attitudes and performance of externals. This conclusion comes from a field study of 85 computer system users in a wide variety of business and government organizations. Externals who had been significantly involved in designing their organization's computer information system had more favourable attitudes towards the system than their external-locus co-workers who had not participated.[55]

Second, locus of control has implications for reward systems. Given that internals have a greater belief that their effort leads to performance, internals likely would prefer and respond more productively to incentives such as merit pay or sales commissions.[56]

Attitudes and Behaviour

Hardly a day goes by without the popular media reporting the results of another attitude survey. The idea is to take the pulse of public opinion. What do we think about candidate X, the war on drugs, the introduction of the Euro, or abortion? In the workplace, meanwhile, managers conduct attitude surveys to monitor such things as job and pay satisfaction.[57] All this attention to attitudes is based on the assumption that attitudes somehow influence behaviour such as voting for someone, working hard, or quitting one's job. In this section, we will examine the connection between attitudes and behaviour.

Attitudes versus Values

Attitude

Learned predisposition towards a given object.

An **attitude** is defined as "a learned predisposition to respond in a consistently favourable or unfavourable manner with respect to a given object."[58] Regarding the matter of consistency, researchers found the *job* attitudes of 5,000 middle-aged male employees to be very stable over a five-year period.[59] Employees with positive attitudes towards the job tended to maintain their positive attitudes. Negative-attitude employees tended to remain negative. Even those who changed jobs or occupations tended to maintain their prior job attitudes. Thus, attitudes tend to be consistent over time *and* across related situations.[60]

Attitudes affect behaviour at a different level than do values. While values represent global beliefs that influence behaviour across *all* situations, attitudes relate only to behaviour directed towards *specific* objects, persons, or situations.[61] Values and attitudes generally, but not always, are in harmony. A manager who strongly values helpful behaviour may have a negative attitude towards helping an unethical co-worker.

Because our cultural backgrounds and experiences vary, our attitudes and behaviour vary. Attitudes are translated into behaviour via behavioural intentions. Let us examine an established model of this important process.

Attitudes and Behavioural Intentions

Behavioural scientists Martin Fishbein and Icek Ajzen developed a comprehensive model of behavioural intentions used widely to explain attitude—behaviour relationships.[62] As depicted in Figure 5–4, an individual's intention to engage in a given behaviour is the best

---

OB EXERCISE   *Where Is Your Locus of Control?*

Circle one letter for each pair of items, in accordance with your beliefs:

1. A. Many of the unhappy things in people's lives are partly due to bad luck.

   B. People's misfortunes result from the mistakes they make.

2. A. Unfortunately, an individual's worth often passes unrecognized no matter how hard he tries.

   B. In the long run, people get the respect they deserve.

3. A. Without the right breaks one cannot be an effective leader.

   B. Capable people who fail to become leaders have not taken advantage of their opportunities.

4. A. I have often found that what is going to happen will happen.

   B. Trusting to fate has never turned out as well for me as making a decision to take a definite course of action.

5. A. Most people don't realize the extent to which their lives are controlled by accidental happenings.

   B. There really is no such thing as "luck."

6. A. In the long run, the bad things that happen to us are balanced by the good ones.

   B. Most misfortunes are the result of lack of ability, ignorance, laziness, or all three.

7. A. Many times I feel I have little influence over the things that happen to me.

   B. It is impossible for me to believe that chance or luck plays an important role in my life.

Note: In determining your score, A = 0 and B = 1.

Arbitrary norms for this shortened version are: External locus of control = 1–3; Balanced internal and external locus of control = 4; Internal locus of control = 5–7.

SOURCE   Excerpted from J B Rotter, "Generalized Expectancies for Internal versus External Control of Reinforcement," *Psychological Monographs*, vol. 80 (Whole no. 609, 1966), pp 11–12. Copyright © 1966 by the American Psychological Association. Reprinted with permission.

predictor of that behaviour. For example, the quickest and possibly most accurate way of determining whether an individual will quit his or her job is to have an objective third party ask if he or she intends to quit. A meta-analysis of 34 studies of employee turnover involving more than 83,000 employees validated this direct approach. The researchers found stated behavioural intentions to be a better predictor of employee turnover than job satisfaction, satisfaction with the work itself, or organizational commitment.[63]

Although asking about intentions enables one to predict who will quit, it does not help explain why an individual would want to quit. Thus, to better understand why employees exhibit certain behaviours, such as quitting their jobs, one needs to consider their relevant attitudes. As shown in Figure 5–4, behavioural intentions are influenced both by one's attitude towards the behaviour and by perceived norms about exhibiting the behaviour. In turn, attitudes and subjective norms are determined by personal beliefs.

Beliefs Influence Attitudes   A person's belief system is a mental representation of his or her relevant surroundings, complete with probable cause-and-effect relationships. Beliefs are the result of direct observation and inferences from previously learned relationships. For example, we tend to infer that a laughing co-worker is happy. In terms of the strength of the relationship between beliefs and attitudes, beliefs do not have equal impacts on attitudes. Research indicates that attitudes are based on salient or important beliefs that may change as relevant information is received. For example, your beliefs about the quality of a particular car may change after hearing the car has been recalled for stability problems, as happened in Sweden to the Mercedes-A-class compact car in November 1997 as a result of the so-called Elk-test.[64]

In Figure 5–4, you can see that an individual will have positive attitudes towards performing a behaviour when he or she believes the behaviour is associated with positive outcomes. An individual is more likely to quit a job when he or she believes quitting will result in a better position and a reduction in job stress. In contrast, negative attitudes towards quitting will be formed when a person believes quitting leads to negative outcomes, such as the loss of money and status.

Beliefs Influence Subjective Norms   Subjective norms refer to perceived social pressure to perform a specific behaviour. As noted by Ajzen and Fishbein, "Subjective norms are also a function of beliefs, but beliefs of a different kind, namely the person's beliefs that specific individuals or groups think he should or should not perform the behaviour."[65] Subjective norms can exert a powerful influence on the behavioural intentions of those who are sensitive to the opinions of respected role models. This effect was observed in a laboratory study of students' intentions to apply for a job at companies that reportedly tested employees for drugs. The students generally had a negative attitude about companies that tested for drugs. But positive statements from influential persons about the need for drug testing tended to strengthen intentions to apply at companies engaged in drug testing.[66]

Thus, as diagrammed in Figure 5–4, both attitudes and subjective norms shape behavioural intentions.

Attitudinal Research and Application

Research has demonstrated that Fishbein and Ajzen's model accurately predicted intentions to buy consumer products, have children, and choose a career versus becoming a homemaker. Weight loss intentions and behaviour, voting for political candidates, attending on-the-job training sessions have also been predicted successfully by the model.[67]

From a practical management standpoint, the behavioural intention model we have just reviewed has important implications. First, managers need to appreciate the dynamic relationships between beliefs, attitudes, subjective norms, and behavioural intentions when attempting to foster productive behaviour Although attitudes are often resistant to

Figure 5 – 4   A Model of Behavioural Intention

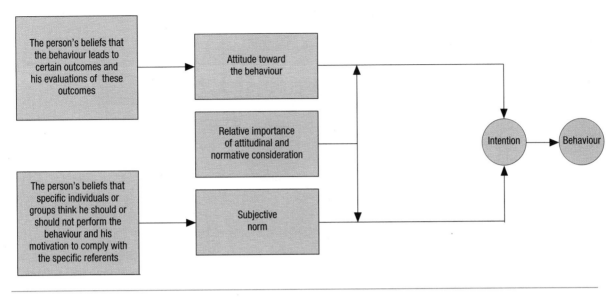

Note: Arrows indicate the direction of influence.

Source: Icek Ajzen and Martin Fishbein, *Understanding Attitudes and Predicting Social Behaviour*, © 1980, p 8. Reprinted by permission of Prentice Hall, Englewood Cliffs, New Jersey.

change, they can be influenced indirectly through education and training experiences that change underlying beliefs. A case in point is a recent study documenting how men's beliefs about gender differences can be reduced by taking a women's studies course.[68] Another tactic involves redirecting subjective norms through clear and credible communication, organizational culture values, and role models. Finally, regular employee-attitude surveys can let managers know if their ideas and changes go with or against the grain of popular sentiment.

Abilities and Performance

Individual differences in abilities and accompanying skills are a central concern for managers because nothing can be accomplished without appropriately skilled personnel. An **ability** represents a broad and stable characteristic responsible for a person's maximum—as opposed to typical—performance on mental and physical tasks. A **skill,** on the other hand, is the specific capacity to physically manipulate objects. Consider this difference as you imagine yourself being the only passenger on a small commuter airplane in which the pilot has just passed out. As the plane nose-dives, your effort and abilities will not be enough to save yourself and the pilot if you do not possess flying skills. As shown in Figure 5–5, successful performance (be it landing an airplane or performing any other job) depends on the right combination of effort, ability, and skill.

Abilities and skills are getting a good deal of attention in management circles these days. Among the many desirable competencies are oral communication, initiative, decisiveness, tolerance, problem solving, and adaptability. Importantly, our earlier cautions about on-the-job personality testing extend to ability, intelligence, and competency testing and certification.

This section explores important cognitive abilities and cognitive styles related to job performance.

Ability

Stable characteristic responsible for a person's maximum physical or mental performance.

Skill

Specific capacity to manipulate objects.

Figure 5 – 5   Performance Depends on the Right Combination of Effort, Ability, and Skill

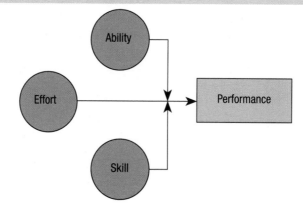

Intelligence and Cognitive Abilities

Intelligence
Capacity for constructive thinking, reasoning, problem solving.

Although experts do not agree on a specific definition, **intelligence** represents an individual's capacity for constructive thinking, reasoning, and problem solving.[69] Historically, intelligence was believed to be an innate capacity, passed genetically from one generation to the next. Research since has shown, however, that intelligence (like personality) also is a function of environmental influences.[70] Organic factors have more recently been added to the formula as a result of mounting evidence of the connection between alcohol and drug abuse by pregnant women and intellectual development problems in their children.[71]

Researchers have produced some interesting findings about abilities and intelligence in recent years. A unique five-year study documented the tendency of people to "gravitate into jobs commensurate with their abilities."[72] This prompts the vision of the labour market acting as a giant sorting or sifting machine, with employees tumbling into various ability bins. Meanwhile, a steady and significant rise in average intelligence among those in developed countries has been observed over the last 70 years. Why? Experts at a recent American Psychological Association conference concluded, "Some combination of better schooling, improved socioeconomic status, healthier nutrition, and a more technologically complex society might account for the gains in IQ scores."[73] So if you think you're smarter than your parents and your teachers, you're probably right!

Two Types of Abilities   Human intelligence has been studied predominantly through the empirical approach. By examining the relationships between measures of mental abilities and behaviour, researchers have statistically isolated major components of intelligence. Using this empirical procedure, pioneering psychologist Charles Spearman proposed in 1927 that all cognitive performance is determined by two types of abilities. The first can be characterized as a general mental ability needed for *all* cognitive tasks. The second is unique to the task at hand.[74] For example, an individual's ability to complete crossword puzzles is a function of his or her broad mental abilities as well as the specific ability to perceive patterns in partially completed words.

Seven Major Mental Abilities   Through the years, much research has been devoted to developing and expanding Spearman's ideas on the relationship between cognitive abilities and intelligence. One research psychologist listed 120 distinct mental abilities. Table 5-3 contains definitions of the seven most frequently cited mental abilities. Of the seven abilities, personnel selection researchers have found verbal ability, numerical ability, spatial ability, and inductive reasoning to be valid predictors of job performance.[75]

Table 5 – 3   Mental Abilities Underlying Performance

ABILITY	DESCRIPTION
1. Verbal comprehension	The ability to understand what words mean and to readily comprehend what is read.
2. Word fluency	The ability to produce isolated words that fulfil specific symbolic or structural requirements (such as all words that begin with the letter b and have two vowels).
3. Numerical	The ability to make quick and accurate arithmetic computations such as adding and subtracting.
4. Spatial	Being able to perceive spatial patterns and to visualize how geometric shapes would look if transformed in shape or position.
5. Memory	Having good rote memory for paired words, symbols, lists of numbers, or other associated items.
6. Perceptual speed	The ability to perceive figures, identify similarities and differences, and carry out tasks involving visual perception.
7. Inductive reasoning	The ability to reason from specifics to general conclusions.

Source: Adapted from M D Dunnette, "Aptitudes, Abilities, and Skills," in *Handbook of Industrial and Organizational Psychology*, ed M D Dunnette (Skokie, IL: Rand McNally, 1976), pp 478–83

Jung's Cognitive Styles Typology

Cognitive style
A perceptual and judgemental tendency, according to Jung's typology.

Within the context of Jung's theory, the term **cognitive style** refers to mental processes associated with how people perceive and make judgments from information. Although the landmark work on cognitive styles was completed in the 1920s by the noted Swiss psychoanalyst Carl Jung, his ideas did not catch on in the study of personality until the 1940s. That was when the mother—daughter team of Katharine C Briggs and Isabel Briggs Myers developed the Myers-Briggs Type Indicator (MBTI), an instrument for measuring Jung's cognitive styles. Today, the MBTI is a widely used personal growth and development tool in schools and businesses.[76]

Four Different Cognitive Styles   According to Jung, two dimensions influence perception and two others affect individual judgement. Perception is based on either sensation, using one's physical senses to interpret situations, or intuition, relying on past experience. In turn, judgements are made by either thinking or feeling. Finally, Jung proposed that an individual's cognitive style is determined by the pairing of one's perception and judgement tendencies. The resulting four cognitive styles are as follows:

- Sensation/thinking (ST).

- Intuition/thinking (NT).

- Sensation/feeling (SF).

- Intuition/feeling (NF).

Characteristics of each style are presented in Figure 5 – 6.[77] (The Personal Awareness and Growth Exercise at the end of this chapter, patterned after the MBTI, will help you determine your cognitive style.)

An individual with an ST style uses senses for perception and rational thinking for judgement. The ST-style person uses facts and impersonal analysis and develops greater abilities in technical areas involving facts and objects. A successful engineer could be expected to exhibit this cognitive style. In contrast, a person with an NT style focuses on possibilities rather than facts and displays abilities in areas involving theoretical or technical development. This style would enhance the performance of a research scientist.

Although an SF person likely is interested in gathering facts, he or she tends to treat others with personal warmth, sympathy, and friendliness. Successful counsellors or teachers probably use this style. Finally, an individual with an NF style tends to exhibit artistic flair while relying heavily on personal insights rather than objective facts (see Figure 5 – 6).

Practical Research Findings   If Jung's cognitive styles typology is valid, then individuals with different cognitive styles should seek different kinds of information when making a decision. A study of 50 MBA students found that those with different cognitive styles did in fact use qualitatively different information while working on a strategic planning problem.[78] Research also has shown that people with different cognitive styles prefer different careers. For example, people who rely on intuition prefer careers in psychology, advertising, teaching, and the arts.

Findings have further shown that individuals who make judgements based on the "thinking" approach have higher work motivation and quality of work life than those who take a "feeling" approach. In addition, individuals with a sensation mode of perception have higher job satisfaction than those relying on intuition.[79] Small business owner/managers with a "thinking" style made more money than their "feeling" counterparts. But no correlation was found between the four Jungian styles and small business owner/manager success.[80] The following conclusion from a recent exhaustive review of management-oriented MBTI studies makes us cautious about these findings: "It is clear that efforts to detect simplistic linkages between type preferences and managerial effectiveness have been disappointing. Indeed, given the mixed quality of research and the inconsistent findings, no definitive conclusions regarding these relationships can be drawn."[81] On balance, we believe Jung's cognitive styles typology and the MBTI are useful for diversity training and management development purposes,[82] but inappropriate for making personnel decisions such as hiring and promotions.

Figure 5 – 6   People Have Different Cognitive Styles and Corresponding Characteristics

	Decision Style			
	ST Sensation/Thinking	**NT** Intuition/Thinking	**SF** Sensation/Feeling	**NF** Intuition/Feeling
Focus of attention	Facts	Possibilities	Facts	Possibilities
Method of handling things	Impersonal analysis	Impersonal analysis	Personal warmth	Personal warmth
Tendency to become	Practical and matter-of-fact	Logical and ingenious	Sympathetic and friendly	Enthusiastic and insightful
Expression of abilities	Technical skills with facts and objects	Theoretical and technical developments	Practical help and services for people	Understanding and communicating with people
Representative occupation	Technician	Planner	Teacher	Artist
		Manager		

Source: W Taggart and D Robey, "Minds and Managers: On the Dual Nature of Human Information Processing and Management," *Academy of Management Review*, April 1981, p 190. Used with permission.

Emotions: An Emerging OB Topic

In the ideal world of management theory, employees pursue organizational goals in a logical and rational manner. Emotional behaviour seldom is factored into the equation. Yet day-to-day organizational life shows us how prevalent and powerful emotions can be. Anger and jealousy, both potent emotions, often push aside logic and rationality in the workplace. Managers use emotions to both motivate and intimidate. Consider the following story:

Although I was a very competent trainer with several years of experience, every course I gave was highly critiqued by my boss. Time after time, verbal abuse would start and my feeling of well-being would evaporate in seconds to be replaced by humiliation and depression. He needed someone to humiliate and I was the usual target. There was no logical reason for his actions. He used me as a verbal punchbag for reasons best known to himself. Over a long time, I lost count of the number of highly personal and offensive remarks he made.

Needless to say, he eventually succeeded in provoking me to hate so much I started to react against him. This was his ploy to eventually get rid of me by telling his superiors I was a problem employee. Mud sticks and I was eventually moved on and made redundant by an even bigger bully manager.[83]

In this final section, our examination of individual differences turns to defining emotions, reviewing a typology of 10 positive and negative emotions, and focusing on the management of anger, a potentially destructive and dangerous emotion.

Positive and Negative Emotions

Emotions
Complex human reactions to personal achievements and setbacks.

Richard S Lazarus, a leading authority on the subject, defines **emotions** as "complex, patterned, organismic reactions to how we think we are doing in our lifelong efforts to survive and flourish and to achieve what we wish for ourselves."[84] The word *organismic* is appropriate because emotions involve the whole person—biological, psychological, and social. As discussed in Chapter 17, emotions play roles in both causing and adapting to stress and its associated biological and psychological problems. The destructive effect of emotional behaviour on social relationships is all too obvious in daily life.

Lazarus's definition of emotions centres on a person's goals. Accordingly, his distinction between positive and negative emotions is goal oriented. Some emotions are triggered by frustration and failure when pursuing one's goals. Lazarus calls these negative emotions. They are said to be goal incongruent. For example, which of the six negative emotions in Figure 5–7 are you likely to experience if you fail the final exam in a required course? Failing the exam would be incongruent with your goal of graduating on time. On the other hand, which of the four positive emotions in Figure 5–7 would you probably experience if you graduated on time and with honours? The emotions you would experience in this situation are positive because they are congruent (or consistent) with an important lifetime goal. The individual's goals, it is important to note, may or may not be socially acceptable. Thus, a positive emotion, such as love/affection, may be undesirable if associated with sexual harassment. Oppositely, slight pangs of guilt, anxiety, and envy can motivate extra effort. On balance, the constructive or destructive nature of a particular emotion must be judged in terms of both its intensity and the person's relevant goal.

More Attention Needed

Emotional behaviour receives less than its fair share of attention in the general business and management literature. Daniel Goleman, author of the bestseller *Emotional Intelligence,*[85] has, however, brilliantly summarized insights in the role of emotions in people's interactions. People who excel in real life, whose intimate relationships flourish, who are stars in the workplace, possess "emotional intelligence," which includes self-awareness, impulse control and self-motivation. The concept of emotional intelligence is applicable to organizations as well as to individuals.[86] Business people and researchers are beginning to find that when understood and managed wisely, emotions can enhance a business. However, if they go unacknowledged or are misunderstood or mismanaged, they set a business back. Many psychologists and business leaders say emotions can help teams work effectively, can create commitment because of the excitement employees feel about their work, can energize workers and can enable them to unleash their creativity.[87] Other recent articles looked at fear of success, fear among trainers and trainees, and conquering fear by learning to trust others in experiential exercises such as falling backwards from an elevated platform into the arms of team members.[88]

The OB research literature is even more sparse. Emotional behaviour is not typically covered as a central variable but rather as a subfactor in discussions of organizational politics, conflict, and stress. One OB researcher recently offered a model of jealousy and envy in the workplace and theorized that the trend towards self-managed work teams would be helpful:

With shared responsibility for task completion and the deliberate elimination of "turf," self-managed teams provide a model that is distinct from traditional, hierarchical work systems. As a consequence, the magnitude of workplace jealousy and envy that may be found in self-managed or semi-autonomous teams may be significantly lower than in traditional settings.[89]

Systematic mood control among a sample of 57 hospital employees touched on emotions in another recent study. Specifically, employees who were given cookies prior to filling out a job satisfaction survey tended to report higher satisfaction than co-workers who did not get cookies.[90] Of course, employees have long known about this tactic (for instance, getting the boss in a good mood before asking for a pay rise). We look forward to more comprehensive OB research on the causes and consequences of emotional behaviour.

Managing Anger

Of all the emotions in Figure 5–7, anger is the one most likely to be downright dangerous. It deserves special attention. Unchecked anger could be a key contributing

---

Figure 5 – 7   Positive and Negative Emotions

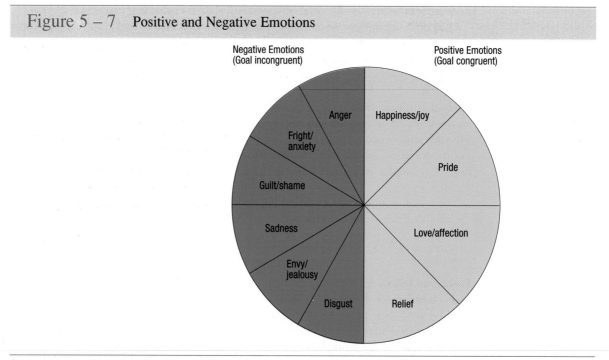

Source: Adapted from discussion in R S Lazarus, *Emotion and Adaptation* (New York: Oxford University Press, 1991), Chs 6, 7.

factor to what one team of researchers calls *organization-motivated aggression.*[91] Worse, uncontrolled anger certainly is a contributor to workplace violence. As awareness of workplace violence increases, employers are installing various security systems and training employees to avoid or diffuse incidents. The European Commission's definition of workplace violence includes "incidents where persons are abused, threatened or assaulted in circumstances relating to their work, involving an explicit challenge to their safety, well-being and health.[92] Anger-management training for all employees, based on the self-control tactics in Table 5–4, could make a positive contribution to reducing workplace violence and improving the general quality of work life. In summary, if the most troublesome emotion—anger—can be managed through learned self-control, then all the emotions can be managed. (See the behavioural self-management model and related techniques in Chapter 15.) Meantime, the workplace remains an emotionally charged environment where too much of either positive or negative emotions is counterproductive.

Table 5 – 4   How to Manage Anger in Yourself and Others

REDUCING CHRONIC ANGER [IN YOURSELF]	RESPONDING TO ANGRY PROVOCATION
GUIDES FOR ACTION	**GUIDES FOR ACTION**
• Appreciate the potentially valuable lessons from anger.	• Expect angry people to exaggerate.
• Use mistakes and slights to learn.	• Recognize the other's frustrations and pressures.
• Recognize that you and others can do well enough without being perfect.	• Use the provocation to develop your abilities
• Trust that most people want to be caring, helpful family members and colleagues.	• Allow the other to let off steam.
• Forgive others and yourself.	• Begin to problem solve when the anger is at moderate levels.
• Confront unrealistic, blame-oriented assumptions.	• Congratulate yourself on turning an outburst into an opportunity to find solutions.
• Adopt constructive, learning-oriented assumptions.	• Share successes with partners.
PITFALLS TO AVOID	**PITFALLS TO AVOID**
• Assume every slight is a painful wound.	• Take every word literally.
• Equate not getting what you want with catastrophe.	• Denounce the most extreme statements and ignore more moderate ones.
• See every mistake and slip as a transgression that must be corrected immediately.	• Doubt yourself because the other does.
• Attack someone for your getting angry.	• Attack because you have been attacked.
• Attack yourself for getting angry.	• Forget the experience without learning from it.
• Try to be and have things perfect.	
• Suspect people's motives unless you have incontestable evidence that people can be trusted.	
• Assume any attempt to change yourself is an admission of failure	
• Never forgive.	

Scource: Reprinted with permission from D Tjosvold, *Learning to Manage Conflict: Getting People to Work Together Productively*, pp 127–29. Copyright © 1993 Dean Tjosvold. First published by Lexington Books. All rights reserved.

Summary of Key Concepts

1. *Explain the nature and determinants of organization-based self-esteem.* Organization-based self-estem (OBSE) is an employee's self-perceived value as an organizational member. People high in OBSE see themselves as important and meaningful within the organization. Three primary determinants of high OBSE are managerial respect and concern, flexible organization structure, and complex and challenging jobs.

2. *Define self-efficacy, and explain its sources.* Self-efficacy involves one's belief about one's ability to accomplish specific tasks. Those extremely low in self-efficacy suffer from learned helplessness. Four sources of self-efficacy beliefs are prior experience, behaviour models, persuasion from others, and assessment of one's physical and emotional states. High self-efficacy beliefs foster constructive and goal-oriented action, whereas low self-efficacy fosters passive, failure-prone activities and emotions.

3. *Contrast high and low self-monitoring individuals, and describe resulting problems each may have.* A high self-monitor strives to make a good public impression by closely monitoring his or her behaviour and adapting it to the situation. Very high self-monitoring can create a "chameleon" who is seen as insincere and dishonest. Low self-monitors do the opposite by acting out their momentary feelings, regardless of their surroundings. Very low self-monitoring can lead to a one-way communicator who seems to ignore verbal and nonverbal cues from others.

4. *Identify and describe the Big Five personality dimensions, and specify which one is correlated most strongly with job performance.* The Big Five personality dimensions are extraversion (social and talkative), agreeableness (trusting and cooperative), conscientiousness (responsible and persistent), emotional stability (relaxed and unworried), and openness to experience (intellectual and curious). Conscientiousness is the best predictor of job performance.

5. *Explain the difference between an internal and external locus of control.* People with an internal locus of control, such as entrepreneurs, believe they are masters of their own fate. Those with an external locus of control attribute their behaviour and its results to situational forces.

6. *Explain how attitudes influence behaviour in terms of the Fishbein and Ajzen model of behavioural intentions.* According to Fishbein and Ajzen's model, beliefs about behaviour–outcome relationships and how one should act influence attitudes and subjective norms. Depending on their relative importance, attitudes and norms together foster a behavioural intention, the best predictor of actual behaviour.

7. *Describe Carl Jung's cognitive styles typology.* By combining two dimensions of perception (sensation and intuition) with two dimensions of judgement (thinking and feeling), Carl Jung identified four cognitive styles. They are sensation/thinking (practical and matter-of-fact), intuition/thinking (logical and ingenious), sensation/feeling (sympathetic and friendly), and intuition/feeling (enthusiastic and insightful).

8. *Distinguish between positive and negative emotions, and explain how they can be judged.* Positive emotions—happiness/joy, pride, love/affection, and relief—are personal reactions to circumstances congruent with one's goals. Negative emotions—anger, fright/anxiety, guilt/shame, sadness, envy/jealousy, and disgust—are personal reactions to circumstances incongruent with one's goals. Both types of emotions need to be judged in terms of intensity and the appropriateness of the person's relevant goal.

Discussion Questions

1. How should the reality of a more diverse workforce affect management's approach to dealing with individual differences?

2. What is your personal experience with organization-based self-esteem?

3. How is someone you know with low self-efficacy, relative to a specified task, "programming themselves for failure?" What could be done to help that individual develop high self-efficacy?

4. Why is high self-monitoring both a good and bad thing in today's workplace?

5. What are the career implications of your self-monitoring score in the second OB Exercise?

6. On scales of Low = 1 to High = 10, how would you rate yourself on the Big Five personality dimensions? Is your personality profile suitable for a managerial position?

7. How would you respond to the following statement? "Whenever possible, managers should hire people with an internal locus of control."

8. How would you respond to a manager who made this statement? "I'm only interested in behaviour. I've never seen an attitude, so why be concerned with attitudes?"

9. According to Jung's typology, which cognitive style do you exhibit? How can you tell? Is it an advantage or a disadvantage?

10. What are your personal experiences with negative emotions being positive and positive emotions being negative?

Personal Awareness and Growth Exercise

What Is Your Cognitive Style?

Objectives

1. To identify your cognitive style, according to Carl Jung's typology.[93]

2. To consider the managerial implications of your cognitive style.

Instructions

Please respond to the 16 items below. There are no right or wrong answers. After you have completed all the items, refer to the scoring key, and follow its directions.

Questionnaire

Part I. Circle the response that comes closest to how you usually feel or act.

1. Are you more careful about:
   A. People's feelings
   B. Their rights

2. Do you usually get along better with:
   A. Imaginative people
   B. Realistic people

3. Which of these two is the higher compliment:
   A. A person has real feeling
   B. A person is consistently reasonable

4. In doing something with many other people, does it appeal more to you:
   A. To do it in the accepted way
   B. To invent a way of your own

5. Do you get more annoyed at:
   A. Fancy theories
   B. People who don't like theories

6. It is higher praise to call someone:
   A. A person of vision
   B. A person of common sense

7. Do you more often let:
   A. Your heart rule your head
   B. Your head rule your heart

8. Do you think it is worse:
   A. To show too much warmth
   B. To be unsympathetic

9. If you were a teacher, would you rather teach:
   A. Courses involving theory
   B. Fact courses

Part II. Which word in each of the following pairs appeals to you more? Circle A or B.

10. A. Compassion
     B. Foresight
11. A. Justice
     B. Mercy
12. A. Production
     B. Design
13. A. Gentle
     B. Firm
14. A. Uncritical
     B. Critical
15. A. Literal
     B. Figurative
16. A. Imaginative
     B. Matter of fact

Scoring Key

To categorize your responses to the questionnaire, count one point for each response on the following four scales, and total the number of points recorded in each column. Instructions for classifying your scores are indicated below.

SENSATION	INTUITION	THINKING	FEELING
2 B _____	2 A _____	1 B _____	1 A _____
4 A _____	4 B _____	3 B _____	3 A _____
5 A _____	5 B _____	7 B _____	7 A _____
6 B _____	6 A _____	8 A _____	8 B _____
9 B _____	9 A _____	10 B _____	10 A _____
12 A _____	12 B _____	11 A _____	11 B _____
15 A _____	15 B _____	13 B _____	13 A _____
16 B _____	16 A _____	14 B _____	14 A _____
Totals = _____	_____	_____	_____

Classifying Total Scores

Write *intuitive* if your intuition score is equal to or greater than your sensation score.
Write *sensation* if sensation is greater than intuition.
Write *feeling* if feeling is greater than thinking.
Write *thinking* if thinking is greater than feeling.
When *thinking* equals feeling, you should write feeling if a male and thinking if a female.

QUESTIONS FOR DICUSSION

1. What is your cognitive style?
    Sensation/thinking (ST)
    Intuition/thinking (NT)
    Sensation/feeling (SF)
    Intuition/feeling (NF)

2. Do you agree with this assessment? Why or why not?

3. Will your cognitive style, as determined in this exercise, help you achieve your career goal(s)?

4. Would your style be an asset or liability for a managerial position involving getting things done through others?

Group Exercise

Anger Control Role Play

Objectives

1. To demonstrate that emotions can be managed.

2. To develop your interpersonal skills for managing both your own and someone else's anger.

Introduction

Personal experience and research tell us that anger begets anger. People do not make their best decisions when angry. Angry outbursts often inflict unintentional interpersonal damage by triggering other emotions (e.g., disgust in observers and subsequent guilt and shame in the angry person). Effective managers know how to break the cycle of negative emotions by defusing anger in themselves and others. This is a role-playing exercise for groups of four. You will have a chance to play two different roles. All the roles are generic, so they can be played as either a woman or a man.

Instructions

Your instructor will divide the class into groups of four. Everyone should read all five roles described. Members of each foursome will decide among themselves who will play which roles. All told, you will participate in two rounds of role playing (each round lasting no longer than 8 minutes). In round one, one person will play Role 1 and another will play Role 3; the remaining two group members will play Role 5. In round two, those who played Role 5 in the first round will play Roles 2 and 4. The other two will switch to Role 5.

ROLE 1: THE ANGRY (OUT-OF-CONTROL) SHIFT SUPERVISOR

You work for a leading electronics company that makes computer chips and other computer-related equipment. Your factory is responsible for assembling and testing the company's most profitable line of computer microprocessors. Business has been good, so your factory is working three shifts. The day shift, which you are now on, is the most desirable one. The night shift, from 11 pm to 7:30 am is the least desirable and least productive. In fact, the night shift is such a mess that your boss, the factory manager, wants you to move to the night shift next week. Your boss just broke this bad news as the two of you are having lunch in the company cafeteria. You are shocked and angered because you are one of the most senior and highly rated shift supervisors in the factory. Thanks to your leadership, your shift has broken all production records during the past year. As the divorced single parent of a 10-year-old child, the radical schedule change would be a major lifestyle burden. Questions swirl through your head. "Why me?" "What kind of reliable child-care will be available when I sleep during the day and work at night?" "Why should I be 'punished' for being a top supervisor?" "Why don't they hire someone for the position?" Your boss asks what you think.

When playing this role, be as realistic as possible without getting so loud that you disrupt the other groups. Also, if anyone in your group would be offended by foul language, please refrain from cursing during your angry outburst.

ROLE 2: THE ANGRY (UNDER-CONTROL) SHIFT SUPERVISOR

Same situation as in Role 1. But this role will require you to read and act according to the tips for reducing chronic anger in the left side of Table 5–4. You have plenty of reason to be frustrated and angry, but you realize the importance of maintaining a good working relationship with the factory manager.

ROLE 3: THE (HARD-DRIVING) FACTORY MANAGER

You have a reputation for having a "short fuse." When someone gets angry with you, you attack. When playing this role, be as realistic as possible. Remember, you are responsible for the entire factory with its 1,200 employees and hundreds of millions of euros of electronics products. A hiring freeze is in place, so you have to move one of your current supervisors. You have chosen your best supervisor because the night shift is your biggest threat to profitable operations. The night-shift supervisor gets a 10 per cent pay premium. Ideally, the move will only be for six months.

ROLE 4: THE (MELLOW) FACTORY MANAGER

Same general situation as in Role 3. However, this role will require you to read and act according to the tips for responding to angry provocation in the right side of Table 5–4. You have a reputation for being results-oriented but reasonable. You are good at taking a broad, strategic view of problems and are a good negotiator.

ROLE 5: SILENT OBSERVER

Follow the exchange between the shift supervisor and the factory manager without talking or getting actively involved. Jot down some notes (for later class discussion) as you observe whether the factory manager did a good job of managing the supervisor's anger.

QUESTIONS FOR DISCUSSION

1. Why is uncontrolled anger a sure road to failure?

2. Is it possible to express anger without insulting others? Explain.

3. Which is more difficult, controlling anger in yourself or defusing someone else's anger? Why?

4. What useful lessons did you learn from this role-playing exercise?

Notes

[1] Adapted and translated from A Münninghoff, *De Stijl van de Leider: Boris Jeltsin, de Omgekeerde Facelift van een Russische Messias,* (Amrop International Noteboom Partners, 1992).

[2] M Duffy, "The State of Bill Clinton," *Time*, February 7, 1994, pp. 24-29.

[3] D Seligman, "The Trouble with Buyouts," *Fortune*, November 30, 1992, p 125.

[4] S I Cheldelin and L A Foritano, "Psychometrics: Their Use in Organisation Development," *Journal of Managerial Psychology*, no. 4, 1989, p 21.

[5] See J Gordon, "Different from What? Diversity as a Performance Issue," *Training*, May 1995, pp 25–34; K Hilderbrand, "Use Leadership Training to Increase Diversity," *HRMagazine*, August 1996, pp 53–58; and S M Paskoff, "Ending the Workplace Diversity Wars," *Training*, August 1996, pp 42–47.

[6] V Gecas, "The Self-Concept," in *Annual Review of Sociology*, eds R H Turner and J F Short, Jr. (Palo Alto, CA: Annual Reviews Inc., 1982), vol. 8, p 3. Also see A P Brief and R J Aldag, "The 'Self' in Work Organizations: A Conceptual Review," *Academy of Management Review*, January 1981, pp 75–88; J J Sullivan, "Self Theories and Employee Motivation," *Journal of Management*, June 1989, pp 345–63; and P Cushman, "Why the Self Is Empty," American Psychologist, May 1990, pp 599–611.

[7] L Festinger, *A Theory of Cognitive Dissonance* (Stanford, CA: Stanford University Press, 1957), p 3.

[8] See J Holt and D M Keats, "Work Cognitions in Multicultural

Interaction," *Journal of Cross-Cultural Psychology*, December 1992, pp 421–43.

[9]A Canadian versus Japanese comparison of self-concept can be found in J D Campbell, P D Trapnell, S J Heine, I M Katz, L F Lavallee, and D R Lehman, "Self-Concept Clarity: Measurement, Personality Correlates, and Cultural Boundaries," *Journal of Personality and Social Psychology*, January 1996, pp 141–56.

[10]See D C Barnlund, "Public and Private Self in Communicating with Japan," *Business Horizons*, March–April 1989, pp 32–40; and the section on "Doing Business with Japan" in P R Harris and R T Moran, *Managing Cultural Differences,* 4th edn (Houston: Gulf Publishing, 1996), pp 267–76.

[11]Based in part on a definition found in Gecas, "The Self Concept."

[12]H W Marsh, "Positive and Negative Global Self-Esteem: A Substantively Meaningful Distinction or Artifacts?" *Journal of Personality and Social Psychology*, April 1996, p 819.

[13]Ibid.

[14]For related research, see R C Liden, L Martin, and C K Parsons, "Interviewer and Applicant Behaviors in Employment Interviews," *Academy of Management Journal*, April 1993, pp 372–86; and M B Setterlund and P M Niedenthal, " 'Who Am I? Why Am I Here?': Self-Esteem, Self-Clarity, and Prototype Matching," *Journal of Personality and Social Psychology*, October 1993, pp 769–80.

[15]See J A Stein, M D Newcomb, and P M Bentler, "The Relative Influence on Vocational Behavior and Family Involvement on Self-Esteem: Longitudinal Analyses of Young Adult Women and Men," *Journal of Vocational Behavior*, June 1990, pp 320–38.

[16]Details may be found in B R Schlenker, M F Weigold, and J R Hallam, "Self-Serving Attributions in Social Context: Effects of Self-Esteem and Social Pressure," *Journal of Personality and Social Psychology*, May 1990, pp 855–63.

[17]See R F Baumeister, L Smart, and J M Boden, "Relation of Threatened Egotism to Violence and Aggression: The Dark Side of High Self-Esteem," *Psychological Review*, January 1996, pp 5–33; and D Seligman, "Down with Esteem," *Fortune*, April 29, 1996, pp 211–14.

[18]For related reading, see M Kaeter, "False Identities," *Business Ethics*, March–April 1994, p 46.

[19]M A Mone, "Relationships between Self-Concepts, Aspirations, Emotional Responses, and Intent to Leave a Downsizing Organization," *Human Resource Management,* Summer 1994, vol. 33 (2), pp 281–298.

[20]E Diener and M Diener, "Cross-Cultural Correlates of Life Satisfaction and Self-Esteem," *Journal of Personality and Social Psychology*, April 1995, p 662.

[21]W J McGuire and C V McGuire, "Enhancing Self-Esteem by Directed-Thinking Tasks: Cognitive and Affective Positivity Asymmetries," *Journal of Personality and Social Psychology*, June 1996, p 1124.

[22]J L Pierce, D G Gardner, L L Cummings, and R B Dunham, "Organization-Based Self-Esteem: Construct Definition, Measurement, and Validation," *Academy of Management Journal*, September 1989, p 625. Also see J L Pierce, D G Gardner, R B Dunham, and L L Cummings, "Moderation by Organization-Based Self-Esteem of Role Condition-Employee Response Relationships," *Academy of Management Journal*, April 1993, pp 271–88.

[23]Practical steps are discussed in M Kaeter, "Basic Self-Esteem," *Training,* August 1993, pp 31–35.

[24]Adapted from discussion in J K Matejka and R J Dunsing, "Great Expectations," *Management World*, January 1987, pp 16–17.

[25]M E Gist, "Self-Efficacy: Implications for Organizational Behavior and Human Resource Management," *Academy of Management Review*, July 1987, p 472. Also see A Bandura, "Self-Efficacy: Toward a Unifying Theory of Behavioral Change," *Psychological Review*, March 1977, pp 191–215; and M E Gist and T R Mitchell, "Self-Efficacy: A Theoretical Analysis of Its

Determinants and Malleability," *Academy of Management Review*, April 1992, pp 183–211.

[26]R Tait, *Roads to the Top* (London: Macmillan Press, 1995).

[27]D Rader, " 'I Knew What I Wanted to Be,'" *Parade Magazine,* November 1, 1992, p 4.

[28]Based on D H Lindsley, D A Brass, and J B Thomas, "Efficacy-Performance Spirals: A Multilevel Perspective," *Academy of Management Review,* July 1995, pp 645–78.

[29]See, for example, V Gecas, "The Social Psychology of Self-Efficacy," in *Annual Review of Sociology*, eds W R Scott and J Blake (Palo Alto, CA: Annual Reviews, Inc., 1989), vol. 15, pp 291–316; C K Stevens, A G Bavetta, and M E Gist, "Gender Differences in the Acquisition of Salary Negotiation Skills: The Role of Goals, Self-Efficacy, and Perceived Control," *Journal of Applied Psychology*, October 1993, pp 723–35; and D Eden and Y Zuk, "Seasickness as a Self-Fulfilling Prophecy: Raising Self-Efficacy to Boost Performance at Sea," *Journal of Applied Psychology*, October 1995, pp 628–35.

[30]For more on learned helplessness, see Gecas, "The Social Psychology of Self-Efficacy," and M J Martinko and W L Gardner, "Learned Helplessness: An Alternative Explanation for Performance Deficits," *Academy of Management Review*, April 1982, pp 195–204.

[31]Research on this connection is reported in R B Rubin, M M Martin, S S Bruning, and D E Powers, "Test of a Self-Efficacy Model of Interpersonal Communication Competence," *Communication Quarterly*, Spring 1993, pp 210–20.

[32]For details, see J Barling and R Beattie, "Self-Efficacy Beliefs and Sales Performance," *Journal of Organizational Behaviour Management*, Spring 1983, pp 41–51.

[33]Based in part on discussion in Gecas, "The Social Psychology of Self-Efficacy."

[34]The positive relationship between self-efficacy and readiness for retraining is documented in L A Hill and J Elias, "Retraining Midcareer Managers: Career History and Self-Efficacy Beliefs," *Human Resource Management*, Summer 1990, pp 197–217. Also see A M Saks, "Longitudinal Field Investigation of the Moderating and Mediating Effects of Self-Efficacy on the Relationship between Training and Newcomer Adjustment," *Journal of Applied Psychology*, April 1995, pp 211–25.

[35]See P C Earley and T R Lituchy, "Delineating Goal and Efficacy Effects: A Test of Three Models," *Journal of Applied Psychology,* February 1991, pp 81–98.

[36]See W S Silver, T R Mitchell, and M E Gist, "Response to Successful and Unsuccessful Performance: The Moderating Effect of Self-Efficacy on the Relationship between Performance and Attributions," *Organizational Behavior and Human Decision Processes*, June 1995, pp 286–99; and R Zemke, "The Corporate Coach," *Training*, December 1996, pp 24–28.

[37]G Sadri and I T Robertson, "Self-efficiency and Work Related Behaviour: A Review and Meta-Analysis," *Applied Psychology,* vol 42, no 2, pp 139–152.

[38]M Snyder and S Gangestad, "On the Nature of Self-Monitoring: Matters of Assessment, Matters of Validity," *Journal of Personality and Social Psychology*, July 1986, p 125.

[39]Data from M Kilduff and D V Day, "Do Chameleons Get Ahead? The Effects of Self-Monitoring on Managerial Careers," *Academy of Management Journal*, August 1994, pp 1047–60.

[40]Data from D B Turban and T W Dougherty, "Role of Protege Personality in Receipt of Mentoring and Career Success," *Academy of Management Journal*, June 1994, pp 688–702.

[41]See F Luthans, "Successful vs. Effective Managers," *Academy of Management Executive*, May 1988, pp 127–32.

[42]A Arkin, "Using people as a force for change," *People Management,* October 19, 1995, pp 34–37.

[43]For related research evidence on self-silencing, see L V Gratch, M

E Bassett, and S L Attra, "The Relationship of Gender and Ethnicity to Self-Silencing and Depression among College Students," *Psychology of Women Quarterly*, December 1995, pp 509–15.

[44]For evidence of the stability of adult personality dimensions, see R R McCrae, "Moderated Analyses of Longitudinal Personality Stability," *Journal of Personality and Social Psychology*, September 1993, pp 577—85. Adult personality changes are documented in L Kaufman Cartwright and P Wink, "Personality Change in Women Physicians from Medical Student to Mid-40s," *Psychology of Women Quarterly*, June 1994, pp 291–308.

[45]The landmark report is J M Digman, "Personality Structure: Emergence of the Five-Factor Model," *Annual Review of Psychology*, vol. 41, 1990, pp 417–40. Also see M R Barrick and M K Mount, "Autonomy as a Moderator of the Relationships between the Big Five Personality Dimensions and Job Performance," *Journal of Applied Psychology*, February 1993, pp 111–18; J A Johnson and F Ostendorf, "Clarification of the Five-Factor Model with the Abridged Big Five Dimensional Circumplex," *Journal of Personality and Social Psychology*, September 1993, pp 563–76; and M Zuckerman, D M Kuhlman, J Joireman, P Teta, and M Kraft, "A Comparison of Three Structural Models for Personality: The Big Three, the Big Five, and the Alternative Five," *Journal of Personality and Social Psychology*, October 1993, pp 757–68.

[46]For a review of research on the relationship between introversion—extraversion, motivation, and performance, see M S Humphreys and W Revelle, "Personality, Motivation, and Performance: A Theory of the Relationship between Individual Differences and Information Processing," *Psychological Review*, April 1984, pp 153–84.

[47]Data from S V Paunonen et al., "The Structure of Personality in Six Cultures," *Journal of Cross-Cultural Psychology,* May 1996, pp 339—53. Also see M S Katigbak, A T Church, and T X Akamine, "Cross-Cultural Generalizability of Personality Dimensions: Relating Indigenous and Imported Dimensions in Two Cultures," *Journal of Personality and Social Psychology,* January 1996, pp 99–114.

[48]See M R Barrick and M K Mount, "The Big Five Personality Dimensions and Job Performance: A Meta-Analysis," *Personnel Psychology,* Spring 1991, pp 1–26. Also see R P Tett, D N Jackson, and M Rothstein, "Personality Measures as Predictors of Job Performance: A Meta-Analytic Review," *Personnel Psychology,* Winter 1991, pp 703–42.

[49]Barrick and Mount, "The Big Five Personality Dimensions and Job Performance: A Meta-Analysis," p 18.

[50]Ibid., p 21.

[51]See S B Gustafson and M D Mumford, "Personal Style and Person-Environment Fit: A Pattern Approach," *Journal of Vocational Behavior*, April 1995, pp 163–88.

[52]For an instructive update, see J B Rotter, "Internal versus External Control of Reinforcement: A Case History of a Variable," *American Psychologist,* April 1990, pp 489—93. A critical review of locus of control and a call for a meta-analysis can be found in R W Renn and R J Vandenberg, "Differences in Employee Attitudes and Behaviors Based on Rotter's (1966) Internal-External Locus of Control: Are They All Valid?" *Human Relations*, November 1991, pp 1161–77.

[53]J Fierman, "What's Luck Got to Do with It?" *Fortune*, October 16, 1995, p 149.

[54]For an overall review of research on locus of control, see P E Spector, "Behavior in Organizations as a Function of Employee's Locus of Control," *Psychological Bulletin*, May 1982, pp 482–97; the relationship between locus of control and performance and satisfaction is examined in D R Norris and R E Niebuhr, "Attributional Influences on the Job Performance—Job Satisfaction Relationship," *Academy of Management Journal*, June 1984, pp 424–31; salary differences between internals and externals were examined by P C Nystrom, "Managers' Salaries and Their Beliefs about Reinforcement Control," *The Journal of Social Psychology,* August 1983, pp 291–92.

[55]See S R Hawk, "Locus of Control and Computer Attitude: The Effect of User Involvement," *Computers in Human Behavior*, no. 3, 1989, pp 199–206. Also see A S Phillips and A G Bedeian, "Leader-Follower Exchange Quality: The Role of Personal and Interpersonal Attributes," *Academy of Management Journal*, August 1994, pp 990–1001.

[56]These recommendations are from Spector, "Behavior in Organizations as a Function of Employee's Locus of Control."

[57]See "What Men Think About," *Training,* March 1995, p 14; and P Cappelli, "Is the 'Skills Gap' Really about Attitudes?" *California Management Review,* Summer 1995, pp 108–24.

[58]M Fishbein and I Ajzen, *Belief, Attitude, Intention and Behavior: An Introduction to Theory and Research* (Reading, MA: Addison-Wesley Publishing, 1975), p 6.

[59]See B M Staw and J Ross, "Stability in the Midst of Change: A Dispositional Approach to Job Attitudes," *Journal of Applied Psychology,* August 1985, pp 469–80.

[60]See J Schaubroeck, D C Ganster, and B Kemmerer, "Does Trait Affect Promote Job Attitude Stability?" *Journal of Organizational Behavior*, March 1996, pp 191–96.

[61]For a discussion of the difference between values and attitudes, see B W Becker and P E Connor, "Changing American Values—Debunking the Myth," *Business*, January—March 1985, pp 56—59.

[62]For a brief overview and update of the model, see M Fishbein and M Stasson, "The Role of Desires, Self-Predictions, and Perceived Control in the Prediction of Training Session Attendance," *Journal of Applied Social Psychology,* February 1990, pp 173–98. Alternative models are discussed in M Sverke and S Kuruvilla, "A New Conceptualization of Union Commitment: Development and Test of an Integrated Theory," *Journal of Organizational Behavior,* Special Issue, 1995, pp 505–32; and R C Thompson and J G Hunt, "Inside the Black Box of Alpha, Beta, and Gamma Change: Using a Cognitive-Processing Model to Assess Attitude Structure," *Academy of Management Review,* July 1996, pp 655–90.

[63]See R P Steel and N K Ovalle II, "A Review and Meta-Analysis of Research on the Relationship between Behavioral Intentions and Employee Turnover," *Journal of Applied Psychology,* November 1984, pp 673–86.

[64]Based on Reuters, "Daimler says has 100,000 A-class orders in hand," *http//www.reuters.com/*, December 10, 1997.

[65]I Ajzen and M Fishbein, *Understanding Attitudes and Predicting Social Behavior* (Englewood Cliffs, NJ: Prentice-Hall, 1980), p 7.

[66]Drawn from J M Grant and T S Bateman, "An Experimental Test of the Impact of Drug-Testing Programs on Potential Job Applicants' Attitudes and Intentions," *Journal of Applied Psychology,* April 1990, pp 127–31.

[67]For an overall review of attitude formation research, see Ajzen and Fishbein, *Understanding Attitudes and Predicting Social Behavior.* Also see S Chaiken and C Stangor, "Attitudes and Attitude Change," in *Annual Review of Psychology,* eds M R Rosenzweig and L W Porter (Palo Alto, CA: Annual Reviews, 1987), pp 575–630; and Fishbein and Stasson, "The Role of Desires, Self-Predictions, and Perceived Control in the Prediction of Training Session Attendance."

[68]Based on evidence in C J Thomsen, A M Basu, and M Tippens Reinitz, "Effects of Women's Studies Courses on Gender-Related Attitudes of Women and Men," *Psychology of Women Quarterly*, September 1995, pp 419–26.

[69]For interesting reading on intelligence, see E Cose, "Teaching Kids to Be Smart," *Newsweek,* August 21, 1995, pp 58–60; A Farnham, "Are You Smart Enough to Keep Your Job?" *Fortune,* January 15, 1996, pp 34–48; D Stamps, "Are We Smart Enough for Our Jobs?" *Training,* April 1996, pp 44–50; and K S Peterson, "Do

New Definitions of Smart Dilute Meaning?" *USA Today,* February 18, 1997, pp 1D–2D.

[70]For an excellent update on intelligence, including definitional distinctions and a historical perspective of the IQ controversy, see R A Weinberg, "Intelligence and IQ," *American Psychologist,* February 1989, pp 98–104.

[71]Ibid.

[72]S L Wilk, L Burris Desmarais, and P R Sackett, "Gravitation to Jobs Commensurate with Ability: Longitudinal and Cross-Sectional Tests," *Journal of Applied Psychology,* February 1995, p 79.

[73]B Azar, "People Are Becoming Smarter—Why?" *APA Monitor,* June 1996, p 20. Also see " 'Average' Intelligence Higher than It Used to Be," *USA Today,* February 18, 1997, p 6D.

[74]For related research, see M J Ree and J A Earles, "Predicting Training Success: Not Much More Than g," *Personnel Psychology,* Summer 1991, pp 321–32.

[75]See F L Schmidt and J E Hunter, "Employment Testing: Old Theories and New Research Findings," *American Psychologist,* October 1981, p 1128.

[76]See I Briggs Myers (with P B Myers), *Gifts Differing* (Palo Alto, CA: Consulting Psychologists Press, 1980).

[77]For a complete discussion of each cognitive style, see J W Slocum, Jr., and D Hellriegel, "A Look at How Managers' Minds Work," *Business Horizons,* July–August 1983, pp 58–68; and W Taggart and D Robey, "Minds and Managers: On the Dual Nature of Human Information Processing and Management," *Academy of Management Review,* April 1981, pp 187–95. Also see M Wood Daudelin, "Learning from Experience through Reflection," *Organizational Dynamics,* Winter 1996, pp 36–48.

[78]See B K Blaylock and L P Rees, "Cognitive Style and the Usefulness of Information," *Decision Sciences,* Winter 1984, pp 74–91.

[79]Additional material on cognitive styles may be found in F A Gul, "The Joint and Moderating Role of Personality and Cognitive Style on Decision Making," *The Accounting Review,* April 1984, pp 264–77; B H Kleiner, "The Interrelationship of Jungian Modes of Mental Functioning with Organizational Factors: Implications for Management Development," *Human Relations,* November 1983, pp 997–1012; and J L McKenney and P G W Keen, "How Managers' Minds Work," *Harvard Business Review,* May–June 1974, pp 79–90.

[80]See G H Rice, Jr., and D P Lindecamp, "Personality Types and Business Success of Small Retailers," *Journal of Occupational Psychology,* June 1989, pp 177–82.

[81]W L Gardner and M J Martinko, "Using the Myers-Briggs Type Indicator to Study Managers: A Literature Review and Research Agenda," *Journal of Management,* no. 1, 1996, p 77.

[82]For example, see F Ramsoomair, "Relating Theoretical Concepts to Life in the Classroom: Applying the Myers-Briggs Type Indicator," *Journal of Management Education,* February 1994, pp 111–16. For related material, see S Shapiro and M T Spence, "Managerial Intuition: A Conceptual and Operational Framework," *Business Horizons,* January–February 1997, pp 63–68.

[83]R Powell, "Put bullies on the spot—Intimidation in the workplace can no longer be tolrerated, writes Rick Powell," *Scotland on Sunday,* November 12, 1995, p 17.

[84]R S Lazarus, *Emotion and Adaptation* (New York: Oxford University Press, 1991), p 6.

[85]D Goleman, *Emotional Intelligence* (Bantam Books, 1995)

[86]A Graham, "Getting smart," *Internal Auditor,* February 1996, p 5.

[87]S Nelton, "Emotions in the workplace," *Nation's Business,* February 1996, pp. 25–30.

[88]See A B Fisher, "Are You Afraid of Success?" *Fortune,* July 8, 1996, pp 108–18; M Hequet, "Fighting Fear," *Training,* July 1996, pp 37–40; and J Taylor Buckley, "Getting into Outdoors Builds Corporate Buddies," *USA Today,* August 19, 1996, pp 1A–2A.

[89]R P Vecchio, "It's Not Easy Being Green: Jealousy and Envy in the Workplace," in *Research in Personnel and Human Resources Management,* ed G R Ferris (Greenwich, CT: JAI Press, 1995), vol. 13, p 222. Also see S Fineman, *Emotion in Organizations* (Newbury Park, CA: Sage, 1993).

[90]Data from A P Brief, A Houston Butcher, and L Roberson, "Cookies, Disposition, and Job Attitudes: The Effects of Positive Mood-Inducing Events and Negative Affectivity on Job Satisfaction in a Field Experiment," *Organizational Behavior and Human Decision Processes,* April 1995, pp 55–62. Also see J A Morris and D C Feldman, "The Dimensions, Antecedents, and Consequences of Emotional Labor," *Academy of Management Review,* October 1996, pp 986–1010.

[91]See A M O'Leary-Kelly, R W Griffin, and D J Glew, "Organization-Motivated Aggression: A Research Framework," *Academy of Management Review,* January 1996, pp 225–53.

[92]E Davies, "How violence at work can hit employers hard," *People Management,* September 12, 1996, pp 50–53.

[93]The questionnaire and scoring key are excerpted from J W Slocum, Jr., and D Hellriegel, "A Look at How Managers' Minds Work," *Business Horizons,* July–August 1983, pp 58–68.

Six

Perception and Attributions

When you finish studying the material in this chapter, you should be able to:

1. Describe perception in terms of the social information processing model.

2. Identify and briefly explain four managerial implications of social perception.

3. Discuss stereotypes and the process of stereotype formation.

4. Summarize the managerial challenges and recommendations of sex-role, age, and race stereotypes.

5. Discuss how the self-fulfilling prophecy is created and how it can be used to improve individual and group productivity.

6. Explain, according to Kelley's model, how external and internal causal attributions are formulated.

7. Review Weiner's model of attribution.

8. Contrast the fundamental attribution bias and the self-serving bias.

Gender stereotyping: secretaries

Secretarial work is not only one of the most highly feminized occupations, but is also surrounded by gender stereotypes. Ninety-nine per cent of secretaries in the United States, Britain, Canada, and Australia are women, 98 per cent in Western Germany and in France. Estimates reveal that there are around 300,000 secretaries in West Germany, 800,000 in France, constituting 11 per cent of the female workforce. In Britain, 10 per cent of all office workers are secretaries. Secretaries thus represent a not inconsiderable section of the female labour force in many countries. Moreover, secretarial work is probably the most persistently female of all occupations. This implies that it is not only carried out primarily by women, but that it has acquired certain stereotypical characteristics that single it out as "women's work." Reference has frequently been made to such stereotypes, including the "domestic nature" of some secretarial tasks, the low status of secretarial work, and the alleged importance of "deference" towards the boss.

What a secretary is, and what a secretary does, is very difficult to define: the secretary is Everywoman, which means that a "good woman" makes a "good secretary." Her job content depends on the whim of the manager. In fact, she works for him, her only function being to case his workload.

All over the world, strong associations are made between secretarial work and what is regarded as "women's work" in general. The secretary's role is to carry out "domestic" duties at work: next to carrying out technical duties, such as typing and filing, the secretary should be "supporting" and "representing" the boss, in the same way as she does at home with her husband. This point of view is strongly criticized by feminist writers who claim that the carrying out of domestic tasks reinforces the patriarchal relations between boss and secretary, thus perpetuating the secretary's inferior position.

Similarly as a wife, the secretary derives her status from her boss, to whom she is a status symbol. The secretary is attached to "her" boss, and four behaviours are encouraged on her part, namely parochialism, timidity, praise-addiction, and emotionality. The close relationship between the boss and the secretary is said to be detrimental to her promotion chances. Moreover, she hardly gets a chance to demonstrate expertise, which limits her upward mobility as well.

A cross-country study involving secretaries from the French, German, and English publishing and management consultancy sector has revealed that making coffee is one of the — custodial — tasks most frequently associated with secretaries. In France, contrary to England and Germany, coffee making does not form an essential part of their jobs. As to personal work, French secretaries reported doing fewer tasks not directly related to work than their English and German colleagues. Those tasks include typing personal letters, going to shops or banks, doing work for their boss's spouse. This trend was confirmed by a boss at a French consultancy: "I think you have to be very reasonable about that, in the sense that you shouldn't mix business matters with personal things."

Theorists have not only drawn parallels between the husband and the wife as to custodial tasks such as coffee making, but also as to deferential behaviour. A majority of secretaries in the three countries said that the gender of their boss would make no difference, as personality was far more important. Bosses regularly mentioned character traits when asked about a good secretary.

The third way in which secretarial work is perceived as women's work is through the status of secretaries within their organizations, which is often described as being contingent upon that of their boss, as a wife's status is contingent upon that of her husband. The question of the status of secretaries is highly complex and ambivalent. On the one hand, secretaries are viewed as having a high status, conferred through their proximity to those in powerful positions and, on the other, a low status through the nature of their role and their gender. [1]

Discussion Question
Do you agree with the statement that the best secretaries are women?

Knowledge about the perceptual process can help organizations and managers alike. The perception process influences our behaviour at work. Read how stereotypes can influence the future hiring of accountants.[2] The future of the accounting profession depends on the qualities of those who are presently joining it. The qualities of those joining the profession are jointly determined by the qualities sought by the recruiters and the qualities offered by the potential recruits. A project was recently carried out that was designed to discover whether recruiters and potential trainees share the same views on what those appropriate qualities are. An analysis of the study's findings suggests that the traditional stereotype of the accountant may have adverse consequences for the next generation of accountants. As employment prospects for business graduates improve, in line with recent economic growth, it will become even more important for each member of the profession to help foster a positive image that will attract the appropriate candidates. Researchers wanted to know whether employees' perceptions of how much an organization valued them affected their behaviour and attitudes. The researchers asked samples of teachers, brokerage-firm clerks, manufacturing workers, insurance representatives, and police officers to indicate their perception of the extent to which their organization valued their contributions and their well-being. Employees who perceived that their organization cared about them reciprocated with reduced absenteeism, increased performance, innovation, and positive work attitudes.[3] This study illustrates the importance of employees' perceptions. Let us now begin our exploration of the perceptual process and its associated outcomes.

To guide our discussion, Figure 6–1 provides an overview of the perception process. As shown, the perceptual process is instigated by the presence of environmental stimuli. These stimuli are selectively perceived and interpreted. In turn, there are perceptual outcomes of stereotypes, self-fulfilling prophecies, and attributions formed, and reinforced, by interpretations of environmental stimuli. Finally, perceptual outcomes directly affect attitudes, motivation, and behaviour.

In this chapter we focus on (1) a social information processing model of perception, (2) stereotypes, (3) the self-fulfilling prophecy, and (4) how causal attributions are used to interpret behaviour

A Social Information Processing Model of Perception

Perception

Process of interpreting one's environment.

Perception is a cognitive process that enables us to interpret and understand our surroundings. Recognition of objects is one of this process's major functions. For example, both people and animals recognize familiar objects in their environments. You would recognize a picture of your best friend; dogs and cats can recognize their food dishes or a favourite toy. Reading involves recognition of visual patterns representing letters in the alphabet. People must recognize objects to meaningfully interact with their environment. But since OB's principal focus is on people, the following discussion emphasizes *social* perception rather than object perception.

The study of how people perceive one another has been labelled *social cognition* and *social information processing*. In contrast to the perception of objects,

Social cognition is the study of how people make sense of other people and themselves. It focuses on how ordinary people think about people and how they think about people.

Research on social cognition also goes beyond naive psychology. The study of social cognition entails a fine-grained analysis of how people think about themselves and others, and it leans heavily on the theory and methods of cognitive psychology.[4]

Moreover, while general theories of perception date back many years, the study of social perception is relatively new, having originated about 1976.

Four-Stage Sequence and a Working Example

Social perception involves a four-stage information processing sequence (hence, the label "social information processing"). Figure 6–2 illustrates a basic social information processing model. Three of the stages in this model—selective attention/comprehension, encoding and simplification, and storage and retention—describe how specific social information is observed and stored in memory. The fourth and final stage, retrieval and response, involves turning mental representations into real-world judgements and decisions.

Keep the following everyday example in mind as we look at the four stages of social perception. Suppose you were thinking of taking a course in, say, personal finance. Three

Figure 6–1   An Overview of the Perception Process

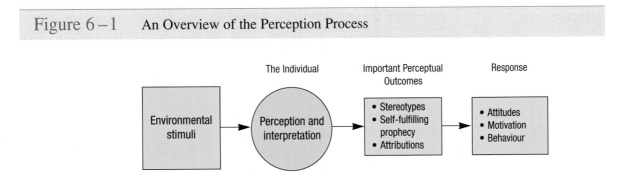

Figure 6–2   Social Perception: A Social Information Processing Model

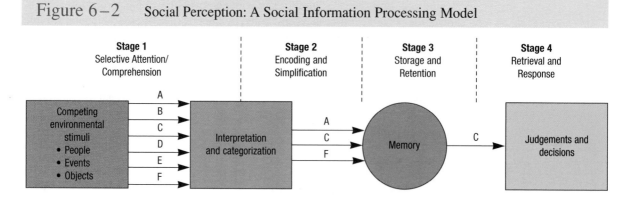

professors teach the same course, using different types of instruction and testing procedures. Through personal experience, you have come to prefer good professors who rely on the case method of instruction and essay tests. According to social perception theory, you would likely arrive at a decision regarding which professor to take as follows:

Stage 1: Selective Attention/Comprehension

People are constantly bombarded by physical and social stimuli in the environment. Since they do not have the mental capacity to fully comprehend all this information, they selectively perceive subsets of environmental stimuli. This is where attention plays a role. **Attention** is the process of becoming consciously aware of something or someone. Attention can be focused on information either from the environment or from memory. Regarding the latter situation, if you sometimes find yourself thinking about totally unrelated events or people while reading a textbook, your memory is the focus of your attention. Research has shown that people tend to pay attention to salient stimuli.

Attention

Being consciously aware of something or someone.

Salient Stimuli   Something is *salient* when it stands out from its context. For example, a 120 kg man would certainly be salient in a women's aerobics class but not at a Weight Watcher's meeting. Social salience is determined by several factors, including

- Being novel (the only person in a group of that race, gender, hair colour, or age).

- Being bright (wearing a yellow shirt).

- Being unusual for that person (behaving in an unexpected way, such as a person with a fear of heights climbing a steep mountain).

- Being unusual for a person's social category (such as a company president driving a motorcycle to work).

- Being unusual for people in general (driving 30 kph in a 100 kph speed zone).

- Being extremely positive (a noted celebrity) or negative (the victim of a bad traffic accident).

- Being dominant in the visual field (sitting at the head of the table).[5]

One's needs and goals often dictate which stimuli are salient. For a driver whose petrol gauge is on empty, a Shell or BP sign is more salient than a McDonald's or Pizza Hut sign. The reverse would be true for a hungry driver with a full petrol tank. Moreover, research shows that people have a tendency to pay more attention to negative than positive information. This leads to a negativity bias.[6] This bias helps explain the gawking factor that slows traffic to a crawl following a car accident.

Back to Our Example   You begin your search for the "right" personal finance professor by asking friends who have taken classes from the three professors. Because you are concerned about the method of instruction and testing procedures, information in those areas is particularly salient to you. Perhaps you even interview the professors to gather still more relevant information. You may even pay more attention to negative information about each professor. Meanwhile, thousands of competing stimuli fail to get your attention.

Stage 2: Encoding and Simplification

Cognitive categories

Mental depositories for storing information.

Observed information is not stored in memory in its original form. Encoding is required; raw information is interpreted or translated into mental representations. To accomplish this, perceivers assign pieces of information to **cognitive categories.** "By *category* we mean a number of objects that are considered equivalent. Categories are generally designated by names, e.g., *dog, animal*."[7] People, events, and objects are interpreted and evaluated by comparing their characteristics with information contained in schemata (or schema in singular form).

Schema

Mental picture of an event or object.

Schemata   According to social information processing theory, a **schema** represents a person's mental picture or summary of a particular event or type of stimulus.[8] For example, your restaurant schema probably is quite similar to the description provided in Table 6–1. Cognitive-category labels are needed to make schemata meaningful. The OB Exercise illustrates this by having you rate the comprehensiveness of a schema both without and with its associated category label. Take a moment to complete this exercise.

Encoding Outcomes   We use the encoding process to interpret and evaluate our environment. Interestingly, this process can result in differing interpretations and

---

Table 6–1   Restaurant Schema

Schema: Restaurant.

Characters: Customers, waiter, chef, cashier.

Scene 1: Entering.
    Customer goes into restaurant.
    Customer finds a place to sit.
        He may find it himself.
        He may be seated by a hostess.
            He asks the hostess for a table.
            She gives him permission to go to the table.

Scene 2: Ordering.
    Customer receives a menu.
    Customer reads it.
    Customer decides what to order.
    Waiter takes the order.
        Waiter sees the customer.
        Waiter goes to the customer.
        Customer orders what he wants.
    Chef cooks the meal.

Scene 3: Eating.
    After some time the waiter brings the meal from the chef.
    Customer eats the meal.

Scene 4: Exiting.
    Customer asks the waiter for the check.
    Waiter gives the check to the customer.
    Customer leaves a tip.
        The size of the tip depends on the goodness of the service.
    Customer pays the cashier.
    Customer leaves the restaurant.

Source: From *Memory, Thought and Behavior* by R W Weisberg. Copyright © 1980 by Oxford University Press, Inc. Reprinted by permission.

evaluations of the same person or event. This occurs for many reasons. First, people possess different information in the schemata used for interpretation. Women and men, for example, have different ideas about what types of behaviour constitute sexual harassment.[9] Second, our moods and emotions influence our focus of attention and evaluations.[10] Third, people tend to apply recently used cognitive categories during encoding. For example, you are more likely to interpret a neutral behaviour exhibited by a professor as positive if you were recently thinking about positive categories and events.[11] Fourth, individual differences influence encoding. Pessimistic or depressed individuals, for instance, tend to interpret their surroundings more negatively than optimistic and happy people.[12] The point is that we should not be surprised when people interpret and evaluate the same situation or event differently. Researchers are currently trying to identify the host of factors that influence the encoding process.

Back to Our Example   Having collected relevant information about the three personal finance professors and their approaches, you compare this information with other details contained in schemata. This leads you to form an impression and evaluation of what it would be like to take a course from each professor. In turn, you may start to prefer one professor over another at this point.

Stage 3: Storage and Retention

This phase involves storage of information in long-term memory. Long-term memory is like an apartment complex consisting of separate units connected to one another. Although different people live in each apartment, they sometimes interact. In addition, large apartment complexes have different wings (such as A, B, and C). Long-term memory similarly consists of separate but related categories. Like the individual apartments inhabited by unique residents, the connected categories contain different types of information. Information also passes among these categories. Finally, long-term memory is made up of three compartments (or wings) containing categories of information about events, semantic materials, and people (see Figure 6 – 3).[13]

Event Memory   This compartment is composed of categories containing information about both specific and general events. These memories describe appropriate sequences of events in well-known situations, such as going to a restaurant (refer back to Table 6 – 1), going for a job interview, going to a supermarket, or going to the cinema.

Semantic Memory   Semantic memory refers to general knowledge about the world. In so doing, it functions as a mental dictionary of concepts. Each concept contains a definition (e.g., a good leader) and associated traits (outgoing), emotional states (happy), physical characteristics (tall), and behaviours (works hard). Just as there are schemata for general events, concepts in semantic memory are stored as schemata.

Given our previous discussion of managing diversity in Chapter 2 and the international OB in Chapter 4, it should come as no surprise that there are cultural

---

Figure 6– 3   The Structure of Memory

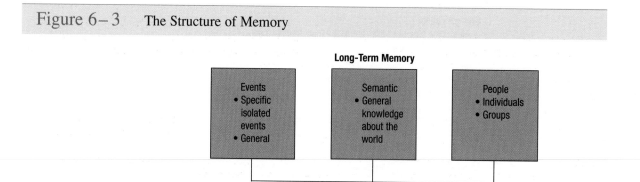

differences in the type of information stored in semantic memory. Gerald Hirshberg, vice president at Nissan Design International Inc., the Japanese car maker's San Diego design shop, learned this lesson when the American Nissan designers competed against the home team in Tokyo for the right to design the Infiniti J30 car (see the International OB).

Person Memory   Categories within this compartment contain information about a single individual (your supervisor) or groups of people (managers).

Back to Our Example   As the time draws near for you to decide which personal finance professor to select, your schemata of them are stored in the three categories of long-term memory. These schemata are available for immediate comparison and/or retrieval.

Stage 4: Retrieval and Response

People retrieve information from memory when they make judgements and decisions. Our ultimate judgements and decisions are either based on the process of drawing on, interpreting, and integrating categorical information stored in long-term memory or on retrieving a summary judgement that was already made.[15]

Concluding our example, it is registration day and you have to choose which professor to take for personal finance. After retrieving from memory your schemata-based impressions of the three professors, you select a good one who uses the case method and gives essay tests. In contrast, you may choose your preferred professor by simply recalling the decision you made two weeks ago.

Managerial Implications

Social cognition is the window through which we all observe, interpret, and prepare our responses to people and events. A wide variety of managerial activities, organizational processes, and quality-of-life issues are thus affected by perception. Consider, for example, the following implications.

Hiring   Interviewers make hiring decisions based on their impression of how an applicant fits the perceived requirements of a job. Inaccurate impressions in either direction produce poor hiring decisions. Moreover, interviewers with racist or sexist

---

OB EXERCISE   *Does a Schema Improve the Comprehension of Written Material?*

Instructions

The purpose of this exercise is to demonstrate the role of schema in encoding. First read the passage shown below. Once done, rate the comprehensiveness of what you read using the scale provided. Next, examine the schema label presented in Reference 14 in the Notes section at the end of the chapter. With this label in mind, reread the passage, and rate its comprehensiveness. Now think about the explanation for why your ratings changed. You just experienced the impact of schema in encoding.

The procedure is actually quite simple. First you arrange things into different groups. Of course, one pile may be sufficient depending on how much there is to do. If you have to go somewhere else due to lack of facilities, that is the next step; otherwise you are pretty well set. It is important not to overdo things. That is, it is better to do too few things at once than too many. In the short run this may not seem important, but complications can easily arise. A mistake can be expensive as well. At first the whole procedure will seem complicated. Soon, however, it will become just another facet of life. It is difficult to foresee any end to the necessity for this task in the immediate future, but then one never can tell. After the procedure is completed, one arranges the materials into different groups again. Then they can be put into their appropriate places. Eventually they will be used once more, and the whole cycle will then have to be repeated. However, that is part of life.

Comprehensive Scale

VERY UNCOMPREHENSIVE	NEITHER 1 — 2 — 3 — 4 — 5	VERY COMPREHENSIVE

SOURCE   J D Bransford and M K Johnson, "Contextual Prerequisite for Understanding: Some Investigations of Comprehension and Recall," *Journal of Verbal Learning and Verbal Behavior*, December 1972, p 722. Reprinted with permission of Academic Press, Inc.

schemata can undermine the accuracy and legality of hiring decisions. Those invalid schemata need to be confronted and improved through coaching and training. Failure to do so can lead to poor hiring decisions. For example, a recent study of 46 male and 66 female financial-institution managers revealed that their hiring decisions were biased by the physical attractiveness of applicants. More attractive men and women were hired over less attractive applicants with equal qualifications.[16] On the positive side, however, a team of researchers demonstrated that a structured behavioural interview reduced sex and race bias and was predictive of successful performers.[17] A Belgian study among 1,724 respondents on the perception of diversity at the workplace revealed that people pretended to be rarely influenced by sex differences when hiring new employees. Age played a more important role: younger people preferred younger people, older respondents chose for their contemporaries. In traditional environments, people chose more traditionally: ethnic minorities and homosexuals had less chances to be recruited.[18]

Performance Appraisal   Faulty schemata about what constitutes good versus poor performance can lead to inaccurate performance appraisals, which erode work motivation, commitment, and loyalty. Therefore, it is important for managers to accurately identify the behavioural characteristics and results indicative of good performance at the beginning of a performance review cycle. These characteristics then can serve as the benchmarks for evaluating employee performance. The importance of using objective rather than subjective measures of employee performance was highlighted in a meta-analysis involving 50 studies and 8,341 individuals. Results revealed that objective and subjective measures of employee performance were only moderately related. The researchers concluded that objective and subjective measures of performance are not interchangeable.[19] Managers are thus advised to use more objectively based measures of performance because subjective indicators are prone to bias and inaccuracy. Furthermore, because memory for specific instances of employee performance deteriorates over time, managers need a mechanism for accurately recalling employee behaviour.[20] Research reveals that individuals can be trained to be more accurate raters of performance.[21]

Leadership   Research demonstrates that employees' evaluations of leader effectiveness are influenced strongly by their schemata of good and poor leaders. A leader will have a difficult time influencing employees when he or she exhibits behaviours contained in employees' schemata of poor leaders. A team of researchers investigated the behaviours contained in our schemata of good and poor leaders. Good leaders were perceived as exhibiting the following behaviours: (1) assigning specific tasks to group members, (2) telling others that they had done well, (3) setting specific goals for the group, (4) letting other group members make decisions, (5) trying to get the group to work as a team, and (6) maintaining definite standards of performance. In contrast, poor leaders were

Visual Perceptions Vary by Culture

When Westerners conjure up an image of a car, he [Hirshberg], says it's a side view. With the Japanese, it's the front. "The Japanese read personality and expression into the 'face' of the car," he says.

All the negotiations between Tokyo and San Diego centered on whether the "eyes" were sleepy or awake and whether the "mouth" gesture was appropriate. "We don't even think of headlights as 'eyes' or the grill as a 'mouth'," Hirshberg says. In the end, San Diego beat out the Tokyo team and got to do the Infiniti—after a compromise: The headlights and grill were redesigned to make for bigger, more expressive "eyes" and a smaller "mouth."

SOURCE   Excerpted from L Armstrong, "It Started with an Egg," *Business Week*, December 2, 1991, p 142.

perceived to exhibit these behaviours: (1) telling others that they had performed poorly, (2) insisting on having their own way, (3) doing things without explaining themselves, (4) expressing worry over the group members' suggestions, (5) frequently changing plans, and (6) letting the details of the task become overwhelming.[22]

Communication   Managers need to remember that social perception is a screening process that can distort communication, both coming and going. Messages are interpreted and categorized according to schemata developed through past experiences and influenced by one's age, gender, and ethnic, geographic, and cultural orientations. Effective communicators try to tailor their messages to the receiver's perceptual schemata. This requires well-developed listening and observation skills and cross-cultural sensitivity.

Self-Perception

Other people may not see us in the way we see ourselves. This is depicted in Figure 6–4, The Johari Window, one of the most famous scheme's in OB. Joe Luft and Harry Ingram (Jo-Hari) conceptualized this as a two-dimensional window.[23] Horizontally, the focus shifts from what is known to what is unknown to oneself. Vertically, the focus shifts from what is known to what is unknown to others. The walls of the window's cells can be shifted to the right and downwards to enlarge the arena or to reduce the unknown. This requests trust, information sharing, and accepting feedback.

The Halo Effect

The term "halo" comes from the Greek *halos,* which means a circle around a shield or a circle around the moon or other celestial body. A halo effect describes the radiation from a single characteristic (the "halo") to the person as a whole. The term "halo effect" was first used by pioneering psychologist Edward L. Thorndike in 1920. Over the years the term "halo effect" has acquired a double meaning. A halo effect occurs when a good or a bad overall impression distorts the perception of another person on specific dimensions. The development of such an overall impression is, however, also called "halo effect".

In practice, a double halo effect can come into play. First, we make a global evaluation of another person based on one single attribute or characteristic. Then, our perception of other specific dimensions is distorted by our initial assessment.

Halo effects play a role in interviews when interviewers base their judgements of specific qualities, such as intelligence or perseverence on "first impressions," which, in turn, are based on very unreliable indications such as dress, handshake, firmness, height, and weight. Halo effects also affect ratings of employee performance, where performance measures such as accuracy or quality of work are highly influenced by the assessment of overall employee effort.

Figure 6 – 4   The Johari Window

	Known to self	Unknown to self
Known to others	**Arena** Openly shared data People see me as I see myself	**Blindspot** People see these aspects of me but I do not
Unknown to others	**Facade** I see these aspects, but I hide them to others	**Unknown** I do not see these aspects of myself, nor do others

Source: J Luft, *Group Processes* (PabloAlto, C A: National Press Books, 1970). Used with permission.

Stereotypes: Perceptions about Groups of People

While it is often true that beauty is in the eye of the beholder, perception does result in some predictable outcomes. Managers aware of the perception process and its outcomes enjoy a competitive edge. The Walt Disney Company, for instance, takes full advantage of perceptual tendencies to influence customers' reactions to waiting in long lines at its theme parks:

In order to make the experience less psychologically wearing, the waiting times posted by each attraction are generously overestimated, so that one comes away mysteriously grateful for having hung around 20 minutes for a 58-second twirl in the Alice in Wonderland teacups.

The lines, moreover, are always moving, even if what looks like the end is actually the start of a second set of switchbacks leading to—oh, no!—a pre-ride waiting area. Those little tricks of the theme park mean a lot.[24]

Likewise, managers can use knowledge of perceptual outcomes to help them interact more effectively with employees. For example, Table 6–2 describes five common perceptual errors. Since these perceptual errors often distort the evaluation of job applicants and of employee performance, managers need to guard against them. This section examines one of the most important and potentially harmful perceptual outcomes associated with person perception: stereotypes. After exploring the process of stereotype formation and maintenance, we discuss sex-role stereotypes, age stereotypes, race stereotypes, and the managerial challenge to avoid stereotypical biases.

Research Evidence

Edwin D. Davidson and Betty Jane Punnet analysed a number of existing studies on gender, race, and international assignment, according to which:

- both ethnic minorities and women tend to be more positive in their attitudes towards ethnic minorities and women as managers

- family and spousal concerns are more important to a woman's performance than to a man's

Table 6–2   Commonly Found Perceptual Errors

PERCEPTUAL ERROR	DESCRIPTION	EXAMPLE
Halo	A rater forms an overall impression about an object and then uses that impression to bias ratings about the object.	Rating a professor high on the teaching dimensions of ability to motivate students, knowledge, and communication because we like him or her.
Leniency	A personal characteristic that leads an individual to consistently evaluate other people or objects in an extremely positive fashion.	Rating a professor high on all dimensions of performance regardless of his or her actual performance. The rater who hates to say negative things about others.
Central tendency	The tendency to avoid all extreme judgements and rate people and objects as average or neutral.	Rating a professor average on all dimensions of performance regardless of his or her actual performance.
Recency effects	The tendency to remember recent information. If the recent information is negative, the person or object is evaluated negatively.	Although a professor has given good lectures for 12 to 15 weeks, he or she is evaluated negatively because lectures over the last 3 weeks were done poorly.
Contrast effects	The tendency to evaluate people or objects by comparing them with characteristics of recently observed people or objects.	Rating a good professor as average because you compared his or her performance with three of the best professors you have ever had in college. You are currently taking courses from the three excellent professors.

• authority and status are seen as affecting both ethnic minorities and women negatively.[25]

These differential perceptions can perhaps be attributed to stereotypes based on historical roles.

Stereotype Formation and Maintenance

Stereotype

Beliefs about the characteristics of a group.

"A **stereotype** is an individual's set of beliefs about the characteristics or attributes of a group."[26] Stereotypes are not always negative. For example, the belief that engineers are good at maths is certainly part of a stereotype. Stereotypes may or may not be accurate. Engineers may in fact be better at maths than the general population. In general, stereotypic characteristics are used to differentiate a particular group of people from other groups.[27]

Consider walking into a business meeting with 10 people seated around a conference table. You notice a male at the head of the table and a woman immediately to his right, taking notes. Due to ingrained stereotypes, you are likely to assume that the man is the top-ranking person in the room and the woman, his secretary. This example highlights how people use stereotypes to interpret their environment and to make judgements about others.

Unfortunately, stereotypes can lead to poor decisions, can create barriers for women and ethnic minorities, and can undermine employee loyalty and job satisfaction. For example, a national survey of 2,958 workers indicated that more than one-fifth of the minority workers perceived that they had been discriminated against. Employees of all kinds also agreed that women and ethnic minorities had lower chances of advancement than white males. Finally, respondents who saw little opportunity for advancement tended to be less loyal, less committed, and less satisfied with their jobs.[28]

Stereotyping is a four-step process. It begins by categorizing people into groups according to various criteria, such as gender, age, race, and occupation. Next, we infer that all people within a particular category possess the same traits or characteristics (e.g., all women are nurturing, older people have more job-related accidents, all blacks are good athletes, all professors are absent-minded). Then, we form expectations of others and interpret their behaviour according to our stereotypes. Finally, stereotypes are maintained by (1) overestimating the frequency of stereotypic behaviours exhibited by others, (2) incorrectly explaining expected and unexpected behaviours, and (3) differentiating minority individuals from oneself.[29] Let us now take a look at different types of stereotypes.

Sex-Role Stereotypes

We would like you to complete the OB Exercise prior to reading this section. The exercise assesses your attitudes towards women executives. Once you have completed the exercise, we will examine the existence and impact of sex-role stereotypes.

Sex-role stereotype

Beliefs about appropriate roles for men and women.

A **sex-role stereotype** is the belief that differing traits and abilities make men and women particularly well suited to different roles. This perceptual tendency was documented in a classic 1972 study. After administering a sex-role questionnaire to 383 women and 599 men, the researchers drew the following conclusion: "Our research demonstrates the contemporary existence of clearly defined sex-role stereotypes for men and women contrary to the phenomenon of 'unisex' currently touted in the media."[30] They further explained:

Women are perceived as relatively less competent, less independent, less objective, and less logical than men; men are perceived as lacking interpersonal sensitivity, warmth, and expressiveness in comparison to women. Moreover, stereotypically masculine traits are more often perceived to be desirable than are stereotypically feminine characteristics. Most importantly, both men and women incorporate both the positive and negative traits of the appropriate stereotype into their self-concepts. Since more feminine traits are negatively valued than are masculine traits, women tend to have more negative self-concepts than do men.[31]

Although more recent research demonstrates that men and women do not systematically differ in the manner suggested by traditional stereotypes,[32] these stereotypes still persist. A recent study compared sex-role stereotypes held by men and women from five countries: China, Japan, Germany, the United Kingdom, and the United States. Males in all five countries perceived that successful managers possessed characteristics and traits more commonly ascribed to men in general than to women in general. Among the females, the same pattern of managerial sex typing was found in all countries except the United States. United States females perceived that males and females were equally likely to possess traits necessary for managerial success.[33] The key question now becomes whether these stereotypes influence the hiring, evaluation, and promotion of people at work.

A meta-analysis of 19 studies comprising 1,842 individuals found no significant relationships between applicant gender and hiring recommendations.[34] A second meta-analysis of 24 experimental studies revealed that men and women received similar performance ratings for the same level of task performance. Stated differently, there was no pro-male bias. These experimental results were further supported in a field study of female and male professors.[35] Unfortunately, results pertaining to promotion decisions are not as promising. Consider the case of Ann Hopkins.

In the spring of 1982, America's Price Waterhouse, an international accounting firm with a large management consulting business, was considering 88 candidates for partnerships. Ann Hopkins was the only woman among the candidates. . . . She had garnered more than $34 million worth of consulting contracts for the firm during her tenure and billed more hours than any of the other 87 candidates in the fiscal year prior to the partnership nominations. At the time of her nomination, Price Waterhouse had 662 senior partners, of which seven were women. . . .

Subsequently, Hopkins' candidacy was placed on a one-year hold, ostensibly on the basis of her poor interpersonal skills and "unfeminine" behaviour. This decision was relayed to Hopkins by

---

OB EXERCISE   *What Are Your Attitudes towards Women Executives?*

Instructions

Read each question and mark your answer by using the rating scale shown below. Remember there are no right or wrong answers. Next, compute a total score by adding your nine responses.

RATING SCALE

1 = Strongly disagree
2 = Disagree
3 = Neither disagree nor agree
4 = Agree
5 = Strongly agree

Females have the capabilities for responsible managerial positions.   1 — 2 — 3 — 4 — 5

A female executive merits the same trust and respect as a male executive.   1 — 2 — 3 — 4 — 5

Women in responsible managerial positions must have the capabilities for their positions and therefore men should honor their decisions.   1 — 2 — 3 — 4 — 5

It's about time we had some women executives in organizations.   1 — 2 — 3 — 4 — 5

Women executives are not ignorant when it comes to highly technical subjects.   1 — 2 — 3 — 4 — 5

It is unfair to say women became top executives by using sexual favours.   1 — 2 — 3 — 4 — 5

A man is not better suited for handling executive responsibility than a woman is.   1 — 2 — 3 — 4 — 5

There are no problems with a male working for a female executive if both are dedicated, competent, and learned workers.   1 — 2 — 3 — 4 — 5

Women are not taking men's positions nowadays.   1 — 2 — 3 — 4 — 5

Total score = _____

NORMS FOR COMPARISON

Unfavourable attitude towards female executives = 9--20; Middle of the road = 21--33; Favourable attitude = 34--45.

SOURCE   Based on P Dubno, J Costas, H Cannon, C Wankel, and H Emin, "An Empirically Keyed Scale for Measuring Managerial Attitudes toward Women Executives," *Psychology of Women Quarterly*, Summer 1979, pp 360–61. (Copyrighted by and reprinted with the permission of Cambridge University Press.)

her male supervisor, who suggested that she should walk more femininely, talk more femininely, dress more femininely, wear makeup, and have her hair styled.[36]

After all appeals were exhausted, the courts held that Price Waterhouse engaged in illegal sex stereotyping. Ms Hopkins was apparently denied a partnership because of inappropriate stereotyping in the way partners were reviewed and evaluated and not for job-related reasons. This case highlights that women and men need to be judged as individuals, when making personnel decisions, not as members of supposedly homogeneous groups. (The same holds true for racial and ethnic minorities.) The existence of sex-role stereotypes may partially explain this finding.

Saville & Holdsworth (UK), asked 3,000 men and women, representative of the UK population, how they rated themselves on 30 attributes, of which 24 are represented in Table 6 – 3. Each score shows the mean on a standard 10 scale for the 34–39 age bracket: in all cases, differences within the sexes were greater than between them, and there was considerable variation over age. The final column shows, across all ages, how small a proportion of the variances (V) are attributable to sex. N/S means no statistical variance. For some, such as detail consciousness and emotional control, there are no real differences, contrary to popular experience. But many more women than men consider themselves "caring" and "artistic"; many more men consider themselves "tough-minded" and "competitive." The role of so-called male characteristics for leading positions is confirmed by Jenifer Rosenberg, founder of a major Marks & Spencer supplier, J & J fashions:

'I'm as tough as any man—possibly tougher" she says.[37]

Table 6 – 3   How Men and Women Differ

	Women	Men	V%
Controlling	5.1	6.1	4.4
Affilliative	5.6	5.2	0.4
Democratic	5.6	5.4	1.2
Caring	5.9	5.1	7.2
Practical	5.2	5.8	5.3
Data rational	5.2	6.2	3.4
Artistic	5.8	5.3	1.8
Behavioural	5.8	5.4	0.9
Conceptual	5.4	6.0	0.6
Relaxed	5.0	6.1	4.1
Worrying	6.0	5.0	4.5
Tough-minded	4.7	6.0	8.7
Emotional control	5.3	5.6	N/S
Active	5.2	5.9	6.5
Competitive	5.0	5.9	4.9
Independent	5.2	5.7	1.3
Modest	5.5	5.6	N/S
Innovative	5.2	5.6	1.5
Conscientious	5.5	5.5	N/S
Critical	5.2	5.9	2.7
Achieving	4.8	5.8	1.7
Decisive	5.4	5.7	2.8
Optimistic	5.6	5.6	N/S
Detail conscious	5.7	5.6	N/S

Source *Management Today,* April 1993, p 46.

Age Stereotypes

Age stereotypes reinforce age discrimination because of their negative orientation. In The Netherlands, a study carried out among 1,182 companies showed that applicants are mainly refused because of their age. This conclusion was confirmed by 75 per cent of the employers questioned.[38] For example, long-standing age stereotypes depict older workers as less satisfied, not as involved with their work, less motivated, not as committed, less productive than their younger co-workers, and more apt to be absent from work. Older employees are also perceived as being more accident prone. As with sex-role stereotypes, these age stereotypes are more fiction than fact.

OB researcher Susan Rhodes sought to determine whether age stereotypes were supported by data from 185 different studies. She discovered that as age increases so do employees' job satisfaction, job involvement, internal work motivation, and organizational commitment. Moreover, older workers were not more accident prone.

Results are not as clear cut regarding job performance. A meta-analysis of 96 studies representing 38,983 people and a cross section of jobs revealed that age and job performance were unrelated.[39] Some OB researchers, however, believe that this finding does not reflect the true relationship between age and performance. They propose that the relationship between age and performance changes as people grow older.[40] This idea was tested on data obtained from 24,219 individuals. In support of this hypothesis, results revealed that age was positively related to performance for younger employees (25 to 30 years of age) and then plateaued: Older employees were not less productive. Age and experience also predicted performance better for more complex jobs than other jobs, and job experience had a stronger relationship with performance than age.[41]

What about turnover and absenteeism? A meta-analysis containing 46 samples and a total of 42,625 individuals revealed that age and turnover were not related. Similarly, another meta-analysis of 34 studies encompassing 7,772 workers indicated that age was inversely related to both voluntary (a day at the beach) and involuntary (sick day) absenteeism.[42] Contrary to stereotypes, older workers are ready and able to meet their job requirements. Moreover, results from the meta-analysis suggest managers should focus more attention on absenteeism among younger workers than among older workers.

Race Stereotypes

There is not a large percentage of ethnic minority managers in Europe. Negative racial stereotypes are one of several potential explanations for this state of affairs. Consider minority women. There appears to be a stereotype that minority women are frequently hired to fulfil equal employment opportunity requirements.

Some research supports this experience. A recent study attempted to determine whether there was a relationship between being labelled an "affirmative action" hire and perceptions of an employee's competence. Results from an experiment using university students and a field test using 184 white men both supported the conclusion that a stigma of incompetence arises when people are hired for supposed "affirmative action" reasons. Consider the case of Kate Redfern:

ETHICS

Kate Redfern, a white teacher, claims to have been sacked—along with three colleagues—from Peckham Rye primary school (UK) as part of an effort to impose race quotas aimed at giving blacks a third of all teaching jobs.[43]

Another study examined the relationship of race to employee attitudes across 814 black managers and 814 white managers. Results demonstrated that blacks, when compared with whites, felt less accepted by their peers, perceived lower managerial discretion on their jobs, reached career plateaus more frequently, noted lower levels of career satisfaction, and received lower performance ratings.[44] Negative findings like these prompted researchers to investigate whether race stereotypes actually bias performance ratings and hiring decisions. Given the increasing number of people of ethnic minorities that will enter the workforce over the next 10 years (recall our discussion in Chapter 3), employers should focus on nurturing and developing women and ethnic minorities as well as increasing managers' sensitivities to invalid racial stereotypes.

Managerial Challenges and Recommendations

Organizations first need to educate themselves about the problem of stereotyping through employee training. The next step entails engaging in a broad effort to reduce stereotypes throughout the organization. The International OB discusses how the Bank of Montreal tried to accomplish this recommendation. Social scientists believe that "quality" interpersonal contact among mixed groups is the best way to reduce stereotypes because it provides people with more accurate data about the characteristics of other groups of people.[45] As such, organizations should create opportunities for diverse employees to meet and work together in cooperative groups of equal status.

Another recommendation is for managers to identify valid individual differences (discussed in Chapter 5) that differentiate between successful and unsuccessful performers. As previously discussed, for instance, research reveals experience is a better predictor of performance than age. Research also shows that managers can be trained to use these valid criteria when hiring applicants and evaluating employee performance.[46]

Removing promotional barriers for men and women and for ethnic minorities is another viable solution to alleviating the stereotyping problem. This can be accomplished by minimizing the differences in job experience across groups of people. Similar experience, coupled with the accurate evaluation of performance, helps managers to make gender, age, and racially blind decisions.

There are several recommendations that can be pursued based on the documented relationship between age and performance:

1. Because performance plateaus with age for noncomplex jobs, organizations may use the variety of job design techniques discussed in Chapter 7 to increase employees' intrinsic motivation.

2. Organizations may need to consider using incentives to motivate employees to upgrade their skills and abilities. This will help avoid unnecessary plateaus.[47]

3. It may be advisable to hire older people in order to acquire their accumulated experience. This is especially useful for highly complex jobs. Moreover, hiring older workers is a good solution for reducing turnover, providing role models for younger

International Organizational Behaviour

Bank of Montreal Proactively Reduces Stereotypes about Women

The Bank of Montreal found that stereotypes were the primary obstacle to women's advancement. In addition to the belief that mothers lack job commitment, the company found that many employees thought women didn't "have the right stuff," or needed more education to qualify for top jobs. Personnel files, however, showed that women in lower-level jobs were better educated than their male peers and that more female employees than men at all levels got top-flight performance ratings.

The company followed up by improving career planning, broadening flexible scheduling, and holding managers accountable for advancing women. Today, 19% of Bank of Montreal's senior executives are women, up from 6% in 1991. The company also monitors the rumor mill, most recently tackling employee talk that "men are an endangered species around here." Again, personnel files revealed men were receiving a fair number of promotions.

SOURCE   S Shellenbarger, "Work & Family: Shedding Light on Women's Records Dispels Stereotypes," *The Wall Street Journal*, December 20, 1995, p B1.

employees, and coping with the current shortage of qualified entry-level workers. Results from a meta-analysis and actual corporate experience both support this recommendation.[48]

A good example is the opening of a new store in Macclesfield, UK, by B&Q, Britain's largest home-improvement chain.[49] The store was staffed entirely with workers aged 50 or older. Consider the results obtained from comparing the Macclesfield store with five B&Q stores with similar employment and sales levels:

- Macclesfield was 18 per cent more profitable than the average of the five comparison B&Q stores.

- Employee turnover at Macclesfield was nearly six times lower than the average of the comparison stores.

- The older workers at Macclesfield were absent 39 per cent less than workers in the other stores.

- Leakage, which is the difference between stock expected in the store and stock actually in the store because of theft, damage, and inventory not received, at Macclesfield is less than half the average of the five comparison stores.

- Extra training has not been required for older workers.

It is important to obtain top management's commitment and support to eliminate the organizational practices that support or reinforce stereotyping and discriminatory decisions. Research clearly demonstrates that top management support is essential to successful implementation of the types of organizational changes being recommended.[50]

Self-Fulfilling Prophecy: The Pygmalion Effect

Self-fulfilling prophecy

People's expectations determine behaviour and performance.

Historical roots of the self-fulfilling prophecy are found in Greek mythology. According to mythology, Pygmalion was a sculptor who hated women yet fell in love with an ivory statue he carved of a beautiful woman. He became so infatuated with the statue that he prayed to the goddess Aphrodite to bring her to life. The goddess heard his prayer, granted his wish, and Pygmalion's statue came to life. The essence of the **self-fulfilling prophecy**, or Pygmalion effect, is that people's expectations or beliefs determine their behaviour and performance, thus serving to make their expectations come true. In other words, we strive to validate our perceptions of reality, no matter how faulty they may be. Thus, the self-fulfilling prophecy is an important perceptual outcome we need to understand better. For example, the self-fulfilling prophecy can dramatically affect people's careers, as explains Cecilia Joseph, a senior lecturer at the UK Civil Service College.

Individuals from ethnic minorities need to be equipped with skills to compete equally in the promotion race. Frequently they fail to understand the politics of promotion and for religious or cultural reasons exclude themselves from socializing which is a necessary part of the work environment.

These employees then become demotivated, work less, and get locked into a vicious circle to that nonpromotion among ethnic minorities becomes a self-fulfilling prophecy. On our courses, delegates begin by talking about the negative perceptions which they believe are held by others, then move on to assess their own skills and how they can improve and market them.[51]

Research and an Explanatory Model

The self-fulfilling prophecy was first demonstrated in an academic environment. After giving a bogus test of academic potential to school students, researchers informed teachers that certain had high potential for achievement. In reality, students were randomly assigned to the "high potential" and "control" (normal potential) groups.

Results showed that students designated as having high potential obtained significantly greater increases in both IQ scores and reading ability than did the control students.[52] The teachers of the supposedly high potential group got better results because their high expectations caused them to give harder assignments, more feedback, and more recognition of achievement. Students in the normal potential group did not excel because their teachers did not expect outstanding results.

Research similarly has shown that by raising instructors' and managers' expectations for individuals performing a wide variety of tasks, higher levels of achievement/productivity can be obtained.[53] Subjects in these field studies included airmen at the United States Air Force Academy Preparatory School, disadvantaged people in job-training programmes, electronics assemblers, trainees in a military command course, US naval personnel, and cadets in a naval officer course in the Israel Defence Forces. There is an interesting trend inherent in research supporting the Pygmalion effect. All studies exclusively involved men.

To overcome this limitation, a recent team of researchers conducted two experimental studies on samples of women and men cadets in the Israel Defence Forces. Results revealed that the self-Pygmalion effect was produced for both women and men cadets, but only when the leader was a male. Female leaders did not produce a significant Pygmalion effect. This finding must be considered in light of the fact that women were rated as better leaders than men in the Israel Defence Forces. The researchers concluded that the Pygmalion effect clearly works on both women and men when the leader is male, but not when the leader is female.[54] Future research is obviously needed to uncover the cause of these gender-based differences.

Figure 6 – 5 presents a model of the self-fulfilling prophecy that helps explain these results. This model attempts to outline how supervisory expectations affect employee performance. As indicated, high supervisory expectancy produces better leadership (linkage 1), which subsequently leads employees to develop higher self-expectations (linkage 2). Higher expectations motivate workers to exert more effort (linkage 3),

| Figure 6 – 5 | A Model of the Self-Fulfilling Prophecy |

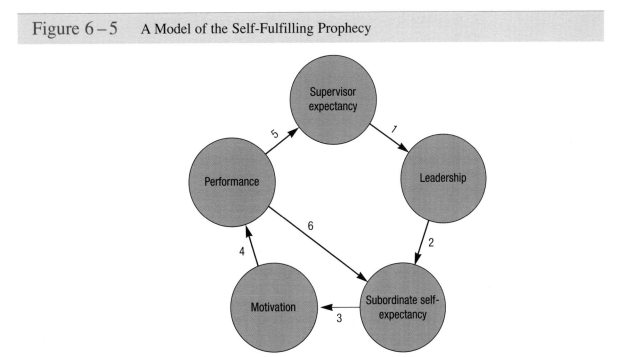

Source: D Eden, "Self-Fulfilling Prophecy as a Management Tool: Harnessing Pygmalion," *Academy of Management Review*, January 1984, p 67. Used with permission.

ultimately increasing performance (linkage 4) and supervisory expectancies (linkage 5). Successful performance also improves an employee's self-expectancy for achievement (linkage 6).

Putting the Self-Fulfilling Prophecy to Work

Largely due to the Pygmalion effect, managerial expectations powerfully influence employee behaviour and performance. Consequently, managers need to harness the Pygmalion effect by building a hierarchical framework that reinforces positive performance expectations throughout the organization.

Employees' self-expectations are the foundation of this framework. In turn, positive self-expectations improve interpersonal expectations by encouraging people to work towards common goals. This cooperation enhances group-level productivity and promotes positive performance expectations within the work group. At Microsoft Corporation, for example, employees routinely put in 75-hour weeks, especially when work groups are trying to meet shipment deadlines for new products. Because Microsoft is known for meeting its deadlines, positive group-level expectations help create and reinforce an organizational culture of high expectancy for success. This process then excites people about working for the organization, thereby reducing turnover.[55]

Because positive self-expectations are the foundation for creating an organization-wide Pygmalion effect, let us consider how managers can create positive performance expectations. This task may be accomplished by using various combinations of the following:

1. Recognize that everyone has the potential to increase his or her performance.
2. Instil confidence in your staff.
3. Set high performance goals.
4. Positively reinforce employees for a job well done.
5. Provide constructive feedback when necessary.
6. Help employees advance through the organization.
7. Introduce new employees as if they have outstanding potential.
8. Become aware of your personal prejudices and nonverbal messages that may discourage others.
9. Encourage employees to visualize the successful execution of tasks.
10. Help employees master key skills and tasks.[56]

Psychologists Jerry May and Richard O'Brien used several of these recommendations to help US athletes compete in the 1996 Olympics:

Olympic psychological consultants spend weeks, months, and years helping athletes put mind over matter. Typically, they emphasize goal-setting, mental imagery, and communication strategies, says May, who has been working with the US sailing team for five years.

"The key to winning is joining mind and body to maximize performance," says May. "Athletes must constantly focus on task and technique." . . .

He [Richard O'Brien] encourages athletes to rehearse their skills until they're rituals—to push themselves until the skill is completely mastered so that their thoughts don't interfere with what their bodies know how to do. He steers their focus away from their anxiety and onto their performance. "Some boxers, for example, get so nervous during the national anthem that they're complete basket cases' by the time it's over," O'Brien says. "Instead, they should think about the punches they will throw in the first five minutes," he said.[57]

Causal Attributions

Attribution theory is based on the premise that people attempt to infer causes for observed behaviour. Rightly or wrongly, we constantly formulate cause-and-effect explanations for

Causal attributions

Suspected or inferred causes of behaviour.

our own and others' behaviour. Attributional statements such as the following are common: "Joe drinks too much because he has no willpower; but I need a couple of drinks after work because I'm under a lot of pressure." Formally defined, **causal attributions** are suspected or inferred causes of behaviour. Even though our causal attributions tend to be self-serving and are often invalid, it is important to understand how people formulate attributions because they profoundly affect organizational behaviour. For example, a supervisor who attributes an employee's poor performance to a lack of effort might reprimand that individual. However, training might be deemed necessary if the supervisor attributes the poor performance to a lack of ability.

Generally speaking, people formulate causal attributions by considering the events preceding an observed behaviour. This section introduces and explores two different widely cited attribution models proposed by Harold Kelley and Bernard Weiner. Attributional tendencies, research, and related managerial implications also are discussed.

Kelley's Model of Attribution

Internal factors

Personal characteristics that cause behaviour.

External factors

Environmental characteristics that cause behaviour.

Current models of attribution, such as Kelley's, are based on the pioneering work of the late Fritz Heider. Heider, the founder of attribution theory, proposed that behaviour can be attributed either to **internal factors** within a person (such as ability) or to **external factors** within the environment (such as a difficult task). This line of thought parallels the idea of an internal versus external locus of control, as discussed in Chapter 5. Building on Heider's work, Kelley attempted to pinpoint major antecedents of internal and external attributions. Kelley hypothesized that people make causal attributions after gathering information about three dimensions of behaviour: consensus, distinctiveness, and consistency.[58] These dimensions vary independently, thus forming various combinations and leading to differing attributions.

Figure 6–6 presents performance charts showing low versus high consensus, distinctiveness, and consistency. These charts are now used to help develop a working knowledge of all three dimensions in Kelley's model.

- *Consensus* involves a comparison of an individual's behaviour with that of his or her peers. There is high consensus when one acts like the rest of the group and low consensus when one acts differently. As shown in Figure 6–6, high consensus is indicated when persons A, B, C, D, and E obtain similar levels of individual performance. In contrast, person C's performance is low in consensus because it significantly varies from the performance of persons A, B, D, and E.

- *Distinctiveness* is determined by comparing a person's behaviour on one task with his or her behaviour on other tasks. High distinctiveness means the individual has performed the task in question in a significantly different manner than he or she has performed other tasks. Low distinctiveness means stable performance or quality from one task to another. Figure 6–6 reveals that the employee's performance on task 4 is highly distinctive because it significantly varies from his or her performance on tasks 1, 2, 3, and 5.

- *Consistency* is determined by judging whether the individual's performance on a given task is consistent over time. High consistency implies that a person performs a certain task the same, time after time. Unstable performance of a given task over time would mean low consistency. The downward spike in performance depicted in the consistency graph of Figure 6–6 represents low consistency. In this case, the employee's performance on a given task varied over time.

It is important to remember that consensus relates to other *people,* distinctiveness relates to other *tasks,* and consistency relates to *time.* The question now is: How does information about these three dimensions of behaviour lead to internal or external attributions?

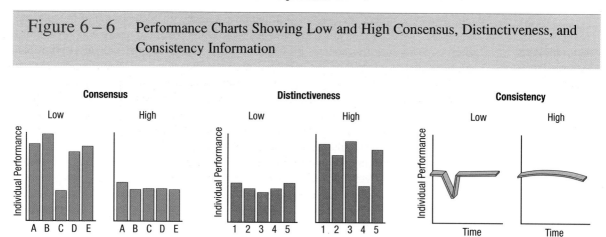

Figure 6 – 6   Performance Charts Showing Low and High Consensus, Distinctiveness, and Consistency Information

Source: K. A. Brown, "Explaining Group Poor Performance: An Attributional Analysis," *Academy of Management Review*, January 1984. p 56. Used with permission.

Kelley hypothesized that people attribute behaviour to *external* causes (environmental factors) when they perceive high consensus, high distinctiveness, and low consistency. *Internal* attributions (personal factors) tend to be made when observed behaviour is characterized by low consensus, low distinctiveness, and high consistency. So, for example, when all employees are performing poorly (high consensus), when the poor performance occurs on only one of several tasks (high distinctiveness), and the poor performance occurs during only one time period (low consistency), a supervisor will probably attribute an employee's poor performance to an external source such as peer pressure or an overly difficult task. In contrast, performance will be attributed to an employee's personal characteristics (an internal attribution) when only the individual in question is performing poorly (low consensus), when the inferior performance is found across several tasks (low distinctiveness), and when the low performance has persisted over time (high consistency). Many studies supported this predicted pattern of attributions.[59]

Weiner's Model of Attribution

Bernard Weiner, a noted motivation theorist, developed an attribution model to explain achievement behaviour and to predict subsequent changes in motivation and performance. In his model, Weiner proposes that ability, effort, task difficulty, luck, and help from others are the primary causes of achievement behaviour (see Figure 6 – 6). In turn, these attributions for success and failure influence how individuals feel about themselves. For instance, a meta-analysis of 104 studies involving almost 15,000 subjects found that people who attributed failure to their lack of ability (as opposed to bad luck) experienced psychological depression. The exact opposite attributions (to good luck rather than to high ability) tended to trigger depression in people experiencing positive events. In short, perceived bad luck took the sting out of a negative outcome, but perceived good luck reduced the joy associated with success.[60]

In further support of Weiner's model, a recent study of 130 male salespeople in the United Kingdom revealed that positive, internal attributions for success were associated with higher sales and performance ratings.[61] A second study examined the attributional processes of 126 employees who were permanently displaced by a plant closing. Consistent with the model, as the explanation for job loss was attributed to internal and stable causes, life satisfaction, self-esteem, and expectations for reemployment diminished. Furthermore, research also shows that when individuals attribute their

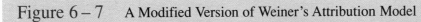

Figure 6 – 7   A Modified Version of Weiner's Attribution Model

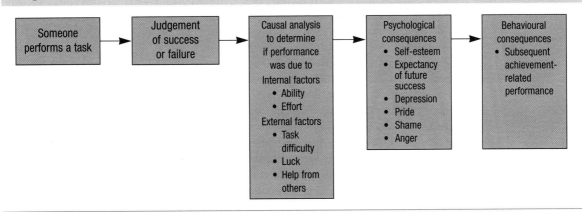

Source: Based in part on B Weiner, "An Attributional Theory of Achievement Motivation and Emotion," *Psychological Review*, October 1985, pp 548-73.

success to internal rather than external factors, they (1) have higher expectations for future success, (2) report a greater desire for achievement, and (3) set higher performance goals.[62]

Attributional Tendencies

Researchers have uncovered two attributional tendencies that distort one's interpretation of observed behaviour—*fundamental attribution bias* and *self-serving bias*.

Fundamental attribution bias

Ignoring environmental factors that affect behaviour.

Fundamental Attribution Bias   The **fundamental attribution bias** reflects one's tendency to attribute another person's behaviour to his or her personal characteristics, as opposed to situational factors. This bias causes perceivers to ignore important environmental forces that often significantly affect behaviour. For example, a study of 145 manufacturing employees demonstrated that upper management attributed the causes of industrial back pain to the individual involved rather than the environment. In contrast, hourly workers attributed back pain to the work environment and not the individual.[63]

Self-serving bias

Taking more personal responsibilty for success than failure.

Self-Serving Bias   The **self-serving bias** represents one's tendency to take more personal responsibility for success than for failure. Referring again to Figure 6–6, employees tend to attribute their successes to internal factors (high ability and/or hard work) and their failures to uncontrollable external factors (tough job, bad luck, unproductive co-workers, or an unsympathetic boss).[64] This self-serving bias is evident in how students typically analyse their performance on exams. Good students are likely to attribute their grade to high ability or hard work. Poor students, meanwhile, tend to pin the blame on factors like an unfair test, bad luck, or unclear lectures. Because of self-serving bias, it is very difficult to pin down personal responsibility for mistakes in today's complex organizations.

Managerial Application and Implications

Attribution models can be used to explain how managers handle poorly performing employees. One study revealed that managers had negative impressions of employees, administered lower levels of rewards, and blamed employees when they attributed their poor performance to internal causes. A second study indicated that managers tended to transfer employees whose poor performance was attributed to a lack of ability. These same managers also decided to take no immediate action when poor performance was attributed to external factors beyond an individual's control.[65]

The preceding situations have several important implications for managers. First, managers tend to disproportionately attribute behaviour to *internal* causes. This can result in inaccurate evaluations of performance, leading to reduced employee motivation. No one likes to be blamed because of factors they perceive to be beyond their control. Further, because managers' responses to employee performance vary according to their attributions, attributional biases may lead to inappropriate managerial actions, including promotions, transfers, layoffs, and so forth. This can dampen motivation and performance. Attributional training sessions for managers are in order. Basic attributional processes can be explained, and managers can be taught to detect and avoid attributional biases. Finally, an employee's attributions for his or her own performance have dramatic effects on subsequent motivation, performance, and personal attitudes such as self-esteem. For instance, people tend to give up, develop lower expectations for future success, and experience decreased self-esteem when they attribute failure to a lack of ability. Fortunately, attributional retraining can improve both motivation and performance. Research shows that employees can be taught to attribute their failures to a lack of effort rather than to a lack of ability.[66] This attributional realignment paves the way for improved motivation and performance.

In summary, managers need to keep a finger on the pulse of employee attributions if they are to make full use of the motivation concepts in the next two chapters.

Summary of Key Concepts

1. *Describe perception in terms of the social information processing model.* Perception is a mental and cognitive process that enables us to interpret and understand our surroundings. Social perception, also known as social cognition and social information processing, is a four-stage process. The four stages are selective attention/comprehension, encoding and simplification, storage and retention, and retrieval and response. During social cognition, salient stimuli are matched with schemata, assigned to cognitive categories, and stored in long-term memory for events, semantic materials, or people.

2. *Identify and briefly explain four managerial implications of social perception.* Social perception affects hiring decisions, performance appraisals, leadership perceptions, and communication processes. Inaccurate schemata or racist and sexist schemata may be used to evaluate job applicants. Similarly, faulty schemata about what constitutes good versus poor performance can lead to inaccurate performance appraisals. Invalid schemata need to be identified and replaced with appropriate schemata through coaching and training. Further, managers are advised to use objective rather than subjective measures of performance. With respect to leadership, a leader will have a difficult time influencing employees when he or she exhibits behaviours contained in employees' schemata of poor leaders. Finally, communication is

influenced by schemata used to interpret any message. Effective communicators try to tailor their messages to the receiver's perceptual schemata.

3. *Discuss stereotypes and the process of stereotype formation.* Stereotypes represent grossly oversimplified beliefs or expectations about groups of people. Stereotyping is a four-step process that begins by categorizing people into groups according to various criteria. Next, we infer that all people within a particular group possess the same traits or characteristics. Then, we form expectations of others and interpret their behaviour according to our stereotypes. Finally, stereotypes are maintained by (a) overestimating the frequency of stereotypic behaviours exhibited by others, (b) incorrectly explaining expected and unexpected behaviours, and (c) differentiating minority individuals from oneself.

4. *Summarize the managerial challenges and recommendations of sex-role, age, and race stereotypes.* The key managerial challenge is to make decisions that are blind to gender, age, and race. Training can be used to educate employees about the problem of stereotyping. Because mixed-group contact reduces stereotyping, organizations should create opportunities for diverse employees to meet and work together in cooperative groups of equal status. Hiring decisions should be based on valid individual differences, and managers can be trained to use

valid criteria when evaluating employee performance. Minimizing differences in job opportunities and experiences across groups of people can help alleviate promotional barriers. Job design techniques can be used to reduce performance plateaus associated with age. Organizations also may need to use incentives to motivate employees to upgrade their skills and abilities, and hiring older workers has many potential organizational benefits. It is critical to obtain top management's commitment and support to eliminate stereotyping and discriminatory decisions.

5. *Discuss how the self-fulfilling prophecy is created and how it can be used to improve individual and group productivity.* The self-fulfilling prophecy, also known as the Pygmalion effect, describes how people behave so that their expectations come true. High managerial expectations foster high employee self-expectations. These, in turn, lead to greater effort and better performance, and yet higher expectations. Conversely, a downward spiral of expectations-performance may occur. Managers are encouraged to harness the Pygmalion effect by building a hierarchical framework that reinforces positive performance expectations throughout the organization.

6. *Explain, according to Kelley's model, how external and internal causal attributions are formulated.* Attribution theory attempts to describe how people infer causes for observed behaviour. According to Kelley's model of causal attribution, external attributions tend to be made when consensus and distinctiveness are high and consistency is low. Internal (personal responsibility) attributions tend to be made when consensus and distinctiveness are low and consistency is high.

7. *Review Weiner's model of attribution.* Weiner's model of attribution predicts achievement behaviour in terms of causal attributions. Attributions of ability, effort, task difficulty, luck, and help from others affect how individuals feel about themselves. In turn, these feelings directly influence subsequent achievement-related performance.

8. *Contrast the fundamental attribution bias and the self-serving bias.* Fundamental attribution bias involves emphasizing personal factors more than situational factors while formulating causal attributions for the behaviour of others. Self-serving bias involves personalizing the causes of one's successes and externalizing the causes of one's failures.

Discussion Questions

1. Why is it important for managers to have a working knowledge of perception and attribution?

2. When you are sitting in class, what stimuli are salient? What is your schema for classroom activity?

3. Have you ever been the victim of a sex-role stereotype? Discuss.

4. Which type of stereotype (sex-role, age, or race) is more pervasive and negative in organizations? Why?

5. What evidence of self-fulfilling prophecies have you seen lately?

6. How might the Pygmalion effect be applied in this class?

7. How would you formulate an attribution, according to Kelley's model, for the behaviour of a classmate who starts arguing in class with your professor?

8. In what situations do you tend to attribute your successes/failures to luck? How well does Weiner's attributional model in Figure 6–7 explain your answers? Explain.

9. Are poor people victimized by a fundamental attribution bias? Explain.

10. What evidence of the self-serving bias have you observed lately?

Personal Awareness and Growth Exercise

What Is Your Attributional Style?

Objectives

1. To assess your attributional style.

2. To consider the personal and managerial implications of your attributional style.

Introduction

People tend to interpret their environments in consistent ways. This tendency is referred to as an attributional style. Attributional style thus represents an individual difference that distinguishes how people interpret and respond to their environments. It is based on determining the extent to which we interpret events as being due to stable, internal, and global causes. A team of researchers developed a novel approach to measure attribution style. It is based on having respondents answer a series of attributional questions about 12 hypothetical events. We have selected four of these situations.[67] To accurately assess your attributional style, it is very important that you vividly imagine yourself in each of these situations.

Instructions

Below are four situations that could possibly happen to you. We want you to imagine that the situation has actually occurred. Analyse each situation, one at a time, by using the following four steps: (1) Read the situation. Be sure to vividly imagine that the situation is actually happening to you. Think about how you would feel if this situation really occurred. (2) Determine the major cause of the situation if it happened to you. Again, you need to put yourself into the situation at hand and then think about why it would have transpired. (3) Write the major cause in the space provided. (4) Answer the three attribution questions that follow the situation by circling your answer on the rating scales that are provided. Now go to the next situation and follow the same four steps. Once you have completed answering the questions for all situations, use the scoring key to compute your attributional style.

SITUATION 1: YOU HAVE BEEN LOOKING FOR A JOB UNSUCCESSFULLY FOR SOME TIME

1. Write down the one major cause:

2. Is the cause of your unsuccessful job search due to something about you or to something about other people or circumstances? (circle one number)

   Totally due to other people or circumstances   1—2—3—4—5—6—7   Totally due to me

3. In the future when looking for a job, will this cause again be present? (circle one number)

   Will never again be present   1—2—3—4—5—6—7   Will always be present

4. Is the cause something that just influences looking for a job or does it also influence other areas of your life? (circle one number)

   Influences just this particular situation   1—2—3—4—5—6—7   Influences all situations in my life

---

SITUATION 2: YOU GET A RAISE AT WORK

1. Write down the one major cause:

2. Is the cause of your rise due to something about you or to something about other people or circumstances? (circle one number)

   Totally due to other people or circumstances   1—2—3—4—5—6—7   Totally due to me

3. When trying to get a rise in the future, will this cause again be present? (circle one number)

   Will never again be present   1—2—3—4—5—6—7   Will always be present

4. Is the cause something that just influences getting a rise or does it also influence other areas of your life? (circle one number)

   Influences just this particular situation   1—2—3—4—5—6—7   Influences all situations in my life

SITUATION 3: YOUR SPOUSE (BOYFRIEND/GIRLFRIEND) HAS BEEN TREATING YOU MORE LOVINGLY

1. Write down the one major cause:

2. Is the cause of being treated more lovingly due to something about you or to something about other people or circumstances? (circle one number)

   Totally due to other people or circumstances   1—2—3—4—5—6—7   Totally due to me

3. In your future relationship with your spouse (boyfriend/girlfriend), will this cause again be present? (circle one number)

   Will never again be present   1—2—3—4—5—6—7   Will always be present

4. Is the cause something that just influences how lovingly your spouse (boyfriend/girlfriend) treats you or does it also influence other areas of your life? (circle one number)

   Influences just this particular situation   1—2—3—4—5—6—7   Influences all situations in my life

---

SITUATION 4: A FRIEND COMES TO YOU WITH A PROBLEM, AND YOU DON'T TRY TO HELP

1. Write down the one major cause:

2. Is the cause of your helping behaviour due to something about you or to something about other people or circumstances? (circle one number)

   Totally due to other people or circumstances   1—2—3—4—5—6—7   Totally due to me

3. When dealing with friends' problems in the future, will this cause again be present? (circle one number)

   Will never again be present   1—2—3—4—5—6—7   Will always be present

4. Is the cause something that just influences your willingness to help friends or does it also influence other areas of your life? (circle onef number)

   Influences just this particular situation   1—2—3—4—5—6—7   Influences all situations in my life

Scoring Key

Your attributional style is based on comparing your average responses to the two positive events (Situations 2 and 3) with the two negative events (Situations 1 and 4). First compute the average attribution score for each situation by calculating the average response for questions 2, 3, and 4 for each situation. Record your answers in the space provided. Now you are ready to compute an average composite score for the positive and negative events. This is done by calculating the average attributional score across Situations 2 and 3 and then across Situations 1 and 4. Record your answers in the space provided. Norms are shown to help you interpret the relative status of your attributional style.

Situation 1 (average score for questions 2–4)   _____
Situation 2 (average score for questions 2–4)   _____
Situation 3 (average score for questions 2–4)   _____
Situation 4 (average score for questions 2–4)   _____
Positive event attribution (average of Situations 2 and 3)   _____
Negative event attribution (average of Situations 1 and 4)   _____

Norms:

	AVERAGE ATTRIBUTIONAL RATING
Situation 1	3.96
Situation 2	5.62
Situation 3	5.11
Situation 4	3.97

QUESTIONS FOR DISCUSSIONS

1. Do you have more of a tendency to interpret positive or negative events to internal, stable, and global causes? What does this pattern suggest about yourself?

2. Using the norms, how would you describe your attributional style towards positive and negative events?

3. Do you see any evidence of the self-serving bias? Explain.

4. What are the implications of your attribution style? Consider how your style might influence hiring, performance appraisal, leadership, and motivating others.

Group Exercise

Using Attribution Theory to Resolve Performance Problems

Objectives

1. To gain experience determining the causes of performance.

2. To decide on corrective action for employee performance.

Introduction

Attributions are typically made to internal and external factors. Perceivers arrive at their assessments by using various informational cues or antecedents. To determine the types of antecedents people use, we have developed a case containing various informational cues about an individual's performance. You will be asked to read the case and make attributions about the causes of performance. To assess the impact of attributions on managerial behaviour, you will also be asked to recommend corrective action.

Instructions

Presented on the following page is a case that depicts the performance of Mary Martin, a computer programmer Please read the case to the right and then identify the causes of her behaviour by answering the questions following the case. After completing this task, decide on the appropriateness of various forms of corrective action. A list of potential recommendations has been developed. The list is divided into four categories. Read each action, and evaluate its appropriateness by using the scale provided. Next, compute a total score for each of the four categories.

Causes of Performance

To what extent was each of the following a cause of Mary's performance? Use the following scale:

THE CASE OF MARY MARTIN

Mary Martin, 30, received her baccalaureate degree in computer science from a reputable state school in the Midwest. She also graduated with above-average grades. Mary is currently working in the computer support/analysis department as a programmer for a nationally based firm. During the past year, Mary has missed 10 days of work. She seems unmotivated and rarely has her assignments completed on time. Mary is usually given the harder programmes to work on.

Past records indicate Mary, on the average, completes programmes classified as "routine" in about 45 hours. Her co-workers, on the other hand, complete "routine" programmes in an average time of 32 hours. Further, Mary finishes programmes considered "major problems," on the average, in about 115 hours. Her co-workers, however, finish these same "major problem" assignments, on the average, in about 100 hours. When Mary has worked in programming teams, her peer performance reviews are generally average to negative. Her male peers have noted she is not creative in attacking problems and she is difficult to work with.

The computer department recently sent a questionnaire to all users of its services to evaluate the usefulness and accuracy of data received. The results indicate many departments are not using computer output because they cannot understand the reports. It was also determined that the users of output generated from Mary's programmes found the output chaotic and not useful for managerial decision making.[68]

	VERY LITTLE			VERY MUCH	
	1 —— 2 ——	3 ——	4 ——	5	
a. High ability	1	2	3	4	5
b. Low ability	1	2	3	4	5
c. Low effort	1	2	3	4	5
d. Difficult job	1	2	3	4	5
e. Unproductive co-workers	1	2	3	4	5
f. Bad luck	1	2	3	4	5

Appropriateness of Corrective Action

Evaluate the following courses of action by using the scale below:

VERY INAPPROPRIATE			VERY APPROPRIATE	
1	2	3	4	5

COERCIVE ACTIONS

a. Reprimand Mary for her performance	1	2	3	4	5
b. Threaten to fire Mary if her performance does not improve	1	2	3	4	5

CHANGE JOB

c. Transfer Mary to another job	1	2	3	4	5
d. Demote Mary to a less demanding job	1	2	3	4	5

NONPUNITIVE ACTIONS

e Work with Mary to help her do the job better	1	2	3	4	5
f. Offer Mary encouragement to help her improve	1	2	3	4	5

NO IMMEDIATE ACTIONS

g. Do nothing	1	2	3	4	5
h. Promise Mary a pay rise if she improves	1	2	3	4	5

Compute a score for the four categories:[69]

Coercive actions = a + b =

Change job = c + d =

Non-punitive actions = e + f =

No immediate actions = g + h =

QUESTIONS FOR DISCUSSIONS

1. How would you evaluate Mary's performance in terms of consensus, distinctiveness, and consistency?

2. Is Mary's performance due to internal or external causes?

3. What did you identify as the top two causes of Mary's performance? Are your choices consistent with Weiner's classification of internal and external factors? Explain.

4. Which of the four types of corrective action do you think is most appropriate? Explain. Can you identify any negative consequences of this choice?

Notes

[1]Based on C Truss, R Goffe, and G Jones, "Segregated Occupations and Gender and Stereotyping: A Study of Secretarial Work in Europe," *Human Relations*, 1995, pp 1331–1355.

[2]K Warnock, "Selecting the Accountants of the Future," *Accountancy Ireland*, June 1997, pp 6–8

[3]Details may be found in R Eisenberger, P Fasolo, and V Davis–LaMastro, "Perceived Organizational Support and Employee Diligence, Commitment, and Innovation," *Journal of Applied Psychology*, February 1990, pp 51–59.

[4]S T Fiske and S E Taylor, *Social Cognition*, 2nd ed (Reading, MA: Addison-Wesley Publishing, 1991), pp 1–2.

[5]Adapted from discussion in Fiske and Taylor, *Social Cognition,* 2nd ed, pp 247–50.

[6]The negativity bias was examined and supported by O Ybarra and W G Stephan, "Misanthropic Person Memory," *Journal of Personality and Social Psychology*, April 1996, pp 691–700; and Y Ganzach, "Negativity (and Positivity) in Performance Evaluation: Three Field Studies," *Journal of Applied Psychology*, August 1995, pp 491–99.

[7]E Rosch, C B Mervis, W D Gray, D M Johnson, and P Boyes-Braem, "Basic Objects in Natural Categories," *Cognitive Psychology,* July 1976, p 383.

[8]A thorough discussion of schema and their role in information processing is presented by S T Fiske and S L Neuberg, "A Continuum of Impression Formation, from Category-Based to Individuating Processes: Influences of Information and Motivation on Attention and Interpretation," in *Advances in Experimental Social Psychology*, ed M P Zanna (New York: Academic Press, 1990), vol. 23, pp 1–74.

[9]See P A Giuffre and C L Williams, "Boundary Lines: Labeling Sexual Harassment in Restaurants," *Gender and Society*, September 1994, pp 378–401.

[10]See A Varma, A S DeNisi, and L H Peters, "Interpersonal Affect and Performance Appraisal: A Field Study," *Personnel Psychology*, Summer 1996, pp 341–60. For a thorough review of mood research, see J P Forgas, "Mood and Judgement: The Affect Infusion Model (AIM)," *Psychological Bulletin*, January 1995, pp 39–66.

[11]See A J Kinicki, P W Hom, M R Trost, and K J Wade, "Effects of Category Prototypes on Performance-Rating Accuracy," *Journal of Applied Psychology*, June 1995, pp 354–70; and J A Bargh, M Chen, and L Burrows, "Automaticity of Social Behaviour: Direct Effects of Trait Construct and Stereotype Activation on Action,"

Journal of Personality and Social Psychology, August 1996, pp 230–44.

[12]For a review of research on the relationship between depression and information processing, see D B Burt, M J Zembar, and G Niederehe, "Depression and Memory Impairment: A Meta-Analysis of the Association, Its Pattern, and Specificity," *Psychological Bulletin*, March 1995, pp 285–305.

[13]For a thorough discussion about the structure and organization of memory, see L R Squire, B Knowlton, and G Musen, "The Structure and Organization of Memory," in *Annual Review of Psychology*, eds L W Porter and M R Rosenzweig (Palo Alto, CA: Annual Reviews Inc., 1993), vol. 44, pp 453–95.

[14]Washing clothes.

[15]A thorough discussion of the reasoning process used to make judgements and decisions is provided by S A Sloman, "The Empirical Case for Two Systems of Reasoning," *Psychological Bulletin*, January 1996, pp 3–22.

[16]Results can be found in C M Marlowe, S L Schneider, and C E Nelson, "Gender and Attractiveness Biases in Hiring Decisions: Are More Experienced Managers Less Biased?" *Journal of Applied Psychology*, February 1996, pp 11–21.

[17]Results from a comprehensive study can be found in S J Motowidlo, G W Cater, M D Dunnette, N Tippins, S Werner, J R Burnett, and M J Vaughan, "Studies of the Structured Behavioural Interview," *Journal of Applied Psychology*, October 1992, p 571–87.

[18]M Buelens, F Debussche, and K Vanderheyden, *Mensen en Verscheidenheid* (Brussels: Vacature, 1997).

[19]Results can be found in W H Bommer, J L Johnson, G A Rich, P M Podsakoff, and S B Mackenzie, "On the Interchangeability of Objective and Subjective Measures of Employee Performance: A Meta-Analysis," *Personnel Psychology*, Autumn 1995, pp 587–605.

[20]See J I Sanchez and P D L Torre, "A Second Look at the Relationship between Rating and Behavioral Accuracy in Performance Appraisal," *Journal of Applied Psychology*, February 1996, pp 3–10; and Kinicki, Hom, Trost, and Wade, "Effects of Category Prototypes on Performance-Rating Accuracy."

[21]The effectiveness of rater training was supported by D V Day and L M Sulsky, "Effects of Frame-of-Reference Training and Information Configuration on Memory Organization and Rating Accuracy," *Journal of Applied Psychology*, February 1995, pp 158–67.

[22]Results can be found in J S Phillips and R G Lord, "Schematic Information Processing and Perceptions of Leadership in Problem-Solving Groups," *Journal of Applied Psychology*, August 1982, pp 486–92.

[23]J Luft, *Group Processes* (CA: PaloAlto: National Press Books, 1970).

[24]C Leerhsen, "How Disney Does It," *Newsweek*, April 3, 1989, p 52.

[25]E D Davidson, and B J Punnett, "International Asignments: Is There a Role for Gender and Race in Decisions?" *International Journal of Human Resource Management*, 1995, vol 6, no 2 pp 411–441.

[26]C M Judd and B Park, "Definition and Assessment of Accuracy in Social Stereotypes," *Psychological Review*, January 1993, p 110.

[27]For a thorough discussion of stereotypes and their accuracy, see Y-T Lee, L J Jussim, and C R McCauley, *Stereotype Accuracy: Toward Appreciating Group Differences* (Washington, DC: American Psychological Association, 1995).

[28]For complete details, see S Shellenbarger, "Work-Force Study Finds Loyalty Is Weak, Division of Race and Gender Are Deep, *The Wall Street Journal*, September 3, 1993, pp B1, B9.

[29]The process of stereotype formation and maintenance is discussed by J W Sherman, "Development and Mental Representation of Stereotypes," *Journal of Personality and Social Psychology*, June 1996, pp 1126–41; and Z Kunda and K C Oleson, "Maintaining Stereotypes in the Face of Disconfirmation: Constructing Grounds for Subtyping Deviants," *Journal of Personality and Social Psychology*, April 1995, pp 565–79.

[30]I K Broverman, S Raymond Vogel, D M Broverman, F E Clarkson, and P S Rosenkrantz, "Sex-Role Stereotypes: A Current Appraisal," *Journal of Social Issues*, 1972, p 75.

[31]Ibid.

[32]See B P Allen, "Gender Stereotypes Are Not Accurate: A Replication of Martin (1987) Using Diagnostic vs. Self-Report and Behavioural Criteria," *Sex Roles*, May 1995, pp 583–600.

[33]Results can be found in V E Schein, R Mueller, T Lituchy, and J Liu, "Think Manager—Think Male: A Global Phenomenon?" *Journal of Organizational Behaviour*, January 1996, pp 33–41.

[34]See J D Olian, D P Schwab, and Y Haberfeld, "The Impact of Applicant Gender Compared to Qualifications on Hiring Recommendations: A Meta-Analysis of Experimental Studies," *Organizational Behaviour and Human Decision Processes*, April 1988, pp 180–95.

[35]Results from the meta-analyses are discussed in K P Carson, C L Sutton, and P D Corner, "Gender Bias in Performance Appraisals: A Meta-Analysis," paper presented at the 49th Annual Academy of Management Meeting, Washington, DC: 1989. Results from the field study can be found in T J Maurer and M A Taylor, "Is Sex by Itself Enough? An Exploration of Gender Bias Issues in Performance Appraisal," *Organizational Behaviour and Human Decision Processes*, November 1994, pp 231–51.

[36]P E kelly, A Oakes Yound, and L S Clark, "Sex Stereotyping in the Workplace: A Manager's Guide", *Business Horizons*, March–April 1993, p 25.

[37]T Lester, "A Women's Place . . . ", *Management Today*, April 1993, pp 46–50.

[38]Based on and translated from "Leeftijd Sollicitant Geeft de Doorslag", *NCR Handelsblad*, May 7, 1997, p 21.

[39]See G M McEvoy, "Cumulative Evidence of the Relationship between Employee Age and Job Performance," *Journal of Applied Psychology*, February 1989, pp 11–17.

[40]A thorough discussion of the relationship between age and performance is contained in D A Waldman and B J Avolio, "Aging and Work Performance in Perspective: Contextual and Developmental Considerations," in *Research in Personnel and Human Resources Management*, ed G R Ferris (Greenwich, CT: JAI Press, 1993), vol. 11, pp 133–62.

[41]For details, see B J Avolio, D A Waldman, and M A McDaniel, "Age and Work Performance in Nonmanagerial Jobs: The Effects of Experience and Occupational Type," *Academy of Management Journal*, June 1990, pp 407–22.

[42]See M C Healy, M Lehman, and M A McDaniel, "Age and Voluntary Turnover: A Quantitative Review," *Personnel Psychology*, Summer 1995, pp 335–45; and J J Martocchio, "Age-Related Differences in Employee Absenteeism: A Meta-Analysis," *Psychology and Aging*, December 1989, pp 409–14.

[43]Based on L Lightfood, "Sacked White Teacher Claims Race Bias", *Sunday Times*, July 10, 1994, p 1.

[44]The affirmative action study was conducted by M E Heilman, and J A Lucas, "Presumed Incompetent? Stigmatization and Affirmative Action Efforts", *Journal of Applied Psychology*, August 1992, pp 536–44. Details of the study on race and attitudes may be found in J H Greenhaus, S Parasuraman, and W M Wormley, "Effects of Race on Organizational Experiences, Job Performance Evaluations, and

Career Outcomes", *Academy of Management Journal*, March 1990, pp 64–86.

[45] See D Bhatnagar and R Swamy, "Attitudes Toward Women as Managers: Does Interaction Make a Difference?" *Human Relations*, November 1995, pp 1285–1307; and B L Hassell and P I Perrewe, "An Examination of Beliefs about Older Workers: Do Stereotypes Still Exist?" *Journal of Organizational Behavior*, September 1995, pp 457–68.

[46] Supporting studies were conducted by A J Kinicki, C A Lockwood, P W Hom, and R W Griffeth, "Interviewer Predictions of Applicant Qualifications and Interviewer Validity," *Journal of Applied Psychology*, October 1990, pp 477–86; and Day and Sulsky, "Effects of Frame-of-Reference Training and Information Configuration on Memory Organization and Rating Accuracy."

[47] Skill based pay is discussed by T P Flannery, D A Hofrichter, P E Platten, *People, Performance, and Pay: Dynamic Compensation for Changing Organizations* (New York: The Free Press, 1996).

[48] Results from the meta-analysis may be found in P W Hom, and R W Griffeth, *Employee Turnover* (Cincinnati, OH: Southwestern, 1994).

[49] "Studies Refute Myths about Older Workers", *Society for Human Resource Management/HR News*, July 1991, p 8.

[50] Research is reviewed by R Rodgers, J E Hunter, and D L Rogers, "Influence of Top Management Commitment on Management Program Success," *Journal of Applied Psychology*, February 1993, pp 151–55.

[51] W Finn, "When race means colour and not competition", *The Times*, February 16, 1995, p SP/XX.

[52] The background and results for this study are presented in R Rosenthal and L Jacobson, *Pygmalion in the Classroom: Teacher Expectation and Pupils' Intellectual Development* (New York: Holt, Rinehart & Winston, 1968).

[53] See D Eden and Y Zuk, "Seasickness as a Self-Fulfilling Prophecy: Raising Self-Efficacy to Boost Performance at Sea," *Journal of Applied Psychology*, October 1995, pp 628–35. For a thorough review of research on the Pygmalion effect, see D Eden, *Pygmalion in Management: Productivity as a Self-Fulfilling Prophecy* (Lexington, MA: Lexington Books, 1990), ch 2.

[54] This study was conducted by T Dvir, D Eden, M L Banjo, "Self-Fulfilling Prophecy and Gender: Can Women Be Pygmalion and Galatea?" *Journal of Applied Psychology*, April 1995, pp 253–70.

[55] See B Schlender, "How Bill Gates Keeps the Magic Going," *Fortune*, June 18, 1990, pp 82–89.

[56] These recommendations were adapted from J Keller, "Have Faith—In You," *Selling Power*, June 1996, pp 84, 86; and R W Goddard, "The Pygmalion Effect," *Personnel Journal*, June 1985, p 10.

[57] B Murray, "More Than 20 American Sport Psychologists—The Most Ever—Will Work with Athletes at the Summer Olympics," *The APA Monitor*, July 1996, p 6.

[58] Kelley's model is discussed in detail in H H Kelley, "The Processes of Causal Attribution," *American Psychologist*, February 1973, pp 107–28.

[59] For recent examples, see D J Hilton, R H Smith, and S H Kim, "Processes of Causal Explanation and Dispositional Attribution,"

Journal of Personality and Social Psychology, March 1995, pp 377–87; and J T Johnson, K R Boyd, and P S Magnani, "Causal Reasoning in the Attribution of Rare and Common Events," *Journal of Personality and Social Psychology*, February 1994, pp 229–42.

[60] See P D Sweeney, K Anderson, and S Bailey, "Attributional Style in Depression: A Meta-Analytic Review," *Journal of Personality and Social Psychology*, May 1986, pp 974–91.

[61] Results can be found in P J Corr and J A Gray, "Attributional Style as a Personality Factor in Insurance Sales Performance in the UK," *Journal of Occupational Psychology*, March 1996, pp 83–87.

[62] Supportive results can be found in J Greenberg, "Forgive Me, I'm New: Three Experimental Demonstrations of the Effects of Attempts to Excuse Poor Performance," *Organizational Behavior and Human Decision Processes*, May 1996, pp 165–78; W S Silver, T R Mitchell, and M E Gist, "Responses to Successful and Unsuccessful Performance: The Moderating Effect of Self-Efficacy on the Relationship between Performance and Attributions," *Organizational Behavior and Human Decision Processes*, June 1995, pp 286–99; and G E Prussia, A J Kinicki, and J S Bracker, "Psychological and Behavioral Consequences of Job Loss: A Covariance Structure Analysis Using Weiner's (1985) Attribution Model," *Journal of Applied Psychology*, June 1993, pp 382–94.

[63] Results can be found in S J Linton and L-E Warg, "Attributions (Beliefs) and Job Satisfaction Associated with Back Pain in an Industrial Setting," *Perceptual and Motor Skills*, February 1993, pp 51–62. The fundamental attribution bias was also demonstrated by J-P Leyens, V Yzerbt, and O Corneille, "The Role of Applicability in the Emergence of the Overattribution Bias," *Journal of Personality and Social Psychology*, February 1996, pp 219–29.

[64] The effect of the self-serving bias was tested and supported by Silver, Mitchell, and Gist, "Responses to Successful and Unsuccessful Performance: The Moderating Effect of Self-Efficacy on the Relationship between Performance and Attributions"; and D Dunning, A Leuenberger, and D A Sherman, "A New Look at Motivated Inference: Are Self-Serving Theories of Success a Product of Motivational Forces?" *Journal of Personality and Social Psychology*, July 1995, pp 58–68.

[65] Details may be found in J M Crant and T S Bateman, "Assignment of Credit and Blame for Performance Outcomes," *Academy of Management Journal*, February 1993, pp 7–27; and E C Pence, W C Pendelton, G H Dobbins, and J A Sgro, "Effects of Causal Explanations and Sex Variables on Recommendations for Corrective Actions Following Employee Failure," *Organizational Behavior and Human Performance*, April 1982, pp 227–40.

[66] For a review of attributional retraining, see F Forsterling, "Attributional Retraining: A Review," *Psychological Bulletin*, November 1985, pp 496–512.

[67] This exercise was adapted from the original procedure and survey contained in C Peterson, A Semmel, C V Baeyer, L Y Abramson, G I Metalsky, and M E P Seligman, "The Attributional Style Questionnaire," *Cognitive Therapy and Research*, September 1982, pp 287–300.

[68] Adapted from A J Kinicki and R W Griffeth, "The Impact of Sex-Role Stereotypes on Performance Ratings and Causal Attributions of Performance," *Journal of Vocational Behavior*, April 1985, pp 155–70.

Seven

Motivation through Needs, Job Design, and Satisfaction

When you finish studying the material in this chapter, you should be able to:

1. Define the term "motivation."

2. Discuss the systems model of motivation and performance.

3. Review the historical roots of modern motivation theories.

4. Contrast Maslow's and McClelland's need theories.

5. Demonstrate your familiarity with scientific management, job enlargement, job rotation, and job enrichment.

6. Explain the practical significance of Herzberg's distinction between motivators and hygiene factors.

7. Describe how internal work motivation is increased by using the job characteristics model.

8. Discuss the causes and consequences of job satisfaction.

The French tollbooth attendants

Bonjour, merci, au revoir. These standard tollbooth phrases can be mumbled, yelled, flatly stated, or even sung. The smile that goes with these them can be neutral or kind, tight, or even absent. The tone of the *bonjour* can be a test, but for the most part it is a simple check. Confined to their small box, the receivers who are handed tickets see at a glance who they'll have to deal with next. *Au premier coup d'oeil* affirms Géraldine, a pretty brunette. "Some lose their temper, because it takes longer in this lane than in another. Others don't even bother to look up; or are even afraid to look up. It regularly happens that the driver starts a quarrel with his wife because she cannot find her purse fast enough."

The Saint-Arnoult tollgate on the south A10 consists of 90 attendants, all of them employed by the motorway's single private company. *Le plus important péage* d'Europe counts 22 million vehicles a year and in an hour one attendant can process 250 transactions.

The high frequency of volatile contacts, most lasting no more than 20 seconds, has turned the attendants into excellent judges of faces. "We have to be on our guard for aggressive drivers. We have witnessed real fights with other attendants, or even between drivers, for trivial reasons such as too long queues or because a driver constantly changes from one queue to another . . ." Nathalie sighs. "And," she continues, "there are the exhibitionists, alone or whole buses of them, showing their buttocks."

"Some drivers have even given up talking, by a simple snap of their fingers they claim a receipt. I then sometimes cannot resist replying *Vous désirez?*" Géraldine says.

"Watch out for dogs! A colleague of mine was bitten on the arm," Nathalie says. She does prefer eccentrics, however: for example, those who cross France with a series of turtle doves neatly aligned on a broomstick in the back seat, or the Englishman who, to resolve the problem of right-seat driving, used a peg fixed to a stick to pass the ticket and the money, and then conjured up a soup ladle to collect the change. "Generally speaking, foreigners are more polite and less hurried than the French," says Jean-Paul Sallé, an attendant at the Orléans-Nord tollgate. "Unfortunately, foreigners have made a habit of reserving their change for us on their way home."

The attendants feel sympathetic towards some of the people they see desperately staying close to Saint-Arnoult's gate after having lost their orientation, or those people who have forgotten to take a ticket at the motorway entry. And often, people will simply start a conversation out of the blue. Géraldine and Nathalie both remember a man who, when hanging up his car phone, opened his heart about his son's poor health, or the lady who confided to them her daughter's anorexia problems. The attendants are also faced everyday with irresponsible driving behaviour. Laurent once had to negotiate with a driver whose car started smoking. *Rien à faire*, he absolutely wanted to continue his journey to the south.

In summer time, the Tarmac lock-keepers have to endure unbearable temperatures (air-conditioners will be installed next year), clouds of dark smoke the lorries leave behind, which obliges the attendant to close the window between two "transactions," and an irregular family life due to inevitable night and Sunday shifts. The attendant's morale sometimes takes a terrible knock, too. One attendant recalls a mother saying to her daughter, "If you don't do your best in school, you will end up here."

Most of the attendants started here as students, or on a temporary basis, but ten years later they are still here. But, time flies. *C'est plutôt bon signe, non?* This hard job is paid rather well (about 9500 FF net, bonuses included), *plutôt bonne*, as the attendants say. There are also the special attractions: stars, politicians, nice cars, or a brief moment of complicity with someone who is in a good mood and who wants to share that mood with the attendant.[1]

Discussion Question

What elements in their job and working environment are (de)motivating the tollbooth attendants?

Effective employee motivation has long been one of management's most difficult and important duties. Success in this endeavour is becoming a more difficult challenge in light of organizational trends to downsize and reengineer and the demands associated with managing a diverse workforce, as discussed in Chapter 2. The purpose of this chapter, as well as the next, is to provide you with a foundation for understanding the complexities of employee motivation.

Specifically, this chapter provides a definitional and theoretical foundation for the topic of motivation so that a rich variety of motivation theories and techniques can be introduced and discussed. Coverage of employee motivation extends to Chapter 8. After providing a conceptual model for understanding motivation, this chapter focuses on (1) need theories of motivation, (2) an overview of job design methods used to motivate employees, (3) a job characteristics approach to job design, and (4) job satisfaction and work-family relationships. In the next chapter, attention turns to equity, expectancy, and goal setting.

What Does Motivation Involve?

Motivation

Psychological processes that arouse and goal-directed behaviour.

The term *motivation* derives from the Latin word *movere,* meaning "to move." In the present context, **motivation** represents "those psychological processes that cause the arousal, direction, and persistence of voluntary actions that are goal directed."[2] Managers need to understand these psychological processes if they are to successfully guide employees toward accomplishing organizational objectives. After considering a conceptual framework for understanding motivation, this section examines the historical roots of motivational concepts and the relationship between motivations and performance.

A Systems Model of Motivation and Performance

A conceptual model for understanding motivation and performance (see Figure 7–1) was created by integrating elements from several of the theories discussed in this book. The foundation of the model is based on systems theory and reinforcement theory. Systems theory is a framework for seeing interrelationships rather than things.[3] It is based on the premise that good performance results from a sequential process of transforming inputs into desired outputs. Systems theory further implies that behaviour is goal directed and that there are natural delays between actions and consequences. Reinforcement theory, the other component of the model, is discussed in Chapter 15. Reinforcement theory involves improving performance with feedback and contingent consequences. Now let us take a closer look at Figure 7–1. Consistent with our definition of motivation, Figure 7–1 shows that motivation is goal directed. There are seven types of inputs that influence your ability to achieve your desired goals: materials and machinery, performance objectives and expectations, individual differences, training, task characteristics, psychological climate,

Figure 7–1   A Systems Model of Motivation and Peformance

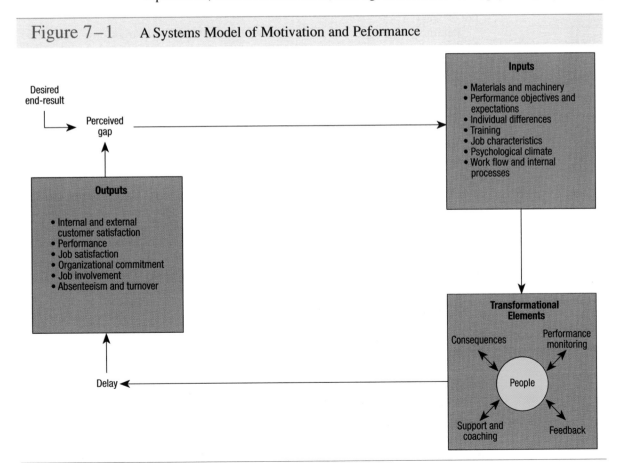

Source: A Kinicki, *Performance Management Systems,* 1992, Kinicki and Associates, Inc., Chandler, AZ pp1-8. Reprinted with permission; all rights reserved.

and work flow and internal processes. Materials and machinery are a fundamental input to performance. It would be very difficult for you to complete a term paper if the hard drive on your computer crashed. Because behaviour is geared towards accomplishing desired end-results, performance goals are a critical input to your performance. Goals and action plans provide you with direction and guidance about how to spend your time on specific tasks. Individual differences represent the self-concepts, motivation, skills, abilities, personality characteristics, values, feelings, and needs that vary among people. These differences can significantly affect your performance. Need theories of motivation are discussed in the next section of this chapter.

Organizations use training to bolster the skills and abilities employees need to effectively perform their jobs. Effective training can enhance performance, while ineffective training or lack of training might impair performance. A recent survey of 350,000 employees in Japan and the United States suggests that US companies manage this input quite differently from their Japanese counterparts. Results revealed that 66 per cent of the US workers reported receiving training that prepared them to do their jobs versus 33 per cent of the Japanese workers. In addition, 37 per cent of Japanese workers said they had sufficient opportunities to attend training compared with 77 per cent of the US employees.[4]

Job characteristics represent the type of tasks you complete at work. The role of job characteristics in employee motivation is discussed later in this chapter. Psychological climate refers to our perceptions about our work environments. A recent study of 162 salespeople, for example, showed that positive climates fostered higher job involvement and effort.[5] Work flow and internal processes, the final input variable, influence performance because they essentially structure the process of transforming raw materials into outputs.

Returning to Figure 7–1, you can see that managers help transform inputs into desired outputs by using performance monitoring, feedback, support and coaching, and consequences. Performance monitoring is used to keep track of performance results, which are then used to conduct feedback and coaching sessions. Support entails supplying employees with adequate resources to get the job done. In addition, coaching involves providing employees with direction, advice, and guidance. These behaviours include effective listening, furnishing employees with successful role models, showing employees how to complete difficult tasks, and helping maintain high self-efficacy and self-esteem.[6] Consequences represent the rewards and recognitions used to reinforce effort, behaviour, and performance.

The output box in Figure 7–1 contains a sample of the many outputs that are important to organizations. Clearly, organizations are interested in maintaining or improving customer satisfaction, performance, job satisfaction, and job involvement. At the same time, companies generally try to reduce both the absenteeism and turnover of good employees. The International OB discusses how Tetsuo Mizuno, head of Square used several inputs and transformational elements from Figure 7–1 to increase sales.

Historical Roots of Modern Motivation Theories

Five methods of explaining behaviour—needs, reinforcement, cognition, job characteristics, and feelings/emotions—underlie the evolution of modern theories of human motivation. As we proceed through this review, remember the objective of each alternative motivation theory is to explain and predict purposeful or goal-directed behaviour. As will become apparent, the differences between theoretical perspectives lie in the causal mechanisms used to explain behaviour.

Needs   Needs theories are based on the premise that individuals are motivated by unsatisfied needs. Dissatisfaction with your social life, for example, should motivate you to participate in more social activities. Henry Murray, a 1930s psychologist, was the first behavioural scientist to propose a list of needs thought to underlie goal-directed behaviour.

From Murray's work sprang a wide variety of need theories, some of which remain influential today. Recognized need theories of motivation are explored in the next section of this chapter.

Reinforcement   Reinforcement theorists, such as Edward L Thorndike and B F Skinner, proposed that behaviour is controlled by its consequences, not by the result of hypothetical internal states such as instincts, drives, or needs. This proposition is based on research data demonstrating that people repeat behaviours followed by favourable consequences and avoid behaviours resulting in unfavourable consequences. Few would argue with the statement that organizational rewards have a motivational impact on job behaviour. However, behaviourists and cognitive theorists do disagree over the role of internal states and processes in motivation.

Cognitions   Uncomfortable with the idea that behaviour is shaped completely by environmental consequences, cognitive motivation theorists contend that behaviour is a function of beliefs, expectations, values, and other mental cognitions. Behaviour is therefore viewed as the result of rational and conscious choices among alternative courses of action. In Chapter 8, we discuss cognitive motivation theories involving equity, expectancies, and goal setting.

International Organizational Behaviour

How a Western Motivation Approach Helped a Japanese Businessman

Square is a small video game software house in Tokyo, that in spite of recession, has seen phenomenal sales of its role-playing games for Nintendo's electronic games hardware. Three out of four games released last year were selling hits, selling more than 1m games. The unprecedented craze for Square's games prompted children and parents to line up outside toy shops, hours before the sixth in its best-selling series reached the shelves last April. The game sold out within hours, and Square posted sales of Y25bn (£160.7m) in a month—almost equal to what it achieved during the whole of last year. Tetsuo Minzu, head of Square broke with traditional Japanese management and his Western approach is the reason for the great success of his company.

Square's unconventional hiring policy is one of the underlying factors in its creative strength. While most leading companies may be losing out on talent by limiting themselves to hiring university graduates, especially from top class schools, Square hires anyone as long as they are inventive and are competent. Some 80 per cent of Square's staff have held other jobs, including teaching, playing in rock bands and acting. Other striking differences are the flexible working hours and the extensive holiday allocation. "Our business is entertainment. How can people have fun playing games made by workers who commute on a crowded train, wear blue suits and are constantly told what to do by their superiors," asks Mizuno. Employees must touch base once a day, but as long as they are productive, do not need to keep set office hours. Long holidays are rare in Japanese companies, which usually only allow employees to take one week off in the summer. Workers may be given a certain amount of paid annual holiday, but they are not really expected to take them. Employees at Square, however, get one month's summer holiday, and an additional 20 days of paid holiday a year. The company encourages employees to travel, especially abroad, and from the second year in the company they can apply for special overseas trips. Mizuno says he wants his employees to enjoy life and to experience different cultures in other countries. "Our games are based on adventures in castles, forests and caves. We want our staff to go and see what these places are really like with their own eyes," he says.

Square evaluates its employees by mixing the western merit approach and the Japanese life-time employment system. While those who help to create a popular game will be compensated, those that have not contributed see a pay rise equal to the cost of inflation. The salary difference between employees who entered the company in the same year can amount to Y4m–Y5m. By providing incentives, the company attempts to increase productivity and morale. Says Mizuno: "You need to ask what people want to be doing in five years. How much they want to be earning, where they want to be living. If workers calculate backwards from such goals, it's clear what they need to do."[7]

Job Characteristics   This theoretical approach is based on the idea that the task itself is the key to employee motivation. Specifically, a boring and monotonous job stifles motivation to perform well, whereas a challenging job enhances motivation. Three ingredients of a more challenging job are variety, autonomy, and decision authority. Two popular ways of adding variety and challenge to routine jobs are job enrichment (or job redesign) and job rotation. These techniques are discussed later in this chapter.

Feelings/Emotions   This most recent addition to the evolution of motivation theory is based on the idea that workers are whole people who pursue goals outside of becoming a high performer.[8] For example, you may want to be a good student, a loving boyfriend or girlfriend, a caring parent, a good friend, a responsible citizen, or a happy person. Work motivation is thus thought to be a function of your feelings and emotions towards the multitude of interests and goals that you have. You are likely to study long and hard if your only interest in life is to go to university and become a doctor. In contrast, a highly motivated professor is likely to stop lecturing and dismiss the class upon receiving a message that his or her child has been seriously hurt in an accident.

A Motivational Puzzle   Motivation theory presents managers with a psychological puzzle composed of alternative explanations and recommendations. There is not any one motivation theory that is appropriate in all situations. Rather, managers need to use a contingency framework to pick and choose the motivational techniques best suited to the people and situation involved. The matrix in Figure 7–2 was created to help managers make these decisions.

Because managers face a variety of motivational problems that can be solved with different theories of motivation, the matrix crosses outcomes of interest with six major motivation theories.[9] Entries in the matrix indicate which theories are best suited for explaining each outcome. For instance, each motivation theory can help managers determine how to increase employee effort. In contrast, need, equity, and job characteristics theories are most helpful in developing programmes aimed at increasing employees' job satisfaction. Managers faced with high turnover are advised to use the reinforcement, equity, expectancy, or job characteristics theory to correct the problem.

You will be better able to apply this matrix after reading the material in this chapter and Chapters 8 and 15. This chapter covers theories related to needs and job characteristics, Chapter 8 focuses on equity, expectancy, and goal setting, and reinforcement theory is reviewed in Chapter 15.

Motivation Is Only One Factor in the Performance Equation

Are performance problems primarily due to a lack of motivation? Not according to the systems model of motivation and performance previously discussed (see Figure 7–1). A

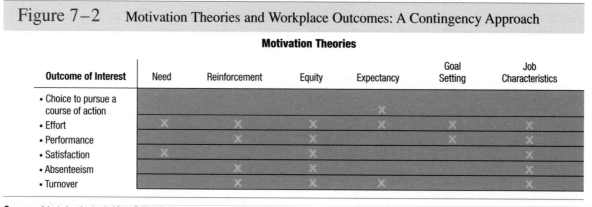

Figure 7–2   Motivation Theories and Workplace Outcomes: A Contingency Approach

Motivation Theories

Outcome of Interest	Need	Reinforcement	Equity	Expectancy	Goal Setting	Job Characteristics
• Choice to pursue a course of action				X		
• Effort	X	X	X	X	X	X
• Performance		X	X		X	X
• Satisfaction	X		X			X
• Absenteeism		X	X			X
• Turnover		X	X	X		X

Source: Adapted and extended from F J Landy and W S Becker, "Motivation Theory Reconsidered," in L L Cummings and B M Staw (eds), *Research in Organizational Behavior* (Greenwich, CT: JAI Press, 1987), vol. 9, p 33.

systems approach suggests that performance problems are due to a combination of individual differences, which include motivation, and characteristics of the system within which an employee works. The following formula for performance helps put this idea into proper perspective:

$$\text{Performance} = \text{Level of ability} \times \text{Level of skill} \times$$
$$\text{Motivation} \times \text{Knowledge about how to complete}$$
$$\text{the task} \times \text{Feelings/emotions} \times \text{Facilitating}$$
$$\text{and inhibiting conditions not under the}$$
$$\text{individual's control}^{[10]}$$

You can see from this equation that motivation is a necessary but insufficient contributor to job performance. The multiplication sign is used to emphasize how a weakness in one factor can negate the others. Drawing a distinction between performance and motivation has its advantages. According to one motivation expert:

The implication is that there probably are some jobs for which trying to influence motivation will be irrelevant for performance. These circumstances can occur in a variety of ways. There may be situations in which ability factors or role expectation factors are simply more important than motivation. For example, the best predictor of high school grades typically is intellectual endowment, not hours spent studying. . . .

Another circumstance may occur in which performance is controlled by technological factors. For example, on an assembly line, given that minimally competent and attentive people are there to do the job, performance may not vary from individual to individual. Exerting effort may be irrelevant for performance.[11]

Managers are better able to identify and correct performance problems when they recognize that poor performance is not due solely to inadequate motivation. This awareness can foster better interpersonal relations in the workplace.

Need Theories of Motivation

Needs

Physiological or psychological deficiencies that arouse behaviour.

Need theories attempt to pinpoint internal factors that energize behaviour. **Needs** are physiological or psychological deficiencies that arouse behaviour. They can be strong or weak and are influenced by environmental factors. Thus, human needs vary over time and place. Two popular need theories are discussed in this section: Maslow's need hierarchy theory and McClelland's need theory.

Maslow's Need Hierarchy Theory

In 1943, psychologist Abraham Maslow published his now-famous need hierarchy theory of motivation. Although the theory was based on his clinical observation of a few neurotic individuals, it has subsequently been used to explain the entire spectrum of human behaviour. Maslow proposed that motivation is a function of five basic needs—physiological, safety, love, esteem, and self-actualization (see Figure 7–3).

Maslow said these five need categories are arranged in a prepotent hierarchy. In other words, he believed human needs generally emerge in a predictable stair-step fashion. Accordingly, when one's physiological needs are relatively satisfied, one's safety needs emerge, and so on up the need hierarchy, one step at a time. Once a need is satisfied it activates the next higher need in the hierarchy. This process continues until the need for self-actualization is activated.[12] In a situation of war, people are not enjoying the satisfaction of higher order needs. They are stuck at lower levels on the need hierarchy trying to survive. Consider the following situation:

A Bosnian couple has to burn its books and furniture to stay warm during cold winter days. The couple goes to bed—fully clothed under a pile of blankets—at about 7 pm, and as the embers

Figure 7–3	Maslow's Need Hierarchy

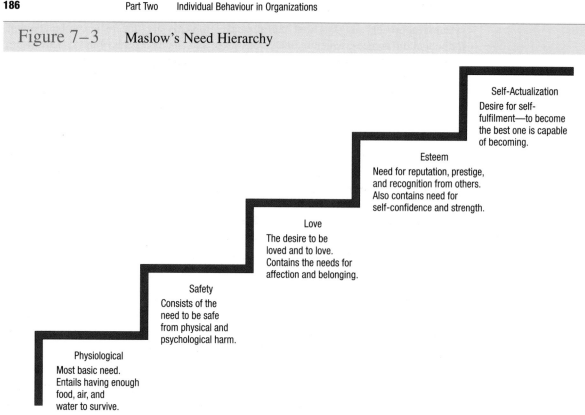

Source: Adapted from descriptions provided by A H Maslow, "A Theory of Human Motivation," *Psychological Review,* July 1943, pp 370–96.

die out the temperature falls to near freezing. . . . There is no running water in Sarajevo—and no electricity or central heating, either—so apartment dwellers must fetch water in buckets from a well two miles away and then haul it stair by stair up to their icy kitchens and bathrooms.[13]

Research Findings on Maslow's Theory   Research does not clearly support this theory because results from studies testing the need hierarchy are difficult to interpret. A well-known motivation scholar summarized the research evidence as follows:

In balance, Maslow's theory remains very popular among managers and students of organizational behaviour, although there are still very few studies that can legitimately confirm (or refute) it. . . . It may be that the dynamics implied by Maslow's theory of needs are too complex to be operationalized and confirmed by scientific research. If this is the case, we may never be able to determine how valid the theory is, or—more precisely—which aspects of the theory are valid and which are not.[14]

Managerial Implications of Maslow's Theory   A satisfied need may lose its motivational potential. Therefore, managers are advised to motivate employees by devising programmes or practices aimed at satisfying emerging or unmet needs. Employees of the Birmingham Midshires Building Society use a recently introduced Flex scheme to achieve such goals as buying dental insurance, health screening or illness cover. The Flex scheme reflects Birmingham Midshire's belief in treating both its customers and its employees as individuals. Giving individuals the opportunity to choose benefits that suit their own lifestyles and needs clearly has the potential to improve motivation and, as HR project leader Claire Pulley points out, well-motivated and satisfied employees have a direct effect on business performance.[15] At the UK's Mortgage Express, the Trustee's Savings Bank's central mortgage lending bank subsidiary, employee involvement, training, and better communication are on the agenda. An important part of the remotivation strategy has been the development of two-way communication channels. Particular emphasis was placed on introducing a staff opinion survey that adequately reflected the needs of the company. Other companies, such as Rank Xerox and Federal Express have introduced benchmarking and 'metaplanning', a technique involving different groups of staff in confidential brainstorming groups.[16]

The same recommendation applies to the context of motivating customers to purchase specific products.

The Ritz-Carlton, as seen in the OB exercise in Chapter 3, believes that customer loyalty and satisfaction are based on satisfying customer needs. The organization attempts to motivate us to stay at its hotels by first gathering detailed information on customer preferences and needs from a variety of sources. This information is then entered into an on-line, nationwide computer system. The Ritz-Carlton then uses this information to satisfy customer needs.[17]

Need theory offers another recommendation for companies undergoing downsizing or large-scale layoffs. Because layoffs create stress and feelings of job insecurity, organizations can implement support programmes and focus groups to help employees cope with their feelings and emotions. Once employees feel secure in their jobs, management might attempt to satisfy esteem needs. This can be done using status symbols, participative management, and positive performance feedback. When employees' esteem needs are satisfied, management can enhance motivation by redesigning jobs to provide more autonomy and responsibility.

McClelland's Need Theory

David McClelland, a well-known psychologist, has been studying the relationship between needs and behaviour since the late 1940s. Although he is most recognized for his research on the need for achievement, he also investigated the needs for affiliation and power. Before discussing each of these needs, let us consider the typical approach used to measure the strength of an individual's needs.

Measuring Need Strength   The Thematic Apperception Test (TAT) is frequently used to measure an individual's motivation to satisfy various needs. In completing the TAT, people are asked to write stories about ambiguous pictures. These descriptions are then scored for the extent to which they contain achievement, power, and affiliation imagery. A meta-analysis of 105 studies demonstrated that the TAT is a valid measure of the need for achievement.[18] At this time, we would like you to examine the picture in the OB Exercise and then write a brief description of what you think is happening to the people in the picture and what you think will happen to them in the future. Use the scoring guide to determine your need strength. What is your most important need?

The Need for Achievement   Achievement theories propose that motivation and performance vary according to the strength of one's need for achievement. For example, a field study of 222 life insurance brokers found a positive correlation between the number of policies sold and the brokers' need for achievement. McClelland's research supported an analogous relationship for societies as a whole. His results revealed that a country's level of economic development was positively related to its overall achievement motivation.[19] The **need for achievement** is defined by the following desires:

Need for achievement

Desire to accomplish something difficult.

To accomplish something difficult. To master, manipulate, or organize physical objects, human beings, or ideas. To do this as rapidly and as independently as possible. To overcome obstacles and attain a high standard. To excel one's self. To rival and surpass others. To increase self-regard by the successful exercise of talent.[20]

This definition reveals that the need for achievement overlaps Maslow's higher order needs of esteem and self-actualization.

Characteristics of High Achievers   Achievement-motivated people share three common characteristics. One is a preference for working on tasks of moderate difficulty. For example, when high achievers are asked to stand wherever they like while tossing rings at a peg on the floor, they tend to stand about 3–6 m from the peg. This distance presents the ring tosser with a challenging but not impossible task. People with a low need for achievement, in contrast, tend to either walk up to the peg and drop the rings on or gamble on a lucky shot from far away. The high achiever's preference for moderately difficult tasks reinforces achievement behaviour by reducing the frequency of failure and increasing the satisfaction associated with successfully completing challenging tasks.

Achievers also like situations in which their performance is due to their own efforts rather than to other factors, such as luck. A third identifying characteristic of high achievers is that they desire more feedback on their successes and failures than do low achievers.[21] Given these characteristics, McClelland proposed that high achievers are more likely to be successful entrepreneurs. A recent review of research on the "entrepreneurial" personality supported this conclusion. Entrepreneurs were found to have a higher need for achievement than nonentrepreneurs.[22]

Years of experience with East Europeans, makes Yale Richmond conclude that Hungarians are high-achievers:

Hungarians have a well-deserved reputation for being high achievers. Faced with adversaries, real and potential, on all sides—Turks, Romanians, Russians, Slovaks, Croats, Serbs

OB EXERCISE *Assess Your Need Strength with a Thematic Apperception Test (TAT)*

What is happening in this picture?

	LOW	MODERATE	HIGH
• Achievement motivation	1——2——3——4——5		
• Power motivation	1——2——3——4——5		
• Affiliation motivation	1——2——3——4——5		

Score *achievement* motivation high if:

- A goal, objective, or standard of excellence is mentioned.

- Words such as good, better, or best are used to evaluate performance.

- Someone in your story is striving for a unique accomplishment.

- Reference is made to career status or being a success in life.

Score *power* motivation high if:

- There is emotional concern for influencing someone else.

- Someone is actively striving to gain or keep control over others by ordering, arguing, demanding, convincing, threatening, or punishing.

- Clear reference is made to a superior–subordinate relationship and the superior is taking steps to gain or keep control over the subordinate.

Score *affiliation* motivation high if:

- Someone is concerned about establishing or maintaining a friendly relationship with another.

- Someone expresses the desire to be liked by someone else.

- There are references to family ties, friendly discussions, visits, reunions, parties, or informal get-togethers.

and Austrians—Hungarians early on developed a militant and competitive spirit, a win at all costs in order to survive as a nation.[23]

The Need for Affiliation   Researchers believe that people possess a basic desire to form and maintain a few lasting, positive, and important interpersonal relationships. A recent summary of research supported this premise. In addition, the researchers noted that both psychological and physical health problems are higher among people who lack social attachments.[24] Just the same, not everyone has a high need to affiliate. People with a high **need for affiliation** prefer to spend more time maintaining social relationships, joining groups, and wanting to be loved. Individuals high in this need are not the most effective managers or leaders because they have a hard time making difficult decisions without worrying about being disliked.

The Need for Power   The **need for power** reflects an individual's desire to influence, coach, teach, or encourage others to achieve. People with a high need for power like to work and are concerned with discipline and self-respect. There is a positive and negative side to this need. The negative face of power is characterized by an "if I win, you lose" mentality. Consider the words of Kevin Maxwell, son of the late publisher Robert Maxwell:

My father was motivated by power rather than money. However, he was also capable of "verbal brutality," bullying, and the public humiliation of staff. As a child I had been in awe and frightened by my father.[25]

In contrast, people with a positive orientation to power focus on accomplishing group goals and helping employees obtain the feeling of competence. More is said about the two faces of power in Chapter 11. Because effective managers must positively influence others, McClelland proposes that top managers should have a high need for power coupled with a low need for affiliation. He also believes that individuals with high achievement motivation are not best suited for top management positions. Several studies support these propositions.[26] A recent study of 60 Australian founder businesswomen revealed three psychological types of female entrepreneurs: the need achiever female entrepreneurs have a high need for achievement, the pragmatic entrepreneur has a high need for power and influence, and the managerial entrepreneur is moderate on both motivations.[27]

Managerial Implications   Given that adults can be trained to increase their achievement motivation,[28] organizations should consider the benefits of providing achievement training for employees. Moreover, achievement, affiliation, and power needs can be considered during the selection process, for better placement. For example, a study revealed that individuals' need for achievement affected their preference to work in different companies. People with a high need for achievement were more attracted to companies that had a pay-for-performance environment than were those with a low achievement motivation.[29] Finally, managers should create challenging task assignments or goals because the need for achievement is positively correlated with goal commitment, which, in turn, influences performance.[30] Moreover, challenging goals should be accompanied with a more autonomous work environment and employee empowerment to capitalize on the characteristics of high achievers.

Need for affiliation
Desire to spend time in social relationships and activities.

Need for power
Desire to influence, coach, teach, or encourage others to achieve.

Historical Approaches to Job Design

Job design
Changing the content and/or process of a specific job to increase job satisfaction and performance.

Job design, also referred to as job redesign, "refers to any set of activities that involve the alteration of specific jobs or interdependent systems of jobs with the intent of improving the quality of employee job experience and their on-the-job productivity."[31] There are two very different routes, one traditional and one modern, that can be taken when deciding how to design jobs. Each is based on a different assumption about people.

The first route entails *fitting people to jobs*. It is based on the assumption that people will gradually adjust and adapt to any work situation. Thus, employee attitudes towards the job are ignored, and jobs are designed to produce maximum economic and technological efficiency. This approach uses the principles of scientific management and work simplification. In contrast, the second route involves fitting jobs to people. It assumes that people are underutilized at work and that they desire more challenges and responsibility. This philosophy is part of the driving force behind the widespread implementation of work teams. Techniques such as job enlargement, job rotation, job enrichment, and job characteristics are used when designing jobs according to this second alternative.

The remainder of this section discusses the first four methods of job design to be widely used in industry. They are scientific management, job enlargement, job rotation, and job enrichment. The next section explores the job characteristics approach to job design.

Scientific Management

Developed by Frederick Taylor, scientific management relied on research and experimentation to determine the most efficient way to perform jobs. Jobs are highly specialized and standardized when they are designed according to the principles of scientific management. This technique was the impetus for the development of assembly line technology and currently is used in many manufacturing and production-oriented firms throughout the world. It has become very popular in the United States and western Europe, but it was also the dominant job design in the former Soviet Union. Taylorism was not only popular with Henry Ford, but also with Vladimir Ilyich Lenin and even with the Italian fascist leader Benito Mussolini.

The Japanese, on the other hand, have always praised themselves for not being tayloristic. Konosuke Matsushita, founder of the giant Matsushita Co., once stated:

We are going to win and the industrial West is going to lose out; there is not much you can do about it because the reasons for your failures are within yourselves. Your firms are built on the Taylor idea—and even worse—so are your minds. Your bosses do the thinking, your workers wield the screwdrivers. . . . We are beyond the Taylor model. The continued existence of business depends on the day-to-day mobilization of every ounce of intelligence.[32]

Designing jobs according to the principles of scientific management has both positive and negative consequences. Positively, employee efficiency and productivity are increased. On the other hand, research reveals that simplified, repetitive jobs also lead to job dissatisfaction, poor mental health, and low sense of accomplishment and personal growth.[33] Further, the principles of scientific management do not apply to professional "knowledge" workers, and they are not consistent with the trend to empower both employees and work teams. These negative consequences paved the way for the development of other job designs. Newer approaches attempt to design intrinsically satisfying jobs.

Job Enlargement

Job enlargement
Putting more variety into a job.

This technique was first used in the late 1940s in response to complaints about tedious and overspecialized jobs. **Job enlargement** involves putting more variety into a worker's job by combining specialized tasks of comparable difficulty. Some call this horizontally loading the job. For instance, the job of installing television picture tubes could be enlarged to include installation of the circuit boards.

Proponents of job enlargement claim it can improve employee satisfaction, motivation, and quality of production. Unfortunately, research reveals that job enlargement, by itself, does not have a significant and lasting positive impact on job performance. Researchers recommend using job enlargement as part of a broader approach that uses multiple job design techniques.[34]

Job Rotation

Job rotation

Moving employees from one specialized job to another.

As with job enlargement, job rotation's purpose is to give employees greater variety in their work. **Job rotation** calls for moving employees from one specialized job to another. Rather than performing only one job, workers are trained and given the opportunity to perform two or more separate jobs on a rotating basis. By rotating employees from job to job, managers believe they can stimulate interest and motivation while providing employees with a broader perspective of the organization.

Other proposed advantages of job rotation include increased worker flexibility and easier scheduling because employees are cross trained to perform different jobs. In turn, this cross training requires employees to learn new skills, which can assist them in upward or lateral mobility. Although some documented cases support the use of job rotation, the promised benefits associated with job rotation programmes have not been adequately researched.[35] It is thus difficult to draw any empirical conclusions about their effectiveness.

Job Enrichment

Job enrichment is the practical application of Frederick Herzberg's motivator–hygiene theory of job satisfaction.[36] After reviewing the foundation of Herzberg's theory, we will discuss its application through job enrichment.

The Legacy of Herzberg's Motivator–Hygiene Theory   Herzberg's theory is based on a landmark study in which he interviewed 203 accountants and engineers. These interviews sought to determine the factors responsible for job satisfaction and dissatisfaction. Herzberg found separate and distinct clusters of factors associated with job satisfaction and dissatisfaction. Job satisfaction was more frequently associated with achievement, recognition, characteristics of the work, responsibility, and advancement. These factors were all related to outcomes associated with the *content* of the task being performed. Herzberg labelled these factors **motivators** because each was associated with strong effort and good performance. He hypothesized that motivators cause a person to move from a state of no satisfaction to satisfaction (see Figure 7–4). Therefore, Herzberg's theory predicts managers can motivate individuals by incorporating "motivators" into an individual's job.

Motivators

Job characteristics associated with job satisfaction.

Herzberg found job *dissatisfaction* to be associated primarily with factors in the work *context* or environment. Specifically, company policy and administration, technical supervision, salary, interpersonal relations with one's supervisor, and working conditions were most frequently mentioned by employees expressing job dissatisfaction. Herzberg labelled this second cluster of factors **hygiene factors.** He further proposed that they were not motivational. At best, according to Herzberg's interpretation, an individual will experience no job dissatisfaction when he or she has no grievances about hygiene factors (refer to Figure 7–4).[37]

Hygiene factors

Job characteristics associated with job dissatisfaction.

A Zero Midpoint   The key to adequately understanding Herzberg's motivator–hygiene theory is recognizing that he does not place dissatisfaction and satisfaction on opposite ends of a single, unbroken continuum. Instead, he believes there is a zero midpoint between dissatisfaction and satisfaction. Conceivably, an organization member who has good supervision, pay, and working conditions but a tedious and unchallenging task with little chance of advancement would be at the zero midpoint. That person would have no dissatisfaction (because of good hygiene factors) and no satisfaction (because of a lack of motivators). Consequently, Herzberg warns managers that it takes more than good pay and good working conditions to motivate today's employees. It takes an "enriched job" that offers the individual opportunity for achievement and recognition, stimulation, responsibility, and advancement. Asda, one of UK's big food retailers, is making

Figure 7–4   Herzberg's Motivator–Hygiene Model

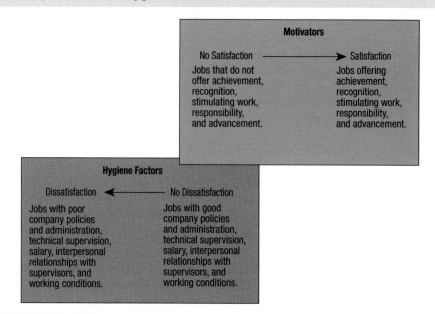

Source: Adapted in part from D A Whitsett and E K Winslow, "An Analysis of Studies Critical of the Motivator-Hygiene Theory," *Personnel Psychology,* Winter 1967, pp 391–415.

employee motivation a big priority, giving staff greater autonomy, more feedback, and incentives to perform.[38]

Unfortunately, a recent study of 600 managers and 900 workers indicated that organizations may not be heeding Herzberg's advice. Results revealed that only 33 per cent feel that their managers know what motivates them, and 60 per cent concluded that they do not receive any sort of recognition or rewards for their work.[39]

International Organizational Behaviour
Work Culture That Brings No Satisfaction

Switzerland has the most contented workers in the world, satisfied with their jobs and admiring of their employers. They are followed in order of satisfaction by workers of Denmark, Austria, Canada, and Norway.

The most discontented employees are apparently the Japanese. So much it seems for *kaizen* work culture and all the supposed virtues of the Japanese ways of organizing work. Or is it that Japanese workers are simply being more honest about what they think of their own employers?

Even the awkward British workers score higher on the employee satisfaction index than those from Japan, although they are the next most dissatisfied—followed by the Italians, Spanish, and French.

These findings are contained in the latest annual international survey of employee attitudes produced by ISR International Survey Research, the independent consultants. The survey sample is based on reports from over 1,200 companies in more

than 60 countries covering 26 million employees. It provides a useful and entertaining—if subjective—view of workplace attitudes in different countries.

To the surprise of the survey organizers, Japanese workers come out consistently bottom in most of the comparative satisfaction tables. Apparently, the Japanese have a lower opinion of their company's operating efficiency, the quality of its management and products, training and information provision, safety and working conditions than those in any other market economy.

Companies may find it hard to draw any practical lessons from these international findings on how to satisfy their employees. But one trend is noticeable in the comparative data. Many of the countries which have more job security, greater individual affluence, and a cradle-to-grave welfare state are likely to have more contented employees than those working in more deregulated, flexible labour markets.[40]

Research on the Motivator–Hygiene Theory   Herzberg's theory generated a great deal of research and controversy. The controversy revolved around whether studies supporting the theory were flawed, and thus invalid.[41] A motivation scholar attempted to sort out the controversy by concluding:

In balance, when we combine all of the evidence with all of the allegations that the theory has been misinterpreted, and that its major concepts have not been assessed properly, one is left, more than twenty years later, not really knowing whether to take the theory seriously, let alone whether it should be put into practice in organizational settings. . . . There is support for many of the implications the theory has for enriching jobs to make them more motivating. But the two-factor aspect of the theory—the feature that makes it unique—is not really a necessary element in the use of the theory for designing jobs, per se.[42]

Applying Herzberg's Model through Vertical Loading   Job enrichment is based on the application of Herzberg's ideas. Specifically, **job enrichment** entails modifying a job such that an employee has the opportunity to experience achievement, recognition, stimulating work, responsibility, and advancement. These characteristics are incorporated into a job through vertical loading.

Job enrichment

Building achievement, recognition, stimulating work, responsibility, and advancement into a job.

Rather than giving employees additional tasks of similar difficulty (horizontal loading), vertical loading consists of giving workers more responsibility. In other words, employees take on chores normally performed by their supervisors. Managers are advised to follow seven principles when vertically loading jobs (see Table 7–1).

Job Characteristics Approach to Job Design

The job characteristics model is a more recent approach to job design. It is a direct outgrowth of job enrichment and attempts to pinpoint those situations and those individuals for which job design is most effective. In this regard, the job characteristics model represents a contingency approach.

Overview of the Job Characteristics Model

Two OB researchers, J Richard Hackman and Greg Oldham, played a central role in developing the job characteristics approach. These researchers tried to determine how work can be structured so that employees are internally (or intrinsically) motivated. **Internal motivation** occurs when an individual is "turned on to one's work because of the positive internal feelings that are generated by doing well, rather than being dependent

Internal motivation

Motivation caused by positive internal feelings.

Table 7 – 1	Principles of Vertically Loading a Job

PRINCIPLE	MOTIVATORS INVOLVED
A. Removing some controls while retaining accountability	Responsibility and personal achievement
B. Increasing the accountability of individuals for their own work	Responsibility and recognition
C. Giving a person a complete natural unit of work (module, division, area, and so on)	Responsibility, achievement, and recognition
D. Granting additional authority to an employee in his activity; job freedom	Responsibility, achievement, and recognition
E. Making periodic reports directly available to the worker himself rather than to the supervisor	Internal recognition
F. Introducing new and more difficult tasks not previously handled	Growth and learning
G. Assigning individuals specific or specialized tasks, enabling them to become experts	Responsibility, growth, and advancement

on external factors (such as incentive pay or compliments from the boss) for the motivation to work effectively."[43] These positive feelings power a self-perpetuating cycle of motivation. As shown in Figure 7–5, internal work motivation is determined by three psychological states. In turn, these psychological states are fostered by the presence of five core job dimensions. As you can see in Figure 7–5, the object of this approach is to promote high internal motivation by designing jobs that possess the five core job characteristics. Let us examine the major components of this model to see how it works.

Experienced meaningfulness
Feeling that one's job is important and worthwhile.

Experienced responsibility
Believing that one is accountable for work outcomes.

Knowledge of results
Feedback about work outcomes.

Critical Psychological States   A group of management experts described the conditions under which individuals experienced the three critical psychological states. They are:

1. **Experienced meaningfulness.** The individual must perceive his work as worthwhile or important by some system of value he accepts.

2. **Experienced responsibility.** He must believe that he personally is accountable for the outcomes of his efforts.

3. **Knowledge of results.** He must be able to determine, on some fairly regular basis, whether or not the outcomes of his work are satisfactory.[44]

These psychological states generate internal work motivation. Moreover, they encourage job satisfaction and perseverance because they are self-reinforcing.

If one of the three psychological states is shortchanged, motivation diminishes. Consider, for example, Joyce Roché's decision to quit her job as vice president of global marketing at Avon:

The decision to ditch a plum, six-figure position in a major corporation where one is highly regarded might strike most people as insane. But Roché's decision grew out of her realization that despite the great title and income (she had a six-figure salary with substantial bonus potential), her job did not hold the level of autonomy or responsibility she initially thought it had.[45]

Joyce Roché's internal motivation was diminished by not feeling the psychological state of "experienced responsibility."

Figure 7 – 5   The Job Characteristics Model

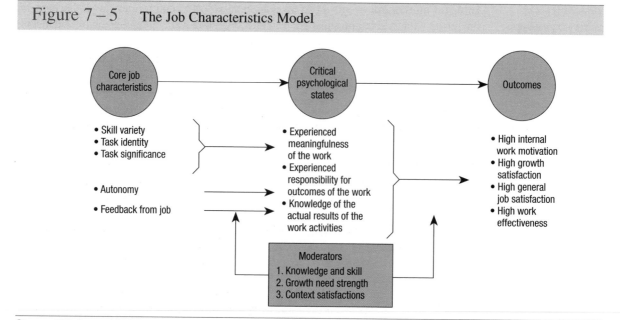

Source: J R Hackman and G R Oldham, *Work Redesign,* © 1980, Addison-Wesley Publishing Co., Reading, MA, p 90. Reprinted with permission.

Core job dimensions
Job characteristics found to various degrees in all jobs.

Core Job Dimensions

In general terms, **core job dimensions** are common characteristics found to a varying degree in all jobs. Once again, five core job characteristics elicit the three psychological states (see Figure 7–5). Three of those job characteristics combine to determine experienced meaningfulness of work. They are

- *Skill variety.* The extent to which the job requires an individual to perform a variety of tasks that require him or her to use different skills and abilities.

- *Task identity.* The extent to which the job requires an individual to perform a whole or completely identifiable piece of work. In other words, task identity is high when a person works on a product or project from beginning to end and sees a tangible result.

- *Task significance.* The extent to which the job affects the lives of other people within or outside the organization.

Experienced responsibility is elicited by the job characteristic of autonomy, defined as follows:

- *Autonomy.* The extent to which the job enables an individual to experience freedom, independence, and discretion in both scheduling and determining the procedures used in completing the job.

Finally, knowledge of results is fostered by the job characteristic of feedback, defined as follows:

- *Feedback.* The extent to which an individual receives direct and clear information about how effectively he or she is performing the job.[46]

Motivating potential score
The amount of internal work motivation associated with a specific job.

Motivating Potential of a Job

Hackman and Oldham devised a self-report instrument to assess the extent to which a specific job possesses the five core job characteristics. With this instrument, which is discussed in the next section, it is possible to calculate a motivating potential score for a job. The **motivating potential score** (MPS) is a summary index that represents the extent to which the job characteristics foster internal work motivation. Low scores indicate that an individual will not experience high internal work motivation from the job. Such a job is a prime candidate for job redesign. High scores reveal that the job is capable of stimulating internal motivation. The MPS is computed as follows:

$$MPS = \frac{\text{Skill variety} + \text{Task identity} + \text{Task significance}}{3} \times \text{Autonomy} \times \text{Feedback}$$

Judging from this equation, which core job characteristic do you think is relatively more important in determining the motivational potential of a job? Since MPS equals zero when autonomy or feedback are zero, you are correct if you said both experienced autonomy and feedback.

Does the Theory Work for Everyone?

As previously discussed, not all people may want enriched work. Hackman and Oldham incorporated this conclusion into their model by identifying three attributes that affect how individuals respond to jobs with a high MPS. These attributes are concerned with the individual's knowledge and skill, growth need strength (representing the desire to grow and develop as an individual), and context satisfactions (see Figure 7–5). Context satisfactions represent the extent to which employees are satisfied with various aspects of their job, such as satisfaction with pay, co-workers, or supervision.

Hackman and Oldham proposed that people will respond positively to jobs with a high MPS when (1) they have the knowledge and skills necessary to do the job, (2) they have high growth needs, and (3) they are satisfied with various aspects of the work context, such as pay and co-workers. Although these recommendations make sense, two studies did not support the moderating influence of an employee's growth needs and context satisfaction.[47] The model worked equally well for employees with high and low growth needs and context satisfaction. Future research needs to examine whether an employee's knowledge and skills are an important moderator of the model's effectiveness.

Applying the Job Characteristics Model

There are three major steps to follow when applying Hackman and Oldham's model. Since the model seeks to increase employee motivation and satisfaction, the first step consists of diagnosing the work environment to determine if a problem exists. Hackman and Oldham developed a self-report instrument for managers to use called the *job diagnostic survey* (JDS).

Diagnosis begins by determining if motivation and satisfaction are lower than desired. If they are, a manager then assesses the MPS of the jobs being examined. National norms are used to determine whether the MPS is low or high.[48] If the MPS is low, an attempt is made to determine which of the core job characteristics is causing the problem. If the MPS is high, managers need to look for other factors eroding motivation and satisfaction. (You can calculate your own MPS in the group exercise at the end of this chapter.) Potential factors may be identified by considering other motivation theories discussed in this book.

Step two consists of determining whether job redesign is appropriate for a given group of employees. Job redesign is most likely to work in a participative environment in which employees have the necessary knowledge and skills

In the third step, managers need to consider how to redesign the job. The focus of this effort is to increase those core job characteristics that are lower than national norms. Managers may want to gain employees' input during this step.

Practical Implications of the Job Characteristics Model

Managers may want to use this model to increase employee job satisfaction. Research overwhelmingly demonstrates a moderately strong relationship between job characteristics and satisfaction.[49] A recent study of 1,563 managerial, technical, and professional employees in manufacturing, services, and government also indirectly supported the job characteristics model. The majority of respondents indicated that being responsible for their work outcomes increased their levels of voluntary effort.[50] Unfortunately, job redesign appears to reduce the quantity of output just as often as it has a positive impact. Caution and situational appropriateness are advised. For example, one study demonstrated that job redesign works better in less complex organizations (small plants or companies).[51] Nonetheless, managers are likely to find noticeable increases in the quality of performance after a job redesign programme. Results from 21 experimental studies revealed that job redesign resulted in a median increase of 28 per cent in the quality of performance.[52] Moreover, two separate meta-analyses support the practice of using the job characteristics model to help managers reduce absenteeism and turnover.[53]

Job characteristics research also underscores an additional implication for companies undergoing reengineering. Reengineering potentially leads to negative work outcomes because it increases job characteristics beyond reasonable levels. This occurs for two reasons: (1) reengineering requires employees to use a wider variety of skills to perform their jobs, and (2) reengineering typically results in downsizing and short-term periods of understaffing.[54] The unfortunate catch is that understaffing was found to produce lower levels of group performance, and jobs with either overly low or high levels of job characteristics were associated with higher stress.[55] Managers are advised to carefully consider the level of perceived job characteristics when implementing reengineering initiatives.

In conclusion, managers need to realize that job redesign is not a panacea for all their employee satisfaction and motivation problems. To enhance their chances of success with this approach, managers need to remember that a change in one job or department can create problems of perceived inequity in related areas or systems within the organization. Managers need to take an open systems perspective when implementing job redesign, as was suggested by Hackman and Oldham. They wrote:

Our observations of work redesign programs suggest that attempts to change jobs frequently run into—and sometimes get run over by—other organizational systems and practices, leading to a diminution (or even a reversal) of anticipated outcomes. . . .

The "small change" effect, for example, often develops as managers begin to realize that radical changes in work design will necessitate major changes in other organizational systems as well.[56]

The Causes and Consequences of Job Satisfaction

An individual's work motivation is related to his or her job satisfaction. Motivation is not independent of an employee's work environment or personal life. For example, your desire to study for your next OB test is jointly affected by how much you like the course and the state of your health at the time you are studying. It is very hard to study when you have a bad cold or the flu. Because of these dynamic relationships, we conclude our discussion of motivation in this chapter by discussing the causes and consequences of job satisfaction. This information will increase your understanding about how to motivate others as well as yourself.

The Causes of Job Satisfaction

Job satisfaction
An affective or emotional response to one's job.

Job satisfaction is an affective or emotional response towards various facets of one's job. This definition means job satisfaction is not a unitary concept. Rather, a person can be relatively satisfied with one aspect of his or her job and dissatisfied with one or more

---

OB EXERCISE   *How Satisfied Are You with Your Present Job?*

	VERY DISSATISFIED				VERY SATISFIED
1. The way I am noticed when I do a good job	1	2	3	4	5
2. The recognition I get for the work I do	1	2	3	4	5
3. The praise I get for doing a good job	1	2	3	4	5
4. How my pay compares with that for similar jobs in other companies	1	2	3	4	5
5. My pay and the amount of work I do	1	2	3	4	5
6. How my pay compares with that of other workers	1	2	3	4	5
7. The way my boss handles employees	1	2	3	4	5
8. The way my boss takes care of complaints brought to him/her by employees	1	2	3	4	5
9. The personal relationship between my boss and his/her employees	1	2	3	4	5

Total score for satisfaction with recognition (add questions 1–3), compensation (add questions 4–6), and supervision (add questions 7–9).

Comparative norms for each dimension of job satisfaction are: Total score of 3–6 = Low job satisfaction; 7–11 = Moderate satisfaction; 12 and above = High satisfaction.

SOURCE: Adapted from D J Weiss, R V Dawis, G W England, and L H Lofquist, *Manual for the Minnesota Satisfaction Questionnaire,* (Minneapolis: Industrial Relations Center, University of Minnesota, 1967). Used with permission

other aspects. For example, researchers at Cornell University developed the Job Descriptive Index (JDI) to assess one's satisfaction with the following job dimensions: work, pay, promotions, co-workers, and supervision.[57] Researchers at the University of Minnesota concluded there are 20 different dimensions underlying job satisfaction. Selected Minnesota Satisfaction Questionnaire (MSQ) items measuring satisfaction with recognition, compensation, and supervision are listed in the OB Exercise. Please take a moment now to determine how satisfied you are with these three aspects of your present or most recent job, and then use the norms to compare your score.[58] How do you feel about your job?

Five predominant models of job satisfaction specify its causes. They are need fulfilment, discrepancy, value attainment, equity, and trait/genetic components. A brief review of these models will provide insight into the complexity of this seemingly simple concept.

Need Fulfilment   These models propose that satisfaction is determined by the extent to which the characteristics of a job allow an individual to fulfil his or her needs. Although these models generated a great degree of controversy, it is generally accepted that need fulfilment is correlated with job satisfaction.[59]

Met expectations

The extent to which one receives what he or she expects from a job.

Discrepancies   These models propose that satisfaction is a result of met expectations. **Met expectations** represent the difference between what an individual expects to receive from a job, such as good pay and promotional opportunities, and what he or she actually receives. When expectations are greater than what is received, a person will be dissatisfied. In contrast, this model predicts the individual will be satisfied when he or she attains outcomes above and beyond expectations. A meta-analysis of 31 studies that included 17,241 people demonstrated that met expectations were significantly related to job satisfaction.[60]

Value attainment

The extent to which a job allows fulfilment of one's work values.

Value Attainment   The idea underlying **value attainment** is that satisfaction results from the perception that a job allows for fulfilment of an individual's important work values.[61] In general, research consistently supports the prediction that value fulfilment is positively related to job satisfaction.[62] Managers can thus enhance employee satisfaction by structuring the work environment and its associated rewards and recognition to reinforce employees' values.[63]

Equity   In this model, satisfaction is a function of how "fairly" an individual is treated at work. Satisfaction results from one's perception that work outcomes, relative to inputs, compare favourably with a significant other's outcomes/inputs. A recent meta-analysis involving data from 30 different organizations and 12,979 people supported this model. Employees perceived fairness of pay and promotions were significantly correlated with job satisfaction.[64] Chapter 8 explores this promising model in more detail.

Trait/Genetic Components   Have you ever noticed that some of your co-workers or friends appear to be satisfied across a variety of job circumstances, whereas others always seem dissatisfied? This model of satisfaction attempts to explain this pattern. Specifically, the trait/genetic model is based on the belief that job satisfaction is partly a function of both personal traits and genetic factors. As such, this model implies that stable individual differences are just as important in explaining job satisfaction as are characteristics of the work environment. Although only a few studies have tested these propositions, results support a positive, significant relationship between personal traits and job satisfaction over a period of time from 2 to 50 years.[65] Genetic factors also were found to significantly predict life satisfaction, well-being, and general job satisfaction.[66] Additional research is needed to test this new model of job satisfaction.

The Consequences of Job Satisfaction

This area has significant managerial implications because thousands of studies have examined the relationship between job satisfaction and other organizational variables.

Table 7 – 2   Correlates of Job Satisfaction

VARIABLES RELATED WITH SATISFACTION	DIRECTION OF RELATIONSHIP	STRENGTH OF RELATIONSHIP
Motivation	Positive	Moderate
Job involvement	Positive	Moderate
Organizational citizenship behaviour	Positive	Moderate
Organizational commitment	Positive	Strong
Absenteeism	Negative	Weak
Tardiness	Negative	Weak
Turnover	Negative	Moderate
Heart disease	Negative	Moderate
Perceived stress	Negative	Strong
Pro-union voting	Negative	Moderate
Job performance	Positive	Weak
Life satisfaction	Positive	Moderate
Mental health	Positive	Moderate

Since it is impossible to examine them all, we will consider a subset of the more important variables from the standpoint of managerial relevance.

Table 7–2 summarizes the pattern of results. The relationship between job satisfaction and these other variables is either positive or negative. The strength of the relationship ranges from weak (very little relationship) to strong. Strong relationships imply that managers can significantly influence the variable of interest by increasing job satisfaction. Let us now consider several of the key correlates of job satisfaction.

Motivation   A recent meta-analysis of nine studies and 2,237 workers revealed a significant positive relationship between motivation and job satisfaction. Because satisfaction with supervision was also significantly correlated with motivation, managers are advised to consider how their behaviour affects employee satisfaction.[67] Managers can potentially enhance employees' motivation through various attempts to increase job satisfaction.

Job Involvement   Job involvement represents the extent to which an individual is personally involved with his or her work role. A recent meta-analysis involving 27,925 individuals from 87 different studies demonstrated that job involvement was moderately related with job satisfaction.[68] Managers are thus encouraged to foster satisfying work environments in order to fuel employees' job involvement.

Organizational Citizenship Behaviour   Organizational citizenship behaviours consist of employee behaviours that are beyond the call of duty. Examples include "such gestures as constructive statements about the department, expression of personal interest in the work of others, suggestions for improvement, training new people, respect for the spirit as well as the letter of housekeeping rules, care for organizational property, and punctuality and attendance well beyond standard or enforceable levels."[69] Managers certainly would like employees to exhibit these behaviours. A recent meta-analysis covering 6,746 people and 28 separate studies revealed a significant and moderately positive correlation between organizational citizenship behaviours and job satisfaction.[70] Moreover, additional research demonstrated that employees' citizenship behaviours were determined more by leadership and characteristics of the work environment than by an employee's personality.[71] It thus appears that managerial behaviour significantly influences an employee's willingness to exhibit citizenship behaviours. This relationship is important to recognize because organizational citizenship behaviours were positively correlated with performance ratings.[72]

Organizational Commitment   Organizational commitment reflects the extent to which an individual identifies with an organization and is committed to its goals. A meta-analysis of 68 studies and 35,282 individuals uncovered a significant and strong relationship between organizational commitment and satisfaction.[73] Managers are advised to increase job satisfaction in order to elicit higher levels of commitment. In turn, higher commitment can facilitate higher productivity.[74] According to the Confederation of British Industry a delicate balance has to be struck between the dual demands of the company to promote loyalty among its employees, but also have the power to respond to increasingly uncertain business pressures. The CBI is uncertain whether loyalty in the company is an outdated concept and if the future employment relationship is moving 'towards specific contracts for a specified job within a specified period.'[75]

Absenteeism   Absenteeism is costly, and managers are constantly on the lookout for ways to reduce it. One recommendation has been to increase job satisfaction. If this is a valid recommendation, there should be a strong negative relationship (or negative correlation) between satisfaction and absenteeism. In other words, as satisfaction increases, absenteeism should decrease. A researcher tracked this prediction by synthesizing three separate meta-analyses containing a total of 74 studies. Results revealed a weak negative relationship between satisfaction and absenteeism.[76] It is unlikely, therefore, that managers will realize any significant decrease in absenteeism by increasing job satisfaction.

Turnover   Turnover is important to managers because it both disrupts organizational continuity and is very costly. A meta-analysis of 49 studies covering 13,722 people demonstrated a moderate negative relationship between satisfaction and turnover.[77] (See Table 7–2.) Given the strength of this relationship, managers would be well advised to try to reduce turnover by increasing employee job satisfaction.

Perceived Stress   Stress can have very negative effects on organizational behaviour. In the UK, about 1.5m working days a year are lost through stress-related illness.[78] The estimated costs of stress for the UK vary from £3.7bn to £11bn a year.[79] Based on a meta-analysis of seven studies covering 2,659 individuals, Table 7–2 reveals that perceived stress has a strong, negative relationship with job satisfaction.[80] A study of 31,000 employees at Boeing supported this finding. Job dissatisfaction was significantly related to complaints of lower back pain.[81] It is hoped that managers would attempt to reduce the negative effects of stress by improving job satisfaction. The results of a study with managers from 44 companies showed that 70.5 per cent believed that employees in their company experienced stress. However, few companies had mechanisms for identifying and helping stressed employees.[82]

Job Performance   One of the biggest controversies within organizational research centres on the relationship between satisfaction and job performance. Some, such as Herzberg, argue that satisfaction leads to higher performance while others contend that high performance leads to satisfaction. In an attempt to resolve this controversy, a meta-analysis accumulated results from 74 studies. Overall, the relationship between job satisfaction and job performance was examined for 12,192 people. It was discovered that satisfaction and performance were only slightly related.[83]

Some researchers claim that this result is misleading and that it understates the true relationship between performance and satisfaction. The rationale for this claim revolves around the accuracy of measuring an individual's performance. If performance ratings do not reflect the actual interactions and interdependencies at work, weak meta-analytic results are partially due to incomplete measures of individual-level performance.[84] Examining the relationship between *aggregate* measures of job satisfaction and organizational performance is one solution to correct this problem. In support of these ideas, a recent study found a significant, positive correlation between organizational performance and employee satisfaction for data collected from 298 schools and 13,808 teachers.[85] Thus, it appears that managers can positively affect performance by increasing employee job satisfaction.

Summary of Key Concepts

1. *Define the term "motivation."* Motivation is defined as those psychological processes that cause the arousal, direction, and persistence of voluntary, goal-oriented actions. Managers need to understand these psychological processes if they are to successfully guide employees towards accomplishing organizational objectives.

2. *Discuss the systems model of motivation and performance.* The foundation of the model is based on systems theory and reinforcement theory. Seven types of inputs affect employees' ability to achieve their desired goals: materials and machinery, performance objectives and expectations, individual differences, training, task characteristics, psychological climate, and work flow and internal processes. Managers help transform inputs into desired outputs by using performance monitoring, feedback, support and coaching, and consequences. The output box contains a sample of the many outputs that are important to organizations. Examples include customer satisfaction, performance, job satisfaction, and job involvement.

3. *Review the historical roots of modern motivation theories.* Five ways of explaining behaviour—needs, reinforcement, cognition, job characteristics, and feelings/emotions—underlie the evolution of modern theories of human motivation. Some theories of motivation focus on internal energizers of behaviour such as needs, satisfaction, and feelings/emotions. Other motivation theories, which deal in terms of reinforcement, cognitions, and job characteristics, focus on more complex person–environment interactions. There is no single, universally accepted theory of motivation.

4. *Contrast Maslow's and McClelland's need theories.* Two well-known need theories of motivation are Maslow's need hierarchy and McClelland's need theory. Maslow's notion of a prepotent or stair-step hierarchy of five levels of needs has not stood up well under research. McClelland believes that motivation and performance vary according to the strength of an individual's need for achievement. High achievers prefer moderate risks and situations where they can control their own destiny. Top managers should have a high need for power coupled with a low need for affiliation.

5. *Demonstrate your familiarity with scientific management, job enlargement, job rotation, and job enrichment.* Each of these techniques is used in the process of job design. Job design involves altering jobs with the intent of increasing employee job satisfaction and productivity. Scientific management designs jobs by using research and experimentation to identify the most efficient way to perform tasks. Jobs are horizontally loaded in job enlargement by giving workers more than one specialized task to complete. Job rotation increases workplace variety by moving employees from one specialized job to another. Job enrichment vertically loads a job by giving employees administrative duties normally performed by their superiors.

6. *Explain the practical significance of Herzberg's distinction between motivators and hygiene factors.* Herzberg believes job satisfaction motivates better job performance. His hygiene factors, such as policies, supervision, and salary, erase sources of dissatisfaction. On the other hand, his motivators, such as achievement, responsibility, and recognition, foster job satisfaction. Although Herzberg's motivator–hygiene theory of job satisfaction has been criticized on methodological grounds, it has practical significance for job enrichment.

7. *Describe how internal work motivation is increased by using the job characteristics model.* The psychological states of experienced meaningfulness, experienced responsibility, and knowledge of results produce internal work motivation. These psychological states are fostered by the presence of five core job characteristics. People respond positively to jobs containing these core job characteristics when they have the knowledge and skills necessary to perform the job, high growth needs, and high context satisfactions.

8. *Discuss the causes and consequences of job satisfaction.* Job satisfaction is an affective or emotional response towards various facets of one's job. Five models of job satisfaction specify its causes. They are need fulfilment, discrepancy, value attainment, equity, and trait/genetic components. Job satisfaction has been correlated with hundreds of consequences. Table 7–2 summarizes the pattern of results found for a subset of the more important variables.

Discussion Questions

1. Why should the average manager be well versed in the various motivation theories?

2. From a practical standpoint, what is a major drawback of theories of motivation based on internal factors such as needs, satisfaction, and feelings/emotions?

3. Are you a high achiever? How can you tell? How will this help or hinder your path to top management?

4. How have hygiene factors and motivators affected your job satisfaction and performance?

5. How might the job characteristics model be used to increase your internal motivation to study?

6. Do you know anyone who would not respond positively to an enriched job? Describe this person.

7. Do you believe that job satisfaction is partly a function of both personal traits and genetic factors? Explain.

8. Do you think job satisfaction leads directly to better job performance? Explain.

9. What are the three most valuable lessons about employee motivation that you have learned from this chapter?

10. How would you respond to a manager who said, "Work-life balance is a personal problem that does not belong in the workplace. If you want to get ahead, be prepared to work a lot of hours and don't complain."

Personal Awareness and Growth Exercise

What Is Your Work Ethic?

Objectives

1. To measure your work ethic.

2. To determine how well your work ethic score predicts your work habits.

Introduction

The work ethic reflects the extent to which an individual values work. A strong work ethic involves the belief that hard work is the key to success and happiness. In recent years, there has been concern that the work ethic is dead or dying. This worry is based on findings from observational studies and employee attitude surveys.

People differ in terms of how much they believe in the work ethic. These differences influence a variety of behavioural outcomes. What better way to gain insight into the work ethic than by measuring your own work ethic and seeing how well it predicts your everyday work habits?

Instructions

To assess your work ethic, complete the eight-item instrument developed by a respected behavioural scientist.[86] Being honest with yourself, circle your responses on the rating scales following each of the eight items. There are no right or wrong answers. Add up your total score for the eight items, and record it in the space provided. *The higher your total score, the stronger your work ethic.*

Following the work ethic scale is a short personal-work-habits questionnaire. Your responses to this questionnaire will help you determine whether your work ethic score is a good predictor of your work habits.

Work Ethic Scale

1. When the workday is finished, people should forget their jobs and enjoy themselves.
   Agree completely   1—2—3—4—5   Disagree completely

2. Hard work does not make an individual a better person.
   Agree completely   1—2—3—4—5   Disagree completely

3. The principal purpose of a job is to provide a person with the means for enjoying his or her free time.
   Agree completely   1—2—3—4—5   Disagree completely

4. Wasting time is not as bad as wasting money.
   Agree completely   1—2—3—4—5   Disagree completely

5. Whenever possible, a person should relax and accept life as it is, rather than always striving for unreachable goals.
   Agree completely   1—2—3—4—5   Disagree completely

6. A person's worth should not be based on how well he or she performs a job.
   Agree completely   1—2—3—4—5   Disagree completely

7. People who do things the easy way are the smart ones.
   Agree completely   1—2—3—4—5   Disagree completely

8. If all other things are equal, it is better to have a job with little responsibility than one with a lot of responsibility.
   Agree completely   1—2—3—4—5   Disagree completely

Group Exercise

Applying the Job Characteristics Model

Objectives

1. To assess the motivating potential score (MPS) of several jobs.

2. To determine which core job characteristics need to be changed for each job.

3. To explore how you might redesign one of the jobs.

Introduction

The first step in calculating the MPS of a job is to complete the job diagnostic survey (JDS). Since the JDS is a long questionnaire, we would like you to complete a subset of the instrument. This will enable you to calculate the MPS and to identify deficient job characteristics.

Instructions

Your instructor will divide the class into groups of four to six. Each group member will first assess the MPS of his or her current job and then will identify which core job characteristics need to be changed. Once each group member completes these tasks, the group will identify the job with the lowest MPS and devise a plan for redesigning it. The following steps should be used.

You should first complete the 12 items from the JDS. For each item, indicate whether it is an accurate or inaccurate description of your current or most recent job by selecting one number from the scale provided. Write your response in the space provided next to each item. After completing the JDS, use the scoring key to compute a total score for each of the core job characteristics.

1 = Very inaccurate   5 = Slightly accurate
2 = Mostly inaccurate   6 = Mostly accurate
3 = Slightly inaccurate   7 = Very accurate
4 = Uncertain

_____1. Supervisors often let me know how well they think I am performing the job.

_____2. The job requires me to use a number of complex or high-level skills.

_____3. The job is arranged so that I have the chance to do an entire piece of work from beginning to end.

_____4. Just doing the work required by the job provides many chances for me to figure out how well I am doing.

_____5. The job is not simple and repetitive.

_____6. This job is one where a lot of other people can be affected by how well the work gets done.

_____7. The job does not deny me the chance to use my personal initiative or judgement in carrying out the work.

_____8. The job provides me the chance to completely finish the pieces of work I begin.

_____9. The job itself provides plenty of clues about whether or not I am performing well.

_____10. The job gives me considerable opportunity for independence and freedom in how I do the work.

_____11. The job itself is very significant or important in the broader scheme of things.

_____12. The supervisors and co-workers on this job almost always give me "feedback" about how well I am doing in my work.

Scoring Key

Compute the *average* of the two items that measure each job characteristic.

Skill variety (2 and 5)   _____
Task identity (3 and 8)   _____
Task significance (6 and 11)   _____
Autonomy (7 and 10)   _____
Feedback from job itself (4 and 9)   _____
Feedback from others (1 and 12)   _____

Now you are ready to calculate the MPS. First, you need to compute a total score for the feedback job characteristic. This is done by computing the average of the job characteristics entitled "feedback from job itself" and "feedback from others." Second, use the MPS formula presented earlier in this chapter to compute the MPS. Finally, use the JDS norms provided to interpret the relative status of the MPS and each individual job characteristic.[87]

Once all group members have finished these activities, convene as a group to complete the exercise. Each group member should present his or her results and interpretations of the strengths and deficiencies of the job characteristics. Next, pick the job within the group that has the lowest MPS. Prior to redesigning this job, however, each group member needs more background information. The individual who works in the lowest MPS job should thus provide a thorough description of the job, including its associated tasks, responsibilities, and reporting relationships. A brief overview of the general working environment is also useful. With this information in hand, the group should now devise a detailed plan for how it would redesign the job.

Norms

	Type of Job			
	PROFESSIONAL/ TECHNICAL	**CLERICAL**	**SALES**	**SERVICE**
Skill variety	5.4	4.0	4.8	5.0
Task identity	5.1	4.7	4.4	4.7
Task significance	5.6	5.3	5.5	5.7
Autonomy	5.4	4.5	4.8	5.0
Feedback from job itself	5.1	4.6	5.4	5.1
Feedback from others	4.2	4.0	3.6	3.8
MPS	154	106	146	152

QUESTIONS FOR DISCUSSION

1. Using the norms, which job characteristics are high, average, or low for the job being redesigned?

2. Which job characteristics did you change? Why?

3. How would you specifically redesign the job under consideration?

4. What would be the difficulties in implementing the job characteristics model in a large organization?

Notes

[1] Translated from J-M Normand, "La drôle de vie des éclusiers du bitume," *Le Monde*, July 28, 1995, p 7.

[2] T R Mitchell, "Motivation: New Direction for Theory, Research, and Practice," *Academy of Management Review,* January 1982, p 81.

[3] A thorough review of the principles of systems is contained in P M Senge, *The Fifth Discipline: The Art & Practice of the Learning Organization* (New York: Doubleday, 1990). A systems model of performance is presented by G Rummler, "In Search of the Holy Performance Grail," *Training & Development*, April 1996, pp 26–32.

[4] Results can be found in H Allerton, "News You Can Use: He(d)gemony: A Global Perspective," *Training & Development,* January 1996, p 18.

[5] This study was conducted by S P Brown and T W. Leigh, "A New Look at Psychological Climate and Its Relationship to Job Involvement, Effort, and Performance," *Journal of Applied Psychology,* August 1996, pp 358–68.

[6] A discussion of coaching is contained in J F Monoky, "Why Do Salespeople Fail?" *Industrial Distribution,* March 1996, p 78; and B W Armentrout, "Make Coaching Your Management Metaphor," *HRFOCUS,* June 1995, p 3.

[7] "Management (The growing Business): a role-play revolution —a Japanese businessman has found that a western approach to motivation has helped deliver spectacular results", *The Financial Times*, June 28, 1994, p 14.

[8] The effects of feelings and emotions on work motivation are discussed by J M George and A P Brief, "Motivational Agendas in the Workplace: The Effects of Feelings on Focus of Attention and Work Motivation," in *Research in Organizational Behavior,* eds B M Staw and L L Cummings (Greenwich, CT: JAI Press, 1996), vol. 18, pp 75–109.

[9] For a complete discussion of the organizational criterion of interest to managers and researchers, see J T Austin and P Villanova, "The Criterion Problem: 1917–1992," *Journal of Applied Psychology,* December 1992, pp 836–74.

[10] This equation was adapted from J P Campbell and R D Pritchard, "Motivation Theory in Industrial and Organizational Psychology," in *Handbook of Industrial and Organizational Psychology,* ed M D Dunnette (Skokie, IL: Rand McNally, 1976), pp 63–130.

[11] Mitchell, "Motivation: New Direction for Theory, Research, and Practice," p 83.

[12] For a complete description of Maslow's theory, see A H Maslow, "A Theory of Human Motivation," *Psychological Review,* July 1943, pp 370–96.

[13] P Maass, "Losing the Battle to Stay Warm and Clean", *Washington Post National Weekly Edition*, January 25–31, 1993, p 18.

[14]C C Pinder, *Work Motivation: Theory, Issues, and Applications* (Glenview, IL: Scott, Foresman, 1984), p 52.

[15]A Arkin, "Mutually Inclusive", *People Management,* 1997, vol 3, no 2, pp 32–34.

[16]T Dickson, "A Question of Motivation - How to Keep Up Staff Morale, *The Financial Times,* September 2, 1994.

[17]Excerpted from W Band, "Targeting Quality Efforts to Build Customer Loyalty," *The Quality Observer,* December 1995, p 34.

[18]Results can be found in W D Spangler, "Validity of Questionnaire and TAT Measures of Need for Achievement: Two Meta-Analyses," *Psychological Bulletin,* July 1992, pp 140–54.

[19]Results can be found in S D Bluen, J Barling, and W Burns, "Predicting Sales Performance, Job Satisfaction, and Depression by Using the Achievement Strivings and Impatience–Irritability Dimensions of Type A Behavior," *Journal of Applied Psychology,* April 1990, pp 212–16; and D C McClelland, *The Achieving Society* (New York: Free Press, 1961).

[20]H A Murray, *Explorations in Personality* (New York: John Wiley & Sons, 1938), p 164.

[21]Recent studies of achievement motivation and behaviour were conducted by R K Deppe and J M Harackiewicz, "Self-Handicapping and Intrinsic Motivation: Buffering Intrinsic Motivation from the Threat of Failure," *Journal of Personality and Social Psychology,* April 1996, pp 868–76; and A J Elliot and J M Harackiewicz, "Approach and Avoidance Achievement Goals and Intrinsic Motivation: A Mediational Analysis," *Journal of Personality and Social Psychology,* March 1996, pp 461–75.

[22]See K G Shaver, "The Entrepreneurial Personality Myth," *Business and Economic Review,* April/June 1995, pp 20–23.

[23]Y Richmond, *From Da to Yes* (Yarmouth: Intercultural Press, 1995)

[24]Research on the affiliative motive can be found in S C O'Connor and L K Rosenblood, "Affiliation Motivation in Everyday Experience: A Theoretical Comparison," *Journal of Personality and Social Psychology,* March 1996, pp 513–22; and R F Baumeister and M R Leary, "The Need to Belong: Desire for Interpersonal Attachments as a Fundamental Human Motivation," *Psychological Bulletin,* May 1995, pp 497–529.

[25]J Mason, "The Maxwell Trial: Publisher's Son Denies Using Shares Dishonestly to Gain Overdraft", *Financial Times,* October 17, 1995, p 10.

[26]See the following series of research reports: A M Harrell and M J Stahl, "A Behavioral Decision Theory Approach for Measuring McClelland's Trichotomy of Needs," *Journal of Applied Psychology,* April 1981, pp 242–47; M J Stahl and A M Harrell, "Evolution and Validation of a Behavioral Decision Theory Measurement Approach to Achievement, Power, and Affiliation," *Journal of Applied Psychology,* December 1982, pp 744–51; and M J Stahl, "Achievement, Power and Managerial Motivation: Selecting Managerial Talent with the Job Choice Exercise," *Personnel Psychology,* Winter 1983, pp 775–89.

[27]J Langan-Fox J., and S Roth, "Achievement Motivation and Female Entrepreneurs", *Journal of Occupational and Organizational Behaviour*, September 1995, pp 209–218.

[28]For a review of the foundation of achievement motivation training, see D C McClelland, "Toward a Theory of Motive Acquisition," *American Psychologist,* May 1965, pp 321–33. Evidence for the validity of motivation training can be found in H Heckhausen and S Krug, "Motive Modification," in *Motivation and Society,* ed A J Stewart (San Francisco: Jossey-Bass, 1982).

[29]Results can be found in D B Turban and T L Keon, "Organizational Attractiveness: An Interactionist Perspective," *Journal of Applied Psychology,* April 1993, pp 184–93.

[30]See D Steele Johnson and R Perlow, "The Impact of Need for Achievement Components on Goal Commitment and Performance," *Journal of Applied Social Psychology,* November 1992, pp 1711–20.

[31]J L Bowditch and A F Buono, *A Primer on Organizational Behavior* (New York: John Wiley & Sons, 1985), p 210.

[32]R N Steck, "The First Efficiency Expert," *D&B Reports,* January/February 1992, p 40.

[33]The relationship between monotonous work and job satisfaction, distress, and absenteeism was investigated by S Melamed, I Ben-Avi, J Luz, and M S Green, "Objective and Subjective Work Monotony: Effects on Job Satisfaction, Psychological Distress, and Absenteeism in Blue-Collar Workers," *Journal of Applied Psychology,* February 1995, pp 29–42.

[34]This type of programme was developed and tested by M A Campion and C L McClelland, "Follow-Up and Extension of the Interdisciplinary Costs and Benefits of Enlarged Jobs," *Journal of Applied Psychology,* June 1993, pp 339–51.

[35]An empirical test of the relationship between job rotation and career-related outcomes was conducted by M A Campion, L Cheraskin, and M J Stevens, "Career-Related Antecedents and Outcomes of Job Rotation," *Academy of Management Journal,* December 1994, pp 1518–42.

[36]See F Herzberg, B Mausner, and B B Snyderman, *The Motivation to Work* (New York: John Wiley & Sons, 1959).

[37]Two tests of Herzberg's theory can be found in I O Adigun and G M Stephenson, "Sources of Job Motivation and Satisfaction among British and Nigerian Employees," *The Journal of Social Psychology,* June 1992, pp 369–76; and E A Maidani, "Comparative Study of Herzberg's Two-Factor Theory of Job Satisfaction Among Public and Private Sectors," *Public Personnel Management,* Winter 1991, pp 441–48.

[38]"Asda adds up," *Financial Times,* June 30, 1995, p 16.

[39]Results are presented in "Are Your Staffers Happy? They're in the Minority," *Supervisory Management,* March 1996, p 11.

[40]R Taylor, "Work Culture That Brings No Satisfaction," *Financial Times,* August 25, 1995, p 8.

[41]Both sides of the Herzberg controversy are discussed by N King, "Clarification and Evaluation of the Two-Factor Theory of Job Satisfaction," *Psychological Bulletin,* July 1970, pp 18–31; and B Grigaliunas and Y Weiner, "Has the Research Challenge to Motivation–Hygiene Theory Been Conclusive? An Analysis of Critical Studies," *Human Relations,* December 1974, pp 839–71.

[42]Pinder, *Work Motivation*: Theory, Issues, and Applications, p 28.

[43]J R Hackman, G R Oldham, R Janson, and K Purdy, "A New Strategy for Job Enrichment," *California Management Review,* Summer 1975, p 58.

[44]Ibid., p 58. (Emphasis added.)

[45]C V Clarke, "Be All You Can Be!" *Black Enterprise,* February 1996, pp 72–73.

[46]Definitions of the job characteristics were adapted from J R Hackman and G R Oldham, "Motivation through the Design of Work: Test of a Theory," *Organizational Behavior and Human Performance,* August 1976, pp 250–79.

[47]Results can be found in R B Tiegs, L E Tetrick, and Y Fried, "Growth Need Strength and Context Satisfactions as Moderators of the Relations of the Job Characteristics Model," *Journal of Management,* September 1992, pp 575–93; and G Johns, J L Xie, and Y Fang, "Mediating and Moderating Effects in Job Design," *Journal of Management,* December 1992, pp 657–76.

[48]The complete JDS and norms for the MPS are presented in J R Hackman and G R Oldham, *Work Redesign* (Reading, MA: Addison-Wesley Publishing, 1980). Studies that revised the JDS

were conducted by J L Cordery and P P Sevastos, "Responses to the Original and Revised Job Diagnostic Survey: Is Education a Factor in Responses to Negatively Worded Items?" *Journal of Applied Psychology,* February 1993, pp 141–43; and J R Idaszak and F Drasgow, "A Revision of the Job Diagnostic Survey: Elimination of a Measurement Artifact," *Journal of Applied Psychology*, February 1987, pp 69–74.

[49] See M Morley and N Heraty, "The High-Performance Organization: Developing Teamwork Where It Counts," *Management Decision,* 1995, pp 56–63; B McAfee, V Quarstein, and A Ardalan, "The Effect of Discretion, Outcome Feedback, and Process Feedback on Employee Job Satisfaction," *Industrial Management & Data Systems,* 1995, pp 7–12; and T Loher, R A Noe, N L Moeller, and M P Fitzgerald, "A Meta-Analysis of the Relation of Job Characteristics to Job Satisfaction," *Journal of Applied Psychology,* May 1985, pp 280–89.

[50] Results can be found in L Morris, "Research Capsules: Employees Not Encouraged to Go Extra Mile," *Training & Development,* April 1996, pp 59–60.

[51] Results can be found in M R Kelley, "New Process Technology, Job Design, and Work Organization: A Contingency Model," *American Sociological Review,* April 1990, pp 191–208.

[52] Productivity studies are reviewed in R E Kopelman, *Managing Productivity in Organizations* (New York: McGraw-Hill, 1986).

[53] Absenteeism results are discussed in Y Fried and G R Ferris, "The Validity of the Job Characteristics Model: A Review and Meta-Analysis," *Personnel Psychology*, Summer 1987, pp 287–322. The turnover meta-analysis was conducted by G M McEvoy and W F Cascio, "Strategies for Reducing Turnover: A Meta-Analysis," *Journal of Applied Psychology,* May 1985, pp 342–53.

[54] A thorough discussion of reengineering and associated outcomes can be found in J Champy, *Reengineering Management: The Mandate for New Leadership* (New York: Harper Business, 1995); and M Hammer and J Champy, *Reengineering the Corporation: A Manifesto for Business Revolution* (New York: Harper Business, 1993).

[55] See D C Ganster and D J Dwyer, "The Effects of Understaffing on Individual and Group Performance in Professional and Trade Occupations," *Journal of Management,* 1995, pp 175–90; and J L Xie and G Johns, "Job Scope and Stress: Can Job Scope Be Too High?" *Academy of Management Journal,* October 1995, pp 1288–1309.

[56] G R Oldham and J R Hackman, "Work Design in the Organizational Context," in *Research in Organizational Behavior,* eds B M Staw and L L Cummings (Greenwich, CT: JAI Press, 1980), pp 248–49.

[57] For a review of the development of the JDI, see P C Smith, L M Kendall, and C L Hulin, *The Measurement of Satisfaction in Work and Retirement* (Skokie, IL: Rand McNally, 1969).

[58] For norms on the MSQ, see D J Weiss, R V Dawis, G W England, and L H Lofquist, *Manual for the Minnesota Satisfaction Questionnaire* (Minneapolis: Industrial Relations Center, University of Minnesota, 1967).

[59] For a review of need satisfaction models, see E F Stone, "A Critical Analysis of Social Information Processing Models of Job Perceptions and Job Attitudes," in *Job Satisfaction: How People Feel about Their Jobs and How It Affects Their Performance,* eds C J Cranny, P Cain Smith, and E F Stone (New York: Lexington Books, 1992), pp 21–52.

[60] See J P Wanous, T D Poland, S L Premack, and K S Davis, "The Effects of Met Expectations on Newcomer Attitudes and Behaviors: A Review and Meta-Analysis," *Journal of Applied Psychology,* June 1992, pp 288–97; and P G Irving and J P Meyer, "On Using Direct Measures of Met Expectations: A Methodological Note," *Journal of*

Management, 1995, pp 1159–75.

[61] A complete description of this model is provided by E A Locke, "Job Satisfaction," in *Social Psychology and Organizational Behavior,* eds M Gruneberg and T Wall (New York: John Wiley & Sons, 1984).

[62] For a test of the value fulfilment model, see J K Butler, Jr., "Value Importance as a Moderator of the Value Fulfillment—Job Satisfaction Relationship: Group Differences," *Journal of Applied Psychology*, August 1983, pp 420–28.

[63] See the related discussion in J Mapes, "Training 101: Lessons from the Rainbow and the Kaleidoscope," *Training & Development,* February 1996, pp 11–14; and D R Spitzer, "Power Rewards: Rewards That Really Motivate," *Management Review*, May 1996, pp 45–50.

[64] Results from the meta-analysis can be found in L A Witt and L G Nye, "Gender and the Relationship between Perceived Fairness of Pay or Promotion and Job Satisfaction," *Journal of Applied Psychology,* December 1992, pp 910–17.

[65] See the following series of studies: D Watson and A Keltner Slack, "General Factors of Affective Temperament and Their Relation to Job Satisfaction over Time," *Organizational Behavior and Human Decision Processes,* March 1993, pp 181–202; T A Judge, "Does Affective Disposition Moderate the Relationship between Job Satisfaction and Voluntary Turnover?," *Journal of Applied Psychology,* June 1993, pp 395–401; and B M Staw and J Ross, "Stability in the Midst of Change: A Dispositional Approach to Job Attitudes," *Journal of Applied Psychology,* August 1985, pp 469–80.

[66] See E Diener and C Diener, "Most People Are Happy," *Psychological Science,* May 1996, pp 181–85; D Lykken and A Tellegen, "Happiness Is a Stochastic Phenomenon," *Psychological Science,* May 1996, pp 186–89; and R D Arvey, T J Bouchard, Jr., N L Segal, and L M Abraham, "Job Satisfaction: Environmental and Genetic Components," *Journal of Applied Psychology,* April 1989, pp 187–92.

[67] This study was completed by A J Kinicki, C A Schriesheim, F M McKee, and K P Carson, "The Construct Validity of the Job Descriptive Index (JDI): Review, Critique, and Analysis," 1997, manuscript submitted for publication.

[68] See S P Brown, "A Meta-Analysis and Review of Organizational Research on Job Involvement," *Psychological Bulletin,* September 1996, pp 235–55.

[69] D W Organ, "The Motivational Basis of Organizational Citizenship Behavior," in *Research in Organizational Behavior,* eds B M Staw and L L Cummings (Greenwich, CT: JAI Press, 1990), p 46.

[70] See D W Organ and K Ryan, "A Meta-Analytic Review of Attitudinal and Dispositional Predictors of Organizational Citizenship Behavior," *Personnel Psychology,* Winter 1995, pp 775–802.

[71] Supportive results can be found in M A Konovsky and D W Organ, "Dispositional and Contextual Determinants of Organizational Citizenship Behavior," *Journal of Organizational Behavior,* May 1996, pp 253–66; and P M Podsakoff, S B MacKenzie, and W H Bommer, "Transformational Leader Behaviors and Substitutes for Leadership as Determinants of Employee Satisfaction, Commitment, Trust, and Organizational Citizenship Behaviors," *Journal of Management,* pp 259–98.

[72] For a review of research on organizational citizenship, see L V Dyne, L L Cummings, and J M Parks, "Extra-Role Behaviors: In Pursuit of Construct and Definitional Clarity (A Bridge over Muddied Waters)" in *Research in Organizational Behavior,* eds L L Cummings and B M Staw (Greenwich, CT: JAI Press, 1995), vol. 17, pp 215–85.

[73]See R P Tett and J P Meyer, "Job Satisfaction, Organizational Commitment, Turnover Intention, and Turnover: Path Analysis Based on Meta-Analytic Findings," *Personnel Psychology*, Summer 1993, pp 259–93.

[74]See J E Mathieu and D Zajac, "A Review and Meta-Analysis of the Antecedents, Correlates, and Consequences of Organizational Commitment," *Psychological Bulletin,* September 1990, pp 171–94.

[75]R Taylor, "Reconciling commitment and flexibility - How can companies maintain employee loyalty when they can no longer promise a job for life?," *Financial Times*, June 1, 1994, p 15.

[76]See R D Hackett, "Work Attitudes and Employee Absenteeism: A Synthesis of the Literature," *Journal of Occupational Psychology,* 1989, pp 235–48.

[77]The results can be found in Tett and Meyer, "Job Satisfaction, Organizational Commitment, Turnover Intention, and Turnover: Path Analysis Based on Meta-Analytic Findings."

[78]"Stress-related illness costs UK 1.5 million working days a year," *Personnel Management*, 1993, vol 25, no 2, p 11.

[79]S Midgley, "Pressure points", *People Management*, 1997, vol 3, no 14, pp 36–39

[80]Results can be found in M A Blegen, "Nurses' Job Satisfaction: A Meta-Analysis of Related Variables," *Nursing Research,* January/February 1993, pp 36–41.

[81]Results from this study were discussed in J Gice, "The Relationship between Job Satisfaction and Workers Compensation Claims," *CPCU Journal,* September 1995, pp 178–84.

[82]M McHugh, "Stress at work, Do managers really count the costs?", *Employee Relations*, 1993, vol 15, no 1, pp 18–32.

[83]The relationship between performance and satisfaction was reviewed by M T Iaffaldano and P M Muchinsky, "Job Satisfaction and Job Performance: A Meta-Analysis," *Psychological Bulletin,* March 1985, pp 251–73.

[84]These issues are discussed by C Ostroff, "The Relationship between Satisfaction, Attitudes, and Performance: An Organizational Level Analysis," *Journal of Applied Psychology*, December 1992, pp 963–74; and R A Katzell, D E Thompson, and R A Guzzo, "How Job Satisfaction and Job Performance Are and Are Not Linked," in *Job Satisfaction: How People Feel about Their Jobs and How It Affects Their Performance,* eds C J Cranny, P Cain Smith, and E F Stone (New York: Lexington Books, 1992), pp 195–217.

[85]See Ostroff, "The Relationship between Satisfaction, Attitudes, and Performance: An Organizational Level Analysis."

[86]Adapted from M R Blood, "Work Values and Job Satisfaction," *Journal of Applied Psychology,* December 1969, pp 456–59.

[87]The JDS and its norms were adapted from Hackman and Oldham, *Work Redesign*, pp 280–81, 317.

Eight

Motivation through Equity, Expectancy, and Goal Setting

LEARNING OBJECTIVES

When you finish studying the material in this chapter, you should be able to:

1. Discuss the role of perceived inequity in employee motivation.

2. Distinguish between positive and negative inequity.

3. Describe the practical lessons derived from equity theory.

4. Explain Vroom's expectancy theory

5. Discuss Porter and Lawler's expectancy theory of motivation.

6. Describe the practical implications of expectancy theory of motivation.

7. Explain how goal setting motivates an individual.

8. Identify five practical lessons from goal-setting research.

9. Specify issues that should be addressed before implementing a motivational programme.

Campbell Soup CEO David Johnson believes in goals, measurement, and linking performance to rewards. This mini-case illustrates how he used these management tools to increase sales and profitability at Campbell.

When he got to Campbell in 1990, Johnson indoctrinated employees with his first fundamental truth—the company's primary purpose is to build shareholder wealth: "The shareholder is the prime, supreme, and first of all stakeholders." That proposition has done wonders for Campbell's stock, which has outperformed both Standard & Poor's food group and the S&P 500, with a five-year compound annual growth rate of 14.2 per cent. Shares are selling these days for about $59, up from $25 when he took over. A study by consultants Stern Stewart, which tracks the amount of market value added, or MVA, that 1,000 companies have created over a decade, ranks Campbell among the top 5 per cent for creating $7.4 billion of shareholder wealth.

The secret behind those numbers? Johnson focuses his people on a single goal—increasing net earnings faster than competitors. Scoreboards comparing Campbell's net-profit increases with other food companies' are scattered throughout the company. Johnson pours much of his excess energy into the gritty task of prodding lieutenants to surpass even the loftiest earnings targets. Wearing a hat more typical of a COO, he drives managers to search for the next big idea that could produce a blockbuster. Typical was a February managers meeting—this *Fortune* reporter was the first outsider ever to attend one—where Johnson flashed a slide showing Wall Street's aggregate 1996 earnings per share estimate for Campbell of $3.10. He compared the figure with estimates for competitors, concluded that Campbell's projection wasn't high enough to finish the year among the top four food companies, and challenged the 23 officers to beat it. "Bring me ideas supported by how much each will add to earnings," he directed.

F Martin Thrasher, president of Campbell's international grocery division, calls this style "loose-tight." Johnson lets subordinates figure out how to pull off minor miracles, but holds them accountable. Taking risks, however, in this era of layoffs is scary for any employee. To reduce the fear factor, Johnson holds celebrations designed to build confidence among the rank and file.

Johnson's cheerleading and exhortation would be so much hot air if they weren't anchored by an obsession with measurement. "Numbers always tell the story," he says, and he neither accepts nor offers excuses when numbers pinpoint weakness. Measurement creates the discipline that prompts general counsel John Coleman to warn, "You can miss your plan and not be shot. But you wouldn't want to miss it twice." Only eight of the 35 officers who were running Campbell when Johnson arrived are still in place. At that time the company was, in the words of senior vice president Robert Bernstock, "at the bottom of the pack, stumbling toward the cellar." Seventeen officers were fired, five retired, and another five "resigned." Johnson doesn't humiliate slackers in front of others. He just bluntly tells them to shape up or they are out. . . .

Many managers, though, put up with Johnson's antics because they're well rewarded for their trouble. About 1,200 employees including Johnson earn bonuses if they meet certain financial hurdles. The CEO himself received $5.5 million last year in salary and bonuses. Currently he's striving to earn a "challenge incentive" worth a million or two and aimed at supercharging the overseas business.

Johnson, who rewards people for thinking like owners, uses a model that Sanford Bernstein analyst Steven Galbraith calls "vastly superior to any I've ever seen in any industry." Campbell requires the top 300 executives to own from one-half to three times their base salaries in stock. Recently hired chief financial officer Basil Anderson—one of two survivors of Albert "Chainsaw" Dunlap's housecleaning at Scott Paper—borrowed $700,000 to fulfill the requirement before he set foot in his new office. The policy extends to the board. Campbell has eliminated directors' benefits. Board members are now required to own 3,000 shares by their third year; 75 per cent of their pay is annual grants of shares and options, and Campbell prohibits repricing options to cushion declining value.[1]

Discussion Question

What do you think of David Johnson's approach to goals, measurement, and rewards? Would you like to work at Campbell Soup?

---

his chapter explores three cognitive theories of work motivation: equity, expectancy, and goal setting. Each theory is based on the premise that employees'cognitions are the key to understanding their motivation. To help you apply what you have learned, we conclude the chapter by highlighting the prerequisites of successful motivational programmes.

Adams's Equity Theory of Motivation

Equity theory
Holds that motivation is a function of fairness in social exchanges.

Defined generally, **equity theory** is a model of motivation that explains how people strive for *fairness* and *justice* in social exchanges or give-and-take relationships. Equity theory is based on cognitive dissonance theory, developed by social psychologist Leon Festinger in the 1950s.[2]

According to Festinger's theory, people are motivated to maintain consistency between their cognitive beliefs and their behaviour. Perceived inconsistencies create cognitive dissonance (or psychological discomfort), which, in turn, motivates corrective action. For example, a cigarette smoker who sees a heavy-smoking relative die of lung cancer probably would be motivated to quit smoking if he or she attributes the death to smoking. Accordingly, when victimized by unfair social exchanges, our resulting cognitive dissonance prompts us to correct the situation. Corrective action may range from a slight change in attitude or behaviour to stealing to the extreme case of trying to harm someone. For example, experts believe that employee theft, which costs American business about $120 billion a year, represents an employee's attempt to even the score.[3]

Psychologist J Stacy Adams pioneered application of the equity principle to the workplace. Central to understanding Adams's equity theory of motivation is an awareness of key components of the individual–organization exchange relationship. This relationship is pivotal in the formation of employees'perceptions of equity and inequity.

The Individual–Organization Exchange Relationship

Adams points out that two primary components are involved in the employee–employer exchange, *inputs* and *outcomes*. An employee's inputs, for which he or she expects a just return, include education, experience, skills, and effort. On the outcome side of the exchange, the organization provides such things as pay, fringe benefits, and recognition. These outcomes vary widely, depending on one's organization and rank. Table 8–1 presents a list of on-the-job inputs and outcomes employees consider when making equity comparisons.

Negative and Positive Inequity

On the job, feelings of inequity revolve around a person's evaluation of whether he or she receives adequate rewards to compensate for his or her contributive inputs. People perform these evaluations by comparing the perceived fairness of their employment exchange to that of relevant others. This comparative process, which is based on an equity norm, was found to generalize across countries.[4] OB scholar Robert Vecchio identified three major categories of relevant others that people use when making equity comparisons:

(1) *Other* (including referent others inside and outside the organization, and referent others in similar or different jobs), (2) *self* (self-comparisons over time and against one's ideal ratio), and

---

Table 8 – 1   Factors Considered When Making Equity Comparisons

INPUTS	OUTCOMES
Time	Pay/bonuses
Education/training	Fringe benefits
Experience	Challenging assignments
Skills	Job security
Creativity	Career advancement/promotions
Seniority	Status symbols
Loyalty to organization	Pleasant/safe working environment
Age	Opportunity for personal growth/development
Personality traits	Supportive supervision
Effort expended	Recognition
Personal appearance	Participation in important decisions

Source: Based in part on J S Adams, "Toward an Understanding of Inequity," *Journal of Abnormal and Social Psychology*, November 1963, pp 422–36.

(3) *system* (based on exchanges between an individual and the organization). In addition to these categorizations, it should be noted that a group or even multiple groups can serve as referents.[5]

People tend to compare themselves to similar others—such as people performing the same job or individuals of the same gender or educational level—rather than dissimilar others.[6]

Three different equity relationships are illustrated in Figure 8–1: equity, negative inequity, and positive inequity. Assume the two people in each of the equity relationships in Figure 8–1 have equivalent backgrounds (equal education, seniority, and so forth) and perform identical tasks. Only their hourly pay rates differ. Equity exists for an individual when his or her ratio of perceived outcomes to inputs is equal to the ratio of outcomes to inputs for a relevant co-worker (see part A in Figure 8–1). Since equity is based on comparing ratios of outcomes to inputs, inequity will not necessarily be perceived just because someone else receives greater rewards. If the other person's additional outcomes are due to his or her greater inputs, a sense of equity may still exist. However, if the comparison person enjoys greater outcomes for similar inputs, **negative inequity** will be perceived (see part B in Figure 8–1). On the other hand, a person will experience **positive inequity** when his or her outcome to input ratio is greater than that of a relevant co-worker (see part C in Figure 8–1).

Let us consider the type of equity associated with the pay gap between chief executive officers and workers:

Negative inequity

Comparison in which another person receives greater outcomes for similar inputs.

Positive inequity

Comparison in which another person receives lesser outcomes for similar inputs.

Figure 8 – 1   Negative and Positive Inequity

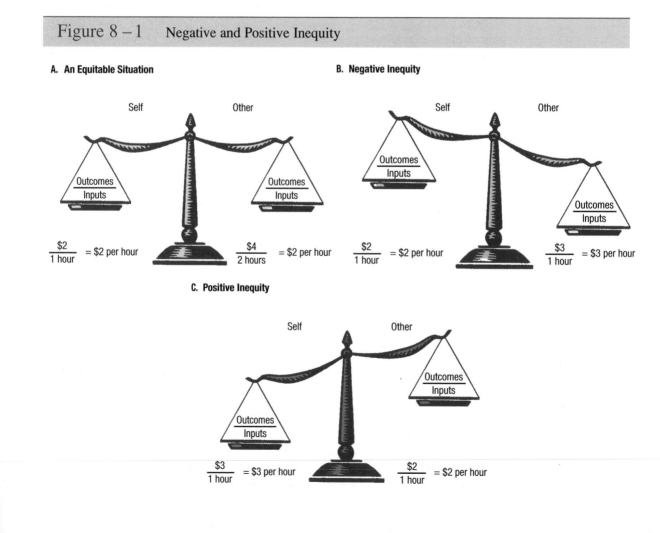

A. **An Equitable Situation**

B. **Negative Inequity**

C. **Positive Inequity**

Last year [1995], CEO salaries and bonuses jumped 10.4%, reflecting a surge in corporate profits, while US wages and benefits inched up just 2.9%. That creates a huge gap: in 1995, 30 chiefs from big companies were paid 212 times more than the average American employee . . . way up from a multiple of 44 in 1965.[7] European top-managers are paid 20 to 50 times more than their employees.[8]

How do you think the typical employee would interpret this situation? Workers are likely to interpret this situation as negative inequity in spite of the increased stress and responsibility associated with being a CEO. In contrast, CEOs like Jack Welch, from General Electric, and Eastman Kodak's George Fisher believe that compensation is fair. An absolute record is the compensation of Walt Disney's chief Michael Eisner who earned $190 million in 1994.[9] When *The Wall Street Journal* asked Welch about his $22 million compensation in 1995, he replied, "This is a market. It's a free market and people have choices." Similarly, George Fisher concluded, "We all should be compensated based on competitive issues. If you want a world-class shortstop, you pay. The good news is that many CEOs are getting well compensated for really good performances."[10] We wonder whether workers also believe that they are being well compensated for really good performance.

Dynamics of Perceived Inequity

Managers can derive practical benefits from Adams's equity theory by recognizing that (1) negative inequity is less tolerable than positive inequity and (2) inequity can be reduced in a variety of ways.

Thresholds of Inequity   People have a lower tolerance for negative inequity than they do for positive inequity. Those who are shortchanged are more powerfully motivated to correct the situation than those who are excessively rewarded. For example, if you have ever been overworked and underpaid, you know how negative inequity can erode your job satisfaction and performance. Perhaps you put forth less effort or quit the job to escape the negative inequity. Hence, it takes much more positive than negative inequity to produce the same degree of motivation. Moreover, a meta-analysis of 12,979 people demonstrated that males and females had equal reactions to negative inequity. There were no gender differences in response to perceived inequity.[11]

Reducing Inequity   Table 8–2 lists eight possible ways to reduce inequity. It is important to note that equity can be restored by altering one's equity ratios behaviourally and/or cognitively. Equity theorists propose that the many possible combinations of behavioural and cognitive adjustments are influenced by the following tendencies:

1. An individual will attempt to maximize the amount of positive outcomes he or she receives.

2. People resist increasing inputs when it requires substantial effort or costs.

3. People resist behavioural or cognitive changes in inputs important to their self-concept or self-esteem.

4. Rather than change cognitions about oneself, an individual is more likely to change cognitions about the comparison other's inputs and outcomes.

5. Leaving the field (quitting) is chosen only when severe inequity cannot be resolved through other methods.[12]

Expanding the Concept of Equity

Distributive justice
The perceived fairness of how resources and rewards are distributed.

Equity was previously defined as a ratio of outcomes to inputs. This definition has recently been expanded to include two separate components. The first, referred to as **distributive justice**, reflects the perceived fairness of how resources and rewards are distributed or allocated. The second is called **procedural justice** and is defined as the

Table 8 – 2	Eight Ways to Reduce Inequity

METHODS	EXAMPLES
1. Person can increase his or her inputs.	Work harder; attend school or a specialized training programme.
2. Person can decrease his or her inputs.	Don't work as hard; take longer breaks.
3. Person can attempt to increase his or her outcomes.	Ask for a rise; ask for a new title; seek outside intervention.
4. Person can decrease his or her outcomes.	Ask for less pay.
5. Leave the field.	Absenteeism and turnover.
6. Person can psychologically distort his or her input and outcomes.	Convince self that certain inputs are not important; convince self that he or she has a boring and monotonous job.
7. Person can psychologically distort the inputs or outcomes of comparison other.	Conclude that other has more experience or works harder; conclude that other has a more important title.
8. Change comparison other.	Pick a new comparison person; compare self to previous job.

Source Adapted from J S Adams, "Toward an Understanding of Inequity," *Journal of Abnormal and Social Psychology*, November 1963, pp 422–36.

Procedural justice

The perceived fairness of the process and procedures used to make allocation decisions.

perceived fairness of the process and procedures used to make allocation decisions. Research shows that positive perceptions of distributive and procedural justice are enhanced by giving employees a "voice" in decisions that affect them.[13] Voice represents the extent to which employees who are affected by a decision can present relevant information about the decision to others.

Equity Research Findings

Different managerial insights have been gained from laboratory and field studies.

Insights from Laboratory Studies   The basic approach used in laboratory studies is to pay an experimental subject more (overpayment) or less (underpayment) than the standard rate for completing a task. People are paid on either an hourly or piece-rate basis. Research findings supported equity theory. Overpaid subjects on a piece-rate system lowered the quantity of their performance and increased the quality of their performance. In contrast, underpaid subjects increased the quantity and decreased the quality of their performance.[14] A study extended this stream of research by examining the effect of underpayment inequity on ethical behaviour. A total of 102 undergraduate students were either equitably paid or underpaid for performing a clerical task. Results indicated that underpaid students stole money to compensate for their negative inequity[15]

Insights from Field Studies   Field studies of equity theory are on the rise. Overall, results support propositions derived from the theory. For example, perceptions of distributive and procedural justice were positively related to pay and benefit satisfaction, job satisfaction, organizational commitment, trust in management, and commitment to support a decision.[16] Other studies further revealed that lower absenteeism, intentions to quit, and turnover were significantly correlated with perceptions of distributive and procedural justice.[17] It thus appears beneficial for managers to equitably distribute monetary rewards and promotions by using a fair and equitable decision-making process. Finally, a study of 20 intact management teams further revealed that the teams' assessment of procedural justice during strategic planning was significantly related to the quality of decisions, commitment to decisions, and trust in the team leader.[18]

Practical Lessons from Equity Theory

Equity theory has at least seven important practical implications. First, equity theory provides managers with yet another explanation of how beliefs and attitudes affect job performance. According to this line of thinking, the best way to manage job behaviour is to adequately understand underlying cognitive processes. Indeed, we are motivated powerfully to correct the situation when our ideas of fairness and justice are offended.

Second, research on equity theory emphasizes the need for managers to pay attention to employees' *perceptions* of what is fair and equitable. No matter how fair management thinks the organization's policies, procedures, and reward system are, each employee's perception of the equity of those factors is what counts. For example, a recent study of 620 white males and 792 white females revealed that resistance to affirmative action programmes and the overt display of accepting and rejecting behaviours were associated with employees' fairness perceptions. People resisted and acted negatively when they reported feelings of injustice.[19] This study underscores the need for managers to make hiring and promotion decisions on merit-based, job-related information.

Third, managers benefit by allowing employees to participate in making decisions about important work outcomes. For example, employees were more satisfied with their performance appraisals and resultant outcomes when they had a "voice" during the appraisal review.[20]

Fourth, employees should be given the opportunity to appeal decisions that affect their welfare. Being able to appeal a decision promotes the belief that management treats employees fairly. In turn, perceptions of fair treatment promote job satisfaction and organizational commitment and help reduce absenteeism and turnover.

Fifth, employees are more likely to accept and support organizational change when they believe it is implemented fairly and when it produces equitable outcomes.[21]

ETHICS

Sixth, managers can promote cooperation and teamwork among group members by treating them equitably. Research reveals that people are just as concerned with fairness in group settings as they are with their own personal interests.[22]

Seventh, treating employees inequitably can lead to litigation and costly court settlements. Employees denied justice at work are turning increasingly to arbitration and the courts. This American trend is clearly shifting to Europe.

Managers can attempt to follow these practical implications by monitoring equity perceptions through informal conversations, interviews, or attitude surveys. Please take a moment now to complete the brief equity/fairness questionnaire in the OB Exercise. If you perceive your work organization as unfair, you are probably dissatisfied and have contemplated quitting. In contrast, your organizational loyalty and attachment are likely greater if you believe you are treated fairly at work.

Expectancy Theory of Motivation

Expectancy theory
Holds that people are motivated to behave in ways that produce valued outcomes.

Expectancy theory holds that people are motivated to behave in ways that produce desired combinations of expected outcomes. Perception plays a central role in expectancy theory because it emphasizes cognitive ability to anticipate likely consequences of behaviour. Embedded in expectancy theory is the principle of hedonism. Hedonistic people strive to maximize their pleasure and minimize their pain. Generally, expectancy theory can be used to predict behaviour in any situation in which a choice between two or more alternatives must be made. For example, it can be used to predict whether to quit or stay at a job; whether to exert substantial or minimal effort at a task; and whether to study management, computer science, accounting, or finance.

This section introduces and explores two expectancy theories of motivation: Vroom's expectancy theory and Porter and Lawler's expectancy theory. Understanding these cognitive process theories can help managers develop organizational policies and practices that enhance rather than inhibit employee motivation.

Vroom's Expectancy Theory

Victor Vroom formulated a mathematical model of expectancy theory in his 1964 book *Work and Motivation*.[23] Vroom's theory has been summarized as follows:

The strength of a tendency to act in a certain way depends on the strength of an expectancy that the act will be followed by a given consequence (or outcome) and on the value or attractiveness of that consequence (or outcome) to the actor.[24]

Motivation, according to Vroom, boils down to the decision of how much effort to exert in a specific task situation. This choice is based on a two-stage sequence of expectations (effort→performance and performance→outcome). First, motivation is affected by an individual's expectation that a certain level of effort will produce the intended performance goal. For example, if you do not believe increasing the amount of time you spend studying will significantly raise your grade on an exam, you probably will not study any harder than usual. Motivation also is influenced by the employee's perceived chances of getting various outcomes as a result of accomplishing his or her performance goal. Finally, individuals are motivated to the extent that they value the outcomes received. Consider the motivation and behaviour of Hans Vermeulen. In 1993 Hans Vermeulen was expelled as a member of the Dutch Stock Exchange (AEX) by the disciplinary committee as a consequence of his misbehaviour in his trade activities. Many considered his punishment too light. Nevertheless, at the end of 1993 Hans Vermeulen became managing director at Leemhuis & Van Loon a Dutch company active on the Dutch Stock Exchange. In 1995, Hans Vemeulen was again discredited for malversations, but nothing happened. In 1997, he was at last arrested for committing fraud and for laundering practices.[25]

OB EXERCISE   *Measuring Perceived Organizational Equity/Fairness*

Instructions
Evaluate your present (or most recent) job according to the following five dimensions.

Norms
Very fair organization = 26–35
Moderately fair organization = 15–25
Unfair organization = 5–14

DIMENSIONS	ITEM	SCORE
		False .... True
1. Pay rules	The rules for granting pay raises in my organization are fair.	1—2—3—4—5—6—7
2. Pay administration	My supervisor rates everyone fairly when considering them for promotion.	1—2—3—4—5—6—7
3. Pay level	My employer pays me more for my work than I would receive from other organizations in this area	1—2—3—4—5—6—7
4. Work pace	My supervisor makes everyone meet their performance standards.	1—2—3—4—5—6—7
5. Rule administration	My supervisor makes everyone come to work on time and adhere to the same rules of conduct.	1—2—3—4—5—6—7
		Total score = _____

SOURCE   Adapted in part from J E Dittrich and M R Carrell, "Organizational Equity Perceptions, Employee Job Satisfaction, and Departmental Absence and Turnover Rates," *Organizational Behavior and Human Performance*, August 1979, pp 29–40.

ETHICS

Based on expectancy theory, we would expect Hans Vermeulen to continue his current behaviour because he values money highly and there are no major consequences for his questionable conduct.

Vroom used a mathematical equation to integrate these concepts into a predictive model of motivational force or strength. For our purposes, however, it is sufficient to define and explain the three key concepts within Vroom's model—*expectancy, instrumentality,* and *valence.*

Expectancy
Belief that effort leads to a specific level of performance.

Expectancy

An **expectancy**, according to Vroom's terminology, represents an individual's belief that a particular degree of effort will be followed by a particular level of performance. In other words, it is an effort→performance expectation. Expectancies take the form of subjective probabilities. As you may recall from a course in statistics, probabilities range from zero to one. An expectancy of zero indicates effort has no anticipated impact on performance.

For example, suppose you do not know how to use a typewriter. No matter how much effort you exert, your perceived probability of typing 30 error-free words per minute would probably be zero. An expectancy of one suggests that performance is totally dependent on effort. If you decided to take a typing course as well as practice a couple of hours a day for a few weeks (high effort), you should be able to type 30 words per minute without any errors. In contrast, if you do not take a typing course and only practice an hour or two per week (low effort), there is a very low probability (say, a 20 per cent chance) of being able to type 30 words per minute without any errors.

The following factors influence an employee's expectancy perceptions:

- Self-esteem.

- Self-efficacy.

- Previous success at the task.

- Help received from a supervisor and subordinates.

- Information necessary to complete the task.

- Good materials and equipment to work with.[26]

Instrumentality
A performance→outcome perception.

Instrumentality

An **instrumentality** is a performance→outcome perception. It represents a person's belief that a particular outcome is contingent on accomplishing a specific level of performance. Performance is instrumental when it leads to something else. For example, passing exams is instrumental to graduating from university.

Instrumentalities range from −1.0 to 1.0. An instrumentality of 1.0 indicates attainment of a particular outcome is totally dependent on task performance. An instrumentality of zero indicates there is no relationship between performance and outcome. For example, most companies link the number of vacation days to seniority, not job performance. Finally, an instrumentality of −1.0 reveals that high performance reduces the chance of obtaining an outcome while low performance increases the chance. For example, in some government agencies promotion depends on a favourable ranking in examinations. The more a civil servant studies during working hours and hence neglects his or her work, the higher the probability of being promoted.

The concept of instrumentality can be seen in action by considering the "Winning Together" reward programme implemented at AlliedSignal's Engineered Materials division in Morristown, New Jersey:

It works something like an airline frequent flier program . . . with employees at manufacturing locations awarded points for meeting specific goals on a quarterly basis. The employees can then accumulate points and cash them in for any of a range of specific noncash rewards.

According to Scott Pitasky, director/compensation for Engineered Materials, all manufacturing facilities establish metrics based on things such as safety, customer satisfaction, and operational excellence, including capacity productivity and cost measures. Large scoreboards are posted indicating where the location stands relative to its goal. Under the "green light" program, progress toward meeting the goal is monitored continuously and summed up with a graph and traffic light symbol—red for underperformance, green for exceeding the goals.[27]

The "Winning Together" programme clearly makes performance instrumental for obtaining rewards.

Valence

The value of a reward or outcome.

Valence   As Vroom used the term, **valence** refers to the positive or negative value people place on outcomes. Valence mirrors our personal preferences.[28] For example, most employees have a positive valence for receiving additional money or recognition. In contrast, job stress and being laid off would likely be negatively valent for most individuals. In Vroom's expectancy model, *outcomes* refer to different consequences that are contingent on performance, such as pay, promotions, or recognition. An outcome's valence depends on an individual's needs and can be measured for research purposes with scales ranging from a negative value to a positive value. For example, an individual's valence towards more recognition can be assessed on a scale ranging from −2 (very undesirable) to 0 (neutral) to +2 (very desirable).

Vroom's Expectancy Theory in Action

Vroom's expectancy model of motivation can be used to analyse a real-life motivation programme. Consider the following performance problem described by Frederick W Smith, founder and chief executive officer of Federal Express Corporation:

. . . we were having a helluva problem keeping things running on time. The airplanes would come in, and everything would get backed up. We tried every kind of control mechanism that you could think of, and none of them worked. Finally, it became obvious that the underlying problem was that it was in the interest of the employees at the cargo terminal—they were college kids, mostly—to run late, because it meant that they made more money. So what we did was give them all a minimum guarantee and say, "Look, if you get through before a certain time, just go home, and you will have beat the system." Well, it was unbelievable. I mean, in the space of about 45 days, the place was way ahead of schedule. And I don't even think it was a conscious thing on their part.[29]

How did Federal Express get its student cargo handlers to switch from low effort to high effort? According to Vroom's model, the student workers originally exerted low effort because they were paid on the basis of time, not output. It was in their best interest to work slowly and accumulate as many hours as possible. By offering to let the student workers *go home early if and when they completed their assigned duties,* Federal Express prompted high effort. This new arrangement created two positively valued outcomes: guaranteed pay plus the opportunity to leave early. The motivation to exert high effort became greater than the motivation to exert low effort.

Judging from the impressive results, the student workers had both high effort→ performance expectancies and positive performance→outcome instrumentalities. Moreover, the guaranteed pay and early departure opportunity evidently had strongly positive valences for the student workers.

Porter and Lawler's Extension

Two OB researchers, Lyman Porter and Edward Lawler III, developed an expectancy model of motivation that extended Vroom's work. This model attempted to (1) identify the source of people's valences and expectancies and (2) link effort with performance and job satisfaction. The model is presented in Figure 8–2.[30]

Predictors of Effort

Effort is viewed as a function of the perceived value of a reward (the reward's valence) and the perceived effort→reward probability (an expectancy). Employees should exhibit more effort when they believe they will receive valued rewards for task accomplishment.

Predictors of Performance   Performance is determined by more than effort. Figure 8–2 indicates that the relationship between effort and performance is moderated by an employee's abilities and traits and role perceptions. That is, employees with higher abilities attain higher performance for a given level of effort than employees with less ability. Similarly, effort results in higher performance when employees clearly understand and are comfortable with their roles. This occurs because effort is channelled into the most important job activities or tasks. For example, stage fright can render an otherwise well prepared actor or speaker ineffective.

Predictors of Satisfaction   Employees receive both intrinsic and extrinsic rewards for performance. Intrinsic rewards are self-granted and consist of intangibles such as a sense of accomplishment and achievement. Extrinsic rewards are tangible outcomes such as pay and public recognition. In turn, job satisfaction is determined by employees' perceptions of the equity of the rewards received. Employees are more satisfied when they feel equitably rewarded. Figure 8–2 further shows that job satisfaction affects employees' subsequent valence of rewards. Finally, employees' future effort→reward probabilities are influenced by past experience with performance and rewards.

Research on Expectancy Theory and Managerial Implications

Many researchers have tested expectancy theory. A summary of 16 studies revealed that expectancy theory correctly predicted occupational or organizational choice 63.4 per cent of the time; this was significantly better than chance predictions. Further, expectancy theory accurately predicted job satisfaction, decisions to retire (80 per cent accuracy), voting behaviour in union representation elections (over 75 per cent accuracy) and the frequency of drinking alcohol. A recent meta-analysis of 77 studies indicated that

---

Figure 8 – 2   Porter and Lawler's Expectancy Model

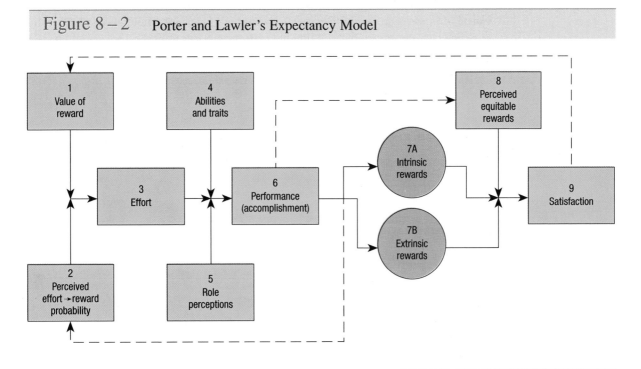

Source: L W Porter and E E Lawler III, *Managerial Attitudes and Performance* (Homewood, IL: Richard D. Irwin, 1968), p 165.

expectancy theory significantly predicted performance, effort, intentions, preferences, and choice.[31]

Nonetheless, expectancy theory has been criticized for a variety of reasons. For example, the theory is difficult to test, and the measures used to assess expectancy, instrumentality, and valence have questionable validity.[32] In the final analysis, however, expectancy theory has important practical implications for individual managers and organizations as a whole (see Table 8–3).

Managers are advised to enhance effort→performance expectancies by helping employees accomplish their performance goals. Managers can do this by providing support and coaching and by increasing employees'self-efficacy. A management expert suggests that managers can effectively coach for success by (1) establishing both individual and team goals, (2) holding individuals and team members accountable for goals, (3) showing employees how to complete difficult assignments and tasks, (4) advising employees on how to overcome performance roadblocks, (5) verbally expressing support, (6) listening to employees and fostering two-way communication, and (7) sharing and recognizing progress.[33]

It also is important for managers to influence employees'instrumentalities and to monitor valences for various rewards. This raises the issue of whether organizations should use monetary rewards as the primary method to reinforce performance. Although money is certainly a positively valent reward for most people, there are three issues to consider when deciding on the relative balance between monetary and non-monetary rewards. First, some research shows that workers value interesting work and recognition more than money.[34] Second, extrinsic rewards can lose their motivating properties over time and may undermine intrinsic motivation.[35] Third, monetary rewards must be large enough to generate motivation. For example, Steven Kerr, chief learning officer at GE, estimates that monetary awards must be at least 10 per cent to 12 per cent above employees'base pay to truly motivate people.[36] Unfortunately, merit pay increases may not be large enough to create long-term motivation. In summary, there is no one best type of reward. Individual differences and need theories tell us that people are motivated by different rewards. Managers should therefore focus on linking employee performance to valued rewards regardless of the type of reward used to enhance motivation.

There are four prerequisites to linking performance and rewards:

Table 8–3   Managerial and Organizational Implications of Expectancy Theory

IMPLICATIONS FOR MANAGERS	IMPLICATIONS FOR ORGANIZATIONS
Determine the outcomes employees value.	Reward people for desired performance, and do not keep pay decisions secret.
Identify good performance so appropriate behaviours can be rewarded.	Design challenging jobs.
Make sure employees can achieve targeted performance levels.	Tie some rewards to group accomplishments to build teamwork and encourage cooperation.
Link desired outcomes to targeted levels of performance.	Reward managers for creating, monitoring, and maintaining expectancies, instrumentalities, and outcomes that lead to high effort and goal attainment.
Make sure changes in outcomes are large enough to motivate high effort.	Monitor employee motivation through interviews or anonymous questionnaires.
Monitor the reward system for inequities.	Accommodate individual differences by building flexibility into the motivation programme.

1. Managers need to develop and communicate performance standards to employees. For instance, a survey of 487 managers indicated that they were not held accountable for increasing quality. In turn, these managers did not set or enforce high performance standards among their employees.[37] Without question, increased motivation will not result in higher performance unless employees know how and where to direct their efforts.

2. Managers need valid and accurate performance ratings with which to compare employees. Inaccurate ratings create perceptions of inequity and thereby erode motivation.

3. Managers need to determine the relative mix of individual versus team contribution to performance and then reward accordingly. If an employee is truly an independent contributor, then recognition and rewards should be based solely on his or her performance. In contrast, many organizations believe that individual performance is partly due to team-level efforts and productivity. For example, a survey of 45 US insurance companies revealed that 13 per cent based part of an employee's pay on team performance, and 44 per cent were considering implementing team-based rewards.[38]

4. Managers should use the performance ratings to differentially allocate rewards among employees. That is, it is critical that managers allocate significantly different amounts of rewards for various levels of performance. As illustrated in the International OB, this practice is just beginning to take hold in Japan. Pay for performance is likely to be met with resistance in Japan because it conflicts with a culture that historically reinforced seniority.

Motivation through Goal Setting

Regardless of the nature of their specific achievements, successful people tend to have one thing in common. Their lives are goal oriented. This is as true for politicians seeking votes as it is for rocket scientists probing outer space. In Lewis Carroll's delightful tale of *Alice's Adventures in Wonderland,* the smiling Cheshire cat advised the bewildered Alice, "If you don't know where you're going, any road will take you there." Goal-oriented managers tend to find the right road because they know where they are going. Within the context of employee motivation, this section explores the theory, research, and practice of goal setting.

Goals: Definition and Background

Goal

What an individual is trying to accomplish.

Edwin Locke, a leading authority on goal setting, and his colleagues define a **goal** as "what an individual is trying to accomplish; it is the object or aim of an action."[39] Expanding this definition, they add:

The concept is similar in meaning to the concepts of purpose and intent. . . . Other frequently used concepts that are also similar in meaning to that of goal include performance standard (a measuring rod for evaluating performance), quota (a minimum amount of work or production), work norm (a standard of acceptable behaviour defined by a work group), task (a piece of work to be accomplished), objective (the ultimate aim of an action or series of actions), deadline (a time limit for completing a task), and budget (a spending goal or limit).[40]

The motivational impact of performance goals and goal-based reward plans has been recognized for a long time. At the turn of the century, Frederick Taylor attempted to scientifically establish how much work of a specified quality an individual should be assigned each day. He proposed that bonuses be based on accomplishing those output standards. More recently, goal setting has been promoted through a widely used

Management by objectives

Management system incorporating participation in decision making, goal setting, and feedback.

management technique called management by objectives (MBO). **Management by objectives** is a management system that incorporates participation in decision making, goal setting, and objective feedback.[41] A meta-analysis of MBO programmes showed productivity gains in 68 of 70 different organizations. Specifically, results uncovered an average gain in productivity of 56 per cent when top-management commitment was high. The average gain was only 6 per cent when commitment was low. A second meta-analysis of 18 studies further demonstrated that employees' job satisfaction was significantly related to top management's commitment to a MBO implementation.[42] These impressive results highlight the positive benefits of implementing MBO and setting goals. To further understand how MBO programmes can increase both productivity and satisfaction, let us examine the process by which goal setting works.

How Does Goal Setting Work?

Despite abundant goal-setting research and practice, goal-setting theories are surprisingly scarce. An instructive model was formulated by Locke and his associates (see Figure 8–3). According to Locke's model, goal setting has four motivational mechanisms.

Goals Direct Attention   Goals that are personally meaningful tend to focus one's attention on what is relevant and important. If, for example, you have a term project due in a few days, your thoughts tend to revolve around completing that project. Similarly, the members of a home appliance salesforce who are told they can win a trip to Hawaii for selling the most refrigerators will tend to steer customers towards the refrigerator display. Veba AG, a German firm, represents a good example of how goals direct attention. The International OB on page 224 describes how the company is beginning to focus its goals on increasing shareholder value. This perspective is quite different from the typical "German model of business, where executives, banks, and labor decide behind closed doors what is best for a company."[43]

Goals Regulate Effort   Not only do goals make us selectively perceptive, they also motivate us to act. The instructor's deadline for turning in your term project would prompt you to complete it, as opposed to going out with friends, watching television, or studying for another course. Generally, the level of effort expended is proportionate to the difficulty of the goal.

I n t e r n a t i o n a l   O r g a n i z a t i o n a l   B e h a v i o u r

Japanese Organizations Begin to Reward Performance Instead of Seniority

Japan's full-time workers, meanwhile, have to work harder for pay. Toyota plans to widen the pay gap among managers of the same rank, allowing strong performers to earn up to $65,000 more than their peers. This will "encourage the competent to do a better job," a spokeswoman says. Honda Motor Corp. will adopt a "tenure" system for managers next year. A government survey finds 45% of companies plan to modify seniority-based pay systems to cut costs.

More than half of companies introducing performance-based salary structures haven't reduced pay for underperformers, says the Japan Productivity Center for Socio-Economic Development.

SOURCE   M Kanabayashi, "More Cracks Appear in Japan's Cradle-to-grave Employment System," *The Wall Street Journal*, August 20, 1996, p A1.

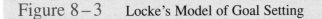

Figure 8–3   Locke's Model of Goal Setting

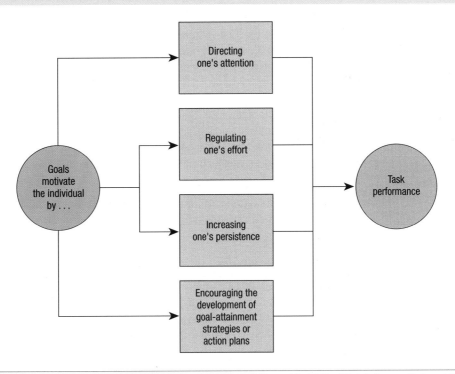

Source: Adapted from discussion in E A Locke and G P Latham, *A Theory of Goal Setting & Task Performance* (Englewood Cliffs, NJ: Prentice-Hall, 1990). Reprinted by permission of Prentice Hall, Inc.

Persistence

Extent to which effort is expended on a task over time.

Goals Increase Persistence   Within the context of goal setting, **persistence** represents the effort expended on a task over an extended period of time. It takes effort to run 100 metres; it takes persistence to run a 42 km marathon. Persistent people tend to see obstacles as challenges to be overcome rather than as reasons to fail. A difficult goal that is important to an individual is a constant reminder to keep exerting effort in the appropriate direction. Astronaut Jim Lovell represents a great example of someone who persisted at his goals. Lovell commanded NASA's ill-fated Apollo 13 mission that almost did not return from deep space. Here is what Lovell had to say about his career during an interview:

"When you look at the end result today," he explains, "it's easy to think that it was nothing but smooth sailing all the way. But perseverance was absolutely essential to getting to where I am… not only did I fail to get into the Naval Academy the first time I tried—I barely made it as the first alternate the second time. Then to be the only one of 32 guys to flunk the physical for the Mercury Program—you can imagine how that sets you back. But I persevered, and that's why I made it when I got the second shot.

"There are three traits that I think are absolutely essential to achieving success, and the first one is perseverance."[44]

Goals Foster Strategies and Action Plans   If you are here and your goal is out there somewhere, you face the problem of getting from here to there. For example, the person who has resolved to lose 9 kg must develop a plan for getting from "here" (his or her present weight) to "there" (9 kg lighter). Goals can help because they encourage people to develop strategies and action plans that enable them to achieve their goals.[45] By virtue of setting a weight-reduction goal, the dieter may choose a strategy of exercising more, eating less, or some combination of the two. For a work-related example, consider the strategies and plans used by Barbara Smith to develop and grow a new restaurant. Smith was a previous cabaret singer, play producer, author, actress, television spokesperson, and the first African-American on the cover of *Mademoiselle*:

> "When I returned to the [United States] from Vienna I decided to really go for it, so I wrote down my goals and figured out exactly how I was going to get there."
>
> Unlike some celebrity restaurateurs who show up for opening night only to follow the paparazzi to the next media event, Smith has been hands-on from the outset. To begin with she talked a prospective partner into letting her work at another restaurant from pre-opening day through its first year of business. Starting out as a hostess, she studied every aspect of running the restaurant, eventually working her way up to being floor manager. At the end of the year Smith had so impressed the prospective boosters with her cost-consciousness, attention to detail, and aptitude for building a customer base that she received the go-ahead to find an appropriate space to locate B Smith's.[46]

Barbara Smith's strategies and plans paid good dividends. This year her New York restaurant celebrated its 10th anniversary and she has since opened a second restaurant in Washington DC.

Insights from Goal-Setting Research

Research consistently has supported goal setting as a motivational technique. Setting performance goals increases individual, group, and organizational performance. Further, the positive effects of goal setting were found in countries or regions such as Australia, Canada, the Caribbean, England, Germany, and Japan. Goal setting works in different cultures. Reviews of the many goal-setting studies conducted over the last couple of decades have given managers five practical insights:

Goal difficulty

The amount of effort required to meet a goal.

1. *Difficult goals lead to higher performance.* **Goal difficulty** reflects the amount of effort required to meet a goal. It is more difficult to sell nine cars a month than it is to sell three cars a month. A meta-analysis spanning 4,000 people and 65 separate studies revealed that goal difficulty was positively related to performance.[47] As illustrated in Figure 8–4, however, the positive relationship between goal difficulty and performance breaks down when goals are perceived to be impossible. Figure 8–4 reveals that performance goes up when employees are given hard goals as opposed to easy or moderate goals (section A). Performance then plateau (section B) and drops (section C) as the difficulty of a goal goes from challenging to impossible.[48]

International Organizational Behaviour

Veba AG Directs Its Attention to Shareholder Value

Ulrich Hartmann, the chief executive of industrial giant Veba AG, is doing something unheard of in Germany: He's worrying about shareholder value.

He has laid off thousands of workers, fired longtime managers, and closed divisions that date back to Veba's beginnings—all in the name of investors. "Our commitment," he said in last year's annual report, "is to create value for you, our shareholders."

The developments at Veba, Germany's fourth-largest company in revenue terms, underscore a trend catching hold in German boardrooms. Mr. Hartmann believes the trend will pick up in Germany if only, he says, because the pursuit of shareholder value is in everyone's interest.

"Satisfying the shareholders is the best way to make sure that other stakeholders are served as well," he says. "It does no good when all the jobs are at sick companies"

SOURCE   G Steinmetz, "Changing Values: Satisfying Shareholders Is a Hot New Concept at Some German Firms," *The Wall Street Journal*, March 6, 1996, p A1.

Figure 8 – 4   Relationship between Goal Difficulty and Performance

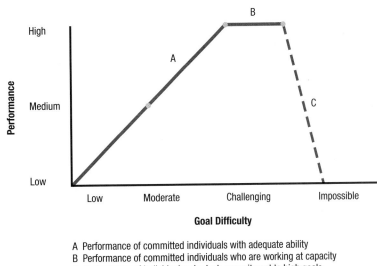

A Performance of committed individuals with adequate ability
B Performance of committed individuals who are working at capacity
C Performance of individuals who lack commitment to high goals

Source: E A Locke and G P Latham, *Goal Setting: A Motivational Technique That Works!* © 1984, p 22. Reprinted by permission of Prentice Hall, Inc., Englewood Cliffs, NJ.

Goal specificity

Quantifiability of a goal.

2. *Specific, difficult goals may or may not lead to higher performance.* **Goal specificity** pertains to the quantifiability of a goal. For example, a goal of selling nine cars a month is more specific than telling a salesperson to do his or her best. In an early review of goal-setting research, 99 of 110 studies (90 per cent) found that specific, hard goals led to better performance than did easy, medium, do-your-best, or no goals. This result was confirmed in a meta-analysis of 70 studies conducted between 1966 and 1984, involving 7,407 people.[49]

In contrast to these positive effects, several recent studies demonstrated that setting specific, difficult goals leads to poorer performance under certain circumstances. For example, a meta-analysis of 125 studies indicated that goal-setting effects were strongest for easy tasks and weakest for complex tasks.[50] There are two explanations for this finding. First, employees are not likely to put forth increased effort to achieve complex goals unless they "buy-in" or support them.[51] Thus, it is important for managers to obtain employee buy-in to the goal-setting process. Second, novel and complex tasks take employees longer to complete. This occurs because employees spend more time thinking about how to approach and solve these tasks. In contrast, employees do not have to spend much time thinking about solutions for easy tasks. Specific difficult goals thus impair performance on novel, complex tasks when employees do not have clear strategies for solving these types of problems. On a positive note, however, a recent study demonstrated that goal setting led to gradual improvements in performance on complex tasks when people were encouraged to explicitly solve the problem at hand.[52]

Finally, positive effects of goal setting also were reduced when people worked on interdependent tasks.[53] Managers need to encourage cooperation and efficient work flow in these situations.

3. *Feedback enhances the effect of specific, difficult goals.* Feedback plays a key role in all of our lives. For example, consider the role of feedback in bowling. Imagine going to the bowling lanes only to find that someone had hung a sheet from the ceiling to the floor in front of the pins. How likely is it that you would reach your goal score or typical bowling average? Not likely, given your inability to see the pins. Regardless of your goal, you would have to guess where to throw your second ball if you did not get a strike on your first shot. The same principles apply at work.

Feedback lets people know if they are headed towards their goals or if they are off course and need to redirect their efforts. Goals plus feedback is the recommended approach.[54] Goals inform people about performance standards and expectations so that they can channel their energies accordingly. In turn, feedback provides the information needed to adjust direction, effort, and strategies for goal accomplishment.

4. *Participative goals, assigned goals, and self-set goals are equally effective.* Both managers and researchers are interested in identifying the best way to set goals. Should goals be participatively set, assigned, or set by the employee him- or herself? A summary of goal-setting research indicated that no single approach was consistently more effective than others in increasing performance.[55]

Managers are advised to use a contingency approach by picking a method that seems best suited for the individual and situation at hand. For example, employees'preferences for participation should be considered. Some employees desire to participate in the process of setting goals, whereas others do not. Employees are also more likely to respond positively to the opportunity to participate in goal setting when they have greater task information, higher levels of experience and training, and greater levels of task involvement. Finally, a participative approach helps reduce employees'resistance to goal setting.

Goal commitment

Amount of commitment to achieving a goal.

5. *Goal commitment and monetary incentives affect goal-setting outcomes.* **Goal commitment** is the extent to which an individual is personally committed to achieving a goal. In general, an individual is expected to persist in attempts to accomplish a goal when he or she is committed to it. Researchers are currently debating the process by which goal commitment affects performance.[56] Some contend that goal commitment moderates the relationship between the difficulty of a goal and performance. That is, difficult goals lead to higher performance only when employees are committed to their goals. Conversely, difficult goals lead to lower performance when people are not committed to their goals. Other researchers contend that goal commitment directly affects performance. Although evidence can be presented to support both positions, recent research supports the prediction that goal commitment moderates the relationship between goal level and performance.[57] A meta-analysis of 78 studies covering 17,607 people also demonstrated that goal commitment did not directly influence performance.[58]

Like goal setting, the use of monetary incentives to motivate employees is seldom questioned. Unfortunately, recent research uncovered some negative consequences when goal achievement is linked to individual incentives. Case studies, for example, reveal that pay should not be linked to goal achievement unless (a) performance goals are under the employees'control; (b) goals are quantitative and measurable; and (c) frequent, relatively large payments are made for performance achievement.[59] Goal-based incentive systems are more likely to produce undesirable effects if these three conditions are not satisfied.

Moreover, empirical studies demonstrated that goal-based bonus incentives produced higher commitment to easy goals and lower commitment to difficult goals. People were reluctant to commit to difficult goals that were tied to monetary incentives. People with high goal commitment also offered less help to their co-workers when they received goal-based bonus incentives to accomplish difficult individual goals. Individuals neglected aspects of the job that were not covered in the performance goals.[60] As another case in point, several studies revealed that quality suffered when employees were given quantity goals.[61]

These findings underscore some of the dangers of using goal-based incentives, particularly for employees in complex, interdependent jobs requiring cooperation. Managers need to consider the advantages, disadvantages, and dilemmas of goal-based incentives prior to implementation.

Practical Application of Goal Setting

There are three general steps to follow when implementing a goal-setting programme. Serious deficiencies in one step cannot make up for strength in the other two. The three steps need to be implemented in a systematic fashion.

Step 1: Set Goals   A number of sources can be used as input during this goal-setting stage. Time and motion studies are one source. Goals also may be based on the average past performance of job holders. Third, the employee and his or her manager may set the goal participatively, through give-and-take negotiation. Fourth, goal setting often is constrained by external factors. For example, the production schedule of a firm with a government contract may be dictated largely by the terms of that agreement. Finally, the overall strategy of a company (e.g., become the lowest-cost producer) may affect the goals set by employees at various levels in the organization.

In accordance with available research evidence, goals should be specific and difficult, yet attainable through persistent effort. For complex tasks, however, managers should train employees in problem-solving techniques and encourage them to develop a performance action plan. Action plans specify the strategies or tactics to be used in order to accomplish the goal.[62]

Goal specificity can be achieved by stating goals in quantitative terms (e.g., units of output, cash, or per cent of desired increase or decrease). With respect to measuring performance, it is important to achieve a workable balance between quantity and quality. Well-conceived goals also have a built-in time limit or deadline. Priorities need to be established in multiple-goal situations.

Finally, because of individual differences in skills and abilities, it may be necessary to establish different goals for employees performing the same job. For example, a study of 91 sales representatives revealed that individuals high in conscientiousness set more difficult goals, were more committed to goals, and achieved greater sales volume than employees low in conscientiousness. A second study demonstrated that more difficult goals were set by individuals with high rather than low task abilities.[63] If an employee has low conscientiousness or lacks the ability to perform the job, then progressively harder developmental goals may be in order. But this practice may create feelings of inequity among co-workers, necessitating other alternatives. For example, inability to perform at the standard may suggest a training deficiency or the need to transfer the individual to another job. In any event, managers need to keep in mind that motivation diminishes when people continually fail to meet their goals.

Step 2: Promote Goal Commitment   Obtaining goal commitment is important because employees are more motivated to pursue goals they view as reasonable, obtainable, and fair. Goal commitment may be increased by using one or more of the following techniques:

1. Provide an explanation for why the organization is implementing a goal-setting programme.

2. Present the corporate goals, and explain how and why an individual's personal goals support them.

3. Have employees establish their own goals and action plans. Encourage them to set challenging, stretch goals. Goals should not be impossible.

4. Train managers in how to conduct participative goal-setting sessions, and train

employees in how to develop effective action plans.

5. Be supportive, and do not use goals to threaten employees.

6. Set goals that are under the employees' control, and provide them with the necessary resources.

7. Provide monetary incentives or other rewards for accomplishing goals.

Step 3: Provide Support and Feedback   Step 3 calls for providing employees with the necessary support elements or resources to get the job done. This includes ensuring that each employee has the necessary abilities and information to reach his or her goals. As a pair of goal-setting experts succinctly stated, "Motivation without knowledge is useless."[64] Training often is required to help employees achieve difficult goals. Moreover, managers should pay attention to employees' perceptions of effort→performance expectancies, self-efficacy, and valence of rewards. Finally, as we discuss in detail in Chapter 9 employees should be provided with timely, specific feedback (knowledge of results) on how they are doing.

Putting Motivational Theories to Work

Successfully designing and implementing motivational programmes is not easy. Managers cannot simply take one of the theories discussed in this book and apply it word for word. Dynamics within organizations interfere with applying motivation theories in "pure" form. According to management scholar Terence Mitchell,

> There are situations and settings that make it exceptionally difficult for a motivational system to work. These circumstances may involve the kinds of jobs or people present, the technology, the presence of a union, and so on. The factors that hinder the application of motivational theory have not been articulated either frequently or systematically.[65]

With Mitchell's cautionary statement in mind, this section uses the systems model of motivation and performance introduced in Chapter 7, which is shown once again in Figure 8–5, to raise issues that need to be addressed before implementing a motivational program. Our intent is not to discuss all relevant considerations but rather to highlight a few important ones.

Assuming a motivational programme is being considered to improve productivity, quality, or customer satisfaction, the first issue revolves around the difference between motivation and performance. As pointed out in Chapter 7, motivation and performance are not one and the same. Motivation is only one of several factors that influence performance. For example, poor performance may be more a function of outdated or inefficient materials and machinery, not having goals to direct one's attention, a monotonous job, feelings of inequity, a negative work environment characterized by political behaviour and conflict, poor supervisory support and coaching, or poor work flow. Motivation cannot make up for deficient inputs (see Figure 8–5) or inappropriate use of the transformational elements. For example, employees are unlikely to identify safety issues if they feel punished for doing so.

Importantly, managers should not ignore the individual differences discussed in Chapter 5. Figure 8–5 clearly indicates that individual differences are an important input that influences performance. Managers are advised to develop and nurture positive employee characteristics, such as self-esteem, self-efficacy, positive emotions, and need for achievement.

Because motivation is goal directed, the process of developing and setting goals should be consistent with our previous discussion. Moreover, the method used to evaluate performance also needs to be considered. Without a valid performance appraisal system,

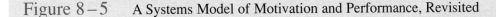

Figure 8–5   A Systems Model of Motivation and Performance, Revisited

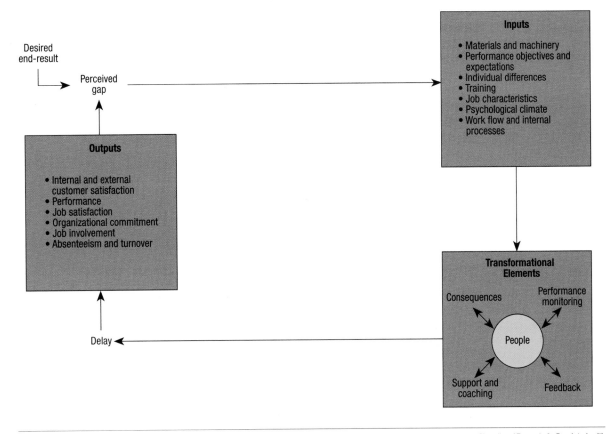

it is difficult, if not impossible, to accurately distinguish good and poor performers. Managers need to keep in mind that both equity and expectancy theory suggest that employee motivation is squelched by inaccurate performance ratings. Inaccurate ratings also make it difficult to evaluate the effectiveness of any motivational programme, so it is beneficial for managers to assess the accuracy and validity of their appraisal systems.

Consistent with expectancy theory and the principles of behaviour modification discussed in Chapter 15 managers should make rewards contingent on performance. In doing so, it is important that managers consider the accuracy and fairness of the reward system. As discussed under expectancy theory, the promise of increased rewards will not prompt higher effort and good performance unless those rewards are clearly tied to performance. Moreover, equity theory tells us that motivation is influenced by employee perceptions about the fairness of reward allocations. Motivation is decreased when employees believe rewards are inequitably allocated. Rewards also need to be integrated appropriately into the appraisal system. If performance is measured at the individual level, individual achievements need to be rewarded. On the other hand, when performance is the result of group effort, rewards should be allocated to the group.

Feedback also should be linked with performance. Feedback provides the information and direction needed to keep employees focused on relevant tasks, activities, and goals. Managers should strive to provide specific, timely, and accurate feedback to employees.

Finally, an organization's culture significantly influences employee motivation and behaviour. A positive self-enhancing culture is more likely to engender higher motivation and commitment than a culture dominated by suspicion, fault finding, and blame.

We end this chapter with the following case on Disneyland Paris:

To improve motivation, morale and quality of service provided to visitors, France's Disneyland Paris has launched "Small World," named after one of its attractions:

The whole idea is to improve motivation through a process of decentralising power, cutting down hierarchy and creating internal competition between different parts of the park—although within certain limits. The park's operations will be split into "small world" units of 30–50 staff, headed by a manager. Each will be given greater responsibility and flexibility than in the past to meet three goals: to achieve management targets, improve visitor satisfaction and get to know and motivate staff. Small world managers may receive up to 10 per cent of their salary in bonuses linked to performance. Other staff will receive nonfinancial rewards, including improved promotion prospects.[66]

Summary of Key Concepts

1. *Discuss the role of perceived inequity in employee motivation.* Equity theory is a model of motivation that explains how people strive for fairness and justice in social exchanges. On the job, feelings of inequity revolve around a person's evaluation of whether he or she receives adequate rewards to compensate for his or her contributive inputs. People perform these evaluations by comparing the perceived fairness of their employment exchange with that of relevant others. Perceived inequity creates motivation to restore equity.

2. *Distinguish between positive and negative inequity.* Equity exists for an individual when his or her ratio of perceived outcomes to inputs is equal to the ratio of outcomes to inputs for a relevant co-worker. If the comparison co-worker enjoys greater outcomes for similar inputs, negative inequity will be perceived. Positive inequity is experienced when an individual's outcome to input ratio is greater than that of a relevant co-worker. People have a lower tolerance for negative inequity than they do for positive inequity.

3. *Describe the practical lessons derived from equity theory.* Equity theory has at least seven practical implications. First, because people are motivated to resolve perceptions of inequity, managers should not discount employees' feelings and perceptions when trying to motivate workers. Second, managers should pay attention to employees' perceptions of what is fair and equitable. It is the employee's view of reality that counts when trying to motivate someone, according to equity theory. Third, employees should be given a voice in decisions that affect them. Fourth, employees should be given the opportunity to appeal decisions that affect their welfare. Fifth, employees are more likely to accept and support organizational change when they believe it is implemented fairly and when it produces equitable outcomes. Sixth, managers can promote cooperation and teamwork among group members by treating them equitably. Finally, treating employees inequitably can lead to litigation and costly court settlements.

4. *Explain Vroom's expectancy theory.* Expectancy theory assumes motivation is determined by one's perceived chances of achieving valued outcomes. Vroom's expectancy model of motivation reveals how effort→performance expectancies and performance→outcome instrumentalities influence the degree of effort expended to achieve desired (positively valent) outcomes.

5. *Discuss Porter and Lawler's expectancy theory of motivation.* Porter and Lawler developed a model of expectancy that expanded upon the theory proposed by Vroom. This model specifies (*a*) the source of people's valences and expectancies and (*b*) the relationship between performance and satisfaction.

6. *Describe the practical implications of expectancy theory of motivation.* Managers are advised to enhance effort→performance expectancies by helping employees accomplish their performance goals. With respect to instrumentalities and valences, managers should attempt to link employee performance and valued rewards. There are four prerequisites to linking performance and rewards: (*a*) managers need to develop and communicate performance standards to employees, (*b*) managers need valid and accurate performance ratings, (*c*) managers need to determine the relative mix of individual versus team contribution to performance and then reward accordingly, and (*d*) managers should use performance ratings to differentially allocate rewards among employees.

7. *Explain how goal setting motivates an individual.* Four motivational mechanisms of goal setting are: (*a*) goals direct one's attention, (*b*) goals regulate effort, (*c*) goals increase one's persistence, and (*d*) goals encourage development of goal-attainment strategies and action plans.

8. *Identify five practical lessons to be learned from goal-setting research.* Difficult goals lead to higher performance than easy or moderate goals: goals should not be impossible to achieve. Second, specific, difficult goals may or may not

lead to higher performance. Third, feedback enhances the effect of specific, difficult goals. Fourth, participative goals, assigned goals, and self-set goals are equally effective. Fifth, goal commitment and monetary incentives affect goal-setting outcomes.

9. *Specify issues that should be addressed before implementing a motivational programme.* Managers need to consider the variety of causes of poor performance and employee misbehaviour. Undesirable employee performance and behaviour may be due to a host of deficient inputs (materials and machinery, performance objectives and expectations, individual differences, training, job characteristics, psychological climate, and work flow and internal processes) and poorly executed transformational elements (performance monitoring, feedback, support and coaching, and consequences). Managers should also recognize that employee motivation and behaviour are influenced by organizational culture.

Discussion Questions

1. Have you experienced positive or negative inequity at work? Describe the circumstances in terms of the inputs and outcomes of the comparison person and yourself.

2. Could a manager's attempt to treat his or her employees equally lead to perceptions of inequity? Explain.

3. What work outcomes (refer to Table 8–1) are most important to you? Do you think different age groups value different outcomes? What are the implications for managers who seek to be equitable?

4. Relative to Table 8–2, what techniques have you relied on recently to reduce either positive or negative inequity?

5. What is your definition of studying hard? What is your expectancy for earning an A on the next exam in this course? What is the basis of this expectancy?

6. If someone who reported to you at work had a low expectancy for successful performance, what could you do to increase this person's expectancy?

7. Do goals play an important role in your life? Explain.

8. How would you respond to a manager who said, "Goals must be participatively set?"

9. Goal-setting research suggests that people should be given difficult goals. How does this prescription mesh with expectancy theory? Explain.

10. How could a professor use equity, expectancy, and goal-setting theory to motivate students? Have you experienced positive or negative inequity at work? Describe the circumstances in terms of the inputs and outcomes of the comparison person and yourself.

Personal Awareness and Growth Exercise

What Outcomes Motivate Employees?

Objectives

1. To determine how accurately you perceive the outcomes that motivate nonmanagerial employees.

2. To examine the managerial implications of inaccurately assessing employee motivators.

Introduction

One thousand employees were given a list of 10 outcomes people want from their work. They were asked to rank these items from most important to least important.[67] We are going to have you estimate how you think these workers ranked the various outcomes. This will enable you to compare your perceptions with the average rankings documented by a researcher. The survey results are presented in note 68 at the end of this chapter. Please do not read them until indicated.

Instructions

Below is a list of 10 outcomes people want from their work. Read the list, and then rank each item according to how you think the typical nonmanagerial employee would rank them. Rank the outcomes from 1 to 10; 1 = Most important and 10 = Least important. (Please do this now before reading the rest of these instructions.) After you have completed your ranking, calculate the discrepancy between your perceptions and the actual results. Take the absolute value of the difference between your ranking and the actual ranking for each item, and then add them to get a total discrepancy score. For example, if you gave job security a ranking of 1, your discrepancy score would be 3 because the actual ranking was 4. The lower your discrepancy score, the more accurate your perception of the typical employee's needs. The actual rankings are shown in note 68. How do you believe the typical nonmanagerial employee would rank these outcomes?

_____ Full appreciation of work done
_____ Job security
_____ Good working conditions
_____ Feeling of being in on things
_____ Good wages
_____ Tactful discipline
_____ Personal loyalty to employees
_____ Interesting work
_____ Sympathetic help with personal problems
_____ Promotion and growth in the organization

1. **Were your perceptions accurate? Why or why not?**

2. **What would expectancy theory suggest you should do?**

3. **Based on the size of your discrepancy, what does the systems model of motivation and performance in Figure 8–5 suggest will happen to satisfaction and commitment?**

4. **Would you generalize the actual survey results to all nonmanagerial employees? Why or why not?**

Group Exercise

The Case of the Missing Form

Objectives

1. To give you practice at diagnosing the causes of a performance problem by using the systems model of motivation and performance.
2. To apply one of the motivation models discussed in Chapters 7 and 8 in order to solve a performance problem.

Introduction

Managers frequently encounter performance problems. These problems might represent incidents such as missed deadlines, poor quality, inadequate levels of performance, excessive time off, cynical or negative behaviour, and lack of cooperation with team members. As we discussed in both this chapter and Chapter 7, motivation is only one factor in these types of performance problems. As such, managers must learn how to diagnose the cause(s) of performance problems prior to trying to solve them. The following case provides you this opportunity. After diagnosing the cause(s) of the performance problem, you will be asked to solve it. The models of motivation presented in Chapters 7 and 8 provide useful frameworks for generating solutions.

Instructions

Your instructor will divide the class into groups of four to six. You should first read the case provided. Once all group members are finished, meet as a group to discuss the case. Begin your discussion by brainstorming a list of potential causes of the performance problem. Use the systems model of motivation and performance shown in Figure 8–5 to conduct this brainstorming activity. Be sure to consider whether each and every input and transformational element are possible causes of the problem. Once the group has identified the causes of the performance problem, the group should answer the discussion questions that follow the case.

The Case of the Missing Form[69]

S	M	T	W	T	F	S
			MAY			
				1	2	3	4
5	6	7	8	9	10	11
12	13	14	15	16	17	18
19	20	21	22	23	24	25
26	27	28	29	30	31	

S	M	T	W	T	F	S
			JUNE			
						1
2	3	4	5	6	7	8
9	10	11	12	13	14	15
16	17	18	19	20	21	22
23	24	25	26	27	28	29
30						

Ann Anders has been manager of Training and Development at TYCO Financial Services for 3 years. (Ann has been with TYCO 21 years.) She has 10 professional level training employees reporting to her.

Her boss, Joyce Davis, Director of Training, asked Ann to put together a new cost benefit analysis package on a project Ann had completed. This was not a requirement for Ann by her previous boss; training has never been measured in terms of money.

Joyce explained that she wanted Ann to document the savings that the "Customer Dispute Resolution" training program had produced so she could share it with her peers in the other divisions of TYCO. She wanted to formalize the practice of preparing a cost benefit analysis (CBA) format because this was something no one else had done. She directed Ann to further research the numbers to validate the findings and put it into a form (Joyce's idea of a form was a page with lines and boxes). It was Wednesday, May 15th; Joyce was leaving for a meeting in New York at 8:00 am Monday, May 20th. She wanted to take this assignment with her. Joyce asked Ann to see her Friday with her progress.

On Thursday, Ann met with the Performance Engineering department at TYCO and shared with Joyce a format they were currently using on their projects. Ann agreed to apply that process to her training project. Joyce was pleased with the progress.

Ann returned to Joyce on Friday, May 17th, with the formula for the training CBA typed on a plain white page. Joyce acknowledged the work to prepare the calculations and again asked if Ann could create a form. Joyce had to catch her airplane first thing Monday morning and knew she would not have time to review a second document. Joyce took the work Ann had completed; however, she decided to stall until the next monthly meeting in June to present the idea.

The following week, on May 27th, Joyce explained to Ann that there was not enough time to discuss her CBA so she would do it next month. Joyce asked Ann for additional information that needed to be gathered to effectively document the project and set a new completion date, June 10th: only one week prior to the June 17th meeting.

Ann returned on June 10th with more calculations that were thoroughly documented. Joyce was happy to see the additional research. However, she was disappointed because the format had not yet been put into a professional "form." Joyce then took out a piece of paper and wrote the sections for Ann so she could better understand what she wanted.

Joyce felt confident that Ann understood what she wanted. Joyce, in order to give Ann the maximum time to get it right this time, said she needed the document no later than the end of the day Friday, June 14th.

The end of the day Friday, June 14th, Ann walked into Joyce's office proudly displaying this neatly typed document. However, there were no lines or boxes as you would see on a traditional business form. Joyce said "This is not in a form! I'll take it home over the weekend and bring you the revision Monday morning, you can then fax me the changes at the meeting."

Joyce then took 15 to 20 minutes Sunday to draw out the lines and reformat the information for ease of reading and to create a professional image for the product. On Monday morning Joyce stopped by and gave the changes to her secretary to finish. Ann faxed the changes. Joyce presented "the form" at the meeting, and it had the positive impact she expected.

After the meeting, Joyce reflected on Ann's problem. After 21 years with this company and 3 years as a manager, why couldn't Ann create something as simple as a business form? Joyce is trying to determine the root cause(s) of Ann's poor performance.

QUESTIONS FOR DISCUSSION

1. What are the causes of Ann's poor performance? Explain your rationale.

2. Based on the causes you identified, how would you keep the problem from happening again?

3. Which of the motivation models discussed in Chapters 7 and 8 are most relevant for solving this problem? Why?

4. How would you use the model identified in question 3 to improve Ann's future performance? Be sure to specifically discuss how you would apply the model.

Notes

[1] Excerpted from L Grant, "Stirring It Up at Campbell," *Fortune,* May 13, 1996, p 82. © 1996 Time Inc. All rights reserved.

[2] See L Festinger, *A Theory of Cognitive Dissonance* (Stanford, CA: Stanford University Press, 1957).

[3] See E Nelson, "Work Week: A Special News Report about Life on the Job—and Trends Taking Shape There," *The Wall Street Journal,* February 6, 1996, p A1.

[4] The generalizability of the equity norm was examined by K I Kim, H-J Park, and N Suzuki, "Reward Allocations in the United States, Japan, and Korea: A Comparison of Individualistic and Collectivistic Cultures," *Academy of Management Journal,* March 1990, pp 188–98.

[5] R P Vecchio, "Models of Psychological Inequity," *Organizational Behavior and Human Performance,* October 1984, p 268. (Emphasis added.)

[6] The choice of a comparison person is discussed by P M Sias and F M Jablin, "Differential Superior-Subordinate Relations, Perceptions of Fairness, and Coworker Communication," *Human Communication Research,* September 1995, pp 5–38; and J Greenberg and C L McCarty, "Comparable Worth: A Matter of Justice," in *Research in Personnel and Human Resources Management,* eds G R Ferris and K M Rowland (Greenwich, CT: JAI Press, Inc., 1990), vol. 8, pp 265–303.

[7] C Duff, "Top Executives Ponder High Pay, Decide They're Worth Every Cent," *The Wall Street Journal,* May 13, 1996, p B1.

[8] Based on and translated from M Buelens, "De schaamte voorbij,"

Trends, March 28, 1996.

[9]Based on and translated from "De miljoenen van de baas," *Knack,* April 26, 1995.

[10]Duff, op.cit.

[11]See R S Lapidus and L Pinketon, "Customer Complaint Situations: An Equity Theory Perspective," *Psychology & Marketing,* March 1995, pp 105–22; and L A Witt and L G Nye, "Gender and the Relationship between Perceived Fairness of Pay or Promotion and Job Satisfaction," *Journal of Applied Psychology,* December 1992, pp 910–17.

[12]Adapted from a discussion in R L Opsahl and M D Dunnette, "The Role of Financial Compensation in Industrial Motivation," *Psychological Bulletin,* August 1966, pp 94–118.

[13]Supportive results can be found in J B Olson-Buchanan, "Voicing Discontent: What Happens to the Grievance Filer After the Grievance?" *Journal of Applied Psychology,* February 1996, pp 52–63; and V Scarpello and F F Jones, "Why Justice Matters in Compensation Decision Making," *Journal of Organizational Behavior,* May 1996, pp 285–99.

[14]Results can be found in R W Griffeth, R P Vecchio, and J W Logan, Jr., "Equity Theory and Interpersonal Attraction," *Journal of Applied Psychology,* June 1989, pp 394–401; and R P Vecchio, "Predicting Worker Performance in Inequitable Settings," *Academy of Management Review,* January 1982, pp 103–10.

[15]See J Greenberg, "Stealing in the Name of Justice: Informational and Interpersonal Moderators of Theft Reactions to Underpayment Inequity," *Organizational Behavior and Human Decision Process,* February 1993, pp 81–103.

[16]See H J Sapienza and M A Korsgaard, "Procedural Justice in Entrepreneur-Investor Relations," *Academy of Management Journal,* June 1996, pp 544–74; C Martin and N Bennett, "The Role of Justice Judgments in Explaining the Relationship between Job Satisfaction and Organizational Commitment," *Group & Organization Management,* March 1996, pp 84–104; and L P Livingstone, J A Roberts, L B Chonko, "Perceptions of Internal and External Equity as Predictors of Outside Salespeoples' Job Satisfaction," *Journal of Personal Selling & Sales Management,* Spring 1995, pp 33–46.

[17]Supporting studies were conducted by P D Sweeney and D B McFarlin, "Workers' Evaluations of the "Ends" and the "Means": An Examination of Four Models of Distributive and Procedural Justice," *Organizational Behavior and Human Decision Processes,* June 1993, pp 23–40; and R C Dailey and D J Kirk, "Distributive and Procedural Justice as Antecedents of Job Dissatisfaction and Intent to Turnover," March 1992, pp 305–18.

[18]This study was conducted by M A Korsgaard, D M Schweiger, and H J Sapienza, "Building Commitment, Attachment, and Trust in Strategic Decision-Making Teams: The Role of Procedural Justice," *Academy of Management Journal,* February 1995, pp 60–84.

[19]Results can be found in J D Leck, D M Saunders, and M Charbonneau, "Affirmative Action Programs: An Organizational Justice Perspective," *Journal of Organizational Behavior,* January 1996, pp 79–89.

[20]See M A Korsgaard and L Roberson, "Procedural Justice in Performance Evaluation: The Role of Instrumental and Non-Instrumental Voice in Performance Appraisal Discussions," *Journal of Management,* 1995, pp 657–69.

[21]The role of equity in organizational change is thoroughly discussed by A T Cobb, R Folger, and K Wooten, "The Role Justice Plays in Organizational Change," *Public Administration Quarterly,* Summer 1995, pp 135–51.

[22]The impact of individual and group values on justice perceptions was examined by J Giacobbe-Miller, "A Test of the Group Values and Control Models of Procedural Justice from the Competing Perspectives of Labor and Management," *Personnel Psychology,* Spring 1995, pp 115–42.

[23]For a complete discussion of Vroom's theory, see V H Vroom, *Work and Motivation* (New York: John Wiley & Sons, 1964).

[24]E E Lawler III, *Motivation in Work Organizations* (Belmont, CA: Wadsworth, 1973), p 45.

[25]Based on and translated from "Amsterdamse Beurs geschokt door grootscheeps fraude onderzoek," *Financieel Economische Tijd,* October 28, 1997, p 7.

[26]See J Chowdhury, "The Motivational Impact of Sales Quotas on Effort," *Journal of Marketing Research,* February 1993, pp 28–41; and C C Pinder, *Work Motivation* (Glenview, IL: Scott, Foresman, 1984), ch 7.

[27]H B Fuller, "Helping Employees Do the Right Thing," *Chemical Week,* May 3, 1995, p 36.

[28]The measurement and importance of valence was investigated by N T Feather, "Values, Valences, and Choice: The Influence of Values on the Perceived Attractiveness and Choice of Alternatives," *Journal of Personality and Social Psychology,* June 1995, pp 1135–5; and A Pecotich and G A Churchill, Jr., "An Examination of the Anticipated-Satisfaction Importance Valence Controversy," Organizational Behavior and Human Performance, April 1981, pp 213–26.

[29]Excerpted from "Federal Express's Fred Smith," *Inc.,* October 1986, p 38.

[30]For a thorough discussion of the model, see L W Porter and E E Lawler III, *Managerial Attitudes and Performance* (Homewood, IL: Richard D. Irwin, 1968).

[31]These results are based on the following studies: J P Wanous, T L Keon, and J C Latack, "Expectancy Theory and Occupational/Organizational Choices: A Review and Test," *Organizational Behavior and Human Performance,* August 1983, pp 66–86; E D Pulakos and N Schmitt, "A Longitudinal Study of a Valence Model Approach for the Prediction of Job Satisfaction of New Employees," *Journal of Applied Psychology,* May 1983, pp 307–12; A J Kinicki, "Predicting Occupational Role Choices for Involuntary Job Loss," *Journal of Vocational Behavior,* October 1989, pp 204–18; T A DeCotiis and J-Y LeLouarn, "A Predictive Study of Voting Behavior in a Representation Election Using Union Instrumentality and Work Perceptions," *Organizational Behavior and Human Performance,* February 1981, pp 103–18; P W Hom, "Expectancy Prediction of Reenlistment in the National Guard," *Journal of Vocational Behavior,* April 1980, pp 235–48; D F Parker and L Dyer, "Expectancy Theory as a Within-Person Behavioral Choice Model: An Empirical Test of Some Conceptual and Methodological Refinements," *Organizational Behavior and Human Performance,* October 1976, pp 97–117; A W Stacy, K F Widaman, and G A Marlatt, "Expectancy Models of Alcohol Use," *Journal of Personality and Social Psychology,* May 1990, pp 918–28; and W van Eerde and H Thierry, "Vroom's Expectancy Models and Work-Related Criteria: A Meta-Analysis," *Journal of Applied Psychology,* October 1996, pp 575–86.

[32]For reviews of the criticisms of expectancy theory, see F J Landy and W S Becker, "Motivation Theory Reconsidered," in *Research in Organizational Behavior,* vol. 9, eds L L Cummings and B M Staw (Greenwich, CT: JAI Press, 1987), pp 1–38; and T R Mitchell, "Expectancy Models of Job Satisfaction, Occupational Preference and Effort: A Theoretical, Methodological, and Empirical Appraisal," *Psychological Bulletin,* December 1974, pp 1053–77.

[33]Components of coaching are discussed by S R Levine, "Performance Coaching: Great Coaching Skills Help Build a Team of Champions," *Selling Power,* July/August 1996, p 46.

[34]Supportive results are presented in L Morris, "Employees Not Encouraged to Go Extra Mile," *Training & Development,* April

1996, pp 59–60; and "Crossed Wires on Employee Motivation," *Training & Development,* July 1995, pp 59–60.

[35] See D R Spitzer, "Power Rewards: Rewards That Really Motivate," *Management Review,* May 1996, pp 45–50; and A Kohn, *Punished by Rewards: The Trouble with Gold Stars, Incentive Plans, A's, Praise, and Other Bribes* (Boston: Houghton Mifflin Company, 1993).

[36] See S Kerr, "Risky Business: The New Pay Game," *Fortune,* July 22, 1996, pp 94–95.

[37] P Ancona, "Nice Bosses Often Don't Get Quality They Want," *The Arizona Daily Star,* February 8, 1993, p 9.

[38] See M Leshner, "Targeting Work Culture Leads to Winning Teams," *Best's Review,* February 1996, pp 51–55.

[39] E A Locke, K N Shaw, L M Saari, and G P Latham, "Goal Setting and Task Performance: 1969–1980," *Psychological Bulletin,* July 1981, p 126.

[40] Ibid.

[41] A thorough discussion of MBO is provided by P F Drucker, *The Practice of Management* (New York: Harper, 1954); and P F Drucker, "What Results Should You Expect? A User's Guide to MBO," *Public Administration Review,* January/February 1976, pp 12–19.

[42] Results from both studies can be found in R Rodgers and J E Hunter, "Impact of Management by Objectives on Organizational Productivity," *Journal of Applied Psychology,* April 1991, pp 322–36; and R Rodgers, J E Hunter, and D L Rogers, "Influence of Top Management Commitment on Management Program Success," *Journal of Applied Psychology,* February 1993, pp 151–55.

[43] G Steinmetz, "Changing Values: Satisfying Shareholders Is a Hot New Concept at Some German Firms," *The Wall Street Journal,* March 6, 1996, p A1.

[44] M Fleschner, "How High Can You Fly?" *Personal Selling Power,* November/December 1995, p 15.

[45] For an example of how to write a good action plan, see G Bachelor, "Your Master Plan of Action," *Selling Power,* September 1996, pp 92–93.

[46] M Fleschner, "Delicious Success: How a Small-Town Girl Turned Her Natural Good Looks and Invincible Spirit into Big City Success," *Selling Power*, April 1996, p 68.

[47] Results can be found in P M Wright, "Operationalization of Goal Difficulty as a Moderator of the Goal Difficulty-Performance Relationship," *Journal of Applied Psychology,* June 1990, pp 227–34. Supportive results from a more recent study can be found in P H White, M M Kjelgaard, S G Harkins, "Testing the Contribution of Self-Evaluation to Goal-Setting Effects," *Journal of Personality and Social Psychology,* July 1995, pp 69–79.

[48] This linear relationship was not supported by P M Wright, J R Hollenbeck, S Wolf, and G C McMahan, "The Effects of Varying Goal Difficulty Operationalizations on Goal Setting Outcomes and Processes," *Organizational Behavior and Human Decision Processes,* January 1995, pp 28–43.

[49] See Locke, Shaw, Saari, and Latham, "Goal Setting and Task Performance: 1969–1980"; and A J Mento, R P Steel, and R J Karren, "A Meta-Analytic Study of the Effects of Goal Setting on Task Performance: 1966–1984," *Organizational Behavior and Human Decision Processes,* February 1987, pp 52–83.

[50] Results from the meta-analysis can be found in R E Wood, A J Mento, and E A Locke, "Task Complexity as a Moderator of Goal Effects: A Meta-Analysis," *Journal of Applied Psychology*, August 1987, pp 416–25.

[51] See E L Deci, "On the Nature and Functions of Motivation Theories," *Psychological Science*, May 1992, pp 167–71.

[52] See R P DeShon and R A Alexander, "Goal Setting Effects on

Implicit and Explicit Learning of Complex Tasks," *Organizational Behavior and Human Decision Processes,* January 1996, pp 18–36.

[53] Results can be found in K H Doerr, T R Mitchell, T D Klastorin, and K A Brown, "Impact of Material Flow Policies and Goals on Job Outcomes," *Journal of Applied Psychology,* April 1996, pp 142–52.

[54] The positive effects of feedback are supported by M E Tubbs, D M Boehne, and J G Dahl, "Expectancy Valence and Motivational Force Functions in Goal-Setting Research: An Empirical Test," *Journal of Applied Psychology,* June 1993, pp 361–73; and Mento, Steel, and Karren, "A Meta-Analytic Study of the Effects of Goal Setting on Task Performance: 1966–1984."

[55] See E A Locke and G P Latham, *A Theory of Goal Setting & Task Performance* (Englewood Cliffs, NJ: Prentice-Hall, 1990).

[56] For a thorough discussion of this debate, see M E Tubbs, "Commitment as a Moderator of the Goal-Performance Relation: A Case for Clearer Construct Definition," *Journal of Applied Psychology,* February 1993, pp 86–97. Also see D A Harrison and L Z Liska, "Promoting Regular Exercise in Organizational Fitness Programs: Health-Related Differences in Motivational Building Blocks," *Personnel Psychology,* Spring 1994, pp 47–72.

[57] See B A Martin and D J Manning, Jr., "Combined Effects of Normative Information and Task Difficulty on the Goal Commitment-Performance Relationship," *Journal of Management,* 1995, pp 65–80.

[58] Results are presented in J C Wofford, V L Goodwin, and S Premack, "Meta-Analysis of the Antecedents of Personal Goal Level and of the Antecedents and Consequences of Goal Commitment," *Journal of Management,* September 1992, pp 595–615.

[59] See the related discussion in T P Flannery, D A Hofrichter, and P E Platten, *People, Performance, & Pay* (New York: The Free Press, 1996).

[60] See P M Wright, J M George, S R Farnsworth, and G C McMahan, "Productivity and Extra-Role Behavior: The Effects of Goals and Incentives on Spontaneous Helping," *Journal of Applied Psychology,* June 1993, pp 374–81; and P M Wright, "An Examination of the Relationships among Monetary Incentives, Goal Level, Goal Commitment, and Performance," *Journal of Management*, December 1992, pp 677–93.

[61] Supporting results can be found in S W Gilliland and R S Landis, "Quality and Quantity Goals in a Complex Decision Task: Strategies and Outcomes," *Journal of Applied Psychology,* October 1992, pp 672–81.

[62] The development of action plans are discussed by W E Goddard, "Making Stretch Goals Happen," *Modern Materials Handling*, March 1996, p 31.

[63] The relationship between conscientiousness and goal setting was examined by M R Barrick, M K Mount, and J P Strauss, "Conscientiousness and Performance of Sales Representatives: Test of the Mediating Effects of Goal Setting," *Journal of Applied Psychology,* October 1993, pp 715–22. Ability and goal difficulty was investigated by R J Vance and A Colella, "Effects of Two Types of Feedback on Goal Acceptance and Personal Goals," *Journal of Applied Psychology,* February 1990, pp 68–76.

[64] E A Locke and G P Latham, *Goal Setting: A Motivational Technique That Works!* (Englewood Cliffs, NJ: Prentice-Hall, 1984), p 79.

[65] T R Mitchell, "Motivation: New Directions for Theory, Research, and Practice," *Academy of Management Review,* January 1982, p 81.

[66] A Jack "Big Stackes in a 'small world' - Andrew Jack looks at the latest to attempt to improve performance at Euro Disney," *The Financial Times* , January 13, 1995, p12.

[67]Results from this study are reported in K A Kovach, "What Motivates Employees? Workers and Supervisors Give Different Answers," *Business Horizons,* September–October 1987, pp 58–65.

[68]Actual survey rankings are as follows: (1) interesting work, (2) full appreciation of work done, (3) feeling of being in on things, (4) job security, (5) good wages, (6) promotion and growth in the organization, (7) good working conditions, (8) personal loyalty to employees, (9) tactful discipline, and (10) sympathetic help with personal problems.

[69]Reprinted by permission of Kinicki and Associates, Inc. "The Case of the Missing Form," by A Kinicki, *Performance Management Systems,* pp 3–34, 3–35. Copyright © 1992 by Kinicki and Associates, Inc.; all rights reserved.

Nine

Improving Job Performance with Feedback and Rewards

LEARNING OBJECTIVES

When you finish studying the material in this chapter, you should be able to:

1. Specify the two basic functions of feedback and three sources of feedback.

2. Discuss how the recipient's characteristics, perceptions, and cognitive evaluations affect how the individual processes feedback.

3. List at least three practical lessons from feedback research.

4. Define upward feedback and 360-degree feedback, and summarize the general tips for giving good feedback.

5. Briefly explain the four different organizational reward norms, and summarize the reasons rewards often fail to motivate employees.

6. Discuss the impact that incentive bonuses have on employee motivation and performance.

7. Distinguish among profit sharing, gainsharing, and team-based pay.

8. Discuss how managers can generally improve pay-for-performance plans.

Management: Turning the Tables

If you want to find out whether a manager is doing a good job, how would you go about it? You could ask their boss, you could ask their colleagues or you could ask their underlings; better still, you could ask all three. The answer may seem obvious, yet it is just dawning on human resource departments all over Europe, and is forcing them to make one of the biggest changes to their appraisal methods in years.

The approach goes under the ugly name of "360° feedback," and so far it has won over companies including BP, BT, Bupa, BMW, United Distillers, WH Smith, Rhône-Poulenc, and Northumbrian Water. It is practised by Will Carling and his England rugby team; in the public sector the Bank of England is gingerly trying it out; the Treasury has said it will introduce it, and Gillian Shephard, education secretary, has plans to make it part of the way headteachers are judged. Last week British Aerospace disclosed that it was going to use 360° feedback for that most sensitive subject of all: the setting of managers' pay.

"The reason that so many companies are looking at 360° feedback is that the new flat hierarchies have made bosses less in touch with their subordinates," says Trevor Toolan of Pilat, a specialist consultancy. 'There are many aspects of behaviour that a boss does not see, for example, how well they communicate and motivate and plan.'

At heart, the idea is simple. It involves inviting views from a broad range of people on a manager's performance. Yet the notion that underlings and peers should have a say presents a fundamental departure for most organizations. "Everybody is talking about it," says Angela Baron of the Institute of Personnel and Development. "But some managers are resisting. They are right to resist. If you don't do it properly it can turn into a knocking session, and be very damaging indeed."

While most people agree that 360° feedback is a good idea in principle, there is considerable disagreement on how best it should be implemented. Some companies are doing it informally, while others have got it down almost to a science.

At the Bank of England, managers are being encouraged to call colleagues into their office and ask point black what they think of them. At the other extreme are companies as United Distillers, WH Smith and Northumbrian Water, which have developed sophisticated tailor-made systems. Each has produced a questionnaire which asks respondents to rank managers up to 30 different counts. The questionnaires are filled in confidentially, and then sent to an independent third party, which processes the results. The manager is then helped through the report either by an occupational psychologist or by a manager who has been specially trained.

"It is important to do things in a constructive way, especially when someone thinks they are supportive and open, but their subordinates say they are bossy and hard to approach," says Fred Bunter, human resource manager at Northumbrian Water.

Despite the potential for upsetting and demotivating managers by exposing them to the pent-up frustrations of their workforce, most 360° feedback programmes are running surprisingly smoothly. "In all the years I have been doing it I have only ever come across two problems," says John Hunt of the London Business School. "In one case, the chairman summoned his team and demanded to know who had written these things about him. The finance director left the meeting and phoned me, and I had to jump into a cab to go to quieten things down."

John Lurie, occupational psychologist at KPMG, argues that problems can be avoided by making the questions as precisely formulated as possible. Otherwise, he warns that a popular but incompetent manager may fare better than one who is highly effective but not particularly pleasant.

There is also disagreement about what the results should be used for. Most companies and consultants feel they should only be used for management development. According to Chris Bones, human resource director of United Distillers, the feedback should be used purely as a personal development tool. He warns against linking it to pay: "You might get a 'halo effect' … as your manager, I'll look after you, if you look after me."

Maury Peiperl of the London Business School disagrees. "My research shows that when the results are tied to pay it works better, as people don't want to spend time on something that has no teeth."

Because the information is so sensitive, most companies are taking great steps to make it anonymous and confidential. According to Toolan this is inevitable. "I'm not going to give negative feedback if it affects how many oysters I eat or how much champagne I can drink," he says. However, others say that anonymous information is a weakness in the system. Kevin Delany of Coopers & Lybrand argues that 360° feedback works best in open organisations where people are confident enough to put their names to their questionnaires.

Whichever route they take, the companies that have been practising 360° feedback claim it has made a marked difference. Lurie argues it helps individual managers improve their skills and also elevates the general importance of management. "In the past people have been valued more for their functional expertise. 360° feedback recognizes that you need to be more of a generalist, which means achieving with or through other people." John Ainley, group personnel manager at WH Smith, goes so far as to say it has been the single most importance piece of cultural change in the organization. "It has changed the balance of power in the company by making a commitment to listen to workers' views," he says.

Companies which have yet to catch on to 360° feedback should be warned that the idea may be obsolete before they get to it. The latest idea from the human resource wizards is to involve customers and suppliers too. And that goes by the even uglier name of 540° feedback.[1]

Discussion Question

Which aspect of 360° feedback is most critical to its success?

Productivity and total quality experts tell us that we need to work smarter, not harder. While it is true that a sound education and appropriate skill training are needed if one is to work smarter, the process does not end there. Today's employees need instructive and supportive feedback and desired rewards if they are to translate their knowledge into improved productivity and superior quality. Figure 9–1 illustrates a learning- and development-focused cycle in which feedback enhances ability, encourages effort, and acknowledges results. Rewards, meanwhile, motivate effort and compensate results. Learning and personal development, according to the authors of the book, *Working Wisdom*, are the key to success at all levels

. . . work can be an enriching experience, a way of developing mastery in the world, a source of valued relationships, and for some—however high-minded this may sound—a path to self-realization. Combining work and learning to promote personal development, as well as a profitable enterprise, is the key. As the pace of change quickens, individuals, companies, and countries that fail to continually learn and adapt to change will be left behind.[2]

Properly administered feedback and rewards can guide, teach, and motivate people in the direction of positive change.

This chapter concludes our discussion of individual behaviour by discussing the impact of feedback and rewards on behaviour and by integrating those insights with what you have learned about individual differences, perception, and various motivational tools such as goal setting.

Understanding the Feedback Process

Achievement-oriented students have a hearty appetite for feedback. Following a difficult exam, for instance, students want to know two things: how they did and how their peers did. By letting students know how their work measures up to grading and competitive standards, an instructor's feedback permits the students to adjust their study habits so they can reach their goals. Likewise, managers in well-run organizations follow up goal setting with a feedback programme to provide a rational basis for adjustment and improvement. For example, consider these two diverse feedback examples:

Figure 9 – 1   Feedback and Rewards Are Important Links in the Job Performance Cycle

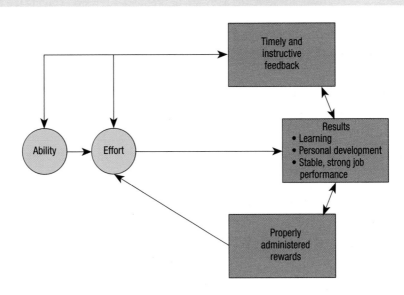

IBM's Raleigh, North Carolina, personal computer factory: "Every day, managers see a fresh . . . number on their screens, telling them how many PCs have been shipped so far this year. . . . every model is broken out so managers can see what's moving and what's not."[3]

A 55,000-employee copper mine in Zambia, Africa: "As largely uneducated workers march into the front entrance, they can't help but spot a 50-foot-high scoreboard that lists monthly and year-to-date financials, from 'copper revenue' to 'corporate depreciation.' "[4]

Although this sort of open book management is becoming popular, feedback too often gets shortchanged. In fact, "poor or insufficient feedback" was the leading cause of deficient performance in a survey of US and European companies.[5]

Feedback
Objective information about performance.

As the term is used here, **feedback** is objective information about individual or collective performance. Subjective assessments such as "You're doing a poor job," "You're too lazy," or "We really appreciate your hard work" do not qualify as objective feedback. But hard data such as units sold, days absent, money saved, projects completed, and quality control rejects are all candidates for objective feedback programmes. Management consultants Chip Bell and Ron Zemke offered this perspective of feedback:

Feedback is, quite simply, any information that answers those "How am I doing?" questions. Good feedback answers them truthfully and productively. It's information people can use either to confirm or correct their performance.

Feedback comes in many forms and from a variety of sources. Some is easy to get and requires hardly any effort to understand. The charts and graphs tracking group and individual performance that are fixtures in many workplaces are an example of this variety. Performance feedback—the numerical type at least—is at the heart of most approaches to total quality management.

Some feedback is less accessible. It's tucked away in the heads of customers and managers. But no matter how well-hidden the feedback, if people need it to keep their performance on track, we need to get it to them—preferably while it's still fresh enough to make an impact.[6]

Two Functions of Feedback

Experts say feedback serves two functions for those who receive it, one is *instructional* and the other *motivational*. Feedback instructs when it clarifies roles or teaches new behaviour. For example, an assistant accountant might be advised to handle a certain entry as a capital item rather than as an expense item. On the other hand, feedback motivates when it serves as a reward or promises a reward.[7] Having the boss tell you that a gruelling project you worked on earlier has just been completed can be a rewarding piece of news. As documented in one study, the motivational function of feedback can be significantly enhanced by pairing *specific*, challenging goals with *specific* feedback about results.[8] We expand upon these two functions in this section by analysing a cognitive model of feedback, and reviewing the practical implications of recent feedback research.

A Cognitive-Processing Model of Performance Feedback

Giving and receiving feedback on the job are popular ideas today. Conventional wisdom says the more feedback organizational members get, the better. An underlying assumption is that feedback works automatically. Managers simply need to be motivated to give it. According to a recent meta-analysis of 23,663 feedback incidents, however, feedback is far from automatically effective. While feedback did, in fact, have a generally positive impact on performance, performance actually *declined* in more than 38 per cent of the feedback incidents.[9] These results are a big caution light for those interested in improving job performance with objective feedback. If feedback is to be effective, managers need to understand the interaction between feedback recipients and their environment. Managers also need to appreciate how employees cognitively or mentally process feedback. This complex process is illustrated in Figure 9–2. Immediately obvious is the fact that

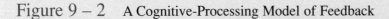

Figure 9 – 2   A Cognitive-Processing Model of Feedback

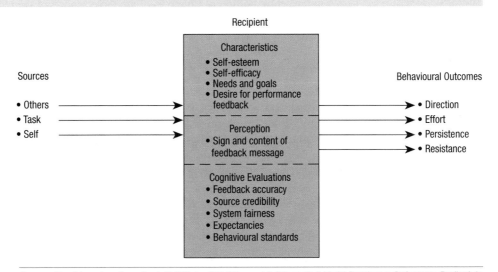

Sources: Based in part on discussion in M S Taylor, C D Fisher, and D R Ilgen, "Individuals' Reactions to Performance Feedback in Organizations: A Control Theory Perspective," in *Research in Personnel and Human Resources Management*, vol. 2, eds K M Rowland and G R Ferris (Greenwich, CT: JAI Press, 1984), pp 81–124; and A N Kluger and A DeNisi, "The Effects of Feedback Interventions on Performance: A Historical Review, a Meta-Analysis, and a Preliminary Feedback Intervention Theory," *Psychological Bulletin*, March 1996, pp 254–84.

feedback must successfully clear many hurdles if the desired behavioural outcomes are to be achieved.

A lighthearted case in point is Scott Adams, the former telephone company employee who draws the popular cartoon strip, Dilbert. According to *The Wall Street Journal,*

. . . he can thank feedback from his readers, who flooded him with comments—about 200 a day—after he published his e-mail address in 1993. They persuaded him to concentrate on workplace issues, which had been a smaller part of the strip, and Dilbert's popularity soared. "There was this huge vein of discontent and nobody was talking about it from the employees' perspective," he says.

Thanks to his experiences in the trenches, and his e-mail army, Mr. Adams has become a walking database of workplace foibles and career frustrations.[10]

Feedback—from customers, in this case—was effective because cartoonist Adams (1) wanted feedback, (2) actively sought feedback, and (3) acted on the feedback. He receives readers' e-mail messages to the tune of 350 a day regaling him with the latest horror stories of corporate life.[11] A step-by-step exploration of the model in Figure 9–2 can help us better understand this sort of feedback–performance relationship.

Sources of Feedback

It almost goes without saying that employees receive objective feedback from others such as peers, supervisors, subordinates, and outsiders. Perhaps less obvious is the fact that the task itself is a ready source of objective feedback. Anyone who has been "hooked into" pumping quarters into a video game can appreciate the power of task-provided feedback. Similarly, skilled tasks such as computer programming or landing a jet airplane provide a steady stream of feedback about how well or poorly one is doing. A third source of feedback is oneself, but self-serving bias and other perceptual problems can contaminate this source. Those high in self-confidence tend to rely on personal feedback more than those with low self-confidence. Although circumstances vary, an employee can be bombarded by feedback from all three sources simultaneously. This is where the gatekeeping functions of perception and cognitive evaluation are needed to help sort things out.

The Recipient of Feedback

Listed in the centre portion of Figure 9 – 2 are three aspects of the recipient requiring our attention. They are the individual's characteristics, perceptions, and cognitive evaluations. As characterized earlier, each recipient variable is a hurdle intended feedback must clear if it is to be effective. Knowing about these recipient hurdles is a big step in the right direction.

The Recipient's Characteristics   Personality characteristics such as self-esteem and self-efficacy can help or hinder one's readiness for feedback.[12] Those having low self-esteem and low self-efficacy generally do not actively seek feedback that, unfortunately, would tend to confirm those problems. Needs and goals also influence one's openness to feedback. In a laboratory study, Japanese psychology students who scored high on need for achievement responded more favourably to feedback than did their classmates who had low need for achievement.[13] This particular relationship likely exists in Western cultures as well. Long-tenured employees from this sample also were less likely to seek feedback than employees with little time on the job.[14] High self-monitors, those chameleonlike people we discussed in Chapter 5, are also more open to feedback because it helps them adapt their behaviour to the situation. Recall from Chapter 5 that high self-monitoring employees were found to be better at initiating relationships with mentors (who typically provide feedback).[15] Low self-monitoring people, in contrast, are tuned into their own internal feelings more than they are to external cues.

OB EXERCISE   *How Strong Is Your Desire for Performance Feedback?*

Instructions
Circle one number indicating the strength of your agreement or disagreement with each statement. Total your responses, and compare your score with our arbitrary norms.

	DISAGREE	AGREE

1. As long as I think that I have done something well, I am not too concerned about how other people think I have done.   5 — 4 — 3 — 2 — 1

2. How other people view my work is not as important as how I view my own work.   5 — 4 — 3 — 2 — 1

3. It is usually better not to put much faith in what others say about your work, regardless of whether it is complimentary or not.   5 — 4 — 3 — 2 — 1

4. If I have done something well, I know it without other people telling me so.   5 — 4 — 3 — 2 — 1

5. I usually have a clear idea of what I am trying to do and how well I am proceeding toward my goal.   5 — 4 — 3 — 2 — 1

6. I find that I am usually a pretty good judge of my own performance.   5 — 4 — 3 — 2 — 1

7. It is very important to me to know what people think of my work.   1 — 2 — 3 — 4 — 5

8. It is a good idea to get someone to check on your work before it's too late to make changes.   1 — 2 — 3 — 4 — 5

9. Even though I may think I have done a good job, I feel a lot more confident of it after someone else tells me so.   1 — 2 — 3 — 4 — 5

10. Since one cannot be objective about their own performance, it is best to listen to the feedback provided by others.   1 — 2 — 3 — 4 — 5

Total score = _____

Arbitrary Norms
10–23 = Low desire for feedback
24–36 = Moderate desire for feedback
37–50 = High desire for feedback

SOURCE   Excerpted and adapted from D M Herold, C K Parsons, and R B Rensvold, "Individual Differences in the Generation and Processing of Performance Feedback," *Educational and Psychological Measurement*, February 1996, Table 1, p 9. Copyright © 1996 by Sage Publications. Reprinted by permission of Sage Publications, Inc.

Researchers have started to focus more directly on the recipient's actual desire for feedback, as opposed to indirectly on personality characteristics, needs, and goals. Everyday experience tells us that not everyone really wants the performance feedback they supposedly seek. Restaurant servers who ask, "How was everything?" while presenting the bill, typically are not interested in a detailed reply. A recent study of 498 supervisors yielded an instrument for measuring desire for performance feedback[16] (see the OB Exercise for a shortened version). Such desire involves *self-reliance* (items 1–3), *self-assessment ability* (items 4–6), and *a preference for external information* (items 7–10). The general contingency approach to management would require different strategies for giving feedback to employees scoring low versus high on the OB Exercise.

The Recipient's Perception of Feedback   The *sign* of feedback refers to whether it is positive or negative. Generally, people tend to perceive and recall positive feedback more accurately than they do negative feedback.[17] But feedback with a negative sign (e.g., being told your performance is below average) can have a *positive* motivational impact. In fact, in one study, those who were told they were below average on a creativity test subsequently outperformed those who were led to believe their results were above average. The subjects apparently took the negative feedback as a challenge and set and pursued higher goals. Those receiving positive feedback apparently were less motivated to do better.[18] Nonetheless, feedback with a negative sign or threatening content needs to be administered carefully to avoid creating insecurity and defensiveness. Self-efficacy also can be damaged by negative feedback, as discovered in a pair of recent experiments with business students. The researchers concluded, "To facilitate the development of strong efficacy beliefs, managers should be careful about the provision of negative feedback. Destructive criticism by managers which attributes the cause of poor performance to internal factors reduces both the beliefs of self-efficacy and the self-set goals of recipients."[19]

The Recipient's Cognitive Evaluation of Feedback   Upon receiving feedback, people cognitively evaluate factors such as its accuracy, the credibility of the source, the fairness of the system (e.g., performance appraisal system), their performance→reward expectancies, and the reasonableness of the standards. Any feedback that fails to clear one or more of these cognitive hurdles will be rejected or downplayed. Personal experience largely dictates how these factors are weighed. For instance, you would probably discount feedback from someone who exaggerates or from someone who performed poorly on the same task you have just successfully completed. In view of the "trust gap," discussed in Chapter 13, managerial credibility is an ethical matter of central importance today. According to the authors of the book *Credibility: How Leaders Gain and Lose It, Why People Demand It*, "without a solid foundation of personal credibility, leaders can have no hope of enlisting others in a common vision."[20] Managers who have proven untrustworthy and not credible have a hard time improving job performance through feedback.[21]

Feedback from a source who apparently shows favouritism or relies on unreasonable behaviour standards would be suspect. Also, as predicted by expectancy motivation theory, feedback must foster high effort→performance expectancies and performance→reward instrumentalities if it is to motivate desired behaviour. For example, many growing children have been cheated out of the rewards of athletic competition because they were told by respected adults that they were too small, too short, too slow, too clumsy, and so forth. Feedback can have a profound and lasting impact on behaviour.

Behavioural Outcomes of Feedback

In Chapter 8, we discussed how goal setting gives behaviour direction, increases expended effort, and fosters persistence. Because feedback is intimately related to the goal-setting process, it involves the same behavioural outcomes: direction, effort, and persistence. However, while the fourth outcome of goal setting involves formulating goal-attainment strategies, the fourth possible outcome of feedback is resistance. Feedback schemes, that smack of manipulation or fail one or more of the perceptual and cognitive evaluation tests just discussed, breed resistance.[22]

Practical Lessons from Feedback Research

After reviewing dozens of laboratory and field studies of feedback, a trio of OB researchers cited the following practical implications for managers:

- The acceptance of feedback should not be treated as a given; it is often misperceived or rejected. This is especially true in intercultural situations.
- Managers can enhance their credibility as sources of feedback by developing their expertise and creating a climate of trust.
- Negative feedback is typically misperceived or rejected.
- Although very frequent feedback may erode one's sense of personal control and initiative, feedback is too infrequent in most work organizations.
- Feedback needs to be tailored to the recipient.
- While average and below-average performers need extrinsic rewards for performance, high performers respond to feedback that enhances their feelings of competence and personal control.[23]

Other research insights about feedback include the following:

- Computer-based performance feedback leads to greater improvements in performance when it is received directly from the computer system rather than via an immediate supervisor.[24]
- Recipients of feedback perceive it to be more accurate when they actively participate in the feedback session versus passively receiving feedback.[25]
- Destructive criticism tends to cause conflict and reduce motivation.[26]
- "The higher one rises in an organization the less likely one is to receive quality feedback about job performance."[27]

Managers who act on these research implications and the trouble signs in Table 9–1 can build credible and effective feedback systems.[28]

Our discussion upto this point has focused on traditional downward feedback. Let us explore a couple of new and interesting approaches to feedback in the workplace.

Nontraditional Feedback: Upward and 360-Degree

Traditional top-down feedback programmes have given way to some interesting variations in recent years. Two newer approaches, discussed in this section, are upward feedback and so-called 360-degree feedback. The latter was discussed in the opening case. Aside from breaking away from a strict superior-to-subordinate feedback loop, these

Table 9 – 1	Six Common Trouble Signs for Organizational Feedback Systems

1. Feedback is used to punish, embarrass, or put down employees.
2. Those receiving the feedback see it as irrelevant to their work.
3. Feedback information is provided too late to do any good.
4. People receiving feedback believe it relates to matters beyond their control.
5. Employees complain about wasting too much time collecting and recording feedback data.
6. Feedback recipients complain about feedback being too complex or difficult to understand.

Source: Adapted from C Bell and R Zemke, "On-Target Feedback," *Training*, June 1992, pp 36–44.

newer approaches are different because they typically involve *multiple sources* of feedback. Instead of getting feedback from one boss, often during an annual performance appraisal, more and more managers are getting structured feedback from superiors, subordinates, peers, and even outsiders such as customers. Nontraditional feedback is growing in popularity for at least five reasons:

1. Traditional performance appraisal systems have created widespread dissatisfaction.

2. Team-based organization structures are replacing traditional hierarchies. This trend requires managers to have good interpersonal skills that are best evaluated by team members.

3. Multiple-rater systems are said to make feedback more valid than single-source feedback.[29]

4. Bottom-up feedback meshes nicely with the trend towards participative management and employee empowerment.

5. Co-workers and subordinates are said to know more about a manager's strengths and limitations than the boss.[30]

Together, these factors make a compelling case for looking at better ways to give and receive performance feedback.

Upward Feedback

Upward feedback

Subordinates evaluate their boss.

Upward feedback stands the traditional approach on its head by having subordinates provide feedback on a manager's style and performance. This type of feedback is generally anonymous. Most students are familiar with upward feedback programmes from years of filling out anonymous teacher evaluation surveys.

Indeed, managers typically resist upward feedback programmes because they believe it erodes their authority. Other critics say anonymous upward feedback can become little more than a personality contest or, worse, be manipulated by managers who make promises or threats. What does the research literature tell us about upward feedback?

Recent Research Insights   Recent studies with diverse samples have given us these useful insights:

- The question of whether upward feedback should be *anonymous* was addressed by a study at a large US insurance company. All told, 183 employees rated the skills and effectiveness of 38 managers. Managers who received anonymous upward feedback received *lower* ratings and liked the process *less* than did those receiving feedback from identifiable employees. This finding confirmed the criticism that employees will tend to go easier on their boss when not protected by confidentiality.[31]

- In another study, 83 supervisors employed by a US government agency were divided into three feedback groups: (1) feedback from both superiors and subordinates, (2) feedback from superiors only, and (3) feedback from subordinates only. Group 1 was most satisfied with the overall evaluation process and responded more positively to upward feedback. "Group 3 expressed more concern that subordinate appraisals would undermine supervisors' authority and that supervisors would focus on pleasing subordinates."[32]

- In a field study of 238 corporate managers, upward feedback had a positive impact on the performance of low to moderate performers.[33]

General Recommendations for Using Upward Feedback   These research findings suggest the practical value of *anonymous* upward feedback used in *combination* with other sources of performance feedback and evaluation. Because of managerial resistance and potential manipulation, using upward feedback as the primary determinant for promotions and pay decisions is *not* recommended. Carefully collected upward feedback is useful for management development programmes.

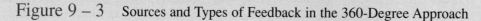

Figure 9 – 3   Sources and Types of Feedback in the 360-Degree Approach

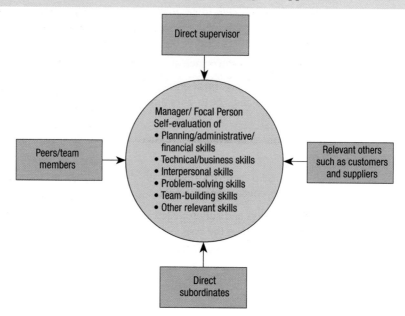

360-Degree Feedback

The concept of giving a manager collective feedback from different levels and categories of co-workers is not new. Training and development specialists have used multirater, multilevel feedback for more than 20 years. As aggressively marketed 360-degree feedback programmes became available in the late 1980s, corporate use mushroomed. Whether 360-degree feedback goes down in history as just another passing fad or an established practice remains to be seen. An unfortunate by-product of sudden popularity is that enthusiastic sellers of 360-degree feedback systems are more interested in advocacy than objective evaluation.[34] Importantly, our goal here is not to provide cookbook instructions in how to administer complex 360-degree reviews. Rather, our purpose is to see if the concept is sound and deserves managerial time and money.

360-degree feedback

Comparison of anonymous feedback from one's superior, subordinates, and peers with self-perceptions.

The concept of **360-degree feedback** involves letting individuals compare their own perceived performance with behaviourally specific (and usually anonymous) performance information from their manager, subordinates, and peers as discussed in the opening case. Even outsiders may be involved in what is sometimes called full-circle feedback (see Figure 9 – 3). *Fortune* offered this humorous yet instructive explanation:

Here's how it works. Everyone from the office screwup to your boss, including your crackerjack assistant and your rival across the hall, will fill out lengthy, anonymous questionnaires about you. You'll complete one too. Are you crisp, clear, and articulate? Abrasive? Spreading yourself too thin? Trustworthy? Off-the-cuff remarks may be gathered too. A week or two later you'll get the results, all crunched and graphed by a computer. Ideally, all this will be explained by someone from your human-resources department or the company that handled the questionnaires, a person who can break bad news gently. You get to see how your opinion of yourself differs from those of the group of subordinates who participated, your peer group, and the boss.[35]

The idea is to let the individual know how their behaviour affects others, with the goal of motivating change.[36] In a 360-degree feedback programme, a given manager will play different roles, including focal person, superior, subordinate, and peer. Of course, the focal person role is played only once. The other roles are played more than once for various other focal persons.

Relevant Research Evidence Because upward feedback is a part of 360-degree feedback programmes, the evidence reviewed earlier applies here as well. As with upward feedback, peer- and self-evaluations, central to 360-degree feedback programmes, also are a significant affront to tradition. But advocates say co-workers and managers themselves are appropriate performance evaluators because they are closest to the action. Generally, research builds a stronger case for peer appraisals than for self-appraisals.[37] Self-serving bias, discussed in Chapter 6, is a problem.

Rigorous research evidence of 360-degree feedback programmes is scarce. A two-year study of 48 managers given 360-degree feedback in a large US public utility company led to these somewhat promising results. According to the researchers, "The group as a whole developed its skills, but there was substantial variability among individuals in how much change occurred."[38] Thus, as with any feedback, individuals vary in their response to 360-degree feedback.

Practical Recommendations for 360-Degree Feedback Programmes Our recommendations for upward feedback, favouring anonymity and discouraging linkage to pay and promotion decisions, apply as well to 360-degree feedback programmes. We believe 360-degree feedback has a place in the development of managerial skills, especially in today's team-based organizations. However, it is important to remember that this complex feedback process is only as strong as its various components:

- Process design and planning.
- Instrument development.
- Instrument design.
- Administration.
- Feedback processing and reporting.
- Action planning as a result of feedback.[39]

It is not a quick-and-easy fix, as some advocates would have us believe.

Some Concluding Tips for Giving Good Feedback

Managers need to keep the following tips in mind when giving feedback:

- Relate feedback to existing performance *goals* and clear *expectations.*
- Give *specific* feedback tied to observable behaviour or measurable results.
- Channel feedback towards *key result areas.*
- Give feedback as *soon* as possible.[40]
- Give positive feedback for *improvement*, not just final results.
- Focus feedback on *performance*, not personalities.
- Base feedback on *accurate* and *credible* information.

Organizational Reward Systems

Rewards are an ever-present and always controversial feature of organizational life.[41] Some employees see their jobs as the source of a paycheque and little else. Others derive great pleasure from their jobs and association with co-workers. Even volunteers who donate their time to charitable organizations, such as the Red Cross, walk away with rewards in the form of social recognition and pride of having given unselfishly of their time. Hence, the subject of organizational rewards includes, but goes far beyond, monetary compensation. This section examines key components of organizational reward systems to provide a conceptual background for discussing the timely topics of pay for performance and team-based pay.

Despite the fact that reward systems vary widely, it is possible to identify and interrelate some common components. The model in Figure 9–4 focuses on four important components: (1) types of rewards, (2) reward norms, (3) distribution criteria, and (4) desired outcomes. Let us examine these components.

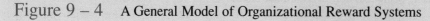

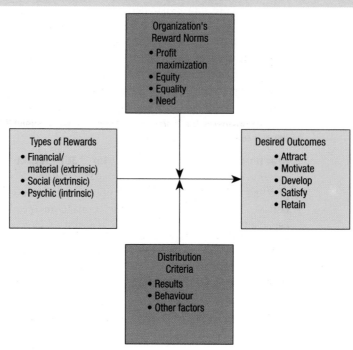

Figure 9 – 4   A General Model of Organizational Reward Systems

Types of Rewards

Including the usual paycheque, the variety and magnitude of organizational rewards boggles the mind—from subsidized lunches to stock options, from boxes of chocolate to golf club membership, from balloon flights to dragon boat racing in Hong Kong. Consider Naf Naf's stock-option plan (France):

In order to reward employees and to establish their loyalty to the company, Naf Naf regularly offers stock-options to a selected number of employees, from packer to executive. Naf Naf's system is very innovative, as its 250 head office and warehouse employees may receive stock-options, whereas most companies reserve this reward system for the top-management.

Beneficiaries are put forward by their immediate superiors who advise the board of directors, taking the final decision. The chosen receive a document by mail from Mr. Gérard Pariente, the company's CEO, giving all information on the use of stock options.

As Naf Naf is a young company, stock-options are an excellent way to directly individualize employees' salaries. "The employees feel their efforts are recognized and they are proud to have contributed to the company's success," says Ms Gwenaëlle Duval, human resource manager.

Naf Naf's system is open to all head office and warehouse employees on condition they have been in the company for the last 6 months. On term, Naf Naf wants to reach 90 per cent of its target group. In case of professional misconduct or departure within three years after reception of the stock-options, they are withdrawn.[42]

In addition to the obvious pay and benefits, there are less obvious social and psychic rewards. Social rewards include praise and recognition from others both inside and outside the organization. Psychic rewards come from personal feelings of self-esteem, self-satisfaction, and accomplishment.

An alternative typology for organizational rewards is the distinction between extrinsic and intrinsic rewards. Financial, material, and social rewards qualify as **extrinsic rewards** because they come from the environment. Psychic rewards, however, are **intrinsic rewards** because they are self-granted. An employee who works to obtain extrinsic rewards, such as money or praise, is said to be extrinsically motivated. One who

Extrinsic rewards
Financial, material, or social rewards from the environment.

Intrinsic rewards
Self-granted, psychic rewards.

derives pleasure from the task itself or experiences a sense of competence or self-determination is said to be intrinsically motivated.[43] The relative importance of extrinsic and intrinsic rewards is a matter of personal values and tastes. Extrinsic rewards cause one big problem: when a person is happy doing a job and receives important extrinsic rewards, he starts thinking that there might be something wrong with the intrinsic aspects of the job. This is the parable of the professional writer:

A professional writer is struggling at home with his next pages. For some days, children had played noisily in the street in front of his study. The noise was highly stressful because it was simultaneously loud, uncontrollable, and unpredictable.

He considered the following solutions (1) ask (politely) that they quieten down or go away; (2) call the police or the parents if you know them; (3) threaten them with force if they don't comply; (4) all of the above in that order.

His job depending on intrinsic motivation, he decided to do something completely different. He went to the children and said that he was so delighted with their games that he was prepared to pay them each £1 a day if they carried on.

Surprised but delighted they accepted his offer. For two days the writer dispensed the cash. But on the third day he explained that because of a "cash-flow" problem he could only give them 50p each. The next day he claimed to be "cash-light" and only handed out 10p.

True to his prediction the children complained and refused to continue. They all left and never came back. Satisfied, the writer went home to continue in silence.[44]

This parable clearly illustrates that through explicit rewards, such as money, employees tend to focus on these rewards, which have to be escalated to maintain satisfaction.

Organizational Reward Norms

As discussed in Chapter 8 under the heading of equity theory, the employe–employee linkage can be viewed as an exchange relationship. Employees exchange their time and talent for rewards. Ideally, four alternative norms dictate the nature of this exchange. In pure form, each would lead to a significantly different reward distribution system. They are as follows:

- *Profit maximization.* The objective of each party is to maximize its net gain, regardless of how the other party fares. A profit-maximizing company would attempt to pay the least amount of wages for maximum effort. Conversely, a profit-maximizing employee would seek maximum rewards, regardless of the organization's financial well-being, and leave the organization for a better deal.

Reward equity norm
Rewards should be tied to contributions.

- *Equity.* According to the **reward equity norm**, rewards should be allocated proportionate to contributions. Those who contribute the most should be rewarded the most. A cross-cultural study of American, Japanese, and Korean students led the researchers to the following conclusion: "Equity is probably a phenomenon common to most cultures, but its strength will vary."[45] Basic principles of fairness and justice, evident in most cultures, drive the equity norm.

Reward equality norm
Everyone should get the same rewards.

- *Equality.* The **reward equality norm** calls for rewarding all parties equally, regardless of their comparative contributions.

- *Need.* This norm calls for distributing rewards according to employees' needs, rather than their contributions.[46]

After defining these exchange norms, a pair of researchers concluded that these contradictory norms are typically intertwined:

We propose that employer–employee exchanges are governed by the contradictory norms of profit maximization, equity, equality, and need. These norms can coexist; what varies is the extent to which the rules for correct application of a norm are clear and the relative emphasis different managements will give to certain norms in particular allocations.[47]

ETHICS

Conflict and ethical debates often arise over the perceived fairness of reward allocations because of disagreement about reward norms.[48] Shareholders might prefer a profit-maximization norm, while technical specialists would like an equity norm, and unionized hourly workers would argue for a pay system based on equality. A reward norm anchored to need might prevail in a family-owned and operated business. Effective reward systems are based on clear and consensual exchange norms.

Reward Distribution Criteria

According to one expert on organizational reward systems, three general criteria for the distribution of rewards are as follows:

- *Performance: results.* Tangible outcomes such as individual, group, or organization performance; quantity and quality of performance.
- *Performance: actions and behaviours.* Such as teamwork, cooperation, risk taking, creativity.
- *Nonperformance considerations.* Customary or contractual, where the type of job, nature of the work, equity, tenure, level in hierarchy, etc., are rewarded.[49]

Desired Outcomes of the Reward System

As listed in Figure 9–4, a good reward system should attract talented people and motivate and satisfy them once they have joined the organization.[50] Further, a good reward system should foster personal growth and development and keep talented people from leaving.

Why Do Rewards Fail to Motivate?

Despite huge investments of time and money for organizational reward systems, the desired motivational impact often is not achieved. A management consultant/writer recently offered these eight reasons:

1. Too much emphasis on monetary rewards.
2. Rewards lack an "appreciation effect."
3. Extensive benefits become entitlements.
4. Counterproductive behaviour is rewarded. (For example, "a pizza delivery company focused its rewards on the on-time performance of its drivers, only to discover that it was inadvertently rewarding reckless driving."[51])
5. Too long a delay between performance and rewards.
6. Too many one-size-fits-all rewards.
7. Use of one-shot rewards with a short-lived motivational impact.
8. Continued use of demotivating practices such as layoffs, across-the-board rises and cuts, and excessive executive compensation.[52]

These stubborn problems have fostered a growing interest in more effective reward and compensation practices. Although we cannot engage in a comprehensive discussion of modern compensation practices in the balance of this chapter, a subject requiring an entire book,[53] we can explore general approaches to boosting the motivational impact of monetary rewards. This is where pay for performance—including profit sharing, gainsharing, and team-based pay—enters the picture.

Pay for Performance

Our discussion of organizational rewards would not be complete without more closely considering the role of *money*. In today's workplace, despite lots of complaints about pay,[54] money remains the central organizational reward. Consequently, we need to address this important underlying OB question: How can managers increase the incentive effect of monetary compensation? Managers who adequately comprehend this issue are in a better position to make decisions about specific compensation plans.

Putting Pay for Performance in Perspective

Pay for performance
Monetary incentives tied to one's results or accomplishments.

Pay for performance is the popular term for monetary incentives linking at least some portion of the paycheque directly to results or accomplishments. Many refer to it simply as *incentive pay*, while others call it *variable pay*.[55] The general idea behind pay-for-performance schemes—including but not limited to merit pay, bonuses, and profit sharing—is to give employees an incentive for working harder and/or smarter. Pay for performance is something extra, compensation above and beyond basic wages and salaries. Proponents of incentive compensation say something extra is needed because hourly wages and fixed salaries do little more than motivate people to show up at work and put in the required hours.[56] The most basic form of pay for performance is the traditional piece-rate plan, whereby the employee is paid a specified amount of money for each unit of work. Sales commissions, whereby a salesperson receives a specified amount of money for each unit sold, is another longstanding example of pay for performance. Today's service economy is forcing management to adapt creatively and go beyond piece-rate and sales commission plans to accommodate greater emphasis on product and service quality, interdependence, and teamwork.

Methods for paying incentives may differ from time to time, but the trend towards variable compensation remains strong.[57] Top executives are routinely granted excessive bonuses. For example, in 1993, Jim Fifield, Thorn EMI's music chief in 1994 received a £13.5m package made up of every kind of bonus, option, free share deal possible.[58]

Preoccupation with the size of executive rewards seems to be a largely Anglo/American phenomenon, but the popularity of share options has spilled into France, where companies have been quick to spot their tax advantages. "Options have become practically the most significant element of executive compensation," says Eduardo de Martino, a partner with accountants Arthur Andersen in Paris. "You can't really recruit or retain a high-quality executive without them."

In the most other European countries, the culture of share options has yet to develop, although bonuses are commonplace. In Italy, for instance, where the small- and medium-sized enterprises, which form the backbone of the Italian economy, are not listed on the stock exchange, top Italian directors may receive up to 25 or 30 per cent of their renumeration in the form of cash bonuses.

Research carried out by the London School of Economics, based on information from more than 1,500 work places with more than 25 employees, observed a positive link between employee involvement, profit sharing and merit pay schemes and productivity and job creation. Cash-based profit sharing schemes are linked to economic outcomes, but not to better industrial relations. The authoritarian workplace—with hardly any employee involvement—has a positive impact on industrial relations (lower turnover and absenteeism rate, …), but a negative one on productivity.[59]

Consider the pay system Whirlpool introduced gradually from 1987 on:[60]

True pay for performance became the foundation of the new system for all employee segments, along with a strong focus on shareholder value creation, including introduction of an all-employee stock option program in November 1991.

Even at the board level, Whirlpool substantially revamped the total compensation program for directors, revising stock option grants so they are awarded only if the company achieves certain performance targets.

At senior management levels, annual bonus opportunity shifted from "unknown" to a clear 50 per cent to 100 per cent of base, depending on achievement of targeted corporate and business unit financial goals and individual performance. Long-term incentives shifted from occasional use of stock options to annual stock options awards plus new plants that incorporated an equity focus. For exempt compensation, base pay was set at 90 per cent of market and total cash compensation at 110 per cent of market payable upon achievement of

Figure 9 – 5   The Double Impact of Incentive Bonuses on Employee Motivation and Performance

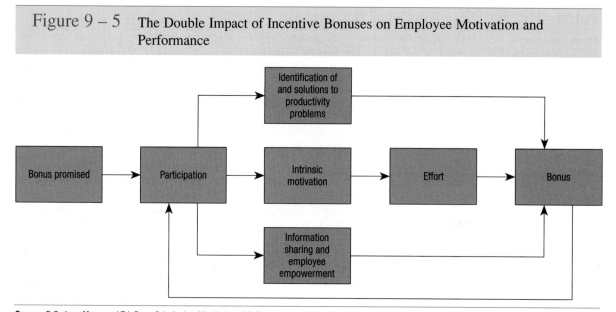

Source: B Graham-Moore and T L Ross, Gainsharing (Washington, DC: The Bureau of National Affairs, 1990), p 13 as adapted from T Hammer, "New Developments in Profit Sharing," in *Productivity in Organizations*, eds J Campbell, R Campbell, and Associates (San Francisco: Jossey-Bass, 1988). Reprinted by permission. Note: Arrows indicate the direction of influence.

stretch targets. (Individual target bonuses range from 10 per cent to 40 per cent of base pay. Depending on various combinations of corporate, business unit and individual performance, actual individual awards or bonuses could range from zero to 11/2 times target.) In non-exempt compensation, Whirlpool eliminated corporate profit sharing (which averaged 7 per cent of pay), substituted a 401(k) plan with a performance match, and introduced gainsharing at plant locations.

The fiercest debates about executive pay, however, are taking place in the US and UK, which both have highly developed stock markets and where the influence of any individual shareholder on company directors is relatively weak.[61]

The fact remains that pay for performance too often falls short of its goal of improved job performance. "Experts say that roughly half the incentive plans they see don't work, victims of poor design and administration."[62] Researchers have found only a weak statistical link between large executive bonuses paid out in good years and subsequent improvement in corporate profitability.[63] Also, in a survey of small business owners, more than half said their commission plans failed to motivate extra effort from their salespeople.[64] Linking teachers' merit pay to student performance, an exciting school reform idea, turned out to be a big disappointment: "The bottom line is that despite high hopes, none of the 13 districts studied was able to use teacher pay incentives to achieve significant, lasting gains in student performance."[65] Clearly, the pay-for-performance trend could stall if constructive steps are not taken.

Incentive Bonuses and Motivation: A Double-Impact Model

A first important step towards improving pay for performance is to better understand the motivational mechanism of bonuses (see Figure 9–5). As the term is used in Figure 9–5, *bonuses* refers to all forms of incentive compensation (in other words, pay for performance). Notice how *participation* plays a central role in this model. When employees fully participate in developing, implementing, and updating the performance-reward standards, three processes are triggered. First, productivity problems are more readily identified and solved. This is particularly true when teamwork techniques, such as the quality circles discussed in Chapter 13 are in force. Second, intrinsic motivation grows as the employee finds greater personal enjoyment and challenge in her or his work. Third, increased two-way information flow between management and employees empowers the

Table 9 – 2	Profit Sharing and Gainsharing Plans

TYPES OF PROFIT-SHARING PLANS

Deferred plan—Credit individuals with periodic earnings, delaying actual distribution until their disability, retirement, or death.

Distribution plan—Fully distributes each period's earned benefits as soon as the profit-sharing pool can be calculated.

Combination plan—Allows employees to receive a portion of each period's earnings in cash, while the remainder awaits future distribution.

TYPES OF GAINSHARING PLANS

Improshare plans—Based on employees' ability to complete assignments in less time than would be expected given the historical productivity base ratio. Work-hours saved are divided between the firm and plan participants according to a set percentage, such as 50 percent. Individuals receive a corresponding percentage increase in gross pay. Although no structural barriers exist, these plans generally do not provide formal participation in decision making.

Rucker plan—Generally limits decision-making participation to a single screening committee or the interface of a production and a screening committee. The Rucker formula assesses the relationship between the value added to produced goods as they pass through the manufacturing process and total labor costs. Unlike the typical Scanlon ratio, this formula enables workers to benefit from savings in production-related materials, supplies, and services. Bonuses result when the current ratio is better than that for the base period. A reserve pool is established to offset bad months. The reserves left over at the end of the year are paid out to employees as an additional bonus.

Scanlon plan—Uses a dual-committee system to foster companywide participation in decision making. Draws upon a historical productivity base ratio relating adjusted sales to total payroll. A bonus pool is created whenever actual output, as measured by adjusted sales, requires lower labor costs than would be expected using the base ratio. Each month, a percentage of the bonus pool is held in reserve to offset deficit months. The remaining funds are divided between the firm and employees. All of the retained funds remaining at year's end are proportionately shared by the parties.

Source: "Analyzing Group Incentive Plans," by Gary W. Florkowski, January 1990. Reprinted with permission of *HR Magazine*, published by the Society for Human Resource Management, Alexandria, VA.

employees. In turn, each of these three processes increases one's chances of earning the promised bonus, via lower costs and/or higher productivity. Intrinsic motivation translates into increased effort. Recalling our discussion of job design in Chapter 7 and expectancy motivation theory in Chapter 8, we can appreciate the motivating potential of properly administered incentive bonuses. This model makes a significant contribution to our thinking about pay for performance by emphasizing the double impact of bonuses. They motivate both when promised and when granted! It is likely that the feedback loop from bonus to participation bolsters the employee's self-efficacy.

With this model in mind as a useful conceptual framework, let us take a closer look at three distinctly different pay-for-performance practices.[66] We then offer some practical recommendations.

Profit Sharing versus Gainsharing

The terms *profit sharing* and *gainsharing* are sometimes used interchangeably. That is not only a conceptual mistake, but a major disservice to gainsharing as well. These two general approaches to pay for performance differ significantly in both method and results.

Profit sharing
Portion of bottom-line economic profits given to employees.

Profit Sharing   Most of today's corporate pay-for-performance plans are profit-sharing schemes. **Profit sharing** occurs when individual employees or work groups are granted a specified portion of any economic profits earned by the business as a whole. These internally distributed profits may be apportioned according to the equality or equity norms discussed earlier. Equity distributions supposedly occur when performance appraisal results are used to gauge who gets how much in the way of merit pay or profit-sharing bonuses. Profit-sharing bonuses may be paid in cash, deferred until retirement (see the top section of Table 9 – 2).

Gainsharing

Bonuses tied to measurable productivity increases.

Gainsharing　　Perhaps because it tends to be used in smaller companies with 500 or fewer employees, gainsharing is not as popularly known as profit sharing. "Gainsharing involves a measurement of productivity combined with the calculation of a bonus designed to offer employees a mutual share of any increases in total organizational productivity. Usually all those responsible for the increase receive the bonus."[67] **Gainsharing** has been around for more than a half century and typically goes by one of the following names: Improshare®, Rucker® plan, or Scanlon plan (see the bottom section of Table 9–2 for details). Distinguishing characteristics of gain sharing include the following:

- An organizational culture based on labour–management cooperation, trust, free-flowing information, and extensive participation.

- Built-in employee involvement structures such as suggestion systems or quality circles.

- Precise measurement and tracking of cost and/or productivity data for comparison purposes.

- The sharing with managerial and non-managerial employees of the proceeds from any productivity gains.[68]

Ideally, a self-perpetuating cycle develops. Communication and participation generate creative suggestions which foster productivity gains that yield bonuses which build motivation and trust.[69]

How Do Profit Sharing and Gainsharing Measure Up?

Profound differences mark these two general approaches to pay for performance. Gainsharing, by definition, is anchored to hard productivity data; profit sharing typically is more loosely linked to performance appraisal results. Thus profit-sharing determinations, like performance appraisals, are readily plagued by bias and misperception. Another significant problem with profit sharing is that bottom-line profits are influenced by many factors beyond the average employee's control. Those factors include strategy, pricing, competition, and fluctuating interest rates, to name just a few. Profit sharing's principal weaknesses are effectively neutralized by gainsharing's major strength, namely, a quantified performance-pay formula.

Critics of profit sharing admit it is generous to share the good times with employees, but they fear profit-sharing bonuses are perceived as a reward for past performance, not as an incentive to work harder in the future. Moreover, gainsharing rewards participation and teamwork while profit sharing generally does not. On the other hand, gainsharing formulas are complex and require extensive communication and training commitments.[70]

So, on balance, which is better? Judging by available research evidence, much of which is subjective, the vote goes to gainsharing. One study of 71 managers and *professionals* in a metals processing company found no significant correlation between *individual* performance and profit-sharing bonuses.[71] Another study of 1,746 manufacturing employees, at seven firms with Scanlon plans and two control firms without Scanlon plans, found higher job satisfaction and commitment among the Scanlon employees. Additionally, participation was a significantly stronger cultural norm in the Scanlon organizations. Scanlon participants quickly passed this norm along to new employees.[72] Gainsharing seems to work best when it becomes embedded in the organization's culture.[73] (See the International OB.) Positive results, in terms of lower costs, improved quality, and improved health and safety conditions, were documented in a recent study of four companies with Scanlon-type plans in force for four or more years.[74]

International Organizational Behaviour

Gainsharing Helps This Swedish-American Joint Venture Thrive

In the early '80s, Ericsson GE was General Electric's Mobile Communications Business and it was in trouble. In 1984 General Electric CEO Jack Welch directed John Trani, then general manager, to close the [Lynchburg, Virginia] division, "fix" it, or sell it.

In attempting to fix the business, Trani cut the workforce to the bone, laying off some 700 line workers in 1984. He froze salaried and hourly workers' pay. But Trani recognized that cuts alone weren't going to save the division, so he also cast about for some way to improve its performance. The seeds of Winshare were sown when Trani brought in consultant Tim Ross in 1986 to create a gainsharing plan that would help fix GE Mobile Communications.

According to Ross, currently the director of Ross Gainsharing Institute in Chapel Hill, NC, there are three ways to design a gainsharing system: The first stresses the gainsharing bonus (the cash incentive employees receive when the company exceeds a targeted profitability) and includes no employee involvement; the second also stresses the bonus, but includes some form of employee involvement; the third, the one Ross recommended to Ericsson, is built around extensive employee involvement and fundamentally changes the way a company manages its people.

Top executives at Lynchburg weren't enthusiastic about the employee-involvement part of the package at first, says Ross. In fact, he virtually had to push them into it.

The gainsharing part of Ericsson's program provided for a quarterly bonus based on the company's performance. If profits rose above a certain level, the employees got a bonus. The employee-involvement part of the program rested on the assumption that the line workers knew best how to do—and how to improve—their jobs. Since the average length of tenure of a line employee at Ericsson GE is 22 years, the premise that workers are qualified to come up with ideas for improvement seemed reasonable. Employees were encouraged to suggest ways to improve production processes, reduce waste, or just make their jobs easier. Instead of submitting these ideas to some committee of managers that might respond to them six months later, employee teams—dubbed Win Teams— were given both the power and the budget to implement the ideas themselves.

Membership on Win Teams is voluntary. Currently, there are 50 teams in the plant, each led by an elected line employee. A team has the authority to accept an idea, spend money on equipment to expedite the change, and implement it without management input. The budgetary limit for each team started out at $250 per year, but has since been increased to $6,000. Managers and exempt employees *can* belong to Win Teams, but only as resource people who do some of the interdepartmental legwork and research to see if an idea is feasible. Final approval and authority lie with the Win Team and its leader.

This may sound like a simple suggestion system with a budgetary twist, and indeed, it started out that way. But because employees took this empowerment effort seriously and because management at all levels supported the change, the Winshare program became a permanent part of the company's culture.

As a result of Trani's cuts and the division concentrating on what it did best (i.e., making mobile radios), the unit became profitable in 1986. Profitability and this new way of doing business attracted the attention of Ericsson, a Swedish company whose core business is mobile communications. Ericsson bought a 60 per cent share of the company at the end of 1989, and GE Mobile Communications Business became Ericsson GE.

This partnership gave Ericsson an American plant and a foot in the door of the US market. Though its name is well-known in Europe, Ericsson wanted the General Electric label on its radios and cellular phones for the recognition value in the United States.

The now-profitable joint venture had sales of $1.1 billion for 1992, and the Lynchburg plant currently employs about 2,000 people. On paper, Ericsson now owns 80 per cent of Ericsson GE while General Electric maintains a 20 per cent share. But it is line employees who actually have taken ownership of the business, in feeling if not in fact. As Jimmy Howerton, an associate who works on the Carfone line, puts it, "It doesn't matter what name is on the gate because this is my company."

SOURCE   Excerpted from B Filipczak, "Ericsson General Electric: The Evolution of Empowerment," *Training*, September 1993, pp 21–27. Reprinted with permission of the September 1993 issue of *Training* Magazine. Copyright 1993. Lakewood Publications, Minneapolis, MN. All rights reserved. Not for resale.

Team-Based Pay

Team-based pay

Linking pay to teamwork behaviour and/or team results.

One very clear trend in today's workplace is the move towards teams (see Chapter 13). There are permanent work teams and temporary project teams. There are cross-functional teams with specialists from different areas such as engineering, production, marketing, and finance. Most recently, there are self-managed teams, where employees take turns handling traditional managerial tasks including staffing, scheduling, training, and record keeping. While the move towards team structure certainly is a promising one, there are many loose ends, a major one being how to reward team members and teamwork.

Team-based pay is defined as incentive compensation that rewards individuals for teamwork and/or rewards the teams for collective results. This definition highlights an important distinction between individual *behaviour* and *team* results. Stated another way, it takes team players to get team results. Any team-oriented pay plan that ignores this distinction almost certainly will fail.

Problems   The biggest single barrier to effective team-based pay is *cultural*, especially in highly individualistic cultures such as the United States, Canada, Norway, and Australia.[75] Individual competition for pay and pay rises has long been the norm in the United States.[76] Entrenched grading schemes in schools and colleges, focused on individual competition and not group achievement, are a good preview of the traditional American workplace. Team-based pay is a direct assault on the cultural tradition of putting the individual above the group. Recall from our discussion in Chapter 4 that collectivist cultures put the group above the individual.

Another culturally rooted problem is a general *lack of teamwork skills*. Members of high-performance teams are skilled communicators, conflict handlers, and negotiators; they are flexible, adaptable, and open to change. Employees accustomed to being paid for personal achievements tend to resent having their pay dependent upon others' performance and problems. The combination of poor interpersonal skills and an individualistic work ethic can breed conflict and excessive peer pressure, as Levi Strauss & Co. learned at its El Paso, Texas, jeans factory. The El Paso plant was one of 27 sewing operations in the United States, where Levi's switched from traditional assembly lines to 20- to 30-worker multitask teams responsible for complete batches of jeans, from start to finish. Eighteen months into the new team structure, orders were being processed in only three days, as opposed to a seven-day turnaround under the old system. But Levi's got more than improved productivity:

Under the team system, a worker's incentive pay is tied to team performance. A poor performer or absent worker affects everybody's paycheck. When someone is perceived to be faking sick days or lollygagging on a sewing machine, tempers flare. Says [team member Salvador] Salas: "Somebody's fooling around, and somebody else calls attention to that, and the first guy will just flip him off." Supervisor Gracie Cortez says that "it gets tough out there." She finds herself intervening to prevent "big fights." Says plant manager Edward Alvarez: "Peer pressure can be vicious and brutal."[77]

Levi's officials eventually realized that only two weeks of "group dynamics" training for plant workers, prior to the shift to teams, was insufficient.

Recommendations   The state of the art in team-based pay is very primitive today. Given the many different types of teams, we can be certain there is no single best approach. However, based on anecdotal evidence from the general management literature and case studies,[78] we can make these five recommendations:

- *Prepare employees* for team-based systems with as much interpersonal skills training as possible. This ongoing effort should include diversity training and skill training in communication, conflict resolution, trust building, group problem solving, and negotiating.

- *Establish teams* and get them running smoothly before introducing team-based pay incentives to avoid overload and frustration.

- Create a pay plan that *blends* individual achievement and team incentives.

- Begin by rewarding teamwork *behaviours* (such as mutual support, cooperation, and group problem solving), and then phase in pay incentives for team *results*.

- When paying for team results, make sure individual team members see a clear connection between their own work and team results. Compensation specialists call this a *clear line of sight*.

Making Pay for Performance Work

From a practical "so what" perspective, the real issue is not profit sharing versus gainsharing versus team-based pay. Rather, the issue is this: How can managers improve the motivational impact of their current pay-for-performance plan? The fact is, most such plans are not pure types. They are hybrids. They combine features of profit sharing, gainsharing, and team approaches.[79] One option is to hire consultants to establish one of the trademarked gainsharing plans or the Scanlon plan. A second, more broadly applicable, option is to build the best characteristics of profit sharing, gainsharing, and team pay plans into the organization's pay-for-performance plan. The following practical recommendations can help in this regard:

- Make pay for performance an integral part of the organization's basic strategy (e.g., pursuit of best-in-the-industry product or service quality).[80]

- Base incentive determinations on objective performance data.

- Have all employees actively participate in the development, implementation, and revision of the performance-pay formulas.

- Encourage two-way communication so problems with the pay-for-performance plan will be detected early.

- Build the pay-for-performance plan around participative structures such as suggestion systems or quality circles.

- Reward teamwork and cooperation whenever possible.

- Actively sell the plan to supervisors and middle managers who may view employee participation as a threat to their traditional notion of authority.

- If annual cash bonuses are granted, pay them in a lump sum to maximize their motivational impact.

Summary of Key Concepts

1. *Specify the two basic functions of feedback and three sources of feedback.* Feedback, in the form of objective information about performance, both instructs and motivates. According to the cognitive-processing model, individuals receive feedback from others, the task, and from themselves.

2. *Discuss how the recipient's characteristics, perceptions, and cognitive evaluations affect how the* individual processes feedback. The recipient's openness to feedback is determined by one's self-esteem, self-efficacy, needs and goals, and desire for feedback. One's perception determines if feedback is viewed positively or negatively. Cognitively, the recipient will tend to act on feedback that is seen as accurate, from a credible source, based on a fair system, and tied to reasonable expectations and behavioural standards.

3. *List at least three practical lessons from feedback research.* Feedback is not automatically accepted as intended, especially negative feedback. Managerial credibility can be enhanced through expertise and a climate of trust. Feedback must not be too frequent or too scarce and must be tailored to the individual. Feedback directly from computers is effective. Active participation in the feedback session helps people perceive feedback as more accurate. The quality of feedback received decreases as one moves up the organizational hierarchy.

4. *Define upward feedback and 360-degree feedback, and summarize the general tips for giving good feedback.* Lower-level employees provide upward feedback (usually anonymous) to their managers. A focal person receives 360-degree feedback from subordinates, the manager, peers, and selected others such as customers or suppliers. Good feedback is tied to performance *goals* and clear *expectations*, linked with *specific* behaviour and/or results, reserved for *key result areas*, given as *soon* as possible, provided for *improvement* as well as for final results, focused on *performance* rather than on personalities, and based on *accurate* and *credible* information.

5. *Briefly explain the four different organizational reward norms, and summarize the reasons rewards often fail to motivate employees.* Maximizing individual gain is the object of the *profit maximization* reward norm. The *equity* norm calls for distributing rewards proportionate to contributions (those who contribute the most should earn the most). Everyone is rewarded equally when the equality reward norm is in force. The *need* reward norm involves distributing rewards based on employees' needs. Reward systems can fail to motivate employees for these reasons: overemphasis on money, no appreciation effect, benefits become entitlements, wrong behaviour is rewarded, rewards are delayed too long, use of one-size-fits-all rewards, one-shot rewards with temporary impact, and demotivating practices such as layoffs.

6. *Discuss the impact that incentive bonuses have on employee motivation and performance.* Incentive bonuses have a double impact on employee motivation and performance because they are first promised and then delivered. Employee participation plays a key role in this process by generating solutions to productivity problems and prompting intrinsic motivation, information sharing, and employee empowerment.

7. *Distinguish among profit sharing, gainsharing, and team-based pay.* Profit-sharing plans give employees a specified portion of the business's economic profits. Gainsharing ties bonuses to documented productivity increases. Team-based pay is incentive pay for engaging in teamwork *behaviours* and/or for team *results*.

8. *Discuss how managers can generally improve pay-for-performance plans.* They need to be strategically anchored, based on quantified performance data, highly participative, actively sold to supervisors and middle managers, and teamwork oriented. Annual bonuses of significant size are helpful.

Discussion Questions

1. How can feedback and rewards *combine* to improve job performance?

2. How has feedback instructed and/or motivated you lately?

3. Relative to your study, which of the three sources of feedback—others, task, self—has the greatest impact on your performance? If you have a job, which source of feedback is most potent in that situation?

4. Which of the five cognitive evaluation criteria for feedback—feedback accuracy, source credibility, system fairness, expectancies, behavioural standards—do you think ranks as most important? Explain.

5. What is the most valuable lesson feedback research teaches us? Explain.

6. How would you summarize the practical benefits and drawbacks of 360-degree feedback?

7. Which of the four organizational reward norms do you prefer? Why?

8. What is your personal experience with failed organizational reward systems and practices?

9. As a modern manager, which pay-for-performance approach do you like better: profit sharing, gainsharing, or team-based pay?

10. How would you respond to a manager who said, "Employees cannot be motivated with money"?

Personal Awareness and Growth Exercise

What Kind of Feedback Are You Getting

Objectives

1. To provide actual examples of on-the-job feedback from three primary sources: organization /supervisor, co-workers, and self/task.

2. To provide a handy instrument for evaluating the comparative strength of positive feedback from these three sources.

Introduction

A pair of researchers from Georgia Tech developed and tested a 63-item feedback questionnaire to demonstrate the importance of both the sign and content of feedback messages.[81] Although their instrument contains both positive and negative feedback items, we have extracted 18 positive items for this self-awareness exercise.

Instructions

Thinking of your current job (or your most recent job), circle one number for each of the 18 items. Alternatively, you could ask one or more other employed individuals to complete the questionnaire. Once the questionnaire has been completed, calculate subtotal and total scores by adding the circled numbers. Then try to answer the discussion questions.

Instrument

How frequently do you experience each of the following outcomes in your present (or past) job?

ORGANIZATIONAL/SUPERVISORY FEEDBACK

		RARELY	OCCASIONALLY	VERY FREQUENTLY

1. My supervisor complimenting me on something I have done. 1—— 2 —— 3 —— 4——5

2. My supervisor increasing my responsibilities. 1—— 2 —— 3 —— 4——5

3. The company expressing pleasure with my performance. 1—— 2 —— 3 —— 4——5

4. The company giving me a rise. 1—— 2 —— 3 —— 4——5

5. My supervisor recommending me for a promotion or rise. 1—— 2 —— 3 —— 4——5

6. The company providing me with favourable data concerning my performance. 1—— 2 —— 3 —— 4——5

Subscore = _____

CO-WORKER FEEDBACK

7. My co-workers coming to me for advice. 1—— 2 —— 3 —— 4——5

8. My co-workers expressing approval of my work. 1—— 2 —— 3 —— 4——5

9. My co-workers liking to work with me. 1—— 2 —— 3 —— 4——5

10. My co-workers telling me that I am doing a good job. 1—— 2 —— 3 —— 4——5

11. My co-workers commenting favourably on something I have done. 1—— 2 —— 3 —— 4——5

12. Receiving a compliment from my co-workers. 1—— 2 —— 3 —— 4——5

Subscore = _____

SELF/TASK FEEDBACK

13. Knowing that the way I go about my duties is superior to most others. 1—— 2 —— 3 —— 4——5

14. Feeling I am accomplishing more than I used to. 1—— 2 —— 3 —— 4——5

15. Knowing that I can now perform or do things which previously were difficult for me. 1—— 2 —— 3 —— 4——5

16. Finding that I am satisfying my own standards for "good work." 1—— 2 —— 3 —— 4——5

17. Knowing that what I am doing "feels right." 1—— 2 —— 3 —— 4——5

18. Feeling confident of
being able to handle all
aspects of my job.   1—— 2 —— 3 —— 4——5

Subscore = _____

Total Score = _____

QUESTIONS FOR DISCUSSION

1. Which items on this questionnaire would you rate
as primarily instructional in function? Are all of
the remaining items primarily motivational?
Explain.
2. In terms of your own feedback profile, which of

the three types is the strongest (has the highest
subscore)? Which is the weakest (has the lowest
subscore)? How well does your feedback profile
explain your job performance and/or satisfaction?

3. How does your feedback profile measure up
against those of your classmates? (Arbitrary
norms, for comparative purposes, are: Deficient
feedback = 18–42; Moderate feedback = 43–65;
Abundant feedback = 66–90.)

4. Which of the three sources of feedback is most
critical to your successful job performance and/or
job satisfaction? Explain.

Group Exercise

Rewards, Rewards, Rewards
Objectives

1. To tap the class's collective knowledge of
organizational rewards.
2. To appreciate the vast array of potential rewards.
3. To contrast individual and group perceptions of
rewards.
4. To practice your group creativity skills.

Introduction

Rewards are a centrepiece of organizational life. Both
extrinsic and intrinsic rewards motivate us to join and
continue contributing to organized effort. But not all
rewards have the same impact on work motivation.
Individuals have their own personal preferences for
rewards. The best way to discover people's reward
preferences is to ask them, both individually and
collectively. This group brainstorming and class
discussion exercise requires about 20 to 30 minutes.

Instructions

Your instructor will divide your class randomly into
teams of five to eight people. Each team will go
through the following four-step process:

1. Each team will have a six-minute brainstorming
session, with one person acting as recorder. The
objective of this brainstorming session is to list as
many different organizational rewards as the group
can think of. Your team might find it helpful to
think of rewards by category (such as rewards from
the work itself, rewards you can spend, rewards you
can eat and drink, rewards you can feel, rewards
you can wear, rewards you can share, rewards you
cannot see, etc.). Remember, good brainstorming
calls for withholding judgements about whether

ideas are good or not. Quantity is wanted. Building
upon other people's ideas also is encouraged.

2. Next, each individual will take four minutes to
write down, in decreasing order of importance, 10
rewards they want from the job. Note: These are
your personal preferences; your "top 10" rewards
that will motivate you to do your best.

3. Each team will then take five minutes to generate a
list of "today's 10 most powerful rewards." List
them in decreasing order of their power to motivate
job performance. Voting may be necessary.

4. A general class discussion of the questions listed
below will conclude the exercise.

QUESTIONS FOR DISCUSSION

1. How did your personal "top 10" list compare with
your group's "top 10" list? If there is a serious
mismatch, how would it affect your motivation?
(To promote discussion, the instructor may ask
several volunteers to read their personal "top 10"
lists to the class.)

2. Which team had the most productive
brainstorming session? (The instructor may
request each team to read its brainstormed list of
potential rewards and "top 10" list to the class.)

3. Were you surprised to hear certain rewards getting
so much attention? Why?

4. How can managers improve the incentive effect of
the rewards most frequently mentioned in class?

5. What is the likely future of organizational reward
plans? Which of today's compensation trends will
probably thrive, and which are probably passing
fads?

Notes

[1]L Kellaway, "Management: Turning the Tables. A Look at a Method of Appraisal which Requires Employees to Assess Their Managers," *The Financial Times*, May 31, 1995, p 16.

[2]R Aubrey and P M Cohen, *Working Wisdom: Timeless Skills and Vanguard Strategies for Learning Organizations* (San Francisco: Jossey-Bass, 1995), p 4.

[3]I Sager, "The Man Who's Rebooting IBM's PC Business," *Business Week*, July 24, 1995, p 70.

[4]J A Byrne, "Management Meccas," *Business Week*, September 18, 1995, p 128.

[5]Data from M Hequet, "Giving Feedback," *Training*, September 1994, pp 72–77.

[6]C Bell and R Zemke, "On-Target Feedback," *Training*, June 1992, p 36.

[7]Both the definition of feedback and the functions of feedback are based on discussion in D R Ilgen, C D Fisher, and M S Taylor, "Consequences of Individual Feedback on Behaviour in Organizations," *Journal of Applied Psychology*, August 1979, pp 349–71; and R E Kopelman, *Managing Productivity in Organizations: A Practical People-Oriented Perspective* (New York: McGraw-Hill, 1986), p 175.

[8]See P C Earley, G B Northcraft, C Lee, and T R Lituchy, "Impact of Process and Outcome Feedback on the Relation of Goal Setting to Task Performance," *Academy of Management Journal*, March 1990, pp 87–105.

[9]Data from A N Kluger and A DeNisi, "The Effects of Feedback Interventions on Performance: A Historical Review, a Meta-Analysis, and a Preliminary Feedback Intervention Theory," *Psychological Bulletin*, March 1996, pp 254–84.

[10]H Lancaster, "Scott Adams Offers Valuable Lessons from Life with Dilbert," *The Wall Street Journal*, August 8, 1995, p B1.

[11]K MacKenzie, "The Man who Made Business to Bash Bosses", *The Financial Times*, November 23–23, 1997, *Weekend FT*, p III.

[12]See P E Levy, M D Albright, B D Cawley, and J R Williams, "Situational and Individual Determinants of Feedback Seeking: A Closer Look at the Process," *Organizational Behavior and Human Decision Processes*, April 1995, pp 23–37; M R Leary, E S Tambor, S K Terdal, and D L Downs, "Self-Esteem as an Interpersonal Monitor: The Sociometer Hypothesis," *Journal of Personality and Social Psychology*, June 1995, pp 518–30; and M A Quinones, "Pretraining Context Effects: Training Assignment as Feedback," *Journal of Applied Psychology*, April 1995, pp 226–38.

[13]See T Matsui, A Okkada, and T Kakuyama, "Influence of Achievement Need on Goal Setting, Performance, and Feedback Effectiveness," *Journal of Applied Psychology*, October 1982, pp 645–48.

[14]S J Ashford, "Feedback-Seeking in Individual Adaptation: A Resource Perspective," *Academy of Management Journal*, September 1986, pp 465–87. Also see D B Fedor, R B Rensvold, and S M Adams, "An Investigation of Factors Expected to Affect Feedback Seeking: A Longitudinal Field Study," *Personnel Psychology*, Winter 1992, pp 779–805.

[15]See D B Turban and T W Dougherty, "Role of Protege Personality in Receipt of Mentoring and Career Success," *Academy of Management Journal*, June 1994, pp 688–702. Also see M E Burkhardt, "Social Interaction Effects Following a Technological Change: A Longitudinal Investigation," *Academy of Management Journal*, August 1994, pp 869–98.

[16]See D M Herold, C K Parsons, and R B Rensvold, "Individual Differences in the Generation and Processing of Performance Feedback," *Educational and Psychological Measurement*, February 1996, pp 5–25.

[17]See B D Bannister, "Performance Outcome Feedback and Attributional Feedback: Interactive Effects on Recipient Responses," *Journal of Applied Psychology*, May 1986, pp 203–10.

[18]For complete details, see P M Podsakoff and J-L Farh, "Effects of Feedback Sign and Credibility on Goal Setting and Task Performance," *Organizational Behavior and Human Decision Processes*, August 1989, pp 45–67. Also see S J Ashford and A S Tsui, "Self-Regulation for Managerial Effectiveness: The Role of Active Feedback Seeking," *Academy of Management Journal*, June 1991, pp 251–80.

[19]W S Silver, T R Mitchell, and M E Gist, "Responses to Successful and Unsuccessful Performance: The Moderating Effect of Self-Efficacy on the Relationship between Performance and Attributions," *Organizational Behavior and Human Decision Processes*, June 1995, p 297.

[20]J M Kouzes and B Z Posner, *Credibility: How Leaders Gain and Lose It, Why People Demand It* (San Francisco: Jossey-Bass, 1993), p 25.

[21]For related research, see J B Vancouver and E Wolfe Morrison, "Feedback Inquiry: The Effect of Source Attributes and Individual Differences," *Organizational Behavior and Human Decision Processes*, June 1995, pp 276–85.

[22]See S H Barr and E J Conlon, "Effects of Distribution of Feedback in Work Groups," *Academy of Management Journal*, June 1994, pp 641–55.

[23]Based on discussion in Ilgen, Fisher, and Taylor, "Consequences of Individual Feedback on Behaviour in Organizations," pp 367–68. Also see J J Martocchio and J Webster, "Effects of Feedback and Cognitive Playfulness on Performance in Microcomputer Software Training," *Personnel Psychology*, Autumn 1992, pp 553–78.

[24]See P C Earley, "Computer-Generated Performance Feedback in the Magazine-Subscription Industry," *Organizational Behavior and Human Decision Processes*, February 1988, pp 50–64.

[25]See M De Gregorio and C D Fisher, "Providing Performance Feedback: Reactions to Alternate Methods," *Journal of Management*, December 1988, pp 605–16.

[26]For details, see R A Baron, "Countering the Effects of Destructive Criticism: The Relative Efficacy of Four Interventions," *Journal of Applied Psychology*, June 1990, pp 235–45. Also see M L Smith, "Give Feedback, Not Criticism," *Supervisory Management*, February 1993, p 4.

[27]C O Longenecker and D A Gioia, "The Executive Appraisal Paradox," *Academy of Management Executive*, May 1992, p 18. Also see "It's Still Lonely at the Top," *Training*, April 1993, p 8.

[28]Practical tips for giving feedback can be found in E Van Velsor and S J Wall, "How to Choose a Feedback Instrument," *Training*, March 1992, pp 47–52; T Lammers, "The Effective Employee-Feedback System," *Inc.*, February 1993, pp 109–11; L Smith, "The Executive's New Coach," *Fortune*, December 27, 1993, pp 126–34; and M Hequet, "Giving Good Feedback," *Training*, September 1994, pp 72–77.

[29]See M R Edwards, A J Ewen, and W A Verdini, "Fair Performance Management and Pay Practices for Diverse Work Forces: The Promise of Multisource Assessment," *ACA Journal*, Spring 1995, pp 50–63.

[30]This list is based in part on discussion in H J Bernardin, "Subordinate Appraisal: A Valuable Source of Information about

Managers," *Human Resource Management*, Fall 1986, pp 421–39.

[31]Data from D Antonioni, "The Effects of Feedback Accountability on Upward Appraisal Ratings," *Personnel Psychology*, Summer 1994, pp 349–56.

[32]H J Bernardin, S A Dahmus, and G Redmon, "Attitudes of First-Line Supervisors toward Subordinate Appraisals," *Human Resource Management*, Summer/Fall 1993, p 315.

[33]Data from J W Smither, M London, N L Vasilopoulos, R R Reilly, R E Millsap, and N Salvemini, "An Examination of the Effects of an Upward Feedback Program Over Time," *Personnel Psychology*, Spring 1995, pp 1–34.

[34]For example, see R Hoffman, "Ten Reasons You Should Be Using 360-Degree Feedback," *HRMagazine*, April 1995, pp 82–85; and "360-Degree Feedback: Will The Circle Be Broken?" *Training*, October 1996, pp 24–25.

[35]B O'Reilly, "360 Feedback Can Change Your Life," *Fortune*, October 17, 1994, p 93.

[36]For background reading on 360-degree feedback, see the entire Summer/Fall 1993 issue of *Human Resource Management*; M London and R W Beatty, "360-Degree Feedback as a Competitive Advantage," *Human Resource Management*, Summer/Fall 1993, pp 353–72; M Maynard, "Evaluations Evolve from Bottom," *USA Today*, August 3, 1994, p 6B; G Yukl and R Lepsinger, "360;dg Feedback," *Training*, December 1995, pp 45–50; and M B N Vinson, "The Pros and Cons of 360-Degree Feedback: Making It Work," *Training & Development*, April 1996, pp 11–12.

[37]See M M Harris and J Schaubroeck, "A Meta-Analysis of Self-Supervisor, Self-Peer, and Peer-Supervisor Ratings," *Personnel Psychology*, Spring 1988, pp 43–62, and J Lane and P Herriot, "Self-Ratings, Supervisor Ratings, Positions and Performance," *Journal of Occupational Psychology*, March 1990, pp 77–88. Also see J R Williams and P E Levy, "The Effects of Perceived System Knowledge on the Agreement between Self-Ratings and Supervisor Ratings," *Personnel Psychology*, Winter 1992, pp 835–47; and R F Martell and M R Borg, "A Comparison of the Behavioral Rating Accuracy of Groups and Individuals," *Journal of Applied Psychology*, February 1993, pp 43–50.

[38]Fisher Hazucha, S A Hezlett, and R J Schneider, "The Impact of 360-Degree Feedback on Managerial Skills Development," *Human Resource Management*, Summer/Fall 1993, p 42.

[39]List quoted from D W Bracken, "Straight Talk about Multirater Feedback," *Training & Development*, September 1994, p 46. Also see D Antonioni, Designing An Effective 360-Degree Appraisal Feedback Process," *Organizational Dynamics*, Autumn 1996, pp 24–38.

[40]For supporting evidence of employees' desire for prompt feedback, see D H Reid and M B Parsons, "A Comparison of Staff Acceptability of Immediate versus Delayed Verbal Feedback in Staff Training," *Journal of Organizational Behavior Management*, no. 2, 1996, pp 35–47.

[41]See B Filipczak, "Can't Buy Me Love," *Training*, January 1996, pp 29–34; and S Kerr, "Risky Business: The New Pay Game," *Fortune*, July 22, 1996, pp 94–95.

[42]Based on and translated from V Giolito, "Naf Naf Étend aux Non-Cadres le Régime des Stock-options," *L'Essentiel du Management*, August 1995, p 46.

[43]For complete discussions, see A P Brief and R J Aldag, "The Intrinsic-Extrinsic Dichotomy: Toward Conceptual Clarity," *Academy of Management Review*, July 1977, pp 496–500; and E L Deci, *Intrinsic Motivation* (New York: Plenum Press, 1975), ch. 2.

[44]Based on A Furnham, "No Need to Reward Good Performance—How To Make Intrinsic Motivation," *The Financial Times*, April 27, 1994, p 19.

[45]See K I Kim, H-J Park, and N Suzuki, "Reward Allocations in the United States, Japan, and Korea: A Comparison of Individualistic and Collectivistic Cultures," *Academy of Management Journal*, March 1990, pp 188–98.

[46]Adapted from J L Pearce and R H Peters, "A Contradictory Norms View of Employer–Employee Exchange," *Journal of Management*, Spring 1985, pp 19–30.

[47]Ibid., p 25.

[48]See D B McFarlin and P D Sweeney, "Distributive and Procedural Justice as Predictors of Satisfaction with Personal and Organizational Outcomes," *Academy of Management Journal*, August 1992, pp 626–37.

[49]M Von Glinow, "Reward Strategies for Attracting, Evaluating, and Retaining Professionals," *Human Resource Management*, Summer 1985, p 193.

[50]Six reward system objectives are discussed in E E Lawler III, "The New Pay: A Strategic Approach," *Compensation & Benefits Review*, July–August 1995, pp 14–22.

[51]D R Spitzer, "Power Rewards: Rewards That Really Motivate," *Management Review*, May 1996, p 47. Also see S Kerr, "An Academy Classic: On the Folly of Rewarding A, while Hoping for B," *Academy of Management Executive*, February 1995, pp 7–14.

[52]List adapted from discussion in Spitzer, "Power Rewards: Rewards that Really Motivate," pp 45–50. Also see R Eisenberger and J Cameron, "Detrimental Effects of Reward: Reality or Myth?" *American Psychologist*, November 1996, pp 1153–1166.

[53]See, for example, T P Flannery, D A Hofrichter, and P E Platten, *People, Performance, and Pay: Dynamic Compensation for Changing Organizations* (New York: The Free Press, 1996).

[54]Among such factors as "relationship with boss" and "job responsibilities," respondents in a survey expressed the least satisfaction with "salary." See "Whistling while They Work," *USA Today*, August 29, 1996, p 1B.

[55]See P K Zingheim and J R Schuster, "How Are the New Pay Tools Being Deployed?" *Compensation & Benefits Review*, July–August 1995, pp 10–13.

[56]See G M Ritzky, "Incentive Pay Programmes That Help the Bottom Line," *HRMagazine*, April 1995, pp 68–74; and I T Kay and D Lerner, "What's Good for the Parts May Hurt the Whole," *HRMagazine*, September 1995, pp 71–77. The case against incentive plans is presented in A Kohn, "Why Incentive Plans Cannot Work," *Harvard Business Review*, September–October 1993, pp 54–63.

[57]See H Gleckman, "Bonus Pay: Buzzword or Bonanza?" *Business Week*, November 14, 1994, pp 62–64; B Wysocki Jr., "Unstable Pay Becomes Ever More Common," *The Wall Street Journal*, December 4, 1995, p A1; and L K Stroh, J M Brett, J P Baumann, and A H Reilly, "Agency Theory and Variable Pay Compensation Strategies," *Academy of Management Journal*, June 1996, pp 751–67.

[58]L Kellaway, "The Pen is Mightier than the Boss," *The Financial Times*, June 27, 1994, p 16.

[59]S Fernie, and D Metcalf, *Participation, Contingent Pay, Representation and Workplace Performance: Evidence from Great Britain* (London: Centre for Economic Performance, 1995).

[60]"How Four Companies Are Redefining the Employment Relationship through Innovative Changes in Compensation and Benefits, Case studies: Whirlpool, Nike, Salamon and PSEG," *Compensation & Benefits Review*, January–February 1995, pp 71–80.

[61]V Houlder, A Hill, A Jack, "Why Do You Deserve To Be Paid So Much? A Look at Moves To Counter Recent Criticism of Big Bonuses by Establishing a Better Link with Performance" *The Financial Times*, November 21, 1994, p 12.

[62]Data from N J Perry, "Here Come Richer, Riskier Pay Plans," *Fortune*, December 19, 1988, p 51. Also see W Zellner, "Trickle-Down Is Trickling Down at Work," *Business Week*, March 18, 1996, p 34.

[63]See M J Mandel, "Those Fat Bonuses Don't Seem to Boost Performance," *Business Week*, January 8, 1990, p 26. Also see J A Byrne, "Deliver—or Else," *Business Week*, March 27, 1995, pp 36–38; R A G Monks, "Stock Options Don't Work. If CEOs Want Shares, Let 'em Buy Some," *Fortune*, September 18, 1995, pp 230–32; and D J Miller, "CEO Salary Increases May Be Rational After All: Referents and Contracts in CEO Pay," *Academy of Management Journal*, October 1995, pp 1361–85.

[64]Based on discussion in R Ricklefs, "Whither the Payoff on Sales Commissions?" *The Wall Street Journal*, June 6, 1990, p B1.

[65]G Koretz, "Bad Marks for Pay-by-Results," *Business Week*, September 4, 1995, p 28.

[66]Another approach to getting employees to think and act like owners of the business, employee stock ownership plans, is given complete coverage in J R Blasi and D L Kruse, *The New Owners: The Mass Emergence of Employee Ownership in Public Companies and What It Means to American Business* (New York: HarperCollins, 1991). Also see N J Perry, "Talk about Pay for Performance," *Fortune*, May 4, 1992, p 77; and S Baker and K L Alexander, "The Owners vs the Boss at Weirton Steel," *Business Week*, November 15, 1993, p 38.

[67]B Graham-Moore, "Review of the Literature," in *Gainsharing*, eds B Graham-Moore and T L Ross (Washington, DC: The Bureau of National Affairs, 1990), p 20 (emphasis added).

[68]Ibid., based largely on pp 3–4. Also see J G Belcher, Jr., "Gainsharing and Variable Pay: The State of the Art," *Compensation & Benefits Review*, May–June 1994, pp 50–60; and T M Welbourne and L R Gomez Mejia, "Gainsharing: A Critical Review and a Future Research Agenda," *Journal of Management*, no. 3, 1995, pp 559–609.

[69]Practical examples of gainsharing can be found in T Ehrenfeld, "Cashing In," *Inc.*, July 1993, pp 69–70; T Ehrenfeld, "Gain-Sharing," *Inc.*, August 1993, pp 87–89; and R L Masternak, "Gainsharing Boosts Quality and Productivity at a BF Goodrich Plant," *National Productivity Review*, Spring 1993, pp 225–38.

[70]For gainsharing success factors and problems, see D O Kim, "Factors Influencing Organizational Performance in Gainsharing Programmes," *Industrial Relations*, April 1996, pp 227–44; D Collins, "Death of a Gainsharing Plan: Power Politics and Participatory Management," *Organizational Dynamics*, Summer 1995, pp 23–38; and D Collins, "Case Study: 15 Lessons Learned from the Death of a Gainsharing Plan," *Compensation & Benefits*

Review, March–April 1996, pp 31–40.

[71]For details, see S E Markham, "Pay-for-Performance Dilemma Revisited: Empirical Example of the Importance of Group Effects," *Journal of Applied Psychology*, May 1988, pp 172–80.

[72]Data from K I Miller, "Cultural and Role-Based Predictors of Organizational Participation and Allocation Preferences," *Communication Research*, December 1988, pp 699–725.

[73]Gainsharing studies are reviewed in W Imberman, "Gainsharing: A Lemon or Lemonade?" *Business Horizons*, January–February 1996, pp 36–40. Also see T M Welbourne, D B Balkin, and L R Gomez Mejia, "Gainsharing and Mutual Monitoring: A Combined Agency-Organizational Justice Interpretation," *Academy of Management Journal*, June 1995, pp 881–99.

[74]Data from D Collins, "How and Why Participatory Management Improves a Company's Social Performance," *Business & Society*, June 1996, pp 176–210.

[75]Ranking based on research evidence in F Trompenaars, *Riding the Waves of Culture: Understanding Diversity in Global Business* (Chicago: Irwin Professional Publishing, 1994), p 52.

[76]See S Caudron, "Tie Individual Pay to Team Success," *Personnel Journal*, October 1994, pp 40–46.

[77]R Mitchell, "Managing by Values," *Business Week*, August 1, 1994, p 50.

[78]For example, see R Sisco, "Put Your Money Where Your Teams Are," *Training*, July 1992, pp 41–45; J L Morris, "Bonus Dollars for Team Players," *HRMagazine*, February 1995, pp 76–83; W J Timmins, "Team-Based Compensation at Recently Reengineered Zeneca Ag Products," *Employment Relations Today*, Summer 1995, pp 43–51; and R L Heneman and C von Hippel, "Balancing Group and Individual Rewards: Rewarding Individual Contributions to the Team," *Compensation & Benefits Review*, July–August 1995, pp 63–68.

[79]See D O'Neill, "Blending the Best of Profit Sharing and Gainsharing, *HRMagazine*, March 1994, pp 66–70.

[80]See Lawler, "The New Pay: A Strategic Approach," pp 14–22.

[81]This exercise is adapted from material in D M Herold and C K Parsons, "Assessing the Feedback Environment in Work Organizations: Development of the Job Feedback Survey," *Journal of Applied Psychology*, May 1985, pp 290–305.

Three

Group and Social Processes

Ten   Group Dynamics

Eleven   Power, Politics, Conflict, and Negotiation

Twelve   Individual and Group Decision Making

Thirteen Teams and Teamwork for the 21st Century

Ten

Group Dynamics

The Wilderness Lab

I found myself on a bus with 18 other refugees from the white-collar world. We all headed for five days of management development in the woods. We were a diverse group representing a variety of organizations from one-person consulting firms to multinational corporations. The participants included wise, understated, seasoned managers as well as bright young travellers on the corporate ladder whose rough edges were softened by the positive energy in their eyes. There were managers whose natural interests in people and leadership ability had taken them up the ranks, and highly skilled technicians, used to being independent contributors, who had recently found themselves in the uncomfortable position of needing to manage others. Ages ranged from 24 to 44, and disciplines included law, engineering, architecture, marketing, and education, among others. Some participants were veterans of many training programs; others were fairly new to the realm of management development.

Most of us wanted to be there. Some had learned of the program themselves and lobbied to go. Others had been sent by their organizations to learn to work more effectively in groups—either because they were normally reticent in groups, or because they tended to dominate and compete. The outdoor medium had been selected by some because it is a more comfortable setting than the traditional classroom. Others had chosen it because it is a substantial step beyond the familiar corporate comfort zone and as such is a ripe environment for testing the ways we plan, solve problems, and work with others.

Most of us were a little scared. Our fears ranged from making fools of ourselves to falling off a cliff. It was hard to determine which of those fears was more serious. . . .

At the top of the hill we found a "trust ladder" nailed to one of the many pines surrounding us. There appeared to be a little more risk here than looking silly. Eric [the course director] explained that we would need to rely on one another under many circumstances in the coming week, and that the object of this exercise was to climb the ladder and fall off backwards into the arms of the group. He showed us how to line up and join hands to catch our falling teammate, and he headed for the ladder before we could ponder the matter too thoroughly. I was afraid that I wouldn't be able to hold him . . . and, of course, I couldn't have alone. One by one we climbed the ladder and thumped down into the waiting arms.

This was the first activity that we analysed. We talked about risk taking, trusting one's support system, communicating needs, and checking to be sure that the support system is ready before relying on it . . . and a little about what's involved in supporting someone effectively.

Our most physical group challenge was a 13-foot wall the entire group had to scale. It was sheer and smooth, with a platform behind it on which one could stand at about waist level with the top of the wall. This platform could be occupied by two people (once we got them up and over) to help haul up the rest of the group. A ladder was provided on the back for climbing down to earth. Thirteen feet had never seemed so imposing. We were given a few safety restrictions, and the stopwatch began ticking. Group planning and problem solving were again germane, with special attention to the first and last people over the wall.

We decided that we needed to boost some strong people up first to help pull the rest up, and keep some powerful boosters on the ground. The middle group would be relatively straightforward, with help from above and below. The final climb appeared to require two key players: someone strong enough to act as a "human rope," facing the wall and hanging with his shoulders looped over the top; and someone light and strong enough to scramble up the wall, using the human rope until he could get a hand from the pullers.

The roles clear, we began to assess our resources. I was proud of the group as we offered up both our strengths and limitations. We had walked past THE WALL several times over the previous two days, and it was the culmination of our group challenges. We

were hungry to do it well, and the chance to play a key role was tantalizing. But the group interdependence in this exercise took on a more serious note. Despite good safety precautions (such as helmets and "spotters" whose job it would be to break anyone's fall) we really did have one another's safety in our hands. It would not do to play the hero here and be unable to come through. Some of our most athletic team members owned up to prohibitive injuries that would keep them in the middle of the progression. Others stepped forward to fill the void, each assessing his or her own capabilities with a balance of commitment and responsibility. Soon we all knew our roles, and the adrenaline began to flow.

The scene that followed was an organized frenzy of push, pull, scramble, encourage, and keep those hands in the air in case someone fell. No one spent a moment uninvolved in the process. We all ached for our last two teammates as they completed the grueling climb. It was a tired and happy group that sat in a circle beneath the wall to talk not only about planning and problem solving but also the dynamics of sensible group risk taking, and the strength of being part of a multitalented, interdependent and mutually supportive team.

As I leaned back against the wall and watched all this with an analytical trainer's eye, I became aware of the powerful lesson I was experiencing at gut level. [White-water canoeing had] . . . left me with a shoulder that chronically dislocates, which not only put me in the center of the progression up the wall, but made me feel like a liability to the group. As I stepped up for my boost, I told the pullers what to expect. "All right, Wayne, you can pull for all you're worth. But Mike, I can't extend this right arm very high, and if I call your name, let go in a hurry." I could feel the spotters move in around me, but I was up and over in a moment with no trouble.

During the debriefing I asked what effect my limitation had on the group, especially Wayne and Mike. "None at all," said Wayne. "None," echoed Mike, "because you told us what your needs were. I could lean down the wall further and put myself into a more vulnerable position with more leverage because I knew you wouldn't be pulling very hard with that arm." I've never been good at making my needs known, but in this situation I felt a responsibility to the group. I thought back to the office and wondered how many projects I had avoided or contributed less than I could have because I didn't give someone the chance to fill in my weak spots.[1]

Discussion Question

Why might the wilderness lab be a better learning environment than the classroom?

I n Part Two, we studied individual and personal factors within organizational settings. Now, in Part Three, our attention turns to the collective or *social* dimensions of organizational behaviour. Because the management of organizational behaviour is above all else a social endeavour, managers need a strong working knowledge of *interpersonal* behaviour. Research consistently reveals the importance of social skills for both individual and organizational success. An ongoing study by the Center for Creative Leadership (involving diverse samplings from Belgium, France, Germany, Italy, the United Kingdom, the United States, and Spain) found four stumbling blocks that tend to derail executives' careers. According to the researchers, "A derailed executive is one who, having reached the general manager level, finds that there is little chance of future advancement due to a misfit between job requirements and personal skills."[2] The four stumbling blocks, consistent across the cultures studied, are as follows:

1. Problems with interpersonal relationships.

2. Failure to meet business objectives.

3. Failure to build and lead a team.

4. Inability to change or adapt during a transition.[3]

Notice how both the first and third career stumbling blocks involve interpersonal skills—the ability to get along and work effectively with others. Managers with interpersonal problems typically were described as manipulative and insensitive. Interestingly, two-thirds of the derailed European managers studied had problems with interpersonal relationships. That same problem reportedly plagued one-third of the derailed US executives.[4] Management, as defined in Chapter 1, involves getting things done with and through others. The job is simply too big to do it alone.

Let us begin by defining the term *group* as a prelude to examining types of groups, functions of group members, and the group development process. Our attention then turns to group roles and norms, the basic building blocks of group dynamics. Impacts of group structure and member characteristics on group outcomes are explored next. Finally, three serious threats to group effectiveness are discussed.

Groups: Definitions, Types, and Functions

Groups and teams are inescapable features of modern life.[5] University students are often teamed with their peers for class projects. Parents serve on community advisory boards at their local school. Managers find themselves on product planning committees and productivity task forces. Productive organizations simply cannot function without gathering individuals into groups and teams.[6] But, as personal experience shows, group effort can bring out both the best and the worst in people. A marketing department meeting, where several people excitedly brainstorm and refine a creative new advertising campaign, can yield results beyond the capabilities of individual contributors. Conversely, committees have become the butt of jokes (e.g., a committee is a place where they take minutes and waste hours; a camel is a horse designed by a committee) because they all too often are plagued by lack of direction and by conflict. Modern managers need a solid understanding of groups and group processes so as to both avoid their pitfalls and tap their vast potential. (Teams and teamwork are discussed in Chapter 13.)

Although other definitions of groups exist, we draw from the field of sociology and define a **group** as two or more freely interacting individuals who share collective norms and goals and have a common identity.[7] Figure 10–1 illustrates how the four criteria in this definition combine to form a conceptual whole. Organizational psychologist Edgar Schein shed additional light on this concept by drawing instructive distinctions between a group, a crowd, and an organization:

Group

Two or more freely interacting people with shared norms and goals and a common identity.

Figure 10 – 1   Four Sociological Criteria of a Group

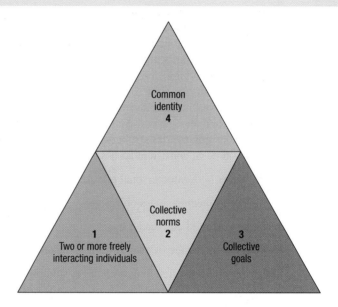

The size of a group is thus limited by the possibilities of mutual interaction and mutual awareness. Mere aggregates of people do not fit this definition because they do not interact and do not perceive themselves to be a group even if they are aware of each other as, for instance, a crowd on a street corner watching some event. A total department, a union, or a whole organization would not be a group in spite of thinking of themselves as "we," because they generally do not all interact and are not all aware of each other. However, work teams, committees, subparts of departments, cliques, and various other informal associations among organizational members would fit this definition of a group.[8]

Take a moment now to think of various groups of which you are a member. Does each of your "groups" satisfy the four criteria in Figure 10-1?

Formal and Informal Groups

Formal group
Formed by the organization.

Informal group
Formed by friends.

Individuals join groups, or are assigned to groups, to accomplish various purposes. If the group is formed by a manager to help the organization accomplish its goals, then it qualifies as a formal group. **Formal groups** typically wear such labels as work group, team, committee, quality circle, or task force. An **informal group** exists when the members' overriding purpose of getting together is friendship. Although formal and informal groups often overlap, such as a team of corporate auditors heading for the tennis

Table 10 – 1   Formal Groups Fulfil Organizational and Individual Functions

ORGANIZATIONAL FUNCTIONS	INDIVIDUAL FUNCTIONS
1. Accomplish complex, interdependent tasks that are beyond the capabilities of individuals.	1. Satisfy the individual's need for affiliation.
2. Generate new or creative ideas and solutions.	2. Develop, enhance, and confirm the individual's self-esteem and sense of identity.
3. Coordinate interdepartmental efforts.	3. Give individuals an opportunity to test and share their perceptions of social reality.
4. Provide a problem-solving mechanism for complex problems requiring varied information and assessments.	4. Reduce the individual's anxieties and feelings of insecurity and powerlessness.
5. Implement complex decisions.	5. Provide a problem-solving mechanism for personal and interpersonal problems.
6. Socialize and train newcomers.	

Source: Adapted from E H Schein, *Organizational Psychology*, 3rd ed (Englewood Cliffs, NJ: Prentice Hall, 1980), pp 149–51.

courts after work, some employees are not friends with their co-workers. The desirability of overlapping formal and informal groups is problematic. Some managers firmly believe personal friendship fosters productive teamwork on the job while others view workplace "gossip"as a serious threat to productivity. Both situations are common, and it is the manager's job to strike a workable balance, based on the maturity and goals of the people involved.

Functions of Formal Groups

Researchers point out that formal groups fulfill two basic functions: *organizational* and *individual.*[9] The various functions are listed in Table 10–1. Complex combinations of these functions can be found in formal groups at any given time.

For example, consider what Mazda's new American employees experienced when they spent a month working in Japan before the opening of the firm's Flat Rock, Michigan, plant:

> After a month of training in Mazda's factory methods, whipping their new Japanese buddies at softball and sampling local watering holes, the Americans were fired up. . . . [A maintenance manager] even faintly praised the Japanese practice of holding group calisthenics at the start of each working day: "I didn't think I'd like doing exercises every morning, but I kind of like it."[10]

While Mazda pursued the organizational functions it wanted—interdependent teamwork, creativity, coordination, problem solving, and training—the American workers benefited from the individual functions of formal groups. Among those benefits were affiliation with new friends, enhanced self-esteem, exposure to the Japanese social reality, and reduction of anxieties about working for a foreign-owned company. In short, Mazda created a workable blend of organizational and individual group functions by training its newly hired American employees in Japan.

The Group Development Process

Groups and teams in the workplace go through a maturation process, such as one would find in any life-cycle situation (e.g., humans, organizations, products). While there is general agreement among theorists that the group development process occurs in identifiable stages, they disagree about the exact number, sequence, length, and nature of those stages.[11] One oft-cited model is the one proposed in 1965 by educational psychologist Bruce W Tuckman. His original model involved only four stages (forming, storming, norming, and performing). The five-stage model in Figure 10–2 evolved when Tuckman and a doctoral student added "adjourning" in 1977.[12] A word of caution is in order. Somewhat akin to Maslow's need hierarchy theory, Tuckman's theory has been repeated and taught so often and for so long that many have come to view it as documented fact, not merely a theory. Even today, it is good to remember Tuckman's own caution that his group development model was derived more from group therapy sessions than from natural-life groups. Still, many in the OB field like Tuckman's five-stage model of group development because of its easy-to-remember labels and common sense appeal.[13]

Five Stages

Let us briefly examine the five stages in Tuckman's model. Notice in Figure 10–2 how individuals give up a measure of their independence when they join and participate in a group. Also, the various stages are not necessarily of the same duration or intensity. For instance, the storming stage may be practically nonexistent or painfully long, depending on the goal clarity and the commitment and maturity of the members. You can make this process come to life by relating the various stages to your own experiences with work groups, committees, athletic teams, social or religious groups, or class project teams.

Figure 10 – 2 Tuckman's Five-Stage Theory of Group Development

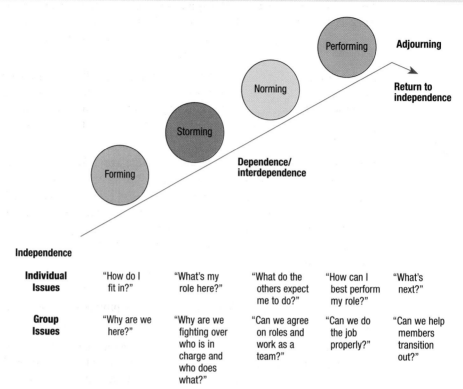

Some group happenings that surprised you when they occurred may now make sense or strike you as inevitable when seen as part of a natural development process.

Stage 1: Forming During this "ice-breaking" stage, group members tend to be uncertain and anxious about such things as their roles, who is in charge, and the group's goals. Mutual trust is low, and there is a good deal of holding back to see who takes charge and how. If the formal leader (e.g., a supervisor) does not assert his or her authority, an emergent leader will eventually step in to fulfil the group's need for leadership and direction. Leaders typically mistake this honeymoon period as a mandate for permanent control. But later problems may force a leadership change.

Stage 2: Storming This is a time of testing. Individuals test the leader's policies and assumptions as they try to determine how they fit into the power structure.[14] Subgroups take shape, and subtle forms of rebellion, such as procrastination, occur. Many groups stall in stage 2 because power politics erupts into open rebellion.

Stage 3: Norming Groups that make it through stage 2 generally do so because a respected member, other than the leader, challenges the group to resolve its power struggles so something can be accomplished. Questions about authority and power are resolved through unemotional, matter-of-fact group discussion. A feeling of team spirit is experienced because members believe they have found their proper roles. **Group cohesiveness**, defined as the "we feeling" that binds members of a group together, is the principal by-product of stage 3.

Group cohesiveness
A "we feeling" binding group members together.

Stage 4: Performing Activity during this vital stage is focused on solving task problems. As members of a mature group, contributors get their work done without hampering others. (See the Personal Awareness and Growth Exercise at the end of this chapter for a way to measure group maturity.) There is a climate of open communication, strong cooperation, and lots of helping behaviour. Conflicts and job boundary disputes are handled constructively and efficiently. Cohesiveness and personal commitment to group goals help the group achieve more than could any one individual acting alone. According to a pair of group development experts,

. . . the group structure can become flexible and adjust to fit the requirements of the situation without causing problems for the members. Influence can shift depending on who has the particular expertise or skills required for the group task or activity. Subgroups can work on special problems or subproblems without posing threats to the authority or cohesiveness of the rest of the group.[15]

Stage 5: Adjourning   The work is done; it is time to move on to other things. Having worked so hard to get along and get something done, many members feel a compelling sense of loss. The return to independence can be eased by rituals celebrating "the end" and "new beginnings." Parties, award ceremonies, graduations, or mock funerals can provide the needed punctuation at the end of a significant group project. Leaders need to emphasize valuable lessons learned in group dynamics to prepare everyone for future group and team efforts.

Group Development: Research and Practical Implications

A growing body of group development research provides managers with some practical insights.

Feedback   One fruitful study was carried out by a pair of Dutch social psychologists. They hypothesized that interpersonal feedback would vary systematically during the group development process. "The unit of feedback measured was a verbal message directed from one participant to another in which some aspect of behaviour was addressed."[16] After collecting and categorizing 1,600 instances of feedback from four different eight-person groups, they concluded the following:

• Interpersonal feedback increases as the group develops through successive stages.

• As the group develops, positive feedback increases and negative feedback decreases.

• Interpersonal feedback becomes more specific as the group develops.

• The credibility of peer feedback increases as the group develops.[17]

These findings hold important lessons for managers. The content and delivery of interpersonal feedback among work group or committee members can be used as a gauge of whether the group is developing properly. For example, the onset of stage 2 (storming) will be signalled by a noticeable increase in *negative* feedback. Effort can then be directed at generating specific, positive feedback among the members so the group's development will not stall. The feedback model discussed in Chapter 9 is helpful in this regard.

Deadlines   Field and laboratory studies found uncertainty about deadlines to be a major disruptive force in both group development and intergroup relations. The practical implications of this finding were summed up by the researcher as follows:

Uncertain or shifting deadlines are a fact of life in many organizations. Interdependent organizational units and groups may keep each other waiting, may suddenly move deadlines forward or back, or may create deadlines that are known to be earlier than is necessary in efforts to control erratic workflows. The current research suggests that the consequences of such uncertainty may involve more than stress, wasted time, overtime work, and intergroup conflicts. Synchrony in group members' expectations about deadlines may be critical to groups' abilities to accomplish successful transitions in their work.[18]

Thus, effective group management involves clarifying not only tasks and goals, but deadlines as well. When group members accurately perceive important deadlines, the pacing of work and timing of interdependent tasks tend to be more efficient.

Leadership Styles   Along a somewhat different line, experts in the area of leadership contend that different leadership styles are needed as work groups develop.

In general, it has been documented that leadership behavior that is active, aggressive, directive, structured, and task-oriented seems to have favorable results early in the group's history. However, when those behaviors are maintained throughout the life of the group, they seem to have a negative impact on cohesiveness and quality of work. Conversely, leadership behavior that is supportive, democratic, decentralized, and participative seems to be related to poorer functioning in the early group development stages. However, when these behaviors are maintained throughout the life of the group, more productivity, satisfaction, and creativity result.[19]

The practical punch line here is that managers are advised to shift from a directive and structured leadership style to a participative and supportive style as the group develops.[20]

Roles and Norms: Social Building Blocks for Group and Organizational Behaviour

Work groups transform individuals into functioning organizational members through subtle yet powerful social forces.[21] These social forces, in effect, turn "I" into "we" and "me" into "us." Group influence weaves individuals into the organization's social fabric by communicating and enforcing both role expectations and norms. We need to understand roles and norms if we are to effectively manage group and organizational behaviour.

Roles

Four centuries have passed since William Shakespeare had his character Jaques speak the following memorable lines in Act II of *As You Like It*: "All the world's a stage, And all the men and women merely players; They have their exits and their entrances; And one man in his time plays many parts. . . ." This intriguing notion of all people as actors in a universal play was not lost on 20th-century sociologists who developed a complex theory of human interaction based on roles. According to an OB scholar, "**roles** are sets of behaviours that persons expect of occupants of a position." [22] Role theory attempts to explain how these social expectations influence employee behaviour. This section explores role theory by analysing a role episode and defining the terms *role overload*, *role conflict*, and *role ambiguity*.

Roles

Expected behaviours for a given position.

Role Episodes   A role episode, as illustrated in Figure 10-3, consists of a snapshot of the ongoing interaction between two people. In any given role episode, there is a role sender and a focal person who is expected to act out the role. Within a broader context, one may be simultaneously a role sender and a focal person. For the sake of social analysis, however, it is instructive to deal with separate role episodes.

Role episodes begin with the role sender's perception of the relevant organization's or group's behavioural requirements. Those requirements serve as a standard for formulating expectations for the focal person's behaviour. The role sender then cognitively evaluates the focal person's actual behaviour against those expectations. Appropriate verbal and nonverbal messages are then sent to the focal person to pressure him or her into behaving as expected.[23] Consider how Westinghouse used a carrot-and-stick approach to communicate role expectations:

The carrot is a plan, that . . . rewarded 134 managers with options to buy 764,000 shares of stock for boosting the company's financial performance.

Figure 10 – 3 A Role Episode

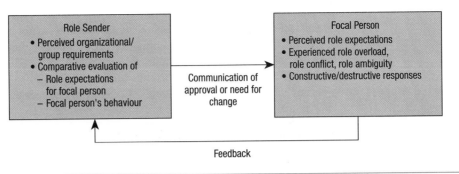

Source: Adapted in part from R L Kohn, D M Wolfe, R P Quinn, and J D Snoek, *Organizational Stress: Studies in Role Conflict and Ambiguity*, 1981 edition (Malabar, FL: Robert E Krieger Publishing, 1964), p 26.

The stick is quarterly meetings that are used to rank managers by how much their operations contribute to earnings per share. The soft-spoken . . . [chairman of the board] doesn't scold. He just charts in green the results of the sectors that have met their goals and charts the laggards in red. Peer pressure does the rest. Shame "is a powerful tool," says one executive.[24]

On the receiving end of the role episode, the focal person accurately or inaccurately perceives the communicated role expectations. Various combinations of role overload, role conflict, and role ambiguity are then experienced. (These three outcomes are defined and discussed in the following sections.) The focal person then responds constructively by engaging in problem solving, for example, or destructively because of undue tension, stress, and strain.[25]

Role overload

Others' expectations exceed one's ability.

Role Overload According to organizational psychologist Edgar Schein, **role overload** occurs when "the sum total of what role senders expect of the focal person far exceeds what he or she is able to do."[26] Students who attempt to handle a full course load and maintain a decent social life while working 30 or more hours a week know full well the consequences of role overload. As the individual tries to do more and more in less and less time, stress mounts and personal effectiveness slips.

Role conflict

Others have conflicting or inconsistent expectations.

Role Conflict Have you ever felt like you were being torn apart by the conflicting demands of those around you? If so, you were a victim of role conflict. **Role conflict** is experienced when "different members of the role set expect different things of the focal person."[27] Managers often face conflicting demands between work and family, for example.[28] Interestingly, however, women experience greater role conflict between work and family than men because women perform the majority of the household duties and child-care responsibilities.[29]

Role conflict also may be experienced when internalized values, ethics, or personal standards collide with others' expectations. For instance, an otherwise ethical production supervisor may be told by a superior to "fudge a little" on the quality control reports so an important deadline will be met. The resulting role conflict forces the supervisor to choose between being loyal but unethical or ethical but disloyal. Tough ethical choices such as this mean personal turmoil, interpersonal conflict, and even resignation. Consequently, experts say business schools should do a better job of weaving ethics training into their course requirements.

Role ambiguity

Others' expectations are unknown.

Role Ambiguity Those who experience role conflict may have trouble complying with role demands, but they at least know what is expected of them. Such is not the case with **role ambiguity**, which occurs when "members of the role set fail to communicate to the focal person expectations they have or information needed to perform the role, either because they do not have the information or because they deliberately withhold it."[30] In short, people experience role ambiguity when they do not know what is expected of them. Organizational newcomers often complain about unclear job descriptions and vague promotion criteria. According to role theory, prolonged role ambiguity can foster job dissatisfaction, erode self-confidence, and hamper job performance.

As might be expected, role ambiguity varies across cultures. In a recent 21-nation study, people in individualistic cultures were found to have higher role ambiguity than people in collectivist cultures.[31] In other words, people in collectivist or "we" cultures had a clearer idea of others' expectations. Collectivist cultures make sure everyone knows their proper place in society. People in individualistic "me" cultures, such as western Europe and the United States, may enjoy more individual discretion, but comparatively less input from others has its price—namely, greater role ambiguity.

Take a moment now to complete the self-assessment exercise in the OB Exercise. See if you can distinguish between sources of role conflict and sources of role ambiguity, as they affect your working life.

Norms

Norm

Shared attitudes, opinions, feelings, or actions that guide social behaviour.

Norms are more encompassing than roles. While roles involve behavioural expectations for specific positions, norms help organizational members determine right from wrong and good from bad. According to one respected team of management consultants: "A **norm** is an attitude, opinion, feeling, or action—shared by two or more people—that guides their behaviour."[33] Although norms are typically unwritten and seldom discussed openly, they have a powerful influence on group and organizational behaviour.[34] PepsiCo Inc., for instance, has evolved a norm that equates corporate competitiveness with physical fitness. According to observers:

OB EXERCISE   *Measuring Role Conflict and Role Ambiguity*

Instructions

Step 1. While thinking of your current (or last) job, circle one response for each of the following statements. Please consider each statement carefully because some are worded positively and some negatively.

Step 2. In the space in the far right column, label each statement with either a "C" for role conflict or an "A" for role ambiguity. (See note 32 for a correct categorization.)

Step 3. Calculate separate totals for role conflict and role ambiguity, and compare them with these arbitrary norms: 5–14 = low; 15–25 = moderate; 26–35 = high.

	VERY FALSE	VERY TRUE	
1. I feel certain about how much authority I have.	7 — 6 — 5 — 4 — 3 — 2 — 1	_____
2. I have to do things that should be done differently.	1 — 2 — 3 — 4 — 5 — 6 — 7	_____
3. I know that I have divided my time properly.	7 — 6 — 5 — 4 — 3 — 2 — 1	_____
4. I know what my responsibilities are.	7 — 6 — 5 — 4 — 3 — 2 — 1	_____
5. I have to buck a rule or policy in order to carry out an assignment.	1 — 2 — 3 — 4 — 5 — 6 — 7	_____
6. I feel certain how I will be evaluated for a rise or promotion.	7 — 6 — 5 — 4 — 3 — 2 — 1	_____
7. I work with two or more groups who operate quite differently.	1 — 2 — 3 — 4 — 5 — 6 — 7	_____
8. I know exactly what is expected of me.	7 — 6 — 5 — 4 — 3 — 2 — 1	_____
9. I do things that are apt to be accepted by one person and not accepted by others.	1 — 2 — 3 — 4 — 5 — 6 — 7	_____
10. I work on unnecessary things.	1 — 2 — 3 — 4 — 5 — 6 — 7	_____

Role conflict score = _____

Role ambiguity score = _____

SOURCE   Adapted from J R Rizzo, R J House, and S I Lirtzman, "Role Conflict and Ambiguity in Complex Organizations," *Administrative Science Quarterly*, June 1970, p 156.

Leanness and nimbleness are qualities that pervade the company. When Pepsi's brash young managers take a few minutes away from the office, they often head straight for the company's physical fitness center or for a jog around the museum-quality sculptures outside of PepsiCo's Purchase, New York, headquarters.[35]

At PepsiCo and elsewhere, group members positively reinforce those who adhere to current norms with friendship and acceptance. On the other hand, nonconformists experience criticism and even **ostracism,** or rejection by group members. Anyone who has experienced the "silent treatment" from a group of friends knows what a potent social weapon ostracism can be. Norms can be put into proper perspective by understanding how they develop and why they are enforced.

Ostracism

Rejection by other group members.

How Norms Are Developed   Experts say norms evolve in an informal manner as the group or organization determines what it takes to be effective. Generally speaking, norms develop in various combinations of the following four ways:

1. *Explicit statements by supervisors or co-workers.* For instance, a group leader might explicitly set norms about not drinking (alcohol) at lunch.

2. *Critical events in the group's history.* At times there is a critical event in the group's history that established an important precedent. (For example, a key recruit may have decided to work elsewhere because a group member said too many negative things about the organization. Hence, a norm against such "sour grapes" behaviour might evolve.)

3. *Primacy.* The first behaviour pattern that emerges in a group often sets group expectations. If the first group meeting is marked by very formal interaction between supervisors and subordinates, then the group often expects future meetings to be conducted in the same way.

4. *Carryover behaviours from past situations.* Such carryover of individual behaviours from past situations can increase the predictability of group members' behaviours in new settings and facilitate task accomplishment. For instance, students and professors carry fairly constant sets of expectations from class to class.[36]

We would like you to take a few moments and think about the norms that are currently in effect in your classroom. List the norms on a sheet of paper. Do these norms help or hinder your ability to learn? Norms can affect performance either positively or negatively.[37]

Why Norms Are Enforced   Norms tend to be enforced by group members when they

- Help the group or organization survive.
- Clarify or simplify behavioural expectations.
- Help individuals avoid embarrassing situations.
- Clarify the group's or organization's central values and/or unique identity.[38]

Working examples of each of these four situations are presented in Table 10–2.

Relevent Research Insights and Managerial Implications

Although instruments used to measure role conflict and role ambiguity have questionable validity,[39] two separate meta-analyses indicated that role conflict and role ambiguity negatively affected employees. Specifically, role conflict and role ambiguity were associated with job dissatisfaction, tension and anxiety, lack of organizational commitment, intentions to quit, and, to a lesser extent, poor job performance.[40]

The meta-analyses results hold few surprises for managers. Generally, because of the negative association reported, it makes sense for management to reduce both role conflict and role ambiguity. In this endeavour, managers can use feedback, formal rules and

Table 10 – 2   Four Reasons Norms Are Enforced

NORM	REASON FOR ENFORCEMENT	EXAMPLE
"Make our department look good in management's eyes."	Group/organization survival	After vigorously defending the vital role played by the top Human Resources Management Department at a divisional meeting, a staff specialist is complimented by her boss.
"Success comes to those who work hard and don't make waves."	Clarification of behavioural expectations	A senior manager takes a young associate aside and cautions him to be a bit more patient with co-workers who see things differently.
"Be a team player, not a star."	Avoidance of embarrassment	A project team member is ridiculed by her peers for dominating the discussion during a progress report to top management.
"Customer service is our top priority."	Clarification of central values/unique identity	Two sales representatives are given a surprise Friday afternoon party for having received prestigious best-in-the-industry customer service awards from an industry association.

procedures, directive leadership, setting of specific (difficult) goals, and participation. Managers can also use the mentoring process discussed in Chapter 3 to reduce role conflict and ambiguity.

Group Structure and Composition

Work groups of varying size are made up of individuals with varying ability and motivation. Moreover, those individuals perform different roles, on either an assigned or voluntary basis. No wonder some work groups are more productive than others. No wonder some committees are tightly knit while others wallow in conflict. In this section, we examine four important dimensions of group structure and composition: (1) functional roles of group members, (2) group size, (3) gender composition, and (4) group member ability. Each of these dimensions alternatively can enhance or hinder group effectiveness, depending on how it is managed.[41]

Functional Roles Performed by Group Members

As described in Table 10–3, both task and maintenance roles need to be performed if a work group is to accomplish anything.[42]

Task roles
Task-oriented group behaviour.

Maintenance roles
Relationship-building group behaviour.

Task versus Maintenance Roles   **Task roles** enable the work group to define, clarify, and pursue a common purpose. Meanwhile, **maintenance roles** foster supportive and constructive interpersonal relationships. In short, task roles keep the group *on track* while maintenance roles keep the group *together.* A group member is performing a task function when he or she stands at a business meeting and says, "What is the real issue here? We don't seem to be getting anywhere." Another individual who says, "Let's hear from those who oppose this plan," is performing a maintenance function. Importantly, each of the various task and maintenance roles may be played in varying combinations and sequences by either the group's leader or any of its members.

Checklist for Managers   The task and maintenance roles listed in Table 10–3 can serve as a handy checklist for managers and group leaders who wish to ensure proper group development. Roles that are not always performed when needed, such as those of coordinator, evaluator, and gatekeeper, can be performed in a timely manner by the formal leader or assigned to other members. The task roles of initiator, orienter, and energizer are especially important because they are *goal-directed* roles. Recent research studies on group goal setting confirm the motivational power of challenging goals. As with individual goal setting (in Chapter 8), difficult but achievable goals are associated with better group results.[43] Also in line with individual goal-setting theory and research, group goals are more effective if group members clearly understand them and are both

Table 10 – 3   Functional Roles Performed by Group Managers

TASK ROLES	DESCRIPTION
Initiator	Suggests new goals or ideas.
Information seeker/giver	Clarifies key issues.
Opinion seeker/giver	Clarifies pertinent values.
Elaborator	Promotes greater understanding through examples or exploration of implications.
Coordinator	Pulls together ideas and suggestions.
Orienter	Keeps group headed towards its stated goal(s).
Evaluator	Tests group's accomplishments with various criteria such as logic and practicality.
Energizer	Prods group to move along or to accomplish more.
Procedural technician	Performs routine duties (e.g., handing out materials or rearranging seats).
Recorder	Performs a "group memory" function by documenting discussion and outcomes.
MAINTENANCE ROLES	**DESCRIPTION**
Encourager	Fosters group solidarity by accepting and praising various points of view.
Harmonizer	Mediates conflict through reconciliation or humour.
Compromiser	Helps resolve conflict by meeting others "half way."
Gatekeeper	Encourages all group members to participate.
Standard setter	Evaluates the quality of group processes.
Commentator	Records and comments on group processes/dynamics.
Follower	Serves as a passive audience.

Source: Adapted from discussion in K D Benne and P Sheats, "Functional Roles of Group Members," *Journal of Social Issues*, Spring 1948, pp 41–49.

individually and collectively committed to achieving them. Initiators, orienters, and energizers can be very helpful in this regard.

International managers need to be sensitive to cultural differences regarding the relative importance of task and maintenance roles. In Japan, for example, cultural tradition calls for more emphasis on maintenance roles, especially the roles of harmonizer and compromiser:

Courtesy requires that members not be conspicuous or disputatious in a meeting or classroom. If two or more members discover that their views differ—a fact that is tactfully taken to be unfortunate—they adjourn to find more information and to work toward a stance that all can accept. They do not press their personal opinions through strong arguments, neat logic, or rewards and threats. And they do not hesitate to shift their beliefs if doing so will preserve smooth interpersonal relations. (To lose is to win.)[44]

Group Size

How many group members is too many? The answer to this deceptively simple question has intrigued managers and academics for years. Folk wisdom says "two heads are better than one" but that "too many cooks spoil the broth." So where should a manager draw the line when staffing a committee? At 3? At 5 or 6? At 10 or more? Researchers have taken two different approaches to pinpointing optimum group size: mathematical modelling and laboratory simulations. Let us briefly review recent findings from these two approaches.

The Mathematical Modelling Approach   This approach involves building a mathematical model around certain desired outcomes of group action such as decision quality. Due to differing assumptions and statistical techniques, the results of this research are inconclusive. Statistical estimates of optimum group size have ranged from 3 to 13.[45]

The Laboratory Simulation Approach   This stream of research is based on the assumption that group behaviour needs to be observed firsthand in controlled laboratory settings. A laboratory study by respected Australian researcher Philip Yetton and his colleague, Preston Bottger, provides useful insights about group size and performance.[46]

A total of 555 subjects (330 managers and 225 management students, of whom 20 per cent were female) were assigned to task teams ranging in size from 2 to 6. The teams worked on the National Aeronautics and Space Administration moon survival exercise. (This exercise involves the rank ordering of 15 pieces of equipment that would enable a spaceship crew on the moon to survive a 320-km trip between a crash-landing site and home base.)[47] After analysing the relationships between group size and group performance, Yetton and Bottger concluded the following:

It would be difficult, at least with respect to decision quality, to justify groups larger than five members. . . . Of course, to meet needs other than high decision quality, organizations may employ groups significantly larger than four or five.[48]

More recent laboratory studies exploring the brainstorming productivity of various size groups (2 to 12 people), in face-to-face versus computer-mediated situations, proved fruitful. In the usual face-to-face brainstorming sessions, productivity of ideas did not increase as the size of the group increased. But brainstorming productivity increased as the size of the group increased when ideas were typed into networked computers.[49] These results suggest that computer networks could help deliver on the promise of productivity improvement through modern information technology.[50]

Managerial Implications   Within a contingency management framework, there is no hard-and-fast rule about group size. It depends on the manager's objective for the group. If a high-quality decision is the main objective, then a three- to five-member group would be appropriate. However, if the objective is to generate creative ideas, encourage participation, socialize new members, engage in training, or communicate policies, then groups much larger than five could be justified. But managers need to be aware of *qualitative* changes that occur when group size increases. A meta-analysis of eight studies found the following relationships: as group size increased, group leaders tended to become more directive, and group member satisfaction tended to decline slightly.[51]

Odd-numbered groups (e.g., three, five, seven members) are recommended if the issue is to be settled by a majority vote. Voting deadlocks (e.g., 2-2, 3-3) too often hamper effectiveness of even-numbered groups. A majority decision rule is not necessarily a good idea. One study found that better group outcomes were obtained by negotiation groups that used a unanimous as opposed to majority decision rule. Individuals' self-interests were more effectively integrated when groups used a unanimous decision criterion.[52]

Effects of Men and Women Working Together in Groups

The increase of women at work brought an increase in the number of organizational committees and teams composed of both men and women. Some profound effects on group dynamics might be expected.[53] Let us see what researchers have found in the way of group gender composition effects and what managers can do about them.[54]

Women Face an Uphill Battle in Mixed-Gender Task Groups   Recent laboratory and field studies paint a picture of inequality for women working in mixed-gender groups. Both women and men need to be aware of these often subtle but powerful group dynamics so that corrective steps can be taken.

In a laboratory study of six-person task groups, a clear pattern of gender inequality was found in the way group members interrupted each other. Men interrupted women significantly more often than they did other men. Women, who tended to interrupt less frequently and less successfully than men, interrupted men and women equally.[55]

A field study of mixed-gender police and nursing teams in the Netherlands found another group dynamics disadvantage for women. These two particular professions—police work and nursing—were fruitful research areas because men dominate the former while women dominate the latter. As women move into male-dominated police forces and men gain employment opportunities in the female-dominated world of nursing, who faces the greatest resistance? The answer from this study was the women police officers. As the representation of the minority gender (either female police officers or male nurses) increased in the work groups, the following changes in attitude were observed:

The attitude of the male majority changes from neutral to resistant, whereas the attitude of the female majority changes from favorable to neutral. In other words, men increasingly want to keep their domain for themselves, while women remain willing to share their domain with men.[56]

Again, managers are faced with the challenge of countering discriminatory tendencies in group dynamics.

According to B A Gutek, social sexual behaviour is influenced by social rules on male and female interactions. Hence, they are inappropriate for occupational gender interactions.[57] Research has shown that sexiness and attractiveness are female stereotypes.[58] This explains why working women are often regarded as sex objects by colleagues and supervisors, which can give way to sexual harassment.[59] The EC Code of Practice defines sexual harassment as follows.

Sexual harassment means unwanted conduct of a sexual nature, or other conduct based on sex affecting the dignity of women and men at work. This can include unwelcome physical, verbal or nonverbal conduct.[60]

Research carried out within the European Union shows the scale of the problem of sexual harassment. The percentage of individuals reporting sexual harassment in the workplace varies from 22 per cent in the Northern Ireland to 84 per cent in Spain with 30 per cent in Belgium, 51 per cent in the UK and 59 per cent in Germany. Between 6 per cent and 8 per cent of women who are dismissed or give up their job do so because of sexual harassment.[61]

Japanese businessmen are for the first time to be offered insurance policies covering sexual harassment. AIU Insurance, the Tokyo-based subsidiary of American International Group offers policies covering expenses and damages related to sexual harassment suits. AIU targets Japanese companies abroad, especially in the US. Male chauvinism is widespread in Japanese society where women commonly suffer a lack of status in the workplace. According to a 1995 survey, 41.3 per cent of Japanese women polled said they had been sexually harassed.[62]

To assess the extent of sexualization in your present or former workplace, take a moment to complete the OB Exercise. What are the ethical implications of your score?[63]

Constructive Managerial Action   Male and female employees can and often do work well together in groups.[64] A survey of 387 male US government employees sought to determine how they were affected by the growing number of female co-workers. The researchers concluded, "Under many circumstances, including inter-gender interaction in work groups, frequent contact leads to cooperative and supportive social relations."[65] Still, managers need to take affirmative steps to ensure that the documented sexualization of work environments does not erode into sexual harassment. Whether perpetrated against women or men, sexual harassment is demeaning, unethical, and appropriately called "work environment pollution."

The European Union has been actively combating sexual harassment since the 1980s, which finally resulted in 1991 in a recommendation and subsequent code of practice on protecting the dignity of women and men at work. This recommendation and this code of practice offer the member states a definition of sexual harassment in the workplace. It includes measures to prevent and combat sexual harassment and a number of recommendations to the parties concerned.

In some states, situations of sexual harassment are combated in the framework of the provisions on nondiscrimination. This is the case in Ireland and the UK. In others, such as Belgium, Denmark, Spain, and France specific legislation has been adopted. In countries such as Italy and Portugal only very general provisions on the civil and/or contractual liability of the employer can be invoked. As sexual harassment is a source of inequality and unfairness, more and more people are arguing for the introduction of specific legislation in every member state.

Beyond avoiding lawsuits by establishing and enforcing anti-discrimination and sexual harassment policies, managers need to take additional steps. C L Cooper and S. Lewis suggest five immediate strategies.

1. Ensure equality of opportunity at work and at home, by introducing family-friendly policies and equal opportunity policies.

2. Provide gender awareness training.

3. Introduce other forms of training, for example assertiveness training.

4. Take steps to avoid and discourage sexual harassment and other behaviour resulting from the perception of women as sex objects.

5. Promote professional behaviour and ambiance throughout the organization.[66]

British Rail introduced tough guidelines to combat sexual harassment in 1994.

According to former chairman Sir Bob Reid

Workplaces free of fear of harassment make a positive contribution to productivity and safety. I place as much emphasis on this as on our attitude to drugs and alcohol.[67]

Individual Ability and Group Effectiveness

Imagine that you are a department manager charged with making an important staffing decision amid the following circumstances. You need to form 8 three-person task teams from a pool of 24 employees. Based on each of the employee's prior work records and

---

OB EXERCISE   *What Is the Degree of Sexualization in Your Work Environment*

Instructions
Describe the work environment at your current (or last) job by selecting one number along the following scale for each question.

	LITTLE OR FEW	MUCH OR MANY

1. How much joking or talking about sexual matters do you hear?   1 — 2 — 3 — 4 — 5

2. How much social pressure are women under to flirt with men?   1 — 2 — 3 — 4 — 5

3. How much social pressure are men under to flirt with women?   1 — 2 — 3 — 4 — 5

4. How much of a problem is sexual harassment in your workplace?   1 — 2 — 3 — 4 — 5

5. How many women dress in a sexually attractive way to men?   1 — 2 — 3 — 4 — 5

6. How many men dress in a sexually attractive way to women?   1 — 2 — 3 — 4 — 5

7. How many women act in sexually seductive ways towards men?   1 — 2 — 3 — 4 — 5

8. How many men act in sexually seductive ways towards women?   1 — 2 — 3 — 4 — 5

Total score =

Norms
8—16   Low degree of sexualization
17—31   Moderate degree of sexualization
32—40   High degree of sexualization

SOURCE   Adapted from B A Gutek, A Gross Cohen, and A M Konrad, "Predicting Social-Sexual Behavior at Work: A Contact Hypothesis," *Academy of Management Journal*, September 1990, p 577.

their scores on ability tests, you know that 12 have high ability and 12 have low ability. The crux of your problem is how to assign the 12 high-ability employees. Should you spread your best talent around by making sure there are both high- and low-ability employees on each team? Then again, you may want to concentrate your best talent by forming four high-ability teams and four low-ability teams. Or should you attempt to find a compromise between these two extremes? What is your decision? Why? One field experiment provided an instructive and interesting answer.

The Israeli Tank-Crew Study   Aharon Tziner and Dov Eden, researchers from Tel Aviv University, systematically manipulated the composition of 208 three-man tank crews. All possible combinations of high- and low-ability personnel were studied (high-high-high; high-high-low; high-low-low; and low-low-low). Ability was a composite measure of (1) overall intelligence, (2) amount of formal education, (3) proficiency in Hebrew, and (4) interview ratings. Successful operation of the tanks required the three-man crews to perform with a high degree of synchronized interdependence.[68] Tank-crew effectiveness was determined by commanding officers during military manoeuvers for the Israel Defence Forces.

As expected, the high-high-high ability tank crews performed the best and the low-low-low the worst. But the researchers discovered an important *interaction effect*:

Each member's ability influenced crew performance effectiveness differently depending on the ability levels of the other two members. A high-ability member appears to achieve more in combination with other uniformly high-ability members than in combination with low-ability members.[69]

The tank crews composed of three high-ability personnel far outperformed all other ability combinations. The interaction effect also worked in a negative direction because the low-low-low ability crews performed far below expected levels. Moreover, as illustrated in Figure 10–4, significantly greater performance gains were achieved by creating high-high-high ability crews than by upgrading low-low-low ability crews with one or two high-ability members.

This returns us to the staffing problem at the beginning of this section. Tziner and Eden recommended the following solution:

Figure 10 – 4 Ability of Israeli Tank-Crew Members and Improvements in Effectiveness

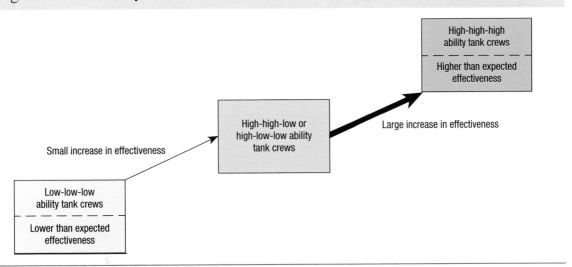

Source: Adapted from B A Gutek, A Gross Cohen, and A M Konrad, "Predicting Social-Sexual Behavior at Work: A Contact Hypothesis," *Academy of Management Journal,* September 1990, p 577.

Our experimental results suggest that the most productive solution would be to allocate six highs and all 12 lows to six teams of high-low-low ability and to assign the six remaining highs to two teams of high-high-high ability. This avoids the disproportionately low productivity of the low-low-low ability combination, while leaving some of the highs for high-high-high ability teams where they are most productive. . . . Our results show that talent is used more effectively when concentrated than when spread around.[70]

A Managerial Interpretation While the real-life aspect of the tank-crew study makes its results fairly generalizable, a qualification is in order. Specifically, modern complex organizations demand a more flexible contingency approach. Figure 10–5 shows two basic contingencies. If management seeks to *improve* the performance of *all* groups or train novices, high-ability personnel can be spread around. This option would be appropriate in a high-volume production operation. But if the desired outcome is to *maximize* performance of the *best* group(s), then high-ability personnel should be concentrated. This second option would be advisable in research and development departments, for example, where technological breakthroughs need to be achieved. Extraordinary achievements require clusters of extraordinary talent.[71]

Threats to Group Effectiveness

Even when managers carefully staff and organize task groups, group dynamics can still go haywire. Prior knowledge of three major threats to group effectiveness—the Asch effect, groupthink, and social loafing—can help managers take necessary preventive steps. Because the first two problems relate to blind conformity, some brief background work is in order.

Very little would be accomplished in task groups and organizations without conformity to norms, role expectations, policies, and rules and regulations. After all, deadlines, commitments, and product/service quality standards have to be established and adhered to if the organization is to survive. But, as pointed out by management consultants Robert Blake and Jane Srygley Mouton, conformity is a two-edged sword:

Social forces powerful enough to influence members to conform may influence them to perform at a very high level of quality and productivity. All too often, however, the pressure to conform stifles creativity, influencing members to cling to attitudes that may be out of touch with organizational needs and even out of kilter with the times.[72]

Figure 10 – 5 A Contingency Model for Staffing Work Groups: Effective Use of Available Talent

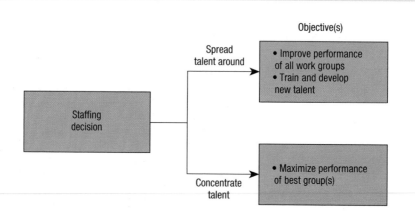

Moreover, excessive or blind conformity can stifle critical thinking, the last line of defence against unethical conduct. Almost daily accounts in the popular media of insider trading scandals, illegal dumping of hazardous wastes, and other unethical practices make it imperative that future managers understand the mechanics of blind conformity.

The Asch Effect

More than 45 years ago, social psychologist Solomon Asch conducted a series of laboratory experiments that revealed a negative side of group dynamics.[73] Under the guise of a "perception test," Asch made groups of seven to nine volunteer college students look at 12 pairs of cards such as the ones in Figure 10–6. The object was to identify the line that was the same length as the standard line. Each individual was told to announce his or her choice to the group. Since the differences among the comparison lines were obvious, there should have been unanimous agreement during each of the 12 rounds. But that was not the case.

A Minority of One   All but one member of each group were Asch's confederates who agreed to systematically select the wrong line during seven of the rounds (the other five rounds were control rounds for comparison purposes). The remaining individual was the naive subject who was being tricked. Group pressure was created by having the naive subject in each group be among the last to announce his or her choice. Thirty-one subjects were tested. Asch's research question was: "How often would the naive subjects conform to a majority opinion that was obviously wrong?"

Only 20 per cent of Asch's subjects remained entirely independent; 80 per cent yielded to the pressures of group opinion at least once! Fifty-eight per cent knuckled under to the "immoral majority" at least twice. Hence, the **Asch effect,** the distortion of individual judgement by a unanimous but incorrect opposition, was documented. (Do you ever turn your back on your better judgement by giving in to group pressure?)

Asch effect

Giving in to a unanimous but wrong opposition.

A Managerial Perspective   Asch's experiment has been widely replicated with mixed results. Both high and low degrees of blind conformity have been observed with various situations and subjects. Replications in Japan and Kuwait have demonstrated that the Asch effect is not unique to the United States.[74] A cross-cultural study, using white British males and white American males showed no significant differences between them. The study confirmed the existence of the Asch effect, but remarked that the effect was significantly weaker than the results S. Asch reported in the 50s.[75] Internationally, collectivist countries, where the group prevails over the individual, produced higher levels of conformity than individualistic countries.[76] The point is not precisely how great the Asch effect is in a given situation or culture, but rather, managers committed to ethical conduct need to be concerned that the Asch effect exists. Even isolated instances of blind, unthinking conformity seriously threaten the effectiveness and integrity of work groups

Figure 10 – 6 The Asch Experiment

Standard Line Card

Comparison Lines Card

1   2   3

and organizations. Functional conflict and assertiveness, discussed in Chapters 11 and 14, can help employees respond appropriately when they find themselves facing an immoral majority. Ethical codes mentioning specific practices also can provide support and guidance.

Groupthink

Why did President Lyndon B Johnson and his group of intelligent White House advisers make some very *unintelligent* decisions that escalated the Vietnam War? How is it possible that in 1995 Robert McNamara, US Secretary of Defense under Kennedy and Johnson, reflecting on the Vietnam war, had to admit "We were wrong, terribly wrong."[77] Those fateful decisions were made despite obvious warning signals, including stronger than expected resistance from the North Vietnamese and withering support at home and abroad. Systematic analysis of the decision-making processes underlying the war in Vietnam and other US foreign policy fiascoes prompted Yale University's Irving Janis to coin the term *groupthink*.[78] Modern managers can all too easily become victims of groupthink, just like President Johnson's staff, if they passively ignore the danger.

Groupthink

Janis's term for a cohesive in-group's unwillingness to realistically view alternatives.

Definition and Symptoms of Groupthink   Janis defines **groupthink** as "a mode of thinking that people engage in when they are deeply involved in a cohesive in-group, when members' strivings for unanimity override their motivation to realistically appraise alternative courses of action."[79] He adds, "Groupthink refers to a deterioration of mental efficiency, reality testing, and moral judgement that results from in-group pressures."[80] Unlike Asch's subjects, who were strangers to each other, members of groups victimized by groupthink are friendly, tightly knit, and cohesive. In short, policy- and decision-making groups can become so cohesive that strong-willed executives are able to gain unanimous support for poor decisions.[81]

Groupthink Research and Prevention   Laboratory studies using college students as subjects validate portions of Janis's groupthink concept. Specifically, it has been found that

- Groups with a moderate amount of cohesiveness produce better decisions than low- or high-cohesive groups.

- Highly cohesive groups victimized by groupthink make the poorest decisions, despite

Figure 10 – 7 Symptoms of Groupthink Lead to Defective Decision Making

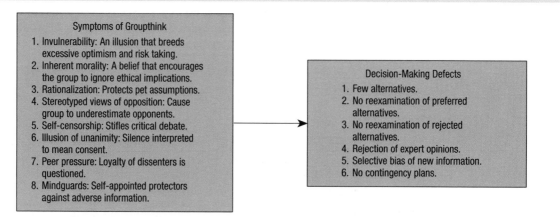

Sources: Symptoms adapted from I L Janis, *Groupthink*, 2nd ed (Boston: Houghton Mifflin, 1982), pp 174—75. Defects excerpted from G Moorhead, "Groupthink: Hypothesis in Need of Testing," *Group & Organization Studies*, December 1982, p 434. Copyright © 1982 by Sage Publications. Reprinted by permission of Sage Publications, Inc.

high confidence in those decisions.[82]

Janis believes prevention is better than cure when dealing with groupthink. He recommends the following preventive measures:

1. Each member of the group should be assigned the role of critical evaluator. This role involves actively voicing objections and doubts.

2. Top-level executives should not use policy committees to rubber-stamp decisions that have already been made.

3. Different groups with different leaders should explore the same policy questions.

4. Subgroup debates and outside experts should be used to introduce fresh perspectives.

5. Someone should be given the role of devil's advocate when discussing major alternatives. This person tries to uncover every conceivable negative factor.

6. Once a consensus has been reached, everyone should be encouraged to rethink their position to check for flaws.[83]

These anti-groupthink measures can help cohesive groups produce sound recommendations and decisions.[84]

Social Loafing

Is group performance less than, equal to, or greater than the sum of its parts? Can three people, for example, working together accomplish less than, the same as, or more than they would working separately? An interesting study conducted more than a half century ago by a French agricultural engineer named Ringelmann found the answer to be "less than."[85] In a rope-pulling exercise, Ringelmann reportedly found that three people pulling together could achieve only two and a half times the average individual rate. Eight pullers achieved less than four times the individual rate. This tendency for individual effort to decline as group size increases has come to be called **social loafing**.[86] Let us briefly analyse this threat to group effectiveness and synergy with an eye towards avoiding it.

Social loafing

Decrease in individual effort as group size increases.

Social Loafing Theory and Research   Among the theoretical explanations for the social loafing effect are (1) equity of effort ("Everyone else is goofing off, so why shouldn't I?"), (2) loss of personal accountability ("I'm lost in the crowd, so who cares?"), (3) motivational loss due to the sharing of rewards ("Why should I work harder than the others when everyone gets the same reward?"), and (4) coordination loss as more people perform the task ("We're getting in each other's way.")

Laboratory studies refined these theories by identifying situational factors that moderated the social loafing effect. Social loafing occurred when

- The task was perceived to be unimportant, simple or not interesting.[87]

- Group members thought their individual output was not identifiable.[88]

- Group members expected their co-workers to loaf.[89]

But social loafing did *not* occur when group members in two laboratory studies expected to be evaluated.[90] Also, recent research suggests that self-reliant "individualists" are more prone to social loafing than are group-oriented "collectivists." But individualists can be made more cooperative by keeping the group small and holding each member personally accountable for results.[91]

Practical Implications   These findings demonstrate that social loafing is not an inevitable part of group effort. Management can curb this threat to group effectiveness by making sure the task is challenging and perceived as important. Additionally, it is a good idea to hold group members personally accountable for identifiable portions of the

Table 10 – 4   How to Avoid Social Loafing in Groups and Teams:
The Stepladder Technique

The stepladder technique is intended to enhance group decision making by structuring the entry of group members into a core group. Increasing or decreasing the number of group members alters the number of steps. In a four-person group, the stepladder technique has three steps. Initially, two group members (the initial core group) work together on the problem at hand. Next, a third member joins the core group and presents his or her preliminary solutions for the same problem. The entering member's presentation is followed by a three-person discussion. Finally, the fourth group member joins the core group and presents his or her preliminary solutions. This is followed by a four-person discussion, which has as its goal the rendering of a final group decision.

The stepladder technique has four requirements. First, each group member must be given the group's task and sufficient time to think about the problem before entering the core group. Second, the entering member must present his or her preliminary solutions before hearing the core group's preliminary solutions. Third, with the entry of each additional member to the core group, sufficient time to discuss the problem is necessary. Fourth, a final decision must be purposely delayed until the group has been formed in its entirety.

Source: Excerpted from S G Rogelberg, J L Barnes-Farrell, and C A Lowe, "The Stepladder Technique: An Alternative Group Structure Facilitating Effective Group Decision Making," *Journal of Applied Psychology*, October 1992, vol 77, p 731. Copyright © 1992 by the American Psychological Association. Reprinted with permission.

group's task. One way to do this is with the *stepladder technique,* a group decision-making process proven effective in recent research (see Table 10—4). Compared with conventional groups, stepladder groups produced significantly better decisions in the same amount of time. "Furthermore, stepladder groups' decisions surpassed the quality of their best individual members' decisions 56 per cent of the time. In contrast, conventional groups' decisions surpassed the quality of their best members' decisions only 13 per cent of the time."[92] The stepladder technique could be a useful tool for organizations relying on self-managed or total quality management (TQM) teams.

Summary of Key Concepts

1. *Identify the four criteria of a group from a sociological perspective.* Sociologically, a *group* is defined as two or more freely interacting individuals who share collective norms and goals and have a common identity.

2. *Identify and briefly describe the five stages in Tuckman's theory of group development.* The five stages in Tuckman's theory are *forming* (the group comes together), *storming* (members test the limits and each other), *norming* (questions about authority and power are resolved as the group becomes more cohesive), *performing* (effective communication and cooperation help the group get things done), and *adjourning* (group members go their own way).

3. *Distinguish between role conflict and role ambiguity.* Organizational *roles* are sets of behaviours persons expect of occupants of a position. One may experience role overload (too much to do in too little time), role

conflict (conflicting role expectations), or role ambiguity (unclear role expectations).

4. *Contrast roles and norms, and specify four reasons norms are enforced in organizations.* While roles are specific to the person's position, norms are shared attitudes that differentiate appropriate from inappropriate behaviour in a variety of situations. Norms evolve informally and are enforced because they help the group or organization survive, clarify behavioural expectations, help people avoid embarrassing situations, and clarify the group's or organization's central values.

5. *Distinguish between task and maintenance functions in groups.* Members of formal groups need to perform both task (goal-oriented) and maintenance (relationship-oriented) roles if anything is to be accomplished.

6. *Summarize the practical contingency management implications for group size and group member ability.* Laboratory simulation studies suggest decision-making groups should be limited to five or fewer members. Larger groups are appropriate when creativity, participation, or socialization are the main objectives. If majority votes are to be taken, odd-numbered groups are recommended to avoid deadlocks. Results of the Israeli tank-crew study prompted researchers to conclude that it is better to concentrate high-ability personnel in separate groups. Within a contingency management perspective, however, there are situations in which it is advisable to spread high-ability people around.

7. *Discuss why managers need to carefully handle mixed-gender task groups.* Women face special group dynamics challenges in mixed-gender task groups. Steps need to be taken to make sure increased sexualization of work environments does not erode into illegal sexual harassment.

8. *Describe groupthink, and identify at least four of its symptoms.* Groupthink plagues cohesive in-groups that shortchange moral judgement while putting too much emphasis on unanimity. Symptoms of groupthink include invulnerability, inherent morality, rationalization, stereotyped views of opposition, self-censorship, illusion of unanimity, peer pressure, and mindguards. Critical evaluators, outside expertise, and devil's advocates are among the preventive measures recommended by Irving Janis, who coined the term *groupthink.*

9. *Define social loafing, and explain how managers can prevent it.* Social loafing involves the tendency for individual effort to decrease as group size increases. This problem can be contained if the task is challenging and important, individuals are held accountable for results and group members expect everyone to work hard. The stepladder technique, a structured approach to group decision making, can reduce social loafing by increasing personal effort and accountability.

Discussion Questions

1. Which of the following would qualify as a sociological group? A crowd watching a football game? One of the football teams? Explain.

2. What is your opinion about employees being friends with their co-workers (overlapping formal and informal groups)?

3. What is your personal experience with groups that failed to achieve stage 4 of group development? At which stage did they stall? Why?

4. Considering your current lifestyle, how many different roles are you playing? What sorts of role conflict and role ambiguity are you experiencing?

5. What norms do university students usually enforce in class? How are they enforced?

6. Which roles do you prefer to play in work groups: task or maintenance? How could you do a better job in this regard?

7. How would you respond to a manager who made the following statement? "When it comes to the size of work groups, the smaller the better."

8. Are women typically at a disadvantage in mixed-gender work groups? Give your rationale.

9. Have you ever been a victim of either the Asch effect or groupthink? Explain the circumstances.

10. Have you observed any social loafing recently? What were the circumstances and what could be done to correct the problem?

Personal Awareness and Growth Exercise

Is This a Mature Work Group or Team

Objectives

1. To increase your knowledge of group processes and dynamics.

2. To give you a tool for assessing the maturity of a work group or task team as well as a diagnostic tool for pinpointing group problems.

3. To help you become a more effective group leader or contributor.

Introduction

Group action is so common today that many of us take it for granted. But are the groups and teams to which we contribute much of our valuable time mature and hence more likely to be effective? Or do they waste our time? How can they be improved? We can and should become tough critical evaluators of group processes.

Instructions

Think of a work group or task team with which you are very familiar (preferably one you worked with in the past or are currently working with). Rate the group's maturity on each of the 20 dimensions.[93] Then add your circled responses to get your total group maturity score. The higher the score, the greater the group's maturity.

	VERY FALSE (OR NEVER)				VERY TRUE (OR ALWAYS)

1. Members are clear about group goals.   1 — 2 — 3 — 4 — 5

2. Members agree with the group's goals.   1 — 2 — 3 — 4 — 5

3. Members are clear about their roles.   1 — 2 — 3 — 4 — 5

4. Members accept their roles and status.   1 — 2 — 3 — 4 — 5

5. Role assignments match member abilities.   1 — 2 — 3 — 4 — 5

6. The leadership style matches the group's developmental level.   1 — 2 — 3 — 4 — 5

7. The group has an open communication structure in which all members participate.   1 — 2 — 3 — 4 — 5

8. The group gets, gives, and uses feedback about its effectiveness and productivity.   1 — 2 — 3 — 4 — 5

9. The group spends time planning how it will solve problems and make decisions.   1 — 2 — 3 — 4 — 5

10. Voluntary conformity is high.   1 — 2 — 3 — 4 — 5

11. The group norms encourage high performance and quality   1 — 2 — 3 — 4 — 5

12. The group expects to be successful.   1 — 2 — 3 — 4 — 5

13. The group pays attention to the details of its work.   1 — 2 — 3 — 4 — 5

14. The group accepts coalition and subgroup formation.   1 — 2 — 3 — 4 — 5

15. Subgroups are integrated into the group as a whole.   1 — 2 — 3 — 4 — 5

16. The group is highly cohesive.   1 — 2 — 3 — 4 — 5

17. Interpersonal attraction among members is high.   1 — 2 — 3 — 4 — 5

18. Members are cooperative.   1 — 2 — 3 — 4 — 5

19. Periods of conflict are frequent but brief.   1 — 2 — 3 — 4 — 5

20. The group has effective conflict-management strategies.   1 — 2 — 3 — 4 — 5

Total score = _____

ARBITRARY NORMS

20—39	"When in doubt, run in circles, scream and shout!"
40—59	A long way to go
60—79	On the right track
80—100	Ready for group dynamics graduate school

QUESTIONS FOR DISCUSSION

1. Does your evaluation help explain why the group or team was successful or not? Explain.

2. Was (or is) there anything *you* could have done (or can do) to increase the maturity of this group? Explain.

3. How will this evaluation instrument help you be a more effective group member or leader in the future?

Group Exercise

A Committee Decision

Objectives

1. To give you firsthand experience with work group dynamics through a role-playing exercise.[94]

2. To develop your ability to evaluate group effectiveness.

Introduction

Please read the following case before going on.

THE JOHNNY ROCCO CASE

Johnny has a grim personal background. He is the third child in a family of seven. He has not seen his father for several years, and his recollection is that his father used to come home drunk and beat up every member of the family; everyone ran when his father came staggering home.

His mother, according to Johnny, wasn't much better. She was irritable and unhappy, and she always predicted that Johnny would come to no good end. Yet she worked when her health allowed her to do so in order to keep the family in food and clothing. She always decried the fact that she was not able to be the kind of mother she would like to be.

Johnny left school at the age of twelve. He had great difficulty conforming to the school routine—-he misbehaved often, was truant frequently, and fought with schoolmates. On several occasions he was picked up by the police and, along with members of his gang, questioned during several investigations into cases of both petty and grand larceny. The police regarded him as "probably a bad one."

The juvenile officer of the court saw in Johnny some good qualities that no one else seemed to sense. Mr. O'Brien took it on himself to act as a "big brother" to Johnny. He had several long conversations with Johnny, during which he managed to penetrate to some degree Johnny's defensive shell. He represented to Johnny the first semblance of personal interest in his life. Through Mr. O'Brien's efforts, Johnny returned to school and obtained a high school diploma. Afterwards, Mr. O'Brien helped him obtain a job.

Now 20, Johnny is a stockroom clerk in one of the laboratories where you are employed. On the whole Johnny's performance has been acceptable, but there have been glaring exceptions. One involved a clear act of insubordination on a fairly unimportant matter. In another, Johnny was accused, on circumstantial grounds, of destroying some expensive equipment. Though the investigation is still open, it now appears the destruction was accidental.

Johnny's supervisor wants to keep him on for at least a trial period, but he wants "outside" advice as to the best way of helping Johnny grow into greater responsibility. Of course, much depends on how Johnny behaves in the next few months. Naturally, his supervisor must follow personnel policies that are accepted in the company as a whole. It is important to note that Johnny is not an attractive young man. He is rather weak and sickly, and he shows unmistakable signs of long years of social deprivation.

A committee is formed to decide the fate of Johnny Rocco. The chairperson of the meeting is Johnny's supervisor and should begin by assigning roles to the group members. These roles [shop steward (representing the union), head of production, Johnny's co-worker, director of personnel, and social worker who helped Johnny in the past] represent points of view the chairperson believes should be included in this meeting. (Johnny is not to be included.) Two observers should also be assigned. Thus, each group will have eight members.

Instructions

After roles have been assigned, each role player should complete the personal preference part of the work sheet, ranking from 1 to 11 the alternatives according to their appropriateness from the vantage point of his or her role.

Once the individual preferences have been determined, the chairperson should call the meeting to order. The following rules govern the meeting: (1) The group must reach a consensus ranking of the alternatives; (2) the group cannot use a statistical aggregation, or majority vote, decision-making process; (3) members should stay "in character" throughout the discussion. Treat this as a committee meeting consisting of members with different backgrounds, orientation, and interests who share a problem.

After the group has completed the assignment, the observers should conduct a discussion of the group process, using the Group Effectiveness Questions here as a guide. Group members should not look at these questions until after the group task has been completed.

Group Effectiveness Questions

A. Referring to Table 10—3, what task roles were performed? By whom?

B. What maintenance roles were performed? By whom?

C. Were any important task or maintenance roles ignored? Which?

D. Was there any evidence of the Asch effect, groupthink, or social loafing? Explain.

QUESTIONS FOR DISCUSSION

1. Did your committee do a good job? Explain.

2. What, if anything, should have been done differently?

3. How much similarity in rankings is there among the different groups in your class? What group dynamics apparently were responsible for any variations in rankings?

Worksheet

PERSONAL PREFERENCE	GROUP DECISION	
_____	_____	Warn Johnny that at the next sign of trouble he will be fired.
_____	_____	Do nothing, as it is unclear if Johnny did anything wrong.
_____	_____	Create strict controls (do's and don'ts) for Johnny with immediate strong punishment for any misbehaviour.
_____	_____	Give Johnny a great deal of warmth and personal attention and affection (overlooking his present behaviour) so he can learn to depend on others.
_____	_____	Fire him. It's not worth the time and effort spent for such a low-level position.
_____	_____	Talk over the problem with Johnny in an understanding way so he can learn to ask others for help in solving his problems.
_____	_____	Give Johnny a well-structured schedule of daily activities with immediate and unpleasant consequences for not adhering to the schedule.
_____	_____	Do nothing now, but watch him carefully and provide immediate punishment for any future behaviour.
_____	_____	Treat Johnny the same as everyone else, but provide an orderly routine so he can learn to stand on his own two feet.
_____	_____	Call Johnny in and logically discuss the problem with him and ask what you can do to help him.
_____	_____	Do nothing now, but watch him so you can reward him the next time he does something good.

Notes

[1] Excerpted from J W Long, "The Wilderness Lab," *Training and Development Journal*, May 1984, pp 58–69. Used with permission.

[2] E Van Velsor and J Brittain Leslie, "Why Executives Derail: Perspectives across Time and Cultures," *Academy of Management Executive*, November 1995, p 62.

[3] Ibid., p 63.

[4] According to a recent survey, "getting along with others who work at the company" was the top-ranked skill believed to be most important for organizational success. See "Gets Along Well with Others," *Training*, August 1996, pp 17–18.

[5] See L G Bolman and T E Deal, *Reframing Organizations* (San Francisco: Jossey-Bass, 1991), ch. 7.

[6] For instructive research overviews, see K L Bettenhausen, "Five Years of Group Research: What We Have Learned and What Needs To Be Addressed," *Journal of Management*, no. 2, 1991, pp 345–81; and R T Mowday and R I Sutton, "Organizational Behavior: Linking Individuals and Groups to Organizational Contexts," in *Annual Review of Psychology*, vol. 44, eds L W Porter and M R Rosenzweig (Palo Alto, CA: Annual Reviews Inc., 1993), pp 195–229. Also see W G Dyer, *Team Building: Current Issues and New Alternatives*, 3rd ed (Reading, MA: Addison-Wesley, 1995).

[7] This definition is based in part on one found in D Horton Smith, "A Parsimonious Definition of 'Group': Toward Conceptual Clarity and Scientific Utility," *Sociological Inquiry*, Spring 1967, pp 141–67.

[8] E H Schein, *Organizational Psychology*, 3rd ed (Englewood Cliffs, NJ: Prentice-Hall, 1980), p 145.

[9] Ibid., pp 149–53.

[10] J Castro, "Mazda U.," *Time*, October 20, 1986, p 65.

[11] For an instructive overview of five different theories of group development, see J P Wanous, A E Reichers, and S D Malik," Organizational Socialization and Group Development: Toward an Integrative Perspective," *Academy of Management Review*, October 1984, pp 670–83.

[12] See B W Tuckman, "Developmental Sequence in Small Groups," *Psychological Bulletin*, June 1965, pp 384–99; and B W Tuckman and M A C Jensen, "Stages of Small-Group Development Revisited," *Group & Organization Studies*, December 1977, pp 419–27. An instructive adaptation of the Tuckman model can be found in L Holpp, "If Empowerment Is So Good, Why Does It Hurt?" *Training*, March 1995, p 56.

[13] Alternative group development models are discussed in L N Jewell and H J Reitz, *Group Effectiveness in Organizations* (Glenview, IL: Scott, Foresman, 1981), pp 15–20, and R S Wellins, W C Byham, and J M Wilson, *Empowered Teams: Creating Self-Directed Work Groups That Improve Quality, Productivity, and Participation* (San Francisco: Jossey-Bass, 1991).

[14] Practical advice on handling a dominating group member can be found in M Finley, "Belling the Bully," *HRMagazine*, March 1992, pp 82–86.

[15] Jewell and Reitz, *Group Effectiveness in Organizations*, p 19.

[16] D Davies and B C Kuypers, "Group Development and Interpersonal Feedback," *Group & Organizational Studies*, June 1985, p 194.

[17] Ibid., pp 184–208.

[18] C J G Gersick, "Marking Time: Predictable Transitions in Task Groups," *Academy of Management Journal*, June 1989, pp 274–309.

[19] D K Carew, E Parisi-Carew, and K H Blanchard, "Group Development and Situational Leadership: A Model for Managing Groups," *Training and Development Journal*, June 1986, pp 48–49. For evidence linking leadership and group effectiveness, see G R Bushe and A L Johnson, "Contextual and Internal Variables Affecting Task Group Outcomes in Organizations," *Group & Organization Studies*, December 1989, pp 462–82.

[20] For an excellent collection of readings on leadership, see F Hesselbein, M Goldsmith, and R Beckhard, eds., *The Leader of the Future: New Visions, Strategies, and Practices for the Next Era* (San Francisco: Jossey-Bass, 1996).

[21]Negative social impact on individuals is documented in G Blau, "Influence of Group Lateness on Individual Lateness: A Cross-Level Examination," *Academy of Management Journal*, October 1995, pp 1483–96.

[22]G Graen, "Role-Making Processes within Complex Organizations," in *Handbook of Industrial and Organizational Psychology*, ed M D Dunnette (Chicago: Rand McNally, 1976), p 1201.

[23]Other role determinants are explored in H Ibarra "Network Centrality, Power, and Innovation Involvement: Determinants of Technical and Administrative Roles," *Academy of Management Journal*, June 1993, pp 471–501.

[24]Excerpted from G L Miles, "Doug Danforth's Plan to Put Westinghouse in the `Winner's Circle,' " *Business Week*, July 28, 1986, p 75.

[25]For a review of research on the role episode model, see L A King and D W King, "Role Conflict and Role Ambiguity: A Critical Assessment of Construct Validity," *Psychological Bulletin*, January 1990, pp 48–64. Consequences of role perceptions are discussed in R C Netemeyer, S Burton, and M W Johnston, "A Nested Comparison of Four Models of the Consequences of Role Perception Variables," *Organizational Behavior and Human Decision Processes*, January 1995, pp 77–93.

[26]Schein, *Organizational Psychology*, p 198. Also see E Van De Vliert and N W Van Yperen, "Why Cross-National Differences in Role Overload? Don't Overlook Ambient Temperature!" *Academy of Management Journal*, August 1996, pp 986–1004.

[27]Ibid.

[28]See A S Wharton and R J Erickson, "Managing Emotions on the Job and at Home: Understanding the Consequences of Multiple Emotional Roles," *Academy of Management Review*, July 1993, pp 457–86; and S Shellenbarger, "Feel Like You Need To Be Cloned? Even That Wouldn't Work," *The Wall Street Journal*, July 10, 1996, p B1.

[29]See D Moore, "Role Conflict: Not Only for Women? A Comparative Analysis of 5 Nations," *International Journal of Comparative Sociology*, June 1995, pp 17–35; and S Shellenbarger, "More Men Move Past Incompetence Defense to Share Housework," *The Wall Street Journal*, February 21, 1996, p B1.

[30]Schein, *Organizational Psychology*, p 198.

[31]Drawn from M Peterson et al., "Role Conflict, Ambiguity, and Overload: A 21-Nation Study," *Academy of Management Journal*, April 1995, pp 429–52.

[32]1 = A; 2 = C; 3 = A; 4 = A; 5 = C; 6 = A; 7 = C; 8 = A; 9 = C; 10 = C.

[33]R R Blake and J Srygley Mouton, "Don't Let Group Norms Stifle Creativity," *Personnel*, August 1985, p 28.

[34]See D Kahneman, "Reference Points, Anchors, Norms, and Mixed Feelings," *Organizational Behavior and Human Decision Processes*, March 1992, pp 296–312.

[35]A Dunkin, "Pepsi's Marketing Magic: Why Nobody Does It Better," *Business Week*, February 10, 1986, p 52.

[36]D C Feldman, "The Development and Enforcement of Group Norms," *Academy of Management Review*, January 1984, pp 50–52.

[37]For more on norms, see K L Bettenhausen and K J Murnigham, "The Development of an Intragroup Norm and the Effects of Intrapersonal and Structural Challenges," *Administrative Science Quarterly*, March 1991, pp 20–35; R I Sutton, "Maintaining Norms about Expressed Emotions; The Case of Bill Collectors," *Administrative Science Quarterly*, June 1991, pp 245–68; and R D Russell and C J Russell, "An Examination of the Effects of Organizational Norms, Organizational Structure, and Environmental Uncertainty on Entrepreneurial Strategy," *Journal of Management*, December 1992, pp 639–56.

[38]Feldman, "The Development and Enforcement of Group Norms."

[39]See R G Netemeyer, M W Johnston, and S Burton, "Analysis of Role Conflict and Role Ambiguity in a Structural Equations Framework," *Journal of Applied Psychology*, April 1990, pp 148–57; and G W McGee, C E Ferguson, Jr., and A Seers, "Role Conflict and Role Ambiguity: Do the Scales Measure These Two Constructs?" *Journal of Applied Psychology*, October 1989, pp 815–18.

[40]See S E Jackson and R S Schuler, "A Meta-Analysis and Conceptual Critique of Research on Role Ambiguity and Role Conflict in Work Settings," *Organizational Behavior and Human Decision Processes*, August 1985, pp 16–78. Also see King and King, "Role Conflict and Role Ambiguity: A Critical Assessment of Construct Validity."

[41]For a comprehensive overview, see H Arrow and J E McGrath, "Membership Dynamics in Groups at Work: A Theoretical Framework," in *Research in Organizational Behavior*, eds L L Cummings and B M Staw (Greenwich, CT: JAI Press, 1995), vol. 17, pp 373–411.

[42]See K D Benne and P Sheats, "Functional Roles of Group Members," *Journal of Social Issues*, Spring 1948, pp 41–49.

[43]See H J Klein and P W Mulvey, "Two Investigations of the Relationships among Group Goals, Goal Commitment, Cohesion, and Performance," *Organizational Behavior and Human Decision Processes*, January 1995, pp 44–53; and D F Crown and J G Rosse, "Yours, Mine, and Ours: Facilitating Group Productivity through the Integration of Individual and Group Goals," *Organizational Behavior and Human Decision Processes*, November 1995, pp 138–50.

[44]A Zander, "The Value of Belonging to a Group in Japan," *Small Group Behavior*, February 1983, pp 7–8. Also see P R Harris and R T Moran, *Managing Cultural Differences*, 4th ed (Houston: Gulf Publishing, 1996), pp 267–76.

[45]For example, see B Grofman, S L Feld, and G Owen, "Group Size and the Performance of a Composite Group Majority: Statistical Truths and Empirical Results," *Organizational Behavior and Human Performance*, June 1984, pp 350–59.

[46]See P Yetton and P Bottger, "The Relationships among Group Size, Member Ability, Social Decision Schemes, and Performance," *Organizational Behavior and Human Performance*, October 1983, pp 145–59.

[47]This copyrighted exercise may be found in J Hall, "Decisions, Decisions, Decisions," *Psychology Today*, November 1971, pp 51–54, 86, 88.

[48]Yetton and Bottger, "The Relationships among Group Size, Member Ability, Social Decision Schemes, and Performance," p 158.

[49]Based on R B Gallupe, A R Dennis, W H Cooper, J S Valacich, L M Bastianutti, and J F Nunamaker, Jr., "Electronic Brainstorming and Group Size," *Academy of Management Journal*, June 1992, pp 350–69.

[50]For encouraging data, see L S Richman, "The Big Payoff from Computers," *Fortune*, March 7, 1994, p 28.

[51]Drawn from B Mullen, C Symons, L-T Hu, and E Salas, "Group Size, Leadership Behavior, and Subordinate Satisfaction," *The Journal of General Psychology*, April 1989, pp 155–69. Also see P Oliver and G Marwell, "The Paradox of Group Size in Collective Action: A Theory of the Critical Mass. Il.," *American Sociological Review*, February 1988, pp 1–8.

[52]Details of this study are presented in L L Thompson, E A Mannix, and M H Bazerman, "Group Negotiation: Effects of Decision Rule, Agenda and Aspiration," *Journal of Personality and Social Psychology*, January 1988, pp 86–95.

[53]For example, see A B Fisher, "Getting Comfortable with Couples

in the Workplace," *Fortune*, October 3, 1994, pp 138–44; A P Baridon and D R Eyler, "Workplace Etiquette for Men and Women," *Training*, December 1994, pp 31—37; J Connelly, "Let's Hear It for the Office," *Fortune*, March 6, 1995, pp 221–22; and M Hequet, "Office Romance," *Training*, February 1996, pp 44–50.

[54]See S G Rogelberg and S M Rumery, "Gender Diversity, Team Decision Quality, Time on Task, and Interpersonal Cohesion," *Small Group Research*, February 1996, pp 79–90.

[55]See L Smith-Lovin and C Brody, "Interruptions in Group Discussions: The Effects of Gender and Group Composition," *American Sociological Review*, June 1989, pp 424–35.

[56]E M Ott, "Effects of the Male-Female Ratio at Work," *Psychology of Women Quarterly*, March 1989, p 53.

[57]B A Gutek, "Sexuality in the Workplace: Key Issues in Social Research and Organisational Practice," in *The Sexuality of Organizations*, eds J Hearn, D L Sheppard, P Tancred-Sheri and G Burrell, (London: Sage, 1989).

[58]J E Williams and D L Best, *Measuring Sex Stereotypes, A Thirty Nation Study* (Beverly Hills, C.A: Sage, 1982)

[59]C L Cooper and S Lewis, "Working Together: Men and Women in Organizations," *Leadership and Organization Development Journal*, vol. 16, no. 5, 1995, pp 29–31

[60]*Measures to Combat Sexual Harassment at the Workplace: Action Taken in the Member States of the European Community* (Luxembourg: European Parliament, 1994), Doc EN/DV/245/245696

[61]Ibid.

[62]J Annells, "Japanese Companies in the US Are Nervous They May Be Sued for Harassment," *The Financial Times*, March 8, 1997, p 24.

[63] Sexual Harassment is discussed as one of 10 ethical landmines in C Cox, "High Explosives," *Business Ethics*, January 1994, pp 33–5.

[64]See S A Lobel, R E Quinn, L St. Clair, and A Warfield, "Love without Sex: The Impact of Psychological Intimacy between Men and Women at Work," *Organizational Dynamics*, Summer 1994, pp 5–16.

[65]S J South, C M Bonjean, W T Markham, and J Corder, "Female Labor Force Participation and the Organizational Experiences of Male Workers," *The Sociological Quarterly*, Summer 1983, p 378.

[66] C L Cooper and S Lewis, "Working Together: Men and Women in Organizations," *Leadership and Organization Development Journal*, vol. 16, no. 5, 1995, pp 30–1.

[67]K Harper, "BR Outlaws Harassment," *The Guardian*, April 25, 1994, p 2.

[68]A former Israeli tank commander's first-hand account of tank warfare in the desert can be found in A Kahalani, "Advice from a Desert Warrior," *Newsweek*, September 3, 1990, p 32.

[69]A Tziner and D Eden, "Effects of Crew Composition on Crew Performance: Does the Whole Equal the Sum of Its Parts?" *Journal of Applied Psychology*, February 1985, p 91.

[70]Ibid.

[71]For related research, see R Saavedra, C P Earley, and L Van Dyne, "Complex Interdependence in Task-Performing Groups," *Journal of Applied Psychology*, February 1993, pp 61–72.

[72]Blake and Mouton, "Don't Let Group Norms Stifle Creativity," p 29.

[73]For additional information, see S E Asch, *Social Psychology* (Englewood Cliffs, NJ: Prentice-Hall, 1952), ch. 16.

[74]See T P Williams and S Sogon, "Group Composition and Conforming Behavior in Japanese Students," *Japanese Psychological Research*, no. 4, 1984, pp 231–34; and T Amir, "The Asch Conformity Effect: A Study in Kuwait," *Social Behavior and Personality*, no. 2, 1984, pp 187–90.

[75]N Nicholson, S G Cole, T Rocklin, "Conformity in the Asch Situation: Acomparison Between Contemporary British and US University Students," *British Journal of Social Psychology*, 1985 Feb, vol. 24, no. 1, pp 59–63.

[76]Data from R Bond and P B Smith, "Culture and Conformity: A Meta-Analysis of Studies Using Asch's (1952b, 1956) Line Judgment Task," *Psychological Bulletin*, January 1996, pp 111–37.

[77]R McNamara, *In Retrospect: The Tragedy and Lessons of Vietnam* (New York: Times Books, 1995).

[78]For an interesting analysis of the presence or absence of groupthink in selected US foreign policy decisions, see C McCauley, "The Nature of Social Influence in Groupthink: Compliance and Internalization," *Journal of Personality and Social Psychology*, August 1989, pp 250–60. Also see G Whyte, "Groupthink Reconsidered," *Academy of Management Review*, January 1989, pp 40–56.

[79]I L Janis, *Groupthink*, 2nd ed (Boston: Houghton Mifflin, 1982), p 9.

[80]Ibid. For an alternative model, see R J Aldag and S Riggs Fuller, "Beyond Fiasco: A Reappraisal of the Groupthink Phenomenon and a New Model of Group Decision Processes," *Psychological Bulletin*, May 1993, pp 533–52. Also see A A Mohamed and F A Wiebe, "Toward a Process Theory of Groupthink," *Small Group Research*, August 1996, pp 416–30.

[81]For an ethical perspective, see R R Sims, "Linking Groupthink to Unethical Behavior in Organizations," *Journal of Business Ethics*, September 1992, pp 651–62.

[82]Details of this study may be found in M R Callaway and J K Esser, "Groupthink: Effects of Cohesiveness and Problem-Solving Procedures on Group Decision Making," *Social Behavior and Personality*, no. 2, 1984, pp 157–64. Also see C R Leana, "A Partial Test of Janis's Groupthink Model: Effects of Group Cohesiveness and Leader-Behavior on Defective Decision Making," *Journal of Management*, Spring 1985, pp 5–17; and G Moorhead and J R Montanari, "An Empirical Investigation of the Groupthink Phenomenon," *Human Relations*, May 1986, pp 399–410.

[83]Adapted from discussion in Janis, *Groupthink*, ch. 11.

[84]An illustrative case study is reported in C P Neck and G Moorhead, "Jury Deliberations in the Trial of U.S. v John DeLorean: A Case Analysis of Groupthink Avoidance and an Enhanced Framework," *Human Relations*, October 1992, pp 1077–91.

[85]Based on discussion in B Latane, K Williams, and S Harkins, "Many Hands Make Light the Work: The Causes and Consequences of Social Loafing," *Journal of Personality and Social Psychology*, June 1979, pp 822–32; and D A Kravitz and B Martin, "Ringelmann Rediscovered: The Original Article," *Journal of Personality and Social Psychology*, May 1986, pp 936–41.

[86]See J A Shepperd, "Productivity Loss in Performance Groups: A Motivation Analysis," *Psychological Bulletin*, no. 1, 1993, pp 67–81; R E Kidwell, Jr., and N Bennett, "Employee Propensity to Withhold Effort: A Conceptual Model to Intersect Three Avenues of Research," *Academy of Management Review*, July 1993, pp 429–56; and S J Karau and K D Williams, "Social Loafing: Meta-Analytic Review and Theoretical Integration," *Journal of Personality and Social Psychology*, October 1993, pp 681–706.

[87]See S J Zaccaro, "Social Loafing: The Role of Task Attractiveness," *Personality and Social Psychology Bulletin*, March 1984, pp 99–106; J M Jackson and K D Williams, "Social Loafing on Difficult Tasks: Working Collectively Can Improve Performance," *Journal of Personality and Social Psychology*,

October 1985, pp 937–42; and J M George, "Extrinsic and Intrinsic Origins of Perceived Social Loafing in Organizations," *Academy of Management Journal*, March 1992, pp 191–202.

[88]For complete details, see K Williams, S Harkins, and B Latane, "Identifiability as a Deterrent to Social Loafing: Two Cheering Experiments," *Journal of Personality and Social Psychology*, February 1981, pp 303–11.

[89]See J M Jackson and S G Harkins, "Equity in Effort: An Explanation of the Social Loafing Effect," *Journal of Personality and Social Psychology*, November 1985, pp 1199–1206.

[90]Both studies are reported in S G Harkins and K Szymanski, "Social Loafing and Group Evaluation," *Journal of Personality and Social Psychology*, June 1989, pp 934–41.

[91]Data from J A Wagner III, "Studies of Individualism-Collectivism: Effects on Cooperation in Groups," *Academy of Management Journal*, February 1995, pp 152–72.

[92]S G Rogelberg, J L Barnes-Farrell, and C A Lowe, "The Stepladder Technique: An Alternative Group Structure Facilitating Effective Group Decision Making," *Journal of Applied Psychology*, October 1992, p 730.

[93]Twenty items excerpted from S A Wheelan and J M Hochberger, "Validation Studies of the Group Development Questionnaire," *Small Group Research*, February 1996, pp 143–70.

[94]From *Developing Management Skills* by D A Whetten and K S Cameron. Copyright © 1984 by Scott, Foresman and Company. Reprinted by permission of Addison Wesley Educational Publishers, Inc.

Eleven

Power, Politics, Conflict, and Negotiation

LEARNING OBJECTIVES

When you finish studying the material in this chapter, you should be able to:

1. Explain the concept of mutuality of interest, and identify the three most effective influence tactics.

2. Identify and briefly describe French and Raven's five bases of power.

3. Explain why delegation is the highest form of empowerment.

4. Define organizational politics, and explain what triggers it.

5. Distinguish between favourable and unfavourable impression management tactics, and explain how to manage organizational politics.

6. Define conflict, and distinguish between functional and dysfunctional conflict.

7. Explain how managers can stimulate functional conflict.

8. Identify the five conflict-handling styles, and explain the contingency approach to managing conflict.

9. Explain the difference between distributive and integrative negotiation, and discuss the concept of added-value negotiation.

Wine cellar, nuclear cellar, and nursery: France's most famous status symbols

At 55, rue du Faubourg-Saint-Honoré, the Elysée Palace, France's presidential palace is situated. It is the most impressive part of the numerous castles, palaces, and territories the president of France inherits at his election. It is not possible to pop in at any time, and when you pass in front of it, the French police kindly ask you to cross the street.

The Elysée Palace hides a world of treasures. It covers 375 rooms, a private apartment of about 300 m^2 and a park of over 20,000 m^2. It once housed the Marquis de Pompadour, in 1815 Napoleon Bonaparte signed his second abdication at the 18th century Palace and in 1848 it was Napoleon III's residence. It has been the official residence of all French presidents since 1873.

The Palace is a mixture of four styles: 18th century, first and second French Empire, and Third Republic. The presidents have no right to change the design thoroughly, but they are entitled to make a choice from the "mobilier national," a stock of furniture, carpets and ornamental objects.

The holiest place, the president's office, is situated on the first floor, his private apartments on the second floor.

The Pompidou family was the first to introduce the 20th century at the Elysée. They asked designer Pierre Paulin to handle their private rooms. The round table with tinted tabletop surrounded by bucket seats in the president's dining room is still evidence of it.

But today's design was introduced by Mitterrand and his entourage. They wanted their apartments to mirror the modern French interior design: Marc Held, Ronald Cecil Sportes, Jean Michel Wilmotte, Philippe Starck, and Tribel were selected for designing the rooms.

Next to salons and offices, the Elysée has a chapel which is cleaned once a month, although the personnel says it has not been used since Giscard.

From the president's nuclear cellar, called Jupiter, there is a direct link with the Ministry of Defence, the prime minister, and the airforce commander in Albion, where France's nuclear missiles are located. From this "bunker," the French president can at any time launch missiles.

A private television studio allows the president to address the French population at any moment. Everything is in perfect order, and only ten minutes after he has decided to do so, the president can be on air. In a private cinema, he can invite special guests to a preview of a new film.

The Elysée's personnel have a sports room at their disposal and a medical cabinet. In 1986, Danielle Mitterrand had a nursery installed for the staff's children.

The presidential household is enormous: the president's secretary-general—his political staff—numbers some 150 advisers and officials. They draw up dozens of notes and speeches for the president daily, they are in touch with the different ministries, they take care of the press contacts and the presidents' public relations and each of them has a certain number of files under his or her authority.

Beside the secretary-general, the president has a cabinet which has a far less political role to fulfil. The cabinet is responsible for audiences, presidential trips, the protocol, the Elysée's financial and material organization, and the president's security.

Finally, the president has a military staff of 30 people. In addition the 188 member Republican Guard looks after the president.

In total, some 800 people work directly for the Elysée, although only a limited budget is reserved for that purpose. The maintenance of the buildings depends on the Ministry of Culture, trips abroad, and receptions on foreign affairs. The majority of personnel members are paid by the Ministries of Defence and Internal Affairs. Nevertheless, the president and the heating specialist are the only two effectively residing at the Elysée.

In the basement, Joël Normand guards over a kitchen of about 600 m^2, 10 chefs and 10 conscripts. He was only 20 years old when he first entered the Elysée as "sous-chef." He remembers the time when Valéry Giscard introduced "nouvelle cuisine." "He enjoyed being innovative," says Normand. Mitterrand did not like game. He preferred beef or lamb, and crustaceans or asparagus as a starter.

The wine cellars, located next to the kitchen, has some 15,000 bottles of wine. For a gala diner of 200 people, 40 bottles of red wine, 20 bottles of white wine and 50 bottles of champagne are served.

The presidential staff also counts a number of specialized people, such as the "lustriers," who are responsible for repairing and maintaining the palace's many crystal chandeliers. The "tapistier," who succeeded his father, guards over the carpets, and the "ébéniste" takes care of the furniture, whereas the watchmaker carefully watches whether the 260 clocks lose time.

More up-to-date are the 10 mechanics and 3 drivers who take care that the sixty cars—Renault, Peugeot and Citroën—function as it should be, the two photographers who always join the president and the Palace's private printer.

The Elysée's payroll includes two florists. "Madame Pompidou did not like violets and carnations," the eldest of the two recalls. "And Giscard wanted us to follow the rhythm of nature. Mitterrand paid more attention to the harmony of colours. He liked red roses."

Six "argentiers" keep an eye on the 10,000 sets of cutlery in solid silver, some 7,000 glasses and decanters, 5,300 plates in china from Sèvres, which costs between 2,000 and 6,000 FF each. Moreover, the dishes are done by hand and…spoons or knives regularly disappear during official banquets…People like to take a small souvenir.[1]

Discussion Question

Is a display of power and status of this kind essential to the presidency?

A t the very heart of interpersonal dealings in today's work organizations is a constant struggle between individual and collective interests. For example, Sid wants a rise, but his company doesn't make enough money to both grant rises and pay minimum shareholder dividends. Preoccupation with self-interest is understandable. After all, each of us was born, not as a cooperating organization member, but as an individual with instincts for self-preservation. It took socialization in family, school, religious, sports, recreation, and employment settings to introduce us to the notion of mutuality of interest. Basically, **mutuality of interest** involves win–win situations in which one's self-interest is served by cooperating actively and creatively with potential adversaries. A pair of

Mutuality of interest

Balancing individual and organizational interests through win–win cooperation.

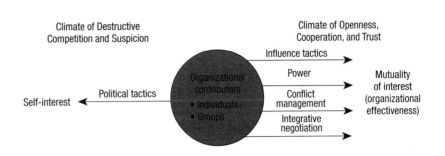

Figure 11 − 1   The Constant Tug-of-War Between Self-Interest and Mutuality of Interest Requires Managerial Action

organization development consultants offered this managerial perspective of mutuality of interest:

Nothing is more important than this sense of mutuality to the effectiveness and quality of an organization's products and services. Management must strive to stimulate a strong sense of shared ownership in every employee, because otherwise an organization cannot do its best in the long run. Employees who identify their own personal self-interest with the quality of their organization's output understand mutuality and strive to maintain it in their jobs and work relations.[2]

Figure 11–1 graphically portrays the constant tug-of-war between employees' self-interest and the organization's need for mutuality of interest. It also serves as an overview model for this chapter, dealing with social influence tactics, social power, organizational politics, and conflict management/negotiation. Notice how political tactics, motivated by self-interest, tend to pull individuals and groups away from mutual self-interest (organizational effectiveness). To counteract this, managers have four tools at their disposal: influence tactics, power, conflict management techniques, and negotiation strategies. At stake in this tug-of-war between individual and collective interests is no less than the ultimate survival of the organization.

Organizational Influence Tactics: Getting One's Way at Work

How do you get others to carry out your wishes? Do you simply tell them what to do? Or do you prefer a less direct approach, such as promising to return the favour? Whatever approach you use, the crux of the issue is *social influence*. A large measure of interpersonal interaction involves attempts to influence others, including parents, bosses, co-workers, spouses, teachers, friends, and children. Even if managers do not expect to get such dramatic results, they need to sharpen their influence skills. A good starting point is familiarity with the following research insights.

Eight Generic Influence Tactics

A particularly fruitful stream of research, initiated by David Kipnis and his colleagues in 1980, reveals how people influence each other in organizations. The Kipnis methodology involved asking employees how they managed to get either their bosses, co-workers, or subordinates to do what they wanted them to do.[3] Statistical refinements and replications by other researchers over a 10-year period eventually yielded eight influence tactics. The eight tactics, ranked in diminishing order of use in the workplace are as follows:

1. *Consultation.* Getting others to participate in decisions and changes.

2. *Rational persuasion.* Trying to convince someone with reason, logic, or facts.

3. *Inspirational appeals.* Trying to build enthusiasm by appealing to others' emotions, ideals, or values.

4. *Ingratiating tactics.* Getting someone in a good mood prior to making a request.

5. *Coalition tactics.* Getting others to support your effort to persuade someone.

6. *Pressure tactics.* Demanding compliance or using intimidation and threats.

7. *Upward appeals.* Trying to persuade someone on the basis of express or implied support from superiors.

8. *Exchange tactics.* Making express or implied promises and trading favours.[4]

These approaches can be considered *generic* influence tactics because they characterize social influence in all directions. Researchers have found this ranking to be fairly consistent regardless of whether the direction of influence is downward, upward, or lateral.

Three Possible Influence Outcomes

Put yourself in this familiar situation. It's Wednesday and a big project you've been working on for your project team is due on Friday. You're behind on the preparation of your computer graphics for your final report and presentation. You catch a friend who is great at computer graphics as he or she heads out of the office at quitting time. You try this *exchange tactic* to get your friend to help you out: "I'm way behind. I need your help. If you could come back in for two to three hours tonight and help me with these graphics, I'll complete those spreadsheets you've been complaining about." According to researchers, your friend will engage in one of three possible influence outcomes:

1. *Commitment.* Your friend enthusiastically agrees and will demonstrate initiative and persistence while completing the assignment.

2. *Compliance.* Your friend grudgingly complies and will need prodding to satisfy minimum requirements.

3. *Resistance.* Your friend will say no, make excuses, stall, or put up an argument.[5]

The best outcome is commitment because the target person's intrinsic motivation will energize good performance. However, managers often have to settle for compliance in today's hectic workplace. Resistance means a failed influence attempt.

Practical Research Insights

Laboratory and field studies have taught us useful lessons about the relative effectiveness of influence tactics along with other instructive insights:

- Commitment is more likely when people rely on consultation, strong rational persuasion, and inspirational appeals and *do not* rely on pressure and coalition tactics.[6] Interestingly, in one study, managers were not very effective at *downward* influence. They relied most heavily on inspiration (an effective tactic), ingratiation (a moderately effective tactic), and pressure (an ineffective tactic).[7]

- A 1996 meta-analysis of 69 studies suggests ingratiating tactics (making the boss feel good) can slightly improve your performance appraisal results and make your boss like you significantly more.[8]

- Commitment is more likely when the influence attempt involves something *important* and *enjoyable* and is based on a *friendly* relationship.[9]

- Another study probed male–female differences in influencing work group members. Many studies have found women to be perceived as less competent and less influential in work groups than men. The researchers had male and female work group leaders engage in either task behaviour (demonstrating ability and task competence) or dominating behaviour (relying on threats). For both women and men, task behaviour was associated with perceived competence and effective influence. Dominating behaviour was not effective. The following conclusion by the researchers has important practical implications for all managers who desire to successfully influence others: "The display of task cues is an effective means to enhance one's status in groups and…the attempt to gain influence in task groups through dominance is an ineffective and poorly received strategy for both men and women."[10]

- Interpersonal influence is culture bound. The foregoing research evidence on influence tactics has a bias in favour of European–North Americans. Much remains to be learned about how to effectively influence others (without unintended insult) in today's diverse labour force and cross-cultural economy.[11]

ETHICS

How to Extend Your Influence by Forming Strategic Alliances

In their book, *Influence without Authority,* Allan R Cohen and David L Bradford extended the concept of corporate strategic alliances to interpersonal influence. Hardly a day goes by without another mention in the business press of a new strategic alliance between two global companies intent on staying competitive. These win–win relationships are based on complementary strengths. According to Cohen and Bradford, managers need to follow suit by forming some strategic alliances of their own with anyone who has a stake in their area. This is particularly true given today's rapid change, cross-functional work teams, and diminished reliance on traditional authority structures.

While admitting the task is not an easy one, Cohen and Bradford recommend the following tips for dealing with potential allies:

1. *Mutual respect.* Assume they are competent and smart.

2. *Openness.* Talk straight to them. It isn't possible for any one person to know everything, so give them the information they need to know to help you better.

3. *Trust.* Assume that no one will take any action that is purposely intended to hurt another, so hold back no information that the other could use, even if it doesn't help your immediate position.

4. *Mutual benefit.* Plan every strategy so that both parties win. If that doesn't happen over time, the alliance will break up. When dissolving a partnership becomes necessary as a last resort, try to do it in a clean way that minimizes residual anger. Some day, you may want a new alliance with that person.[12]

Reciprocity

Widespread belief that people should be paid back for their positive and negative acts.

True, these tactics involve taking some personal risks. But the effectiveness of interpersonal strategic alliances is anchored to the concept of reciprocity. "**Reciprocity** is the almost universal belief that people should be paid back for what they do—that one good (or bad) turn deserves another."[13] In short, people tend to get what they give when attempting to influence others.

By demonstrating the rich texture of social influence, the foregoing research evidence and practical advice whet our appetite for learning more about how today's managers can and do reconcile individual and organizational interests. Let us focus on social power.

Social Power and Empowerment

The term *power* evokes mixed and often passionate reactions. Citing recent instances of government corruption and corporate misconduct, many observers view power as a sinister force. By 1992, the figure had reached 71 per cent.[14] To these sceptics, Lord Acton's time-honoured statement that "power corrupts and absolute power corrupts absolutely" is as true as ever. However, OB specialists remind us that, like it or not, power is a fact of life in modern organizations. According to one management writer:

> Power must be used because managers must influence those they depend on. Power also is crucial in the development of managers' self-confidence and willingness to support subordinates. From this perspective, power should be accepted as a natural part of any organization. Managers should recognize and develop their own power to coordinate and support the work of subordinates; it is powerlessness, not power, that undermines organizational effectiveness.[15]

> Bullying apart from sexual harassment, workplace bullying is another growing trend which goes along with abuse of power. Bullying is no longer confined to primary school pupils, but it has become an adult virus crossing all sectors and ranks, white collar as well as blue collar environments. Resulting from macho management style, bullying is likely to result in demoralization, stress-related absenteeism and higher staff-turnover. Bullying is directly linked to power over others. Remove the bullier's power, and the bullying will cease to exist. Bulliers may have been victims bullying before. Some companies are aware of the seriousness of bullies and have taken action to stop or prevent it by introducing an anti-bullying policy.[16]

Social power

Ability to get things done with human, informational, and material resources.

Thus, power is a necessary and generally positive force in organizations. As the term is used here, **social power** is defined as "the ability to marshal the human, informational, and material resources to get something done."[17] Power is, however, a strong weapon, which can be used to get things done, as illustrated in the following example of pyramid sales:

> In some form of Hollywood spectacle, Titan, a Hamburg-based company, tries to convince people to 'invest' 4,500 German marks. By recruiting three others to invest the same amount, you advance on the Titan-ladder and you are paid out a commission. All power lies in the hands of the fluent person on the podium, who uses all his capacities to talk the audience into the system.[18]

> According to one ex-distributor of Amway, a system equal to Titan, pyramid selling is based on pure indoctrination. Competition is stirred up through sophisticated systems of rewards and bonuses.[19]

Dimensions of Power

The use of power is associated to the Italian statesman and writer, Niccolò Machiavelli, who lived in Florence from 1469 to 1527. With his principal work *The Prince* (*Il Principe*, 1513), dedicated to Lorenzo de Medici who ruled over Florence from 1513, Machiavelli wanted to contribute to Italy's unification. His great hope was to obtain a post at Lorenzo's court, but in vain.

The Prince can be considered as a guideline for ruling. Machiavelli discusses the causes of the rise and fall of states and the statesman's role in this process. The state is a goal in itself and the ruler must if necessary be prepared to make use of reprehensible methods to maintain his power. The interests of the state take precedence over all other considerations. Political ends justify the means. The ruler can either rule by exercising absolute power or by surrounding himself with independent lords. In the first case, all others are his subjects, while in the latter, the lord's power is derived from his birth.

Absolute power for Machiavelli was the only alternative to chaos and anarchy. By imposing laws and rules, a balance of power is installed, which will finally result in a republican society such as the Roman Empire. A government can only be successful if a legal system is installed which bans arbitrariness, which guarantees equality of all civilians, and in which appeal is possible.

Machiavelli was the first political philosopher to separate political thought from religious considerations: religion only has importance if it influences politics. This line of thought was in sharp contrast with medieval society, where power was considered as divine. Machiavelli has been reproached repeatedly for encouraging the use of immoral means to gain power. He is often blamed for being cruel and interested only in power. Hence the term machiavellianism is used derogatorily for immoral politics and pure self-interest.

While power may be an elusive concept to the casual observer, social scientists view power as having reasonably clear dimensions. Two dimensions of power that deserve our attention are (1) socialized versus personalized power and (2) the five bases of power.

Two Types of Power   Behavioural scientists such as David McClelland contend that one of the basic human needs is the need for power (n Pwr). Because this need is learned and not innate, the need for power has been extensively studied. Historically, need for power was scored when subjects interpreted TAT pictures in terms of one person attempting to influence, convince, persuade, or control another, as discussed in Chapter 7. More recently, however, researchers have drawn a distinction between **socialized power** and **personalized power.**

> **Socialized power**
> Directed at helping others.

> **Personalized power**
> Directed at helping oneself.

There are two subscales or "faces" in n Pwr. One face is termed "socialized" (s Pwr) and is scored in the Thematic Apperception Test (TAT) as "plans, self-doubts, mixed outcomes and concerns for others, . . ." while the second face is "personalized" power (p Pwr), in which expressions of power for the sake of personal aggrandizement become paramount.[20]

This distinction between socialized and personalized power helps explain why power has a negative connotation for many people.[21] Managers and others who pursue personalized power for their own selfish ends give power a bad name. But a series of interviews with 25 American women elected to public office found a strong preference for socialized power. The following comments illustrate their desire to wield power effectively and ethically:

- "Power in itself means nothing. . . . I think power is the opportunity to really have an impact on your community."

- "My goal is to be a powerful advocate on the part of my constituents."[22]

Five Bases of Power   A popular classification scheme for social power traces back nearly 40 years to the work of John French and Bertram Raven. They proposed that power arises from five different bases: reward power, coercive power, legitimate power, expert power, and referent power.[23] Each involves a different approach to influencing others:

> **Reward power**
> Obtaining compliance with promised or actual rewards.

- *Reward power.* A manager has **reward power** to the extent that he or she obtains compliance by promising or granting rewards. On-the-job behaviour modification, for example, relies heavily on reward power.

> **Coercive power**
> Obtaining compliance through threatened or actual punishment.

- *Coercive power.* Threats of punishment and actual punishment give an individual **coercive power**. A sales manager who threatens to fire any salesperson who uses a company car for family holidays is relying on coercive power.

> **Legitimate power**
> Obtaining compliance through formal authority.

- *Legitimate power.* This base of power is anchored to one's formal position or authority. Thus, individuals who obtain compliance primarily because of their formal authority to make decisions have **legitimate power**. Legitimate power may express itself in either a positive or negative manner in managing people. Positive legitimate power focuses constructively on job performance. Negative legitimate power tends to be threatening and demeaning to those being influenced. Its main purpose is to build the power holder's ego.

> **Expert power**
> Obtaining compliance through one's knowledge or information.

- *Expert power.* Valued knowledge or information gives an individual **expert power** over those who need such knowledge or information. The power of supervisors is enhanced because they know about work schedules and assignments before their subordinates do. Skilful use of expert power played a key role in the effectiveness of team leaders in a recent study of three physician medical diagnosis teams.[24] Knowledge *is* power in today's high-tech workplaces.

Referent power

Obtaining compliance through charisma or personal attraction.

- *Referent power.* Also called charisma, **referent power** comes into play when one's personality becomes the reason for compliance. Role models have referent power over those who identify closely with them.[25]

Shipley and Egan invested the relationship between brewers and their tenants in the UK. They concluded that brewers apply the wrong types of power in the wrong way and consequently these brewers generate too little channel co-operation and to much conflict.

Most tenants are small independent business persons contracted for a short period (three years). These short tenancy contracts give brewers substantial power to apply coercive power by threatening nonrenewal. Conversely, tenants have little or no countervailing power. The results showed that tenants are not well-motivated and its concluded that this is because brewers use coercive power excessively and reward power insufficiently.[26]

To further your understanding of these five bases of power and to assess your self-perceived power, please take a moment to complete the questionnaire in the OB Exercise. Think of your present job or your most recent job when responding to the various items. What is your power profile?

Research Insights about Social Power

In one study, a sample of 94 male and 84 female nonmanagerial and professional employees in Denver, Colorado, completed TAT tests. The researchers found that the male and female employees had similar needs for power (n Pwr) and personalized power (p Pwr). But the women had a significantly higher need for socialized power (s Pwr) than did their male counterparts.[27] This bodes well for today's work organizations where women are playing an ever greater administrative role. Unfortunately, as women gain power in the workplace, greater tension between men and women has been observed. *Training* magazine offered this perspective:

. . . observers view the tension between women and men in the workplace as a natural outcome of power inequities between the genders. Their argument is that men still have most of the power

---

OB EXERCISE   *What Is Your Self-Perceived Power?*

Instructions

Score your various bases of power for your current (or former) job, using the following scale:

1 = Strongly disagree   4 = Agree

2 = Disagree   5 = Strongly agree

3 = Slightly agree

REWARD POWER SCORE = _____

1. I can reward persons at lower levels. _____

2. My review actions affect the rewards gained at lower levels. _____

3. Based on my decisions, lower level personnel may receive a bonus. _____

COERCIVE POWER SCORE = _____

1. I can punish employees at lower levels. _____

2. My work is a check on lower level employees. _____

3. My diligence reduces error. _____

LEGITIMATE POWER SCORE = _____

1. My position gives me a great deal of authority. _____

2. The decisions made at my level are of critical importance. _____

3. Employees look to me for guidance. _____

EXPERT POWER SCORE = _____

1. I am an expert in this job. _____

2. My ability gives me an advantage in this job. _____

3. Given some time, I could improve the methods used on this job. _____

REFERENT POWER SCORE = _____

1. I attempt to set a good example for other employees. _____

2. My personality allows me to work well in this job. _____

3. My fellow employees look to me as their informal leader. _____

Arbitrary norms for each of the five bases of power are: 3–6 = Weak power base; 7–11 = Moderate power base; 12–15 = Strong power base.

SOURCE   Adapted and excerpted in part from D L Dieterly and B Schneider, "The Effect of Organizational Environment on Perceived Power and Climate: A Laboratory Study," *Organizational Behavior and Human Performance*, June 1974, pp 316–37.

and are resisting any change as a way to protect their power base. [Consultant Susan L] Webb asserts that sexual harassment has far more to do with exercising power in an unhealthy way than with sexual attraction. Likewise, the glass ceiling, a metaphor for the barriers women face in climbing the corporate ladder to management and executive positions, is about power and access to power.[28]

Accordingly, "powerful women were described more positively by women than by men" in a recent study of 140 female and 125 male college students in Sydney, Australia.[29]

A reanalysis of 18 field studies that measured French and Raven's five bases of power uncovered "severe methodological shortcomings."[30] After correcting for these problems, the researchers identified the following relationships between power bases and work outcomes such as job performance, job satisfaction, and turnover:

- Expert and referent power had a generally positive impact.

- Reward and legitimate power had a slightly positive impact.

- Coercive power had a slightly negative impact.

The same researcher, in a 1990 follow-up study involving 251 employed business seniors, looked at the relationship between influence styles and bases of power. This was a bottom-up study. In other words, subordinate perceptions of managerial influence and power were examined. Rational persuasion was found to be a highly acceptable managerial influence tactic. Why? Because subordinates perceived it to be associated with the three bases of power they viewed positively: legitimate, expert, and referent.[31]

In summary, expert and referent power appear to get the best *combination* of results and favourable subordinate reactions.[32]

The following situation of coercive power forced an employee to take sick leave and finally to give up her job because of the resulting total lack of self-confidence.

When returning back to work after a day off because of migraine, I was called into my boss's office. He threw my doctor's certificate across the desk and said 'Stress! That's not going to help your application for senior product manager, is it?' I told him that if he checked my records he would see I had taken less than 3 weeks' sick leave in the 5 years I had been with the company.

He then tossed a newspaper across the desk. A job advert had been circled; the senior products' manager job that he knew I wanted. "I think you'll find you don't meet the criteria," he said.

I could swear he was actually enjoying taunting me. I bit my tongue and said: "Thank you, anyway. Is that it or is there something else?" He did not answer, so I got up and walked to the door. "Where the hell are you going, come back here," he shouted. I walked back to his desk but refused to sit down. He then indicated I could go. Presumably he had finished his little power game for the moment.[33]

Responsible Management of Power through Empowerment

If managers are to use their various bases of power effectively and ethically, they need to strive for commitment rather than mere compliance and understand the difference between power sharing and power distribution.

From Compliance to Commitment   Responsible managers strive for socialized power while avoiding personalized power. In fact, in a recent survey, organizational commitment was higher among US federal government executives whose superiors exercised socialized power than among colleagues with "power-hungry" bosses. The researchers used the appropriate terms *uplifting power* versus *dominating power*.[34] How does this relate to the five bases of power? As with influence tactics, managerial power has three possible outcomes: commitment, compliance, or resistance. Reward, coercive, and negative legitimate power tend to produce *compliance* (and sometimes, resistance). On the other hand, positive legitimate power, expert power, and referent power tend to foster *commitment.* Once again, commitment is superior to compliance because it is driven by internal or intrinsic motivation.[35] Employees who merely comply require frequent "jolts" of power from the boss to keep them headed in a productive direction. Committed employees tend to be self-starters who do not require close supervision—a key success factor in today's flatter, team-oriented organizations.

According to research cited earlier, expert and referent power have the greatest potential for improving job performance and satisfaction and reducing turnover. Formal education, training, and self-development can build a manager's expert power. At the same time, one's referent power base can be strengthened by forming and developing the strategic alliances discussed earlier under the heading of influence tactics.

Empowerment

Sharing power with nonmanagers through participative management.

Empowerment: From Power Sharing to Power Distribution   An exciting trend in today's organizations centres on **empowerment**.[36] Other labels attached to this trend are "participative management," "participative decision making," and "delegation." Regardless of the term one prefers, the underlying process is the same. Namely, the decentralization of power (see International OB).

The concept of empowerment requires some adjustments in traditional thinking. First, power is not a zero-sum situation where one person's gain is another's loss. Social power is unlimited. This requires win–win thinking.

The second adjustment to traditional thinking involves seeing empowerment as *a matter of degree* not as an either-or proposition.[37] Figure 11–2 illustrates how power can be shifted to the hands of nonmanagers step by step. The overriding goal is to increase productivity and competitiveness in leaner organizations. Each step in this evolution increases the power of organizational contributors who traditionally had little or no legitimate power. Consider this recent example of mid-range empowerment involving a combination of influence sharing (consultation) and power sharing (participation):

Long ladders don't seem to have much to do with saving jet fuel. But when United Airlines Inc. brought together its pilots, ramp workers, and managers for the first time to brainstorm about fuel conservation, the answer was just that simple. The idea was to use electricity instead of jet fuel to power planes idling at gates. But ramp workers couldn't plug cables into the aircraft because their ladders were often too short. "In the past, we would have sent out an edict and nothing would have changed," [said a United Airlines executive]. . . . Now, equipped with taller ladders, the carrier will save $20 million in fuel costs [annually].[38]

Figure 11 – 2   The Evolution of Power: From Domination to Delegation

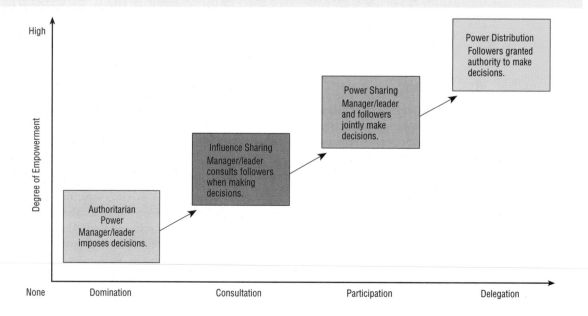

Delegation

Granting decision-making authority to people at lower levels.

The highest degree of empowerment is **delegation**, the process of granting decision-making authority to lower-level employees. This amounts to *power distribution*. Delegation has long been the recommended way to lighten the busy manager's load while at the same time developing employees' abilities. Importantly, delegation gives non-managerial employees more than simply a voice in decisions. It empowers them to make their own decisions. A prime example is the Ritz-Carlton Hotel chain:

At Ritz-Carlton, every worker is authorized to spend up to $2,000 to fix any problem a guest encounters. Employees do not abuse the privilege. "When you treat people responsibly, they act responsibly," said Patrick Mene, the hotel chain's director of quality.[39]

Not surprising, then, that Ritz-Carlton has won national service quality awards.

International Organizational Behaviour

Mercedes-Benz to Employees: Do Your Own Reorganizing

... it's possible to eliminate jobs without writing off the future. The first step is delegating re-engineering efforts to those who know best where to cut: the people actually doing the work. The second step is comforting them with a guarantee: Anyone bold enough to eliminate his own job will receive a new job—and probably a better one—helping to create new growth.

That is one of the principles behind a revolution under way at Mercedes-Benz Credit Corp., the US finance unit of Germany's Daimler-Benz. "It was absolutely essential to establish a no-fear element in this whole change process," says Georg Bauer, president of the US affiliate. Having done so, he adds, released the full creativity—and objectivity—of the people leading the process.

Reared in Bavaria, Mr. Bauer is a 44-year-old hybrid of modern management. He started out in an American corporation (Citibank) in Germany, only to wind up heading a German company in America.

When he arrived here in 1992, the future was uncertain; the era of factory-subsidized auto financing was ending, throwing Mercedes-Benz Credit onto a level playing field with the biggest US lenders.

In a commodity business—money being the ultimate commodity—customer service becomes the sole basis for competition. Alas, Mr. Bauer found the service mind-set lacking. German companies, he says, emphasize perfection in the product, but the US customer demands something harder to provide. The US customer demands sincerity and efficiency in the delivery of the product.

Mr. Bauer began by realigning the field operations. Customer-service functions from far-flung offices were centralized (in Dallas, where Mr. Bauer found the labor pool to be particularly personable) and expanded (to 100 people). Training and performance measurements were standardized—all calls answered within three rings, for instance, and 90% of all problems handled without transferring the caller.

But the people on the front lines could aid customers only as quickly as they received support from the home office here, which readily proved the larger challenge. Fiefdoms abounded. An eight-layer hierarchy slowed decisions. Everything happened on paper, yet memos could be signed only by a certain rank.

So to the shock (and skepticism) of his superiors in Stuttgart, Mr. Bauer delegated the problem of streamlining to groups of employees and managers, partly in the cold calculation that a grassroots effort would help workers "buy in" and partly in the sincere belief that the best ideas would come from outside the executive suite.

The outcome shook the operation to its core. Managers proposed reducing or even wiping out their own departments through automation or restructuring. Four entire layers of management vanished. Employees were assigned to functional teams with almost complete authority to execute decisions.

The very look of the place changed radically. Private offices gave way to conference rooms, cubicles to clusters of desks, plaster walls to glass. "Discussion databases" helped speed the spread of ideas.

But the adjustment was traumatic for many. Busted managers nursed their career disappointments. Teams looking upward for decisions or approval found that the calls were theirs to make. "It was utter chaos," says Doug Rozman of the communications team. Some people quit.

In time, though, people could see that information and decisions were traveling along much shorter paths and that the company was winning customers as a consequence. Soon, entirely new business lines were being dreamed up—a wholesaling operation to dispose of lease returns, for instance.

Mr. Bauer was soon basking in the numbers—a 31% increase in assets (to $7.6 billion) between 1992 and last year, plus several new operations, all on a 19% increase in staff (to 475). J D Power & Associates last year ranked Mercedes-Benz Credit first in customer satisfaction among import captive-finance companies.

SOURCE | Excerpted from T Petzinger Jr., "Georg Bauer Put Burden of Downsizing into Employees' Hands," *The Wall Street Journal,* May 10, 1996, p B1. Reprinted by permission of *The Wall Street Journal,* © 1996 Dow Jones & Company, Inc. All Rights Reserved Worldwide.

Empowerment: The Research Record and Practical Advice Most agree that empowerment is a good idea. But does it actually work? Research results to date are mixed and a bit disappointing.[40]

- According to a field study of 26 insurance claims supervisors, employees who enjoyed a greater degree of delegation processed more insurance claims at lower cost.[41]

- A study of 297 service employees led the researchers to conclude: "Empowerment may contribute to an employee's job satisfaction, but not as profoundly shape work effort and performance."[42]

- When the job performance of 81 empowered employees at the home office of a Canadian life insurance company was compared with a control group of 90 employees, the researchers found "minimal support" for empowerment.[43]

We believe empowerment has more promise than these research results suggest. Empowerment is a sweeping concept with many different definitions. Consequently, researchers use inconsistent measurements, and cause–effect relationships are fuzzy. Managers committed to the idea of employee empowerment need to follow the path of continuous improvement, learning from their successes and failures. Eight years of research with 10 "empowered" companies led consultant W Alan Randolph to formulate the three-pronged empowerment plan in Figure 11–3. Notice how open-book management and active information sharing are needed to build the necessary foundation of trust. Beyond that, clear goals and lots of relevant training are needed. While noting that the empowerment process can take several years to unfold, Randolph offered this perspective:

While the keys to empowerment may be easy to understand, they are hard to implement. It takes tremendous courage to start sharing sensitive information. It takes true strength to build more structure just at the point when people want more freedom of action. It takes real growth to allow teams to take over the management decision-making process. And above all, it takes perseverance to complete the empowerment process.[44]

Figure 11 – 3   Randolph's Empowerment Model

The Empowerment Plan

Share Information
- Share company performance information.
- Help people understand the business.
- Build trust through sharing sensitive information.
- Create self-monitoring possibilities.

Create Autonomy Through Structure
- Create a clear vision and clarify the little pictures.
- Clarify goals and roles collaboratively.
- Create new decision-making rules that support empowerment.
- Establish new empowering performance management processes.
- Use heavy doses of training.

Let Teams Become The Hierarchy
- Provide direction and training for new skills.
- Provide encouragement and support for change.
- Gradually have managers let go of control.
- Work through the leadership vacuum stage.
- Acknowledge the fear factor.

**Remember: Empowerment is not magic;
it consists of a few simple steps and a lot of persistence.**

Source: "Navigating the Journey to Empowerment," by W Alan Randolph. Reprinted by permission of the publisher from *Organizational Dynamics*, Spring 1995.© 1995 American Management Association. All rights reserved.

Organizational Politics and Impression Management

Most students of OB find the study of organizational politics intriguing. Perhaps this topic owes its appeal to the antics of television series such as 'Dallas' or 'The Bold and the Beautiful' whose heroes get their way by stepping on anyone and everyone. As we will see, however, organizational politics includes, but is not limited to, dirty dealing. Organizational politics is an ever-present and sometimes annoying feature of modern work life. "According to 150 executives from large US companies, office politics wastes an average of 20 per cent of their time; that's 10 weeks a year."[45] On the other hand, organizational politics is often a positive force in modern work organizations. Skilful and well-timed politics can help you get your point across, neutralize resistance to a key project, or get a choice job assignment.

Roberta Bhasin, a district manager for US West, put organizational politics into perspective by observing the following:

Most of us would like to believe that organizations are rationally structured, based on reasonable divisions of labor, a clear hierarchical communication flow, and well-defined lines of authority aimed at meeting universally understood goals and objectives.

But organizations are made up of *people* with personal agendas designed to win power and influence. The agenda—the game—is called corporate politics. It is played by avoiding the rational structure, manipulating the communications hierarchy, and ignoring established lines of authority. The rules are never written down and seldom discussed.

For some, corporate politics are second nature. They instinctively know the unspoken rules of the game. Others must learn. Managers who don't understand the politics of their organizations are at a disadvantage, not only in winning raises and promotions, but even in getting things *done.*[46]

We explore this important and interesting area by (1) defining the term *organizational politics,* (2) identifying three levels of political action, (3) discussing eight specific political tactics, (4) considering a related area called *impression management,* and (5) examining relevant research and practical implications.

Definition and Domain of Organizational Politics

Organizational politics
Intentional enhancement of self-interest.

ETHICS

"**Organizational politics** involves intentional acts of influence to enhance or protect the self-interest of individuals or groups."[47] An emphasis on *self-interest* distinguishes this form of social influence. Managers are endlessly challenged to achieve a workable balance between employees' self-interests and organizational interests. When a proper balance exists, the pursuit of self-interest may serve the organization's interests. Political behaviour becomes a negative force when self-interests erode or defeat organizational interests. For example, researchers have documented the political tactic of filtering and distorting information flowing up to the boss. This self-serving practice put the reporting employees in the best possible light.[48]

Uncertainty Triggers Political Behaviour   Political manoeuvering is triggered primarily by *uncertainty.* Five common sources of uncertainty within organizations are

1. Unclear objectives.

2. Vague performance measures.

3. Ill-defined decision processes.

4. Strong individual or group competition.[49]

5. Any type of change.

Regarding this last source of uncertainty, organization development specialist Anthony Raia noted, "Whatever we attempt to change, the political subsystem becomes active.

Vested interests are almost always at stake and the distribution of power is challenged."[50]

Thus, we would expect a field sales representative, striving to achieve an assigned quota, to be less political than a management trainee working on a variety of projects. While some management trainees stake their career success on hard work, competence, and a bit of luck, many do not. These people attempt to gain a competitive edge through some combination of the political tactics discussed below. Meanwhile, the salesperson's performance is measured in actual sales, not in terms of being friends with the boss or taking credit for others' work. Thus, the management trainee would tend to be more political than the field salesperson because of greater uncertainty about management's expectations.

Three Levels of Political Action   Although much political manoeuvering occurs at the individual level, it also can involve group or collective action. Figure 11–4 illustrates three different levels of political action: the individual level, the coalition level, and the network level.[51] Each level has its distinguishing characteristics. At the individual level, personal self-interests are pursued by the individual. The political aspects of coalitions and networks are not so obvious, however.

People with a common interest can become a political coalition by fitting the following definition. In an organizational context, a **coalition** is an informal group bound together by the *active* pursuit of a *single* issue. Coalitions may or may not coincide with formal group membership. When the target issue is resolved (a sexually harassing supervisor is fired, for example), the coalition disbands. Experts note that political coalitions have "fuzzy boundaries," meaning they are fluid in membership, flexible in structure, and temporary in duration.[52]

A third level of political action involves networks. Unlike coalitions, which pivot on specific issues, networks are loose associations of individuals seeking social support for their general self-interests. Politically, networks are people-oriented, while coalitions are issue-oriented. Networks have broader and longer term agendas than do coalitions.

Coalition

Temporary groupings of people who actively pursue a single issue.

Political Tactics

Anyone who has worked in an organization has firsthand knowledge of blatant politicking. Blaming someone else for your mistake is an obvious political ploy. But other political tactics are more subtle. Researchers have identified a range of political behaviour.

One landmark study, involving in-depth interviews with 87 managers from 30 electronics companies in Southern California, identified eight political tactics. Top-, middle-, and low-level managers were represented about equally in the sample. According to the researchers: "Respondents were asked to describe organizational political tactics and personal characteristics of effective political actors based upon their

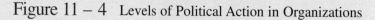

Figure 11 – 4   Levels of Political Action in Organizations

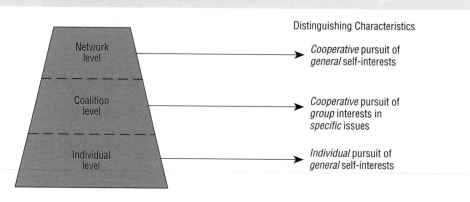

accumulated experience in *all* organizations in which they had worked."[53] Listed in descending order of occurrence, the eight political tactics that emerged were

1. Attacking or blaming others.

2. Using information as a political tool.

3. Creating a favourable image. (Also known as *impression management.*)[54]

4. Developing a base of support.

5. Praising others (ingratiation).

6. Forming power coalitions with strong allies.

7. Associating with influential people.

8. Creating obligations (reciprocity).

Table 11–1 describes these political tactics and indicates how often each reportedly was used by the interviewed managers.

The researchers distinguished between reactive and proactive political tactics. Some of the tactics, such as scapegoating, were *reactive* because the intent was to *defend* one's self-interest. Other tactics, such as developing a base of support, were *proactive* because they sought to *promote* the individual's self-interest.

What is your attitude towards organizational politics? How often do you rely on the various tactics in Table 11–1? You can get a general indication of your political tendencies by comparing your behaviour with the characteristics in Figure 11–5. Would you characterize yourself as politically *naive,* politically *sensible,* or a political *shark?* How do you think others view your political actions? What are the career, friendship, and ethical implications of your political tendencies? (For a more detailed analysis of your political tendencies, see the Personal Awareness and Growth Exercise at the end of this chapter.)

Table 11 – 1   Eight Common Political Tactics in Organizations

POLITICAL TACTIC	PERCENTAGE OF MANAGERS MENTIONING TACTIC	BRIEF DESCRIPTION OF TACTIC
1. Attacking or blaming others	54%	Used to avoid or minimize association with failure. Reactive when scapegoating is involved. Proactive when goal is to reduce competition for limited resources.
2. Using information as a political tool	54	Involves the purposeful withholding or distortion of information. Obscuring an unfavourable situation by overwhelming superiors with information.
3. Creating a favourable image (impression management)	53	Dressing/grooming for success. Adhering to organizational norms and drawing attention to one's successes and influence. Taking credit for others' accomplishments.
4. Developing a base of support	37	Getting prior support for a decision. Building others' commitment to a decision through participation.
5. Praising others (ingratiation)	25	Making influential people feel good ("apple polishing").
6. Forming power coalitions with strong allies	25	Teaming up with powerful people who can get results.
7. Associating with influential people	24	Building a support network both inside and outside the organization.
8. Creating obligations (reciprocity)	13	Creating social debts ("I did you a favour, so you owe me a favour").

Source: Adapted from R W Allen, D L Madison, L W Porter, P A Renwick, and B T Mayes, "Organizational Politics: Tactics and Characteristics of Its Actors," *California Management Review*, Fall 1979, pp 77—83.

Figure 11 – 5   Are You Politically Naive, Politically Sensible, or a Political Shark?

Characteristics	Naive	Sensible	Sharks
Underlying attitude	Politics is unpleasant.	Politics is necessary.	Politics is an opportunity.
Intent	Avoid at all costs.	Further departmental goals.	Self-serving and predatory.
Techniques	Tell it like it is.	Network; expand connections; use system to give and receive favors.	Manipulate; use fraud and deceit when necessary.
Favorite tactics	None—the truth will win out.	Negotiate, bargain.	Bully; misuse information; cultivate and use "friends" and other contacts.

Source: Reprinted from J K Pinto and O P Kharbanda, "Lessons for an Accidental Profession," *Business Horizons*, March–April 1995, p 45. © 1998 by the Foundation for the School of Business at Indiana University. Used with permission.

Impression Management

Impression management
Getting others to see us in a certain manner.

Impression management is defined as "the process by which people attempt to control or manipulate the reactions of others to images of themselves or their ideas."[55] This encompasses how one talks, behaves, and looks. Most impression management attempts are directed at making a *good* impression on relevant others. But, as we will see, some employees strive to make a *bad* impression. For purposes of conceptual clarity, we will focus on *upward* impression management (trying to impress one's immediate supervisor) because it is most relevant for managers. Still, it is good to remember that *anyone* can be the intended target of impression management. Parents, teachers, peers, subordinates, and customers are all fair game when it comes to managing the impressions of others.

A Conceptual Crossroads   Impression management is an interesting conceptual crossroads involving self-monitoring, attribution theory, and organizational politics.[56] Perhaps this explains why impression management has received active research attention in recent years. High self-monitoring employees ("chameleons" who adjust to their surroundings) are likely to be more inclined to engage in impression management than would low self-monitors. Impression management also involves the systematic manipulation of attributions. For example, a bank president will look good if the board of directors is encouraged to attribute organizational successes to her efforts and attribute problems and failures to factors beyond her control. Impression management definitely fits into the realm of organizational politics because of an overriding focus on furthering one's *self-interests*.

Making a Good Impression   If you "dress for success," project an upbeat attitude at all times, and avoid offending others, you are engaging in favourable impression management—particularly so if your motive is to improve your chances of getting what you want in life. Former British Airways chairman, Lord King, admitted he had underestimated his casually dressed rival (Richard Branson, Virgin Atlantic chairman). 'If Richard Branson had worn a pair of steelrimmed glasses, a double-breasted suit and shaved off his beard, I would have taken him seriously. As it was, I couldn't. I underestimated him.'[57] On the lighter side, the trends towards more casual dress codes has working men and women rethinking what it means to dress for success. *Newsweek* recently framed the irony this way:

Guys, it's your turn. As women are liberated from some of the meaner dictates of dress, men are losing a certain brand of fashion freedom. Sure, you may no longer have to wear a suit and tie to work. But there's the rub. With so many offices gone "casual," the corporate uniform is gone. You have to consider not only when to dress up or down, but a whole new vocabulary of texture, pattern, and fabric. And that mandate dreaded by some females of the species now applies to you, too: accessorize! Can I wear a silk-crepe tie with denim? Bucks with dress pants?[58]

No one ever said impression management was easy!

A statistical factor analysis of the influence attempts reported by a sample of 84 bank employees (including 74 women) identified three categories of favourable upward impression management tactics.[59] As labelled in the OB Exercise, favourable upward impression management tactics can be *job-focused* (manipulating information about one's job performance), *supervisor-focused* (praising and doing favours for one's supervisor), and *self-focused* (presenting oneself as a polite and nice person). Take a short break from your studying to complete the OB Exercise. How did you do? A moderate amount of upward impression management is a necessity for the average employee today. Too little, and busy managers are liable to overlook some of your valuable contributions when they make job assignment, pay, and promotion decisions. Too much, and you run the risk of being branded a "schmoozer," a "phony," and other unflattering things by your co-workers. Excessive flattery and ingratiation can backfire by embarrassing the target person and damaging one's credibility. Also, the risk of unintended insult is very high when impression management tactics cross gender, racial, ethnic, and cultural lines.[60] International management experts warn:

The impression management tactic is only as effective as its correlation to accepted norms about behavioral presentation. In other words, slapping a Japanese subordinate on the back with a rousing "Good work, Hiro!" will not create the desired impression in Hiro's mind that the expatriate intended. In fact, the behavior will likely create the opposite impression.[61]

Making a Poor Impression   At first glance, the idea of consciously trying to make a bad impression in the workplace seems absurd. But an interesting new line of impression management research has uncovered both motives and tactics for making oneself look *bad*. In a survey of the work experiences of business students at a large northwestern US university, more than half "reported witnessing a case of someone intentionally looking bad at work."[62] Why? Four motives came out of the study:

(1) *Avoidance:* Employee seeks to avoid additional work, stress, burnout, or an unwanted transfer or promotion. (2) *Obtain concrete rewards:* Employee seeks to obtain a pay raise or a desired transfer, promotion, or demotion. (3) *Exit:* Employee seeks to get laid off, fired, or suspended, and perhaps also to collect unemployment or workers' compensation. (4) *Power:* Employee seeks to control, manipulate, or intimidate others, get revenge, or make someone else look bad.[63]

Within the context of these motives, unfavourable upward impression management makes sense.

Five unfavourable upward impression management tactics identified by the researchers are as follows:

- *Decreasing performance*—restricting productivity, making more mistakes than usual, lowering quality, neglecting tasks.

- *Not working to potential*—pretending ignorance, having unused capabilities.

- *Withdrawing*—being tardy, taking excessive breaks, faking illness.

- *Displaying a bad attitude*—complaining, getting upset and angry, acting strangely, not getting along with co-workers.

- *Broadcasting limitations*—-letting co-workers know about one's physical problems and mistakes (both verbally and nonverbally).[64]

Recommended ways to manage employees who try to make a bad impression can be found throughout this book. They include more challenging work, greater autonomy, better feedback, supportive leadership, clear and reasonable goals, and a less stressful work setting.[65]

Research Evidence on Organizational Politics and Impression Management

Recent field research involving employees in real organizations rather than students in contrived laboratory settings has yielded these useful insights:

- In a study of 514 nonacademic university employees in the southwestern United States, white men had a greater understanding of organizational politics than did racial and ethnic minorities and white women. The researchers endorsed the practice of using mentors to help women and minorities develop their political skills.[66]

- Impression management attempts can either positively or negatively impact one's performance appraisal results.[67] The researchers in one study of 67 manager–employee pairs concluded, "Subordinates who were friendly and reasonable were perceived as amiable, and favorably evaluated."[68] However, subordinates who relied on ingratiation (making the boss feel good) did not get better performance appraisals.[69]

OB EXERCISE   *How Much Do You Rely on Upward Impression Management Tactics?*

Instructions
Rate yourself on each item according to how you behave on your current (or most recent) job. Add your circled responses to calculate a total score. Compare your score with our arbitrary norms.

JOB-FOCUSED TACTICS	RARELY	VERY OFTEN
1. I play up the value of my positive work results and make my supervisor aware of them.	1 — 2 — 3 — 4 — 5	
2. I try to make my work appear better than it is.	1 — 2 — 3 — 4 — 5	
3. I try to take responsibility for positive results, even when I'm not solely responsible for achieving them.	1 — 2 — 3 — 4 — 5	
4. I try to make my negative results not as severe as they initially appear to my supervisor.	1 — 2 — 3 — 4 — 5	
5. I arrive at work early and/or work late to show my supervisor I am a hard worker	1 — 2 — 3 — 4 — 5	

SUPERVISOR-FOCUSED TACTICS

6. I show an interest in my supervisor's personal life.   1 — 2 — 3 — 4 — 5

7. I praise my supervisor on his/her accomplishments.   1 — 2 — 3 — 4 — 5

8. I do personal favours for my supervisor that I'm not required to do.   1 — 2 — 3 — 4 — 5

9. I compliment my supervisor on her/his dress or appearance.   1 — 2 — 3 — 4 — 5

10. I agree with my supervisor's major suggestions and ideas.   1 — 2 — 3 — 4 — 5

SELF-FOCUSED TACTICS

11. I am very friendly and polite around my supervisor.   1 — 2 — 3 — 4 — 5

12. I try to act as a model employee around my supervisor.   1 — 2 — 3 — 4 — 5

13. I work harder when I know my supervisor will see the results.   1 — 2 — 3 — 4 — 5

Total score = _____

Arbitrary norms
13—26	Free agent
27—51	Better safe than sorry
52—65	Hello, Hollywood

SOURCE   Adapted from S J Wayne and G R Ferris, "Influence Tactics, Affect, and Exchange Quality in Supervisor-Subordinate Interactions: A Laboratory Experiment and Field Study," *Journal of Applied Psychology*, October 1990, pp 487—99.

Managing Organizational Politics

Organizational politics cannot be eliminated. A manager would be naive to expect such an outcome. But political manoeuvering can and should be managed to keep it constructive and within reasonable bounds. Harvard's Abraham Zaleznik put the issue this way: "People can focus their attention on only so many things. The more it lands on politics, the less energy—emotional and intellectual—is available to attend to the problems that fall under the heading of real work." [70]

ETHICS

An individual's degree of politicalness is a matter of personal values, ethics, and temperament. People who are either strictly nonpolitical or highly political generally pay a price for their behaviour. The former may experience slow promotions and feel left out, while the latter may run the risk of being called self-serving and lose their credibility. People at both ends of the political spectrum may be considered poor team players. A moderate amount of prudent political behaviour generally is considered a survival tool in complex organizations. Experts remind us that

. . . political behavior has earned a bad name only because of its association with politicians. On its own, the use of power and other resources to obtain your objectives is not inherently unethical. It all depends on what the preferred objectives are.[71]

With this perspective in mind, the practical steps in Table 11–2 are recommended. Notice the importance of reducing uncertainty through standardized performance evaluations and clear performance–reward linkages.[72] Measurable objectives are management's first line of defence against negative expressions of organizational politics.

Women and Organizational Politics

It is widely known that women have far more difficulty in reaching a higher position on the career ladder, which is closely related to women's reluctance to engage in politics. By recognizing the importance of politics in organizations, women can multiply their chances on the career ladder.

According to T Arroba and K James[73] women are less engaged in politics than men because (1) they think they are not competent enough, (2) they lack confidence, and (3) they dislike political activity. To overcome these impediments, Sandi Mann[74] proposes:

1. Overcoming the socialization process, by commanding their rights.
2. Changing the stereotyped image of women as self-effacing, nurturing selfless people.
3. Recognizing the value of politics as a powerful force in organizations.

Table 11 – 2   Some Practical Advice on Managing Organizational Politics

TO REDUCE SYSTEM UNCERTAINTY
Make clear what are the bases and processes for evaluation.
Differentiate rewards among high and low performers.
Make sure the rewards are as immediately and directly related to performance as possible.

TO REDUCE COMPETITION
Try to minimize resource competition among managers.
Replace resource competition with externally oriented goals and objectives.

TO BREAK EXISTING POLITICAL FIEFDOMS
Where highly cohesive political empires exist, break them apart by removing or splitting the most dysfunctional subgroups.
If you are an executive, be keenly sensitive to managers whose mode of operation is the personalization of political patronage. First, approach these persons with a directive to "stop the political maneuvering." If it continues, remove them from the positions and, preferably, the company.

TO PREVENT FUTURE FIEFDOMS
Make one of the most important criteria for promotion an apolitical attitude that puts organizational ends ahead of personal power ends.

Source: D R Beeman and T W Sharkey, "The Use and Abuse of Corporate Politics," *Business Horizons*, March–April 1987, p 30.

Managing Interpersonal and Intergroup Conflict

Mention the term *conflict* and most people envision fights, riots, or war. In fact, on virtually every day of every year one can find approximately two dozen armed combat situations somewhere in the world.[75] But these extreme situations represent only the most overt and violent expressions of conflict. During the typical workday, managers encounter more subtle and nonviolent types of opposition such as arguments, criticism, and disagreement. Conflict, like power and organizational politics, is an inevitable and sometimes positive force in modern work organizations. For example, a sincere dissenting opinion by a member of an executive planning committee might prevent the group from falling victim to groupthink. A recent comprehensive review of the conflict management literature yielded this consensus definition: "**conflict** is a process in which one party perceives that its interests are being opposed or negatively affected by another party."[76] Conflict can escalate (strengthen) or deescalate (weaken) over time. "The conflict process unfolds in a context, and whenever conflict, escalated or not, occurs the disputants or third parties can attempt to manage it in some manner."[77] Consequently, current and future managers need to understand the mechanics of conflict and know how to handle it effectively.

Conflict
One party perceives its interests are being opposed or set back by another party.

Conflict occurs at two levels within organizations: interpersonal and intergroup.[78] This section addresses both levels of conflict by (1) distinguishing between functional and dysfunctional conflict; (2) identifying antecedents of conflict; (3) explaining how to promote functional conflict; (4) examining alternative styles of handling conflict, along with discussing negotiation and third-party interventions; (5) reviewing relevant research evidence; and (6) discussing a contingency approach to managing conflict.

A Conflict Continuum

Ideas about managing conflict have undergone an interesting evolution during this century. Initially, scientific management experts such as Frederick W Taylor believed all conflict ultimately threatened management's authority and thus had to be avoided or quickly resolved. Later, human relationists recognized the inevitability of conflict and advised managers to learn to live with it. Emphasis remained on resolving conflict whenever possible, however. Beginning in the 1970s, OB specialists realized conflict had both positive and negative outcomes, depending on its nature and intensity. This perspective introduced the revolutionary idea that organizations could suffer from *too little* conflict. Figure 11–6 illustrates the relationship between conflict intensity and outcomes.

Work groups, departments, or organizations that experience too little conflict tend to be plagued by apathy, lack of creativity, indecision, and missed deadlines. Excessive conflict, on the other hand, can erode organizational performance because of political infighting, dissatisfaction, lack of teamwork, and turnover. Workplace aggression and violence are manifestations of excessive conflict.[79] Appropriate types and levels of conflict energize people in constructive directions.

Functional versus Dysfunctional Conflict

Functional conflict
Serves organization's interests.

Dysfunctional conflict
Threatens organization's interests.

The distinction between **functional conflict** and **dysfunctional conflict** pivots on whether the organization's interests are served. According to one conflict expert,

Some [types of conflict] support the goals of the organization and improve performance; these are functional, constructive forms of conflict. They benefit or support the main purposes of the organization. Additionally, there are those types of conflict that hinder organizational performance; these are dysfunctional or destructive forms. They are undesirable and the manager should seek their eradication.[80]

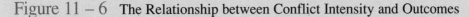

Figure 11 – 6   The Relationship between Conflict Intensity and Outcomes

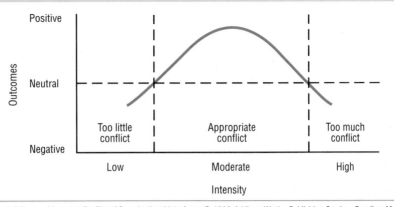

Source: L D Brown, *Managing Conflict of Organizational Interfaces*, © 1986, Addison-Wesley Publishing Co., Inc., Reading, Massachusetts. Figure 1.1 on page 8. Reprinted with permission.

Functional conflict is commonly referred to in management circles as constructive or cooperative conflict.[81]

Managers such as Fred Ackman, former chairman of Superior Oil Corporation, foster dysfunctional conflict by dealing with personalities rather than with issues:

Employees say Ackman proved thoroughly autocratic, refusing even to discuss staff suggestions. He tended to treat disagreement as disloyalty. Many were put off by Ackman's abusive temper, which together with his stature (5 feet 8 inches) and red hair earned him the nickname "Little Red Fred." Says a former subordinate, "He couldn't stand it when somebody disagreed with him, even in private. He'd eat you up alive, calling you a dumb S.O.B. or asking if you had your head up your ass. It happened all the time."[82]

Not surprisingly, of 13 top executives at Superior Oil, 9 left within one year after Ackman joined the company.

Antecedents of Conflict

Certain situations produce more conflict than others. By knowing the antecedents of conflict, managers are better able to anticipate conflict and take steps to resolve it if it becomes dysfunctional. Among the situations that tend to produce either functional or dysfunctional conflict are

- Incompatible personalities or value systems.

- Overlapping or unclear job boundaries.

- Competition for limited resources.

- Inadequate communication.

- Interdependent tasks (e.g., one person cannot complete his or her assignment until others have completed their work).

- Organizational complexity (conflict tends to increase as the number of hierarchical layers and specialized tasks increase).

- Unreasonable or unclear policies, standards, or rules.

- Unreasonable deadlines or extreme time pressure.

- Collective decision making (the greater the number of people participating in a decision, the greater the potential for conflict).

- Decision making by consensus.

- Unmet expectations (employees who have unrealistic expectations about job assignments, pay, or promotions are more prone to conflict).

- Unresolved or suppressed conflicts.[83]

Proactive managers carefully read these early warnings and take appropriate action. For example, group conflict can be reduced by making decisions on the basis of a majority vote rather than seeking a consensus.

Sometimes committees and decision-making groups become so bogged down in details and procedures that nothing substantive is accomplished. Carefully monitored functional

International Organizational Behaviour
Conflict-Handling in an International Context

In a continuously globalizing world, people are increasingly confronted with different cultures. Within organizations, multinationals in particular, this confrontation often results in serious conflicts. Jan Pieter van Oudenhoven and Lonneke Mechelse took a closer look at conflict-handling in five European countries. Their respondents were Belgian, Danish, English, Dutch, and Spanish managers working for the same multinational. Their research is based on Hofstede (discussed in Chapter 2) and Tjosvold. Hofstede, on the one hand, made cross-cultural comparisons along power distance, individualism–collectivism, masculinity–femininity, and uncertainty avoidance. Tjosvold, on the other hand, presents a conflict handling approach called "constructive controversy". Constructive controversy is a productive discussion of mutual differences, resulting from open conflict handling. This implies that conflicts have a positive influence on organizations. Constructive controversy is based on the following points:

- Differences should not be avoided, but respected; an open confrontation of opinions is essential.

- Employees should be oriented towards the same goals. Although they may not agree on the way the goals are reached, mutual differences may have a positive influence if oriented towards the same one.

- It is important to make sure the others feel competent. This creates an atmosphere with room for open discussions of all possible ideas and opinions.

- Through feedback and discussion it should be possible to learn and reflect in each stage of the conflict.

Constructive controversy enhances the organization's efficiency and management's decision-making processes. Jan Pieter van Oudenhoven and Lonneke Mechelse assume that constructive controversy has a positive influence on

international cooperation. Differences in background may lead to misinterpretations of behaviour in other cultures. A constructive, open discussion of opposing points of view can be essential for the solution of conflicts resulting from different culturally programmed thinking.

Managers from different cultures handle conflicts differently. According to Hofstede, in countries with low power distance, people are cooperative, they prefer a consultative management style, there is more harmony between the powerful and the powerless. When high power distance prevails, employees will trust each other less and people will prefer a more autocratic management style. Moreover, a hidden conflict is observed between higher and lower ranked.

In cases of low uncertainty avoidance, conflicts are considered as being natural and constructive, whereas in situations of high uncertainty avoidance, conflicts are unwelcome and avoided if possible.

Low power distance and low uncertainty avoidance are a good starting point for constructive conflict handling: people are free to express their opinions and they are not afraid to be faced with conflicts.

The results of the study confirmed the statement that managers from countries with low power distance countries and low uncertainty avoidance (Denmark, the UK, and The Netherlands) prefer open communication with their superior, whereas communication becomes less open when uncertainty avoidance and power distance increases (Spain and Belgium). The Dutch managers are the most willing to reach a consensus, immediately followed by the Spanish.[84]

Stimulating Functional Conflict

conflict can help get the creative juices flowing once again. Managers basically have two options. They can fan the fires of naturally occurring conflict—but this approach can be unreliable and slow. Alternatively, managers can resort to programmed conflict. Experts in the field define **programmed conflict** as "conflict that raises different opinions *regardless of the personal feelings of the managers.*"[85] The trick is to get contributors to either defend or criticize ideas based on relevant facts rather than on the basis of personal preference or political interests. This requires disciplined role playing. Two programmed conflict techniques with proven track records are devil's advocacy and the dialectic method. Let us explore these two ways of stimulating functional conflict.

Programmed conflict
Encourages different opinions without protecting management's personal feelings.

Devil's Advocacy   This technique gets its name from a traditional practice within the Roman Catholic Church. When someone's name came before the College of Cardinals for elevation to sainthood, it was absolutely essential to ensure that he or she had a spotless record. Consequently, one individual was assigned the role of *devil's advocate* to uncover and air all possible objections to the person's canonization. In accordance with this practice, **devil's advocacy** in today's organizations involves assigning someone the role of critic.[86] Recall from the last chapter, Irving Janis recommended the devil's advocate role for preventing groupthink.

Devil's advocacy
Assigning someone the role of critic.

In the left half of Figure 11–7 note how devil's advocacy alters the usual decision-making process in steps 2 and 3. This approach to programmed conflict is intended to generate critical thinking and reality testing.[87] It is a good idea to rotate the job of devil's advocate so no one person or group develops a strictly negative reputation. Moreover, periodic devil's advocacy role playing is good training for developing analytical and communicative skills.

The Dialectic Method   Like devil's advocacy, the dialectic method is a time-honoured practice. This particular approach to programmed conflict traces back to the dialectic school of philosophy in ancient Greece. Plato and his followers attempted to synthesize truths by exploring opposite positions (called thesis and antithesis). Court systems in the United States and elsewhere rely on directly opposing points of view for determining guilt or innocence. Accordingly, today's **dialectic method** calls for managers to foster a structured debate of opposing viewpoints prior to making a decision.[88] Steps 3 and 4 in the right half of Figure 11–7 set the dialectic approach apart from the normal decision-making process. Here is how Anheuser-Busch's corporate policy committee uses the dialectic method:

Dialectic method
Fostering a debate of opposing viewpoints to better understand an issue.

When the policy committee . . . considers a major move—getting into or out of a business, or making a big capital expenditure—it sometimes assigns teams to make the case for each side of the question. There may be two teams or even three. Each is knowledgeable about the subject; each has access to the same information. Occasionally someone in favour of the project is chosen to lead the dissent, and an opponent to argue for it. Pat Stokes, who heads the company's beer empire, describes the result: "We end up with decisions and alternatives we hadn't thought of previously," sometimes representing a synthesis of the opposing views. "You become a lot more anticipatory, better able to see what might happen, because you have thought through the process."[89]

A major drawback of the dialectic method is that "winning the debate" may overshadow the issue at hand. Also, the dialectic method requires more skill training than does devil's advocacy. Regarding the comparative effectiveness of these two approaches to stimulating functional conflict, however, a laboratory study ended in a tie. Compared with groups that strived to reach a consensus, decision-making groups using either devil's advocacy or the dialectic method yielded equally higher quality decisions.[90] But, in a more recent laboratory study, groups using devil's advocacy produced more potential

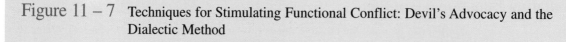

Figure 11 – 7   Techniques for Stimulating Functional Conflict: Devil's Advocacy and the Dialectic Method

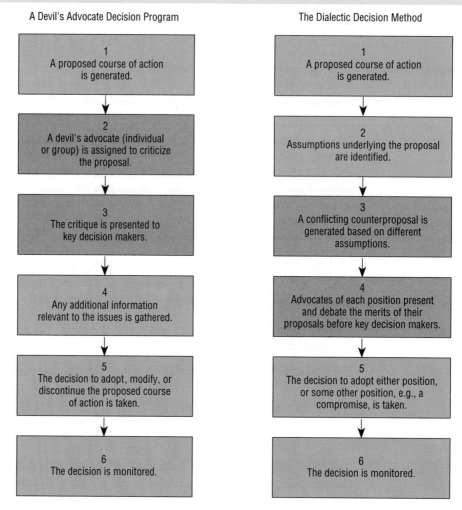

Source: R A Cosier and C R Schwenk, "Agreement and Thinking Alike: Ingredients for Poor Decisions," *Academy of Management Executive*, February 1990, pp 72–73. Used with permission.

solutions and made better recommendations for a case problem than did groups using the dialectic method.[91] In light of this mixed evidence, managers have some latitude in using either devil's advocacy or the dialectic method for pumping creative life back into stalled deliberations. Personal preference and the role players' experience may well be the deciding factors in choosing one approach over the other. The important thing is to actively stimulate functional conflict when necessary (such as when the risk of blind conformity or groupthink is high).

Alternative Styles for Handling Dysfunctional Conflict

People tend to handle negative conflict in patterned ways referred to as *styles.* Several conflict styles have been categorized over the years. According to conflict specialist Afzalur Rahim's model, five different conflict-handling styles can be plotted on a 2 x 2 grid. High to low concern for *self* is found on the horizontal axis of the grid while low to high concern for *others* forms the vertical axis (see Figure 11 – 8). Various combinations of these variables produce the five different conflict-handling styles: integrating, obliging, dominating, avoiding, and compromising.[92] There is no single best style; each has strengths and limitations and is subject to situational constraints.

Integrating (Problem Solving)   In this style, interested parties confront the issue and cooperatively identify the problem, generate and weigh alternative solutions, and select a solution. Integrating is appropriate for complex issues plagued by misunderstanding. However, it is inappropriate for resolving conflicts rooted in opposing value systems. Its primary strength is its longer lasting impact because it deals with the underlying problem rather than merely with symptoms. The primary weakness of this style is that it is very time consuming.

Obliging (Smoothing)   "An obliging person neglects his or her own concern to satisfy the concern of the other party."[93] This style, often called smoothing, involves playing down differences while emphasizing commonalities. Obliging may be an appropriate conflict-handling strategy when it is possible to eventually get something in return. But it is inappropriate for complex or worsening problems. Its primary strength is that it encourages cooperation. Its main weakness is that it's a temporary fix that fails to confront the underlying problem.

Dominating (Forcing)   High concern for self and low concern for others encourages "I win, you lose" tactics. The other party's needs are largely ignored. This style is often called forcing because it relies on formal authority to force compliance. Dominating is appropriate when an unpopular solution must be implemented, the issue is minor, or a deadline is near. It is inappropriate in an open and participative climate. Speed is its primary strength. The primary weakness of this domineering style is that it often breeds resentment.

Avoiding   This tactic may involve either passive withdrawal from the problem or active suppression of the issue. Avoidance is appropriate for trivial issues or when the costs of confrontation outweigh the benefits of resolving the conflict. It is inappropriate for difficult and worsening problems. The main strength of this style is that it buys time in unfolding or ambiguous situations. The primary weakness is that the tactic provides a temporary fix that sidesteps the underlying problem.

Compromising   This is a give-and-take approach involving moderate concern for both self and others. Compromise is appropriate when parties have opposite goals or possess equal power. But compromise is inappropriate when overuse would lead to inconclusive action (e.g., failure to meet production deadlines). The primary strength of this tactic is that the democratic process has no losers, but it is a temporary fix that can stifle creative

Figure 11 – 8   Five Conflict-Handling Styles

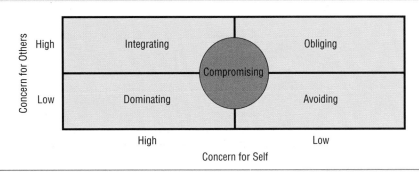

Source: M A Rahim, "A Strategy for Managing Conflict in Complex Organizations, *Human Relations*, January 1985, p 84. Used with author's permission.

problem solving.

To reinforce your knowledge of these conflict styles and learn more about yourself, take a few moments to complete the self-quiz in the OB Exercise.

Handling Intergroup Conflict with Negotiation and Third-Party Intervention

Although the conflict handling styles just discussed can be used for all types of conflict, the model primarily targets interpersonal conflict. But what about *intergroup* conflict that is increasingly common in today's team- and project-oriented organizations? And what about *interorganizational* conflict often encountered in today's world of organizational alliances and partnerships? Negotiation and third-party interventions can be helpful in these areas.

Negotiation

Give-and-take process between conflicting interdependent parties.

Negotiation   Formally defined, **negotiation** is a give-and-take decision-making process involving interdependent parties with different preferences.[94] Common examples include labour-management negotiations over wages, hours, and working conditions and negotiations between purchasing agents and vendors involving price, delivery schedules, and credit terms. Self-managed work teams with overlapping task boundaries also need to rely on negotiated agreements.[95] Negotiating skills are more important than ever today.[96]

OB EXERCISE   *What Is Your Primary Conflict-Handling Style?*

Instructions

For each of the 15 items, indicate how often you rely on that tactic by circling the appropriate number. After you have responded to all 15 items, complete the scoring key below.

CONFLICT-HANDLING TACTICS	RARELY	ALWAYS
1. I argue my case with my co-workers to show the merits of my position.	1—2—3—4—5	
2. I negotiate with my co-workers so that a compromise can be reached.	1—2—3—4—5	
3. I try to satisfy the expectations of my co-workers.	1—2—3—4—5	
4. I try to investigate an issue with my co-workers to find a solution acceptable to us.	1—2—3—4—5	
5. I am firm in pursuing my side of the issue.	1—2—3—4—5	
6. I attempt to avoid being "put on the spot" and try to keep my conflict with my co-workers to myself.	1—2—3—4—5	
7. I hold on to my solution to a problem.	1—2—3—4—5	
8. I use "give and take" so that a compromise can be made.	1—2—3—4—5	
9. I exchange accurate information with my co-workers to solve a problem together.	1—2—3—4—5	
10. I avoid open discussion of my differences with my co-workers.	1—2—3—4—5	
11. I accommodate the wishes of my co-workers.	1—2—3—4—5	
12. I try to bring all our concerns out in the open so that the issues can be resolved in the best possible way.	1—2—3—4—5	

13. I propose a middle ground for breaking deadlocks.   1—2—3—4—5

14. I go along with the suggestions of my co-workers.   1—2—3—4—5

15. I try to keep my disagreements with my co-workers to myself in order to avoid hard feelings.   1—2—3—4—5

Scoring Key

INTEGRATING		OBLIGING		DOMINATING	
Item	Score	Item	Score	Item	Score
4. ____		3. ____		1. ____	
9. ____		11. ____		5. ____	
12. ____		14. ____		7. ____	
Total = ____		Total = ____		Total = ____	

AVOIDING		COMPROMISING	
Item	Score	Item	Score
6. ____		2. ____	
10. ____		8. ____	
15. ____		13. ____	
Total = ____		Total = ____	

Your primary conflict-handling style is: _____
(The category with the highest total.)

Your backup conflict-handling style is: _____
(The category with the second highest total.)

SOURCE   Adapted and excerpted in part from M A Rahim, "A Measure of Styles of Handling Interpersonal Conflict," *Academy of Management Journal*, June 1983, pp 368–76.

Negotiation experts distinguish between two types of negotiation—*distributive* and *integrative*. Understanding the difference requires a change in traditional "fixed-pie" thinking.:

A *distributive* negotiation usually involves a single issue—a "fixed-pie"—in which one person gains at the expense of the other. For example, haggling over the price of a rug in a bazaar is a distributive negotiation. In most conflicts, however, more than one issue is at stake, and each party values the issues differently. The outcomes available are no longer a fixed-pie divided among all parties. An agreement can be found that is better for both parties than what they would have reached through distributive negotiation. This is an *integrative* negotiation.

However, parties in a negotiation often don't find these beneficial trade-offs because each *assumes* its interests *directly* conflict with those of the other party. "What is good for the other side must be bad for us" is a common and unfortunate perspective that most people have. This is the mind-set we call the *mythical* "fixed-pie."[97]

Distributive negotiation involves traditional win–lose thinking. Integrative negotiation calls for a progressive win–win strategy,[98] such as the one in Figure 11–9. In a recent laboratory study of joint venture negotiations, teams trained in integrative tactics achieved better outcomes for *both* sides than did untrained teams.[99] However, another study involving 700 employees from 11 cultures discovered the integrative (or problem-

---

Figure 11 – 9   An Integrative Approach: Added-Value Negotiation

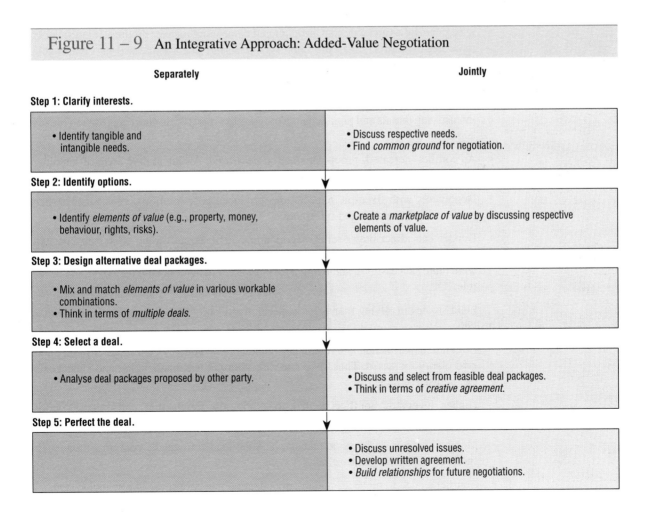

	Separately	**Jointly**
Step 1: Clarify interests.	• Identify tangible and intangible needs.	• Discuss respective needs. • Find *common ground* for negotiation.
Step 2: Identify options.	• Identify *elements of value* (e.g., property, money, behaviour, rights, risks).	• Create a *marketplace of value* by discussing respective elements of value.
Step 3: Design alternative deal packages.	• Mix and match *elements of value* in various workable combinations. • Think in terms of *multiple deals*.	
Step 4: Select a deal.	• Analyse deal packages proposed by other party.	• Discuss and select from feasible deal packages. • Think in terms of *creative agreement*.
Step 5: Perfect the deal.		• Discuss unresolved issues. • Develop written agreement. • *Build relationships* for future negotiations.

Source: Adapted from K Albrecht and S Albrecht, "Added Value Negotiating," *Training*, April 1993, pp 26–29.

solving) approach to negotiation was *not* equally effective across cultures.[100] North American negotiators generally are too short-term oriented and poor relationship builders when negotiating in Asia, Latin America, and the Middle East.[101]

Third-Party Intervention   Sometimes, when conflicting parties do not have the desire or ability to complete their own negotiation process, a third party may have to intervene. Briefly, there are three types of third-party interventions:

* *Consultation*—an impartial third party helps the conflicting parties analyse the situation and their relationship so they can get on with productive negotiation.

* *Mediation*—a trusted third party facilitates the negotiating process and suggests alternatives.[102]

* *Arbitration*—the conflicting parties agree to abide by the decision of a mutually acceptable third party.

Conflict and Negotiation Research Evidence

Laboratory studies, relying on university students as subjects, uncovered the following insights about organizational conflict:

* People with a high need for affiliation tended to rely on a smoothing (obliging) style while avoiding a forcing (dominating) style.[103] Thus, personality traits affect how people handle conflict.

* Disagreement expressed in an arrogant and demeaning manner produced significantly more negative effects than the same sort of disagreement expressed in a reasonable manner.[104] In other words, *how* you disagree with someone is very important in conflict situations.

* Threats and punishment, by one party in a disagreement, tended to produce intensifying threats and punishment from the other party.[105] In short, aggression breeds aggression.

* As conflict increased, group satisfaction decreased. An integrative style of handling conflict led to higher group satisfaction than did an avoidance style.[106]

* Negotiators with fixed-pie expectations produced poor joint outcomes because they restricted and mismanaged information.[107]

* Gender can affect buyer-seller negotiation outcomes, according to a study of 248 business students at a midwestern US university. ". . . when paired with females, males were more successful in achieving a favourable settlement in both the buyer and seller role."[108]

Field studies involving managers and real organizations have given us the following insights:

* Both intradepartmental and interdepartmental conflict decreased as goal difficulty and goal clarity increased. Thus, as is the case with politics, challenging and clear goals can defuse conflict.

* Higher levels of conflict tended to erode job satisfaction and internal work motivation.[109]

* Men and women at the same managerial level tended to handle conflict similarly. In short, there was no gender effect.[110]

* Conflict tended to move around the organization in a case study of a school system.[111] Thus, managers need to be alerted to the fact that conflict often originates in one area

or level and becomes evident somewhere else. Conflict needs to be traced back to its source if there is to be lasting improvement.

Conflict Management: A Contingency Approach

Three realities dictate how organizational conflict should be managed. First, conflict is inevitable because it is triggered by a wide variety of antecedents. Second, too little conflict may be as counterproductive as too much. Third, there is no single best way of resolving conflict. Consequently, conflict specialists recommend a contingency approach to managing conflict. Antecedents of conflict and actual conflict need to be monitored. If signs of too little conflict such as apathy or lack of creativity appear, then functional conflict needs to be stimulated. This can be done by nurturing appropriate antecedents of conflict and/or programming conflict with techniques such as devil's advocacy and the dialectic method. On the other hand, when conflict becomes dysfunctional, the appropriate conflict-handling style needs to be enacted. Realistic training involving role playing can prepare managers to try alternative conflict styles.

Integrative or added-value negotiation is appropriate for intergroup and interorganizational conflict. The key is to get the conflicting parties to abandon traditional fixed-pie thinking and their win–lose expectations. Third-party interventions are necessary when conflicting parties are unwilling and/or unable to engage in conflict resolution or integrative negotiation.

Managers can keep from getting too deeply embroiled in conflict by applying three lessons from recent research: (1) establish challenging and clear goals, (2) disagree in a constructive and reasonable manner, and (3) refuse to get caught in the aggression-breeds-aggression spiral.

Summary of Key Concepts

1. *Explain the concept of mutuality of interest, and identify the three most effective influence tactics.* Managers are constantly challenged to foster mutuality of interest (a win–win situation) between individual and organizational interests. Organization members need to actively and creatively cooperate with potential adversaries. The three most commonly used and most effective influence tactics are consultation, rational persuasion, and inspirational appeals.

2. *Identify and briefly describe French and Raven's five bases of power.* French and Raven's five bases of power are reward power (rewarding compliance), coercive power (punishing noncompliance), legitimate power (relying on formal authority), expert power (providing needed information), and referent power (relying on personal attraction).

3. *Explain why delegation is the highest form of empowerment.* An exciting and promising trend in today's organizations is the decentralization of power. In short, power is shifting to nonmanagerial employees

as a way of boosting productivity and competitiveness. The highest evolution of power is delegation. Delegation gives employees more than a participatory role in decision making. It allows them to make their own work-related decisions.

4. *Define organizational politics, and explain what triggers it.* Organizational politics is defined as intentional acts of influence to enhance or protect the self-interests of individuals or groups. Uncertainty triggers most politicking in organizations. Political action occurs at individual, coalition, and network levels. Coalitions are informal, temporary, and single-issue alliances.

5. *Distinguish between favourable and unfavourable impression management tactics, and explain how to manage organizational politics.* Favourable upward impression management can be job-focused (manipulating information about one's job performance), supervisor-focused (praising or doing favours for the boss), or self-focused (being polite and nice). Unfavourable upward impression management

tactics include decreasing performance, not working to potential, withdrawing, displaying a bad attitude, and broadcasting one's limitations. Since organizational politics cannot be eliminated, managers need to learn to deal with it. Uncertainty can be reduced by evaluating performance and linking rewards to performance. Measurable objectives are key. Participative management also helps.

6. *Define conflict, and distinguish between functional and dysfunctional conflict.* Conflict is a process in which one party perceives that its interests are being opposed or negatively affected by another party. It is inevitable and not necessarily destructive. Too little conflict, as evidenced by apathy or lack of creativity, can be as great a problem as too much conflict. Functional conflict enhances organizational interests while dysfunctional conflict is counterproductive.

7. *Explain how managers can stimulate functional conflict.* There are many antecedents of conflict—including incompatible personalities, competition for limited resources, and unrealized expectations—that need to be monitored. Functional conflict can be stimulated by permitting selected antecedents of conflict to persist and/or programming conflict during decision making with devil's advocates or the dialectic method.

8. *Identify the five conflict-handling styles, and explain the contingency approach to managing conflict.* They are integrating (problem solving), obliging (smoothing), dominating (forcing), avoiding, and compromising. There is no single best style. Antecedents of conflict need to be monitored and stimulated if too little conflict is a problem. Functional conflict can be programmed with techniques such as devil's advocacy and the dialectic method. An appropriate conflict-handling style needs to be employed when conflict becomes dysfunctional. Intergroup conflict can be managed through integrative negotiation.

9. *Explain the difference between distributive and integrative negotiation, and discuss the concept of added-value negotiation.* Distributive negotiation involves fixed-pie and win–lose thinking. Integrative negotiation is a win–win approach to better results for both parties. The five steps in added value negotiation are as follows: Step 1—Clarify interests; Step 2—Identify options; Step 3—Design alternative deal packages; Step 4—Select a deal; and Step 5—Perfect the deal. Elements of value, multiple deals, and creative agreement are central to this approach.

Discussion Questions

1. Of the eight generic influence tactics, which do you use the most when dealing with friends, parents, your boss, or your professors? Would other tactics be more effective?

2. Before reading this chapter, did the term *power* have a negative connotation for you? Do you view it differently now? Explain.

3. What base(s) of power do you rely on in your daily affairs? (Use the OB Exercise on page 306 to assess your power bases at work.) Do you handle power effectively and responsibly?

4. What are the main advantages and drawbacks of the trend toward increased delegation?

5. Why do you think organizational politics is triggered primarily by uncertainty?

6. What personal experiences have you had with coalitions? Explain any positive or negative outcomes.

7. According to the OB Exercise, how heavily do you rely on upward impression management tactics? What are the career implications of your approach to impression management?

8. What examples of functional and dysfunctional conflict have you encountered?

9. According to the OB Exercise on page 324, what is your primary conflict-handling style? Would this help or hinder your effectiveness as a manager?

10. How could added-value negotiation make your life a bit easier? Explain in terms of a specific problem, conflict, or deadlock.

Personal Awareness and Growth Exercise

How Political Are You?

Objectives

1. To get to know yourself a little bit better.

2. Within an organizational context, to assess your political tendencies.

3. To consider the career implications of your political tendencies.

Introduction

Organizational politics is an unavoidable feature of modern organizational life. Your career success, job performance, and job satisfaction can hinge on your political skills. But it is important to realize that some political tactics can cause ethical problems.

Instructions

For each of the 10 statements, select the response that best characterizes your behaviour. You do not have to engage in the behaviour at all times to answer true.[112]

1. You should make others feel important through an open appreciation of their ideas and work.	True	False
2. Because people tend to judge you when they first meet you, always try to make a good first impression.	True	False
3. Try to let others do most of the talking, be sympathetic to their problems, and resist telling people that they are totally wrong.	True	False
4. Praise the good traits of the people you meet and always give people an opportunity to save face if they are wrong or make a mistake.	True	False
5. Spreading false rumours, planting misleading information, and backstabbing are necessary, if somewhat unpleasant, methods to deal with your enemies.	True	False
6. Sometimes it is necessary to make promises that you know you will not or cannot keep.	True	False
7. It is important to get along with everybody, even with those who are generally recognized as windbags, abrasive, or constant complainers.	True	False
8. It is vital to do favours for others so that you can call in these IOUs at times when they will do you the most good.	True	False
9. Be willing to compromise, particularly on issues that are minor to you, but important to others.	True	False
10. On controversial issues, it is important to delay or avoid your involvement if possible.	True	False

Scoring and Interpretation

The author of this quiz recommends the following scoring system:

A confirmed organizational politician will answer "true" to all 10 questions. Organizational politicians with fundamental ethical standards will answer "false" to Questions 5 and 6, which deal with deliberate lies and uncharitable behaviour. Individuals who regard manipulation, incomplete disclosure, and self-serving behaviour as unacceptable will answer "false" to all or almost all of the questions.[113]

QUESTIONS FOR DISCUSSION

1. Did this instrument accurately assess your tendencies towards organizational politics? Explain.

2. Do you think a confirmed organizational politician would answer this quiz honestly? Explain.

3. Will your political tendencies help or hinder your career? Explain.

4. Are there any potential ethical problems with any of your answers? Which ones?

5. How important is political behaviour for career success today? Explain, relative to the industry or organization you have in mind.

Group Exercise

Bangkok Blowup (A Role-Playing Exercise)

Objectives

1. To further your knowledge of interpersonal conflict and conflict-handling styles.

2. To give you a firsthand opportunity to try the various styles of handling conflict.

Introduction

This is a role-playing exercise intended to develop your ability to handle conflict. There is no single best way to resolve the conflict in this exercise. One style might work for one person, while another gets the job done for someone else.

Instructions

Read the following short case, "Can Larry Fit In?" Pair up with someone else and decide which of you will play the role of Larry and which will play the role of Melissa, the office manager. Pick up the action from where the case leaves off. Try to be realistic and true to the characters in the case. The manager is primarily responsible for resolving this conflict situation. Whoever plays Larry should resist any unreasonable requests or demands and cooperate with any personally workable solution. *Note:* To conserve time, try to resolve this situation in less than 15 minutes.

CASE: "CAN LARRY FIT IN?"[114]

MELISSA, OFFICE MANAGER

You are the manager of an auditing team sent to Bangkok, Thailand, to represent a major international accounting firm headquartered in New York. You and Larry, one of your auditors, were sent to Bangkok to set up an auditing operation. Larry is about seven years older than you and has five more years seniority in the firm. Your relationship has become very strained since you were recently designated as the office manager. You feel you were given the promotion because you have established an excellent working relationship with the Thai staff as well as a broad range of international clients. In contrast, Larry has told other members of the staff that your promotion simply reflects the firm's heavy emphasis on affirmative action. He has tried to isolate you from the all-male accounting staff by focusing discussions on sports, local night spots, and so forth.

You are sitting in your office reading some complicated new reporting procedures that have just arrived from the home office. Your concentration is suddenly interrupted by a loud knock on your door. Without waiting for an invitation to enter, Larry bursts into your office. He is obviously very upset, and it is not difficult for you to surmise why he is in such a nasty mood.

You recently posted the audit assignments for the coming month, and you scheduled Larry for a job you knew he wouldn't like. Larry is one of your senior auditors, and the company norm is that they get the choice assignments. This particular job will require him to spend two weeks away from Bangkok in a remote town, working with a company whose records are notoriously messy.

Unfortunately, you have had to assign several of these less-desirable audits to Larry recently because you are short of personnel. But that's not the only reason. You have received several complaints from the junior staff (all Thais) recently that Larry treats them in a condescending manner. They feel he is always looking for an opportunity to boss them around, as if he were their supervisor instead of an experienced, supportive mentor. As a result, your whole operation works more smoothly when you can send Larry out of town on a solo project for several days. It keeps him from coming into your office and telling you how to do your job, and the morale of the rest of the auditing staff is significantly higher.

Larry slams the door and proceeds to express his anger over this assignment.

LARRY, SENIOR AUDITOR

You are really ticked off! Melissa is deliberately trying to undermine your status in the office. She knows that the company norm is that senior auditors get the better jobs. You've paid your dues, and now you expect to be treated with respect. And this isn't the first time this has happened. Since she was made the office manager, she has tried to keep you out of the office as much as possible. It's as if she doesn't want her rival for leadership of the office around. When you were asked to go to Bangkok, you assumed that you would be made the office manager because of your seniority in the firm. You are certain that the decision to pick Melissa is yet another indication of reverse discrimination against white males.

In staff meetings, Melissa has talked about the need to be sensitive to the feelings of the office staff as well as the clients in this multicultural setting. "Where does she come off preaching about sensitivity! What about my feelings, for heaven's sake?" you wonder. This is nothing more than a straightforward power play. She is probably feeling insecure about being the only female accountant in the office and being promoted over someone with more experience. "Sending me out of town," you decide, "is a clear case of 'out of sight, out of mind.'"

Well, it's not going to happen that easily. You are not going to roll over and let her treat you unfairly. It's time for a showdown. If she doesn't agree to change this assignment and apologize for the way she's been treating you, you're going to register a formal complaint with her boss in the New York office. You are prepared to submit your resignation if the situation doesn't improve.

QUESTIONS FOR DISCUSSION

1. What antecedents of conflict appear to be present in this situation? What can be done about them?

2. Having heard how others handled this conflict, did one particular style seem to work better than the others?

3. Did influence tactics, power, politics, or impression management enter into your deliberations? Explain.

Notes

[1]Translated from P Vandermeersch, "Chirac erft wijnkelder, atoombunker en peutertuin," *De Standaard*, May 16, 1995, p 4.

[2]H Malcolm and C Sokoloff, "Values, Human Relations, and Organization Development," in *The Emerging Practice of Organizational Development*, eds W Sikes, A Drexler, and J Gant (San Diego: University Associates, 1989), p 64.

[3]See D Kipnis, S M Schmidt, and I Wilkinson, "Intraorganizational Influence Tactics: Explorations in Getting One's Way," *Journal of Applied Psychology*, August 1980, pp 440–52. Also see C A Schriesheim and T R Hinkin, "Influence Tactics Used by Subordinates: A Theoretical and Empirical Analysis and Refinement of the Kipnis, Schmidt, and Wilkinson Subscales," *Journal of Applied Psychology*, June 1990, pp 246–57.

[4]Based on G Yukl and C M Falbe, "Influence Tactics and Objectives in Upward, Downward, and Lateral Influence Attempts," *Journal of Applied Psychology*, April 1990, pp 132–40.

[5]Based on discussion in G Yukl, H Kim, and C M Falbe, "Antecedents of Influence Outcomes," *Journal of Applied Psychology*, June 1996, pp 309–17.

[6]Data from Ibid.

[7]Data from G Yukl and J B Tracey, "Consequences of Influence Tactics Used with Subordinates, Peers, and the Boss," *Journal of Applied Psychology*, August 1992, pp 525–35. Also see C M Falbe and G Yukl, "Consequences for Managers of Using Single Influence Tactics and Combinations of Tactics," *Academy of Management Journal*, August 1992, pp 638–52.

[8]Data from R A Gordon, "Impact of Ingratiation on Judgments and Evaluations: A Meta-Analytic Investigation," *Journal of Personality and Social Psychology*, July 1996, pp 54–70. Also see S J Wayne, R C Liden, and R T Sparrowe, "Developing Leader–Member Exchanges," *American Behavioral Scientist*, March 1994, pp 697–714; and A Oldenburg, "These Days, Hostile Is Fitting for Takeovers Only," *USA Today*, July 22, 1996, pp 8B, 10B.

[9]Data from Yukl, Kim, and Falbe, "Antecedents of Influence Outcomes."

[10]J E Driskell, B Olmstead, and E Salas, "Task Cues, Dominance Cues, and Influence in Task Groups," *Journal of Applied Psychology*, February 1993, p 51.

[11]For example, see P Rosenfeld, S Booth-Kewley, J E Edwards, and D L Alderton, "Linking Diversity and Impression Management: A Study of Hispanic, Black, and White Navy Recruits," *American Behavioral Scientist*, March 1994, pp 672–81; and K F Dunn and G Cowan, "Social Influence Strategies among Japanese and American College Women," *Psychology of Women Quarterly*, March 1993, pp 39–52.

[12]A R Cohen and D L Bradford, *Influence Without Authority*, (New York: John Wiley & Sons, 1990), pp 23–24.

[13]Ibid., p 28. Another excellent source on this subject is R B Cialdini, *Influence* (New York: William Morrow, 1984).

[14]Based on H Collingwood, "That Shut-Out Feeling," *Business Week*, January 18, 1993, p 40.

[15]D Tjosvold, "The Dynamics of Positive Power," *Training and Development Journal*, June 1984, p 72. Also see T A Stewart, "Get with the New Power Game," *Fortune*, January 13, 1997, pp 58–62.

[16]Based on Cunningham, J. "Real Lives: Fearing the Work — Workplace bullies are a growing trend, causing enough concern to prompt a TUC debate," *The Guardian*, September 13, 1995, p.4; "Politics: Managers warned bullying in workplace does not pay," *The Herald*, November 14, 1995, p. 4.

[17]M W McCall, Jr., *Power, Influence, and Authority: The Hazards of Carrying a Sword*, Technical Report No. 10 (Greensboro, NC: Center for Creative Leadership, 1978), p 5. For an excellent update on power, see E P Hollander and L R Offermann, "Power and Leadership in Organizations," *American Psychologist*, February 1990, pp 179–89. Also see E Lesly, "Manager See, Manager Do," *Business Week*, April 3, 1995, pp 90–91.

[18]Based on and translated from M Hensen, "De Polonaise van het Grote Gelds," *De Standaard*, January 20–21, 1996, p 19.

[19]Translated from K Van Wichelen, "De Vloek van de Farao," *Humo*, February 27, 1996, pp 146–9.

[20]L H Chusmir, "Personalized versus Socialized Power Needs among Working Women and Men," *Human Relations*, February 1986, p 149.

[21]See B Lloyd, "The Paradox of Power," *The Futurist*, May–June 1996, p 60.

[22]D W Cantor and T Bernay, *Women in Power: The Secrets of Leadership* (Boston: Houghton Mifflin, 1992), p 40.

[23]See J R P French and B Raven, "The Bases of Social Power," in *Studies in Social Power*, ed D Cartwright (Ann Arbor: University of Michigan Press, 1959), pp 150–67.

[24]Data from J R Larson, Jr., C Christensen, A S Abbott, and T M Franz, "Diagnosing Groups: Charting the Flow of Information in Medical Decision-Making Teams," *Journal of Personality and Social Psychology*, August 1996, pp 315–30.

[25]See D A Morand, "Forms of Address and Status Leveling in Organizations," *Business Horizons*, November–December 1995, pp 34–39; and H Lancaster, "A Father's Character, Not His Success, Shapes Kids' Careers," *The Wall Street Journal*, February 27, 1996, p B1.

[26]D Shipley and C Egan, "Power, Conflict and Co-operation in Brewer-Tenant Distribution Channels," *International Journal of Service Industry Management*, 1992, vol. 3, no 4, pp 44–62.

[27]Details may be found in Chusmir, "Personalized vs. Socialized Power Needs among Working Women and Men," pp 149—59. For a review of research on individual differences in the need for power, see R J House, "Power and Personality in Complex Organizations," in *Research in Organizational Behavior*, ed B M Staw and L L Cummings (Greenwich, CT: JAI Press, 1988), pp 305–57.

[28]B Filipczak, "Is It Getting Chilly in Here?" *Training*, February 1994, p 27.

[29]Data from J Onyx, R Leonard, and K Vivekananda, "Social Perception of Power: A Gender Analysis," *Perceptual and Motor Skills*, February 1995, pp 291–96.

[30]P M Podsakoff and C A Schriesheim, "Field Studies of French and Raven's Bases of Power: Critique, Reanalysis, and Suggestions for Future Research," *Psychological Bulletin*, May 1985, p 388. Also see M A Rahim and G F Buntzman, "Supervisory Power Bases, Styles of Handling Conflict with Subordinates, and Subordinate Compliance and Satisfaction," *Journal of Psychology*, March 1989, p 195–210; D Tjosvold, "Power and Social Context in Superior-Subordinate Interaction," *Organizational Behavior and Human Decision Processes*, June 1985, pp 281–93; and C A Schriesheim, T R Hinkin, and P M Podsakoff, "Can Ipsative and Single-Item Measures Produce Erroneous Results in Field Studies of French and Raven's (1950) Five Bases of Power? An Empirical Investigation," *Journal of Applied Psychology*, February 1991, pp 106–14.

[31]See T R Hinkin and C A Schriesheim, "Relationships between Subordinate Perceptions and Supervisor Influence Tactics and

Attributed Bases of Supervisory Power," *Human Relations,* March 1990, pp 221–37. Also see D J Brass and M E Burkhardt, "Potential Power and Power Use: An Investigation of Structure and Behavior," *Academy of Management Journal,* June 1993, pp 441–70.

[32]See H E Baker III, " 'Wax On—Wax Off:' French and Raven at the Movies," *Journal of Management Education,* November 1993, pp 517–19.

[33]"The tyranny of fear: working for a bully," *Sunday Times,* July 16, 1995.

[34]Based on P A Wilson, "The Effects of Politics and Power on the Organizational Commitment of Federal Executives," *Journal of Management,* Spring 1995, pp 101–18. For related research, see J B Arthur, "Effects of Human Resource Systems on Manufacturing Performance and Turnover," *Academy of Management Journal,* June 1994, pp 670–87.

[35]For related research, see L G Pelletier and R J Vallerand, "Supervisors' Beliefs and Subordinates' Intrinsic Motivation: A Behavioral Confirmation Analysis," *Journal of Personality and Social Psychology,* August 1996, pp 331–40.

[36]See L Holpp, "If Empowerment Is So Good, Why Does It Hurt?" *Training,* March 1995, pp 52–57; R C Liden and S Arad, "A Power Perspective of Empowerment and Work Groups: Implications for Human Resources Management Research," in *Research in Personnel and Human Resources Management,* ed G R Ferris (Greenwich, CT: JAI Press, 1996), vol. 14, pp 205–51; and G M Spreitzer, "Social Structural Characteristics of Psychological Empowerment," *Academy of Management Journal,* April 1996, pp 483–504.

[37]See R C Ford and M D Fottler, "Empowerment: A Matter of Degree," *Academy of Management Executive,* August 1995, pp 21–31.

[38]S Chandler, "United We Own," *Business Week,* March 18, 1996, p 96.

[39]M Memmott, "Managing Government Inc.," *USA Today,* June 28, 1993, p 2B.

[40]See J A Belasco and R C Stayer, "Why Empowerment Doesn't Empower: The Bankruptcy of Current Paradigms," *Business Horizons,* March–April 1994, pp 29–41.

[41]For complete details, see C R Leana, "Power Relinquishment versus Power Sharing: Theoretical Clarification and Empirical Comparison of Delegation and Participation," *Journal of Applied Psychology,* May 1987, pp 228–33.

[42]M D Fulford and C A Enz, "The Impact of Empowerment on Service Employees," *Journal of Managerial Issues,* Summer 1995, p 172.

[43]Data from A J H Thorlakson and R P Murray, "An Empirical Study of Empowerment in the Workplace," *Group & Organization Management,* March 1996, pp 67–83.

[44]W A Randolph, "Navigating the Journey to Empowerment," *Organizational Dynamics,* Spring 1995, p 31.

[45]C Pasternak, "Corporate Politics May Not Be a Waste of Time," *HRMagazine,* September 1994, p 18.

[46]R Bhasin, "On Playing Corporate Politics," *Pulp & Paper,* October 1985, p 175. Also see N Gupta and G D Jenkins, Jr., "The Politics of Pay," *Compensation & Benefits Review,* March–April 1996, pp 23–30.

[47]R W Allen, D L Madison, L W Porter, P A Renwick, and B T Mayes, "Organizational Politics: Tactics and Characteristics of Its Actors," *California Management Review,* Fall 1979, p 77. Also see K M Kacmar and G R Ferris, "Politics at Work: Sharpening the Focus of Political Behavior in Organizations," *Business Horizons,* July–August 1993, pp 70–74. For related discussion, see A G Bedeian, "Workplace Envy," *Organizational Dynamics,* Spring

1995, pp 49–56.

[48]See P M Fandt and G R Ferris, "The Management of Information and Impressions: When Employees Behave Opportunistically," *Organizational Behavior and Human Decision Processes,* February 1990, pp 140–58.

[49]First four based on discussion in D R Beeman and T W Sharkey, "The Use and Abuse of Corporate Politics," *Business Horizons,* March–April 1987, pp 26–30.

[50]A Raia, "Power, Politics, and the Human Resource Professional," *Human Resource Planning,* no. 4, 1985, p 203.

[51]This three-level distinction comes from A T Cobb, "Political Diagnosis: Applications in Organizational Development," *Academy of Management Review,* July 1986, pp 482–96.

[52]An excellent historical and theoretical perspective of coalitions can be found in W B Stevenson, J L Pearce, and L W Porter, "The Concept of 'Coalition' in Organization Theory and Research," *Academy of Management Review,* April 1985, pp 256–68.

[53]Allen, Madison, Porter, Renwick, and Mayes, "Organizational Politics: Tactics and Characteristics of Its Actors," p 77.

[54]See W L Gardner III, "Lessons in Organizational Dramaturgy: The Art of Impression Management," *Organizational Dynamics,* Summer 1992, pp 33–46.

[55]A Rao, S M Schmidt, and L H Murray, "Upward Impression Management: Goals, Influence Strategies, and Consequences," *Human Relations,* February 1995, p 147.

[56]See P M Fandt and G R Ferris, "The Management of Information and Impressions: When Employees Behave Opportunistically," *Organizational Behavior and Human Decision Processes,* February 1990, pp 140—58; C A Riordan, T Gross, and C C Maloney, "Self-Monitoring, Gender, and the Personal Consequences of Impression Management," *American Behavioral Scientist,* March 1994, pp 715–25; and K S Crittenden and H Bae, "Self-Effacement and Social Responsibility: Attribution as Impression Management in Asian Cultures," *American Behavioral Scientist,* March 1994, pp 653–71.

[57]A Arkin, "Tailoring clothes to suit the image," *People Management,* August 24, 1995, pp 18–21.

[58]J Solomon, "Why Worry About Pleat Pull and Sloppy Socks?" *Newsweek,* September 30, 1996, p 51.

[59]See S J Wayne and G R Ferris, "Influence Tactics, Affect, and Exchange Quality in Supervisor-Subordinate Interactions: A Laboratory Experiment and Field Study," *Journal of Applied Psychology,* October 1990, pp 487–99. For another version, see Table 1 (p 246) in S J Wayne and R C Liden, "Effects of Impression Management on Performance Ratings: A Longitudinal Study," *Academy of Management Journal,* February 1995, pp 232–60.

[60]See P Rosenfeld, R A Giacalone, and C A Riordan, "Impression Management Theory and Diversity: Lessons for Organizational Behavior," *American Behavioral Scientist,* March 1994, pp 601–04; and R A Giacalone and J W Beard, "Impression Management, Diversity, and International Management," *American Behavioral Scientist,* March 1994, pp 621–36.

[61]M E Mendenhall and C Wiley, "Strangers in a Strange Land: The Relationship between Expatriate Adjustment and Impression Management," *American Behavioral Scientist,* March 1994, pp 605–20.

[62]T E Becker and S L Martin, "Trying to Look Bad at Work: Methods and Motives for Managing Poor Impressions in Organizations," *Academy of Management Journal,* February 1995, p 191.

[63]Ibid., p 181.

[64]Adapted from Ibid., pp 180–81.

[65]Based on discussion in Ibid., pp 192–93.

[66]Data from G R Ferris, D D Frink, D P S Bhawuk, J Zhou, and D C Gilmore, "Reactions of Diverse Groups to Politics in the Workplace," *Journal of Management,* no. 1, 1996, pp 23–44. For other findings from the same database, see G R Ferris, D D Frink, M C Galang, J Zhou, K M Kacmar, and J L Howard, "Perceptions of Organizational Politics: Prediction, Stress-Related Implications, and Outcomes," *Human Relations,* February 1996, pp 233–66.

[67]See S J Wayne and R C Liden, "Effects of Impression Management on Performance Ratings: A Longitudinal Study," *Academy of Management Journal,* February 1995, pp 232–60.

[68]Rao, Schmidt, and Murray, "Upward Impression Management: Goals, Influence Strategies, and Consequences," p 165.

[69]Also see A Tziner, G P Latham, B S Price, and R Haccoun, "Development and Validation of a Questionnaire for Measuring Perceived Political Considerations in Performance Appraisal," *Journal of Organizational Behavior,* March 1996, pp 179–90.

[70]A Zaleznik, "Real Work," *Harvard Business Review,* January–February 1989, p 60.

[71]C M Koen, Jr., and S M Crow, "Human Relations and Political Skills," *HR Focus,* December 1995, p 11.

[72]For more on workplace politics, see "Smart Workplace Politics," *Supervisory Management,* September 1994, pp 11–12; J A Byrne, "How to Succeed: Same Game, Different Decade," *Business Week,* April 17, 1995, p 48; and M Moats Kennedy, "Political Mistakes of the Newly Promoted," *Across the Board,* October 1995, pp 53–54.

[73]T Arroba and K James, "Are politics palatable to women managers," *Women in Management Review,* vol 3, no 3, p 23.

[74]S Mann, "Politics and powder in organizations: Why women lose out," *Leadership & Organization Development Journal,* 1995, vol 16, no 2, pp 9–15.

[75]Data from M Ingwerson, "Clinton Will Inherit Bush Legacy of Military Use 'Without Formulas,' " *The Christian Science Monitor,* January 7, 1993, pp 1, 4.

[76]J A Wall, Jr., and R Robert Callister, "Conflict and Its Management," *Journal of Management,* no. 3, 1995, p 517.

[77]Ibid., p 544.

[78]Intergroup conflict is discussed in N N Thalhofer, "Intergroup Differentiation and Reduction of Intergroup Conflict," *Small Group Research,* February 1993, pp 28–43; and R J Fisher, "Generic Principles for Resolving Intergroup Conflict," *Journal of Social Issues,* no. 1, 1994, pp 47–66.

[79]See A M O'Leary-Kelly, R W Griffin, and D J Glew, "Organization-Motivated Aggression: A Research Framework," *Academy of Management Review,* January 1996, pp 225–53.

[80]S P Robbins, " 'Conflict Management' and 'Conflict Resolution' Are Not Synonymous Terms," *California Management Review,* Winter 1978, p 70.

[81]Cooperative conflict is discussed in D Tjosvold, *Learning to Manage Conflict: Getting People to Work Together Productively* (New York: Lexington Books, 1993). Also see A C Amason, K R Thompson, W A Hochwarter, and A W Harrison, "Conflict: An Important Dimension in Successful Management Teams," *Organizational Dynamics,* Autumn 1995, pp 20–35; and A C Amason, "Distinguishing the Effects of Functional and Dysfunctional Conflict on Strategic Decision Making: Resolving a Paradox for Top Management Teams," *Academy of Management Journal,* February 1996, pp 123–48.

[82]S Flax, "The Toughest Bosses in America," *Fortune,* August 6, 1984, p 21.

[83]Adapted in part from discussion in A C Filley, *Interpersonal Conflict Resolution* (Glenview, IL: Scott, Foresman, 1975), pp 9–12; and B Fortado, "The Accumulation of Grievance Conflict," *Journal of Management Inquiry,* December 1992, pp 288–303.

[84]Based on and translated from van J P Oudenhoven, L Mechelse, "Conflicthantering in vijf Europese landen," *Negotiation Magazine,* 1995, no 1, pp. 3–12.

[85]R A Cosier and C R Schwenk, "Agreement and Thinking Alike: Ingredients for Poor Decisions," *Academy of Management Executive,* February 1990, p 71. Also see J P Kotter, "Kill Complacency," *Fortune,* August 5, 1996, pp 168–70.

[86]For example, see "Facilitators as Devil's Advocates," *Training,* September 1993, p 10.

[87]Good background reading on devil's advocacy can be found in C R Schwenk, "Devil's Advocacy in Managerial Decision Making," *Journal of Management Studies,* April 1984, pp 153–68.

[88]See G Katzenstein, "The Debate on Structured Debate: Toward a Unified Theory," *Organizational Behavior and Human Decision Processes,* June 1996, pp 316–32.

[89]W Kiechel III, "How to Escape the Echo Chamber," *Fortune,* June 18, 1990, p 130.

[90]See D M Schweiger, W R Sandberg, and P L Rechner, "Experiential Effects of Dialectical Inquiry, Devil's Advocacy, and Consensus Approaches to Strategic Decision Making," *Academy of Management Journal,* December 1989, pp 745–72.

[91]See J S Valacich and C Schwenk, "Devil's Advocacy and Dialectical Inquiry Effects on Face-to-Face and Computer-Mediated Group Decision Making," *Organizational Behavior and Human Decision Processes,* August 1995, pp 158–73.

[92]A recent statistical validation for this model can be found in M A Rahim and N R Magner, "Confirmatory Factor Analysis of the Styles of Handling Interpersonal Conflict: First-Order Factor Model and Its Invariance Across Groups," *Journal of Applied Psychology,* February 1995, pp 122–32.

[93]M A Rahim, "A Strategy for Managing Conflict in Complex Organizations," *Human Relations,* January 1985, p 84.

[94]Based on a definition in M A Neale and M H Bazerman, "Negotiating Rationally: The Power and Impact of the Negotiator's Frame," *Academy of Management Executive,* August 1992, pp 42–51.

[95]See L Thompson, E Peterson, and S E Brodt, "Team Negotiation: An Examination of Integrative and Distributive Bargaining," *Journal of Personality and Social Psychology,* January 1996, pp 66–78.

[96]See D A Whetten and K S Cameron, *Developing Management Skills,* 3rd ed (New York: HarperCollins, 1995), pp 425–30.

[97]M H Bazerman and M A Neale, *Negotiating Rationally* (New York: The Free Press, 1992), p 16.

[98]Good win-win negotiation strategies can be found in R R Reck and B G Long, *The Win-Win Negotiator: How to Negotiate Favorable Agreements That Last* (New York: Pocket Books, 1987); R Fisher and W Ury, *Getting to YES: Negotiating Agreement Without Giving In* (Boston: Houghton Mifflin, 1981); and R Fisher and D Ertel, *Getting Ready to Negotiate: The Getting to YES Workbook* (New York: Penguin Books, 1995).

[99]See L R Weingart, E B Hyder, and M J Prietula, "Knowledge Matters: The Effect of Tactical Descriptions on Negotiation Behavior and Outcome," *Journal of Personality and Social Psychology,* June 1996, pp 1205–17.

[100]Data from J L Graham, A T Mintu, and W Rodgers, "Explorations of Negotiation Behaviors in Ten Foreign Cultures Using a Model Developed in the United States," *Management Science,* January 1994, pp 72–95.

[101]For practical advice, see K Kelley Reardon and R E Spekman, "Starting Out Right: Negotiation Lessons for Domestic and Cross-Cultural Business Alliances," *Business Horizons,* January–February 1994, pp 71–79.

[102]The distinction between consultation and mediation adapted from discussion in L Keashly, R J Fisher, and P R Grant, "The Comparative Utility of Third Party Consultation and Mediation within a Complex Simulation of Intergroup Conflict," *Human Relations,* March 1993, pp 371–93. Also see A R Elangovan, "Managerial Third-Party Dispute Intervention: A Prescriptive Model of Strategic Selection," *Academy of Management Review,* October 1995, pp 800–30. An empirically derived list of 43 third-party mediation tactics can be found in R G Lim and P J D Carnevale, "Contingencies in the Mediation of Disputes," *Journal of Personality and Social Psychology,* February 1990, pp 259–72.

[103]See R E Jones and B H Melcher, "Personality and the Preference for Modes of Conflict Resolution," *Human Relations,* August 1982, pp 649–58.

[104]See R A Baron, "Reducing Organizational Conflict: An Incompatible Response Approach," *Journal of Applied Psychology,* May 1984, pp 272–79.

[105]See G A Youngs, Jr., "Patterns of Threat and Punishment Reciprocity in a Conflict Setting," *Journal of Personality and Social Psychology,* September 1986, pp 541–46.

[106]For more details, see V D Wall, Jr., and L L Nolan, "Small Group Conflict: A Look at Equity, Satisfaction, and Styles of Conflict Management," *Small Group Behavior,* May 1987, pp 188–211.

[107]Based on R L Pinkley, T L Griffith, and G B Northcraft, " 'Fixed Pie' a la Mode: Information Availability, Information Processing, and the Negotiation of Suboptimal Agreements," *Organizational Behavior and Human Decision Processes,* April 1995, pp 101–12.

[108]W C King, Jr., and T D Hinson, "The Influence of Sex and Equity Sensitivity on Relationship Preferences, Assessment of Opponent, and Outcomes in a Negotiation Experiment," *Journal of Management,* Fall 1994, p 618.

[109]See M E Schnake and D S Cochran, "Effect of Two Goal-Setting Dimensions on Perceived Intraorganizational Conflict," *Group & Organization Studies,* June 1985, pp 168–83.

[110]Drawn from L H Chusmir and J Mills, "Gender Differences in Conflict Resolution Styles of Managers: At Work and at Home," *Sex Roles,* February 1989, pp 149–63.

[111]See K K Smith, " The Movement of Conflict in Organizations: The Joint Dynamics of Splitting and Triangulation," *Administrative Science Quarterly,* March 1989, pp 1–20.

[112]Ten quiz items quoted from J F Byrnes, "Connecting Organizational Politics and Conflict Resolution," *Personnel Administrator,* June 1986, p 49.

[113]Scoring system quoted from Ibid.

[114]This case is quoted from *Developing Management Skills,* by David A. Whetten and Kim S Cameron. Copyright © 1984 by Scott, Foresman and Company. Reprinted by permission of Addison Wesley Educational Publishers, Inc.

Twelve

Individual and Group Decision Making

According to the report of the Presidential Commission on the Space Shuttle Challenge Accident, the debate over whether to launch on January 28, 1986 unfolded as follows: Shortly after 1 PM ET on January 27, the National Aeronautic and Space Administration's (NASA) booster rocket manager in Cape Canaveral Larry Wear asks officials of rocket maker Morton Thiokol in Utah whether cold weather on the 28th would present a problem for launch.

By 2 PM, NASA's top managers are discussing how temperatures in the 30s at the launch pad might affect the shuttle's performance. In Utah, an hour later, Thiokol engineer Roger Boisjoly learns of the forecast for the first time.

By late afternoon, midlevel NASA managers at the Cape are on the phone with Thiokol managers, who point out that the booster's rubbery O-rings, which seal in hot gases, might be affected by cold.

That concern brings in officials from NASA's Marshall Space Flight Center in Huntsville, Alabama, which buys the rockets from Thiokol and readies them for launch.

Marshall managers decide that a three-way telephone conference call is needed, linking NASA and Thiokol engineers and managers in Alabama, Florida, and Utah.

The first conference call begins about 5:45 PM, and Thiokol tells NASA it believes launch should be delayed until noon or afternoon, when the weather turns warmer. It is decided a second conference call would be needed later that evening.

Marshall deputy project manager Judson Lovingood tells shuttle projects manager Stan Reinartz at the Cape that if Thiokol persists, NASA should not launch. Top NASA managers at Marshall are told of Thiokol's concern.

At 8:45 PM, the second conference call begins, involving 34 engineers and managers from NASA and Thiokol at the three sites.

Thiokol engineers Boisjoly and Arnie Thompson present charts showing a history of leaking O-ring joints from tests and previous flights.

The data show that the O-rings perform worse at lower temperatures and that the worst leak of hot gases came in January 1985, when a shuttle launched with the temperature at 12°C. Thiokol managers recommend not flying Challenger at temperatures colder than that.

NASA's George Hardy says he's "appalled" at Thiokol's recommendation. Larry Mulloy, Marshall's booster rocket manager, complains that Thiokol is setting down new launch criteria and exclaims, "My God, Thiokol, when do you want me to launch, next April?"

Thiokol Vice President Joe Kilminster asks for five minutes to talk in private. The debate continues for 30 minutes. Boisjoly, Thompson, engineer Bob Ebeling, and others are overruled by Thiokol management, who decide to approve the launch.

At 11 PM, Kilminster tells NASA that Thiokol has changed its mind: Temperature is stil a concern, but the data are inconclusive. He recommends launch. Thiokol's concerns that cold weather could hurt the booster joints are not passed up NASA's chain of command beyond officials at the Marshall Space Flight Center.

Challenger is launched at 11:38 AM January 28 in a temperature of 2.5°C.[1]

Shortly after launch on January 28, 1986, Challenger was engulfed in a fiery explosion that led to the deaths of six astronauts and teacher-in-space Christa McAuliffe. As a shocked world watched great billows of smoke trail over the Atlantic, it was clear to those involved that launching Challenger in 2.5-degree weather was a catastrophic decision.[2]

... Ten Years Later

Two who argued the longest and loudest against launch were Thiokol engineers Roger Boisjoly and Arnie Thompson. But their lives took widely differing paths after the accident.

Boisjoly remembers the prelaunch debate this way: "When NASA created the pressure, they all buckled."

He became nationally known as the primary whistle-blower. Thiokol removed Boisjoly from the investigation team and sent him home after he testified before a presidential commission that the company ignored evidence that the booster rocket seals would fail in cold weather.

Boisjoly, 57, says he was blackballed by the industry and run out of town by Thiokol.

For a time, he sought psychiatric help. "It just became unbearable to function," says Boisjoly, who now lives with his wife and daughter in a small mountain town in Utah. He spoke on condition that the town not be named because he fears for his family's safety.

Boisjoly is convinced he is a marked man because some former co-workers believe his testimony contributed to resulting layoffs at Thiokol.

After the accident, he says, drivers would try to run him off the road when he was out on a walk. He got threatening phone calls. Someone tried to break into his house.

"It became so uncomfortable for me that I went out and bought a .38 revolver," he says.

Now retired, Boisjoly earns $1,500 for speeches to universities and business groups. He also runs his own engineering company and teaches Sunday school in the Mormon church, something he says he never would have dreamed of doing before the accident.

Says Thompson, the other voice against launch: "There were the two of us that didn't want to fly and we were defeated. A lot of my top managers were not happy with me."

Yet, with longer ties to Thiokol than Boisjoly, Thompson was promoted to manager and stayed on through the shuttle's redesign.

He retired three years ago at the end of a 25-year-career. Now 66, he spends his time building a small office building in Brigham City, Utah.

"My attitude was, I wanted to stay on and redesign the bird and get back into the air," says Thompson. "I had a personal goal to get flying again." . . .

Thiokol's Bob Ebeling was so sure that Challenger was doomed, he asked his daughter, Leslie, then 33, to his office to watch "a super colossal disaster" unfold on live TV.

When it exploded, "I was in the middle of a prayer for the Lord to do his will and let all these things come to a happy ending and not let this happen," says Ebeling, who managed the rocket ignition system for Thiokol. "We did our level best but it wasn't good enough."

The fact that he foresaw disaster and could not stop it has tortured him since.

Ebeling, 69, says that within a week of the accident he became impotent and suffered high stress and constant headaches, problems he still has today. After 40 years of engineering experience, Thiokol "put me out to pasture on a medical" retirement, he says.

Ebeling still feels "the decision to recommend a launch was pre-ordained by others, by NASA leaning on our upper management. The deck was stacked."

One of those who overruled Ebeling and the others was Jerry Mason, the senior Thiokol manager on the conference call. He took an early retirement from Thiokol five months after the disaster, ending a 25-year career in aerospace.

"I was basically responsible for the operation the day it happened," says Mason, 69. "It was important to the company to put that behind them and get going on the recovery and it would be hard to do that with me sitting there. So I left."

In Mason's case, that meant going abruptly from corporate chieftain to unpaid volunteer. He helped set up a local economic development board and now chairs the Utah Wildlife Federation.

"I had a pretty successful career, and would liked to have gone out with the feeling that I really had done very well all the time instead of having to go out feeling I'd made a mistake at the end."

For Judson Lovingood, the loss was more personal.

Formerly one of NASA's deputy managers for the shuttle project, he wonders still if Challenger contributed to the breakup of his marriage.

"I think (Challenger) had an effect on my personal life," says Lovingood, "a long-term effect."

After the accident, he went to work for Thiokol in Huntsville and retired as director of engineering in 1993. Now remarried, he spends his time puttering in the yard of his Gurley, Alabama, home.

"Sometimes when I think about the seven people (aboard the shuttle), it's pretty painful," says Lovingood.

Besides McAuliffe, on board Challenger were commander Dick Scobee, pilot Mike Smith, and astronauts Ron McNair, Ellison Onizuka, Judy Resnik, and Greg Jarvis.

Their families settled with the government and Thiokol for more than $1.5 billion. Still, "I think people should hold us collectively responsible as a group," Lovingood says. "Every person in that meeting the night before the launch shared in the blame." . . .

Investigations of the Challenger explosion placed much of the blame on NASA's George Hardy, a senior engineering manager.

By saying he was "appalled" by Thiokol's fears of flying in cold weather, critics charged, Hardy pressured Thiokol into approving the launch.

But Hardy refuses to shoulder the blame. "If Thiokol had stuck to their position, there wasn't any way we were going to launch," he says.

Hardy left NASA four months after the accident. Now 65, he runs a small aerospace consulting company in Athens, Alabama.

Whatever else the last decade brought, many of the recollections return to that pressure-packed conference call on the eve of launch.

Discussion Question
Do you think decision-making is more of a logical or random process?

Decision making is one of the primary responsibilities of being a manager. The quality of a manager's decisions is important for two principal reasons. First, the quality of a manager's decisions directly affects his or her career opportunities, rewards, and job satisfaction. Second, managerial decisions contribute to the success or failure of an organization.

Decision making

Identifying and choosing solutions that lead to a desired end result.

Decision making is a means to an end. It entails identifying and choosing alternative solutions that lead to a desired state of affairs. The process begins with a problem and ends when a solution has been chosen. To gain an understanding of how managers can make better decisions, this chapter focuses on (1) models of decision making, (2) the dynamics of decision making, (3) group decision making, and (4) creativity.

Models of Decision Making

There are several models of decision making. Each is based on a different set of assumptions and offers unique insight into the decision-making process. This section reviews three key historical models of decision making. They are (1) the rational model, (2) Simon's normative model, and (3) the garbage can model. Each successive model assumes that the decision-making process is less and less rational. Let us begin with the most orderly or rational explanation of managerial decision making.

The Rational Model

Rational model

Logical four-step approach to decision making.

The **rational model** proposes that managers use a rational, four-step sequence when making decisions: (1) identifying the problem, (2) generating alternative solutions, (3) selecting a solution, and (4) implementing and evaluating the solution. According to this model, managers are completely objective and possess complete information to make a decision. Despite criticism for being unrealistic, the rational model is instructive because it analytically breaks down the decision-making process and serves as a conceptual anchor for newer models.[3] Let us now consider each of these four steps.

Problem

Gap between an actual and desired situation.

Identifying the Problem   A **problem** exists when the actual situation and the desired situation differ. For example, a problem exists when you have to pay rent at the end of the month and don't have enough money. Your problem is not that you have to pay rent. Your problem is obtaining the needed funds. Consider the situation occurring at Boeing Co. Boeing is receiving a large increase in new orders for airliners from around the world.

The problem is that Boeing is right in the midst of a huge revamping of its engineering processes, a changeover that it had counted on having another 30 months to complete. Yet the company—which invited its first-ever discounts of up to 10%—is in no mood to turn away any orders now that they are finally arriving, even if they are so huge that they threaten to overwhelm its current capacity.

So the world's largest airliner manufacturer finds itself struggling with an uncharacteristic run of factory glitches. . . . The problems are evident in the assembly line for the 777, a hot-selling model. The line producing wings for the plane has fallen badly behind schedule. Three weeks ago, one of the huge wings had to be pulled back up the line for a weekend of costly reworking after harried mechanics misdrilled a main connection.[4]

Boeing's problem is the difference between how many high-quality planes it can produce per month and the number promised for delivery. Potential causes of the problem include excess demand from price discounts and the major revamping of its engineering processes.

How do companies such as Boeing know when a problem exists or is going to occur in the near future? One expert proposed that managers use one of three methods to identify problems: historical cues, planning, and other people's perceptions:[5]

1. Using historical cues to identify problems assumes that the recent past is the best estimate of the future. Thus, managers rely on past experience to identify discrepancies (problems) from expected trends. For example, a sales manager may conclude that a problem exists because the first-quarter sales are less than they were a year ago. This method is prone to error because it is highly subjective.

Scenario technique
Speculative forecasting method.

2. A planning approach is more systematic and can lead to more accurate results. This method consists of using projections or scenarios to estimate what is expected to occur in the future. A time period of one or more years is generally used. The **scenario technique** is a speculative, conjectural forecast tool used to identify future states, given a certain set of environmental conditions. Once different scenarios are developed, companies devise alternative strategies to survive in the various situations. This process helps to create contingency plans far into the future. Companies such as Royal Dutch/Shell, IBM, and Pfizer are increasingly using the scenario technique as a planning tool.[6]

3. A final approach to identifying problems is to rely on the perceptions of others. A restaurant manager may realize that his or her restaurant provides poor service when a large number of customers complain about how long it takes to receive food after placing an order. In other words, customers' comments signal that a problem exists. Interestingly, companies frequently compound their problems by ignoring customer complaints or feedback. This is precisely what happened to Ford Motor Co. when it decided to ignore customer feedback about the design of the Windstar minivan:

But Ford's biggest product blunder during the past five years is probably the 1995 Windstar minivan, which the company had hoped would lead it to the top of the lucrative minivan market. At December's [1995] close, Ford had a whopping 100-day plus supply of Windstars on dealer lots across the country. Why? Ford built the Windstar with only three doors, ignoring the company's own internal market data that showed about a third of the consumers it surveyed wanted another sliding door on the new van. Chrysler didn't ignore such data and offered an extra sliding door on its redesigned 1996 models. Today, Chrysler finds most of its minivan customers want the extra door, as it continues to sell nearly one-third more minivans than Ford.[7]

Generating Solutions   After identifying a problem, the next logical step is generating alternative solutions. For repetitive and routine decisions such as deciding when to send customers a bill, alternatives are readily available through decision rules. For example, a company might routinely bill customers three days after shipping a product. This is not the case for novel and unstructured decisions. Because there are no cut-and-dried procedures for dealing with novel problems, managers must creatively generate alternative solutions. Managers can use a number of techniques to stimulate creativity. Techniques to increase creativity are discussed later in this chapter.

Selecting a Solution   Optimally, decision makers want to choose the alternative with the greatest value. Decision theorists refer to this as maximizing the expected utility of an outcome. This is no easy task. First, assigning values to alternatives is complicated and prone to error. Not only are values subjective, but they also vary according to the preferences of the decision maker. For example, research demonstrates that people vary in their preferences for safety or risk when making decisions.[8] Further, evaluating alternatives assumes they can be judged according to some standards or criteria. This further assumes that (1) valid criteria exist, (2) each alternative can be compared against these criteria, and (3) the decision maker actually uses the criteria. As you know from making your own key life decisions, people frequently violate these assumptions.

Implementing and Evaluating the Solution   Once a solution is chosen, it needs to be implemented. Before implementing, though, managers need to do their homework. For example, three ineffective managerial tendencies have been observed frequently during the initial stages of implementation (see Table 12—1). Skilful managers try to avoid these

Table 12 – 1   Three Managerial Tendancies Reduce the Effectiveness of Implementation

MANAGERIAL TENDENCY	RECOMMENDED SOLUTION
The tendency not to ensure that people understand what needs to be done.	Involve the implementors in the choice-making step. When this is not possible, a strong and explicit attempt should be made to identify any misunderstanding, perhaps by having the implementor explain what he or she thinks needs to be done and why.
The tendency not to ensure the acceptance or motivation for what needs to be done.	Once again, involve the implementors in the choice-making step. Attempts should also be made to demonstrate the payoffs for effective implementation and to show how completion of various tasks will lead to successful implementation.
The tendency not to provide appropriate resources for what needs to be done.	Many implementations are less effective than they could be because adequate resources, such as time, staff, or information, were not provided. In particular, the allocations of such resources across departments and tasks are assumed to be appropriate because they were appropriate for implementing the previous plan. These assumptions should be checked.

Source: Modified from G P Huber, *Managerial Decision Making* (Glenview, IL: Scott, Foresman, 1980), p 19.

tendencies. Table 12–1 indicates that to promote necessary understanding, acceptance, and motivation, managers should involve implementators in the choice-making step.

After the solution is implemented, the evaluation phase assesses its effectiveness. If the solution is effective, it should reduce the difference between the actual and desired states that created the problem. If the gap is not closed, the implementation was not successful, and one of the following is true: Either the problem was incorrectly identified, or the solution was inappropriate. Assuming the implementation was unsuccessful, management can return to the first step, problem identification. If the problem was correctly identified, management should consider implementing one of the previously identified, but untried, solutions. This process can continue until all feasible solutions have been tried or the problem has changed.[9]

Summarizing the Rational Model   The rational model is based on the premise that managers optimize when they make decisions. **Optimizing** involves solving problems by producing the best possible solution. This assumes that managers

Optimizing

Choosing the best possible solution.

- Have knowledge of all possible alternatives.

- Have complete knowledge about the consequences that follow each alternative.

- Have a well-organized and stable set of preferences for these consequences.

- Have the computational ability to compare consequences and to determine which one is preferred.[10]

As noted by Herbert Simon, a decision theorist who in 1978 earned the Nobel Prize for his work on decision making: "The assumptions of perfect rationality are contrary to fact. It is not a question of approximation; they do not even remotely describe the processes that human beings use for making decisions in complex situations."[11] Thus, the rational model is at best an instructional tool. Since decision makers do not follow these rational procedures, Simon proposed a normative model of decision making.

Simon's Normative Model

This model attempts to identify the process that managers actually use when making decisions. The process is guided by a decision maker's bounded rationality. Bounded rationality represents the notion that decision makers are "bounded" or restricted by a variety of constraints when making decisions. These constraints include any personal or environmental characteristics that reduce rational decision making. Examples are the limited capacity of the human mind, problem complexity and uncertainty, amount and timeliness of information at hand, criticality of the decision, and time demands.[12]

As opposed to the rational model, Simon's normative model suggests that decision making is characterized by (1) limited information processing, (2) the use of rules of thumb or shortcuts, and (3) satisficing. Each of these characteristics is now explored.

Limited Information Processing   Managers are limited by how much information they process because of bounded rationality. This results in the tendency to acquire manageable rather than optimal amounts of information. In turn, this practice makes it difficult for managers to identify all possible alternative solutions. In the long run, the constraints of bounded rationality cause decision makers to fail to evaluate all potential alternatives.

Use of Rules of Thumb or Shortcuts   Decision makers use rules of thumb or shortcuts to reduce information-processing demands. Since these shortcuts represent knowledge gained from past experience, they help decision makers evaluate current problems. For example, recruiters may tend to hire applicants receiving degrees from the same university attended by other successful employees. In this case, the "school attended" criterion is used to facilitate complex information processing associated with employment interviews. Unfortunately, these shortcuts can result in biased decisions.[13]

Satisficing

Choosing a solution that meets a minimum standard of acceptance.

Satisficing   People satisfice because they do not have the time, information, or ability to handle the complexity associated with following a rational process. This is not necessarily undesirable. **Satisficing** consists of choosing a solution that meets some minimum qualifications, one that is "good enough." Satisficing resolves problems by producing solutions that are satisfactory, as opposed to optimal. Finding a radio station to listen to in your car is a good example of satisficing. You cannot optimize because it is impossible to listen to all stations at the same time. You thus stop searching for a station when you find one playing a song you like or do not mind hearing.

The Garbage Can Model

As is true of Simon's normative model, this approach grew from the rational model's inability to explain how decisions are actually made. It assumes that decision making does not follow an orderly series of steps. In fact, organizational decision making is said to be such a sloppy and haphazard process that the garbage can label is appropriate. This contrasts sharply with the rational model, which proposed that decision makers follow a sequential series of steps beginning with a problem and ending with a solution. According to the **garbage can model**, decisions result from a complex interaction between four independent streams of events: problems, solutions, participants, and choice opportunities.[14] The interaction of these events creates "a collection of choices looking for problems, issues and feelings looking for decision situations in which they might be aired, solutions looking for issues to which they might be the answer, and decision makers looking for work."[15] The garbage can model attempts to explain how these events interact and lead to a decision. After discussing the streams of events and how they interact, this section highlights managerial implications of the garbage can model.

Garbage can model

Holds that decision making is sloppy and haphazard.

Streams of Events   The four streams of events—problems, solutions, participants, and choice opportunities—represent independent entities that flow into and out of organizational decision situations (see Figure 12–1). Because decisions are a function of the interaction among these independent events, the stages of problem identification and problem solution may be unrelated. For instance, a solution may be proposed for a problem that does not exist. On the other hand, some problems are never solved. Each of the four events in the garbage can model deserves a closer look.

- *Problems.* As defined earlier, problems represent a gap between an actual situation and a desired condition. But problems are independent from alternatives and solutions. The problem may or may not lead to a solution.

Figure 12 – 1   Garbage Can Model of Organizational Decision Making

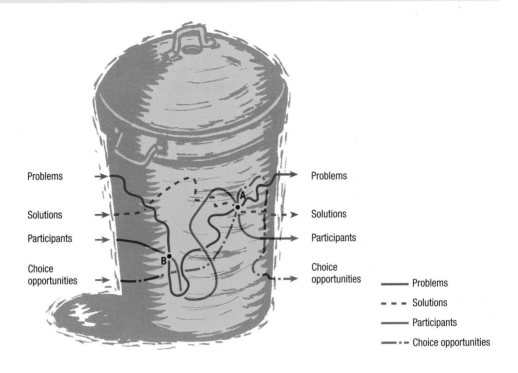

- *Solutions.* Solutions are answers looking for questions. They represent ideas constantly flowing through an organization. Contrary to the classical model, however, solutions are used to formulate problems rather than vice versa. This is predicted to occur because managers often do not know what they want until they have some idea of what they can get.

- *Participants.* Participants are the organizational members who come and go throughout the organization. They bring different values, attitudes, and experiences to a decision-making situation. Time pressures limit the extent to which participants are involved in decision making.

- *Choice opportunities.* Choice opportunities are occasions in which an organization is expected to make a decision. While some opportunities, such as hiring and promoting employees, occur regularly, others do not because they result from some type of crisis or unique situation.

Interactions among the Streams of Events   Because of the independent nature of the streams of events, they interact in a random fashion. This implies that decision making is more a function of chance encounters than a rational process. Thus, the organization is characterized as a "garbage can" in which problems, solutions, participants, and choice opportunities are all mixed together (see Figure 12–1). Only when the four streams of events happen to connect, such as at point A in Figure 12–1, is a decision made. Since these connections randomly occur among countless combinations of streams of events, decision quality generally depends on *timing*. (Some might use the term *luck*.) In other words, good decisions are made when these streams of events interact at the proper time. This explains why problems do not necessarily relate to solutions (point B in Figure 12–1) and why solutions do not always solve problems. In support of the garbage can model, one study indicated that decision making in the textbook publishing industry followed a garbage can process. Moreover, knowledge of this process helped the researchers to identify a variety of bestselling textbooks.[16]

Garbage Can Process in Action   International OB presents a detailed example of a garbage can process underlying Triton Energy Corporation's oil strike in Colombia. After reading it, try to identify the constellation of problems, solutions, participants, and choice opportunities floating around in the garbage can. Did you notice the problems of Triton's reputation, geography, guerrillas attacking crews, underground pressure, wells closing up, lack of funding, and mud? Some of the key participants in this case include Triton, British Petroleum, Norsk Hydro, Exxon Corp., Royal Dutch/Shell Group, DuPont, Thorleif Enger, President Ernesto Samper, and, of course, James Edwards and John Tatum from Triton. The choice opportunities of whether to invest in the Soviet Union, Asia, or

---

International Organizational Behaviour

A Garbage Can Process Leads Triton Energy Corp. to Strike Oil in Yopal, Columbia

For oil companies, there have been few places on Earth more formidable than Colombia's Cusiana field, nestled near here in the rugged Andes. The treacherous mountains stymie all but the most intrepid explorers, the area's geology is often impenetrable, and guerrillas attack crews in the fields.

So Cusiana was passed over by almost every company in the oil patch.

Save for one. Triton Energy Corp., a small and, for many years, undercapitalized exploration firm based in Dallas, endeavored for more than a decade to line up the money and support needed to get at the oil its executives were convinced was beneath Cusiana. . . .

That the main promoter of Cusiana was Triton—which before this project had a reputation among many as a small-change operator prone to hype—did little to inspire early investment by the industry's giants. The company has been around since 1962 and has explored sites around the globe—but with mixed results.

Now, in a testament to its unfailing faith—and some good luck—Triton's fortunes have turned. Cusiana is the largest oil strike in the Western Hemisphere in more than 20 years, the biggest since Alaska's Prudhoe Bay. And it looks like the investment by Triton and its partners—a gamble of some $6 billion—is going to pay off.

"Everybody would like to be sitting on a Cusiana," says Thorleif Enger, president of exploration and production for Norsk Hydro, a huge Norwegian firm that considered and rejected Colombia as a prospect before the Cusiana find was declared.

Mr. Enger wasn't alone in bypassing Colombia. In recent years, most big oil producers put their money on new fields in Asia and the former Soviet Union, even as Triton and its

partners pushed on here. . . .

For Colombia itself—a nation plagued by poverty, political chaos, guerrilla warfare, and drug trafficking—Cusiana is a vital part of the government's plan to bolster the economy. "For years, I asked myself why all the oil [in Latin America] was found in Venezuela," says President Ernesto Samper. "God made the world in a slanted way. Now in my dream for Colombia, oil will ultimately be one of the leading sectors" of the economy. . . .

But Cusiana and Cupiagua eluded everyone. As early as the 1960s, major oil companies were combing geological data in the area. BP [British Petroleum], now the operator of Cusiana, drilled a well just south of the field in 1973, says Roger Herrera, BP's chief geologist in Colombia during that period. That well collapsed. Also in the mid-1970s, Ecopetrol, the state-owned oil company that is now part of the Triton team, drilled two wells directly into Cusiana. Yet, neither well showed significant amounts of oil.

Sometimes, the crews just didn't drill deep enough. In other cases, the underground pressure that created the majestic Andes caused so much shifting of rock that wells closed up during drilling.

As a result, "Big Oil wrote off the area," explains Nick De'Ath, a Triton executive who was then BP's representative in Colombia.

None of the problems stopped two mid-level Triton executives, James Edwards and John Tatum, from singling out Cusiana as the most interesting geological opportunity in South America in 1981. Both were helping the company sweep through Latin America for the best geology they could find.

Colombia also played a significant role for the companies involved in this case. Interestingly, British Petroleum passed on the first opportunity to invest in the Cusiana field. Finally, Union Texas Petroleum Holdings' unsuccessful decision to drill in the flatlands portion of the lease played a big role in the case. It surely affected Edwards and Tatum's subsequent solution of drilling in the foothills, and it provided British Petroleum with a second opportunity to invest in the project. Although the oil strike in Colombia appears lucky, chaotic, and disorderly, the garbage can model suggests that there are patterns underlying the confusion.

Managerial Implications   The garbage can model of organizational decision making has four practical implications.[17] First, many decisions will be made by oversight or the presence of a salient opportunity. Second, political motives frequently guide the process by which participants make decisions. Participants tend to make decisions that promise to

International Organizational Behaviour

Concluded

The two pored over maps and other documents Ecopetrol had stowed in its library. The maps, Mr. Edwards recalls, showed promising features in the foothills near the town of Yopal. And the seismic information indicated a substantial oil trap. Then, too, there were the earlier Ecopetrol tests, which hadn't shown large quantities of crude in Cusiana but suggested some oil was there.

The two men wondered if most of the oil somehow leaked out of the field over time.

One way to answer that, they figured, was to go look. So they rented a truck and drove through the countryside around the Cusiana prospect. They hiked obscure trails into the hills.

Finally, after a couple of days, they decided the oil probably was still sealed underground. And Triton, in turn, applied for a permit to drill Cusiana.

At this point, DuPont Co.'s Conoco unit also began sniffing around Cusiana. But it was Triton that managed to obtain the approvals to explore the field.

This was the first step. Triton, strung out for cash, needed help. After approaching at least 70 potential partners, three companies led by Union Texas Petroleum Holdings Inc. joined Triton in 1983. But the newcomers insisted on drilling the flatlands portion of the lease rather than the foothills where Triton's people believed oil was most likely to be found. . . .

The two wells drilled by the small consortium were unsuccessful, the group broke up, and Triton was forced to search for partners again.

This time, it was tougher. Triton had to explain why it had struck out with Union Texas, as well as play down decades of negative assessments on Cusiana by other oil companies.

Triton executives flew around the world—London, Paris, Tokyo—pleading for participation from more than 80 oil companies, including Exxon Corp. and Royal Dutch/Shell Group.

"They told us it was too risky, too expensive, and that the geological features were too young," Mr. Edwards says. "We knew it was a leap of faith, but we still believed."

BP finally signed on in 1987. Known as a swashbuckler among major oil companies, BP already had been over the area almost 20 years earlier with its own people. At one time, it even owned a concession for part of what ultimately became Cusiana, but the company relinquished it in the early 1970s, Mr. Herrera says.

Now, however, the British company was willing to try again, based upon Triton's presentations and its own reassessment. Paris-based Total joined, and BP took on the role as operator, or lead partner. . . .

The group sunk its first exploratory well in late 1987, and work proceeded rapidly. But activity stopped early Sunday morning, January 16, 1988. Mr. De'Ath was awakened from a deep sleep in Bogota. Guerrillas had overrun the exploration camp and set the rig afire. They had detonated sticks of dynamite, and topped off the attack with a flurry of grenades. No one was hurt, but there was nothing left of the site.

It was months before work started again, and it wasn't until early 1989 that a major gas discovery was made. Even that didn't come off without a hitch. Crews had to rejigger everything from the pipes and valves to the consistency of the mud used to keep the bore hole open during drilling. Finally, after four tests, bingo—the gas strike was made.

source   Excerpted from A Sullivan, "Striking It Rich: Where Others Feared to Drill, One Group Hits a Gusher of Oil," *The Wall Street Journal*, January 2, 1996, pp A1, A6. Reprinted by permission of *The Wall Street Journal* © 1996 Dow Jones & Company, Inc. All Rights Reserved Worldwide.

increase their status. Third, the process is sensitive to load. That is, as the number of problems increases, relative to the amount of time available to solve them, problems are less likely to be solved. Finally, important problems are more likely to be solved than unimportant ones because they are more salient to organizational participants.[18]

Dynamics of Decision Making

Decision making is part science and part art. Accordingly, this section examines two dynamics of decision making—contingency considerations and the problem of escalation of commitment—that affect the "science" component. An understanding of these dynamics can help managers make better decisions.

Selecting Solutions: A Contingency Perspective

The previous discussion of decision-making models noted that managers typically satisfice when they select solutions. However, we did not probe how managers actually evaluate and select solutions. Let us explore the model in Figure 12–2 to better understand how individuals make decisions.

Strategies for Selecting a Solution   What procedures do decision makers use to evaluate the costs and benefits of alternative solutions? According to management experts Lee Roy Beach and Terence Mitchell, one of three approaches is used: aided-analytic, unaided-analytic, and nonanalytic.[19] Decision makers systematically use tools such as mathematical equations, calculators, or computers to analyse and evaluate alternatives within an **aided-analytic** approach. DecideRight is an example of a decision-making tool that managers can use to make aided-analytic decisions:

Aided-analytic
Using tools to make decisions.

Figure 12 – 2   A Contingency Model for Selecting a Solution

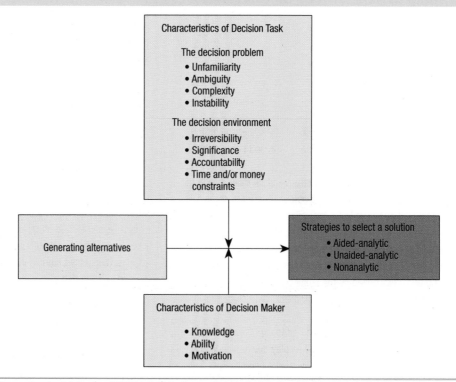

Source: Based on L R Beach and T R Mitchell, "A Contingency Model for the Selection of Decision Strategies," *Academy of Management Review*, July 1978, pp 439–44.

DecideRight is nothing less than an all-purpose decision-making system. It works both for business decisions, such as which applicant to hire or which location is best for a new store, and for personal ones, such as which car to buy or which colleges to pursue.

It does a far better job of organizing your options in a decision, and then ranking them by criteria you choose, than the traditional yellow legal pad with columns labeled "pro" and "con"— the method used by millions.

It's actually easier to use if you're comfortable at the computer. And unlike the paper method, DecideRight constantly computes a ranking of your choices no matter how often you re-evaluate them.[20]

In addition to using decision-making tools, managers may hire consultants to conduct a formal study of the problem at hand.

In contrast, decision makers rely on the confines of their minds when using an **unaided-analytic** strategy. In other words, the decision maker systematically compares alternatives, but the analysis is limited to evaluating information that can be directly processed in his or her head. Decision-making tools such as a personal computer are not used. Finally, a **nonanalytic** strategy consists of using a simple preformulated rule to make a decision. Examples are flipping a coin, habit, normal convention ("we've always done it that way"), using a conservative approach ("better safe than sorry"), or following procedures offered in instruction manuals. Both the cost and level of sophistication decrease as one moves from an aided-analytic to a nonanalytic strategy.

Determining which approach to use depends on two sets of contingency factors: characteristics of the decision task and characteristics of the decision maker (refer again to Figure 12–2).

Characteristics of the Decision Task   This set of contingency factors reflects the demands and constraints a decision maker faces. These characteristics are divided into two components: those pertaining to the specific problem and those related to the general decision environment. In general, the greater the demands and constraints encountered by a decision maker, the higher the probability that an aided-analytic approach will be used. This conclusion is consistent with results from two recent studies.

The first study conducted a series of experiments with 18–19-year-old-students. Findings revealed that the students made less consistent decisions in less predictable and unstable situations. Aided-analytic methods could have helped these individuals make more consistent decisions. The second study examined the strategic decision-making process within 24 organizations with annual sales ranging from euros 1.5 million to more than euros 3 billion. Results demonstrated that more effective decisions were made by managers who collected information and used analytical techniques than by managers who did not.[21]

The environment also restricts the type of analysis used. For instance, a study of 75 MBA students revealed that they purchased and used less information for decision making as the cost of information increased. In contrast, they purchased and used more information when they were rewarded for making good decisions. These results suggest that both the cost of information and one's accountability for a decision affect the type of analysis used to solve a problem.[22] Moreover, time constraints influence selection of a solution. Poorer decisions are bound to be made in the face of severe time pressure.

Characteristics of the Decision Maker   Chapter 5 highlighted a variety of individual differences that affect employee behaviour and performance. In the present context, knowledge, ability, and motivation affect the type of analytical procedure used by a decision maker. In general, research supports the prediction that aided-analytic strategies are more likely to be used by competent and motivated individuals.[23]

Contingency Relationships   There are many ways in which characteristics of the decision task and decision maker can interact to influence the strategy used to select a solution.[24] In choosing a strategy, decision makers compromise between their desire to make correct

Unaided-analytic

Analysis is limited to processing information in one's mind.

Nonanalytic

Using preformulated rules to make decisions.

Table 12 – 2 Contingency Relationships in Decision Making

1. Analytic strategies are used when the decision problem is unfamiliar, ambiguous, complex, or unstable.

2. Nonanalytic methods are employed when the problem is familiar, straightforward, or stable.

3. Assuming there are no monetary or time constraints, analytic approaches are used when the solution is irreversible and significant and when the decision maker is accountable.

4. Nonanalytic strategies are used when the decision can be reversed and is not very significant or when the decision maker is not held accountable.

5. As the probability of making a correct decision goes down, analytic strategies are used.

6. As the probability of making a correct decision goes up, nonanalytic strategies are employed.

7. Time and money constraints automatically exclude some strategies from being used.

8. Analytic strategies are more frequently used by experienced and educated decision makers.

9. Nonanalytic approaches are used when the decision maker lacks knowledge, ability, or motivation to make a good decision.

Source: Adapted from L R Beach and T R Mitchell, "A Contingency Model for the Selection of Decision Strategies," *Academy of Management Review,* July 1978, pp 439–44.

decisions and the amount of time and effort they put into the decision-making process. Table 12 – 2 lists contingency relationships that help reconcile these competing demands. As shown in this table, analytic strategies are more likely to be used when the problem is unfamiliar and irreversible. In contrast, nonanalytic methods are employed on familiar problems or problems in which the decision can be reversed.

Escalation of Commitment

Prior to reading any further, we would like you to read the scenario in the OB Exercise and answer the diagnostic question. The scenario describes an escalation situation. Escalation situations involve circumstances in which things have gone wrong but where the situation can possibly be turned around by investing additional time, money or effort.[25]

Escalation of commitment

Sticking to an ineffective course of action too long.

Let us return to the scenario in the OB Exercise. What was your answer? If you responded yes, you experienced what researchers call escalation of commitment. **Escalation of commitment** refers to the tendency to stick to an ineffective course of action when it is unlikely that the bad situation can be reversed. Personal examples include investing more money into an old or broken car, waiting an extremely long time for a bus to take you somewhere that you could have walked just as easily, or trying to save a disruptive interpersonal relationship that has lasted 10 years. Case studies also indicate that escalation of commitment is partially responsible for some of the worst financial losses experienced by organizations. For example, from 1966 to 1989 the Long Island Lighting Company's investment in the Shoreham nuclear power plant escalated from $65 million to $5 billion, despite a steady flow of negative feedback. The plant was never opened.[26] Actor and co-producer Kevin Kostner and producer Kevin Reynolds saw

OB EXERCISE *Making a Decision in an Escalation Situation*

As the president of an airline company, you have invested $10 million of the company's money into a research project. The purpose was to build a plane that would not be detected by conventional radar, in other words, a radar-blank plane. When the project is 90% completed, another firm begins marketing a plane that cannot be detected by radar. Also, it is apparent that

their plane is much faster and far more economical than the plane your company is building. The question is: Should you invest the last 10% of the research funds to finish your radar-blank plane?

Answer: Yes, invest the money.
No, drop the project.

Source H R Arkes and C Blumer, "The Psychology of Sunk Cost," *Organizational Behavior and Human Decision Processes,* February 1985, p 129.

how the original budget of the movie *Waterworld* escalated from $65 million to $175 million, equivalent to $1.3 million for 1 minute entertainment. *Waterworld* became the most expensive movie, at that moment (1995), ever made in history.[27] In 1997, the block-buster *Titanic* took over as the most expensive movie.

OB Researchers Jerry Ross and Barry Staw identified four reasons for escalation of commitment (see Figure 12–3). They involve psychological and social determinants, organizational determinants, project characteristics, and contextual determinants.[28]

Psychological and Social Determinants   Ego defence and individual motivations are the key psychological contributors to escalation of commitment. Individuals "throw good money after bad" because they tend to (1) bias facts so that they support previous decisions, (2) take more risks when a decision is stated in negative terms (to recover losses) rather than positive ones (to achieve gains), and (3) get too ego-involved with the project. Because failure threatens an individual's self-esteem or ego, people tend to ignore negative signs and push forward.[29]

Social pressures can make it difficult for a manager to reverse a course of action. For instance, peer pressure makes it difficult for an individual to drop a course of action when he or she publicly supported it in the past. Further, managers may continue to support bad decisions because they don't want their mistakes exposed to others. For example, a recent study showed that decision-making groups escalated their commitment to a failing course of action more when they were responsible for the initial investment than when they were not.[30]

Organizational Determinants   Breakdowns in communication, workplace politics, and organizational inertia cause organizations to maintain bad courses of action.

Project Characteristics   Project characteristics involve the objective features of a project. They have the greatest impact on escalation decisions. For example, because most projects do not reap benefits until some delayed time period, decision makers are motivated to stay with the project until the end. Thus, there is a tendency to attribute setbacks to temporary causes that are correctable with additional expenditures.[31]

Contextual Determinants   These causes of escalation are due to external political forces outside an organization's control. For instance, the continuance of the previously discussed Shoreham nuclear power plant was partially influenced by pressures from other public utilities interested in nuclear power, representatives of the nuclear power industry, and people in the federal government pushing for the development of nuclear power.[32]

Reducing Escalation of Commitment   It is important to reduce escalation of commitment because it leads to poor decision making for both individuals and groups.[33] Barry Staw and Jerry Ross, the researchers who originally identified the phenomenon of escalation, recommended several ways to reduce it:

- Set minimum targets for performance, and make decision makers compare their performance with these targets.

- Let different individuals make the initial and subsequent decisions about a project.

- Encourage decision makers to become less ego-involved with a project.

- Provide more frequent feedback about project completion and costs.

- Reduce the risk or penalties of failure.

- Make decision makers aware of the costs of persistence.[34]

Moreover, a recent study further revealed that people are more likely to escalate commitment when they fail to set budgets and when expenses are difficult to track.[35] Managers should thus be encouraged to develop and monitor project budgets.

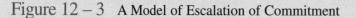

Figure 12 – 3   A Model of Escalation of Commitment

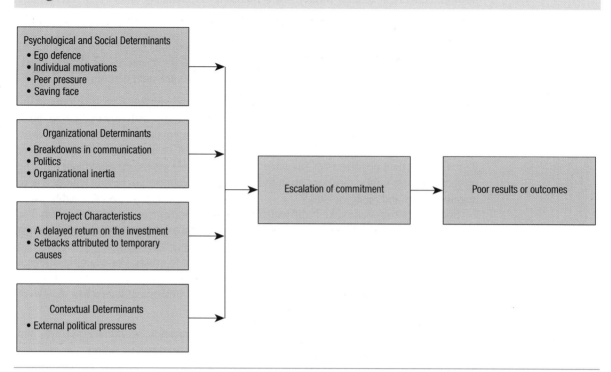

Source: Based on discussion in J Ross and B M Staw, "Organizational Escalation and Exit: Lessons from the Shoreham Nuclear Power Plant," *Academy of Management Journal,* August 1993, pp 701–32

Group Decision Making

Chapter 10 examined the unique dynamics that arise when individuals work together in groups. Groups such as committees, task forces, or review panels often play a key role in the decision-making process. Are two or more heads always better than one? Do all employees desire to have a say in the decision-making process? When and how should a manager use group decision making? This section provides the background for answering these questions, essential for gaining maximum benefits from group decision making. We discuss (1) advantages and disadvantages of group-aided decision making, (2) participative management, (3) when to use groups in decision making, and (4) group problem-solving techniques.

Advantages and Disadvantages of Group-Aided Decision Making

Including groups in the decision-making process has both pros and cons (see Table 12 – 3). On the positive side, groups contain a greater pool of knowledge, provide more varied perspectives, create more comprehension of decisions, increase decision acceptance, and create a training ground for inexperienced employees. These advantages must be balanced, however, with the disadvantages listed in Table 12–3. In doing so, managers need to determine the extent to which the advantages and disadvantages apply to the decision situation. The following three guidelines may then be applied to help decide whether groups should be included in the decision-making process:

1. If additional information would increase the quality of the decision, managers should involve those people who can provide the needed information.

2. If acceptance ȷs important, managers need to involve those individuals whose acceptance and commitment are important.

3. If people can be developed through their participation, managers may want to involve those whose development is most important.[36]

Group versus Individual Performance   Before recommending that managers involve groups in decision making, it is important to examine whether groups perform better or worse than individuals. After reviewing 61 years of relevant research, a decision-making expert concluded that "Group performance was generally qualitatively and quantitatively superior to the performance of the average individual."[37] Although subsequent research of small-group decision making generally supported this conclusion, there are five important issues to consider when using groups to make decisions:

1. Groups were less efficient than individuals. This suggests that time constraints are an important consideration in determining whether to involve groups in decision making.

2. Groups were more confident about their judgements and choices than individuals. Because group confidence is not a surrogate for group decision quality, this overconfidence can fuel groupthink—recall the discussion in Chapter 10—and a resistance to consider alternative solutions proposed by individuals outside the group.

3. Group size affected decision outcomes. Decision quality was negatively related to group size.[38]

4. Decision-making accuracy was higher when (*a*) groups knew a great deal about the issues at hand and (*b*) group leaders possessed the ability to effectively weight the group members' opinions and judgements. Groups need to give more weight to relevant and accurate judgements while downplaying irrelevant or inaccurate judgements made by its members.[40]

5. The composition of a group affects its decision-making processes and ultimately performance. For example, groups of familiar people are more likely to make better decisions when members possess a lot of unique information. In contrast, unacquainted group members should outperform groups of friends when most group members possess common knowledge.[40]

Table 12 – 3   Advantages and Disadvantages of Group-Aided Decision Making

ADVANTAGES	DISADVANTAGE
1. *Greater pool of knowledge.* A group can bring much more information and experience to bear on a decision or problem than can an individual acting alone.	1. *Social pressure.* Unwillingness to "rock the boat" and pressure to conform may combine to stifle the creativity of individual contributors.
2. *Different perspectives.* Individuals with varied experience and interests help the group see decision situations and problems from different angles.	2. *Minority domination.* Sometimes the quality of group action is reduced when the group gives in to those who talk the loudest and longest.
3. *Greater comprehension.* Those who personally experience the give-and-take of group discussion about alternative courses of action tend to understand the rationale behind the final decision.	3. *Logrolling.* Political wheeling and dealing can displace sound thinking when an individual's pet project or vested interest is at stake.
4. *Increased acceptance.* Those who play an active role in group decision making and problem solving tend to view the outcome as "ours" rather than "theirs."	4. *Goal displacement.* Sometimes secondary considerations such as winning an argument, making a point, or getting back at a rival displace the primary task of making a sound decision or solving a problem
5. *Training ground.* Less experienced participants in group action learn how to cope with group dynamics by actually being involved.	5. *"Groupthink."* Sometimes cohesive "in-groups" let the desire for unanimity override sound judgment when generating and evaluating alternative courses of action.

Source: R Kreitner, *Management*, 4th ed (Boston: Houghton Mifflin, 1989) p 238.

Additional research suggests that managers should use a contingency approach when determining whether to include others in the decision-making process. Let us now consider these contingency recommendations.

Practical Contingency Recommendations   If the decision occurs frequently, such as deciding on promotions or who qualifies for a loan, use groups because they tend to produce more consistent decisions than do individuals.[41] Given time constraints, let the most competent individual, rather than a group, make the decision. In the face of environmental threats such as time pressure and potential serious impact of a decision, groups use less information and fewer communication channels. This increases the probability of a bad decision.[42] This conclusion underscores a general recommendation that managers should keep in mind: because the quality of communication strongly affects a group's productivity, on complex tasks it is essential to devise mechanisms to enhance communication effectiveness.

Participative Management

An organization needs to maximize its workers' potential if it wants to successfully compete in the global economy. As noted by Jack Welch, CEO of General Electric, "Only the most productive companies are going to win. If you can't sell a top-quality product at the world's lowest price, you're going to be out of the game. In that environment, 6 per cent annual improvement in productivity may not be good enough anymore; you may need 8 per cent to 9 per cent."[43] Participative management and its associated employee involvement are highly touted methods for meeting this productivity challenge. Interestingly, employees also seem to desire or recognize the need for participative management. A survey of 2,408 employees, for example, revealed that almost 66 per cent desired more influence or decision-making power in their jobs.[44]

Participative management
Involving employees in various forms of decision making.

Confusion exists about the exact meaning of participative management (PM). One management expert clarified this situation by defining **participative management** as the process whereby employees play a direct role in (1) setting goals, (2) making decisions, (3) solving problems, and (4) making changes in the organization. Without question, participative management entails much more than simply asking employees for their ideas or opinions.[45]

Advocates of PM claim employee participation increases employee satisfaction, commitment, and performance. To get a fuller understanding of how and when participative management works, we begin by discussing a model of participative management.

A Model of Participative Management   Consistent with both Maslow's need theory and the job characteristics model of job design (see Chapter 7), participative management is predicted to increase motivation because it helps employees fulfil three basic needs: (1) autonomy, (2) meaningfulness of work, and (3) interpersonal contact. Satisfaction of these needs enhances feelings of acceptance and commitment, security, challenge, and satisfaction. In turn, these positive feelings supposedly lead to increased innovation and performance.[46]

Participative management does not work in all situations. The design of work, the level of trust between management and employees, and the employees' readiness to participate represent three factors that influence the effectiveness of PM. With respect to the design of work, individual participation is counterproductive when employees are highly interdependent on each other, as on an assembly line. The problem with individual participation in this case is that interdependent employees generally do not have a broad understanding of the entire production process. Participative management also is less likely to succeed when employees do not trust management. Finally, PM is more effective when employees are properly trained, prepared, and interested in participating.[47]

Research and Practical Suggestions for Managers Participative management can significantly increase employee job involvement, organizational commitment, and creativity. It can also lower role conflict and ambiguity.[48] A meta-analysis further demonstrates that participation only has a small but significant impact on both job performance and job satisfaction. This finding questions the practical value of using participative management to influence performance or satisfaction at work.[49]

So what is a manager to do? We believe that PM is not a quick-fix solution for low productivity and motivation, as some enthusiastic supporters claim. Nonetheless, since participative management is effective in certain situations, managers can increase their chances of obtaining positive results by using once again a contingency approach.[50] For example, the effectiveness of participation depends on the type of interactions between managers and employees as they jointly solve problems. Effective participation requires a constructive interaction that fosters cooperation and respect, as opposed to competition and defensiveness.[51] Managers are advised not to use participative programmes when they have destructive interpersonal interactions with their employees.

Experiences of companies implementing participative management programmes suggest three additional practical recommendations. First, supervisors and middle managers tend to resist participative management because it reduces their power and authority. It is important to gain the support and commitment from employees who have managerial responsibility. Second, a longitudinal study of *Fortune* 1000 firms in 1987, 1990, and 1993 indicated that employee involvement was more effective when it was implemented as part of a broader total quality management programme.[52] This study suggests that organizations should use participative management and employee involvement as vehicles to help them meet their strategic and operational goals as opposed to using these techniques as ends in and of themselves. Third, the process of implementing participative management must be monitored and managed by top management.[53]

When Groups should Participate in Decision Making: The Vroom/Yetton/Jago Model

Victor Vroom and Philip Yetton developed a model in 1973 to help managers determine the degree of group involvement in the decision-making process. It was later expanded by Vroom and Arthur Jago.[54] The model is prescriptive in that it specifies decision-making styles that should be effective in different situations.

Vroom and Jago's model is represented as a decision tree. The manager's task is to move from left to right along the various branches of the tree. A specific decision-making style is prescribed at the end point of each branch. Before we apply the model, however, it is necessary to consider the different decision styles managers ultimately choose from and an approach for diagnosing the problem situation.

Five Decision-Making Styles Vroom and Yetton identified five distinct decision-making styles. In Table 12–4, each style is represented by a letter. The letter indicates the basic thrust of the style. For example, A stands for *autocratic,* C for *consultive,* and G for *group.* There are several important issues to consider as one moves from an AI style to a GII style:

- The problem or decision is discussed with more people.

- Group involvement moves from merely providing data to recommending solutions.

- Group "ownership" and commitment to the solution increases.

- As group commitment increases, so does the time needed to arrive at a decision.[55]

Style choice depends on the type of problem situation.

Table 12 – 4	Management Decision Styles

AI   You solve the problem or make the decision yourself, using information available to you at that time.

AII   You obtain the necessary information from your subordinate(s), then decide on the solution to the problem yourself. You may or may not tell your subordinates what the problem is in getting the information from them. The role played by your subordinates in making the decision is clearly one of providing the necessary information to you rather than generating or evaluating solutions.

CI   You share the problem with relevant subordinates individually, getting their ideas and suggestions without bringing them together as a group. Then you make the decision that may or may not reflect your subordinates' influence.

CII   You share the problem with your subordinates as a group, collectively obtaining their ideas and suggestions. Then you make the decision that may or may not reflect your subordinates' influence.

GII   You share a problem with your subordinates as a group. Together you generate and evaluate alternatives and attempt to reach agreement (consensus) on a solution. Your role is much like that of a chairman. You do not try to influence the group to adopt "your" solution, and you are willing to accept and implement any solution that has the support of the entire group.

Source: "A New Look at Managerial Decision Making" by V H Vroom. Reprinted by permission of publisher from *Organizational Dynamics,* Spring 1973, p 67, © 1973 American Management Association, New York. All rights reserved.

Matching the Situation to Decision-Making Style   Vroom and Jago developed eight problem attributes that managers can use to diagnose a situation. They are shown at the top of the decision tree presented in Figure 12–4 and are expressed as questions. Answers to these questions lead managers along different branches, pointing the way to potentially effective decision-making styles.

Applying the Model   Because Vroom and Jago developed four decision trees, the first step is to choose one of the trees. Each tree represents a generic type of problem that managers frequently encounter. They are (1) an individual-level problem with time constraints, (2) an individual-level problem in which the manager wants to develop an employee's decision-making abilities, (3) a group-level problem in which the manager wants to develop employees' decision-making abilities, and (4) a time-driven group problem[56] (illustrated in Figure 12–4).

To use the model in Figure 12–4, start at the left side and move towards the right by asking yourself the questions associated with each decision point (represented by a box in the figure) encountered. A decision-making style is prescribed at the end of each branch.

Let us track a simple example through Figure 12–4. Suppose you have to determine the work schedule for a group of part-time workers who report to you. The first question is "How important is the technical quality of this decision?" It seems rather low. This leads us to the second question: "How important is subordinate commitment to the decision?" Assuming acceptance is important, this takes us along the branch leading to the question about commitment probability (CP). If you were to make the decision by yourself, is it reasonably certain that your subordinate(s) would be committed to the decision? A yes answer suggests you should use an AI decision-making style (see Table 12–4) and a GII style if you answered no.

Research Insights and Managerial Implications   Very little research has tested the predictive accuracy of this model. Nonetheless, research does support the earlier model developed by Vroom and Yetton in 1973.[57] For example, a study of 36 departments in a large retail department store indicated that group productivity was higher when managers used decision-making styles consistent with the model.[58] Managers thus are advised to use different decision-making styles to suit situational demands.

Figure 12 – 4   Vroom and Jago's Decision-Making Model

QR	Quality Requirement	How important is the technical quality of this decision?
CR	Commitment Requirement	How important is subordinate commitment to the decision?
LI	Leader's Information	Do you have sufficient information to make a high-quality decision?
ST	Problem Structure	Is the problem well structured?
CP	Commitment Probability	If you were to make the decision by yourself, is it reasonably certain that your subordinate(s) would be committed to the decision?
GC	Goal Congruence	Do subordinates share the organizational goals to be attained in solving this problem?
CO	Subordinate Conflict	Is conflict among subordinates over preferred solutions likely?
SI	Subordinate Information	Do subordinates have sufficient information to make a high-quality decision?

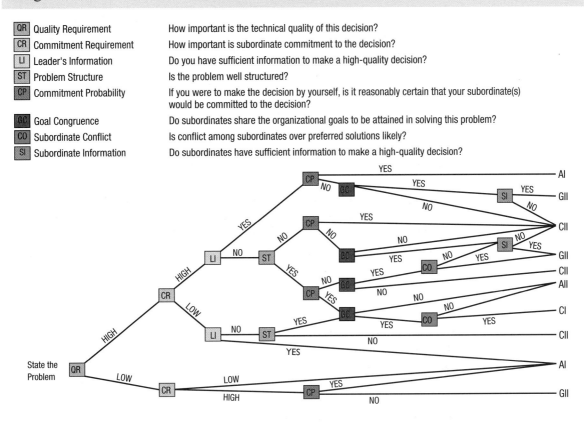

Scource: V H Vroom and A G Jago, *The New Leadership: Managing Participation in Organizations* (Englewood Cliffs, NJ: Prentice-Hall, 1988), p 184.

Also, the model can help managers determine when, and to what extent, they should involve employees in decision making. By simply being aware of the eight diagnostic questions, managers can enhance their ability to structure ambiguous problems. This should ultimately enhance the quality of managerial decisions.

Group Problem-Solving Techniques

Consensus

Presenting opinions and gaining agreement to support a decision.

Using groups to make decisions generally requires that they reach a consensus. According to a decision-making expert, a **consensus** "is reached when all members can say they either agree with the decision or have had their 'day in court' and were unable to convince the others of their viewpoint. In the final analysis, everyone agrees to support the outcome."[59] This definition indicates that consensus does not require unanimous agreement because group members may still disagree with the final decision, but are willing to work towards its success.

Groups can experience roadblocks when trying to arrive at a consensus decision. For one, groups may not generate all relevant alternatives to a problem because an individual dominates or intimidates other group members. This is both overt and/or subtle. For instance, group members who possess power and authority, such as a CEO, can be intimidating, regardless of interpersonal style, simply by being present in the room. Moreover, shyness inhibits the generation of alternatives. Shy or socially anxious individuals may withhold their input for fear of embarrassment or through lack of confidence.[60] Satisficing is another hurdle to effective group decision making. As previously noted, groups satisfice due to limited time, information, or ability to handle large amounts of information.[61] A management expert offered the following "do's" and "don'ts" for successfully achieving consensus: Groups should use active listening skills, involve as many members as possible, seek out the reasons behind arguments, and dig for the facts. At the same time, groups should not horse trade (I'll support you on this decision because you supported me on the last one), vote, or agree just to avoid "rocking the boat."[62] Voting is not encouraged because it can split the group into winners and losers.

Decision-making experts have developed three group problem-solving techniques—brainstorming, the nominal group technique, and the Delphi technique—to reduce the above roadblocks. Knowledge of these techniques can help current and future managers to use group-aided decision making more effectively. Further, the advent of computer-aided decision making enables managers to use these techniques to solve complex problems with large groups of people.

Brainstorming
Process to generate a quantity of ideas.

Brainstorming   Brainstorming was developed by A F Osborn, an advertising executive, to increase creativity.[63] **Brainstorming** is used to help groups generate multiple ideas and alternatives for solving problems. This technique is effective because it helps reduce interference caused by critical and judgemental reactions to one's ideas from other group members.

When brainstorming, a group is convened, and the problem at hand is reviewed. Individual members then are asked to silently generate ideas/alternatives for solving the problem. Silent idea generation is recommended over the practice of letting group members randomly shout out their ideas because it leads to a greater number of unique ideas.[64] Next, these ideas/alternatives are solicited and written on a board or flip chart. A second session is used to review and evaluate the alternatives. Managers are advised to follow four rules when brainstorming:

1. *Freewheeling is encouraged.* Group members are advised to offer any and all ideas they have. The wilder, the better.

2. *Criticism is discouraged.* Don't criticize during the initial stage of idea generation. Phrases such as "we've never done it that way," "it won't work," "it's too expensive," and "the boss will never agree" should not be used.

3. *Quantity of ideas is encouraged.* Managers should try to generate and write down as many ideas as possible.

4. *Combination and improvement of ideas is pursued.* Group members are advised to "piggyback" onto the ideas of others.

Brainstorming is an effective technique for generating new ideas/alternatives. It is not appropriate for evaluating alternatives or selecting solutions.

Nominal group technique
Process to generate ideas and evaluate solutions.

The Nominal Group Technique   The **nominal group technique** (NGT) helps groups generate ideas and evaluate and select solutions. NGT is a structured group meeting that follows this format:[65]

A group is convened to discuss a particular problem or issue. After the problem is understood, individuals silently generate ideas in writing. Each individual, in round-robin fashion, then offers one idea from his or her list. Ideas are recorded on a blackboard or flip chart; they are not discussed at this stage of the process. Once all ideas are elicited, the group discusses them. Anyone may criticize or defend any item. During this step, clarification is provided as well as general agreement or disagreement with the idea. The "30-second soap box" technique, which entails giving each participant a maximum of 30 seconds to argue for or against any of the ideas under consideration, can be used to facilitate this discussion. Finally, group members anonymously vote for their top choices with a weighted voting procedure (e.g., 1st choice = 3 points; 2nd choice = 2 points; 3rd choice = 1 point). The group leader then adds the votes to determine the group's choice.

Prior to making a final decision, the group may decide to discuss the top-ranked items and conduct a second round of voting.

The nominal group technique reduces the roadblocks to group decision making by (1) separating brainstorming from evaluation, (2) promoting balanced participation among group members, and (3) incorporating mathematical voting techniques in order to reach consensus. NGT has been successfully used in many different decision-making situations.

The Delphi Technique   This problem-solving method was originally developed by the Rand Corporation for technological forecasting.[66] It is now used as a multipurpose planning tool. The **Delphi technique** is a group process that anonymously generates ideas or judgements from physically dispersed experts. Unlike the NGT, experts' ideas are obtained from questionnaires as opposed to face-to-face group discussions.

Delphi technique
Process to generate ideas from physically dispersed experts.

A manager begins the Delphi process by identifying the issue(s) he or she wants to investigate. For example, a manager might want to enquire about customer demand, customers' future preferences, or the impact of locating a plant in a certain region of the country. Next, participants are identified and a questionnaire is developed. The questionnaire is sent to participants and returned to the manager. In today's computer networked environments, this often means that the questionnaires are e-mailed to participants. The manager then summarizes the responses and sends feedback to the participants. At this stage, participants are asked to (1) review the feedback, (2) prioritize the issues being considered, and (3) return the survey within a specified time period. This cycle repeats until the manager obtains the necessary information.

The Delphi technique is useful when face-to-face discussions are impractical, when disagreements and conflict are likely to impair communication, when certain individuals might severely dominate group discussion, and when groupthink is a probable outcome of the group process (recall our discussion in Chapter 10).[67]

Computer-Aided Decision Making   The purpose of computer-aided decision making is to reduce consensus roadblocks while collecting more information in a shorter period of time. There are two types of computer-aided decision-making systems: chauffeur driven and group driven.[68] Chauffeur-driven systems ask participants to answer predetermined questions on electronic keypads or dials. Live television audiences are frequently polled with this system. The computer system tabulates participants' responses in a matter of seconds.

Group-driven meetings are conducted in special facilities equipped with individual computer workstations that are networked to each other. Instead of talking, participants type their input, ideas, comments, reactions, or evaluations on their keyboards. The input simultaneously appears on a large projector screen at the front of the room, thereby enabling all participants to see all input. This computer-driven process reduces consensus roadblocks because input is anonymous, everyone gets a chance to contribute, and no one can dominate the process.

Computers basically serve three functions.

1. Access to information (databases)—group decisions support systems (GDSS) can generate information or can help in evaluating information.

2. Process structuring: computers can offer a structured format for discussions. GDSS will very often "slow down" discussions, so that more time is devoted to all the different steps and phases—GDSS can organize information.

3. A means of communication between the different group members—GDSS can communicate information.

Computers can create virtual teams, where team members are geographically dispersed and/or interact asynchronously, i.e., at different moments.

Many people resist computer-assisted decision making in groups because it lacks the richness of the face-to-face communication, with nonverbal and paraverbal cues. Literature findings on the effects on GDSS are still preliminary and the effects of GDSS are not very clear. Based on meta-analyses of experimental studies, one can conclude the following.[69]

1. It takes longer to perform the task.

2. There is more equal participation (the discussions are more 'democratic') due to an overall decrease in the participation of all members, resulting in smaller differences between highly talkative and more silent members

3. Computer groups generate more ideas of higher quality. However, imposing on a face-to-face group the same structure as the computer systems, ends in even better results.

4. Task processes are made more explicit, resulting in higher levels of conflict. Only when these conflicts can be integrated will the final results be superior to face-to-face groups.

5. GDSS are still inferior to well-trained process facilitators, although the best results are obtained when GDSS and process facilitator work together.[70]

6. Most results of laboratory studies are contingent on factors such as the group size, task structures and type of facilitation. Research has demonstrated that computer-aided decisions making produces a greater quality and quantity of ideas than either traditional brainstorming or the nominal group technique for large groups of people.[71]

Field studies reveal a much more positive picture:[72] almost all studies show a positive effect of GDSS.

Research on Group Problem-Solving Techniques

Contrary to common belief, natural face-to-face groups are not very effective in problem solving. "Face-to-face meetings are a very time-consuming feature of organizational life and, as numerous studies have concluded, have a large time-wasting potential."[73]

Research on group problem solving shows that nominal groups mostly outperform face-to-face groups.[74] In a meta-analysis nominal groups exceeded interactive groups by approximately two-thirds of a standard deviation.[75] Research particularly contradicts the belief that brainstorming is an effective technique for generating creative solutions. Brainstorming research has shown an "illusion of group effectivity." Nominal groups produce more ideas than interactive groups; the ideas are at least of the same quality. Nominal groups outperform brainstorming groups by a margin of nearly two to one.[76] Brainstorming groups have one clear advantage: members enjoy them.

Research demonstrated that computer-aided decision making produced greater quality and quantity of ideas than either traditional brainstorming or the nominal group technique for large groups of people. There were no significant advantages to group-aided decision making with groups of four to six.[77] Moreover, a recent study demonstrated that computer-aided decision making produced more ideas as group size increased from 5 to 10 members. The positive benefits of larger groups, however, were more pronounced for heterogeneous as opposed to homogeneous groups.[78]

Creativity

In light of today's need for fast-paced decisions, an organization's ability to stimulate the creativity and innovation of its employees is becoming increasingly important. Some organizations are successfully meeting this challenge; others are not. Consider the creativity and innovation occurring at Rubbermaid, ranked as the most admired company in the United States by *Fortune* in 1995:

Rubbermaid is a veritable juggernaut when it comes to putting out new products: 365 a year, or almost two new products every workday. Each year it improves over 5,000 existing products. Wolfgang Schmitt, Rubbermaid's CEO, has established lofty objectives for the firm: He wants Rubbermaid to enter a new-product category every 12 to 18 months . . . to obtain a third of its sales from products introduced within the past five years; and to obtain 25% of its revenues from markets outside the United States by the year 2000, up from the current 18%. To achieve these objectives, Schmitt will continue to pursue Rubbermaid's long-established strategy of innovation. . . .

Rubbermaid has taught its employees to think in terms of letting new products flow from the firm's core competencies—the things it does well. It encourages its managers to find out what's happening in the rest of the company, continually looking at processes and technologies.[79]

Rubbermaid is clearly meeting the challenge to innovate. This example also highlights the point that creativity and innovation are fuelled by an organization's culture and goals.[80]

To gain further insight into managing the creative process, we begin by defining creativity and highlighting the stages underlying individual creativity. This section then presents a model of organizational creativity and innovation.

Definition and Stages

Creativity

Process of developing something new or unique.

Although many definitions have been proposed, **creativity** is defined here as the process of using imagination and skill to develop a new or unique product, object, process, or thought.[81] It can be as simple as locating a new place to hang your car keys or as complex as developing a pocket-size microcomputer. This definition highlights three broad types of creativity. One can create something new (creation), one can combine or synthesize things (synthesis), or one can improve or change things (modification).

Early approaches to explaining creativity were based on differences between the left and right hemispheres of the brain. Researchers thought the right side of the brain was responsible for creativity. More recently, however, researchers have questioned this explanation:

"The left brain/right brain dichotomy is simplified and misleading," says Dr. John C Mazziotta, a researcher at the University of California at Los Angeles School of Medicine.

What scientists have found instead is that creativity is a feat of mental gymnastics engaging the conscious and subconscious parts of the brain. It draws on everything from knowledge, logic, imagination, and intuition to the ability to see connections and distinctions between ideas and things.[82]

Let us now examine the stages underlying the creativity process.

Researchers are not absolutely certain how creativity takes place. Nonetheless, we do know that creativity involves "making remote associations" between unconnected events, ideas, information stored in memory (recall our discussion in Chapter 6), or physical objects. Figure 12–5 depicts five stages underlying this process.[83]

The *preparation* stage reflects the notion that creativity starts from a base of knowledge. Experts suggest that creativity involves a convergence between tacit or implied knowledge and explicit knowledge. It was Ikujiro Nonaka who first expounded on the difference between tacit and explicit knowledge.[84] Notice how these two forms of knowledge converged to help create a new product at Matsushita Electric (see International OB).

During the *concentration* stage, an individual focuses on the problem at hand. Interestingly, Japanese companies are noted for encouraging this stage as part of a quality improvement process more than American companies. For example, the average number of suggestions per employee for improving quality and productivity is significantly lower in the typical US company than in comparable Japanese firms.[85]

Incubation is done unconsciously. During this stage, people engage in daily activities while their minds simultaneously mull over information and make remote associations.

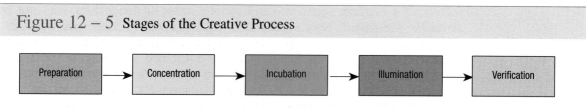

Figure 12 – 5   Stages of the Creative Process

Preparation → Concentration → Incubation → Illumination → Verification

These associations ultimately are generated in the *illumination* stage. Finally, *verification* entails going through the entire process to verify, modify, or try out the new idea.

Let us examine the stages of creativity to determine why Japanese organizations propose and implement more ideas than do American companies. To address this issue, a creativity expert visited and extensively interviewed employees from five major Japanese companies. He observed that Japanese firms have created a management infrastructure that encourages and reinforces creativity. People were taught to identify problems (discontents) on their first day of employment. In turn, discontents were referred to as "golden eggs" to reinforce the notion that it is good to identify problems.

These organizations also promoted the stages of incubation, illumination, and verification through teamwork and incentives. For example, some companies posted the golden eggs on large wall posters in the work area; employees were then encouraged to interact with each other to execute the final three stages of the creative process. Employees eventually received monetary awards for any suggestions that passed all five phases of this process.[86] This research underscores the conclusion that creativity can be enhanced by effectively managing the creativity process.

A Model of Organizational Creativity and Innovation

Organizational creativity and innovation are relatively unexplored topics within the field of OB despite their importance for organizational success. Rather than focus on group and organizational creativity, researchers historically examined the predictors of individual creativity. This final section examines a process model of organizational creativity. Knowledge of its linkages can help you to facilitate and contribute to organizational creativity.

Figure 12–6 illustrates the process underlying organizational creativity and

---

International Organizational Behaviour

Matsushita Electric Creates Breadmaker by Combining Tacit and Explicit Knowledge

In Japan, Matsushita Electric used to be known as *maneshita*, which means "copycat." Big and successful but not an innovator. That changed dramatically with the introduction of the Home Bakery, the first automatic breadmaker. A software engineer, a woman named Tanaka, recognized that with Westernization, the time had come for a breadmaker in Japan. But she knew almost nothing about baking. So she apprenticed herself to a master baker. He had all the knowledge in his fingertips, but it was very hard for him to verbalize. After watching him for two or three weeks, she went back to Matsushita to write up a set of specifications for the machine, translating his tacit knowledge into something explicit.

They made a prototype, but the bread tasted terrible. So Tanaka-san brought a group of her peers to observe the baker again. Finally, they realized that what the machine lacked was the twisting motion the baker used when kneading his dough. Incorporating that understanding enabled them to develop a hugely successful product.

The breadmaker changed the corporate culture at Matsushita. People in other divisions said, "Why can't we do that?"

Source   S Sherman, "Hot Products from Hot Tubs, or How Middle Managers Innovate," *Fortune*, April 29, 1996, pp 165–66. © 1996 Time Inc. All rights reserved.

Figure 12 – 6 A Model of Organizational Creativity and Innovation

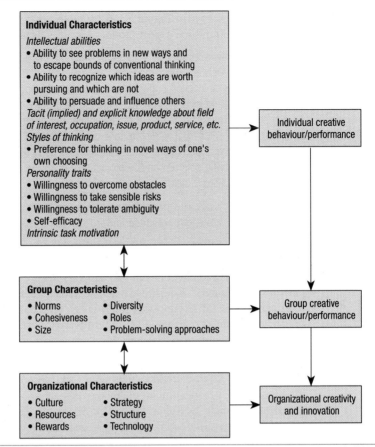

Sources: Based on discussion in R J Sternberg and R I Lubart, "Investing in Creativity," *American Psychologist*, July 1996, pp 677–88; and R W Woodman, J E Sawyer, and R W Griffin, "Toward a Theory of Organizational Creativity," *Academy of Management Review*, April 1993, pp 293–321.

innovation. It shows that organizational creativity is directly influenced by organizational characteristics and the amount of creative behaviour that occurs within work groups. In turn, a group's creative behaviour is influenced by group characteristics and the individual creative behaviour/performance of its members. Individual creative behaviour is directly affected by a variety of individual characteristics. The double-headed arrows between individual and group and between group and organizational characteristics indicate that the various characteristics all influence each other. Let us now consider the model's major components.

Individual Characteristics[87] Creative people typically march to the beat of a different drummer. They are highly motivated individuals who spend considerable time developing both tacit (implied) and explicit knowledge about their field of interest or occupation. But contrary to stereotypes, creative people are not necessarily geniuses or introverted nerds. In addition, they are not *adaptors*. "Adaptors are those who seek to solve problems by 'doing things better.' They prefer to resolve difficulties or make decisions in such a way as to have the least impact upon the assumptions, procedures, and values of the organization. . . ."[88] In contrast, creative individuals are dissatisfied with the status quo. They look for new and exciting solutions to problems. Because of this, creative organizational members can be perceived as disruptive and hard to get along with. Further, research indicates that male and female managers do not differ in levels of creativity, and there are a host of personality characteristics that are associated with creativity. These characteristics include, but are not limited to, those shown in Figure 12–6. This discussion comes to life by considering the following example.

The Post-It Notes story represents a good illustration of how the individual characteristics shown in Figure 12-6 promote creative behaviour/performance. Post-It Notes are a $200 million-a-year product for 3M Corporation:

The idea originated with Art Fry, a 3M employee who used bits of paper to mark hymns when he sat in his church choir. These markers kept falling out of the hymn books. He decided that he needed an adhesive-backed paper that would stick as long as necessary but could be removed easily. He soon found what he wanted in the 3M laboratory, and the Post-It Note was born.

Fry saw the market potential of his invention, but others did not. Market-survey results were negative; major office-supply distributors were skeptical. So he began giving samples to 3M executives and their secretaries. Once they actually used the little pieces of adhesive paper, they were hooked. Having sold 3M on the project, Fry used the same approach with other executives throughout the United States.[89]

Notice how Fry had to influence others to try out his idea. Figure 12–6 shows that creative people have the ability to persuade and influence others.

Group Characteristics   Figure 12–6 also lists six characteristics that influence the level of creative behaviour/performance exhibited by a work group. In general, group creativity is fueled by a cohesive environment that supports open interactions, diverse viewpoints, and playful surroundings.[90] Kodak, for example, created a humour room where employees can relax and have creative brainstorming sessions. The room contains joke books, videotapes of comedians, stress-reducing toys, and software for creative decision making.[91] Structured problem-solving procedures such as those previously discussed and supportive supervision also enhance creativity.[92]

Organizational Characteristics   Research and corporate examples clearly support the importance of organizational characteristics in generating organizational creativity. Organizations such as Rubbermaid, 3M, Microsoft, The Body Shop, and DuPont are all known as innovative companies that encourage creativity via the organizational characteristics shown in Figure 12–6. Consider the approach used by Anita Roddick, founder of The Body Shop, and Edgar Woolard, chairman of DuPont.

The Body Shop, which was founded in 1976, has more than 400 personal-care products being sold in 600 retail outlets worldwide:

Roddick says her organization cultivates creativity most strongly through education. Franchisees and store managers participate in extensive training at corporate headquarters in England, while managers are taught in training sessions to unleash the passions of their staff. To support this training effort, The Body Shop launches its search for creative staffers during the recruitment process.[93]

DuPont created the Center for Creativity and Innovation in 1991. Its mission is to encourage creativity throughout the organization:

Although the center is staffed by only three full-time employees, it has the support of 10 facilitators—creativity-training "volunteers" who hold full-time DuPont jobs outside the center. In this way, DuPont conducts creativity training in-house. This has two important advantages: First, the company has fewer security concerns; and second, training costs are lower.

Top management support for the center is visible and continuous. A senior manager sponsors each creative problem-solving workshop and attends as a full participant, not just an observer. The company's support for creativity training is expressed by Edgar Woolard, chairman: "We intend to provide hero status to those who show us how to get products to the marketplace more promptly and more creatively."[94]

In 1990, Lars Kolind (CEO Oticon A/S, a Danish manufacturer of high-quality hearing aids) described a new Oticon organization that would ensure future competitive advantage through creativity, innovation, and flexibility. His "spaghetti" organization had no formal structure, the only structure was provided by projects with the additional dimension that all staff were multiskilled. The results ? Lars Kolind explains:

I believe that we managed a breakthrough in creativity. We cut down our product development cycle, our time to market, by 50 per cent. Our best competitor requires a couple of years to produce a new product, but we can do it in less than 12 months.[95]

These three examples illustrate the point that organizational creativity requires resources, commitment, and a reinforcing organizational culture. Table 12–5 presents a number of suggestions that may be used to help create this culture.

Table 12 – 5   Suggestions for Improving Employee Creativity

Develop an environment that supports creative behaviour.
Try to avoid using an autocratic style of leadership.
Encourage employees to be more open to new ideas and experiences.
Keep in mind that people use different strategies, like walking around or listening to music, to foster their creativity.
Provide employees with stimulating work that creates a sense of personal growth.
Encourage employees to view problems as opportunities.
Don't let your decision-making style stifle those employees who have a different style.
Guard against employees being too involved with putting out fires and dealing with urgent short-term problems.
Make sure creative people are not bogged down with specific tasks all day long.
Allow employees to have fun and play around.
Encourage an open environment that is free from defensive behaviour.
Treat errors and mistakes as opportunities for learning.
Let employees occasionally try out their pet ideas. Provide a margin of error.
Be a catalyst instead of an obstacle.
Avoid using a negative mindset when an employee approaches you with a new idea.
Encourage creative people to communicate with one another.
Welcome diverse ideas and opinions.
Send yourself and your employees to creativity training.
Reward creative behaviour.

Source: Adapted from discussion in E Raudsepp, "101 Ways to Spark Your Employees' Creative Potential," *Office Administration and Automation,* September 1985, pp 38, 39–43, 56.

Summary of Key Concepts

1. *Discuss the four steps of the rational model of decision making.* The rational decision-making model consists of identifying the problem, generating alternative solutions, evaluating and selecting a solution, and implementing and evaluating the solution. Research indicates that decision makers do not follow the series of steps outlined in the rational model.

2. *Contrast Simon's normative model and the garbage can model of decision making.* Simon's normative model is guided by a decision maker's bounded rationality. Bounded rationality means that decision makers are bounded or restricted by a variety of constraints when making decisions. The normative model suggests that decision making is characterized

by (*a*) limited information processing, (*b*) the use of rules of thumb or shortcuts, and (*c*) satisficing.

The garbage can model of decision making assumes that decision making does not follow an orderly series of steps. In a garbage can process, decisions result from the interaction among four independent streams of events: problems, solutions, participants, and choice opportunities.

3. *Discuss the contingency relationships that influence the three primary strategies used to select solutions.* Decision makers use either an aided-analytic, unaided-analytic, or nonanalytic strategy when selecting a solution. The choice of a strategy depends on the characteristics of the decision task and the characteristics of the decision maker. In general, the

greater the demands and constraints faced by a decision maker, the higher the probability that an aided-analytic approach will be used. Aided-analytic strategies are more likely to be used by competent and motivated individuals. Ultimately, decision makers compromise between their desire to make correct decisions and the amount of time and effort they put into the decision-making process.

4. *Describe the model of escalation of commitment.* Escalation of commitment refers to the tendency to stick to an ineffective course of action when it is unlikely that a bad situation can be reversed. Psychological and social determinants, organizational determinants, project characteristics, and contextual determinants cause managers to exhibit this decision-making error.

5. S*ummarize the pros and cons of involving groups in the decision-making process.* There are both pros and cons to involving groups in the decision-making process. Although research shows that groups typically outperform the average individual, there are five important issues to consider when using groups to make decisions.
(*a*) Groups are less efficient than individuals.
(*b*) A group's overconfidence can fuel groupthink.
(*c*) Decision quality is negatively related to group size.
(*d*) Groups are more accurate when they know a great deal about the issues at hand and when the leader possesses the ability to effectively weight the group members' opinions and judgements.
(*e*) The composition of a group affects its decision-making processes and performance. In the final analysis, managers are encouraged to use a contingency approach when determining whether to include others in the decision-making process.

6. *Explain how participative management affects performance.* Participative management reflects the extent to which employees participate in setting goals, making decisions, solving problems, and making changes in the organization. Participative management is expected to increase motivation because it helps employees fulfil three basic needs: (*a*) autonomy, (*b*) meaningfulness of work, and (*c*) interpersonal contact. Participative management does not work in all situations. The design of work and the level of trust between management and employees influence the effectiveness of participative management.

7. *Review Vroom and Jago's decision-making model.* Vroom, Yetton, and Jago developed a model to help managers determine the extent to which they should include groups in the decision-making process. Through the use of decision trees, the model identifies appropriate decision-making styles for various types of managerial problems. The styles range from autocratic to highly participative.

8. *Contrast brainstorming, the nominal group technique, the Delphi technique, and computer-aided decision making.* Group problem-solving techniques facilitate better decision making within groups. Brainstorming is used to help groups generate multiple ideas and alternatives for solving problems. The nominal group technique assists groups both to generate ideas and to evaluate and select solutions. The Delphi technique is a group process that anonymously generates ideas or judgments from physically dispersed experts. The purpose of computer-aided decision making is to reduce consensus roadblocks while collecting more information in a shorter period of time.

9. *Describe the stages of the creative process.* Creativity is defined as the process of using imagination and skill to develop a new or unique product, object, process, or thought. It is not adequately explained by differences between the left and right hemispheres of the brain. There are five stages of the creative process: preparation, concentration, incubation, illumination, and verification.

10. *Explain the model of organizational creativity and innovation.* Organizational creativity is directly influenced by organizational characteristics and the creative behaviour that occurs within work groups. In turn, a group's creative behaviour is influenced by group characteristics and the individual creative behaviour/performance of its members. Individual creative behaviour is directly affected by a variety of individual characteristics. Finally, individual, group, and organizational characteristics all influence each other within this process.

Discussion Questions

1. What role do emotions play in decision making?

2. Do you think people are rational when they make decisions? Under what circumstances would an individual tend to follow a rational process?

3. Describe a situation in which you satisficed when making a decision. Why did you satisfice instead of optimize?

4. Do you think the garbage can model is a realistic representation of organizational decision making? Explain your rationale.

5. What is the most valuable lesson about selecting solutions through a contingency perspective? Explain.

6. Describe a situation in which you exhibited escalation of commitment. Why did you escalate a losing situation?

7. Do you prefer to solve problems in groups or by yourself? Why?

8. Given the intuitive appeal of participative management, why do you think it fails as often as it succeeds? Explain.

9. Do you think you are creative? Why or why not?

10. What advice would you offer a manager who was attempting to improve the creativity of his or her employees? Explain.

Personal Awareness and Growth Exercise

What Is Your Decision-Making Style?

Objectives

1. To assess your decision-making style.

2. To consider the managerial implications of your decision-making style.

Introduction

A pair of researchers developed a 25-item survey to measure an individual's decision-making style. They defined decision-making style as a learned or habitual manner of responding to a decision situation. Rather than being a personality trait, decision-making style is a habit-based propensity to respond in a certain way when making decisions. The instrument measures four decision styles. A rational decision-making style reflects the use of a thorough search and evaluation of alternatives. An intuitive decision-making style reflects the tendency to rely on hunches and feelings. A dependent decision-making style is illustrated by a search for advice, input, and direction from others. An avoidant *decision-making style* reflects the avoidance of decision making.[96] We have extracted 16 of the 25 items for this self-awareness exercise.

Instructions

The following statements reflect various ways people go about making *important* decisions. For each statement, indicate the extent to which you agree or disagree with it by selecting one number from the scale provided. Circle your response for each statement.

Remember, there are no right or wrong answers. After completing the survey, use the scoring key to compute a total score for each decision-making style.

1 = Strongly disagree
2 = Disagree
3 = Neither agree nor disagree
4 = Agree
5 = Strongly agree

1. I double-check my information sources to be sure I have the right facts before making decisions.	1—2—3—4—5
2. When making decisions, I rely upon my instincts.	1—2—3—4—5
3. I often need the assistance of other people when making important decisions.	1—2—3—4—5
4. I avoid making important decisions until the pressure is on.	1—2—3—4—5
5. I make decisions in a logical and systematic way.	1—2—3—4—5
6. When I make decisions, I tend to rely on my intuition.	1—2—3—4—5
7. I rarely make important decisions without consulting other people.	1—2—3—4—5
8. I often procrastinate when it comes to making important decisions.	1—2—3—4—5
9. My decision making requires careful thought.	1—2—3—4—5
10. I generally make decisions that feel right to me.	1—2—3—4—5
11. If I have the support of others, it is easier for me to make important decisions.	1—2—3—4—5

12. I generally make important decisions at the last minute.   1—2—3—4—5

13. When making a decision, I consider various options in terms of a specific goal.   1—2—3—4—5

14. When I make a decision, I trust my inner feelings and reactions.   1—2—3—4—5

15. I use the advice of other people in making my important decisions.   1—2—3—4—5

16. I put off making many decisions because thinking about them makes me uneasy.   1—2—3—4—5

Scoring Key

Compute a total score for each decision-making style:

Rational decision making	(1, 5, 9, and 13)	_____
Intuitive decision making	(2, 6, 10, and 14)	_____
Dependent decision making	(3, 7, 11, and 15)	_____
Avoidant decision making	(4, 8, 12, and 16)	_____

QUESTIONS FOR DISCUSSION

1. In terms of your decision-making profile, which of the four styles best represents your decision-making style (has the highest subscore)? Which is the least reflective of your style (has the lowest subscore)?

2. Do you agree with this assessment? Explain.

3. What are the advantages and disadvantages of your decision-making profile?

4. Which decision-making styles are most consistent and inconsistent with your own? How would this affect your ability to make decisions with others?

Group Exercise

Applying the Vroom/Yetton/Jago Decision-Making Model

Introduction

Vroom and Jago extended an earlier model by Vroom and Yetton to help managers determine the extent to which they should include groups in the decision-making process. To enhance your understanding of this model, we would like you to use it to analyse a brief case. You will be asked to read the case and use the information to determine an appropriate decision-making style. This will enable you to compare your solution with that recommended by Vroom and Jago. Since their analysis is presented at the end of this exercise, please do not read it until indicated.

Instructions

Your instructor will divide the class into groups of four to six. Once the group is assembled, each member should read the case presented. It depicts a situation faced by the manufacturing manager of an electronics plant.[97] The group should then use Vroom and Jago's model (refer to Figure 12–4 and Table 12–4) to arrive at a solution. At this point, it might be helpful for the group to reread the material that explains how to apply the model. Keep in mind that you move towards a solution by asking yourself the questions (at the top of Figure 12–4) associated with each relevant decision point. After the group completes its analysis, compare your solution with the one offered by Vroom and Jago.

LEADERSHIP CASE

You are a manufacturing manager in a large electronics plant. The company's management has recently installed new machines and put in a new simplified work system, but to the surprise of everyone, yourself included, the expected increase in productivity was not realized. In fact, production has begun to drop, quality has fallen off, and the number of employee separations has risen.

You do not believe that there is anything wrong with the machines. You have had reports from other companies that are using them, and they confirm this opinion. You have also had representatives from the firm that built the machines go over them, and they report that they are operating at peak efficiency.

You suspect that some parts of the new work system may be responsible for the change, but this view is not widely shared among your immediate subordinates, who are four first-line supervisors, each in charge of a section, and your supply manager. The drop in production has been variously attributed to poor training of the operators, lack of an adequate system of financial incentives, and poor morale. Clearly, this is an issue about which there is considerable depth of feeling within individuals and potential disagreement among your subordinates.

This morning you received a phone call from your division manager. He had just received your production figures for the last six months and was calling to express his concern. He indicated that the problem was yours to solve in any way that you think best, but that he would like to know within a week what steps you plan to take.

You share your division manager's concern with the falling productivity and know that your [people] are also concerned. The problem is to decide what steps to take to rectify the situation.

QUESTIONS FOR DISCUSSION

1. What decision-making style from Table 12—4 do you recommend?

2. Did you arrive at the same solution as Vroom and Jago? If not, what do you think caused the difference?

3. Based on this experience, what problems would a manager encounter in trying to apply this model?

VROOM AND JAGO'S ANALYSIS AND SOLUTION

Question:
(QR: quality requirement) = Critical/high importance
(CR: commitment requirement) = High importance
(LI: leader's information) = Probably no
(ST: problem structure) = No
(CP: commitment probability) = Probably no
(GC: goal congruence) = Probably yes
(CO: subordinate conflict) = Not a consideration for this problem.
(SI: subordinate information) = Maybe [but probably not]
        Decision-making style = CII

Notes

[1]P Hoverston, "Thiokol Wavers, Then Decides to Launch," *USA Today*, January 22, 1996, p 2A.

[2]This paragraph and the balance of the case are excepted from P Hoversten, P Edmonds, and H El Nasser, "Debate Raged Before Doomed Launch," *USA Today*, January 22, 1996, pp 1A–2A.

[3]For a review of research on the rational model, see R Lipshitz and O Bar-Ilan, "How Problems Are Solved: Reconsidering the Phase Theorem," *Organizational Behavior and Human Decision Processes*, January 1996, pp 48–60.

[4]J Cole, "Sleepless in Seattle: Onslaught of Orders Has Boeing Scrambling to Build Jets Faster," *The Wall Street Journal*, July 24, 1996, p A1.

[5]See W F Pounds, "The Process of Problem Finding," *Industrial Management Review*, Fall 1969, pp 1–19.

[6]Scenario planning is discussed by C M Perrottet, "Scenarios for the Future," *Management Review*, January 1996, pp 43–46.

[7]O Suris, "Dearborn Distress: Ford's Rebates Spell Trouble as New Models Fail to Excite Buyers," *The Wall Street Journal*, January 10, 1996, p A1.

[8]Risk preferences in decision making were investigated by M Zeelenberg, J Beattie, J Van Der Plight, and N K DeVries, "Consequences of Regret Aversion: Effects of Expected Feedback on Risky Decision Making," *Organizational Behavior and Human Decision Processes*, February 1996, pp 148–58; and Y B McDougal, "Decision Making Under Risk: Risk Preference, Monetary Goals and Information Search," *Personality & Individual Differences*, June 1995, pp 771–82.

[9]The implementation process and its relationship to decision outcomes is discussed by S J Miller, D J Hickson, and D C Wilson, "Decision-Making in Organizations," in *Handbook of Organization Studies*, eds S R Clegg, C Hardy, and W R Nord (London: Sage Publications, 1996), pp 293–312.

[10]For a review of these assumptions, see H A Simon, "A Behavioral Model of Rational Choice," *The Quarterly Journal of Economics*, February 1955, pp 99–118.

[11]H A Simon, "Rational Decision Making in Business Organizations," *The American Economic Review*, September 1979, p 510.

[12]For a complete discussion of bounded rationality, see H A Simon, *Administrative Behavior*, 2nd ed (New York: Free Press, 1957); J G March and H A Simon, *Organizations* (New York: Wiley, 1958); and H A Simon, "Altruism and Economics," *American Economic Review*, May 1993, pp 156–61.

[13]Biases associated with using shortcuts in decision making are discussed by A Tversky and D Kahneman, "Judgment under Uncertainty: Heuristics and Biases," *Science*, September 1974, pp 1124–31; and D Stahlberg, F Eller, A Maass, and D Frey, "We Knew It All Along: Hindsight Bias in Groups," *Organizational Behavior and Human Decision Processes*, July 1995, pp 46–58.

[14]The model is discussed in detail in M D Cohen, J G March, and J P Olsen, "A Garbage Can Model of Organizational Choice," *Administrative Science Quarterly*, March 1971, pp 1–25.

[15]Ibid., p 2.

[16]Results can be found in B Levitt and C Nass, "The Lid on the Garbage Can: Institutional Constraints on Decision Making in the Technical Core of College-Text Publishers," *Administrative Science Quarterly*, June 1989, pp 190–207.

[17]This discussion is based on material presented by J G March and R Weissinger-Baylon, *Ambiguity and Command* (Marshfield, MA: Pitman Publishing, 1986), pp 11–35.

[18]Simulated tests of the garbage can model were conducted by M Masuch and P LaPotin, "Beyond Garbage Cans: An AI Model of Organizational Choice," *Administrative Science Quarterly*, March 1989, pp 38–67; and M B Mandell, "The Consequences of Improving Dissemination in Garbage-Can Decision Processes," *Knowledge: Creation, Diffusion, Utilization*, March 1988, pp 343–61.

[19]For a complete discussion, see L R Beach and T R Mitchell, "A Contingency Model for the Selection of Decision Strategies," *Academy of Management Review*, July 1978, pp 439–44.

[20]W S Mossberg, "Personal Technology: In Time for Elections, Software to Help You Make Up Your Mind," *The Wall Street Journal*, February 8, 1996, p B1.

[21]Results can be found in N Harvey, "Why Are Judgments Less Consistent in Less Predictable Task Situations?" *Organizational Behavior and Human Decision Processes*, September 1995, pp 247–63; and J W Dean, Jr., and M P Sharfman, "Does Decision Process Matter? A Study of Strategic Decision-Making Effectiveness," *Academy of Management Journal*, April 1996, pp 368–96.

[22]Results from this study can be found in S W Gilliland, N Schmitt, and L Wood, "Cost-Benefit Determinants of Decision Process and Accuracy," *Organizational Behavior and Human Decision Processes*, November 1993, pp 308–30.

[23]See P E Johnson, S Graziolo, K Jamal, and I A Zualkernan, "Success and Failure in Expert Reasoning," *Organizational Behavior and Human Decision Processes*, November 1992, pp 173–203.

[24]Two recent studies were conducted by S B Sitkin and L R Weingart, "Determinants of Risky Decision-Making Behavior: A Test of the Mediating Role of Risk Perceptions and Propensity," *Academy of Management Journal*, December 1995, pp 1573–92; and D J Devine and S W J Kozlowski, "Domain-Specific Knowledge and Task Characteristics in Decision Making," *Organizational Behavior and Human Decision Processes*, December 1995, pp 294–306.

[25]A thorough discussion of escalation situations can be found in B M Staw and J Ross, "Behavior in Escalation Situations: Antecedents, Prototypes, and Solutions," in *Research in*

Organizational Behavior, vol 9, eds L L Cummings and B M Staw (Greenwich, CT: JAI Press, 1987), pp 39–78

[26]The details of this case are discussed in J Ross and B M Staw, "Organizational Escalation and Exit: Lessons from the Shoreham Nuclear Power Plant," *Academy of Management Journal,* August 1993, pp 701–32.

[27]Based on and translated from "Een Slag in Het Water," *Knack,* 1995, October 18, p 84.

[28]See Ross and Staw, "Organizational Escalational and Exit: Lessons from the Shoreham Nuclear Power Plant."

[29]Psychological determinants of escalation are discussed by J Brockner, "The Escalation of Commitment to a Failing Course of Action: Toward Theoretical Progress," *Academy of Management Review,* January 1992, pp 39–61; and J Schaubroeck and S Williams, "Type A Behavior Pattern and Escalating Commitment," *Journal of Applied Psychology,* October 1993, pp 862–67.

[30]Results can be found in R W Rutledge, "Escalation of Commitment in Groups and the Moderating Effects of Information Framing," *Journal of Applied Business Research,* Spring 1995, pp 17–23.

[31]See H Garland, C A Sandefur, and A C Rogers, "De-Escalation of Commitment in Oil Exploration: When Sunk Costs and Negative Feedback Coincide," *Journal of Applied Psychology,* December 1990, pp 721–27; and H Garland, "Throwing Good Money after Bad: The Effect of Sunk Costs on the Decision to Escalate Commitment to an Ongoing Project," *Journal of Applied Psychology,* December 1990, pp 728–32.

[32]See Ross and Staw, "Organizational Escalation and Exit: Lessons from the Shoreham Nuclear Power Plant."

[33]Escalation among individuals and groups was examined by J Schaubroeck and E Davis, "Prospect Theory Predictions When Escalation Is Not the Only Chance to Recover Sunk Costs," *Organizational Behavior and Human Decision Processes,* January 1994, pp 59–82; and G Whyte, "Escalating Commitment in Individual and Group Decision Making: A Prospect Theory Approach," *Organizational Behavior and Human Decision Processes,* April 1993, pp 430–55.

[34]See Staw and Ross, "Behavior in Escalation Situations: Antecedents, Prototypes, and Solutions"; and W S Silver and T R Mitchell, "The Status Quo Tendency in Decision Making," *Organizational Dynamics,* Spring 1990, pp 34–36.

[35]See C Heath, "Escalation and De-escalation of Commitment in Response to Sunk Costs: The Role of Budgeting in Mental Accounting," *Organizational Behavior and Human Decision Processes,* April 1996, pp 38–54.

[36]These guidelines were derived from G P Huber, *Managerial Decision Making* (Glenview, IL: Scott, Foresman, 1980), p 149.

[37]G W Hill, "Group versus Individual Performance: Are N + 1 Heads Better than One?" *Psychological Bulletin,* May 1982, p 535.

[38]These conclusions were based on the following studies: J H Davis, "Some Compelling Intuitions about Group Consensus Decisions, Theoretical and Empirical Research, and Interpersonal Aggregation Phenomena: Selected Examples, 1950–1990," *Organizational Behavior and Human Decision Processes,* June 1992, pp 3–38; and J A Sniezek, "Groups Under Uncertainty: An Examination of Confidence in Group Decision Making," *Organizational Behavior and Human Decision Processes,* June 1992, pp 124–55.

[39]Supporting results can be found in J R Hollenbeck, D R Ilgen, D J Sego, J Hedlund, D A Major, and J Phillips, "Multilevel Theory of Team Decision Making: Decision Performance in Teams Incorporating Distributed Expertise," *Journal of Applied Psychology,* April 1995, pp 292–316.

[40]See D H Gruenfeld, E A Mannix, K Y Williams, and M A Neale, "Group Composition and Decision Making: How Member Familiarity and Information Distribution Affect Process and Performance," *Organizational Behavior and Human Decision Processes,* July 1996, pp 1–15.

[41]This finding was obtained by P Chalos and S Pickard, "Information Choice and Cue Use: An Experiment in Group Information Processing," *Journal of Applied Psychology,* November 1985, pp 634–41.

[42]See D L Gladstein and N P Reilly, "Group Decision Making under Threat: The Tycoon Game," *Academy of Management Journal,* September 1985, pp 613–27.

[43]"Jack Welch's Lessons for Success," *Fortune,* January 25, 1993, p 86.

[44]Results are presented in J T Delaney, "Workplace Cooperation: Current Problems, New Approaches," *Journal of Labor Research,* Winter 1996, pp 45–61.

[45]See D Pojidaeff, "Human Productivity and Pride in Work: The Core Principles of Participative Management," *Journal for Quality and Participation,* December 1995, pp 44–47; and N A Holland, "A Pathway to Global Competitiveness and Total Quality: Participative Management," *Journal for Quality and Participation,* September 1995, pp 58–62.

[46]For an extended discussion of this model, see M Sashkin, "Participative Management Is an Ethical Imperative," *Organizational Dynamics,* Spring 1984, pp 4–22.

[47]Employee involvement training was investigated by P E Tesluk, J L Farr, J E Mathieu, and R J Vance, "Generalization of Employee Involvement Training to the Job Setting: Individual and Situational Effects," *Personnel Psychology,* Autumn 1995, pp 607–32.

[48]Supporting results can be found in C R Leana, R S Ahlbrandt, and A J Murrell, "The Effects of Employee Involvement Programs on Unionized Workers' Attitudes, Perceptions, and Preferences in Decision Making," *Academy of Management Journal,* October 1992, pp 861–73; and D Plunkett, "The Creative Organization: An Empirical Investigation of the Importance of Participation in Decision Making," *The Journal of Creative Behavior,* Second Quarter 1990, pp 140–48. Results pertaining to role conflict and ambiguity can be found in C S Smith and M T Brannick, "A Role and Expectancy Model of Participative Decision Making: A Replication and Theoretical Extension," *Journal of Organizational Behavior,* March 1990, pp 91–104.

[49]See J A Wagner III, "Participation's Effects on Performance and Satisfaction: A Reconsideration of Research Evidence," *Academy of Management Review,* April 1994, pp 312–30.

[50]See E A Locke, D M Schweiger, and G R Latham, "Participation in Decision Making: When Should It Be Used?" *Organizational Dynamics,* Winter 1986, pp 65–79.

[51]A thorough discussion of this issue is provided by W A Randolph, "Navigating the Journey to Empowerment," *Organizational Dynamics,* Spring 1995, pp 19–32.

[52]Results can be found in S A Mohrman, E E Lawler III, and G E Ledford, Jr., "Organizational Effectiveness and the Impact of Employee Involvement and TQM Programs: Do Employee Involvement and TQM Programs Work?" *Journal for Quality and Participation,* January/February 1996, pp 6–10.

[53]See R Rodgers, J E Hunter, and D L Rogers, "Influence of Top Management Commitment on Management Program Success," *Journal of Applied Psychology,* February 1993, pp 151–55.

[54]See V H Vroom and P W Yetton, *Leadership and Decision Making* (Pittsburgh, PA: University of Pittsburgh Press, 1973); and V H Vroom and A G Jago, *The New Leadership: Managing Participation in Organizations* (Englewood Cliffs, NJ: Prentice-Hall, 1988), p 184.

[55]See N B Wright, "Leadership Styles: Which Are Best When?" *Business Quarterly,* Winter 1984, pp 20–23.

[56]For a complete discussion of these decision trees, see Vroom and Jago, *The New Leadership: Managing Participation in Organizations.*

[57]Supportive results can be found in R H G Field and R J House, "A Test of the Vroom–Yetton Model Using Manager and Subordinate Reports," *Journal of Applied Psychology,* June 1990, pp 362–66; and A Crouch and P Yetton, "Manager Behaviour, Leadership Style, and Subordinate Performance: An Empirical Extension of the Vroom–Yetton Conflict Rule," *Organizational Behavior and Human Decision Processes,* June 1987, pp 384–96.

[58]See R J Paul and Y M Ebadi, "Leadership Decision Making in a Service Organization: A Field Test of the Vroom–Yetton Model," *Journal of Occupational Psychology,* September 1989, pp 201–11.

[59]G M Parker, *Team Players and Teamwork: The New Competitive Business Strategy* (San Francisco, CA: Jossey-Bass, 1990).

[60]Results can be found in L M Camacho and P B Paulus, "The Role of Social Anxiousness in Group Brainstorming," *Journal of Personality and Social Psychology,* June 1995, pp 1071–80.

[61]Methods for increasing group consensus were investigated by R L Priem, D A Harrison, and N K Muir, "Structured Conflict and Consensus Outcomes in Group Decision Making," *Journal of Management,* 1995, pp 691–710.

[62]These recommendations were obtained from Parker, *Team Players and Teamwork: The New Competitive Business Strategy.*

[63]See A F Osborn, *Applied Imagination: Principles and Procedures of Creative Thinking,* 3rd ed (New York: Scribners, 1979).

[64]See P B Paulus, T S Larey, and A H Ortega, "Performance and Perceptions of Brainstormers in an Organizational Setting," *Basic and Applied Social Psychology,* August 1995, pp 249–65; and R Zemke, "In Search of . . .: Are Your Quality Teams Getting Tired of Using Traditional Brainstorming to Solve Problems? It's Not the Only Way to Generate Creative Solutions," *Training,* January 1993, pp 46–52.

[65]A complete description of the nominal group technique can be found in A L Delbecq, A H Van de Ven, and D H Gustafson, *Group Techniques for Program Planning: A Guide to Nominal Group and Delphi Processes* (Glenview, IL: Scott, Foresman, 1975).

[66]See N C Dalkey, D L Rourke, R Lewis, and D Snyder, *Studies in the Quality of Life: Delphi and Decision Making* (Lexington, MA: Lexington Books: D C Heath and Co, 1972).

[67]Benefits of the Delphi technique are discussed by N I Whitman, "The Committee Meeting Alternative: Using the Delphi Technique," *Journal of Nursing Administration,* July/August 1990, pp 30–36.

[68]A thorough description of computer-aided decision-making systems is provided by M C Er and A C Ng, "The Anonymity and Proximity Factors in Group Decision Support Systems," *Decision Support Systems,* May 1995, pp 75–83; and A LaPlante, "Brainstorming," *Forbes,* October 25, 1993, pp 45–61.

[69]I Benbasat and L Lim, "The Effects of Group, Task, Context and Technology Variables on the Usefulness of Group Support Systems," *Small Group Research,* vol 24, no 4, 1993, pp 430–62.

[70]For further information on group and process facilitators, see R Anson, R Bostrom, and B Wynne, "An Experiment Assessing Group Support System and Facilitator Effects on Meeting Outcomes," *Management Science,* vol 41, no 2, 1995, pp 189–208.

[71]The results can be found in RB Gallupe, W H Cooper, M Grise, and L M Bastianutti, "Blocking Electronic Brainstorms," *Journal of Applied Psychology,* February 1994, pp 77–86; A R Dennis and J S Valacich, Computer brainstorms: more heads are better than one, *Journal of Applied Psychology,* August 1993, pp 531–7; and R B Gallupe, A R Dennis, W H Cooper, J S Vlacich, L M Bastianutti, and J F Nunamaker, Jr, "Electronic Brainstorming and Group Size," *Academy of Management Journal,* June 1992, pp 350–69.

[72]R B Gallupe et al."Electronic Brainstorming and Group Sizing."

[73]For further information on group or process facilitators, see R Anson, R Bostrom, and B Wynne, "An Experiment Assessing Group Support System and Facilitator Effects on Meeting Outcomes," *Management Science,* vol 41, no 2, 1995, pp 189–208.

[74]For more information, see M Diehl, and W Stroebe, "Productivity Loss in Brainstorming Groups: toward the Solution of a Riddle," *Journal of Personality and Social Psychology,* vol 53, 1987, pp 497–509; and R A Guzzo, "Group Decision Making and Group Effectiveness in Organizations," in ed P. S. Goodman, *Design Effective Work Groups* (San Francisco: Jossey-Bass, 1986), pp 34–71.

[75]B Mullen, C Johnson, and E Salas, "Productivity Loss in Brainstorming Groups: A Meta-Analytic Integration," *Basic and Applied Social Psychology,* vol 12, 1991, pp 3–23.

[76]For more information, see M Diehl and W Stroebe, "Productivity loss in brainstorming groups: toward the solution of a riddle," *Journal of Personality and Social Psychology,* vol 53, pp 497–509; and R A Guzzo, "Group Decision Making and Group Effectiveness in Organizations," in *Design Effective Work Groups* (ed P. S. Goodman, San Francisco: Jossey-Bass, 1986), pp 34–71.

[77]Results can be found in J S Valacich and C Schwenk, "Devil's Advocacy and Dialectical Inquiry Effects on Face-to-Face and Computer-Mediated Group Decision Making," *Organizational Behavior and Human Decision Processes,* August 1995, pp 158–73; R B Gallupe, W H Cooper, M Grise, and L M Bastianutti, "Blocking Electronic Brainstorms," and A R Dennis and J S Valacich, "Computer Brainstorms: More Heads Are Better than One," *Journal of Applied Psychology,* August 1993, pp 531–37.

[78]This study was conducted by J S Valacich, B C Wheeler, B E Mennecke, R Wachter, "The Effects of Numerical and Logical Group Size on Computer-Mediated Idea Generation," *Organizational Behavior and Human Decision Processes,* June 1995, pp 318–29.

[79]J M Higgins, "Innovate or Evaporate: Seven Secrets of Innovative Corporations," *The Futurist,* September–October 1995, pp 42–43.

[80]The relationship between organizational culture and creativity is discussed by D Dougherty, "Organizing for Innovation," in *Handbook of Organization Studies,* eds S R Clegg, C Hardy, and W R Nord (London: Sage Publications, 1996), pp 424–39; O Harari, "Mind Matters," *Management Review,* January 1996, pp 47–49; and L K Gundry, J R Kickul, and C W Prather, "Building the Creative Organization," *Organizational Dynamics,* Spring 1994, pp 22–36.

[81]This definition was adapted from one provided by R K Scott, "Creative Employees: A Challenge to Managers," *Journal of Creative Behavior,* First Quarter, 1995, pp 64–71.

[82]E T Smith, "Are You Creative?" *Business Week,* September 30, 1985, pp 81–82. For a review of research about the left and right hemispheres of the brain, see T Hines, "Left Brain/Right Brain Mythology and Implications for Management and Training," *Academy of Management Review,* October 1987, pp 600–6.

[83]These stages are thoroughly discussed by E Glassman, "Creative Problem Solving," *Supervisory Management,* January 1989, pp 21–26.

[84]I Nonaka and H Takeuchi, *The Knowledge Creating Company* (London: Oxford University Press, 1995); I Nonaka, "A Dynamic Theory of Organizational Knowledge Creation," *Organization Science,* vol 5, no 1, February 1994, pp 14–37; R R Nelson and S G Winter, *An Evolutionary Theory of Economic Change*

(Cambridge, MA: The Belknap Press of Harvard University Press, 1982); and L Prusak, *Knowledge in Organizations* (Boston: Butterworth-Heinemann, 1997)

[85]Details of this study can be found in M Basadur, "Managing Creativity: A Japanese Model," *Academy of Management Executive,* May 1992, pp 29–42.

[86]Ibid.

[87]This discussion is based on research reviewed by R J Sternberg and T I Lubart, "Investing in Creativity," *American Psychologist,* July 1996, pp 677–88; and R W Woodman, J E Sawyer, and R W Griffin, "Toward a Theory of Organizational Creativity," *Academy of Management Review,* April 1993, pp 293–321.

[88]T A Matherly and R E Goldsmith, "The Two Faces of Creativity," *Business Horizons,* September–October 1985, p 9.

[89]Higgins, "Innovate or Evaporate: Seven Secrets of Innovative Corporations," p 46.

[90]See Woodman, Sawyer, and Griffin, "Toward a Theory of Organizational Creativity"; and R Henkoff, "Jamming: The Road to Creativity," *Fortune,* September 9, 1996, p 183.

[91]See S Caudron, "Humor Is Healthy in the Workplace," *Personnel Journal,* June 1992, pp 63–66.

[92]See G R Oldham and A Cummings, "Employee Creativity: Personal and Contextual Factors at Work," *Academy of Management Journal,* June 1996, pp 607–34; P L Roth, L L F Schleifer, and F S Switzer, "Nominal Group Technique–An Aid in Implementing TQM," *CPA Journal,* May 1995, pp 68–69.

[93]L K Gundry, J R Kickul, and C W Prather, "Building the Creative Organization," *Organizational Dynamics,* Spring 1994, p 26.

[94]Gundry, Kickul, and Prather, "Building the Creative Organization," p 32.

[95]"The Revolution at Oticon: Creating a 'Spaghetti' Organization," *Research-Technology-Management*, 1996, September–October, vol 39, no 5, pp 54.

[96]The survey was adapted from S G Scott and R A Bruce, "Decision-Making Style: The Development and Assessment of a New Measure," *Educational and Psychological Measurement,* October 1995, pp 818–31. Copyright © 1995 by Sage Publications. Reprinted by permission of Sage Publications, Inc.

[97]Reprinted by permission of the publisher, "A New Look at Managerial Decision Making," V H Vroom, *Organizational Dynamics,* Spring 1973, p 72,©1973 American Management Association, New York. All rights reserved.

Thirteen

Teams and Teamwork for the 21st Century

LEARNING OBJECTIVES

When you finish studying the material in this chapter, you should be able to:

1. Explain how a work group becomes a team.

2. Identify and describe the four types of work teams.

3. Explain the ecological model of work team effectiveness.

4. Discuss why teams fail.

5. List at least three things managers can do to build trust.

6. Distinguish two types of group cohesiveness, and summarize cohesiveness research findings.

7. Contrast quality circles and self-managed teams.

8. Discuss what must be done to set the stage for self-managed teams.

9. Describe high-performance teams.

Geert Goethals is head of the "Vehicle Design" department at Volvo Europe Truck in Belgium. He emphasizes the importance of continually being one step ahead of the competitors. His department saw an increase in the frequency of adjustments made to the models over the past few years. In order to get the job done in a more efficient way Aeropa, a consulting bureau was asked to analyse and improve the development process. They suggested a dramatic change, a time reduction of 50 per cent was possible but only when "concurrent engineering" was applied.

Concurrent engineering is an organizational technique that enables the company to parallel the different development stages, instead of using a traditional sequential order. All parties involved are gathered from the beginning of the project: Development, production, marketing departments, and even the suppliers work together at the same time. "It is absolutely essential that all the product specifications can be frozen by the ending of the pre-study," says Geert Goethals. "It is also important that a multidisciplinary team, with a far reaching decision competence, is put in charge of the operation. By doing so, one can simplify the communication structure. It's evident that top management must fully support the concept of concurrent engineering and place all necessary means at its disposal."[1]

Concurrent engineering contrasts sharply with the traditional approach to designing new products, in which plans and drawings originate in the engineering department, pass on to production, then to marketing, and so on. This is commonly referred to as the "throwing it over the wall" method of building a new product, meaning little communication goes on between each department as the product travels from function to function. In fact, if you ever end up at a cocktail party full of engineers, you'll win instant recognition as a savvy player if you deplore the fuzzy-headed thinking of the "throwing it over the wall" approach. (Don't laugh, it could happen.)

The problem with throwing it over the wall was that designers sometimes created a widget on paper that couldn't actually be built by the production department. Then they had to go back to the drawing board, as it were, and keep fine-tuning the widget until the production department was happy. This repetitive, or iterative, process was a lot like taking two steps forward and one step back. It was expensive, inefficient, and often did not result in well-made, well-designed products that customers wanted.

In concurrent engineering, on the other hand, all the players from different departments get together to design a product. The design engineers, the production engineers, the quality-assurance experts, the reliability specialists, and the marketing professionals decide together what the product will look like. From an engineering perspective, that seems like a logical and simple solution to the problems created by the traditional approach. Of course, when you add humans to the mix, it can get messy.

If you suspect that any product coming out of a concurrent-engineering team is doomed to resemble a camel—the infamous horse designed by committee—that hasn't proven to be the case in practice. Part of the reason may be that engineers tend to keep teams on a pragmatic path. Also, getting everyone's input doesn't always mean the group has to reach consensus, though that is often the objective. "In some cases, you don't even try for consensus," says Floyd Williams, organization adviser for Boeing's 777 project, in which the company used concurrent engineering to design a new jetliner. When teams hit an impasse, he adds, the team member responsible for that part of the design is the final authority.

Concurrent-engineering teams tend to be small groups; typically, they are made up of between 8 and 15 people, depending on the complexity of the product or project. The trick is hitting the right balance. The pertinent specialists must be on the team, but the group can't be so big that people can't work together well.[2]

Discussion Question

What is the link between team-based concurrent engineering and product quality?

T*eams* and *teamwork* are popular terms in management circles these days. Cynics might dismiss teamwork as just another management fad or quick-fix gimmick. But a closer look reveals a more profound and durable trend. For instance, former English professor Martin Jack Rosenblum finds fulfilment in Harley-Davidson's motorcycle operations where teamwork is a central feature:

What Rosenblum found at Harley was camaraderie, teamwork, and the sense of accomplishment that made him feel like a contributor to his microcosm. Says Rosenblum, a bearded long-hair who likes to wear snakeskin boots and cowboy shirts to his job as the archivist at Harley's Milwaukee headquarters: "For the first time in my life I feel like I'm part of a community. Harley is the university I've always been looking for."

When Rosenblum was a professor at the University of Wisconsin, he hated all the politics and backstabbing and despaired at all the ineffectual intellectual banter. It was, he says, diametrically opposed to effective teamwork. During those years in the 1980s, he developed an ulcer that nearly killed him. But once he found a more open, goal-oriented environment at Harley, his life improved.[3]

The team approach to managing organizations is having diverse and substantial impacts on organizations and individuals. Teams promise to be a cornerstone of progressive management for the foreseeable future. According to management expert Peter Drucker, tomorrow's organizations will be flatter, information based, and organized around teams.[4] This means managers will need to polish their team skills. This opinion was bolstered by a 1995 survey of human resource executives in which 44 per cent called for *more teamwork* as a change employees need to make to achieve today's business goals.[5]

Examples of the trend towards teams and teamwork abound. Consider this global sampling from recent business articles:

- *Siemens, the euros 60-billion-a-year German manufacturing company.* "... a new generation of managers is fostering cooperation across the company: They are setting up teams to develop products and attack new markets. They are trying hiking expeditions and weekend workshops to spur ideas and new work methods."[6]

- *Motorola's walkie-talkie plants in Penang, Malaysia, and Plantation, Florida.* "The goal, pursued by Motorola worldwide, is to get employees at all levels to forget narrow job titles and work together in teams to identify and act on problems that hinder quality and productivity. . . . New applicants are screened on the basis of their attitude toward 'teamwork.' " [7]

- *Fiat's new auto plant in Melfi, Italy.* "Fiat slashed the layers between plant managers and workers and spent euros 64 million training its 7,000 workers and engineers to work in small teams. Now, the 31 independent teams—with 15 to 100 workers apiece—oversee car-assembly tasks from start to finish."[8]

Like Siemens and Motorola, Fiat has staked its future competitiveness on teams and total quality management.

Emphasis in this chapter is on tapping the full and promising potential of work groups. We will (1) identify different types of work teams, (2) introduce a model of team effectiveness, (3) discuss keys to effective teamwork—such as trust, (4) explore applications of the team concept, and (5) review team-building techniques.

Work Teams: Types, Effectiveness, and Stumbling Blocks

A general typology of teams

Jon R Katzenbach and Douglas K Smith, management consultants at McKinsey & Company, say it is a mistake to use the terms *group* and *team* interchangeably. After studying many different kinds of teams—from athletic to corporate to military—they concluded that successful teams tend to take on a life of their own. Katzenbach and Smith define a **team** as "a small number of people with complementary skills who are committed to a common purpose, performance goals, and approach for which they hold themselves mutually accountable."[9] Relative to Tuckman's theory of group development in Chapter 10—forming, storming, norming, performing, and adjourning—teams are task groups that have matured to the *performing* stage. Because of conflicts over power and authority and unstable interpersonal relations, many work groups never qualify as a real team.[10] Katzenbach and Smith clarified the distinction this way: "The essence of a team is common commitment. Without it, groups perform as individuals; with it, they become a powerful unit of collective performance."[11] (See Table 13–1.)

Team

Small group with complementary skills who hold themselves mutually accountable for common purpose, goals, and approach.

When Katzenbach and Smith refer to "a small number of people" in their definition, they mean between 2 and 25 team members. They found effective teams to typically have fewer than 10 members. This conclusion was echoed in a recent survey of 400 workplace team members in the United States and Canada: "The average North American team consists of 10 members. Eight is the most common size."[12]

Goals   Setting performance goals increases performance. To what extent is this valid for groups? Do groups with difficult and specific goals perform better than groups with easy

Table 13 – 1   The Evolution of a Team

A work group becomes a team when

1. *Leadership* becomes a shared activity.
2. *Accountability* shifts from strictly individual to both individual and collective.
3. The group develops its own *purpose* or mission.
4. *Problem solving* becomes a way of life, not a part-time activity.
5. *Effectiveness* is measured by the group's collective outcomes and products.

Source: Condensed and adapted from J R Katzenbach and D K Smith, *The Wisdom of Teams: Creating the High-Performance Organization* (Boston: Harvard Business School Press, 1993), p 214.

or vague goals? A meta-analysis of 26 effect sizes, derived from 10 different studies, showed that the mean performance of groups with goals was one standard deviation higher than the performance of groups without goals.[13]

Qualitative reviews find a positive effect of group goals on group performance in 93 per cent of the studies. Goal specificity seems to be the most important characteristic: 95 per cent of the studies using specific goals find positive results, but only 50 per cent of the studies not clarifying goal specificity yielded positive effects.[14]

Team Types   Work teams are created for various purposes and thus face different challenges. Managers can deal more effectively with those challenges when they understand how teams differ. A helpful way of sorting things out is to consider a typology of work teams developed by Eric Sundstrom and his colleagues.[15] Four general types of work teams listed in Table 13 – 2 are (1) advice, (2) production, (3) project, and (4) action. Each of these labels identifies a basic *purpose*. For instance, advice teams generally make recommendations for managerial decisions. Less commonly do they actually make final decisions. In contrast, production and action teams carry out management's decisions.

Four key variables in Table 13 – 2 deal with technical specialization, coordination, work cycles, and outputs. Technical specialization is low when the team draws upon members' general experience and problem-solving ability. It is high when team members are required to apply technical skills acquired through higher education and/or extensive training. The degree of coordination with other work units is determined by the team's relative independence (low coordination) or interdependence (high coordination). Work cycles are the amount of time teams need to discharge their missions. The various outputs listed in Table 13 – 2 are intended to illustrate real-life impacts. A closer look at each type of work team is in order.[16]

Advice Teams   As their name implies, advice teams are created to broaden the information base for managerial decisions. Quality circles, discussed later, are a prime example because they facilitate suggestions for quality improvement from volunteer production or service workers. Advice teams tend to have a low degree of technical specialization. Coordination is also low because advice teams work pretty much on their own. Ad hoc committees (e.g., the annual picnic committee) have shorter life cycles than standing committees (e.g., the grievance committee).

Production Teams   This second type of team is responsible for performing day-to-day operations. Minimal training for routine tasks accounts for the low degree of technical specialization. But coordination typically is high because work flows from one team to another. For example, railroad maintenance crews require fresh information about needed repairs from train crews.

Project Teams   Projects require creative problem solving, often involving the application of specialized knowledge. For example, Boeing's 777 jumbo jet was designed by project teams consisting of engineering, manufacturing, marketing, finance, and customer service specialists. State-of-the-art computer modelling programmes allowed

Table 13 – 2   Four General Types of Work Teams and Their Outputs

TYPES AND EXAMPLES	DEGREE OF TECHNICAL SPECIALIZATION	DEGREE OF COORDINATION WITH OTHER WORK UNITS	WORK CYCLES	TYPICAL OUTPUTS
ADVICE Committees Review panels, boards Quality circles Employee involvement groups Advisory councils	Low	Low	Work cycles can be brief or long; one cycle can be team life span.	Decisions Selections Suggestions Proposals Recommendations
PRODUCTION Assembly teams Manufacturing crews Mining teams Flight attendant crews Data processing groups Maintenance crews	Low	High	Work cycles typically repeated or continuous process; cycles often briefer than team life span.	Food, chemicals Components Assembles Retail sales Customer service Equipment repairs
PROJECT Research groups Planning teams Architect teams Engineering teams Development teams Task forces	High	Low (for traditional units) or High (for cross-functional units)	Work cycles typically differ for each new project; one cycle can be team life span.	Plans, designs Investigations Presentations Prototypes Reports, findings
ACTION Sports team Entertainment groups Expeditions Negotiating teams Surgery teams Cockpit crews Military platoons and squads	High	High	Brief performance events, often repeated under new conditions, requiring extended training and/or preparation	Combat missions Expeditions Contracts, lawsuits Concerts Surgical operations Competitive events

Source: Excerpted and adapted from E Sundstrom, K P De Meuse, and D Futrell, "Work Teams," *American Psychologist*, February 1990, p 125.

the teams to assemble three-dimensional computer models of the new aircraft. Design and assembly problems were ironed out in project team meetings before production workers started cutting any metal for the first 777. Boeing's 777 design teams required a high degree of coordination among organizational subunits because they were cross-functional.[17] A pharmaceutical research team of biochemists, on the other hand, would interact less with other work units because it is relatively self-contained.

The creation of a project team at Blue Circle, a British company, resulted in a totally new product on the European market.

When Blue Circle wanted to introduce a standardized boiler for the European market, a design team was composed of British, French, German, and Dutch specialists. Their task was to adapt the huge variations in the different European housing, climate, and plumbing demands. The team was based in the United Kingdom. English was its working language. The team's efforts finally resulted in a condensing boiler which could be sold anywhere rather than only to a particular country.[18]

Action Teams   This last type of team is best exemplified by a sports teams, airline cockpit crews, hospital surgery teams, mountain-climbing expeditions, rock groups, management /trade union negotiating committees and policy interventions teams, among others. A unique challenge for action teams is to exhibit peak performance on demand. Some companies use action groups as training tools to promote the team spirit.

The Dutch Culinair Centrum regularly welcomes management teams from Fuji, Rabobank and Philips to participate in cooking sessions. After a business meeting, all participants set to work in the kitchen. Because doing the cooking enhances the team spirit and in the kitchen everybody is equal. After dinner, all participants have a feeling of we-ness: "We have fixed this by joining forces."[19]

This four-way typology of work teams is dynamic and changing, not static. Some teams evolve from one type to another.

Team member types   Even if a team has all the necessary information, know-how and expertise, it can completely fail. Different group members must perform different group roles. Imagine a group where all the members want to perform the leader role. Dr Meredith Belbin of Brunel University in London has developed a highly influential typology of team roles.

Belbin identified nine different team types. An ideal team should be composed of several of the following team types.

1. *Coordinator*: mature, confident, and balanced.

2. *Plant*: creative, imaginative, and unorthodox.

3. *Resource investigator*: extravert, enthusiastic, and exploratory.

4. *Shaper*: dynamic, challenging, and outgoing.

5. *Monitor-evaluator*: serious, strategic, and discerning.

6. *Teamworker*: mild, perceptive, and accommodating.

7. *Co-implementer*: disciplined, reliable, and efficient.

8. *Completer*: painstaking, careful, and conscientious.

9. *Specialist*: single-minded, self-starter, and dedicated.

By putting together coordinator, plant and implementer, bright ideas, practicality and direction are combined. When using the Belbin team types it is, however, necessary to realize that people rarely correspond exactly to one of Belbin's team types.[20]

Work Team Effectiveness: An Ecological Model

The effectiveness of athletic teams is a straightforward matter of wins and losses. Things become more complicated, however, when the focus shifts to work teams in today's organizations.[21] Figure 13–1 lists two effectiveness criteria for work teams: performance and viability. According to Sundstrom and his colleagues: "*Performance* means acceptability of output to customers within or outside the organization who receive team products, services, information, decisions, or performance events (such as presentations or competitions)."[22] While the foregoing relates to satisfying the needs and expectations of outsiders such as clients, customers, and fans, another team-effectiveness criterion arises. Namely, **team viability**, defined as team member satisfaction and continued willingness to contribute. Are the team members better or worse off for having contributed to the team effort? A work team is not truly effective if it gets the job done but self-destructs in the process.[23]

Figure 13–1 is an *ecological* model because it portrays work teams within their organizational environment. In keeping with the true meaning of the word *ecology*—the study of interactions between organisms and their environments—this model emphasizes that work teams need an organizational life-support system. Six critical organizational context variables are listed in Figure 13–1. Work teams have a much greater chance of being effective if they are nurtured and facilitated by the organization. The team's purpose needs to be in concert with the organization's strategy. Similarly, team participation and autonomy require an organizational culture that values those processes. Team members

Team viability
Team members satisfied and willing to contribute.

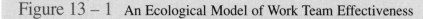

Figure 13 – 1   An Ecological Model of Work Team Effectiveness

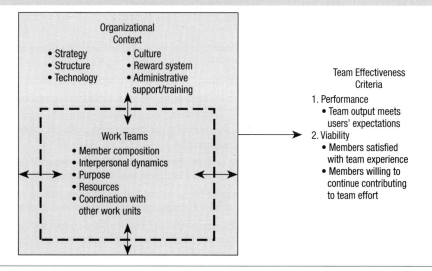

Source: Adapted in part from E Sundstrom, K P De Meuse, and D Futrell, "Work Teams," *American Psychologist*, February 1990, pp 120—33.

also need appropriate technological tools and training. Teamwork needs to be reinforced by the organizational reward system. Such is not the case when pay and bonuses are tied solely to individual output.

Regarding the internal processes of work teams, five important factors are listed in Figure 13 – 1. Table 13 – 3 contains an expanded list of characteristics of effective teams that can be useful for evaluating task teams both in school and on the job.

Why Do Work Teams Fail?

Not all OB specialists are happy with the strong emphasis on teams. Teams have become a panacea for all managerial diseases. Teams are overused. They are used for problems where technology change, radical decisions, or individual excellence would be a better solution. No wonder that A T Kearny, a consultancy firm, found that nearly 7 out of 10 teams do not produce the expected results.[24] The frequent failure of teamwork has nothing to do with the introduction of teams, but with poor team management: a failure to set clear objectives, not changing the reward systems from individual to team rewards, lack of training in group dynamics, or too much time spent on this training, lack of support from top management, unclear boundaries, and so on.[25]

According to Professor Edward Lawler : "People are very naive about how easy it is to create a team. Teams are the Ferraris of work design. They're high performance but high maintenance and expensive."[26]

While exact statistics are not available, teams can and often do fail. Anyone contemplating the use of team structures in the workplace needs a balanced perspective of advantages and limitations.

Team advocates may find these words harsh, but they challenge us to reject the myth that teams can magically replace traditional authority and accountability links. If teams are to be effective, both management and team members must make a concerted effort to think and do things differently.

Common Management Mistakes with Teams   The main threats to team effectiveness, according to the centre of Figure 13 – 2, are *unrealistic expectations* leading to *frustration*. Frustration, in turn, encourages people to abandon teams. Both managers and team members can be victimized by unrealistic expectations.[27]

On the left side of Figure 13 – 2 is a list of common management mistakes. These

Table 13 – 3   Characteristics of an Effective Team

1. Clear purpose	The vision, mission, goal, or task of the team has been defined and is now accepted by everyone. There is an action plan.
2. Informality	The climate tends to be informal, comfortable, and relaxed. There are no obvious tensions or signs of boredom.
3. Participation	There is much discussion, and everyone is encouraged to participate.
4. Listening	The members use effective listening techniques such as questioning, paraphrasing, and summarizing to get out ideas.
5. Civilized disagreement	There is disagreement, but the team is comfortable with this and shows no signs of avoiding, smoothing over, or suppressing conflict.
6. Consensus decisions	For important decisions, the goal is substantial but not necessarily unanimous agreement through open discussion of everyone's ideas, avoidance of formal voting, or easy compromises.
7. Open communication	Team members feel free to express their feelings on the tasks as well as on the group's operation. There are few hidden agendas. Communication takes place outside of meetings.
8. Clear roles and work assignments	There are clear expectations about the roles played by each team member. When action is taken, clear assignments are made, accepted, and carried out. Work is fairly distributed among team members.
9. Shared leadership	While the team has a formal leader, leadership functions shift from time to time depending on the circumstances, the needs of the group, and the skills of the members. The formal leader models the appropriate behaviour and helps establish positive norms.
10. External relations	The team spends time developing key outside relationships, mobilizing resources, and building credibility with important players in other parts of the organization.
11. Style diversity	The team has a broad spectrum of team-player types including members who emphasize attention to task, goal setting, focus on process, and questions about how the team is functioning.
12. Self-assessment	Periodically, the team stops to examine how well it is functioning and what may be interfering with its effectiveness.

Source: G M Parker, *Team Players and Teamwork: The New Competitive Business Strategy* (San Francisco: Jossey-Bass, 1990), Table 2, p 33. Copyright 1990 by Jossey-Bass Inc., Publishers.

mistakes generally involve doing a poor job of creating a supportive environment for teams and teamwork. Recalling our discussion of team-based rewards in Chapter 9, reward plans that encourage individuals to compete with one another erode teamwork. As mentioned earlier, teams need a good organizational life-support system.

Problems for Team Members   The right portion of Figure 13 – 2 lists common problems for team members. Contrary to critics' Theory X contention about employees lacking the motivation and creativity for real teamwork, it is common for teams to take on too much too quickly and to drive themselves too hard for fast results. Important group dynamics and team skills get lost in the rush for results. Consequently, team members' expectations need to be given a reality check by management and team members themselves. Also, teams need to be counselled against quitting when they run into an unanticipated obstacle. Failure is part of the learning process with teams, as it is elsewhere in life. Comprehensive training in interpersonal skills can prevent many common teamwork problems.

Additional insights lie ahead as we turn our attention to cooperation, trust, and cohesiveness.

Effective Teamwork through Cooperation, Trust, and Cohesiveness

As competitive pressures intensify, experts say organizational success increasingly will depend on teamwork rather than individual stars. In fact, companies such as Microsoft and Xerox have gone so far as to fill the position of corporate president with a team of executives instead of an individual. According to Xerox's Chairman Paul Allaire, cooperation from top to bottom is the goal:

Figure 13 – 2   Why Work Teams Fail

Mistakes typically made by management

- Teams cannot overcome weak strategies and poor business practices.
- Hostile environment for teams (command-and-control culture; competitive/individual reward plans; management resistance).
- Teams adopted as a fad, a quick-fix; no long-term commitment.
- Lessons from one team not transferred to others (limited experimentation with teams).
- Vague or conflicting team assignments.
- Inadequate team skills training.
- Poor staffing of teams.
- Lack of trust.

Unrealistic expectations resulting in frustration

Problems typically experienced by team members

- Team tries to do too much too soon.
- Conflict over differences in personal work styles (and/or personality conflicts).
- Too much emphasis on results, not enough on team processes and group dynamics.
- Unanticipated obstacle causes team to give up.
- Resistance to doing things differently.
- Poor interpersonal skills (aggressive rather than assertive communication, destructive conflict, win–lose negotiation).
- Poor interpersonal chemistry (loners, dominators, self-appointed experts do not fit in).
- Lack of trust.

Sources: Adapted from discussion in S R Rayner, "Team Traps: What They Are, How to Avoid Them," *National Productivity Review*, Summer 1996, pp 101–15; L Holpp and R Phillips, "When Is a Team Its Own Worst Enemy?" *Training*, September 1995, pp 71–82; and B Richardson, "Why Work Teams Flop—and What Can Be Done About It," *National Productivity Review*, Winter 1994/95, pp 9–13.

"I would hope that we have been clear enough that one of the criteria of this new organization is working together," he says. To underscore the issue, he says future Xerox leaders will be drawn only from those who can cooperate: "Anyone who isn't a team player would be automatically excluded from succession," he says.[28]

In Brazil, Semco's directors or counselors rotate every 6 months because "it increases knowledge and collaboration and shares responsibility."[29]

If this sort of commitment to teamwork has a familiar ring, it is because sports champions generally say they owe their success to it. Whether in the athletic arena or the world of business, three components of teamwork receiving the greatest attention are cooperation, trust, and cohesiveness. Let us explore the contributions each can make to effective teamwork.

Cooperation

Individuals are said to be cooperating when their efforts are systematically *integrated* to achieve a collective objective. The greater the integration, the greater the degree of cooperation.

Already in the 1940s Morton Deutch showed how people's beliefs are related to their interdependence. In cooperation, they believe that goal attainment by other people will also foster their own goals. In competition, however, people believe that goal attainment by others ("Competitors") will diminish their own. "When others fail I succeed." Independent people see no relationship between their own results and the results of the others.[30]

In practice, most team members find themselves in a 'mixed motive' situation. Just think of the football player who can score himself, but sees a teammate who is better placed and has a higher chance of scoring the winning goal. John Kay, British economist and dean of the Oxford management school, illustrates this with the following analysis of Liverpool Football Club.

If we where to build a model of the game of football, it would recognize that every time a player has the ball he faces the alternative of shooting for goal or passing to a better placed player. If he passes to a player of similar calibre to himself, he will score fewer goals but the team will score more. If everyone in the team plays a passing game, every member of it can expect to score more goals than if their normal instinct is to shoot. That choice is repeated every few minutes in every match the team plays and there are two equilibria—a passing game or a shooting game. Liverpool is well known for its passing game. Many of its opponents adopt a more individualistic style.

Liverpool illustrates the principal ways in which architecture can form the basis of a distinctive capability. The club has created an intangible asset—the organizational knowledge of the club—which, although it is derived from the contributions of the individual members, belongs to the firm and not to the individual members and cannot be appropriated by them. There are organizational routines—complex manoeuvres, perfected through repeated trial, in which each player fulfils his own role without needing or necessarily having, a picture of the whole. And there is the "passing game," the cooperative ethic, in which the player's instinct is to maximize the number of goals the club scores rather than the number of goals he scores. Each of these sources of sporting success has it precise business analogies.[31]

Cooperation versus Competition   A widely held assumption among American managers is that "competition brings out the best in people." From an economic standpoint, business survival depends on staying ahead of the competition. But from an interpersonal standpoint, critics contend competition has been overemphasized, primarily at the expense of cooperation.[32] According to Alfie Kohn, a strong advocate of greater emphasis on cooperation in classrooms, offices, and factories,

My review of the evidence has convinced me that there are two . . . important reasons for competition's failure. First, success often depends on sharing resources efficiently, and this is nearly impossible when people have to work against one another. Cooperation takes advantage of all the skills represented in a group as well as the mysterious process by which that group becomes more than the sum of its parts. By contrast, competition makes people suspicious and hostile toward one another and actively discourages this process. . . .

Second, competition generally does not promote excellence because trying to do well and trying to beat others simply are two different things. Consider a child in class, waving his arm wildly to attract the teacher's attention, crying, "Oooh! Oooh! Pick me!" When he is finally recognized, he seems befuddled. "Um, what was the question again?" he finally asks. His mind is focused on beating his classmates, not on the subject matter.[33]

Research Support for Cooperation   After conducting a meta-analysis of 122 studies encompassing a wide variety of subjects and settings, one team of researchers concluded that

1. Cooperation is superior to competition in promoting achievement and productivity.

2. Cooperation is superior to individualistic efforts in promoting achievement and productivity.

3. Cooperation without intergroup competition promotes higher achievement and productivity than cooperation with intergroup competition.[34]

Given the size and diversity of the research base, these findings strongly endorse cooperation in modern organizations. Cooperation can be encouraged by reward systems that reinforce teamwork as well as individual achievement.

Research suggests that managers can enhance equal employment opportunity and diversity programmes by encouraging *voluntary* helping behaviour in interracial work teams.[35] Accordingly, it is reasonable to conclude that voluntary helping behaviour could build cooperation in mixed-gender teams and groups as well. Remember the material studied in Chapter 2, diversity should include more than racial or gender differences alone. Asea Brown Boveri Canada Inc. applied this statement when composing a team responsible for the design of a new factory.

"I put together a seven-member design team, composed of two workers from manufacturing, three from engineering, one from finance. One team member was a female and one of the males was a person of color. Their ages ranged from 23 to 49 years. Their company service ranged from 4 months to 12 years. They held positions from a single mother to a father with teenage children. In short, they were a representative cross-section of business and modern lifestyles.

"Each member brought something unique to the team and each got something different from the experience," says B Randall Palef, ABB switchgeard Division's Human Resources Manager at the time of the project.[36]

Trust

These have not been good times for trust in the world. Years of mergers, downsizings, layoffs, bloated executive bonuses, and broken promises have left many employees justly cynical about trusting management. A recent survey of over 1,000 employees in six companies in Britain (including ICL, BT and British Aerospace), concluded that trust is the missing factor: only 13 per cent think that the people they work with feel valued by the company; 9 per cent think that top management has a sincere interest in the welfare of its employees and hardly 8 per cent are convinced that management gives fair deals.[37]

Lower-level employees also rate trust highly. In a 1995 American Management Association survey, organizational team members ranked "intragroup trust" first among eight desired changes in the workplace.[38]

In this section, we examine the concept of trust and introduce six practical guidelines for building trust.

Trust
Reciprocal faith in others' intentions and behaviour

A Cognitive Leap   **Trust** is defined as reciprocal faith in others' intentions and behaviour. Experts on the subject explain the reciprocal (give-and-take) aspect of trust as follows:

When we see others acting in ways that imply that they trust us, we become more disposed to reciprocate by trusting in them more. Conversely, we come to distrust those whose actions appear to violate our trust or to distrust us.[39]

In short, we tend to give what we get: trust begets trust; distrust begets distrust.

A recently proposed model of organizational trust includes a personality trait called **propensity to trust**. The developers of the model explain:

Propensity to trust
A personality trait involving one's general willingness to trust others.

Propensity might be thought of as the *general willingness to trust others.* Propensity will influence how much trust one has for a trustee prior to data on that particular party being available. People with different developmental experiences, personality types, and cultural backgrounds vary in their propensity to trust. . . . An example of an extreme case of this is what is commonly called blind trust. Some individuals can be observed to repeatedly trust in situations that most people would agree do not warrant trust. Conversely, others are unwilling to trust in most situations, regardless of circumstances that would support doing so.[40]

What is your propensity to trust? How did you develop that personality trait? (See the trust questionnaire in the Personal Awareness and Growth Exercise at the end of this chapter.)

Trust involves "a cognitive 'leap' beyond the expectations that reason and experience alone would warrant"[41] (see Figure 13–3). For example, suppose a member of a newly formed class project team works hard, based on the assumption that her teammates also are working hard. That assumption, on which her trust is based, is a cognitive leap that goes beyond her actual experience with her teammates. When you trust someone, you have *faith* in their good intentions. The act of trusting someone, however, carries with it the inherent risk of betrayal.[42] Progressive managers believe that the benefits of interpersonal trust far outweigh any risks of betrayed trust.

How to Build Trust   Management professor/consultant Fernando Bartolomé offers the following six guidelines for building and maintaining trust:

1. *Communication.* Keep team members and employees informed by explaining policies and decisions and providing accurate feedback. Be candid about one's own problems and limitations. Tell the truth.[43]

2. *Support.* Be available and approachable. Provide help, advice, coaching, and support for team members' ideas.

3. *Respect.* Delegation, in the form of real decision-making authority, is the most important expression of managerial respect. Actively listening to the ideas of others is a close second.

4. *Fairness.* Be quick to give credit and recognition to those who deserve it. Make sure all performance appraisals and evaluations are objective and impartial.

5. *Predictability.* As mentioned previously, be consistent and predictable in your daily affairs. Keep both expressed and implied promises.

6. *Competence.* Enhance your credibility by demonstrating good business sense, technical ability, and professionalism.[44]

Trust needs to be earned; it cannot be demanded.[45] The importance of these six guidelines in the team-building process is illustrated by Colgate-Palmolive Corp. in central Europe's Czechoslovakia, Romania, and Poland. The communist regime had destroyed employee initiative, eliminated trust, and created lazy workers who spent their careers in a vacuum. They had no information about organizational goals. They knew nothing about sales. They had no idea what it costs to produce products. And because they were used to working in a communist system, they had no understanding of marketing or free enterprise.

To help employees understand their new jobs, Colgate's HR managers gave them information about the business, invested in new skills training, set goals for employees, and gave them ongoing feedback on how they were meeting those goals. "In short, we treated them like adults," say Philip Berry, the company's director of HR for Central Europe.[46]

Cohesiveness

Cohesiveness
A sense of "we-ness" helps group stick together.

Cohesiveness is a process whereby "a sense of 'we-ness' emerges to transcend individual differences and motives."[47] Members of a cohesive group stick together. They are reluctant to leave the group. Cohesive group members stick together for one or both of the following reasons: (1) because they enjoy each others' company or (2) because they need each other to accomplish a common goal. Accordingly, two types of group cohesiveness, identified by sociologists, are socio-emotional cohesiveness and instrumental cohesiveness.[48]

Socio-emotional cohesiveness
Sense of togetherness based on emotional satisfaction.

Socio-Emotional and Instrumental Cohesiveness   **Socio-emotional cohesiveness** is a sense of togetherness that develops when individuals derive emotional satisfaction from group participation. Most general discussions of group cohesiveness are limited to this type. However, from the standpoint of getting things accomplished in task groups and teams, we cannot afford to ignore instrumental cohesiveness. **Instrumental cohesiveness** is a sense of togetherness that develops when group members are mutually dependent on

Figure 13 – 3   Interpersonal Trust Involves a Cognitive Leap

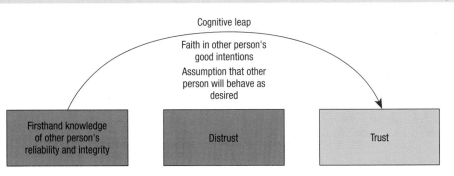

Instrumental cohesiveness

Sense of togetherness based on mutual dependency needed to get the job done.

one another because they believe they could not achieve the group's goal by acting separately. A feeling of "we-ness" is *instrumental* in achieving the common goal. Team advocates generally assume both types of cohesiveness are essential to productive teamwork. But is this really true?

Lessons from Group Cohesiveness Research   What is the connection between group cohesiveness and performance? A recent landmark meta-analysis of 49 studies involving 8,702 subjects provided these insights:

- There is a small but statistically significant cohesiveness→performance effect.

- The cohesiveness→performance effect was stronger for smaller and real groups (as opposed to contrived groups in laboratory studies).

- The cohesiveness→performance effect becomes stronger as one moves from nonmilitary real groups to military groups to sports teams.

- Commitment to the task at hand (meaning the individual sees the performance standards as legitimate) has the most powerful impact on the cohesiveness→performance linkage.

- The performance→cohesiveness linkage is stronger than the cohesiveness→performance linkage. Thus, success tends to bind group or team members together rather than closely knit groups being more successful.

- Contrary to the popular view, cohesiveness is not "a 'lubricant' that minimizes friction due to the human 'grit' in the system."[49]

- All this evidence led the researchers to this practical conclusion: "Efforts to enhance group performance by fostering interpersonal attraction or 'pumping up' group pride are not likely to be effective."[50]

A second meta-analysis found no significant relationship between cohesiveness and the quality of group decisions. However, support was found for Janis's contention that *groupthink* tends to afflict cohesive in-groups with strong leadership. Groups whose members liked each other a great deal tended to make poorer quality decisions.[51]

Getting Some Positive Impact from Group Cohesiveness   Research tells us that group cohesiveness is no "secret weapon" in the quest for improved group or team performance. The trick is to keep task groups small, make sure performance standards and goals are clear and accepted, achieve some early successes, and follow the tips in Table 13–4. A good example is Renault's restructured factory at Douai, France. A new production system was introduced for the construction of the Mégane, based on strong employee involvement. Those who were involved in the project from the beginning were responsible for the training of 200 colleagues, who, in turn, instructed their peers. This

Table 13 – 4	Steps Managers Can Take to Enhance the Two Types of Group Cohesiveness

SOCIO-EMOTIONAL COHESIVENESS
Keep the group relatively small.
Strive for a favourable public image to increase the status and prestige of belonging.
Encourage interaction and cooperation.
Emphasize members' common characteristics and interests.
Point out environmental threats (e.g., competitors' achievements) to rally the group.

INSTRUMENTAL COHESIVENESS
Regularly update and clarify the group's goal(s).
Give every group member a vital "piece of the action."
Channel each group member's special talents toward the common goal(s).
Recognize and equitably reinforce every member's contributions.
Frequently remind group members they need each other to get the job done.

training system enhanced employee cooperation.[52]

Self-selected work teams (in which people pick their own teammates) and off-the-job social events can stimulate socio-emotional cohesiveness.[53] The fostering of socio-emotional cohesiveness needs to be balanced with instrumental cohesiveness. The latter can be encouraged by making sure everyone in the group recognizes and appreciates each member's vital contribution to the group goal. While balancing the two types of cohesiveness, managers need to remember that groupthink theory and research cautions against too much cohesiveness.

Teams in Action: From Quality Circles to Self-Managed Teams

This section strives to bring the team approach to life for present and future managers. It does so by exploring two different team formats found in the workplace today: quality circles and self-managed teams. We have chosen these two particular applications of teamwork, out of a growing variety,[54] for three reasons. First, they are sharply contrasting approaches to teamwork. Managers can gain valuable insights about work teams by understanding their basic differences. Second, each is established enough to be generally recognizable. Third, both approaches have been evaluated by OB researchers.

Table 13 – 5 provides a conceptual foundation for this section by highlighting important distinctions between quality circles and self-managed teams. Quality circles involve limited empowerment in the form of consultation. Thus, they qualify as *advice* teams (as described in Table 13-2). Self-managed teams, in contrast, enjoy a high degree of empowerment through delegation. Production, project, and/or action teams may be self-managed because decision authority can be delegated to teams in virtually any part of the organization. Regarding membership, quality circles rely on volunteers while employees are assigned to self-managed teams or selected by the team itself. Another vital distinction involves the team's relationship to the organization's structure and hierarchy. Quality circles are called parallel structures[55] because they exist outside normal channels of authority and communication. Self-managed teams, on the other hand, are integrated into the basic organizational structure. Quality circles make recommendations to management, which retains all decision-making authority. Self-managed teams, meanwhile, make and implement their own decisions. Finally, quality circles primarily influence production and service operations at the lowest levels. Self-managed teams tend to have much broader influence because of greater reliance on technical and staff specialists throughout the organization.

Keeping these conceptual distinctions in mind, let us examine quality circles and self-managed teams more closely.

Table 13 – 5   Some Basic Distinctions between Quality Circles and Self-Managed Teams

	QUALITY CIRCLES	SELF-MANAGED TEAMS
Type of team (see Table 13—2)	Advice	Production, project, or action
Type of empowerment (see Figure 11—2)	Consultation	Delegation
Basis of membership	Voluntary	Assigned
Relationship to organization structure	Parallel	Integrated
Focus of influence	Lower level operations	Possibly all organizational levels and functions, depending on makeup of team

Quality Circles

Quality circles

Small groups of volunteers who strive to solve quality-related problems.

Quality circles are small groups of people from the same work area who voluntarily get together to identify, analyse, and recommend solutions for problems related to quality, productivity, and cost reduction. Some prefer the term *quality control circles*. With an ideal size of 10 to 12 members, they typically meet for about 60 to 90 minutes on a regular basis. Some companies allow meetings during work hours, others encourage quality circles to meet after work on employees' time. Once a week or twice a month are common schedules. Management facilitates the quality circle programme through skills training and listening to periodic presentations of recommendations. Monetary rewards for suggestions tend to be the exception rather than the rule. Intrinsic motivation, derived from learning new skills and meaningful participation, is the primary payoff for quality circle volunteers.

The Quality Circle Movement   American quality control experts helped introduce the basic idea of quality circles to Japanese industry soon after World War II. The idea eventually returned to the United States, was exported to Europe, and reached fad proportions during the 1970s and 1980s. Proponents made zealous claims about how quality circles were the key to higher productivity, lower costs, employee development, and improved job attitudes. At its zenith during the mid-1980s, the quality circle movement claimed millions of employee participants around the world.[56] Hundreds of companies and government agencies adopted the idea under a variety of labels.[57] Dramatic growth of quality has been attributed to (1) a desire to replicate Japan's industrial success, (2) a penchant for business fads, especially in the United State, and (3) the relative ease of installing quality circles without restructuring the organization.[58] All too often, however, early enthusiasm gave way to disappointment, apathy, and abandonment.[59]

But quality circles, if properly administered and supported by management, can be much more than a management fad seemingly past its prime. According to researchers Edward E Lawler and Susan A Mohrman, "quality circles can be an important first step toward organizational effectiveness through employee involvement."[60] As we will see later, quality circles can be a stepping-stone to self-managed teams.

A life-cycle perspective of quality circles helps us better appreciate their promises and pitfalls.

A Life-Cycle Perspective of Quality Circle Programmes   The six-phase life-cycle model in Figure 13– 4 makes two important contributions to management's thinking. First, it portrays an organization's quality circle programme as a step-by-step evolution rather than a one-shot deal. Second, it warns of potentially fatal problems during each phase. By systematically anticipating and addressing each set of problems along the bottom of Figure 13– 4, managers can reach and prolong phase 5 (the expansion phase).

Management's first significant hurdle is to sell the idea to suspicious and possibly mistrusting employees. Remember, *volunteers* are the lifeblood of quality circles. This can be a particularly hard sell with militant union members. This sort of opposition to quality circles or any other form of teamwork needs to be overcome with training,

Figure 13 – 4 A Life-Cycle Model of Quality Circle Programs

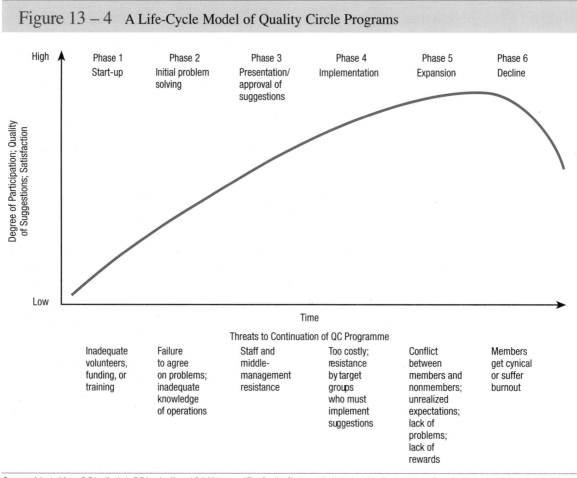

	Phase 1 Start-up	Phase 2 Initial problem solving	Phase 3 Presentation/ approval of suggestions	Phase 4 Implementation	Phase 5 Expansion	Phase 6 Decline

Y-axis: Degree of Participation; Quality of Suggestions; Satisfaction (High / Low)

X-axis: Time

Threats to Continuation of QC Programme

Inadequate volunteers, funding, or training	Failure to agree on problems; inadequate knowledge of operations	Staff and middle- management resistance	Too costly; resistance by target groups who must implement suggestions	Conflict between members and nonmembers; unrealized expectations; lack of problems; lack of rewards	Members get cynical or suffer burnout

Source: Adapted from G E Ledford, Jr, E E Lawler III, and S A Mohrman, "The Quality Circle and Its Variations," in *Productivity in Organizations*, eds J P Campbell, R J Campbell and Associates (San Francisco: Jossey-Bass, 1988), pp 255–94.

honesty, and patience.[61] Monetary rewards can help, too. Beyond overcoming resistance, quality circle members need to be adequately trained in problem-solving and presentation skills. A good working knowledge of company operations also is a must. Otherwise, unrealistic recommendations will be made. Resistance from supervisors and middle managers, who sometimes view employee participation as a threat to their authority, needs to be neutralized. This can be accomplished through their personal involvement and recognition of benefits for management.

Another problem, encountered in phase 4, relates to quality circles being outside the normal hierarchy. Just because one group of managers has endorsed a proposal made during a quality circle presentation, prompt implementation by other managers does not automatically follow. The parallel or ad hoc structure of quality circles makes implementation very problematic. In phase 5, a whole host of problems can arise. Not the least being that the quality circle can work itself out of business by running out of problems. If the threats to success during phases 1 through 5 are allowed to accumulate, then cynicism and burnout will eventually kill the programme.

Insights from Field Research on Quality Circles A body of objective field research on quality circles is growing. Still, much of what we know comes from testimonials and case histories from managers and consultants who have a vested interest in demonstrating the technique's success. Although documented failures are scarce, one expert concluded that quality circles have failure rates of more than 60 per cent.[62] Poor implementation is probably more at fault than the quality circle concept itself.[63]

To date, field research on quality circles has been inconclusive. Lack of standardized variables is the main problem, as it typically is when comparing the results of field studies.[64] Team participation programmes of all sizes and shapes have been called quality circles. Here is what we have learned to date. A case study of military and civilian personnel found a positive relationship between quality circle participation and a desire to continue working for the organization. The observed effect on job performance was slight. A longitudinal study spanning 24 months revealed that quality circles had only a marginal impact on employee attitudes, but had a positive impact on productivity. In a more recent study, utility company employees who participated in quality circles received significantly better job performance ratings and were promoted more frequently than nonparticipants. This suggests that quality circles live up to their billing as a good employee development technique.[65]

Overall, quality circles are a promising participative management tool, *if they are carefully implemented and supported by all levels of management during the first five phases of the programme life cycle.*

Strengthening Quality Circles   In addition to doing a better job of implementing and supporting quality circles during later phases of the life cycle, management can take other constructive steps as well. Lawler and Mohrman recommend the following changes:

The most important of the changes is probably the development of a gainsharing formula that will let everyone participate in the benefits of performance improvement. Other possible approaches include improved information and education for circle members and the use of training, appraisal, and rewards to develop participative supervision. The suggested reward, information, and education system changes involve changing the work organization in some important ways. In essence, they call for making it a more active organization for lower-level participants by giving them new kinds of knowledge, information, supervision, and rewards. This reinforces the fact that an organization that wants to sustain a participative parallel structure must become more participative in its day-to-day business.[66]

Self-Managed Teams

Have you ever thought you could do a better job than your boss? Well, if the trend towards self-managed work teams continues to grow as predicted, you just may get your chance. Entrepreneurs and artisans often boast of not having a supervisor. The same generally cannot be said for employees working in organizational offices and factories. But things are changing. According to a British survey published by the Industrial Society 10 per cent out of 500 personnel managers polled, said that most teams in their company were self-managed, Nearly 40 per cent declared that their organization operated at least some self-managed teams.[67] For example, consider the following situations:

In the late 1980s, the Rover Group's production departments were radically changed by the elimination of the position of the works supervisor (foreman).[68]

Body Shop experimented with an autonomous team existing of 30 full time employees, all with equal status. Each member was paid the same salary. This group operated as a single self-managed team with the collective authority of a branch manager, rotating the four departmental teams and managerial responsibilities. Although some adjustments were carried out, the experiment was a great success.[69]

This section explores self-managed teams by looking at their past, present, and future.

What Are Self-Managed Teams?   Something much more complex is involved than this apparently simple label suggests. The term *self-managed* does not mean simply turning workers loose to do their own thing. Indeed, as we will see, an organization embracing self-managed teams should be prepared to undergo revolutionary changes in management philosophy, structure, staffing and training practices, and reward systems. Moreover, the traditional notions of managerial authority and control are turned on their heads. Not surprisingly, many managers strongly resist giving up the reins of power to people they view as subordinates. They see self-managed teams as a threat to their job security. Texas Instruments has constructively dealt with this problem at its Malaysian factory by making former production supervisors part of the all-important training function.

Self-managed teams find their roots in socio-technical systems thinking,[70] which tries to optimize and integrate both the social and technical requirements of a work system. This joint optimization is made possible through a shift from Taylorist individualistic approaches to team-based work methods. Employees work in teams based on the natural sequences in the workflow processes. Autonomous groups were pioneered in the United Kingdom and Sweden, but never became very popular. In the first half of the 1990s, self-managed teams became so popular in the United States that they might be considered another fad in modern management.

Self-managed teams

Groups of employees granted administrative oversight for their work.

Self-managed teams are defined as groups of workers who are given administrative oversight for their task domains. Administrative oversight involves delegated activities such as planning, scheduling, monitoring, and staffing. These are chores normally performed by managers. In short, employees in these unique work groups act as their own supervisor.[71] Self-managed teams are variously referred to as semiautonomous work groups, autonomous work groups, and superteams. A common feature of self-managed teams, particularly among those above the shop-floor or clerical level, is **cross-functionalism**.[72] In other words, specialists from different areas are put on the same team. Maxus Energy goes even further. This US oil company has built a cross-functional team that consists of different cultures, languages, locations, and time zones.

Cross-functionalism

Team made up of technical specialists from different areas.

To maximize oil and gas production, two Maxus groups formed a cross-functional and cross-cultural unit. Teaming up were Americans, Dutch, British, and Indonesians. Some of these people believe in individualism, others believe in collectivism; some believe in equal opportunity based on achievement, others believe status is inherited. Politically, culturally, and religiously, this group was composed of disparate elements.

Working together, the team not only stabilized production and avoided the expected 15 per cent reduction, but even levelled-off production and helped the companies add oil reserves to their stock piles—an almost unprecedented achievement.[73]

Extensive coverage in the popular media in recent years has created the impression that self-managed teams have become the norm. The fact is they still are not very far beyond the experimental stage. Among the companies with self-managed teams, the most commonly delegated tasks were work scheduling and dealing directly with outside customers (see Table 13–6). The least common team chores were hiring and firing. Most of today's self-managed teams remain bunched at the shop-floor level in factory settings. Experts predict growth of the practice in the managerial ranks and in service operations.[74]

Historical and Conceptual Roots of Self-Managed Teams

Self-managed teams are an outgrowth of a blend of behavioural science and management practice.[75] Group dynamics research of variables such as cohesiveness initially paved the way. A later stimulus was the socio-technical systems approach in which first British, and then American researchers, tried to harmonize social and technical factors. Their goal was to simultaneously increase productivity and employees' quality of work life. More recently, the idea of self-managed teams has been given a strong boost from job design and participative management advocates. Recall our discussion of Hackman and Oldham's job characteristics model in Chapter 7. According to their model, internal motivation, satisfaction, and performance can be enhanced through five core job characteristics. Of those five core factors, increased *autonomy* is a major benefit for members of self-managed teams. Three types of autonomy are method, scheduling, and criteria autonomy (see the OB Exercise). Members of self-managed teams score high on group autonomy. Autonomy empowers those who are ready and able to handle added responsibility. How did you score? Finally, the social learning theory of self-management, as discussed in Chapter 15, has helped strengthen the case for self-managed teams.

Table 13 – 6   Survey Evidence: What Self-Managing Teams Manage

PERCENTAGE OF COMPANIES SAYING THEIR SELF-MANAGING TEAMS PERFORM THESE TRADITIONAL MANAGEMENT FUNCTIONS BY THEMSELVES:

Schedule work assignments	67%
Work with outside customers	67
Conduct training	59
Set production goals/quotas	56
Work with suppliers/vendors	44
Purchase equipment/services	43
Develop budgets	39
Do performance appraisals	36
Hire co-workers	33
Fire co-workers	14

Source: Adapted from "1996 Industry Report: What Self-Managing Teams Manage," *Training*, October 1996, p 69.

The net result of this confluence is the continuum in Figure 13–5. The traditional clear-cut distinction between manager and managed is being blurred as nonmanagerial employees are delegated greater authority and granted increased autonomy. Importantly, self-managed teams do not eliminate the need for all managerial control (see the upper right-hand corner of Figure 13–5. Semiautonomous work teams represent a balance between managerial and group control.[76]

Are Self-Managed Teams Effective? Research Evidence   As with quality circles, much of what we know about self-managed teams comes from testimonials and case studies. Fortunately, a body of higher quality field research is slowly developing. A review of three meta-analyses covering 70 individual studies concluded that self-managed teams had

- A positive impact on productivity.
- A positive impact on specific attitudes relating to self-management (e.g., responsibility and control).

OB EXERCISE   *Measuring Work Group Autonomy*

Instructions

Think of your current (or past) job and work groups. Characterize the group's situation by circling one number on the following scale for each statement. Add your responses for a total score:

STRONGLY
DISAGREE

STRONGLY
AGREE

1 — 2 — 3 — 4 — 5 — 6 — 7

WORK METHOD AUTONOMY

1. My work group decides how to get the job done.   _____

2. My work group determines what procedures to use.   _____

3. My work group is free to choose its own methods when carrying out its work.   _____

WORK SCHEDULING AUTONOMY

4. My work group controls the scheduling of its work.   _____

5. My work group determines how its work is sequenced.   _____

6. My work group decides when to do certain activities.   _____

WORK CRITERIA AUTONOMY

7. My work group is allowed to modify the normal way it is evaluated so some of our activities are emphasized and some deemphasized.   _____

8. My work group is able to modify its objectives (what it is supposed to accomplish).   _____

9. My work group has some control over what it is supposed to accomplish.   _____

Total score = _____

NORMS

9 — 26 = Low autonomy
27 — 45 = Moderate autonomy
46 — 63 = High autonomy

SOURCE   Adapted from an individual autonomy scale in J A Breaugh, "The Work Autonomy Scales: Additional Validity Evidence," *Human Relations*, November 1989, pp 1033–56.

Figure 13 – 5   The Evolution of Self-Managed Work Teams

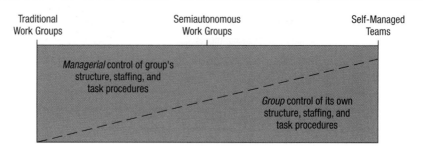

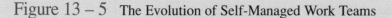

- No significant impact on general attitudes (e.g., job satisfaction and organizational commitment).
- No significant impact on absenteeism or turnover.[77]

Although encouraging, these results do not qualify as a sweeping endorsement of self-managed teams. Nonetheless, experts say the trends towards self-managed work teams will continue upwards. Managers need to be prepared for the resulting shift in organizational administration.

Setting the Stage for Self-Managed Teams   Experience shows that it is better to build a new production or service facility around self-managed teams than to attempt to convert an existing one. The former approach involves so-called "green field sites." Green field sites give management the advantage of selecting appropriate technology and carefully screening job applicants likely to be good team players.

But the fact is, most organizations are not afforded green field opportunities. They must settle for introducing self-managed teams into an existing organization structure.[78] This is where Lawler and Mohrman's transitional model is helpful (see Figure 13– 6). Even though their model builds a bridge specifically from quality circles to team organization, their recommendations apply to the transition from any sort of organization structure to teams. As mentioned earlier, quality circles are a good stepping-stone from a nonparticipative organization to one driven by self-managed teams. A brief overview of this multidimensional transition programme is in order.

Making the Transition to Self-Managed Teams   Extensive *management training and socialization* are required to deeply embed Theory Y and participative management values in the organization's culture. This new logic necessarily has to start with top management and filter down. Otherwise, resistance among middle- and lower-level managers will block the transition to teams.[79] Some turnover can be expected among managers who refuse to adjust to broader empowerment. Both *technical and organizational redesign* are necessary. Self-managed teams may require special technology. Volvo's team-based auto assembly plant, for example, relies on portable assembly platforms rather than traditional assembly lines. Structural redesign of the organization must take place because self-managed teams are an integral part of the organization, not patched on to it as in the case of quality circles. For example, in one of Texas Instruments' computer chip factories a hierarchy of teams operates within the traditional structure. Four levels of teams are responsible for different domains. Reporting to the steering team that deals with strategic issues are quality-improvement, corrective-action, and effectiveness teams. TI's quality-improvement and corrective-action teams are cross-functional teams made up of middle managers and functional specialists such as accountants and engineers. Production workers make up the effectiveness teams. The corrective-action teams are unique because they are formed to deal with short-term

Figure 13 – 6   Making the Transition between Quality Circles and Self-Managed Teams

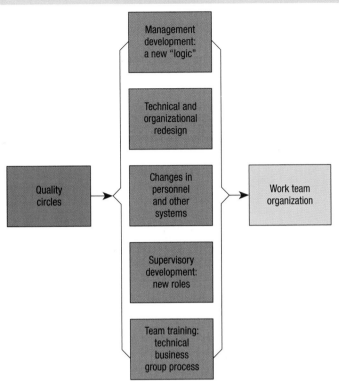

problems and are disbanded when a solution is found. All the other teams are long-term assignments.[80]

In turn, *personnel and reward systems* need to be adapted to encourage teamwork. Staffing decisions may shift from management to team members who hire their own co-workers. Individual bonuses must give way to team bonuses. *Supervisory development workshops* are needed to teach managers to be facilitators rather than order givers.[81] Finally, extensive *team training* is required to help team members learn more about technical details, the business as a whole, and how to be team players. This is where team building enters the picture.

Team Building

Team building

Experiential learning aimed at better internal functioning of groups.

Team building is a catch-all term for a whole host of techniques aimed at improving the internal functioning of work groups. Whether conducted by company trainers or outside consultants, team-building workshops strive for greater cooperation, better communication, and less dysfunctional conflict. Experiential learning techniques such as interpersonal trust exercises, conflict-handling role play sessions, and interactive games are common. For example, Germany's Opel uses Lego blocks to teach its car workers the tight teamwork necessary for just-in-time production.[82] In the mountains of British Columbia, Canada, DowElanco employees try to overcome fear and build trust as they help each other negotiate a difficult tree-top rope course.[83] Meanwhile, in the United States, the Target department store chain makes its salesclerks learn cooperation and teamwork with this exercise: "employees linked in a human chain must each wriggle through two Hula-Hoops moving in opposite directions, without breaking the chain or letting the hoops touch the ground."[84] And in Prescott, Arizona, trainees at Motorola's Advanced Leadership Academy polish their teamwork skills by trying to make music with an odd assortment of percussion instruments.[85]

Rote memorization and lecture/discussion are discouraged by team-building experts who prefer this sort of *active* versus passive learning. Greater emphasis is placed on *how* work groups get the job done than on the job itself. Team building generally is carried out in the name of organization development (OD). According to the *Training* magazine survey cited earlier, 67 per cent of the companies polled in 1996 used team building.[86] The extensive use of team building appears to be justified at least in the United States. In a survey of human resource development managers from 179 *Fortune* 500 companies, team building reportedly was the most successful management technique.[87]

Complete coverage of the many team-building techniques would require a separate book. Consequently, the scope of our current discussion is limited to the purposes of team building and the day-to-day development of self-management skills. This foundation is intended to give you a basis for selecting appropriate team-building techniques from the many you are likely to encounter in the years ahead.[88]

The Purpose of Team Building/High-Performance Teams

According to Richard Beckhard, a respected authority on organization development, the four purposes of team building are

- To set goals and/or priorities.
- To analyse or allocate the way work is performed.
- To examine the way a group is working and its processes (such as norms, decision making, and communication).
- To examine relationships among the people doing the work.[89]

Trainers achieve these objectives by allowing team members to wrestle with simulated or real-life problems. Outcomes are then analysed by the group to determine what group processes need improvement. Learning stems from recognizing and addressing faulty group dynamics. Perhaps one subgroup withheld key information from another, thereby hampering group progress. With cross-cultural teams becoming commonplace in today's global economy, team building is more important than ever (see the International OB).

Most OB specialists agree on a few basic characteristics of effective teams.[90]

1. A clear sense of purpose. Better teams have clear goals and a strong sense of purpose. All team members are committed to a common objective. At Germany's Bosch spark plug factory in Bamberg, teamwork has improved employee involvement and identification with the product and the production goal has increased.[91]

2. A wide range of team roles, skills, and know-how. Teams succeed because they use all the available skills and know-how needed to realize their goal. The better teams represent a wide variety of content–information, expertise, perspectives, background, and process (different team roles). Effective teams combine this diversity into a focused task accomplishment. This is easier in smaller than in large teams.

3. A small number of members. Teams must be large enough to take advantage of the required variety, but large groups seldom form teams. Teams must be staffed with the smallest number of members able to perform the task.

Chris Bonington, who has climbed Mount Everest several times, compares team building to mountain climbing. Some of the above mentioned attributes can be identified in his words.

This [team spirit] means the feeling of involvement in the original planning and a sense of ownership of that plan are all the more important. The other key factor is a sense of trust in the leader, so changes in the plan are accepted and their reactions understood.

When I went to Everest in 1985 as a member of a Norwegian expedition, I asked everyone a series of questions. One of them was "How important is it to you, personally, to reach the summit of Everest?"[92]

A nationwide survey of team members from many organizations, by Wilson Learning Corporation, provides a useful model or benchmark of what OD specialists expect of teams. The researchers' question was simply: "What is a high-performance team?"[93] The respondents were asked to describe their peak experiences in work teams. Analysis of the survey results yielded the following eight attributes of high-performance teams:

1. *Participative leadership.* Creating an interdependency by empowering, freeing up, and serving others.

2. *Shared responsibility.* Establishing an environment in which all team members feel as responsible as the manager for the performance of the work unit.

3. *Aligned on purpose.* Having a sense of common purpose about why the team exists and the function it serves.

4. *High communication.* Creating a climate of trust and open, honest communication.

5. *Future focused.* Seeing change as an opportunity for growth.

6. *Focused on task.* Keeping meetings focused on results.

7. *Creative talents.* Applying individual talents and creativity.

8. *Rapid response.* Identifying and acting on opportunities.[94]

These attributes effectively combine many of today's most progressive ideas on management,[95] among them being participation, empowerment, service ethic, individual responsibility and development, self-management, trust, active listening, and envisioning. But patience and diligence are required. According to a manager familiar with work teams, "high-performance teams may take three to five years to build."[96] Let us keep this inspiring model of high-performance teams in mind as we conclude our discussion of team building.

Developing Team Members' Self-Management Skills

Self-management leadership
Process of leading others to lead themselves.

A promising dimension of team building has emerged in recent years. It is an extension of the behavioural self-management approach discussed in Chapter 15. Proponents call it **self-management leadership**, defined as the process of leading others to lead themselves. An underlying assumption is that self-managed teams are likely to fail if team members are not expressly taught to engage in self-management behaviours. This makes sense because it is unreasonable to expect employees who are accustomed to being managed and led to suddenly manage and lead themselves. Transition training is required, as discussed in the previous section. A key transition to self-management involves *current managers* engaging in self-management leadership behaviours. This is team building in the fullest meaning of the term.

Six self-management leadership behaviours were isolated in a field study of a manufacturing company organized around self-managed teams. The observed behaviours were

1. *Encourages self-reinforcement* (e.g., getting team members to praise each other for good work and results).

2. *Encourages self-observation/evaluation* (e.g., teaching team members to judge how well they are doing).

3. *Encourages self-expectation* (e.g., encouraging team members to expect high performance from themselves and the team).

4. *Encourages self-goal-setting* (e.g., having the team set its own performance goals).

5. *Encourages rehearsal* (e.g., getting team members to think about and practice new tasks).

6. *Encourages self-criticism* (e.g., encouraging team members to be critical of their own poor performance).[97]

According to the researchers, Charles Manz and Henry Sims, this type of leadership is a dramatic departure from traditional practices such as giving orders and/or making sure everyone gets along. Empowerment, not domination, is the overriding goal.

International Organizational Behaviour
The Wild World of Cross-Cultural Team Building

Brussels—Anyone can talk about cultural differences. Fons Trompenaars tries to make his students feel them.

To do that, the Dutch leader of workshops on "multicultural" management teaches his students (mostly executives) to play a game invented by one of his colleagues, L J P Brug. The object: building towers made of paper.

Mr. Trompenaars, a 39-year-old former Royal Dutch/Shell executive, divides a group of several dozen Swedish managers into two groups. Four are designated as "international experts" in building paper towers. Everyone else becomes a native of a make-believe village called Derdia.

"Your culture loves towers but doesn't know how to build them," Mr. Trompenaars tells the Derdians. "It's a bit like the British car industry."

The experts are sent out of the room to learn to make paper towers and prepare to pass that skill on to Derdia. Meanwhile, Mr. Trompenaars initiates the Swedes into the strange customs of Derdia.

Derdians' greetings involve kissing one another on the shoulder. Holding out a hand to someone means "Please go away." If they disagree, Derdians say "Yes!" and nod their heads vigorously.

What's more, Derdian women have a taboo against using paper or scissors in the presence of men, while men would never use a pencil or a ruler in front of women.

The Swedes, reserved a moment ago, throw themselves into the task of acting like Derdians. They merrily tap one another, kiss shoulders and bray "Yessss!"

Soon, two "experts" are allowed back into the room for a brief study of Derdian culture. The Derdians flock to the experts and gleefully kiss their shoulders. The experts turn red. They seem lost already.

"Would you please sit?" asks Hans Olav Friberg, a young "expert" who, back home in Sweden, works for a company that makes flooring.

"Yessss!" the Derdians say in a chorus. But they don't sit down.

"Who is in charge here?" Mr. Friberg inquires. "Yessss!" the Derdians reply.

Mr. Friberg leaves the room to confer with his fellow experts. "They didn't understand us," he tells them. But fellow expert Hakan Kalmermo isn't about to be deterred by strange habits. He is taking charge. As he briskly practices making a paper tower, Mr. Kalmermo says firmly to the other experts: "The target is to have them produce one tower."

The four experts carry paper and other supplies to the adjoining room, now known as Derdia. They begin to explain the process to the Derdians very slowly, as if speaking to small children. When one of the Derdians shows he understands the workings of a scissors, Mr. Kalmermo exclaims: "Good boy!"

Although Mr. Kalmermo works hard at making himself clear, the Derdians' customs and taboos obstruct progress. The men won't use rulers as long as women are around but don't explain this behaviour to the experts. The answer to every question seems to be "yes." At the end of 30 minutes, no tower has been completed.

The game is over; now comes the self-criticism. "They treated us like idiots," protests one of the Derdians.

The lessons are clear, but Mr. Trompenaars drives them home: If you don't figure out basics of a foreign culture, you won't get much accomplished. And if your biases lead you to think of foreign ways as childish, the foreigners may well respond by acting childish.

Still, Mr. Kalmermo, the take-charge expert, thinks his team was on the right track. "If we'd had another hour," he says, "I think we would have had 15 towers built."

Source B Hagerty, "Learning to Turn the Other Shoulder," *The Wall Street Journal*, June 14, 1993, pp B1, B3. Reprinted by permission of *The Wall Street Journal*, © 1993 Dow Jones & Company, Inc. All Rights Reserved Worldwide.

Summary of Key Concepts

1. *Explain how a work group becomes a team.* A team is a mature group where leadership is shared, accountability is both individual and collective, the members have developed their own purpose, problem solving is a way of life, and effectiveness is measured by collective outcomes.

2. *Identify and describe the four types of work teams.* Four general types of work teams are advice, production, project, and action teams. Each type has its characteristic degrees of specialization and coordination, work cycle, and outputs.

3. *Explain the ecological model of work team effectiveness.* According to the ecological model, two effectiveness criteria for work teams are performance and viability. The performance criterion is met if the group satisfies its clients/customers. A work group is viable if its members are satisfied and continue contributing. An ecological perspective is appropriate because work groups require an organizational life-support system. For instance, group participation is enhanced by an organizational culture that values employee empowerment.

4. *Discuss why teams fail.* Teams fail because unrealistic expectations cause frustration and failure. Common management mistakes include weak strategies, creating a hostile environment for teams, faddish use of teams, not learning from team experience, vague team assignments, poor team staffing, inadequate training, and lack of trust. Team members typically try too much too soon, experience conflict over differing work styles and personalities, ignore important group dynamics, resist change, exhibit poor interpersonal skills and chemistry, and display a lack of trust.

5. *List at least three things managers can do to build trust.* Six recommended ways to build trust are through communication, support, respect (especially delegation), fairness, predictability, and competence.

6. *Distinguish two types of group cohesiveness, and summarize cohesiveness research.* Cohesive groups have a shared sense of togetherness or a "we" feeling. Socio-emotional cohesiveness involves emotional satisfaction. Instrumental cohesiveness involves goal-directed togetherness. There is a small but significant relationship between cohesiveness and performance. The effect is stronger for smaller groups. Commitment to task among group members strengthens the cohesiveness →performance linkage. Success can build group cohesiveness. Cohesiveness is not a cure-all for group problems. Too much cohesiveness can lead to groupthink.

7. *Contrast quality circles and self-managed teams.* Quality circles are groups of volunteers, usually at the lowest operating levels, who meet periodically to identify and solve quality and productivity problems. Based on Japan's success with quality circles, the practice grew to fad proportions in the United States during the 1970s and 1980s. Sloppy implementation too often led to unrealized expectations and disappointment.

   Self-managed teams, barely beyond the experimentation stage, hold great promise for tapping the full potential of today's employees by increasing their autonomy. They call for nonmanagerial employees to take over traditional managerial duties such as planning, scheduling, and even hiring.

8. *Discuss what must be done to set the stage for self-managed teams.* Management must embed a new Theory Y logic in the organization's culture. Technology and the organization need to be redesigned to accommodate self-managed teams. Personnel changes and reward systems that reinforce teamwork are necessary. Supervisory training helps managers learn to be facilitators rather than traditional order givers. Team members need lots of training and team building to make them cooperative team players.

9. *Describe high-performance teams.* Eight attributes of high-performance teams are (*a*) participative leadership, (*b*) shared responsibility, (*c*) aligned on purpose, (*d*) high communication, (*e*) future focused for growth, (*f*) focused on task, (*g*) creative talents applied, and (*h*) rapid response.

Discussion Questions

1. Do you agree or disagree with Drucker's vision of more team-oriented organizations? Explain your assumptions and reasoning.

2. Which of the factors listed in Table 13–1 is most crucial to a successful team? Explain.

3. Why bother taking an ecological perspective of work-team effectiveness?

4. In your personal friendships, how do you come to trust someone? How fragile is that trust? Explain.

5. Why is delegation so important to building organizational trust?

6. Why should a group leader strive for both socio-emotional and instrumental cohesiveness?

7. Which threats during the life cycle of the quality circle programme deserve management's closest attention? Explain.

8. Would you like to work on a self-managed team? Explain.

9. How would you respond to a manager who said, "Why should I teach my people to manage themselves and work myself out of a job?"

10. Have you ever been a member of a high-performing team? If so, explain the circumstances and success factors.

Personal Awareness and Growth Exercise

How Trusting Are You?

Objectives

1. To introduce you to different dimensions of interpersonal trust.

2. To measure your trust in another person.

3. To discuss the managerial implications of your propensity to trust.

Introduction

The trend towards more open and empowered organizations, where teamwork and self-management are vital, requires heightened interpersonal trust. Customers need to be able to trust organizations producing the goods and services they buy, managers need to trust nonmanagers to carry out the organization's mission, and team members need to trust each other in order to get the job done. As with any other interpersonal skill, we need to be able to measure and improve our ability to trust others. This exercise is a step in that direction.

Instructions[98]

Think of a specific individual who currently plays an important role in your life (e.g., present or future spouse, friend, supervisor, co-worker, team member, etc.), and rate his or her trustworthiness for each statement according to the following scale. Total your responses, and compare your score to the arbitrary norms provided.

STRONGLY DISAGREE   **STRONGLY AGREE**

1 — 2 — 3 — 4 — 5 — 6 — 7 — 8 — 9 — 10

OVERALL TRUST   **SCORE**

1. I can expect this person to play fair. _____

2. I can confide in this person and know she/he desires to listen. _____

3. I can expect this person to tell me the truth. _____

4. This person takes time to listen to my problems and worries. _____

EMOTIONAL TRUST

5. This person would never intentionally misrepresent my point of view to other people. _____

6. I can confide in this person and know that he/she will not discuss it with others. _____

7. This person responds constructively and caringly to my problems. _____

RELIABLENESS

8. If this person promised to do me a favour, she/he would carry out that promise. _____

9. If I had an appointment with this person, I could count on him/her showing up. _____

10. I could lend this person money and count on getting it back as soon as possible. _____

11. I do not need a backup plan because I know this person will come through for me. _____

Total score = _____

QUESTIONS FOR DISCUSSION

1. Which particular items in this trust questionnaire are most central to your idea of trust? Why?

2. Does your score accurately depict the degree to which you trust (or distrust) the target person?

3. Why do you trust (or distrust) this individual?

4. If you trust this person to a high degree, how hard was it to build that trust? Explain. What would destroy that trust?

5. Based on your responses to this questionnaire, how would you rate your "propensity to trust"? Low? Moderate? High?

6. What are the managerial implications of your propensity to trust?

Group Exercise

Student Team Development Project

Objectives

1. To help you better understand the components of teamwork.

2. To give you a practical diagnostic tool to assess the need for team building.

3. To give you a chance to evaluate and develop an actual group/team.

Introduction

Student teams are very common in today's university classrooms. They are an important part of the move towards cooperative and experiential learning. In other words, learning by doing. Group dynamics and teamwork are best learned by doing. Unfortunately, many classroom teams wallow in ambiguity, conflict, and ineffectiveness. This team development questionnaire can play an important role in the life cycle of your classroom team or group. All members of your team can complete this evaluation at one or more of the following critical points in your team's life cycle: (1) when the team reaches a crisis point and threatens to break up, (2) about halfway through the life of the team, and (3) at the end of the team's life cycle. Discussion of the results by all team members can enhance the group's learning experience.

Instructions

Either at the prompting of your instructor or by group consensus, decide at what point in your team's life cycle this exercise should be completed. *Tip:* Each team member should write their responses to the 10 items on a sheet of paper with no names attached. This will permit the calculation of a group mean score for each item and for all 10 items. Attention should then turn to the discussion questions provided to help any team development problems surface and to point the way towards solutions.

(An alternative to these instructions is to evaluate a team or work group you are associated with in your current job. You may also draw from a group experience in a past job.)

Questionnaire[99]

1. To what extent do I feel a real part of the team?

5	4	3	2	1
Completely a part all the time.	A part most of the time.	On the edge—sometimes in, sometimes out.	Generally outside except for one or two short periods.	On the outside, not really part of the team.

2. How safe is it in this team to be at ease, relaxed, and myself?

5	4	3	2	1
I feel perfectly safe to be myself; they won't hold mistakes against me.	I feel most people would accept me if I were completely myself but there are some I am not sure about.	Generally one has to be careful what one says or does in this team.	I am quite fearful about being completely myself this team.	I am not a fool; I would never be myself team.

3. To what extent do I feel "under wraps," that is, have private thoughts, unspoken reservations, or unexpressed feelings and opinions that I have not felt comfortable bringing out into the open?

1	2	3	4	5
Almost completely under and wraps.	Under wraps many times.	Slightly more free and expressive than under wraps.	Quite free and expressive much of the time.	Almost completely free expressive.

4. How effective are we, in our team, in getting out and using the ideas, opinions, and information of all team members in making decisions?

1	2	3	4	5
We don't really encourage everyone to share their ideas, opinions, and information with the team in making decisions.	Only the ideas, opinions, and information of a few members are really known and used in making decisions.	Sometimes we hear the views of most members before making decisions, and sometimes we disregard most members.	A few are sometimes hesitant about sharing their opinions, but we generally have good participation in making decisions.	Everyone feels his or her ideas, opinions, and information are given a fair hearing before decisions are made.

5. To what extent are the goals the team is working towards understood, and to what extent do they have meaning for you?

5	4	3	2	1
I feel extremely good about goals of our team.	I feel fairly good, but some things are not too clear or meaningful.	A few things we are doing are clear and meaningful.	Much of the activity is not clear or meaningful ti me.	I really do not understand or feel involved in the goals of the team.

6. How well does the team work at its tasks?

1	2	3	4	5
Coasts, loafs, makes no progress.	Makes a little progress, but most members loaf.	Progress is slow; spurts of effective work.	Above average in progress and pace of work.	Works well; achieves definite progress.

7. Our planning and the way we operate as a team are largely influenced by:

1	2	3	4	5
One or two team members.	A clique.	Shifts from one person or clique to another.	Shared by most of the members, but some are left out.	Shared by all members of the team.

8. What is the level of responsibility for work in our team?

5	4	3	2	1
Each person assumes personal responsibility for getting work done.	A majority of the members assume responsibility for getting work done.	About half assume responsibility; about half do not.	Only a few assume responsibility for getting work done.	Nobody (except perhaps one) really assumes responsibility for getting work done.

9. How are differences or conflicts handled in our team?

1	2	3	4	5
Differences or conflicts are denied, supressed, or avoided at all costs.	Differences or conflicts are recognized but remain mostly unresolved.	Differences or conflicts are recognized, and some attempts are made to work them through by some members, often outside the team meetings.	Differences and conflicts are recognized and some attempts are made to deal with them in our team.	Differences and conflicts are recognized, and the team usually is working them through satisfactorily.

10. How do people relate to the team leader, chairperson, or "boss"?

1	2	3	4	5
The leader dominates the team, and people are often fearful or passive.	The leader tends to control thy team, although people generally agree with the leader's direction.	There is some give and take between the leader and the team members.	Team members relate easily to the leader and usually are able to influence leader decisions.	Team members respect the leader, but they work together as a unified team, with everyone participating and no one dominant.

Total score =

QUESTIONS FOR DISCUSSION

1. Have any of the items on the questionnaire helped you better understand why your team has had problems? What problems?

2. Based on Table 13–1, are you part of a group or team? Explain.

3. How do your responses to the items compare with the average responses from your group? What insights does this information provide?

4. Refer back to Tuckman's five-stage model of group development in Figure 10–2. Which stage is your team at? How can you tell?

5. If you are part way through your team's life cycle, what steps does your team need to take to become more effective?

6. If this is the end of your team's life cycle, what should your team have done different?

7. What lasting lessons about teamwork have you learned from this exercise?

Notes

[1] Based on and translated from J Verbeeck "Samen Gaat Het Sneller," *Belgian Business & Industrie Nederlands*, 1995, October 5.

[2] Excerpted from B Filipczak, "Concurrent Engineering: A Team by Any Other Name?" *Training*, August 1996, pp 55–56. Reprinted with permission from the August 1996 issue of *Training* magazine. Copyright 1996 Lakewood Publications, Minneapolis, MN. All rights reserved. Not for resale.

[3] B Dumaine, "Why Do We Work?" *Fortune*, December 26, 1994, p 202.

[4] See P F Drucker, "The Coming of the New Organization," *Harvard Business Review*, January—February 1988, pp 45–53.

[5] Data from "HR Data Files," *HRMagazine*, June 1995, p 65.

[6] K Lowry Miller, "Siemens Shapes Up," *Business Week*, May 1, 1995, p 52.

[7] P Engardio and G DeGeorge, "Importing Enthusiasm," *Business Week*, 1994 Special Issue: 21st Century Capitalism, p 122.

[8] J Rossant, "The Man Who's Driving Fiat Like a Ferrari," *Business Week*, January 23, 1995, p 82.

[9] J R Katzenbach and D K Smith, *The Wisdom of Teams: Creating the High-Performance Organization* (Boston: Harvard Business School Press, 1993), p 45.

[10] See L G Bolman and T E Deal, "What Makes a Team Work?" *Organizational Dynamics*, Autumn 1992, pp 34–44.

[11] J R Katzenbach and D K Smith, "The Discipline of Teams," *Harvard Business Review*, March–April 1993, p 112.

[12] "A Team's-Eye View of Teams," *Training*, November 1995, p 16.

[13] A M O'Leary-Kelly, J J Martocchio, and D D Frink, "A Review of the Influence of Group Goals on Group Performance," *Academy of Management Journal*, vol 37, no 5, 1994, pp 1285–303.

[14] E A Locke and G P A Latham, *Theory of Goal Setting and Task Performance* (Englewood Cliffs, N J: Prentice-Hall, 1990)

[15] See E Sundstrom, K P DeMeuse, and D Futrell, "Work Teams," *American Psychologist*, February 1990, pp 120–33.

[16] For an alternative typology of teams, see S G Cohen, "New Approaches to Teams and Teamwork," in *Organizing for the Future: The New Logic for Managing Complex Organizations*, eds J R Galbraith, E E Lawler III and Associates (San Francisco: Jossey-Bass, 1993), ch. 8, pp 194–226.

[17] For a good update, see A Reinhardt and S Browder, "Boeing," *Business Week*, September 30, 1996, pp 119–25.

[18] Based on P Marsch, "Managment: Down in the Boiler Room—Peter Marsch Explains How Blue Circle Developed a Standardised Product for the European market," *The Financial Times*, August 21, 1995, p 8.

[19] Based on and translated from F Krijnen, "De Schuimspaan als Management-tool," *Management Team*, May 19, 1995, pp 123–3

[20] Based on "How to build Effective Teams," *People Management*, February 23, 1995, pp 40–41.

[21] An instructive overview of group effectiveness models can be found in P S Goodman, E Ravlin, and M Schminke, "Understanding Groups in Organizations," in *Research in Organizational Behavior*, eds L L Cummings and B M Staw (Greenwich, CT: JAI Press, 1987), vol 9, pp 121–73. Also see D Dunphy and B Bryant, "Teams: Panaceas or Prescriptions for Improved Performance?" *Human Relations*, May 1996, pp 677–99.

[22] Sundstrom, De Meuse, and Futrell, "Work Teams," p 122.

[23] For a winning football coach's advice on teamwork, see R Rapaport, "To Build a Winning Team: An Interview with Head Coach Bill Walsh," *Harvard Business Review*, January–February 1993, pp 111–20. Also see M A Campion, G J Medsker, and A C Higgs, "Relations between Work Group Characteristics and Effectiveness: Implications for Designing Effective Work Groups," *Personnel Psychology*, Winter 1993, pp 823–50; and K K Reiste and A Hubrich, "How to Implement Successful Work Teams: Learning from the Frigidaire Experience," *National Productivity Review*, Autumn 1995, pp 45–55.

[24] "The trouble with Teams," *The Economist*, January 14, 1995, p 69.

[25] Based on ibid. and B Dumaine, "The Trouble with Teams," *Fortune*, September 5, 1994, pp 76–82.

[26] B. Dumaine, ibid.

[27] Team problems are revealed in L Holpp, "The Betrayal of the American Work Team," *Training*, May 1996, pp 38–42; S Wetlaufer, "The Team That Wasn't," *Harvard Business Review*, November—December 1994, pp 22–38; "More Trouble with Teams," *Training*, October 1996, p 21; and E Neuborne, "Companies Save, But Workers Pay," *USA Today*, February 25, 1997, pp 1B–2B.

[28] A Bennett, "Firms Run by Executive Teams Can Reap Rewards, Incur Risks," *The Wall Street Journal*, February 5, 1992, p B1.

[29] R Heller, "Several Heads are Better than One," *Management Today*, November 1995, p 33.

[30] M Deutch, *The Resolution of Conflict* (New Haven, CT: Yale University Press, 1973).

[31] J Kay, *Foundations of Corporate Success* (New York: Oxford University Press, 1993), pp 70–1.

[32] See "Work Teams Have Their Work Cut Out for Them," *HR Focus*, January 1993, p 24; W F Fechter, "The Competitive Myth," *Quality Progress*, May 1993, pp 87–88; and K G Salwen, "To Some Small Firms, Idea of Cooperating with Labor Is Foreign," *The Wall Street Journal*, July 27, 1993, pp A1–A6. Also see J T Delaney, "Workplace Cooperation: Current Problems, New Approaches," *Journal of Labor Research*, Winter 1996, pp 45–61; H Mintzberg, D Dougherty, J Jorgensen, and F Westley, "Some Surprising Things about Collaboration—Knowing How People Connect Makes It Work Better," *Organizational Dynamics*, Spring 1996, pp 60–71; R Crow, "Institutionalized Competition and Its Effects on Teamwork," *Journal for Quality and Participation*, June 1995, pp 46–54; and K G Smith, S J Carroll, and S J Ashford, "Intra- and Interorganizational Cooperation: Toward a Research Agenda," *Academy of Management Journal*, February 1995, pp 7–23.

[33] A Kohn, "How to Succeed without Even Vying," *Psychology Today*, September 1986, pp 27—28. Sports psychologists discuss

"cooperative competition" in S Sleek, "Competition: Who's the Real Opponent?" *APA Monitor,* July 1996, p 8.

[34]D W Johnson, G Maruyama, R Johnson, D Nelson, and L Skon, "Effects of Cooperative, Competitive, and Individualistic Goal Structures on Achievement: A Meta-Analysis," *Psychological Bulletin,* January 1981, pp 56–57. An alternative interpretation of the foregoing study that emphasizes the influence of situational factors can be found in J L Cotton and M S Cook, "Meta-Analysis and the Effects of Various Reward Systems: Some Different Conclusions from Johnson et al.," *Psychological Bulletin,* July 1982, pp 176–83. Also see A E Ortiz, D W Johnson, and R T Johnson, "The Effect of Positive Goal and Resource Interdependence on Individual Performance," *The Journal of Social Psychology,* April 1996, pp 243–49.

[35]S W Cook and M Pelfrey, "Reactions to Being Helped in Cooperating Interracial Groups: A Context Effect," *Journal of Personality and Social Psychology,* November 1985, p 1243.

[36]B Randall Palef, "The Team and Me: Reflections of a Design Group," *Personnel Journal*, February 1994, p 48.

[37]Cruise and R O'Brien, "Is Trust a Calculable Asset in the Firm," *Business Strategy Review,* Winter 1995, pp 39–54.

[38]Data from "HR Data File," *HRMagazine,* November 1995, p 47.

[39]J D Lewis and A Weigert, "Trust as a Social Reality," *Social Forces,* June 1985, p 971.

[40]R C Mayer, J H Davis, and F D Schoorman, "An Integrative Model of Organizational Trust," *Academy of Management Review,* July 1995, p 715.

[41]Lewis and Weigert, "Trust as a Social Reality," p 970. Also see S G Goto, "To Trust or Not to Trust: Situational and Dispositional Determinants," *Social Behavior and Personality,* no. 2, 1996, pp 119–32; T Tyler, P Degoey, and H Smith, "Understanding Why the Justice of Group Procedures Matters: A Test of the Psychological Dynamics of the Group-Value Model," *Journal of Personality and Social Psychology,* May 1996, pp 913–30; S C Currall and T A Judge, "Measuring Trust between Organizational Boundary Role Persons," *Organizational Behavior and Human Decision Processes,* November 1995, pp 151–70; L T Hosmer, "Trust: The Connecting Link between Organizational Theory and Philosophical Ethics," *Academy of Management Review,* April 1995, pp 379–403; and D J McAllister, "Affect- and Cognition-Based Trust as Foundations for Interpersonal Cooperation in Organizations," *Academy of Management Journal,* February 1995, pp 24–59.

[42]For an interesting trust exercise, see G Thompson and P F Pearce, "The Team-Trust Game," *Training & Development Journal,* May 1992, pp 42–43.

[43]For interesting new theory and research on telling lies, see B M DePaulo, D A Kashy, S E Kirkendol, M M Wyer, and J A Epstein, "Lying in Everyday Life," *Journal of Personality and Social Psychology,* May 1996, pp 979–95; and D A Kashy and B M DePaulo, "Who Lies?" *Journal of Personality and Social Psychology,* May 1996, pp 1037–51.

[44]Adapted from F Bartolomé, "Nobody Trusts the Boss Completely—Now What?" *Harvard Business Review,* March–April 1989, pp 135–42. Also see M A Korsgaard, D M Schweiger, and H J Sapienza, "Building Commitment, Attachment, and Trust in Strategic Decision-Making Teams: The Role of Procedural Justice," *Academy of Management Journal,* February 1995, pp 60–84.

[45]Additional trust-building tips and five "trustbusters" are reported in "You Probably Won't Believe This, But. . . .," *Training,* September 1995, pp 19–20.

[46]Based on S Caudron, "Create an Empowering Environment," *Personnel Journal,* September 1995, pp 28–36.

[47]W Foster Owen, "Metaphor Analysis of Cohesiveness in Small

Discussion Groups," *Small Group Behavior,* August 1985, p 416. Also see J Keyton and J Springston, "Redefining Cohesiveness in Groups," *Small Group Research,* May 1990, pp 234–54.

[48]This distinction is based on discussion in A Tziner, "Differential Effects of Group Cohesiveness Types: A Clarifying Overview," *Social Behavior and Personality,* no. 2, 1982, pp 227–39.

[49]B Mullen and C Copper, "The Relation between Group Cohesiveness and Performance: An Integration," *Psychological Bulletin,* March 1994, p 224.

[50]Ibid. Additional research evidence is reported in T Kozakaï, S Moscovici, and B Personnaz, "Contrary Effects of Group Cohesiveness in Minority Influence: Intergroup Categorization of the Source and Levels of Influence," *European Journal of Social Psychology,* November–December 1994, pp 713–18.

[51]Based on B Mullen, T Anthony, E Salas, and J E Driskell, "Group Cohesiveness and Quality of Decision Making: An Integration of Tests of the Groupthink Hypothesis," *Small Group Research,* May 1994, pp 189–204.

[52]Translated and adapted from Ph Tranchart, "Révolution Culturelle' Chez Renault," *Enterprises-formation,* December 1995, pp 10–11.

[53]See, for example, P Jin, "Work Motivation and Productivity in Voluntarily Formed Work Teams: A Field Study in China," *Organizational Behavior and Human Decision Processes,* 1993, pp 133–55.

[54]For example, see M Bassin, "From Teams to Partnerships," *HRMagazine,* January 1996, pp 84–86; B Geber, "Virtual Teams," *Training,* April 1995, pp 36–40; and J Nirenberg, "From Team Building to Community Building," *National Productivity Review,* Winter 1994–95, pp 51–62.

[55]Based on discussion in E E Lawler III and S A Mohrman, "Quality Circles: After the Honeymoon," *Organizational Dynamics,* Spring 1987, pp 42–54. Also see B Sheehy, "Understanding Q Levels—From Quality Circles to Federal Budgets," *National Productivity Review,* Winter 1992–93, pp 3–7.

[56]For a report on 8,000 quality circles in Mexico, see R Carvajal, "Its Own Reward," *Business Mexico,* Special edition 1996, pp 26–28.

[57]The historical development of quality circles is discussed by C Stohl, "Bridging the Parallel Organization: A Study of Quality Circle Effectiveness," in *Organizational Communication,* ed M L McLaughlin (Beverly Hills, CA: Sage Publications, 1987), pp 416–30; T Li-Ping Tang, P Smith Tollison, and H D Whiteside, "The Effect of Quality Circle Initiation on Motivation to Attend Quality Circle Meetings and on Task Performance," *Personnel Psychology,* Winter 1987, pp 799–814; and N Kano, "A Perspective on Quality Activities in American Firms," *California Management Review,* Spring 1993, pp 12–31. Also see the discussion of quality circles in J B Keys, L T Denton, and T R Miller, "The Japanese Management Theory Jungle—Revisited," *Journal of Management,* Summer 1994, pp 373–402.

[58]Based on discussion in K Buch and R Spangler, "The Effects of Quality Circles on Performance and Promotions," *Human Relations,* June 1990, pp 573–82.

[59]See G R Ferris and J A Wagner III, "Quality Circles in the United States: A Conceptual Reevaluation," *The Journal of Applied Behavioral Science,* no. 2, 1985, pp 155–67.

[60]Lawler and Mohrman, "Quality Circles: After the Honeymoon," p 43. Also see E E Lawler III, "Total Quality Management and Employee Involvement: Are They Compatible?" *Academy of Management Executive,* February 1994, pp 68–76.

[61]A good case study of resistance to team empowerment can be found in M Levinson, "Playing with Fire," *Newsweek,* June 21,

1993, pp 46–48.

[62]See M L Marks, "The Question of Quality Circles," *Psychology Today,* March 1986, pp 36–38, 42, 44, 46.

[63]See A K Naj, "Some Manufacturers Drop Effort to Adopt Japanese Techniques," *The Wall Street Journal,* May 7, 1993, p A1.

[64]See E E Adam, Jr., "Quality Circle Performance," *Journal of Management,* March 1991, pp 25–39.

[65]See R P Steel and R F Lloyd, "Cognitive, Affective, and Behavioral Outcomes of Participation in Quality Circles: Conceptual and Empirical Findings," *The Journal of Applied Behavioral Science,* no. 1, 1988, pp 1–17; M L Marks, P H Mirvis, E J Hackett, and J F Grady, Jr., "Employee Participation in a Quality Circle Program: Impact on Quality of Work Life, Productivity, and Absenteeism," *Journal of Applied Psychology,* February 1986, pp 61–69; and Buch and Spangler, "The Effects of Quality Circles on Performance and Promotions." Additional research is reported in T Li-Ping Tang, P Smith Tollison, and H D Whiteside, "Differences between Active and Inactive Quality Circles in Attendance and Performance," *Public Personnel Management,* Winter 1993, pp 579–90; and C Doucouliagos, "Worker Participation and Productivity in Labor-Managed and Participatory Capitalist Firms: A Meta-Analysis," *Industrial and Labor Relations Review,* October 1995, pp 58–77.

[66]Lawler and Mohrman, "Quality Circles: After the Honeymoon," p 52.

[67]L Wood, "Increase in Self-managed Teams: Industry," *The Financial Times,* June 26, 1995, p 11.

[68]M Arthur, "Rover Managers Learn to Take a Back Seat," *Personnel Management,* October 1994, pp 58–63.

[69]"Industrial Relations Services, Autonomy in Store: Self-Management at the Body Shop," *Industrial Relations Review and Report,* 583, June 1993.

[70]Good background discussions can be found in work cited in note 74 and in C Lee, "Beyond teamwork," *Training,* June 1990, pp 25–32.

[71]For example, see M Selz, "Testing Self-Managed Teams, Entrepreneur Hopes to Lose Job," *The Wall Street Journal,* January 11, 1994, pp B1–B2. Also see "Even in Self-Managed Teams There Has to Be a Leader," *Supervisory Management,* December 1994, pp 7–8.

[72]See D R Denison, S L Hart, and J A Kahn, "From Chimneys to Cross-Functional Teams: Developing and Validating a Diagnostic Model," *Academy of Management Journal,* August 1996, pp 1005–23.

[73]Based on C M Solomon, "Global Teams: The Ultimate Collaboration," *Personnel Journal,* September 1995, pp 49–58.

[74]See P S Goodman, R Devadas, and T L Griffith Hughson, "Groups and Productivity: Analyzing the Effectiveness of Self-Managing Teams," in *Productivity in Organizations,* eds J P Campbell, R J Campbell and Associates (San Francisco: Jossey-Bass, 1988), pp 295–327.

[75]Good background discussions can be found in work cited in note 74 and in C Lee, "Beyond Teamwork," *Training,* June 1990, pp 25–32. Also see S G Cohen, G E Ledford, Jr, and G M Spreitzer, "A Predictive Model of Self-Managing Work Team Effectiveness," *Human Relations,* May 1996, pp 643–76.

[76]For an instructive continuum of work team autonomy, see R D Banker, J M Field, R G Schroeder, and K K Sinha, "Impact of Work Teams on Manufacturing Performance: A Longitudinal Field Study," *Academy of Management Journal,* August 1996, pp 867–90.

[77]Drawn from Goodman, Devadas, and Hughson, "Groups and Productivity: Analyzing the Effectiveness of Self-Managing Teams." Also see E F Rogers, W Metlay, I T Kaplan, and T Shapiro,

"Self-Managing Work Teams: Do They Really Work?" *Human Resource Planning,* no. 2, 1995, pp 53–57.

[78]For useful tips, see L Holpp, "Five Ways to Sink Self-Managed Teams," *Training,* September 1993, pp 38–42.

[79]See B Dumaine, "The New Non-Manager Managers," *Fortune,* February 22, 1993, pp 80–84. Also see "Easing the Fear of Self-Directed Teams," *Training,* August 1993, pp 14, 55–56.

[80]See Dumaine, "Who Needs a Boss?" pp 55, 58; and J Hillkirk, "Self-Directed Work Teams Give TI Lift," *USA Today,* December 20, 1993, p 8B. A good contingency model for empowering teams is presented in R C Liden, S J Wayne, and L Bradway, "Connections Make the Difference," *HRMagazine,* February 1996, pp 73–79.

[81]For an instructive case study on this topic, see C C Manz, D E Keating, and A Donnellon, "Preparing for an Organizational Change to Employee Self-Management: The Managerial Transition," *Organizational Dynamics,* Autumn 1990, pp 15–26.

[82]Based on K Lowry Miller, "GM's German Lessons," *Business Week,* December 20, 1993, pp 67–68.

[83]See J T Buckley, "Getting into Outdoors Builds Corporate Buddies," *USA Today,* August 19, 1996, pp 1A–2A; and J T Taylor, "Participants Learn the Ropes of Team Building," *USA Today,* August 19, 1996, p 7B. For more on outdoor experiential learning, see H Campbell, "Adventures in Teamland," *Personnel Journal,* May 1996, pp 56–62.

[84]R Henkoff, "Companies that Train Best," *Fortune,* March 22, 1993, p 73.

[85]See M J McCarthy, "A Management Rage: Beating the Drums for the Company," *The Wall Street Journal,* August 13, 1996, pp A1, A6.

[86]Data from "1996 Industry Report: Specific Types of Training," *Training,* October 1996, p 59.

[87]Data from E Stephan, G E Mills, R W Pace, and L Ralphs, "HRD in the Fortune 500: A Survey," *Training and Development Journal,* January 1988, pp 26–32.

[88]An excellent resource is W G Dyer, *Team Building: Current Issues and New Alternatives,* 3rd ed (Reading, MA: Addison-Wesley, 1995).

[89]R Beckhard, "Optimizing Team-Building Efforts," *Journal of Contemporary Business,* Summer 1972, p 24.

[90]Based on Solomon (note 73); J R Katzenbach and D K Smith, "The Discipline of Teams," *Harvard Business Review,* March–April 1993, pp 111–20; D J McNerney, "The Facts of Live for Teambuilding," *HR Focus,* December 1994, pp 12–13; M A Campion, G J Medsker and A C Higgs, "Relations Between Work Groups," *Personnel Psychology,* 46, 1993, pp 823–50.

[91]R Yale Bergstrom, "Teams: Dedicated Players," *Production,* March 1994, pp 58–60.

[92]C Bonington, "The Heights of Teamwork," *Personnel Management,* October 1994, pp 44–7.

[93]S Bucholz and T Roth, *Creating the High-Performance Team* (New York: John Wiley & Sons, 1987), p xi.

[94]Ibid., p 14.

[95]See S Caminiti, "What Team Leaders Need to Know," *Fortune,* February 20, 1995, pp 93–100; K Labich, "Elite Teams Get the Job Done," *Fortune,* February 19, 1996, pp 90–99; and E Hart, "Top Teams," *Management Review,* February 1996, pp 43–47.

[96]P King, "What Makes Teamwork Work?" *Psychology Today,* December 1989, p 17.

[97]Adapted from C C Manz and H P Sims, Jr., "Leading Workers to Lead Themselves: The External Leadership of Self-Managing Work Teams," *Administrative Science Quarterly,* March 1987, pp 106–29. Also see C C Manz, "Beyond Self-Managing Work Teams: Toward

Self-Leading Teams in the Workplace," in *Research in Organizational Change and Development,* vol. 4, eds R W Woodman and W A Pasmore (Greenwich, CT: JAI Press, 1990), pp 273–99; C C Manz, "Self-Leading Work Teams: Moving Beyond Self-Management Myths," *Human Relations,* no. 11, 1992, pp 1119–40; and C C Manz, *Mastering Self-Leadership: Empowering Yourself for Personal Excellence* (Englewood Cliffs, NJ: Prentice-Hall, 1992).

[98]Questionnaire items adapted from C Johnson-George and W C Swap, "Measurement of Specific Interpersonal Trust: Construction and Validation of a Scale to Assess Trust in a Specific Other," *Journal of Personality and Social Psychology,* December 1982, pp 1306–17; and D J McAllister, "Affect- and Cognition-Based Trust as Foundations for Interpersonal Cooperation in Organizations," *Academy of Management Journal,* February 1995, pp 24–59.

[99]Ten questionnaire items excerpted from W G Dyer, *Team Building: Current Issues and New Alternatives,* 3rd ed (Reading, MA: Addison-Wesley, 1995), pp 96–99.

Four

Organizational Processes

Fourteen   Organizational Communication in the
Computerized Workplace

Fifteen   Behaviour Modification and
Self-Management

Sixteen   Leadership

Seventeen   Managing Occupational Stress

Fourteen

Organizational Communication in the Computerized Workplace

LEARNING OBJECTIVES

When you finish studying the material in this chapter, you should be able to:

1. Describe the perceptual process model of communication.

2. Explain the contingency approach to media selection.

3. Contrast the communication styles of assertiveness, aggressiveness, and nonassertiveness.

4. Discuss the primary sources of both nonverbal communication and listener comprehension.

5. Identify and give examples of the three different listening styles, and review the 10 keys to effective listening.

6. Describe the communication differences between men and women, and explain the source of these differences.

7. Discuss patterns of hierarchical communication and the grapevine.

8. Demonstrate your familiarity with four antecedents of communication distortion between managers and employees.

9. Explain the information technology of Internet/Intranent, e-mail, collaborative computing, and videoconferencing, and explain the related use of telecommuting.

10. Describe the process, personal, physical, and semantic barriers to effective communication.

The Intranet Revolution

Imagine that your company has 20 sites and 1000 people who need timely access to company news, corporate policy changes, human resource procedures — even simple, but crucial, documents such as phone books, product specifications and, pricing information.

Normally, you use printed matter, such as employee handbooks, price lists, sales guides, etc. This printed material is both expensive and time consuming to produce, as well as not contributing directly to the bottom line. Once created, there is the question of distribution and dissemination. How can you guarantee that all your people have received exactly what they need? How can you be sure they have the latest and correct versions? How can you ensure that they even know that important policy details or other information have changed or are now available? The simple answer is, with existing technology, you can't.

Add to this the problem that, due to the changing nature of any organization in today's frenetic business world, the shelf life of any internal printed matter is reducing so rapidly that, in many cases, it is out of date before it reaches the people that need it. Many corporate hours are lost just confirming and verifying the validity of information.

Then we can start to consider the direct cost of preparation, typesetting, production, distribution, and mailing. Add labour costs and overheads and the fact that during any financial year most documents require reprinting with ever-increasing frequency. For example a standard price book may cost in the region of £15 each to produce. Add the distribution cost and multiply this by the number of people who need it, and then by the number of times per year it is produced. We can very easily see the substantial cost that is required to deliver just a single, accurate document to one of our employees to allow them to perform their job. But if you also add the hidden cost of the people verifying accuracy and quality of the information the cost becomes even more astronomical. And this is just one document!

The above example assumed 20 sites and 1,000 employees, but the reality is that this problem is equally important to a single site with 20 people. Accurate, timely communication and information flow is essential in today's world.

The solution to this problem is provided by just one of the technologies available under the generic heading of "the Internet." Different problems require different solutions, which is why the use of the full spectrum of Internet technologies within an organization will generate one of the biggest corporate IT revolutions as the birth of the Intranet becomes a reality.

In simple terms, the Intranet is the descriptive term being used for the implementation of Internet technologies within a corporate organization, rather than for external connection to the global Internet. This implementation is performed in such a way as to transparently deliver the immense informational resources of an organization to each individual's desktop with minimal cost, time and effort.

"Intranets in Europe are going up even faster, around 25 percent faster than commercial Internet services," says Netscape European director Didier Benchimol. Ford Motor Co. has for example created an intranet link between American, Asian, European design centres for the 1996 creation of the Taurus.[1]

Discussion Question
Do you think intranets will create a corporate revolution?

Management is communication. Every managerial function and activity involves some form of direct or indirect communication. Whether planning and organizing or directing and leading, managers find themselves communicating with and through others. Managerial decisions and organizational policies are ineffective unless they are understood by those responsible for enacting them. Management experts also note that effective communication is a cornerstone of ethical organizational behaviour:

Communication by top executives keeps the firm on its ethical course, and top executives must ensure that the ethical climate is consistent with the company's overall objectives. Communication is important in providing guidance for ethical standards and activities that provide integration between the functional areas of the business. A vice president of marketing, for example, must communicate and work with regional sales managers and other marketing employees to make sure that all agree on what constitutes certain unethical activities such as bribery, price collusion, and deceptive sales techniques. Top corporate executives must also communicate with managers at the operations level (in production, sales, and finance, for example) and enforce overall ethical standards within the organization.[2]

Moreover, effective communication is critical for both managerial and organizational success. For example, a study involving 65 savings and loan employees and 110 manufacturing employees revealed that employee satisfaction with organizational communication was positively and significantly correlated with both job satisfaction and performance. The quality of organizational communication also was found to play a significant role in employees' acceptance of organizational change.[3] Finally, a recent survey of 300 executives underscored the importance of communication. Results demonstrated that 71 per cent and 68 per cent of the respondents believed that written communication skills and interpersonal communication skills, respectively, were critical competencies that needed enhancement via training. These executives believed the lack of communication skills had resulted in increased costs.[4]

This chapter will help you better understand how managers can both improve their communication skills and design more effective communication programmes. We discuss (1) basic dimensions of the communication process, focusing on a perceptual process model and a contingency approach to selecting media; (2) interpersonal communication; (3) organizational communication patterns; and (4) the dynamics of modern communications.

Basic Dimensions of the Communication Process

Communication

Interpersonal exchange of information and understanding.

Communication is defined as "the exchange of information between a sender and a receiver, and the inference (perception) of meaning between the individuals involved."[5] Analysis of this exchange reveals that communication is a two-way process consisting of consecutively linked elements (see Figure 14–1). Managers who understand this process can analyse their own communication patterns as well as design communication programmes that fit organizational needs. This section reviews a perceptual process model of communication and discusses a contingency approach to choosing communication media.

A Perceptual Process Model of Communication

The communication process historically has been described in terms of a *conduit* model. This traditional model depicts communication as a pipeline in which information and meaning are transferred from person to person. Recently, however, communication scholars have criticized the conduit model for being based on unrealistic assumptions. For example, the conduit model assumes communication transfers *intended meanings* from person to person.[6] If this assumption were true, miscommunication would not exist and there would be no need to worry about being misunderstood. We could simply say or write what we want and assume the listener or reader accurately understands our intended meaning.

As we all know, communicating is not that simple or clear-cut. Communication is fraught with miscommunication. In recognition of this, researchers have begun to examine communication as a form of social information processing (recall the discussion in

Figure 14–1   A Perceptual Model of Communication

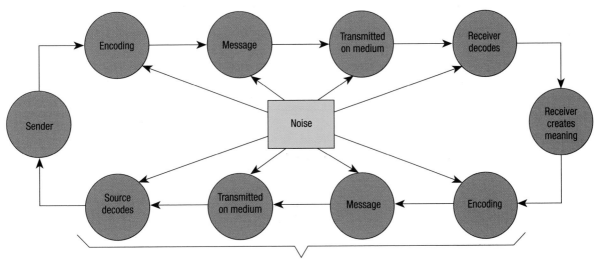

Feedback Loop

Perceptual model of communication

Consecutively linked elements within the communication process.

Chapter 6) in which receivers interpret messages by cognitively processing information. This view led to development of a **perceptual model of communication** that depicts communication as a process in which receivers create meaning in their own minds. Let us briefly examine the elements of the perceptual process model shown in Figure 14–1.

Sender   The sender is an individual, group, or organization that desires or attempts to communicate with a particular receiver. Receivers may be individuals, groups, or organizations.

Encoding   Communication begins when a sender encodes an idea or thought. Encoding translates mental thoughts into a code or language that can be understood by others. Managers typically encode using words, numbers, gestures, nonverbal cues such as facial expressions, or pictures. Moreover, different methods of encoding can be used to portray similar ideas. The following short exercise highlights this point.

On a piece of paper, draw a picture of the area currently surrounding you. Now, write a verbal description of the same area. Does the pictorial encoding portray the same basic message as the verbal description? Which mode was harder to use and which more effective? Interestingly, a growing number of management consultants recommend using visual communication, such as drawings, to analyse and improve group interaction and problem solving and to reduce stress.

The Message   The output of encoding is a message. There are two important points to keep in mind about messages. First, they contain more than meets the eye. Messages may contain hidden agendas as well as trigger affective or emotional reactions. For example, comparisons of internal and external documents within the forest products industry over a 10-year period demonstrated that executives' private and public evaluative statements about events and situations were inconsistent. These executives apparently wanted to convey different messages to the public and to internal employees.[7] The second point to consider about messages is that they need to match the medium used to transmit them. How would you evaluate the match between the message of letting someone know they have been laid off and the communication medium used in the following examples?

A man finds out he has been let go when a restaurant won't accept his company credit card. A woman manager gets the news via a note placed on her chair during lunch. Employees at a high-tech firm learn of their fate when their security codes no longer open the front door of their office building.[8]

These horrible mismatches reveal how thoughtless managers can be when they do not carefully consider the interplay between a message and the medium used to convey it. More is said about this issue in the next section.

Selecting a Medium   Managers can communicate through a variety of media. Potential media include face-to-face conversations, telephone calls, electronic mail, voice mail, written memos or letters, photographs or drawings, meetings, bulletin boards, computer output, and charts or graphs. Choosing the appropriate media depends on many factors, including the nature of the message, its intended purpose, the type of audience, proximity to the audience, time horizon for disseminating the message, and personal preferences.

All media have advantages and disadvantages. Face-to-face conversations, for instance, are useful for communicating about sensitive or important issues and those requiring feedback and intensive interaction. Telephones are convenient, fast, and private, but lack nonverbal information. Although writing memos or letters is time consuming, it is a good medium when it is difficult to meet with the other person, when formality and a written record are important, and when face-to-face interaction is not necessary to enhance understanding. More is said later in this chapter about choosing media.

Decoding   Decoding is the receiver's version of encoding. Decoding consists of translating verbal, oral, or visual aspects of a message into a form that can be interpreted.

Receivers rely on social information processing to determine the meaning of a message during decoding. Decoding is a key contributor to misunderstanding in interracial and intercultural communication because decoding by the receiver is subject to social values and cultural values that may not be understood by the sender.

Learning about cultural values and norms is the key to improving communication across diverse cultures. Consider in this context the problems Western organizations are faced with when starting up a business in former communist societies:

When Siemens chose Poland and the Czech Republic for the production of wire harnesses that connect all the electronic parts of a car, it had to conclude that the habits of a lifetime can be difficult to break. People don't believe they should have to move for a job, so Siemens has to bus workers to its Czech wire harness plant from 60 km away.

Danube Knitwear, set up in southern Hungary by private Western investors to export T-shirts, gives bonuses for attendance to rid its workers of the communist penchant for sneaking out to do errands. "People have to move faster than they are used to," says CEO Michael Smolens.[9]

Creating Meaning   In contrast to the conduit model's assumption that meaning is directly transferred from sender to receiver, the perceptual model is based on the belief that a receiver creates the meaning of a message in his or her mind. A receiver's interpretation of a message will often differ from that intended by the sender. In turn, receivers act according to their own interpretations, not the communicator's. A communication expert concluded the following after considering this element of the communication process:

Miscommunication and unintentional communication are to be expected, for they are the norm. Organizational communicators who take these ideas seriously would realize just how difficult successful communication truly is. Presumably, they would be conscious of the constant effort needed to communicate in ways most closely approximating their intentions. . . . Communication is fraught with unintentionality and, thereby, great difficulty for communicators.[10]

Managers are encouraged to rely on *redundancy* of communication to reduce this unintentionality. This can be done by transmitting the message over multiple media. For example, a production manager might follow up a phone conversation about a critical schedule change with a memo.

Feedback   The receiver's response to a message is the crux of the feedback loop. At this point in the communication process, the receiver becomes a sender. Specifically, the receiver encodes a response and then transmits it to the original sender. This new message is then decoded and interpreted. As you can see from this discussion, feedback is used as a comprehension check. It gives senders an idea of how accurately their message is understood.

Noise

Interference with the transmission and understanding of a message.

Noise   Noise represents anything that interferes with the transmission and understanding of a message. It affects all linkages of the communication process. Noise includes factors such as a speech impairment, poor telephone connections, illegible handwriting, inaccurate statistics in a memo or report, poor hearing and eyesight, and physical distance between sender and receiver. Managers can improve communication by reducing noise. Growing diversity in the workforce is one example of a significant source of noise that managers need to manage. According to Kazu Chiba, Japanese ambassador to Britain, language is one of the reasons why Japanese companies choose Britain over its other European parts to establish themselves: "It is much easier for a Japanese manager to understand what the workers are saying in Britain, be that in Wales or Scotland, than elsewhere in Europe."[11]

Choosing Media: A Contingency Perspective

Managers need to determine which media to use for both obtaining and disseminating information. If an inappropriate medium is used, managerial decisions may be based on

Figure 14–2	Characteristics of Information Richness for Different Media

INFORMATION RICHNESS	MEDIUM	FEEDBACK	CHANNEL	TYPE OF COMMUNICATION	LANGUAGE SOURCE
High	Face-toFace	Immediate	Visual, audio	Personal	Body, natural
▲	Telephone	Fast	Audio	Personal	Natural
	Personal written	Slow	Limited visual	Personal	Natural
	Formal written	Very slow	Limited visual	Impersonal	Natural
Low	Formal numeric	Very slow	Limited visual	Impersonal	Numeric

Source: Adapted from R L Daft and R H Lengel, "Information Richness: A New Approach to Managerial Behavior and Organization Design," in *Research in Organizational Behavior,* eds B M Staw and L L Cummings (Greenwich, CT: JAI Press, 1984), p 197.

inaccurate information and/or important messages may not reach the intended audience. Media selection therefore is a key component of communication effectiveness. This section explores a contingency model designed to help managers select communication media in a systematic and effective manner. Media selection in this model is based on the interaction between information richness and complexity of the problem/situation at hand.

Information richness

Information-carrying capacity of data.

Information Richness   Respected organizational theorists Richard Daft and Robert Lengel define **information richness** in the following manner:

Richness is defined as the potential information-carrying capacity of data. If the communication of an item of data, such as a wink, provides substantial new understanding, it would be considered rich. If the datum provides little understanding, it would be low in richness.[12]

As this definition implies, alternative media possess levels of information richness that vary from high to low.

Information richness is determined by four factors: (1) feedback (ranging from immediate to very slow), (2) channel (ranging from a combined visual and audio to limited visual), (3) type of communication (personal versus impersonal), and (4) language source (body, natural, or numeric). In Figure 14-2, the information richness of five different media is categorized in terms of these four factors.

Face-to-face is the richest form of communication. It provides immediate feedback, which serves as a comprehension check. Moreover, it allows for the observation of multiple language cues, such as body language and tone of voice, over more than one channel. Although high in richness, the telephone is not as informative as the face-to-face medium. Formal numeric media such as quantitative computer printouts or video displays possess the lowest richness. Feedback is very slow, the channel involves only limited visual information, and the numeric information is impersonal.

Complexity of the Managerial Problem/Situation   Managers face problems and situations that range from low to high in complexity. Low-complexity situations are routine, predictable, and managed by using objective or standard procedures. Calculating an employee's pay is an example of low complexity. Highly complex situations, like a corporate reorganization, are ambiguous, unpredictable, hard to analyse, and often emotionally laden. Managers spend considerably more time analysing these situations because they rely on more sources of information during their deliberations. There are no set solutions to complex problems or situations.

Contingency Recommendations   The contingency model for selecting media is graphically depicted in Figure 14–3. As shown, there are three zones of communication effectiveness. Effective communication occurs when the richness of the medium is matched appropriately with the complexity of the problem or situation. Media low in richness—formal numeric or formal written—are better suited for simple problems, while media high in richness—telephone or face-to-face—are appropriate for complex

Figure 14 – 3   A Contingency Model for Selecting Communication Media

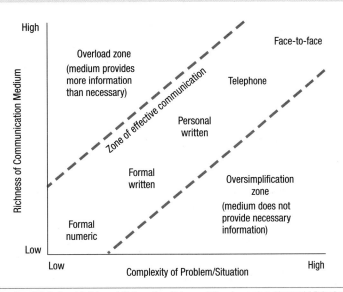

Source: Adapted from R L Daft and R H Lengel, "Information Richness: A New Approach to Managerial Behavior and Organization Design," in *Research in Organizational Behavior,* eds B M Staw and L L Cummings (Greenwich, CT: JAI Press, 1984), p 199. Used with permission.

problems or situations. Consider, for example, how The Body Shop maintains communication with its many shops:

[Anita] Roddick [The Body Shop's head] constantly worked at communications within the company. Every shop had a bulletin board, a fax machine and a video player through which she bombarded staff with information.[13]

Conversely, ineffective communication occurs when the richness of the medium is either too high or too low for the complexity of the problem or situation. Extending the preceding example, a district sales manager would fall into the *overload zone* if he or she communicated monthly sales reports through richer media. Conducting face-to-face meetings or telephoning each salesperson would provide excessive information and take more time than necessary to communicate monthly sales data. The oversimplification zone represents another ineffective choice of communication medium. In this situation, media with inadequate richness are used to communicate complicated problems

Effective communicators need to use rich media for an extended period of time to prepare employees for mergers and reorganizations.

Research Evidence   The relationship between media richness and problem/situation complexity has not been researched extensively because the underlying theory is relatively new. Available evidence indicates that managers used richer sources when confronted with ambiguous and complicated events.[14] Moreover, a meta-analysis of more than 40 studies revealed that media usage was significantly different across organizational levels. Upper-level executives/managers spent more time in face-to-face meetings than did lower-level managers.[15] This finding is consistent with recommendations derived from the contingency model just discussed.

Interpersonal Communication

The quality of interpersonal communication within an organization is very important. People with good communication skills helped groups make better decisions and were promoted more frequently than individuals with less developed abilities.[16] Although there

**Communication
competence**

Ability to effectively use
communication behaviours in
a given context.

is no universally accepted definition of **communication competence,** it is a performance-based index of an individual's ability to effectively use communication behaviours in a given context.[17]

Communication competence is determined by three components: communication abilities and traits, situational factors, and the individuals involved in the interaction (see Figure 14–4). Cross-cultural awareness, for example, is an important communication ability/trait. As a case in point, the International OB illustrates how a lack of cross-cultural awareness can negatively affect business negotiations.

Individuals involved in an interaction also affect communication competence. For example, people are likely to withhold information and react emotionally or defensively when interacting with someone they dislike or do not trust. You can improve your communication competence through five communication styles/abilities/traits under your control: assertiveness, aggressiveness, nonassertiveness, nonverbal communication, and active listening. We conclude this section by discussing gender differences in communication.

Assertiveness, Aggressiveness, and Nonassertiveness

Assertive style

Expressive and self-enhancing, but does not take advantage of others.

Aggressive style

Expressive and self-enhancing, but takes unfair advantage of others.

Nonassertive style

Timid and self-denying behaviour.

The saying, "You can attract more bees with honey than with vinegar," captures the difference between using an assertive communication style and an aggressive style. Research studies indicate that assertiveness is more effective than aggressiveness in both work-related and consumer contexts.[18] An **assertive style** is expressive and self-enhancing and is based on the "ethical notion that it is not right or good to violate our own or others' basic human rights, such as the right to self-expression or the right to be treated with dignity and respect."[19] In contrast, an **aggressive style** is expressive and self-enhancing and strives to take unfair advantage of others. A **nonassertive style** is characterized by timid and self-denying behaviour. Nonassertiveness is ineffective because it gives the other person an unfair advantage.

Managers may improve their communication competence by trying to be more assertive and less aggressive or nonassertive. This can be achieved by using the appropriate nonverbal and verbal behaviours listed in Table 14–1. For instance, managers should attempt to use the nonverbal behaviours of good eye contact, a strong, steady, and

Figure 14–4   Communication Competence Affects Upward Mobility

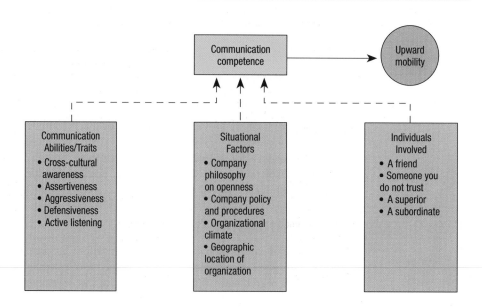

Table 14 – 1   Communication Styles

COMMUNICATION STYLE	DESCRIPTION	NONVERBAL BEHAVIOUR PATTERN	VERBAL BEHAVIOUR PATTERN
Assertive	Pushing hard without attacking; permits others to influence outcome; expressive and self-enhancing without intruding on others	Good eye contact Comfortable but firm posture Strong, steady, and audible voice Facial expressions matched to message Appropriately serious tone Selective interruptions to ensure understanding	Direct and unambiguous language No attributions or evaluations of other's behaviour Use of "I" statements and cooperative "we" statements
Aggressive	Taking advantage of others; expressive and self-enhancing at other's expense	Glaring eye contact Moving or leaning too close Threatening gestures (pointed finger; clenched fist) Loud voice Frequent interruptions	Swear words and abusive language Attributions and evaluations of other's behaviour Sexist or racist terms Explicit threats or put-downs
Nonassertive	Encouraging others to take advantage of us; inhibited; self-denying	Little eye contact Downward glances Slumped posture Constantly shifting weight Wringing hands Weak or whiny voice	Qualifiers ("maybe"; "kind of") Fillers ("uh," "you know," "well") Negaters ("It's not really that important"; "I'm not sure")

Source: Adapted in part from J A Waters, "Managerial Assertiveness," *Business Horizons*, September–October 1982, pp 24–29.

International Organizational Behaviour

Cross-Cultural Awareness Affects Business Negotiations

It's often assumed that the more you talk the better you communicate—though this is perhaps less true of the British than of the French, Italians and Americans. Yet anyone who has done business in countries where words are used sparingly will appreciate that silence can be used to just as good effect. In Asia — and especially Japan — the protracted pause is often as eloquent as speech. In Europe, the Swedes and Finns can be similarly mute — the latter, in particular, excel at it.

The reason is perhaps partly geographic. Sandwiched for centuries between Swedish and Russian bosses in a cold climate, the Finn had little incentive to open his mouth unless he was asked. Not only was it prudent to remain quiet but it suited his view of society. "Those who know, do not speak; those who speak, do not know" is an ancient Chinese proverb to which the Finns, like the Japanese, adhere. Silence is not seen as a failure to communicate but as an integral part of interaction; what is not said is important. Silence means that you listen and learn; verbosity merely expresses cleverness, egoism and arrogance. Silence also protects privacy and shows respect for others. In Finland and Japan it is considered impolite to force one's opinions on others.

In the Anglo-Saxon world and Latin and Middle Eastern countries, talking has another function. The British habit of discussing the weather with neighbours or even strangers shows both a preoccupation with climate and a desire to show solidarity and friendliness. Sociable discourse is even more evident in the US, Canada and Australia, where speech is a vital tool for establishing rapidly. In France, fluency is an important social attribute; to the Finn, the Frenchman may seem to babble — or be pushy and intruding — but to compatriots he appears intelligent and coherent. The American habit of "thinking aloud," the French stage performance, the Italian baring of the soul, Arabic rhetoric — all are

attempts to gain the confidence of the listener and share ideas which can then be discussed and modified. The Finns and the Japanese, meanwhile, listen to such outpourings with a kind of horror: in their countries a statement is a commitment to stand by, not to change, twist or contradict in the very next breath.

It is a view of language that sets Finland and Japan apart. In both countries the whispers are the same: "Foreigners talk so fast; we are slow by comparison; we can't learn languages; our pronunciation is terrible; our own language is so difficult; foreigners are more experienced than us; they are cleverer and often deceive; they don't mean what they say", hence, "we can't rely on them."

In Japan what is actually said has no significance whatsoever. Language is used as a tool of communication, but the words and sentences themselves give no indication of what the speaker is saying. What they want and how they feel is conveyed by the way in which they address their conversation partner: smiles, pauses, sighs, grunts, nods and eye movements convey everything. The Japanese executive leaves his fellow Japanese knowing perfectly well what has been agreed, no matter what was said. The foreigner leaves the Japanese with a completely different idea. If he thinks all has gone well it is often only because the Japanese would never offend him by saying anything negative or unpleasant.

Of course, in negotiation, the protracted pause can trap the unwary — particularly the bewildered and easily embarrassed Briton who, having had his initial offer met with silence, rushes into fill it. "The Japanese stared at his feet for five minutes and I could feel my opportunity slipping away," recalls one visitor. I came down another 3% and got the order."

SOURCE | R Lewis, "Sometimes It's Right to Remain Silent," *Management Today*, May 1995, pp 95–96.

audible voice, and selective interruptions. They should avoid nonverbal behaviours such as glaring or little eye contact, threatening gestures, slumped posture, and a weak or whiny voice. Appropriate verbal behaviours include direct and unambiguous language and the use of "I" messages instead of "you" statements. For example, when you say, "Mike, I was disappointed with your report because it contained typographical errors," rather than "Mike, your report was poorly done," you reduce defensiveness. "I" statements describe your feelings about someone's performance or behaviour instead of laying blame on the person.[20]

Remember that nonverbal and verbal behaviours should complement and reinforce each other. James Waters, a communication expert, further recommends that assertiveness can be enhanced by using various combinations of the following assertiveness elements:

1. *Describe* the situation or the behaviour of people to which you are reacting.

2. *Express* your feelings, and/or *explain* what impact the other's behaviour has on you.

3. *Empathize* with the other person's position in the situation.

4. *Specify* what changes you would like to see in the situation or in another's behaviour, and offer to *negotiate* those changes with the other person.

5. *Indicate,* in a nonthreatening way, the possible consequences that will follow if change does not occur.[21]

Waters offers managers the following situational advice when using the various assertiveness elements: (1) *empathize* and *negotiate* with superiors or others on whom you are dependent, (2) *specify* with friends and peers, and (3) *describe* to strangers.

Sources of Nonverbal Communication

Nonverbal communication
Messages sent outside the written or spoken word.

Nonverbal communication is "Any message, sent or received independent of the written or spoken word . . . [It] includes such factors as use of time and space, distance between persons when conversing, use of colour, dress, walking behaviour, standing, positioning, seating arrangement, office locations and furnishing."[22]

Communication experts estimate that nonverbal communication is responsible for up to 60 per cent of a message being communicated. It is thus important to ensure that your nonverbal signals are consistent with your intended verbal messages. Inconsistencies create noise and promote miscommunications[23] Because of the prevalence of nonverbal communication and its significant impact on organizational behaviour (including, but not limited to, perceptions of others, hiring decisions, work attitudes, and turnover),[24] it is important that managers become consciously aware of the sources of nonverbal communication.

Body Movements and Gestures   Body movements, such as leaning forwards or backwards, and gestures, such as pointing, provide additional nonverbal information. Open body positions such as leaning backwards, communicate *immediacy,* a term used to represent openness, warmth, closeness, and availability for communication. *Defensiveness* is communicated by gestures such as folding arms, crossing hands, and crossing one's legs. Judith Hall, a communication researcher, conducted a meta-analysis of gender differences in body movements and gestures. Results revealed that women nodded their heads and moved their hands more than men. Leaning forwards, large body shifts, and foot and leg movements were exhibited more frequently by men than women.[25] Although it is both easy and fun to interpret body movements and gestures, it is important to remember that body-language analysis is subjective, easily misinterpreted, and highly dependent on the context and cross-cultural differences.[26] Thus, managers need to be careful when trying to interpret body movements. Inaccurate interpretations can create additional "noise" in the communication process. Make for example a circle by putting the tip of your middle finger on top of your thumb. What does it mean to you? In English-speaking countries this usually means OK, good. In France its means zero, bad. In the eastern Mediterranean it is obscene.

Even the simple handshake is different from country to country. Anglo-Saxons are taught to look the other person in the eye and use a firm grip. But to many people that can feel like a challenge, an invitiation to arm-wrestle. In central Europe and parts of Scandinavia you nod the head in respect, a gesture which can appear to others as a head-butt. In Mediterranean countries the handshake can be accompanied by an arm squeeze with other hand, a vestigial embrace.[27]

Touch   Touching is another powerful nonverbal cue. People tend to touch those they like. A meta-analysis of gender differences in touching indicated that women do more touching during conversations than men.[28] Of particular note, however, is the fact that men and women interpret touching differently. Sexual harassment claims might be reduced by keeping this perceptual difference in mind.

Moreover, norms for touching vary significantly around the world. Consider the example of two males walking across campus holding hands. In the Middle East, this behaviour would be quite normal for males who are friends or have great respect for each other. In contrast, this behaviour is not commonplace elsewhere. The International OB presents cross-cultural norms for nonverbal behaviour, including touching, across Asia.

Facial Expressions   Facial expressions convey a wealth of information. Smiling, for instance, typically represents warmth, happiness, or friendship, whereas frowning conveys dissatisfaction or anger. Do you think these interpretations apply to different cross-cultural groups? If you said yes, it supports the view that there is a universal recognition of emotions from facial expressions. If you said no, this indicates you believe the relationship between facial expressions and emotions varies across cultures. A recent summary of relevant research revealed that the association between facial expressions and emotions varies across cultures.[29] A smile, for example, does not convey the same emotion in different countries. Therefore, managers need to be careful in interpreting facial expressions among diverse groups of employees.

I n t e r n a t i o n a l   O r g a n i z a t i o n a l   B e h a v i o u r

Norms for Touching Vary across Countries

China
- Hugging or taking someone's arm is considered inappropriate.
- Winking or beckoning with one's index finger is considered rude.

The Philippines
- Handshaking and a pat on the back are common greetings.

Indonesia
- Handshaking and head nodding are customary greetings.

Japan
- Business cards are exchanged before bowing or handshaking.
- A weak handshake is common.
- Lengthy or frequent eye contact is considered impolite.

Malaysia
- It is considered impolite to touch someone casually, especially on the top of the head.
- It is best to use your right hand to eat and to touch people and things.

South Korea
- Men bow slightly and shake hands, sometimes with two hands; women refrain from shaking hands.
- It is considered polite to cover your mouth while laughing.

Thailand
- Public displays of temper or affection are frowned on.
- It is considered impolite to point at anything using your foot or to show the soles of your feet.

SOURCE   Guidelines taken from R E Axtell, *Gestures: The Do's and Taboos of Body Language Around the World* (New York: Wiley, 1991)

Eye Contact   Eye contact is a strong nonverbal cue that serves four functions in communication. First, eye contact regulates the flow of communication by signalling the beginning and end of conversation. There is a tendency to look away from others when beginning to speak and to look at them when done. Second, gazing (as opposed to glaring) facilitates and monitors feedback because it reflects interest and attention. Third, eye contact conveys emotion. People tend to avoid eye contact when discussing bad news or providing negative feedback. Fourth, gazing relates to the type of relationship between communicators.

As is also true for body movements, gestures, and facial expressions, norms for eye contact vary across cultures. Westerners are taught at an early age to look at their parents when spoken to. In contrast, Asians are taught to avoid eye contact with a parent or superior in order to show obedience and subservience.[30]

Eye contact is something that is not easy for the shyer type of Briton or Swede, whereas a Spaniard is capable of transfixing you with his stare. The Hungarian is, too, as Zsuzsanna Ardó points out : "Ongoing eye contact, gazing openly and honestly into the other's eye, is considered imperative, especially for the more manipulative discourses and transactions."[31] Once again, managers should be sensitive to different orientations towards maintaining eye contact with diverse employees.

Practical Tips   A communication expert offers the following advice to improve nonverbal communication skills:

- Positive nonverbal actions that help to communicate include:
- Maintaining eye contact.
- Occasionally nodding the head in agreement.
- Smiling and showing animation.
- Leaning toward the speaker.
- Speaking at a moderate rate, in a quiet, assuring tone. . . .

Here are some actions . . . to avoid:
- Looking away or turning away from the speaker.
- Closing your eyes.
- Using an unpleasant voice tone.
- Speaking too quickly or too slowly.
- Yawning excessively.[32]

Practice these tips by turning the sound off while watching television and then trying to interpret emotions and interactions. Honest feedback from your friends about your nonverbal communication style also may help.

Active Listening

Some communication experts contend that listening is the keystone communication skill for today's managers. Estimates suggest that managers typically spend about 9 per cent of a working day reading, 16 per cent writing, 30 per cent talking, and 45 per cent listening.[33] Unfortunately, research evidence suggests that most people are not very good at listening. For example, communication experts estimate that people generally comprehend about 25 per cent of a typical verbal message.[34] Interestingly, this problem is partly due to the fact that we can process information faster than most people talk. The average speaker communicates 125 words per minute while we can process 500 words per minute. Poor listeners use this information processing gap to daydream and think about other things, thereby missing important parts of what is being communicated.[35]

Listening

Actively decoding and interpreting verbal messages.

Listening involves much more than hearing a message. Hearing is merely the physical component of listening. **Listening** is the process of *actively* decoding and interpreting verbal messages. Listening requires cognitive attention and information processing; hearing does not. With these distinctions in mind, we will examine a model of listener comprehension, listening styles, and some practical advice for becoming a more effective listener.

Listener Comprehension Model   Listener comprehension represents the extent to which an individual can recall factual information and draw accurate conclusions and inferences from a verbal message. It is a function of listener, speaker, message, and environmental characteristics (see Figure 14–5). Communication researchers Kittie Watson and Larry Barker conducted a global review of listening behaviour research and arrived at the following conclusions. Listening comprehension is positively related to high mental and reading abilities, academic achievements, a large vocabulary, being ego-involved with the speaker, having energy, being female, extrinsic motivation to pay attention, and being able to take good notes. Speakers who talk too fast or too slow, possess disturbing accents or speech patterns, are not visible to the audience, lack credibility, or are disliked have a negative impact on listening comprehension. In contrast, clear messages stated in the active voice increase listening comprehension. The same is true of messages containing viewpoints similar to the listener's or those that disconfirm expectations. Finally, comfortable environmental characteristics and compact seating arrangements enhance listening comprehension.[36]

Listening Styles   A pair of communication experts identified three different listening styles.[37] Their research indicated that people prefer to hear information that is suited to their own listening style. People also tend to speak in a style that is consistent with their own listening style. Because inconsistent styles represent a barrier to effective listening, it is important for managers to understand and respond to the different listening styles.

Figure 14–5   Listener Comprehension Model

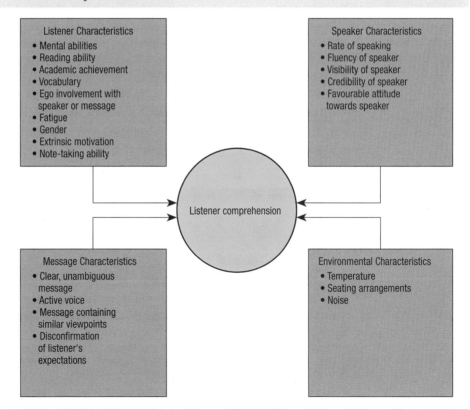

Source: Adapted from discussion in K W Watson and L L Barker, "Listening Behavior: Definition and Measurement," in *Communication Yearbook 8*, ed R N Bostrom (Beverly Hills, CA: Sage Publications, 1984), pp 178–97.

The three listening styles are called "results," "reasons," and "process."

Results-style
Interested in hearing the bottom line or result of a message.

Results-style listeners don't like any beating around the bush. They are interested in hearing the bottom line or result of the communication message first, and then like to ask questions. These behaviours identify a results-style listener:

- They sound direct. Everything is right out front, so you never have to wonder. They may sound blunt or even rude sometimes.
- They are action oriented.
- They are present oriented.
- They love to problem solve. Because of their love of fixing things and their action orientation, they are usually good crisis managers.
- Their first interest is the bottom line.[38]

Reasons-style
Interested in hearing the rationale behind a message.

Reasons-style listeners want to know the rationale for what someone is saying or proposing. They must be convinced about a point of view before accepting it. Typical behaviours exhibited by a reasons-style listener include:

- They are most concerned with whether or not a solution is practical, realistic, and reasonable for the situation.
- They weigh and balance everything. . . .
- If asked a direct question, they frequently answer, "It depends."
- They argue, out loud or internally.
- They expect people to present ideas in an organized way. They have little tolerance and no respect for a "disorderly" mind.
- Their first concern is "Why?"[39]

Process-style
Likes to discuss issues in detail.

Process-style listeners like to discuss issues in detail. They prefer to receive background information prior to having a thorough discussion and like to know why an issue is important in the first place. You can identify process-style listeners by watching for these behaviours:

- They are people oriented. They have a high concern for relationships, believing that people and relationships are the keys to long-term success.
- They like to know the whole story before making a decision.
- They have a high concern for quality and will hold out for a quality solution to a problem, even if it seems unrealistic to others.
- They are future oriented. They are not only concerned about the future, but they predict what may happen in the future as a result of decisions made today.
- They have ongoing conversations. They continue subjects from one conversation to the next.
- Their language and messages tend to be indirect. They imply rather than state the bottom line.
- Their primary interests are *how* and *benefits*.[40]

Managers can gain greater acceptance of their ideas and proposals by adapting the *form* and *content* of a message to fit a receiver's listening style:

1. For a results-style listener, for instance, the sender should present the bottom line at the beginning of the discussion.
2. Explain your rationale to a reasons-style listener.
3. For a process-style listener, describe the process and the benefits.

Becoming a More Effective Listener In addition to following the preceding recommendations, you can improve your listening skills by avoiding the 10 habits of bad listeners while cultivating the 10 good listening habits (see Table 14–2). Stephen Covey, author of the bestseller *The 7 Habits of Highly Effective People,* offers another good piece of advice about becoming a more effective listener. He concludes that we should "seek first to understand, then to be understood."[41] In conclusion, it takes awareness, effort, and practice to improve one's listening comprehension. Listening is not a skill that will improve on its own. Is anyone listening?

Women and Men Communicate Differently

Women and men have communicated differently since the dawn of time. These differences can create communication problems that undermine productivity and interpersonal communication. For example, surveys identified five common communication problems between women and men: (1) men were too authoritarian, (2) men did not take women seriously, (3) women were too emotional, (4) men did not accept women as co-workers or bosses, and (5) women did not speak up enough.[42]

Gender-based differences in communication are partly caused by linguistic styles commonly used by women and men. Deborah Tannen, a communication expert, defines **linguistic style** as follows:

Linguistic style

A person's typical speaking pattern.

Linguistic style refers to a person's characteristic speaking pattern. It includes such features as directness or indirectness, pacing and pausing, word choice, and the use of such elements as jokes, figures of speech, stories, questions, and apologies. In other words, linguistic style is a set of culturally learned signals by which we not only communicate what we mean but also interpret others' meaning and evaluate one another as people.[43]

Linguistic style not only helps explain communication differences between women and men, but it also influences our perceptions of others' confidence, competence, and abilities. Increased awareness of linguistic styles can thus improve communication accuracy and your communication competence. This section strives to increase your understanding of interpersonal communication between women and men by discussing alternative explanations for differences in linguistic styles, various communication

Table 14–2   The Keys to Effective Listening

KEYS TO EFFECTIVE LISTENING	THE BAD LISTENER	THE GOOD LISTENER
1. Capitalize on thought speed	Tends to daydream	Stays with the speaker, mentally summarizes the speaker, weighs evidence, and listens between the lines
2. Listen for ideas	Listens for facts	Listens for central or overall ideas
3. Find an area of interest	Tunes out dry speakers or subjects	Listens for any useful information
4. Judge content, not delivery	Tunes out dry or monotone speakers	Assesses content by listening to entire message before making judgements
5. Hold your fire	Gets too emotional or worked up by something said by the speaker and enters into an argument	Withholds judgement until comprehension is complete
6. Work at listening	Does not expend energy on listening	Give the speaker full attention
7. Resist distractions	Is easily distracted	Fights distractions and concentrates on the speaker
8. Hear what is said	Shuts out or denies unfavourable information	Listens to both favourable and unfavourable information
9. Challege yourself	Resist listening to presentations of difficult subject matter	Treats complex presentations as exercise for the mind
10.Use handouts, overheads, or other visual aids	Does not take notes or pay attention to visual aids	Takes notes as required and uses visual aids to enhance understanding of the presentation

Source: Derived from G Manning, K Curtis, and S McMillen, *Building the Human Side of Work Community* (Cincinnati, OH: Thomson Executive Press, 1996), pp 127–54; and P Slizewski, "Tips for Active Listening," *HRFocus,* May 1995, p 7.

differences between women and men, and recommendations for improving communication between the sexes.

Why Do Linguistic Styles Vary between Women and Men?   Although researchers do not completely agree on the cause of communication differences between women and men, there are two competing explanations that involve the well-worn debate between *nature* and *nurture*. Some researchers believe that interpersonal differences between women and men are due to inherited biological differences between the sexes. More specifically, this perspective, which also is called the "Darwinian perspective" or "evolutionary psychology," attributes gender differences in communication to drives, needs, and conflicts associated with reproductive strategies used by women and men. For example, proponents would say that males communicate more aggressively, interrupt others more than women, and hide their emotions because they have an inherent desire to possess features attractive to females in order to compete with other males for purposes of mate selection. Although males are certainly not competing for mate selection during a business meeting, evolutionary psychologists propose that men cannot turn off their biologically based determinants of their behaviour.[44]

In contrast, social role theory is based on the idea that females and males learn ways of speaking as children growing up. Research shows that girls learn conversational skills and habits that focus on rapport and relationships, whereas boys learn skills and habits that focus on status and hierarchies. Accordingly, women come to view communication as a network of connections in which conversations are negotiations for closeness. This orientation leads women to seek and give confirmation and support more so than men. Men, on the other hand, see conversations as negotiations in which people try to achieve and maintain the upper hand. It thus is important for males to protect themselves from others' attempts to put them down or push them around. This perspective increases a male's need to maintain independence and avoid failure.[45]

Gender Differences in Communication   Research demonstrates that women and men communicate differently in a number of ways. Table 14–3 illustrates seven different communication patterns that vary between women and men. Women, for example, are more likely to share credit for success, to ask questions for clarification, to tactfully give feedback by mitigating criticism with praise, and to indirectly tell others what to do. In contrast, men are more likely to boast about themselves, to bluntly give feedback, to withhold compliments, and are less likely to ask questions and to admit fault or weaknesses.

Table 14–3   Communication Differences between Women and Men

LINGUISTIC CHARACTERISTIC	MEN	WOMEN
Taking credit	Greater use of "I" statements (e.g., "I did this" and "I did that"); more likely to boast about their achievements	Greater use of "We" statements (e.g., "We did this" and "We did that"); less likely to boast about their achievements
Displaying confidence	Less likely to indicate that they are uncertain about an issue	More likely to indicate a lack of uncertainty about an issue
Asking questions	Less likely to ask questions (e.g., asking for directions)	More likely to ask questions
Conversation rituals	Avoid making apologies because it puts them in a one-down position	More frequently say "I'm sorry"
Giving feedback	More direct and blunt	More tactful; tend to temper criticism with praise
Giving compliments	Stingy with praise	Pay more compliments than men
Indirectness	Indirect when it comes to admitting fault or when they don't know something	Indirect when telling others what to do

Source: Derived from D Tannen, "The Power of Talk: Who Gets Heard and Why," *Harvard Business Review*, September–October 1995, pp 138–48; and D Tannen, *You Just Don't Understand: Women and Men in Conversation* (New York: Ballantine Books, 1990).

There are two important issues to keep in mind about the trends identified in Table 14–3. First, the trends identified in the table cannot be generalized to include all women and men. Some men are less likely to boast about their achievements while some women are less likely to share the credit. The point is that there are always exceptions to the rule. Second, your linguistic style influences perceptions about your confidence, competence, and authority. These judgements may, in turn, affect your future job assignments and subsequent promotability. Consider, for instance, linguistic styles displayed by Greg and Mindy. Greg downplays any uncertainties he has about issues and asks very few questions. He does this even when he is unsure about an issue being discussed. In contrast, Mindy is more forthright at admitting when she does not understand something, and she tends to ask a lot of questions. Some people may perceive Greg as more competent than Mindy because he displays confidence and acts as if he understands the issues being discussed.

Genderflex

Temporarily using communication behaviours typical of the other gender.

Improving Communication between the Sexes   Author Judith Tingley suggests that women and men should learn to genderflex. **Genderflex** entails the temporary use of communication behaviours typical of the other gender in order to increase the potential for influence.[46] For example, a female manager might use sports analogies to motivate a group of males. She believes that this approach increases understanding and sensitivity between the sexes. Research has not yet investigated the effectiveness of this approach.

In contrast, Deborah Tannen recommends that everyone needs to become aware of how linguistic styles work and how they influence our perceptions and judgements. She believes that knowledge of linguistic styles helps to ensure that people with valuable insights or ideas get heard. Consider how gender-based linguistic differences affect who gets heard at a meeting:

Those who are comfortable speaking up in groups, who need little or no silence before raising their hands, or who speak out easily without waiting to be recognized are far more likely to get heard at meetings. Those who refrain from talking until it's clear that the previous speaker is finished, who wait to be recognized, and who are inclined to link their comments to those of others will do fine at a meeting where everyone else is following the same rules but will have a hard time getting heard in a meeting with people whose styles are more like the first pattern. Given the socialization typical of boys and girls, men are more likely to have learned the first style and women the second, making meetings more congenial for men than for women.[47]

Knowledge of these linguistic differences can assist managers in devising methods to ensure that everyone's ideas are heard and given fair credit both in and out of meetings. Furthermore, it is useful to consider the organizational strengths and limitations of your linguistic style. You may want to consider modifying a linguistic characteristic that is a detriment to perceptions of your confidence, competence, and authority. In conclusion, communication between the sexes can be improved by remembering that women and men have different ways of saying the same thing.

Organizational Communication Patterns

Examining organizational communication patterns is a good way to identify factors contributing to effective and ineffective management. For example, research reveals that employees do not receive enough information from their immediate supervisors. It is therefore no surprise to learn that a lot of employees use the grapevine as a source for information.[48] This section promotes a working knowledge of three important communication patterns: hierarchical communication, the grapevine, and communication distortion.

Hierarchical Communication

Hierarchical communication is defined as "those exchanges of information and influence between organizational members, at least one of whom has formal (as defined

Hierarchical communication

Exchange of information between managers and employees.

by official organizational sources) authority to direct and evaluate the activities of other organizational members."[49] This communication pattern involves information exchanged downward from manager to employee and upward from employee to manager. Managers provide five types of information through downward communication: job instructions, job rationale, organizational procedures and practices, feedback about performance, and indoctrination of goals. Employees, in turn, communicate information upwards about themselves, co-workers and their problems, organizational practices and policies, and what needs to be done and how to do it. Managers are encouraged to foster two-way communication among all employees. If this fails, then management needs to devise alternative methods for obtaining employee feedback. Pillsbury, for instance, is trying to open the channels of communication between employees and top management by getting employees to anonymously telephone a third party:

> Ask employees to identify the biggest problem in the company and invariably they say poor communication. Yet even when management pleads for feedback, the silence is deafening. . . . Pillsbury and a few other companies have discovered the glimmer of a solution: getting employees to telephone a third party anonymously. Every word of every call is transcribed. Every transcript reaches the hand of Pillsbury Chief Executive Paul Walsh. And in small but numerous ways, Pillsbury is changing how it does business as a result.
>
> "This is not some warm and fuzzy human-resource program," says Lou de Ocejo, Pillsbury's personnel chief. By giving people the chance to end-run the chain of command, the system exposes inefficiencies, douses brush fires, and, most important, motivates employees to keep calling. "People know it gets read," he says, "and they know it will get action."[50]

The Grapevine

Grapevine

Unofficial communication system of the informal organization.

The term *grapevine* originated from the American Civil War practice of stringing battlefield telegraph lines between trees. Today, the **grapevine** represents the unofficial communication system of the informal organization. Information travelling along the grapevine supplements official or formal channels of communication. Although the grapevine can be a source of inaccurate rumours, it functions positively as an early warning signal for organizational changes, a medium for creating organizational culture, a mechanism for fostering group cohesiveness, and a way of informally bouncing ideas off others.[51] Evidence indicates that the grapevine is alive and well in today's workplaces. It has been estimated that people in offices spend 18 per cent of their working week gossiping with each other.[52] Gossip is intrinsic to organizational life. Analysis of gossip in organizations helps to clarify an understanding of the social organization of work. Although gossip is an informal process, it has important ramifications for the relationships and formal structures at work. It protects organizations by offering individuals both informal social mobility/influence and escapism. It is facile to believe that gossip can be eliminated and futile for managers to attempt to do so.[53] In a recent study 57 per cent of the respondents said that the grapevine is the only means for them to learn about the things that are happening in their organizations.[54]

A national survey of the readers of *Industry Week,* a professional management magazine, revealed that employees used the grapevine as their most frequent source of information.[55] Contrary to general opinion, the grapevine is not necessarily counterproductive. Plugging into the grapevine can help employees, managers, and organizations alike achieve desired results. To enhance your understanding of the grapevine, we will explore grapevine patterns and research and managerial recommendations for monitoring this often-misunderstood system of communication.

Grapevine Patterns   Communication along the grapevine follows predictable patterns (see Figure 14–6). The most frequent pattern is not a single strand or gossip chain, but the cluster pattern.[56] In this case, person A passes along a piece of information to three people,

Figure 14 – 6   Grapevine Patterns

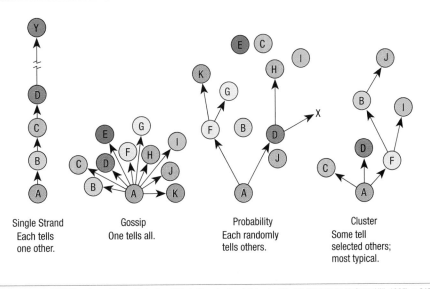

Single Strand	Gossip	Probability	Cluster
Each tells	One tells all.	Each randomly	Some tell
one other.		tells others.	selected others;
			most typical.

Source: K Davis and J W Newstrom, *Human Behavior at Work: Organizational Behavior*, 7th edn (New York: McGraw-Hill, 1985), p 317. Used with permission.

one of whom—person F—tells two others, and then one of those two—person B—tells one other. As illustrated in Figure 14 – 6, only certain individuals repeat what they hear when the cluster pattern is operating. People who consistently pass along grapevine information to others are called **liaison individuals** or "gossips":

Liaison individuals

Consistently pass along grapevine information to others.

About 10% of the employees on an average grapevine will be highly active participants. They serve as liaisons with the rest of the staff members who receive information but spread it to only a few other people. Usually these liaisons are friendly, outgoing people who are in positions that allow them to cross departmental lines. For example, secretaries tend to be liaisons because they can communicate with the top executive, the janitor, and everyone in between without raising eyebrows.[57]

Effective managers monitor the pulse of work groups by regularly communicating with known liaisons.

Organizational moles

Use the grapevine to enhance their power and status.

In contrast to liaison individuals, **organizational moles** use the grapevine for a different purpose. They obtain information, often negative, in order to enhance their power and status. They do this by secretly reporting their perceptions and hearsay about the difficulties, conflicts, or failure of other employees to powerful members of management. This enables a mole to divert attention away from him- or herself and to position him- or herself as more competent than others. Management should attempt to create an open, trusting environment that discourages mole behaviour because moles can destroy teamwork, create conflict, and impair productivity.[58]

Research and Practical Implications   Although research activity on this topic has slowed in recent years, past research about the grapevine provided the following insights: (1) it is faster than formal channels; (2) it is about 75 per cent accurate; (3) people rely on it when they are insecure, threatened, or faced with organizational changes; and (4) employees use the grapevine to acquire the majority of their on-the-job information.[59]

The key managerial recommendation is to *monitor* and *influence* the grapevine rather than attempt to control it. Effective managers accomplish this by openly sharing relevant information with employees. For example, managers can increase the amount of communication by both keeping in touch with liaison individuals and making sure information travels to people "isolated" from the formal communication system. Providing advance notice of departmental or organizational changes, carefully listening to employees, and selectively sending information along the grapevine are other ways to influence and monitor the grapevine. Keith Davis, who has studied the grapevine for more than 30 years, offers this final piece of advice:

No administrator in his right mind would try to abolish the management grapevine. It is as permanent as humanity is. Nevertheless, many administrators have abolished the grapevine from their own minds. They think and act without giving adequate weight to it or, worse, try to ignore it. This is a mistake. The grapevine is a factor to be reckoned with in the affairs of management. The administrator should analyze it and should consciously try to influence it.[60]

Communication Distortion between Managers and Employees

Communication distortion
Purposely modifying the content of a message.

Communication distortion occurs when an employee purposely modifies the content of a message, thereby reducing the accuracy of communication between managers and employees. Employees tend to engage in this practice because of workplace politics, a desire to manage impressions, or fear of how a manager might respond to a message.[61] Communication experts point out the organizational problems caused by distortion:

Distortion is an important problem in organizations because modifications to messages cause misdirectives to be transmitted, nondirectives to be issued, incorrect information to be passed on, and a variety of other problems related to both the quantity and quality of information.[62]

Knowledge of the antecedents or causes of communication distortion can help managers avoid or limit these problems.

Antecedents of Distortion   Studies have identified four situational antecedents of distortion in upward communication (see Figure 14 – 7). Distortion tends to increase when supervisors have high upward influence and/or power. Employees also tend to modify or distort information when they aspire to move upwards and when they do not trust their supervisors.[63] Because managers generally do not want to reduce their upward influence or curb their subordinates' desire for upward mobility, they can reduce distortion in several ways:

1. Managers can deemphasize power differences between themselves and their subordinates.

Figure 14 – 7   Sources of Distortion in Upward Communication

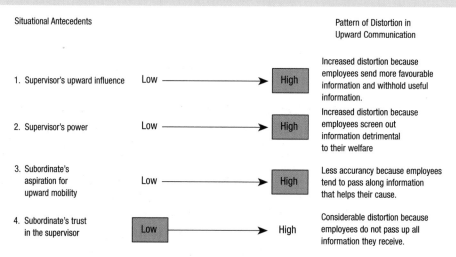

Source: Adapted in part from J Fulk and S Mani, "Distortion of Communication in Hierarchical Relationships," in *Communication Yearbook 9*, ed M L McLaughlin (Beverly Hills, CA: Sage Publications, 1986).

2. They can enhance trust through a meaningful performance review process that rewards actual performance.

3. Managers can encourage staff feedback by conducting smaller, more informal meetings.

4. They can establish performance goals that encourage employees to focus on problems rather than personalities.

5. Distortion can be limited by encouraging dialogue between those with opposing viewpoints.

What Is Your Potential for Communication Distortion? To assess the communication pattern between you and your immediate supervisor, please take a moment to complete the survey in the OB Exercise. Think of your current (or last) job when responding to the various items. Do your responses to the first three statements suggest low or high potential for distortion? How does this assessment mesh with your responses to the last three statements, which measure three outcomes of distortion?

Dynamics of Modern Communications

Effective communication is the cornerstone of survival in today's competitive business environment. This is particularly true for companies that operate or compete worldwide or those undertaking significant organizational change. Operation Centurion at Philips and Phoenix at KLM are two examples of major change processes in The Netherlands:

Former Philips head Jan Timmer deliberately entered into contact with his employees, to stress that changes have to come from them. According to him, changes which come from the personnel usually lead to radical solutions. "Town-meetings," mass meetings with delegates from each level were organized to make an inventory of the existing problems on the floor and to find solutions locally. Thanks to that communication strategy, there was less resistance to the changes.

At KLM, the Dutch national airline, the change process was accompanied by extra video bulletins, information gathering, special Phoenix bulletin boards, newsletters and posters and finally a staff magazine.[64]

Managers who effectively use information technology and are sensitive to various communication barriers are more likely to contribute to organizational success.

Communication in the Computerized Information Age

Organizations are increasingly using information technology as a lever to improve productivity and customer and employee satisfaction. In turn, communication patterns at work are radically changing.

Almost 60 per cent of the IBM Belgium employees work in shared offices. They may use a Thinkpad portable and work at home or with the customer, going into the company for such things as meetings. When they want to work there, they can use special prepared rooms which have all the necessary infrastructure available; they don't have their own offices.[65]

Alcatell Bell uses telecottages. These decentralized offices are connected with the central one. People who live at a distance can simply go to the nearest telecottage, and are thus spared a lot of time travelling and sitting in traffic jams.[66]

Like other companies, IBM Belgium and Alcatel Bell are using information technology to change the way people work. This section explores five components: Internet/Intranet, electronic mail, collaborative computing, videoconferencing, and telecommuting. All five are elements of communicating in a computerized workplace.

Internet

A global network of computer networks.

Internet/Intranet   The Internet is more than a computer network. It is a network of computer networks. Very simply, "the **Internet** is a global collection of independently operating, but interconnected, computers."[67] The Internet connects everything from supercomputers, to large mainframes contained in businesses, government, and universities, to the personal computers in our homes and offices.

Intranet

An organization's private Internet.

An **Intranet** is nothing more than an organization's private Internet. Intranets also have *firewalls* that block outside Internet users from accessing internal information. This is done to protect the privacy and confidentiality of company documents. The Intranet is a relatively new application not yet widely used by organizations.[68]

The primary benefit of both the Internet and Intranet is that they can enhance the ability of employees to find, create, manage, and distribute information. The effectiveness of the Internet/Intranet, however, depends on how employees use the acquired information because information by itself cannot solve or do anything; information is knowledge or a thing.[69] To date no rigorous research studies have been conducted that directly demonstrate productivity increases from using the Internet/Intranet. There are, however, case studies that reveal other organizational benefits. Cop Volmac (a software company) connected 4,000 employees in one intranet: 3,000 Belgian employees and 1,000 Dutch employees. By doing so the company supports interactive communication between employees. The Net will also be used for videoconferencing. In the future, the communication on paper will decrease by 90 per cent.[70] In contrast, other reports detail stories of people spending hours surfing the Net only to find themselves overwhelmed with information. Using the Internet can be very time consuming because it is an unstructured repository of information that is becoming increasingly slow to access.[71] Only the future will tell whether the Internet is more useful as a marketing/sales tool, a device to conduct personal transactions such as banking or ordering videos, or a management vehicle that enhances employee motivation and productivity.

OB EXERCISE   *A Self-Assessment of Antecedents and Outcomes of Distortion in Upward Communication*

Instructions

Circle your response to each question by using the following scale:

    1 = Strongly disagree
    2 = Disagree
    3 = Neither agree nor disagree
    4 = Agree
    5 = Strongly agree

SUPERVISOR'S UPWARD INFLUENCE

In general, my immediate supervisor can have a big impact on my career in this organization.   1—2—3—4—5

ASPIRATION FOR UPWARD MOBILITY

It is very important for me to progress upward in this organization.   1—2—3—4—5

SUPERVISORY TRUST

I feel free to discuss the problems and difficulties of my job with my immediate supervisor without jeopardizing my position or having it "held against" me later.   1—2—3—4—5

WITHHOLDING INFORMATION

I provide my immediate supervisor with a small amount of the total information I receive at work.   1—2—3—4—5

SELECTIVE DISCLOSURE

When transmitting information to my immediate supervisor, I often emphasize those aspects that make me look good.   1—2—3—4—5

SATISFACTION WITH COMMUNICATION

In general, I am satisfied with the pattern of communication between my supervisor and me.   1—2—3—4—5

Arbitrary Norms

Low = 1–2
Moderate = 3
High = 4–5

SOURCE   Adapted and excerpted in part from K H Roberts and C A O'Reilly III, "Measuring Organizational Communication," *Journal of Applied Psychology*, June 1974, p 323.

Electronic mail

Uses the Internet/Intranet to send computer-generated text and documents.

Electronic Mail   **Electronic mail** or e-mail uses the Internet/Intranet to send computer-generated text and documents between people.

1. E-mail reduces the cost of distributing information to a large number of employees

2. E-mail is a tool for increasing teamwork. It enables employees to send messages quickly to colleagues on the next floor, in another building, or in another country. In support of this benefit, a study of 375 managers indicated they used e-mail for three dominant reasons: (*a*) to keep others informed, (*b*) to follow up an earlier communication, and (*c*) to communicate the same thing to many people.[72]

3. E-mail reduces the costs and time associated with print duplication and paper distribution.

4. E-mail fosters flexibility. This is particularly true for employees with a portable computer because they can log on to e-mail whenever and wherever they want.

There are three additional issues to consider when using e-mail: (1) e-mail only works when the party you desire to communicate with also uses it. E-mail may not be a viable communication medium in all cases. (2) The speed of getting a response to an e-mail message is dependent on how frequently the receiver examines his or her messages. It is important to consider this issue when picking a communication medium. (3) Many companies do not have policies for using e-mail, which can lead to misuse and potential legal liability. For instance, Credit Suisse First Boston dismissed five temporary personnel and censured five permanent staff in its London office after a routine audit of the firm's electronic mail system turned up lewd jokes and inappropriate messages the individuals had been circulating inside and outside the firm.[73] Do not assume that your e-mail messages are private and confidential. Organizations are advised to develop policies regarding the use of e-mail.[74]

Collaborative computing

Using computer software and hardware to help people work better together.

Collaborative Computing   **Collaborative computing** entails using state-of-the-art computer software and hardware to help people work better together. Collaborative systems enable people to share information without the constraints of time and space. This is accomplished by utilizing computer networks to link people across a room or across the globe. Collaborative applications include messaging and e-mail systems, calendar management, videoconferencing, computer teleconferencing, electronic whiteboards, and the type of computer-aided decision-making systems discussed in Chapter 12.[75]

Organizations that use fully-fledged collaborative systems are referred to as "virtual companies" because people can communicate with anyone at anytime. However, there are potential drawbacks to the type of workplace. Research reveals that employees may feel socially disconnected and experience more role overload, interference, and stress.[76] This environment can also fuel conflict between remote and on-site workers. William Pape, co-founder of VeriFone, a virtual company, suggested that managers should adhere to the following recommendations when implementing a virtual system:[77]

1. Make sure your senior managers operate virtually at least part of the time.

2. Visit your remote offices frequently. The CEO and senior managers at VeriFone meet face-to-face for one week every six to eight weeks.

3. Make sure that employees have a work space that promotes productivity. Pape suggests creating written guidelines for home offices.

4. Help remote workers form strong ties to people at the central office.

5. Find ways to compensate for the loss of daily face-to-face contact.

6. Counteract the sense among remote workers that they're missing out on key business advances.

Videoconferencing   Videoconferencing is an application of collaborative computing. It uses video and audio links to connect people at different locations. This enables employees to conduct long-distance meetings and training classes without leaving their office. The results are substantial cost savings. Therefore, it is not surprising that the use of videoconferencing is on the rise.[78] For example, the Royal Bank of Scotland has employed video conferencing techniques since 1985, as face-to-face meetings have to take place every day and the participants are separated by 400 miles.

"Users at the bank have grown to love it — it's very practical and we're hooked on the thing. We've expanded the initial service to include four suites here in Edinburgh, three in London and one in Manchester," says Mr James of the Edinburgh bank.[79]

Telecommuting

Receiving and sending work from home to the office by using the phone or a computer link.

Telecommuting   **Telecommuting** involves receiving and sending work from home via phone or by using a modem to link a home computer to an office computer. The average telecommuter works at home about one week a month. Telecommuting is more common for jobs that involve computer work, writing, and phone or brain work that requires concentration and limited interruptions.[80] Today, 150,000 Germans, 560,000 Britons, 215,000 Frenchmen, and 80,000 Italians already work through teleworking. By the end of this century, the European Union wants to see 10 million people working as teleworkers.[81] Proposed benefits of telecommuting include the following:

1. *Reduction of capital costs.* The London Borough of Enfield has calculated that its home-based employees cost between £500 and £1,000 less a year than their office equivalents.[82]

2. *Increased flexibility and autonomy for workers.*

3. *Competitive edge in recruitment.* The Traveler's Insurance Company and the federal government used telecommuting to increase their ability to keep and attract qualified personnel.

4. *Increased job satisfaction.* Employees like telecommuting because it helps resolve work–family conflicts. A study revealed that homeworkers at British Telecom coped better with the daily stresses of working life than the bureau-bound operators.[83] The productivity of teleworkers, according to time-based output measures used by SW 2000, can show gains of up to 45 per cent when compared to that of office-based staff.[84]

5. *Increased productivity.*

6. *Tapping nontraditional labour pools* (such as prison inmates and home-bound disabled persons).[85]

Although telecommuting represents an attempt to accommodate employee needs and desires, it requires adjustments and is not for everybody. Many people thoroughly enjoy the social camaraderie that exists within an office setting. These individuals probably would not like to telecommute. Others lack the self-motivation needed to work at home. Finally, organizations must be careful to implement telecommuting in a non-discriminatory manner. Organizations can easily and unknowingly violate one of several antidiscrimination laws.[86]

Barriers to Effective Communication

Communication noise is a barrier to effective communication because it interferes with the accurate transmission and reception of a message. Management awareness of these barriers is a good starting point to improve the communication process. There are four key barriers to effective communication: (1) process barriers, (2) personal barriers, (3) physical barriers, and (4) semantic barriers.

Process Barriers   Every element of the perceptual model of communication shown in Figure 14–1 is a potential process barrier. Consider the following examples:

1. *Sender barrier.* A customer gets incorrect information from a customer service agent because he or she was recently hired and lacks experience.

2. *Encoding barrier.* An employee for whom English is a second language has difficulty explaining why a delivery was late.

3. *Message barrier.* An employee misses a meeting for which he or she never received a confirmation memo.

4. *Medium barrier.* A salesperson gives up trying to make a sales call when the potential customer fails to return three previous phone calls.

5. *Decoding barrier.* An employee does not know how to respond to a manager's request to stop exhibiting "passive aggressive" behaviour.

6. *Receiver barrier.* A student who is talking to his or her friend during a lecture asks the professor the same question that was just answered.

7. *Feedback barrier.* The nonverbal head nodding of an interviewer leads an interviewee to think that he or she is doing a great job answering questions.

Barriers in any of these process elements can distort the transfer of meaning. Reducing these barriers is essential but difficult given the current diversity of the workforce.

Personal Barriers   There are many personal barriers to communication. We highlight eight of the more common ones. The first is our *ability to effectively communicate.* As highlighted throughout this chapter, people possess varying levels of communication skills. The *way people process and interpret information* is a second barrier. Chapter 6 highlighted the fact that people use different frames of reference and experiences to interpret the world around them. We also learned that people selectively attend to various stimuli. All told, these differences affect both what we say and what we think we hear. Third, the *level of interpersonal trust between people* can either be a barrier or enabler of effective communication. Communication is more likely to be distorted when people do not trust each other. *Stereotypes and prejudices* are a fourth barrier. They can powerfully distort what we perceive about others. Our *egos* are a fifth barrier. Egos can cause political battles, turf wars, and pursuit of power, credit, and resources. Egos influence how people treat each other as well as our receptiveness to being influenced by others. *Poor listening skills* are a sixth barrier.[87]

Carl Rogers, a renowned psychologist, identified the seventh and eighth barriers that interfere with interpersonal communication.[88] The seventh barrier is a *natural tendency to evaluate or judge a sender's message.* To highlight the natural tendency to evaluate, consider how you might respond to the statement "I like the book you are reading." What would you say? Your likely response is to approve or disapprove the statement. You may say, "I agree," or alternatively, "I disagree, the book is boring." The point is that we all tend to evaluate messages from our own point of view or frame of reference. The tendency to evaluate messages is greatest when one has strong feelings or emotions about the issue being discussed. An *inability to listen with understanding* is the eighth personal barrier to effective communication. Listening with understanding occurs when a receiver can "see the expressed idea and attitude from the other person's point of view, to sense how it feels to him, to achieve his frame of reference in regard to the thing he is talking about."[89] Listening with understanding reduces defensiveness and improves accuracy in perceiving a message.

Physical Barriers   The distance between employees can interfere with effective communication. It is hard to understand someone who is speaking to you from 20 metres away. Time zone differences around the world also represent physical barriers. Work and office noise are additional barriers. The quality of telephone lines or crashed computers represent physical barriers that impact our ability to communicate with information technology.

In spite of the general acceptance of physical barriers, they can be reduced. Distracting or inhibiting walls also can be torn down. It is important that managers attempt to manage this barrier by choosing a medium that optimally reduces the physical barrier at hand.

Semantic Barriers   *Semantics* is the study of words. Semantic barriers show up as encoding and decoding errors because these phases of communication involve transmitting and receiving words and symbols. These barriers occur very easily. Consider the following statement: Crime is ubiquitous.

Do you understand this message? Even if you do, would it not be simpler to say that "crime is all around us" or "crime is everywhere"? Choosing our words more carefully is the easiest way to reduce semantic barriers. This barrier can also be decreased by attentiveness to mixed messages and cultural diversity. Mixed messages occur when a person's words imply one message while his or her actions or nonverbal cues suggest something different. Obviously, understanding is enhanced when a person's actions and nonverbal cues match the verbal message.

Summary of Key Concepts

1. *Describe the perceptual process model of communication.* Communication is a process of consecutively linked elements. Historically, this process was described in terms of a conduit model. Criticisms of this model led to development of a perceptual process model of communication that depicts receivers as information processors who create the meaning of messages in their own mind. Because receivers' interpretations of messages often differ from those intended by senders, miscommunication is a common occurrence.

2. *Explain the contingency approach to media selection.* Selecting media is a key component of communication effectiveness. Media selection is based on the interaction between the information richness of a medium and the complexity of the problem/situation at hand. Information richness ranges from low to high and is a function of four factors: speed of feedback, characteristics of the channel, type of communication, and language source. Problems/situations range from simple to complex. Effective communication occurs when the richness of the medium matches the complexity of the problem/situation. From a contingency perspective, richer media need to be used as problems/situations become more complex.

3. *Contrast the communication styles of assertiveness, aggressiveness, and nonassertiveness.* An assertive style is expressive and self-enhancing but does not violate others' basic human rights. In contrast, an aggressive style is expressive and self-enhancing but takes unfair advantage of others. A nonassertive style is characterized by timid and self-denying behaviour. An assertive communication style is more effective than either an aggressive or nonassertive style.

4. *Discuss the primary sources of both nonverbal communication and listener comprehension.* There are several identifiable sources of nonverbal communication effectiveness. Body movements and gestures, touch, facial expressions, and eye contact are important nonverbal cues. The interpretation of these nonverbal cues significantly varies across cultures. Listening is the process of actively decoding and interpreting verbal messages. Listener characteristics, speaker characteristics, message characteristics, and environmental characteristics influence listener comprehension.

5. *Identify and give examples of the three different listening styles, and review the 10 keys to effective listening.* Communication experts identified three

unique types of listening styles. A results-style listener likes to hear the bottom line or result of a communication at the beginning of a conversation. Reasons-style listeners want to know the rationale for what someone is saying or proposing. Process-style listeners like to discuss issues in detail. Good listeners use the following 10 listening habits: (*a*) capitalize on thought speed by staying with the speaker and listening between the lines, (*b*) listen for ideas rather than facts, (*c*) identify areas of interest between the speaker and listener, (*d*) judge content and not delivery, (e) do not judge until the speaker has completed his or her message, (*f*) put energy and effort into listening, (*g*) resist distractions, (*h*) listen to both favourable and unfavourable information, (*i*) read or listen to complex material to exercise the mind, and (*j*) take notes when necessary and use visual aids to enhance understanding.

6. *Describe the communication differences between men and women, and explain the source of these differences.* Women and men vary in terms of how they give and take credit, display confidence, ask questions, make apologies, give feedback, give compliments, and provide direct versus indirect comments. There are two competing explanations for these differences. The biological perspective attributes gender differences in communication to inherited drives, needs, and conflicts associated with reproductive strategies used by women and men. The second explanation, which is based on social role theory, is based on the idea that females and males learn different ways of speaking as children growing up.

7. *Discuss the patterns of hierarchical communication and the grapevine.* Hierarchical communication patterns describe exchanges of information between managers and the employees they supervise. Managers provide five types of downward communication: job instructions, job rationale, organizational procedures and practices, feedback about performance, and indoctrination of goals. Employees communicate information upwards about themselves, co-workers and their problems, organizational practices and policies, and what needs to be done and how to do it.

The grapevine is the unofficial communication system of the informal organization. Communication along the grapevine follows four predictable patterns: single strand, gossip, probability, and cluster. The cluster pattern is the most common.

8. *Demonstrate your familiarity with four antecedents of communication distortion between managers and employees.* Communication distortion is a common problem that consists of modifying the content of a message. Employees distort upward communication when their supervisor has high upward influence and/or power. Distortion also increases when employees aspire to move upwards and when they do not trust their supervisor.

9. *Explain the information technology of Internet/Intranet, e-mail, collaborative computing, and videoconferencing, and explain the related use of telecommuting.* The Internet is a global network of computer networks. An Intranet is an organization's private Internet. It contains a firewall that blocks outside Internet users from accessing private internal information. The primary benefit of both the Internet and Intranet is that they can enhance the ability of employees to find, create, manage, and distribute information. E-mail uses the Internet/Intranet to send computer-generated text and documents between people. Collaborative computing entails using state-of-the-art computer software and hardware to help people work better together. Information is shared across time and space by linking people with computer networks. Videoconferencing is an application of collaborative computing. It uses video and audio links to connect people at different locations. Telecommuting involves receiving and sending work from home by using a modem to link a home computer to an office computer.

10. *Describe the process, personal, physical, and semantic barriers to effective communication.* Every element of the perceptual model of communication is a potential process barrier. There are eight personal barriers that commonly influence communication: (*a*) the ability to effectively communicate, (*b*) the way people process and interpret information, (*c*) the level of interpersonal trust between people, (*d*) the existence of stereotypes and prejudices, (*e*) the egos of the people communicating, (*f*) the ability to listen, (*g*) the natural tendency to evaluate or judge a sender's message, and (*h*) the inability to listen with understanding. Physical barriers pertain to distance, physical objects, time, and work and office noise. Semantic barriers show up as encoding and decoding errors because these phases of communication involve transmitting and receiving words and symbols. Cultural diversity is a key contributor to semantic barriers.

Discussion Questions

1. Describe a situation where you had trouble decoding a message. What caused the problem?

2. What are some sources of noise that interfere with communication during a class lecture, an encounter with a professor in his or her office, and a film?

3. Which of the three zones of communication in Figure 14–3 (overload, effective, oversimplification) do you think is most common in today's large organizations? What is your rationale?

4. Would you describe your prevailing communication style as assertive, aggressive, or nonassertive? How can you tell? Would your style help or hinder you as a manager?

5. Are you good at reading nonverbal communication? Give some examples.

6. What is your listening style? Give behavioural examples to support your assessment.

7. Describe a miscommunication that occurred between you and someone of the opposite sex. Now, explain how genderflexing might have been used to improve this interaction.

8. What is your personal experience with the grapevine? Do you see it as a positive or negative factor in the workplace? Explain.

9. Have you ever distorted upward communication? What was your reason? Was it related to one of the four antecedents of communication distortion? Explain.

10. Which barrier to effective communication is more difficult to reduce? Explain

Personal Awareness and Growth Exercise

Assessing Your Listening Skills

Objectives

1. To assess your listening skills.
2. To develop a personal development plan aimed at increasing your listening skills.

Introduction

Listening is a critical component of effective communication. Unfortunately, research and case studies suggest that many of us are not very good at actively listening. This is particularly bad in light of the fact that managers spend more time listening than they do speaking or writing. This exercise provides you the opportunity to assess your listening skills and develop a plan for improvement.

Instructions

The following statements reflect various habits we use when listening to others. For each statement, indicate the extent to which you agree or disagree with it by selecting one number from the scale provided. Circle your response for each statement. Remember, there are no right or wrong answers. After completing the survey, add up your total score for the 17 items, and record it in the space provided.

Listening Skills Survey

1 = Strongly disagree
2 = Disagree
3 = Neither agree nor disagree
4 = Agree
5 = Strongly agree

1. I daydream or think about other things when listening to others. 1—2—3—4—5

2. I do not mentally summarize the ideas being communicated by a speaker. 1—2—3—4—5

3. I do not use a speaker's body language or tone of voice to help interpret what he or she is saying. 1—2—3—4—5

4. I listen more for facts than overall ideas during classroom lectures. 1—2—3—4—5

5. I tune out dry speakers. 1—2—3—4—5

6. I have a hard time paying attention to boring people. 1—2—3—4—5

7. I can tell whether someone has anything useful to say before he or she finishes communicating a message. 1—2—3—4—5

8. I quit listening to a speaker when I think he or she has nothing interesting to say. 1—2—3—4—5

9. I get emotional or upset when speakers make jokes about issues or things that are important to me. 1—2—3—4—5

10. I get angry or distracted when speakers use offensive words. 1—2—3—4—5

11. I do not expend a lot of energy when listening to others. 1—2—3—4—5

12. I pretend to pay attention to others even when I'm not really listening. 1—2—3—4—5

13. I get distracted when listening to others. 1—2—3—4—5

14. I deny or ignore information and comments that go against my thoughts and feelings. 1—2—3—4—5

15. I do not seek opportunities to challenge
my listening skills. 1—2—3—4—5

16. I do not pay attention to the visual aids
used during lectures. 1—2—3—4—5

17. I do not take notes on handouts when
they are provided. 1—2—3—4—5

Total Score = _____

Preparing a Personal Development Plan

1. Use the following norms to evaluate your listening skills:
   17–34 = Good listening skills
   35–53 = Moderately good listening skills
   54–85 = Poor listening skills.
   How would you evaluate your listening skills?

2. Do you agree with the assessment of your listening skills? Why or why not?

3. The 17-item listening skills survey was developed to assess the extent to which you use the keys to effective listening presented in Table 14–2. Use Table 14–2 and the development plan format shown opposite to prepare your development plan. First, identify the five statements from the listening skills survey that received your highest ratings—high ratings represent low skills. Record the survey numbers in the space provided in the development plan. Next, compare the content of these survey items to the descriptions of bad and good listeners shown in Table 14–2. This comparison will help you identify the keys to effective listening being measured by each survey item. Write down the keys to effective listening that correspond to each of the five items you want to improve. Finally, write down specific actions or behaviours that you can undertake to improve the listening skill being considered.

Development Plan

SURVEY ITEMS	KEY TO EFFECTIVE LISTENING I WANT TO IMPROVE	ACTION STEPS REQUIRED (WHAT DO YOU NEED TO DO TO BUILD LISTENING SKILLS FOR THIS LISTENING CHARACTERISTIC?)
#		
#		
#		
#		
#		

Group Exercise

Practising Different Styles of Communication

Objectives

1. To demonstrate the relative effectiveness of communicating assertively, aggressively, and nonassertively.

2. To give you hands-on experience with different styles of communication.

Introduction

Research shows that assertive communication is more effective than either an aggressive or nonassertive style. This *role-playing exercise* is designed to increase your ability to communicate assertively. Your task is to use different communication styles while attempting to resolve the work-related problems of a poor performer.

Instructions

Divide into groups of three, and read the "Poor Performer" and "Store Manager" roles provided here. Then decide who will play the poor performer role, who will play the managerial role, and who will be the observer. The observer will be asked to provide feedback to the manager after each role play. When playing the managerial role, you should first attempt to resolve the problem by using an aggressive communication style. Attempt to achieve your objective by using the nonverbal and verbal behaviour patterns associated with the aggressive style shown in Table 14–1. Take about four to six minutes to act out the instructions. The observer should give feedback to the manager after completing the role play. The observer should comment on how the employee responds to the aggressive behaviours displayed by the manager.

After feedback is provided on the first role play, the person playing the manager should then try to resolve the problem with a nonassertive style. Observers once again should provide feedback. Finally, the manager should confront the problem with an assertive style. Once again, rely on the relevant nonverbal and verbal behaviour patterns presented in Table 14–1, and take four to six minutes to act out each scenario. Observers should try to provide detailed feedback on how effectively the manager exhibited nonverbal and verbal assertive behaviours. Be sure to provide positive and constructive feedback.

After completing these three role plays, switch roles: manager becomes observer, observer becomes poor performer, and poor performer becomes the manager. When these role plays are completed, switch roles once again.

ROLE: POOR PERFORMER

You sell shoes full-time for a national chain of shoe shops. During the last month you have been absent three times without giving your manager a reason. The quality of your work has been slipping. You have a lot of creative excuses when your boss tries to talk to you about your performance.

When playing this role, feel free to invent a personal problem that you may eventually want to share with your manager. However, make the manager dig for information about this problem. Otherwise, respond to your manager's comments as you normally would.

ROLE: STORE MANAGER

You manage a store for a national chain of shoe shops. In the privacy of your office, you are talking to one of your salespeople who has had three unexcused absences from work during the last month. (This is excessive, according to company guidelines, and must be corrected.) The quality of his or her work has been slipping. Customers have complained that this person is rude, and co-workers have told you this individual isn't carrying his or her fair share of the work. You are fairly sure this person has some sort of personal problem. You want to identify that problem and get him or her back on the right track.

QUESTIONS FOR DISCUSSION

1. What drawbacks of the aggressive and nonassertive styles did you observe?
2. What were major advantages of the assertive style?
3. What were the most difficult aspects of trying to use an assertive style?
4. How important was nonverbal communication during the various role plays? Explain with examples.

Notes

[1] Based on "The Intranet: A Corporate Revolution," *www.intranet.co.uk/intranet/intranet.html*, March 1993.

[2] O C Ferrell and John Fraedrich, *Business Ethics: Ethical Decision Making and Cases* (Boston: Houghton Mifflin, 1991), p 143.

[3] See B Nixon, "Employee Relations during Times of Change," *America's Community Banker,* July 1995, pp 26–32; and P G Clampitt and C W Downs, "Employee Perceptions of the Relationship between Communication and Productivity: A Field Study," *Journal of Business Communication,* 1993, pp 5–28.

[4] Results can be found in D Fenn, "Benchmark: What Drives the Skills Gap?" *Inc.,* May 1996, p 111.

[5] J L Bowditch and A F Buono, *A Primer on Organizational Behavior* (New York: Wiley , 1994), p 132.

[6] For a review of these criticisms see L L Putnam, N Phillips, and P Chapman, "Metaphors of Communication and Organization," in *Handbook of Organization Studies,* eds S R Clegg, C Hardy, and W R Nord (London: Sage Publications, 1996), pp 375–408.

[7] Results of this study can be found in C M Fiol, "Corporate Communications: Comparing Executives' Private and Public Statements," *Academy of Management Journal,* April 1995, pp 522–36.

[8] L Labich, "How to Fire People and Still Sleep at Night," *Fortune,* June 10, 1996, p 65.

[9] Based on K Lowry Miller, P Simpson, and T Smart, "Europe, The Push East," *Business Week*, November 7, 1994, p 26–29.

[10] S R Axley, "Managerial and Organizational Communication in Terms of the Conduit Metaphor," *Academy of Management Review,* July 1984, pp 428–37.

[11] P Popham, "Rise of the British Kogaisha," *Management Today*, May 1995, p 86–92.

[12] R L Daft and R H Lengel, "Information Richness: A New Approach to Managerial Behavior and Organizational Design," in *Research in Organizational Behavior,* eds B M Staw and L L Cummings (Greenwich, CT: JAI Press, 1984), p 196.

[13] C A Barlett, K Elderkin, K McQuade, and M Hart, "The Body Shop International," in (eds.) R D Buzzell, J A Quelch, and C A Bartlett, *Global Marketing Management: Cases and Readings* (Reading: Addison-Wesley Publishing Company, 1995), p 619.

[14] Supporting results can be found in J Webster and L K Trevino, "Rational and Social Theories as Complementary Explanations of Communications Media Choices: Two Policy-Capturing Studies," *Academy of Management Journal,* December 1995, pp 1544–72, and J Fulk, "Social Construction of Communication Technology," *Academy of Management Journal,* October 1993, pp 921–50.

[15] See R E Rice and D E Shook, "Relationships of Job Categories and Organizational Levels to Use of Communication Channels, Including Electronic Mail: A Meta-Analysis and Extension," *Journal of Management Studies,* March 1990, pp 195–229.

[16] Results can be found in B Davenport Sypher and T E Zorn, Jr., "Communication-Related Abilities and Upward Mobility: A Longitudinal Investigation," *Human Communication Research,* Spring 1986, pp 420–31.

[17] The causes and consequences of communication competence are discussed by J W Haas and C L Arnold, "An Examination of the Role of Listening in Judgments of Communication Competence in Co-Workers," *Journal of Business Communication,* April 1995, pp 123–39.

[18] See E Raudsepp, "Are You Properly Assertive?" *Supervision,* June 1992, pp 17–18; and D A Infante and W I Gorden, "Superiors' Argumentativeness and Verbal Aggressiveness as Predictors of Subordinates' Satisfaction," *Human Communication Research,* Fall 1985, pp 117–25.

[19] J A Waters, "Managerial Assertiveness," *Business Horizons,* September–October 1982, p 25.

[20]The application of "I" messages is discussed by L Hildula, "Improving Employee Empowerment," *The CPA Journal,* January 1996, p 70; and L Carbone, "How to Communicate Effectively," *Restaurant Hospitality,* June 1995, p 32.

[21]Ibid., p 27.

[22]W D St. John, "You Are What You Communicate," *Personnel Journal,* October 1985, p 40.

[23]The importance of nonverbal communication is discussed by D Arthur, "The Importance of Body Language," *HRFocus,* June 1995, pp 22–23; and N M Grant, "The Silent Shout: Build Bridges, Not Barriers," *HRFocus,* April 1995, p 16.

[24]The impact of nonverbal cues on hiring decisions was examined by G E Wright and K D Multon, "Employer's Perceptions of Nonverbal Communication in Job Interviews for Persons with Physical Disabilities," *Journal of Vocational Behavior,* October 1995, pp 214–27; and R C Liden, C L Martin, and C K Parsons, "Interviewer and Applicant Behaviors in Employment Interviews," *Academy of Management Journal,* April 1993, pp 372–86.

[25]Related research is summarized by J A Hall, "Male and Female Nonverbal Behavior," in *Multichannel Integrations of Nonverbal Behavior,* eds A W Siegman and S Feldstein (Hillsdale, NJ: Lawrence Erlbaum, 1985), pp 195–226.

[26]A thorough discussion of cross-cultural differences is provided by R E Axtell, Gestures: *The Do's and Taboos of Body Language Around the World* (New York: Wiley, 1991). Problems with body language analysis also are discussed by C L Karrass, "Body Language: Beware the Hype," *Traffic Management,* January 1992, p 27; and M Everett and B Wiesendanger, "What Does Body Language Really Say?" *Sales & Marketing Management,* April 1992, p 40.

[27]J Mole, *Mind Your Manners* (London: Nicholas Brealey Publishing, 1992).

[28]Results can be found in Hall, "Male and Female Nonverbal Behavior."

[29]See J A Russell, "Facial Expressions of Emotion: What Lies Beyond Minimal Universality?" *Psychological Bulletin,* November 1995, pp 379–91.

[30]Norms for cross-cultural eye contact are discussed by C Engholm, *When Business East Meets Business West: The Guide to Practice and Protocol in the Pacific Rim* (New York: Wiley, 1991).

[31]R Hill, *We Europeans* (Brussels: Euro Publications, 1995).

[32]St. John, "You Are What You Communicate," p 43.

[33]Estimates are provided in both J Hart Seibert, "Listening in the Organizational Context," in *Listening Behavior: Measurement and Application,* ed R N Bostrom (New York: The Guilford Press, 1990), pp 119–27; and D W Caudill and R M Donaldson, "Effective Listening Tips for Managers," *Administrative Management,* September 1986, pp 22–23.

[34]See C G Pearce, "How Effective Are We as Listeners?" *Training & Development,* April 1993, pp 79–80; and R A Luke, Jr., "Improving Your Listening Ability," *Supervisory Management,* June 1992, p 7.

[35]See the discussion on listening in G Manning, K Curtis, and S McMillen, *Building Community: The Human Side of Work* (Cincinnati, OH: Thomson Executive Press, 1996), pp 127–54.

[36]For a summary of supporting research, see K W Watson and L L Barker, "Listening Behavior: Definition and Measurement," in *Communication Yearbook 8,* ed R N Bostrom (Beverly Hills, CA: Sage Publications, 1984); and R W Preiss and L R Wheeles, "Affective Responses in Listening: A Meta-Analysis of Receiver Apprehension Outcomes," in *Listening Behavior: Measurement and Application,* ed R N Bostrom (New York: The Guilford Press, 1990), pp 91–118.

[37]For a thorough discussion of the different listening styles, see R T Bennett and R V Wood, "Effective Communication via Listening Styles," *Business,* April–June 1989, pp 45–48.

[38]Ibid., p 46.

[39]Ibid., p 47.

[40]Ibid., p 46.

[41]See S R Covey, *The 7 Habits of Highly Effective People* (New York: Simon & Schuster, 1989).

[42]Results are presented in J C Tingley, *Genderflex: Men & Women Speaking Each Other's Language at Work* (New York: American Management Association, 1994).

[43]D Tannen, "The Power of Talk: Who Gets Heard and Why," *Harvard Business Review,* September–October 1995, p 139.

[44]For a thorough review of the evolutionary explanation of sex differences in communication, see J Archer, "Sex Differences in Social Behavior: Are the Social Role and Evolutionary Explanations Compatible?" *American Psychologist,* September 1996, pp 909–17.

[45]See D Tannen, *You Just Don't Understand: Women and Men in Conversation* (New York: Ballantine Books, 1990); and K K Reardon, *They Don't Get It, Do They: Communication in the Workplace–Closing the Gap between Women and Men* (New York: Little, Brown, 1995).

[46]This definition was taken from Tingley, *Genderflex: Men & Women Speaking Each Other's Language at Work,* p 16.

[47]Tannen, "The Power of Talk: Who Gets Heard and Why," pp 147–48.

[48]Supporting results are presented in Manning, Curtis, and McMillen, *Building Community: The Human Side of Work,* pp 328–46.

[49]C Redding, *Communication within the Organization: An Interpretive Review of Theory and Research* (New York: Industrial Communication Council, 1972).

[50]T Petzinger Jr., "The Front Lines: Two Executives Cook Up Way to Make Pillsbury Listen," *The Wall Street Journal,* September 27, 1996, p B1.

[51]Organizational benefits of the grapevine are discussed by T Galpin, "Pruning the Grapevine," *Training & Development,* April 1995, pp 28–32; and J Smythe, "Harvesting the Office Grapevine," *People Management,* September 1995, pp 24–27.

[52]C Dawson, "Shop Talk," *Sunday Times,* October 16, 1994, p 8–9.

[53]M Noon, and R Delbridge, "News From Behind My Hand: Gossip in Organizations," *Organization Studies,* vol 14, no 1, 1993, p 23–36.

[54]"Did You Hear It Through the Grapevine," *Training & Development,* October 1994, p 20.

[55]Results can be found in S J Modic, "Grapevine Rated Most Believable," *Industry Week,* May 15, 1989, pp 11, 14.

[56]See K Davis, "Management Communication and the Grapevine," *Harvard Business Review,* September–October 1953, pp 43–49.

[57]H B Vickery III, "Tapping into the Employee Grapevine," *Association Management,* January 1984, pp 59–60.

[58] A thorough discussion of organizational moles is provided by J G Bruhn and A P Chesney, "Organizational Moles: Information Control and the Acquisition of Power and Status," *Health Care Supervisor,* September 1995, pp 24–31.

[59] Earlier research is discussed by Davis, "Management Communication and the Grapevine"; and R Rowan, "Where Did That Rumor Come From?" *Fortune,* August 13, 1979, pp 130–31, 134, 137. The most recent research is discussed in "Pruning the Company Grapevine," *Supervision,* September 1986, p 11; and R Half, "Managing Your Career: 'How Can I Stop the Gossip?' " *Management Accounting,* September 1987, p 27.

[60] Davis, "Management Communication and the Grapevine," p 49.

[61] For a thorough discussion of communication distortion, see E W Larson and J B King, "The Systematic Distortion of Information: An Ongoing Challenge to Management," *Organizational Dynamics,* Winter 1996, pp 49–61.

[62] J Fulk and S Mani, "Distortion of Communication in Hierarchical Relationships," in *Communication Yearbook 9,* ed M L McLaughlin (Beverly Hills, CA: Sage Publications, 1986), p 483.

[63] For a review of this research, see Fulk and Mani, "Distortion of Communication in Hierarchical Relationships," pp 483–510.

[64] Based on and translated from M Bosma, "Interne Communicatie: Het Nut van Tweerichtingsverkeer," *Management Team,* November 17, 1995, p 99–102.

[65] Based on and translated from C Huge, "De Nomaden van IBM," *Belgian Business & Industrie,* September 19, 1997.

[66] Based on and translated from R Baguette, "Ver Werken, Meer Werken," *Trends,* May 8, 1997.

[67] B J Finch, *The Management Guide to Internet Resources, 1997 Edition* (New York: McGraw-Hill, 1997), p 2.

[68] A discussion of the Intranet is provided by L Stevens, "The Intranet: Your Newest Training Tool," *Personnel Journal,* July 1996, pp 27–32.

[69] This conclusion is discussed by O Edwards, "Inflammation Highway," *Forbes,* February 26, 1996, p 120.

[70] Based on and translated from "Intranet bij Cap Volmac," *Belgian Business & Industrie,* August 23, 1996.

[71] Problems with the Internet are discussed by B Ziegler, "Slow Crawl on the Internet: Massive Amounts of Data Clog System Studded with Roadblocks," *The Wall Street Journal,* August 23, 1996, p B1.; and W S Mossberg, "Personal Technology: Good News for You: Web, On-Line Services Are All Tangled Up," *The Wall Street Journal,* May 30, 1996, p B1.

[72] Results can be found in M L Markus, "Electronic Mail as the Medium of Managerial Choice," *Organization Science,* November 1994, pp 502–27.

[73] M Bender, "CSFB Fires Five for Dirty Jokes on E-mail System," *Investment Dealers Digest,* vol 63, no 36, p 8–10.

[74] For information regarding the issue of organizational E-mail policies, see J A Van Doren, "E-Mail Monitoring Policies—A Must for Employers," *Supervisory Management,* February 1996, p 5; B D Weiss, "Four Black Holes in Cyberspace," *American Management Association,* January 1996, pp 30–32; and R Posch, "E-Mail and Voice Mail: Basic Legal Issues for Corporate Management," *Direct Marketing,* January 1996, pp 54–56.

[75] Collaborative computing is discussed by A Field, "Group Think," *Inc. Technology,* 1996, pp 38–44; and E Teicholz, "Exciting New Communications Technology," *Buildings,* March 1996, pp 44–46.

[76] See L E Duxbury, C A Higgins, D R Thomas, "Work and Family Environments and the Adoption of Computer-Supported Supplemental Work-at-Home," *Journal of Vocational Behavior,* August 1996, pp 1–23.

[77] These recommendations were taken from W R Pape, "Remote Control," *Inc. Technology*, 1996, pp 25–26.

[78] Videoconferencing is discussed by L Parker, "Make the Most of Teleconferencing," *Training & Development*, February 1996, pp 28–29; and W M Bulkeley, "Picture-Phone Marketers Target the Home PC," *The Wall Street Journal,* February 27, 1996, pp B1, B6.

[79] M Demsey, "Scottish Pace-Setter — For a Decade, the Royal Bank Has pioneered in Video," *The Financial Times*, November 1, 1995, p IX.

[80] See L K Romei, "Your Home Office: A Multiplicity of Choices," *Managing Office Technology*, January 1996, pp 25–26; and "Home Work Pays Off," *Via Fedex*, Spring 1996, p 11.

[81] L Vervenne, "Tele-Flexibiliteit," *Belgian Business & Industry*, November 3, 1994, p 62.

[82] "The Profits of Progress," *The Times*, March 12, 1994, p18.

[83] Ibid.

[84] D Pancucci, "Remote Conrol," *Management Today*, April 1995, p 78–80.

[85] Supporting evidence is presented in G Piskurich, "Making Telecommuting," *Training & Development*, February 1996, pp 20–27; D T Prystash, "Corporate Attitudes and Commitments to Telecommuting," *IEE Transactions on Professional Communication*, June 1995, pp 95–99; and W E Snizek, "Virtual Offices: Some Neglected Considerations," *Communications of the ACM*, September 1995, pp 15–17.

[86] The legal considerations of telecommuting are discussed by B A Hartstein and M L Schulman, "Telecommuting: The New Workplace of the 90s," *Employee Relations L. J.,* Spring 1996, pp 179–88.

[87] The preceding barriers are discussed by J P Scully, "People: The Imperfect Communicators," *Quality Progress*, April 1995, pp 37–39.

[88] For a thorough discussion of these barriers, see C R Rogers and F J Roethlisberger, "Barriers and Gateways to Communication," *Harvard Business Review*, July–August 1952, pp 46–52.

[89] Rogers and Roethlisberger, "Barriers and Gateways to Communication," p 47.

Fifteen

Behaviour Modification and Self-Management

Incentives to work safely

When workers constructing the new Glaxo Medicines Research Centre in Stevenage (UK) recently clocked up a million-man-hours without losing time through serious injury, they had every cause to celebrate. This was the tenth time the site had reached the one million-hour milestone since 1991 and, as on previous occasions, a new car was the first prize in a raffle held to mark the event.

The draw which saw Claidon Ferrairo become the latest winner of a white Volvo 440—a car chosen for its safety features—took place at a pig roast to which the whole workforce was invited. By holding this huge feast and drawing the winning ticket so publicly, the site's management was able to underline the importance attached to safety, while also allaying any suspicions that the draw might be a fix.

With six runners-up standing to win prizes worth £4,000 and the rest of the workforce receiving smaller rewards for their part in the site's achievement, the prize draw has provided workers with a powerful incentive to make safety a priority. It is, however, only one element of a safety motivation programme that has helped the 72-acre building site achieve a safety record roughly 10 times better than the construction industry's national average.

Incentive schemes have long been used to motivate and reward sales staff. But LMK, the Laing-Morrison, Knudsen consortium acting as Glaxo's management contractor at the Stevenage site, is one of a growing number of companies now using these schemes to change attitudes and improve efficiency in a wide range of areas, including customer care, teamwork and safety performance.

The incentives are used to reward real effort rather than token compliance with safety procedures. Even a relatively trivial accident before the million-hour target has been reached can result in the clock being turned back to zero. The last time this happened was when a worker had to take more than three days off work after tripping on some steps on his way to the toilet.

While the prize draw encourages all operatives to contribute to the site's safety, another element of the motivation scheme is targeted at smaller teams on this vast building project, which at its height employed 3,000 people. Monthly safety league tables are used to rate all sub-contractors, not in terms of accident rates but of more positive measures such as training, safe working systems, supervision and attitudes. These tables are considered the most safety conscious.

Coming top of one of these tables carries its own reward, while coming at or near the bottom can do wonders for a sub-contractor's motivation. As LMK safety manager John Scott explains: "One of the most effective ways of getting sub-contractors to improve is for visiting managers to tell resident managers that they don't want to see their company's name at the bottom of the league table again."

While LMK motivates and rewards its largely migrant workforce with prizes worth set amounts of money, companies with more stable workforces sometimes allow individuals to build up merit points that can be exchanged for gifts of varying value. This was the system adopted by Luxfer UK Ltd, a subsidiary of British Alcan that produces gas cylinders.

Administered by Motivforce, the same organisation that helped LMK set up its motivation programme, Luxfer's "Spotlight on safety" (SOS) scheme aims to promote both safety awareness and teamwork. Members of each team in the company's two plants are awarded so many merit points for going a whole month without a lost-time accident, with production teams in potentially hazardous areas eligible for up to 1,000 points a month, compared with 300 points for office-based teams.

In the first two-and-a-half years the SOS programme had been running at Luxfer, the number of "lost time accidents" at the firm's Nottingham and west Midlands plants had fallen from an average of 12 or 13 a year to just four.

"We've reduced accidents by about two-thirds, but I wouldn't want to say that the incentive scheme was the only reason for that reduction," says Luxfer's personnel manager Peter Brock. "A lot of other things have been going on on the safety front as well. There are various auditing systems that we use to focus attention on safety, as well as training."

Training, in fact, is a crucial element in the success of any incentive scheme, not only those aiming to promote safety awareness. John Chalker, chief executive of the motivation and performance improvement consultancy Maritz Ltd, argues that incentive programmes introduced independently of training schemes can actually reward incompetence. "If a person is doing a job and you put in an incentive programme without looking at how they do that job, you may well find that all you are making them do is continue to repeat a number of errors with more and more customers."

Chalker views incentive awards primarily as a way of giving recognition to people who have changed the way they work. "It's less about the awards themselves and more about communicating what you require individuals to do, giving them the skills to do that task more effectively, and then thanking them for responding to the communication and the training."[1]

Discussion Question
Would you like to work in an organization where incentives are given to change your working patterns?

magine you are the general manager of the public transportation authority in a large city, and one of your main duties is overseeing the city's bus system. During the past several years, you have noted with growing concern the increasing number and severity of bus accidents. In the face of mounting public and administrative pressure, it is clear that a workable accident-prevention programme must be enacted. Large pay rises for the bus drivers and other expensive options are impossible because of a tight city budget. Based on what you read in Part Two about motivation, what remedial action do you propose? (Please take a moment now to jot down some ideas.)

Since these facts have been drawn from a real-life field study, we can see what happened.[2] Management tried to curb the accident rate with some typical programmes, including yearly safety awards, stiffer enforcement of a disciplinary code, complimentary coffee and doughnuts for drivers who had a day without an accident, and a comprehensive training programme. Despite these remedial actions, the accident rate kept climbing. Finally, management agreed to a behaviour modification experiment that directly attacked unsafe driver behaviour.

One hundred of the city's 425 drivers were randomly divided into four experimental teams of 25 each. The remaining drivers served as a control group. During an 18-week period, the drivers received daily feedback on their safety performance on a chart posted in their lunchroom. An accident-free day was noted on the chart with a green dot, while a driver involved in an accident found a red dot posted next to his or her name. At two-week intervals, members of the team with the best competitive safety record received their choice of incentives averaging $5 in value (e.g., cash, free petrol, free bus passes). Teams that went an entire two-week period without an accident received double incentives.

Unlike previous interventions, the behaviour modification programme reduced the accident rate. Compared with the control group, the experimental group recorded a 25 per cent lower accident rate. During an 18-week period following termination of the incentive programme, the experimental group's accident rate remained a respectable 16 per cent better than the control group's. This indicated a positive, long-term effect. Moreover, the programme was cost effective. The incentives cost the organization $2,033.18, while it realized a savings of $9,416.25 in accident settlement expenses (a 1:4.6 cost/benefit ratio).

Why did this particular programme work, while earlier attempts failed? It worked because a specific behaviour (safe driving) was modified through *systematic* management of the drivers' work environment. If the posted feedback, team competition, and rewards had been implemented in traditional piecemeal fashion, they probably would have failed to reduce the accident rate. However, when combined in a coordinated and systematic fashion, these common techniques produced favourable results. Research in Finland has demonstrated that B Mod techniques reduced accidents by as much as 80 per cent.[3]

This chapter introduces two systematic ways to manage job *behaviour:* behaviour modification and behavioural self-management. Both areas have a common theoretical heritage, behaviourism. In the concluding section, we go beyond behaviourism to explore an array of useful techniques for self-improvement.

What Is Behaviour Modification?

Behaviour modification

Making specific behaviour occur more or less often by managing its cues and consequences.

Behaviour modification (or B Mod) involves making specific behaviour occur more or less often by systematically managing its cues and consequences.[4] On-the-job behaviour modification has been variously labelled *organizational behaviour modification* (OB Mod), *organizational behaviour management,* and *performance management.*[5] The generic term *behaviour modification* is used here to avoid unnecessary confusion. B Mod traces back to the work of two pioneering psychologists, E L Thorndike and B F Skinner.

Thorndike's Law of Effect

During the early 1900s, Edward L Thorndike observed in his psychology laboratory that a cat would behave randomly and wildly when placed in a small box with a secret trip lever

Law of effect

Behaviour with favourable consequences is repeated; behaviour with unfavourable consequences disappears.

that opened a door. However, once the cat accidentally tripped the lever and escaped, the animal would go straight to the lever when placed back in the box. Hence, Thorndike formulated his famous **law of effect,** which says *behaviour with favourable consequences tends to be repeated, while behaviour with unfavourable consequences tends to disappear.*[6] This was a dramatic departure from the prevailing notion nearly a century ago that behaviour was the product of inborn instincts.

Skinner's Operant Conditioning Model

Skinner refined Thorndike's conclusion that behaviour is controlled by its consequences. Skinner's work became known as *behaviourism* because he dealt strictly with observable behaviour.[7] As a behaviourist, Skinner believed it was pointless to explain behaviour in terms of unobservable inner states such as needs, drives, attitudes, or thought processes.[8] He similarly put little stock in the idea of self-determination.

Respondent behaviour

Skinner's term for unlearned stimulus–response reflexes.

In his 1938 classic, *The Behavior of Organisms,* Skinner drew an important distinction between the two types of behaviour: respondent and operant behaviour.[9] He labelled unlearned reflexes or stimulus–response (S–R) connections **respondent behaviour.** This category of behaviour was said to describe a very small proportion of adult human behaviour. Examples of respondent behaviour would include shedding tears while peeling onions and reflexively withdrawing one's hand from a hot stove. Skinner attached the label **operant behaviour** to behaviour that is learned when one "operates on" the environment to produce desired consequences. Some call this the response–stimulus (R–S) model. Years of controlled experiments with pigeons in "Skinner boxes" helped Skinner develop a sophisticated technology of behaviour control, or operant conditioning. For example, he taught pigeons how to pace figure-eights and how to bowl by reinforcing the underweight (and thus hungry) birds with food whenever they more closely approximated target behaviours. Skinner's work has significant implications for OB because the vast majority of organizational behaviour falls into the operant category.[10]

Operant behaviour

Skinner's term for learned, consequence-shaped behaviour.

Principles of Behaviour Modification

Although B Mod interventions in the workplace often involve widely used techniques such as goal setting, feedback, and rewards, B Mod is unique in its adherence to Skinner's operant model of learning.[11] To review, operant theorists assume it is more productive to deal with observable behaviour and its environmental determinants than with personality traits, perception, or inferred internal causes of behaviour such as needs or cognitions. The purpose of this section is to introduce important concepts and terminology associated with B Mod. Subsequent sections explore B Mod application and research and some issues, pro and con.

A→B→C Contingencies

Behavioural contingencies

Antecedent→behaviour→ consequence (A→B→C) relationships.

To adequately understand the operant learning process, one needs a working knowledge of **behavioural contingencies,** as characterized by the A→B→C model. The initials stand for Antecedent→Behaviour→Consequence. When person–environment interaction is reduced to A→B→C terms (as in Figure 15–1), a **functional analysis** has taken place.[12]

Functional analysis

Reducing person– environment interaction to A→B→C terms.

Within the context of B Mod, *contingency* means the antecedent, behaviour, and consequence in a given A→B→C relationship are connected in "if-then" fashion. If the antecedent is present, then the behaviour is more likely to be displayed. If the behaviour is displayed, then the consequence is experienced. Furthermore, as learned from Thorndike's law of effect, if the consequence is pleasing, the behaviour will be strengthened (meaning it will occur more often). According to a pair of writers, one a clinical psychologist and the other a manager:

Some contingencies occur automatically; others we set up by linking our behavior with the behavior of others in an attempt to design an environment that will best serve our purposes. Setting up a contingency involves designating behaviors and assigning consequences to follow.

Figure 15–1   Productive Job Behaviour Requires Supportive Antecedents and Consequences

ANTECEDENT→	BEHAVIOUR→	CONSEQUENCE→	BEHAVIOUR OUTCOME
Manager: "I suppose you haven't finished the payroll report yet."	*Payroll clerk:* "No way! I'm behind schedule because the supervisors didn't submit their payroll cards on time."	*Manager:* "I'm sure everyone will enjoy getting their paycheque late again!"	The payroll clerk continues to make excuses while missing important deadlines because of the manager's negative antecedents and sarcastic consequences.
Manager: "How are you coming along on this week's payroll report?"	*Payroll clerk:* "I'm a little behind schedule. But if I work during my lunch hour, I'll have it in on time."	*Manager:* "I appreciate the extra effort! How would you like to spend tomorrow working on that bonus-pay project you suggested last week?"	The payroll clerk continues to meet important deadlines because of the manager's nonthreatening antecedents and rewarding consequences.

We design contingencies for children fairly simply ("If you finish your homework, I'll let you watch television"), but influencing the behavior of people in the workforce is more difficult. As a result, managers often fail to use contingencies to their full advantage.[13]

Let us look more closely at antecedents, behaviour, and consequences to fully understand A→B→C contingencies.

The Role of Antecedents   Unlike the S in the reflexive stimulus–response (S–R) model, antecedents *cue* rather than cause behaviour. For example, in classic S–R fashion, a blistering hot piece of pizza *causes* you to quickly withdraw it from your mouth. In contrast, a yellow traffic light *cues* rather than causes you to step on the brake. Because many motorists step on the gas when green traffic signals change to yellow, traffic signals have probable rather than absolute control over driving behaviour. Antecedents get the power to cue certain behaviours from associated consequences. For instance, if you have just received a summons for going through a red light, you will probably step on the brake when encountering the next few amber traffic signals.

Focusing on Behaviour   True to Skinnerian behaviourism, B Mod proponents emphasize the practical value of focusing on *behaviour.* They caution against references to unobservable psychological states and general personality traits when explaining job performance (e.g., see Table 15–1). Phil's behavioural descriptions (the italicized

Table 15–1   Behaviourists Explain How Managers Should Describe Job Behaviour: *A Brief Case Study*

THE WRONG WAY: Subjective appraisal of the **person,** rather than objective information about **performance.**

Phil Oaks, the department manager, describes his subordinate, Joe Scott, as follows:

Well, Joe is just not easy to get along with. He's so disagreeable and negative all the time. He's very aggressive and disruptive. When he's unhappy he just sulks a lot, and he daydreams. He's also insubordinate and doesn't follow the rules. I don't know if he's immature, not intelligent, or irrational. Overall, his motivation is very low. He lacks drive and is generally hostile. I suspect that there may be a home problem also.

THE RIGHT WAY: Objective information about **observable performance behaviours,** rather than subjective appraisal of the person.

In contrast, if Phil had training in pinpointing behaviours, he might describe Joe as follows:

Well, whenever Joe is given some direction, he responds by immediately *telling you why it can't be done.* He frequently *threatens other employees* and has even been in one or two *fights.* He *leaves his own work area to tell jokes* to other workers. Sometimes he just *sits in a corner, or stares out the window* for several minutes.

He has violated several company rules such as *smoking in a nonsmoking zone, working without safety goggles, and parking in a fire lane.* He can't seem to tell *right-handed prints from left-handed prints.* Also, he *arrived late for work* 10 times in the last month, and *returned from his break* late on 12 occasions.

Source: Performance descriptions excerpted from C C Manz and H P Sims, Jr., *SuperLeadership: Leading Others to Lead Themselves* (New York: Prentice-Hall, 1989), pp 66–67.

portions in the bottom half of the table) give him a solid foundation for modifying Joe's behavioural performance problems.

ETHICS

When managers focus exclusively on behaviour, without regard for personality traits or cognitive processes, their approach qualifies as radical behaviourism.[14] As one might suspect, this extreme perspective has stirred debate and controversy, complete with philosophical and ethical implications.

Contingent Consequences

Contingent consequences, according to Skinner's operant theory, control behaviour in four ways: positive reinforcement, negative reinforcement, punishment, and extinction.[15] These contingent consequences are managed systematically in B Mod programmes. To avoid the all-too-common mislabelling of these consequences, let us review some formal definitions.

Positive reinforcement

Making behaviour occur more often by contingently presenting something positive.

Positive Reinforcement Strengthens Behaviour   **Positive reinforcement** is the process of strengthening a behaviour by contingently presenting something pleasing. (Remember that a behaviour is strengthened when it increases in frequency and weakened when it decreases in frequency.) A young design engineer who works overtime because of praise and recognition from the boss is responding to positive reinforcement. Similarly, people tend to return to restaurants where they are positively reinforced with good food and friendly, high-quality service.[16]

Negative reinforcement

Making behaviour occur more often by contingently withdrawing something negative.

Negative Reinforcement Also Strengthens Behaviour   **Negative reinforcement** is the process of strengthening a behaviour by contingently withdrawing something displeasing. For example, an army sergeant who stops yelling when a recruit jumps out of bed has negatively reinforced that particular behaviour. Similarly, the behaviour of clamping our hands over our ears when watching a jumbo jet take off is negatively reinforced by relief from the noise. Negative reinforcement is often confused with punishment. But the two strategies have opposite effects on behaviour. Negative reinforcement, as the word *reinforcement* indicates, strengthens a behaviour because it provides relief from an unpleasant situation.

Punishment

Making behaviour occur less often by contingently presenting something negative or withdrawing something positive.

Punishment Weakens Behaviour   **Punishment** is the process of weakening behaviour through either the contingent presentation of something displeasing (see the International OB) or the contingent withdrawal of something positive. A manager assigning a tardy employee to a dirty job exemplifies the first type of punishment. Docking a tardy employee's pay is an example of the second type of punishment, called "response cost" punishment. Legal fines involve response cost punishment. Salespeople who must make

---

Figure 15–2   Contingent Consequences in Behaviour Modification

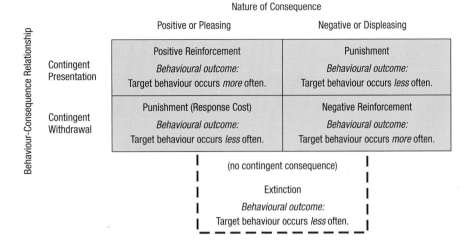

up any cash register shortages out of their own pockets are being managed through response cost punishment. Ethical questions can and should be raised about this type of on-the-job punishment.

ETHICS

Extinction

Making behaviour occur less often by ignoring or not reinforcing it.

Extinction Also Weakens Behaviour   **Extinction** is the weakening of a behaviour by ignoring it or making sure it is not reinforced. Getting rid of a former boyfriend or girlfriend by refusing to answer their phone calls is an extinction strategy. A good analogy for extinction is to imagine what would happen to your houseplants if you stopped watering them. Like a plant without water, a behaviour without occasional reinforcement eventually dies. Although very different processes, both punishment and extinction have the same weakening effect on behaviour.

How to Properly Categorize Contingent Consequences   In B Mod, consequences are defined in terms of their demonstrated impact on behaviour (see Figure 15–2), not subjectively or by their intended impact. For example, notice how one expert in the field distinguishes between reinforcement and rewards:

Reinforcement is distinguished from reward in that a reward is something that is perceived to be desirable and is delivered to an individual after performance. An increase in pay, a promotion, and a comment on good work performance may all be rewards. But rewards are not necessarily reinforcers. Reinforcers are defined by the increase in the rate of behaviour.[17]

A promotion is both a reward and a positive reinforcer if the individual's performance subsequently improves.[18] On the other hand, *apparent* rewards may turn out to be the opposite.[19] For example, consider Tampa Electric Company's successful "positive discipline" programme, which gives misbehaving employees a paid day off!

It works like this: employees who come in late, do a sloppy job, or mistreat a colleague first get an oral "reminder" rather than a "reprimand." Next comes a written reminder, then the paid day off—called a "decision-making leave day."

After a pensive day on the beach, naughty employees must agree in writing—or orally, at some union shops—that they will be on their best behaviour for the next year. The paid day off is a one-shot chance at reform. If the employee doesn't shape up, it's curtains. The process is documented, so employees often have little legal recourse.[20]

Contingent consequences are always categorized "after the fact" by answering the following two questions: (1) Was something contingently presented or withdrawn? and (2) Did the target behaviour subsequently occur more or less often? Using these two

Table 15–2 Schedules of Reinforcement

SCHEDULE	DESCRIPTION	PROBABLE EFFECTS ON RESPONDING
Continuous (CRF)	Reinforcer follows every response.	Steady high rate of performance as long as reinforcement continues to follow every response. High frequency of reinforcement may lead to early satiation. Behaviour weakens rapidly (undergoes extinction) when reinforcers are withheld. Appropriate for newly emitted, unstable, or low-frequency responses.
Intermittent	Reinforcer does not follow every response.	Capable of producing high frequencies of responding. Low frequency of reinforcement precludes early satiation. Appropriate for stable or high-frequency responses.
Fixed ratio (FR)	A fixed number of responses must be emitted before reinforcement occurs.	A fixed ratio of 1:1 (reinforcement occurs after every response); the same as a continuous schedule. Tends to produce a high rate of response, which is vigorous and steady.
Variable ratio (VR)	A varying or random number of responses must be emitted before reinforcement occurs.	Capable of producing a high rate of response, which is vigorous, steady, and resistant to extinction.
Fixed interval (FI)	The first response after a specific period of time has elapsed is reinforced.	Produces an uneven response pattern varying from a very slow, unenergetic response immediately following reinforcement to a very fast, vigorous response immediately preceding reinforcement.
Variable interval (VI)	The first response after varying or random periods of time have elapsed is reinforced.	Tends to produce a high rate of response, which is vigorous, steady, and resistant to extinction.

Source: F Luthans and R Kreitner, *Organizational Behavior Modification and Beyond: An Operant and Social Learning Approach* (Glenview, IL: Scott, Foresman, 1985), p 58. Used with authors' permission.

diagnostic questions, can you figure out why Tampa Electric's apparent reward turned out to be punishment for employees? Referring to the upper-right-hand quadrant in Figure 15–2, something was contingently presented, and the target behaviour (tardiness, sloppy work, etc.) was weakened. Hence, it was a punishment contingency.

Schedules of Reinforcement

As just illustrated, contingent consequences are an important determinant of future behaviour. The *timing* of behavioural consequences can be even more important. Based on years of tedious laboratory experiments with pigeons in highly controlled environments, Skinner and his colleagues discovered distinct patterns of responding for various schedules of reinforcement.[21] Although some of their conclusions can be generalized to negative reinforcement, punishment, and extinction, it is best to think only of positive reinforcement when discussing schedules.

Continuous reinforcement

Reinforcing every instance of a behaviour.

Continuous Reinforcement As indicated in Table 15–2, every instance of a target behaviour is reinforced when a **continuous reinforcement** (CRF) schedule is in effect. For instance, when your television set is operating properly, you are reinforced with a picture every time you turn it on (a CRF schedule). But, as with any CRF schedule of reinforcement, the behaviour of turning on the television will undergo rapid extinction if the set breaks.

Intermittent reinforcement

Reinforcing some but not all instances of behaviour.

Intermittent Reinforcement Unlike CRF schedules, **intermittent reinforcement** involves reinforcement of some but not all instances of a target behaviour. Four subcategories of intermittent schedules, described in Table 15–2, are fixed and variable ratio schedules and fixed and variable interval schedules. Reinforcement in *ratio* schedules is contingent on the number of responses emitted. *Interval* reinforcement is tied to the passage of time. Some common examples of the four types of intermittent reinforcement are as follows:

- *Fixed ratio*—piece-rate pay; bonuses tied to the sale of a fixed number of units.

- *Variable ratio*—slot machines that pay off after a variable number of lever pulls; lotteries that pay off after the purchase of a variable number of tickets.

- *Fixed interval*—hourly pay; annual salary paid on a regular basis.

- *Variable interval*—random supervisory praise and pats on the back for employees who have been doing a good job. (See the OB Exercise.)

Scheduling Is Critical   The schedule of reinforcement can more powerfully influence behaviour than the magnitude of reinforcement. Although this proposition grew out of experiments with pigeons, subsequent on-the-job research confirmed it. Consider, for example, a field study of 12 unionized beaver trappers employed by a lumber company to keep the large rodents from eating newly planted tree seedlings.[23]

The beaver trappers were randomly divided into two groups that alternated weekly between two different bonus plans. Under the first schedule, each trapper earned his regular $7 per hour wage plus $1 for each beaver caught. Technically, this bonus was paid on a CRF schedule. The second bonus plan involved the regular $7 per hour wage plus a one-in-four chance (as determined by rolling the dice) of receiving $4 for each beaver trapped. This second bonus plan qualified as a variable ratio (VR-4) schedule. In the long run, both incentive schemes averaged out to a $1-per-beaver bonus. Surprisingly, however, when the trappers were under the VR-4 schedule, they were 58 per cent more productive than under the CRF schedule, despite the fact that the net amount of pay averaged out the same for the two groups during the 12-week trapping season.

Work Organizations Typically Rely on the Weakest Schedule   Generally, variable ratio and variable interval schedules of reinforcement produce the strongest behaviour that is most resistant to extinction. As gamblers will attest, variable schedules hold the promise of reinforcement after the next target response. For example, the following drama at a Laughlin, Nevada, gambling casino is one more illustration of the potency of variable ratio reinforcement:

OB EXERCISE   *A Test of How Well You Know the Schedules of Reinforcement*

Company
Drakenfeld Colors, Ciba-Geigy Corporation, Washington, Pennsylvania

Target behavior
Absenteeism

Instructions
Read the following case incident, select one of the answers listed below, and then check the interpretation in footnote 22 at the end of this chapter.

Drakenfeld had a population of about 250 employees with an absenteeism rate of only 0.89%. In fact, a full 44% of its employees had perfect attendance records in 1987. . . .

Because of the significant population of perfect attendees, it was decided to capitalize upon the strengths and to not only reward these people but to showcase them to the organization-at-large. This included a monetary bonus of $50 at six months and again at 12, with an additional $25 bonus for a full-calendar year of perfect attendance. Such an incentive alone may not sound as though it would induce someone to crawl out of bed on a day he or she might not otherwise do so, but the majority of the workforce already had a strong work ethic, and that root behavior was still dominant.

In order to make the program visible and exciting, employees with perfect attendance were entered into a sweepstakes drawing to take place at a special awards banquet with employees, spouses, and management. The winner would receive an all-expenses paid trip for two to a resort location. The cost/benefit ratio of this incentive is obvious. . . .

Response to . . . [this] aspect of the program was extremely well received, with perfect attendance increasing from an already impressive 44% to a new high of 62% in the first year (1988).

Which schedules of reinforcement were used in this case?

1. Fixed interval plus variable interval.
2. Variable ratio plus variable interval.
3. Fixed ratio plus fixed interval.
4. Variable interval plus fixed ratio.
5. Fixed ratio plus variable ratio.

SOURCE   Case incident excerpted from "Attendance Management and Control," by J Putzier and F T Nowak, August 1989. Reprinted with the permission of *HR Magazine,* published by the Society for Human Resource Management, Alexandria, VA.

An elderly woman with a walker had lost her grip on the slot [machine] handle and had collapsed on the floor.

"Help," she cried weakly.

The woman at the machine next to her interrupted her play for a few seconds to try to help her to her feet, but all around her the army of slot players continued feeding coins to the machines.

A security man arrived to soothe the woman and take her away.

"Thank you," she told him appreciatively. "But don't forget my winnings."[24]

Organizations without at least some variable reinforcement are less likely to prompt this type of dedication to task. Despite the trend toward this sort of pay-for-performance, time-based pay schemes such as hourly wages and yearly salaries that rely on the weakest schedule of reinforcement (fixed interval) are still the rule in today's workplaces.

Behaviour Shaping

Have you ever wondered how trainers at aquarium parks manage to get bottle-nosed dolphins to do flips, killer whales to carry people on their backs, and seals to juggle balls? The results are seemingly magical. Actually, a mundane learning process called shaping is responsible for the animals' antics.

Two-ton killer whales, for example, have a big appetite, and they find buckets of fish very reinforcing. So if the trainer wants to ride a killer whale, he or she reinforces very basic behaviours that will eventually lead to the whale being ridden. The killer whale is contingently reinforced with a few fish for coming near the trainer, then for being touched, then for putting its nose in a harness, then for being straddled, and eventually for swimming with the trainer on its back. In effect, the trainer systematically raises the behavioural requirement for reinforcement. Thus, **shaping** is defined as the process of reinforcing closer and closer approximations to a target behaviour.

Shaping

Reinforcing closer and closer approximations to a target behaviour.

Shaping works very well with people, too, especially in training and quality programmes involving continuous improvement. Praise, recognition, and instructive and credible feedback cost managers little more than moments of their time.[25] Yet, when used in conjunction with a behaviour-shaping programme, these consequences can efficiently foster significant improvements in job performance.[26] The key to successful behaviour shaping lies in reducing a complex target behaviour to easily learned steps and then faithfully (and patiently) reinforcing any improvement. For example, Continental Airlines used a cash bonus programme to improve its on-time arrival record from one of the worst in the industry to one of the best. Employees originally were promised a $65 bonus each month Continental earned a top-five ranking. Now it takes a second- or third-place ranking to earn the $65 bonus and a $100 bonus awaits employees when they achieve a No. 1 ranking.[27] (Table 15–3 lists practical tips on shaping.)

A Model for Modifying Job Behaviour

Someone once observed that children and pets are the world's best behaviour modifiers. In fact, one of your authors responds obediently to his cats, while the other jumps to satisfy contingencies arranged by his dog! Despite their ignorance of operant theory, children and pets are good behaviour modifiers because they (1) know precisely what behaviour they want to elicit, (2) provide clear antecedents, and (3) wield situationally appropriate and powerful contingent consequences. Let us learn from these "masters" of behaviour modification and examine a four-step B Mod process for managing on-the-job behaviour[28] (see Figure 15–3). A review of practical implications follows.

Step 1: Identify Target Behaviour

Managers who strictly follow the operant principle of focusing on observable behaviour rather than on inferred internal states, have two alternatives in step 1. They can pinpoint a *desirable* behaviour that occurs too *seldom* (e.g., contributing creative ideas at staff

Table 15–3   Ten Practical Tips for Shaping Job Behaviour

1. *Accommodate the process of behavioural change.* Behaviours change in gradual stages, not in broad, sweeping motions.

2. *Define new behaviour patterns specifically.* State what you wish to accomplish in explicit terms and in small amounts that can be easily grasped.

3. *Give individuals feedback on their performance.* A once-a-year performance appraisal is not sufficient.

4. *Reinforce behaviour as quickly as possible.*

5. *Use powerful reinforcement.* To be effective, rewards must be important to the employee—not to the manager.

6. *Use a continuous reinforcement schedule.* New behaviours should be reinforced every time they occur. This reinforcement should continue until these behaviours become habitual.

7. *Use a variable reinforcement schedule for maintenance.* Even after behaviour has become habitual, it still needs to be rewarded, though not necessarily every time it occurs.

8. *Reward teamwork—not competition.* Group goals and group rewards are one way to encourage cooperation in situations in which jobs and performance are interdependent.

9. *Make all rewards contingent on performance.*

10. *Never take good performance for granted.* Even superior performance, if left unrewarded, will eventually deteriorate.

Source: Adapted from A T Hollingsworth and D Tanquay Hoyer, "How Supervisors Can Shape Behavior," *Personnel Journal,* May 1985, pp 86, 88.

meetings), or they can focus on an *undesirable* behaviour that occurs too *often* (e.g., making disruptive comments at staff meetings).[29] Organizational behaviour modification proponents prefer the first alternative because it requires managers to see things in a positive, growth-oriented manner instead of in a negative, punitive manner. As a case in point, researchers have documented the benefits of "well pay" versus the costs of traditional sick pay.[30] In short, every undesirable behaviour has a desirable opposite. Just a few of many possible examples are being absent/being on time, having an accident/working safely, remaining aloof/participating actively, procrastinating/completing assignments on time, competing destructively/being a team player.

Pointers for Identifying Behaviour According to the former editor of the *Journal of Organizational Behavior Management,* a journal devoted to the study of B Mod in the workplace, too many B Mod programmes focus on process (rule following) rather than on accomplishments. Thus, he offers the following three pointers for identifying target behaviours:

1. The primary focus should be on accomplishments or outcomes. These accomplishments should have *significant* organizational impact.

2. The targeting of process behaviours (rule adherence, etc.) should only occur when that behaviour can be functionally related to a significant organizational accomplishment.

3. There should be broad participation in the development of behavioural targets.[31]

These pointers are intended to prevent managers from falling victim to charges of unethical manipulation.

Figure 15–3   Modifying On-the-Job Behaviour

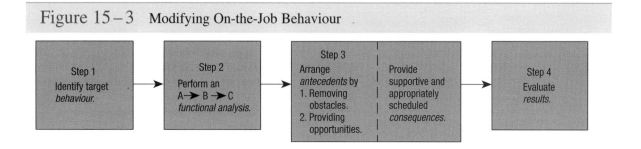

A Word of Caution about Shifting the Focus from Behaviour to Results In laboratory settings or highly controlled situations such as classrooms or machine shops, it is possible to directly observe and record the frequency of specific behaviours. Asking a question in class, arriving late at work, and handing in an error-free report are all observable behavioural events. However, in today's complex organizations, it is not always possible (or desirable) to observe and record work behaviours firsthand. For example, top-level managers and technical specialists often spend time alone in closed offices. When work behaviour cannot be monitored firsthand, the next-best alternative is to track results. Examples include number of units sold, number of customer complaints, degree of goal attainment, and percentage of projects completed. Managers who build contingencies around results need to keep in mind that those contingencies will be less precise than ones anchored to observable behavioural events.[32] For instance, the wrong person could be reinforced because organizational politicians sometimes take credit for others' results.

Step 2: Functionally Analyse the Situation

Any behaviours occurring on a regular basis necessarily have their own supportive cues and consequences. Thus, it is important for managers to identify existing A→B→C contingencies before trying to rearrange things. For example, it is important to know that a recently uncooperative employee is being pressured by co-workers to vote in a particular way in a union ballot.

Step 3: Arrange Antecedents and Provide Consequences

In this step, analysis gives way to action. An instructive way to discuss step 3 is to explore separately antecedent management and consequence management. In practice, antecedent and consequence management are closely intertwined.

Managing Antecedents As specified in step 3 of Figure 15–3, antecedent management involves two basic strategies: (1) removing obstacles and/or (2) providing opportunities. Some practical suggestions are listed in Table 15–4. Based on the discussion of goal setting in Chapter 8, challenging objectives that specify what and when something is to be accomplished are probably the most potent antecedent management tool. For instance, supervisors in one study handed in their weekly reports more promptly when they were given specific target dates.[33]

By rearranging apparently insignificant antecedents, significant results can be achieved. Importantly, these must be *contingent* antecedents, as identified through an A→B→C functional analysis. For example, a telephone company was losing an estimated $250,000 annually because its telephone installers were not reporting the installation of "ceiling drops." A ceiling drop involves installing extra wiring to compensate for a lowered ceiling. Despite comprehensive training on how to install and report ceiling

Table 15–4   Paving the Way for Good Job Performance with Helpful Antecedents

REMOVE OBSTACLES	PROVIDE OPPORTUNITIES
Eliminate unrealistic plans, schedules, and deadlines.	Formulate difficult but attainable goals.
Identify and remedy skill deficiencies through training.	Provide clear instructions.
Eliminate confusing or contradictory rules.	Give friendly reminders, constructive suggestions, and
Avoid conflicting orders and priorities.	helpful tips.
Remove distracting co-workers.	Ask nonthreatening questions about progress.
	Display posters with helpful advice.
	Rely on easy-to-use forms.
	Build enthusiasm and commitment through participation
	and challenging work assignments.
	Promote personal growth and development through
	training.

drops, a large percentage of ceiling drops remained unreported and thus unbilled by the company. The following turn of events then took place:

A specialist in training design was called in to find out why the training had failed. She noted a curious thing. The form that the installers were required to fill out was extremely complicated and the part dealing with ceiling drops was even more complicated. . . .

One small change was made by adding a box where the installer could merely check "ceiling drop installed." Now the installer no longer had to fill out an extensive explanation of what took place in the house. Within one week after the change in the form, the number of ceiling drops reported and charged back to the customers had increased dramatically, far above what it was immediately after the training sessions.[34]

Summarizing, from a B Mod perspective the telephone installers did not have an attitude or motivation problem. Nor did they have a knowledge deficiency requiring more training. They simply did not report ceiling drops because it was too complicated to do so. The streamlined reporting form presented the installers with an opportunity to behave properly, whereas the old form was an obstacle to good performance. In A→B→C terms, the streamlined reporting form became an antecedent that efficiently cued the desired behaviour.

Managing Consequences   Step 3 in Figure 15–3 calls for providing supportive and appropriately scheduled consequences. Six guidelines for successfully managing consequences during B Mod are as follows:

1. *Reinforce improvement, not just final results.* Proper shaping cannot occur if the behavioural requirement for reinforcement is too demanding. Behaviour undergoes extinction when it is not shaped in achievable step-by-step increments.

2. *Fit the consequences to the behaviour.* A pair of B Mod scholars interpreted this guideline as follows:

   Overrewarding a worker may make him feel guilty and certainly reinforces his current performance level. If the performance level is lower than that of others who get the same reward, he has no reason to increase his output. When a worker is underrewarded, he becomes angry with the system. His behavior is being extinguished and the company may be forcing the good employee (under-rewarded) to seek employment elsewhere while encouraging the poor employee (overrewarded) to stay on.[35]

   Note how this recommendation is consistent with the discussion of equity theory in Chapter 8.

Natural rewards
Normal social interactions such as praise or recognition.

3. *Emphasize natural rewards over contrived rewards.* **Natural rewards** are potentially reinforcing consequences derived from day-to-day social and administrative interactions. Typical natural rewards include supervisory praise, assignment to favoured tasks, early time off with pay, flexible work schedules, and extended breaks. Contrived rewards include money and other tangible rewards. Regarding this distinction, it has been pointed out that

   Natural social rewards are potentially the most powerful and universally applicable reinforcers. In contrast to contrived rewards, they do not generally lead to satiation (people seldom get tired of compliments, attention, or recognition) and can be administered on a very contingent basis.[36]

4. *Provide individuals with objective feedback whenever possible.* As discussed in Chapter 9, objective feedback can have a positive impact on future behaviour. This is particularly true when people have the opportunity to keep track of their own performance.[37] The three-way marriage of goal setting, objective feedback, and positive reinforcement for improvement can be fruitful indeed. For example, a field

study of hockey players demonstrated that a B Mod intervention of goal setting, feedback, and praise increased the team's winning percentage by almost 100 per cent for two consecutive years.[38]

5. *Emphasize positive reinforcement; deemphasize punishment.* Proponents of B Mod in the workplace, as mentioned earlier, recommend building up good behaviour with positive reinforcement instead of tearing down bad behaviour with punishment.[39] For instance, the authors of the best seller, *The One Minute Manager,* told their readers to "catch them doing something right!"[40] In other words, managers who focus on what's right with job performance unavoidably end up emphasizing positive reinforcement.

Regarding the use of punishment, operant researchers found it tends to suppress undesirable behaviour only temporarily while prompting emotional side effects. For example, a computer programmer who is reprimanded publicly for failing to "debug" an important programme may get even with the boss by skilfully sabotaging another programme. Moreover, those punished come to fear and dislike the person administering the punishment.[41] Thus, it is unlikely that punitive managers can build the climate of trust so necessary for success in today's TQM-oriented organizations. For example, the "giant retailer W T Grant, which went bankrupt in 1975, made it a practice to cut the tie of any sales manager who did not meet his quota."[42]

Constructive and positive feedback is a proven alternative to punishment (e.g., see the International OB).

6. *Schedule reinforcement appropriately.* Once again, immature behaviour requires the nurture of continuous reinforcement. Established or habitual behaviour, in contrast, can be maintained with fixed or variable schedules of intermittent reinforcement.

International Organizational Behaviour

Organizational Behaviour Modification (OB Mod) Successfully Exported to Russia

The Setting*

The study was conducted at the largest textile mill in Russia. The mill employed about 8,000 employees at the time of the study, late spring of 1990. This was after Gorbachev's perestroika (economic and political restructuring) had been implemented, but before the breakup of the Soviet Union. The factory is located in Tver (formerly Kalinin), about 150 kms northwest of Moscow.

The Intervention**

The supervisors were instructed on examples of specific functional and dysfunctional performance behaviours and were encouraged to ask clarifying questions. The researchers then instructed the supervisors to administer recognition and praise when workers performed the functional behaviours and to provide specific

feedback to them about these behaviours. The supervisors were also instructed to give reminders and make corrections when they observed the dysfunctional behaviours but were specifically told not to give negative reprimands or punishment.

The Results*

First, the introduction of an OB Mod intervention led to an increase in functional behaviour and a decrease in dysfunctional behaviour among the [33] workers in this study. Second, the impact was more immediate and distinctive for eliminating undesired behaviours than for increasing desired behaviours. Third, both the functional and dysfunctional behaviours failed to reverse after the withdrawal of the intervention.

SOURCES   *Excerpted from D H B Welsh, F Luthans, and S M Sommer, "Organizational Behavior Modification Goes to Russia: Replicating an Experimental Analysis Across Cultures and Tasks," *Journal of Organizational Behavior Management,* no 2, 1993, pp 15–35.

**Excerpted from D H B Welsh, F Luthans, and S M Sommer, "Managing Russian Factory Workers: The Impact of US-Based Behavioral and Participative Techniques," *Academy of Management Journal,* February 1993, pp 58–79.

Step 4: Evaluate Results

B Mod intervention is effective if (1) a desirable target behaviour occurs more often or (2) an undesirable target behaviour occurs less often. Since *more* or *less* are relative terms, managers need a measurement tool that provides an objective basis for comparing preintervention with postintervention data. This is where baseline data and behaviour charting can make a valuable contribution.

Baseline data
Preintervention data collected by someone other than the target person.

Baseline data are preintervention behavioural data collected without the target person's knowledge. This "before" measure later provides a basis for assessing an intervention's effectiveness.

Behaviour chart
Programme evaluation graph with baseline and intervention data.

A **behaviour chart** is a B Mod programme evaluation tool that includes both preintervention baseline data and postintervention data. The vertical axis of a behaviour chart can be expressed in terms of behaviour frequency, percentage, or results attained. A time dimension is typically found on the horizontal axis of a behaviour chart. When a goal is included, as shown in Figure 15 – 4, a behaviour chart quickly tells the individual where his or her performance has been, is, and should be. As the successful bus driver safety programme discussed at the opening of this chapter illustrates, posted feedback can be a very effective management tool. Moreover, a behaviour chart provides an ongoing evaluation of a B Mod programme.

Some Practical Implications

ETHICS

Some believe B Mod does not belong in the workplace.[43] They see it as blatantly manipulative and demeaning. Although even the severest critics admit it works, they rightly point out that on-the-job applications of B Mod have focused on superficial rule-following behaviour such as getting to work on time. Indeed, B Mod is still in transition from highly controlled and simple laboratory and clinical settings to loosely controlled and complex organizational settings.[44] A promising application of B Mod in recent years has been in the area of employee safety and accident prevention.[45] Despite the need for more B Mod research and application in complex organizations, some practical lessons already have been learned.

Figure 15 – 4   Behaviour Charts Help Evaluate B Mod Programmes and Provide Feedback

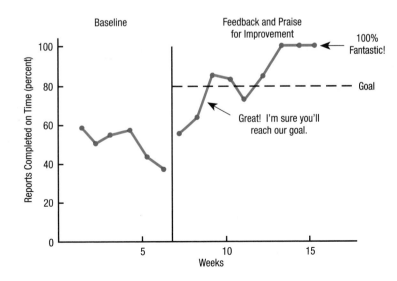

First, it is very difficult and maybe impossible to change organizational behaviour without systematically managing antecedents and contingent consequences. Second, even the best-intentioned reward system will fail if it does not include clear behaviour–consequence contingencies. Third, behaviour shaping is a valuable developmental technique. Fourth, goal setting, objective feedback, and positive reinforcement for improvement, when combined in systematic A→B→C fashion, are a powerful management tool. Finally, because formal programme evaluation is fundamental to B Mod, those who use it on the job can be held accountable.

Why OB Mod is so Unpopular in Europe

Behavioural modification with its emphasis on "rewards for good behaviour" seems to fit excellently with American values, such as individualism, competition, profit-orientation,

European OB specialists, on the contrary, loathe behavioural modification for at least one of the following reasons:[46]

1. European management is humanistic, structuralistic, and phenomenological. It emphasizes human dignity, social structures, and meaningful behaviour by actors who define their social reality. B Mod is fundamentally opposed to these three tendencies.

    "Behaviour is shaped by its consequences" seems to deny that behaviour is shaped by free choice, intention, or purposes. Employees do not have an array of behaviour at their disposal to choose from. Rather they are led into an increasingly narrowing number of options, i.e., behaviours rewarded by management. This deprives employees of their dignity and freedom of choice and is the opposite of the notion of empowerment.[47] Skinner's most popular book on behaviourism bears the title *Beyond Freedom and Dignity*,[48] as a kind of direct attack on European values.

    OB Mod is controlling and is based on an old-fashioned command and control management style where management is responsible for defining results and desired behaviour. Employees are nothing more than well-trained performing artists who will not take any initiatives or show any form of creativity.

2. Behavioural modification is overtly manipulative and its techniques can be so strong and effective that they are arouse serious ethical questions. It is very easy for people to get addicted to gambling. Is it acceptable to use the same techniques as casinos do to "motivate" employees? The ethical questions are described in Anthony Burgess's novel *A Clockwork Orange*[49] where the leading character, Alex, is used as a guinea pig for an OB Mod experiment, loosing his free will. Can the use of techniques initially designed for the treatment of mental disorders be justified in the workplace? An alternative strategy to improve safety at the workplace is presented by Ricky Gilby, a specialist in the field of safety. According to her, accidents are multicausal, and it only takes a trigger to make them happen. As an example, she takes the Zeebrugge example, the capsizing of the *Herald of Free Enterprise*, which was caused by a chain of events: the bosun being asleep, design failures, management failures, the culture of the owning company, . . . Instead of using the behaviour-based approach, she proposes develop a positive "safety culture".[50]

3. Behavioural modification shifts the attention from intrinsic to extrinsic motivation. Why do we have to reinforce employees with extrinsic rewards for behaviour that should be intrinsically rewarded? This system may imply that management no longer seeks to enrich the tasks, that jobs that could have been made meaningful remain dull and monotonous. Employees, on the other hand, may start thinking that there is something wrong with their jobs, as management has to reward and punish.

The Anthroposophic Movement

The anthroposophic movement, launched by the Austrian philosopher Rudolf Steiner, is a philosophy which holds that people should be paid according to their needs, and not according to how senior they are in the organization, or to the job they carry out. Paying according to need leads to a totally different relationship between people and their work.

People have a sense of responsibility for the whole organization, and relationships between people are much freer. The status hierarchy arises out of the nature of people and their wisdom, not from a given structure. Glenn Saunders, managing director of Mercury Provident Bank in the UK states why his staff is prepared to be paid according to the anthroposophic principles:

There are reasons for working that go beyond the drudgery of earning a living. And the more you have responsibility for the direction of the organization, the more important these reasons are. People make a definite and positive decision to work here because they believe in what we do.[51]

Behavioural Self-Management

Judging from the number of diet books appearing on bestseller lists each year, self-control seems to be in rather short supply. Historically, when someone sought to wage the war of self-control, he or she was told to exercise willpower, be self-disciplined, resist temptation, or seek divine guidance. Although well-intentioned, this advice gives the individual very little to go on relative to actually changing his or her behaviour. Fortunately, behavioural scientists formulated step-by-step self-management models that have helped individuals conquer serious behavioural problems. Typical among those problems are alcohol and drug abuse, overeating, cigarette smoking, phobias, and antisocial behaviour. True to its interdisciplinary nature, the field of OB has recently translated self-management theory and techniques from the clinic to the workplace.

Behavioural
self-management
Modifying one's own
behaviour by managing
cues, cognitive processes,
and consequences.

Formally defined, **behavioural self-management** (BSM) is the process of modifying one's own behaviour by systematically managing cues, cognitive processes, and contingent consequences. The term *behavioural* signifies that BSM focuses primarily on modifying behaviour, rather than on changing values, attitudes, or personalities. At first glance, BSM appears to be little more than self-imposed B Mod. But BSM differs from B Mod in that cognitive processes are considered in BSM while ignored in B Mod. This adjustment reflects the influence of Albert Bandura's extension of operant theory into social learning theory.

In this section, we discuss Bandura's social learning theory, from which BSM has evolved. Next, a brief overview of the managerial context for BSM is presented. A social learning model of self-management is then introduced and explored, followed by some practical implications of relevant research findings.

Bandura's Social Learning Theory

Albert Bandura built on Skinner's work by initially demonstrating how people acquire new behaviour by imitating role models (called vicarious learning) and later exploring the cognitive processing of cues and consequences. (Recall our discussion of the Stanford psychologist's ideas about self-efficacy in Chapter 5.) Like Skinner's operant model, Bandura's approach makes observable behaviour the primary unit of analysis. Bandura also goes along with Skinner's contention that behaviour is controlled by environmental cues and consequences. However, Bandura has extended Skinner's operant model by emphasizing that cognitive or mental processes affect how one responds to surroundings. In short, Bandura considers factors *inside* the individual, whereas the operant model stays outside the person. This extension is called social learning theory.[52]

A Managerial Context for Behavioral Self-Management

ETHICS

OB scholars Fred Luthans and Tim Davis developed the managerial context for BSM as follows:

Research and writing in the management field have given a great deal of attention to managing societies, organizations, groups, and individuals. Strangely, almost no one has paid any attention to managing oneself more effectively. . . . Self-management seems to be a basic prerequisite for effective management of other people, groups, organizations, and societies.[53]

Moreover, some have wrapped BSM in ethical terms: "Proponents of self-control contend that it is more ethically defensible than externally imposed behaviour control techniques when used for job enrichment, behaviour modification, management by objectives, or organization development."[54] Others have placed self-management within a managerial context by discussing it as a substitute for hierarchical leadership.[55] Behavioural self-management also meshes well with today's emphasis on empowerment, self-managed teams, and total quality management (TQM).[56] Recall that *everyone* is responsible for product and service quality in a TQM environment.

Social Learning Model of Self-Management

Bandura has put self-management into a social learning context by noting the following:

[A] distinguishing feature of social learning theory is the prominent role it assigns to self-regulatory capacities. By arranging environmental inducements, generating cognitive supports, and producing consequences for their own actions people are able to exercise some measure of control over their own behavior.[57]

In other words, to the extent that you can control your environment and your cognitive representations of your environment, you are the master of your own behaviour. The practical BSM model displayed in Figure 15–5 is derived from social learning theory.

Figure 15–5   A Social Learning Model of Self-Management

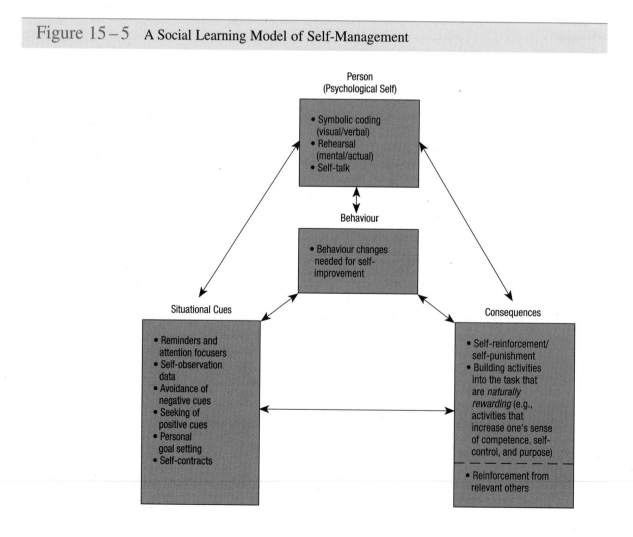

Reflecting Bandura's extension of Skinner's basic A→B→C model, the BSM model includes the person's psychological self. The two-headed arrows reflect Bandura's contention, discussed previously, that the individual has a degree of control over his or her own antecedent cues, behaviour, and consequences. Each of the four major components of this BSM model requires a closer look. Since this is a *behavioural* model, let us begin our examination with the behaviour component in the centre of the triangle.

An Agenda for Self-Improvement   Self-improvement and self-development are more important than ever considering the *new employment contract* discussed in Chapter 1. Corporate handholding up each rung of a well-defined career ladder has become a thing of the past. Now, employees are told they "own their own employability." They must make the best of themselves and any opportunities that may come along. A brochure at Intel Corp., the computer chip giant, tells employees: "No one is more interested or qualified when it comes to evaluating your individual interests, values, skills, and goals than you are."[58] The new age of *career self-management* challenges you to do a better job of setting personal goals, having clear priorities, being well organized, skilfully managing your time, and developing a self-learning programme.[59]

Fortunately, Stephen R Covey, in his bestselling book *The 7 Habits of Highly Effective People,* has given managers a helpful agenda for improving themselves (see Table 15–5). Covey refers to the seven habits, practised by truly successful people, as "principle-centered, character-based."[60] The first step for those practising BSM is to pick one or more of the seven habits that are personal trouble spots and translate them to specific behaviours. For example, "think win–win" might remind a conflict-prone manager to practise cooperative teamwork behaviours with co-workers. Habit number five might prompt another manager to stop interrupting others during conversations.

As a procedural note, behaviour charts can be used in BSM to evaluate progress towards one's goals, but baseline data ideally should be collected by someone else to ensure objectivity.

Managing Situational Cues   When people try to give up a nagging habit such as smoking, the cards are stacked against them. Many people (friends who smoke) and situations (after dinner, when under stress at work, or when relaxing) serve as subtle yet powerful cues telling the individual to light up. If the behaviour is to be changed, the cues need to be rearranged so as to trigger the alternative behaviour. Six techniques for managing situational cues are listed in the left column of Figure 15–5.

Table 15–5   Covey's Seven Habits: An Agenda for Managerial Self-Improvement

1. *Be proactive.* Choose the right means and ends in life, and take personal responsibility for your actions. Make timely decisions and make positive progress.

2. *Begin with the end in mind.* When all is said and done, how do you want to be remembered? Be goal oriented.

3. *Put first things first.* Establish firm priorities that will help you accomplish your mission in life. Strike a balance between your daily work and your potential for future accomplishments.

4. *Think win–win.* Cooperatively seek creative and mutually beneficial solutions to problems and conflicts.

5. *Seek first to understand, then to be understood.* Strive hard to become a better listener.

6. *Synergize.* Because the whole is greater than the sum of its parts, you need to generate teamwork among individuals with unique abilities and potential. Value interpersonal differences.

7. *Sharpen the saw.* "This is the habit of self-renewal, which has four elements. The first is mental, which includes reading, visualizing, planning, and writing. The second is spiritual, which means value clarification and commitment, study, and meditation. Third is social/emotional, which involves service, empathy, synergy, and intrinsic security. Finally, the physical element includes exercise, nutrition, and stress management."

Sources: Adapted from discussion in S R Covey, *The 7 Habits of Highly Effective People* (New York: Simon & Schuster, 1989). Excerpt from "Q & A with Stephen Covey," *Training,* December 1992, p 38.

Reminders and attention focusers do just that. For example, many students and managers cue themselves about deadlines and appointments with Post-it Notes stuck all over their work areas, refrigerators, and dashboards. Self-observation data, when compared against a goal or standard, can be a potent cue for improvement. Those who keep a weight chart near their bathroom scale will attest to the value of this tactic. Successful self-management calls for avoiding negative cues while seeking positive cues. Managers in Northwestern Mutual Life Insurance Company's new business department appreciate the value of avoiding negative cues: "On Wednesdays, the department shuts off all incoming calls, allowing workers to speed processing of new policies. On those days, the unit averages 23 per cent more policies than on other days."[61]

Goals, as repeatedly mentioned in this text, are the touchstone of good management. So it is with challenging yet attainable personal goals and effective self-management. Goals simultaneously provide a target and a measuring stick of progress.[62] Finally, a self-contract is an "if-then" agreement with oneself. For example, if you can define all the key terms in this chapter, treat yourself to something special.

Arranging Cognitive Supports   This component makes BSM distinctly different from conventional behaviour modification. Referring to the *person* portion of the self-management model in Figure 15–5, three cognitive supports for behaviour change are symbolic coding, rehearsal, and self-talk. These amount to psychological, as opposed to environmental, cues. Yet, according to Bandura, they prompt appropriate behaviour in the same manner. Each requires brief explanation:

• *Symbolic coding:* From a social learning theory perspective, the human brain stores information in visual and verbal codes. For example, a sales manager could use the visual picture of a man chopping down a huge tree to remember Woodman, the name of a promising new client. In contrast, people commonly rely on acronyms to recall names, rules for behaviour, and other information. An acronym (or verbal code) that is often heard in managerial circles is the KISS principle, standing for "Keep It Simple, Stupid."

• *Rehearsal:* While it is true that practice often makes perfect, mental rehearsal of challenging tasks also can increase one's chances of success. Importantly, experts draw a clear distinction between systematic visualization of how one should proceed and daydreaming about success.

The big difference between daydreaming and visualizing is that "visualizing is much more specific and detailed," says Philadelphia consultant Judith Schuster. "A daydream typically has gaps in it—we jump immediately to where we want to wind up. In visualization, we use building blocks and, step-by-step, construct the result we want."[63]

This sort of visualization has been recommended for use in managerial planning.[64]

Managers stand to learn a great deal about mental rehearsal and visualization from successful athletes. Mary Lou Retton, 1984 Olympic gold medal gymnast, is an inspiring example:

"Before I dropped off to sleep inside the Olympic Village, I did what I always do before a major competition—mind-scripted it completely. I mentally ran through each routine, every move, imagining everything done perfectly," recalls Retton.[65]

Job-finding seminars are very popular on university campuses today because they typically involve mental and actual rehearsal of tough job interviews. This sort of manufactured experience can build the confidence and self-efficacy necessary for real-world success.[66]

Self-talk

Evaluating thoughts about oneself.

• *Self-talk:* According to an expert on the subject, "**self-talk** is the set of evaluating thoughts that you give yourself about facts and events that happen to you."[67] Personal experience tells us that self-talk tends to be a self-fulfilling prophecy. Negative self-talk tends to pave the way for failure, whereas positive self-talk often facilitates success.

Replacing negative self-talk ("I'll never get a rise") with positive self-talk ("I deserve a rise and I'm going to get it") is fundamental to better self-management.[68] One business writer, while urging salespeople to be their own cheerleaders, offered this advice for handling difficult situations:

Tell yourself there's a positive side to everything and train yourself to focus on it. At first your new self-talk will seem forced and unnatural, but stick with it. Use mental imagery to help you concentrate on the benefits of what you think is a bad situation. If you don't like cold calling, for example, think of how good you'll feel when you're finished, knowing you have a whole list of new selling opportunities. Forming a new habit isn't easy, but the effort will pay off.[69]

Self-Reinforcement   The satisfaction of self-contracts and other personal achievements calls for self-reinforcement. According to Bandura, three criteria must be satisfied before self-reinforcement can occur:

1. The individual must have *control over desired reinforcers.*

2. Reinforcers must be *self-administered on a conditional basis.* Failure to meet the performance requirement must lead to self-denial.

3. *Performance standards must be adopted* to establish the quantity and quality of target behaviour required for self-reinforcement.[70]

In view of the following realities, self-reinforcement strategies need to be resourceful and creative:

Self-granted rewards can lead to self-improvement. But as failed dieters and smokers can attest, there are short-run as well as long-run influences on self-reinforcement. For the overeater, the immediate gratification of eating has more influence than the promise of a new wardrobe. The same sort of dilemma plagues procrastinators. Consequently, one needs to weave a powerful web of cues, cognitive supports, and internal and external consequences to win the tug-of-war with status-quo payoffs. Primarily because it is so easy to avoid, self-punishment tends to be ineffectual. As with managing the behaviour of others, positive instead of negative consequences are recommended for effective self-management.[71]

In addition, it helps to solicit positive reinforcement for self-improvement from supportive friends, co-workers, and relatives.

Research and Managerial Implications

There is ample evidence that behavioural self-management works. For example, in one controlled study of 20 university students, 17 were able to successfully modify their own behaviour problems involving smoking, lack of assertiveness, poor study habits, overeating, sloppy housekeeping, lack of exercise, and moodiness.[72] Research on self-monitoring, discussed in Chapter 5, may help explain why BSM works for some but not for others.[73] High self-monitors are likely to have an advantage over low self-monitors because they are more concerned about their social behaviour and tend to be more adaptable.

Because BSM has only recently been transplanted from clinical and classroom applications to the workplace, on-the-job research evidence is limited. One pair of researchers reported successful BSM interventions with managerial problems, including overdependence on the boss, ignoring paperwork, leaving the office without notifying anyone, and failing to fill out expense reports.[74] Also, absenteeism of unionized state government employees was significantly reduced with BSM training.[75] A survey of 36 organization development consultants found positive applications of mental imagery and visualization for organizational problem solving.[76] These preliminary studies need to be supplemented by research of how, why, and under what conditions BSM does or does not work.[77] In the meantime, current and future managers can fine-tune their own behaviour by taking lessons from proven self-management techniques.

Summary of Key Concepts

1. **State Thorndike's "law of effect," and explain Skinner's distinction between respondent and operant behaviour.** According to Edward L Thorndike's law of effect, behaviour with favourable consequences tends to be repeated, while behaviour with unfavourable consequences tends to disappear. B F Skinner called unlearned stimulus–response reflexes respondent behaviour. He applied the term operant behaviour to all behaviour learned through experience with environmental consequences.

2. **Define the term behaviour modification, and explain the A→B→C model.** Behaviour modification (B Mod) is defined as the process of making specific behaviour occur more or less often by systematically managing (*a*) antecedent cues and (*b*) contingent consequences. B Mod involves managing person–environment interactions that can be functionally analysed into antecedent→behaviour→consequence (A→B→C) relationships. Antecedents cue rather than cause subsequent behaviour. Contingent consequences, in turn, either strengthen or weaken that behaviour.

3. **Demonstrate your knowledge of positive reinforcement, negative reinforcement, punishment, and extinction.** Positive and negative reinforcement are consequence management strategies that strengthen behaviour, whereas punishment and extinction weaken behaviour. These strategies need to be defined objectively in terms of their actual impact on behaviour frequency, not subjectively on the basis of intended impact.

4. **Distinguish between continuous and intermittent schedules of reinforcement, and specify which schedules are most resistant to extinction.** Every instance of a behaviour is reinforced with a continuous reinforcement (CRF) schedule. Under intermittent reinforcement schedules—fixed and variable ratio or fixed and variable interval—some, rather than all, instances of a target behaviour are reinforced. Variable schedules produce the most extinction-resistant behaviour.

5. **Demonstrate your knowledge of behaviour shaping.** Behaviour shaping occurs when closer and closer approximations of a target behaviour are reinforced. In effect, the standard for reinforcement is made more difficult as the individual learns. The process begins with continuous reinforcement, which gives way to intermittent reinforcement when the target behaviour becomes strong and habitual.

6. **Identify and briefly explain each step in the four-step B Mod process.** On-the-job behaviour can be modified with the following four-step model: (*a*) identify target behaviour, (*b*) functionally analyse the situation, (*c*) arrange antecedents and provide consequences, and (*d*) evaluate results. Behaviour charts, with baseline data for before-and-after comparison, are a practical way of evaluating the effectiveness of a B Mod programme.

7. **Specify the six guidelines for managing consequences during B Mod.** (*a*) Reinforce improvement, not just final results. (*b*) Fit the consequences to the behaviour. (*c*) Emphasize natural rewards over contrived rewards. (*d*) Provide individuals with objective feedback whenever possible. (*e*) Emphasize positive reinforcement; deemphasize punishment. (*f*) Schedule reinforcement appropriately.

8. **Give three reasons why OB Mod is unpopular in Europe.** (1) OB Mod is fundamentally opposed to the European humanistic, structuralistic and phenomenological management approach; (2) OB Mod is overtly manipulative, which gives way to ethical questions; (3) OB Mod shifts the attention from intrinsic to extrinsic motivation.

9. **Explain the social learning model of self-management.** Behaviour results from interaction among four components: (a) situational cues, (b) the person's psychological self, (c) the person's behaviour, and (d) consequences. Behaviour, such as Covey's seven habits of highly effective people, can be developed by relying on supportive cognitive processes such as mental rehearsal and self-talk. Carefully arranged cues and consequences also help in the self-improvement process.

Discussion Questions

1. What would an A→B→C functional analysis of your departing your residence on time for school or work look like? How about a functional analysis of your leaving late?

2. Why is the term contingency central to understanding the basics of B Mod?

3. What real-life examples of positive reinforcement, negative reinforcement, both forms of punishment, and extinction can you draw from your recent experience? Were these strategies appropriately or inappropriately used?

4. From a schedule of reinforcement perspective, why do people find gambling so addictive?

5. What sort of behaviour shaping have you engaged in lately? Explain your success or failure.

6. Regarding the six guidelines for successfully managing consequences, which do you think ranks as the most important? Explain your rationale.

7. Why is valid baseline data essential in a B Mod programme?

8. What sort of luck have you had with self-management recently? Which of the self-management techniques discussed in this chapter would help you do better?

9. Do you agree with the assumption that managers need to do a good job with self-management before they can effectively manage others? Explain.

10. What importance would you attach to self-talk in self-management? Explain.

Personal Awareness and Growth Exercise

How Are Your B Mod Skills?

Objectives

1. To better understand the principles of behaviour modification through firsthand experience.
2. To improve your own or someone else's behaviour by putting to use what you have learned in this chapter.

Introduction

Because the areas of B Mod and BSM are application oriented, they need to be put to practical use if they are to be fully appreciated. In a general sense, everyone is a behaviour modifier. Unfortunately, those without a working knowledge of behavioural principles tend to manage their own and others' behaviour rather haphazardly. They tend to unwittingly reinforce undesirable behaviour, put desirable behaviour on extinction, and rely too heavily on punishment and negative reinforcement. This exercise is designed to help you become a more systematic manager of behaviour.

Instructions

Selecting the target behaviour of your choice, put the four-step behaviour modification model in Figure 15–3 into practice. The target may be your own behaviour (e.g., studying more, smoking fewer cigarettes, eating less or eating more nutritionally, or one of Covey's seven habits in Table 15–5) or someone else's (e.g., improving a roommate's

housekeeping behaviour). Be sure to construct a behaviour chart (as in Figure 15–4) with the frequency of the target behaviour on the vertical axis and time on the horizontal axis. It is best to focus on a behaviour that occurs daily so a three- or four-day baseline period can be followed by a one- to two-week intervention period. Make sure you follow as many of the six consequence management guidelines as possible.

You will find it useful to perform an A→B→C functional analysis of the target behaviour to identify its supporting (or hindering) cues and consequences. Then you will be in a position to set a reasonable goal and design an intervention strategy involving antecedent and consequence management. When planning a self-management intervention, give careful thought to how you can use cognitive supports. Make sure you use appropriate schedules of reinforcement.

QUESTIONS FOR DISCUSSION

1. Did you target a specific behaviour (e.g., eating) or an outcome (e.g., pounds lost)? What was the advantage or disadvantage of tracking that particular target?
2. How did your B Mod or BSM programme turn out? What did you do wrong? What did you do right?
3. How has this exercise increased your working knowledge of B Mod and/or BSM?

Group Exercise

Human Resource Problem-Solving Team

Objectives

1. To continue developing your teamwork and group problem-solving skills.
2. To think creatively about solving common "people problems."
3. To put your knowledge of B Mod to work.

Introduction

People may be an organization's most important resource, but they also are the source of management's most vexing and troublesome problems. Deviant behaviour is wide ranging, and managers need the skills to deal with it. This exercise introduces a useful typology of deviant behaviour as a stepping stone towards developing B Mod interventions. A 30-minute

small group session will be followed by brief oral reports to the entire class. Total time needed for this exercise is about 45 to 50 minutes.

Instructions

Your instructor will divide the class randomly into five- to seven-person teams. Each team will act as a human resource problem-solving team for a typical large organization. Step 1 for each team is to take five minutes to discuss the Typology of Deviant Workplace Behaviour provided and to brainstorm at least two additional deviant behaviours for each of the four categories. Step 2 calls for the group to select one behaviour from each of the four categories to serve as targets for behaviour modification. Step 3 involves developing a behaviour modification strategy for each of the four targeted deviant behaviours.

Tips: Be sure to rearrange antecedents and consequences for each target behaviour (making realistic assumptions about existing A→B→C relationships). Use behaviour charts whenever possible. Assign one team member the job of summarizing and reporting the team's B Mod strategies to the class.

Here are some things to keep in mind during step 3. Don't forget the common practice in B Mod of reinforcing a positive behaviour (e.g., good attendance) rather than punishing its reciprocal deviant behaviour (e.g., absenteeism). Of course, some of the deviant behaviours in the typology are so bad that termination of employment will be necessary. Your job as a human resource problem-solving team is to decide which behaviours warrant swift and sure punishment and which can be turned around with positive or negative reinforcement or extinction strategies.

QUESTIONS FOR DISCUSSION

1. Did your team do a good job of interpreting deviant behaviours as reinforceable productive behaviours (e.g., blaming co-workers versus owning up to one's mistakes)? Explain.
2. How difficult was it for your team to agree to fire someone for serious misconduct? Explain.
3. How realistic are the various B Mod strategies shared in class? Explain.
4. What situations were encountered where an approach other than B Mod would be best? Which approach?
5. In terms of the group and social processes material in Part Three of this book, how effective was your team? Explain.

Typology of Deviant Workplace Behaviour[78]

Organizational

Production Deviance
- Leaving early
- Taking excessive breaks
- Intentionally working slow
- Wasting resources
- _____
- _____

Property Deviance
- Sabotaging equipment
- Accepting kickbacks
- Lying about hours worked
- Stealing from company
- _____
- _____

Minor ← → Serious

Political Deviance
- Showing favouritism
- Gossiping about co-workers
- Blaming co-workers
- Competing nonbeneficially
- _____
- _____

Personal Aggression
- Sexual harassment
- Verbal abuse
- Stealing from co-workers
- Endangering co-workers
- _____
- _____

Interpersonal

Notes

[1] Excerpted from A Arkin, "Incentives to Work Safely," *Personnel Management*, September 1994, p 48–52.

[2] Complete details of this field study may be found in R S Haynes, R C Pine, and H G Fitch, "Reducing Accident Rates with Organizational Behavior Modification," *Academy of Management Journal*, June 1982, pp 407–16. A related study in The Netherlands is reported in S Siero, M Boon, G Kok, and F Siero, "Modification of Driving Behavior in a Large Transport Organization: A Field Experiment," *Journal of Applied Psychology*, June 1989, pp 417–23.

[3] J Saari, "When does behaviour modification prevent accidents," *Leadership and Organization Development Journal*, vol 15, 1994, p 11–15.

[4] Based on a similar definition in R Kreitner, "The Feed-forward and Feedback Control of Job Performance through Organizational Behavior Management (OBM)," *Journal of Organizational Behavior Management*, no. 3, 1982, pp 3–20. Three excellent resources, relative to B Mod in the workplace, are L W Frederiksen, ed, *Handbook of Organizational Behavior Management* (New York: John Wiley & Sons, 1982); F Andrasik, "Organizational Behavior Modification in Business Settings: A Methodological and Content

Review," *Journal of Organizational Behavior Management,* no. 1, 1989, pp 59–77; and G A Merwi, Jr., J A Thomason, and E E Sanford, "A Methodology and Content Review of Organizational Behavior Management in the Private Sector: 1978–1986," *Journal of Organizational Behavior Management,* no. 1, 1989, pp 39–57.

[5]For a good background article on performance management, see G Rummler, "In Search of the Holy Performance Grail," *Training & Development,* April 1996, pp 26–32.

[6]See E L Thorndike, *Educational Psychology: The Psychology of Learning, Vol. II* (New York: Columbia University Teachers College, 1913).

[7]Discussion of an early behaviourist who influenced Skinner's work can be found in P J Kreshel, "John B Watson at J Walter Thompson: The Legitimation of 'Science' in Advertising,' *Journal of Advertising,* no. 2, 1990, pp 49–59. Recent discussions involving behaviourism include M R Ruiz, "B F Skinner's Radical Behaviourism: Historical Misconstructions and Grounds for Feminist Reconstructions," *Psychology of Women Quarterly,* June 1995, pp 161–79; J A Nevin, "Behavioral Economics and Behavioral Momentum," *Journal of the Experimental Analysis of Behavior,* November 1995, pp 385–95; and H Rachlin, "Can We Leave Cognition to Cognitive Psychologists? Comments on an Article by George Loewenstein," *Organizational Behavior and Human Decision Processes,* March 1996, pp 296–99.

[8]For recent discussion, see J W Donahoe, "The Unconventional Wisdom of B F Skinner: The Analysis-Interpretation Distinction," *Journal of the Experimental Analysis of Behavior,* September 1993, pp 453–56.

[9]See B F Skinner, *The Behavior of Organisms* (New York: Appleton-Century-Crofts, 1938).

[10]For interesting discussions of Skinner and one of his students, see M B Gilbert and T F Gilbert, "What Skinner Gave Us," *Training,* September 1991, pp 42–48; and "HRD Pioneer Gilbert Leaves a Pervasive Legacy," *Training,* January 1996, p 14.

[11]For an instructive overview of learning, see G S Odiorne, "Four Magic Moments in Changing Behavior," *Training,* June 1991, pp 43–46.

[12]Complete discussion of the A→B→C model may be found in F Luthans and R Kreitner, *Organizational Behavior Modification and Beyond: An Operant and Social Learning Approach* (Glenview, IL: Scott, Foresman, 1985), pp 46–49.

[13]D H Ruben and M J Ruben, "Behavioral Principles on the Job: Control or Manipulation?" *Personnel,* May 1985, p 61.

[14]See P A Lamal, "The Continuing Mischaracterization of Radical Behaviorism," *American Psychologist,* January 1990, p 71.

[15]See Luthans and Kreitner, *Organizational Behavior Modification and Beyond,* pp 49–56.

[16]See D H B Welsh, D J Bernstein, and F Luthans, "Application of the Premack Principle of Reinforcement to the Quality Performance of Service Employees," *Journal of Organizational Behavior Management,* no. 1, 1992, pp 9–32.

[17]L M Miller, *Behavior Management: The New Science of Managing People at Work* (New York: John Wiley & Sons, 1978), p 106.

[18]For a unique psychobiological interpretation of reinforcement, see N M White and P M Milner, "The Psychobiology of Reinforcers," *Annual Review of Psychology,* vol. 43, 1992, pp 443–71.

[19]A useful resource on rewards is B Nelson, *1001 Ways to Reward Employees* (New York: Workman Publishing, 1994).

[20]L Baum, "Punishing Workers with a Day Off," *Business Week,* June 16, 1986, p 80.

[21]See C B Ferster and B F Skinner, *Schedules of Reinforcement* (New York: Appleton-Century-Crofts, 1957).

[22]Our choice is e. Of course, the correct answer to this challenging exercise is a matter of interpretation. There is plenty of room for honest disagreement. Our interpretation is based on the belief that the passage of time is not the primary criterion for granting reinforcement. The first reinforcement schedule, involving cash bonuses at the end of 6-month and 12-month periods for perfect attendance, is anchored to a specific number of complete work days. Every employee, regardless of his or her attendance record, does not automatically receive the cash bonuses at 6- and 12-month intervals (as would be the case with a fixed interval schedule). Hence, it is a fixed ratio schedule.

The second reinforcement schedule is anchored to whether or not one is eligible to enter the drawing. Again, the criterion is a specific set of behaviors, not the passage of time. This second reinforcement schedule qualifies as variable ratio, because the chance to win a reward is tied to a perfect attendance *quota.* Maintaining perfect attendance to qualify for the drawing each year is just like playing a slot machine. Together, these two schedules of reinforcement are a good incentive for perfect attendance.

[23]See L M Saari and G P Latham, "Employee Reactions to Continuous and Variable Ratio Reinforcement Schedules Involving a Monetary Incentive," *Journal of Applied Psychology,* August 1982, pp 506–8.

[24]P Brinkley-Rogers and R Collier, "Along the Colorado, the Money's Flowing," *The Arizona Republic,* March 4, 1990, p A12.

[25]The topic of managerial credibility is covered in J M Kouzes and B Z Posner, *Credibility* (San Francisco: Jossey-Bass, 1993).

[26]See, for example, J C Bruening, "Shaping Workers' Attitudes toward Safety," *Occupational Hazards,* March 1990, pp 49–51.

[27]Data from K L Alexander, "Continental Airlines Soars to New Heights," *USA Today,* January 23, 1996, p 4B.

[28]An alternative five-step model––pinpoint, record, involve, coach, evaluate––may be found in K Blanchard and R Lorber, *Putting the One Minute Manager to Work* (New York: Berkley Books, 1984), p 58.

[29]For related reading, see L J Rifkind and L F Harper, "Conflict Management Strategies for the Equal Opportunity Difficult Person in the Sexually Harassing Workplace," *Public Personnel Management,* Fall 1994, pp 487–500.

[30]For example, see B H Harvey, J A Schultze, and J F Rogers, "Rewarding Employees for Not Using Sick Leave," *Personnel Administrator,* May 1983, pp 55–59. Also see J C Landau, "The Impact of a Change in an Attendance Control System on Absenteeism and Tardiness," *Journal of Organizational Behavior Management,* no. 2, 1993, pp 51–70; and "High-Risk Employees Often Require Coaxing to Watch Their Health," *The Wall Street Journal,* September 24, 1996, p A1.

[31]L W Frederiksen, "The Selection of Targets for Organizational Interventions," *Journal of Organizational Behavior Management,* no 4, 1981–1982, p 4. Also see M E Furman, "Reverse the 80-20 Rule," *Management Review,* January 1997, pp 18–21.

[32]For related discussion, see W Wilhelm, "Changing Corporate Culture---or Corporate Behavior? How to Change Your Company," *Academy of Management Executive,* November 1992, pp 72–77.

[33]See J Conrin, "A Comparison of Two Types of Antecedent Control over Supervisory Behavior," *Journal of Organizational Behavior*

Management, Fall–Winter 1982, pp 37–47. For a report of the positive impact of antecedents on consumer behavior, see M J Martinko, J D White, and B Hassell, "An Operant Analysis of Prompting in a Sales Environment," *Journal of Organizational Behavior Management,* no. 1, 1989, pp 93–107. Antecedent control of safety behavior is reported in F M Streff, M J Kalsher, and E S Geller, "Developing Efficient Workplace Safety Programs: Observations of Response Covariation," *Journal of Organizational Behavior Management,* no. 2, 1993, pp 3–14.

[34]T K Connellan, *How to Improve Human Performance: Behaviorism in Business and Industry* (New York: Harper & Row, 1978), p 27. Effective antecedent control is reported in G Koretz, "'No Smoking' Is Working," *Business Week,* July 8, 1996, p 24.

[35]W C Hamner and E P Hamner, "Behavior Modification on the Bottom Line," *Organizational Dynamics,* Spring 1976, p 8.

[36]Luthans and Kreitner, *Organizational Behavior Modification and Beyond,* p 128. Incentive programs are critiqued in B Filipczak, "Why No One Likes Your Incentive Program," *Training,* August 1993, pp 19–25; and A Kohn, "Why Incentive Plans Cannot Work," *Harvard Business Review,* September–October 1993, pp 54–63.

[37]See "At Emery Air Freight: Positive Reinforcement Boosts Performance," *Organizational Dynamics,* Winter 1973, pp 41–50.

[38]See D C Anderson, C R Crowell, M Doman, and G S Howard, "Performance Posting, Goal Setting, and Activity-Contingent Praise as Applied to a University Hockey Team," *Journal of Applied Psychology,* February 1988, pp 87–95.

[39]An alternative perspective of punishment is presented in L Klebe Trevino, "The Social Effects of Punishment in Organizations: A Justice Perspective," *Academy of Management Review,* October 1992, pp 647–76.

[40]K Blanchard and S Johnson, *The One Minute Manager* (New York: Berkley Books, 1982), p 39. Interestingly, managers were given this identical bit of advice, "Catch them doing something right!" five years earlier by R Kreitner, "People Are Systems, Too: Filling the Feedback Vacuum," *Business Horizons,* November 1977, pp 54–58.

[41]For a review of this research, see Luthans and Kreitner, *Organizational Behavior Modification and Beyond,* pp 139–44. An alternative view of the benefits of punishment is discussed by R D Arvey and J M Ivancevich, "Punishment in Organizations: A Review, Propositions, and Research Suggestions," *Academy of Management Review,* January 1980, pp 123–32.

[42]S Narod, "Off-Beat Company Customs," *Dun's Business Month,* November 1984, p 66.

[43]For example, see F L Fry, "Operant Conditioning in Organizational Settings: Of Mice or Men?" *Personnel,* July–August 1974, pp 17–24, and E A Locke, "The Myths of Behavior Mod in Organizations," *Academy of Management Review,* 1977, pp 543–53.

[44]Evidence of constructive applications of B Mod in the workplace can be found in K O'Hara, C M Johnson, and T A Beehr, "Organizational Behavior Management in the Private Sector: A Review of Empirical Research and Recommendations for Further Investigation," *Academy of Management Review,* October 1985, pp 848–64. Also see recent issues of *Journal of Organizational Behavior Management,* particularly the special issue: "Promoting Excellence through Performance Management," *Journal of Organizational Behavior Management,* no 1, 1990; and W C Byham and A Pescuric, "Behavior Modeling at the Teachable Moment," *Training,* December 1996, pp 50–56.

[45]See R A Reber, J A Wallin, and D L Duhon, "Preventing Occupational Injuries through Performance Management," *Public Personnel Management,* Summer 1993, pp 301–11; R Ceniceros, "Safety Rewards Can Lead to Real Change," *Business Insurance,* May 1, 1995, p 21; and M A Hofmann, "Behavior Modification at Work," *Business Insurance,* April 29, 1996, p 18.

[46]Most European textbooks do not devote much attention to the subject (for an exception see J Arnold, C L Cooper, and I T Robertson, *Work Psychology* (London: Pitman Publishing, 1995). and even the reasons why European OB specialists do not like OB mod are not well documented.

[47]R Gilby, "Bogus Behavior," *The Safety and Health Practiner,* August 1996, p 13–15.

[48]B F Skinner, *Beyond Freedom and Dignity* (New York: Knopf, 1971).

[49]A Burgess, *A Clockwork Orange* (Harmondsworth: Penguin, 1972).

[50]Gilby, *op. cit.,* p13.

[51]E Fursland, "More to work than a pay check," *People Management,* August 24, 1995, p 36–37.

[52]See A Bandura, *Social Learning Theory* (Englewood Cliffs, NJ: Prentice-Hall, 1977).

[53]F Luthans and T R V Davis, "Behavioral Self-Management—The Missing Link in Managerial Effectiveness," *Organizational Dynamics,* Summer 1979, p 43.

[54]Luthans and Kreitner, *Organizational Behavior Modification and Beyond,* p 158.

[55]See, for example, C C Manz and H P Sims, Jr., "Self-Management as a Substitute for Leadership: A Social Learning Theory Perspective," *Academy of Management Review,* July 1980, pp 361–67; C C Manz, The Art of Self-Leadership (Englewood Cliffs, NJ: Prentice-Hall, 1983); C C Manz, "Self-Leadership: Toward an Expanded Theory of Self-Influence Processes in Organizations," *Academy of Management Review,* July 1986, pp 585–600; and C C Manz and H P Sims, Jr., SuperLeadership: Leading Others to Lead Themselves (New York: Prentice-Hall, 1989). An application of the social learning model is discussed in A M O'Leary-Kelly, R W Griffin, and D J Glew, "Organization-Motivated Aggression: A Research Framework," *Academy of Management Review,* January 1996, pp 225–53.

[56]For example, see R Kelley and J Caplan, "How Bell Labs Creates Star Performers," *Harvard Business Review,* July–August 1993, pp 128–39; E E Lawler III, "Total Quality Management and Employee Involvement: Are They Compatible?" *Academy of Management Executive,* February 1994, pp 68–76; and M J Stevens and M A Campion, "The Knowledge, Skill, and Ability Requirements for Teamwork: Implications for Human Resource Management, *Journal of Management,* Summer 1994, pp 503–30.

[57]Bandura, *Social Learning Theory,* p 13.

[58]"Career Self-Management," *Industry Week,* September 5, 1994, p 36.

[59]For more, see J Davidson, "Overworked Americans or Overwhelmed Americans?" *Business Horizons,* January–February 1994, pp 62–66; S Sherman, "What Software Should I Use to Organize My Life?" *Fortune,* October 16, 1995, pp 102–12; H Lancaster, "Is Your Messy Desk a Sign You're Busy or Just Disorganized?" *The Wall Street Journal,* January 30, 1996, p B1; L Sandler, "Walden Wisdom," *Training,* July 1990, pp 44–48; S Shellenbarger, "Good Time-Managers Try Not to Manage All of Their Time," *The Wall Street Journal,* October 9, 1996, p B1; P

Buhler, "Time Management Is Really Self-Management," *Supervision,* March 1996, pp 24–26; H Lancaster, "Procrastinators: Mend Your Ways Before Your Job Stalls," *The Wall Street Journal,* May 7, 1996, p B1; R Aubrey and P M Cohen, "Learning for Survival," *Working Wisdom: Timeless Skills and Vanguard Strategies for Learning Organizations* (San Francisco: Jossey-Bass, 1995), Ch. 1; and M O'Brien, "Personal Mastery: The New Executive Curriculum," *Training,* July 1996, p 82.

[60]S R Covey, *The 7 Habits of Highly Effective People* (New York: Simon & Schuster, 1989), p 42. Also see J Hillkirk, "Golden Rules Promoted for Work Success," *USA Today,* August 20, 1993, pp 1B–2B; L Bongiorno, "Corporate America, Dr. Feelgood Will See You Now," *Business Week,* December 6, 1993, p 52; and T K Smith, "What's So Effective About Stephen Covey?" *Fortune,* December 12, 1994, pp 116–26.

[61]"Labor Letter: A Special News Report on People and their Jobs in Offices, Fields, and Factories," *The Wall Street Journal,* October 15, 1985, p 1.

[62]Helpful instructions on formulating career goals may be found in D Heide and E N Kushell, "I Can Improve My Management Skills by:" *Personnel Journal,* June 1984, pp 52–54. Also see B Farber, "A Winning Attitude," *Selling Power,* April 1996, pp 70–71.

[63]R McGarvey, "Rehearsing for Success," *Executive Female,* January/February 1990, p 36.

[64]See W P Anthony, R H Bennett, III, E N Maddox, and W J Wheatley, "Picturing the Future: Using Mental Imagery to Enrich Strategic Environmental Assessment," *Academy of Management Executive,* May 1993, pp 43–56.

[65]McGarvey, "Rehearsing for Success," p 36.

[66]For excellent tips on self-management, see C P Neck, "Managing Your Mind," *Internal Auditor,* June 1996, pp 60–63.

[67]C Zastrow, *Talk to Yourself: Using the Power of Self-Talk* (Englewood Cliffs, NJ: Prentice-Hall, 1979), p 60. Also see Manz and Sims, *SuperLeadership,* pp 41–43; and C C Manz and C P Neck, "Inner Leadership: Creating Productive Thought Patterns," *Academy of Management Executive,* August 1991, pp 87–95.

[68]See C C Manz and C P Neck, "Inner Leadership: Creating

Productive Thought Patterns," pp 87–95.

[69]E Franz, "Private Pep Talk," *Selling Power,* May 1996, p 81.

[70]Drawn from discussion in A Bandura, "Self-Reinforcement: Theoretical and Methodological Considerations," *Behaviorism,* Fall 1976, pp 135–55.

[71]R Kreitner and F Luthans, "A Social Learning Approach to Behavioral Management: Radical Behaviorists 'Mellowing Out,'" *Organizational Dynamics,* Autumn 1984, p 63.

[72]See R F Rakos and M V Grodek, "An Empirical Evaluation of a Behavioral Self-Management Course in a College Setting," *Teaching of Psychology,* October 1984, pp 157–62.

[73]S J Zaccaro, R J Foti, and D A Kenny, "Self-Monitoring and Trait-Based Variance in Leadership: An Investigation of Leader Flexibility across Multiple Group Situations," *Journal of Applied Psychology,* April 1991, p 309.

[74]Luthans and Davis, "Behavioral Self-Management—The Missing Link in Managerial Effectiveness," pp 52–59.

[75]Results are presented in C A Frayne and G P Latham, "Application of Social Learning Theory to Employee Self-Management of Attendance," *Journal of Applied Psychology,* August 1987, pp 387–92. Follow-up data are presented in G P Latham and C A Frayne, "Self-Management Training for Increasing Job Attendance: A Follow-Up and a Replication," *Journal of Applied Psychology,* June 1989, pp 411–16.

[76]See M A Howe, "Using Imagery to Facilitate Organizational Development and Change," *Group & Organizational Studies,* March 1989, pp 70–82.

[77]See C A Frayne and J M Geringer, "Self-Management Training for Joint Venture General Manager's," *Human Resource Planning,* no 4, 1992, pp 69–85.

[78]S L Robinson and R J Bennett, "A Typology of Deviant Workplace Behaviours: a Multidimensional Scaling Study," *Acadamy of Management Journal,* April 1995, p 565.

Sixteen

Leadership

LEARNING OBJECTIVES

When you finish studying the material in this chapter, you should be able to:

1. Define the term leadership, and explain the difference between leading versus managing.

2. Review trait theory research, and discuss the idea of one best style of leadership, using the Ohio State studies and the Leadership Grid® as points of reference.

3. Explain, according to Fiedler's contingency model, how leadership style interacts with situational control.

4. Discuss House's path–goal theory, and Hersey and Blanchard's situational leadership theory.

5. Define and differentiate transactional and charismatic leadership.

6. Explain how charismatic leadership transforms followers.

7. Summarize the managerial implications of charismatic leadership.

8. Explain Graen's leader–member exchange model of leadership.

9. Describe the substitutes for leadership, and explain how they substitute for, neutralize, or enhance the effects of leadership.

10. Describe superleadership and coaching.

Anita Roddick: The Body Shop's flamboyant head

"1996 and January has been crazy. Here are a few things that keep me breathless with enthusiasm. The launch of Biz:Ed on the Web — a site dedicated to providing specific educational information to students of business. As I see it, business education must contain the language and action of social justice, human rights, community economics and the development of the human spirit." With those words, Anita Roddick, founder and managing director of The Body Shop opens her site on the Internet. They are an extension of her personal philosophy and convictions, which characterize the way she has been doing business since 1976.

On her travels round the world, she had met all kinds of different people from whom she learned to take care of the human body by pure natural products. When, in 1976, her husband decided to travel through South America by horse for two years, Anita had to provide a daily income for herself and her two daughters: the first Body Shop was opened in Brighton, selling 25 naturally based skin and hair care products. Eight months later, she opened a second shop in Chichester. Today, The Body Shop has over 1,300 branches in 45 countries throughout the Americas, Europe, and Asia, selling over 550 different products and a similar number of accessories.

Although Anita Roddick's first goal was survival, she is now well known because of her strong feeling for ethical entrepreneurship. In the course of the years she has become world famous for having created a cosmetics company with a human rights department, a rigid environmental policy, an alliance with Greenpeace (Save the Whales campaign), giving charitable donations and acting against animal testing. She even launched a "Trade Not Aid" policy: a part of the ingredients of the cosmetic products are imported from third world communities who get a fair price for their products. "Trade Not Aid" was followed by a similar policy in Britain: in 1987 a soap factory was created in one of Britain's regions putting part of the region's chronically unemployed to work.

Roddick's ethical approach is not limited to The Body Shop's product development, production and marketing strategies. It is a way of life which she tries to pass over to her staff by offering attractive working conditions. She spends much of her time on internal communication and a journey abroad is always coupled to a visit to the local Body Shop. Dressed in casual wear and hardly made up she enters the shop issuing compliments and critiques on the way the products are presented. Enthusiastically she motivates her staff by a "Brilliant!" or "Fantastic!". Innovative suggestions are rewarded, employees are encouraged to "think frivolously".

To enhance communication, every shop is equipped with a bulletin board, a fax machine and a video player. The video player is a strong tool she uses to inform the staff on new products, new tendencies, her new projects, . . . All suggestions are welcome at DODGI (the Department of Damned Good Ideas), meetings between a cross-section of staff are held regularly and through a "Red Letter" system any employee can communicate directly with a director. When asked if her company's globalization does not hamper internal communication, Anita Roddick says "We do not behave as a large company. The shops are small individual companies. The only thing that bothers me is that I do not know every employee by name."

At the company's headquarters in Littlehampton, there is a pleasant atmosphere. Visitors are coming in and out, mothers with children come to take a look, there are crazy statues all over the place. According to Anita Roddick, creativity is the result of a series of absurd and passionate ideas.

Named Business Woman of the Year in 1985, awarded an Order of the British Empire in 1988 and ranked with the richest women of Britain, Anita Roddick is said to have a plain lifestyle. She always travels economy class, stays at ordinary hotels, and does not invest in expensive clothes.[1]

Discussion Question
Would you like to work at The Body Shop? Explain

S omeone once observed that a leader is a person who finds out which way the parade is going, jumps in front of it, and yells "Follow me!" The plain fact is that this approach to leadership has little chance of working in today's rapidly changing world. Admired leaders, such as Mahatma Ghandi, John Kennedy, Richard Branson, and Microsoft's Bill Gates, led people in bold new directions. They envisioned how things could be improved, rallied followers, and refused to accept failure. In short, successful leaders are those individuals who can step into a difficult situation and make a noticeable difference. But how much of a difference can leaders make in modern organizations?

OB researchers have discovered that leaders can make a difference. One study, for example, tracked the relationship between net profit and leadership in 167 companies from 13 industries. It also covered a time span of 20 years. Higher net profits were earned by companies with effective leaders.[2] In a carefully controlled study of Icelandic fishing ships, it was found that differences in skippers accounted for one-third up to half of the catch.[3] Leadership makes a difference!

On the other hand, subordinates are generally not very pleased with their leaders, as can be found in Table 16-1.

After formally defining the term leadership, this chapter focuses on the following areas: (1) trait and behavioural approaches to leadership, (2) alternative situational theories of leadership, (3) charismatic leadership, and (4) additional perspectives on leadership. Because there are many different leadership theories within each of these areas, it is impossible to discuss them all. This chapter is based on reviewing those theories with the most research support, with the exception of the part on coaching, for the simple reason that the topic is highly relevant for modern thinking on leadership. But even the research data are not very conclusive. Peter Wright, a British OB-specialist, concludes as follows in his book on managerial leadership:

Most research findings, even when significant, account for a relatively small amount of the variance in subordinates' work perfomance and satisfaction. Similarly, there are a great many alternative approaches to leadership theory, the different theories within any one approach often contradict each other, and none is without flaws or limitations.[4]

Leadership is culturally bound. Americans are the only people who talk so openly — sometimes obsessively— about the very notion of leadership. In America, leadership has become something of a cult concept. The French, tellingly, have no adequate word of their own for it. Germans have perfectly good words for leader and leadership; Hitler rendered them politically incorrect (though Helmut Kohl has started occasionally to extol the virtues of *Führerschaft*). Mussolini similarly stigmatized the word *duce*.[5] The situation is even more extreme in The Netherlands or the Scandinavian countries, where leaders don't behave like leaders at all, at least not like leaders described in American textbooks.[6]

An excellent example of informal leadership, is the way Ingvar Kamprad manages IKEA, the world's largest home furnishing chain. The patriarchal way in which he treats his customers and staff reflects his philosophy of life. He is blessed with a genuine warmth and interest in people, which is undoubtedly one of the most important reason for his success. Thanks to his influence, the company has an informal atmosphere stressing simplicity. It is reflected in the neat but casual dress of the employees—jeans and sweaters—and in the relaxed office atmosphere with practically everyone sitting in an open-plan office.[7]

This culturally bound phenomenon is not only restricted to charismatic leaders or to top management. The tendency to rely on supervision is clearly much stronger in English-

Table 16 – 1	What the Successful Business Leader Should Have and What He Really Has		
		WHAT HE/SHE SHOULD HAVE	**WHAT MY PRESENT CEO HAS**
Able to build effective teams		96%	50%
Knows how to listen		93%	44%
Capable of making decisions on his own		87%	66%
Knows how to retain good people		86%	39%
Energetic		85%	62%
Innovative		83%	47%
Visionary		79%	45%
Has high ethical standards		76%	53%
Strong-willed		70%	65%
Charismatic		54%	34%
Motivated by power		35%	59%
Motivated by money		17%	40%
Ruthless		10%	28%
Paternalistic		6%	24%

Source: "Leadership," *Management Centre Europe,* 1988, p11.

speaking countries, especially in the United States than in any other country. Figure 16–1 gives a survey of the intensity of supervision in a number of European countries and in the United States. Supervision varies from very low in Switzerland to very high in the United States.

What Does Leadership Involve?

Because the topic of leadership has fascinated people for centuries, definitions abound. This section presents a definition of leadership and highlights the similarities and differences between leading versus managing.

What Is Leadership?

Disagreement about the definition of leadership stems from the fact that it involves a complex interaction among the leader, the followers, and the situation. For example, some researchers define leadership in terms of personality and physical traits, while others believe leadership is represented by a set of prescribed behaviours. In contrast, other researchers believe that the concept of leadership doesn't really exist.[8] There is a common thread, however, among the different definitions of leadership. The common thread is social influence.

Leadership

Influencing employees to voluntarily pursue organizational goals.

As the term is used in this chapter, **leadership** is defined as "a social influence process in which the leader seeks the voluntary participation of subordinates in an effort to reach organizational goals."[9] Tom Peters and Nancy Austin, authors of the bestseller, *A Passion for Excellence,* describe leadership in broader terms:

Leadership means vision, cheerleading, enthusiasm, love, trust, verve, passion, obsession, consistency, the use of symbols, paying attention as illustrated by the content of one's calendar, out-and-out drama (and the management thereof), creating heroes at all levels, coaching,

---

Figure 16–1   The Intensity of Supervision in 16 Countries

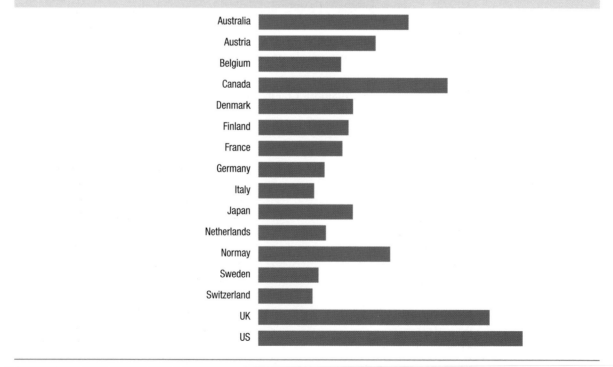

Source: D Gordon, "Boxes of Different Stripes: A Cross National Perspective on Monitoring and Supervision," *AEA Papers and Proceedings,* May 1994, p376.

effectively wandering around, and numerous other things. Leadership must be present at all levels of the organization. It depends on a million little things done with obsession, consistency, and care, but all of those million little things add up to nothing if the trust, vision, and basic belief are not there.[10]

As you can see from this definition, leadership clearly entails more than wielding power and exercising authority.

Figure 16–2 provides a conceptual framework for understanding leadership. It was created by integrating components of the different theories and models discussed in this chapter. Figure 16–2 indicates that certain leader characteristics/traits are the foundation of effective leadership. In turn, these characteristics affect an individual's ability to carry out various managerial behaviours/roles. Effective leadership also depends on various situational variables. These variables are important components of the contingency leadership theories discussed later in this chapter. Finally, leadership is results oriented. This conclusion is best summarized by Neville Bain, Coats Viyella Plc's Groups Chief Executive (UK):

You give your team freedom but there are some guiding principles they need to understand. The captain of the team decides the team he is going to field, the strategy against the opposition, and motivates his team to do their best.[11]

Leading versus Managing

It is important to appreciate the difference between leadership and management to fully understand what leadership is all about. Bernard Bass, a leadership expert, concluded that "leaders manage and managers lead, but the two activities are not synonymous."[12] Bass tells us that although leadership and management overlap, each entails a unique set of activities or functions. Broadly speaking, managers typically perform functions associated with planning, investigating, organizing, and control, and leaders deal with the interpersonal aspects of a manager's job. Leaders inspire others, provide emotional support, and try to get employees to rally around a common goal. Leaders also play a key role in creating a vision and strategic plan for an organization. Managers, in turn, are charged with implementing the vision and strategic plan. Table 16–2 summarizes the key differences found between leaders and managers.

International Organizational Behaviour

Yotari Kobayashi

Although 62 years old, Yotari Kobayashi, Fuji Xerox' boss cannot be said to be a typical Japanese leader. He obtained an MBA from the American Wharton Business School and studied Plato, Aristotle and the Bible at the American Aspen Institute, which served as an example for the Armagi Institute he founded to introduce Japanese business people to a range of thinkers. His American background also influences the way he is dressed: in striking pinstripes and not in the traditional blue suits most Japanese men wear.

To Kobayashi, personal contact is essential in business. "Only by meeting a person face to face — not once but several times — can you sense their qualities." To enhance interaction with others, he takes part in conversations on a variety of subjects, from religion to management issues. He tries to participate as much time as possible in off-work activities. In this way, he tries to lift the aura of majesty and mystery that usually surrounds leaders. Much to his regret, however, the expansion his company takes creates a gap between himself and his employees, who are more likely to see him on TV than at the company.

As to business, Kobayashi advises his staff to be interested in other people, especially now that the market is globalizing and the future will force us to deal with other cultures all over the world. Not only frontiers between countries are breaking down, but those between the organizational hierarchies as well. Kobayashi welcomes this evolution and he encourages Fuji Xerox's middle managers to make strategic decisions, and to become acquainted with history and culture, next to pure business matters.[13]

Figure 16–2   A Conceptual Framework for Understanding Leadership

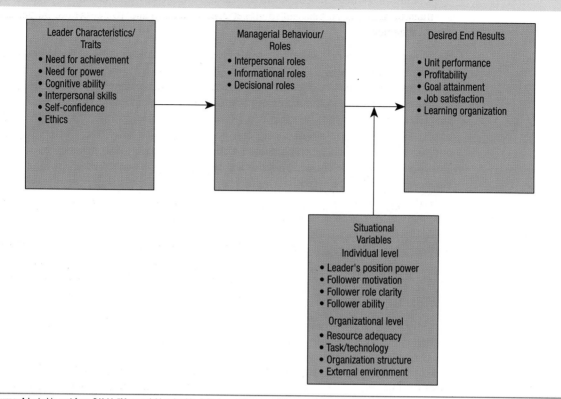

Source: Adapted in part from G Yukl, "Managerial Leadership: A Review of Theory and Research," *Journal of Management,* June 1989, p 274.

The distinction between leaders and managers is more than a semantic issue for four reasons:

1. It is important from a hiring standpoint. Because leaders and managers perform a subset of unique functions, it is important to recruit and select people who have the required intellectual abilities, experience, and job-relevant knowledge to perform their jobs.[14]

2. Differences may affect group effectiveness. Work group performance can be increased by staffing a productive mix of leaders and managers.

3. Successful organizational change is highly dependent upon effective leadership

Table 16–2   Differences Between Leaders and Managers

LEADERS	**MANAGERS**
Innovate	Administer
Develop	Maintain
Inspire	Control
Long-term view	Short-term view
Ask what and why	Ask how and when
Originate	Initiate
Challenge the status quo	Accept the status quo
Do the right things	Do things right

Source: Distinctions were taken from W G Bennis, *On Becoming a Leader* (Reading, MA: Addison-Wesley, 1989).

throughout an organization. Senior executives cannot create change on their own. According to organizational change expert John Kotter, successful organizational transformation is 70 per cent to 90 per cent leadership and 10 per cent to 30 per cent management.[15]

4. Distinctions between leading and managing highlight the point that leadership is not restricted to people in particular positions or roles. Anyone from the bottom to the top of an organization can be a leader. Many informal leaders have contributed to organizational effectiveness. Consider the behaviour exhibited by Skip Tobey, an employee at America West Airlines.

"I'm not just an aircraft cleaner," the 36-year-old said. "That's my title, but that's not the end of my job."

Tobey said he looks for ways to help passengers, lending a hand to young families maneuvering strollers through narrow aircraft aisles and assisting elderly travelers.

"My satisfaction is tied into quality, helping the passengers," he said. "No matter what it takes, if it means going to the furthest extreme, I'll do it."[16]

Skip's behaviour is not only inspirational, but it supports leadership expert Warren Bennis's conclusion about leaders and managers. Bennis characterized managers as people who do things right and leaders as individuals who do the "right" things. Skip Tobey is clearly doing the "right" things to help America West provide excellent customer service.

Trait and Behavioural Theories of Leadership

This section examines the two earliest approaches used to explain leadership. Trait theories focused on identifying the personal traits that differentiated leaders from followers. Behavioural theorists examined leadership from a different perspective. They tried to uncover the different kinds of leader behaviours that resulted in higher work group performance. Both approaches to leadership can teach current and future managers valuable lessons about leading.

Trait Theory

Leader trait

Personal characteristics that differentiate leaders from followers.

At the turn of the 20th century, the prevailing belief was that leaders were born, not made. Selected people were thought to possess inborn traits that made them successful leaders. A **leader trait** is a physical or personality characteristic that can be used to differentiate leaders from followers.

Before World War II, hundreds of studies were conducted to pinpoint the traits of successful leaders. Dozens of leadership traits were identified. During the postwar period, however, enthusiasm was replaced by widespread criticism. Studies conducted by Ralph Stogdill in 1948 and by Richard Mann in 1959, which sought to summarize the impact of traits on leadership, caused the trait approach to fall into disfavour.

Stogdill's and Mann's Findings   Based on his review, Stogdill concluded that five traits tended to differentiate leaders from average followers: (1) intelligence, (2) dominance, (3) self-confidence, (4) level of energy and activity, and (5) task-relevant knowledge.[17] However, these five traits did not accurately predict which individuals became leaders in organizations. People with these traits often remained followers.

Mann's review was similarly disappointing for the trait theorists. Among the seven categories of personality traits he examined, Mann found intelligence was the best predictor of leadership. However, Mann warned that all observed positive relationships between traits and leadership were weak (correlations averaged about 0.15).[18]

Together, Stogdill's and Mann's findings dealt a near deathblow to the trait approach. But now, decades later, leadership traits are once again receiving serious research attention.

Contemporary Trait Research   Two OB researchers concluded in 1983 that past trait data may have been incorrectly analysed. By applying modern statistical techniques to an old database, they demonstrated that the majority of a leader's behaviour could be attributed to stable underlying traits.[19] Unfortunately, their methodology did not single out specific traits.

A 1986 meta-analysis by Robert Lord and his associates remedied this shortcoming. Based on a reanalysis of Mann's data and subsequent studies, Lord concluded that people have leadership *prototypes* that affect our perceptions of who is and who is not an effective leader. Your **leadership prototype** is a mental representation of the traits and behaviours that you believe are possessed by leaders. We thus tend to perceive that someone is a leader when he or she exhibits traits or behaviours that are consistent with our prototypes.[20] Lord's research demonstrated that people are perceived as being leaders when they exhibit the traits associated with intelligence, masculinity, and dominance.[21]

More recently, a pair of leadership researchers asked the following open-ended question to more than 20,000 people around the world: "What values (personal traits or characteristics) do you look for and admire in your superiors?" The top four traits included honesty, forward-looking, inspiring, and competent.[22] The researchers concluded that these four traits constitute a leader's credibility. This research suggests that people want their leaders to be credible and to have a sense of direction.[23]

Leadership prototype

Mental representation of the traits and behaviours possessd by leaders.

Gender and Leadership   The increase of women in the workforce has generated much interest in understanding the similarities and differences in female and male leaders. Important issues concern whether women and men (1) assume varying leadership roles within work groups, (2) use different leadership styles, (3) are relatively more or less effective in leadership roles, and (4) whether there are situational differences that produce gender differences in leadership effectiveness. Three meta-analyses were conducted to summarize research pertaining to these issues.

The first meta-analysis demonstrated that men and women differed in the type of leadership roles they assumed within work groups. Men were seen as displaying more overall leadership and task leadership. In contrast, women were perceived as displaying more social leadership.[24] Results from the second meta-analysis revealed that leadership styles varied by gender. Women used a more democratic or participative style than men. Men employed a more autocratic and directive style than women.[25] Finally, a recent meta-analysis of more than 75 studies uncovered three key findings: (1) Female and male leaders were rated as equally effective. This is a very positive outcome because it suggests that despite barriers and possible negative stereotypes towards female leaders, female and male leaders were equally effective. (2) Men were rated as more effective leaders than women when their roles were defined in more masculine terms, and women were more effective than men in roles defined in less masculine terms. (3) Gender differences in leadership effectiveness were associated with the percentage of male leaders and male subordinates. Specifically, male leaders were seen as more effective than females when there was a greater percentage of male leaders and male subordinates. Interestingly, a similar positive bias in leadership effectiveness was not found for women.[26] Research carried out in the UK by Hay Management Consultants on 15 male, 20 female and 191 male and female subordinates concludes as follows:

The styles that female managers use are not working as effectively with their male subordinates. The men do not see female managers doing such things as giving clear directions, explaining decisions and monitoring task performance. The authoritative style is an effective and important one. If women are not seen as using it by men this may not only affect their team's effectiveness but could influence their visibility with colleagues and bosses.[27]

Trait Theory in Perspective   We can no longer afford to ignore the implications of leadership traits. Traits play a central role in how we perceive leaders. Recalling the Chapter 6 discussion of social perception, it is important to determine the traits embodied in people's schemata (or mental pictures) for leaders. If those traits are inappropriate (i.e., foster discriminatory selection and invalid performance appraisals), they need to be corrected through training and development. Moreover, organizations may find it beneficial to consider selected leadership traits when choosing among candidates for leadership positions.[28] Gender should not be used as one of these traits. The International OB outlines the relevant leadership traits of Russian leaders from the 1400s to the present time. As you can see, Russian organizations need to nurture and develop a similar but different set of leadership traits.

Behavioural Styles Theory

This phase of leadership research began during World War II as part of an effort to develop better military leaders. It was an outgrowth of two events: the seeming inability of trait theory to explain leadership effectiveness and the human relations movement, an outgrowth of the Hawthorne Studies. The thrust of early behavioural leadership theory was to focus on leader behaviour, instead of on personality traits. It was believed that leader behaviour directly affected work group effectiveness. This led researchers to identify patterns of behaviour (called leadership styles) that enabled leaders to effectively influence others.

The Ohio State Studies   Researchers at Ohio State University began by generating a list of behaviours exhibited by leaders. At one point, the list contained 1,800 statements that described nine categories of leader behaviour. Ultimately, the Ohio State researchers concluded there were only two independent dimensions of leader behaviour: consideration and initiating structure. **Consideration** involves leader behaviour associated with creating mutual respect or trust and focuses on a concern for group members' needs and desires. Illustrative in this respect is the leadership style of Penny Hughes, former president of Coca Cola Company Great Britain and Ireland. According to a close colleague of hers:

> Penny is really excellent at establishing rapport with people and encouraging them to be more open, more challenging. To an unusual and refreshing degree she genuinely values people and is totally fair with them. She often walks around the office, sits on the back of a chair and shares a joke with us. There is always lots of laughter![29]

Initiating structure is leader behaviour that organizes and defines what group members should be doing to maximize output. These two dimensions of leader behaviour were oriented at right angles to yield four behavioural styles of leadership (see Figure 16–3).

Consideration
Creating mutual respect and trust with followers.

Initiating structure
Organizing and defining what group members should be doing.

Figure 16 – 3   Four Leadership Styles Derived from The Ohio State Studies

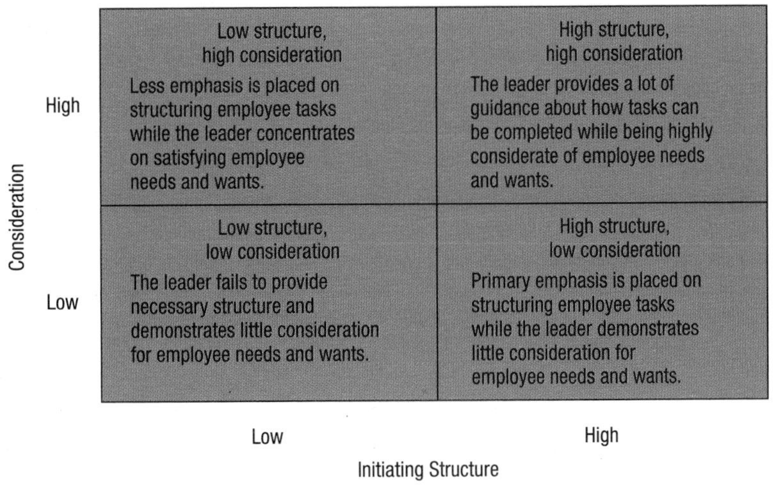

	Low	High
High	Low structure, high consideration. Less emphasis is placed on structuring employee tasks while the leader concentrates on satisfying employee needs and wants.	High structure, high consideration. The leader provides a lot of guidance about how tasks can be completed while being highly considerate of employee needs and wants.
Low	Low structure, low consideration. The leader fails to provide necessary structure and demonstrates little consideration for employee needs and wants.	High structure, low consideration. Primary emphasis is placed on structuring employee tasks while the leader demonstrates little consideration for employee needs and wants.

Consideration (vertical axis)

Initiating Structure (horizontal axis)

It initially was hypothesized that a high-structure, high-consideration style would be the one best style of leadership. Through the years, the effectiveness of the high–high style has been tested many times. Overall, results have been mixed. Researchers thus concluded that there is not one best style of leadership.[30] Rather, it is argued that effectiveness of a given leadership style depends on situational factors.

University of Michigan Studies As in the Ohio State studies, this research sought to identify behavioural differences between effective and ineffective leaders. Researchers identified two different styles of leadership: one was employee centred, the other was job centred. These behavioural styles parallel the consideration and initiating-structure styles identified by the Ohio State group. In summarizing the results from these studies, one management expert concluded that effective leaders (1) tend to have supportive or employee-centred relationships with employees, (2) use group rather than individual methods of supervision, and (3) set high performance goals.[31]

Blake and Mouton's Managerial/Leadership Grid® Perhaps the most widely known behavioural styles model of leadership is the Managerial Grid®. Behavioural scientists Robert Blake and Jane Srygley Mouton developed and trademarked the grid. They use it to demonstrate that there *is* one best style of leadership. Blake and Mouton's Managerial Grid® (renamed the **Leadership Grid®** in 1991) is a matrix formed by the intersection of two dimensions of leader behaviour (see Figure 16–4). On the horizontal axis is "concern for production." "Concern for people" is on the vertical axis.

Blake and Mouton point out that "the variables of the Managerial Grid® are *attitudinal and conceptual*, with *behaviour* descriptions derived from and connected with

Leadership Grid®

Represents four leadership styles found by crossing concern for production and concern for people.

International Organizational Behaviour
Russian Leadership Traits in Three Eras

LEADERSHIP TRAIT	TRADITIONAL RUSSIAN SOCIETY (1400S TO 1917)	THE RED EXECUTIVE (1917 TO 1991)	THE MARKET-ORIENTED MANAGER (1991 TO PRESENT)
LEADERSHIP MOTIVATION			
Power	Powerful autocrats	Centralized leadership stifled grass-roots democracy	Shared power and ownership
Responsibility	Centralization of responsibility	Micromanagers and macropuppets	Delegation and strategic decision making
DRIVE			
Achievement motivation	Don't rock the boat	Frustrated pawns	The sky's the limit
Ambition	Equal poverty for all	Service to party and collective good	Overcoming the sin of being a winner
Initiative	Look both ways	Meticulous rule following and behind-the-scenes finessing	Let's do business
Energy	Concentrated spasms of labour	"8-hour day," 8 to 8, firefighting	8-day week, chasing opportunities
Tenacity	Life is a struggle	Struggling to accomplish the routine	Struggling to accomplish the new
HONESTY AND INTEGRITY			
Dual ethical standard	Deception in dealings, fealty in friendship	Two sets of books, personal integrity	Wild capitalism, personal trust
Using connections (*blat*)	Currying favour with landowners	Greasing the wheels of the state	Greasing palms, but learning to do business straight
SELF-CONFIDENCE			
	From helplessness to bravado	From inferior quality to "big is beautiful"	From cynicism to overpromising

SOURCE | S M Puffer, "Understanding the Bear: A Portrait of Russian Business Leaders," *Academy of Management Executive*, February 1994, p 42. Used with permission.

Figure 16 – 4   The Leadership Grid®

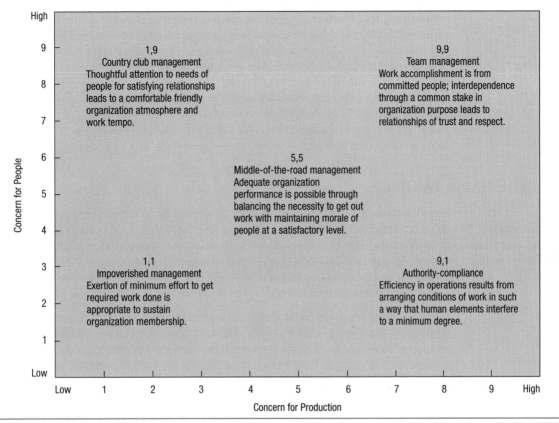

the thinking that lies behind action."[32] In other words, concern for production and concern for people involve attitudes and patterns of thinking, as well as specific behaviours. By scaling each axis of the grid from 1 to 9, Blake and Mouton were able to plot five leadership styles. Because it emphasizes teamwork and interdependence, the 9,9 style is considered by Blake and Mouton to be the best, regardless of the situation.

In support of the 9,9 style, Blake and Mouton cite the results of a study in which 100 experienced managers were asked to select the best way of handling 12 managerial situations. Between 72 per cent and 90 per cent of the managers selected the 9,9 style for each of the 12 situations.[33] Moreover, Blake and Mouton report, "The 9,9, orientation … leads to productivity, satisfaction, creativity, and health."[34] Critics point out that Blake and Mouton's research may be self-serving. At issue is the grid's extensive use as a training and consulting tool for diagnosing and correcting organizational problems.

Behavioural Styles Theory in Perspective By emphasizing leader *behaviour,* something that is learned, the behavioural style approach makes it clear that leaders are made, not born. This is the opposite of the trait theorists' traditional assumption. Given what we know about behaviour shaping and model-based training, leader *behaviours* can be systematically improved and developed. For example, a study demonstrated that employee creativity was increased when leaders were trained to (1) help employees identify problems and (2) enhance employees feelings of self-efficacy.[35]

Behavioural styles research also revealed that there is no one best style of leadership. The effectiveness of a particular leadership style depends on the situation at hand. For instance, employees prefer structure over consideration when faced with role ambiguity.[36]

At this time we would like you to complete the OB exercise. The exercise gives you the opportunity to test the behavioural styles theory by assessing your teacher's leadership style and your associated class satisfaction and role clarity. Are you satisfied with this class? If yes, the behavioural styles approach is supported if your teacher displayed both high consideration and initiating structure. In contrast, the behavioural style approach is not supported if you are satisfied with this class and your teacher exhibits something other than the standard high–high style. Do your results support the proposition that there is one best style of leadership? Are your results consistent with past research that showed leadership behaviour depends on the situation at hand? The answer is yes if you prefer initiating structure over consideration when faced with high role ambiguity. The answer is also yes if you prefer consideration over structure when role ambiguity is low. We now turn our attention to discussing alternative situational theories of leadership.

Situational Theories

Situational theories

Propose that leader styles should match the situation at hand.

Situational leadership theories grew out of an attempt to explain the inconsistent findings about traits and styles. **Situational theories** propose that the effectiveness of a particular style of leader behaviour depends on the situation. As situations change, different styles become appropriate. This directly challenges the idea of one best style of leadership. Liam Strong, Sears plc's chief executive (UK) believes that there is not such thing as a born leader, that leadership is contextual and therefore no single model can be provided:

It's difficult to put your finger on the qualities of leadership because the oddest people can be very good leaders and they can lead in all sorts of different ways. Some people lead from the middle, some from behind, some from the front and some from the side. What you are looking for is someone who can actually build a group of people, and get them to perform. One does well by virtue of working with a number of people, and therefore it is not really appropriate to think in terms of individual success.[37]

Let us closely examine three alternative situational theories of leadership that reject the notion of one best leadership style.

Fiedler's Contingency Model

Fred Fiedler, an OB scholar, developed a situational model of leadership. It is the oldest and one of the most widely known models of leadership. Fiedler's model is based on the following assumption:

The performance of a leader depends on two interrelated factors: (1) the degree to which the situation gives the leader control and influence—that is, the likelihood that [the leader] can successfully accomplish the job; and (2) the leader's basic motivation—that is, whether [the leader's] self-esteem depends primarily on accomplishing the task or on having close supportive relations with others.[38]

With respect to a leader's basic motivation, Fiedler believes that leaders are either task motivated or relationship motivated. These basic motivations are similar to initiating structure/concern for production and consideration/concern for people

Fiedler's theory also is based on the premise that leaders have one dominant leadership style that is resistant to change. He suggests that leaders must learn how to match their leadership style to the amount of control within a leadership situation. After discussing the components of situational control and the leadership matching process, we review relevant research and managerial implications.[39]

Situational Control   Situational control refers to the amount of control and influence the leader has in her or his immediate work environment. Situational control ranges from high to low. High control implies that the leader's decisions will produce predictable results because the leader has the ability to influence work outcomes. Low control implies that the leader's decisions may not influence work outcomes because the leader has very little influence. There are three dimensions of situational control: leader—member relations, task structure, and position power. These dimensions vary independently, forming eight combinations of situational control (see Figure 16–5).

The three dimensions of situational control are defined as follows:

Leader—member relations
Extent that leader has the support, loyalty, and trust of work group.

- **Leader–member relations** reflect the extent to which the leader has the support, loyalty, and trust of the work group. This dimension is the most important component of situational control. Good leader–member relations suggest that the leader can depend on the group, thus ensuring that the work group will try to meet the leader's goals and objectives.

Task structure
Amount of structure contained within work tasks.

- **Task structure** is concerned with the amount of structure contained within tasks performed by the work group. For example, a managerial job contains less structure than that of a bank teller. Since structured tasks have guidelines for how the job should be completed, the leader has more control and influence over employees performing such tasks. This dimension is the second most important component of situational control.

Position power
Degree to which leader has formal power.

- **Position power** refers to the degree to which the leader has formal power to reward, punish, or otherwise obtain compliance from employees.[40]

Linking Leadership Motivation and Situational Control   Fiedler's complete contingency model is presented in Figure 16–5. The horizontal axis breaks out the eight control

---

OB EXERCISE   *Assessing Teacher Leadership Style, Class Satisfaction, and Student Role Clarity*

Instructions
A team of researchers converted a set of leadership measures for application in the classroom. For each of the items shown here, use the following rating scale to circle the answer that best represents your feelings. Next, use the scoring key to compute scores for your teacher's leadership style and your class satisfaction and role clarity.

1 = Strongly disagree
2 = Disagree
3 = Neither agree nor disagree
4 = Agree
5 = Strongly agree

1. My instructor behaves in a manner which is thoughtful of my personal needs.   1—2—3—4—5
2. My instructor maintains a friendly working relationship with me.   1—2—3—4—5
3. My instructor looks out for my personal welfare.   1—2—3—4—5
4. My instructor gives clear explanations of what is expected of me.   1—2—3—4—5
5. My instructor tells me the performance goals for the class.   1—2—3—4—5
6. My instructor explains the level of performance that is expected of me.   1—2—3—4—5
7. I am satisfied with the variety of class assignments.   1—2—3—4—5

8. I am satisfied with the way my instructor handles the students.   1—2—3—4—5
9. I am satisfied with the spirit of cooperation among my fellow students.   1—2—3—4—5
10. I know exactly what my responsibilities are.   1—2—3—4—5
11. I am given clear explanations of what has to be done.   1—2—3—4—5

Scoring Key
Teacher consideration (1, 2, 3)   _____
Teacher initiating structure (4, 5, 6)   _____
Class satisfaction (7, 8, 9)   _____
Role clarity (10, 11)   _____

Arbitrary Norms
Low consideration = 3—8
High consideration = 9—15
Low structure = 3—8
High structure = 9—15
Low satisfaction = 3—8
High satisfaction = 9—15
Low role clarity = 2—5
High role clarity = 6—10

SOURCE   The survey was adapted from A J Kinicki and C A Schriesheim, "Teachers as Leaders: A Moderator Variable Approach," *Journal of Educational Psychology,* 1978, pp 928–35.

Figure 16 – 5 Representation of Fiedler's Contingency Model

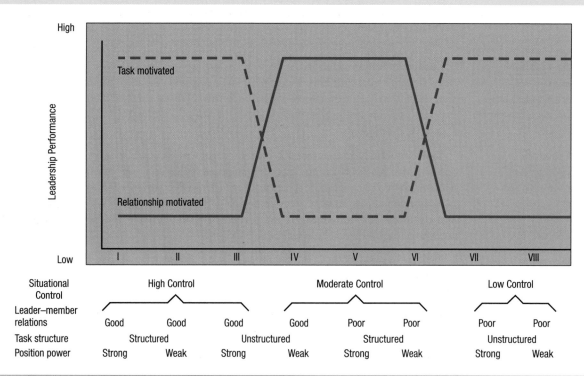

Source: Adapted from F E Fiedler, "Situational Control and a Dynamic Theory of Leadership," in *Managerial Control and Organizational Democracy*, eds B King, S Streufert and F E Fiedler (New York: John Wiley & Sons, 1978), p 114. Used with permission.

situations. Each situation represents a unique combination of leader–member relations, task structure, and position power. The vertical axis indicates the level of leader effectiveness. Plotted on the resulting quadrant are lines indicating those situations in which task-motivated (dotted line) and relationship-motivated (solid line) leaders are predicted to be effective.

For those situations in which the leader has high control (situations I, II, and III), task-motivated leaders are hypothesized to be more effective than relationship-motivated leaders. Under conditions of moderate control (situations IV, V, and VI), relationship-motivated leaders are expected to be more effective. Finally, the results orientation of task-motivated leaders is predicted to be more effective under conditions of low control (situations VII and VIII).

Research and Managerial Implications The overall accuracy of Fiedler's contingency model was tested through a meta-analysis of 35 studies containing 137 leader style—performance relations. According to the researchers' findings, (1) the contingency theory was correctly induced from studies on which it was based; (2) for laboratory studies testing the model, the theory was supported for all leadership situations except situation II; and (3) for field studies testing the model, three of the eight situations (IV, V, and VII) produced completely supportive results, while partial support was obtained for situations I, II, III, VI, and VIII.[41] A more recent meta-analysis of data obtained from 1,282 groups also provided mixed support for the contingency model. These findings suggest that Fiedler's model needs theoretical refinement.[42]

The major contribution of Fiedler's model is that it prompted others to examine the contingency nature of leadership. This research, in turn, reinforced the notion that there is no one best style of leadership. Leaders are advised to alter their task and relationship orientation to fit the demands of the situation at hand.

Path–Goal Theory

Path–goal theory is based on the expectancy theory of motivation discussed in Chapter 8. Expectancy theory proposes that motivation to exert effort increases as one's effort → performance→outcome expectations improve. Path–goal theory focuses on how leaders influence followers' expectations.

Robert House originated the path–goal theory of leadership. He proposed a model that describes how expectancy perceptions are influenced by the contingent relationships among four leadership styles and various employee attitudes and behaviours (see Figure 16–6).[43] According to the path–goal model, leader behaviour is acceptable when employees view it as a source of satisfaction or as paving the way to future satisfaction. In addition, leader behaviour is motivational to the extent it (1) reduces roadblocks that interfere with goal accomplishment, (2) provides the guidance and support needed by employees, and (3) ties meaningful rewards to goal accomplishment. Because the model deals with pathways to goals and rewards, it is called the path–goal theory of leadership. House sees the leader's main job as helping employees stay on the right paths to challenging goals and valued rewards.

Leadership Styles   House believes leaders can exhibit more than one leadership style. This contrasts with Fiedler, who proposes that leaders have one dominant style. The four leadership styles identified by House are as follows:

- *Directive leadership.* Providing guidance to employees about what should be done and how to do it, scheduling work, and maintaining standards of performance.

- *Supportive leadership.* Showing concern for the well-being and needs of employees, being friendly and approachable, and treating workers as equals.

- *Participative leadership.* Consulting with employees and seriously considering their ideas when making decisions.

Figure 16–6   A General Representation of House's Path–Goal Theory

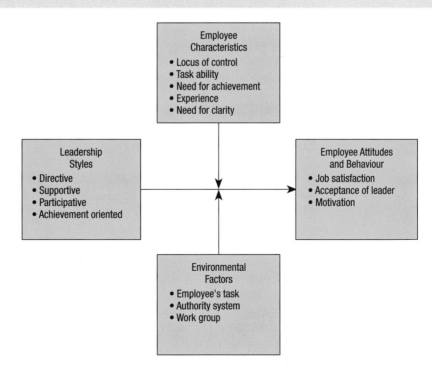

• *Achievement-oriented leadership.* Encouraging employees to perform at their highest level by setting challenging goals, emphasizing excellence, and demonstrating confidence in employee abilities.[44]

Research evidence supports the idea that leaders exhibit more than one leadership style.[45] Descriptions of business leaders reinforce these findings. For example:

Percy Barnevik, (former) ABB (Asea Brown Boveri) CEO, uses multiple leadership styles. When he introduced a matrix organization and seriously reduced the staff, he preferred to communicate directly with the 206,000 staff members: "You cannot hide up there in an ivory tower. You have to be out there." Although he prefers a persuasive approach in conflicts, he had to adopt a severe approach when he was faced with stubborn unions in the 1980s. It was only by issuing an ultimatum that Barnevik achieved the cuts he wanted.[46]

Contingency Factors   **Contingency factors** are situational variables that cause one style of leadership to be more effective than another. In this context, these variables affect expectancy or path–goal perceptions. This model has two groups of contingency variables (see Figure 16–6). They are employee characteristics and environmental factors. Five important employee characteristics are locus of control, task ability, need for achievement, experience, and need for clarity. Three relevant environmental factors are (1) the employee's task, (2) the authority system, and (3) the work group. All these factors have the potential for hindering or motivating employees.

Research has focused on determining whether the various contingency factors influence the effectiveness of different leadership styles. A recent summary of this research revealed that only 138 of 562 (25 per cent) contingency relationships tested confirmed the theory. Although these results were greater than chance, they provided limited support for the moderating relationships predicted within path–goal theory. On the positive side, however, the *task characteristics* of autonomy, variety, and significance and the *employee characteristics* of ability, experience, training and knowledge, professional orientation, indifference to organizational rewards, and need for independence obtained results that were semiconsistent with the theory.[47]

Managerial Implications   There are two important managerial implications. First, leaders possess and use more than one style of leadership. Managers thus should not be hesitant to try new behaviours when the situation calls for them. Second, a small set of task and employee characteristics are relevant contingency factors. Managers are encouraged to modify their leadership style to fit these various task and employee characteristics. For example, supportive and achievement leadership are more likely to be satisfying when employees have a lot of ability and experience.

Hersey and Blanchard's Situational Leadership Theory

Situational leadership theory (SLT) was developed by management writers Paul Hersey and Kenneth Blanchard.[48] According to the theory, effective leader behaviour depends on the readiness level of a leader's followers. **Readiness** is defined as the extent to which a follower possesses the ability and willingness to complete a task. Willingness is a combination of confidence, commitment, and motivation.

The SLT model is summarized in Figure 16–7. The appropriate leadership style is found by cross-referencing follower readiness, which varies from low to high, with one of four leadership styles. The four leadership styles represent combinations of task and relationship-oriented leader behaviours (S_1 to S_4). Leaders are encouraged to use a "telling style" for followers with low readiness. This style combines high task-oriented leader behaviours, such as providing instructions, with low relationship-oriented behaviours, such as close supervision (see Figure 16–7). As follower readiness increases, leaders are advised to gradually move from a telling, to a selling, to a participating, and, ultimately, to a delegating style. In the most recent description of this model, the four leadership styles depicted in Figure 16–7 are referred to as telling or directing (S_1), persuading or

Contingency factors
Variables that influence the appropriateness of a leadership style.

Readiness
Follower's ability and willingness to complete a task.

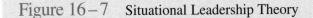

Figure 16–7   Situational Leadership Theory

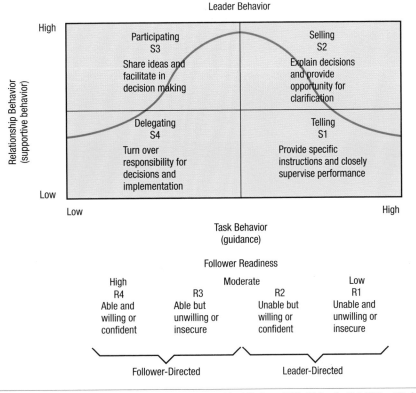

coaching (S_2), participating or supporting (S_3), and delegating (S_4).[49]

Although SLT is widely used as a training tool, it is not strongly supported by scientific research. For instance, leadership effectiveness was not attributable to the predicted interaction between follower readiness and leadership style in a recent study of 459 salespeople.[50] Moreover, a study of 303 teachers indicated that SLT was accurate only for employees with low readiness. This finding is consistent with a survey of 57 chief nurse executives in California. These executives did not delegate in accordance with SLT.[51] Finally, researchers have concluded that the self-assessment instrument used to measure leadership style and follower readiness is inaccurate and should be used with caution.[52] In summary, managers should exercise discretion when using prescriptions from SLT.

A Competing Value Approach to Leadership

Modern management is paradoxal. It is geared by contradictory and paradoxal forces. Table 16–3 gives a survey of paradoxes organizations are faced with. Modern management is not either . . . or . . . but and . . . and . . .[53] Criteria, values and suppositions from which "actors" or stakeholders judge organizations often are conflicting, opposite, or excluding one another. Organizations have to be innovative and flexible, but under control from the manager's point of view. On the one hand employees expect development opportunities, but on the other hand, formalized planning systems are welcomed as well.

The modern organization has created these paradoxes. Opposing forces need to be integrated: general global thinking, but local handling; formal and informal systems; flexible planning; dynamic equilibrium; freedom to labour for a preconceived objective.

Table 16 – 3   Paradoxes Organizations are Faced With

Competition - Partnership
Formal - Informal
Vision - Reality
Analysis - Intuition
Delegation - Control
Individuality - Teamwork
Action - Reflection
Top-down - Bottom-up
Tolerance - Forthrightness
Flexibility - Focus

Source: P Evans, and Y Doz, "The Dualistic Organizations," in *Human Resource Management in International Firms*, eds P Evans, Y Doz, and A Laurant (London: Macmillan, 1989) pp 219–420.

This implies Janusian thinking: one has to be capable to keep in mind two opposing ideas, without going insane. Organizations and their managers are faced with diverging, even opposing demands. Many situations are paradoxal.

Robert Quinn has successfully translated this starting point into a competing value approach of leadership. Table 16–4 gives Quinn's central concept of leadership roles, based on the underlying dimensions: stability versus flexibility and internal versus external focus.[54]

From Transactional to Charismatic Leadership

New perspectives of leadership theory have emerged in the past 15 years, variously referred to as "charismatic," "heroic," "transformational," or "visionary" leadership.[55] These competing but related perspectives have created confusion among researchers and practising managers. Fortunately, Robert House and Boas Shamir have given us a

Table 16 – 4   Quinn's Central Concept of Leadership Roles

	FLEXIBILITY	EXTERNAL FOCUS	STABILITY	INTERNAL FOCUS	CHARACTERISTICS
Innovator Role	XX	X			Creative favours change
Broker Role	X	XX			Politically clever maintains external contacts
Producer Role		XX	X		Task-oriented
Director Role		X	XX		Goal-setting establishes clear expectations
Coordinator Role			XX	X	Maintains structures coordinating
Monitor Role			X	XX	Collects and distributes information Provides Continuity
Facilitator Role	X			XX	Encourages dialogue
Mentor Role	XX	X			Fair encourages the individual
XX = Strong X = Weak					

Source: E Quinn, *Beyond Rational Management* (San Francisco: Jossey–Bass, 1988)

practical, integrated theory. It is referred to as *charismatic leadership.*

This section begins by highlighting the differences between transactional and charismatic leadership. We then discuss a model of the charismatic leadership process and its research and management implications.

What Is the Difference between Transactional and Charismatic Leadership?

Transactional leadership
Focuses on interpersonal interactions between managers and employees.

Most of the models and theories previously discussed in this chapter represent transactional leadership. **Transactional leadership** focuses on the interpersonal transactions between managers and employees. Leaders are seen as engaging in behaviours that maintain a quality interaction between themselves and followers. The two underlying characteristics of transactional leadership are that (1) leaders use contingent rewards to motivate employees and (2) leaders exert corrective action only when subordinates fail to obtain performance goals.

Charismatic leadership
Transforms employees to pursue organizational goals over self-interests.

In contrast, **charismatic leadership** emphasizes "symbolic leader behaviour, visionary and inspirational messages, nonverbal communication, appeal to ideological values, intellectual stimulation of followers by the leader, display of confidence in self and followers, and leader expectations for follower self-sacrifice and for performance beyond the call of duty."[56]

Let us now examine how charismatic leadership transforms followers.

How Does Charismatic Leadership Transform Followers?

Charismatic leaders transform followers by creating changes in their goals, values, needs, beliefs, and aspirations. They accomplish this transformation by appealing to followers' self-concepts—namely, their values and personal identity. Figure 16–8 presents a model of how charismatic leadership accomplishes this transformation process.

Charismatic leaders first engage in three key sets of leader behaviour. If done effectively, these behaviours positively affect followers' self-concepts. In turn, a positive self-concept propels employee motivation towards a host of personal outcomes such as personal commitment to the leader and vision, self-sacrificial behaviour, organizational commitment, task meaningfulness and satisfaction, intrinsic motivation, and increased performance.

Charismatic Leader Behaviour   The first set of charismatic leader behaviours involves establishing a common vision of the future. A vision is "a realistic, credible, attractive future for your organization."[57] According to Burt Nanus, a leadership expert, the "right" vision unleashes human potential because it serves as a beacon of hope and common purpose. It does this by attracting commitment, energizing workers, creating meaning in employees' lives, establishing a standard of excellence, promoting high ideals, and bridging the gap between an organization's present problems and its future goals and aspirations.[58] In contrast, the "wrong" vision can be very damaging to an organization. Consider what happened to Saatchi and Saatchi, once Britain's and the world's most famous publicity agency:

Strengthened by successive successful publicity campaigns, including former prime minister Margaret Thatcher's in the eighties, Maurice Saatchi's unrestrained ambition pulled down the entire business. Thanks to a positive evelution on the stock market, he suddenly had an enormous budget at his disposal which prompted him to buy publicity agencies, marketing companies, public relations agencies, and publishing houses. He was game for everything. His wild buying binge led to pure megalomania, as in 1987 he decided to take over Britain's number one bank, Hill Samuel and then the Midland Bank.

Mismanagement and disorganization, followed by a crash, resulted in the break up of the company.[59]

As you can see, Maurice Saatchi's vision produced disastrous results. This highlights the fact that charismatic leaders do more than simply establish a vision. They also must gain input from others in developing an effective implementation plan. For example, Johnson & Johnson obtained input about its vision and implementation plan by surveying all of its 80,000 employees.[60]

The second set of leader behaviours involves two key components:

1. Charismatic leaders set high performance expectations and standards because they know challenging, attainable goals lead to greater productivity.

2. Charismatic leaders need to publicly express confidence in the followers' ability to meet high performance expectations. This is essential because employees are more likely to pursue difficult goals when they believe they can accomplish what is being asked of them.

The third and final set of leader behaviours involves being a role model. Through their actions, charismatic leaders model the desired values, traits, beliefs, and behaviours needed to realize the vision.

Effects on Follower Self-Concepts   Figure 16–8 also shows that charismatic leadership affects three aspects of a follower's self-concept:

1. It enhances follower motivation, achievement motivation, and goal pursuit.

2. It increases the extent to which followers identify with the leader's values, goals, and aspirations and with the collective interests of all employees.

3. Follower self-esteem and self-efficacy are heightened by charismatic leader behaviour.

In contrast, followers' self-concepts are negatively affected by destructive charismatic leadership.

Motivational Mechanisms   Charismatic leadership positively affects employee motivation (see Figure 16–8). One way in which this occurs is by increasing the intrinsic

Figure 16 – 8   A Charismatic Model of Leadership

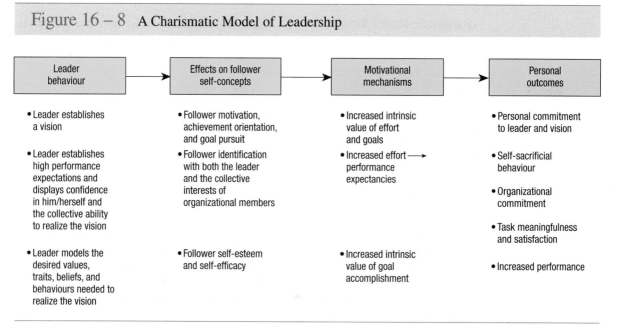

Sources: Based in part on B Shamir, R J House, and M B Arthur, "The Motivational Effects of Charismatic Leadership: A Self-Concept Based Theory," *Organization Science*, November 1993, pp 577–94; and R J House and B Shamir, "Toward the Integration of Transformation, Charismatic, and Visionary Theories," in *Leadership Theory and Research: Perspectives and Directions*, eds M M Chemers and R Ayman (New York: Academic Press, 1993), pp 81–107.

value of an employee's effort and goals. Leaders do this by emphasizing the symbolic value of effort; that is, charismatic leaders convey the message that effort reflects important organizational values and collective interests. Followers come to learn that their level of effort represents a moral statement. For example, high effort represents commitment to the organization's vision and values, whereas low effort reflects a lack of commitment.

Charismatic leadership also increases employees' effort→performance expectancies by positively contributing to followers' self-esteem and self-efficacy. Leaders also increase the intrinsic value of goal accomplishment by explaining the organization's vision and goals in terms of the personal values they represent. This helps employees to personally connect with the organization's vision. Charismatic leaders further increase the meaningfulness of actions aimed towards goal accomplishment by showing how goals move the organization towards its positive vision, which then gives followers a sense of "growth and development," both of which are important contributors to a positive self-concept.

Research and Managerial Implications

The charismatic model of leadership presented in Figure 16–8 was supported by an experiment in which 282 business students performed a simulated assembly task. Results revealed that charismatic leadership positively influenced students' quality and quantity goals and their self-efficacy, which, in turn, enhanced the quality and quantity of performance.[61] A recent meta-analysis of 54 studies further indicated that charismatic leaders were viewed as more effective leaders by both supervisors and followers and had followers who exerted more effort and reported higher levels of job satisfaction than noncharismatic leaders.[62] Other studies showed that followers trusted charismatic leaders more than noncharismatic ones, and charismatic leaders had higher project quality and budget/schedule performance ratings and were identified as more effective role models.[63] Two additional studies demonstrated that both charismatic and transactional leadership were positively associated with a variety of important employee outcomes.[64] Finally, a study of 31 presidents of the United States indicated that charisma significantly predicted presidential performance.[65]

These results underscore four important managerial implications. First, the best leaders are not just charismatic, they are both transactional and charismatic. Leaders should attempt these two types of leadership while avoiding a "laissez-faire" or "wait-and-see" style. Laissez-faire leadership is the most ineffective leadership style.[66]

Second, charismatic leadership is not applicable in all organizational situations. According to a team of experts, charismatic leadership is most likely to be effective when

1. The situation offers opportunities for "moral" involvement.

2. Performance goals cannot be easily established and measured.

3. Extrinsic rewards cannot be clearly linked to individual performance.

4. There are few situational cues or constraints to guide behaviour.

5. Exceptional effort, behaviour, sacrifices, and performance are required of both leaders and followers.[67]

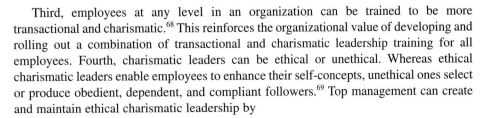

Third, employees at any level in an organization can be trained to be more transactional and charismatic.[68] This reinforces the organizational value of developing and rolling out a combination of transactional and charismatic leadership training for all employees. Fourth, charismatic leaders can be ethical or unethical. Whereas ethical charismatic leaders enable employees to enhance their self-concepts, unethical ones select or produce obedient, dependent, and compliant followers.[69] Top management can create and maintain ethical charismatic leadership by

1. Creating and enforcing a clearly stated code of ethics.

2. Recruiting, selecting, and promoting people with high morals and standards.

3. Developing performance expectations around the treatment of employees—these expectations can then be assessed in the performance appraisal process.

4. Training employees to value diversity.

5. Identifying, rewarding, and publicly praising employees who exemplify high moral conduct.[70]

Additional Perspectives on Leadership

This section examines four additional approaches to leadership: leader–member exchange theory, substitutes for leadership, superleadership and coaching. We spend more time discussing leader–member exchange theory and substitutes for leadership because they have been more thoroughly investigated.

Graen's Leader–Member Exchange (LMX) Model of Leadership

George Graen, an industrial psychologist, believes popular theories of leadership are based on an incorrect assumption. Theories such as the Leadership Grid® and Fiedler's contingency model assume that leader behaviour is characterized by a stable or average leadership style. In other words, these models assume a leader treats all subordinates in about the same way. This traditional approach to leadership is shown in the left side of Figure 16–9. In this case, the leader (designated by the circled L) is thought to exhibit a similar pattern of behaviour towards all employees (E_1 to E_5). In contrast, Graen contends that leaders develop unique one-to-one relationships with each of the people reporting to them. Behavioural scientists call this sort of relationship a *vertical dyad*. The forming of vertical dyads is said to be a naturally occurring process, resulting from the leader's attempt to delegate and assign work roles. As a result of this process, Graen predicts that one of two distinct types of leader–member exchange relationships will evolve.[71]

One type of leader–member exchange is called the **in-group exchange**. In this relationship, leaders and followers develop a partnership characterized by reciprocal

In-group exchange

A partnership characterized by mutual trust, respect, and liking.

Figure 16 – 9   A Role-Making Model of Leadership

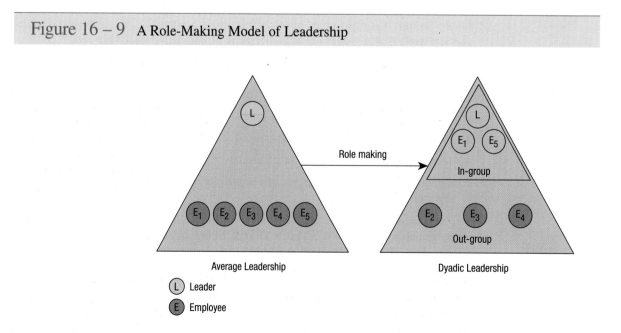

Average Leadership

Dyadic Leadership

Ⓛ Leader
Ⓔ Employee

Source: Adapted from F Dansereau, Jr., G Graen, and W J Haga, "A Vertical Dyad Linkage Approach to Leadership within Formal Organizations," *Organizational Behavior and Human Performance*, February 1975, p 72.

Out-group exchange
A partnership characterized by a lack of mutual trust, respect, and liking

influence, mutual trust, respect and liking, and a sense of common fates. Figure 16—9 shows that E_1 and E_5 are members of the leader's in-group. In the second type of exchange, referred to as an **out-group exchange**, leaders are characterized as overseers who fail to create a sense of mutual trust, respect, or common fate.[72] E_2, E_3, and E_4 are members of the out-group on the right side of Figure 16–9.

Research Findings   If Graen's model is correct, there should be a significant relationship between the type of leader–member exchange and job-related outcomes. Research supports this prediction. For example, in-group members were found to have higher organizational commitment, job satisfaction, and job performance than did employees in the out-group.[73] Positive leader–member exchange also was associated with greater levels of perceived environmental control, supervisory fairness, and satisfaction with leadership.[74] The type of leader–member exchange was found to predict not only turnover among nurses and computer analysts, but also career outcomes, such as promotability, salary level, and receipt of bonuses over a seven-year period.[75] Finally, a recent study sought to determine the demographic and organizational characteristics that foster the quality of an LMX. Results revealed that LMX was of lower quality when leaders and followers had different genders. The quality of an LMX also was negatively associated with the number of employees reporting to a manager and the work load.[76]

Managerial Implications   Graen's model underscores the importance of training managers to improve leader–member relations. Ideally, this should enhance the job satisfaction and performance of employees and also reduce turnover. A large US government installation in the Midwest conducted such a training programme. Results indicated a 19 per cent increase on an objective measure of productivity. This improvement resulted in an estimated annual cost savings of more than $5 million.[77] In addition to training, OB researcher Robert Vecchio offers the following tips to both followers and leaders for improving the quality of leader–member exchanges:

1. New employees should offer their loyalty, support, and cooperativeness to their manager.

2. If you are an out-group member, either accept the situation, try to become an in-group member by being cooperative and loyal, or quit.

3. Managers should consciously try to expand their in-groups.

4. Managers need to give employees ample opportunity to prove themselves.[78]

Substitutes for Leadership

Virtually all leadership theories assume that some sort of formal leadership is necessary, whatever the circumstances. But this basic assumption is questioned by this model of leadership. Specifically, some OB scholars propose that there are a variety of situational variables that can substitute for, neutralize, or enhance the effects of leadership. These situational variables are referred to as substitutes for leadership.[79] Substitutes for leadership can thus increase or diminish a leader's ability to influence the work group. For example, leader behaviour that initiates structure would tend to be resisted by independent-minded employees with high ability and vast experience. Consequently, such employees would be guided more by their own initiative than by managerial directives.

Kerr and Jermier's Substitutes for Leadership Model   According to Steven Kerr and John Jermier, the OB researchers who developed this model, the key to improving leadership effectiveness is to identify the situational characteristics that can either substitute for, neutralize, or improve the impact of a leader's behaviour. Table 16–5 lists the various substitutes for leadership. Characteristics of the subordinate, the task, and the organization can act as substitutes for traditional hierarchical leadership. Further, different

Table 16 – 5   Substitutes for Leadership

CHARACTERISTIC	RELATIONSHIP-ORIENTED OR CONSIDERATE LEADER BEHAVIOUR IS UNNECESSARY	TASK-ORIENTED OR INITIATING STRUCTURE LEADER BEHAVIOUR IS UNNECESSARY
OF THE SUBORDINATE		
1. Ability, experience, training, knowledge		X
2. Need for independence	X	X
3. "Professional" orientation	X	X
4. Indifference toward organizational rewards	X	X
OF THE TASK		
5. Unambiguous and routine		X
6. Methodologically invariant		X
7. Provides its own feedback concerning accomplishment		X
8. Intrinsically satisfying	X	
OF THE ORGANIZATION		
9. Formalization (explicit plans, goals, and areas of responsibility)		X
10. Inflexibility (rigid, unbending rules and procedures)		X
11. Highly specified and active advisory and staff functions		X
12. Closely knit, cohesive work groups	X	X
13. Organizational rewards not within the leader's control	X	X
14. Spatial distance between superior and subordinates	X	X

Source: Adapted from S Kerr and J M Jermier, "Substitutes for Leadership: Their Meaning and Measurement," *Organizational Behavior and Human Performance*, December 1978, pp 375–403.

characteristics are predicted to negate different types of leader behaviour. For example, tasks that provide feedback concerning accomplishment, such as taking a test, tend to negate task-oriented but not relationship-oriented leader behaviour (see Table 16–5). Although the list in Table 16–5 is not all-inclusive, it shows that there are more substitutes for task-oriented leadership than for relationship-oriented leadership.

Research and Managerial Implications   Two different approaches have been used to test this model. The first is based on the idea that substitutes for leadership are contingency variables that moderate the relationship between leader behaviour and employee attitudes and behaviour.[80] A recent summary of this research revealed that only 318 of 3,741 (9 per cent) contingency relationships tested supported the model.[81] This demonstrates that substitutes for leadership do not moderate the effect of a leader's behaviour as suggested by Steve Kerr and John Jermier. The second approach to test the substitutes model examined whether substitutes for leadership have a direct effect on employee attitudes and behaviours. A recent meta-analysis of 36 different samples revealed that the combination of substitute variables and leader behaviours significantly explained a variety of employee attitudes and behaviours. Interestingly, the substitutes for leadership were more important than leader behaviours in accounting for employee attitudes and behaviours.[82]

The key implication is that managers should be attentive to the substitutes listed in Table 16–5 because they directly influence employee attitudes and performance. Managers can positively influence the substitutes through employee selection, job design, work group assignments, and the design of organizational processes and systems.[83]

Superleadership

Superleader
Someone who leads others to lead themselves.

A **superleader** is someone who leads others to lead themselves. You may recall that we already discussed this approach to leadership in Chapter 13 with respect to developing team members' self-management skills. We briefly highlight it again because superleadership is equally relevant within teams as well as any general leadership situation. Superleaders empower followers by acting as a teacher and coach rather than as a dictator and autocrat. The need for this form of leadership is underscored by a recent survey of 1,046 Americans. Results demonstrated that only 38 per cent of the respondents ever had an effective coach or mentor.[84]

Productive thinking is the cornerstone of superleadership. Specifically, managers are encouraged to teach followers how to engage in productive thinking.[85] This is expected to increase employees feelings of personal control and intrinsic motivation. Superleadership has the potential to free up a manager's time because employees are encouraged to manage themselves. Future research is needed to test the validity of recommendations derived from this new approach to leadership.

Coaching

Modern management thinking is no longer characterized by dominant and authoritarian leadership, but by coaching.[86] A good coach has the following characteristics:

- *Commitment.* The professional manager directs from a distance, whereas the coach acts directly with his or her team. A coach is present on the field to support the team, and is present at the moment of action, which he or she experiences actively. The coach does not get engrossed in files or participating in long-lasting meetings. Action happens in the field. A real coach is not afraid of hard work. The rational, cool and, distant manager has to make place for the enthusiastic coach, who trusts the team and knows the members personally, and is conscious of their weaknesses and is capable of getting the best out of them. Day after day, the coach tries to improve his or her staff's performance and possibilities.

- *Skill building.* The coach invests much in the employees' skill building, and is aware of the fact that they are the driving force of the organization. He or she will see to it that they improve their professional skills, that they can organize their work themselves, directed towards a common goal.

- *Support.* The coach will principally support the team, and enable the members to show results.

- *Team builder.* The coach is a team builder, bringing people together with different skills, interests, and backgrounds to create a solid team. A struggle for power and political conflict has to be replaced by mutual respect. He or she is successful in transforming internal into external competition, directed towards the real competitors.

- *Result oriented.* The coach's efforts are not aimed at creating a cosy environment, but at getting results.

Summary of Key Concepts

1. *Define the term leadership, and explain the difference between leading versus managing.* Leadership is defined as a social influence process in which the leader tries to obtain the voluntary participation of employees in an effort to reach organizational objectives. Leadership entails more

than having authority and power. Although leadership and management overlap, each entails a unique set of activities or functions. Managers typically perform functions associated with planning, investigating, organizing, and control, and leaders deal with the interpersonal aspects of a manager's job. Table 16–2 summarizes the differences between leading and managing.

2. *Review trait theory research, and discuss the idea of one best style of leadership, using the Ohio State studies and the Leadership Grid ® as points of reference.* Historical leadership research did not support the notion that effective leaders possessed unique traits from followers. However, teams of researchers reanalysed this historical data with modern-day statistical procedures. Results revealed that individuals tend to be perceived as leaders when they possess one or more of the following traits: intelligence, dominance, and masculinity. A recent study further demonstrated that employees value credible leaders. Credible leaders are honest, forward-looking, inspiring, and competent. Research also examined the relationship between gender and leadership. Results demonstrated that (*a*) men and women differed in the type of leadership roles they assume, (*b*) leadership styles varied by gender, and (*c*) gender differences in ratings of leadership effectiveness were associated with the percentage of male leaders and male subordinates. The Ohio State studies revealed that there were two key independent dimensions of leadership behaviour: consideration and initiating structure. Authors of the Leadership Grid® proposed that leaders should adopt a style that demonstrates high concern for production and people. Research did not support the premise that there is one best style of leadership.

3. *Explain, according to Fiedler's contingency model, how leadership style interacts with situational control.* Fiedler believes leader effectiveness depends on an appropriate match between leadership style and situational control. Leaders are either task motivated or relationship motivated. Situation control is composed of leader—member relations, task structure, and position power. Task-motivated leaders are effective under situations of both high and low control. Relationship-motivated leaders are more effective when they have moderate situational control.

4. *Discuss House's path–goal theory and Hersey and Blanchard's situational leadership theory.* According to path–goal theory, leaders alternately can exhibit directive, supportive, participative, or achievement-oriented styles of leadership. The effectiveness of

these styles depends on various employee characteristics and environmental factors. Path–goal theory has received limited support from research. There are two important managerial implications: (*a*) leaders possess and use more than one style of leadership, and (*b*) managers are advised to modify their leadership style to fit a small subset of task and employee characteristics. According to situational leadership theory (SLT), effective leader behaviour depends on the readiness level of a leader's followers. As follower readiness increases, leaders are advised to gradually move from a telling to a selling to a participating and, finally, to a delegating style. Research does not support SLT.

5. *Define and differentiate transactional and charismatic leadership.* There is an important difference between transactional and charismatic leadership. Transactional leaders focus on the interpersonal transactions between managers and employees. Charismatic leaders motivate employees to pursue organizational goals above their own self-interests. Both forms of leadership are important for organizational success.

6. *Explain how charismatic leadership transforms followers.* Charismatic leaders transform followers by creating changes in their goals, values, needs, beliefs, and aspirations. Leaders accomplish this by first engaging in three key sets of leader behaviour. These leader behaviours, in turn, positively affect followers' self-concepts. A positive self-concept then unleashes employee motivation towards achieving a host of preferred outcomes.

7. *Summarize the managerial implications of charismatic leadership.* There are four managerial implications: (*a*) The best leaders are both transactional and charismatic. (*b*) Charismatic leadership is not applicable in all organizational situations. (*c*) Employees at any level in an organization can be trained to be more transactional and charismatic. (*d*) Top management needs to promote and reinforce ethical charismatic leadership because charismatic leaders can be ethical or unethical.

8. *Explain Graen's leader–member exchange model of leadership.* George Graen believes that leaders develop unique one-to-one relationships, referred to as vertical dyads, with each employee. These leader–member exchanges qualify as either in-group or out-group relationships. Research supports this model of leadership.

9. *Describe the substitutes for leadership, and explain how they substitute for, neutralize, or enhance the*

effects of leadership. There are 14 substitutes for leadership (see Table 16–5) that can substitute for, neutralize, or enhance the effects of leadership. These substitutes contain characteristics of the subordinates, the task, and the organization. Research shows that substitutes directly influence employee attitudes and performance.

10. *Describe superleadership and coaching.* Superleaders empower followers by acting as a teacher and coach rather than as a dictator and autocrat. A good coach has the following characteristics: commitment, skill builder, supporter, team builder and result oriented.

Discussion Questions

1. Is everyone cut out to be a leader? Explain.

2. Has your university education helped you develop any of the traits that characterize leaders?

3. Should organizations change anything in response to research pertaining to gender and leadership? If yes, describe your recommendations.

4. What leadership traits and behavioural styles are possessed by the prime minister of your country?

5. Does it make more sense to change a person's leadership style or the situation? How would Fred Fiedler and Robert House answer this question?

6. Describe how a university professor might use House's path–goal theory to clarify student's path–goal perceptions.

7. Identify three charismatic leaders, and describe their leadership traits and behavioural styles.

8. Have you ever worked for a charismatic leader? Describe how he or she transformed followers.

9. Have you ever been a member of an in-group or out-group? For either situation, describe the pattern of interaction between you and your manager.

10. In your view, which leadership theory has the greatest practical application? Why?

Personal Awareness and Growth Exercise

How Ready Are You To Assume the Leadership Role?

Objectives

1. To assess your readiness for the leadership role.

2. To consider the implications of the gap between your career goals and your readiness to lead.

Introduction

Leaders assume multiple roles. Roles represent the expectations that others have of occupants of a position. It is important for potential leaders to consider whether they are ready for the leadership role because mismatches in expectations or skills can derail a leader's effectiveness. This exercise assesses your readiness to assume the leadership role.[87]

Instructions

For each statement, indicate the extent to which you agree or disagree with it by selecting one number from the scale provided. Circle your response for each statement. Remember, there are no right or wrong answers. After completing the survey, add your total score for the 20 items, and record it in the space provided.

1 = Strongly disagree
2 = Disagree
3 = Neither agree nor disagree
4 = Agree
5 = Strongly agree

1. It is enjoyable having people count on me for ideas and suggestions.   1—2—3—4—5

2. It would be accurate to say that I have inspired other people.   1—2—3—4—5

3. It's a good practice to ask people provocative questions about their work.   1—2—3—4—5

4. It's easy for me to compliment others.   1—2—3—4—5

5. I like to cheer people up even when my own spirits are down.   1—2—3—4—5

6. What my team accomplishes is more important than my personal glory.　　1—2—3—4—5

7. Many people imitate my ideas.　　1—2—3—4—5

8. Building team spirit is important to me.　　1—2—3—4—5

9. I would enjoy coaching other members of the team.　　1—2—3—4—5

10. It is important to me to recognize others for their accomplishments.　　1—2—3—4—5

11. I would enjoy entertaining visitors to my firm even if it interfered with my completing a report.　　1—2—3—4—5

12. It would be fun for me to represent my team at gatherings outside our department.　　1—2—3—4—5

13. The problems of my teammates are my problems too.　　1—2—3—4—5

14. Resolving conflict is an activity I enjoy.　　1—2—3—4—5

15. I would cooperate with another unit in the organization even if I disagreed with the position taken by its members.　　1—2—3—4—5

16. I am an idea generator on the job.　　1—2—3—4—5

17. It's fun for me to bargain whenever I have the opportunity.　　1—2—3—4—5

18. Team members listen to me when I speak.　　1—2—3—4—5

19. People have asked me to assume the leadership of an activity several times in my life.　　1—2—3—4—5

20. I've always been a convincing person.　　1—2—3—4—5

Total score: _____

Norms for Interpreting the Total Score[88]

90—100 = High readiness for the leadership role
60—89 = Moderate readiness for the leadership role
40—59 = Some uneasiness with the leadership role
39 or less = Low readiness for the leadership role

QUESTIONS FOR DISCUSSION

1. Do you agree with the interpretation of your readiness to assume the leadership role? Explain why or why not.

2. If you scored below 60 and desire to become a leader, what might you do to increase your readiness to lead? To answer this question, we suggest that you study the statements carefully—particularly those with low responses—to determine how you might change either an attitude or a behaviour so that you can realistically answer more questions with a response of "agree" or "strongly agree."

3. How might this evaluation instrument help you to become a more effective leader?

Group Exercise

Exhibiting Leadership Within the Context of Running a Meeting[89]

Objectives

1. To consider the types of problems that can occur when running a meeting.

2. To identify the leadership behaviours that can be used to handle problems that occur in meetings.

Introduction

Managers often find themselves playing the role of formal or informal leader when participating in a planned meeting (e.g., committees, work groups, task forces, etc.). As a leader, individuals must often handle a number of interpersonal situations that have the potential of reducing the group's productivity. For example, if an individual has important information that is not shared with the group, the meeting will be less productive. Similarly, two or more individuals who engage in conversational asides could disrupt the normal functioning of the group. Finally, the group's productivity will also be threatened by two or more individuals who argue or engage in personal attacks on one another during a meeting. This exercise is designed to help you practise some of the behaviours necessary to overcome these problems and at the same time share in the responsibility of leading a productive group.[90]

Instructions

Your instructor will divide the class into groups of four to six. Once the group is assembled, briefly summarize the types of problems that can occur when running a meeting—start with the material presented in the preceding introduction. Write your final list on a piece of paper. Next, for each problem on the group's list, the group should brainstorm a list of appropriate leader behaviours that can be used to handle the problem. Use the guidelines for brainstorming discussed in Chapter

12. Try to arrive at a consensus list of leadership behaviours that can be used to handle the various problems encountered in meetings.

QUESTIONS FOR DISCUSSION

1. What type of problems that occur during meetings are most difficult to handle? Explain.

2. Are there any particular leader behaviours that can be used to solve multiple problems during meetings? Discuss your rationale.

3. Was there a lot of agreement about which leader behaviours were useful for dealing with specific problems encountered in meetings? Explain.

Notes

[1] Based on P Elmer-Dewitt, "Anita the Agitator," *Time*, January 25, 1993, pp. 44–46; T Moerkerke, "Anita Roddick: Kennis die uit het hart komt, is niet gevaarlijk," *Knack,* ; C A Barlett, K Elderkin, K McQuade, and M Hart, "The Body Shop International," in (eds.) R D Buzzell, J A Quelch, and C A Bartlett, Global Marketing Management: Cases and Readings (Reading: Addison and Sesley Publishing Company) 1995, pp 608–631.

[2] See S Lieberson and J F O'Connor, "Leadership and Organizational Performance: A Study of Large Corporations," *American Sociological Review,* April 1972, pp 117–30.

[3] T Thorlindson, *The Skipper Effect in Icelandic Herring Fishing* (Reykjavik: University of Iceland, 1987), in M Smith, and C Cooper, "Leadership and Stress," *Leadership and Organization Development Journal*, vol 15, no 2, 1994, pp 3–7.

[4] P Wright, *Managerial Leadership.* (London: Routledge, 1996)

[5] "The American Survey," *The Economist*, December, 9, 1995, pp 53-54.

[6] In the UK, John Adair has become very popular as an expert on leadership training. See a.o. J Adair, *Effective Leadership. (*London: Pan Books, 1988.)

[7] Based on C A Bartlett, and A Nanda, "Ingvar Kamprad and IKEA," in R Buzzell, J Quelch, and C A Bartlett, *Global Marketing Management: Cases and Readings* (Reading: Addison-Wesley Publishing Company,), pp 69–95; and on B Enström, "The Well Tempered Viking," *Scanorama*, June 1989, pp 64–72.

[8] See J R Meindl, S B Ehrlich, and J M Dukerich, "The Romance of Leadership," *Administrative Science Quarterly,* March 1985, pp 78–102.

[9] C A Schriesheim, J M Tolliver, and O C Behling, "Leadership Theory: Some Implications for Managers," *MSU Business Topics,* Summer 1978, p 35.

[10] T Peters and N Austin, *A Passion for Excellence* (New York: Random House, 1985), pp 5–6.

[11] R Tait, *Roads to the Top* (Basingstoke: Macmillan Press Ltd., 1995) p 105.

[12] B M Bass, *Bass & Stogdill's Handbook of Leadership: Theory, Research, and Managerial Applications,* 3rd ed, (New York: Free Press, 1990), p 383.

[13] Based on "The Heavier-Than-Air Manager," *The Economist*, December 23, 1995, p 88; and S Sherman, "How Tomorrow Leaders are Learning Their Stuff," *Fortune*, November 27, 1995, pp 64–72.

[14] See the related discussion in F E Fiedler, "Research on Leadership Selection and Training: One View of the Future," *Administrative Science Quarterly*, June 1996, pp 241–50.

[15] These statistics were obtained from J P Kotter, *Leading Change* (Boston: Harvard Business School Press, 1996).

[16] K Western, "No Matter What It Takes, I'll Do It," *The Arizona Republic,* August 1, 1993, p F1.

[17] For complete details, see R M Stogdill, "Personal Factors Associated with Leadership: A Survey of the Literature," *Journal of Psychology,* 1948, pp 35–71; and R M Stogdill, *Handbook of Leadership* (New York: Free Press, 1974).

[18] See R D Mann, "A Review of the Relationships between Personality and Performance in Small Groups," *Psychological Bulletin,* July 1959, pp 241–70.

[19] See D A Kenny and S J Zaccaro, "An Estimate of Variance Due to Traits in Leadership," *Journal of Applied Psychology,* November 1983, pp 678–85. Results from a more recent verification can be found in S J Zaccaro, R J Foti, and D A Kenny, "Self-Monitoring and Trait-Based Variance in Leadership: An Investigation of Leader Flexibility across Multiple Group Situations," *Journal of Applied Psychology,* April 1991, pp 308–15.

[20] See A J Kinicki, P W Hom, M R Trost, and K J Wade, "Effects of Category Prototypes on Performance-Rating Accuracy," *Journal of Applied Psychology,* June 1995, pp 354–70; J S Phillips and R G Lord, "Schematic Information Processing and Perceptions of Leadership in Problem-Solving Groups," *Journal of Applied Psychology,* August 1982, pp 486–92; and R J Foti, S L Fraser, and R G Lord, "Effects of Leadership Labels and Prototypes on Perceptions of Political Leaders," *Journal of Applied Psychology,* June 1982, pp 326–33.

[21] See R G Lord, C L De Vader, and G M Alliger, "A Meta-Analysis of the Relation between Personality Traits and Leadership Perceptions: An Application of Validity Generalization Procedures," *Journal of Applied Psychology,* August 1986, p 407.

[22] Results can be found in J M Kouzes and B Z Posner, *The Leadership Challenge* (San Francisco: Jossey-Bass, 1995).

[23] See J M Kouzes and B Z Posner, *Credibility* (San Francisco: Jossey-Bass, 1993).

[24] Gender and the emergence of leaders was examined by A H Eagly and S J Karau, "Gender and the Emergence of Leaders: A Meta-Analysis," *Journal of Personality and Social Psychology,* May 1991, pp 685–710.

[25] See A H Eagly, S J Karau, and B T Johnson, "Gender and Leadership Style among School Principals: A Meta-Analysis," *Educational Administration Quarterly,* February 1992, pp 76–102.

[26] Results can be found in A H Eagly, S J Karau, and M G Makhijani, "Gender and the Effectiveness of Leaders: A Meta-Analysis," *Psychological Bulletin,* January 1995, pp 125–45.

[27] Hay Management Consultants.

[28] For recommendations on how to hire the best leaders, see T R Horton, "Selecting the Best for the Top," *American Management*

Association, January 1996, pp 20–23.

[29]R Tait, *op cit.,* p 21.

[30]This research is summarized and critiqued by Bass, *Bass & Stogdill's Handbook of Leadership: Theory, Research, and Managerial Applications,* ch. 24.

[31]See V H Vroom, "Leadership," in *Handbook of Industrial and Organizational Psychology,* ed M D Dunnette (Chicago: Rand McNally, 1976).

[32]R R Blake and J S Mouton, "A Comparative Analysis of Situationalism and 9,9 Management by Principle," *Organizational Dynamics,* Spring 1982, p 23.

[33]Ibid., pp 28–29. Also see R R Blake and J S Mouton, "Management by Grid Principles or Situationalism: Which?" *Group & Organization Studies,* December 1981, pp 439–55.

[34]Ibid., p 21.

[35]Results can be found in M R Redmond, M D Mumford, and R Teach, "Putting Creativity to Work: Effects of Leader Behavior on Subordinate Creativity," *Organizational Behavior and Human Decision Processes,* June 1993, pp 120–51.

[36]See Bass, *Bass & Stogdill's Handbook of Leadership: Theory, Research, and Managerial Applications,* ch. 20–25.

[37]R Tait, *Roads to the Top* (Basingstoke: Macmillan Press Ltd, 1995), p 105.

[38]F E Fiedler, "Job Engineering for Effective Leadership: A New Approach," *Management Review,* September 1977, p 29.

[39]For more on this theory, see F E Fiedler, "A Contingency Model of Leadership Effectiveness," in *Advances in Experimental Social Psychology,* vol. 1, ed L Berkowitz (New York: Academic Press, 1964); F E Fiedler, *A Theory of Leadership Effectiveness* (New York: McGraw-Hill, 1967).

[40]Additional information on situational control is contained in F E Fiedler, "The Leadership Situation and the Black Box in Contingency Theories," in *Leadership Theory and Research: Perspectives and Directions,* eds M M Chemers and R Ayman (New York: Academic Press, 1993), pp 2–28.

[41]See L H Peters, D D Hartke, and J T Pohlmann, "Fiedler's Contingency Theory of Leadership: An Application of the Meta-Analyses Procedures of Schmidt and Hunter," *Psychological Bulletin,* March 1985, pp 274–85.

[42]The meta-analysis was conducted by C A Schriesheim, B J Tepper, and L A Tetrault, "Least Preferred Co-Worker Score, Situational Control, and Leadership Effectiveness: A Meta-Analysis of Contingency Model Performance Predictions," *Journal of Applied Pyschology,* August 1994, pp 561–73. Also see A Bryman, "Leadership in Organizations," in *Handbook of Organization Studies,* eds S R Clegg, C Hardy, and W R Nord (London: Sage, 1996), pp 276–92.

[43]For more detail on this theory, see R J House, "A Path–Goal Theory of Leader Effectiveness," *Administrative Science Quarterly,* September 1971, pp 321–38.

[44]Adapted from R J House and T R Mitchell, "Path–Goal Theory of Leadership," *Journal of Contemporary Business,* Autumn 1974, p 83.

[45]See R Hooijberg, "A Multidirectional Approach toward Leadership: An Extension of the Concept of Behavioral Complexity," *Human Relations,* July 1996, pp 917–46.

[46]Based on A Brown, "Top of the Bosses," *International Management,* April 1994, pp 26–31.

[47]Results can be found in P M Podsakoff, S B MacKenzie, M Ahearne, and W H Bommer, "Searching for a Needle in a Haystack: Trying to Identify the Illusive Moderators of Leadership Behaviors," *Journal of Management,* 1995, pp 422–70.

[48]A thorough discussion of this theory is provided by P Hersey and K H Blanchard, *Management of Organizational Behavior: Utilizing*

Human Resources, 5th ed (Englewood Cliffs, NJ: Prentice-Hall, 1988).

[49]A comparison of the original theory and its latent version is provided by P Hersey and K Blanchard, "Great Ideas Revisited," *Training & Development,* January 1996, pp 42–47.

[50]Results can be found in J R Goodson, G W McGee, and J F Cashman, "Situational Leadership Theory," *Group & Organization Studies,* December 1989, pp 446–61.

[51]The first study was conducted by R P Vecchio, "Situational Leadership Theory: An Examination of a Prescriptive Theory," *Journal of Applied Psychology,* August 1987, pp 444–51. Results from the study of nurse executives can be found in C Adams, "Leadership Behavior of Chief Nurse Executives," *Nursing Management,* August 1990, pp 36–39.

[52]See D C Lueder, "Don't Be Misled by LEAD," *Journal of Applied Behavioral Science,* May 1985, pp 143–54; and C L Graeff, "The Situational Leadership Theory: A Critical View," *Academy of Management Review,* April 1983, pp 285–91.

[53]C Hampden-Turner, *Charting the Corporate Mind* (Oxford: Basil Blackwell, 1990)

[54]Based on D R Denison, R Hooijberg, and E Quinn, "Paradox and Performance: Toward a Theory of Behavioral Complexity in Managerial Leadership," *Organization Science,* September–October 1995, pp 524–540; Quinn, R. *Beyond Rational Management* (San Francisco: Jossey-Bass, 1988)

[55]For details on these different theories, see J McGregor Burns, *Leadership* (New York: Harper & Row, 1978); N M Tichy and M A Devanna, *The Transformational Leader* (New York: John Wiley & Sons, 1986); J M Kouzes and B Z Posner, *The Leadership Challenge: How to Get Extraordinary Things Done in Organizations* (San Francisco: Jossey-Bass, 1990); B Bass and B J Avolio, "Transformational Leadership: A Response to Critiques," in *Leadership Theory and Research: Perspectives and Directions,* eds M M Chemers and R Ayman (New York: Academic Press, 1993), pp 49–80; B Nanus, *Visionary Leadership* (San Francisco: Jossey-Bass, 1992); and B Shamir, R J House, and M B Arthur, "The Motivational Effects of Charismatic Leadership: A Self-Concept Based Theory," *Organization Science,* November 1993, pp 577–94.

[56]Shamir, House, and Arthur, "The Motivational Effects of Charismatic Leadership: A Self-Concept Based Theory," p 578.

[57]Nanus, *Visionary Leadership,* p 8.

[58]See Ibid; and L Larwood, C M Falbe, M P Kriger, P Miesing, "Structure and Meaning of Organizational Vision," *Academy of Management Journal,* June 1995, pp 740–69.

[59]Based on and translated from J Grobben, "Tien voor Twee," *Knack,* February 2, 1995, pp 40–42.

[60]See G Fuchsberg, " `Visioning' Missions Becomes Its Own Mission," *The Wall Street Journal,* January 7, 1994, p B1.

[61]Results can be found in S A Kirkpatrick and E A Locke, "Direct and Indirect Effects of Three Core Charismatic Leadership Components on Performance and Attitudes," *Journal of Applied Psychology,* February 1996, pp 36–51.

[62]Results can be obtained from T G DeGroot, D S Kiker, and T C Cross, "A Meta-Analysis to Review the Consequences of Charismatic Leadership," paper presented at the annual meeting of the Academy of Management, Cincinnati, Ohio, 1996.

[63]Supporting research can be found in P M Podsakoff, S B MacKenzie, and W H Bommer, "Transformational Leader Behaviors and Substitutes for Leadership as Determinants of Employee Satisfaction, Commitment, Trust, and Organizational Citizenship Behaviors," *Journal of Management,* 1996, pp 259–98; M A Jolson, A J Dubinsky, F J Yammarino, and L B Comer, "Transforming the Salesforce with Leadership," *Sloan Management Review,* Spring 1993, pp 95–106; and R T Keller, "Transformation

Leadership and the Performance of Research and Developmental Project Groups," *Journal of Management,* September 1992, pp 489–501.

[64]See P Bycio, R D Hackett, and J S Allen, "Further Assessments of Bass's (1985) Conceptualization of Transactional and Transformational Leadership," *Journal of Applied Psychology,* August 1995, pp 468–78; and A J Dubinsky, F J Yammarino, M A Jolson, and W D Spangler, "Transformational Leadership: An Initial Investigation in Sales Management," *Journal of Personal Selling & Sales Management,* Spring 1995, pp 17–31.

[65]Results can be found in R J House, W D Spangler, and J Woycke, "Personality and Charisma in the US Presidency: A Psychological Theory of Leader Effectiveness," *Administrative Science Quarterly,* September 1991, pp 364–96.

[66]See B M Bass, "Does the Transactional-Transformational Leadership Paradigm Transcend Organizational and National Boundaries?" *American Psychologist,* Febuary 1997, pp 130–39.

[67]See B Shankar Pawar and K K Eastman, "The Nature and Implications of Contextual Influences on Transformational Leadership: A Conceptual Examination," *Academy of Management Review,* January 1997, pp 80–109; and P Sellers, "What Exactly Is Charisma?" *Fortune,* January 15, 1996, pp 68–75.

[68]Supporting research is summarized by Bass and Avolio, "Transformation Leadership: A Response to Critiques," pp 49–80. The effectiveness of leadership training is discussed by J Huey, "The Leadership Industry," *Fortune,* February 21, 1994, pp 54–56.

[69]The ethics of charismatic leadership is discussed by D Sankowsky, "The Charismatic Leader as Narcissist: Understanding the Abuse of Power," *Organizational Dynamics,* Spring 1995, pp 57–71.

[70]These recommendations were derived from J M Howell and B J Avolio, "The Ethics of Charismatic Leadership: Submission or Liberation," *The Executive,* May 1992, pp 43–54.

[71]See F Dansereau, Jr., G Graen, and W Haga, "A Vertical Dyad Linkage Approach to Leadership within Formal Organizations," *Organizational Behavior and Human Performance,* February 1975, pp 46–78; and R M Dienesch and R C Liden, "Leader–Member Exchange Model of Leadership: A Critique and Further Development," *Academy of Management Review,* July 1986, pp 618–34.

[72]These descriptions were taken from D Duchon, S G Green, and T D Taber, "Vertical Dyad Linkage: A Longitudinal Assessment of Antecedents, Measures, and Consequences," *Journal of Applied Psychology,* February 1986, pp 56–60.

[73]Supporting evidence can be found in A J Kinicki and R P Vecchio, "Influences on the Quality of Supervisor-Subordinate Relations: The Role of Time Pressure, Organizational Commitment, and Locus of Control," *Journal of Organizational Behavior,* January 1994, pp 75–82; and R C Liden, S J Wayne, and D Stilwell, "A Longitudinal Study on the Early Development of Leader–Member Exchanges," *Journal of Applied Psychology,* August 1993, pp 662–74.

[74]See T Keller and F Dansereau, "Leadership and Empowerment: A Social Exchange Perspective," *Human Relations,* February 1995, pp 127–46.

[75]Turnover studies were conducted by G B Graen, R C Liden, and W Hoel, "Role of Leadership in the Employee Withdrawal Process," *Journal of Applied Psychology,* December 1982, pp 868–72; G R Ferris, "Role of Leadership in the Employee Withdrawal Process: A Constructive Replication," *Journal of Applied Psychology,* November 1985, pp 777–81. The career progress study was conducted by M Wakabayashi and G B Graen, "The Japanese Career Progress Study: A 7-Year Follow-Up," *Journal of Applied Psychology,* November 1984, pp 603–14.

[76]S G Green, S E Anderson, and S L Shivers, "Demographic and Organizational Influences on Leader–Member Exchange and Related Work Attitudes," *Organizational Behavior and Human Decision Processes,* May 1996, pp 203–14.

[77]See T A Scandura and G B Graen, "Moderating Effects of Initial Leader–Member Exchange Status on the Effects of a Leadership Intervention," *Journal of Applied Psychology,* August 1984, pp 428–36.

[78]These recommendations are from R P Vecchio, "Are You In or Out with Your Boss?" *Business Horizons,* November–December 1986, pp 76–78.

[79]For an expanded discussion of this model, see S Kerr and J Jermier, "Substitutes for Leadership: Their Meaning and Measurement," *Organizational Behavior and Human Performance,* December 1978, pp 375–403.

[80]See J P Howell, P W Dorfman, and S Kerr, "Moderator Variables in Leadership Research," *Academy of Management Review,* January 1986, pp 88–102.

[81]Results can be found in Podsakoff, MacKenzie, Ahearne, and Bommer, "Searching for a Needle in a Haystack: Trying to Identify the Illusive Moderators of Leadership Behaviors."

[82]For details of this study, see P M Podsakoff, S B MacKenzie, and W H Bommer, "Meta-Analysis of the Relationship between Kerr and Jermier's Substitutes for Leadership and Employee Job Attitudes, Role Perceptions, and Performance," *Journal of Applied Psychology,* August 1996, pp 380–99.

[83]Ibid.

[84]See E McShulskis, "HRM Update: Coaching Helps, But Is Not Often Used," *HRMagazine,* March 1966, pp 15–16; and L McDermott, "Wanted: Chief Executive Coach," *Training & Development,* May 1996, pp 67–70.

[85]For a discussion of superleadership, see C C Manz and H P Sims, Jr., *Superleadership: Leading Others to Lead Themselves* (New York: Berkley Books, 1989).

[86]Based on T Peters, N Austin, *A Passion for Excellence* (Glasgow: Collins, 1985); C D Orth, H E Wilkinson, R C Benfari, "The Manager's Role as Coach and Mentor," *Organizational Dynamics,* 1987, vol 15, no 4, pp 66–74; R D Evered, J C Selman, "Coaching and the Art of Management," *Organizational Dynamics,* 1989, vol 18, pp 16–32.

[87]The scale used to assess readiness to assume the leadership role was taken from A J DuBrin, *Leadership: Research Findings, Practice, and Skills* (Boston: Houghton Mifflin Company, 1995), pp 10–11.

[88]The norms were taken from Ibid.

[89]This exercise was based on one contained in L W Mealiea, *Skills for Managers in Organizations* (Burr Ridge, IL: Irwin, 1994), pp 96–97.

[90]The introduction was quoted from Ibid., p 96.

Seventeen

Managing Occupational Stress

LEARNING OBJECTIVES

When you finish studying the material in this chapter, you should be able to:

1. Define the term *stress*.

2. Describe the three approaches to stress.

3. Describe Matteson and Ivancevich's model of occupational stress.

4. Discuss four reasons why it is important for managers to understand the causes and consequences of stress.

5. Describe spill-over.

6. Explain how stressful life events create stress.

7. Review the model of burnout, and highlight the managerial solutions to reduce it.

8. Explain the mechanisms of social support.

9. Describe the coping process.

10. Discuss the personality characteristic of hardiness.

11. Discuss the Type A behaviour pattern and its management implications.

12. Contrast the four dominant stress-reduction techniques.

Alternative Ways to Take Out Stress

Employees in the cable industry are under intense pressure. At the forefront of the information superhighway, technology is advancing rapidly and staff have to adapt constantly to innovations.

At Cable Midlands (UK), which has been supplying cable TV, telephone and information services in the Black Country and Telford areas for four years, frequent changes in working practices reflect shifting priorities. The company is also experiencing rapid growth, having recently won the franchises to provide cable services in the Worcester and Redditch areas. It expects its 580 staff on five sites to increase to around 700 by the end of this year. In addition, the company's recent merger with Telewest Communications Group, the largest cable operator in the UK, has raised the subject of cultural change.

As HR manager, I was aware that Cable needed to take steps to alleviate employee stress, particularly in the light of the Walker vs. Northumberland County Council case. Stress was increasingly becoming a problem. It was clear that if the organization was to achieve more demanding business objectives, it was going to have to provide practical help for all employees.

In September 1995, after reviewing the options for an employee assistance programme, the HR team decided to test the water by offering stress management courses. The company decided that traditional assistance programmes offering a free telephone enquiry line and, usually, a limited number of free counselling sessions, did not go far enough. So our team of internal training consultants began to consider the alternatives.

Steve Miller, a training consultant and stress management specialist, argued that "employee assistance" should be more widely interpreted. He recognized the need for a range of support mechanisms so that staff could pick and choose those most useful to them.

Miller, who had previously implemented stress management workshops in a health service trust, was eager to offer similar workshops at Cable. He also advised that while there was a place for time management, assertiveness training and other traditional methods of dealing with employee stress, the company could benefit from a range of complementary therapies.

Senior management was sceptical of the workshops at first, and the pilot sessions, diplomatically entitled "Managing pressure to maximize performance," were initially offered only to managers. However, the reaction at this level was so positive that we decided to open up the programme to nonmanagers, as stress was affecting people at all levels of the organization, particularly those dealing directly with customers.

Around 120 employees have now attended the stress workshops, which are held twice a month. The results have been encouraging. Managers feel that the sessions have raised awareness of the need to manage stress and offer practical measures to support staff in their roles. The company hopes that by the end of this year half of the workforce will have attended one of these workshops.

Meanwhile, Miller and Gina Crighton, his fellow training consultant, explored a range of therapies that would help people to cope with stress outside work, but at the same time would add value to the company.

One of the pilot schemes allowed managers to spend two days assessing their own stress levels, identifying stress symptoms and exploring strategies to manage stressful circumstances in the future. These strategies included clinical hypnosis.

Mind over matter

The employee assistance programme has now been developed further. It includes a range of both conventional and complementary approaches. Miller has introduced training sessions in clinical hypnosis to teach individuals practical relaxation techniques to complement the workshops.

Pointing out that stress-related illness is a major concern for business, Chris Guest, Cable's network design supervisor, says of one of the sessions: "Hypnosis helped us to move into a deep state of relaxation, something we all need in a fast-moving business." Other employees have claimed that hypnosis has boosted their confidence and self-esteem and even helped them to quit smoking. Some have bought hypnosis tapes for use at home. Aromatherapy and reflexology, also used to aid relaxation and relieve stress, are now offered to staff and managers at lunchtimes as well as in the workshops. Employees can learn about the use of aromatic oils and

massage to reduce muscular tension, while reflexology uses pressure points on the feet to relieve stress. These two techniques have proved popular. Many employees have decided to make appointments with aromatherapists and reflexologists in their own time.

Confidential counselling, along the lines of more conventional employee assistance programmes, is also available to any employee. Individuals are allowed up to six sessions with a counsellor from the South Birmingham Mental Health Trust staff support department. If more time is needed, the trust will provide this with the company's permission, while still guaranteeing confidentiality.

The HR team rejected the idea of a telephone helpline in the belief that true counselling means a face-to-face experience and that staff must be made to feel comfortable within a supportive environment. Although an individual has to ring up the counsellors to arrange a meeting, no advice is offered over the telephone. The personal approach also means that employees can speak to the same counsellor every time they seek help. Over several weeks, the consistency of this approach provides more effective counselling than a telephone helpline can provide.

Cable also offers its employees technical awareness training. Mick Taggart, a technical training consultant, claims that inability to understand new technology is a major cause of stress in the workplace. He has helped to develop a training centre where employees are coached to understand the key technical areas of the business.

Cable now plans to offer yoga and exercise classes, as well as sessions on healthy eating and creating a positive image. Other events planned for the future include a follow-up stress management course for staff who attended the initial sessions. These "Stress 2" programmes will help participants to focus on the psychological aspects of managing stress.

Steve Miller is also planning to look at techniques for maintaining creativity and managing perception. He believes that negative thought processes are a common source of stress. "If we control and programme our thoughts from the negative to the positive, it will help us to overcome the difficult situations often faced in work," he says.

All these classes will take place during lunchtimes, so staff will be able to sample a variety of alternative approaches to maintaining health and well-being.

The team hopes to recoup the investment by reducing levels of sickness absence by 2 per cent over the next 18 months and by reducing staff turnover.

The latest signs are that the programme is well on its way to achieving these goals. Sickness absence has been reduced by about 1 per cent over the past six months, while staff turnover in certain departments has also fallen. There is a genuine feeling that the company cares about the welfare of its employees.[1]

Discussion Question
Are you open to alternative stress programmes?

Work not only provides us with income, recognition, or other positive outcomes. It can also be a source of conflict, overload, burnout and tension. Due to increased competition, employees are being asked to deliver a better quality and a greater quantity of work in less time and with fewer resources. The triad quality–speed–flexibility might contribute to the organization's well-being, but it might be very detrimental to the employee's physical and psychological health as well.

Work is the major cause of stress, according to a survey of more than 5,000 office workers in 16 countries. More than half of respondents said stress levels had risen over the past two years and almost one in five took time off because of stress.[2]

The biggest contributor to work stress revolves around fundamental changes occurring in many organizations. Technological advancements make it harder for employees to completely disconnect from the office. Pagers, fax machines, e-mail, and cellular phones make it easy to disrupt our free time while at home or during vacations. Finally, the dynamics of modern life make it difficult to balance the demands between work and home. Research demonstrates that work stress spills over into one's personal life and vice versa.[3]

All told, the incidence of stress is rising. This trend is supported by the dramatic growth in the number of published articles, magazines, and self-help books on the topic of stress. The amount of published material doubled between 1980 and 1990.[4] Figure 17–1 shows the stress rates in the EC's 1991 twelve member states.

Although stress cannot be completely eliminated, it can be reduced and managed. With this end in mind, this chapter discusses the foundation of stress, examines stressors and burnout, highlights four moderators of occupational stress, and explores a variety of stress-reduction techniques.

Defining Stress

Stress

Behavioural, physical, or psychological response to stressors.

Formally defined, **stress** is "an adaptive response, mediated by individual characteristics and/or psychological processes, that is a consequence of any external action, situation, or event that places special physical and/or psychological demands upon a person."[5] This definition is not as difficult as it seems when we reduce it to three interrelated dimensions of stress: (1) environmental demands, referred to as stressors, that produce (2) an adaptive response that is influenced by (3) individual differences.

One can look at stress from at least three different viewpoints: the medical, the clinical and OB.

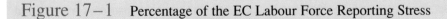

Figure 17–1   Percentage of the EC Labour Force Reporting Stress

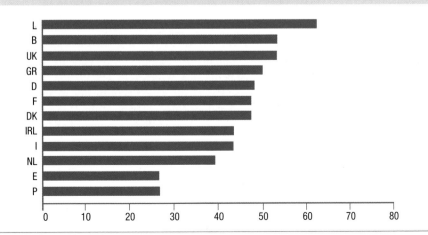

Source: Commission to the European Communities, 1998.

The Medical Approach to Stress

The medical model of stress gives us an idea of the physical changes our body goes through when under stress. It focuses on physical stressors, such as heat or noise or biological stressors, like contagious diseases. The outcomes are primarily physical: hormonal changes or higher blood pressure can be measured. The body has excellent physiological mechanisms to respond to sudden short-term physical emergencies. Researchers in the medical tradition conclude that stress triggers one of two basic reactions: active fighting or passive flight (running away or acceptance), the so-called **fight-or-flight response**[6]. Physiologically, this stress response is a biochemical "passing gear" involving hormonal changes that mobilize the body for extraordinary demands.

Fight-or-flight response
To either confront stressors or try to avoid them.

Imagine how our prehistoric ancestors responded to the stress associated with a charging sabre-toothed tiger. To avoid being eaten, they could stand their ground and fight the beast or run away. In either case, their bodies would have been energized by an identical hormonal change, involving the release of adrenaline into the bloodstream. According to stress specialist Robert M. Sapolsky:

You and I are more likely to get an ulcer than a zebra is. For animals, like zebras, the most upsetting things in life are acute physical stressors. You are that zebra, a lion has just leapt out and ripped your stomach open, you've managed to get away, and now you have to spend the next hour evading the lion as its continues to stalk you. Or, perhaps just as stressfully, you are that lion, half starved, and you had better be able to sprint across the savanna at top speed and grab something to eat or you won't survive. These are extremely stressful events, and they demand immediate physiological adaptations if you are going to live. Your body's responses are brilliantly adapted for handling this sort of emergency.[7]

In today's hectic, urbanized and industrialized society, charging beasts have been replaced by problems such as deadlines, role conflict and ambiguity, financial responsibilities, traffic congestion, noise and air pollution, family problems, and work overload. As with our ancestors, our response to stress may or may not trigger negative side effects, including headaches, ulcers, insomnia, heart attacks, high blood pressure, and strokes. The same stress response that helped our prehistoric ancestors survive has too often become a factor that seriously impairs our daily lives. Consider the following three examples:

An advertising salesman treated by Bruce Yaffe, a New York internist, screamed so loudly when he argued with his boss that he punctured a lung. Another patient, an office receptionist, had such severe stress-induced vomiting that she eventually had to quit her job. And a third, a Wall Street broker treated by physician Larry Lerner for hypertension, was so certain his death was imminent that he refused to take his children to the park for fear they would be abandoned when he died.[8]

Hans Selye, considered the father of the modern concept of stress, started the stress-research within this paradigm. A Prague physician, who had emigrated to Canada, Selye was struck as a medical student by the fact that patients suffering from the most diverse diseases had so many symptoms in common: losing appetite, energy, weight. He felt sure that the syndrome of just being sick, which is essentially the same no matter what disease we have, could be analysed and expressed scientifically. Years later, trying to find a new sex hormone in rats, he developed the concept of the General Adaptation Syndrome or GAS. His experiments with rats showed that continuous exposure to any noxious agent— high and low temperatures, shocks, intense noises—was always followed by a stage of adaption or resistance.

According to Selye, whatever creates the stress, the body reacts in the same way: only the organs that break down differ from body to body. In other words, the origin of the stressors is unimportant: they may originate in life events, in social relationships, or in private events.

The GAS encompasses three stages. During the alarm stage, the individual responds to a signal by going into a state of alarm: breathing rate and heart rate both accelerate. Next, the body enters into the stage of resistance: through various coping mechanisms, the body adapts itself to the new situation and appears to resist the stressors. If those stressors are repeated, or if they are prolonged because of recurring problems, they may cause irreversible physiological damage. At that moment, the body enters into the third stage of the GAS: the exhaustion stage. Resistance is no longer possible. Exhaustion creates diseases of adaptation: such as cardiovascular and kidney diseases, which may be followed by death. Moreover, Selye emphasized that both positive and negative events can trigger a stress response. He also noted that

- Stress is not merely nervous tension.

- Stress can have positive consequences.

- Stress is not something to be avoided.

- The complete absence of stress is death.[9]

Selye was right in pointing to the positive aspects of stress. All learning implies at least a moderate amount of stress. Regular exposure to a manageable amount of stress keeps us fit. With too little stress we feel bored. Although a moderate amount of stress seems to be beneficial, research is especially. focused on 'excessive' stress. What conditions cause excessive stress and how can it be alleviated or even be eliminated?[10]

The Clinical Approach to Stress

The clinical approach differs only in one respect from the medical: physical stressors and outcomes are replaced by psychological ones. This approach stresses the psychological adaptations of our body when submitted to stressors. Neither the medical nor the clinical approach was initially geared towards organizational stressors. They have, however, been applied increasingly in an occupational context, notably in a substantial number of Employee Assistance Programs. EAPs are discussed on p 523.

The fundamental premise is Shakespeare's: "There is nothing either good or bad, but thinking makes it so:"[11] stressors are not an objective fact, but are perceived as such. People evaluate the same stressors differently. For example, some individuals perceive unemployment as a positive, liberating experience, whereas others perceive it as a negative, debilitating one.[12]

Cognitive appraisal reflects an individual's overall evaluation of a situation or stressor and results in a categorization of the situation or stressor as either harmful, threatening, or challenging. It is important to understand the differences among these appraisals because they influence how people react. This idea will play a key role in what we will discuss under Coping, (p 515).

A second basic idea in the clinical approach is that stress is the difference between demands and resources, between load or burden and capacity or strength. Stress is then presented as a balance, where the weights of the stressors should be counterbalanced by the person's resilience. For that reason, stress management consists of two basic endeavours: reducing the demands and strengthening the resources.

The OB Approach to Stress

Contrary to both the medical and the clinical model, the OB approach interprets stress in a wider context: it not only includes physical or psychological elements, but also organizational ones. As illustrated in Figure 17–2, stressors lead to stress, which, in turn, produces a variety of outcomes. The model also specifies several individual differences that *moderate* the stressor–stress–outcome relationship. A moderator is a variable that causes the relationship between two variables—such as stress and outcomes—to be stronger for some people and weaker for others.

Figure 17–2   A Model of Occupational Stress

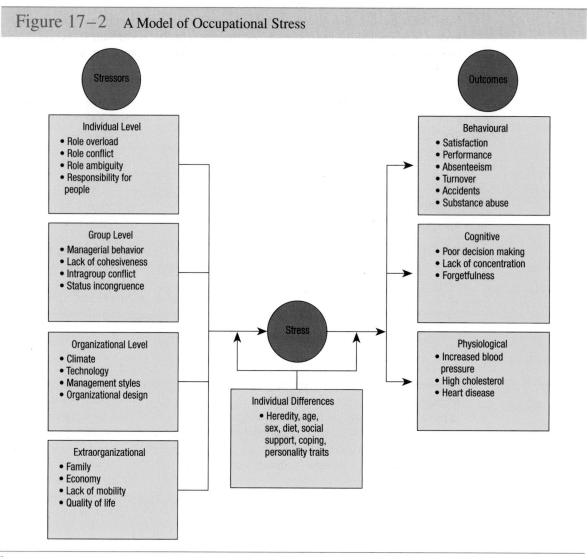

Source: Adapted from M T Matteson and J M Ivancevich, "Organizational Stress and Heart Disease: A Research Model," *Academy of Management Review*, July 1979, p 350. Used with permission.

For example, a study of 256 employees in a business office of a large retail organization investigated whether allowing workers to use personal-stereo headsets influenced the relationship between job characteristics and a variety of work outcomes. Results revealed that employees who used stereo headsets had significant improvements in performance, turnover intentions, job satisfaction, and mood. Use of personal-stereo headsets moderated the effects of stress.[13]

Stressors

Environmental factors that produce stress.

Stressors   **Stressors** are environmental factors that produce stress. Stated differently, stressors are a prerequisite to experiencing the stress response. Figure 17–2 shows the four major types of stressors: individual, group, organizational, and extraorganizational. Individual-level stressors are those directly associated with a person's job duties. For example, experts estimate that in the US alone more than 10 million workers have computer-related vision problems each year that require a trip to an optometrist. Forty per cent of these people use special glasses while working with video display terminals.[14] The most common examples of stressors are workload, role conflict, and role ambiguity. As discussed in Chapter 10, these role characteristics create stress because they make people feel both overworked and uncertain about what they should be doing.[15] Managers can reduce these stressors by providing direction and support for their employees. Finally, job security is a potent stressor that significantly influences employee attitudes and behaviour. Recent surveys indicate that employees frequently worry about being laid off.[16] Job security is an important stressor to manage because it can result in reduced job satisfaction, organizational commitment, and performance.[17]

Group-level stressors are caused by group dynamics (recall our discussion in Chapter 10) and managerial behaviour. Managers create stress for employees by (1) exhibiting inconsistent behaviours, (2) failing to provide support, (3) showing lack of concern, (4) providing inadequate direction, (5) creating a high productivity environment, and (6) focusing on negatives while ignoring good performance.[18]

As Shirley Fisher, Strathclyde University, states:

"People are putting the screws on other people, to get things done quickly with less financial burden. They want more output for less cost. It doesn't work. What happens is people go off sick and they don't come back to work quickly because they want some time off to relieve the pressure."[19]

Sexual harassment experiences represent another group-level stressor. Studies show that harassing experiences are negatively associated with work, supervision, and promotion satisfaction and are positively related to ambiguity, conflict, and stress.[20]

Organizational stressors affect large numbers of employees. Organizational culture, which was discussed in Chapter 3 is a prime example. For instance, a high-pressure environment that places chronic work demands on employees fuels the stress response.[21] In contrast, research provides preliminary support for the idea that participative management can reduce organizational stress.[22] The office design and general office environment are important organizational-level stressors. Research demonstrates that poor lighting, loud noise, improper placement of furniture, and a dirty or smelly environment are responsible for the creation of stress.[23] Managers are advised to monitor and eliminate stressors.

Extraorganizational stressors are those caused by factors outside the organization. For instance, conflicts associated with balancing one's career and family life are stressful. Consider the situation faced by the following couple:

For the past three years, Arthur and Mary have cared for dying relatives. First it was Mary's mother, who was dying of emphysema. She was unable to care for herself, so the couple took her into their home. She had no health insurance, so the couple was forced to foot her medical expenses, too.

Six months after her mother died, Mary's grandmother got cancer, and Arthur and Mary found themselves caring for another dying relative.

During this time, Mary gave birth to a daughter and a son, one of which was unplanned. She stays home to care for the children; day care is just too expensive. Arthur toils at a Scottsdale [Arizona] resort. On his days off, he cares for the children, while Mary tries to earn some extra money cleaning homes.

Like other working-class people, the couple's anxious quest to make ends meet is a primary concern.[24]

Stress from Arthur and Mary's home life surely impacts on their attitudes and performance at work. Socio-economic status is another extraorganizational stressor. Stress is higher for people with lower socio-economic status, which represents a combination of (1) economic status, as measured by income, (2) social status, assessed by education level, and (3) work status, as indexed by occupation.[25] These stressors are likely to become more important in the future.

The Work–Family Interface   Boundaries between work and family life being very fluid, the separation of work stress and life stress is artificial. The boundaries between work and family are very permeable. Moreover, the conflictual demands of family and role works are one of the strongest stressors.

In theory, the relationship between work and family can take one of three forms:

- Separation.
- Segmentation.
- Spill-over: work problems invade private life and vice versa: family strains adversely affect work outcomes.

In the case of separation, work and family are two totally different things: they take place in a separate world, there is no spill-over. In the case of segmentation, work and family are separated strictly, but work does influence private life as the person involved experiences mental or emotional spill-over. Although segmentators deliberately try to avoid spill-over—for example by doing overtime—unconscious spill-over manifests itself through fatigue, irritability, or a relatively long adaptation period.

The notion of negative spill-over has been the dominant theme in the research area, and especially the asymmetrical character of spill-over: family life is much more disturbed by occupational stress than work by domestic stress. According to estimates, the effect of work on family is three times as intensive as the other way around.

Different elements, positive or negative, are taken from one world to the other, such as attitudes, emotions, and skills. Both worlds demand time and energy. Conflicts seem unavoidable but have an important negative impact on life satisfaction.[26]

Consider the following example:

With family-related issues high on the list of concerns of its relatively young workforce (average age 33) Nike has responded with a number of initiatives with an innovative twist. On 1 April 1994 Nike introduced LifeTrek, a new benefit and compensation program designed around what employees most want and need. One of the items on the program is "Taking care of your family" which consists of a dependent care spending account to which Nike contributes up to 30% of the employee's account balance for employees with household incomes of less than $60,000 annually, a child education savings account to which Nike matches 25 cents for every dollar saved by the employee during a child's four high school years and the Nike Scholarship Fund, which provides renewable undergraduate scholarships ranging from $500 to $3,000 annually, based on academic achievement and financial need.[27]

Outcomes   Theorists contend that stress has behavioural, cognitive, and physiological consequences or outcomes. A large body of research supports the conclusion that stress produces harmful physiological outcomes.[28] But researchers have only begun to examine the relationship between stress and work-related behavioural and cognitive outcomes. These studies indicate that stress is negatively related to job satisfaction, organizational commitment, and performance and positively related to turnover.[29]

Individual Differences   People do not experience the same level of stress or exhibit similar outcomes for a given type of stressor. As discussed later, stressors are less apt to produce stress for people with a strong social support network and those who employ a variety of coping strategies. *Perception* of a stressor is another important moderator. If a stressor is perceived as threatening, an individual tends to experience greater stress and more negative outcomes.

Finally, the personality trait of chronic hostility or cynicism also moderated stress. Research demonstrated that people who were chronically angry, suspicious, or mistrustful were twice as likely to have coronary artery blockages. We all can protect our hearts by learning to avoid these tendencies.[30] In summary, even though researchers have been able to identify several important moderators, a large gap still exists in identifying relevant individual differences.

Important Stressors and Stress Outcomes

As we have seen, stressors trigger stress, which, in turn, leads to a variety of outcomes. This section explores an important category of *extraorganizational* stressors: stressful life events. Burnout, another especially troublesome stress-related outcome, is also examined.

Stressful Life Events

Stressful life events
Life events that disrupt daily routines and social relationships.

Events such as experiencing the death of a family member, being assaulted, moving, ending an intimate relationship, being seriously ill, or taking a big test can create stress. These events are stressful because they involve significant changes that require adaptation and often social readjustment. Accordingly, **stressful life events** are defined as nonwork-related changes that disrupt an individual's lifestyle and social relationships. They have been the most extensively investigated extraorganizational stressors.

Thomas Holmes and Richard Rahe conducted pioneering research on the relationship between stressful life events and subsequent illness. During their research, they developed a widely used questionnaire to assess life stress.[31]

Assessing Stressful Life Events   The *Social Readjustment Rating Scale* developed by Holmes and Rahe, is the dominant method for assessing an individual's cumulative stressful life events. As shown in the OB Exercise, the rating scale consists of 43 life events. Each event has a corresponding value, called a life change unit, representing the degree of social readjustment necessary to cope with the event. The larger the value, the more stressful the event. These values were obtained from a convenience sample of 394 people, who evaluated the stressfulness of each event. (Please take a moment to complete the social readjustment rating scale, and calculate your total life stress score.)

Research revealed a positive relationship between the total score on the social readjustment rating scale and subsequent illness. The interpretative norms reveal that low scores are associated with good health, and larger scores are related to increased chances for illness. A word of caution is in order, however. If you scored above 150, don't head for a sterile cocoon. High scores on the social readjustment rating scale do not guarantee you will become ill. Rather, a high score simply increases one's statistical risk of illness.[32]

Research and Practical Implications   Numerous studies have examined the relationship between life stress and both illness and job performance. Subjects with higher scores on the social readjustment rating scale had significantly more problems with chronic headaches, sudden cardiac death, pregnancy and birth complications, tuberculosis, diabetes, anxiety, depression, and a host of minor physical ailments. Meanwhile, academic and work performance declined as scores on the social readjustment rating scale increased.[33] *Negative* (as opposed to positive) personal life changes were associated with greater susceptibility to colds, job stress, and psychological distress, and lower levels of job satisfaction and organizational commitment.[34] Finally, life events that were *uncontrollable* (e.g., death of spouse), rather than controllable (such as marriage) were more strongly associated with subsequent illness and depression.[35]

The key implication is that employee illness and job performance are affected by extraorganizational stressors, particularly those that are negative and uncontrollable. Because employees do not leave their personal problems at the office door or factory gate, management needs to be aware of external sources of employee stress. As Cary Cooper of the Manchester School of Management argues: "Employers have a duty of care in respect of how they manage not only their equipment or physical environment but also their people, including their workload, their hours of work and perhaps their careers."[36] Once identified, alternative work schedules, training programmes, and/or counselling can be used to help employees cope with these stressors. This may not only reduce costs associated with illnesses and absenteeism, but may also lead to positive work attitudes, better job performance, and reduced turnover, as seen in the opening case on Cable Midlands.

In addition, by acknowledging that work outcomes are affected by extraorganizational stressors, managers may avoid the trap of automatically attributing poor performance to low motivation or lack of ability. Such awareness is likely to engender positive reactions from employees and lead to resolution of problems, not just symptoms. For individuals

OB EXERCISE *The Holmes and Rahe Social Readjustment Rating Scale*

Instructions

Place a check mark next to each event you experienced within the past year. Then add the life change units associated with the various events to derive your total life stress score.

LIFE EVENT	LIFE CHANGE UNIT
_____ Death of spouse	100
_____ Divorce	73
_____ Marital separation from mate	65
_____ Detention in jail or other institution	63
_____ Death of a close family member	63
_____ Major personal injury or illness	53
_____ Marriage	50
_____ Being fired at work	47
_____ Marital reconciliation with mate	45
_____ Retirement from work	45
_____ Major change in the health or behaviour of a family member	44
_____ Pregnancy	40
_____ Sexual difficulties	39
_____ Gaining a new family member (e.g., through birth, adoption, oldster moving in)	39
_____ Major business readjustment (e.g., merger, reorganization, bankruptcy)	39
_____ Major change in financial state (e.g., a lot worse off or a lot better off than usual)	38
_____ Death of a close friend	37
_____ Changing to a different line of work	36
_____ Major change in the number of arguments with spouse (e.g., either a lot more or a lot less than usual regarding childbearing, personal habits)	35
_____ Taking out a mortgage or loan for a major purchase (e.g., for a home, business)	31
_____ Foreclosure on a mortgage or loan	30
_____ Major change in responsibilities at work (e.g., promotion, demotion, lateral transfer)	29
_____ Son or daughter leaving home (e.g., marriage, attending college)	29
_____ Trouble with in-laws	29
_____ Outstanding personal achievement	28
_____ Wife beginning or ceasing work outside the home	26
_____ Beginning or ceasing formal schooling	26
_____ Major change in living conditions (e.g., building a new home, remodeling, deterioration of home or neighborhood)	25
_____ Revision of personal habits (dress, manners, association)	24
_____ Troubles with the boss	23
_____ Major change in working hours or conditions	20
_____ Change in residence	20
_____ Changing to a new school	20
_____ Major change in usual type and/or amount of recreation	19
_____ Major change in church activities (e.g., a lot more or a lot less than usual)	19
_____ Major change in social activities (e.g., clubs, dancing, movies, visiting)	18
_____ Taking out a mortgage or loan for a lesser purchase (e.g., for a car, TV, freezer)	17
_____ Major change in sleeping habits (a lot more or a lot less sleep, or change in part of day when asleep)	16
_____ Major change in number of family get-togethers (e.g., a lot more or a lot less than usual)	15
_____ Major change in eating habits (a lot more or a lot less food intake, or very different meal hours or surroundings)	15
_____ Vacation	13
_____ Christmas	12
_____ Minor violations of the law (e.g., traffic tickets, jaywalking, disturbing the peace)	11

Total score = _____

Interpretative Norms:

Less than 150 = Odds are you will experience good health next year

150--300 = 50% chance of illness next year

Greater than 300 = 70% chance of illness next year

with a high score on the social readjustment rating scale, it would be best to defer controllable stressors, such as moving or buying a new car, until things settle down.

Burnout

Burnout

A condition of emotional exhaustion and negative attitudes.

Burnout is a chronic affective response to very extreme demands from the work environment, especially pressures and conflicts arising from direct contact with and care of other people.[37] Burnout is a stress-induced problem common among members of "helping" professions, such as teaching, social work, employee relations, nursing, and police work. It does not involve a specific feeling, attitude, or physiological outcome anchored to a specific point in time. Rather, **burnout** is a condition that occurs over time and is characterized by physical fatigue, emotional exhaustion, and cognitive weariness[38] and a combination of negative attitudes. Typical negative attitudes are withdrawal and less job involvement, the latter mainly being noticed by highly involved people. Table 17–1 describes 10 attitudinal characteristics of burnout. Experts say a substantial number of people suffer from this problem. For example, a recent national study of 28,000 Americans indicated that more than 50 per cent were burned out.[39] This result implies that burnout is not limited to people working in the helping professions. A study of 180 software professionals from 19 German and Swiss companies revealed a positive association of burnout measures, especially lack of identification, and job stressors and lack of positive features in the work situation, such as control at work, complexity at work, or openness to criticism within the team.[40] To promote better understanding of this important stress outcome, we turn our attention to a model of the burnout process and highlight relevant research and techniques for its prevention.

A Model of Burnout   A model of burnout is presented in Figure 17–3. The fundamental premise underlying the model is that burnout develops in phases. The three key phases are emotional exhaustion, depersonalization, and feeling a lack of personal accomplishment.[41] As shown in Figure 17–3, emotional exhaustion is due to a combination of personal stressors and job and organizational stressors.[42] People who expect a lot from themselves and the organizations in which they work tend to create more internal stress, which, in turn, leads to emotional exhaustion. Similarly, emotional exhaustion is fuelled by having too much work to do, by role conflict, and by the type of interpersonal interactions encountered at work. Frequent, intense face-to-face interactions that are emotionally charged are associated with higher levels of emotional exhaustion.

Over time, emotional exhaustion leads to depersonalization, which is a state of psychologically withdrawing from one's job. This ultimately results in a feeling of being

Table 17–1	Attitudinal Characteristics of Burnout	

ATTITUDE	DESCRIPTION
Fatalism	A feeling that you lack control over your work.
Boredom	A lack of interest in doing your job.
Discontent	A sense of being unhappy with your job.
Cynicism	A tendency to undervalue the content of your job and the rewards received.
Inadequacy	A feeling of not being able to meet your objectives.
Failure	A tendency to discredit your performance and conclude that you are ineffective.
Overwork	A feeling of having too much to do and not enough time to complete it.
Nastiness	A tendency to be rude or unpleasant to your co-workers.
Dissatisfaction	A feeling that you are not being justly rewarded for your efforts.
Escape	A desire to give up and get away from it all.

Source: Adapted from D P Rogers, "Helping Employees Cope with Burnout," *Business,* October–December 1984, p 4.

Figure 17–3   A Model of Burnout

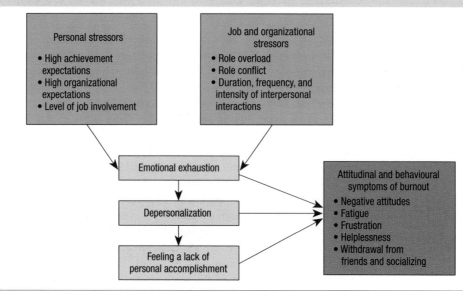

Source: Based in part on C L Cordes and T W Dougherty, "A Review and an Intergration of Research on Job Burnout," *Academy of Management Review*, October 1993, p 641.

unappreciated, ineffective, or inadequate. The additive effect of these three phases is a host of negative attitudinal and behavioural outcomes. Consider the case of Bob Kok:

Former director of internal and external payments of the Dutch bank ABN-AMRO, Bob Kok arrived at the company's health service after a total blackout during an evening meeting. That evening, he suddenly felt a total stranger, although he was in a familiar environment and surrounded by familiar faces. He had no idea what the meeting was about. He even did not recognize his colleagues any more.

He had not anticipated this, in spite of a series of physical warnings. "Only afterwards did I recognize the link between my high blood pressure, pain in the breast, in the hips, loss of sight and my constant fight against fatigue."

After six months of almost permanent sleep, Kok tried to resume his former job, and finally handed in his resignation.[43]

Research Findings and Prevention   A recent meta-analysis of 61 studies covering several thousand people uncovered three important conclusions.[44] First, burnout was positively related to job stressors and turnover intentions and negatively associated with the receipt of supportive resources (e.g., social support and team cohesion), job enhancement opportunities, performance-contingent rewards, organizational commitment, and job satisfaction. Second, the different phases of burnout shown in Figure 17–3 obtained differential relationships with a variety of behavioural and attitudinal symptoms of burnout. This supports the idea that burnout develops in phases. Nonetheless, researchers do not yet completely agree on the order of these phases.[45] Finally, burnout was more strongly related to employees' work demands than it was to the resources people received at work. This suggests that organizations should be particularly sensitive to employees' workloads. The International OB discusses how Zeneca Pharmaceuticals, which is located in the United Kingdom, tried to adhere to this recommendation.

Removing personal stressors and job and organizational stressors is the most straightforward way to prevent burnout. Managers also can reduce burnout by buffering its effects. **Buffers** are resources or administrative changes that alleviate the symptoms of burnout. Potential buffers include extra staff or equipment at peak work periods, support from top management, increased freedom to make decisions, recognition for

Buffers

Resources or administrative changes that reduce burnout.

accomplishments, time off for personal development or rest, and equitable rewards. Decreasing the quantity and increasing the *quality* of communications is another possible buffer. Finally, managers can change the content of an individual's job by adding or eliminating responsibilities, increasing the amount of participation in decision making, altering the pattern of interpersonal contacts, or assigning the person to a new position.[46] There also are two long-term strategies for reducing burnout that are increasingly being used by companies. In the United States, Apple Computer, American Express, IBM, McDonald's Corporation, and Intel, for instance, use sabbaticals to replenish employees' energy and desire to work. These programmes allow employees to take a designated amount of time off from work after being employed a certain number of years. McDonald's grants paid sabbaticals after 10 years of employment; for Intel, it is eight weeks off with pay after seven years for every full-time employee. An employee retreat is the second long-term strategy. Retreats entail sending employees to an offsite location for three to five days. While there, everyone can relax, reflect, or engage in team and relationship building activities. Hallmark Cards uses retreats to help in the fight against burnout.[47] Companies in Canada, Australia and Israel too use sabbaticals to prevent stress and burnout, whereas Europe does not have a sabbatical culture. In The Netherlands, the organization "Stichting Sabbatical Leave" argues that a sabbatical leave should be a right for every employee. When a number of large Dutch companies, such as PTT Telecom, Randstad, and KLM were asked if they were planning to introduce sabbatical leaves in the future, they did not seem to be very enthusiastic.[48]

Organizational Outcomes and Economic Costs of Stress

Some outcomes are of primary importance to the organization. Typical examples are: profits, sales, and innovation. Those organizational performance criteria have not often been related to stress, although on a macrolevel organizational indicators such as absenteeism, turnover, and job performance seem to be strongly correlated with job stress. US industry loses approximately 550 million working days each year due to absenteeism. In terms of job and organizational generated problems, it has been estimated that 54 per cent of these absences are in some way stress-related, that is, created by an unhealthy work environment. Recent figures released by the Confederation of British Industry calculate that in the UK, 360 million working days are lost annually through sickness, at a cost to organisations of £8 billion. Again, it has been estimated by the UK Health and Safety Executive that at least half of these lost days are related to workplace stress.[49] About 80m working days are lost every year because of stress, according to Department of Health figures published at the Confederation of British Industry conference in 1994. Mental health troubles, such as headaches, irritability and indecision, are estimated to cost the UK economy £3.7bn annually. [50]

But researchers have only begun to examine the relationship between stress and work-related outcomes. These studies indicate a negative relationship between stress and turnover, job satisfaction, and performance.[51]

Moderators of Occupational Stress

Social support

One of the most recurring themes in stress-management is the role of social support. There is a widespread conviction that "misery loves company" and the literature on the positive effects of social support on well-being is impressive. But what exactly is social support?

Intuitively one will equate social support with emotional support: a warm, caring, empathic, listening presence. But there are many different manifestations of social support, ranging from simply being there to therapeutic counselling. There are at least four types of social support.[52]

1. *Instrumental social support.* Providing tangible help, financial aid, material resources, or needed services. It is material helping in solve the problems causing the stress.
2. *Emotional support.* Providing sympathy, listening and warm feelings, and accepting and respecting the other person, despite any problems or inadequacies.
3. *Informational support.* Providing information and advice in defining, understanding and solving problems.
4. *Social companionship.* Spending time with others in leisure and recreational activities.

If social support is perceived as available, an individual then decides whether to use it.[53] Generally, support is used for one or both of two purposes. The first purpose is very broad in scope. **Global social support,** encompassing the total amount of support available from the four sources, is applicable to any situation at any time. The narrower **functional social support** buffers the effects of stressors or stress in specific situations. When relied on in the wrong situation, functional social support is not very helpful. For example, if you lost your job, unemployment compensation (instrumental support) would be a better buffer than sympathy from a bartender. On the other hand, social companionship would be more helpful than instrumental support in coping with loneliness. After social support is engaged for one or both of these purposes, its effectiveness can be determined. If consolation or relief is not experienced, it may be that the type of support was inappropriate. The feedback loop in Figure 17–4, from effect of social support back to perceived availability, reflects the need to fall back on other sources of support when necessary.

Global social support

The total amount of social support available.

Functional social support

Support sources that buffer stress in specific situations.

Research Findings and Managerial Lessons   Research shows that global social support is negatively related to physiological processes and mortality. In other words, people with low social support tend to have poorer cardiovascular and immune system functioning and tend to die earlier than those with strong social support networks.[54] Further, global support protects against depression, psychological well-being, pregnancy complications, anxiety, high blood pressure, and a variety of other ailments. In contrast, negative social support, which amounts to someone undermining another person, negatively affects one's mental health.[55] We would all be well advised to avoid people who try to undermine us. Moreover, there is no clear pattern of results regarding the buffering effects of both global and functional social support. It appears that social support does buffer against stress, but we do not know precisely when or why.[56] Additional research is needed to figure out this inconsistency. Finally, as suggested in Figure 17–4, global social support is positively related to the availability of support resources; that is, people who interact with a greater number of friends, family, or co-workers have a wider base of social support to draw upon during stressful periods.[57]

International Organizational Behaviour

Zeneca Pharmaceuticals Helps Employees Manage Their Workloads

In the mid-1980s, when the company was still part of ICI, there was a sharp increase in the number of employees suffering from stress-related illness. . . .

In response to these findings, the company introduced measures to help staff avoid stress-related illness. These ranged from one-day workshops to an assessment of mental health as part of employees' medical screening. The company also decided to use its appraisal system to review workload and draft individual development plans, so that staff would have opportunities to develop knowledge and skills matching the demands of their jobs.

Pivotal to the success of these efforts to prevent excessive pressure on employees was a letter from the company's chief executive urging managers to keep track of individuals' workloads, set staff reasonable timescales, and make sure that they had "enough free time for outside pursuits."

Source: A Arkin, "HSE Guide Helps Stress Victims Claim Damages," *People Management,* June 15, 1996, p 10.

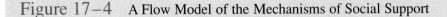

Figure 17–4   A Flow Model of the Mechanisms of Social Support

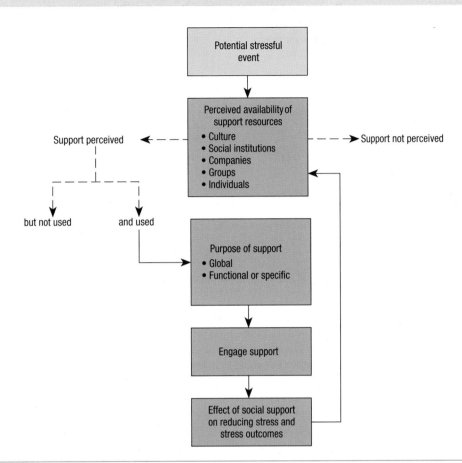

Sources: Portions adapted from S Cohen and T A Wills, "Stress, Social Support, and the Buffering Hypothesis," *Psychological Bulletin,* September 1985, pp 310–57; and J G Bruhn and B U Philips, "Measuring Social Support: A Synthesis of Current Approaches," *Journal of Behavioral Medicine,* June 1984, pp 151–69.

One practical recommendation is to keep employees informed about external and internal social support systems. Internally, managers can use esteem and informational support while administering daily feedback and coaching.[58] Further, participative management programmes and company-sponsored activities that make employees feel they are an important part of an "extended family" can be rich sources of social support. Employees need time and energy to adequately maintain their social relationships. If organizational demands are excessive, employees' social relationships and support networks will suffer, resulting in stress-related illness and decreased performance. Also, the positive effects of social support are enhanced when functional support is targeted precisely.

Coping

Coping

Process of managing stress and stressors.

Coping is "the process of managing demands (external or internal) that are appraised as taxing or exceeding the resources of the person."[59] Because effective coping helps reduce the impact of stressors and stress, your personal life and managerial skills can be enhanced by better understanding this process. Figure 17–5 depicts an instructive model of coping.

The coping process has three major components: (1) situational and personal factors, (2) cognitive appraisals of the stressor, and (3) coping strategies. As shown in Figure

Figure 17–5 A Model of the Coping Process

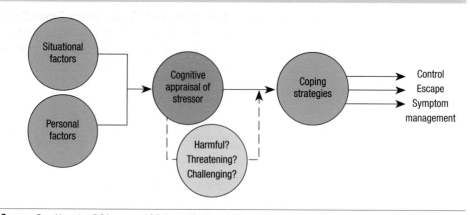

Source: Based in part on R S Lazarus and S Folkman, "Coping and Adaptation," in *Handbook of Behavioral Medicine*, ed W D Gentry (New York: The Guilford Press, 1984), pp 282–325.

17–5, both situational and personal factors influence the appraisal of stressors. In turn, appraisal directly influences the choice of coping strategies. Each of the major components of this model deserves a closer look.

Situational and Personal Factors Situational factors are environmental characteristics that affect how people interpret (appraise) stressors. For example, the ambiguity of a situation—such as walking down a dark street at night in an unfamiliar area—makes it difficult to determine whether a potentially dangerous situation exists. Ambiguity creates differences in how people appraise and subsequently cope with stressors. Other situational factors are the frequency of exposure to a stressor and social support networks.

Personal factors are personality traits and personal resources that affect the appraisal of stressors. For instance, because being tired or sick can distort the interpretation of stressors, an extremely tired individual may appraise an innocent question as a threat or challenge. Traits such as locus of control, self-esteem, self-efficacy (recall our discussion in Chapter 4), and work experience were also found to affect the appraisal of stressors.[60]

Cognitive Appraisal of Stressors Cognitive appraisal reflects an individual's overall evaluation of a situation or stressor. Appraisal is an important component within the stress process because people appraise the same stressors differently. For example, some individuals perceive unemployment as a positive, liberating experience, whereas others perceive it as a negative, debilitating one.[61]

Cognitive appraisal results in a categorization of the situation or stressor as either harmful, threatening, or challenging. It is important to understand the differences among these appraisals because they influence how people cope. "'Harm' (including loss) represents damage already done; 'threat' involves the potential for harm; and 'challenge' means the potential for significant gain under difficult odds."[62] Coping with harm usually entails undoing or reinterpreting something that occurred in the past because the damage is already done. In contrast, threatening situations engage anticipatory coping. That is, people cope with threat by preparing for harm that may occur in the future. Challenge also activates anticipatory coping. In contrast with threat, an appraisal of challenge results in coping that focuses on what can be gained rather than what may be lost.

Coping Strategies Coping strategies are characterized by the specific behaviours and cognitions used to cope with a situation. People use a combination of three approaches to cope with stressors and stress (see Figure 17–5). The first, called a **control strategy,** consists of using behaviours and cognitions to directly anticipate or solve problems. A control strategy has a take-charge tone. Consider the control strategy used by President

Control strategy

Coping strategy that directly confronts or solves problems.

Clinton and his White House senior adviser George Stephanopoulos in October 1993, when Clinton was delivering a televised speech to the nation:

> Minutes before speech time, White House Senior Advisor George Stephanopoulos rushed in with the final version, but the aide running the TelePrompTer accidentally hit the wrong computer button, merging the new speech with the February economic address to Congress, still in the system. No one realized the mistake until Clinton himself reached the podium and saw the old speech on the TelePrompTer. With a stricken look, he turned to Al Gore and said, "We have to get this fixed." Gore alerted Stephanopoulos. . . . Stephanopoulos quickly found White House word whiz David Dreyer, who had a copy on a floppy disk in his laptop computer. When aides couldn't load it into the system, Steph says, he momentarily "went numb." It took a full seven minutes to get it straightened out. Reading from a written text, Clinton scarcely stumbled until the TelePrompTer caught up with him.[63]

Escape strategy

Coping strategy that avoids or ignores stressors and problems.

In contrast to tackling the problem head-on, an **escape strategy** amounts to avoiding the problem. Behaviours and cognitions are used to avoid or escape situations. Individuals use this strategy when they passively accept stressful situations or avoid them by failing to confront the cause of stress (an obnoxious co-worker, for instance). Finally, a *symptom management strategy* consists of using methods such as relaxation, meditation, or medication to manage the symptoms of occupational stress.[64]

Research Findings and Managerial Recommendations   As suggested by the model in Figure 17–5, an individual's appraisal of a stressor correlates with the choice of a coping strategy.[65] In further support of the coping model, personal factors, appraisal, and coping all significantly predicted psychological symptoms of stress. Nonetheless, research has not clearly identified which type of coping strategy—control, escape, or symptom management—is most effective. It appears that the best coping strategy depends on the situation at hand.[66] Escaping stress—by going on vacation, for example—is sometimes better than confronting a stressor with a control-oriented coping strategy. Researchers are currently trying to determine these contingency relationships.

The preceding results suggest that employees should be taught a contingency approach to coping with organizational stressors. This might begin by helping employees identify those stressors that they perceive as harmful or threatening. Training or managerial support can then be used to help employees manage and possibly eliminate the most serious stressors. The final section of this chapter describes specific techniques for that purpose.

Hardiness

Hardiness

Personality characteristic that neutralizes stress.

Suzanne Kobasa, a behavioural scientist, identified a collection of personality characteristics that neutralize occupational stress. This collection of characteristics, referred to as **hardiness,** involves the ability to perceptually or behaviourally transform negative stressors into positive challenges. Hardiness embraces the personality dimensions of commitment, locus of control, and challenge.[67]

Personality Characteristics of Hardiness   *Commitment* reflects the extent to which an individual is involved in whatever he or she is doing. Committed people have a sense of purpose and do not give up under pressure because they tend to invest themselves in the situation. The extent of commitment, however, is culturally determined, observes Cary Cooper:

> "A UK manager who takes work home is said to be committed to his job. A German manager who did the same would be thought of as incompetent, because part of his job as a manager is to manage his time."[68]

As discussed in Chapter 4, individuals with an *internal locus of control* believe they can influence the events that affect their lives. People possessing this trait are more likely to foresee stressful events, thereby reducing their exposure to anxiety-producing situations. Moreover, their perception of being in control leads "internals" to use proactive coping strategies.

Challenge is represented by the belief that change is a normal part of life. Hence, change is seen as an opportunity for growth and development rather than a threat to security.

Hardiness Research and Application A five-year study of 259 managers from a public utility revealed that hardiness—commitment, locus of control, and challenge—reduced the probability of illness following exposure to stress.[69] The three components of hardiness also were found to directly influence how 276 members of the Israeli Defence Forces appraised stressors and ultimately coped with them. Hardy individuals interpreted stressors less negatively and were more likely to use control coping strategies than unhardy people.[70] Furthermore, additional research demonstrated that hardy individuals displayed lower stress, burnout, and psychological distress and higher job satisfaction than their less hardy counterparts.[71] Finally, a study of 73 pregnant women revealed that hardy women had fewer problems during labour and more positive perceptions about their infants than unhardy women.[72]

One practical offshoot of this research is organizational training and development programmes that strengthen the characteristics of commitment, personal control, and challenge. Because of cost limitations, it is necessary to target key employees or those most susceptible to stress (e.g., air traffic controllers). The hardiness concept also meshes nicely with job design. Enriched jobs are likely to fuel the hardiness components of commitment and challenge. A final application of the hardiness concept is as a diagnostic tool. Employees scoring low on hardiness would be good candidates for stress-reduction programmes.

Type A Behaviour Pattern

Cardiovascular disease is the leading cause of death among adults in Western industrialized countries. Because Type A behaviour was linked to cardiovascular disease, researchers devoted significant effort in identifying Type A characteristics and situations that elicit this behavior pattern.

Type A behaviour pattern
Aggressively involved in a chronic, determined struggle to accomplish more in less time.

Type A Behaviour Defined According to Meyer Friedman and Ray Rosenman (the cardiologists who isolated the Type A syndrome in the 1950s):

Type A behaviour pattern is an action-emotion complex that can be observed in any person who is aggressively involved in a chronic, incessant struggle to achieve more and more in less and less time, and if required to do so, against the opposing efforts of other things or persons. It is not psychosis or a complex of worries or fears or phobias or obsessions, but a socially acceptable—indeed often praised—form of conflict. Persons possessing this pattern also are quite prone to exhibit a free-floating but extraordinarily well-rationalized hostility. As might be expected, there are degrees in the intensity of this behavior pattern.[73]

Since Type A behaviour is a matter of degree, it is measured on a continuum. This continuum has the hurried, competitive Type A behaviour pattern at one end and the more relaxed Type B behaviour pattern at the other. Take a moment to complete the Type A survey in the OB Exercise. This exercise will help you better understand the characteristics of the Type A behaviour pattern. Where did you fall on the Type A continuum?

Type A Characteristics While labelling Type A behaviour as "hurry sickness," Friedman and Rosenman noted that Type A individuals frequently tend to exhibit most of the behaviours listed in Table 17–2. In high-pressure, achievement-oriented schools and work environments, Type A behaviour is unwittingly cultivated and even admired.

The next section highlights the pros and cons of being Type A.

Type A Research and Management Implications OB research has demonstrated that Type A employees tend to be more productive than their Type B co-workers. For instance, Type

Table 17–2   Type A Characteristics

1. Hurried speech; explosive accentuation of key words.
2. Tendency to walk, move, and eat rapidly.
3. Constant impatience with the rate at which most events take place (e.g., irritation with slow-moving traffic and slow-talking and slow-to-act people).
4. Strong preference for thinking of or doing two or more things at once (e.g., reading this text and doing something else at the same time).
5. Tendency to turn conversations around to personally meaningful subjects or themes.
6. Tendency to interrupt while others are speaking to make your point or to complete their train of thought in your own words.
7. Guilt feelings during periods of relaxation or leisure time.
8. Tendency to be oblivious to surroundings during daily activities.
9. Greater concern for things worth having than with things worth being.
10. Tendency to schedule more and more in less and less time; a chronic sense of time urgency.
11. Feelings of competition rather than compassion when faced with another Type A person.
12. Development of nervous tics or characteristic gestures.
13. A firm belief that success is due to the ability to get things done faster than the other guy.
14. A tendency to view and evaluate personal activities and the activities of other people in terms of "numbers" (e.g., number of meetings attended, telephone calls made, visitors received).

Source: Adapted from M Friedman and R H Rosenman, *Type A Behavior and Your Heart* (Greenwich, CT: Fawcett Publications, 1974), pp 100–102.

OB EXERCISE *Where Are You on the Type A–B Behaviour Continuum?*

Instructions

For each question, indicate the extent to which each statement is true of you.

	NOT AT ALL TRUE OF ME	NEITHER VERY TRUE NOR VERY UNTRUE OF ME	VERY TRUE OF ME

1. I hate giving up before I'm absolutely sure that I'm licked.   1 —— 2 —— 3 —— 4 —— 5
2. Sometimes I feel that I shouldn't be working so hard, but something drives me on.   1 —— 2 —— 3 —— 4 —— 5
3. I thrive on challenging situations. The more challenges I have, the better.   1 —— 2 —— 3 —— 4 —— 5
4. In comparison to most people I know, I'm very involved in my work.   1 —— 2 —— 3 —— 4 —— 5
5. It seems as if I need 30 hours a day to finish all the things I'm faced with.   1 —— 2 —— 3 —— 4 —— 5
6. In general, I approach my work more seriously than most people I know.   1 —— 2 —— 3 —— 4 —— 5
7. I guess there are some people who can be nonchalant about their work, but I'm not one of them.   1 —— 2 —— 3 —— 4 —— 5
8. My achievements are considered to be significantly higher than those of most people I know.   1 —— 2 —— 3 —— 4 —— 5
9. I've often been asked to be an officer of some group or groups.   1 —— 2 —— 3 —— 4 —— 5

Total score = _____

Arbitrary Norms

Type B	= 9--22
Balanced Type A and Type B	= 23--35
Type A	= 36--45

SOURCE   Taken from R D Caplan, S Cobb, J R P French, Jr., R Van Harrison, and S R Pinneau, Jr., *Job Demands and Worker Health* (HEW Publication No. [NIOSH] 75-160), (Washington, DC: US Department of Health, Education, and Welfare, 1975), pp 253–54.

A behaviour yielded a significant and positive correlation with 766 students' grade point averages, the quantity and quality of 278 university professors' performance, and sales performance of 222 life insurance brokers.[74] On the other hand, Type A behaviour is associated with some negative consequences.

A meta-analysis of 99 studies revealed that Type A individuals had higher heart rates, diastolic blood pressure, and systolic blood pressure than Type B people. Type A people also showed greater cardiovascular activity when they encountered the following situations:

1.   Receipt of positive or negative feedback.

2.   Receipt of verbal harassment or criticism.

3.   Tasks requiring mental as opposed to physical work.[75]

Unfortunately for Type A individuals, these situations are frequently experienced at work. A second meta-analysis of 83 studies further demonstrated that the hard-driving and competitive aspects of Type A are related to coronary heart disease, but the speed and impatience and job involvement aspects are not. This meta-analysis also showed that feelings of anger, hostility, and aggression were more strongly related to heart disease than was Type A behaviour.[76]

Do these results signal the need for Type A individuals to quit working so hard? Not necessarily. First, the research indicated that feelings of anger, hostility, and aggression were more detrimental to our health than being Type A. We should all attempt to reduce these negative emotions.

Second, researchers have developed stress-reduction techniques to help Type A people pace themselves more realistically and achieve better balance in their lives; they are discussed in the next section of this chapter. Management can help Type A people, however, by not overloading them with work despite their apparent eagerness to take an ever-increasing work load. Managers need to actively help rather than unthinkingly exploit Type A individuals because the premature disability or death of valued employees poses fundamental questions.

Stress-Reduction Techniques

It is, therefore, not surprising that organizations are increasingly implementing a variety of stress-reduction programs to help employees cope with modern-day stress. Consider the following examples:

A letter from the CEO and the active support of high management levels enhanced the staff's credibility in the strategy. A fall in the number of stress cases, continuing growth in profitability and improved commitment and efficiency prove that it has paid off.[77] In a radical change of direction some [senior managers] are looking to meditation, therapy, breathing work, complementary medicine and psychological profiling to keep themselves going on the daily treadmill. [. . .] In fact, companies including IBM, British Airways, BT, Shell, Barclays Bank and BP are turning to innovative ways of boosting the performance of their staff.[78]

There are many different stress-reduction techniques available. The four most frequently used approaches are muscle relaxation, biofeedback, meditation, and cognitive restructuring. Each method involves somewhat different ways of coping with stress (see Table 17–3).

Stress interventions can focus on the individual, the organization or on the interface between individual and organization (e.g. through participation)[79] Most workplace stress initiatives focus on individual stress management training, relaxation techniques, or counselling[80] and not on reducing the sources of organizational stress, e.g., by redesigning tasks. The different stress reduction therapies that are available can be

Table 17–3   Stress-Reduction Techniques

TECHNIQUE	DESCRIPTIONS	ASSESSMENT
Muscle relaxation	Uses slow deep breathing, systematic muscle tension reduction, and an altered state of consciousness to reduce stress.	Inexpensive and easy to use; may require a trained professional to implement.
Biofeedback	A machine is used to train people to detect muscular tension; muscle relaxation is then used to alleviate this symptom of stress.	Expensive due to costs of equipment; however, equipment can be used to evaluate effectiveness of other stress-reduction programs.
Meditation	The relaxation response is activated by redirecting one's thoughts away from oneself; a four-step procedure is used.	Least expensive, simple to implement, and can be practiced almost anywhere.
Cognitive restructuring	Irrational or maladaptive thoughts are identified and replaced with those that are rational or logical.	Expensive because it requires a trained psychologist or counselor.
Holistic wellness	A broad, interdisciplinary approach that goes beyond stress reduction by advocating that people strive for personal wellness in all aspects of their lives.	Involves inexpensive but often behaviorally difficult lifestyle changes.

classified as somatic, cognitive, or behavioural. Some techniques deal almost exclusively with the bodily, somatic aspects, while other concentrate on the cognitive restructuring, a third group concentrating on the so-called coping behaviours.

Each new day sees its newest stress reduction technique, from music to aerobic exercise.

Muscle Relaxation

Tension and relaxation do not match. A deliberate and successful attempt to relax will therefore decrease tensions, including psychological strain. The relaxation response is the physiological opposite of the fight-or-flight response. Importantly, however, the relaxation response must be learned and consciously activated, whereas the stress response is automatically engaged. The common denominators of various muscle relaxation techniques are slow and deep (abdominal) breathing, a conscious effort to relieve muscle tension and a change in the brainwaves, which is experienced as an altered state of consciousness. Among the variety of techniques available, progressive relaxation—first devised by Edmund Jacobson in 1938—is probably the most frequently used, and is very popular among psychotherapists. The classical Jacobsonian method teaches the trainee to recognize and control the most subtle muscular tonus. Abbreviated methods focus on the active creation of relaxation, in combination with the use of some hypnotic-like relaxation suggestions. In practice, it consists of repeatedly tensing and relaxing muscles beginning at the feet and progressing to the face. Relaxation is achieved by concentrating on the warmth and calmness associated with relaxed muscles. Consider the following ad for Office ROMance:

Turn off the lights, switch on your computer, make sure that the office door is firmly closed. Enter the world of Digital Love, the creation of Hex, a small London-based multimedia company. Digital Love is a CD-ROM relaxation programme that uses ambient sounds and hypnotic visuals to take the viewer into what is claimed to be a meditative state. Ten minutes of digitally included trance a day, its maker claims, will lower the heart rate and ease the stress of even the most anxious executive.

Unsurprisingly, Hex's products (described as Eyepopping Rave and NarcoVideo) are not aimed at the business market. Director Robert Peperell admits that it might be too weird for the average

British business person and expects most sales to come from home PC users and the more open-minded youtï

"It's not a normal way to use a computer and people don't quite know how to react on it," Peperell notes. "All the same," he adds, "I hope that a few brave people in business will discover that it is not embarrassing and, more to the point, that it works."[81]

Biofeedback

Biofeedback makes somatic information available to the person. A biofeedback machine is used to train people to detect and control stress-related symptoms such as tense muscles and elevated blood pressure. The machine measures the physiological tension. The result is shown to the person by means of a flashing light, a beeper, or simply a measurement. Based on this information one can learn to relax that group of muscles. Gradually the person learns to recognize bodily tension and to relax without the aid of the machine. Being highly specific, biofeedback is usually combined with more general techniques.

Meditation

Relaxation response
State of peacefulness.

Meditation is an intrinsic part of the Eastern practice of Yoga, which in its turn is an essential component of the Hindu culture for over 2000 years. In the West therapists have westernized the meditation procedures, removing them from the Hindu philosophy and making them more technicial and efficient. Meditation activates a relaxation response by redirecting one's thoughts away from oneself. The **relaxation response** is the physiological and psychological opposite of the fight-or-flight stress response. Importantly, however, the relaxation response must be learned and consciously activated, whereas the stress response is automatically engaged. Herbert Benson, a Harvard medical doctor, analysed many meditation programmes and derived a four-step relaxation response. The four steps are (1) find a *quiet environment,* (2) use a *mental device* such as a peaceful word or pleasant image to shift the mind from externally oriented thoughts, (3) disregard distracting thoughts by relying on a *passive attitude,* and (4) assume a *comfortable position*—preferably sitting erect—to avoid undue muscular tension or going to sleep. Benson emphasizes that the most important factor is a passive attitude.[82] Maximum benefits supposedly are obtained by following this procedure once or twice a day for 10 to 20 minutes, preferably just before breakfast and dinner. People following this advice experienced favourable reductions in blood pressure and anxiety levels and slept better.[83] For example, a recent study of 36 men and women between the ages of 55 to 85 showed that blood pressure significantly dropped from 145/94 after using transcendental meditation for three months.[84]

Cognitive Restructuring

Because the clinical approach emphasizes the perception and interpretation of the situation as the central element in the process, it is obvious that one looks for a solution in changing the beliefs.

A two-step procedure is followed. First, irrational or maladaptive thought processes that create strain are identified. For example type A individuals may believe that working is a competition with only a few winners, but many losers, which explains why teamwork can create strain for the Type A person. The second step consists of replacing these irrational thoughts with more rational or reasonable ones. Rational problem solving and effective communication are two basic components of cognitive restructuring. Cognitive restructuring would alleviate the problems by encouraging the person to adopt a more reasonable belief about the outcomes of teamwork. For instance, the person might be encouraged to adopt the belief that criticism in teamwork does not mean hostility. The person will then stop accusing others and creating a stressful environment.

Employment Assistance Programmes (EAPs)

These difficulties are not left behind when an employee comes to work. "Frequently stress in domestic life has knock-on effects at work," says Dr. Michael Turner, chief medical officer at the UK's Texaco, the oil company. To help workers deal with personal and professional anxieties, more than 80 per cent of the companies in the UK offer some form of stress counselling. Approximately 4 per cent now use specialized external counselling services, known as employment assistance programmes.[85]

EAPs are a counselling service for employees and their families. They provide counselling both over work-related and personal problems. One company providing as EAP is the UK brewery Whitbread: a Freefone line can be consulted by staff, their partner, and children up to 21 living at home. They can discuss any problem, because any problem impacts on the employee's efficacy. According to Whitbread's Ian Anderson, "it nips problems in the bud."[86]

Legal Liabilities of Stress

Along with an increase in occupational stress cases, the number of stress-related claims will rise as well. A survey of 65 leading companies, such as Pepsi-Cola International, Trebor-Bassett, Westinghouse Cable, Duracell UK, Du Pont Chemicals, and Lukas Braking Systems has revealed that workload is one of the major causes of stress. This results in increased absenteeism and illness and reduced work performance.[87] According to Jeremy Rutledge from the Association of British Insurers, stress-related claims against employers will take over from repetitive strain injury as the main cause of concern for companies providing employers' liability cover.[88] The companies should be aware of this situation and ensure that their health policies cover stress reduction programmes as well. If they fail to take care of their employees' well-being, they will probably be faced with expensive court cases. Consider the case of John Walker:

John Walker worked for the Northumberland County Council as an area social services officer for 17 years. He led a team of social service field workers in an area of Northumberland with a particularly high child care problem. He came under intense pressure in the 1980s because of a population increase in the area, which produced more child care cases. He asked his employers for more staff and management guidance, but neither was forthcoming.

At the end of 1986, he had a nervous breakdown and was off work until March 1987. He had no previous history of mental disorder. It was common ground that this illness was attributable to his work's impact on his personality.

He returned to work, but in spite of assurances by his superior that the pressure of the job would be relieved, it was not, in any substantial sense. In 1987 he suffered a second nervous breakdown and was obliged to retire from his post. He then brought a claim against his employer for negligence in failing to provide a safe system of work.

The judge found that, although the plaintiff's personality was normal, he had been driven to the point of despair by the defendants' failure to provide him with sufficient resources to satisfy the urgent needs of the people in his area and thereby alleviate the work pressure. He had been trapped in a situation where, on the one hand, he was unable to persuade superior management to increase staff or give management guidance on work distribution or prioritisation. The judge decided that the first breakdown was not reasonably foreseeable, but in respect of the second breakdown he was in no doubt that in the circumstances the superior authorities ought to have foreseen that if the plaintiff were once again exposed to the same workload, there was a risk of another breakdown, likely to result in the end of his social services career. It should have been appreciated that the plaintiff was a man distinctly more vulnerable to psychiatric damage than he had been on the previous occasion.

The additional assistance ought to have been provided, notwithstanding that the defendants could have expected a disruptive effect on the provision of services to the public.

Damages have yet to be assessed, but compensation of £200,000 is being sought by Unison, Mr. Walker's union.[89]

Reacting to the Walker case, organizations are advised by the UK's major employment lawyers to fire employees with stress-related complaints: a judgement by an industrial tribunal for "unfair dismissal" will always turn out cheaper than the damages to be paid for a nervous breakdown.[90]

A recent survey, carried out by the Confederation of British Industry, however, has shown that, although more than 90 per cent of companies claim to take care of the mental health of their staff, only 12 per cent have a programme to deal with it.

Summary of Key Concepts

1. *Define the term* stress. Stress is an adaptive reaction to environmental demands or stressors that triggers a fight-or-flight response. This response creates hormonal changes that mobilize the body for extraordinary demands.

2. *Describe the three approaches to stress.* The medical approach to stress focuses on physical or biological stressors. The clinical approach focuses on psychological stressors and outcomes. The OB approach to stress regards stress as a process, in which stressors produces a variety of outcomes, which can, however, be moderated.

3. *Describe Matteson and Ivancevich's model of occupational stress.* Matteson and Ivancevich's model of occupational stress indicates that stress is caused by four sets of stressors: individual level, group level, organizational level, and extraorganizational. In turn, stress has behavioural, cognitive, and physiological outcomes. Several individual differences moderate relationships between stressors, stress, and outcomes.

4. *Discuss four reasons why it is important for managers to understand the causes and consequences of stress.* First, from a quality-of-work life perspective, workers are more satisfied when they are not under a lot of stress. Second, a moral imperative suggests that managers should reduce stress because it leads to negative outcomes. The third reason relates to the significant economic costs associated with stress. Fourth, because stress-related illnesses may be covered under worker's compensation laws, employers can be sued for exposing employees to undue stress.

5. *Describe spill-over.* Spill-over implies that work problems invade private life and vice versa: family strains adversely affect work outcomes.

6. *Explain how stressful life events create stress.* Stressful life events are changes that disrupt an individual's lifestyle and social relationships. Holmes and Rahe developed the Social Readjustment Rating Scale to assess an individual's cumulative stressful life events. A positive relationship exists between the scores on the social readjustment rating scale and illness. Uncontrollable events that are negative create the most stress.

7. *Review the model of burnout, and highlight the managerial solutions to reduce it.* Burnout develops in phases. The three key phases are emotional exhaustion, depersonalization, and feeling a lack of personal accomplishment. Emotional exhaustion, the first phase, is due to a combination of personal stressors and job and organizational stressors. The additive effect of the burnout phases is a host of negative attitudinal and behavioural outcomes. Managers can reduce burnout by buffering its effects; potential buffers include extra staff or equipment, support from top management, increased freedom to make decisions, recognition for accomplishments, time off, equitable rewards, and increased communication from management. Managers can also change the content of an individual's job or assign the person to a new position. Sabbaticals and employee retreats also are used to reduce burnout.

8. *Explain the mechanisms of social support.* Social support, an important moderator of relationships between stressors, stress, and outcomes, represents the amount of perceived helpfulness derived from social relationships. Cultural norms, social institutions, companies, groups, and individuals are sources of social support. These sources provide four types of support: esteem, informational, social companionship, and instrumental.

9. *Describe the coping process.* Coping is the management of stressors and stress. Coping is directly affected by the cognitive appraisal of stressors, which, in turn, is influenced by situational and personal factors. People cope by using control, escape, or symptom management strategies. Because research has not identified the most effective method of coping, a contingency approach to coping is recommended.

10. *Discuss the personality characteristic of hardiness.* Hardiness is a collection of personality characteristics that neutralizes stress. It includes the characteristics of commitment, locus of control, and challenge. Research has demonstrated that hardy individuals respond less negatively to stressors and stress than unhardy people. Unhardy employees would be good candidates for stress-reduction programs.

11. *Discuss the Type A behaviour pattern and its management implications.* The Type A behaviour pattern is characterized by someone who is aggressively involved in a chronic, determined struggle to accomplish more and more in less and less time. Type B is the opposite of Type A. Although there are several positive outcomes associated with being Type A, Type A behaviour is positively correlated with coronary heart disease. Management can help Type A individuals by not overloading them with work despite their apparent eagerness to take on an ever-increasing work load.

12. *Contrast the four dominant stress-reduction techniques.* Muscle relaxation, biofeedback, meditation, and cognitive restructuring are predominant stress-reduction techniques. Slow and deep breathing, a conscious effort to relieve muscle tension, and altered consciousness are common denominators of muscle relaxation. Biofeedback relies on a machine to train people to detect bodily signs of stress. This awareness facilitates proactive coping with stressors. Meditation activates the relaxation response by redirecting one's thoughts away from oneself. Cognitive restructuring entails identifying irrational or maladaptive thoughts and replacing them with rational or logical thoughts.

Discussion Questions

1. What are the key stressors encountered by students? Which ones are under their control?

2. Describe the behavioural and physiological symptoms you have observed in others when they are under stress.

3. Why do uncontrollable events lead to more stress than controllable events?

4. Why would people in the helping professions become burned out more readily than people in other occupations?

5. Which of the five sources of social support is most likely to provide individuals with social support? Explain.

6. Why would people have difficulty using a control coping strategy to cope with the aftermath of a natural disaster like an earthquake or flood?

7. How can someone increase their hardiness and reduce their Type A behaviour?

8. Have you used any of the stress-reduction techniques? Evaluate their effectiveness.

9. What is the most valuable lesson you learned from this chapter? Explain.

Personal Awareness and Growth Exercise

ARE YOU BURNED OUT?

Objectives

1. To determine the extent to which you are burned out.
2. To determine if your burnout scores are predictive of burnout outcomes.
3. To identify specific stressors that affect your level of burnout.

Introduction

An OB researcher named Christina Maslach developed a self-report scale measuring burnout. This scale assesses burnout in terms of three phases: depersonalization, personal accomplishment, and emotional exhaustion. To determine if you suffer from burnout in any of these phases, we would like you to complete an abbreviated version of this scale. Moreover, because burnout has been found to influence a variety of behavioural outcomes, we also want to determine how well burnout predicts three important outcomes.

Instructions

To assess your level of burnout, complete the following 18 statements developed by Maslach.[91] Each item probes how frequently you experience a particular feeling or attitude. If you are currently working, use your job as the frame of reference for responding to each statement. If you are a full-time student use your role as a student as your frame of reference. After you have completed the 18 items, refer to the score key and follow its directions. Remember, there are no right or wrong answer. Indicate your answer for each statement by circling one number from the following scale:

1 = A few times a year

2 = Monthly

3 = A few times a month

4 = Every week

5 = A few times as week

6 = Every day

BURNOUT INVENTORY

1. I've become more callous towards people since I took this job.   1—2—3—4—5

2. I worry that this job is hardening me emotionally.   1—2—3—4—5

3. I don't really care what happens to some of the people who need my help.   1—2—3—4—5

4. I feel that people who need my help blame me for some their problems.   1—2—3—4—5

5. I deal very effectively with the problems of those peple who need my help.   1—2—3—4—5

6. I feel I'm positively influencing other people's lives through my work   1—2—3—4—5

7. I feel very energetic.   1—2—3—4—5

8. I can easily create a relaxed atmosphere with those people who need my help.   1—2—3—4—5

9. I feel exhilarated after working closely with those who need my help.   1—2—3—4—5

10. I have accomplished many worthwhile things in this job.   1—2—3—4—5

11. In my work, I deal with emotional problems very calmly.   1—2—3—4—5

12. I feel emotionally drained from my work.   1—2—3—4—5

13. I feel used up at the end of the workday.   1—2—3—4—5

14. I feel fatigued when I get up in the morning.   1—2—3—4—5

15. I feel frustrated by my job.   1—2—3—4—5

16. I feel I'm working too hard on my job.   1—2—3—4—5

17. Working with people directly puts too much stress on me.   1—2—3—4—5

18. I feel like I'm at the end of my rope.   1—2—3—4—5

Scoring

Compute the average of those itmes measuring each phase of burnout.

Depersonalization (questions 1–4)

Personal accomplishment (questions 5–11)

Emotional exhaustion (questions 12–18)

Assessing Burnout Outcomes

1. How many times were you absent from work over the last three months (indicate the number of absences from classes last semester if using the student role)?

    __ absences

2. How satisfied are you with your job (or role as a student)? Circle one.

    | Very dissatisfied | Dissatisfied | Neutral | Satisfied | Very satisfied |

2. Do you have trouble sleeping? Circle one.

    Yes   No

QUESTIONS FOR DISCUSSION

1. To what extent are you burned out in terms of depersonalization and emotional exhaustion?

    Low   = 1–2.99
    Moderate = 3–4.99
    High   = 5 or above

2. To what extent are you burned out in terms of personal accomplishment?

    Low   = 5 or above
    Moderate = 3–4.99
    High   = 1–1.299

3. How well do your burnout scores predict your burnout outcomes?

4. Do your burnout scores suggest that burnout follows a sequence going from depersonalization, to feeling a lack of personal accomplishment, to emotional exhaustion? Explain.

5. Which of the unique burnout stressors illustrated in Figure 17–2 are affecting your level of burnout?

Group Exercise

Reducing the Stressors in Your Environment

Objectives

1. To identify the stressors in your environment.

2. To evaluate the extent to which each stressor is a source of stress.

3. To develop a plan for reducing the impact of stressors in your environment.

Introduction

Stressors are environmental factors that produce stress. They are prerequisites to experiencing the symptoms of stress. As previously discussed in this chapter, people do not appraise stressors in the same way. For instance, having to complete a challenging assignment may be motivational for one person and threatening to another. This exercise was designed to give you the opportunity to identify the stressors in your environment, to evaluate the extent to which these stressors create stress in your life, and to develop a plan for reducing the negative effects of these stressors.

Instructions

Your instructor will divide the class into groups of four to six. Once the group is assembled, the group should brainstorm and record a list of stressors that they believe exist in their environments. Use the guidelines for brainstorming discussed in Chapter 12. After recording all the brainstormed ideas on a piece of paper, remove redundancies and combine like items so that the group has a final list of unique stressors. Next, each group member should individually determine the extent to which each stressor is a source of stress in his or her life. For the purpose of this exercise, stress is defined as existing whenever you experience feelings of pressure, strain, or emotional upset. The stress evaluation is done by first indicating the frequency with which each stressor is a source of stress to you. Use the six-point rating scale provided. Once everyone has completed their individual ratings, combine the numerical judgments to compute an average stress score for each stressor. Next, identify the five stressors with the highest average stress ratings. Finally, the group should develop a plan for coping with each of these five stressors. Try to make your recommendations as specific as possible.

Rating Scale

Answer the following question for each stressor: To what extent is the stressor a source of stress?

1 = Never

2 = Rarely

3 = Occasionally

4 = Often

5 = Usually

6 = Always

QUESTIONS FOR DISCUSSION

1. Are you surprised by the type of stressors that were rated as creating the most stress in your lives? Explain.

2. Did group members tend to agree or disagree when evaluating the extent to which the various stressors created stress in their lives? What is the source of the different appraisals?

3. Did your coping plans include more forms of control or escape-oriented coping strategies? Explain.

Notes

[1] S Butler, "Alternative ways to take out stress," *People Management*, May 16, 1996, p 43–44.

[2] "World News in brief: Stress Study," *The Financial Times*, November 16, 1994, p1.

[3] See F Jones and B C Fletcher, "Taking Work Home: A Study of Daily Fluctuations in Work Stressors, Effects on Moods and Impacts on Marital Partners," *Journal of Occupational and Organizational Psychology,* March 1996, pp 89–106; and S Parasuraman, Y S Purohit, V M Godshalk, and N J Beutell, "Work and Family Variables, Entrepreneurial Career Success, and Psychological Well-Being," *Journal of Vocational Behavior,* June 1996, pp 275–300.

[4] See S R Barley, and D B Knight, "Toward a Cultural Theory of Stress Complaints," in *Research in Organizational Behavior,* eds B M Staw, and L L Cummings (Greenwich, CT: JAI Press, 1992),p 1–48.

[5] J M Ivancevich and M T Matteson, *Stress and Work: A Managerial Perspective* (Glenview, IL: Scott, Foresman, 1980), pp 8–9.

[6] The stress response is thoroughly discussed by H Selye, *Stress Without Distress* (New York: Lippincott, 1974).

[7] R Salolsky, *Why Zebras Don't Get Ulcers: A Guide to Stress, Stress-Related Diseases, and Coping* (New York: Freeman, 1994), p 5.

[8] T F O'Boyle, "Fear and Stress in the Office Take Toll," *The Wall Street Journal*, November 6, 1990, p B1.

[9] H Selye, op. cit.

[10]M P Driscoll, and C L Cooper, "Sources and Management of Excessive Job Stress and Burnout," In P Warr, *Psychology at Work.* (Harmondsworth: Peguin, 1996), p 189.

[11]W Shakespeare, *Hamlet,* Act II, Sc. II.

[12]For a thorough review of research on coping with unemployment, see J Lattack, A J Kinicki, and S E Prussia, "An Integrative Process Model of Coping with Job Loss," *Academy of Management Review,* April 1995, pp 311–41.

[13]This study was conducted by G R Oldham, A Cummings, L J Mischel, J M Schmidtke, J Zhou, "Listen While You Work? Quasi-Experimental Relations between Personal-Stereo Headset Use and Employee Work Responses," *Journal of Applied Psychology,* October 1995, pp 547–64.

[14]See R Sharpe, "Work Week: Special Report about Life on the Job–And Trends Taking Shape There," *The Wall Street Journal,* April 9, 1996, p A1.

[15]See R G Netemeyer, S Burton, and M W Johnston, "A Nested Comparison of Four Models of the Consequences of Role Perception Variables," *Organizational Behavior and Human Decision Processes,* January 1995, pp 77–93.

[16]Supportive results can be found in T D Schellhardt, "Company Memo to Stressed-Out Employees: 'Deal With It'," *The Wall Street Journal,* October 2, 1996, pp B1, B4.

[17]See J A Davy, A J Kinicki, and C L Scheck, "A Test of Job Security's Direct and Mediated Effects on Withdrawal Cognitions," *Journal of Organizational Behavior,* 1997, in press.

[18]See T D Wall, P R Jackson, S Mullarkey, and S K Parker, "The Demands-Control Model of Job Strain: A More Specific Test," *Journal of Occupational and Organizational Psychology,* June 1996, pp 153–66; and R C Barnett and R T Brennan, "The Relationship between Job Experiences and Psychological Distress: A Structural Equation Approach," *Journal of Organizational Behavior,* May 1995, pp 250–76.

[19]M Vaughan, "Overload in the Workplace," *The Herald,* October 27, 1995, p 15.

[20]Results can be found in P C Morrow, J C McElroy, and C M Phillips, "Sexual Harassment Behaviors and Work Related Perceptions and Attitudes," *Journal of Vocational Behavior,* December 1994, pp 295–309.

[21]The relationship between chronic work demands and stress was investigated by J Schaubroeck and D C Ganster, "Chronic Demands and Responsivity to Challenge," *Journal of Applied Psychology,* February 1993, pp 73–85.

[22]See J M Plas, *Person-Centered Leadership: An American Approach to Participatory Management* (Thousand Oaks, CA: Sage, 1996).

[23]See G Stern, "Take a Bite, Do Some Work, Take a Bite," *The Wall Street Journal,* January 17, 1994, pp B1, B2; R F Bettendorf, "Curing the New Ills of Technology: Proper Ergonomics Can Reduce Cumulative Trauma Disorders among Employees," *HRMagazine,* March 1990, pp 35–36, 80; and S Overman, "Prescriptions for a Healthier Office," *HRMagazine,* February 1990, pp 30–34.

[24]Amparano, "On-Job Stress Is Making Workers Sick," *The Arizona Republic,* August 4, 1996, p A12.

[25]Supporting evidence is presented in N E Adler, T Boyce, M A Chesney, S Cohen, S Folkman, R L Kahn, and S L Syme, "Socioeconomic Status and Health: The Challenge of the Gradient," *American Psychologist,* January 1994, pp 15–24.

[26]See B N Uchino, J T Cacioppo, W Malarkey, and G Raser, "Individual Differences in Cardiac Sympathetic Control Predict Endocrine and Immune Responses to Acute Psychological Stress," *Journal of Personality and Social Psychology,* October 1995, pp 736–43.

[27]R W Rice, M R Frone, and D B McFarlin, "Work–nonwork Conflict and the Perceived Quality of Life," *Journal of Organizational Behavior,* 1992, 13, 2, 155–68.

[28]"How Four Companies are Redefining the Employment Relationship through Innovative Changes in Compensation and Benefits. Case studies: Whirlpool, Nike, Salomon and PSEG," *Compensation & Benefits Review,* January–Febraury 1995, p 71–80.

[29]This research is reviewed by A J Kinicki, F M McKee, and K J Wade, "Annual Review, 1991–1995: Occupational Health," *Journal of Vocational Behavior,* October 1996, pp 190–220; and A L Kristof, "Person-Organization Fit: An Integrative Review of Its Conceptualizations, Measurement, and Implications," *Personnel Psychology,* Spring 1996, pp 1–49.

[30]Research on chronic hostility is discussed by "Healthy Lives: A New View of Stress," *University of California, Berkeley Wellness Letter,* June 1990, pp 4–5. Also see R S Jorgensen, B T Johnson, M E Kolodziej, and G E Schreer, "Elevated Blood Pressure and Personality: A Meta-Analytic Review," *Psychological Bulletin,* September 1996, pp 293–320.

[31]This landmark study was conducted by T H Holmes and R H Rahe, "The Social Readjustment Rating Scale," *Journal of Psychosomatic Research,* August 1967, pp 213–18.

[32]Normative predictions are discussed in O Behling and A L Darrow, "Managing Work-Related Stress," in *Modules in Management,* eds J E Rosenzweig and F E Kast (Chicago: Science Research Associates, 1984).

[33]This research is discussed by G De Benedittis, A Lorenzetti, and A Pieri, "The Role of Stressful Life Events in the Onset of Chronic Primary Headache," *Pain,* January 1990, pp 65–75; and R S Bhagat, "Effects of Stressful Life Events on Individual Performance Effectiveness and Work Adjustment Processes within Organizational Settings: A Research Model," *Academy of Management Review,* October 1983, pp 660–71.

[34]See D R Pillow, A J Zautra, and I Sandler, "Major Life Events and Minor Stressors: Identifying Mediational Links in the Stress Process," *Journal of Personality and Social Psychology,* February 1996, pp 381–94; R C Barnett, S W Raudenbush, R T Brennan, J H Pleck, and N L Marshall, "Change in Job and Marital Experiences and Change in Psychological Distress: A Longitudinal Study of Dual-Earner Couples," *Journal of Personality and Social Psychology,* November 1995, pp 839–50; and S Cohen, D A J Tyrell, and A P Smith, "Negative Life Events, Perceived Stress, Negative Affect, and Susceptibility to the Common Cold," *Journal of Personality and Social Psychology,* January 1993, pp 131–40.

[35]The influence of perceived control over stressors on stress outcomes is examined by E A Skinner, "A Guide to Constructs of Control," *Journal of Personality and Social Psychology,* September 1996, pp 549–70; and S J Ashford and J S Black, "Proactivity during Organizational Entry: The Role of Desire for Control," *Journal of Applied Psychology,* April 1996, pp 199–214.

[36]R Bruce, "Experienced and on the Move," *Accountancy,* March 1995, p 62.

[37]M P O'Driscoll and C L Cooper, "Sources and Management of Excessive Job Stress and Burnout."

[38]A Shirom, "Burnout in Work Organizations," *International Review of Industrial and Organizational Psychology,* 1989, p 25–48.

[39]Results are presented in T D Schellhardt, "Off the Track: Is Your Job Going Nowhere? That May Be Natural, but It Doesn't Have to Be Permanent," *The Wall Street Journal* (Eastern Edition), February 26, 1996, p R4.

[40]S Sonnentag, F C Brodbeck, T Heinbokel, and W Stolte, "Stressor-Burnout Relationship on Software Development teams," *Journal of Occupational and Organizational Psychology,* 1994, vol 67, p 327–341.

[41]The phases are thoroughly discussed by C Maslach, *Burnout: The Cost of Caring* (Englewood Cliffs, NJ: Prentice-Hall, 1982).

[42]The discussion of the model is based on C L Cordes and T W Dougherty, "A Review and Integration of Research on Job Burnout," *Academy of Management Review,* October 1993, pp 621–56.

[43]Translated from J Moerkamp, "Burnout," *Management Team,* March 3, 1996, p 18.

[44]Results and conclusions can be found in R T Lee and B E Ashforth, "A Meta-Analytic Examination of the Correlates of the Three Dimensions of Burnout," *Journal of Applied Psychology,* April 1996, pp 123–33.

[45]See Ibid.; and R T Lee and B E Ashforth, "A Longitudinal Study of Burnout among Supervisors and Managers: Comparisons between the Leiter and Maslach (1988) and Golembiewski et al. (1986) Models," *Organizational Behavior and Human Decision Processes,* April 1993, pp 369–98.

[46]Recommendations for reducing burnout are discussed by M Wylie, "Preventing Worker Burnout while Supporting the Users," *MacWeek,* October 4, 1993, pp 12–14; and "How To Avoid Burnout," *Training,* February 1993, pp 15, 16, 70.

[47]These examples and techniques are discussed by R L Rose, "Time Out: At the Menninger Clinic, Executives Learn More About Themselves–And Why They're So Unhappy," *The Wall Street Journal* (Eastern Edition), February 26, 1996, p R5; and L Landon, "Pump Up Your Employees," *HRMagazine,* May 1990, pp 34–37.

[48]Based on and translated from E Verdegaal, "Sabbatical Leave: Prima, maar Niet in de Tijd Van de Baas," *Management Team,* November 17, 1995, p 111–114.

[49]C L Cooper, and S Williams, *Creating Healthy Work Organizations* (Chichester: Wiley, 1994) pp 1–2.

[50]R Wolffe, "Macho Managers Are Bad For Health, Say Guidelines," *The Financial Times*, December 30, 1994, p 1.

[51]See C S Smith and J Tisak, "Discrepancy Measures of Role Stress Revisited: New Perspectives on Old Issues,"p 285–307; J R Edwards and R Van Harrison, "Job Demands and Worker Health: Three Dimensional Reexamination of the Relationship Between Person-Environmant Fit and Strain," pp 628–48, and M Jamal, "Job Stress and Job Performance Controversy: An Empirical Assessment," *Organizational Behavior and Human Performance,* February 1984, pp 1–21; T A Beehr, *Psychological Stress in the Workplace* (New York: Routledge, 1995).

[52]Types of support are discussed by S Cohen and T A Wills, "Stress, Social Support, and the Buffering Hypothesis," *Psychological Bulletin,* September 1985, pp 310–57.

[53]The perceived availability and helpfulness of social support was examined by F H Norris and K Kaniasty, "Received and Perceived Social Support in Times of Stress: A Test of the Social Support Deterioration Deterrence Model," *Journal of Personality and Social Psychology,* September 1996, pp 498–511; and B Lakey, K M McCabe, S A Fisicaro, and J B Drew, "Environmental and Personal Determinants of Support Perceptions: Three Generalizability Studies," *Journal of Personality and Social Psychology,* June 1996, pp 1270–80.

[54]See B N Uchino, J T Cacioppo, and J K Kiecolt-Glaser, "The Relationship between Social Support and Physiological Processes: A Review with Emphasis on Underlying Mechanisms and Implications for Health," *Psychological Bulletin,* May 1996, pp 488–531; and H Benson and M Stark, *Timeless Healing: The Power and Biology of Belief* (New York: Scribner, 1996).

[55]Supporting results can be found in W Stroebe, M Stroebe, G Abakoumkin, and H Schut, "The Role of Loneliness and Social Support in Adjustment to Loss: A Test of Attachment versus Stress Theory," *Journal of Personality and Social Psychology,* June 1996, pp 1241–49; J I Sanchez, W P Korbin, and D M Viscarra, "Corporate Support in the Aftermath of a Natural Disaster: Effects on Employee Strains," *Academy of Management Journal,* April 1995, pp 504–21; and N L Scrimshaw, "Social Support in Pregnancy: Psychosocial Correlates of Birth Outcomes and Postpartum Depression," *Journal of Personality and Social Psychology,* December 1993, pp 1243–58.

[56]See Kinicki, McKee, and Wade, "Annual Review, 1991—1995: Occupational Health"; R E Harlow and N Cantor, "To Whom Do People Turn When Things Go Poorly? Task Orientation and Functional Social Contacts," *Journal of Personality and Social Psychology,* August 1995, pp 329–40; and T Matsui, T Ohsawa, and M L Onglatco, "Work-Family Conflict and the Stress-Buffering Effects of Husband Support and Coping Behavior among Japanese Married Working Women," *Journal of Vocational Behavior,* October 1995, pp 178–92.

[57]For details, see B P Buunk, B J Doosje, L G J M Jans, and L E M Hopstaken, "Perceived Reciprocity, Social Support, and Stress at Work: The Role of Exchange and Communal Orientation," *Journal of Personality and Social Psychology,* October 1993, pp 801–11; and C E Cutrona, "Objective Determinants of Perceived Social Support," *Journal of Personality and Social Psychology,* February 1986, pp 349–55.

[58]The relationship between managerial behavior and organizational policies and the receipt of social support was investigated by I P Erera, "Social Support Under Conditions of Organizational Ambiguity," *Human Relations,* March 1992, pp 247–64.

[59]R S Lazarus and S Folkman, "Coping and Adaptation," in *Handbook of Behavioral Medicine,* ed W D Gentry (New York: The Guilford Press, 1984), p 283.

[60]The antecedents of appraisal were investigated by B C Long and R W Schutz, "Temporal Stability and Replicability of a Workplace Stress and Coping Model for Managerial Women: A Multiwave Panel Study," *Journal of Counseling Psychology,* July 1995, pp 266–78; and P P Heppner, D J Walther, and G E Good, "The Differential Role of Instrumentality, Expressivity, and Social Support in Predicting Problem-Solving Appraisal in Men and Women," *Sex Roles,* January 1995, pp 91–108.

[61]For a thorough review of research on coping with unemployment, see J C Latack, A J Kinicki, and G E Prussia, "An Integrative, Process Model of Coping with Job Loss," *Academy of Management Review,* April 1995, pp 311–42.

[62]Lazarus and Folkman, "Coping and Adaptation," p 289.

[63]"The President: Tale of the TelePrompTer," *Newsweek*, October 4, 1993, p 4.

[64]Descriptions of coping strategies are provided by D T Terry, "Determinants of Coping: The Role of Stable and Situational Factors," *Journal of Personality and Social Psychology,* May 1994, pp 895–910.

[65]See C A Smith and R S Lazarus, "Appraisal Components, Core Relational Themes, and the Emotions," *Cognition and Emotion,* May 1993, pp 233–69; and E J Peacock, P T P Wong, and G T Reker, "Relations between Appraisals and Coping Schemas: Support for the Congruence Model," *Canadian Journal of Behavioral Science,* January 1993, pp 64–80.

[66]See the discussion in Kinicki, McKee, and Wade, "Annual Review, 1991–1995: Occupational Health."

[67]This pioneering research is presented in S C Kobasa, "Stressful Life Events, Personality, and Health: An Inquiry into Hardiness," *Journal of Personality and Social Psychology,* January 1979, pp 1–11.

[68]"Burning the Midnight Oil," *Management Today*, February 1995, p 11–12.

[69]See S C Kobasa, S R Maddi, and S Kahn, "Hardiness and Health: A Prospective Study," *Journal of Personality and Social Psychology,* January 1982, pp 168–77.

[70]Results can be found in V Florian, M Mikulincer, and O Taubman, "Does Hardiness Contribute to Mental Health during a Stressful Real-Life Situation? The Roles of Appraisal and Coping," *Journal of Personality and Social Psychology,* April 1995, pp 687–95.

[71]See "Basic Behavioral Science Research for Mental Health," *American Psychologist,* January 1996, pp 22–28; and M C Rush, W A Schoel, and S M Barnard, "Psychological Resiliency in the Public Sector: `Hardiness' and Pressure for Change," *Journal of Vocational Behavior,* February 1995, pp 17–39.

[72]B Priel, N Gonik, and B Rabinowitz, "Appraisals of Childbirth Experience and Newborn Characteristics: The Role of Hardiness and Affect," *Journal of Personality,* September 1993, pp 299–315.

[73]M Friedman and R H Rosenman, *Type A Behavior and Your Heart* (Greenwich, CT: Fawcett Publications, 1974), p 84. (Boldface added.)

[74]See C Lee, L F Jamieson, and P C Earley, "Beliefs and Fears and Type A Behavior: Implications for Academic Performance and Psychiatric Health Disorder Symptoms," *Journal of Organizational Behavior,* March 1996, pp 151–77; S D Bluen, J Barling, and W Burns, "Predicting Sales Performance, Job Satisfaction, and Depression by Using the Achievement Strivings and Impatience-Irritability Dimensions of Type A Behavior," *Journal of Applied Psychology,* April 1990, pp 212–16; and M S Taylor, E A Locke, C Lee and M E Gist, "Type A Behavior and Faculty Research Productivity: What Are the Mechanisms?" *Organizational Behavior and Human Performance,* December 1984, pp 402–18.

[75]Results from the meta-analysis are contained in S A Lyness, "Predictors of Differences between Type A and B Individuals in Heart Rate and Blood Pressure Reactivity," *Psychological Bulletin,* September 1993, pp 266–95.

[76]See S Booth-Kewley and H S Friedman, "Psychological Predictors of Heart Disease: A Quantitative Review" *Psychological Bulletin,* May 1987, pp 343–62. More recent results can be found in T Q Miller, T W Smith, C W Turner, M L Guijarro, A J Hallet, "A Meta-Analytic Review of Research on Hostility and Physical Health," *Psychological Bulletin,* March 1996, pp 322–48.

[77]Based on C L Cooper, and S Williams, *Creating Healthy Work Organizations* (Chichester: John Wiley and Sons, 1994), pp 133–65.

[78]C Barrie, and J Confino, "Mobile phones are out, shrinks are in," *The Guardian*, August 13, 1994, p 34.

[79]R S DeFrank, and C L Cooper, "Worksite Stress Management Interventions: Their Effectiveness and Conceptualization," *Journal of Management Psychology*, vol 2, pp 4–10.

[80]C L Cooper, and S Cartwright, (1994) Healthy Mind, Healthy Organization: A Proactive Approach to Occultional Stress," *Human Relations*, vol 47, no 4, pp 455–471.

[81]"Office ROMance," *Management Today*, February 1994, p 89.

[82]See H Benson, *The Relaxation Response* (New York: William Morrow and Co., 1975).

[83]Research pertaining to the relaxation response is discussed by W P Smith, W C Compton, and W B West, "Meditation as an Adjunct to a Happiness Enhancement Program," *Journal of Clinical Psychology,* March 1995, pp 269–73; and Benson and Stark, *Timeless Healing: The Power and Biology of Belief.*

[84]Results are presented in "Your Blood Pressure: Think it Down" *Cooking Light*, October, p 24.

[85]R Motoko, "Working life: outside help for troubled workers—jobs," *The Financial Times*, June 6, 1994, p 17.

[86]Based on M Coles, "Employers join fight to control stress," *Sunday Times*, June 18, 1995.

[87]Adapted from K Harper, "Stress Survey Shows Big Load on Industry's Mind," *The Guardian*, November 1, 1994, p 11.

[88]Adapted from M Scott, "Stress Claims Give Insurers Headache," *The Observer*, February 6, 1994, p 1.

[89]D Keenan, "Safe System of Work and Psychiatric Damage," *Accountancy*, January 1995, pp 93–94.

[90]Based on B Clement, "Just Sack Them Before They Sue: Bosses Urged to Fire Stress Victims," *Independent on Sunday*, November 27, 1994, p 2.

[91]Adapted from C Maslach and S E Jackson, "The Measurement of Experienced Burnout," *Journal of Occupational Behavior,* April 1981, pp 99–113.

Five

The Evolving Organization

Eighteen Organizations: Structure and Effectiveness

Nineteen Organizational Life Cycles and Design

Twenty Managing Change in Learning Organizations

Eighteen

Organizations: Structure and Effectiveness

In 1994 Air France implemented the first phase of an aggressive recovery plan for 1994 to 1997 that calls for increasing productivity by 30 per cent and sales by 14 per cent during the period, as well as reducing personnel costs by 10 per cent each year.

"We are in an emergency situation — we now must work at supersonic speed," Christian Blanc, the chairman and chief executive told employees and union delegates at the time of the introduction of the first phase in 1994. "Air France workers must prepare for a 'cultural revolution' and adopt a new spirit," he added.

On the face of it the strategy is straightforward. The principal steps have comprised a diagnosis of the airline's ailments, an attempt to win the support of the workers, and the implementation of recovery measures. But the scale of the task has prompted Blanc and his team to resort to methods which have often proved innovative and occasionally desperate. The innovations started immediately. A team of sociologists from SMG, a consultancy group, was called in to help identify the airline's problems. It was led by Francois Dupuy, a colleague of Professor Michel Crozier, a pioneer in the study of bureaucratic organizations.

"What we found was a profound inadaptation of the organization." Like many state-owned companies Air France had a hierarchical and centralized structure with little co-ordination between activities. It had technical excellence but no commercial excellence. An example he cites to demonstrate the lack of coordination between the various divisions was the last evening flight from Stockholm. The aircraft would park near the hanger for overnight maintenance, despite the fact that this added almost 30 minutes to the time it took passengers to reach the terminal. "People were only concerned with their own job, there was no consideration for the final product."

To gain support for the necessary reforms, Blanc resorted to a second innovation — a referendum. Faced with opposition from the majority of the airline's 14 unions to a rescue package which included 5,000 job cuts, a pay freeze, and measures to raise productivity by 30 per cent by the end of 1997, the chairman appealed directly to the company's 40,000 employees. It was a big gamble, but it paid off. More than 80 per cent of the 30,000 employees who responded to the referendum gave their approval. All but two of the trade unions, anxious at having been outflanked in this manner, have subsequently given their approval to the package, allowing Blanc to proceed with the implementation of cost-cutting measures.

The economies, however, are a relatively easy part of the task. "There is no magic on the cost side," says one official at the airline. "You just need commitment and determination." It is much harder to revive revenues and the quality of service. This is where the real battle is being waged and where a revolution is being attempted. At the thick of this battle lies a reorganization of the company structure. "We realized that we could not remedy the organization in place, so we would have to rebuild it," says Olivennes. This has involved breaking up the previous structure into separate profit centres. Instead of a handful of large management structures, such as the personnel division, which covered the flight crews, and the commercial division, which was responsible for ticket sales and marketing, Air France now comprises 11 profit centres. Five cover geographical markets, such as the Americas and France, while others include freight, maintenance, and the Paris airport services. Each centre includes parts of the previous structures, so the Americas profit centre, for example, contains personnel, commercial, airport, and transport responsibilities.

For Christian Kozar, head of the profit centre for airport operations in Paris and a close aide to Blanc, the guiding principle behind the strategy is decentralization and coordination. "We had to make the organization units of a human size and bring decisions to ground level. We also had to improve connections between activities."

The dogma of decentralization might sound banal. It has, after all, been the management creed of many companies over the past decade. At an airline, however, it is not so ordinary. "To my knowledge no other major airline has attempted this kind of decentralization before," says one senior industry executive.

For Olivennes, the only previous experiment has been at Iberia — hardly a happy example given its struggle against bankruptcy. He argues, however, that the lesson from the Spanish airline does not invalidate the idea of decentralization but shows that it must be balanced.

"They had profit centres competing against each other, such as separate ticket offices for different regions in the same town," he says. "If passengers on a Paris-Madrid flight don't go afterwards from Madrid to New York then you lose money. There has to be cooperation and coordination between profit centres because airlines are essentially a network."

If there are risks to be avoided, what are the benefits to be reaped? Most immediately there is something constructive in the destruction of the previous system. "It is an intelligent way to break the bureaucracy," says one industry analyst. "It shakes things up and facilitates a change in thinking and attitudes which is absolutely essential."

By making managers identifiable and responsible for results it also assists efficiency. "We have a 2.5bn euros revenue business and we are absolutely answerable for it," says Louise Roy, the head of the profit centre for the Americas. Efficiencies are also created by the client/supplier relationship between the profit centres.

For Kozar, one of the principal advantages of the new structure is that it has stripped out layers of managers. "Hierarchical management is finished. We have cut the management levels in our profit centres from eight to three and have created a much more responsive operation."

At the airports under his control this means that employees are divided into units for each terminal, usually numbering about 500. There is one chief manager for each terminal and one permanently manned command post. "Before, like other airlines, we had a huge transport division which managed all of the airports and destinations. But how can someone sitting in Paris do

this properly?"

Kozar and the management team are convinced that the new organization is a necessary condition for survival. But they know it is not sufficient. "We can't say today whether it will work," says Olivennes. "But we have moved in the right direction."

Whether the airline can move far enough will depend on the extent to which Blanc's shake-up and reorganization change attitudes and culture within the company. "I am worried because most of you do not have an economic culture," the chairman told an audience of managers last year. Dupuy believes that the restructuring of the company has helped. "It has sent a powerful message of change. But you can't alter attitudes just by redrawing the company organization chart."

Part of the problem stems from contradictions involved in reforming a bureaucratic company. "To fundamentally reform a big company you need the confidence and enthusiasm of the workforce. But if the company is in crisis then you don't have that confidence," says Olivennes.

At the same time, he argues, it has been hard to persuade some employees of the need to change. "There has been a myth that Air France, as the national carrier, could not fail." For Dupuy, a further obstacle lies in the fact that bureaucracies are characterized by orders coming from above. "People often wait to be told what to do rather than develop their initiative. There are many people who are unable or unwilling to change their attitudes."

The response to these obstacles has been to increase the incentives for employees and also to change the personnel themselves. On the first count, the company this month completed a scheme whereby employees could take shares in the company in return for salary cuts. About 30 per cent of the staff signed up, providing the twin benefits of an immediate cut in staff costs and motivation to maximize the value of the shares received.

There have been losers. "A lot of the old barons had to leave or to find other jobs," says one executive. For example, the former manager for "technical affairs" who used to have 17,000 employees under his control has been put in charge of studies relating to the recovery project.

Not surprisingly, Blanc and his team believe they will succeed. And there are precedents for cheering recovery stories in the French public sector. The most encouraging is Renault, which transformed itself from the sick man of the European car industry to one of its most profitable members.

Dupuy cites several parallels between the two cases. "Renault used to have a very rigid structure. To take an example, there was no cooperation between the design and manufacturing divisions. They changed this entirely, and Air France must do the same."

The trouble, however, lies in the timetable. Renault took eight years or so to turn itself around. With the liberalization of Europe's airline market scheduled for 1997 and with competitive gains at rivals such as British Airways and Lufthansa, Air France is facing a daunting race against the clock.[1]

Discussion Question

Will these measures make Air France competitive for today's high-speed, global economy?

Virtually every aspect of life is affected at least indirectly by some type of organization.[2] We look to organizations to feed, clothe, house, educate, and employ us. Organizations attend to our needs for entertainment, police and fire protection, insurance, recreation, national security, transportation, news and information, legal assistance, and health care. Many of these organizations seek a profit, others do not. Some are extremely large, others are tiny family operations. Despite this mind-boggling diversity, modern organizations have one basic thing in common. They are the primary context for *organizational* behaviour. In a manner of speaking, organizations are the chessboard upon which the game of organizational behaviour is played. Therefore, present and future managers need a working knowledge of modern organizations to improve their chances of making the right moves when managing people at work.

This chapter explores the structure and effectiveness of modern organizations. We begin by defining the term *organization*, discussing important dimensions of organization charts, and analysing fundamental models of organization. Next, a way of dealing with the recent wave of corporate reorganizations is examined. We conclude this chapter with criteria for assessing the effectiveness of organizations. These concepts provide a useful foundation of understanding for our discussion of modern organization trends and design options in the next chapter.

Defining and Charting Organizations

As a necessary springboard for this chapter, we need to formally define the term organization and clarify the meaning of organization charts.

What Is an Organization?

Organization
System of consciously coordinated activities of two or more people.

According to Chester I. Barnard's classic definition, an **organization** is "a system of consciously coordinated activities or forces of two or more persons."[3] Embodied in the conscious coordination aspect of this definition are four common denominators of all organizations: coordination of effort, a common goal, division of labour, and a hierarchy of authority[4] (see Figure 18–1). Organization theorists refer to these factors as the organization's structure.[5]

Coordination of effort is achieved through formulation and enforcement of policies, rules, and regulations. Division of labour occurs when the common goal is pursued by individuals performing separate but related tasks. The hierarchy of authority, also called the chain of command, is a control mechanism dedicated to making sure the right people do the right things at the right time. Historically, managers have maintained the integrity of the hierarchy of authority by adhering to the unity of command principle. The **unity of command principle** specifies that each employee should report to only one manager. Otherwise, the argument goes, inefficiency would prevail because of conflicting orders and lack of personal accountability.[6] (Indeed, these are problems in today's more fluid and flexible organizations that are relying on innovations such as cross-functional and self-managed teams.) Managers in the hierarchy of authority also administer rewards and punishments. When the four factors in Figure 18–1 operate in concert, the dynamic entity called an organization exists.

Unity of command principle
Each employee should report to a single manager.

Organization Charts

Organization chart
Boxes-and-lines illustration showing chain of formal authority and division of labour.

An **organization chart** is a graphic representation of formal authority and division of labour relationships. To the casual observer, the term *organization chart* is exemplified by the family tree of boxes and lines posted on workplace walls. Within each box one usually finds the names and titles of current position holders. To organization theorists, however, organization charts reveal much more. The partial organization chart in Figure 18–2 reveals four basic dimensions of organizational structure: (1) hierarchy of authority (who reports to whom), (2) division of labour, (3) spans of control, and (4) line and staff positions.

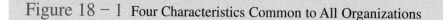

Figure 18 − 1   Four Characteristics Common to All Organizations

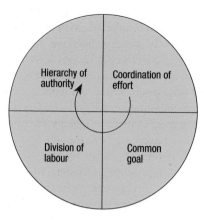

Hierarchy of Authority

As Figure 18−2 illustrates, there is an unmistakable hierarchy of authority.[7] Working from bottom to top, the 10 directors report to the two executive directors who report to the president who reports to the chief executive officer. Ultimately, the chief executive officer answers to the hospital's board of directors. The chart in Figure 18−2 shows strict unity of command up and down the line. A formal hierarchy of authority also delineates the official communication network.

Division of Labour

In addition to showing the chain of command, the sample organization chart indicates extensive division of labour. Immediately below the hospital's president, one executive director is responsible for general administration while another is responsible for medical affairs. Each of these two specialties is further subdivided as indicated by the next layer of positions. At each successively lower level in the organization, jobs become more specialized.

Span of control
The number of people reporting directly to a given manager.

Spans of Control

The span of control refers to the number of people reporting directly to a given manager.[8] Spans of control can range from narrow to wide. For example, the president in Figure 18−2 has a narrow span of control of two. (Staff assistants usually are not included in a manager's span of control.) The executive administrative director in Figure 18−2 has a wider span of control of five. Spans of control exceeding 30 can be found in assembly-line operations where machine-paced and repetitive work substitutes for close supervision. Historically, spans of five to six were considered best. Despite years of debate, organization theorists have not arrived at a consensus regarding the ideal span of control.

Generally, the narrower the span of control, the closer the supervision and the higher the administrative costs as a result of a higher manager-to-worker ratio. Recent emphasis on leanness and administrative efficiency dictates spans of control as wide as possible but guarding against inadequate supervision and lack of coordination. Wider spans also complement the trend towards greater worker autonomy.

Staff personnel
Provide research, advice, and recommendations to line managers.

Line managers
Have authority to make organizational decisions.

Line and Staff Positions

The organization chart in Figure 18−2 also distinguishes between line and staff positions. Line managers such as the president, the two executive directors, and the various directors occupy formal decision-making positions within the chain of command. Line positions generally are connected by solid lines on organization charts. Dotted lines indicate staff relationships. Staff personnel do background research and provide technical advice and recommendations to their line managers, who have the authority to make decisions. For example, the cost-containment specialists in the sample organization chart merely advise the president on relevant matters. Apart from supervising

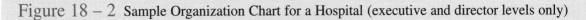

Figure 18 – 2 Sample Organization Chart for a Hospital (executive and director levels only)

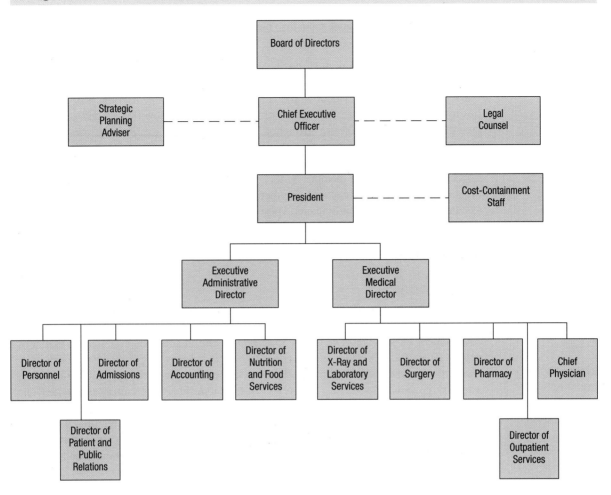

the work of their own staff assistants, they have no line authority over other organizational members. Modern trends such as cross-functional teams and reengineering are blurring the distinction between line and staff.

According to a study of 207 police officers in Israel, line personnel exhibited greater job commitment than did their staff counterparts.[9] This result was anticipated because the line managers' decision-making authority empowered them and gave them comparatively more control over their work situations.

The Evolution of Organizational Metaphors

The complexity of modern organizations makes them somewhat difficult to describe. Consequently, organization theorists have resorted to the use of metaphors.[10] A metaphor is a figure of speech that characterizes one object in terms of another object. Good metaphors help us comprehend complicated things by describing them in everyday terms. For example, consider the following metaphor that envisions the modern organization as an orchestra:

The system can be thought of as a large modern orchestra with a number of professionals playing quite different instruments and performing separate—and often very difficult—tasks. Each instrumentalist, like so many in large organizations, is indeed a specialist in a particular field whose work must be integrated with the work of others to make up the whole.

The manager's job is more than what the concert-goer sees. It includes planning the performance, helping to select those numbers that the orchestra can best perform, presiding at rehearsals, and doing many of the things that are required to make the final concert notable. The manager's contribution is much more than being the one with the baton, and what the audience sees should be understood in that context.[11]

OB scholar Kim Cameron sums up the value of organizational metaphors as follows: "Each time a new metaphor is used, certain aspects of organizational phenomena are uncovered that were not evident with other metaphors. In fact, the usefulness of metaphors lies in their possession of some degree of falsehood so that new images and associations emerge."[12] With the orchestra metaphor, for instance, one could come away with an exaggerated picture of harmony in large and complex organizations. On the other hand, it realistically encourages us to view managers as facilitators rather than absolute dictators.

Four organizational metaphors that have evolved over the years characterize organizations alternatively as military/mechanical systems, biological systems, cognitive systems, and ecosystem participants. These four metaphors can be plotted on a continuum ranging from simple closed systems to complex open systems (see Figure 18–3). We need to clarify the important distinction between closed and open systems before exploring the metaphors.

Closed versus Open Systems

Closed system
A relatively self-sufficient entity.

Open system
Organism that must constantly interact with its environment to survive.

A **closed system** is said to be a self-sufficient entity. It is "closed" to the surrounding environment. In contrast, an **open system** depends on constant interaction with the environment for survival. The distinction between closed and open systems is a matter of degree. Since every worldly system is partly closed and partly open, the key question is: How great a role does the environment play in the functioning of the system? For instance, a battery-powered clock is a relatively closed system. Once the battery is inserted, the clock performs its time-keeping function hour after hour until the battery goes dead. The human body, on the other hand, is a highly open system because it requires a constant supply of life-sustaining oxygen from the environment. Nutrients also are imported from the environment. Open systems are capable of self-correction, adaptation, and growth, thanks to characteristics such as homeostasis and feedback control.

Figure 18 – 3 Four Contrasting Organizational Metaphors

	Closed Systems		Open Systems	
	MILITARY/MECHANICAL MODEL (Bureaucracy)	**BIOLOGICAL MODE (Resource Transformation System)**	**COGNITIVE MODEL (Interpretation and Meaning System)**	**ECOSYSTEM MODEL (Life and Death Struggle in Organizational Communities)**
Metaphorical comparison	Precision military unit/well-oiled machine	Human body	Human mind	Natural ecosystems; Darwin's theory of natural selection (survival of the fittest)
Assumption about organization's environment	Predictable (controllable impacts)	Uncertain (filled with surprises)	Uncertain and ambiguous	Primary determinant of success/failure
Organization's primary goal	Maximum economic efficiency through rigorous planning and control	Survival through adaptation to environmental constraints and opportunities	Growth and survival through environmental scanning, interpretation, and learning	Growth and survival through opportunistic cooperation and competition

The traditional military/mechanical metaphor is a closed-system model because it largely ignores environmental influences. It gives the impression that organizations are self-sufficient entities. Conversely, the biological, cognitive, and ecosystem metaphors emphasize interaction between organizations and their environments. These newer models are based on open-system assumptions. A closer look at the four organizational metaphors reveals instructive insights about organizations and how they work. Each perspective offers something useful.

Organizations as Military/Mechanical Bureaucracies

A major by-product of the Industrial Revolution was the factory system of production. People left their farms and cottage industries to operate steam-powered machines in centralized factories. The social unit of production evolved from the family to formally managed organizations encompassing hundreds or even thousands of people. Managers sought to maximize the economic efficiency of large factories and offices by structuring them according to military principles. At the turn of the century, a German sociologist, Max Weber, formulated what he termed the most rationally efficient form of organization.[13] He patterned his ideal organization after the vaunted Prussian army and called it **bureaucracy.**

Bureaucracy

Max Weber's idea of the most rationally efficient form of organization.

Weber's Bureaucracy   According to Weber's theory, the following four factors should make bureaucracies the epitome of efficiency:

1. Division of labour (people become proficient when they perform standardized tasks over and over again).

2. A hierarchy of authority (a formal chain of command ensures coordination and accountability).

3. A framework of rules (carefully formulated and strictly enforced rules ensure predictable behaviour).

4. Administrative impersonality (personnel decisions, such as hiring and promoting, should be based on competence, not favouritism).[14]

How the Term _Bureaucracy_ Became a Synonym for Inefficiency   All organizations possess varying degrees of these characteristics. Thus, every organization is a bureaucracy to some extent. In terms of the ideal metaphor, a bureaucracy should run like a well-oiled machine, and its members should perform with the precision of a polished military unit. But practical and ethical problems arise when bureaucratic characteristics become extreme or dysfunctional. For example, extreme expressions of specialization, rule following, and impersonality can cause a bureaucrat to treat a client as a number rather than as a person.[15]

Weber would probably be surprised and dismayed that his model of rational efficiency has become a synonym for inefficiency.[16] Today, bureaucracy stands for being put on hold, waiting in long lines, and getting shuffled from one office to the next. (See the International OB.) This irony can be explained largely by the fact that organizations with excessive or dysfunctional bureaucratic tendencies become rigid, inflexible, and resistant to environmental demands and influences.[17]

Organizations as Biological Systems

Drawing upon the field of general systems theory that emerged during the 1950s,[18] organization theorists suggested a more dynamic model for modern organizations. As noted in Figure 18–3, this metaphor likens organizations to the human body. Hence, it has been labelled the _biological model_. In his often-cited organization theory text, _Organizations in Action_, James D Thompson explained the biological model of organizations in the following terms:

Approached as a natural system, the complex organization is a set of interdependent parts which together make up a whole because each contributes something and receives something from the whole, which in turn is interdependent with some larger environment. Survival of the system is taken to be the goal, and the parts and their relationships presumably are determined through evolutionary processes. . . .

Central to the natural-system approach is the concept of homeostasis, or self-stabilization, which spontaneously, or naturally, governs the necessary relationships among parts and activities and thereby keeps the system viable in the face of disturbances stemming from the environment.[19]

Unlike the traditional military/mechanical theorists who downplayed the environment, advocates of the biological model stress organization–environment interaction. As Figure 18–4 illustrates, the biological model characterizes the organization as an open system that transforms inputs into various outputs. The outer boundary of the organization is permeable. People, information, capital, and goods and services move back and forth across this boundary. Moreover, each of the five organizational subsystems—goals and values, technical, psychosocial, structural, and managerial—is dependent on the others. Feedback about such things as sales and customer satisfaction or dissatisfaction enables the organization to self-adjust and survive despite uncertainty and change.[20] In effect, the organization is alive.

International Organizational Behaviour
The Mugama: *Egypt's Bureaucratic Legacy*

Cairo—In Egypt, the bureaucracy is not just an engine of policy, or even a state of mind. It is a semicircular concrete behemoth in the center of this city's central square.

In this towering edifice—the Mugama ("Uniting") Central Government Complex—office opens onto office, crumbling stairway onto stairway, and the circular corridors that wheel 14 stories high around a dusky inner courtyard seem to have no end. . . .

The Mugama holds 20,000 public employees in 1,400 rooms. It is headquarters to 14 government departments. So deep is its reach into the everyday life of Cairenes that most adult city dwellers will find themselves forced to visit it several times a year. Upward of 45,000 people pass through its portals each day.

Perhaps unrivaled anywhere in the world as a symbol of government dithering and public despair, it is at once the most feared and hated structure in Egypt and the evolutionary product of millennia of bureaucracy on the shores of the Nile.

Twelve hapless clients of the Mugama have hurled themselves from its broken windows or from the soaring circular balconies that ring the central lobby up to the 13th-floor dome. A generation of Arab social engineers, who threw off a monarchy and seized Egypt in the name of its poor and unrepresented, planted their dreams in the Mugama's corridors and largely watched them die there. . . .

"The Mugama is to Egypt generally a symbol of 4,000 years of bureaucracy, and for the average Egyptian, it means all that is negative about the bureaucracy: routine, slow paperwork, complicated paperwork, a lot of signatures, impersonality. It is a Kafka building," said political sociologist Saad Eddin Ibrahim.

"You enter there, you can get the job done—the same job—in five minutes, in five days, in five months, or five years," Ibrahim said. "You can never predict what might happen to you in that building. Anybody who has dealt with that building for whatever reason knows the uncertainty of his affairs there."

In Egypt, the legacy of bureaucracy dates back to the time of the pharaohs. Temple walls and statues depict countless scribes, papyrus and pen in hand, taking down for the files of posterity everything from the deeds of the Pharaoh to the tax man's inventory. Subsequent French, Turkish, and British occupiers refined Egyptian red tape to a fine art.

Today, it takes 11 different permits for a foreign resident to buy an apartment in downtown Cairo. A bride wishing to join her husband working abroad in the Persian Gulf region must get stamps and signatures from the Foreign Ministry, the Ministry of Justice, the prosecutor general, the local court in her district, and the regional court, a process that one Cairo newspaper referred to as "legalized torture."

One young physician recently left the Mugama in tears after three days of trying to resign from her government job.

"They told me finally it would be easier if I just took a long sick leave," she said with a sigh. "But I'm leaving the country for a year!"

SOURCE   "Woe Awaits in Tower of Babble" by Kimberly Murphy, published May 24, 1993. Copyright, 1993, *Los Angeles Times.* Reprinted by permission.

Organizations as Cognitive Systems

A more recent metaphor characterizes organizations in terms of mental functions. According to respected organization theorists Richard Daft and Karl Weick,

This perspective represents a move away from mechanical and biological metaphors of organizations. Organizations are more than transformation processes or control systems. To survive, organizations must have mechanisms to interpret ambiguous events and to provide meaning and direction for participants. Organizations are meaning systems, and this distinguishes them from lower-level systems. . . .

Almost all outcomes in terms of organization structure and design, whether caused by the environment, technology, or size, depend on the interpretation of problems or opportunities by key decision makers. Once interpretation occurs, the organization can formulate a response.[21]

This interpretation process, carried out at the top-management or strategic level, leads to organizational learning and adaptation.

In fact, the concept of the learning organization,[22] discussed in detail in Chapter 20, is very popular in management circles these days. In a learning organization, structures must be developed to capture and share learning. As an example, the structure at Asea Brown Boveri, the Zurich-based industrial engineering firm, is designed to capture and share learning and knowledge systematically.

Figure 18 – 4   The Organization as an Open System: The Biological Model

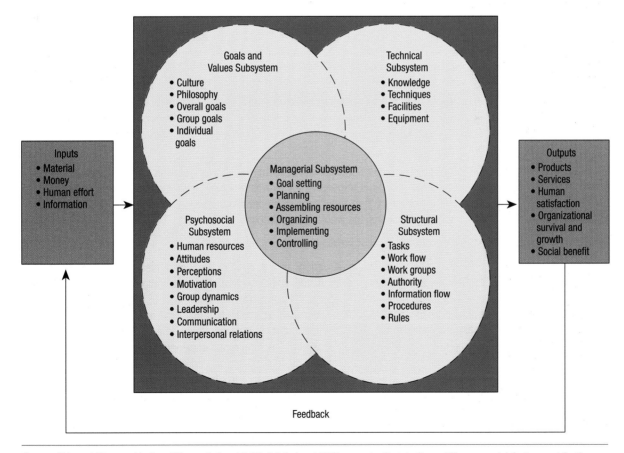

Source: This model is a combination of Figures 5–2 and 5–3 in F E Kast and J E Rosenzweig, *Organization and Management: A Systems and Contingency Approach,* 4th ed (New York: McGraw-Hill, 1986), pp 112, 114. Used with permission.

With $30 billion in annual sales and nearly 200,000 employees, ABB is made up of 5,000 autonomous profit centers averaging 50 employees each. Employees at each profit centre are divided into 10-person multifunctional teams. The centres capture knowledge through contacts with customers, and the structure of 65 business areas supports and coordinates learning and sharing. The result is a rapid transfer of information to empowered employees engaged in teamwork and networking on a global scale.

Support systems. Sound systems for performance support and performance management provide rewards that promote learning and knowledge by (1) providing indicators of the organization's progress; (2) identifying areas for improvement and (3) tracking employees' individual development and contributions. [23]

Organizations as Ecosystem Participants

Organizational ecologists

Those who study the impact of environmental factors on organizational success/failure and interrelationships among populations and communities of organizations.

Managers have long joked about organizational life being a "jungle" where it is "dog eat dog." According to the newest organizational metaphor, it is indeed a jungle out there. Organizational ecology parallels the study of earth's natural ecosystems. Ecologists are interested in the interaction between an organism and its environment. For instance, consider the fate of birds of prey—eagles, ospreys, and falcons—in recent years. The pesticide DDT in the food chain caused these magnificent birds to lay eggs with shells too thin to make it through the incubation period. Thanks largely to the banning of DDT, the birds of prey are making a strong comeback. [24] So, too, organizations live or die depending on the health and supportiveness of their environment, according to this metaphor. A recent review of the field produced this definition: "**Organizational ecologists** seek to explain how social, economic, and political conditions affect the relative abundance and diversity of organizations and attempt to account for their changing composition." [25] Thus, organizational ecologists study organizational foundings, failures, changes, and interrelationships within the context of environmental factors. They talk in terms of *populations* (groups of similar organizations) and *communities* (networks of differing organizations).

Inherent in the ecological metaphor, as indicated in Figure 18–3, is Darwin's theory of natural selection. In the natural world, the fittest members of each species survive because their environment makes them stronger. James F Moore, in his bestselling book, *The Death of Competition: Leadership and Strategy in the Age of Business Ecosystems*, offers this example:

Take the caribou and the wolf. The wolf culls the weaker caribou, which strengthens the herd. But with a stronger herd, it is imperative for wolves to evolve and become stronger themselves to succeed. And so the pattern is not simply competition or cooperation, but coevolution. Over time, as coevolution proceeds, the whole system becomes more hardy. [26]

Moving from the natural world to organizations, Moore goes on to explain:

Business ecosystems span a variety of industries. The companies within them coevolve capabilities around the innovation and work cooperatively and competitively to support new products, satisfy customer needs, and incorporate the next round of innovation. Microsoft, for example, anchors an ecosystem that traverses at least four major industries: personal computers, consumer electronics, information, and communications. Centered on innovation in microprocessing, the Microsoft ecosystem encompasses an extended web of suppliers including Intel and Hewlett-Packard and myriad customers across market segments.

. . . shaping cohesive strategy in the new order starts by defining an opportunity environment. Within such an environment, strategy-making revolves around devising novel ways to seize opportunities and create viable networks with other business ecosystems. [27]

Importantly, Moore believes the key to organizational survival today is learning how to selectively cooperate with one's competitors. The joint ventures, strategic partnerships, and corporate alliances we read about today are steps in the right direction.

Organizational Metaphors in Perspective (towards Postmodern Organizations)

In newly industrialized nations with poorly educated workers, the military/mechanical approach was widely applicable. Narrowly defined jobs, militarylike discipline, and strict chains of command enabled factory and office managers to control their employees and meet production quotas. As things grew more complex, however, the military/mechanical model was found lacking. Thanks to modern open-system thinking, we now see organizations as more than internally focused control mechanisms.

A useful model of modern organizations emerges when we integrate the biological, cognitive, and ecological metaphors. Conceptually, the organization's body and head need to be connected. One cannot function without the other. Managers of today's productive organizations are responsible for transforming factors of production into needed goods and services (the body). Yet they can remain competitive only if they wisely interpret environmental opportunities and obstacles (the head). Another job for the thinking/learning organization, according to the ecological model, is to coevolve with other organizations through balanced competition and cooperation.

Postmodern organizations

Flexible organizations that are decentralized, computer linked, and less hierarchical than bureaucracies.

This sort of open-system thinking has turned managers away from rigid bureaucracies and towards what organization theorists call postmodern organizations. **Postmodern organizations** are flexible and responsive organizations characterized by decentralized decision making, computer-linked units, and less emphasis on hierarchy (more emphasis on empowerment and teamwork).[28] We will explore the changing role of hierarchy in the next section and nontraditional organizations in Chapter 19.

The Role of Hierarchy in Today's Downsized, Reengineered Organizations

As we documented and discussed in Chapter 1, the downsizing movement during the 1980s and 1990s yielded stunning layoff statistics but disappointing productivity improvement. Millions of employees were laid off as big companies attempted to become leaner and more responsive global competitors.[29] In recent years, the ranks of middle managers have been particularly hard hit by so-called delayering. When Ford, in 1995, merged its North American and European operations into a single "global" structure, it was halved from an average of 14 levels to 7.[30] At Tungsram, the Hungarian light-bulb manufacturer, layers of management were cut from 11 to 3.[31] And just when the downsizing/delayering era seemed to be nearing an end, the idea of reengineering caught the fancy of large company executives. **Reengineering** involves the radical redesign of the entire organization to achieve dramatically improved results. "Reengineers start from the future and work backwards, as if unconstrained by existing methods, people, or departments. In effect they ask, 'If we were a new company, how would we run this place?'"[32]

Reengineering

Radical redesign of entire organization for dramatic improvement.

Three years and countless lost jobs later, reengineering looks like another overpromised and undelivered management fad.[33] Sceptics in the workplace call reengineering "two jobs for the price of one," referring to the plight of layoff *survivors*, who end up doing twice as much work for no extra pay.[34] Ethics specialists say their worst fears about the human toll of ill-conceived reengineering programmes have become reality.

Putting things in perspective, this reorganization revolution of downsizing, delayering, and reengineering is nothing less than a frontal assault on the once-unquestioned notion of hierarchy. The chain of command concept, discussed earlier as an element common to all organizations, will never be the same.

France is known as a very hierarchical society, which is reflected in its organizations, as states Robert Pingeon of Cigna Insurance Company:

Table 18 – 1   Organizational Hierarchies: Pro and Con

PRO	CON
Elliot Jacques	*Edward E Lawler III*
Bureaucracy is a dirty word even among bureaucrats, and in business there is a widespread view that managerial hierarchy kills initiative, crushes creativity, and has therefore seen its day. Yet 35 years of research have convinced me that managerial hierarchy is the most efficient, the hardiest, and in fact the most natural structure ever devised for large organizations. Properly structured, hierarchy can release energy and creativity, rationalize productivity, and actually improve morale. Moreover, I think most managers know this intuitively and have only lacked a workable structure and a decent intellectual justification for what they have always known could work and work well....	More and more organizations are concluding that they simply cannot afford the salary and other costs of maintaining an extensive hierarchy.... In a real sense, all members of the organizational hierarchy above the people who produce the organization's products or services produce nothing of value. Their only purpose is facilitating the performance of those involved in making the organization's products or delivering the organization's services. Thus they constitute an overhead expense whether they are in line or staff positions. They are worth having only if they add significant value to what is done by the people who actually produce the organization's products or services....
The hierarchical kind of organization we call bureaucracy did not emerge accidentally. It is the only form of organization that can enable a company to employ large numbers of people and yet preserve unambiguous accountability for the work they do. And that is why, despite its problems, it has so doggedly persisted.	Without a thorough redesign of the organization, however, it is unlikely that a significant part of the hierarchy can be made unnecessary. Hierarchies perform some very important organizational functions that must be done in some way if coordinated, organized behavior is to take place. On the other hand, if an organization design is adopted that includes work teams, new reward systems, extensive training, and ... various other practices ..., organizations can operate effectively with substantially less hierarchy.

Sources: Excerpted from E Jacques, "In Praise of Hierarchy," *Harvard Business Review,* January–February 1990, p 127; and "Substitutes for Hierarchy" by E E Lawler III. Reprinted by permission of publisher from *Organizational Dynamics,* Summer 1988 © 1988. American Management Association, New York. All rights reserved.

The French business scene does have its particularities and special rituals. Americans like myself are struck by the importance of hierarchy and the proliferation of job titles. I recall first reading the collective bargaining agreement of our industry, which listed 28 distinct grades, each one with a clarifying letter coefficient ... *"chef", "sous-chef b", "chef-adjoint c,"* etc. I felt as if I was studying the reorganization chart of an American Indian tribe. Trying to match French titles with our relatively simple numeric grade system ultimately required a special computer program."[35]

How Necessary Is Hierarchy?

According to the traditional chain-of-command concept, adapted from the military, supervisors are needed to assign, monitor, motivate, and control the work of subordinates. But workers and workplaces have changed.[36] Knowledge workers in our service-oriented economy are better educated and hungry for responsibility. Tasks are more complex. And the trend toward fewer organizational layers is gaining momentum. Consequently, management's traditional heavy reliance on hierarchical control is subject to debate (see Table 18–1). According to Lawler's side of the argument, less emphasis on hierarchy is better. In other words, the best management may be self-management. Lawler's contingency model deserves careful consideration because it is a necessary tool for getting the most out of today's organizations that have fewer layers of management.

Substitutes for Hierarchy: A Contingency Approach

Keuning and Opheij's model of substitutes for hierarchy is portrayed in Table 18–2. The 12 supervisory functions in the left-hand column are vital and need to be performed.

Table 18 – 2   Substitutes for Hierarchy

Roles of middle management	Organize around processes	Work in broad task groups	Promote internal entrepre-eurship	Develop process controlling information systems	Introduce flexible reward structure	Award contracts to suppliers/ customers	Change personnel selection and training	Promote behaviour changes
Motivate	X	X		X	X	X	X	X
Measure	X			X				
Coordinate	X	X	X	X	X	X	X	X
Assign work		X		X				
Look after personnel matters		X	X				X	
Provide expertise		X		X			X	
Set goals	X	X	X		X	X	X	X
Plan								
Linking communications	X	X	X		X			X
Train		X	X					
Control	X			X	X			
Provide leadership		X	X					

Source: Keuning and Opheij, *Delayering Organizations* (London: Pitman Publishing, 1994), p 149. Keuning and Opheij's overview is partly based on E E Lawler, III, Substitutes for hierarchy, *Organizational Dynamics*, Summer 1988, p 12.

Substitutes for hierarchy

Organizational factors such as computer networks and self-management training that reduce the need for direct supervision.

However, thanks to various combinations of the eigtht **substitutes for hierarchy** (organize around processes, work in broad task groups, and so on), the need for direct supervisory control can be reduced or perhaps eliminated. For instance, the X in the upper-left corner indicates the motivational power of organizing around processes. Notice that there is no perfect substitute for hierarchy capable of handling all 12 supervisory functions (work in broad task groups comes closest). Brief descriptions of each substitute for hierarchy follow:

- *Organize around processes.* Organizing around processes is a structural measure which requires fewer managers.

- *Work in broad task groups.* Organizational units are developed in which teams are responsible.

- *Promote internal entrepreneurship.* By organizing work around processes and by developing teams, people become responsible for the results of the team they are part of. As a result, internal entrepreneurship will be created.

- *Develop process controlling information systems.* This includes networked personal computers. Free access to vital information empowers employees.

- *Introduce flexible reward structure.* Rewards need to be adapted to the new work systems.

- *Award contracts to suppliers/customers.* Awards have a positive effect on motivation, coordination and goal setting.

- *Change personnel selection and training.* By changing the working methods, other technical skills are required. When new employees are recruited, it is important to know if they will fit in to the new working conditions.

- *Promote behaviour changes.* In many organizations, a change in behaviour is necessary to adapt to the new working environment.

According to Lawler, who first introduced the notion of substitutes for hierarchy: "Technology, work interdependence, work complexity, and required knowledge clearly influence the opportunities for adopting an organizational approach that is based on minimal hierarchy and high involvement."[37] But employees must want to take greater control of their organizational lives. If they do, and the effectiveness criteria discussed next are met, today's compressed hierarchies can be both productive and satisfying.

Organizational Effectiveness

How effective are you? If someone asked you this apparently simple question, you would probably ask for clarification before answering. For instance, you might want to know if they were referring to your exam results, annual income, actual accomplishments, ability to get along with others, public service, or perhaps something else entirely. So it is with modern organizations. Effectiveness criteria abound. According to the survey of Europe's Most Respected Companies carried out by *The Financial Times* and Price Waterhouse, the most important attributes of business performance are:

- Consistent growth.

- Long-term profitability.

- Quality of staff.

- Leadership.

- Vision.

- Customer service.

ABB, the Swiss engineering multinational, ranked top in the Survey of Europe's Most Respected Companies for the second time in 1995, followed by Nestlé, British Airways, BMW, Shell, and Marks and Spencer. There are, however, huge variations in priorities from country to country. Whereas France prefers good products, services and new technologies, Germany gives priority to clear leadership, "Führerschaft." In The Netherlands, the UK and Spain, global markets rank highly.[38] In France, car maker Citroën has gained a reputation for over-complex innovations.[39]

International Organizational Behaviour

French Bureaucracy: Le systéme "D"

Now for the big A — tackling that citadel of power known as *l' Administration.* There is no way around the French bureaucracy in some form or other, if you stay for any length of time. You need good nerves, determination, patience and a great sense of identity. You need time, lots of time. The big A is Them with capital T. The good news is that Them are people too, and that France is about personal relationships. Figuring it out with the other French people, you deal with in one way or another is a great warm-up for the big A. But not quite.

First you must master that tool with is indispensable in handling things at the Big A, the *système D. "D"* comes from *débrouiller*, meaning to untangle, to sort out. *So débrouiller* is to extricate yourself from difficulties. This can take many forms, from convincing a civil servant in the Adminstration to abridge certain procedures involved in issuing you a document, to driving down a one way street the wrong way to escape a traffic jam. It is *not* about doing something illegal. People who think it is inevitably end up in deep trouble. However, it can be convincing a policeman, as a French lawyer explained it to me, "that you have an exceptional reason why the application of the law can be suspended in this parpticular case." In other words, you can defend yourself.

SOURCE   P Platt, *French or Foe* (London: Culture Crossings, 1995).

Assessing organizational effectiveness is an important topic for an array of people, including managers, shareholders, government agencies, and OB specialists. The purpose of this final section is to introduce a widely applicable and useful model of organizational effectiveness.

Generic Organizational-Effectiveness Criteria

A good way to better understand this complex subject is to consider four generic approaches to assessing an organization's effectiveness (see Figure 18–5). These effectiveness criteria apply equally well to large or small and profit or not-for-profit organizations. Moreover, as denoted by the overlapping circles in Figure 18–5, the four effectiveness criteria can be used in various combinations. The key thing to remember is "no single approach to the evaluation of effectiveness is appropriate in all circumstances or for all organization types."[40] What do Coca-Cola and Exxon, for example, have in common, other than being large profit-seeking corporations? Because a multidimensional approach is required, we need to look more closely at each of the four generic effectiveness criteria.

Goal Accomplishment   Goal accomplishment is the most widely used effectiveness criterion for organizations. Key organizational results or outputs are compared with previously stated goals or objectives. Deviations, either plus or minus, require corrective action. This is simply an organizational variation of the personal goal-setting process discussed in Chapter 8. Effectiveness, relative to the criterion of goal accomplishment, is gauged by how well the organization meets or exceeds its goals.

Figure 18 – 5 Four Ways to Assess Organizational Effectiveness

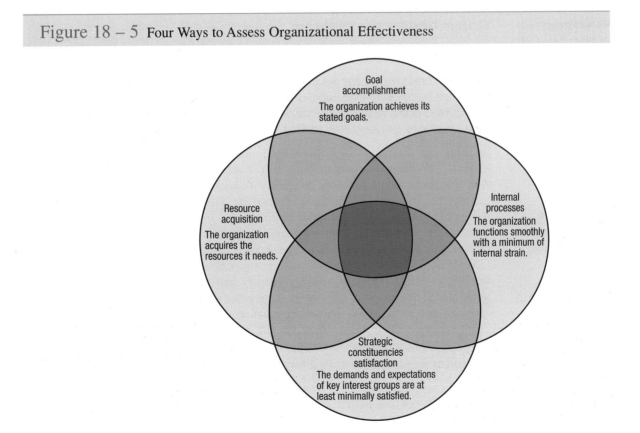

Source: Adapted from discussion in K Cameron, "Critical Questions in Assessing Organizational Effectiveness," *Organizational Dynamics*, Autumn 1980, pp 66–80; and K S Cameron, "Effectiveness as Paradox: Consensus and Conflict in Conceptions of Organizational Effectiveness," *Management Science*, May 1986, pp 539–53.

Productivity improvement, involving the relationship between inputs and outputs, is a common organization-level goal.[41] Goals also may be set for organizational efforts such as minority recruiting, pollution prevention, and quality improvement. Given today's competitive pressures, innovation and speed are very important organizational goals worthy of measurement and monitoring. An excellent example of an organization using speed as a competitive advantage is the Dutch department store Albert Heijn's "Today-Before-Tomorrow" concept:

At the very moment a product is scanned by the cashier, an enormous logistic chain reaction is launched: when a product is sold, it is immediately registered by the supplier, who no longer delivers on a weekly basis, but within 18 hours. In the long run, Albert Heijn even wants the shelves to be replenished within four hours.[42]

Resource Acquisition   This second criterion relates to inputs rather than outputs. An organization is deemed effective in this regard if it acquires necessary factors of production such as raw materials, labour, capital, and managerial and technical expertise. Charitable organizations judge their effectiveness in terms of how much money they raise from private and corporate donations.

Internal Processes   Some refer to this third effectiveness criterion as the "healthy systems" approach. An organization is said to be a healthy system if information flows smoothly and if employee loyalty, commitment, job satisfaction, and trust prevail. Goals may be set for any of these internal processes. Healthy systems, from a behavioural standpoint, tend to have a minimum of dysfunctional conflict and destructive political manoeuvering.

Strategic constituency

Any group of people with a stake in the organization's operation or success.

Strategic Constituencies Satisfaction   Organizations both depend on people and affect the lives of people. Consequently, many consider the satisfaction of key interested parties to be an important criterion of organizational effectiveness.

A strategic constituency is any group of individuals who have some stake in the organization—for example, resource providers, users of the organization's products or services, producers of the organization's output, groups whose cooperation is essential for the organization's survival, or those whose lives are significantly affected by the organization.[43]

Strategic constituencies (or *stakeholders*) generally have competing or conflicting interests.[44] For instance, stock investors who want higher dividends and consumers who seek low prices would probably disagree with a union's demand for a wage increase. Strategic constituents or stakeholders can be identified systematically through a stakeholder's audit.[45] A **stakeholder audit** enables management to identify all parties significantly impacted by the organization's performance. Conflicting interests and relative satisfaction among the listed stakeholders can then be dealt with.

Stakeholder audit

Systematic identification of all parties likely to be affected by the organization.

Frederick W. Julien and James C. Lampe, two scholars in the field of internal auditing working at Arthur Andersen, identify primary and secondary stakeholders.[46] Primary stakeholders have formal, official or contractual relationships and have direct and necessary economic impact on the organization. Secondary stakeholders, on the other hand, are not directly involved in the organization's economic activities. Both key stakeholders can in turn be classified into four categories:

1. *Supportive*, cooperative and actively involved in the organization.

2. *Adverse*, hindering and actively involved in the organization.

3. *Marginal*, not cooperative and not actively involved in the organization.

4. *Mixed*, cooperative and hindering, but not actively involved in the organization.

A never-ending challenge for management is to strike a workable balance among stakeholders so as to achieve at least minimal satisfaction on all fronts. McDonald's is an interesting and compelling case in point. After the smoke had cleared from the riots in south central Los Angeles in April 1992, observers were amazed to find every McDonald's restaurant in the area untouched by arsonists. But that outcome was not surprising to McDonald's:

> For Edward H Rensi, president and CEO of McDonald's USA, the explanation of what happened, or didn't happen, in South Central LA was simple: "Our businesses there are owned by African-American entrepreneurs who hired African-American managers who hired African-American employees who served everybody in the community, whether they be Korean, African American, or Caucasian."[47]

Corporate governance

Organization's roles in a larger context and the way those roles are carried out.

Corporate Governance   In the last two decades, corporate governance has recurrently been discussed in newspapers and journals, both in the USA and in Europe, more particularly in the UK and Germany. **Corporate governance** includes organizations' roles in a larger context (director's ethics, conflicts of interests, and codes of conduct) and the way they carry out those roles (the operation, composition, information, and liability of the boards of directors and stakeholder strategy). According to John Kay and Aubrey Silberston, two British economists, corporate managers are not responsible for shareholders alone, but for all stakeholders. This vision should be reflected in company law, to ensure that directors balance the interests of all stakeholders: shareholders, workers, customers, and suppliers.

The subject of corporate governance is a hot topic today because of recent disclosures of huge corporate collapses (Rolls-Royce and Barings) and corporate fraud (Didier Pineau-Valenciennes and Bernard Tapie in France, Italy's Carlo De Benedetti). Even after being declared incapable of directing a public company, Robert Maxwell went on to plunder the assets of several more.[48] The Bank of Credit and Commerce International covered a fraud network. The above-mentioned fiascos, and many other illegal situations, raised serious questions about company law, the appointment and remuneration of executives, their accountability and auditors' responsibility.

As an answer to this, Kay and Silberston propose their alternative, the stakeholder company, in which directors respresent all stakeholders. Moreover, they argue that chief executives should be appointed for a limited period of four years, and that their remunerations should be established by outsiders.[49] In the UK, prime minister Tony Blair in particular supports the idea of the stakeholder approach. He proposes to reform the economy by giving all people a new "stake" in its development.

Multiple Effectiveness Criteria: Some Practical Guidelines

Experts on the subject recommend a multidimensional approach to assessing the effectiveness of modern organizations. This means no single criterion is appropriate for all stages of the organization's life cycle (the organizational life cycle concept is covered in Chapter 19). Nor will a single criterion satisfy competing stakeholders. Well-managed organizations mix and match effectiveness criteria to fit the unique requirements of the situation.[50] Managers need to identify and seek input from strategic constituencies. This information, when merged with the organization's stated mission and philosophy, enables management to derive an appropriate combination of effectiveness criteria. The following guidelines are helpful in this regard:

- The goal accomplishment approach is appropriate when "goals are clear, consensual, time-bounded, measurable."[51]

- The resource acquisition approach is appropriate when inputs have a traceable impact on results or output. For example, the amount of money the Red Cross receives through donations dictates the level of services provided.

- The internal processes approach is appropriate when organizational performance is strongly influenced by specific processes (e.g., cross-functional teamwork).

- The strategic constituencies approach is appropriate when powerful stakeholders can significantly benefit or harm the organization.[52]

Keeping these basic concepts of organizational structure and effectiveness in mind, we turn our attention in Chapter 19 to the building of effective organizations.

Summary of Key Concepts

1. Describe the four *characteristics common to all organizations.* They are coordination of effort (achieved through policies and rules), a common goal (a collective purpose), division of labour (people performing separate but related tasks), and a hierarchy of authority (the chain of command).

2. *Explain the difference between closed and open systems.* These are relative terms. Closed systems, such as a battery-powered clock, are relatively self-sufficient. Open systems, such as the human body, are highly dependent on the environment for survival. Organizations are said to be open systems.

3. *Contrast the following organizational metaphors: military/mechanical, biological, and cognitive systems.* According to the military/mechanical model, a relatively closed system perspective, the organization seeks to maximize economic efficiency in a predictable environment. The biological metaphor views the organization as a living organism striving to survive in an uncertain environment. In terms of the cognitive metaphor, an organization is like the human mind, capable of interpreting and learning from uncertain and ambiguous situations.

4. *Describe the ecosystem model of organizations, and define the term* postmodern organization. Organizations are characterized as being in a life-and-death struggle for survival in an environment that presents opportunities to both compete and cooperate. Strategic emphasis needs to be on building cooperative relationships and exploiting opportunities within diverse organizational communities. The postmodern organization is decentralized, computer networked, and less hierarchical than traditional organizations.

5. *Explain the term* reengineering, *and discuss its record to date.* Reengineering is a blank-sheet-of-paper approach to radically redesigning the entire organization for dramatically improved performance. Ill-conceived or haphazard reengineering programmes are an ethical issue. Reengineering has not lived up to early expectations. It will probably be remembered as just another management fad. Still, it challenged us to think differently about organizational hierarchies.

6. *Identify Keuning and Opheij's substitutes for hierarchy, and explain their significance for managing today's flatter organizations.* Their eight substitutes for hierarchy reduce or even eliminate the need for direct supervision. They (1) organize around processes, (2) work in broad task groups, (3) promote internal entrepreneurship, (4) develop process-controlling information systems, (5) introduce flexible reward structures, (6) award contracts to suppliers/customers, (7) change personnel selection and training, and (8) promote behaviour changes.

7. *Describe the four generic organizational effectiveness criteria.* They are goal accomplishment (satisfying stated objectives), resource acquisition (gathering the necessary productive inputs), internal processes (building and maintaining healthy organizational systems), and strategic constituencies satisfaction (achieving at least minimal satisfaction for all key stakeholders).

8. *Explain why a multidimensional approach to organizational effectiveness is recommended.* Because no two industries or organizations are exactly alike, managers need to mix and match effectiveness criteria in a manner appropriate to the situation. Moreover, different effectiveness criteria become important as the organization moves through its life cycle.

Discussion Questions

1. How many organizations directly affect your life today? List as many as you can.

2. What would an organization chart of your current (or last) place of employment look like? Does the chart you have drawn reveal the hierarchy (chain of command), division of labor, span of control, and line—staff distinctions? Does it reveal anything else? Explain.

3. Why is it appropriate to view modern organizations as open systems?

4. How would you respond to a person who said, "All bureaucracies are useless"?

5. Why is it instructive to characterize today's complex organizations as cognitive (learning) systems?

6. How important is hierarchy in today's typical organization?

7. Which of Lawler's eight substitutes for hierarchy do you think has the greatest promise? Why?

8. How would you respond to a manager who claimed the only way to measure a business's effectiveness is in terms of how much profit it makes?

9. What role can stakeholder audits play in assessing organizational effectiveness?

10. Why do you suppose goal accomplishment is the most widely used effectiveness criterion?

Personal Awareness and Growth Exercise

Imagine you are a consultant asked to evaluate the effectiveness of the French-run Doctors without Borders. What model would you develop to chart this NGO?

QUESTIONS FOR DISCUSSION

1. How do your effectiveness criteria measure up to those suggested by your classmates? Did you overlook any important factors? Explain.

2. Are there any inherent conflicts among your effectiveness criteria? How can these conflicts be resolved?

3. Did your personal ethics and values play a role in how you determined the effectiveness criteria in this case? Explain.

Group Exercise

Stakeholders Audit Team

Objectives

1. To continue developing your group interaction and teamwork skills.

2. To engage in open-system thinking.

3. To conduct a stakeholder audit and thus more fully appreciate the competing demands placed on today's managers.

4. To establish priorities and consider trade-offs for modern managers.

Introduction

According to open-system models of organizations, environmental factors—social, political, legal, technological, and economic—greatly affect what managers can and cannot do. This exercise gives you an opportunity to engage in open-system thinking within a team setting. It requires a team meeting of about 20 to 25 minutes followed by a 10- to 15-minute general class discussion. Total time required for this exercise is about 30 to 40 minutes.

Instructions

Your instructor will randomly assign you to teams with five to eight members each. Choose one team member to act as recorder/spokesperson. Either at your instructor's prompting or as a team, choose one of these options:

1. Identify an organization that is familiar to everyone on your team (it can be a local business, your college or university, or a well-known organization such as McDonald's, Royal Dutch Shell, or British Airways.

2. Use BT's dress code in the opening case in Chapter 3, p 55.

Next do a *stakeholder audit* for the organization in question. This will require a team brainstorming session followed by brief discussion. Your team will need to make reasonable assumptions about the circumstances surrounding your target organization.

Finally, your team should select the three (or more) *high-priority* stakeholders on your team's list. Rank them number one, number two, and so on. (*Tip*: A top-priority stakeholder is one with the greatest short-term impact on the success or failure of your target organization.) Be prepared to explain to the entire class your rationale for selecting each high-priority stakeholder.

QUESTIONS FOR DISCUSSION

1. How does this exercise foster open-system thinking? Give examples.

2. Did this exercise broaden your awareness of the complexity of modern organizational environments? Explain.

3. Why do managers need clear priorities when it comes to dealing with organizational stakeholders?

4. How many trade-offs (meaning one party gains at another's expense) can you detect in your team's list of stakeholders? Specify them.

5. Does your experience with doing a stakeholder audit strengthen or weaken the validity of the ecosystem model of organizations? Explain.

6. How difficult was it for your team to complete this assignment? Explain.

Notes

[1]Excerpted from P Sparaco, "Air France Chief Seeks Cultural Revolution," *Aviation Week and Space Technology*, 1994, January 10, pp. 32–33 and from Ridding, J. "Tough Schedule for Take-Off," *The Financial Times*, 1995, January 16, p. 8.

[2]See P F Drucker, "The New Society of Organizations," *Harvard Business Review*, September–October 1992, pp 95–104; J R Galbraith, E E Lawler III, and Associates, eds, *Organizing for the Future: The New Logic for Managing Complex Organizations*, (San Francisco: Jossey-Bass, 1993); and B J Hodge, W P Anthony, and L M Gales, *Organization Theory: A Strategic Approach*, 5th ed (Upper Saddle River, NJ: Prentice-Hall, 1996).

[3]C I Barnard, The Functions of the Executive (Cambridge, MA: Harvard University Press, 1938), p 73. Also see M C Suchman, "Managing Legitimacy: Strategic and Institutional Approaches," *Academy of Management Review*, July 1995, pp 571–610.

[4]Drawn from E H Schein, *Organizational Psychology*, 3rd ed (Englewood Cliffs, NJ: Prentice-Hall, 1980), pp 12–15.

[5]For interesting and instructive insights about organization structure, see G Morgan, *Images of Organization* (Newbury Park, CA: Sage, 1997); G Morgan, *Creative Organization Theory: A Resource Book* (Newbury Park, CA: Sage, 1989); G Hofstede, "An American in Paris: The Influence of Nationality on Organization Theories," *Organization Studies*, no. 3, 1996, pp 525–37; and J G March, "Continuity and Change in Theories of Organizational Action," *Administrative Science Quarterly*, June 1996, pp 278–87.

[6]For related research, see S Finkelstein and R A D'Aveni, "CEO Duality as a Double-Edged Sword: How Boards of Directors Balance Entrenchment Avoidance and Unity of Command," *Academy of Management Journal*, October 1994, pp 1079–1108.

[7]For an interesting historical perspective of hierarchy, see P Miller and T O'Leary, "Hierarchies and American Ideals, 1900–1940," *Academy of Management Review*, April 1989, pp 250–65.

[8]For an excellent overview of the span of control concept, see D D Van Fleet and A G Bedeian, "A History of the Span of Management," *Academy of Management Review*, July 1977, pp 356–72. Also see E E Lawler III and J R Galbraith, "New Roles for the Staff: Strategic Support and Service," in *Organizing for the Future: The New Logic for Managing Complex Organizations*, eds J R Galbraith, E E Lawler III, and Associates, (San Francisco: Jossey-Bass, 1993), pp 65–83.

[9]M Koslowsky, "Staff/Line Distinctions in Job and Organizational Commitment," *Journal of Occupational Psychology*, June 1990, pp 167–73.

[10]See, for example, R J Marshak, "Managing the Metaphors of Change," *Organizational Dynamics*, Summer 1993, pp 44–56; R Garud and S Kotha, "Using the Brain as a Metaphor to Model Flexible Production Systems," *Academy of Management Review*, October 1994, pp 671–98; and R W Keidel, "Rethinking Organizational Design," *Academy of Management Executive*, November 1994, pp 12–30.

[11]D S Brown, "Managers' New Job Is Concert Building," *HRMagazine*, September 1990, p 42.

[12]K S Cameron, "Effectiveness as Paradox: Consensus and Conflict in Conceptions of Organizational Effectiveness," *Management Science*, May 1986, pp 540–41. Also see S Sackmann, "The Role of Metaphors in Organization Transformation," *Human Relations*, June 1989, pp 463–84; and H Tsoukas, "The Missing Link: A Transformational View of Metaphors in Organizational Science," *Academy of Management Review*, July 1991, pp 566–85.

[13]See W R Scott, "The Mandate Is Still Being Honored: In Defense of Weber's Disciples," *Administrative Science Quarterly*, March 1996, pp 163–71.

[14]Based on M Weber, *The Theory of Social and Economic Organization*, translated by A M Henderson and T Parsons (New York: Oxford University Press, 1947). An instructive analysis of the mistranslation of Weber's work may be found in R M Weiss, "Weber on Bureaucracy: Management Consultant or Political Theorist?" *Academy of Management Review*, April 1983, pp 242–48.

[15]For a critical appraisal of bureaucracy, see R P Hummel, *The Bureaucratic Experience*, 3rd ed (New York: St. Martin's Press, 1987). The positive side of bureaucracy is presented in C T Goodsell, *The Case for Bureaucracy: A Public Administration Polemic* (Chatham, NJ: Chatham House Publishers, 1983).

[16]See G Pinchot and E Pinchot, "Beyond Bureaucracy," *Business Ethics*, March–April 1994, pp 26–29; and O Harari, "Let the Computers Be the Bureaucrats," *Management Review*, September 1996, pp 57–60.

[17]For examples of what managers are doing to counteract bureaucratic tendencies, see B Dumaine, "The Bureaucracy Busters," *Fortune*, June 17, 1991, pp 36–50; and C J Cantoni, "Eliminating Bureaucracy–Roots and All," *Management Review*, December 1993, pp 30–33.

[18]A management-oriented discussion of general systems theory—an interdisciplinary attempt to integrate the various fragmented sciences—may be found in K E Boulding, "General Systems Theory—The Skeleton of Science," *Management Science*, April 1956, pp 197–208.

[19]J D Thompson, *Organizations in Action* (New York: McGraw-Hill, 1967), pp 6–7. Also see A C Bluedorn, "The Thompson Interdependence Demonstration," *Journal of Management Education*, November 1993, pp 505–09.

[20]For more on this subject, see V-W Mitchell, "Organizational Homoeostasis: A Role for Internal Marketing," *Management Decision*, no. 2, 1992, pp 3–7.

[21]R L Daft and K E Weick, "Toward a Model of Organizations as Interpretation Systems," *Academy of Management Review*, April 1984, p 293.

[22]For background reading, see M E McGill, J W Slocum, Jr., and D Lei, "Management Practices in Learning Organizations," *Organizational Dynamics*, Summer 1992, pp 5–17; D A Garvin, "Building a Learning Organization," *Harvard Business Review*, July–August 1993, pp 78–91; and F Kofman and P M Senge, "Communities of Commitment: The Heart of Learning Organizations," *Organizational Dynamics*, Autumn 1993, pp 5–23. The entire Autumn 1993 issue of Organizational Dynamics is devoted to organizational learning. Also see R Recardo, K Molloy, and J Pellegrino, "How the Learning Organization Manages Change," *National Productivity Review*, Winter 1995–96, pp 7–13; R French and J Bazalgette, "From 'Learning Organization' to 'Teaching-Learning Organization?'" *Management Learning*, March 1996, pp 113–28; and D Miller, "A Preliminary Typology of Organizational Learning: Synthesizing the Literature," *Journal of Management*, no 3, 1996, pp 485–505.

[23]*Training and development*, 1996, vol 50, issue 12, p 34.

[24]See J F Moore, *The Death of Competition: Leadership and Strategy in the Age of Business Ecosystems* (New York: HarperBusiness, 1996), pp 153–54.

[25]J A C Baum, "Organizational Ecology," in *Handbook of Organization Studies*, eds S R Clegg, C Hardy, and W R Nord (Thousand Oaks, CA: Sage Publications, 1996), p 77. (Emphasis added.)

[26]Moore, *The Death of Competition*, pp 11–12.

[27]Ibid., pp 15–16. (Emphasis added.)

[28]Based on discussion in S R Clegg and C Hardy, "Introduction: Organizations, Organization and Organizing," in *Handbook of Organization Studies*, eds S R Clegg, C Hardy, and W R Nord (Thousand Oaks, CA: Sage Publications, 1996), pp 1–28. Also see B Ettorre, "A Conversation with Charles Handy: On the Future of Work and an End to the 'Century of the Organization'," *Organizational Dynamics*, Summer 1996, pp 15–26.

[29]For 1993 layoff data, see J Schmit, "AMR Quarterly Loss Totals $253 Million," *USA Today*, January 20, 1994, p 2B. Also see K Maney, "High Price of Layoffs," *USA Today*, March 24, 1994, p 6B; J A Byrne, "The Pain of Downsizing," *Business Week*, May 9, 1994, pp 60–68; T Brown, "The Human Side of Downsizing," *Management Review*, August 1996, p 15; and B Ettorre, "Constructive Downsizing?" *Management Review*, September 1996, p 8.

[30]C Lorenz, "Management: Ford's Global Matrix Gamble," *The Financial Times*, December1994, 16, p 13.

[31]M Syrett, and K Kingston, "GE's Hungarian Light Switch," *Management Today*, April 1995, p 57–59.

[32]T A Stewart, "Reengineering: The Hot New Managing Tool," *Fortune*, August 23, 1993, p 41. Also see M Hammer and J Champy, *Reengineering the Corporation: A Manifesto for Business Revolution* (New York: HarperBusiness, 1993); and J Champy, *Reengineering Management: The Mandate for New Leadership* (New York: HarperBusiness, 1995).

[33]See O Harari, "Why Did Reengineering Die?" Management Review, June 1996, pp 49–52; and E Geisler, "Cleaning Up after Reengineering," *Business Horizons*, September–October 1996, pp 71–78.

[34]See J C Latack, A J Kinicki, and G E Prussia, "An Integrative Process Model of Coping with Job Loss," *Academy of Management Review*, April 1995, pp 311–42; R T King, Jr., "Seven Office-Mates at a Dying Bank Ask: Who Will Survive?" *The Wall Street Journal*, October 9, 1996, pp A1, A10; and C Albrecht, Jr., "Career Centers Promote Employability," *HRMagazine*, August 1996, pp 105–08.

[35]P Platt, *French or Foe?* (London: Culture Crossings, 1994).

[36]Instructive critiques of hierarchy can be found in J Gordon,"The Team Troubles That Won't Go Away," *Training*, August 1994, pp 25–34; W E Halal, "From Hierarchy to Enterprise: Internal Markets Are the New Foundation of Management," *Academy of Management Executive*, November 1994, pp 69–83; and H Lancaster, "Those Rotten Things You Say about Work May Be True After All," *The Wall Street Journal*, February 20, 1996, p B1.

[37]E E Lawler III, "Substitutes for Hierarchy," *Organizational Dynamics*, Summer 1988, p 13.

[38]G De Jonquières, "Survey of Europe's Most Respected Companies (1): ABB tops the super league," *The Financial Times*, September 19, 1995, p 1.

[39] "Producer power," *The Economist*, March 4, 1995, p. 78.

[40]K Cameron, "Critical Questions in Assessing Organizational Effectiveness," *Organizational Dynamics*, Autumn 1980, p 70. Also see J Pfeffer, "When It Comes to 'Best Practices'—Why Do Smart Organizations Occasionally Do Dumb Things?" *Organizational Dynamics*, Summer 1996, pp 33–44; and R R Rehder, "Is Saturn Competitive?" Business *Horizons*, March–April 1994, pp 7–15.

[41]See, for example, R O Brinkerhoff and D E Dressler, *Productivity Measurement: A Guide for Managers and Evaluators* (Newbury Park, CA: Sage Publications, 1990).

[42]Based on and translated from E Verdegaal, "De Ahold-Greep: Hoe Albert Heijn zijn eigen boodschappen doet," *Management Team*, April 5, 1996, pp 20–28.

[43]Cameron, "Critical Questions in Assessing Organizational Effectiveness," p 67.

[44]T Donaldson and L E Preston, "The Stakeholder Theory of the Corporation: Concepts, Evidence, and Implications," *Academy of Management Review*, January 1995, pp 65–91.

[45]See N C Roberts and P J King, "The Stakeholder Audit Goes Public," *Organizational Dynamics*, Winter 1989, pp 63–79.

[46]F W Julien, J C Lampe "Managing Internal Audit Stakeholders," *Internal Auditing*, Spring 1994, pp 51–57.

[47]E M Reingold, "America's Hamburger Helper," *Time*, June 29, 1992, p 66.

[48]J Kay and J Silberston, "Corporate Governance," *National Institute Economic Review*, August, 1995, p 84.

[49]Ibid., p. 84–95.

[50]See C Ostroff and N Schmitt, "Configurations of Organizational Effectiveness and Efficiency," *Academy of Management Journal*, December 1993, pp 1345–61.

[51]K S Cameron, "Effectiveness as Paradox: Consensus and Conflict in Conceptions of Organizational Effectiveness," *Management Science*, May 1986, p 542.

[52]Alternative effectiveness criteria are discussed in Ibid.; A G Bedeian, "Organization Theory: Current Controversies, Issues, and Directions," in *International Review of Industrial and Organizational Psychology*, eds C L Cooper and I T Robertson (New York: John Wiley & Sons, 1987), pp 1–33; and M Keeley, "Impartiality and Participant-Interest Theories of Organizational Effectiveness," *Administrative Science Quarterly*, March 1984, pp 1–25.

Nineteen

Organizational Life Cycles and Design

LEARNING OBJECTIVES

When you finish studying the material in this chapter, you should be able to:

1. Identify and briefly explain the three stages of the organizational life cycle .

2. Discuss organizational decline relative to the organizational life cycle.

3. Explain what the contingency approach to organization design involves.

4. Describe the relationship between differentiation in effective organizations.

5. Disuss Burns and Stalker's findings regarding mechanistic and organic organizations.

6. Define and briefly explain the practical significance of centralization and decentralization.

7. Discuss the effective management of organizational size.

8. Discuss horizontal, hourglass, network organizations, and the shamrock organization.

Radical Organizational Surgery at a Swedish Hospital

Like many state-funded hospitals in Europe, prestigious Karolinska Hospital in Stockholm faced financial difficulties in 1992, in its case a reduction of funding by about 20%. Karolinska's then chief executive, Jan Lindsten, dreaded the prospect: He felt the hospital had already cut as much as it could without impairing the quality of care. When he turned to the hospital's professional advisory board, which includes the CEOs of companies like Volvo, they suggested trying Boston Consulting Group's Time Based Management methods to radically change the way work was done. BCG promptly set about reorganizing work at the hospital around patient flow. Instead of bouncing a patient from department to department, BCG advised, look at illness to recovery as a process with pit stops in admission, surgery, and a recovery ward.

What this means in practice is that patients now meet a surgeon and a doctor of internal medicine together, for instance, rather than separately, which results in better care and fewer hospital visits. Says Mikael Lövgren, a BCG consultant who worked with Karolinska: "Hospitals don't think along the patient dimension. They think only in terms of specializations"—not unlike many companies that manage only their functions and thereby obscure their line of vision to customers.

Karolinska's problems as it began to transform itself into a horizontal organization were compounded by the fact that it had recently been through a major decentralization, which had created 47 departments marching to their own drums. Tribalism is the human condition, it seems, within hospitals as well as corporations. Lindsten had brought the number down to 11, but coordination was still woefully haphazard. Patients had to scale the high walls between functions, often making multiple all-day visits to the hospital for tests. A patient with an enlarged prostate gland spent, on average, an astounding 255 days after his first contact with the hospital before it was treated; only 2% of that time involved actual treatment—the rest was passed waiting for appointments, shuttling between departments, and so on.

To manage patient flow, most departments in the hospital created a new position, that of "nurse coordinator," whose responsibilities include minimizing the number of visits a patient must make. Nurse coordinators—one might call them "process doctors"—look for situations where the baton is dropped in the handoff between or within departments. The position has also created a career track for nurses, who can aspire to become administrative heads of various departments. Departments have a medical chief as well, who is responsible for the professional expertise that is so obviously important in a hospital. Says Sonia Wallin, a nurse coordinator, who has worked at Karolinska since 1981: "I report to a nurse who is over the doctors. A few years ago that would have been impossible."

Not all the doctors are entirely comfortable reporting to nurses, even on purely administrative matters. The new structure has been sold to physicians as a way to free them from scheduling and other drudgery. They can concentrate instead on their clinical work and research. Some departments at Karolinska have taken to the concept of patient flow faster than others—orthopedic and plastic surgery share a ward, for example—yet hospital managers are sanguine. Says Einar Areklett, a senior manager: "Running a hospital is like running an opera house. You have a lot of Pavarottis. It takes a few years before you have everyone with you."

One of the clear lessons managers involved in similar transitions can take away from Karolinska is the need for what Reengineering Management author James Champy calls "honest eloquence." Lindsten, who has since left to take charge of a similar redesign of a hospital in Copenhagen, consistently framed his exhortations for change in the context of the hostile external environment the hospital faced. Staff moved quickly from disbelief to action. Waiting times for surgery have been cut from six or eight months to three weeks. Three of 15 operating theaters have been closed, yet 3,000 more operations are performed annually, a 25% increase. Says Dr. Sten Lindahl, head of the department of anesthesiology and intensive care: "We would hate to go back to the lazy days."[1]

Discussion Question

Why was Karolinska's staff generally receptive to the new horizontal structure?

O rganizations are much more than the familiar pattern of boxes and lines we see on organization charts. Charts may be a necessary starting point, but we need to know more if we are to understand and manage organizations adequately. Organization design scholar and consultant Robert W Keidel put it this way:

Our historical preoccupation with organization charts—hierarchical displays of reporting relationships—is counterproductive. Organizational design is far more a matter of charting direction and navigating among autonomy, control, and cooperation than of moving boxes around. The process is never-ending.[2]

Indeed, organizations take on a life of their own. As has been said many times, organizations are more than the sum of their parts. This chapter explores important dynamics of organizations including the life-cycle perspective, with special emphasis on decline, and the contingency approach to organization design. Our underlying challenge is to learn how to build organizations capable of thriving in an environment characterized by rapid change and rugged global competition.[3]

Organizational Life Cycles

Like the people who make up organizations, organizations themselves go through life cycles. Organizations are born and, barring early decline, eventually grow and mature. If decline is not reversed, the organization dies. Just as you will face new problems and challenges during different phases of your lifetime, so do organizations. Thus, managers need a working knowledge of organizational life cycles and the closely related topic of organizational decline. According to a pair of experts on the subject: "A consistent pattern of development seems to occur in organizations over time, and organizational activities and structures in one stage are not the same as the activities and structures present at another stage. This implies that the criteria used to evaluate an organization's success in one stage of development also may be different from criteria used to evaluate success at another stage of development."[4] This section examines stages of the organizational life-cycle concept and discusses the threat of organizational decline.

Organizational Life-Cycle Stages

Although the organizational life-cycle concept has been around for a long time, it has enjoyed renewed interest among respected researchers in recent years. Many life-cycle models have been proposed.[5] One point of agreement among the competing models is that organizations evolve in a predictable sequence of identifiable stages. Table 19–1 presents a basic organizational life-cycle model. Stages 1 through 3 of the model are inception, high growth, and maturity. Changes during these three stages can be summed up in the following rule: *As organizations mature, they tend to become larger, more formalized, and more differentiated (fragmented).* Differentiation increases because of added levels in the hierarchy, further division of labour, and formation of political coalitions.

Life-Cycle Timing and Type of Change

Two key features of this life-cycle model address the timing and type of changes experienced by the organization. Relative to timing, the duration of each phase is highly variable, depending on a host of organizational and environmental factors. This explains why there is no time frame in Table 19–1. Some organizations have short life cycles, with abbreviated or missing stages.

Regarding the type of change that organizations undergo from one stage to the next, Indiana University researchers noted: "The very nature of the firm changes as a business grows in size and matures. These are not changes in degree; rather, they are fundamental changes in kind."[6] This sort of *qualitative* change helps explain the unexpected departure of founder Mitchell D Kapor from Lotus Development Corporation, maker of the

Table 19–1   Stages of the Organizational Life Cycle

CHARACTERISTICS	STAGE I: INCEPTION	STAGE 2: HIGH GROWTH	STAGE 3: MATURITY – – – – – – – – DECLINE	
Type of organizational structure	No formal structure	Centralized Formal	Decentralized Formal	Rigid, top-heavy, overly complex
Communication process and planning	Informal Face-to-face Little planning	Moderately formal Budgets	Very formal Five-year plans Rules and regulations	Communication breakdown Blind adherence to "success formula"
Method of decision making	Individual judgment Entrepreneurial	Professional management Analytical tools	Professional management Bargaining	Emphasis on form rather than substance Self-serving politics
Organizational growth rate	Inconsistent but improving	Rapid positive growth	Growth slowing or declining	Declining
Organizational age and size	Young and small	Larger and older	Largest or once large and oldest	Variable age and shrinking

Sources: Characteristics and first three stages excerpted from K G Smith, T R Mitchell, and C E Summer, "Top Level Management Priorities in Different Stages of the Organizational Life Cycle," *Academy of Management Journal*, December 1985, p 802. Organizational decline portion adapted from discussion in P Lorange and R T Nelson, "How to Recognize—and Avoid—Organizational Decline," *Sloan Management Review*, Spring 1987, pp 41–48.

innovative and once successful 1–2–3® computer spreadsheet program. When asked by *Inc.* magazine why he walked away from it all, Kapor replied:

If you look at Lotus as it started and as it is today, I think you'll see more differences than similarities. In the beginning, it was classically entrepreneurial; a small group of people trying to break into a market with a new product around which they hoped to build a company and achieve market share for the company and financial success, for themselves and their investors. Today, Lotus is a company of 1,350 people with diversified, worldwide operations, with the organizational structure and challenges of a $275 million company. And so the nature of the challenges facing the company, and facing the people in it—and, facing me—is radically different.[7]

Entrepreneurs tend to miss the inception-stage excitement and risk as their organizations move into the high-growth and maturity stages.[8] Some entrepreneurs become liabilities because they fail to grow with their organizations. Others wisely turn the reins over to professional managers who possess the ability and desire to manage large and complex organizations. Managerial skills needed during one stage of the organization's life cycle may be inappropriate or inadequate during a later stage.

The Ever-Present Threat of Decline   While decline is included in the model, it is not a distinct stage with predictable sequencing (hence the broken line between maturity and decline in Table 19–1). Organizational decline is a *potential,* rather than automatic, outcome that can occur any time during the life cycle. Stage 1 and stage 2 organizations are as readily victimized by the forces of decline as mature stage 3 organizations According to a study by Dun & Bradstreet, 205,588 companies failed in 1992 in Europe.[9] Most of the failed businesses experience decline after an extended inception stage or an abbreviated high-growth stage. While noting "decline is almost unavoidable unless deliberate steps are taken to prevent it,"[10] specialists on the subject have alerted managers to 14 early-warning signs of organizational decline:

1. Excess personnel.

2. Tolerance of incompetence.

3. Cumbersome administrative procedures.

4. Disproportionate staff power (e.g., technical staff specialists politically overpower line managers, whom they view as unsophisticated and too conventional).

5. Replacement of substance with form (e.g., the planning process becomes more important than the results achieved).

6. Scarcity of clear goals and decision benchmarks.

7. Fear of embarrassment and conflict (e.g., formerly successful executives may resist new ideas for fear of revealing past mistakes).

8. Loss of effective communication.

9. Outdated organizational structure.[11]

10. Increased scapegoating by leaders.

11. Resistance to change.

12. Low morale.

13. Special interest groups are more vocal.

14. Decreased innovation.[12]

Managers who monitor these early warning signs of organizational decline are better able to reorganize in a timely and effective manner.[13] However, recent research has uncovered a troublesome perception tendency among entrenched top management teams. In companies where there had been little if any turnover among top executives, there was a tendency to attribute organizational problems to *external* causes (e.g., competition, the government, technology shifts). Oppositely, *internal* attributions tended to be made by top management teams with *many* new members. Thus, proverbial "new blood" at the top appears to be a good insurance policy against misperceiving the early-warning signs of organizational decline.[14]

Preventing Organizational Decline   The time to start doing something about organizational decline is when everything is going *right*. For it is during periods of high success that the seeds of decline are sown.[15] *Complacency* is the number one threat because it breeds overconfidence and inattentiveness:[16]

GM [General Motors] is an example of a firm that grew so rich and powerful that it became oblivious to the signals of changing times. Despite the oil crises of the 1970s and the Japanese challenge of the '80s, GM never put its heart into developing smaller, high-quality cars. It took a new division, Saturn, to develop GM's first winning US small car. "When you're on top of the heap, there's a disdain for change, a disdain for new ideas," says Lawrence Hrebiniak, a professor at the Wharton School. "It just goes with the territory, because you are No. 1."[17]

Total quality management advocates remind us that *continuous improvement* is the first line of defence against organizational decline. Japan's Toyota is a world leader in this regard and an instructive counterpoint to General Motors' situation:

Of all the slogans kicked around Toyota City, the key one is *kaizen*, which means "continuous improvement" in Japanese. While many other companies strive for dramatic breakthroughs, Toyota keeps doing lots of little things better and better. . . .

One consultant calls Toyota's strategy "rapid inch-up": Take enough tiny steps and pretty soon you outdistance the competition. . . .

In short, Toyota is the best carmaker in the world. And it keeps getting better. Says Iwao Isomura, chief of personnel: "Our current success is the best reason to change things." Extensive interviews with Toyota executives in the US and Japan demonstrate the company's total dedication to continuous improvement. What is often mistaken for excessive modesty is, in fact, an expression of permanent dissatisfaction—even with exemplary performance.[18]

Organizational Life-Cycle Research and Practical Implications

The best available evidence in this area comes from the combination of a field study and a laboratory simulation. Both studies led researchers to the same conclusions. In the field study, 38 top-level electronics industry managers from 27 randomly selected companies were presented with a decision-making scenario. They then were asked to complete a questionnaire about priorities. It was found that priorities shifted across the three life-cycle stages introduced in Table 19–1. As the organization matured from stage 1 to stages 2 and 3, top management's priorities shifted as follows:

- A strong emphasis on technical efficiency grew even stronger.

- The desire for personal power and commitment from subordinates increased significantly.

- The desire for organizational integration (coordination and cooperation) decreased significantly.[19]

In a separate but related study, researchers examined the relationship between life-cycle stages and effectiveness criteria. This five-year case study of a New York State mental health agency revealed that top management's effectiveness criteria changed during the organization's life cycle. Early emphasis on flexibility, resource acquisition, and employee development/satisfaction gave way to formalization as the agency matured. Formalization criteria encompassed increased attention to factors such as goal setting, information management, communication, control, productivity, and efficiency.[20]

This research reveals that different stages of the organizational life cycle are associated with distinctly different managerial responses. It must be noted, however, that management's priorities and effectiveness criteria in the foregoing studies were not necessarily the *right* ones. Much research remains to be done to identify specific contingencies. Still, the point remains that managers need to be flexible and adaptive as their organizations evolve through the various life-cycle stages.[21] As learned the hard way by General Motors, IBM, Air France, and Apple, yesterday's formula for success can be today's formula for noncompetitiveness and decline.[22]

The Contingency Approach to Organization Design

Contingency approach to organization design
Creating an effective organization–environment fit.

According to the **contingency approach to organization design,** organizations tend to be more effective when they are structured to fit the demands of the situation.[23] A contingency approach can be put into practice by first assessing the degree of environmental uncertainty.[24] Next, the contingency model calls for using various organization design configurations to achieve an effective organization–environment fit. This section presents an environmental uncertainty model along with two classic contingency design studies.

Assessing Environmental Uncertainty

Robert Duncan proposed a two-dimensional model for classifying environmental demands on the organization (see Figure 19–1). On the horizontal axis is the simple→ complex dimension. This dimension "focuses on whether the factors in the environment considered for decision making are few in number and similar or many in number and different."[25] On the vertical axis of Duncan's model is the static→dynamic dimension. "The static–dynamic dimension of the environment is concerned with whether the factors of the environment remain the same over time or change."[26] When combined, these two dimensions characterize four situations that represent increasing uncertainty for organizations. According to Duncan, the complex–dynamic situation of highest uncertainty is the most common organizational environment today.

Figure 19–1 A Four-Way Classification of Organizational Environments

	Simple	Complex
Static	Low perceived uncertainty • Small number of factors and components in the environment • Factors and components are somewhat similar to one another • Factors and components remain basically the same and are not changing • Example: Soft drink industry 1	2 Moderately low perceived uncertainty • Large number of factors and components in the environment • Factors and components are not similar to one another • Factors and components remain basically the same • Example: Food products
Dynamic	3 Moderately high perceived uncertainty • Small number of factors and components in the environment • Factors and components are somewhat similar to one another • Factors and components of the environment are in continual process of change • Example: Fast-food industry	4 High perceived uncertainty • Large number of factors and components in the environment • Factors and components are not similar to one another • Factors and components of environment are in a continual process of change • Examples: Commercial airline industry Telephone communications (AT&T)

Source: "What Is the Right Organization Structure Decision Tree Analysis Provides the Answer" by Robert Duncan. Reprinted by permission of the publisher from *Organizational Dynamics*, Winter 1979, © 1979. American Management Association, New York. All rights reserved.

Amid these fast-paced times, nothing stands still. Not even in the simple–static quadrant. For example, during the first 94 years of the history of the Coca-Cola Company (through 1980), only one soft drink bore the company's name. Just six years later, Coke had its famous name on seven soft drinks, including Coca-Cola Classic, Coke, and Cherry Coke. Despite operating in an environment characterized as simple and static, the Coca-Cola Company has had to become a more risk-taking, entrepreneurial company.[27] This means organizations facing moderate to high uncertainty (quadrants 3 and 4 in Figure 19–1) have to be highly flexible, responsive, and adaptive today.[28] Contingency organization design is more important than ever because it helps managers structure their organizations to fit the key situational factors discussed next.

Differentiation and Integration: The Lawrence and Lorsch Study

In their classic text, *Organization and Environment,* Harvard researchers Paul Lawrence and Jay Lorsch explained how two structural forces simultaneously fragment the organization and bind it together. They cautioned that an imbalance between these two forces—labelled *differentiation* and *integration*—could hinder organizational effectiveness.

Differentiation
Division of labour and specialization that causes people to think and act differently.

Differentiation Splits the Organization Apart **Differentiation** occurs through division of labour and technical specialization. A behavioural outcome of differentiation is that technical specialists such as computer programmers tend to think and act differently than specialists in, say, accounting or marketing. Excessive differentiation can cause the organization to bog down in miscommunication, conflict, and politics. Thus, differentiation needs to be offset by an opposing structural force to ensure needed *coordination*. This is where integration enters the picture (see Figure 19–2).

Figure 19–2   Differentiation and Integration Are Opposing Structural Forces

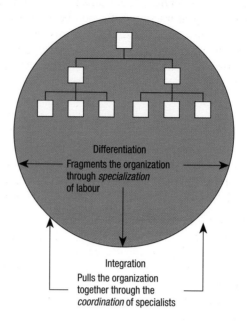

Integration

Cooperation among specialists to achieve common goal.

Integration Binds the Organization Together   Integration occurs when specialists cooperate to achieve a common goal. According to the Lawrence and Lorsch model, integration can be achieved through various combinations of the following six mechanisms: (1) a formal hierarchy; (2) standardized policies, rules, and procedures; (3) departmentalization; (4) committees and cross-functional teams; (5) human relations training, and (6) individuals and groups acting as liaisons between specialists.

Achieving the Proper Balance   When Lawrence and Lorsch studied successful and unsuccessful companies in three industries, they concluded the following: *As environmental complexity increased, successful organizations exhibited higher degrees of both differentiation and integration.* In other words, an effective balance was achieved. Unsuccessful organizations, in contrast, tended to suffer from an imbalance of too much differentiation and not enough offsetting integration. This outcome was confirmed by the life-cycle research discussed earlier. As the organization matured, management's desire for integration became a significantly less important priority. Managers need to fight this tendency if their growing and increasingly differentiated organizations are to be coordinated.

Lawrence and Lorsch also discovered that "the more differentiated an organization, the more difficult it is to achieve integration."[29] Managers of today's complex organizations need to strive constantly and creatively to achieve greater integration.[30] For example, how does 3M Company, with its dozens of autonomous divisions and more than 60,000 products, successfully maintain its competitive edge in technology? Among other things, 3M makes sure its technical specialists frequently interact with one another so cross-fertilization of ideas takes place. Art Fry, credited with inventing the now ubiquitous Post-It Notes, actually owes much of his success to colleague Spencer Silver, an engineer down the hall who created an apparently useless semiadhesive. If Fry and Silver had worked in a company without a strong commitment to integration, we probably would not have Post-It Notes. 3M does not leave this sort of cross-fertilization to chance. It organizes for integration with such things as a Technology Council that regularly convenes researchers from various divisions and an annual science fair at which 3M scientists enthusiastically hawk their new ideas, not to customers, but to each other![31]

Mechanistic versus Organic Organizations

Mechanistic organizations
Rigid, command-and-control bureaucracies.

A second landmark contingency design study was reported by a pair of British behavioural scientists, Tom Burns and G M Stalker. In the course of their research, they drew a very instructive distinction between what they called mechanistic and organic organizations. **Mechanistic organizations** are rigid bureaucracies with strict rules, narrowly defined tasks, and top-down communication. For example, when *Business Week* correspondent Kathleen Deveny spent a day working in a McDonald's restaurant, she found a very mechanistic organization:

> Here every job is broken down into the smallest of steps, and the whole process is automated. . . .
>
> Anyone could do this, I think. But McDonald's restaurants operate like Swiss watches, and the minute I step behind the counter I am a loose part in the works. . . .
>
> I bag French fries for a few minutes, but I'm much too slow. Worse, I can't seem to keep my station clean enough. Failing at French fries is a fluke, I tell myself. . . .
>
> I try to move faster, but my co-workers are playing at 45 rpm, and I'm stuck at 33⅓.[32]

Organic organizations
Fluid and flexible network of multitalented people.

This sort of mechanistic structure is necessary at McDonald's because of the competitive need for uniform product quality, speedy service, and cleanliness. Oppositely, **organic organizations** are flexible networks of multitalented individuals who perform a variety of tasks.[33] W L Gore & Associates, The Newark, Delaware, maker of waterproof Gore-Tex fabric, is a highly organic organization because it lacks job descriptions and a formalized hierarchy and deemphasizes titles and status.[34] (See the International OB.)

A Matter of Degree   Importantly, as illustrated in Figure 19–3, each of the mechanistic-organic characteristics is a matter of degree. Organizations tend to be *relatively* mechanistic or *relatively* organic. Pure types are rare because divisions, departments, or units in the same organization may be more or less mechanistic or organic. From an employee's standpoint, which organization structure would you prefer?

Centralized decision making
Top managers make all key decisions.

Decentralized decision making
Lower-level managers are empowered to make important decisions.

Different Approaches to Decision Making   Decision making tends to be centralized in mechanistic organizations and decentralized in organic organizations. **Centralized decision making** occurs when key decisions are made by top management. **Decentralized decision making** occurs when important decisions are made by middle- and lower-level managers. Generally, centralized organizations are more tightly controlled while decentralized organizations are more adaptive to changing situations.[35] Each has its appropriate use.

Figure 19–3   Characteristics of Mechanistic and Organic Organizations

CHARACTERISTIC	MECHANISTIC ORGANIZATION		ORGANIC ORGANIZATION
1. Task definition and knowledge required	Narrow; technical	→	Broad; general
2. Linkage between individual's contribution and organization's purpose	Vague or indirect	→	Clear or direct
3. Task flexibility	Rigid; routine	→	Flexible; varied
4. Specification of techniques, obligations, and rights	Specific	→	General
5. Degree of hierarchical control	High	→	Low (self-control emphasized)
6. Primary communication pattern	Top-down	→	Lateral (between peers)
7. Primary decision-making style	Authoritarian	→	Democratic; participative
8. Emphasis on obedience and loyalty	High	→	Low

Source: Adapted from discussion in T Burns and G M Stalker, *The Management of Innovation* (London: Tavistock, 1961), pp 119–25.

Experts on the subject warn against extremes of centralization or decentralization. The challenge is to achieve a workable balance between the two extremes. A management consultant put it this way:

The modern organization in transition will recognize the pull of two polarities: a need for greater centralization to create low-cost shared resources; and, a need to improve market responsiveness with greater decentralization. Today's winning organizations are the ones that can handle the paradox and tensions of both pulls. These are the firms that analyze the optimum

---

International Organizational Behaviour
W L Gore's Organic Structure Thrives in Scotland

Associates at W L Gore in Scotland's "Silicon Glen" note with wry satisfaction the number of big companies that are now talking about self-management, empowerment, the flattened hierarchy, and so on. Their company was founded on those principles more than 30 years ago, and they believe they know a thing or two about them. As "associates" . . . rather than managers, employees, staff, or simply workers, they enjoy a freedom of action which would arouse envy in some, concern in others.

"People think we're a philanthropic organization," says one associate, "but in fact, we're very profit-oriented." The five Scottish plants, like the US ones, are managing pretty well to follow founder Bill Gore's precepts for self-realization, avoidance of hierarchy, as well as to "make money and have fun." Exactly how much money the company prefers not to disclose, and, since it is private and registered in Delaware, is not easy for outsiders to discover. But worldwide sales are around $950 million, derived from four main divisions—the well-known Gore-Tex fabrics, electronic connectors, medical patches and implants, industrial filters and other specialized products. The company claims that it would rank 75th in the Fortune 500 league based on a 10-year rate of return to investors. Innovation is its strong point, and its ample cash resources empower the associates in a practical way ignored by most of the textbooks.

The freedom that Gore offers its associates is not an unmixed blessing. Associates are always encouraged to join a team with particular responsibilities, but they also have the opportunity—and encouragement—to pursue ideas and projects of their own choosing, particularly those which might lead to new applications and markets for the product. Much of the company's growth has come from finding new uses for their applications.

PTFE [polytetraflouroethylene] is a good electrical insulator, which provided the basis for Bill Gore's original business. His son Bob, now president of the company, discovered how to expand PTFE film so that it "breathes"—i.e., allows vapor to pass through it, but not liquids. Bonded to a fabric, expanded PTFE is used in rainwear, sportswear, and other forms of clothing, also in medical patches and filters.

Many of the company's most successful ideas are attributable to individuals. "If you demonstrate ability, others give you the opportunity to expand, and you can change roles quite dramatically across disciplines," says Arthur Punchard, the UK fabric plant's leader. "But there's almost an equal amount of freedom to do nothing, if there's no clear statement of intent from the organization. You either thrive on it or you don't."

Most associates encounter difficulties when they first join because of the unaccustomed freedom, because they are uncertain about who does what in the organization, and how to get things done. They wonder, "should I ask, or should I just do it?" The answers require "networking in a real, personal sense," says John Kennedy, responsible for UK fabric marketing, and for the consumer fabrics business across Europe. "Finding the people who really matter is the most difficult bit, but you eventually learn who they are." Kennedy, like Punchard, is more closely associated than most, and would therefore figure on most associates' list of those who matter. . . .

Among newcomers, the company finds, doubts and depression commonly begin to set in about a year after they first join. The advice and support of sponsors can then be invaluable. If they survive that period they usually stay a long time. But not always. Gore has recently been tightening up its selection process to reduce the drop-out rate.

SOURCE   "The Gore's Happy Family." Reproduced from an article by Tom Lester in the Febuary 1993 issue of *Management Today* with the kind permission of the copyright owner, Management Publications, Ltd.

organizational solution in each particular circumstance, without prejudice for one type of organization over another. The result is, almost invariably, a messy mixture of decentralized units sharing cost-effective centralized resources.[36]

Germany's Daimler Benz, maker of Mercedes-Benz cars and trucks, recently reorganized to achieve a better balance between centralization and decentralization:

In just 18 months as Daimler Benz's CEO, Chief Executive Jurgen E Schrempp has engineered a remarkable turnaround at Germany's biggest industrial company. In place of the top-heavy holding-company structure he inherited, Schrempp carved the conglomerate into 36 operating units, each reporting directly to the Daimler board on strategy and profit goals.[37]

Managers of the 36 operating units will have some latitude (decentralization) in how they achieve the strategies and profit goals orchestrated by headquarters (centralization). Centralization and decentralization are not an either-or proposition; they are an *and-also* balancing act.

Relevant Research Findings   When they classified a sample of actual companies as either mechanistic or organic, Burns and Stalker discovered one type was not superior to the other. Each type had its appropriate place, depending on the environment. When the environment was relatively *stable and certain,* the successful organizations tended to be *mechanistic. Organic* organizations tended to be the successful ones when the environment was *unstable and uncertain.*[38]

In a more recent study of 103 department managers from eight manufacturing firms and two aerospace organizations, managerial skill was found to have a greater impact on a global measure of department effectiveness in organic departments than in mechanistic departments. This led the researchers to recommend the following contingencies for management staffing and training:

If we have two units, one organic and one mechanistic, and two potential applicants differing in overall managerial ability, we might want to assign the more competent to the organic unit since in that situation there are few structural aids available to the manager in performing required responsibilities. It is also possible that managerial training is especially needed by managers being groomed to take over units that are more organic in structure.[39]

Another interesting finding comes from a study of 42 voluntary church organizations. As the organizations became more mechanistic (more bureaucratic) the intrinsic motivation of their members decreased. Mechanistic organizations apparently undermined the volunteers' sense of freedom and self-determination. Additionally, the researchers believe their findings help explain why bureaucracy tends to feed on itself: "A mechanistic organizational structure may breed the need for a more extremely mechanistic system because of the reduction in intrinsically motivated behavior."[40] Thus, bureaucracy begets greater bureaucracy.

Most recently, field research in two factories, one mechanistic and the other organic, found expected communication patterns. Command-and-control (downwards) communication characterized the mechanistic factory. Consultative or participative (two-way) communication prevailed in the organic factory.[41]

Both Mechanistic and Organic Structures Are Needed   Although achievement-oriented students of OB typically express a distaste for mechanistic organizations, not all organizations or subunits can or should be organic. For example, as mentioned earlier, McDonald's could not achieve its admired quality and service standards without extremely mechanistic restaurant operations. Imagine the food and service you would get if McDonald's employees used their own favorite ways of doing things and worked at their own pace! On the other hand, mechanistic structure alienates some employees because it erodes their sense of self-control.

Three Important Contingency Variables: Technology, Size, and Strategic Choice

Both contingency theories just discussed have one important thing in common. Each is based on an "environmental imperative," meaning the environment is said to be the primary determinant of effective organizational structure. Other organization theorists disagree. They contend that factors such as the organization's core technology, size, and corporate strategy hold the key to organizational structure. This section examines the significance of these three additional contingency variables.

The Impact of Technology on Structure (Woodward and Beyond)

Joan Woodward proposed a *technological imperative* in 1965 after studying 100 small manufacturing firms in southern England. She found distinctly different structural patterns for effective and ineffective companies based on technologies of low, medium, or high *complexity*. Effective organizations with either low- or high-complexity technology tended to have an organic structure. Effective organizations based on a technology of medium complexity tended to have a mechanistic structure. Woodward concluded that technology was the overriding determinant of organizational structure.[42]

Since Woodward's landmark work, many studies of the relationship between technology and structure have been conducted. Unfortunately, disagreement and confusion have prevailed. For example, a comprehensive review of 50 studies conducted between 1965 and 1980 found six technology concepts and 140 technology-structure relationships.[43] A statistical analysis of those studies prompted the following conclusions:

- The more the technology requires *interdependence* between individuals and/or groups, the greater the need for integration (coordination).

- "As technology moves from routine to nonroutine, subunits adopt less formalized and [less] centralized structures."[44]

Additional insights can be expected in this area as researchers coordinate their definitions of technology and refine their methodologies.[45]

Organizational Size and Performance

Size is an important structural variable subject to two schools of thought. According to the first school, economists have long extolled the virtues of economies of scale. This approach, often called the "bigger is better" model, assumes the per-unit cost of production decreases as the organization grows. In effect, bigger is said to be more efficient. For example, on an annual basis, General Motors supposedly can produce its 100,000th car less expensively than its 10th car.

The second school of thought pivots on the law of diminishing returns. Called the "small is beautiful" model,[46] this approach contends that oversized organizations and subunits tend to be plagued by costly behavioural problems. Large and impersonal organizations are said to breed apathy and alienation, with resulting problems such as turnover and absenteeism. Two strong advocates of this second approach are the authors of the bestselling *In Search of Excellence:*

In the excellent companies, small in almost every case is beautiful. The small facility turns out to be the most efficient; its turned-on, motivated, highly productive worker, in communication (and competition) with his peers, outproduces the worker in the big facilities time and again. It holds for plants, for project teams, for divisions—for the entire company.[47]

Is Complexity the Issue? (A Case against Mergers?) Recent research suggests that when designing their organizations, managers should follow a middle ground between "bigger is better" and "small is beautiful" because both models have been oversold. Indeed, a newer perspective says *complexity,* not size, is the central issue.[48] A thought-provoking case in point is Japan's Mitsubishi, the world's largest company:

Mitsubishi's revenues [$176 billion] are bigger than those of AT&T, Du Pont, Citicorp, and Procter & Gamble combined. In serving its 45,000 customers, Mitsubishi moves as many as 100,000 products, from kernels of corn to huge power generators, around the world. Among the dozens of properties it owns outright are all or parts of cattle feedlots and coal mines in Australia, pulp mills and iron ore mines in Canada, copper mines in Chile, a resort in Hawaii, and the liquefied natural gas fields off the coast of Brunei. . . .

Now here's the pin that punctures the balloon. . . . Mitsubishi is scraping by on meager earnings of $219 million. That translates into a pintsize profit margin of just 0.12%. The other big trading companies, or *sogo shosha* as they are known in Japan, suffer similarly.[49]

So, is Mitsubishi unprofitable because it is too big or because its global web of diverse enterprises has become too complex to manage? We do not have a definite answer, but the excessive complexity argument is compelling. This argument may also help explain why many mergers have been disappointing in recent years. According to *Business Week,* the "historic surge of consolidations and combinations is occurring in the face of strong evidence that mergers and acquisitions, at least over the past 35 years or so, have hurt more than helped companies and shareholders."[50]

Research Insights   Researchers measure the size of organizations and organizational subunits in different ways. Some focus on financial indicators such as total sales or total asset value. Others look at the number of employees, transactions (such as the number of students in a school district), or capacity (such as the number of beds in a hospital). A meta-analysis[51] of 31 studies conducted between 1931 and 1985 that related organizational size to performance found:

- Larger organizations (in terms of assets) tended to be more productive (in terms of sales and profits).

- There were "no positive relationships between organizational size and efficiency, suggesting the absence of net economy of scale effects."[52]

- There were zero to slightly negative relationships between *subunit* size and productivity and efficiency.

- A more recent study examined the relationship between organizational size and employee turnover over a period of 65 months. Turnover was unrelated to organizational size.[53]

Striving for Small Units in Big Organizations   In summary, bigger is not necessarily better and small is not necessarily beautiful.[54] Hard-and-fast numbers regarding exactly how big is too big or how small is too small are difficult to come by. Management consultants offer some rough estimates (see Table 19–2). Until better evidence is available, the best that managers can do is monitor the productivity, quality, and efficiency of divisions, departments, and profit centres. Unwieldy and overly complex units need to be promptly broken into ones of more manageable size. The trick is to *create smallness within bigness.*[55] According to Gerard Fairtlough, author of a book called "*Creative Compartments,*" the future will force large organisations to create interlinked creative compartments of about 100 people each. Benetton is an excellent example of such a structure, he says. Benetton's thousands of subcontractors remain separate firms, although they only sell Benetton products. Fairtlough writes:

The subcontractors are of various kinds - firms controlled by Benetton, firms set up by former Benetton managers, some independent firms and even homeworkers.[56]

Table 19–2   Organizational Size: Management Consultants Address the Question of "How Big Is Too Big?"

Peter F Drucker, well-known management consultant:

The real growth and innovation in this country has been in medium-sized companies that employ between 200 and 4,000 workers. If you are in a small company, you are running all out. You have neither the time nor the energy to devote to anything but yesterday's crisis.

A medium-sized company has the resources to devote to new products and markets, and it's still small enough to be flexible and move fast. And these companies now have what they once lacked—they've learned how to manage.

Thomas J Peters and Robert H Waterman, Jr., bestselling authors and management consultants:

A rule of thumb starts to emerge. We find that the lion's share of the top performers keep their division size between $50 and $100 million, with a maximum of 1,000 or so employees each. Moreover, they grant their divisions extraordinary independence—and give them the functions and resources to exploit.

Sources: Excerpted from J A Byrne, "Advice from the Dr. Spock of Business," *Business Week*, September 28, 1987, p 61; and T J Peters and R H Waterman, Jr., *In Search of Excellence* (New York: Harper & Row, 1982), pp 272–73.

Strategic Choice and Organizational Structure

In 1972, British sociologist John Child rejected the environmental imperative approach to organizational structure. He proposed a *strategic choice* model based on behavioural rather than rational economic principles.[57] Child believed structure resulted from a political process involving organizational power holders. According to the strategic choice model that has evolved from Child's work,[58] an organization's structure is determined largely by a dominant coalition of top-management strategists.[59]

A Strategic Choice Model   As Figure 19–4 illustrates, specific strategic choices or decisions reflect how the dominant coalition perceives environmental constraints and the organization's objectives. These strategic choices are tempered by the decision makers' personal beliefs, attitudes, values, and ethics.[60] More and more organizations become aware of their ethical obligations in society. IKEA, for example, no longer sells carpets if they have no guarantee that they are not made by children. C&A, a store chain in The Netherlands, has agreed to establish a code of conduct to abolish child labour, and German rug-importers recently launched Rugmark, a label which guarantees the rugs have not been made by children.[61]

ETHICS

Research and Practical Lessons   In a study of 97 small and medium-sized companies in Quebec, Canada, strategy and organizational structure were found to be highly interdependent. Strategy influenced structure and structure influenced strategy. This was particularly true for larger, more innovative, and more successful firms.[62]

Strategic choice theory and research teach managers at least two practical lessons. First, the environment is just one of many codeterminants of structure. Second, like any other administrative process, organization design is subject to the byplays of interpersonal power and politics.

The Shape of Tomorrow's Organizations

Organizations are basically tools invented to get things done through collective action. As any carpenter or plumber knows, different jobs require different tools. So it is with organizations. When the situation changes significantly, according to contingency thinking, a different type of organization may be appropriate. The need for new organizations is greater than ever today because managers face revolutionary changes. *Fortune* magazine offered this perspective:

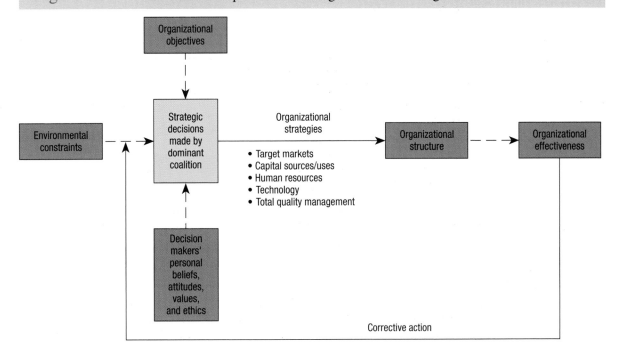

Figure 19–4   The Relationship between Strategic Choice and Organizational Structure

We all sense that the changes surrounding us are not mere trends but the workings of large, unruly forces; the globalization of markets; the spread of information technology and computer networks; the dismantling of hierarchy, the structure that has essentially organized work since the mid-19th century. Growing up around these is a new, information-age economy, whose fundamental sources of wealth are knowledge and communication rather than natural resources and physical labor.[63]

What sorts of organizations will prosper in the information-age economy? Will they be adaptations of the traditional pyramid-shaped organization? Or will they be radically different?[64] Let us put our imaginations to work by envisioning the shape of tomorrow's organizations.

New-Style versus Old-Style Organizations

Organization theorists Jay R Galbraith and Edward E Lawler III have called for a "new logic of organizing."[65] They recommend a whole new set of adjectives to describe organizations (see Table 19–3). Traditional pyramid-shaped organizations, conforming to the old-style pattern, tend to be too slow and inflexible today. Leaner, more organic organizations are needed to accommodate today's strategic balancing act between cost, quality, and speed.[66] These new-style organizations will embrace the total quality management (TQM) principles discussed in Chapter 1. This means they will be customer focused, dedicated to continuous improvement and learning, and structured around teams. These qualities, along with computerized information technology, hopefully will enable big organizations to mimic the speed and flexibility of small organizations.[67]

Four New Organizational Patterns

Figure 19–5 illustrates four radical departures from the traditional pyramid-shaped organization. Each is the logical result of various trends that are evident today. In other words, we have exaggerated these new organizations for instructional purposes. You will probably encounter various combinations of these pure types in the years ahead. Let us

Table 19–3   Profiles of the New-Style and Old-Style Organizations

NEW	OLD
Dynamic, learning	Stable
Information rich	Information is scarce
Global	Local
Small and large	Large
Product/customer oriented	Functional
Skills oriented	Job oriented
Team oriented	Individual oriented
Involvement oriented	Command/control oriented
Lateral/networked	Hierarchical
Customer oriented	Job requirements oriented

Source: J R Galbraith and E E Lawler III, "Effective Organizations: Using the New Logic of Organizing," p. 298 in *Organizing for the Future: The New Logic for Managing Complex Organizations*, eds J R Galbraith, E E Lawler III, and Associates. Copyright 1993 Jossey-Bass Inc. Publishers. Used with permission.

imagine life in the organizations of tomorrow.[68] (Importantly, these characterizations are not intended to be final answers. We simply seek to stimulate thoughtful debate.)

Horizontal Organizations   In the last chapter we pondered the prospect of reengineering becoming just another passing management fad. Even if that turns out to be the case, the reengineering movement still is likely to have a lasting impact on organization design. Namely, it helped refine the concept of a horizontally oriented organization. Unlike traditional vertically oriented organizations with functional units such as production, marketing, and finance, horizontal organizations are flat and built around core processes aimed at satisfying customers. *Fortune* magazine characterized horizontal organizations this way:

The horizontal corporation includes these potent elements: Teams will provide the foundation of organizational design. They will not be set up inside departments, like marketing, but around core processes, such as new-product development. Process owners, not department heads, will be the top managers, and they may sport wonderfully weird titles.

Rather than focusing single-mindedly on financial objectives or functional goals, the horizontal organization emphasizes customer satisfaction. Work is simplified and hierarchy flattened by combining related tasks—for example, an account-management process that subsumes the sales, billing, and service functions—and eliminating work that does not add value. Information zips along an internal superhighway: The knowledge worker analyzes it, and technology moves it quickly across the corporation instead of up and down, speeding up and improving decision making.

Okay, so some of this is derivative; the obsession with process, for example, dates back to Total Quality Management. Part of the beauty of the horizontal corporation is that it distills much of what we know about what works in managing today. Its advocates call it an "actionable model"—jargon for a plan you can work with—that allows companies to use ideas like teams, supplier-customer integration, and empowerment in ways that reinforce each other. A key virtue, says Pat Hoye, dealer-service support manager at Ford Motor, is that the horizontal corporation is the kind of company a customer would design. The customer, after all, doesn't care about the service department's goals or the dealer's sales targets; he just wants his car fixed right and on time—so the organization makes those objectives paramount. In most cases, a horizontal organization requires some employees to be organized functionally where their expertise is considered critical, as in human resources or finance. But those departments are often pared down and judiciously melded into a design where the real authority runs along process lines.[69]

What will it be like to work in a horizontal organization?[70] It will be a lot more interesting than traditional bureaucracies with their functional ghettos. Most employees will be *close to the customer* (both internal and external)—asking questions, getting feedback, and

Figure 19–5   The Shape of Tomorrow's Organizations

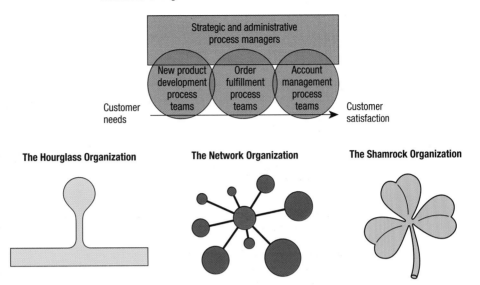

The Horizontal Organization

Strategic and administrative
process managers

New product
development
process
teams

Order
fulfillment
process
teams

Account
management
process
teams

Customer
needs

Customer
satisfaction

The Hourglass Organization   **The Network Organization**   **The Shamrock Organization**

jointly solving problems. Constant challenge also will come from being on cross-functional teams where co-workers with different technical specialties work side-by-side on projects. Sometimes people will find themselves dividing their time among several projects. Blurred and conflicting lines of authority will break the traditional unity-of-command principle. Project goals and deadlines will tend to replace the traditional supervisor role. Training in both technical and teamwork skills will be a top priority. Multiskilled employees at all levels will find themselves working on different teams and various projects during the year. Paradoxically, self-starters and team players will thrive. Due to the flatness of the organization, lateral transfers will be more common than traditional vertical promotions.[71] This will be a source of discontent for many of those who want to move upwards. Constant change will take its toll in terms of interpersonal conflict, personal stress, and burnout. Skill-based pay will supplement pay-for-performance.

Hourglass Organizations   This pattern gets its name from the organization's pinched middle. Thanks to modern information technology, a relatively small executive group will be able to coordinate the efforts of numerous operating personnel who make goods or render services.[72] Multiple and broad layers of middle managers who served as conduits for information in old-style organizations will be unnecessary in hourglass organizations. Competition for promotions among operating personnel will be intense because of the restricted hierarchy. Lateral transfers will be more common. Management will compensate for the lack of promotion opportunities with job rotation, skill training, and pay-for-performance. What few middle managers there are will be cross-functional problem solvers who also possess a number of technical skills. The potential for alienation between the executive elite and those at the base of the hourglass will be great, thus giving labour unions an excellent growth opportunity.

Network Organizations   Actually, this configuration will be a fluid family of several interdependent organizations. Tasks commonly performed by employees in old-style organizations—including, but not limited to, product design, manufacturing, human resource management, training, accounting, data processing, packaging, warehousing, and delivery—will be contracted out to other companies. At the centre of the network will be an entrepreneurial individual or team and a small, comparatively low-paid clerical staff. Andersen Consulting Paris is an excellent example of the virtual office:

By moving its offices to a new location, Andersen Consulting has introduced a totally new working system. Individual desks have been replaced by open spaces. Desks are available, but only if reserved for the time needed. In return, Andersen's consultants have the most advanced tools at their disposal: video-conferencing, portable computers and telephones, . . . By eliminating the personal desk, employees become frail individuals in the system, which will enhance their productivity.[73]

Here is what we envision about life in this sort of network organization. Things will be very interesting and potentially profitable for the elite core of entrepreneurs and engineers. Turnover among the "have nots," the clerical staff who do the routine administrative chores, could be a problem because of glaring inequities. Telephones, fax machines, computer networks, overnight delivery services, and contract lawyers will be crucial linking resources among network participants. Independent contractors will belong to many different network organizations. The length of their membership in a given network will be determined by their performance. Working conditions at some of the small contractors will make them little more than information-age sweatshops. Companies living from one contract to another will offer little in the way of job security. Network companies will employ a wide variety of compensation plans, ranging from very generous to very unfair. Opportunities to start new businesses will be numerous.

Shamrock Organizations   The idea of the shamrock organization was first introduced by Charles Handy.[74] This organizational type has the typical form of a shamrock: three leaves which are, however, still linked. Each leaf represents a workforce type involved in a common business. The types of workforce are the core workforce, the contractual fringe, and the flexible labour force. The core workforce consists of those employees indispensable to the organization. They are very expensive, hence limited in numbers (e.g., technicians). The contractual fringe are the specialist organizations outside the organization (e.g., consultants). The flexible labour force are those who want to keep flexibility in their lives (part-time and temporary workers). Each leaf of the shamrock organization is vital, each is different and each is part of the larger organization

Summary of Key Concepts

1. *Identify and briefly explain the three stages of the organizational life cycle.* They are inception (small, informal, entrepreneurial), high growth (centralized, formal, and large and growing), and maturity (decentralized, formal, slowing growth).

2. *Discuss organizational decline relative to the organizational life cycle.* Decline is an ever-present threat during the organizational life cycle, with complacency during periods of success particularly troublesome. A culture of continuous improvement can avoid organizational decline.

3. *Explain what the contingency approach to organization design involves.* The contingency approach to organization design calls for fitting the organization to

the demands of the situation. Environmental uncertainty can be assessed in terms of various combinations of two dimensions: (*a*) simple or complex and (*b*) static or dynamic.

4. *Describe the relationship between differentiation and integration in effective organizations.* Harvard researchers Lawrence and Lorsch found that successful organizations achieved a proper balance between the two opposing structural forces of differentiation and integration. Differentiation forces the organization apart. Through a variety of mechanisms—including hierarchy, rules, teams, and liaisons—integration draws the organization together.

5. *Discuss Burns and Stalker's findings regarding mechanistic and organic organizations.* British researchers Burns and Stalker found that mechanistic (bureaucratic, centralized) organizations tended to be effective in stable situations. In unstable situations, organic (flexible, decentralized) organizations were more effective. These findings underscored the need for a contingency approach to organization design.

6. *Define and briefly explain the practical significance of centralization and decentralization.* Because key decisions are made at the top of centralized organizations, they tend to be tightly controlled. In decentralized organizations, employees at lower levels are empowered to make important decisions. Contingency design calls for a proper balance.

7. *Discuss the effective management of organizational size.* Regarding the optimum size for organizations, the challenge for today's managers is to achieve smallness within bigness by keeping subunits at a manageable size.

8. *Describe horizontal, hourglass, network, and shamrock organizations.* Horizontal organizations are flat structures built around core processes aimed at identifying and satisfying customer needs. Cross-functional teams and empowerment are central to horizontal organizations. Hourglass organizations have a small executive level, a short and narrow middle-management level (because information technology links the top and bottom levels), and a broad base of operating personnel. Network organizations actually are families of interdependent companies. They are contractual and fluid in nature. Shamrock organizations consist of three vital, but different types of workforce. The core workforce consists of those employees indispensable to the organization. The contractual fringe are the specialist organizations outside the organization. The flexible labour force are those who want to keep flexibility in their lives.

Discussion Questions

1. Why is it instructive to view organizations from a life-cycle perspective?

2. Which phase of the organizational life cycle—inception, high growth, maturity—do you think would be the most difficult for management?

3. How does decline relate to organizational life cycles?

4. Why is it important to focus on the role of complacency in organizational decline?

5. In a nutshell, what does contingency organization design entail?

6. What evidence of integration can you find in your current (or last) place of employment?

7. What is wrong with an organization having too much differentiation and too little integration?

8. If organic organizations are popular with most employees, why can't all organizations be structured in an organic fashion?

9. How can you tell if an organization (or subunit) is too big?

10. Which of the three new organizational configurations probably will be most prevalent 10 to 15 years from now? Why?

Personal Awareness and Growth Exercise

Organization Design Field Study

Objectives
1. To get out into the field and talk to a practising manager about organizational structure.

2. To increase your understanding of the important distinction between mechanistic and organic organizations.

3. To broaden your knowledge of contingency design, in terms of organization–environment fit.

Introduction
A good way to test the validity of what you have just read about organizational design is to interview a practising manager. (Note: If you are a manager, simply complete the questionnaire yourself.)

Instructions
Your objective is to interview a manager about aspects of organizational structure, environmental uncertainty,

and organizational effectiveness. A *manager* is defined as anyone who supervises other people in an organizational setting. The organization may be small or large and for-profit or not-for-profit. Higher-level managers are preferred, but middle managers and first-line supervisors are acceptable. If you interview a lower-level manager, be sure to remind him or her that you want a description of the overall organization, not just an isolated subunit. Your interview will centre on the adaptation of Figure 19–3, as discussed below.

When conducting your interview, be sure to explain to the manager what you are trying to accomplish. But assure the manager that his or her name will not be mentioned in class discussion or any written projects. Try to keep side notes during the interview for later reference.

Questionnaire

The following questionnaire, adapted from Figure 19–3, will help you determine if the manager's organization is relatively mechanistic or relatively organic in structure. Note: For items 1 and 2 on the following questionnaire, have the manager respond in terms of the average nonmanagerial employee. (Circle one number for each item.)

CHARACTERISTICS

1. Task definition and knowledge required	Narrow; technical	1 — 2 — 3 — 4 — 5 — 6 — 7	Broad; general
2. Linkage between individual's contribution and organization's purpose	Vague or indirect	1 — 2 — 3 — 4 — 5 — 6 — 7	Clear or direct
3. Task flexibility	Rigid; routine	1 — 2 — 3 — 4 — 5 — 6 — 7	Flexible; varied
4. Specification of techniques, obligations, and rights	Specific	1 — 2 — 3 — 4 — 5 — 6 — 7	General
5. Degree of hierarchical control	High	1 — 2 — 3 — 4 — 5 — 6 — 7	Low (self-control emphasized)
6. Primary communication pattern	Top-down	1 — 2 — 3 — 4 — 5 — 6 — 7	Lateral (between peers)
7. Primary decision-making style	Authoritarian	1 — 2 — 3 — 4 — 5 — 6 — 7	Democratic; participative
8. Emphasis on obedience and loyalty	High	1 — 2 — 3 — 4 — 5 — 6 — 7	Low

Total score = _____

ADDITIONAL QUESTION ABOUT THE ORGANIZATION'S ENVIRONMENT

This organization faces an environment that is (circle one number):

Stable and certain   1—-2—-3—-4—-5—-6—-7—-8—-9—-10   Unstable and uncertain

ADDITIONAL QUESTIONS ABOUT THE ORGANIZATION'S EFFECTIVENESS

1. Profitability (if a profit-seeking business):

Low   1—-2—-3—-4—-5—-6—-7—-8—-9—-10   High

2. Degree of organizational goal accomplishment:

Low   1—-2—-3—-4—-5—-6—-7—-8—-9—-10   High

3. Customer or client satisfaction:

Low   1—-2—-3—-4—-5—-6—-7—-8—-9—-10   High

4. Employee satisfaction:

Low   1—-2—-3—-4—-5—-6—-7—-8—-9—-10   High

Total effectiveness score =
(Add responses from above)

QUESTIONS FOR DISCUSSION

1. Using the following norms, was the manager's organization relatively mechanistic or organic?

8—24 = Relatively mechanistic
25—39 = Mixed
40—56 = Relatively organic

2. In terms of Burns and Stalker's contingency theory, does the manager's organization seem to fit its environment? Explain.

3. Does the organization's degree of effectiveness reflect how well it fits its environment? Explain.

Group Exercise

Getting Business Colleges to Swallow Their Own Medicine

Objectives

1. To continue developing your group and teamwork skills.

2. To develop your ability to think like a management consultant, someone who sees the big picture.

3. To help solve an organization design problem in a familiar organization.

Introduction

Universities in general, and colleges of business in particular, have been criticized for being resistant to change and unresponsive to undergraduate students. While profit-seeking companies have been in the midst of a reorganizing revolution in recent years, including downsizing, delayering, and process reengineering, most colleges of business are still structured the way they were 30 years ago. Historically, business colleges have been organized along functional lines (e.g., management departments, finance departments, accounting departments, marketing departments, information systems departments, and so on). Students follow a curriculum compartmentalized along the same functional lines and are taught by specialists in each functional department. Too often, however, students complain about getting a disjointed view of business.

Here is a good opportunity to help make things better. This group exercise puts you in the role of a management consultant faced with the challenge of reorganizing a college of business (or other college or university unit your instructor may specify). At the very minimum, 40 to 60 minutes of team discussion is needed, followed by 15 to 20 minutes of general class discussion. *Tips:* One team member should serve as recorder/reporter. Be sure to draw an organization chart for your new design.

Instructions

You have a great deal of latitude in this group problem-solving exercise. There are better and worse answers, but no precise right answers. Here are some tips to get you headed in a productive direction:

- Review what you read in this chapter about integration, organic organizations, new-style organizations in Table 19–3, and horizontal organizations.

- Think in terms of skills students need in today's workplace.

- Think about the university's or college's basic mission and priorities (e.g., research, graduate education, undergraduate education, community service, etc.).

- Think in terms of cross-functional teaching teams.

- Think in terms of a student-centred organization structure.

- Think about recruiters and the general community as ultimate customers.

- Think about how the curriculum (course requirements) will have to change.

- Think of school administrators, professors, and students as partners in the learning process rather than adversaries with conflicting interests. Think win-win.

- Be practical in terms of budgets and funding requirements for your new organization.

QUESTIONS FOR DISCUSSION

1. Is your target organization already up to date or still organized along functional lines? What is good or bad about this situation?

2. What does your new organization look like on paper? Is it realistic in terms of student workloads, instructor workloads, and budgets?

3. What problems or sources of conflict will be likely to arise in your new organization? How should they be handled?

4. How hard will it be to implement your new structure? Why? Who will most be likely to resist the new structure, and why? What can be done to overcome their resistance?

5. What would you say to someone who made this statement? "Creating a student-centred college is like letting the neighbourhood kids run the local sweet shop." In other words, can high academic standards be maintained in your new organization?

Notes

[1] Excerpted from Jacob, "The Struggle to Create an Organization for the 21st Century," *Fortune*, April , 1995, pp 98–99.

[2] R W Keidel, "Triangular Design: A New Organizational Geometry," *Academy of Management Executive*, November 1990, p 35.

[3] For instructive background and examples, see T A Stewart, "Welcome to the Revolution," *Fortune*, December 13, 1993, pp 66–77.

[4] R E Quinn and K Cameron, "Organizational Life Cycles and Shifting Criteria of Effectiveness: Some Preliminary Evidence," *Management Science*, January 1983, p 40.

[5] Ten organizational life-cycle models are reviewed in Ibid., pp 34–41. Also see R K Kazanjian and R Drazin, "A Stage-Contingent Model of Design and Growth for Technology-Based New Ventures," *Journal of Business Venturing*, 1990, pp 137–50; R Drazin and R K Kazanjian, "A Reanalysis of Miller and Friesen's Life Cycle Data," *Strategic Management Journal*, May–June 1990, pp 319–25; A C Bluedorn, "Pilgrim's Progress: Trends and Convergence in Research on Organizational Size and Environments," *Journal of Management*, Summer 1993, pp 163–91; and I Adizes, "The 10 Stages of Corporate Life Cycles," *Inc.*, October 1996, pp 95–98.

[6] R A Cosier and D R Dalton, "Search for Excellence, Learn from Japan—Are These Panaceas or Problems?" *Business Horizons*, November–December 1986, p 67.

[7] R A Mamis and S Pearlstein, " '1—2—3' Creator Mitch Kapor," *Inc.*, January 1987, p 31. (Kapor retained a seat on Lotus's board of directors and 1.6 million shares of the firm's stock.)

[8] Good collections of entrepreneur profiles can be found in C Burck, "The Real World of the Entrepreneur," *Fortune*, April 5, 1993, pp 62–81; and M Warshaw, "Never Say Die," *Success*, July–August 1996, pp 35–44.

[9] Translated from "Aantal Faillissementen Bereikte Vorig Jaar in Europa een Rekordhoogte," *Financieel Economische Tijd*, April, 1993.

[10] P Lorange and R T Nelson, "How to Recognize—and Avoid—Organizational Decline," *Sloan Management Review*, Spring 1987, p 47.

[11] Excerpted from Ibid., pp 43–45. Also see E E Lawler III and J R Galbraith, "Avoiding the Corporate Dinosaur Syndrome," *Organizational Dynamics*, Autumn 1994, pp 5–17; and K Labich, "Why Companies Fail," *Fortune*, November 14, 1994, pp 52–68.

[12] For details, see K S Cameron, M U Kim, and D A Whetten, "Organizational Effects of Decline and Turbulence," *Administrative Science Quarterly*, June 1987, pp 222–40.

[13] Twelve dysfunctional consequences of decline are discussed and empirically tested in K S Cameron, D A Whetten, and M U Kim, "Organizational Dysfunctions of Decline," *Academy of Management Journal*, March 1987, pp 126–38. Also see D K Hurst, *Crisis and Renewal: Meeting the Challenge of Organizational Change* (Boston: Harvard Business School Press, 1995).

[14] Data from V L Barker III and P W Patterson, Jr., "Top Management Team Tenure and Top Manager Causal Attributions at Declining Firms Attempting Turnarounds," *Group & Organization Management*, September 1996, pp 304–36.

[15] Additional scholarly treatment of organizational decline can be found in R I Sutton and T D'Aunno, "Decreasing Organizational Size: Untangling the Effects of Money and People," *Academy of Management Review*, April 1989, pp 194–212; and R I Sutton, "Organizational Decline Processes: A Social Psychological Perspective," in *Research in Organizational Behavior*, vol. 12, eds B M Staw and L L Cummings (Greenwich, CT: JAI Press, 1990), pp 205–54.

[16] A culture of "entitlement" also hastens organizational decline. See J M Bardwick, *Danger in the Comfort Zone: From Boardroom to Mailroom—How to Break the Entitlement Habit That's Killing American Business* (New York: AMACOM, 1991). Also see D W Organ, "Argue with Success," *Business Horizons*, November–December 1995, pp 1–2; and J P Kotter, "Kill Complacency," *Fortune*, August 5, 1996, pp 168–70.

[17] J Greenwald, "Are America's Corporate Giants a Dying Breed?" *Time*, December 28, 1992, p 28. Procter & Gamble's fight against decline is discussed in B Saporito, "Behind the Tumult at P&G," *Fortune*, March 7, 1994, pp 74–82. Also see B Saporito, "The Eclipse of Mars," *Fortune*, November 28, 1994, pp 82–92.

[18] Excerpted from A Taylor III, "Why Toyota Keeps Getting Better and Better and Better," *Fortune*, November 19, 1990, pp 66–67. ©1996 Time Inc. All rights reserved.

[19] Based on K G Smith, T R Mitchell, and C E Summer, "Top Level Management Priorities in Different Stages of the Organizational Life Cycle," *Academy of Management Journal*, December 1985, pp 799–820.

[20] Additional details may be found in Quinn and Cameron, "Organizational Life Cycles and Shifting Criteria of Effectiveness: Some Preliminary Evidence," pp 33–51.

[21] For an instructive conceptual model of the relationship between organizational politics, strategy, and organizational life cycles, see B Gray and S S Ariss, "Politics and Strategic Change across Organizational Life Cycles," *Academy of Management Review*, October 1985, pp 707–23. Practical advice regarding the organizational life cycle can be found in J Mayers, "How to Withstand a Merger," *Management Review*, October 1986, pp 39–42; and B G Posner and B Burlingham, "Getting to Prime," *Inc.*, January 1991, pp 27–33.

[22] See K Kerwin, "Can Jack Smith Fix GM?" *Business Week*, November 1, 1993, pp 126–31; R Henkoff, "Getting Beyond Downsizing," *Fortune*, January 10, 1994, pp 58–64; M Magnet, "Let's Go for Growth," *Fortune*, March 7, 1994, pp 60–72; and I Sager, "Lou Gerstner Unveils His Battle Plan," *Business Week*, April 4, 1994, pp 96–98.

[23] For updates, see J M Pennings, "Structural Contingency Theory: A Reappraisal," *Research in Organizational Behavior* (Greenwich, CT: JAI Press, 1992), vol. 14, pp 267–309; A D Meyer, A S Tsui, and C R Hinings, "Configurational Approaches to Organizational Analysis," *Academy of Management Journal*, December 1993, pp 1175–95; and D H Doty, W H Glick, and G P Huber, "Fit, Equifinality, and Organizational Effectiveness: A Test of Two Configurational Theories," *Academy of Management Journal*, December 1993, pp 1196–1250.

[24] An interesting distinction between three types of environmental uncertainty can be found in F J Milliken, "Three Types of Perceived Uncertainty about the Environment: State, Effect, and Response Uncertainty," *Academy of Management Review*, January 1987, pp 133–43.

[25] R Duncan, "What Is the Right Organization Structure?" *Organizational Dynamics*, Winter 1979, p 63.

[26] Ibid.

[27]See J Huey, "The World's Best Brand," *Fortune,* May 31, 1993, pp 44–54; M T Moore, "Coke Spins Bottle for Classic Look," *USA Today,* March 28, 1994, pp 1B—2B; and P Sellers, "How Coke Is Kicking Pepsi's Can," *Fortune,* October 28, 1996, pp 70–84.

[28]See M Iansiti, "Shooting the Rapids: Managing Product Development in Turbulent Environments," *California Management Review,* Fall 1995, pp 37–58.

[29]P R Lawrence and J W Lorsch, *Organization and Environment* (Homewood, IL: Richard D Irwin, 1967), p 157.

[30]Pooled, sequential, and reciprocal integration are discussed in J W Lorsch, "Organization Design: A Situational Perspective," *Organizational Dynamics,* Autumn 1977, pp 2–14. Also see J E Ettlie and E M Reza, "Organizational Integration and Process Innovation," *Academy of Management Journal,* October 1992, pp 795–827.

[31]See R Mitchell, "Masters of Innovation," *Business Week,* April 10, 1989, pp 58–63; and B Dumaine, "Ability to Innovate," *Fortune,* January 29, 1990, pp 43, 46.

[32]K Deveny, "Bag Those Fries, Squirt That Ketchup, Fry That Fish," *Business Week,* October 13, 1986, p 86.

[33]See D A Morand, "The Role of Behavioral Formality and Informality in the Enactment of Bureaucratic versus Organic Organizations," *Academy of Management Review,* October 1995, pp 831–72.

[34]See J Huey, "The New Post-Heroic Leadership," *Fortune,* February 21, 1994, pp 42–50; and F Shipper and C C Manz, "Employee Self-Management without Formally Designated Teams: An Alternative Road to Empowerment," *Organizational Dynamics,* Winter 1992, pp 48–61.

[35]See G P Huber, C C Miller, and W H Glick, "Developing More Encompassing Theories about Organizations: The Centralization-Effectiveness Relationship as an Example," *Organization Science,* no. 1, 1990, pp 11–40; and C Handy, "Balancing Corporate Power: A New Federalist Paper," *Harvard Business Review,* November–December 1992, pp 59–72. Also see W R Pape, "Divide and Conquer," *Inc. Technology,* no. 2, 1996, pp 25–27; and J Schmidt, "Breaking Down Fiefdoms," *Management Review,* January 1997, pp 45–49.

[36]P Kaestle, "A New Rationale for Organizational Structure," *Planning Review,* July–August 1990, p 22.

[37]J Templeman, "Daimler Has a New Curve to Negotiate," *Business Week,* November 4, 1996, p 64.

[38]Details of this study can be found in T Burns and G M Stalker, *The Management of Innovation* (London: Tavistock, 1961).

[39]D J Gillen and S J Carroll, "Relationship of Managerial Ability to Unit Effectiveness in More Organic versus More Mechanistic Departments," *Journal of Management Studies,* November 1985, pp 674–75.

[40]J D Sherman and H L Smith, "The Influence of Organizational Structure on Intrinsic versus Extrinsic Motivation," *Academy of Management Journal,* December 1984, p 883.

[41].See J A Courtright, G T Fairhurst, and L E Rogers, "Interaction Patterns in Organic and Mechanistic Systems," *Academy of Management Journal,* December 1989, pp 773–802.

[42]See J Woodward, *Industrial Organization: Theory and Practice* (London: Oxford University Press, 1965); and P D Collins and F Hull, "Technology and Span of Control: Woodward Revisited," *Journal of Management Studies,* March 1986, pp 143–64.

[43].See L W Fry, "Technology-Structure Research: Three Critical Issues," *Academy of Management Journal,* September 1982, pp 532–52.

[44].Ibid., p 548. Also see R Reese, "Redesigning for Dial Tone: A Socio-Technical Systems Case Study," *Organizational Dynamics,* Autumn 1995, pp 80–90.

[45]For example, see C C Miller, W H Glick, Y-D Wang, and G P Huber, "Understanding Technology-Structure Relationships: Theory Development and Meta-Analytic Theory Testing," *Academy of Management Journal,* June 1991, pp 370–99; and K H Roberts and M Grabowski, "Organizations, Technology and Structuring," in *Handbook of Organization Studies,* eds S R Clegg, C Hardy, and W R Nord (Thousand Oaks, CA: Sage Publications, 1996), pp 409–23.

[46]The phrase "small is beautiful" was coined by the late British economist E F Schumacher. See E F Schumacher, *Small Is Beautiful: Economics as If People Mattered* (New York: Harper & Row, 1973).

[47]T J Peters and R H Waterman, Jr., *In Search of Excellence* (New York: Harper & Row, 1982), p 321. Also see T Peters, "Rethinking Scale," *California Management Review,* Fall 1992, pp 7–29.

[48]See, for example, W McKinley, "Decreasing Organizational Size: To Untangle or Not to Untangle?" *Academy of Management Review,* January 1992, pp 112–23; W Zellner, "Go-Go Goliaths," *Business Week,* February 13, 1995, pp 64–70; T Brown, "Manage `BIG!' " *Management Review,* May 1996, pp 12–17; and E Shapiro, "Power, Not Size, Counts," *Management Review,* September 1996, p 61.

[49]L Smith, "Does the World's Biggest Company Have a Future?" *Fortune,* August 7, 1995, p 124.

[50]P L Zweig, "The Case against Mergers," *Business Week,* October 30, 1995, p 122. Also see A B Fisher, "How to Make a Merger Work," *Fortune,* January 24, 1994, pp 66–70; D A Andelman, "The Urge to Merge," *Management Review,* December 1995, pp 33–35; and O Harari, "Curing the M&A Madness," *Management Review,* February 1996, pp 29–32.

[51]R Z Gooding and J A Wagner III, "A Meta-Analytic Review of the Relationship between Size and Performance: The Productivity and Efficiency of Organizations and Their Subunits," *Administrative Science Quarterly,* December 1985, pp 462–81.

[52]Ibid., p 477.

[53]Results are presented in P G Benson, T L Dickinson, and C O Neidt, "The Relationship between Organizational Size and Turnover: A Longitudinal Investigation," *Human Relations,* January 1987, pp 15–30. Also see M Yasai-Ardekani, "Effects of Environmental Scarcity and Munificence on the Relationship of Context to Organizational Structure," *Academy of Management Journal,* March 1989, pp 131–56.

[54]The comparative advantages of large and small companies are presented in J O'Toole and W Bennis, "Our Federalist Future: The Leadership Imperative," *California Management Review,* Summer 1992, pp 73–90.

[55]See V Sathe, "Fostering Entrepreneurship in the Large, Diversified Firm," *Organizational Dynamics,* Summer 1989, pp 20–32; J R Galbraith and E E Lawler III, "Effective Organizations: Using the New Logic of Organizing," in *Organizing for the Future: The New Logic for Managing Complex Organizations,* eds J R Galbraith, E E Lawler III, and Associates (San Francisco: Jossey-Bass, 1993), pp 290–92; and J Kim, "Welch Thinks Small, Acts Big," *USA Today,* February 26, 1993, p 2B.

[56]R Donkin, "Natural Selection and Corporate Survival—Organization in the Natural World May Provide Valuable Lessons for the Way We Work", *The Financial Times* , February 1, 1995, p 26.

[57]See J Child, "Organizational Structure, Environment and Performance: The Role of Strategic Choice," *Sociology,* January 1972, pp 1–22.

[58]See J Galbraith, *Organization Design* (Reading, MA: Addison-Wesley Publishing, 1977); J R Montanari, "Managerial Discretion: An Expanded Model of Organization Choice," *Academy of Management Review,* April 1978, pp 231–41; and H R Bobbitt, Jr.,

and J D Ford, "Decision-Maker Choice as a Determinant of Organizational Structure," *Academy of Management Review,* January 1980, pp 13–23.

[59]For an alternative model of strategy making, see S L Hart, "An Integrative Framework for Strategy-Making Processes," *Academy of Management Review,* April 1992, pp 327–51. Also see F E Harrison and M A Pelletier, "A Typology of Strategic Choice," *Technological Forecasting and Social Change,* November 1993, pp 245–63; and H Mintzberg, "The Rise and Fall of Strategic Planning," *Harvard Business Review,* January–February 1994, pp 107–14.

[60]See A Bhide, "How Entrepreneurs Craft Strategies That Work," *Harvard Business Review,* March–April 1994, pp 150–61; and J W Dean, Jr., and M P Sharfman, "Does Decision Process Matter? A Study of Strategic Decision-Making Effectiveness," *Academy of Management Journal,* April 1996, pp 368–96; R L Osborne, "Strategic Values: The Corporate Performance Engine," *Business Horizons,* September–October 1996, pp 41–47; and B Ettorre, "When Patience Is a Corporate Virtue," *Management Review,* November 1996, pp 28–32.

[61]"Ethical Shopping," *The Economist,* June 3, 1995, pp 65–71

[62]Details may be found in D Miller, "Strategy Making and Structure: Analysis and Implications for Performance," *Academy of Management Journal,* March 1987, pp 7–32. Also see J B Thomas and R R McDaniel, Jr., "Interpreting Strategic Issues: Effects of Strategy and the Information-Processing Structure of Top Management Teams," *Academy of Management Journal,* June 1990, pp 286–306. Contrary evidence is presented in M I A At-Twaijri and J R Montanari, "The Impact of Context and Choice on the Boundary-Spanning Process: An Empirical Extension," *Human Relations,* December 1987, pp 783–98. A related study is reported in W Q Judge, Jr., and C P Zeithaml, "Institutional and Strategic Choice Perspectives on Board Involvement in the Strategic Decision Process," *Academy of Management Journal,* October 1992, pp 766–94. For more, see T L Amburgey and T Dacin, "As the Left Foot Follows the Right? The Dynamics of Strategic and Structural Change," *Academy of Management Journal,* December 1994, pp 1427–52; and M W Peng and P S Heath, "The Growth of the Firm in Planned Economies in Transition: Institutions, Organizations, and Strategic Choice," *Academy of Management Review,* April 1996, pp 492–528.

[63]T A Stewart, "Welcome to the Revolution," *Fortune,* December 13, 1993, p 66.

[64]For instructive reading, see I I Mitroff, R O Mason, and C M Pearson, "Radical Surgery: What Will Tomorrow's Organizations Look Like?" *Academy of Management Executive,* May 1994, pp 11–21; T Clancy, "Radical Surgery: A View from the Operating Theater," *Academy of Management Executive,* May 1994, pp 73–78; R E Miles, H J Coleman, Jr., and W E D Creed, "Keys to Success in Corporate Redesign," *California Management Review,* Spring 1995, pp 128–45; G G Dess, A M A Rasheed, K J McLaughlin, and R L Priem, "The New Corporate Architecture," *Academy of Management Executive,* August 1995, pp 7–20; R Ashkenas, D Ulrich, T Jick, and S Kerr, *The Boundaryless Organization: Breaking the Chains of Organizational Structure* (San Francisco: Jossey-Bass, 1995); and J B Quinn, P Anderson, and S Finkelstein, "Leveraging Intellect," *Academy of Management Executive,* August 1996, pp 7–27.

[65]See Galbraith and Lawler, "Effective Organizations: Using the New Logic of Organizing," pp 285–99.

[66]See J P Womack and D T Jones, "From Lean Production to the Lean Enterprise," *Harvard Business Review,* March–April 1994, pp 93–103; and M A Gephart, "Research Reports: Evidence from the Auto Industry," *Training & Development,* June 1995, pp 32–33.

[67]See H Bahrami, "The Emerging Flexible Organization: Perspectives from Silicon Valley," *California Management Review,* Summer 1992, pp 33–52.

[68]For a parallel discussion, see W Kiechel III, "How We Will Work in the Year 2000," *Fortune,* May 17, 1993, pp 38–52.

[67]R Jacob, "The Struggle to Create an Organization for the 21st Century," *Fortune,* April 3, 1995, pp 91–92.

[70]See S Sonnesyn Brooks, "Managing a Horizontal Revolution," *HRMagazine,* June 1995, pp 52–58.

[71].See M Hequet, "Flat and Happy," *Training,* April 1995, pp 29–34.

[72]For related discussion, see B Filipczak, "The Ripple Effect of Computer Networking," *Training,* March 1994, pp 40–47.

[73]Based on and translated from M Jasor, "Andersen Consulting: Finis les Bureaux Individuels: Vive l'Espace à la Carte," *L'Essentiel du Management,* April 1996, pp 54–58

[74]C Handy, *Inside Organisations* (London: BBC Books, 1990).

Twenty

Managing Change in Learning Organizations

LEARNING OBJECTIVES

When you finish studying the material in this chapter, you should be able to:

1. Discuss the external and internal forces that create the need for organizational change.

2. Describe Lewin's change model and the systems model of change.

3. Discuss Kotter's eight steps for leading organizational change.

4. Demonstrate your familiarity with the four identifying characteristics of organization development (OD).

5. Discuss the 10 reasons employees resist change.

6. Identify alternative strategies for overcoming resistance to change.

7. Define a learning organization.

8. Discuss the process organizations use to build their learning capabilities.

9. Review the reasons organizations naturally resist learning.

10. Discuss the role of leadership in creating a learning organization.

In the early 1980s the UK cement industry was threatened by increasing world competition and Blue Circle was determined to meet this challenge by improving efficiency and productivity. Using the opportunities presented by major capital investment at two of its UK cement works, Cauldon in Staffordshire and Dunbar in Scotland, BCI's UK cement division aimed to develop a business unit culture for the whole organization that would be at the leading edge of best work practice, labour relations and productivity.

This was achieved by developing broader, more challenging jobs and creating a work environment which provided job satisfaction and better rewards while greatly increasing the performance and effectiveness of the business. This meant the involvement of employees throughout the organization—treating people as assets with skills, knowledge, experience, and commitment.

Fifteen years ago the UK cement industry was characterized by high manning levels, relatively low wages, restrictive working practices and strict demarcation. Additional payments were made for unsocial hours and working in adverse conditions. Under this system, the more breakdowns occurred, the more overtime had to be worked and the more employees earned. Not surprisingly, productivity was low, supervision high, more poor, and conflict common. Management and employee relationships were characterized by low levels of trust. All change was regarded with intense suspicion, and the situation required radical changes to ensure long-term

The programme adopted involved a complete overhaul of working practices, reward systems and, not least, company culture. The benefits included a flexible, multi-skilled workforce, higher productivity and lower unit costs—all reflected in the financial results. The programme enabled management/employee relations to move from a 'them and us' adversarial culture to one of employee involvement and shared goals. This has been manifested in improved business awareness, increased job involvement, and enhanced quality of working life.

The first step was the formulation of a new vision; the next to ensure it was acceptable to the trade unions. The elements of the new vision included a highly skilled workforce with greater flexibility, working in integrated teams with the most up-to-date technology; the introduction of a simple pay structure with the elimination of paid overtime and bonuses; an increased basic wage; a significant reduction in manning levels; and a cut in labour costs.

The new working practices would be developed into an employment package called 'integrated working'. An essential aim of integrated working was to provide motivation and job interest and improve attitudes. A second key element was to move away from narrowly defined jobs to larger, broader roles based on team working and total flexibility. In order to increase mobility and reduce problems of pay differentials, traditional job specifications and job descriptions were eliminated and a three-grade structure of process operator, senior process operator and craftsman was introduced. A large investment in skills training was made to ensure that employees acquired four additional skills. With more skills, they would be able to contribute elsewhere in the production process. The third key element in the new package was the move to a continuous seven-shift system. This allowed total cover to be provided and worked well with the annual hours contract.

Finally, the ability of everyone to work together with mutual respect was considered essential to the evolution of the new culture, and an extensive training programme on team working was introduced to help break down the entrenched attitudes based on a lifetime of demarcation and suspicion of management motives.

Together with the investment in new equipment and technology, the new working practices provided the foundation which was necessary for real involvement of employees. In addition they dramatically improved productivity and efficiency. They were self-financing—with reduced staffing levels and labour costs and increased output per employee; this resulted in higher wages and an average reduction in working time of eight hours per week.

Of course, all this did not happen overnight, and the company has spent the past 10 years seeking ways to improve on these foundations; it would be wrong to say it was easy or that the changes were readily accepted by everyone. It demanded careful planning, close consultation, and cooperation, but the real bottom-line results have been dramatic. The themes and lessons that emerged from the BCI experience of managing cultural change are relevant to any organization trying to improve performance through its people.

As a tribute to the real impact of these changes, it is perhaps most fitting to end with a quote from a union shop steward: 'We work in an industry where it is no longer a matter of them and us. We can now get fully involved in the business, where mutual respect is the norm. We feel appreciated for what we do. Results are shared, there is more job satisfaction and a better service to customers—and all these have led to improvements in the bottom line.[1]

Discussion Question

What was the most important contribution to successful change at BCI?

ncreased international competition is forcing companies to shape up or ship out. Customers are demanding greater value and lower prices. The rate of organizational and societal change is clearly accelerating.[2] For example, a recent survey of 750 corporations revealed that all of them were involved in at least one organizational change programme. Another survey of 259 executives indicated that 84 per cent had one change initiative under way, while nearly 50 per cent had three or more change programs being implemented.[3]

Companies no longer have a choice—they must change to survive. Unfortunately, people tend to resist change. It is not easy to change an organization, let alone an individual. This puts increased pressure on management to learn the subtleties of change. This final chapter was written to help managers navigate the journey of change.

Specifically, we discuss the forces that create the need for organization change, models of planned change, resistance to change, and creating a learning organization.

Forces of Change

How do organizations know when they should change? What cues should an organization look for? Although there are no clear-cut answers to these questions, the "cues" that signal the need for change are found by monitoring the forces for change.

Organizations encounter many different forces for change. These forces come from external sources outside the organization and from internal sources. This section examines the forces that create the need for change. Awareness of these forces can help managers determine when they should consider implementing an organizational change. The external and internal forces for change are presented in Figure 20–1.

External Forces

External forces for change
Originate outside the organization.

External forces for change originate outside the organization. Because these forces have global effects, they may cause an organization to question the essence of what business it is in and the process by which products and services are produced. There are four key external forces for change: demographic characteristics, technological advancements, market changes, and social and political pressures. Each is now discussed.

Demographic Characteristics   Chapter 2 provided a detailed discussion of the demographic changes occurring in the workforce. Two key trends identified in this discussion were that (1) the workforce is more diverse and (2) there is a business imperative to effectively manage diversity. Organizations need to effectively manage diversity if they are to receive maximum contribution and commitment from employees.

Technological Advancements   Both manufacturing and service organizations are increasingly using technology as a means to improve productivity and market competitiveness. Manufacturing companies, for instance, have automated their operations with robotics, computerized numerical control (CNC), which is used for metal cutting operations, and computer-aided design (CAD). CAD is a computerized process of drafting and designing engineering drawings of products. Companies have just begun to work on computer-integrated manufacturing (CIM). This highly technical process attempts to integrate product design with product planning, control, and operations. In contrast to these manufacturing technologies, the service sector is using office automation. Office automation consists of a host of computerized technologies that are used to obtain, store, analyse, retrieve, and communicate information.[4]

Market Changes   The emergence of a global economy is forcing companies to change the way they do business. For example, South African banks are finding that they need to establish banking locations in remote areas of the country if they wish to grow and remain national banks (see the International OB). European companies are also forging new partnerships and alliances with their suppliers and potential competitors. For example among the airline companies there are some major alliances due to the

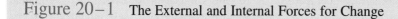

Figure 20–1   The External and Internal Forces for Change

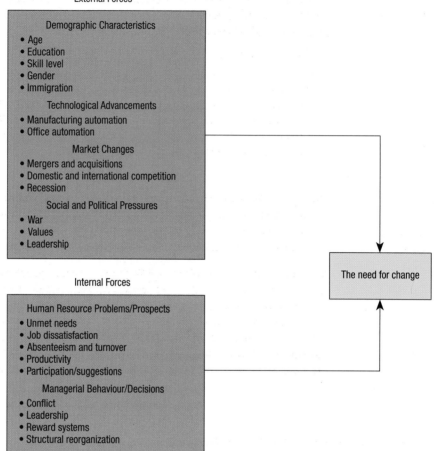

deregulation in the airline business. In 1997, the major alliances were Sabena and
Swissair; Swissair, Delta AirLines, and Singapore Airlines; KLM and Northwest; British
Airways and American Airlines, and United Airlines and Lufthansa. These alliances were
necessary for the airline companies to survive in the deregulated market. The alliances
offer for the involved companies the access to new markets, a higher turnover and some
economics of scale.

The goal is to build a worldwide alliance by connecting the already formed alliances
to one worldwide global network. No company can do this alone, since no company has
the financial strength or time. Airline companies that will not join this global network
might not survive, unless they focus and become specialists in a very narrow market. The
dark side of deregulation and globalization is the danger of ending with a handful of
powerful airline companies controlling the market.[5]

Moreover, organizations and unions are also beginning to pursue collaborative,
win–win relationships rather than adversarial ones. As found by Xerox, this change can
significantly reduce costs and increase quality:

In the early 1980s, Xerox was losing market share to the Japanese and closing plants. Fearing
the worst, union leaders offered to explore ways to improve quality and efficiency. When they sat
down with management, they busted a bunch of old shop taboos. To avoid the periodic layoffs
and rehiring that follow manufacturing cycles, they agreed to let Xerox hire temporary workers for

specified tasks, as long as their number did not exceed 10% of the workforce and they worked for no more than six months. In exchange, management granted union members job security for the duration of their contract. The union also agreed to something called "no-fault termination": If a worker is absent on four occasions for two or more hours per year, he or she may be terminated. . . . Our absenteeism has fallen from 8.5% to 2.5%. Union members threw themselves into the task of making Xerox a world-beating competitor.[6]

Social and Political Pressures   These forces are created by social and political events. For example, tobacco companies are experiencing a lot of pressure to alter the way they market their products. This pressure is being exerted through legislative bodies. Political events can create substantial change. For instance, the collapse of the Berlin Wall and communism in Russia created many new business opportunities. Although it is difficult for organizations to predict changes in political forces, many organizations hire lobbyists and consultants to help them detect and respond to social and political changes.

Internal Forces

Internal forces for change
Originate inside the organization.

Internal forces for change come from inside the organization. These forces may be subtle, such as low job satisfaction, or can manifest in outward signs, such as low productivity and conflict. Internal forces for change come from both human resource problems and managerial behaviour/decisions.

Human Resource Problems/Prospects   These problems stem from employee perceptions about how they are treated at work and the match between individual and organization needs and desires. Chapter 7 highlighted the relationship between an employee's unmet needs and job dissatisfaction. Dissatisfaction is a symptom of an underlying employee problem that should be addressed. Unusual or high levels of absenteeism and turnover also represent forces for change. Organizations might respond to these problems by using the various approaches to job design discussed in Chapter 7,

---

International   Organizational   Behaviour
Banks Try to Penetrate Untapped Markets in South Africa

Khayelitsha Township, South Africa—Ntombizanele King has seen many things here: intractable poverty, sickness, raging fires, police raids, political upheaval, muggings.

Yet nothing quite prepared the 50-something child-care worker for what happens to her on a recent sunny Saturday morning: After less than 10 minutes in line, she, for the first time in her life, opens a bank account.

A teller, speaking Xhosa (pronounced KOH-zah), her tribal dialect, pulls up an application on a computer screen, fills it out by asking simple questions, and presses a button that instantly spits out a shiny bank card with Ms. King's name on it. Then, with a Xhosa-speaking assistant to help her manage her first attempt at an automated-teller machine, she deposits 50 rand (about $12), hidden in her clothes. This is better, she says, than the jar she has hidden in a cranny of her shack. If the *tsotsis,*

or robbers, come, as they often do here, Ms. King's money will be safe.

"A bank here? I never dreamed of such a thing," says Ms. King, who has walked with her neighbor Faltein Mncedisi to a branch recently opened by the E Bank affiliate of Standard Bank of South Africa, South Africa's second-largest bank.

As change rolls slowly across the landscape of the new South Africa, banks are popping up in improbable places to serve a market—essentially 80% of the population—that was largely shunned as too poor or illiterate to be of value to banks in the old South Africa. The effort, in time, holds the promise of tapping a huge pool of untapped capital while fundamentally changing the way ordinary black South Africans feel about the economy, and themselves.

by reducing employees' role conflict, overload, and ambiguity (recall our discussion in Chapter 10), and by removing the different stressors discussed in Chapter 17. Prospects for positive change stem from employee participation and suggestions.

Managerial Behaviour/Decisions   Excessive interpersonal conflict between managers and their subordinates is a sign that change is needed. Both the manager and the employee may need interpersonal skills training, or the two individuals may simply need to be separated. For example, one of the parties might be transferred to a new department. Inappropriate leader behaviours such as inadequate direction or support may result in human resource problems requiring change. As discussed in Chapter 16, leadership training is one potential solution for this problem. Inequitable reward systems—recall our discussion in Chapters 8 and 9—and the type of structural reorganizations discussed in Chapter 18 are additional forces for change.

Models and Dynamics of Planned Change

Many managers are criticized for emphasizing short-term, quick-fix solutions to organizational problems. When applied to organizational change, this approach is doomed from the start. Quick-fix solutions do not really solve underlying problems, and they have little staying power. Researchers and managers alike have thus tried to identify effective ways to manage the change process. This section sheds light on their insights. After discussing different types of organizational changes, we review Lewin's change model, a systems model of change, Kotter's eight-stages for leading organizational change, and organizational development.

Types of Change

A useful three-way typology of change is displayed in Figure 20–2.[7] This typology is generic because it relates to all sorts of change, including both administrative and technological changes. Adaptive change is lowest in complexity, cost, and uncertainty. It involves reimplementation of a change in the same organizational unit at a later time or imitation of a similar change by a different unit. For example, an adaptive change for a department store would be to rely on 12-hour days during the annual inventory week. The store's accounting department could imitate the same change in work hours during tax preparation time. Adaptive changes are not particularly threatening to employees because they are familiar.

Innovative changes fall midway on the continuum of complexity, cost, and uncertainty. An experiment with flexible work schedules by a farm supply warehouse company qualifies as an innovative change if it entails modifying the way other firms in the industry already use it. Unfamiliarity, and hence greater uncertainty, make fear of change a problem with innovative changes.

At the high end of the continuum of complexity, cost, and uncertainty are radically innovative changes. Changes of this sort are the most difficult to implement and tend to be the most threatening to managerial confidence and employee job security.[8] They can tear the fabric of an organization's culture. Resistance to change tends to increase as changes go from adaptive to innovative to radically innovative.

Lewin's Change Model

Most theories of organizational change originated from the landmark work of social psychologist Kurt Lewin. Lewin developed a three-stage model of planned change which explained how to initiate, manage, and stabilize the change process.[9] The three stages are unfreezing, changing, and refreezing. Before reviewing each stage, it is important to highlight the assumptions that underlie this model:[10]

1. The change process involves learning something new, as well as discontinuing current attitudes, behaviours, or organizational practices.

2. Change will not occur unless there is motivation to change. This is often the most difficult part of the change process.

3. People are the hub of all organizational changes. Any change, whether in terms of structure, group process, reward systems, or job design, requires individuals to change.

4. Resistance to change is found even when the goals of change are highly desirable.

5. Effective change requires reinforcing new behaviours, attitudes, and organizational practices.

Let us now consider the three stages of change.

Unfreezing   The focus of this stage is to create the motivation to change. In so doing, individuals are encouraged to replace old behaviours and attitudes with those desired by management. Managers can begin the unfreezing process by disconfirming the usefulness or appropriateness of employees' present behaviours or attitudes. In other words, employees need to become dissatisfied with the old way of doing things. **Benchmarking** is a technique that can be used to help unfreeze an organization. Benchmarking "describes the overall process by which a company compares its performance with that of other companies, then learns how the strongest-performing companies achieve their results."[11] For example, one company for which we consulted discovered through benchmarking that their costs to develop a computer system were twice as high as the best companies in the industry, and the time it took to get a new product to market was four times longer than the benchmarked organizations. These data were ultimately used to unfreeze employees' attitudes and motivate people to change the organization's internal processes in order to remain competitive.[12] Managers also need to devise ways to reduce the barriers to change during this stage.

Changing   Because change involves learning, this stage entails providing employees with new information, new behavioural models, or new ways of looking at things. The purpose is to help employees learn new concepts or points of view. Role models, mentors, experts, benchmarking results, and training are useful mechanisms to facilitate change. Experts recommend that it is best to convey the idea that change is a continuous learning process rather than a one-time event.[13]

Refreezing   Change is stabilized during refreezing by helping employees integrate the changed behaviour or attitude into their normal way of doing things. This is accomplished by first giving employees the chance to exhibit the new behaviours or attitudes. Once

Benchmarking
Process by which a company compares its performance with that of high-performing organizations.

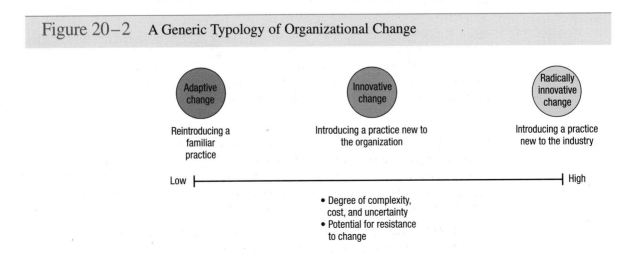

Figure 20–2   A Generic Typology of Organizational Change

Adaptive change — Reintroducing a familiar practice

Innovative change — Introducing a practice new to the organization

Radically innovative change — Introducing a practice new to the industry

Low ———————————————————————— High

• Degree of complexity, cost, and uncertainty
• Potential for resistance to change

exhibited, positive reinforcement is used to reinforce the desired change (recall our discussion in Chapter 15). Additional coaching and modelling are also used at this point to reinforce the stability of the change.[14]

A Systems Model of Change

A systems approach takes a "big picture" perspective of organizational change. It is based on the notion that any change, no matter how large or small, has a cascading impact throughout an organization. For example, promoting an individual to a new work group affects the group dynamics in both the old and new groups. Similarly, creating project or work teams may necessitate the need to revamp compensation practices. These examples illustrate that change creates additional change. Today's solutions are tomorrow's problems. A systems model of change offers managers a framework to understand the broad complexities of organizational change.[15] The three main components of a systems model are inputs, target elements of change, and outputs (see Figure 20–3).

Mission statement
Summarizes "why" an organization exists.

Inputs All organizational changes should be consistent with an organization's mission, vision, and resulting strategic plan. **A mission statement** represents the "reason" an organization exists. In Chapter 3 we defined an organization's *vision* as a long-term goal that describes "what" an organization wants to become. Consider how the difference between mission and vision affects organizational change. Your university probably has a mission to educate people. This mission does not necessarily imply anything about change. It simply defines the university's overall purpose. In contrast, the university may have a vision to be recognized as the "best" university in the country. This vision requires the organization to benchmark itself against other world-class universities and to create plans for achieving the vision. Unilever's corporate purpose, for example, is meeting high standards on several fields:

Our purpose in Unilever is to meet the everyday needs of people everywhere—to anticipate the aspirations of our customers and to respond creatively and competitively with branded products and services which raise the quality of life.

Our deep roots in local cultures and markets around the world are our unparalleled inheritance and the foundation for our future growth. We will bring our wealth of knowledge and international expertise to the service of local customers—a truly multilocal multinational.

Our long-term success requires a total commitment to exceptional standards of performance and productivity, to working together effectively and to a willingness to embrace new ideas and learn continuously.

We believe that to succeed requires the highest standards of corporate behaviour towards our employees, consumers and the societies and world in which we live.

This is Unilever's road to sustainable, profitable growth for our business and long-term value creation for our shareholders and employees.[16]

While vision statements point the way, strategic plans contain the detail needed to create organizational change.

Strategic plan
A long-term plan outlining actions needed to achieve planned results.

A **strategic plan** outlines an organization's long-term direction and actions necessary to achieve planned results.[17] Strategic plans are based on considering an organization's strengths and weaknesses relative to its environmental opportunities and threats. This comparison results in developing an organizational strategy to attain desired outputs such as profits, customer satisfaction, quality, adequate return on investment, and acceptable levels of turnover and employee commitment (see Figure 20–3). In summary, organizations tend to commit resources to counterproductive or conflicting activities when organizational changes are not consistent with its strategic plan.

Target Elements of Change **Target elements of change** represent the components of an organization that may be changed. As shown in Figure 20–3, change can be directed at

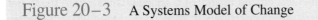

Figure 20–3   A Systems Model of Change

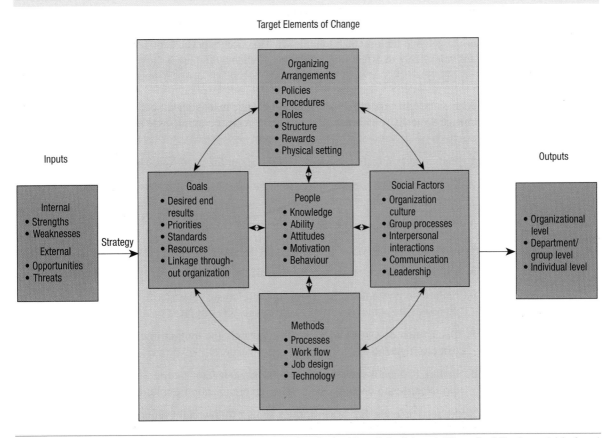

Source: Adapted from D R Fuqua and D J Kurpius, "Conceptual Models in Organizational Consultation," *Journal of Counseling & Development,* July–August 1993, pp 602–18; and D A Nadler and M L Tushman, "Organizational Frame Bending: Principles for Managing Reorientation," *Academy of Management Executive,* August 1989, pp 194–203.

Target elements of change

Components of an organization that may be changed.

realigning organizing arrangements, social factors, methods, goals, and people.[18] The choice is based on the strategy being pursued or the organizational problem at hand. For example, if lack of cooperation or teamwork is causing low productivity, change might be geared towards people or tasks. Moreover, the double-headed arrows among the target elements of change indicate that a change in one organizational component affects the others.

Consider how multiple target elements of change were affected by a reorganization at recently merged Krupp Hoesch (Germany):

Gerhard Cromme, Krupp Hoesch's chief executive introduced the 4K programme, which stands for Kunden (clients), Kosten (costs), Kreativität (creativity) and Kommunikation (communication): the company's major future points of interest. Along with the introduction of the 4K programme, the company's offices were seriously restructured too, so that relevant employees are now located next to each other. Before, the people taking new orders and those processing them worked in completely different buildings which hindered communication.[19]

This example highlights that change begets change. Specifically, a change in organizing arrangements—a new customer-service organization—led to additional changes in social factors, methods, and goals. Finally, Figure 20–3 underscores the assumption that people are the hub of all change. Change will not succeed unless individuals embrace it in one way or another.

Outputs   Output represents the desired end results of a change. Once again, these end results should be consistent with an organization's strategic plan. Figure 20–3 indicates that change may be directed at the organizational level, department/group level, or individual level. Change efforts are more complicated and difficult to manage when they are targeted at the organizational level. This occurs because organizational-level changes are more likely to affect multiple target elements of change shown in the model.

Kotter's Eight Steps for Leading Organizational Change

John Kotter, an expert in leadership and change management, believes that organizational change typically fails because senior management commits one or more of the following errors:[20]

1. Failure to establish a sense of urgency about the need for change.

2. Failure to create a powerful-enough guiding coalition that is responsible for leading and managing the change process.

3. Failure to establish a vision that guides the change process.

4. Failure to effectively communicate the new vision.[21]

5. Failure to remove obstacles that impede the accomplishment of the new vision.

6. Failure to systematically plan for and create short-term wins. Short-term wins represent the achievement of important results or goals.

7. Declaration of victory too soon. This derails the long-term changes in infrastructure that are frequently needed to achieve a vision.

8. Failure to anchor the changes into the organization's culture. It takes years for long-term changes to be embedded within an organization's culture.

Kotter recommends that organizations should follow eight sequential steps to overcome these problems (see Table 20–1).

Each of the steps shown in Table 20–1 is associated with the eight fundamental errors just discussed. These steps also subsume Lewin's model of change. The first four steps represent Lewin's "unfreezing" stage. Steps 5, 6, and 7 represent "changing," and step 8 corresponds to "refreezing." The value of Kotter's steps is that it provides specific recommendations about behaviours that managers need to exhibit to successfully lead organizational change. It is important to remember that Kotter's research reveals that it is ineffective to skip steps and that successful organizational change is 70 per cent to 90 per cent leadership and only 10 per cent to 30 per cent management. Senior managers are thus advised to focus on leading rather than managing change.[22]

Organization Development

Organization development (OD) is an applied field of study and practice. A pair of OD experts defined organization development as follows:

Organization development
A set of techniques or tools that are used to implement organizational change.

Organization development is concerned with helping managers plan change in organizing and managing people that will develop requisite commitment, coordination, and competence. Its purpose is to enhance both the effectiveness of organizations and the well-being of their members through planned interventions in the organization's human processes, structures, and systems, using knowledge of behavioural science and its intervention methods.[23]

As you can see from this definition, OD constitutes a set of techniques or interventions that are used to implement organizational change. These techniques or interventions apply to each of the change models discussed in this section. For example, OD is used during Lewin's "changing" stage. It also is used to identify and implement targeted elements of

Table 20–1   Steps to Leading Organizational Change

STEP	DESCRIPTION
1. Establish a sense of urgency	Unfreeze the organization by creating a compelling reason for why change is needed.
2. Create the guiding coalition	Create a cross-functional, cross-level group of people with enough power to lead the change.
3. Develop a vision and strategy	Create a vision and strategic plan to guide the change process.
4. Communicate the change vision	Create and implement a communication strategy that consistently communicates the new vision and strategic plan.
5. Empower broad-based action	Eliminate barriers to change, and use target elements of change to transform the organization. Encourage risk taking and creative problem solving.
6. Generate short-term wins	Plan for and create short-term "wins" or improvements. Recognize and reward people who contribute to the wins.
7. Consolidate gains and produce more change	The guiding coalition uses credibility from short-term wins to create more change. Additional people are brought into the change process as change cascades throughout the organization. Attempts are made to reinvigorate the change process.
8. Anchor new approaches in the culture	Reinforce the changes by highlighting connections between new behaviours and processes and organizational success. Develop methods to ensure leadership development and succession.

Scource: The steps were developed by J P Kotter, *Leading Change* (Boston: Harvard Business School Press, 1996).

change within the systems model of change. Finally, OD might be used during Kotter's steps 1, 3, 5, 6, and 7. In this section, we briefly review the four identifying characteristics of OD and its research and practical implications.[24]

OD Involves Profound Change   Change agents using OD generally desire deep and long-lasting improvement. OD consultant Warner Burke, for example, who strives for fundamental *cultural* change, wrote: "By fundamental change, as opposed to fixing a problem or improving a procedure, I mean that some significant aspect of an organization's culture will never be the same."[25]

OD Is Value-Loaded   Owing to the fact that OD is rooted partially in humanistic psychology, many OD consultants carry certain values or biases into the client organization. They prefer cooperation over conflict, self-control over institutional control, and democratic and participative management over autocratic management.[26]

OD Is a Diagnosis/Prescription Cycle   OD theorists and practitioners have long adhered to a medical model of organization. Like medical doctors, internal and external OD consultants approach the "sick" organization, "diagnose" its ills, "prescribe" and implement an intervention, and "monitor" progress.[27]

OD Is Process-Oriented   Ideally, OD consultants focus on the form and not the content of behavioural and administrative dealings. For example, product design engineers and market researchers might be coached on how to communicate more effectively with one another without the consultant knowing the technical details of their conversations. In addition to communication, OD specialists focus on other processes, including problem solving, decision making, conflict handling, trust, power sharing, and career development.

OD Research and Practical Implications   Before discussing OD research, it is important to note that many of the topics contained in this book are used during OD interventions. For example, role analysis, which was discussed in Chapter 10, is used to enhance cooperation among work group members by getting them to discuss their mutual expectations. Team building also is commonly used as an OD technique. It is used to improve the functioning of work groups and was reviewed in Chapter 13. The point is that OD research has practical implications for a variety of OB applications previously discussed. OD-related interventions produced the following insights:

- A meta-analysis of 18 studies indicated that employee satisfaction with change was higher when top management was highly committed to the change effort.[28]

- A meta-analysis of 52 studies provided support for the systems model of organizational change. Specifically, varying one target element of change created changes in other target elements. Also, there was a positive relationship between individual behaviour change and organizational-level change.[29]

- A meta-analysis of 126 studies demonstrated that multifaceted interventions using more than one OD technique were more effective in changing job attitudes and work attitudes than interventions that relied on only one human-process or technostructural approach.[30]

There are three practical implications derived from this research. First, planned organization change works. However, management and change agents are advised to rely on multifaceted interventions. As indicated elsewhere in this book, goal setting, feedback, recognition and rewards, training, participation, and challenging job design have good track records relative to improving performance and satisfaction. Second, change programmes are more successful when they are geared towards meeting both short-term and long-term results. Managers should not engage in organizational change for the sake of change. Change efforts should produce positive results.[31] Finally, organizational change is more likely to succeed when top management is truly committed to the change process and the desired goals of the change programme. This is particularly true when organizations pursue large-scale transformation.

Understanding and Managing Resistance to Change

We are all creatures of habit. It is generally difficult for people to try new ways of doing things. It is precisely because of this basic human characteristic that most employees do not have enthusiasm for change in the workplace. Rare is the manager who does not have several stories about carefully cultivated changes that died on the vine because of resistance to change. It is important for managers to learn to manage resistance because failed change efforts are costly. Costs include decreased employee loyalty, lowered probability of achieving corporate goals, a waste of money and resources, and difficulty in fixing the failed change effort.[32] This section examines employee resistance to change, relevant research, and practical ways of dealing with the problem.

Why People Resist Change in the Workplace

Resistance to change
Emotional/behavioural response to real or imagined work changes.

No matter how technically or administratively perfect a proposed change may be, people make or break it. Individual and group behaviour following an organizational change can take many forms (see Figure 20–4). The extremes range from acceptance to active resistance. **Resistance to change** is an emotional/behavioural response to real or imagined threats to an established work routine.

Figure 20–4 shows that resistance can be as subtle as passive resignation and as overt as deliberate sabotage. Managers need to learn to recognize the manifestations of resistance both in themselves and in others if they want to be more effective in creating and supporting change. For example, managers can use the list in Figure 20–4 to prepare answers and tactics to combat the various forms of resistance.

Now we have examined the signs of resistance to change, let us consider the reasons employees resist change in the first place. Ten of the leading reasons are listed here:[33]

1. *An individual's predisposition towards change.* This predisposition is highly personal and deeply ingrained. It is an outgrowth of how one learns to handle change and ambiguity as a child. Consider the hypothetical examples of Mary and Jim. Mary's parents were patient, flexible, and understanding. From the time Mary was weaned from a bottle, she was taught that there were positive compensations for the loss of

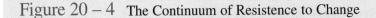

Figure 20 – 4   The Continuum of Resistence to Change

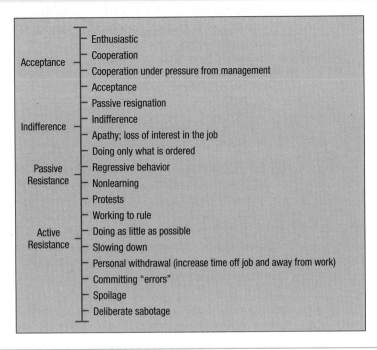

Source: A S Judson, *Changing Behavior in Organizations: Minimizing Resistance to Change* (Cambridge, MA: Basil Blackwell, Inc., 1991), p 48. Used with permission.

immediate gratification. She learned that love and approval were associated with making changes. In contrast, Jim's parents were unreasonable, unyielding, and forced him to comply with their wishes. They forced him to take piano lessons even though he hated them. Changes were demands for compliance. This taught Jim to be distrustful and suspicious of change. These learned predispositions ultimately affect how Mary and Jim handle change as adults.[34]

2. *Surprise and fear of the unknown.* When innovative or radically different changes are introduced without warning, affected employees become fearful of the implications. Grapevine rumours fill the void created by a lack of official announcements. Harvard's Rosabeth Moss Kanter recommends appointing a transition manager charged with keeping all relevant parties adequately informed.[35]

3. *Climate of mistrust.* Trust, as discussed in Chapter 13, involves reciprocal faith in others' intentions and behaviour. Mutual mistrust can doom to failure an otherwise well-conceived change. Mistrust encourages secrecy, which begets deeper mistrust. Managers who trust their employees make the change process an open, honest, and participative affair. Employees who, in turn, trust management are more willing to expend extra effort and take chances with something different.

4. *Fear of failure.* Intimidating changes on the job can cause employees to doubt their capabilities. Self-doubt erodes self-confidence and cripples personal growth and development.

5. *Loss of status and/or job security.* Administrative and technological changes that threaten to alter power bases or eliminate jobs generally trigger strong resistance. For example, most corporate restructuring involves the elimination of managerial jobs. One should not be surprised when middle managers resist restructuring and participative management programmes that reduce their authority and status.

6. *Peer pressure.* Someone who is not directly affected by a change may actively resist it to protect the interest of his or her friends and co-workers.

7. *Disruption of cultural traditions and/or group relationships.* Whenever individuals are transferred, promoted, or reassigned, cultural and group dynamics are thrown into disequilibrium.

8. *Personality conflicts.* Just as a friend can get away with telling us something we would resent hearing from an adversary, the personalities of change agents can breed resistance.

9. *Lack of tact and/or poor timing.* Undue resistance can occur because changes are introduced in an insensitive manner or at an awkward time.

10. *Nonreinforcing reward systems.* Individuals resist when they do not foresee positive rewards for changing. For example, an employee is unlikely to support a change effort that is perceived as requiring him or her to work longer with more pressure.

Research on Resistance to Change

The classic study of resistance to change was reported in 1948 by Lester Coch and John R P French. They observed the introduction of a new work procedure in a garment factory. The change was introduced in three different ways to separate groups of workers. In the "no participation" group, the garment makers were simply told about the new procedure. Members of a second group, called the "representative" group, were introduced to the change by a trained co-worker. Employees in the "total participation" group learned of the new work procedure through a graphic presentation of its cost-saving potential. Mixed results were recorded for the representative group. The no participation and total participation groups, meanwhile, went in opposite directions. Output dropped sharply for the no participation group, while grievances and turnover climbed. After a small dip in performance, the total participation group achieved record-high output levels while experiencing no turnover.[36] Since the Coch and French study, participation has been the recommended approach for overcoming resistance to change.[37]

Empirical research uncovered five additional personal characteristics related to resistance to change. A recent study of 305 college students and 15 university staff members revealed that attitudes toward a specific change were positively related to respondents' general attitudes towards change and content within their change schema. You may recall from Chapter 6 that a change schema relates to various perceptions, thoughts, and feelings that people have when they encounter organizational change.[38] High self-efficacy and an internal locus of control also were negatively associated with resistance to change.[39] Finally, a study of 284 nonmanagerial office personnel (43 per cent male) showed that hands-on experience with computers fostered more positive attitudes toward working with computers.[40]

Alternative Strategies for Overcoming Resistance to Change

Before recommending specific approaches to overcome resistance, there are three key conclusions that should be kept in mind. First, an organization must be ready for change. Just as a table must be set before you can eat, so must an organization be ready for change before it can be effective.[41] The OB exercise contains a survey that assesses an organization's readiness for change. Use the survey to evaluate a company that you worked for or are familiar with that undertook a change effort. What was the company's readiness for change, and how did this evaluation relate to the success of the change effort?

Second, organizational change is less successful when top management fails to keep employees informed about the process of change. Third, employees' perceptions or interpretations of a change significantly affect resistance. Employees are less likely to resist when they perceive that the benefits of a change overshadow the personal costs. At a minimum then, managers are advised to (1) provide as much information as possible to employees about the change, (2) inform employees about the reasons/rationale for the change, (3) conduct meetings to address employees' questions regarding the change, and (4) provide employees the opportunity to discuss how the proposed change might affect them.[42] These recommendations underscore the importance of communicating with employees throughout the process of change.

In addition to communication, employee participation in the change process is another generic approach for reducing resistance. The acquisition of Rover by British Aerospace resulted in the company's key priorities changing, from working with government departments to commercial performance as a part of a public limited company and a greater focus on providing customer satisfaction. This involved the development of total quality principles and practice. Self-development and involvement of the employees through suggestion schemes, discussion groups, quality action teams and workshops is Rover's strategy to stimulate changes on a broad front. Nearly 40 per cent of employees put forward their own ideas via the suggestion scheme, giving almost 30,000 valuable contributions in the first two years. Another two years later there was more than one suggestion per employee. One hundred discussion groups (Rover's name for quality circles) are in operation and, additionally, 500 management-led quality action teams. This means that over 20,000 employees are freely, willingly and enthusiastically contributing their ideas in some formal way, as well as those already treating such inputs as part of the job.

New suggestions in 1992 saved Rover over £10 million in the year and combined with ongoing suggestions still effective from previous years raised that figure to almost £20 million.[43] In spite of positive results like those found by Rover, organizational change experts have nonetheless criticized the tendency to treat participation as a cure-all for

OB EXERCISE   *Assessing an Organization's Readiness for Change*

Instructions

Circle the number that best represents your opinions about the company being evaluated.

3 = Yes
2 = Somewhat
1 = No

1. Is the change effort being sponsored by a senior-level executive (CEO, COO)?   3—2—1

2. Are all levels of management committed to the change?   3—2—1

3. Does the organization culture encourage risk taking?   3—2—1

4. Does the organization culture encourage and reward continuous improvement?   3—2—1

5. Has senior management clearly articulated the need for change?   3—2—1

6. Has senior management presented a clear vision of a positive future?   3—2—1

7. Does the organization use specific measures to assess business performance?   3—2—1

8. Does the change effort support other major activities going on in the organization?   3—2—1

9. Has the organization benchmarked itself against world-class companies?   3—2—1

10. Do all employees understand the customers' needs?   3—2—1

11. Does the organization reward individuals and/or teams for being innovative and for looking for root causes of organizational problems?   3—2—1

12. Is the organization flexible and cooperative?   3—2—1

13. Does management effectively communicate with all levels of the organization?   3—2—1

14. Has the organization successfully implemented other change programmes?   3—2—1

15. Do employees take personal responsibility for their behaviour?   3—2—1

16. Does the organization make decisions quickly?   3—2—1

Total Score: _____

Arbitrary Norms

40—48 = High readiness for change
24—39 = Moderate readiness for change
16—23 = Low readiness for change

SOURCE   Based on the discussion contained in T A Stewart, "Rate Your Readiness to Change," *Fortune*, February 7, 1994, pp 106–10.

Table 20–2   Six Strategies for Overcoming Resistance to Change

APPROACH	COMMONLY USED IN SITUATIONS	ADVANTAGES	DRAWBACKS
Education + Communication	Where there is a lack of information or inaccurate information and analysis.	Once persuaded, people will often help with the implementation of the change.	Can be very time consuming if lots of people are involved.
Participation + Involvement	Where the initiators do not have all he information they need to design the change and where others have considerable power to resist.	People who participate will be committed to implementing change, and any relevant information they have will be integrated into the change plan.	Can be very time consuming if participators design an inappropriate change.
Facilitation + Support	Where people are resisting because of adjustment problems.	No other approach works as well with adjustment problems.	Can be time consuming, expensive, and still fail.
Negotiation + Agreement	Where someone or some group will clearly lose out in a change and where that group has considerable power to resist.	Sometimes it is a relatively easy way to avoid major resistance.	Can be too expensive in many cases if it alerts others to negotiate for compliance.
Manipulation + Cooptation	Where other tactics will not work or are too expensive.	It can be a relatively quick and inexpensive solution to resistance problems.	Can lead to future problems if people feel manipulated.
Explicit+ Implicit coercion	Where speed is essential and where the change initiators possess considerable power.	It is speedy and can overcome any kind of resistance.	Can be risky if it leaves people mad at the initiators.

Source: Reprinted by permission of the *Harvard Business Review.* An exhibit from "Choosing Strategies for Change" by J P Kotter and L A Schlesinger (March/April 1979). Copyright ©1979 by the President and Fellows of Harvard College; all rights reserved.

resistance to change. They prefer a contingency approach because resistance can take many forms and, furthermore, because situational factors vary (see Table 20–2). As seen in Table 20–2, Participation + Involvement does have its place, but it takes time that is not always available. Also as indicated in Table 20–2, each of the other five methods has its situational niche, advantages, and drawbacks. In short, there is no universal strategy for overcoming resistance to change. Managers need a complete repertoire of change strategies.[44]

Creating a Learning Organization

Organizations are finding that yesterday's competitive advantage is becoming the minimum entrance requirement for staying in business. This puts tremendous pressure on organizations to learn how best to improve and stay ahead of competitors. In fact, both researchers and practising managers agree that an organization's capability to learn is a key strategic weapon.[45] A 1996 survey of almost 200 German companies, conducted by DEKRA Akademie with the Mainsberger and Partner consulting firm, found that 90 per cent consider themselves to be a learning organization, or in the process of becoming one.[46] It is therefore important for organizations to enhance and nurture their capability to learn. The basic knowledge for creating a learning organization is present in every organization, argues Herman Van den Broeck, author of a book on learning management

Everybody has a stock of knowledge, background information, experience and know-how on the organization, information on clients, etc. It is essential that managers make use of their own and their staff's hidden knowledge, to manage learning processes.[47]

So how do organizations create a learning organization? It is not easy! To help clarify what this process entails, this section begins by defining a learning organization. We then present a model of how to build an organization's learning capability and discuss some reasons organizations naturally resist learning. The chapter concludes by reviewing new roles and skills required of leaders to create a learning organization and several management practices that must be unlearned.

Defining a Learning Organization

Peter Senge, a professor at the Massachusetts Institute of Technology, popularized the term *learning organization* in his bestselling book entitled *The Fifth Discipline*. He described learning organizations as places "where people continually expand their capacity to create the results they truly desire, where new and expansive patterns of thinking are nurtured, where collective aspiration is set free, and where people are continually learning how to learn together."[48] A practical interpretation of these ideas results in the following definition. A **learning organization** is one that proactively creates, acquires, and transfers knowledge and that changes its behaviour on the basis of new knowledge and insights.[49]

Learning organization
Proactively creates, acquires, and transfers knowledge throughout the organization.

By breaking this definition into its three component parts, we can clearly see the characteristics of a learning organization. First, new ideas are a prerequisite for learning. Learning organizations actively try to infuse their organizations with new ideas and information. They do this by constantly scanning their external environments, hiring new talent and expertise when needed, and by devoting significant resources to train and develop their employees. Second, new knowledge must be transferred throughout the organization. Learning organizations strive to reduce structural, process, and interpersonal barriers to the sharing of information, ideas, and knowledge among organizational members. Finally, behaviour must change as a result of new knowledge. Learning organizations are results oriented. They foster an environment in which employees are encouraged to use new behaviours and operational processes to achieve corporate goals.[50]

Before you read on, first consider the following case:

At Oral-B, we define a world-class manufacturer as a learning organization that achieves total quality through "employee energizing."

A self-learning culture has to find ways to use learning processes to promote lateral thinking and so mobilize employees' creative potential. The results of learning are seen in continuous improvements in process efficiencies. One of the more striking examples is the way in which a project team translated lateral thinking into a new product, Ultra-floss, which was launched worldwide. This "brushy" floss is produced by a machine originally designed for a totally different purpose. They may not have an R&D department, but they do have bright people prepared to work hard.

Oral-B Ireland's success did not happen overnight. Since the first day of operation, quality awareness was instilled in the working systems, and they have since succeeded in taking quality for granted. Quality awareness is achieved when employees progress to actually seeing it, then caring enough to do something to improve it. Success means better product quality, better work ethics a greater employee commitment to improved customer service.

At Oral-B Ireland, the idea of partnership with customers—rather than being customer driven—is central to the approach to total quality management. The difference between the two is that, in a partnership, mutual respect and understanding develops, leading to the discovery of "latent requirements." The objective is to learn from the process of building partnerships. If it can be learned exactly what the customers expect, and they can learn exactly what Oral-B offers, Oral-B will be able to respond faster than the competitors to customer needs, and to inevitable problems. The focus is on two issues in particular: the gap between customer expectations and the provider's understanding of these; and the gap between the customer's experiences and memories of what was delivered, and those of the provider. These gaps occur not only in actual outcomes, such as product delivery, but also in the "soft" areas of communication, empathy and problem solving.

This requires the learning development of all employees. It is not enough to have just a few bright technocrats. But Oral-B is not a training organization—the goal is not to train but to support learning, and the level of learning has increased substantially over the past few years. The primary needs are to equip employees with the necessary learning skills, plus the ability to apply what they have learnt.

Each employee receives modular training in basic statistics and problem-solving techniques.

Figure 20–5   Building an Organization's Learning Capability

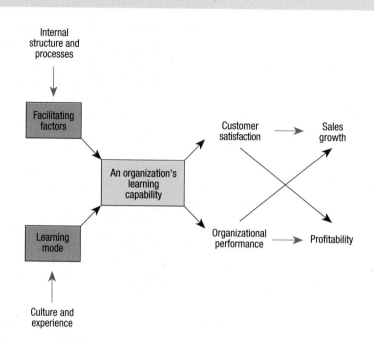

An "improvement road map and dashboard," which contains summary problem-solving tools and key project measures, is distributed to all employees. These simple, yet effective, initiatives demonstrate how they have learned from assessing their past actions. More advanced courses in the design of experiments, using real, practical problems, are given to engineers, chemists, and technicians. Wherever possible, training is designed to help employees learn more about the processes to which they are a supplier, for which they are responsible, or of which they are a customer. In other words, learning is viewed as a powerful factor in creating a climate where continuous improvement takes place naturally.[51]

Building an Organization's Learning Capability

Learning capabilities
The set of core competencies and internal processes that enable an organization to adapt to its environment.

Figure 20–5 presents a model of how organizations build and enhance their learning capability. **Learning capabilities** represent the set of core competencies, which are defined as the special knowledge, skills, and technological know-how that differentiate an organization from its competitors, and processes that enable an organization to adapt to its environment.[52] The general idea underlying Figure 20–5 is that learning capabilities are the fuel for organizational success. Just like gasoline enables a car's engine to perform, learning capabilities equip an organization to foresee and respond to internal and external changes. This capability, in turn, increases the chances of satisfying customers and boosting sales and profitability.[53] Let us now consider the two major contributors to an organization's learning capability: facilitating factors and learning mode.

Facilitating Factors   *Facilitating factors* represent "the internal structure and processes that affect how easy or hard it is for learning to occur and the amount of effective learning that takes place."[54] Table 20–3 contains a list of 10 key facilitating factors. Keep in mind as you read them that these factors can either enable or impede an organization's ability to respond to its environment. Consider, for example, the "concern for measurement" factor. A survey of 203 executives compared companies that did and did not focus on measurement-management. Results revealed that those companies who focused on measurement-management were identified as industry leaders, had financial performance

Table 20–3	Factors That Facilitate Organizational Learning Capabilities

1.	Scanning imperative	Interest in external happenings and in the nature of one's environment. Valuing the processes of awareness and data generation. Curious about what is "out there" as opposed to "in here."
2.	Performance gap	Shared perception of a gap between actual and desired state of performance. Disconfirming feedback interrupts a string of successes. Performance shortfalls are seen as opportunities for learning.
3.	Concern for measurement	Spend considerable effort in defining and measuring key factors when venturing into new areas; strive for specific, quantifiable measures; discourse over metrics is seen as a learning activity.
4.	Experimental mindset	Support for trying new things; curiosity about how things work; ability to "play" with things. Small failures are encouraged, not punished. See changes in work processes, policies, and structures as a continuous series of graded tryouts.
5.	Climate of openness	Accessibility of information; relatively open boundaries. Opportunities to observe others; problems/errors are shared, not hidden; debate and conflict are acceptable.
6.	Continuous education	Ongoing commitment to education at all levels; support for growth and development of members.
7.	Operational variety	Variety exists in response modes, procedures, systems; significant diversity in personnel. Pluralistic rather than monolithic definition of valued internal capabilities.
8.	Multiple advocates	Top-down and bottom-up initiatives are possible; multiple advocates and gatekeepers exist.
9.	Involved leadership	Leadership at significant levels articulates vision and is very actively engaged in its actualization; takes ongoing steps to implement vision; "hands-on" involvement in educational and other implementation steps.
10.	Systems perspective	Strong focus on how parts of the organization are interdependent; seek optimization of organizational goals at the highest levels; see problems and solutions in terms of systemic relationships.

Source: Reprinted by permission of Sage Publications Ltd. from A J DiBella, E C Nevis, and J M Gould, "Organizational Learning Style as a Core Capability," in *Organizational Learning and Competitive Advantage*, eds B Moingeon and A Edmondson (Thousand Oaks, CA: Sage,© 1996), p 43

that put them in the top third of their industry, and were more successful at implementing and managing major change initiatives.[55] This study suggests that concern for measurement enhanced these organizations' learning capabilities.

Learning modes

The various ways in which organizations attempt to create and maximize their learning.

Learning Mode   **Learning modes** represent the various ways in which organizations attempt to create and maximize their learning. Figure 20–5 shows that learning modes are directly influenced by an organization's culture and experience or past history. OB researcher Danny Miller reviewed the literature on organizational learning and identified six dominant modes of learning:[56]

1. *Analytic learning.* Learning occurs through systematic gathering of internal and external information. Information tends to be quantitative and analysed via formal systems. The emphasis is on using deductive logic to numerically analyse objective data.

2. *Synthetic learning.* Synthetic learning is more intuitive and generic than the analytic mode. It emphasizes the synthesis of large amounts of complex information by using systems thinking. That is, employees try to identify interrelationships between issues, problems, and opportunities.

3. *Experimental learning.* This mode is a rational methodological approach that is based on conducting small experiments and monitoring the results.

4. *Interactive learning.* This mode involves learning-by-doing. Rather than using systematic methodological procedures, learning occurs primarily through the exchange of information. Learning is more intuitive and inductive.

5. *Structural learning.* This mode is a methodological approach that is based on the use of organizational routines. Organizational routines represent standardized processes and procedures that specify how to carry out tasks and roles. People learn from routines because they direct attention, institutionalize standards, and create consistent vocabularies.

6. *Institutional learning.* This mode represents an inductive process by which organizations share and model values, beliefs, and practices either from their external environments or from senior executives. Employees learn by observing environmental examples or senior executives. Socialization and mentoring play a significant role in institutional learning.

How Facilitating Factors and Learning Modes Produce Learning Capability

Researchers suspect there is some type of optimal matching between the facilitating factors and learning modes that affects learning capability.[57] For example, the "experimental mindset" facilitating factor should enhance the learning capability of a company that predominately uses an "experimental learning" mode. In contrast, the inconsistency between an "experimental mindset" and a "structural learning" mode would most likely impede organizational learning. Because the concept of a learning organization is very new to the field of OB, we really do not know how the facilitating factors combine with learning modes to influence an organization's learning capability. Future empirical research is needed to examine this issue. Nonetheless, we do know that an organization's learning capability is an important contributor to organizational effectiveness.[58] Managers are thus advised to develop, nurture, and reinforce their organizations' learning capabilities. Let us now consider the reasons organizations unfortunately have a natural tendency to resist learning.

Organizations Naturally Resist Learning

You may be wondering why any rational person or organization would resist learning. It just does not make sense. Well, organizations do not consciously resist learning. They do it because of three fundamental problems that plague society at large: focusing on fragmentation rather than systems, emphasizing competition over collaboration, and a tendency to be reactive rather than proactive.[59] Overcoming these problems requires a fundamental shift in how we view the world.

Focusing on Fragmentation rather than Systems

Fragmentation involves the tendency to break down a problem, project, or process into smaller pieces. For example, as students you are taught to memorize isolated facts, study abstract theories, and learn ideas and concepts that bear no resemblance to your personal life experiences. This reinforces the use of an analytic strategy that entails solving complex problems by studying subcomponents rather than wholes. Unfortunately, modern-day problems such as runaway health care costs or national debt cannot be solved with piecemeal linear approaches.

In organizations, fragmentation creates functional "walls" or "silos" that separate people into independent groups. In turn, this results in creating specialists who work within specific functional areas. It also generates internal fiefdoms that battle over power, resources, and control. Learning, sharing, cooperation, and collaboration are ultimately lost on the battlefield.

Emphasizing Competition over Collaboration

Competition is a dominant societal and management paradigm: A **paradigm** represents a generally accepted way of viewing the world. Although nothing is intrinsically wrong with competition, this paradigm results in employees competing with the very people with whom they need to collaborate for success. Moreover, it creates an overemphasis on looking good rather than being good,

Paradigm
A generally accepted way of viewing the world.

which prohibits learning because people become reluctant to admit when they do not know something. This is especially true of leaders. In turn, employees hesitate to accept tasks or assignments that they are not good at. Finally, competition produces a fixation on short-term measurable results rather than on long-term solutions to root causes of problems.

Being Reactive rather than Creative and Proactive   People are accustomed to changing only when they need to because life is less stressful and frustrating when we stay within our comfort zones. This contrasts with the fundamental catalyst of real learning. The drive to learn is fuelled by personal interest, curiosity, aspiration, imagination, experimentation, and risk taking. The problem is that all of us have been conditioned to respond and react to others' directions and approval. This undermines the intrinsic drive to learn. When this tendency is coupled with management by fear, intimidation, and crisis, people not only resist learning, they become paralysed by the fear of taking risks.

Effective Leadership Is the Solution

There is hope! Effective leadership chisels away at these natural tendencies and paves the way for organizational learning. Leaders can create an organizational culture that promotes systems thinking over fragmentation, collaboration and cooperation over competition, and innovation and proaction over reactivity. Leaders must, however, adopt new roles and associated activities to create a learning organization.

Specifically, leaders perform three key functions in building a learning organization: (1) building a commitment to learning, (2) working to generate ideas with impact, and (3) working to generalize ideas with impact.[60] Table 20–4 contains a list of leadership activities needed to support each role.

Building a Commitment to Learning   Leaders need to instil an intellectual and emotional commitment to learning by using the ideas shown in Table 20–4.

For example, Unilever has included "continuous learning" in its mission statement. Leaders can promote the value of learning by modelling the desired attitudes and behaviours. They can attend seminars as presenters or participants, share effective managerial practices with peers, and disseminate readings, videos, and other educational materials. ICL is an excellent example of promoting self-managed learning.

ICL is a successful European information technology company and a major "investor in people." People own their own development as key to maintain competitive advantage. A variety of self-development/self-managed learning methodologies were used to develop people. Self-managed learning is more effective than imposed teaching. However, it is not easy to change people's instincts, and often the learning consultants find themselves inclined to tell people the best way to go about something, to design for the employees a seminar, to take the lead in a discussion, etc.

Some of the self-development programmes have follow-on learning sets which are a definite part of the structure. In others it is the "expected" norm and in one (run with managers and their teams) it is left to them to continue after the initial event on managing their own development. One of four programmes expects participants to identify a mentor and helps in the identification of needs, while in other programmes this has not been seen as adding value. Some are voluntary, while in others everyone in a division must attend.[61]

Working to Generate Ideas with Impact   Ideas with impact are those that add value to one or more of an organization's three key stakeholders: employees, customers, and shareholders. The leadership activities shown in Table 20–4 reveal six ways to generate ideas with impact.

Working to Generalize Ideas with Impact   Leaders must make a concerted effort to reduce interpersonal, group, and organizational barriers to learning. This can be done by

Table 20-4   Leadership Roles and Activities for Building a Learning Organization

LEADERSHIP ACTIVITIES	ROLE 1: BUILD A COMMITMENT TO LEARNING	ROLE 2: WORK TO GENERATE IDEAS WITH IMPACT	ROLE 3: WORK TO GENERALIZE IDEAS WITH IMPACT
Make learning a component of the vision and strategic objectives	X		
Invest in learning	X		
Publicly promote the value of learning	X		
Measure, benchmark, and track learning	X		
Create rewards and symbols of learning	X		
Implement continuous improvement programmes		X	
Increase employee competence through training, or buy talent from outside the organization		X	
Experiment with new ideas, processes, and structural arrangements		X	
Go outside the organization to identify world-class ideas and processes		X	
Identify mental models of organizational processes		X	
Instil systems thinking throughout the organization		X	
Create an infrastructure that moves ideas across organizational boundaries			X
Rotate employees across functional and divisional boundaries			X

Source: Based in part on D Ulrich, T Jick, and M Von Glinow, "High-Impact Learning: Building and Diffusing Learning Capability," *Organizational Dynamics*, Autumn 1993, pp 52–66.

creating a learning infrastructure. This is a large-scale effort that includes the following activities:

- Measuring and rewarding learning.
- Increasing open and honest dialogue among organizational members.
- Reducing conflict.
- Increasing horizontal and vertical communication.
- Promoting teamwork.
- Rewarding risk taking and innovation.
- Reducing the fear of failure.
- Increasing the sharing of successes, failures, and best practices across organizational members.
- Reducing stressors and frustration.
- Reducing internal competition.
- Increasing cooperation and collaboration.
- Creating a psychologically safe and comforting environment.[62]

Unlearning the Organization

In addition to implementing the ideas listed in Table 20–4, organizations must concurrently unlearn organizational practices and paradigms that made them successful. Quite simply, traditional organizations and the associated organizational behaviours they created have outlived their usefulness. Management must seriously question and challenge the ways of thinking that worked in the past if they want to create a learning organization. For example, the old management paradigm of planning, organizing, and control might be replaced with one of vision, values, and empowerment. The time has come for management and employees to think as owners, not as "us" and "them" adversaries.

Let us close our study of organizational behaviour by considering a mission statement that promotes this new managerial paradigm:

ETHICS

> This is a company of owners, of partners, of businesspeople. We are in business together. Our economic figure—which is to say, our jobs and our financial security—depend not on management's generosity ("them") or on the strength of a union ("us") but on our collective success in the marketplace. We will share in the rewards just as—by definition—we share in the risks.
>
> No one in this company is just an employee. People have different jobs, make different salaries, have different levels of authority. But all workers will see the same basic information and will have a voice in matters affecting them. And it will be everyone's responsibility to understand how the business operates, to keep track of its results, and to make decisions that contribute to its success in the marketplace.[63]

Summary of Key Concepts

1. *Discuss the external and internal forces that create the need for organizational change.* Organizations encounter both external and internal forces for change. There are four key external forces for change: demographic characteristics, technological advancements, market changes, and social and political pressures. Internal forces for change come from both human resource problems and managerial behaviour/decisions.

2. *Describe Lewin's change model and the systems model of change.* Lewin developed a three-stage model of planned change that explained how to initiate, manage, and stabilize the change process. The three states were *unfreezing,* which entails creating the motivation to change, *changing,* and stabilizing change through *refreezing.* A systems model of change takes a big picture perspective of change. It focuses on the interaction among the key components of change. The three main components of change are inputs, target elements of change, and outputs. The target elements of change represent the components of an organization that may be changed. They include organizing arrangements, social factors, methods, goals, and people.

3. *Discuss Kotter's eight steps for leading organizational change.* John Kotter believes that organizational change fails for one or more of eight common errors.

He proposed eight steps that organizations should follow to overcome these errors. The eight steps are as follows:

(*a*) establish a sense of urgency, (*b*) create the guiding coalition, (*c*) develop a vision and strategy, (*d*) communicate the change vision, (*e*) empower broad-based action, (*f*) generate short-term wins, (*g*) consolidate gains and produce more change, and (*h*) anchor new approaches in the culture.

4. *Demonstrate your familiarity with the four identifying characteristics of organization development (OD).* The identifying characteristics of OD are that it (*a*) involves profound change, (*b*) is value loaded, (*c*) is a diagnosis/prescription cycle, and (*d*) is process oriented.

5. *Discuss the 10 reasons employees resist change.* Resistance to change is an emotional/behavioural response to real or imagined threats to an established work routine. Ten reasons employees resist change are (*a*) an individual's predisposition towards change, (*b*) surprise and fear of the unknown, (*c*) climate of mistrust, (*d*) fear of failure, (*e*) loss of status and/or job security, (*f*) peer pressure, (*g*) disruption of cultural traditions and/or group relationships, (*h*) personality conflicts, (*i*) lack of tact and/or poor timing, and (*j*) nonreinforcing reward systems.

6. *Identify alternative strategies for overcoming resistance to change.* Organizations must be ready for change. Assuming an organization is ready for change, the alternative strategies for overcoming resistance to change are education + communication, participation + involvement, facilitation + support, negotiation + agreement, manipulation + cooptation, and explicit + implicit coercion. Each has its situational appropriateness and advantages and drawbacks.

7. *Define a learning organization.* A learning organization is one that proactively creates, acquires, and transfers knowledge and changes its behaviour on the basis of new knowledge and insights.

8. *Discuss the process organizations use to build their learning capabilities.* Learning capabilities represent the set of core competencies and processes that enable an organization to adapt to its environment. Learning capabilities are directly affected by organizational facilitating factors and learning modes. Facilitating factors constitute the internal structure and processes that either encourage or impede learning within an organization. Learning modes represent the various ways by which organizations attempt to create and maximize their learning. Researchers believe that there is some type of optimal matching between the facilitating factors and learning modes that affects learning capability.

9. *Review the reasons organizations naturally resist learning.* There are three underlying reasons. The first involves the tendency to focus on fragmentation rather than systems. Fragmentation involves the tendency to break down a problem, project, or process into smaller pieces. It reinforces a linear analytic strategy that examines subcomponents rather than wholes. A dominant management paradigm that emphasizes competition over collaboration is the second reason. The third reason organizations naturally resist learning is that people have a tendency to be reactive rather than creative and proactive. This tendency stems from the fact that all of us have been conditioned to respond and react to others' directions and approval.

10. *Discuss the role of leadership in creating a learning organization.* Leaders perform three key functions in building a learning organization: (*a*) building a commitment to learning, (*b*) working to generate ideas with impact, and (*c*) working to generalize ideas with impact. There are 13 different leadership activities needed to support each role (see Table 20–4).

Discussion Questions

1. Which of the external forces for change do you believe will prompt the greatest change between now and the year 2010?

2. Have you worked in an organization where internal forces created change? Describe the situation and the resulting change.

3. How would you respond to a manager who made the following statement? "Unfreezing is not important, employees will follow my directives."

4. What are some useful methods that can be used to refreeze an organizational change?

5. Have you ever observed the systems model of change in action? Explain what occurred.

6. Have you ever resisted a change at work? Explain the circumstances and your thinking at the time.

7. Which source of resistance to change do you think is the most common? Which is the most difficult for management to deal with?

8. Does the company you work for act like a learning organization? Explain your rationale.

9. Which of the three reasons for organizations' natural resistance to learning is the most powerful? Explain.

Personal Awareness and Growth Exercise

Applying the Systems Model of Change

Objectives

1. To help you understand the diagnosis step of planned organizational change.

2. To give you a practical diagnostic tool to assess which target elements of change in Figure 20–3 should be changed during a change process.

Introduction

Diagnosis is the first step in planned organizational change. It is used to identify past or current organizational problems that inhibit organizational effectiveness. As indicated in Figure 20–3, there are five organizational areas in which to look for problems: organizing arrangements, social factors, methods, goals, and people. In this exercise, you will be asked to complete a brief survey assessing these five areas of an organization.

Instructions

If you currently have a full- or part-time job, think of your organization and describe it by circling an appropriate response for each of the following 18 statements. Calculate a total score for each diagnostic area. Then connect the set of points for your organization in a vertical profile. If you are not currently employed, describe the last organization you worked for. If you have never worked, use your current university or school as your frame of reference.

After completing the survey, think of an "ideal" organization: an organization that you believe would be most effective. How do you believe this organization would stand in terms of the five diagnostic areas? We would like you to assess this organization with the same diagnostic survey. Circle your responses with a different colour or marking. Then vertically connect the set of points for your "ideal" organization. Calculate a total score for each diagnostic area.

Organizational Diagnostic Survey

1 = Strongly disagree

2 = Disagree

3 = Neutral

4 = Agree

5 = Strongly agree

ORGANIZING ARRANGEMENTS

1. The company has the right recognition and rewards in place to support its vision and strategies. 1—2—3—4—5

2. The organizational structure facilitates goal accomplishment. 1—2—3—4—5

3. Organizational policies and procedures are administered fairly. 1—2—3—4—5

Total Organizing Arrangements score = _____ _____

SOCIAL FACTORS

4. The culture promotes adaptability and flexibility. 1—2—3—4—5

5. Interpersonal and group conflict are handled in a positive manner. 1—2—3—4—5

6. Horizontal and vertical communication is effective. 1—2—3—4—5

7. Leaders are good role models and decision makers. 1—2—3—4—5

Total Social Factors score = _____ _____

METHODS

8. The work flow promotes higher quality and quantity of performance. 1—2—3—4—5

9. Technology is effectively utilized. 1—2—3—4—5

10. People focus on solving root cause problems rather than symptoms. 1—2—3—4—5

Total Methods score = _____ _____

GOALS

11. I am aware of the organization's vision and strategic goals. 1—2—3—4—5

12. I have all the tools and resources I need to do my job. 1—2—3—4—5

13. Corporate goals are cascaded down the organization. 1—2—3—4—5

14. I am evaluated against specific standards of performance. 1—2—3—4—5

Total Goals score = _____ _____

PEOPLE

15. This organization inspires the very best in me in the way of job performance. 1—2—3—4—5

16. I understand my job duties and responsibilities. 1—2—3—4—5

17. I like working in this company. 1—2—3—4—5

18. People are motivated to do the best job they can. 1—2—3—4—5

Total People score = _____ _____

1. Based on your evaluation of your current organization, which diagnostic area(s) is most in need of change?

2. Based on a comparison of your current and ideal organizations, which diagnostic area(s) is most in need of

change? If your answer is different from the first question, explain the difference.

3. What sort of intervention would be appropriate for your work group or organization? Give details.

Group Exercise

Creating Personal Change Through Force-Field Analysis[64]

Objectives

1. To apply force-field analysis to a behaviour or situation you would like to change.

2. To receive feedback on your strategies for bringing about change.

Introduction

The theory of force-field analysis is based on the premise that people resist change because of counteracting positive and negative forces. Positive forces for change are called *thrusters*. They propel people to accept change and modify their behaviour. In contrast, *counterthrusters* or *resistors* are negative forces that motivate an individual to maintain the status quo. People frequently fail to change because they experience equal amounts of positive and negative forces to change.

Force-field analysis is a technique used to facilitate change by first identifying the thrusters and resistors that exist in a specific situation. To minimize resistance to change, it is generally recommended to first reduce or remove the negative forces to change. Removing counterthrusters should create increased pressure for an individual to change in the desired direction. Managers can also further increase motivation to change by following up the reduction of resistors with an increase in the number of positive thrusters of change.

Instructions

Your instructor will pair you up with another student. The two of you will serve as a team that evaluates the completeness of each other's force-field analysis and recommendations. Once the team is assembled, each individual should independently complete the Force-Field Analysis Form presented after these instructions. Once both of you complete this activity, one team member should present results from steps 2 through 5 from the five-step Force-Field Analysis Form. The partner should then evaluate the results by considering

the following questions with his or her team member:

1. Are there any additional thrusters and counterthrusters that should be listed? Add them to the list.

2. Do you agree with the "strength" evaluations of thrusters and counterthrusters in step 4? Ask your partner to share his or her rationale for the ratings. Modify the ratings as needed.

3. Examine the specific recommendations for change listed in step 5, and evaluate whether you think they will produce the desired changes. Be sure to consider whether the focal person has the ability to eliminate, reduce, or increase each thruster and counterthruster that is the basis for a specific recommendation. Are there any alternative strategies you can think of?

4. What is your overall evaluation of your partner's intervention strategy?

FORCE-FIELD ANALYSIS FORM[65]

STEP 1

In the space provided, please identify a number of personal problems you would like to solve or aspects of your life you would like to change. Be as imaginative as possible. You are not limited to school situations. For example, you may want to consider your work environment if you are currently employed, family situation, interpersonal relationships, club situations, and so forth. It is important that you select some aspects of your life that you would like to change but which up to now have made no effort to do.

_____

_____

_____

_____

_____

_____

_____

STEP 2

Review in your mind the problems or aspects listed in step 1. Now select one that you would really like to change and which you believe lends itself easily to force-field analysis. Select one that you will feel comfortable talking about to other people.

STEP 3

On the form following step 4, indicate existing forces that are pushing you in the direction of change. Thrusters may be forces internal to the self (pride, regret, and fear) or they may be external to the self (friends, the boss, a professor). Also list existing forces that are preventing you from changing. Again, the counterthruster may be internal to the self (uncertainty, fear) or external to the self (poor instruction, limited resources, lack of support mechanisms).

STEP 4

In the space to the right of your list of thrusters and counterthrusters indicate the irrelative strength. For consistency, use a scale of 1 to 10, with 1 indicating a weak force and 10 indicating a high force.

THRUSTERS   **STRENGTH**

_____   _____
_____   _____
_____   _____
_____   _____
_____   _____
_____   _____

COUNTERTHRUSTERS   **STRENGTH**

_____   _____
_____   _____
_____   _____
_____   _____

STEP 5

Analyze your thrusters and counterthrusters, and develop a strategy for bringing about the desired change. Remember that it is possible to produce the desired results by strengthening existing thrusters, introducing new thrusters, weakening or removing counterthrusters, or some combination of these. Consider the impact of your change strategy on the system's internal stress (i.e., on yourself and others), the likelihood of success, the availability of resources, and the long-term consequences of planned changes. Be prepared to discuss your recommendations with the partner in your group.

_____
_____
_____
_____
_____

QUESTIONS FOR DICUSSION

1. What was your reaction to doing a force-field analysis? Was it insightful and helpful?

2. Was it valuable to receive feedback about your force-field analysis from a partner? Explain.

3. How would you assess the probability of effectively implementing your recommendations?

Notes

[1]Exerpted from K Orrell-Jones, "How 'Them and Us' Became We," *Management Today,* May 1996 p 5.

[2]C Schock, "Facing Change and Making It Work for You," *Women in Business,* March/April 1996, pp 32–34.

[3]These statistics were taken from J A Lopez, "Corporate Change: You Can Count on It," *The Arizona Republic,* March 3, 1996, pp D1, D3; and J J Laabs, "Expert Advice on How to Move Forward with Change," *Personnel Journal,* July 1996, pp 54–63.

[4]For a thorough discussion of technological advancements in office automation, see the special insert "Telecommunications," *The Wall Street Journal Reports,* February 11, 1994, pp R1–28.

[5]S De Boe "Van Nationale Lunchtvaartmaatschappijen naar Global Airlines," *Financieel Economische Tijd*, August 23, 1997.

[6]P Nulty, "Look What the Unions Want Now," *Fortune,* February 8, 1993, p 132.

[7]This three-way typology of change was adapted from discussion in P C Nutt, "Tactics of Implementation," *Academy of Management Journal,* June 1986, pp 230–61.

[8]Radical organizational change is discussed by T E Vollmann, *The Transformational Imperative* (Boston: Harvard Business School Press, 1996); and J A Neal and C L Tromley, "From Incremental Change to Retrofit: Creating High-Performance Work Systems," *Academy of Management Executive,* February 1995, pp 42–53.

[9]For a thorough discussion of the model, see K Lewin, *Field Theory in Social Science* (New York: Harper & Row, 1951).

[10]These assumptions are discussed in E H Schein, *Organizational Psychology,* 3rd ed (Englewood Cliffs, NJ: Prentice-Hall, 1980).

[11]C Goldwasser, "Benchmarking: People Make the Process," *Management Review,* June 1995, p 40.

[12]Benchmark data for "America's Best Plants" can be found in J H Sheridan, "Lessons from the Best," *Industry Week,* February 1996, pp 13–20.

[13]The role of learning within organizational change is discussed by C Hendry, "Understanding and Creating Whole Organizational Change through Learning Theory," *Human Relations,* May 1996, pp 621–41; and D Ready, "Mastering Leverage, Leading Change," *Executive Excellence,* March 1995, pp 18–19.

[14]Top management's role in implementing change according to Lewin's model is discussed by E H Schein, "The Role of the CEO in the Management of Change: The Case of Information Technology," in *Transforming Organizations,* eds T A Kochan and M Useem (New York: Oxford University Press, 1992), pp 80–95.

[15]Systems models of change are discussed by D R Newhouse and I D Chapman, "Organizational Transformation: A Case Study of Two Aboriginal Organizations," *Human Relations,* July 1996, pp 995–1011; and D R Fuqua and D J Kurpius, "Conceptual Models in Organizational Consultation," *Journal of Counseling & Development,* July/August 1993, pp 607–18.

[16]http:*www.unilever.com/corporate/to/general/intro/english/corp.htm.*

[17]The process of strategic planning is discussed by J C Picken and G G Dess, *Mission Critical: The 7 Strategic Traps That Derail Even the Smartest Companies* (Burr Ridge, IL: Irwin Professional

Publishing, 1996).

[18] A thorough discussion of the target elements of change can be found in M Beer and B Spector, "Organizational Diagnosis: Its Role in Organizational Learning," *Journal of Counseling & Development,* July/August 1993, pp 642–50; and P Dainty, "Organizational Change: A Strategy for Successful Implementation," *Journal of Business and Psychology,* Summer 1990, pp 463–81.

[19] M Lindemann, "Harnessing the Merger's 'Energies'," *The Financial Times,* March 14, 1996, p 16.

[20] These errors are discussed in detail by J P Kotter, "Leading Change: Why Transformation Efforts Fail," *Harvard Business Review,* March–April 1995, pp 59–67.

[21] The role of communication in organizational change is thoroughly discussed by J D Ford and L W Ford, "The Role of Conversations in Producing Intentional Change in Organizations," *Academy of Management Review,* July 1995, pp 541–70; and B Quirke, *Communicating Change* (New York: McGraw-Hill, 1995).

[22] The type of leadership needed during organizational change is discussed by J P Kotter, *Leading Change* (Boston: Harvard Business School Press, 1996); and B Ettorre, "Making Change," *Management Review,* January 1996, pp 13–18.

[23] M Beer and E Walton, "Developing the Competitive Organization: Interventions and Strategies," *American Psychologist,* February 1990, p 154.

[24] An historical overview of the field of OD can be found in J Sanzgiri and J Z Gottlieb, "Philosophic and Pragmatic Influences on the Practice of Organization Development, 1950–2000," *Organizational Dynamics,* Autumn 1992, pp 57–69.

[25] W W Burke, *Organization Development: A Normative View* (Reading, MA: Addison-Wesley Publishing, 1987), p 9.

[26] The role of values and ethics in OD is discussed by M McKendall, "The Tyranny of Change: Organizational Development Revisited," *Journal of Business Ethics,* February 1993, pp 93–104.

[27] An example of using employee surveys to conduct OD is provided by B Schneider, S D Ashworth, A C Higgs, and L Carr, "Design, Validity, and Use of Strategically Focused Employee Attitude Surveys," *Personnel Psychology,* Autumn 1996, pp 695–705.

[28] See R Rodgers, J E Hunter, and D L Rogers, "Influence of Top Management Commitment on Management Program Success," *Journal of Applied Psychology,* February 1993, pp 151–55.

[29] Results can be found in P J Robertson, D R Roberts, and J I Porras, "Dynamics of Planned Organizational Change: Assessing Empirical Support for a Theoretical Model," *Academy of Management Journal,* June 1993, pp 619–34.

[30] Results from the meta-analysis can be found in G A Neuman, J E Edwards, and N S Raju, "Organizational Development Interventions: A Meta-Analysis of Their Effects on Satisfaction and Other Attitudes," *Personnel Psychology,* Autumn 1989, pp 461–90.

[31] The importance of results-oriented change efforts is discussed by R J Schaffer and H A Thomson, "Successful Change Programs Begin with Results," *Harvard Business Review,* January–February 1992, pp 80–89.

[32] Costs of failed change efforts are discussed by J Iacovini, "The Human Side of Organization Change," *Training & Development,* January 1993, pp 65–68.

[33] Adapted in part from B W Armentrout, "Have Your Plans for Change Had a Change of Plan?" *HRFOCUS,* January 1996, p 19; and A S Judson, *Changing Behavior in Organizations: Minimizing Resistance to Change* (Cambridge, MA: Blackwell, Inc., 1991).

[34] See "Vulnerability and Resilience," *American Psychologist,* January 1996, pp 22–28.

[35] See R Moss Kanter, "Managing Traumatic Change: Avoiding the `Unlucky 13,'" *Management Review,* May 1987, pp 23–24.

[36] See L Coch and J R P French, Jr., "Overcoming Resistance to Change," *Human Relations,* 1948, pp 512–32.

[37] For a thorough review of the role of participation in organizational change, see W A Pasmore and M R Fagans, "Participation, Individual Development, and Organizational Change: A Review and Synthesis," *Journal of Management,* June 1992, pp 375–97.

[38] Results can be found in C-M Lau and R W Woodman, "Understanding Organizational Change: A Schematic Perspective," *Academy of Management Journal,* April 1995, pp 537–54.

[39] L Morris, "Research Capsules," *Training & Development,* April 1992, pp 74–76; and T Hill, N D Smith, and M F Mann, "Role of Efficacy Expectations in Predicting the Decision to Use Advanced Technologies: The Case of Computers," *Journal of Applied Psychology,* May 1987, pp 307–14.

[40] Complete details may be found in A Rafaeli, "Employee Attitudes toward Working with Computers," *Journal of Occupational Behavior,* April 1986, pp 89–106.

[41] Readiness for change is discussed by B Trahant and W W Burke, "Traveling through Transitions," *Training & Development,* February 1996, pp 37–41.

[42] Advice on how to reduce the resistance to change can be found in S C Longo, "Change: What Is Gained Is Clearly Better than What Is Lost," *The CPA Journal,* January 1996, p 69; and R F Recardo, "Overcoming Resistance to Change," *National Productivity Review,* Spring 1995, pp 5–12.

[43] D G Bower, "The Learning Organization: A Rover Perspective," *Executive Development,* 1993, pp 3–6.

[44] Additional strategies for managing resistance are discussed by T J Galpin, *The Human Side of Change: A Practical Guide to Organizational Redesign* (San Francisco: Jossey-Bass, 1996); and D May and M Kettelhut, "Managing Human Issues in Reengineering Projects," *Journal of Systems Management,* January/February 1996, pp 4–11.

[45] See G Hamel and C K Prahalad, *Competing for the Future* (Boston: Harvard Business School, 1994).

[46] M Gephart, V Marsick, M van Buren and M Spiro, "Learning Organizations Come Alive," *Training and Development,* December 1996, pp 34–36.

[47] Translated from J L Bauwens, "Anders gaan managen," *Trends,* January 9, 1995, p 28.

[48] P M Senge, *The Fifth Discipline* (New York: Doubleday, 1990), p 1.

[49] This definition was based on D A Garvin, "Building a Learning Organization," *Harvard Business Review,* July/August 1993, pp 78–91.

[50] Organizational learning is discussed by A S Miner and S J Mezias, "Ugly Duckling No More: Pasts and Futures of Organizational Learning Research," *Organization Science,* January–February 1996, pp 88–99; and R P Mai, *Learning Partnerships: How Leading American Companies Implement Organizational Learning* (Chicago, IL: Irwin, 1996).

[51] J Ryan, "Giving the People the Chance to Sparkle," *People Management,* June 29, 1995, pp 40–42.

[52] Definitions of learning capabilities and core competencies were derived from C Long and M Vickers-Koch, "Using Core Capabilities to Create Competitive Advantage," *Organizational Dynamics,* Summer 1995, pp 7–22.

[53] The relationship between organizational learning and various effectiveness criteria is discussed by S F Slater and J C Narver, "Market Orientation and the Learning Organization," *Journal of*

Marketing, July 1995, pp 63–74.

[54] A J DiBella, E C Nevis, and J M Gould, "Organizational Learning Style as a Core Capability," in *Organizational Learning and Competitive Advantage,* eds B Moingeon and A Edmondson (Thousand Oaks, CA: Sage, 1996), pp 41–42.

[55] Details of this study can be found in J H Lingle and W A Schiemann, "From Balanced Scorecard to Strategic Gauges: Is Measurement Worth It?" *American Management Association,* March 1996, pp 56–61.

[56] This discussion and definitions are based on D Miller, "A Preliminary Typology of Organizational Learning: Synthesizing the Literature," *Journal of Management,* 1996, pp 485–505.

[57] See the related discussion in DiBella, Nevis, and Gould, "Organizational Learning Style as a Core Capability."

[58] See D Collis, "Organizational Capability as a Source of Profit," in *Organizational Learning and Competitive Advantage,* eds B Moingeon and A Edmondson (Thousand Oaks, CA: Sage, 1996), pp 139–63.

[59] This discussion is based on material presented in J B Keys, R M Fulmer, and S A Stumpf, "Microworlds and Simuworlds: Practice Fields for the Learning Organization," *Organizational Dynamics,* Spring 1996, pp 36–49; and F Kofman and P M Senge, "Communities of Commitment: The Heart of Learning Organizations," *Organizational Dynamics,* Autumn 1993, pp 5–23.

[60] The role of leadership in building a learning organization is discussed by D M Noer, *Breaking Free: A Prescription for Personal and Organizational Change* (San Francisco: Jossey-Bass, 1996); S F Slater, "Learning to Change," *Business Horizons,* November–December 1995, pp 13–20; and D Ulrich, T Jick, and M Von Glinow, "High-Impact Learning: Building and Diffusing Learning Capability," *Organizational Dynamics,* Autumn 1993, pp 52–66.

[61] C Kennedy, "Re-engineering: The Human costs and Benefits," *Long Range Planning,* October 1994, pp 64–72.

[62] See N A Wishart, J J Elam, D Robey, "Redrawing the Portrait of a Learning Organization: Inside Knight-Ridder, Inc.," *Academy of Management Executive,* February 1996, pp 7–20; C Argyris, "Good Communication That Blocks Learning," *Harvard Business Review,* July–August 1994, pp 77–85; and D A Garvin, "Building a Learning Organization," *Harvard Business Review,* July–August 1993, pp 78–91.

[63] J Case, "A Company of Businesspeople," *Inc.,* April 1993, p 86.

[64] This exercise is based on a group exercise contained in L W Mealiea, *Skills for Managers in Organizations* (Burr Ridge, IL: Irwin, 1994), pp 198–201.

[65] The force-field analysis form was quoted directly from Ibid, pp 199, 201.

Glossary

Ability Stable characteristic responsible for a person's maximum physical or mental performance.

Accountability practices Focus on treating diverse employees fairly.

Adaptive perspective Assumes that adaptive cultures enhance a firm's financial performance.

Affirmative action Focuses on achieving equality of opportunity in an organization.

Aggressive style Expressive and self-enhancing, but takes unfair advantage of others.

Aided-analytic Using tools to make decisions.

Asch effect Giving in to a unanimous but wrong opposition.

Assertive style Expressive and self-enhancing, but does not take advantage of others.

Attention Being consciously aware of something or someone.

Attitude Learned predisposition towards a given object.

Baseline data Preintervention data collected by someone other than the target person.

Behaviour chart Programme evaluation graph with baseline and intervention data.

Behaviour modification Making specific behaviour occur more or less often by managing its cues and consequences.

Behavioural contingencies Antecedent;→ behaviour;→ consequence (A→B→C) relationships.

Behavioural self-management Modifying one's own behaviour by managing cues, cognitive processes, and consequences.

Benchmarking Process by which a company compares its performance with that of high-performing organizations.

Bounded rationality Constraints that restrict decision making.

Brainstorming Process to generate a quantity of ideas.

Buffers Resources or administrative changes that reduce burnout.

Bureaucracy Max Weber's idea of the most rationally efficient form of organization.

Burnout A condition of emotional exhaustion and negative attitudes.

Care perspective Involves compassion and an ideal of attention and response to need.

Career plateauing The end result when the probability of being promoted is very small.

Case study In-depth study of a single person, group, or organization.

Causal attributions Suspected or inferred causes of behaviour.

Centralized decision making Top managers make all key decisions.

Charismatic leadership Transforms employees to pursue organizational goals over self-interests.

Closed system A relatively self-sufficient entity.

Coalition Temporary groupings of people who actively pursue a single issue.

Coercive power Obtaining compliance through threatened or actual punishment.

Cognitions A person's knowledge, opinions, or beliefs.

Cognitive categories Mental depositories for storing information.

Cognitive style A perceptual and judgemental tendency, according to Jung's typology.

Cohesiveness A sense of 'we-ness' helps group stick together.

Collaborative computing Using computer software and hardware to help people work better together.

Communication Interpersonal exchange of information and understanding.

Communication competence Ability to effectively use communication behaviours in a given context.

Communication distortion Purposely modifying the content of a message.

Conflict One party perceives its interests are being opposed or set back by another party.

Consensus Presenting opinions and gaining agreement to support a decision.

Consideration Creating mutual respect and trust with followers.

Contingency approach Using management tools and techniques in a situationally appropriate manner; avoiding the one-best-way mentality.

Contingency approach to organization design Creating an effective organization–environment fit.

Contingency factors Variables that influence the appropriateness of a leadership style.

Continuous reinforcement Reinforcing every instance of a behaviour.

Control strategy Coping strategy that directly confronts or solves problems.

Coping Process of managing stress.

Core job dimensions Job characteristics found to various degrees in all jobs.

Creativity Process of developing something new or unique.

Cross-cultural management Understanding and teaching behavioural patterns in different cultures.

Cross-cultural training Structured experiences to help people adjust to a new culture/country.

Cross-functionalism Team made up of technical specialists from different areas.

Culture Socially derived, taken-for-granted assumptions about how to think and act.

Culture shock Anxiety and doubt caused by an overload of new expectations and cues.

Decentralized decision making Lower-level managers are empowered to make important decisions.

Decision making Identifying and choosing solutions that lead to a desired end result.

Delegation Granting decision-making authority to people at lower levels.

Delphi technique Process to generate ideas from physically dispersed experts.

Development practices Focus on preparing diverse employees for greater responsibility and advancement.

Devil's advocacy Assigning someone the role of critic.

Dialectic method Fostering a debate of opposing viewpoints to better understand an issue.

Differentiation Division of labour and specialization that causes people to think and act differently.

Distributive justice The perceived fairness of how resources and rewards are distributed.

Diversity The host of individual differences that make people different from and similar to each other.

Dysfunctional conflict Threatens organization's interests.

Electronic mail Uses the Internet/Intranet to send computer-generated text and documents.

Emotions Complex human reactions to personal achievements and setbacks.

Employment contract Mutual written and implied expectations between employer and employee.

Empowerment Sharing power with nonmanagers through participative management.

Equity theory Holds that motivation is a function of fairness in social exchanges.

Escalation of commitment Sticking to an ineffective course of action too long.

Escape strategy Coping strategy that avoids or ignores stressors and problems.

Ethics Study of moral issues and choices.

Ethnocentrism Belief that one's native country, culture, language, and behaviour are superior.

Expatriate Anyone living or working in a foreign country.

Expectancy Belief that effort leads to a specific level of performance.

Expectancy theory Holds that people are motivated to behave in ways that produce valued outcomes.

Experienced meaningfulness Feeling that one's job is important and worthwhile.

Experienced responsibility Believing that one is accountable for work outcomes.

Expert power Obtaining compliance through one's knowledge or information.

External factors Environmental characteristics that cause behaviour.

External forces for change Originate outside the organization.

External locus of control Attributing outcomes to circumstances beyond one's control.

Extinction Making behaviour occur less often by ignoring or not reinforcing it.

Extrinsic rewards Financial, material, or social rewards from the environment.

Feedback Objective information about performance.

Field study Examination of variables in real-life settings.

Fight-or-flight response To either confront stressors or try to avoid them.

Fit perspective Assumes that culture must align with its business or strategic context.

Formal group Formed by the organization.

Functional analysis Reducing person–environment interaction to A→B→C terms.

Functional conflict Serves organization's interests.

Functional social support Support sources that buffer stress in specific situations.

Fundamental attribution bias Ignoring environmental factors that affect behaviour.

Gainsharing Bonuses tied to measurable productivity increases.

Garbage can model Holds that decision making is sloppy and haphazard.

Genderflex Temporarily using communication behaviours typical of the other gender.

Global social support The total amount of social support available.

Goal What an individual is trying to accomplish.

Goal commitment Amount of commitment to achieving a goal.

Goal difficulty The amount of effort required to meet a goal.

Goal specificity Quantifiability of a goal.

Grapevine Unofficial communication system of the informal organization.

Group Two or more freely interacting people with shared norms and goals and a common identity.

Group cohesiveness A 'we feeling' binding group members together.

Groupthink Janis's term for a cohesive in-group's unwillingness to realistically view alternatives.

Hardiness Personality characteristic that neutralizes stress.

Hierarchical communication Exchange of information between managers and employees.

High-context cultures Primary meaning derived from nonverbal situational cues.

Holistic wellness approach Advocates personal responsibility in reducing stressors and stress.

Hygiene factors Job characteristics associated with job dissatisfaction.

Impression management Getting others to see us in a certain manner.

Informal group Formed by friends.

Information richness Information-carrying capacity of data.

In-group exchange A partnership characterized by mutual trust, respect, and liking.

Initiating structure Organizing and defining what group members should be doing.

Instrumental cohesiveness Sense of togetherness based on mutual dependency needed to get the job done.

Instrumentality A performance;→outcome perception.

Integration Cooperation among specialists to achieve common goal.

Intelligence Capacity for constructive thinking, reasoning, problem solving.

Intermittent reinforcement Reinforcing some but not all instances of behaviour.

Internal factors Personal characteristics that cause behaviour.

Internal forces for change Originate inside the organization.

Internal locus of control Attributing outcomes to one's own actions.

Internal motivation Motivation caused by positive internal feelings.

Internet A global network of computer networks.

Intranet An organization's private Internet.

Intrinsic rewards Self-granted, psychic rewards.

Job design Changing the content and/or process of a specific job to increase job satisfaction and performance.

Job enlargement Putting more variety into a job.

Job enrichment Building achievement, recognition, stimulating work, responsibility, and advancement into a job.

Job rotation Moving employees from one specialized job to another.

Job satisfaction An affective or emotional response to one's job.

Justice perspective Based on the ideal of reciprocal rights and driven by rules and regulations.

Knowledge of results Feedback about work outcomes.

Laboratory study Manipulation and measurement of variables in contrived situations.

Law of effect Behaviour with favourable consequences is repeated; behaviour with unfavourable consequences disappears.

Leader trait Personal characteristics that differentiate leaders from followers.

Leader–member relations Extent that leader has the support, loyalty, and trust of work group.

Leadership Influencing employees to voluntarily pursue organizational goals.

Leadership Grid ® Represents four leadership styles found by crossing concern for production and concern for people.

Leadership prototype Mental representation of the traits and behaviours possessed by leaders.

Learned helplessness Debilitating lack of faith in one's ability to control the situation.

Learning capabilities The set of core competencies and internal processes that enable an organization to adapt to its environment.

Learning modes The various ways in which organizations attempt to create and maximize their learning.

Learning organization Proactively creates, acquires, and transfers knowledge throughout the organization.

Legitimate power Obtaining compliance through formal authority.

Liaison individuals Consistently pass along grapevine information to others.

Line managers Have authority to make organizational decisions.

Linguistic style A person's typical speaking pattern.

Listening Actively decoding and interpreting verbal messages.

Low-context cultures Primary meaning derived from written and spoken words.

Maintenance roles Relationship-building group behaviour.

Management Process of working with and through others to achieve organizational objectives efficiently and ethically.

Management by objectives Management system incorporating participation in decision making, goal setting, and feedback.

Managing diversity Creating organizational changes that enable all people to perform up to their maximum potential.

Mechanistic organizations Rigid, command-and-control bureaucracies.

Mentoring Process of forming and maintaining developmental relationships between a mentor and a junior person.

Met expectations The extent to which one receives what he or she expects from a job.

Meta-analysis Pools the results of many studies through statistical procedure.

Mission statement Summarizes 'why' an organization exists.

Monochronic time Preference for doing one thing at a time because time is limited, precisely segmented, and schedule driven.

Motivating potential score The amount of internal work motivation associated with a specific job.

Motivation Psychological processes that arouse and direct goal-directed behaviour.

Motivators Job characteristics associated with job satisfaction.

Mutuality of interest Balancing individual and organizational interests through win–win cooperation.

Natural rewards Normal social interactions such as praise or recognition.

Need for achievement Desire to accomplish something difficult.

Need for affiliation Desire to spend time in social relationships and activities.

Need for power Desire to influence, coach, teach, or encourage others to achieve.

Needs Physiological or psychological deficiencies that arouse behaviour.

Negative inequity Comparison in which another person receives greater outcomes for similar inputs.

Negative reinforcement Making behaviour occur more often by contingently withdrawing something negative.

Negotiation Give-and-take process between conflicting interdependent parties.

Noise Interference with the transmission and understanding of a message.

Nominal group technique Process to generate ideas and evaluate solutions.

Nonanalytic Using preformulated rules to make decisions.

Nonassertive style Timid and self-denying behaviour.

Nonverbal communication Messages sent outside of the written or spoken word.

Normative beliefs Thoughts and beliefs about expected behaviour and modes of conduct.

Norm Shared attitudes, opinions, feelings, or actions that guide social behaviour.

Open system Organism that must constantly interact with its environment to survive.

Operant behaviour Skinner's term for learned, consequence-shaped behaviour.

Optimizing Choosing the best possible solution.

Organic organizations Fluid and flexible network of multitalented people.

Organization System of consciously co-ordinated activities of two or more people.

Organization chart Boxes-and-lines illustration showing chain of formal authority and division of labour.

Organization development A set of techniques or tools that are used to implement organizational change.

Organizational behaviour Interdisciplinary field dedicated to better understanding and managing people at work.

Organizational culture Shared values and beliefs that underlie a company's identity.

Organizational ecologists Those who study the impact of environmental factors on organizational success/failure and interrelationships among populations and communities of organizations.

Organizational moles Use the grapevine to enhance their power and status.

Organizational politics Intentional enhancement of self-interest.

Organizational socialization Process by which employees learn an organization's values, norms, and required behaviours.

Organization-based self-esteem An organization member's self-perceived value.

Ostracism Rejection by other group members.

Out-group exchange A partnership characterized by a lack of mutual trust, respect, and liking.

Paradigm A generally accepted way of viewing the world.

Participative management Involving employees in various forms of decision making.

Pay for performance Monetary incentives tied to one's results or accomplishments.

Perception Process of interpreting one's environment.

Perceptual model of communication Consecutively linked elements within the communication process.

Persistence Extent to which effort is expended on a task over time.

Personality Stable physical and mental characteristics responsible for a person's identity.

Personalized power Directed at helping oneself.

Polychronic time Preference for doing more than one thing at a time because time is flexible and multidimensional.

Position power Degree to which leader has formal power.

Positive inequity Comparison in which another person receives lesser outcomes for similar inputs.

Positive reinforcement Making behaviour occur more often by contingently presenting something positive.

Postmodern organizations Flexible organizations that are decentralized, computer linked, and less hierarchical than bureaucracies.

Primary dimensions of diversity Personal characteristics that exert an important and sustained impact throughout our lives.

Problem Gap between an actual and desired situation.

Procedural justice The perceived fairness of the process and procedures used to make allocation decisions.

Process-style Likes to discuss issues in detail.

Profit sharing Portion of bottom-line economic profits given to employees.

Programmed conflict Encourages different opinions without protecting management's personal feelings.

Propensity to trust A personality trait involving one's general willingness to trust others.

Proxemics Hall's term for the study of cultural expectations about interpersonal space.

Punishment Making behaviour occur less often by contingently presenting something negative or withdrawing something positive.

Quality circles Small groups of volunteers who strive to solve quality-related problems.

Rational model Logical four-step approach to decision making.

Readiness Follower's ability and willingness to complete a task.

Realistic job preview Presents both positive and negative aspects of a job.

Reality shock A newcomer's feeling of surprise after experiencing unexpected situations or events.

Reasons-style Interested in hearing the rationale behind a message.

Reciprocity Widespread belief that people should be paid back for their positive and negative acts.

Recruitment practices Attempts to attract qualified, diverse employees at all levels.

Reengineering Radical redesign of entire organization for dramatic improvement.

Referent power Obtaining compliance through charisma or personal attraction.

Relaxation response State of peacefulness.

Resistance to change Emotional/behavioural response to real or imagined work changes.

Respondent behaviour Skinner's term for unlearned stimulus–response reflexes.

Results-style Interested in hearing the bottom line or result of a message.

Reward equality norm Everyone should get the same rewards.

Reward equity norm Rewards should be tied to contributions.

Reward power Obtaining compliance with promised or actual rewards.

Role ambiguity Others' expectations are unknown.

Role conflict Others have conflicting or inconsistent expectations.

Role overload Others' expectations exceed one's ability.

Roles Expected behaviours for a given position.

Sample survey Questionnaire responses from a sample of people.

Satisficing Choosing a solution that meets a minimum standard of acceptance.

Scenario technique Speculative forecasting method.

Schema Mental picture of an event or object.

Secondary dimensions of diversity Personal characteristics that people acquire, discard, and/or modify throughout their lives.

Self-concept Person's self-perception as a physical, social, spiritual being.

Self-efficacy Belief in one's ability to do a task.

Self-esteem One's overall self-evaluation.

Self-fulfilling prophecy People's expectations determine behaviour and performance.

Self-managed teams Groups of employees granted administrative oversight for their work.

Self-management leadership Process of leading others to lead themselves.

Self-monitoring Observing one's own behaviour and adapting it to the situation.

Self-serving bias Taking more personal responsibility for success than failure.

Self-talk Evaluating thoughts about oneself.

Sex-role stereotype Beliefs about appropriate roles for men and women.

Shaping Reinforcing closer and closer approximations to a target behaviour.

Situational theories Propose that leader styles should match the situation at hand.

Skill Specific capacity to manipulate objects.

Social loafing Decrease in individual effort as group size increases.

Social power Ability to get things done with human, informational, and material resources.

Social support Amount of helpfulness derived from social relationships.

Socialized power Directed at helping others.

Socio-emotional cohesiveness Sense of togetherness based on emotional satisfaction.

Span of control The number of people reporting directly to a given manager.

Spillover model Describes the reciprocal relationship between job and life satisfaction.

Staff personnel Provide research, advice, and recommendations to line managers.

Stakeholder audit Systematic identification of all parties likely to be affected by the organization.

Stereotype Beliefs about the characteristics of a group.

Strategic constituency Any group of people with a stake in the organization's operation or success.

Strategic plan A long-term plan outlining actions needed to achieve planned results.

Strength perspective Assumes that the strength of corporate culture is related to a firm's financial performance.

Stress Behavioural, physical, or psychological response to stressors.

Stressful life events Life events that disrupt daily routines and social relationships.

Stressors Environmental factors that produce stress.

Substitutes for hierarchy Organizational factors such as computer networks and self-management training that reduce the need for direct supervision.

Substitutes for leadership Situational variables that can substitute for, neutralize, or enhance the effects of leadership.

Superleader Someone who leads others to lead themselves.

Target elements of change Components of an organization that may be changed.

Task roles Task-oriented group behaviour.

Task structure Amount of structure contained within work tasks.

Team Small group with complementary skills who hold themselves mutually accountable for common purpose, goals, and approach.

Team building Experiential learning aimed at better internal functioning of groups.

Team viability Team members satisfied and willing to contribute.

Team-based pay Linking pay to teamwork behaviour and/or team results.

Telecommuting Receiving and sending work from home to the office by using the phone or a computer link.

Theory A story defining key terms, providing a conceptual framework, and explaining why something occurs.

Theory Y McGregor's modern and positive assumptions about employees being responsible and creative.

360-degree feedback Comparison of anonymous feedback from one's superior, subordinates, and peers with self-perceptions.

Total quality management An organizational culture dedicated to training, continuous improvement, and customer satisfaction.

Transactional leadership Focuses on interpersonal interactions between managers and employees.

Trust Reciprocal faith in others' intentions and behaviour.

Type A behaviour pattern Aggressively involved in a chronic, determined struggle to accomplish more in less time.

Unaided-analytic Analysis is limited to processing information in one's mind.

Underemployment The result of taking a job that requires less education, training, or skills than possessed by a worker.

Unity of command principle Each employee should report to a single manager.

Upward feedback Subordinates evaluate their boss.

Valence The value of a reward or outcome.

Value attainment The extent to which a job allows fulfilment of one's work values.

Value system Pattern of values within an organization.

Values Enduring belief in a mode of conduct or end-state.

Valuing diversity Emphasizes the awareness, recognition, understanding, and appreciation of human differences.

Vision Long-term goal describing 'what' an organization wants to become.

Workforce demographics Statistical profiles of adult workers.

Name Index

A

Abakoumkin, G, 529
Abbott, A S, 331
Abma, H, 52
Abraham, L M, 207
Abramson, L Y, 177
Adair, J, 497
Adam, E E Jr, 403
Adams, C, 498
Adams, G A, 53
Adams, S M, 263
Adent Hoecklin, L, 83
Adigun, I O, 206
Adizes, I, 578
Adler, N E, 528
Adler, N J, 112, 113
Ahearne, M, 498, 499
Ahlbrandt, R S, 368
Ajzen, I, 145
Akamine, T X, 145
Albrecht, C Jr, 554
Albright, M D, 263
Aldag, R J, 143, 264, 296
Alderman, L, 113
Alderton, D L, 331
Aldrich, H E, 25
Alexander, K L, 265, 465
Alexander, R A, 235
Ali, A H, 113
Allen, B P, 176
Allen, J S, 499
Allen, R W, 332
Allerton, H, 205
Alliger, G M, 497
Amason, A C, 333
Amburgey, T L, 580
Amir, T, 296
Amparano, J, 528
Amundson, S D, 83
Ancona, P, 235
Andelman, D A, 579
Anderson, D C, 466
Anderson, K, 177
Anderson, P, 580
Anderson, S E, 499
Andrasik, F, 464
Anfuso, D, 82
Annells, J, 296
Anson, R, 369
Anthony, T, 402
Anthony, W P, 467, 553
Antonioni, D, 264
Arad, S, 332
Archer, J, 437

Ardalan, A, 206
Argyris, C, 611
Ariss, S S, 578
Arkin, A, 144, 205, 332, 464
Armentrout, B W, 205, 610
Arnold, C L, 436
Arnold, J, 466
Arroba, T, 333
Arrow, H, 295
Arthur, D, 437
Arthur, J B, 332
Arthur, M, 403
Arthur, M B, 498
Arvey, R D, 207, 466
Aryee, S, 113
Asch, S E, 296
Ashford, S J, 263, 401, 528
Ashforth, B E, 83, 529
Ashkenas, R, 580
Ashworth, S D, 610
Attanucci, J, 84
Attra, S L, 145
At-Twaijri, M I A, 580
Aubrey, R, 263, 467
Austin, J T, 205
Austin, N, 497, 499
Avolio, B J, 176, 498, 499
Axley, S R, 436
Axtell, R E, 437
Ayman, R, 498
Azar, B, 146

B

Bachelor, G, 235
Bae, H, 332
Baeyer, C V, 177
Baguette, R, 438
Bahrami, H, 580
Bailey, S, 177
Baker, H E III, 332
Baker, S, 265
Baligh, H H, 112
Balkin, D B, 264
Band, W, 205
Bandura, A, 144, 466, 467
Banjo, M L, 177
Banker, R D, 403
Bannister, B D, 263
Bar-Ilan, O, 367
Bardwick, J M, 578
Bargh, J A, 175
Baridon, A P, 296
Barker, L L, 437
Barker, V L III, 578
Barlett, C A, 436

Barley, S R, 527
Barling, J, 144, 205, 530
Barnard, C I, 554
Barnard, S M, 529
Barnes-Farrell, J L, 297
Barnett, R C, 528
Barnlund, D C, 112, 144
Baron, R A, 263, 334
Barr, S H, 263
Barrick, M R, 145, 235
Barrie, C, 530
Barsoux, J L, 26, 82
Bartholomew, S, 112
Bartlett, C A, 113, 436, 497
Bartol, K M, 26
Bartolomé, F, 402
Basadur, M, 370
Bass, B, 498
Bass, B M, 497, 499
Bassett, M E, 144-5
Bassin, M, 402
Bastianutti, L M, 295, 369
Basu, A M, 145
Bateman, T S, 145, 177
Bates, K A, 83
Bauer, T N, 83
Baum, L, 465
Baumann, J P, 264
Baumeister, R F, 144, 205
Baumohl, B, 25
Bauwens, J L, 610
Bavetta, A G, 144
Bazalgette, J, 553
Bazerman, M H, 295, 333
Beach, L R, 367
Beard, J W, 332
Beattie, J, 367
Beattie, R, 144
Beatty, R W, 264
Becker, B W, 145
Becker, T E, 332
Becker, W S, 234
Beckhard, R, 294, 403
Bedeian, A G, 145, 332, 553, 554
Beehr, T A, 466, 529
Beeman, D R, 332
Beer, M, 610
Behling, O C, 497, 528
Belasco, J A, 332
Belcher, J G Jr, 265
Bell, C, 263
Bemowski, K, 83
Ben-Avi, I, 205
Benbasat, I, 369

Bender, M, 438
Benders, J, 25
Benfari, R C, 499
Benne, K D, 295
Bennett, A, 401
Bennett, N, 234, 296
Bennett, R H III, 467
Bennett, R J, 467
Bennett, R T, 437
Bennis, W, 579
Benson, H, 529, 530
Benson, P G, 579
Bentler, P M, 144
Berkowitz, L, 498
Bernardin, H J, 263
Bernay, T, 331
Bernstein, D J, 465
Berra, R, 25
Besmo, M, 53
Best, D L, 296
Bettendorf, R F, 528
Bettenhausen, K L, 294, 295
Beutell, N J, 527
Beyer, J M, 26, 82
Bhagat, R S, 528
Bhasin, R, 332
Bhatnagar, D, 177
Bhawuk, D P S, 53, 333
Bhide, A, 580
Bigley, G A, 82
Black, J S, 112, 113, 528
Blake, J, 144
Blake, R R, 295, 296, 498
Blanchard, K H, 294, 465, 466, 498
Blasi, J R, 265
Blau, G, 295
Blaylock, B K, 146
Blegen, M A, 207
Bloemer, J, 53
Blood, M R, 207
Bluedorn, A C, 112, 553, 578
Bluen, S D, 205, 530
Bobbitt, H R Jr, 579
Boden, J M, 144
Boehne, D M, 235
Bolman, L G, 294, 401
Bolton, A A, 25
Bommer, W H, 176, 207, 498, 499
Bond, M H, 113
Bond, R, 296
Bongiorno, L, 467
Bonington, C, 403
Bonjean, C M, 296

Bonvillian, G, 112
Boon, M, 464
Booth-Kewley, S, 331, 530
Borg, M R, 264
Bosma, M, 438
Bostrom, R N, 369, 437
Bottger, P, 295
Bouchard, T J Jr, 207
Boulding, K E, 553
Bowditch, J L, 205, 436
Bowen, D E, 26
Bower, D G, 610
Boyce, T, 528
Boyd, K R, 177
Boyes-Braem, P, 175
Bracken, D W, 264
Bracker, J S, 177
Bradford, D L, 331
Bradway, L, 403
Brady, R, 112
Brannick, M T, 368
Brass, D A, 144
Brass, D J, 332
Brennan, R T, 528
Brett, J M, 264
Brief, A P, 143, 146, 205, 264
Briggs Myers, I, 146
Briner, B, 26
Brinkerhoff, R O, 554
Brinkley-Rogers, P, 465
Brittain Leslie, J, 294
Brittan, S, 113
Broadwell, M M, 25
Brockner, J, 368
Brodbeck, F C, 528
Brodt, S E, 333
Brody, C, 296
Broeijer, C, 53
Bronw, A, 498
Broverman, D M, 176
Broverman, I K, 176
Browder, S, 401
Brown, D S, 553
Brown, K A, 235
Brown, S P, 205, 207
Brown, T, 554, 579
Bruce, R, 528
Bruce, R A, 370
Bruening, J C, 465
Bruhn, J G, 438
Bruning, S S, 144
Bryant, B, 401
Bryman, A, 498
Buch, K, 402, 403
Bucholz, S, 403
Buckingham, L, 53
Buckley, J T, 403
Buelens, M, 176, 233
Buhler, P, 466
Bulkeley, W M, 438
Buntzman, G F, 331
Buono, A F, 205, 436
Burck, C, 578
Burgess, A, 466

Burke, W W, 610
Burkhardt, M E, 263, 332
Burlingham, B, 578
Burnett, J R, 176
Burns, T, 579
Burns, W, 205, 530
Burrell, G, 296
Burris Desmarais, L, 146
Burrows, L, 175
Burt, D B, 176
Burton, S, 295, 528
Bushe, G R, 294
Butler, J K Jr, 206
Butler, S, 527
Buunk, B P, 529
Buzzell, R D, 436, 497
Bycio, P, 499
Byham, W C, 294, 466
Byrne, J A, 83, 263, 265, 333, 554
Byrnes, J F, 334
Byron, W J, 25

C

Cacioppo, J T, 528, 529
Cain Smith, P, 206, 207
Callaway, M R, 296
Calori, R, 113
Camacho, L M, 369
Cameron, J, 264
Cameron, K S, 297, 333, 334, 553, 554, 578
Caminiti, S, 403
Campbell, D, 52, 53
Campbell, H, 403
Campbell, J D, 144
Campbell, J P, 205, 403
Campbell, R J, 403
Campion, M A, 206, 401, 403, 466
Cantoni, C J, 553
Cantor, D W, 331
Cantor, N, 529
Caplan, J, 466
Cappelli, P, 145
Carbone, L, 437
Carew, D K, 294
Carnegy, H, 52
Carnevale, P J D, 334
Carr, L, 610
Carroll, S J, 401, 579
Carson, K P, 176, 207
Cartwright, D, 331
Cartwright, L K, 145
Cartwright, S, 530
Carvajal, R, 402
Cascio, W F, 25, 206
Case, J, 611
Cashman, J F, 498
Castro, J, 294
Cater, G W, 176
Caudill, D W, 437
Caudron, S, 82, 265, 370, 402
Cawley, B D, 263

Ceniceros, R, 466
Chaiken, S, 145
Chalos, P, 368
Champy, J, 25, 206, 554
Chandler, A Z, 53
Chandler, S, 332
Chao, G T, 83
Chapman, I D, 609
Chapman, P, 436
Chapman, R, 52
Charbonneau, M, 234
Charlier, M, 53
Chay, Y W, 113
Cheldelin, S I, 143
Chemers, M M, 83, 498
Chen, C C, 26
Chen, M, 175
Cheraskin, L, 206
Chesney, A P, 438
Chesney, M A, 528
Cheung, F, 113
Chew, J, 113
Child, J, 579
Chonko, L B, 234
Chowdhury, J, 234
Christensen, C, 331
Christensen, S L, 52
Church, A T, 145
Churchill, G A Jr, 234
Chusmir, L H, 331, 334
Cialdini, R B, 331
Clampitt, P G, 436
Clancy, T, 580
Clark, L S, 176
Clarke, C V, 206
Clarkson, F E, 176
Clegg, S R, 367, 369, 436, 498, 553, 554, 579
Clement, B, 52, 530
Cobb, A T, 234, 332
Coch, L, 610
Cochran, D S, 334
Cohen, A R, 331
Cohen, M D, 367
Cohen, P M, 263, 467
Cohen, S, 528, 529
Cohen, S G, 401, 403
Coil, J H, 52
Cole, J, 367
Cole, S G, 296
Colella, A, 83, 235
Coleman, H J Jr, 580
Coles, M, 530
Collier, R, 465
Collingwood, H, 52, 331
Collins, D, 264, 265
Collins, P D, 579
Collis, D, 611
Comer, L B, 498
Compton, W C, 530
Confino, J, 530
Conlon, E J, 263
Connellan, T K, 466
Connelly, J, 296

Connor, P E, 145
Conrin, J, 465
Cook, S W, 402
Cooke, M S, 402
Cooke, R A, 82, 83
Cooper, C, 497
Cooper, C L, 296, 466, 528, 529, 530, 554
Cooper, W H, 295, 369
Copper, C, 402
Corder, J, 296
Cordery, J L, 206
Cordes, C L, 528
Corneille, O, 177
Corner, P D, 176
Corr, P J, 177
Cose, E, 145
Cosier, R A, 333, 578
Costanzo, M A, 83
Cotton, J L, 402
Courtis, J, 53
Courtright, J A, 579
Covey, S R, 437, 467
Cowan, G, 331
Cox, C, 296
Cox, T H Jr, 83, 84
Crabb, S, 53
Cranny, C J, 206, 207
Crant, J M, 177
Creed, W E D, 580
Crittenden, K S, 332
Cross, T C, 498
Crouch, A, 369
Crow, R, 401
Crow, S M, 333
Crowell, C R, 466
Crown, D F, 295
Cummings, A, 370, 528
Cummings, L L, 52, 144, 205, 206, 207, 234, 295, 331, 368, 401, 436, 527, 578
Cunningham, J, 331
Currall, S C, 402
Curtis, K, 437
Cushman, P, 143
Cutrona, C E, 529

D

Dacin, T, 580
Daft, R L, 26, 436, 553
Dahl, J G, 235
Dahmus, S A, 264
Dailey, R C, 234
Dainty, P, 610
Dalkey, N C, 369
Dallas, S, 113
Dalton, D R, 578
Dansereau, F, 499
Dansereau, F Jr, 499
Darch, M, 52
Darrow, A L, 528
D'Aunno, T, 578
D'Aveni, R A, 553
Davenport Sypher, B, 436

Davidson, E D, 176
Davidson, J, 466
Davies, D, 294
Davies, E, 146
Davis, E, 368
Davis, J H, 368, 402
Davis, K, 437
Davis, K S, 206
Davis, T R V, 438, 466, 467
Davis-LaMastro, V, 175
Davy, J A, 84, 528
Dawis, R V, 206
Dawson, C, 437
Dawson, L M, 84
Day, D V, 144, 176, 177
De Backer, P, 113
De Benedittis, G, 528
De Gregorio, M, 263
De Jonquières, G, 554
De Kerkhofs, J, 84
De Vader, C L, 497
Deal, T E, 82, 83, 294, 401
Dean, J W Jr, 367, 580
Debussche, F, 176
Deci, E L, 235, 264
DeCotiis, T A, 234
DeFrank, R S, 530
DeGeorge, G, 401
Degoey, P, 402
DeGroot, T G, 498
DeLaney, J T, 84, 368, 401
Delbecq, A L, 369
Delbridge, R, 437
Demarie, S M, 26
DeMeuse, K P, 401
Deming, W E, 26
Demsey, M, 438
DeNisi, A S, 175, 263
Denison, D R, 82, 403, 498
Dennis, A R, 295, 369
Denton, D K, 26
Denton, L T, 402
DePaulo, B M, 402
Deppe, R K, 205
DeShon, R P, 235
Dess, G G, 25, 580, 609
Deutch, M, 401
Devadas, R, 403
Devanna, M A, 498
Deveny, K, 579
Devine, D J, 367
DeVries, N K, 367
DiBella, A J, 611
Dickinson, T L, 579
Dickson, T, 84, 205
Diehl, M, 369
Diener, C, 207
Diener, E, 144, 207
Diener, M, 144
Dienesch, R M, 499
Digman, J M, 145
DiTomaso, N, 82
Dobbins, G H, 177
Dobson, J, 84

Dodds, I, 53
Doerr, K H, 235
Doman, M, 466
Donahoe, J W, 465
Donaldson, R M, 437
Donaldson, T, 554
Donkin, R, 113, 579
Donnellon, A, 403
Doosje, B J, 529
Dorfman, P W, 499
Doty, D H, 578
Doucouliagos, C, 403
Dougherty, D, 369, 401
Dougherty, T W, 144, 263, 528
Downs, C W, 436
Downs, D L, 263
Drasgow, F, 206
Drazin, R, 578
Dreher, G F, 83, 84
Dressler, D E, 554
Drew, J B, 529
Drexler, A, 331
Driscoll, M P, 528
Driskell, J E, 331, 402
Drucker, P F, 235, 401, 553
Dubin, R, 83
Dubinsky, A J, 498, 499
DuBrin, A J, 499
Duchon, D, 499
Duff, C, 233, 234
Duffy, M, 143
Dufour, B, 113
Dugan, S, 113
Duhon, D L, 466
Dukerich, J M, 497
Dumaine, B, 83, 113, 401, 403, 554, 579
Duncan, R, 578
Dunham, R B, 144
Dunkin, A, 295
Dunlap Godsey, K, 112
Dunn, K F, 331
Dunnette, M D, 25, 176, 205, 234, 295
Dunning, D, 177
Dunphy, D, 401
Dunsing, R J, 144
Duxbury, L E, 438
Dvir, T, 177
Dwyer, D J, 206
Dyer, L, 234
Dyer, W G, 294, 403, 404
Dyne, L V, 207

E

Eagly, A H, 25, 497
Earles, J A, 146
Earley, C P, 296
Earley, P C, 113, 144, 263, 530
Eastman, K K, 499
Eastman, K L, 113
Ebadi, Y M, 369
Ebrahimi, B, 26

Eden, D, 144, 177, 296
Edmonds, P, 367
Edmondson, A, 611
Edwards, J E, 331, 610
Edwards, J R, 529
Edwards, M R, 263
Edwards, O, 438
Egan, C, 331
Egan, G, 82
Eggers, L M, 53
Ehrenfeld, T, 265
Ehrlich, S B, 497
Eisenberger, R, 175, 264
Eisenhardt, K M, 26
El Nasser, H, 367
Elam, J J, 611
Elangovan, A R, 334
Elderkin, K, 436, 497
Elias, J, 144
Eller, F, 367
Elliot, A J, 205
Elman, N S, 84
Elmer-Dewitt, P, 497
Elsass, P M, 113
Engardio, P, 401
Engen, J R, 113
Engholm, C, 437
England, G W, 206
Enström, B, 25, 497
Enz, C A, 332
Epstein, J A, 402
Er, M C, 369
Erera, I P, 529
Erickson, R J, 295
Ertel, D, 333
Esser, J K, 296
Ettlie, J E, 579
Ettorre, B, 25, 553, 554, 580, 610
Evered, R D, 499
Everett, M, 437
Ewen, A J, 263
Eyler, D R, 296

F

Fagans, M R, 610
Fairhurst, G T, 579
Falbe, C M, 331, 498
Fandt, P M, 332
Fang, Y, 206
Farber, B, 467
Farh, J-L, 263
Farkas, C M, 113
Farnham, A, 145
Farnsworth, S R, 235
Farr, J L, 368
Farson, R, 25
Fasolo P, 175
Feather, N T, 234
Fechter, W F, 401
Fedor, D B, 263
Fedor, K J, 112
Feld, S L, 295
Feldman, D C, 83, 146, 295

Feldstein, S, 437
Fenn, D, 436
Ferguson, C E Jr, 295
Fernie, S, 264
Ferraro, G P, 113
Ferrell, O C, 436
Ferris, G R, 53, 83, 146, 176, 206, 233, 332, 333, 402, 499
Ferster, C B, 465
Festinger, L, 143, 233
Fiedler, F E, 497, 498
Field, A, 438
Field, J M, 403
Field, R H G, 369
Fierman, J, 145
Fijneman, Y A, 113
Filipczak, B, 264, 331, 401, 466, 580
Filley, A C, 333
Finch, B J, 438
Finegan, J, 84
Fineman, S, 146
Finkelstein, S, 553, 580
Finley, M, 294
Finn, W, 177
Fiol, C M, 436
Fishbein, M, 145
Fisher, A B, 146, 296, 579
Fisher, C D, 263
Fisher, R J, 333, 334
Fisicaro, S A, 529
Fiske, S T, 175
Fitch, H G, 464
Fitzgerald, M P, 206
Flannery, T P, 177, 235, 264
Flax, S, 333
Fleschner, M, 235
Fletcher, B C, 527
Florian, V, 529
Folger, R, 234
Folkman, S, 528, 529
Fondas, N, 25
Ford, J D, 580, 610
Ford, L W, 610
Ford, R C, 332
Forgas, J P, 175
Foritano, L A, 143
Forster, N, 113
Forsterling, P, 177
Fortado, B, 333
Foster Owen, W, 402
Foti, R J, 467, 497
Fottler, M D, 332
Fraedrich, J, 436
Franke, R H, 25
Franz, E, 467
Franz, T M, 331
Fraser, S L, 497
Frayne, C A, 467
Frederiksen, L W, 464, 465
French, J R P, 331
French, J R P Jr, 610
French, R, 554
Frey, D, 367

Fried, Y, 206
Friedman, H S, 530
Friedman, M, 529
Frijnen, F, 401
Frink, D D, 53, 333, 401
Frone, M R, 528
Fry, F L, 466
Fry, L W, 579
Fuchsberg, G, 498
Fulford, M D, 332
Fulk, J, 436, 438
Fuller, H B, 234
Fullerton, J, 52, 53
Fulmer, R M, 611
Fuqua, D R, 609
Furman, M E, 465
Furnham, A, 82, 84, 264
Futrell, D, 401

G

Galagan, P A, 52
Galang, M C, 333
Galbraith, J R, 401, 553, 578, 579, 580
Gales, L M, 553
Gallupe, R B, 295, 369
Galpin, T, 83, 437
Galpin, T J, 84, 610
Galuszka, P, 112
Gangestad, S, 144
Ganster, D C, 53, 145, 206, 528
Gant, J, 331
Ganzach, Y, 175
Gardner, D G, 144
Gardner, P D, 83
Gardner, W L III, 25, 144, 146, 332
Garland, H, 368
Garner Stead, J, 84
Garud, R, 554
Garvin, D A, 553, 611
Geber, B, 402
Gecas, V, 143, 144
Gehani, R R, 26
Geisler, E, 554
Geller, E S, 466
Gentry, W D, 529
George, J M, 205, 235, 297
Gephart, M A, 580, 610
Geringer, J M, 467
Gersick, C J G, 294
Ghoshal, S, 113
Giacalone, R A, 332
Giacobbe-Miller, J, 234
Gibson, C B, 113
Gice, J, 207
Gilbert, M B, 465
Gilbert, T F, 465
Gilby, R, 466
Gillen, D J, 579
Gilligan, C, 84
Gilliland, S W, 235, 367
Gillis, D M, 26

Gilmore, D C, 53, 333
Gioia, D A, 263
Giolito, V, 264
Gist, M E, 144, 177, 263, 530
Giuffre, P A, 175
Gladstein, D L, 368
Glaser, R, 528
Glaser, S R, 83
Glassman, E, 369
Gleckman, H, 264
Glew, D J, 146, 333, 466
Glick, W H, 578, 579
Gobeli, D, 26
Goddard, R W, 177
Goddard, W E, 235
Godshalk, V M, 527
Goffe, R, 175
Goldsmith, M, 294
Goldsmith, R E, 370
Goldstein, H W, 83
Goldwasser, C, 609
Goleman, D, 146
Golembiewski, 529
Gomez Mejia, L R, 264, 265
Gonik, N, 529
Good, G E, 529
Gooding, R Z, 579
Goodman, P S, 369, 401, 403
Goodsell, C T, 553
Goodson, J R, 498
Goodwin, V L, 235
Gorden, W I, 436
Gordon, G G, 82
Gordon, J, 143, 554
Gordon, M E, 26
Gordon, R A, 331
Gorissen, P, 52
Goto, S G, 402
Gottlieb, J Z, 610
Gould, J M, 611
Gouttefarde, C, 112
Grabowski, M, 579
Grady, J F Jr, 403
Graeff, C L, 498
Graen, G B, 295, 499
Graham, A, 146
Graham, J L, 333
Graham-Moore, B, 265
Grant, J M, 145
Grant, L, 233
Grant, N M, 437
Grant, P R, 334
Gratch, L V, 144
Gray, B, 578
Gray, J A, 177
Gray, W D, 175
Graziolo, S, 367
Green, M S, 205
Green, S G, 83, 499
Greenberg, J, 26, 177, 233, 234
Greenhaus, J H, 52, 176
Greenwald, J, 578
Greenwood, R A, 25
Greenwood, R G, 25

Greer, C R, 112
Gregersen, H B, 112, 113
Griffeth, R W, 177, 234
Gist, M E, 146, 333, 370, 466
Griffith Hughson, T L, 403
Griffith, T L, 334
Grigaliunas, B, 206
Grise, M, 369
Grobben, J, 498
Grodek, M V, 467
Grofman, B, 295
Gross, T, 332
Gruenfeld, D H, 368
Gruneberg, M, 206
Guijarro, M L, 530
Gul, F A, 146
Gundry, L K, 369, 370
Gupta, N, 332
Gustafson, D H, 369
Gustafson, D J, 113
Gustafson, L T, 26
Gustafson, S B, 145
Gutek, B A, 296
Guzzo, R A, 207, 369

H

Haas, J W, 436
Haberfeld, Y, 176
Haccoun, R, 333
Hackett, E J, 403
Hackett, R D, 207, 499
Hackman, J R, 206, 207
Haenen, M, 113
Haga, W, 499
Hagerty, B, 113
Halal, W E, 554
Half, R, 438
Hall, E T, 112, 113
Hall, J A, 25, 295, 437
Hallam, J R, 144
Hallet, A J, 530
Hamel, G, 610
Hammer, M R, 25, 113, 206, 554
Hamner, E P, 466
Hamner, W C, 466
Hampden, C, 498
Handy, C, 579, 580
Harackiewicz, J M, 205
Harari, O, 369, 553, 554, 579
Hardy, C, 367, 369, 436, 498, 553, 554, 579
Harkins, S G, 235, 296, 297
Harlow, R E, 529
Harpaz, I, 113
Harper, K, 53, 296, 530
Harper, L F, 465
Harrell, A M, 205
Harris, M M, 264
Harris, P R, 112, 113, 144, 295
Harris, S G, 83
Harrison, A W, 333

Harrison, D A, 235, 369
Harrison, F E, 580
Harrison, J K, 113
Hart, E, 403
Hart, M, 436, 497
Hart, S L, 403, 580
Hart Seibert, J, 437
Hartke, D D, 498
Hartstein, B A, 438
Harvey, B H, 465
Harvey, N, 367
Hassell, B, 466
Hassell, B L, 177
Hawk, S R, 145
Haynes, R S, 464
Hazucha, F, 264
Healy, M C, 176
Hearn, J, 296
Heath, C, 368
Heath, P S, 580
Heck, R H, 83
Heckhausen, H, 205
Hedlund, J, 368
Heenan, D A, 112
Heide, D, 467
Heilman, M E, 52, 176
Heinbokel, T, 528
Heine, S J, 144
Heller, R, 401
Hellriegel, D, 146
Henderson, A M, 553
Henderson, G, 52
Hendry, C, 609
Hendry, J, 82
Heneman, R L, 265
Henkoff, R, 25, 370, 403, 578
Hensen, M, 331
Heppner, P P, 529
Hequet, M, 146, 263, 296, 580
Heraty, N, 206
Herold, D M, 263, 265
Herriot, P, 264
Herrmann, D, 113
Hersey, P, 498
Herzberg, F, 206
Heskett, J L, 82, 83
Hesselbein, F, 294
Hezlett, S A, 264
Hickson, D J, 367
Higgins, C A, 438
Higgins, J M, 82, 369, 370
Higgs, A C, 401, 403, 610
Hilderbrand, K, 143
Hildula, L, 437
Hill, A, 264
Hill, G W, 368
Hill, L A, 144
Hill, R, 112, 113, 437
Hill, T, 610
Hillkirk, J, 26, 403, 467
Hilton, D J, 177
Hines, T, 369
Hinings, C R, 83, 578
Hinkin, T R, 331, 332

Hinson, T D, 334
Hochberger, J M, 297
Hochwarter, W A, 333
Hodge, B J, 553
Hodgetts, R, 113
Hodgson, K, 84
Hoel, W, 499
Hoffman, R, 264
Hofmann, M A, 466
Hofrichter, D A, 177, 235, 264
Hofstede, G, 26, 113, 554
Holland, L, 52
Holland, N A, 368
Hollander, E P, 331
Hollenbeck, J R, 235, 368
Holmes, T H, 528
Holpp, L, 294, 332, 401, 403
Holt, J, 84, 143
Hom, P W, 175, 176, 177, 234, 497
Hooijberg, R, 498
Hope, V, 82
Hopstaken, L E M, 529
Horton Smith, D, 294
Horton, T R, 497
Hosmer, L T, 402
Houlder, V, 113, 264
House, R J, 331, 369, 498, 499
Houston Butcher, A, 146
Hoverston, P, 367
Howard, G S, 466
Howard, J L, 333
Howe, M A, 467
Howell, J M, 499
Howell, J P, 499
Hu, L-T, 295
Huber, G P, 368, 578, 579
Hubiak, W A, 113
Hubrich, A, 401
Huey, J, 499, 579
Huge, C, 438
Hui, C H, 113
Hulin, C L, 206
Hull, F, 579
Hummel, R P, 554
Humphreys, M S, 145
Hunt, J G, 145
Hunter, J E, 26, 146, 177, 235, 368, 610
Hurst, D K, 578
Hutter Epstein, R, 26
Hyder, E B, 333
Hymowitz, C, 52

I

Iacovini, J, 610
Iaffaldano, M T, 207
Iansiti, M, 579
Ibarra, H, 53, 295
Idaszak, J R, 206
Ilgen, D R, 263, 368
Imberman, W, 264
Infante, D A, 436

Ingwerson, M, 333
Irving, P G, 206
Ivancevich, J M, 466, 527

J

Jablin, F M, 233
Jack, A, 235, 264
Jackson, D N, 145
Jackson, G B, 26
Jackson, J M, 296, 297
Jackson, P R, 528
Jackson, S E, 295, 530
Jacob, R, 82, 578, 580
Jacobson, L, 177
Jacobus, S, 113
Jago, A G, 368, 369
Jamal, K, 367
Jamal, M, 529
James, K, 333
Jamieson, L F, 530
Janis, I L, 296
Jans, L G J M, 529
Janson, R, 206
Jasor, M, 580
Jenkins, G D J Jr, 332
Jensen, M A C, 294
Jermier, J, 499
Jewell, L N, 294
Jiang, W Y, 84
Jick, T, 580, 611
Jin, P, 402
Johns, G, 206
Johnson, A L, 294
Johnson, B T, 25, 497, 528
Johnson, C, 369
Johnson, C M, 466
Johnson, D M, 175
Johnson, D W, 402
Johnson, J A, 145
Johnson, J H Jr, 84
Johnson, J L, 176
Johnson, J T, 177
Johnson, P E, 367
Johnson, R, 402
Johnson, R T, 402
Johnson, S, 466
Johnson-George, C, 404
Johnston, D K, 84
Johnston, M W, 295, 528
Joireman, J, 145
Jolson, M A, 498, 499
Jones, D, 25
Jones, D T, 580
Jones, F, 527
Jones, F F, 234
Jones, G, 175
Jones, R E, 334
Jorgensen, J, 401
Jorgensen, R S, 528
Joseph-Dezaize, G, 82
Judd, C M, 176
Judge, T A, 207, 402
Judge, W Q Jr, 580
Judson, A S, 610

Julian, F W, 554
Jussim, L J, 176

K

Kabanoff, B, 84
Kacmar, K M, 332, 333
Kaestle, P, 579
Kaeter, M, 144
Kahalani, A, 296
Kahn, J A, 403
Kahn, R L, 528
Kahn, S, 529
Kahneman, D, 295, 367
Kakuyama, T, 263
Kalsher, M J, 466
Kandola, R, 52, 53
Kaniasty, K, 529
Kano, N, 402
Kaplan, I T, 403
Karau, S J, 296, 497
Karrass, C L, 437
Karren, R J, 235
Kashy, D A, 402
Kaspar, H, 53
Kast, F E, 528
Katigbak, M S, 145
Katz, I M, 144
Katzell, R A, 207
Katzenbach, J R, 401, 403
Katzenstein, G, 333
Kaufman, C F, 112
Kaufman, L, 145
Kaul, J D, 25
Kay, I T, 264
Kay, J, 82, 401, 554
Kazanjian, R K, 578
Kazi-Ferrouillet, K, 52
Keashly, L, 334
Keating, D E, 403
Keats, D M, 143
Keeley, M, 555
Keen, P G W, 146
Keenan, D, 530
Keidel, R W, 554, 578
Kellaway, L, 263, 264
Keller, J, 177
Keller, R T, 498
Keller, T, 499
Kelley, H H, 177
Kelley, M R, 206
Kelley, R, 466
Kelley Reardon, K, 333
Kelly, J R, 112
Kelly, P E, 176
Keltner Slack, A, 207
Kemmerer, B, 145
Kendall, L M, 206
Kennedy, A A, 82, 83
Kennedy, C, 611
Kenny, D A, 467, 497
Keon, T L, 205, 234
Kerkhofs, J, 25
Kerr, S, 235, 264, 499, 580
Kerwin, K, 578

Kettelhut, M, 610
Keys, J B, 402, 611
Keyton, J, 402
Kickul, J R, 369, 370
Kidwell, R E Jr, 296
Kiechel, W III, 25, 333, 580
Kiecolt-Glaser, J K, 529
Kiker, D S, 498
Kikkert, O, 52
Kikulis, L M, 83
Kilduff, M, 144
Kim, D O, 265
Kim, H, 331
Kim, J, 579
Kim, K I, 233, 264
Kim, M U, 578
Kim, S H, 177
King, D W, 295
King, J B, 438
King, L A, 295
King, N, 206
King, P, 403
King, P J, 554
King, R T Jr, 554
King, W C Jr, 334
Kingston, K, 555
Kinicki, A J, 53, 84, 175, 176, 177, 207, 234, 236, 497, 499, 528, 529, 555
Kipnis, D, 331
Kirk, D J, 234
Kirkendol, S E, 402
Kirkpatrick, S A, 498
Kiser, K J, 26
Kjelgaard, M M, 235
Klastorin, T D, 235
Klebe Trevino, L, 466
Klein, H J, 295
Klein, R L, 82
Kleiner, B H, 146
Kluger, A N, 263
Knight, D B, 527
Knotts, R, 112
Knowlton, B, 176
Kobasa, S C, 529
Kochan, T A, 609
Koen, C M Jr, 333
Kofman, F, 554, 611
Kohn, A, 235, 264, 401, 466
Kok, G, 464
Kolodziej, M E, 528
Kompier, M, 52
Konovsky, M A, 207
Kopelman, R E, 206, 263
Kopp, R, 112, 113
Korbin, W P, 529
Koretz, G, 265, 466
Korgaard, M A, 234, 402
Koslowsky, M, 553
Kotha, S, 554
Kotter, J P, 82, 83, 84, 333, 497, 578, 610
Kouzes, J M, 263, 465, 497, 498

Kovach, K A, 236
Kozakaï, T, 402
Kozan, M K, 113
Kozlowski, S W J, 83, 367
Kraft, M, 145
Kram, K E, 53, 83, 84
Kraut, A I, 25
Kravitz, D A, 296
Kreitner, R, 464, 465, 466, 467
Kreshel, P J, 465
Kriger, M P, 498
Kristof, A L, 528
Krug, S, 205
Kruse, D L, 265
Kuehl, C, 84
Kuhlman, D M, 145
Kunda, Z, 176
Kurke, L B, 25
Kurpius, D J, 609
Kuruvilla, S, 145
Kushell, E N, 467
Kuypers, B C, 294

L

Laabs, J J, 609
Labich, K, 403, 578
Labich, L, 436
Lakey, B, 529
Lamal, P A, 465
Lammers, T, 263
Lampe, J C, 554
Lancaster, H, 83, 112, 263, 331, 467, 554
Landau, J C, 465
Landis, R S, 235
Landon, L, 529
Landy, F J, 234
Lane, J, 264
Lane, P M, 112
Langan-Fox, J, 205
Lapidus, R S, 234
LaPlante, A, 369
LaPotin, P, 367
Larey, T S, 369
Larson, E W, 438
Larson, J R Jr, 331
Larsson, R, 26
Larwood, L, 498
Latack, J C, 234, 529, 554
Latane, B, 296, 297
Latham, G P, 235, 333, 401, 465, 467
Latham, G R, 368
Lattack, J, 528
Lau, C-M, 610
Lavallee, L F, 144
Lawler, E E III, 26, 234, 264, 265, 368, 401, 402, 403, 466, 553, 554, 578, 579, 580
Lawrence, B S, 25
Lawrence, P R, 579
Lazarus, R S, 146, 529
Leana, C R, 296, 332, 368

Leary, M R, 205, 263
Leck, J D, 234
Ledford, G E Jr, 368, 403
Lee, A S, 26
Lee, C, 25, 263, 403, 530
Lee, R T, 529
Lee, Y-T, 176
Leerhsen, C, 176
Lehman, D R, 144
Lehman, M, 176
Lei, D, 553
Leigh, T W, 205
Leiter, 529
LeLouarn, J-Y, 234
Lemmeck, J, 53
Lengel, R H, 436
Leonard, R, 331
Lepsinger, R, 264
Lerner, D, 264
Leshner, M, 235
Leslie, J B, 25
Lesly, E, 331
Lester, T, 83, 176
Leuenberger, A, 177
Levine, S R, 234
Levinson, M, 402
Levitt, B, 367
Levy, P E, 263, 264
Lewin, K, 609
Lewis, J D, 402
Lewis, P V, 84
Lewis, R, 369
Lewis, S, 296
Leyens, J-P, 177
Liden, R C, 144, 331, 332, 333, 403, 437, 499
Lieberson, S, 497
Lightfood, L, 176
Lim, L, 369
Lim, R G, 334
Lindecamp, D P, 146
Lindemann, M, 610
Lindsley, D H, 144
Lingle, J H, 611
Linowes, R G, 83
Linton, S J, 177
Li-Ping Tang, T, 402, 403
Lipshitz, R, 367
Liska, L Z, 235
Lituchy, T R, 144, 176, 263
Liu, J, 176
Livingstone, L P, 234
Lloyd, B, 331
Lloyd, R F, 403
Lobel, S A, 296
Locke, E A, 206, 235, 368, 401, 466, 498, 530
Lockwood, C A, 177
Loden, M, 52, 53
Lofquist, L H, 206
Logan, J W Jr, 234
Loher, T, 206
London, M, 264
Long, B C, 529

Long, B G, 333
Long, J W, 294
Longenecker, C O, 263
Longo, S C, 610
Lopez, J A, 609
Lorange, P, 578
Lorber, R, 465
Lord, R G, 176, 497
Lorenz, C, 554
Lorenzetti, A, 528
Lorsch, J W, 579
Lowe, C A, 297
Lowry Miller, K, 401, 403, 436
Lubart, T I, 370
Lublin, J S, 53, 112, 113
Lucas, J A, 176
Lueder, D C, 498
Luke, R A Jr, 437
Luthans, F, 25, 112, 113, 144, 465, 466, 467
Luz, J, 205
Lykken, D, 207
Lyness, S A, 530

M

Maass, A, 367
Maass, P, 205
Maastricht, N L, 53
Mabry, M, 112
McAfee, B, 206
McAllister, D J, 402, 404
McCabe, K M, 529
McCall, M W Jr, 331
McCarthy, M J, 403
McCartney, S, 83, 112
McCarty, C L, 233
McCauley, C, 296
McCauley, C D, 53
McCauley, C R, 176
McClelland, C L, 206
McClelland, D C, 205
McCrae, R R, 145
McDaniel, M A, 176
McDaniel, R R Jr, 580
McDermott, L, 499
McDougal, Y B, 367
McElroy, J C, 528
McEvoy, G M, 176, 206
McFarlin, D B, 234, 264, 528
McGarvey, R, 467
McGee, G W, 295, 498
McGill, M E, 554
McGrath, J E, 112, 295
McGregor Burns, J, 498
McGregor, D, 25
McGuire, C V, 144
McGuire, W J, 144
McHenry, R, 25
McHugh, M, 207
Mack, N R, 112
McKee, F M, 207, 528, 529
McKendall, M, 610
McKenna, D D, 25

McKenney, J L, 146
MacKenzie, K, 263
Mackenzie, S B, 176, 207, 498, 499
McKinley, W, 579
McKittrick, D, 52
McLagan, P, 26
McLaughlin, K J, 25, 580
McLaughlin, M L, 402, 438
McMahan, G C, 235
McMillen, S, 437
McNamara, R, 296
McNerney, D J, 403
McQuade, K, 436, 497
McShulskis, E, 499
Maddi, S R, 529
Maddox, E N, 467
Madison, D L, 332
Magnani, P S, 177
Magner, N R, 333
Magnet, M, 578
Mai, R P, 610
Maidani, E A, 206
Main, J, 112
Major, D A, 83, 368
Makhijani, M G, 497
Malarkey, W, 528
Malcolm, H, 331
Malik, S D, 83, 294
Maloney, C C, 332
Mamis, R A, 578
Mandel, M J, 265
Mandell, M B, 367
Maney, K, 554
Mani, S, 438
Mann, M F, 610
Mann, R D, 497
Mann, S, 333
Manning, D J Jr, 235
Manning, G, 437
Mannix, E A, 295, 368
Manrai, A K, 112
Manrai, L A, 112
Manz, C C, 403, 404, 466, 467, 499, 579
Mapes, J, 206
Marbach, W D, 112
March, J G, 367, 553
Marcoulides, G A, 113
Markham, S E, 265
Markham, W T, 296
Marks, M L, 403
Markus, M L, 438
Marlatt, G A, 234
Marlowe, C M, 176
Marren, J, 82
Marsch, P, 401
Marsh, H W, 144
Marshak, R J, 553
Marshall, N L, 528
Marsick, V, 610
Martell, R F, 264
Martin, B, 296
Martin, B A, 235

Martin, C, 234
Martin, C L, 437
Martin, D C, 26
Martin, J N, 113
Martin, L, 144
Martin, M M, 144
Martin, S L, 332
Martinko, M J, 25, 144, 146, 466
Martins, L L, 52
Martocchio, J J, 26, 176, 263, 401
Maruyama, G, 402
Marwell, G, 295
Maslach, C, 528, 529, 530
Maslow, A H, 205
Mason, J, 205
Mason, R O, 580
Masternak, R L, 265
Masuch, M, 367
Matejka, J K, 144
Matherly, T A, 370
Mathieu, J, 84
Mathieu, J E, 207, 368
Matsui, T, 263, 529
Matteson, M T, 527
Maurer, T J, 176
Mausner, B, 206
May, D, 610
Mayer, R C, 402
Mayers, J, 578
Mayes, B T, 332
Maynard, M, 264
Mealiea, L W, 499, 611
Mears, P, 26
Mechelse, L, 333
Medsker, G J, 401, 403
Meindl, J R, 497
Melamed, S, 205
Melcher, B H, 334
Memmott, M, 332
Mendenhall, M E, 112, 113, 332
Mennecke, B E, 369
Mento, A J, 235
Mervis, C B, 175
Merwi, G A Jr, 465
Metalsky, G I, 177
Metcalf, D, 264
Metlay, W, 403
Meyer, A D, 578
Meyer, J P, 206, 207
Michaelson, G A, 113
Midgley, S, 207
Miesing, P, 498
Mikulincer, M, 529
Miles, G L, 295
Miles, R E, 580
Miller, C C, 579
Miller, D, 553, 580, 611
Miller, D J, 265
Miller, K I, 265
Miller, L M, 465
Miller, P, 554

Miller, S J, 367
Miller, T Q, 530
Miller, T R, 402
Milliken, F J, 52, 578
Mills, G E, 403
Mills, J, 334
Millsap, R E, 264
Milner, P M, 465
Miner, J B, 25, 26
Mintu, A T, 333
Mintzberg, H, 25, 401, 580
Mirvis, P H, 403
Mischel, L J, 528
Mishra, A K, 82
Mitchell, R, 265, 579
Mitchell, T R, 144, 177, 205, 234, 235, 263, 367, 368, 498, 578
Mitchell, V-W, 553
Mitroff, I I, 580
Moats Kennedy, M, 333
Modic, S J, 437
Moeller, N L, 206
Moerkamp, J, 528
Moerkerke, T, 497
Mohamed, A A, 296
Mohrman, S A, 368, 402, 403
Moingeon, B, 611
Mole, J, 112, 113, 437
Molloy, K, 553
Mone, M A, 144
Monks, R A G, 265
Monoky, J F, 205
Montanari, J R, 296, 579, 580
Montei, M S, 53
Moore, D, 295
Moore, J F, 553, 554
Moore, M T, 579
Moore, R W, 112
Moorhead, G, 296
Moran, R T, 112, 113, 144, 295
Morand, D A, 331, 579
Morden, T, 112
Morgan, G, 553
Morgan, R B, 84
Morley, M, 206
Morris, A, 53
Morris, J A, 146
Morris, J L, 265
Morris, L, 206, 234, 610
Morris, W T, 83
Morrison, A M, 52, 53
Morrison, E W, 83
Morrow, P C, 528
Moscovici, S, 402
Moss Kanter, R, 610
Mossberg, W S, 367, 438
Mossholder, K W, 83
Motoko, R, 530
Motowidlo, S J, 176
Mount, M K, 145, 235
Mouton, J S, 296, 498
Mowday, R T, 294

Muchinsky, P M, 207
Muelenaer, G, 53
Mueller, R, 176
Muir, N K, 369
Mullane, J V, 26
Mullarkey, S, 528
Mullen, B, 295, 369, 402
Multon, K D, 437
Mulvey, P W, 295
Mumford, M D, 145, 498
Münninghoff, A, 143
Munter, M, 112
Murnigham, K J, 295
Murray, B, 177
Murray, H A, 205
Murray, L H, 332
Murray, R P, 332
Murrell, A J, 368
Musen, G, 176
Myers, P B, 146

N

Naj, A K, 403
Nanda, A, 497
Nanus, B, 498
Narod, S, 466
Nass, C, 367
Neal, J A, 609
Neale, M A, 333, 368
Neck, C P, 296, 467
Neely Martinez, M, 53
Neidt, C O, 579
Nel, C, 26
Nelson, B, 465
Nelson, C E, 176
Nelson, D, 402
Nelson, E, 233
Nelson, R R, 369
Nelson, R T, 578
Nelton, S, 146
Nemetz, P L, 52
Netemeyer, R G, 295, 528
Neuberg, S L, 175
Neuborne, E, 401
Neuman, G A, 610
Nevin, J A, 465
Nevis, E C, 611
Newcomb, M D, 144
Newhouse, D R, 609
Newman, B, 113
Ng, A C, 369
Nicholson, N, 296
Niebuhr, R E, 145
Niedenthal, P M, 144
Niederehe, G, 176
Nijhof, W, 52
Nimgade, A, 113
Nirenberg, J, 402
Nixon, B, 436
Noe, R A, 206
Noer, D M, 611
Nolan, L L, 334
Nonaka, I, 369
Noon, M, 437

Nord, W R, 367, 369, 436, 498, 553, 554, 579
Normand, J-M, 205
Norris, D R, 145
Norris, F H, 529
Northcraft, G B, 263, 334
Nowlin, W A, 112
Nulty, P, 609
Nunamaker, J F Jr, 295, 369
Nutt, P C, 609
Nye, L G, 207, 234
Nystrom, P C, 145

O

Oakes Yound, A, 176
O'Boyle, T F, 527
O'Brien, C, 402
O'Brien, M, 467
O'Brien, R, 402
O'Connor, J F, 497
O'Connor, S C, 205
Odiorne, G S, 465
O'Donnell, S J, 113
O'Driscoll, M P, 528
Offermann, L R, 331
O'Hara, K, 466
Ohlott, P J, 53
Ohsawa, T, 529
Okkada, A, 263
Oldenburg, A, 331
Oldham, G R, 206, 207, 370, 528
O'Leary, T, 554
O'Leary-Kelly, A M, 146, 333, 401, 466
Oleson, K C, 176
Olian, J D, 176
Oliver, P, 295
Olivia, P, 53
Olmstead, B, 331
Olsen, J P, 367
Olson-Buchanan, J B, 234
O'Meara, D P, 84
O'Neill, D, 265
Onglatco, M L, 529
Onyx, J, 331
Opsahl, R L, 234
O'Reilly, B, 264
Organ, D W, 207, 578
Orpen, C, 83
Orrell-Jones, K, 609
Ortega, A H, 369
Orth, C D, 499
Ortiz, A E, 402
Osborn, A F, 369
Osborne, R L, 580
Oskamp, S, 83
Ostendorf, F, 145
Ostroff, C, 207
O'Toole, J, 579
Ott, E M, 296
Otten, A L, 52
Ouchi, W G, 82
Ovalle, N K, 145

Overell, S, 52
Overman, S, 528
Owen, G, 295
Owtroff, C, 554

P

Pace, R W, 403
Palmer, J, 52
Pancucci, D, 438
Paoli, P, 52
Pape, W R, 438, 579
Parasuraman, S, 52, 176, 527
Parisi-Carew, E, 294
Park, B, 176
Park, H-J, 233, 264
Parker, D F, 234
Parker Follett, M, 25
Parker, G M, 369
Parker, L, 438
Parker, S K, 528
Parker, V A, 84
Parks, J M, 207
Parsons, C K, 144, 263, 265, 437
Parsons, M B, 264
Parsons, T, 553
Pascale, R, 84
Paskoff, S M, 143
Pasmore, W A, 404, 610
Pasternak, C, 332
Patrick, R R, 112
Patterson, P W Jr, 578
Paul, R J, 369
Paulus, P B, 369
Paunonen, S V, 145
Peacock, E J, 529
Pearce, C G, 437
Pearce, J L, 264, 332
Pearce, P F, 402
Pearlstein, S, 578
Pearson, C M, 580
Pecotich, A, 234
Pedigo, P R, 25
Pelfrey, M, 402
Pellegrino, J, 553
Pelletier, L G, 332
Pelletier, M A, 580
Pence, E C, 177
Pendelton, W C, 177
Peng, M W, 580
Pennings, J M, 578
Perlmutter, H V, 112
Perlow, R, 205
Perrewe, P I, 177
Perrottet, C M, 367
Perry, N J, 264, 265
Personnaz, B, 402
Pescuric, A, 466
Peters, L H, 175, 498
Peters, R H, 264
Peters, T, 497, 499, 579
Peters, T J, 82, 579
Peterson, C, 177
Peterson, E, 333

Peterson, K S, 146
Peterson, M, 295
Petzinger, T Jr, 437
Pfeffer, J, 554
Phillips, A, 53
Phillips, A S, 145
Phillips, C M, 528
Phillips, J, 368
Phillips, J S, 176, 497
Phillips, N, 436
Pianko, D, 113
Pickard, S, 368
Picken, J C, 609
Pierce, J L, 144
Pieri, A, 528
Pillow, D R, 528
Pinchot, E, 553
Pinchot, G, 553
Pinder, C C, 205, 206, 234
Pine, R C, 464
Pinketon, L, 234
Pinkley, R L, 334
Piskurich, G, 438
Plas, J M, 528
Platt, P, 83, 554
Platten, P E, 177, 235, 264
Pleck, J H, 528
Plunkett, D, 368
Podsakoff, P M, 176, 207, 263, 331, 498, 499
Pohlmann, J T, 498
Pojidaeff, D, 368
Poland, T D, 206
Poortinga, Y H, 113
Popham, P, 436
Porras, J I, 610
Port, O, 113
Porter, L W, 145, 176, 234, 294, 332
Posch, R, 438
Posner, B G, 578
Posner, B Z, 263, 465, 497, 498
Pounds, W F, 367
Powell, R, 146
Powers, D E, 144
Prahalad, C K, 610
Prasad, B, 26
Prasad, S B, 112
Prather, C W, 369, 370
Preiss, R W, 437
Premack, S L, 206. 235
Preston, L E, 554
Price, B S, 333
Priel, B, 529
Priem, R L, 25, 369, 580
Prietula, M J, 333
Pritchard, R D, 205
Prusak, L, 370
Prussia, G E, 177, 529, 554
Prussia, S E, 528
Prystash, D T, 438
Puka, B, 84
Pulakos, E D, 234

Punnett, B J, 176
Purdy, K, 206
Purohit, Y S, 527
Putnam, L L, 436

Q

Quarstein, V, 206
Quelch, J A, 436, 497
Quinn, E, 498
Quinn, J B, 580
Quinn, E, 498
Quinn, R E, 296, 578
Quinones, M A, 263
Quirke, B, 610

R

Rabinowitz, B, 529
Rachlin, H, 465
Rader, D, 144
Rafaeli, A, 610
Ragins, B R, 83, 84
Rahe, R H, 528
Rahim, M A, 331, 333
Raia, A, 332
Raju, N S, 610
Rakos, R F, 467
Ralphs, L, 403
Ralston, D A, 113
Ramsoomair, F, 146
Randall Palef, B, 402
Randolph, W A, 332, 368
Rao, A, 332, 333
Rapaport, R, 401
Rasheed, A M A, 25, 580
Raudenbush, S W, 528
Raudsepp, E, 436
Raven, B, 331
Ravlin, E, 401
Raybeck, D, 113
Ready, D, 609
Reardon, K K, 437
Reber, R A, 466
Recardo, R F, 554, 610
Rechner, P L, 333
Reck, R R, 333
Redding, C, 437
Redmon, G, 264
Redmund, M R, 498
Ree, M J, 146
Reeder, J A, 112
Rees, L P, 146
Reese, R, 579
Reger, R K, 26
Rehder, R R, 554
Reichers, A E, 83, 294
Reid, D H, 264
Reilly, A H, 264
Reilly, N P, 368
Reilly, R R, 264
Reingold, E M, 554
Reinhardt, A, 401
Reiste, K K, 401
Reitz, H J, 294
Reker, G T, 529

Renn, R W, 145
Rensvold, R B, 263
Renwick, P A, 332
Reuter, 145
Revelle, W, 145
Reza, E M, 579
Rice, C M, 52
Rice, G H Jr, 146
Rice, R E, 436
Rice, R W, 528
Rich, G A, 176
Richman, L S, 295
Richmond, Y, 84, 112, 205
Ricklefs, R, 265
Ridding, J, 554
Rienzo, T F, 26
Rifkind, L J, 465
Riggs Fuller, S, 296
Riordan, C A, 332
Ritzky, G M, 264
Robbins, S P, 333
Roberson, L, 146, 234
Robert Callister, R, 333
Roberts, D R, 610
Roberts, J A, 234
Roberts, K H, 82, 579
Roberts, L, 52
Roberts, N C, 554
Robertson, I T, 144, 466, 554
Robertson, P J, 610
Robey, D, 146, 611
Robinson, S L, 467
Rocklin, T, 296
Roddick, A, 25
Rodgers, R, 177, 235, 368, 610
Rodgers, W, 333
Rodrigues, C A, 113
Roethlisberger, F J, 438
Rogelberg, S G, 296, 297
Rogers, A C, 368
Rogers, C R, 438
Rogers, D L, 177, 235, 368, 610
Rogers, E F, 403
Rogers, J F, 465
Rogers, L E, 579
Romei, L K, 438
Rosch, E, 175
Rose, R L, 529
Rosenblood, L K, 205
Rosener, J B, 25
Rosenfeld, P, 331, 332
Rosenkrantz, P S, 176
Rosenman, R H, 529
Rosenthal, R, 177
Rosenzweig, J E, 528
Rosenzweig, M R, 145, 176, 294
Rosenzweig, P M, 113
Ross, J, 145, 207, 367, 368
Ross, T L, 265
Rossant, J, 401
Rosse, J G, 295

Roth, P L, 370
Roth, S, 205
Roth, T, 403
Rothstein, M, 145
Rotter, J B, 145
Rourke, D L, 369
Rowan, R, 438
Rowland, K M, 83, 233
Ruben, D H, 465
Ruben, M J, 465
Rubin, R B, 144
Ruderman, M N, 53
Ruiz, M R, 465
Rumery, S M, 296
Rummler, G, 205, 465
Rush, M C, 529
Russell, C J, 295
Russell, J A, 437
Russell, R D, 295
Rutledge, R W, 368
Ryan, J, 610
Ryan, K, 207

S

Saari, J, 464
Saari, L M, 235, 465
Saavedra, R, 296
Sackett, P R, 146
Sackmann, S, 553
Sadri, G, 144
Sager, I, 263, 578
St. Clair, L, 296
St. John, W D, 437
Saks, A M, 83, 144
Salas, E, 295, 331, 369, 402
Salvemini, N, 264
Salwen, K G, 401
Sanchez, J I, 176, 529
Sandberg, W R, 333
Sandefur, C A, 368
Sandler, I, 528
Sandler, L, 466
Sanford, E E, 465
Sankowsky, D, 499
Sanzgiri, J, 610
Sapienza, H J, 234, 402
Sapolsky, R, 527
Saporito, B, 578
Sashkin, M, 26, 368
Sathe, V, 579
Saunders, D M, 234
Sawyer, J E, 370
Scandura, T A, 499
Scarpello, V, 234
Schaffer, R J, 610
Schaubroeck, J, 145, 264, 368,
    528
Scheck, C L, 84, 528
Schein, E H, 82, 83, 112, 294,
    295, 553, 609
Schein, V E, 176
Schellhardt, T D, 528
Schiemann, W A, 611
Schleifer, L L F, 370

Schlender, B, 177
Schlenker, B R, 144
Schmidt, F L, 26, 146
Schmidt, J, 579
Schmidt, S M, 331, 332, 333
Schmidtke, J M, 528
Schminke, M, 401
Schmit, J, 554
Schmitt, N, 26, 234, 367, 554
Schnake, M E, 334
Schneider, B, 83, 610
Schneider, R J, 264
Schneider, S C, 26, 82
Schneider, S L, 176
Schock, C, 609
Schoel, W A, 529
Schonberger, R J, 26
Schoorman, F D, 402
Schreer, G E, 528
Schriesheim, C A, 207, 331,
    332, 497, 498
Schroeder, R G, 83, 403
Schuler, R S, 295
Schulman, M L, 438
Schultze, J A, 465
Schumacher, E F, 579
Schuster, J R, 264
Schut, H, 529
Schutz, R W, 529
Schwab, D P, 176
Schwartz, S H, 84
Schweiger, D M, 234, 333,
    368, 402
Schwenk, C, 369
Schwenk, C R, 333
Scott, M, 530
Scott, R K, 369
Scott, S G, 370
Scott, W R, 144, 553
Scrimshaw, N L, 529
Scully, J P, 438
Seers, A, 295
Segal, N L, 207
Sego, D J, 368
Seligman, D, 143, 144
Seligman, M E P, 177
Sellers, P, 499, 579
Selman, J C, 499
Selye, H, 527
Selz, M, 403
Semmel, A, 177
Senge, P M, 205, 553, 611
Setterlund, M B, 144
Sevastos, P P, 206
Seymour, J, 84
Sgro, J A, 177
Shackleton, V J, 113
Shakespeare, W, 528
Shamir, B, 498
Shankar Pawar, B, 499
Shapiro, E, 579
Shapiro, S, 146
Shapiro, T, 403
Sharfman, M P, 367, 580

Sharkey, T W, 332
Sharma, C L, 112
Sharpe, R, 528
Shaver, K G, 205
Shaw, K N, 235
Shea, J, 26
Sheats, P, 295
Sheehy, B, 402
Shellenbarger, S, 176, 295,
    466
Sheppard, D L, 296
Shepperd, J A, 296
Sheridan, J E, 83
Sheridan, J H, 609
Sherman, D A, 177
Sherman, J D, 579
Sherman, J W, 176
Sherman, S, 466, 497
Shilling, M, 113
Shipley, D, 331
Shipper, F, 25, 579
Shirom, A, 528
Shivers, S L, 499
Shook, D E, 436
Short, J F Jr, 143
Shostak, A B, 25
Sias, P M, 233
Siberaton, J, 554
Siegman, A W, 437
Siero, F, 464
Siero, S, 464
Sikes, W, 331
Silver, W S, 144, 177, 263,
    368
Simon, H A, 367
Simonian, H, 84
Simpson, P, 436
Sims, H P Jr, 403, 466, 467,
    499
Sims, R R, 296
Singh, H, 113
Sinha, K K, 403
Sisco, R, 265
Sitkin, S B, 367
Skinner, B F, 465, 466
Skinner, E A, 528
Skon, L, 402
Slack, T, 83
Slade, L A, 26
Slater, S F, 611
Sleek, S, 402
Slocum, J W Jr, 26, 146, 553
Sloman, S A, 176
Smart, L, 144
Smart, T, 436
Smircich, L, 82
Smith, A P, 528
Smith, C A, 529
Smith, C S, 368, 529
Smith, D B, 83
Smith, D K, 401, 403
Smith, E T, 369
Smith, H, 402
Smith, H L, 579

Smith, K G, 401, 578
Smith, K K, 334
Smith, L, 112, 263, 579
Smith, M, 497
Smith, M L, 263
Smith, N D, 610
Smith, N R, 26
Smith, P B, 113, 296
Smith, P C, 206
Smith, R H, 177
Smith, T K, 467
Smith, T W, 530
Smith Tollison, P, 402, 403
Smith, W P, 530
Smith-Lovin, L, 296
Smither, J W, 264
Smulders, P, 52
Smythe, J, 437
Sniezek, J A, 368
Snizek, W E, 438
Snyder, D, 369
Snyder, M, 144
Snyderman, B B, 206
Sogon, S, 296
Sokoloff, C, 331
Solomon, C M, 403
Solomon, J, 332
Sommer, S M, 113
Sonnenfeld, J A, 25
Sonnentag, S, 528
Sonnesyn Brooks, S, 580
South, S J, 296
Spangler, R, 402, 403
Spangler, W D, 205, 499
Sparaco, P, 553
Sparrowe, R T, 331
Spector, B, 610
Spector, P E, 145
Spekman, R E, 333
Spence, M T, 146
Spiro, M, 610
Spitzer, D R, 206, 235, 264
Spragins, E E, 53
Spreitzer, G M, 332, 403
Springston, J, 402
Squire, L R, 176
Srygley Mouton, J, 295
Stacy, A W, 234
Stahl, M J, 205
Stahlberg, D, 367
Stalker, G M, 579
Stamps, D, 145
Stanger, T, 112
Stangor, C, 145
Stark, M, 529, 530
Stasson, M, 145
Staw, B M, 52, 145, 205, 206,
    207, 234, 295, 331, 367,
    368, 401, 436, 527, 578
Stayer, R C, 332
Stead, W E, 84
Steck, R N, 205
Steel, R P, 145, 235, 403
Steele Johnson, D, 205

Stein, J A, 144
Steinmetz, G, 235
Stephan, E, 403
Stephan, W G, 175
Stephens, G K, 112
Stephenson, G M, 206
Stern, G, 528
Sternberg, R J, 370
Stevens, C K, 144
Stevens, L, 438
Stevens, M J, 206, 466
Stevenson, W B, 332
Stewart, A J, 205
Stewart, R, 25, 112
Stewart, T A, 331, 554, 578, 580
Stilwell, D, 499
Stogdill, R M, 497
Stohl, C, 402
Stolte, W, 528
Stone, E F, 206, 207
Strauss, J P, 235
Streff, F M, 466
Stroebe, M, 529
Stroebe, W, 369, 529
Stroh, L K, 264
Stuller, J, 25
Stumpf, S A, 611
Suchman, M C, 553
Sullerot, E, 52
Sullivan, J J, 143
Sulsky, L M, 176, 177
Summer, C E, 578
Summers, R J, 83
Sumner, G A, 112
Sundstrom, E, 401
Suris, O, 367
Sutton, C L, 176
Sutton, R I, 294, 295, 578
Suzuki, N, 233, 264
Sverke, M, 145
Swamy, R, 177
Swap, W C, 404
Sweeney, P D, 177, 234, 264
Switzer, F S, 370
Syme, S L, 528
Symonds, C, 295
Syrett, M, 25, 554
Szumal, J L, 82, 83
Szymanski, K, 297

T

Taber, T D, 499
Taggart, W, 146
Tait, R, 144, 497, 498
Takeuchi, H, 369
Tambor, E S, 263
Tancred-Sheri, P, 296
Tannen, D, 437
Taubman, O, 529
Taylor, A III, 578
Taylor Buckley, J, 146
Taylor, J T, 403
Taylor, M A, 176

Taylor, M S, 263, 530
Taylor, R, 206, 207
Taylor, S E, 175
Teach, R, 498
Teagarden, M B, 113
Teicholz, E, 438
Tellegen, A, 207
Templeman, J, 579
Tepper, B J, 84, 498
Terdal, S K, 263
Terpstra, R H, 113
Terry, D T, 529
Tesluk, P E, 368
Teta, P, 145
Tetrault, L A, 498
Tetrick, L E, 206
Tett, R P, 145, 207
Thalhofer, N N, 333
Thibault, L, 83
Thierry, H, 234
Thomas, D R, 438
Thomas, J B, 144, 580
Thomas, L T, 53
Thomas, R R Jr, 52
Thomason, J A, 465
Thompson, D E, 207
Thompson, G, 402
Thompson, J D, 554
Thompson, K R, 333
Thompson, L, 333
Thompson, L L, 295
Thompson, R C, 145
Thomsen, C J, 145
Thomson, H A, 610
Thorlakson, A J H, 332
Thorlindson, T, 497
Thorndike, E L, 465
Thumin, F J, 84
Tichy, N M, 498
Tiegs, R B, 206
Timmins, W J, 265
Tingley, J C, 437
Tippens Reinitz, M, 145
Tippins, N, 176
Tisak, J, 529
Tjosvold, D, 331, 333
Tolliver, J M, 497
Torre, P D L, 176
Tosi, H L Jr, 26
Tracey, J B, 331
Trahant, B, 610
Tranchart, Ph, 402
Trapnell, P D, 144
Trevino, L K, 436
Trice, H M, 26, 82
Tromley, C L, 609
Trompenaars, F, 112, 113, 265
Trost, M R, 175, 176, 497
Trumbull, M, 26
Truss, C, 175
Tsoukas, H, 553
Tsui, A S, 263, 578
Tubbs, M E, 235
Tuckman, B W, 294

Tully, S, 82
Tung, R L, 113
Turban, D B, 144, 205, 263
Turner, C W, 530
Turner, R H, 143
Tversky, A, 367
Tyler, T, 402
Tyrell, D A J, 528
Tziner, A, 296, 333, 402

U

Uchino, B N, 528, 529
Ulrich, D, 580, 611
Ury, W, 333
Useem, M, 609
Usher, R, 84

V

Valacich, J S, 295, 333, 369
Vallerand, R J, 332
Van Buren, M, 610
Van de Looy, F, 25
Van de Ven, A H, 369
Van De Vliert, E, 295
Van Der Plight, J, 367
Van Doren, J A, 438
Van Dyne, L, 296
Van Eerde, W, 234
Van Fleet, D D, 554
Van Harrison, R, 529
Van Maanen, J, 83
Van Oudenhoven, J P, 333
Van Poppel, A, 52
Van Velsor, E, 25, 263, 294
Van Wichelen, K, 331
Van Yperen, N W, 295
Vance, R J, 235, 368
Vancouver, J B, 263
Vandenberg, R J, 145
Vanderheyden, K, 176
Vandermeersch, P, 331
Varma, A, 175
Vasilopoulos, N L, 264
Vaughan, M, 528
Vaughan, M J, 176
Vecchio, R P, 146, 233, 234, 498, 499
Verbeeck, J, 401
Verdegaal, E, 554
Verdini, W A, 263
Vervenne, L, 438
Vezina, R, 53
Vickery, H B III, 437
Villanova, P, 205
Vincent, A, 84
Vinson, M B N, 264
Viscarra, D M, 529
Vivekananda, K, 331
Vogel, D, 84
Vogel, R S, 176
Vollmann, T E, 83, 609
Von Glinow, M, 264, 611
Von Hippel, C, 265

Vroom, V H, 234, 368, 369, 370, 498
Vuga, F, 112

W

Wachtel, J M, 26
Wachter, R, 369
Wade, K J, 175, 176, 497, 528, 529
Wagner, J A III, 297, 368, 402, 579
Wakabayashi, M, 499
Waldman, D A, 176
Wall, J A Jr, 333
Wall, S J, 263
Wall, T, 206
Wall, T D, 528
Wall, V D Jr, 334
Wallin, J A, 466
Walther, D J, 529
Walton, E, 610
Walton, M, 26
Walz, P M, 83
Wang, Y-D, 579
Wanous, J P, 83, 206, 234, 294
Warfield, A, 296
Warg, L-E, 177
Warnock, K, 175
Warshaw, M, 578
Waterman, R H Jr, 82, 579
Waters, J A, 436
Watson, D, 207
Watson, K W, 437
Waung, M, 83
Wayne, S J, 331, 332, 333, 403, 499
Weber, J G, 112
Weber, M, 553
Webster, J, 263, 436
Weick, K E, 26, 553
Weigert, A, 402
Weigold, M F, 144
Weinberg, R A, 146
Weiner, Y, 206
Weingart, L R, 333, 367
Weiss, B D, 438
Weiss, D J, 206
Weiss, R M, 553
Weissinger-Baylon, R, 367
Welbourne, T M, 264, 265
Welch, J, 368
Wellins, R S, 294
Welsh, D H B, 113, 465
Werner, S, 176
Werther, W B Jr, 112
West, W B, 530
Western, K, 497
Westley, F, 401
Wetlaufer, S, 401
Wharton, A S, 295
Wheatley, W J, 467
Wheelan, S A, 297
Wheeler, B C, 369
Wheeles, L R, 437

Whetten, D A, 26, 297, 333, 334, 578
White, J, 84
White, J D, 466
White, N M, 465
White, P H, 235
Whiteside, H D, 402, 403
Whitman, N I, 369
Whyte, G, 296, 368
Widaman, K F, 234
Wiebe, F A, 296
Wiesendanger, B, 437
Wiesner, W H, 83
Wiley, C, 332
Wilhelm, W, 465
Wilk, S L, 146
Wilkinson, H E, 499
Wilkinson, I, 331
Willemsen, M E, 113
Williams, C L, 175
Williams, J E, 296
Williams, J R, 263, 264
Williams, K, 296, 297
Williams, K D, 296
Williams, K Y, 368
Williams, S, 368, 529, 530

Williams, T P, 296
Wills, T A, 529
Wilson, D C, 367
Wilson, J A, 84
Wilson, J M, 294
Wilson, P A, 332
Wink, P, 145
Winter, S G, 369
Wishart, N A, 611
Witt, L A, 207, 234
Wofford, J C, 235
Wolf, S, 235
Wolfe Morrison, E, 263
Wolffe, R, 529
Womack, J P, 580
Wong, P T P, 529
Wood Daudelin, M, 146
Wood, L, 367, 403
Wood, R E, 235
Wood, R V, 437
Woodman, R W, 370, 404, 610
Woodward, J, 579
Wooten, K, 234
Wormley, W M, 52, 176
Worrell, D L, 84
Woycke, J, 499

Wright, G E, 437
Wright, N B, 368
Wright, P, 497
Wright, P M, 235
Wyer, M M, 402
Wylie, M, 529
Wynne, B, 369
Wysocki, B Jr, 264

X

Xenikou, A, 82, 84
Xie, J L, 206

Y

Yale Bergstrom, R, 403
Yammarino, F J, 498, 499
Yasai-Ardekani, M, 579
Ybarra, O, 175
Yee, C, 113
Yetton, P, 295, 369
Yetton, P W, 368
Youngs, G A Jr, 334
Yu, K C, 26
Yukl, G, 264, 331
Yzerbt, V, 177

Z

Zaccaro, S J, 296, 467, 497
Zajac, D, 84, 207
Zaleznik, A, 333
Zamanou, S, 83
Zander, A, 295
Zanna, M P, 84, 175
Zastrow, C, 467
Zautra, A J, 528
Zeelenberg, M, 367
Zeithaml, C P, 580
Zeller, T L, 26
Zellner, W, 264, 579
Zembar, M J, 176
Zemke, R, 25, 144, 263, 369
Zhou, J, 333, 528
Ziegler, B, 438
Zingheim, P K, 264
Zorn, T E Jr, 436
Zualkernan, I A, 367
Zuckerman, M, 145
Zuk, Y, 144, 177
Zweig, P L, 579

Subject Index

A

A→B→C contingencies, 444-446, 452
Abilities, 133-136
  defined, 133
Absenteeism, 199-200
Accountability practices, 45
Achievement/ascription cultures, 103-104
Achievement-motivated people, 188
Achievement motivation, managerial implications, 189
Achievement-oriented leadership, 484
Action teams, 377
Active listening, 418-421
Adams's equity theory of motivation, 210-215
Adaptive change, 588
Adaptive culture, 63-64
Adaptive perspective, 63
Adaptors, 361
Added-value negotiation, 327
Ad hoc committees, 376
Advice teams, 376, 377
Affirmative action, 34-36
Age stereotype, 162-163
Ageing workforce, 39-40
Aggressive style, 414-415
Agreeableness, 128
Aided-analytic strategy, 346-347
Analytic learning, 601
Anger, 138-139
Antecedents, 444-445, 452
Anthroposophic movement, 456-457
Arbitration, 326
Asch effect, 287-288
Assertive style, 414-415
Attention, 152
Attitude, 131-133
  defined, 131
  employee, 40
  ethics, 131
Attribution
  Kelly's model, 167-168
  tendencies, 169
  theory, 166-170
  Weiner's model, 168
Autonomy, 195
Avoidance in conflict management, 323

B

Bandura's social learning theory, 457
Baseline data, 455
Behaviour, focusing on, 445-446
Behaviour chart, 455
Behaviour modification, 440-467
  A→B→C model, 444-446, 452
  behaviour shaping, 450
  behavioural self-management, 457-461
  classical music, 446
  contingent consequences, 446, 447
  defined, 443
  European attitude, 456
  four-step model, 450-455
  schedules of reinforcement, 448-450, 454
  Skinner's operant conditioning model, 444
  Thorndike's law of effect, 443-444
Behaviour of Organisms, The, 444, 465
Behaviour shaping, 450
Behavioural contingencies, 444-446
Behavioural intentions, 131-132 model, 133
Behavioural self-management (BSM), 457-461
Behavioural styles theory, 499-502
Behaviourism, 444
Beliefs, 132
Benchmarking, 589
Biofeedback, 521, 522
Biological model of organization, 538, 539, 541
Body movements and gestures, 416-417
Bonuses, 253, 254, 255
Bounded rationality, 341
Brainstorming, 356
Buffers, 512
Bureaucracy, 539
Burnout, 511-513

C

Care perspective, 76
Career plateau, 41
Case study, 18

Causal attributions, 166-170
  managerial applications and implications, 169-170
Central tendency error, 158
Centralized decision making, 565
Challenge, 518
Change, 582-611
  external forces, 585-587
  generic typology, 589
  internal forces, 587-588
  Kotter's steps for leading, 592
  Lewin's change model, 588-590
  managerial behaviour/decisions, 588
  organization development, 592-594
  process of changing, 589
  resistance to, 594-598
  systems model, 590-592
  target elements, 591
  types of, 588
Charisma, 306
Charismatic leadership, 486-489
Chauffeur-driven decision-making systems, 357
Chinese Value Survey (CVS), 100
Closed system, 538
Coaching, 493
Coalition, 312
  tactics, 302
Codes of ethics, 76
Coercive power, 305
Cognitions, 183
  defined, 120
Cognitive abilities, 134-135
Cognitive categories, 153
Cognitive dissonance theory, 211
Cognitive model of organization, 538, 541
Cognitive-processing model of feedback, 242-243
Cognitive restructuring, 521, 522-523
Cognitive styles, 135-136
Cohesiveness, teams, 384-386
Collaboration, 602
Collaborative computing, 429
Collectivism, 102, 103
Collegial value system, 77
Combination profit sharing plan, 255

Commissions, 253
Commitment, 302, 307, 517
  escalation, 348-350
Committees, 287
  see also Groups
Communication, 96-99, 157, 406-438
  barriers, 430-432
  collaborative computing, 429
  competence, 414
  computerized, 427-432
  conduit model, 409
  defined, 409
  distortion, 426-428
  gender differences, 421-423
  hierarchical, 423-424
  interpersonal, 413-423
  listening, 418-421
  media selection, 411-413
  modern dynamics, 427-432
  nonverbal, 416-418
  organizational patterns, 423-427
  perceptual process model, 409-411
  personal barriers, 431
  physical barriers, 431-432
  process barriers to, 430
  semantic barriers, 432
  styles, 414-416
  see also specific aspects, methods and equipment
Compensation effect, 209
Competencies, 134
Competition, 318, 382, 602
Competitive advantage, 39-40
Complacency, 561
Compliance, 302, 307
Comprehension, 152, 155
Compromise in conflict management, 323
Computer-aided decision making, 357
Computer-aided design (CAD), 585
Computer-integrated manufacturing (CIM), 585
Computerized numerical control (CNC), 585
Computers, communication, 427-432
Concurrent engineering, 373
Conduit model, 409
Conflict
  continuum, 318
  defined, 317

Conflict-handling styles
  in conflict management, 105, 322-327
  managing across cultures, 105
Conflict management, 318-327
  antecedents of conflict, 319
  conflict-handling styles, 105, 322-327
  contingency approach, 327
  cross-cultural issues, 106
  functional vs. dysfunctional conflict, 318-319
  intergroup/interorganizational conflict, 324-326
  practical advice, 318
  stimulating functional conflict, 321-322, 322
Conscientiousness, 128
Consensus, 167-168, 355
Consideration, 477
Consistency, 167-168
Consultation, 302, 326
Contingency approach to organization design, 562-567
  to organizational behaviour, 16
Contingency factors, 484
Contingent consequences, 446, 447
Continuous improvement, 7, 561
Continuous reinforcement (CRF), 448
Contrast effects error, 158
Control strategy, 516-517
Cooperation, 380-383
Coping, 515-517
Core job dimensions, 194
Corporate Cultures: The Rites and Rituals of Corporate Life, 62
Corporate governance, 549
Creativity, 42-43, 358-363
  concentration stage, 359
  defined, 359
  employee, 363
  group characteristics, 362
  illumination stage, 359
  incubation stage, 359
  organizational characteristics, 362-363
  organizational model, 360-363
  preparation stage, 359
  stages in process, 359-360
  verification stage, 359
Credibility: How Leaders Gain and Lose It, Why People Demand It, 245
Cross-cultural issues. *See* Managing across cultures
Cross-functionalism, 390

Cultural insensitivity, 40
Cultural perceptions of time, 94-95
Culture
  defined, 95
  see also Managing across cultures; Organizational culture
Culture shock, 108

D

Death of Competition: Leadership and Strategy in the Age of Business Ecosystems, The, 542
Decentralized decision making, 565
DecideRight, 346-347
Decision making, 336-370
  centralized vs. decentralized, 565
  contingency perspective, 346-348
  defined, 339
  dynamics, 346-349
  escalation of commitment, 348-350
  garbage can model, 342-346
  group, 350-358
  implementation, 341
  models, 339-346
  rational model 339-
  Simon's normative model, 341-342
  Vroom/Yetton/Jago model, 353-355, 366-367
Decoding, 410-411
Deferred profit sharing plan, 255
Delegation, 308, 309
Delphi technique, 357
Demographic issues, 36-40, 585
Derailed executive, 286
Development practices, 45, 46
Deviant workplace behaviour, 464
Devil's advocacy, 321, 322
Dialectic method, 321, 322
Differentiation, 563-564
Directive leadership, 483
Distinciveness, 167-168
Distribution profit sharing plan, 255
Distributive justice, 213
Distributive negotiation, 325
Diversity, *see also* Managing diversity
Division of labour, 536
Dominating power, 307, 308
Domination in conflict management, 323
Downsizing, 543-546
Dysfunctional conflict, 318, 322-327

E

Ecosystem model of organization, 538, 542
Egypt's bureaucratic legacy, 540
85-15 rule, 15
Electronic mail (E-mail), 429
Elite value system, 77
Emotional Intelligence, 137
Emotional stability, 128
Emotional support, 514
Emotions, 137-139, 184
Employee attitudes, 40
Employee loyalty, 9-10
Employment contract, 8-10
  implications for organizations, 9
  implications for the individual, 9
Empowerment, 303-310
  culture, 46-47
  model, 310
Encoding, 410
  outcomes, 153
Environmental uncertainty, 562-563
Equal opportunities, 39
Equity concept, expanding, 213-214
Equity research findings, 214-215
Equity theory, 210-215
  managerial implications, 215
Escalation of commitment, 348-350
Escape strategy, 517
Ethics
  affirmative action, 34-36
  and organizational behaviour, 74-76
  attitudes, 131
  beliefs, 132
  defined, 74
  ethnocentrism, 91
  gender differences, 76
  healthy organizations, 573
  improving ethical climate, 76
  model of ethical behaviour, 74-75
  organizational culture, 57
  organizational politics, 317
  self-esteem, 121-122
  self-monitoring, 126-127
  societal culture, 90
Ethnic map of Europe, 92-93
Ethnic minorities, 38, 162-163
Ethnocentrism, 91
Europe, ethnic map of, 92-93
Event memory, 154
Exchange tactics, 302
Expatriate, defined, 105
Expectancy, 217

Expectancy model of motivation, Porter and Lawler's extension, 218-219
Expectancy theory of motivation, 215-221
  research and managerial implications, 219-220
  Vroom's, 216-218
Experienced meaningfulness, 194
Experienced responsibility, 194
Experimental learning, 601
Expert power, 305
External factors, 167
External forces for change, 585-587
External locus of control, 130
Extinction, 447
Extraversion, 128
Eye contact, 418

F

Facial expressions, 417
Facilitating factors, 599, 601, 602
Fact-based knowledge thrust, 5
Failure rate in foreign assignments, 105-106
Fairness, 210
Feedback, 225, 241-249
  360-degree, 248-249
  behaviour charts, 455
  behavioural outcomes of, 245-246
  cognitive processing model, 242-243
  communication, 411
  defined, 195, 242
  functions of, 242
  group development process, 275
  non-traditional, 246-249
  practical lessons, 246, 249
  recipient, 244-245
  sources of, 243
  trouble signs, 246-247
  upward, 247
Feelings, 184
Fiedler's contingency model, 480-482
Field study, 18
Fifth Discipline, The, 599
Fight-or-flight stress response, 503, 522
Financial performance enhancement, 63
Firewalls, 428
Fit perspective, 63
Fixed interval, 449
Fixed-pie thinking, 325
Fixed ratio, 448
Foreign assignments, 105-111
  failure rate in, 105-106

re-entry shock, 109
support, 108-109
Foreign language skills, 97
4-P cycle of continuous
improvement, 7
Fragmentation, 602
Functional analysis, 444-445
Functional conflict, 318, 321-322
Functional social support, 514
Fundamental attribution bias, 169

G

Gainsharing, 254-256
Garbage can model, 342-346
managerial implications, 345-346
Gender
communication, 421-423
ethics, 76
leadership, 476
linguistic style, 422
mixed-gender task groups, 282-284
moral principles, 76
organizational politics, 215-217
power, 307
sex-role stereotypes, 159-161, 163
Genderflex, 423
General Adaptation Syndrome (GAS), 504-505
Gestures, 417
Global managers, 106-109
Global social support, 514
Goal accomplishment approach, 547-549
Goal commitment, 226
Goal difficulty, 224
Goal setting, 222
Locke's model, 223
motivation through, 221-228
practical application, 227-228
Goal specificity, 225
Goals, 375-376, 460
definition and background, 221-222
Golden Step award, 64
Graen's leader–member exchange (LMX) model of leadership, 490-491
Grapevine, 424-426
Graphology, 129
Groups, 268-297
adjourning, 275
Asch effect, 287-288
autonomy, 391
cohesiveness, 275
composition, 280-286
conformity, 286-287
creativity characteristics, 362

deadlines, 275
decision making, 350-358
defined, 271
degree of sexualization, 284
development process, 273-276
development process feedback, 291
formal, 272-273
forming, 275
functional roles performed by group managers, 281
functions, 271-273
group member ability, 284, 285
groupthink, 288-289
informal, 272-273
laboratory simulation approach, 297
leadership, 276
managerial implications, 282, 286, 287
mathematical modeling approach, 297
norming, 275
norms, 278-280
ostracism, 279
performing, 275-276
role ambiguity, 277-278
role conflict, 277, 278, 293
role episodes, 276, 293
role overload, 277
role theory, 276
roles, 276-278
sexual harassment, 283-284
size, 281-282
social loafing, 289
stepladder technique, 290
storming, 275
structure, 280
task vs. maintenance roles, 280
threats to effectiveness, 286-290
Tuckman's five-stage model of development, 273-275
types, 271-273
voting deadlocks, 298
see also Teams
Groupthink, 288-289, 385

H

Halo effect, 157
Halo error, 158
Handwriting analysis, 129
Hardiness, 517-518
Healthy systems approach, 548
Herzberg's motivator–hygiene theory, 191, 192
Hierarchical communication, 423-424

Hierarchy of authority, 536
High-context cultures, 91-92
Hiring, 155
Hofstede-Bond cross-cultural studies, 100-101
Holistic wellness approach, 521
Horizontal loading, 190
Horizontal organizations, 572, 573
Host country sponsors, 108
Hourglass organizations, 573
Human Problems of an Industrial Civilization, The, 12
Human relations movement, 12, 12-13
Human resource development thrust, 5
Human resource problems/prospects, 587-588
Human Side of Enterprise, The, 12
Hygiene factors, 191

I

Impression management, 314-316
dress, 314-315
upward, 214-216
Improshare plans, 255
In Search of Excellence, 62, 568
Incentive pay, 253, 267
Individual differences, 116-146
conceptual model, 119
self-efficacy, 127-130
Individual level stressors, 530
Individualism, 102, 103
Inductive reasoning, 135
Influence outcomes, 302
Influence tactics, 301-303
Influence without Authority, 303
Information richness for communication media, 432
Informational support, 514
Ingratiating tactics, 302
In-group exchange, 490
Initiating structure, 477-478
Innovation, 42-43, 358-363
Innovative changes, 618
Inspirational appeals, 302
Institutional learning, 602
Instrumental cohesiveness, 384-385
Instrumental social support, 514
Instrumentality, 217-218
Integration, 564
in conflict management, 323
Integrative negotiation, 325, 327
Integrity tests, 129

Intelligence, 134
Interactive learning, 601
Intergroup/interorganizational conflict, 324-326
Intermittent reinforcement, 448-449
Internal factors, 167
Internal forces for change, 587-588
Internal locus of control, 129, 517
Internal motivation, 193
Internal processes approach, 548, 549
International manager, 98-99
Internet, 428
Interpersonal communication, 413-423
Interpersonal space, 95-96
Intimate distance, 95
Intranet, 407-408, 428
Intuition/feeling, 136
Intuition/thinking, 136
Israeli tank-crew study, 285

J

Job behaviour
case study, 445
model for modifying, 450-457
Job characteristics, 182, 184
model, 193-196
Job Descriptive Index (JDI), 197
Job design, 190-191, 193-196
Job diagnostic survey (JDS), 195
Job dissatisfaction, 191, 200
Job enlargement, 190
Job enrichment, 193
Job involvement, 199
Job performance, 200
Job-related values in Europe, 13
Job rotation, 191
Job satisfaction, 197-200, 200
Johari Window, 157
Justice, 210
perspective, 76

K

KISS principle, 460
Knowledge of results, 194
Kotter's steps for leading change, 592

L

Laboratory study, 18
Laissez-faire leadership, 512
Language, 96-100
managing across cultures, 96-100
Law of effect, 444
Leader–member exchange theory, 512-514
Leader–member relations, 481

Leader trait, 475
Leadership, 468-499
   and organizational learning,
     603-604
   and social perception, 156
   behavioural styles theory,
     477-480
   charismatic, 486-489
   conceptual framework,
     474, 495
   cross-cultural contingency
     model, 104-105
   cross-cultural issues, 107
   defined, 472-473
   Fielder's contingency
     model, 480-482
   gender differences, 476
   Graen's leader–member
     exchange (LMX) model,
     490-491
   groups, 276
   managerial implications,
     482-484
   path-goal theory, 483-489
   prototype, 476
   role-making model, 490
   roles, Quinn's central
     concept, 486
   Russian traits, 478
   self-management, 395
   situational theories, 480-486
   styles, 477, 483-484
   substitutes for, 491-492
   superleadership, 493
   trait theory, 475-477
   transactional, 486-489
   value system, 77
   vs. managing, 473-475
Leadership Grid, 478, 479
Learned helplessness, 124
Learning capabilities, 600-602
Learning modes, 601-602
Learning organization, 541,
   598-605
   defined, 599
   resistance to learning, 602-
     603
Legal liabilities, stress, 523-524
Legitimate power, 305
Leniency error, 158
Lewin's change model, 588-
   590
Liaison individuals, 425
Line managers, 536
Linguistic style, 421-423
Listener comprehension model,
   419
Listening, 418-421
   effective, 420-421
   styles, 419-421
LMX model of leadership,
   490-491
Locke's model, goal setting,
   223
Locus of control, 129-130

Long-term memory, 154
Low-context cultures, 92

M

McClelland's need theory,
   187-189
Management by objectives
   (MBO), 222
Management process, 6
Management style,
   interorganizational
   organizational behaviour, 15
Managerial Grid, 478
Managers
   21st-century, 10, 11
   global skills, 106-109
   new employment contract,
     8-10
   role of, 6
   skills profile, 7, 8
   stereotyping, 163-164
   stumbling blocks, 286
Managing across cultures, 86-
   113
   communication, 96-99
   conflict-handling styles,
     105, 105
   foreign assignments, 106-
     111
   high-context/low-context
     cultures, 91-93
   interpersonal space, 95-96
   language, 96-100
   leadership, 104-107
   leadership contingency
     model, 106
   negotiation, 415, 417
   research, 100-105
   time, 94-95
   training, 108
Managing diversity, 28-53
   affirmative action/valuing
     diversity, compared,
     34-36
   attitude towards, 49
   barriers/challenges, 47
   business case for, 36-43
   competitive advantage, 39-
     40
   defined, 36
   demographic trends, 36-40
   dimensions of diversity, 32
   diversity, defined, 32-33
   generic action options, 43-
     44
   organizational practices,
     43-47
   specific diversity initiatives,
     44-47
Market changes, 585-587
Maslow's need hierarchy
   theory, 193-195
Mechanistic organizations,
   565-567
Mediation, 326

Meditation, 521, 522
Memory, 135, 154-155
Mental abilities, 135
Mental rehearsal, 460, 461
Mentoring, 69-72
Meritocratic calue system, 77
Met expectations, 198
Meta-analysis, 18
Metaphor, 537-543
Military/mechanical model of
   organization, 538, 539
Minnesota Satisfaction
   Questionnaire (MSQ), 197
Mission statement, 590
Monochronic time, 94
Moral principles, 76-77
   magnificent seven, 77
Motivation, 22, 181-190
   and job satisfaction, 199
   defined, 181
   equity theory, 210-215
   expectancy model,
     Porter/Lawler's, 218-219
   expectancy theory, 215-221
   goal setting, 221-228
   historical roots of modern
     theory, 182-184
   implementing motivational
     system, 228-230
   job enrichment, 191
   need theories, 182-183,
     185-190
   potential score (MPS), 195
   scientific management, 190
   systems model, 181-182,
     229
Motivator-hygiene theory,
   191-193
Motivators, 191-193
Muscle relaxation, 521-522
Mutual benefit, 303
Mutual respect, 303
Mutuality of interest, 300-301
Mythical fixed-pie, 325

N

Need for achievement, 187
Need for affiliation, 189
Need for power, 189
Need fulfilment, 198
Need hierarchy, Maslow's
   theory, 185-187
Need strength, 187
Need theories, 182-183, 185-
   190
of motivation, McClelland's,
   187-189
Negative emotions, 137-138
Negative inequity, 211-212
Negative reinforcement, 446
Negotiation
   cross-cultural awareness in,
     415, 417
   in conflict management,
     324-327

Network organizations, 573-
   574
Networks, 312
Neutral/affective relationships,
   102-103
New-style organizations, 570-
   574
Noise, 411
Nominal group technique
   (NGT), 356-357
Non-analytic, 347
Nonassertive style, 414-416,
   436
Nonverbal communication,
   416-418
Normative beliefs, 66
Numerical ability, 135

O

Obliging in conflict
   management, 323
Occupational stress. *See* Stress
Ohio State studies, 477
Open book management, 242
Open system, 538, 541
Openness, 303
   to experience, 128
Operant behaviour, 444
Optimizing, 341
Organic organizations, 565-
   567
Organization and Environment,
   563
Organization-based self-esteem
   (OBSE), 122-127
Organization chart, 535-537
Organization development
   (OD), 592-594
Organization-motivated
   aggression, 139
Organizational behaviour
   contingency approach, 16
   cultural influences, 90
   European attitude, 456
   model, 20
   past and present, 10-16
   practice, 19-20
   research, 18-19
   theory, 17-18
Organizational change. *See*
   Change
Organizational citizenship
   behaviours, 199, 207
Organizational commitment,
   199-200
Organizational communication
   patterns, 423-427
Organizational culture
   defined, 57
   embedding culture in
     organization, 65-66
   ethics, 74-76
   foundation, 57-63
   functions of, 58-60
   high-performance cultures,

63-66
manifestations of, 57, 60
mentoring, 69-72
model, 90
model for interpreting, 57-58
research, 61-63
socialization process, 66-69
types, 60, 61
values, 72-78
Organizational decline, 560-561
Organizational design,
contingency approach,
562-567
Organizational effectiveness,
546-549
assessment, 547
generic criteria, 547-549
Organizational environments,
562-563
Organizational hierarchies,
543-546
Organizational learning, 598-605
Organizational life-cycle, 556-580
Organizational metaphors,
537-543
Organizational moles, 425
Organizational politics, 311-317
ethics, 317
Organizational reward systems.
See Reward systems
Organizational socialization,
66-69
Organizational stress. *See* Stress
Organizational values, 72-78
Organizations
biological model, 538, 541
cognitive model, 538, 541
cognitive systems, 541
common characteristics,
561
defined, 535
ecosystem model, 542
environmental demands,
562-563
horizontal, 572, 573
hourglass, 573
mechanistic, 565-567
military/mechanical
bureaucracies, 538,
539, 564
network, 573-574
new style vs. old style,
570-574
organic, 565-567
pyramid-shaped, 571
shamrock, 574
size and performance, 568-570
strategic choice model of,
570
technology impact, 568
Organizations in Action, 539

Ostracism, groups, 279
Out-group exchange, 491

P

Paradigm, defined, 632
Participative leadership, 483
Participative management
(PM), 352
model, 352
research and practical
suggestions, 353
Particularism, 102
Passion for Excellence, A, 472
Path–goal theory, 483-484
Pay for peformance, 252-259
Perceived inequity, 213
Perception, 151-171
causal attributions, 166-170
defined, 151
four-stage sequence, 151-155
information processing
model, 151-158
overview of process, 151
self-fulfilling prophecy,
164-166
stereotypes, 158-164
Perceptual errors, 158
Perceptual model of
communication, 409-411
Perceptual speed, 135
Performance, 133-136
appraisal, 156
systems model, 181-182,
229
Performance-based rewards,
interorganizational
organizational
behaviour, 222
Persistence, 223
Person memory, 155
Personal awareness and growth
exercise, 22-23
Personal distance, 95
Personality, 128-130
Big Five dimensions, 128-129
testing, 129
Personalized power, 305
Piece rate plan, 267
Political action, 312
Political pressures for change,
587
Political tactics, 312-313
Polychronic Attitude Index, 94
Polychronic time, 94
Porter and Lawler's expectancy
model of motivation, 218-219
Position power, 481
Positive emotions, 137-138
Positive inequity, 211-212
Positive reinforcement, 446,
454
Post-It Notes story, 362
Postmodern organizations, 543

Power, 303-310
dimensions, 304-306
distribution, 308
evolution, 308
self-perceived, 306
types, 304
see also Empowerment
Predictors of effort, 218
Predictors of performance,
219
Predictors of satisfaction, 219
Pressure tactics, 302
Primary dimensions of
diversity, 32, 33
Problem
defined, 339
identifying, 339-340
Problem solving, 323
Procedural justice, 213
Process-style listeners, 420
Production teams, 376, 377
Profit maximization, 251
Profit sharing, 254-256
Programmed conflict, 321
Project teams, 376-377
Proxemics, 95
Public distance, 95
Punishment, 446
Pygmalion effect, 164-166
Pyramid-shaped organizations,
571, 601

Q

Quality
aided analytic decision-
making tools, 365
behaviour shaping, 472
mechanistic organizations,
593
pay for performance, 268
see also Total quality
management (TQM)
Quality circles, 376, 386-389

R

Race stereotypes, 162-163
Racial equality, 39
Rational model, 339-341
Rational persuasion, 302
Readiness, 484
Realistic job preview (RJP),
66, 107-108
Reality shock, 66
Reasons-style listeners, 420
Recency effects error, 158
Reciprocity, 303
Recruitment practices, 41, 45,
46
Reengineering, 196, 309, 543-546, 572
Re-entry shock, 109
Referent power, 305
Refreezing, 589-590
Rehearsal, 460, 461
Reinforcement, 183

Relativists, 96
Relaxation response, 522
Repatriate, defined, 105
Resistance, 302
Resistance to change, 594-598
Resource acquisition approach,
548, 549
Respondent behaviour, 444
Results-oriented managerial
thrust, 5
Results-style listeners, 420
Reward power, 305
Reward systems, 241, 249-259, 393
desired outcomes, 252
distribution criteria, 252
equality norm, 251
equity norm, 251
extrinsic rewards, 250-251
gainsharing, 255-257
general model, 250
hybrid plans, 259
intrinsic rewards, 250-251
natural vs. contrived, 453-454
pay for performance, 252-259
performance-based, 222
practical recommendations,
259
profit sharing, 255
psychic rewards, 250
reward norms, 251-252
social rewards, 250
team-based pay, 258-259
types of rewards, 250-251
Rucker plan, 255
Russian leadership traits, 478

S

Sales and market share, 41-42
Sales commissions, 253
Salient stimuli, 152
Sample survey, 18
Satisficing, 342
Scanlon plan, 256
Scenario technique, 340
Schedules of reinforcement,
448-450
Schema, 153, 155
Scientific management, 190
Secondary dimensions of
diversity, 32, 33
Self-concept, 120-127
defined, 120
Self-disclosure, 120, 124
Self-efficacy, 123-126
Self-esteem, 121-123
Self-fulfilling prophecy, 164-166
Self-improvement
agenda, 459
managerial implications,
457-458
Self-interests, 301, 314
Self-managed teams, 389-393

Self-management
  behavioural, 457-461
  managerial implications,
    461-462
  social learning model, 458-461
Self-management leadership,
  395
Self-monitoring, 126-127
Self-perception, 157
Self-reinforcement, 461
Self-serving bias, 169
Self-talk, 460-461
Semantic memory, 154
Semantics, 432
Sensation/feeling, 136
Sensation/thinking, 136
7 Habits of Highly Effective
  People, The, 421, 459
Sex-role stereotype, 159-161,
  163
Sexual harassment, 283-284,
  417, 507
Shamrock organizations, 574
Shaping, 450
Shareholder value, 224
Simon's normative model,
  341-342
Situational control, 480-481
Situational cues, 459-460
Situational leadership theory
  (SLT), 484-486
Situational theories, 480-486
Skill, defined, 133
Skill variety, 195
Skinner's operant conditioning
  model, 444
Social cognition, 151, 155
Social companionship, 514
Social distance, 95
Social influence, 301
Social information processing,
  151
Social learning model, self-
  management, 458-461
Social learning theory, 483
  Bandura's, 457
Social loafing, 289
Social perception. See
  Perception
Social power, 304, 306
Social pressures for change, 587
Social Readjustment Rating
  Scale, 509-511
Social support, 513-515
Socialization research, 68
Socialized power, 305
Societal cultures
  high-context, 91-92
  low-context, 92
  model, 90
Socio-emotional cohesiveness,
  384-385
South Africa, banking in, 587
Space bubbles, 96

Span of control, 536, 563
Spatial ability, 135
Specific/diffuse relationships,
  103
Staff personnel, 536
Stakeholder audit, 548
Stepladder technique, 290
Stereotypes
  age, 162-163
  defined, 159
  formation and maintenance,
    159
  managerial challenges and
    recommendations, 163
  perception, 158-164
Stimulus–response (S–R)
  model, 444
Strategic alliances, 303
Strategic choice model of
  organizational structure,
  599
Strategic constituency, 548,
  549, 574
Strategic plan, 590
Strength perspective, 63
Stress, 200, 500-530
  burnout, 511-513
  clinical approach, 505
  coping, 515-517
  defined, 503
  economic costs, 513
  hardiness, 517-518
  legal liabilities, 523-524
  medical approach, 528
  moderators, 513-520
  OB approach, 505-508
  organizational outcomes,
    513
  reducing, 520-524
  social support, 513-515
  stressful life events, 509-511
  Type A behaviour, 518-520
  Type B behaviour, 518
Stress-reduction techniques,
  520-524
Stressful life events, 509-511
Stressors, 507
  cognitive appraisal, 516
  extraorganizational, 507,
    508
  group level, 507
  individual differences, 508
  organizational, 531
  outcomes, 508
Structural learning, 602
Subjective norms, 132
Substitutes for hierarchy, 543-546
Substitutes for leadership, 515
Superleader, 492-493
Supervisory development
  workshops, 393
Supportive leadership, 483
Symbolic coding, 460

Symptom management strategy,
  517
Synthetic learning, 601
Systems model of motivation and
  performance, 181-182, 229

T

Tank-crew study, 285
Target elements of change,
  591
Targets, 39
Task
  identity, 195
  significance, 195
  structure, 481
Team-based pay, 258-259
Teams, 372-404
  cohesiveness, 384-386,
    403
  cooperation, 380-383
  cross-functionalism, 390
  defined, 375
  ecological model of team
    effectiveness, 378-379
  effectiveness, 378-379
  evolution, 376
  failure, 379-381
  goals, 375-376
  high performance, 394
  members' problems, 380
  self-managed, 389-393
  team building, 393-396
  training, 393
  trust, 383-384
  types, 376-378
  viability, 378
  see also Groups; Quality
    circles
Technology
  and change, 585
  impact on organizational
    structure, 568
Telecommuting, 430, 451
Thematic Apperception Test
  (TAT), 187, 188, 322
Theory X, 12, 13
Theory Y, 12, 13
Theory Z: How American
  Business Can Meet the
  Japanese Challenge, 62
Third-party intervention in
  conflict management, 326
Thorndike's law of effect,
  443-444
Time, cultural perceptions of,
  94-95
Total quality management
  (TQM), 13-16, 561, 571,
  572
Touching, cross-cultural norms,
  417
Training, 182
  teams, 393
Trait/genetic components, 198
Transactional leadership, 486-

  489
Trust, 303, 383-384
Tuckman's five-stage model of
  group development, 273-275
Turnover, 200
Type A behaviour pattern,
  518-520
Type B behaviour pattern, 518

U

Unaided-analytic strategy, 347
Uncertainty, 311, 317
Unity of command principle,
  535
Universalism, 102
Universalists, 96
University of Michigan studies,
  478
Uplifting power, 307
Upward appeals, 302

V

Valance, 218
Value attainment, 198
Values
  and value system, 72
  questionnaire, 78
Valuing diversity, 35-36
Variable interval, 449
Variable pay, 267
Variable ratio, 448
Verbal comprehension, 135
Vertical dyad, 490
Vertical loading, 193
Vicarious learning, 457
Videoconferencing, 430
Vision, 63
Visual perceptions, 156
Visualization, 460, 461
Vroom/Yetton/Jago decision-
  making model, 353-355,
  366-367
Vroom's expectancy theory,
  216-218

W

We Europeans, 92
Whirlpool pay system, 256
Women
  and organizational politics,
    317
  in mixed-gender task
    groups, 282-284
  in workforce, 37-38
  stereotyping, 159-161, 163
  see also Gender
Word fluency, 135
Work and Motivation, 228
Workforce demographics, 36-40
Working Wisdom, 241

Z

Zero midpoint, 191